Foreign Relations of the
United States, 1961–1963

Volume XXV

Organization of
Foreign Policy;
Information Policy;
United Nations;
Scientific Matters

Editors	Paul Claussen
	Evan M. Duncan
	Jeffrey A. Soukup
General Editor	David S. Patterson

United States Government Printing Office
Washington
2001

DEPARTMENT OF STATE PUBLICATION 10864

OFFICE OF THE HISTORIAN

BUREAU OF PUBLIC AFFAIRS

For sale by the Superintendent of Documents, U.S. Government Printing Office
Internet: bookstore.gpo.gov   Phone: (202) 512-1800   Fax: (202) 512-2250
Mail: Stop SSOP, Washington, DC 20402-0001

ISBN 0-16-050885-1

Preface

The *Foreign Relations of the United States* series presents the official documentary historical record of major foreign policy decisions and significant diplomatic activity of the United States Government. The Historian of the Department of State is charged with the responsibility for the preparation of the *Foreign Relations* series. The staff of the Office of the Historian, Bureau of Public Affairs, plans, researches, compiles, and edits the volumes in the series. Official regulations codifying specific standards for the selection and editing of documents for the series were first promulgated by Secretary of State Frank B. Kellogg on March 26, 1925. These regulations, with minor modifications, guided the series through 1991.

A new statutory charter for the preparation of the series was established by Public Law 102–138, the Foreign Relations Authorization Act, Fiscal Years 1992 and 1993, which was signed by President George Bush on October 28, 1991. Section 198 of P.L. 102–138 added a new Title IV to the Department of State's Basic Authorities Act of 1956 (22 USC 4351, *et seq.*).

The statute requires that the *Foreign Relations* series be a thorough, accurate, and reliable record of major United States foreign policy decisions and significant United States diplomatic activity. The volumes of the series should include all records needed to provide comprehensive documentation of major foreign policy decisions and actions of the United States Government. The statute also confirms the editing principles established by Secretary Kellogg: the *Foreign Relations* series is guided by the principles of historical objectivity and accuracy; records should not be altered or deletions made without indicating in the published text that a deletion has been made; the published record should omit no facts that were of major importance in reaching a decision; and nothing should be omitted for the purposes of concealing a defect in policy. The statute also requires that the *Foreign Relations* series be published not more than 30 years after the events recorded.

Structure and Scope of the Foreign Relations Series

This volume is the final volume to be published in a subseries of volumes of the *Foreign Relations* series that documents the most important issues in the foreign policy of the administration of John F. Kennedy (1961–1963). The subseries presents in 25 print volumes and 5 microfiche supplements a documentary record of major foreign policy decisions and actions of President Kennedy's administration. This volume documents the organization and management of U.S. foreign policy; U.S. information policy; U.S. policy toward the United Nations; and various global issues such as human rights, refugees, and international scientific matters.

Focus of Research and Principles of Selection for Foreign Relations, 1961–1963, Volume XXV

The editors of the volume sought to present documentation illuminating responsibility for major foreign policy decisions in the U.S. Government, with emphasis on the President and his advisers. The documents include memoranda and records of discussions that set forth policy issues and options and show decisions or actions taken. The emphasis is on the development of U.S. policy and on major aspects and repercussions of its execution rather than on the details of policy execution.

The first section of this volume deals with the organization and administration of foreign policy. Following the 1960 election, President-elect John F. Kennedy and his transition advisers focused on various proposals for modifying and streamlining the structure of the National Security Council apparatus. Documentation is presented on the interdepartmental review of foreign policy, the abolition of the Operations Coordinating Board, the use of Country Teams in the planning process, and enhanced involvement of the Vice President in national security affairs. A focus on the need for crisis management led to the establishment of the Department of State Operations Center to deal with emergencies on an interdepartmental basis. President Kennedy redefined and expanded the role of U.S. Ambassadors, emphasizing the need for leadership, decision-making authority, and responsibility for overseas representatives of other departments and agencies. Organizational changes included the establishment of several new foreign affairs departments and agencies: the U.S. Agency for International Development (AID), the Peace Corps, and the U.S. Arms Control and Disarmament Agency (ACDA).

This section also provides documentation on organizational changes in the Department of State, such as combining the positions of Counselor and Chairman of the Policy Planning Council, upgrading the Bureau of Educational and Cultural Affairs and the Bureau of Intelligence and Research, abolishing 109 intra- and inter-departmental committees, closing marginal consular posts, improving the reporting system, and planning for the use of automation to expedite Department operations. President Kennedy held an off-the-record meeting on March 30, 1962, in the new Department of State Auditorium with policy officers of the Department down to the desk level. Secretary of State

Dean Rusk urged a broadening of the recruitment process for the Department of State and the Foreign Service, and he criticized discrimination and the slowness of the Department in recruiting minorities for "responsible positions."

Another part of this section covers the organization and administration of the Intelligence Community. During its last month, the Eisenhower administration considered the report of the Joint Study Group on the Foreign Intelligence Activities of the U.S. Government. The Kennedy administration subsequently adopted many of the Joint Study Group's recommendations. One of the most far-reaching was the need for modernizing and streamlining the military intelligence system, which led to the creation of the Defense Intelligence Agency in August 1961. President Kennedy assigned new duties to John McCone as Director of Central Intelligence in January 1962, spelling out his role both as the government's principal foreign intelligence officer, responsible for coordination of the total U.S. intelligence effort, and as head of the Central Intelligence Agency. Documentation is included on the establishment of the National Reconnaissance Program (NRP), consisting of all satellite and overflight activities, and on the increased role of the Bureau of the Budget in the coordination and management of intelligence operations.

The documents on information policy presented in the volume illustrate the U.S. Information Agency's initiatives in seeking to cooperate more closely with the State Department and other U.S. Government agencies, to present U.S. foreign policy objectives to the world in a positive manner, and to assess more accurately foreign opinion of the United States and its policies.

President John F. Kennedy and his advisers took a keen interest in United Nations affairs. This volume includes documentation on the summer strategy sessions that discussed themes that the President would use when addressing the UN General Assembly. In the United Nations, U.S. policy shifted from supporting a "moratorium" on considering the question of Chinese representation to declaring it to be an "important question." Under this formula, a two-thirds majority in the General Assembly would be necessary to admit the People's Republic of China and to expel the Republic of China. Other major topics include the election of U Thant of Burma as Secretary-General after the death of Dag Hammarskjöld, and the financing of UN operations in general and of peacekeeping operations in particular in view of Soviet opposition to paying for UN activities that it opposed. The United Nations was at this time the principal forum for U.S. consideration of human rights conventions, international assistance to refugees, and the international control of narcotic drugs. Lyndon B. Johnson quickly reaffirmed his support for the United Nations after he became President.

Also presented are documents on Department of State involvement in the U.S. space program, U.S. cooperation with the Soviet Union in scientific research in outer space, support for UN resolutions concerning the peaceful uses of outer space, and the Department's role in the organization of space-based communications systems. Despite the initial Soviet advantage in manned space flight, President Kennedy and Soviet Premier Khrushchev sought areas of scientific cooperation between the United States and the Soviet Union in space-related research.   This led to the signature in Rome of a memorandum of understanding between the National Aeronautics and Space Administration and the Soviet Academy of Sciences on March 20, 1963. Vice President Johnson chaired the National Aeronautics and Space Council during this period.

Documentation in the volume on international scientific issues includes coverage of the organization of science-related activities in the Department of State, population, international programs in atmospheric science, consultative meetings under the Antarctic Treaty, preparations to implement the international inspection system that the treaty provided for, and U.S. policy on a proposed multilateral convention on Law of the Sea.

Editorial Methodology

The documents are presented chronologically according to Washington time or, in the case of conferences, in the order of individual meetings. Memoranda of conversation are placed according to the time and date of the conversation, rather than the date the memorandum was drafted.

Editorial treatment of the documents published in the *Foreign Relations* series follows Office style guidelines, supplemented by guidance from the General Editor and the chief technical editor. The source text is reproduced as exactly as possible, including marginalia or other notations, which are described in the footnotes.   Texts are transcribed and printed according to accepted conventions for the publication of historical documents in the limitations of modern typography. A heading has been supplied by the editors for each document included in the volume. Spelling, capitalization, and punctuation are retained as found in the source text, except that obvious typographical errors are silently corrected. Other mistakes and omissions in the source text are corrected by bracketed insertions: a correction is set in italic type; an addition in roman type.   Words or phrases underlined in the source text are printed in italics.   Abbreviations and contractions are preserved as found in the source text, and a list of abbreviations is included in the front matter of each volume.

Bracketed insertions are also used to indicate omitted text that deals with an unrelated subject (in roman type) or that remains classified after declassification review (in italic type). The amount of material not declassified has been noted by indicating the number of lines or pages of source text that were omitted. Entire documents withheld for declassification purposes have been accounted for and are listed with headings, source notes, and number of pages not declassified in their chronological place. All brackets that appear in the source text are so identified by footnotes.

The first footnote to each document indicates the source of the document, original classification, distribution, and drafting information. This note also provides the background of important documents and policies and indicates whether the President or his major policy advisers read the document.

Editorial notes and additional annotation summarize pertinent material not printed in the volume, indicate the location of additional documentary sources, provide references to important related documents printed in other volumes, describe key events, and provide summaries of and citations to public statements that supplement and elucidate the printed documents. Information derived from memoirs and other first-hand accounts has been used when appropriate to supplement or explicate the official record.

The numbers in the index refer to document numbers rather than to page numbers.

Advisory Committee on Historical Diplomatic Documentation

The Advisory Committee on Historical Diplomatic Documentation, established under the *Foreign Relations* statute, reviews records, advises, and makes recommendations concerning the *Foreign Relations* series. The Advisory Committee monitors the overall compilation and editorial process of the series and advises on all aspects of the preparation and declassification of the series. The Advisory Committee does not attempt to review the contents of individual volumes in the series, but it makes recommendations on problems that come to its attention.

The Advisory Committee has not reviewed this volume.

Declassification Review

The Information Response Branch of the Office of IRM Programs and Services, Bureau of Administration, Department of State, conducted the declassification review for the Department of State of documents published in this volume. The review was conducted in accordance with the standards set forth in Executive Order 12958 on Classified National Security Information and applicable laws.

The principle guiding declassification review is to release all information, subject only to the current requirements of national security as embodied in law and regulation. Declassification decisions entailed concurrence of the appropriate geographic and functional bureaus in the Department of State, other concerned agencies of the U.S. Government, and the appropriate foreign governments regarding specific documents of those governments.

The final declassification review of this volume, which began in 1997 and was completed in 2000, resulted in the decision to withhold about .9 percent of the documentation proposed for publication; 3 documents were withheld in full.

Acknowledgments

The editors wish to acknowledge the assistance of officials at the John F. Kennedy Library of the National Archives and Records Administration, especially Suzanne Forbes, who provided key research assistance. The editors also wish to acknowledge the assistance of historians at the Central Intelligence Agency.

Evan M. Duncan collected, selected, and edited the compilations on United Nations affairs and international scientific matters; Jeffrey A. Soukup the compilation on information policy; and Paul Claussen those on the organization of U.S. foreign policy. David S. Patterson, General Editor of the *Foreign Relations* series, oversaw and coordinated the preparation of the volume. Rita M. Baker and Vicki E. Futscher did the copy and technical editing, and Susan C. Weetman coordinated the final declassification review. Max Franke prepared the index.

Marc J. Susser
The Historian
Bureau of Public Affairs

September 2001

Kennedy Administration Volumes

Following is a list of the volumes in the *Foreign Relations* series for the administration of President John F. Kennedy. The year of publication is in parentheses after the title.

Print Volumes

I	Vietnam, 1961 (1988)
II	Vietnam, 1962 (1990)
III	Vietnam, January–August 1963 (1991)
IV	Vietnam, August–December 1963 (1991)
V	Soviet Union (1998)
VI	Kennedy Khrushchev Exchanges (1996)
VII	Arms Control and Disarmament (1995)
VIII	National Security Policy (1996)
IX	Foreign Economic Policy (1995)
X	Cuba, January 1961–September 1962 (1997)
XI	Cuba, October 1962–December 1963 (1997)
XII	American Republics (1996)
XIII	Western Europe and Canada (1994)
XIV	Berlin Crisis, 1961–1962 (1994)
XV	Berlin Crisis, 1962–1963 (1994)
XVI	Eastern Europe; Cyprus; Greece; Turkey (1994)
XVII	Near East, 1961–1962 (1995)
XVIII	Near East, 1962–1963 (1995)
XIX	South Asia (1996)
XX	Congo Crisis (1995)
XXI	Africa (1996)
XXII	Northeast Asia (1996)
XXIII	Southeast Asia (1995)
XXIV	Laos Crisis (1994)
XXV	Organization of Foreign Policy; Information Policy; United Nations; Scientific Matters (2001)

Microfiche Supplements

Arms Control; National Security; Foreign Economic Policy (Volumes VII, VIII, IX) (1997)
Cuba; American Republics (Volumes X, XI, XII) (1998)
Western Europe; Berlin (Volumes XIII, XIV, XV) (1995)
Near East; Congo; Africa (Volumes XVII, XVIII, XX, XXI) (1997)
Northeast Asia; Laos (XXII, XXIV) (1996)

Contents

Sources

Sources for the Foreign Relations Series

The *Foreign Relations* statute requires that the published record in the *Foreign Relations* series include all records needed to provide comprehensive documentation on major U.S. foreign policy decisions and significant U.S. diplomatic activity. It further requires that government agencies, departments, and other entities of the U.S. Government engaged in foreign policy formulation, execution, or support cooperate with the Department of State Historian by providing full and complete access to records pertinent to foreign policy decisions and actions and by providing copies of selected records. Many of the sources consulted in the preparation of this volume have been declassified and are available for review at the National Archives and Records Administration.

The editors of the *Foreign Relations* series have complete access to all the retired records and papers of the Department of State: the central files of the Department; the special decentralized files ("lot files") of the Department at the bureau, office, and division levels; the files of the Department's Executive Secretariat, which contain the records of international conferences and high-level official visits, correspondence with foreign leaders by the President and Secretary of State, and memoranda of conversations between the President and Secretary of State and foreign officials; and the files of overseas diplomatic posts. All the Department's indexed central files for these years have been permanently transferred to the National Archives and Records Administration at College Park, Maryland (Archives II). Almost all the Department's decentralized office (or lot) files covering this period, which the National Archives deems worthy of permanent retention, have been transferred or are in the process of being transferred from the Department's custody to Archives II. During the period in which this volume was compiled, some lot files were kept in the Washington National Records Center at Suitland, Maryland.

The editors of the *Foreign Relations* series also have full access to the papers of President Kennedy and other White House foreign policy records. Presidential papers maintained and preserved at the Presidential libraries include some of the most significant foreign affairs-related documentation from the Department of State and other Federal agencies including the National Security Council, the Central Intelligence Agency, the Department of Defense, and the Joint Chiefs of Staff.

Sources for Foreign Relations, 1961–1963, Volume XXV

In preparing this volume, the editors made use of the Presidential papers and other White House records at the John F. Kennedy Library. Most of the relevant documents were found in the Departments and Agencies Series or the Subjects Series of the National Security Files. The papers of Assistant Secretary of State for International Organization Affairs Harlan Cleveland, and the papers of Special Assistant to the President Arthur Schlesinger, Jr. were also consulted. Vice President Lyndon B. Johnson was Chairman of the National Aeronautics and Space Council; therefore documents from the Vice Presidential Files and the Vice President's Science File in the Lyndon B. Johnson Library were consulted. Research was also done in the Papers of Ambassador Adlai E. Stevenson in the Princeton University Library.

The records of the Department of State were of primary importance in the compilations on the United Nations and general international issues. The Department's central files contain the cable traffic between the Department and the U.S. Mission to the United Nations, U.S. representatives to other UN agencies, and U.S. diplomatic missions; memoranda of diplomatic conversations; and memoranda proposing action or providing information. Some important documents are found only in the Department's lot files. The conference files maintained by the Executive Secretariat contain briefing materials as well as records of conversations. Lot files of the Bureau of International Organization Affairs and of the Office of International Scientific and Technological Affairs were especially useful.

Records of the U.S. Information Agency and the U.S. Arms Control and Disarmament Agency, the USIA Historical Collection, and the Historical Reference Collection of the National Aeronautics and Space Administration supplemented the State Department records.

Department of State historians also have access to records of the Department of Defense, particularly the records of the Secretaries of Defense and their major assistants and the Joint Chiefs of Staff.

The Central Intelligence Agency provides the Department of State historians access to intelligence documents from records in its custody and at the Presidential libraries. This access is arranged and facilitated by the CIA's History Staff, part of the Center for the Study of Intelligence, pursuant to a May 1992 memorandum of understanding.

In the course of preparing this volume, the editors proposed to include the texts of 15 documents and summaries of several others regarding the activities of the President's Foreign Intelligence Advisory Board. The Board, which was established by Executive Order 10938 in May 1961, advised the President "with respect to the objectives and conduct of foreign intelligence and related activities of the United States which are required in the interests of foreign policy and national defense and security." Access for Department of State historians to PFIAB's records was established by an agreement of 1996. The Board subsequently suspended the research access for Department historians for security reasons in February 2000, and, at PFIAB's request, the Historian's Office returned to PFIAB all copies of documents obtained from PFIAB files, before declassification of any of those records was approved by PFIAB. Because there was no likelihood that the access agreement with PFIAB would soon be reinstated, the Historian's Office decided to proceed with the publication of this volume without PFIAB documents. PFIAB documents relative to the Kennedy presidency will continue to be sought for inclusion in the *Foreign Relations* series and, when obtained and declassified, will be published in a subsequent volume.

Almost all of this documentation has been made available for use in the *Foreign Relations* series thanks to the consent of the agencies mentioned, the assistance of their staffs, and especially the cooperation and support of the National Archives and Records Administration.

The following list identifies the particular files and collections used in the preparation of this volume. The declassification and transfer to the National Archives of the Department of State records is in process, and most of these records are already available for public review at the National Archives. The declassification review of other records is going forward in accordance with the provisions of Executive Orders 12958 and 13142, under which all records over 25 years old, except file series exemptions requested by agencies and approved by the President, should be reviewed for declassification by 2003.

Unpublished Sources

Department of State

Central Files. See National Archives and Records Administration below.

Lot Files. These files may be transferred to the National Archives and Records Administration at College Park, Maryland, Record Group 59.

USIA Historical Collection
   Reference works, visual materials, transcripts of oral histories, and copies of official records documenting the activities and history of the USIA and its predecessor agencies

National Archives and Records Administration

Record Group 59, Records of the Department of State

Central Files. In February 1963 the Department of State switched from a decimal file number to a subject-numeric system for its Central Files.

110.10: Organization, functions, rules, and regulations of the Department of State
301: United Nations
303: Admission of new members into the United Nations
310 and subseries: United Nations: charter; membership; delegations
320 and subseries: United Nations General Assembly
324.8411: United Nations High Commissioner's Office for Refugees
330 and subseries: United Nations Security Council
341.7: United Nations Human Rights Commission
341.9: United Nations Narcotic Drugs Commission
345.2: United Nations Narcotic Drug Supervisory Body
399.731: Law of the Sea
611.61: Political relations between the United States and the Soviet Union
701.022: U.S. policy toward outer space
701.56311: U.S. space tracking stations
702 and subseries: Antarctica
911.802: Communications, United States, space travel and artificial satellites
ORG 1: Organization and administration, general policy, plans, coordination
ORG 1 OSD–STATE: General policy, plans, coordination, Office of the Secretary of Defense and the Department of State
ORG 8: Organization and administration: establishment, functions, reorganization
POL 10 UN: Political affairs and relations, colonialism and imperialism
POL 27–4 UN: Political affairs and relations, use of international forces
REF 3 UN: Refugees and migration, organizations and conferences
SCI 11–1 ANT: Science and technology, area research programs, Antarctica
SOC 11–5: Social conditions, narcotic drugs
SOC 14: Social conditions, human rights and race relations
SOC 14 ECOSOC: Social conditions, human rights and race relations, UN Economic and Social Council
SOC 14 UN: Social conditions, human rights and race relations, United Nations
SP 1–1 US–USSR: Space and astronautics, international cooperation, United States and the Soviet Union
SP 6 UN: Space and astronautics, peaceful uses of space
SP 10: Space and astronautics, space flight and exploration
SP 10 US: Space and astronautics, space flight and exploration, United States
SP 10 US/MERCURY: Space flight and exploration, U.S. Project Mercury
SP 10 US/GEMINI: Space flight and exploration, U.S. Project Gemini
SP 10 US/USSR: Space flight and exploration, United States and the Soviet Union
SP 16: Space and astronautics, fragments, unidentified flying objects
UN 3 GA: United Nations General Assembly, meetings and sessions
UN 3 SC: United Nations Security Council, meetings and sessions
UN 3–1: United Nations, meetings, sessions, agenda
UN 6 CHICOM: United Nations, membership and association, Communist China
UN 8: United Nations, structure and functions
UN 8 SC: United Nations, structure and functions, Security Council
UN 10: United Nations, budget and finance
UN 10–4: United Nations, budget and finance, contributions

Lot Files

Conference Files: Lot 65 D 366
>   Records of official visits by heads of government and foreign ministers to the United States, and international conferences attended by the President or Secretary of State, 1961, maintained by the Executive Secretariat

Conference Files: Lot 65 D 533
    Records of official visits by heads of government and foreign ministers to the United States, and international conferences attended by the President or Secretary of State, 1962, maintained by the Executive Secretariat

Conference Files: Lot 66 D 110
    Records of official visits by heads of government and foreign ministers to the United States, and international conferences attended by the President or Secretary of State, 1961–1964, maintained by the Executive Secretariat

IO Files: Lot 64 D 191
    Woodruff Wallner Subject Files

IO Files: Lot 67 D 378
    Deputy Assistant Secretary of State Richard N. Gardner's files, 1961–1965

IO/OES Files: Lot 68 D 379
    Files of the Office of International Economic and Social Affairs, Bureau of International Organization Affairs, Communications Satellites, 1962–1967

IO/OES Files: Lot 69 D 169
    Files of the Office of International Economic and Social Affairs, Bureau of International Organization Affairs, including records pertaining to Antarctica

IO/UNP Files: Lot 71 D 504
    Division of Political and Security Affairs, Office of UN Political Affairs, Bureau of International Organization Affairs, UN General Assembly Position Papers, 1953–1967

IO/UNP/ODA Files: Lot 69 D 130
    Files of the Division of Dependent Area Affairs, Office of UN Political Affairs, Bureau of International Organization Affairs

Management Staff Files: Lot 69 D 434
    Miscellaneous Subject Files of the Management Staff, Deputy Under Secretary of State for Administration and Deputy Assistant Secretary of State for Organization and Management; includes Interagency Liaison Files, 1962–1968

Presidential Correspondence: Lot 66 D 204
    Exchanges of correspondence between the President and the heads of foreign governments for 1953–1964, maintained by the Executive Secretariat

President's Memoranda of Conversation: Lot 66 D 149
    Cleared memoranda of Presidential conversations with foreign visitors, 1956–1964, maintained by the Executive Secretariat

Rusk Files: Lot 72 D 192
    Files of Secretary of State Dean Rusk, 1961–1969, including texts of speeches, miscellaneous correspondence files, White House correspondence, chronological files, and memoranda of telephone conversations

SCI Files: Lot 65 D 473
    Central Files of the Office of International Scientific and Technological Affairs, September 1962–December 1963

S/P Files: Lot 67 D 548
    Subject files, country files, chronological files, documents, drafts, and related correspondence of the Policy Planning Staff, 1957–1961

S/P Files: Lot 70 D 199
  Files of the Policy Planning Council for 1963–1964

S/S–NSC Files: Lot 70 D 265
  Master set of papers pertaining to National Security Council meetings, including policy papers, position papers, and administration for 1961–1966, maintained by the Executive Secretariat

S/S–NSC Files: Lot 72 D 316
  Master file of National Security Action Memoranda (NSAMs), 1961–1968, maintained by the Executive Secretariat

S/S–NSC (Miscellaneous) Files: Lot 66 D 95
  Administrative and miscellaneous National Security Council files, including NSC Records of Action, for 1947–1963, maintained by the Executive Secretariat

Washington National Records Center, Suitland, Maryland

Record Group 306, Records of the U.S. Information Agency

USIA Files: Lot 64 D 171
  Chronological Files of the Director (Edward R. Murrow)

USIA Files: Lot 67 D 317
  Files of the Office of the Director, 1961

USIA Files: Lot 67 D 333
  Files maintained by the Office of the Director, 1962

USIA Files: Lot 68 D 393
  Director's Staff Meeting Notes

USIA Files: Lot 68 A 4933

USIA Files: Lot 70 D 449
  Records maintained by the Office of the Director, 1963

USIA Files: Lot 88 A 18

Record Group 383, Records of the Arms Control and Disarmament Agency

ACDA/DD Files: FRC 77 A 17
  Files of Deputy Director Adrian S. Fisher for 1961–1969

National Aeronautics and Space Administration

Historical Reference Collection
  Correspondence relating to the meetings between Deputy Administrator Hugh L. Dryden and Soviet Academician A. A. Blagonravov during 1962 and 1963

Central Intelligence Agency

DCI (McCone) Files, Job 80–B01285A

DCI (Dulles) Files, Job 80–B1676R

Dwight D. Eisenhower Library, Abilene, Kansas

Gordon Gray Papers

President's Office Files

Records of the Special Assistant for National Security Affairs

White House Office Files
    Project Clean Up

Whitman File
    Presidential Transition Series
    NSC Records

John F. Kennedy Library, Boston, Massachusetts

Cleveland Papers
    Papers of Harlan Cleveland, Assistant Secretary of State for International
    Organization Affairs, 1961–1965

National Security Files
    Bundy Chron Files
    Bundy Files
    Bundy Memoranda to the President
    Departments and Agencies Series
    Meetings and Memoranda Series
    Subjects Series

President's Appointment Books

President's Office Files
    Staff Memos

Arthur M. Schlesinger Papers
    Papers of Arthur Schlesinger, Jr., Special Assistant to President Kennedy, 1961–1963

Wiesner Papers

White House Central Subject Files

Lyndon B. Johnson Library, Austin, Texas

Vice Presidential File

Vice President's Science File

Office Files of Bill D. Moyers

National Security File
    Subject File

Rusk Appointment Book

Princeton University, Seeley G. Mudd Manuscript Library,
Princeton, New Jersey

Stevenson Papers
    Papers of Adlai E. Stevenson, includes his tenure as U.S. Ambassador to the United
    Nations, 1961–1965

Abbreviations

A-A, African and Asian
AAUN, American Association for the United Nations
ACABQ, Advisory Committee on Administrative and Budgetary Questions, United Nations
ACDA, Arms Control and Disarmament Agency
ACDA/DD, Office of the Deputy Director, Arms Control and Disarmament Agency
ACDA/IR, Office of the Assistant Director for International Relations, Arms Control and Disarmament Agency
AEC, Atomic Energy Commission
AES, Adlai E. Stevenson
AF, Bureau of African Affairs, Department of State
AFRTS, Armed Forces Radio and Television Service
AICBM, anti-intercontinental ballistic missile
AID, Agency for International Development
Amb, Ambassador
AmEmbassy, American Embassy
ARA, Bureau of Inter-American Affairs, Department of State
ARPA, Advanced Research Projects Agency
ASAF, Asian-African, Asia-Africa
AT&T, American Telephone and Telegraph Company

BBC, British Broadcasting Corporation
BMEWS, Ballistic Missile Early Warning System
BNSP, basic national security policy

CA, circular airgram
CBS, Columbia Broadcasting System
CCF, Cooperative Commonwealth Federation (Canadian political party)
CENTO, Central Treaty Organization
CEPT, European Conference of Postal and Telecommunications Administrations
ChiComs, Chinese Communists
ChiRep, Chinese representation
CIA, Central Intelligence Agency
CINCCARIB, Commander in Chief, Caribbean
cirtel, circular telegram
comite, committee
cmte, committee
CORE, Congress on Racial Equality
COSPAR, Committee on Space Research
CTF, Commander Task Force

DCI, Director of Central Intelligence
del, delegation
DelOff, delegation officer
Depcirtel, Department of State circular telegram
Dept, Department
Deptel, Department of State telegram
DIA, Defense Intelligence Agency
DOD, Department of Defense

ECOSOC, Economic and Social Council, United Nations
EE, Eastern Europe
ELDO, European Launcher Development Organization
ELINT, electronic intelligence
ENDC, Eighteen-Nation Disarmament Conference
ERM, Edward R. Murrow
ESRO, European Space Research Organization
EUR, Bureau of European Affairs, Department of State
ExtAff, External Affairs

FAA, Federal Aviation Administration
FAO, Food and Agricultural Organization
FCC, Federal Communications Commission
FE, Bureau of Far Eastern Affairs, Department of State
FonMin, Foreign Minister, Foreign Ministry
FonOff, Foreign Office
FR, Federal Register
FRG, Federal Republic of Germany
FSO, Foreign Service officer
FSR, Foreign Service Reserve
FY, fiscal year
FYI, for your information

G, Deputy Under Secretary of State for Political Affairs
GA, United Nations General Assembly
GATT, General Agreement on Tariffs and Trade
GDR, German Democratic Republic
GNP, gross national product
GOP, Government of Portugal
GOT, Government of Turkey
G/PM, Office of the Deputy Assistant Secretary of State for Politico-Military
Affairs
GPO, General Post Office, United Kingdom
GRC, Government of the Republic of China

HEW, Department of Health, Education and Welfare

I, Office of the Deputy Director, U.S. Information Agency
IAEA, International Atomic Energy Agency
IAS, Office of the Soviet Union and Eastern Europe, U.S. Information Agency

IASP, International Atmospheric Science Program
IAU, International Astronomical Union
IBRD, International Bank for Reconstruction and Development
ICA, International Cooperation Administration
ICAO, International Civil Aviation Organization
ICBM, intercontinental ballistic missile
ICC, International Control Commission
ICEM, Intergovernmental Committee for European Migration
ICJ, International Court of Justice
ICSU, International Council of Scientific Unions
ICWRY, International Conference for World Refugee Year
IGY, International Geophysical Year
ILC, International Law Commission
ILO, International Labor Organization
IMF, International Monetary Fund
IMG, Informational Media Guaranty
IMSP, International Meteorological Service Program
IMS, Motion Picture Service, U.S. Information Agency
INR, Bureau of Intelligence and Research, Department of State
IO, Bureau of International Organization Affairs, Department of State
IO/OIA, Office of International Administration, Bureau of International
    Organization Affairs, Department of State
IO/OES, Office of International Economic and Social Affairs, Bureau of
    International Organization Affairs, Department of State
IO/UNP, Office of United Nations Political and Security Affairs, Bureau of
    International Organization Affairs, Department of State; later Office of
    United Nations Political Affairs
IOP, Office of Policy and Plans, U.S. Information Agency
IPS, Press and Publications Service, U.S. Information Agency
IRBM, intermediate-range ballistic missile
IRI, Office of Research and Analysis, U.S. Information Agency
IRR, Research and Reference Service, U.S. Information Agency
IRS, Director of the Information Research Service, U.S. Information Agency
ISA, Office of International Scientific Affairs, Department of State
IT&T, International Telephone and Telegraph Corporation
ITU, International Telecommunications Union

JCS, Joint Chiefs of Staff

KW, kilowatt

L, Office of the Legal Adviser, Department of State
LA, Latin America or Latin American
LDCs, less-developed countries
L/SFP, Assistant Legal Adviser for Special Functional Problems, Department
    of State
L/UNA, Assistant Legal Adviser for United Nations Affairs, Department of
    State

M, Under Secretary of State for Political Affairs
MA, Mercury-Atlas
memcon, memorandum of conversation
MOA, Ministry of Aviation (United Kingdom)
MODS, Military Orbital Development System
MSTS, Military Sea Transport Service

NAACP, National Association for the Advancement of Colored People
NAC, North Atlantic Council
NACA, National Advisory Committee on Aeronautics
Narcom, UN Commission on Narcotic Drugs
NASA, National Aeronautics and Space Administration
NASC, National Aeronautics and Space Council
NATO, North Atlantic Treaty Organization
NCS, National Communications System
NMCC, National Military Command Center
NMCS, National Military Command System
NGO, non-governmental organization
NOA, new obligational authority
NSAM, National Security Action Memorandum
NSF, National Science Foundation
NEA, Bureau of Near Eastern and South Asian Affairs, Department of State
Niact, night action; communications indicator requiring attention by the recipient at any hour of the day or night
NRO, National Reconnaissance Office
NRP, National Reconnaissance Program
NSC, National Security Council

OAS, Organization of American States
OCB, Operations Coordinating Board
OECD, Organization for Economic Cooperation and Development
OEEC, Organization for European Economic Cooperation
OEP, Office of Emergency Preparedness
OM/MS, Office of Management, Department of State
ONUC, United Nations Operations in the Congo
OST, Office of Science and Technology

P, Bureau of Public Affairs, Department of State
PAG, Personnel Advisory Group
PCC, Palestine Conciliation Commission
PCI, Partito Comunista Italiano (Italian Communist Party)
PFIAB, President's Foreign Intelligence Advisory Board
P.L., Public Law
POL, petroleum, oil, and lubricants
POLAD, political adviser
PSAC, President's Science Advisory Committee
PTT, Ministry of Posts, Telegraphs, and Telephones (France)
PX, post exchange

R&D, research and development
RCA, Radio Corporation of America
reftel, reference telegram
rep, representative
res(es), resolution(s)
RFE, Radio Free Europe
RG, Record Group
RIAS, Radio in the American Sector, West Berlin
RL, Radio Liberty
ROK, Republic of Korea
R-U, Ruanda-Urundi

S/AE, Office of the Special Assistant for Atomic Energy and Outer Space, Department of State
S/AL, Ambassador at Large
SANE, National Committee for a Sane Nuclear Policy
SAR, search and rescue
SC, Security Council, United Nations
SCA/ORM, Bureau of Security and Consular Affairs, Office of Refugee and Migration Affairs, Department of State
SCAR, Special Committee on Antarctic Research
SCI, Office of International Scientific Affairs, Department of State
SEATO, Southeast Asia Treaty Organization
Secdel, Secretary of State's delegation
Secto, series indicator for telegrams from the Secretary of State (or his delegation) at international conferences to the Department of State
SNAP, Systems for Nuclear Auxiliary Power
Sov, Soviet
SPA, Office of Southwest Pacific Affairs, Bureau of Far Eastern Affairs, Department of State
S/P, Policy Planning Council, Department of State
SPC, Special Political Committee, United Nations
SR, Southern Rhodesia
S/S, Executive Secretariat, Department of State
S/SA, Office of the Science Adviser, Department of State
SSR, Soviet Socialist Republic
SWA, Southwest Africa
SYG, Secretary-General of the United Nations

TC, Trusteeship Council, United Nations
TFX, Tactical fighter, experimental
TIAS, Treaties and International Agreements of the United States

UAM, Union Africaine et Malagache (African and Malagasy Union)
UAR, United Arab Republic
UCMJ, Uniform Code of Military Justice
U/FW, Special Assistant for Fisheries and Wildlife, Department of State
UK, United Kingdom
UKDel, United Kingdom Delegation at the United Nations

UN, United Nations
UNCTAD, United Nations Conference on Trade and Development
UNDA, United Nations Development Authority
UNEF, United Nations Emergency Force (in the Middle East)
UNESCO, United Nations Educational, Scientific and Cultural Organization
UNGA, United Nations General Assembly
UNHCR, United Nations High Commissioner for Refugees
UNICEF, United Nations Childrens' Fund
UNOC, United Nations Operations in the Congo
unodir, unless otherwise directed
UNRRA, United Nations Relief and Rehabilitation Administration
UNRWA, United Nations Relief and Works Agency for Arab Refugees from
    Palestine
UNTS, United Nations Treaty Series
UNTSO, United Nations Truce Supervision Organization
UNYOM, United Nations Observation Group in Yemen
UPU, Universal Postal Union
urtel, your telegram
USAF, United States Air Force
USC, United States Code
USDel, United States Delegation
USEP, United States Escapee Program
USG, United States Government
USGADel, United States Delegation to the UN General Assembly
USIA, United States Information Agency
USIB, United States Intelligence Board
USIS, United States Information Service
USNR, U.S. Naval Reserve
USOM, United States Operations Mission
USSR, Union of Soviet Socialist Republics
UST, United States Treaties and Other International Agreements
USUN, United States Mission at the United Nations

VIPs, very important persons
VOA, Voice of America
VUNC, Voice of the UN Command in Korea

WE, Western European
WHO, World Health Organization
WMO, World Meteorological Organization
WWW, World Weather Watch

Persons

Abram, Morris, U.S. representative, Sub-Commission on Prevention of Discrimination and Protection of Minorities, UN Commission on Human Rights

Acheson, Dean, former Secretary of State, 1949–1953

Adebo, S. O., Permanent Representative of Nigeria at the United Nations

Aga Khan, Sadruddin, Deputy UN High Commissioner for Refugees from February 1, 1962

Aiken, George D., Republican Senator from Vermont

Akalovsky, Alexander, Officer in Charge of General Disarmament Negotiations, U.S. Disarmament Administration

Algard, Ole, Counselor, Norwegian Mission at the United Nations, 1962

Alphand, Herve, French Ambassador to the United States

Amadeo, Mario, Permanent Representative of Argentina at the United Nations, 1961

Anderson, William O., Officer in Charge, Multilateral Political Relations, Office of Soviet Union Affairs, Bureau of European Affairs, Department of State, August 1961–August 1963

Anslinger, Harvey J., Commissioner of Narcotics, Department of the Treasury

Arkadev, Georgy P., Under Secretary-General for Political and Security Council Affairs, United Nations

Armstrong, Willis C., Director, Office of British Commonwealth and Northern European Affairs, Bureau of European Affairs, Department of State, from September 1962

Bacher, Robert F., Chairman of an ad hoc group in the Office of the President's Special Assistant for Science and Technology, 1961

Baker, William O., Member, Sub-Committee on Communications, National Security Council

Ball, George W., Under Secretary of State for Economic Affairs, January 30, 1961–December 3, 1961; thereafter Under Secretary of State

Banerji, B. N., Indian Representative to the 18th Session of the United Nations Commission on Narcotic Drugs

Bates, Charles C., U.S. Antarctic Observer, 1963–1964

Battle, Lucius D., Executive Secretary, Department of State, March 16, 1961–May 2, 1962; thereafter Assistant Secretary of State for Educational and Cultural Affairs

Beam, Jacob D., Assistant Director for International Relations, Arms Control and Disarmament Agency, from 1962

BeLieu, Kenneth, Member, Ad Hoc Committee on Space

Belk, Samuel E., Member, National Security Council Staff

Bell, David E., Administrator, Agency for International Development, from December 17, 1961

Bell, James D., Director, Office of Southwest Pacific Affairs, Bureau of Far Eastern Affairs, Department of State, from June 1960

Benhima, Ahmed Taibi, Permanent Representative of Morocco at the United Nations, 1963

Benites, Leopoldo, Permanent Representative of Ecuador at the United Nations

Bennett, Lowell, Director, Office of Public Information, U.S. Information Agency

Benton, William, U.S. member of the UNESCO Executive Board, 1963

Berard, Armand, Permanent Representative of France at the United Nations, 1961

Bevans, Charles I., Assistant Legal Adviser for Treaty Affairs, Department of State

Bindzi, Benoit, Deputy Representative of Cameroon at the United Nations, 1961; Permanent Representative, 1962–1963

Bingham, Jonathan B., U.S. Representative at the United Nations Trusteeship Council

Black, Eugene, President of the International Bank for Reconstruction and Development until January 1, 1963

Blagonravov, Anatoliy Arkadievich, Chairman of the Commission on Exploration and Utilization of Outer Space, Academy of Sciences of the USSR

Blumenthal, W. Michael, Deputy Assistant Secretary of State for Economic Affairs; Chairman, Special Subcommittee on Communications Satellites, National Security Council

Bohlen, Charles E., Special Assistant to the Secretary of State, 1961; Ambassador to France from September 4, 1962

Boland, Frederick H., Permanent Representative of Ireland at the United Nations; President of the 15th Session of the UN General Assembly

Boone, Admiral W. F., Deputy Associate Administrator for Defense Affairs, National Aeronautics and Space Administration

Bowles, Chester, Under Secretary of State, January 24–December 3, 1961

Brady, Leslie S., Assistant Director (Soviet Union and Eastern Europe), U.S. Information Agency

Bronk, Detlev W., President of the National Academy of Sciences, 1950–1962

Brooke, Edgar D., Director of Media Content, U.S. Information Agency, 1961

Brown, Harold, Director of Research and Engineering, Department of Defense

Brown, Richard R., Chief of the U.S. Delegation, Executive Committee of the Program of the UN High Commissioner for Refugees, October 1960 and May 1962; Director, Office of Refugee and Migration Affairs, Department of State, 1961

Brubeck, William H., Executive Secretary, Department of State, May 14, 1962–July 20, 1963; thereafter Member, National Security Council Staff

Bruce, David K. E., Ambassador to the United Kingdom from February 22, 1961

Buckley, John L., U.S. Antarctic Observer, 1963–1964

Buffum, William B., Deputy Director, Office of United Nations Political and Security Affairs, Bureau of International Organization Affairs, Department of State, from August 1961

Bugayev, Victor Antonovich, Director, Central Institute of Weather Forecasting, State Administration of the Hydrometeorological Service, Council of Ministers of the Soviet Union

Bunche, Ralph J., Under Secretary-General of the United Nations for Special Political Affairs

Bundy, McGeorge, President's Special Assistant for National Security Affairs

Bundy, William P., Deputy Assistant Secretary of Defense for International Security Affairs

Burdett, William C., Deputy Assistant Secretary of State for European Affairs from September 1962

Burnett, F. W., Representative, U.S. Weather Bureau, Meeting of U.S.-USSR Bilateral Working Groups on Space Science Cooperation

Butler, R.A., British Foreign Secretary from October 20, 1963

Butterworth, W. Walton, Ambassador to Canada from October 4, 1962

Cadieux, Marcel, Canadian Deputy Under Secretary of State for External Affairs, 1961–1963

Cargo, William I., Director, Office of United Nations Political and Security Affairs, Bureau of International Organization Affairs, Department of State, until June 1961

Carlson, Delmar R., Officer in Charge, Canadian Affairs, Bureau of European Affairs, Department of State, until September 1963

Carter, Lieutenant General Marshall S., Deputy Director, Central Intelligence Agency; Acting Director, May 1962

Carter, William G., Special Assistant for International Space Communications, Bureau of Economic Affairs, Department of State, October 1962–July 1963

Chapman, Daniel A., Director, Division of Narcotic Drugs, United Nations, from June 1963

Charyk, Joseph V., Under Secretary of the Air Force; later President, Communications Satellite Corporation

Chayes, Abram, Legal Adviser of the Department of State from February 6, 1961

Ch'en Ch'eng, Vice President and Prime Minister of the Republic of China

Chiang Kai-shek, President of the Republic of China

Cleveland, Harlan M., Assistant Secretary of State for International Organization Affairs from February 20, 1961

Cline, Ray S., Deputy Director (Intelligence), Central Intelligence Agecy

Coerr, Wymberley DeR., Deputy Assistant Secretary of State for Inter-American Affairs until March 1962

Cohn, Aline, U.S. Representative, UN High Commissioner for Refugees, 1961

Coombs, Philip R., Assistant Secretary of State for Educational and Cultural Affairs, March 23, 1961–June 4, 1962

Cordier, Andrew W., Executive Assistant and Under Secretary-General in Charge of General Assembly and Related Affairs of the United Nations

Coulibaly, Sori, Permanent Representative of Mali at the United Nations, 1963

Daddah, Moktar Ould, President of Mauritania

Dadgar, M., Iranian Representative to the 18th Session of the UN Commission on Narcotic Drugs

D'Arcy, Jean, Director of Radio and Visual Services Division, UN Office of Public Information

Davis, Richard H., Deputy Assistant Secretary of State for European Affairs from December 1959; Principal Deputy Assistant Secretary of State for European Affairs from September 1962

De Gaulle, Charles, President of France

Dean, Sir Patrick, Permanent Representative of the United Kingdom at the United Nations

Devine, James T., Minister, U.S. Mission to International Organizations, Geneva; Chairman, U.S. Delegation to the Eighth Session of the Executive Committee of the UN High Commissioner for Refugees Program, 1963

Deyine, Sidi Mohamed, Mauritanian Foreign Minister

Diallo, Telli, Permanent Representative of Guinea at the United Nations

Drumwright, Everett F., Ambassador to the Republic of China until March 8, 1962

Dryden, Hugh L., Deputy Administrator, National Aeronautics and Space Administration

Duke, Angier Biddle, Chief of Protocol, Department of State, from January 24, 1961

Dumont, Donald, United Nations Adviser, Bureau of African Affairs, Department of State, from January 1961; Deputy Director, Office of Western African and Malagasy Affairs, September 1961–October 1962

Dutton, Frederick G., Assistant Secretary of State for Congressional Relations from November 29, 1961

Eisenhower, Dwight D., President of the United States until January 20, 1961

Evans, Allan, Deputy Director for Research, Bureau of Intelligence and Research, Department of State

Evseyev, Petr Karpovich, Director, Weather Computing Center, State Hydrometeorological Service, Council of Ministers of the Soviet Union

Falk, Elmer M., Director, Office of Refugee and Migration Affairs, Department of State from November 1962

Farley, Philip J., Special Assistant for Atomic Energy and Outer Space, Department of State, August 1961–March 1962

Fedorenko, Nikolai Trofimovich. T., Permanent Representative of the Soviet Union at the United Nations, 1963

Feldman, Myer, Member, National Security Council Staff

Fennemore, George M., Office of International Economic and Social Affairs, Bureau of International Organization Affairs, Department of State, from December 1962

Field, Winston, Southern Rhodesian Prime Minister from December 17, 1962

Finger, Seymour M., Chief, Economic and Social Affairs Section, U.S. Mission at the United Nations

Fisher, Adrian S., Deputy Director, Arms Control and Disarmament Agency

Fisher, Wayne W., Office of the Special Assistant for Antarctic Affairs, Bureau of International Organizations, Department of State, to September 1961

Flores Avendano, Colonel Guillermo, Permanent Representative of Guatemala at the United Nations, 1962–1963

Flues, A. Gilmore, Assistant Secretary of the Treasury; Special Consultant to the Secretary of the Treasury, 1962

Foster, William C., Director of the U.S. Arms Control and Disarmament Agency from October 5, 1961

Fredericks, J. Wayne, Deputy Assistant Secretary of State for African Affairs from May 1961

Freund, Richard B., Deputy Assistant Director for International Relations, Arms Control and Disarmament Agency from April 1963

Frutkin, Arnold W., Director, Office of International Programs, National Aeronautics and Space Administration; later Assistant Administrator for International Affairs

Fulbright, J. William, Democratic Senator from Arkansas and Chairman of the Senate Foreign Relations Committee

Fulton, James G., Republican Congressman from Pennsylvania

Furnas, Howard, Deputy Special Assistant for Atomic Energy and Outer Space, Department of State, April 1961–July 1962

Galbraith, John Kenneth, Ambassador to India, March 29, 1961–July 12, 1963

Gardner, Richard N., Deputy Assistant Secretary of State for International Organization Affairs from April 1961

Gardner, Trevor, Member, Ad Hoc Committee on Space

Garthoff, Raymond L., Special Assistant for Politico–Military Affairs, Department of State from February 1962

Gates, Thomas S., Jr., Secretary of Defense until January 20, 1961

Gathright, Wreatham E., Office of the Special Assistant for Atomic Energy and Outer Space, Department of State from March 1961; Chief, Political Research and Analysis Division, Arms Control and Disarmament Agency from April 1962

Gilpatric, Roswell L., Deputy Secretary of Defense

Gilruth, Robert R., Director, Manned Space Flight Center, National Aeronautics and Space Administration

Giordano, Henry L., Deputy Commissioner of Narcotics, Department of the Treasury

Glenn, Colonel John H., first U.S. astronaut to orbit the Earth, February 20, 1962

Goodpaster, General Andrew, Special Assistant to the Chairman of the Joint Chiefs of Staff

Goodwin, Harold L., Science Adviser, U.S. Information Agency

Gordon, Kermit, Director, Bureau of the Budget; Member of the President's Council of Economic Advisers

Gray, Gordon, President's Special Assistant for National Security Affairs to January 20, 1961

Green, Howard C., Canadian Secretary of State for External Affairs to April 22, 1963

Greenhill, Denis A., Counselor, British Embassy in the United States

Gromyko, Andrei A., Soviet Foreign Minister

Guthrie, John C., Director, Office of Soviet Union Affairs, Bureau of European Affairs, Department of State from June 1961; U.S. Antarctic Observer, 1963–1964

Hagen, John P., Director, Office for the UN Conference, National Aeronautics and Space Administration, 1961; Associate Director for Science and Applications, 1962

Hammarskjöld, Dag, Secretary-General of the United Nations until September 17, 1961

Harriman, W. Averell, Assistant Secretary of State for Far Eastern Affairs, November 29, 1961–April 3, 1963; thereafter Under Secretary of State for Political Affairs

Hartley, Virginia F., Special Assistant, Office of United Nations Political Affairs, Bureau of International Organization Affairs, Department of State, 1963

Hartman, Arthur A., Special Assistant to the Under Secretary of State, January 1962–July 1963

Haseganu, Mihail, Permanent Representative of Romania at the United Nations, 1962–1963

Haskins, Charles A., Member, National Security Council Staff

Hawkins, Richard H., Jr., U.S. Antarctic Observer, 1963–1964

Heeney, Arnold D.P., Canadian Ambassador to the United States to May 1962

Hefner, Frank K., Director, Office of International Administration, Bureau of International Organization Affairs, Department of State, January 1962–June 1963

Hendrick, James P., Deputy Assistant Secretary of the Treasury, 1962

Herrington, William C., Special Assistant for Fisheries and Wildlife, Department of State

Herter, Christian A., Secretary of State until January 20, 1961

Hickenlooper, Bourke B., Republican Senator from Iowa

Hilliker, Grant G., Deputy Executive Secretary from April 1963

Hilsman, Roger, Jr., Director of the Bureau of Intelligence and Research, Department of State, February 19, 1961–April 25, 1963; thereafter Assistant Secretary of State for Far Eastern Affairs

Hoare, Sir Samuel, British Representative to the UN Commission on Human Rights

Hoffman, Paul, Managing Director, United Nations Special Fund

Hollomon, J. Herbert, Assistant Secretary of Commerce for Science and Technology

Holmes, Brainerd, Deputy Associate Administrator for Manned Space Flight Centers, National Aeronautics and Space Administrator

Home, Lord (Alexander Frederick Douglas-Home), British Foreign Secretary, July 27, 1960–October 20, 1963; thereafter Prime Minister

Hornig, Donald F., Member, Ad Hoc Committee on Space; Chairman, Ad Hoc Mercury Panel, 1961

Irvin, Admiral William, Vice Chairman, National Communications Systems Working Group

Ivy, Michel, U.S. Antarctic Observer, 1963–1964

Jackson, Elmore, Special Assistant for UN Planning, Bureau of International Organization Affairs, Department of State from July 1961

Jackson, Henry M., Democratic Senator from Washington; member, Joint Committee on Atomic Energy

Jaffe, Leonard, Director of Communications Systems, National Aeronautics and Space Administration

Jha, C. S., Permanent Representative of India at the United Nations, 1961; Chairman of the UN Human Rights Commission, 1961

Johnson, G. Griffith, Assistant Secretary of State for Economic Affairs, May 12, 1962–May 1, 1965

Johnson, Lyndon B., Vice President of the United States, January 20, 1961–November 22, 1963; thereafter President of the United States

Johnson, U. Alexis, Deputy Under Secretary of State for Political Affairs from April 27, 1961

Johnson, David S., Representative, U.S. Weather Bureau, Meeting of U.S.-USSR Bilateral Working Groups on Space Science Cooperation

Jones, Thomas O., Antarctic Program Director, Office of Special International Programs, National Science Foundation

Jorden, William J., Special Assistant to the Under Secretary of State for Political Affairs

Kalinin, Yuri Dmitrievich, Assistant Director, Institute of Earth Magnetism, Ionosphere and Radio Wave Propagation, Academy of Sciences of the USSR

Kavanau, Lawrence, Special Assistant (Space) to the Director, Defense Research and Engineering, Department of Defense

Kaysen, Carl, Deputy Special Assistant to the President for National Security Affairs

Keldysh, Mstislav V., President, Academy of Sciences of the USSR

Kennan, George F., Ambassador to Yugoslavia, March 7, 1961–July 28, 1963

Kennedy, John F., President of the United States, January 20, 1961–November 22, 1963

Kennedy, Robert F., Attorney General of the United States

Kerley, Ernest L., Assistant Legal Adviser for United Nations Affairs, Department of State, 1963

Khrushchev, Nikita Sergeyevich, First Secretary, Communist Party of the Soviet Union; also Chairman, Soviet Council of Ministers

Killian, James R., Jr., Chairman, President's Foreign Intelligence Advisory Board

Kirk, Alan G., Ambassador to the Republic of China, June 7, 1962–January 18, 1963

Kiselev, E.D., Under Secretary-General of the United Nations for Political and Security Council Affairs, 1962

Kistiakowsky, George B., President's Special Assistant for Science and Technology and Director of the White House Office of Science and Technology

Kitchen, Jeffrey C., Deputy Assistant Secretary of State for Politico-Military Affairs from May 1961

Klutznick, Philip M., U.S. Representative and Chairman of the U.S. Delegation to the Economic and Social Council of the United Nations to December 21, 1962

Kohler, Foy D., Assistant Secretary of State for European Affairs, December 11, 1959–August 19, 1962

Komer, Robert, Member, National Security Council Staff

Kornienko, Georgi M., Counselor of the Embassy of the Soviet Union

Kotschnig, Walter, Director, Office of International Economic and Social Affairs, Bureau of International Organization Affairs, Department of State, to September 1962; Alternate U.S. Representative to the UN Economic and Social Council, 1961

Kozyrev, Semyon Pavlovich, Soviet Ambassador to Italy

Kretzmann, Edwin M. J., Deputy Director, Office of International Scientific Affairs, Department of State, from July 1962

Krishnamoorthy, E. S., Indian Representative to the 18th Session of the UN Commission on Narcotic Drugs, 1963

Land, Edwin H., Member, Ad Hoc Committee on Space

Lande, Adolf, Secretary, Permanent Central Opium Board, United Nations, from June 1963

Lausche, Frank J., Democratic Senator from Ohio

Lehrer, Maxwell, Member, Ad Hoc Committee on Space

Lemnitzer, General Lyman L., Chairman of the Joint Chiefs of Staff until September 30, 1962

Lewis, Commander Price, Jr., member, U.S. delegation to the Consultative Meeting on the Antarctic Treaty, Canberra, Australia, July 1961

Lewis, Samuel W., Special Assistant to the Under Secretary of State, May 1961–February 1962

Liang, C. K., Chinese Representative to the 16th Session of the United Nations Commission on Narcotic Drugs, 1961

Liem, Channing, Permanent Observer of the Republic of Korea at the United Nations

Lindt, Auguste, UN High Commissioner for Refugees, 1951–1960

Liu Chieh, Permanent Representative of the Republic of China at the United Nations, 1962–1963

Lodge, Henry Cabot, Ambassador to Vietnam after August 26, 1963

Loomis, Henry, Director, Broadcasting Service, U.S. Information Agency

Lovell, Sir Bernard, Director, Jodrell Bank Observatory, University of Manchester, England

Ludlow, James M., United Nations Adviser, Bureau of Near Eastern and South Asian Affairs, Department of State

Macmillan, Harold, British Prime Minister until October 20, 1963

Malalasekera, G. P., Permanent Representative of Ceylon at the United Nations, 1962

Malone, Thomas, Representative, National Academy of Sciences, Soviet-American Negotiations on Cooperation in the Field of the Peaceful Utilization of Space

Manning, Robert J., Assistant Secretary of State for Public Affairs, April 4, 1962–July 31, 1964

Martin, Edwin M., Assistant Secretary of State for Inter-American Affairs from May 12, 1962

Martin, Paul, Canadian Secretary of State for External Affairs from April 22, 1963

Matsch, Franz, Permanent Representative of Austria at the United Nations; Chairman, United Nations Committee on the Peaceful Uses of Outer Space

McConaughy, Walter P., Assistant Secretary of State for Far Eastern Affairs, April 18–December 3, 1961

McCone, John A., Director of Central Intelligence from November 29, 1961

McGhee, George C., Counselor and Chairman of the Policy Planning Council, Department of State, February 13–December 3, 1961; Under Secretary of State for Political Affairs, December 4, 1961–March 27, 1963

McMillan, Brockway, Assistant Secretary of the Air Force for Research and Development

McNamara, Robert S., Secretary of Defense

McNutt, Louise, United Nations Adviser, Bureau of Far Eastern Affairs, Department of State, from July 1963

Meeker, Leonard C., Deputy Legal Adviser, Department of State

Meloy, Francis E., Jr., Special Assistant to the Deputy Under Secretary of State for Political Affairs, January 1960–June 1962; thereafter Director of the Office of Western European Affairs

Merchant, Livingston T., Ambassador to Canada, February 20, 1961–May 26, 1962

Miller, George P., Democratic Congressman from California

Milovidov, Igor Viktorovich, Scientific Secretary, Commission on the Research and Utilization of Space, Academy of Sciences of the USSR

Minnich, L. Arthur, Director, Secretariat to the U.S. National Commission for UNESCO, 1963

Morozov, Platon Dmitrievich, Deputy Permanent Representative of the Soviet Union at the United Nations, 1963; Soviet Representative to the UN Scientific and Technical Subcommittee on the Peaceful Uses of Outer Space; also delegate to the United Nations Commission on Human Rights

Mulliken, Otis, Deputy Director, Office of Economic and Social Affairs, Bureau of International Organization Affairs, Department of State

Mundt, Karl E., Republican Senator from South Dakota

Murphy, Robert D., Under Secretary of State for Political Affairs, August–December 1959

Murrow, Edward R., Director, United States Information Agency

Narasimhan, C. V., Under Secretary-General for Special Political Affairs of the United Nations

Newell, Homer E., Director, Office of Space Sciences, National Aeronautics and Space Administration; Chief, U.S. Delegation to the Second Session of the Scientific and Technical Subcommittee of the UN Committee on the Peaceful Uses of Outer Space, May 1963

Nikolic, D., Yugoslav Representative to the 16th Session of the UN Commission on Narcotic Drugs, 1961

Nitze, Paul H., Assistant Secretary of Defense (International Security Affairs)

Noyes, Charles P., Counselor, U.S. Mission to the United Nations from July 1961

Okasaki, Katsuo, Permanent Representative of Japan at the United Nations, 1962–1963

Ormsby-Gore, David, British Ambassador to the United States from October 26, 1961

Orrick, William H. Jr., Deputy Under Secretary of State for Management, July 3, 1962–June 7, 1963; Chairman, Subcommittee on Communications, National Security Council from October 1962

Ostrovski, Y. A., Soviet Alternative Representative, UN Commission on Human Rights, 18th Session, 1962

Owen, George H., Special Assistant for Antarctica Affairs, Bureau of International Organization Affairs, Department of State, March 1959–September 1962

Packard, Robert F., Chief, Outer Space Section, Office of the Special Assistant for Atomic Energy and Outer Space, Department of State January–September 1962; thereafter Officer in Charge of Outer Space Affairs, Office of International Scientific Affairs

Pedersen, Richard F., Senior Adviser, Political Affairs Section, U.S. Mission to the United Nations

Pelcovits, Nathan A., Officer in Charge of United Nations Political Affairs, Bureau of International Organization Affairs, Department of State, August 1961–August 1963; thereafter Special Assistant, Office of United Nations Political Affairs

Persons, General Wilton B., Assistant to President Eisenhower

Peterson, Avery F., Deputy Assistant Secretary of State for Economic Affairs

Phleger, Herman, former Legal Adviser of the Department of State, 1953–1957

Plimpton, Francis, Deputy U.S. Representative to the United Nations Security Council from March 1961

Plimsoll, James, Permanent Representative of Australia at the United Nations

Porter, Richard, U.S. representative at U.S.–Soviet talks on space cooperation, 1962

Purcell, Edward M., Member, Ad Hoc Committee on Space

Quaison-Sackey, Alex, Permanent Representative of Ghana at the United Nations

Rae, S.F., Minister, Canadian Embassy, to May 1962; thereafter Canadian Ambassador and Permanent Representative to the European Office of the United Nations in Geneva

Ramsey, Henry C., Special Assistant to the Deputy Under Secretary of State for Political Affairs from February 1963

Rathjens, George W., U.S. Antarctic Observer, 1963–1964

Read, Benjamin H., Executive Secretary of the Department of State from August 3, 1963

Reed, James A., Assistant Secretary of the Treasury, 1962

Reedy, Rear Admiral. James R., Commanding Officer, U.S. Naval Support Force, Antarctica from November 26, 1962

Reis, Herbert, Office of the Assistant Legal Adviser for United Nations Affairs, Department of State

Rewinkel, Milton C., Acting Director, Office of British Commonwealth and Northern European Affairs, Bureau of European Affairs, Department of State, September 1961–September 1962

Riad, Mahmoud, Permanent Representative of the United Arab Republic at the United Nations

Rice, Edward E., Deputy Assistant Secretary of State for Far Eastern Affairs from January 1962

Ritchie, Charles S. A., Canadian Ambassador from May 25, 1962

Roberts, Ralph S., Deputy Assistant Secretary of State for Management, 1961

Robichaud, Hedard, Canadian Minister of Fisheries, 1963

Robinson, David, Office of the President's Special Assistant for Science and Technology

Robinson, H. Basil, Minister of the Canadian Embassy in the United States

Robinson, Marvin W., Office of International Programs, National Aeronautics and Space Administration

Roe, Arthur, Head, Office of International Science Activities, National Science Foundation

Rollefson, Ragnar, Director, Office of International Scientific Affairs, Department of State, from September 14, 1962

Rossi, Bruno B., Member, Ad Hoc Committee on Space

Rostow, Walt W., Deputy Special Assistant to the President; Counselor and Chairman of the Policy Planning Council, Department of State, November 29, 1961–March 31, 1966

Rowan, Carl, Ambassador to Finland to February 1964; thereafter Director of the U.S. Information Agency

Ruina, J. P., U.S. Antarctic Observer, 1963–1964

Rusk, Dean, Secretary of State from January 21, 1961

Salinger, Pierre, Press Secretary to the President

Sandys, Duncan, British Secretary of State for Commonwealth Relations and Secretary of State for the Colonies

Sastroamidjojo, Ali, former Permanent Representative of Indonesia at the United Nations, 1957–1960

Schaetzel, J. Robert, Special Assistant to the Under Secretary of State for Economic Affairs

Scheffer, Victor B., U.S. Antarctic Observer, 1963–1964

Schlesinger, Arthur M., Jr., Special Assistant to the President

Schmidt, G. Lewis, Assistant Director (Administration), U.S. Information Agency, 1961

Schnyder, Felix, UN High Commissioner for Refugees from February 1, 1961

Schurmann, C. W. A., Permanent Representative of the Netherlands at the United Nations

Schwartz, Abba P., Administrator of the Bureau of Security and Consular Affairs, Department of State

Schwebel, Stephen M., Assistant Legal Adviser for United Nations Affairs, Department of State, from April 1962

Scoville, Herbert, Jr., Deputy Director for Science and Technology, Central Intelligence Agency

Seaborg, Glenn T., Chairman, Atomic Energy Commission

Seamans, Robert C., Jr., Associate Administrator, National Aeronautics and Space Administration, 1962

Seydoux, Roger, Permanent Representative of France at the United Nations, 1962–1963

Shen Chang-huan, Foreign Minister of the Republic of China

Simsarian, James, Officer in Charge of Cultural and Human Rights Affairs, Bureau of International Organization Affairs, Department of State, until September 1962; thereafter Officer in Charge of International Scientific Organizations

Sisco, Joseph J., Director, Office of United Nations Political and Security Affairs, Bureau of International Organization Affairs, Department of State; Deputy Assistant Secretary of State for International Organization Affairs from November 1963

Siscoe, Frank G., Director, Soviet and East European Exchanges Staff, Bureau of European Affairs, Department of State; U.S. Antarctic Observer, 1963–1964

Slim, Mongi, Permanent Representative of Tunisia at the United Nations, 1961; President of the 16th Session of the UN General Assembly; acting as Secretary-General of the United Nations, September 21–November 3, 1961

Smith, Bromley, Executive Secretary, National Security Council

Solodovnikov, Vasily Grigoryevich, Deputy Permanent Representative of the Soviet Union at the United Nations, 1963

Sorensen, Theodore, Special Counsel to the President

Sorensen, Thomas C., Deputy Director for Policy and Plans, U.S. Information Agency, 1961

Sosa Rodriguez, Carlos, Permanent Representative of Venezuela at the United Nations; President of the 18th Session of the UN General Assembly

Sparkman, John J., Democratic Senator from Alabama

Speak, Ralph E., Staff Director, Emergency Planning Committee, National Security Council

Springsteen, George S., Special Assistant to the Under Secretary of State from August 1962

Staats, Elmer B., Deputy Director, Bureau of the Budget

Starbird, Lieutenant General Alfred D., Vice Chairman, Subcommittee on Communications, National Security Council

Stephens, Oren M., Director, Office of Research and Analysis (later Office of Research and Reference), U.S. Information Agency

Stevens, George, Jr., Director, Motion Picture Service, U.S. Information Agency

Stevenson, Adlai E., U.S. Representative at the United Nations, January 21, 1961–July 14, 1965

Stewart, Irvin, Special Assistant to the President for Telecommunications

Strong, Curtis C., United Nations Adviser, Bureau of African Affairs, Department of State, from April 1963

Sullivan, William H., United Nations Adviser, Bureau of Far Eastern Affairs, Department of State, September 1960–April 1963; thereafter Special Assistant to the Under Secretary of State for Political Affairs

Talbot, Phillips, Assistant Secretary of State for Near Eastern and South Asian Affairs from April 18, 1961

Talyzin, Nikolai Vladimirovich, Senior Scientific Adviser, Ministry of Communications, USSR

Tasca, Henry J., Deputy Assistant Secretary of State for African Affairs

Taylor, General Maxwell D., Chairman of the Joint Chiefs of Staff from October 1, 1962

Tepper, Morris, Chairman, Director of Meteorological Systems, National Aeronautics and Space Administration

Thant, U, Permanent Representative of Burma at the United Nations; Acting Secretary-General from November 3, 1961

Thompson, Llewellyn E., Ambassador at Large from October 3, 1962

Townsend, Dr. John W., Jr., Assistant Director, Goddard Space Flight Center, National Aeronautics and Space Administration

Tree, Marietta F., U.S. Representative to the UN Commission on Human Rights

Truman, Harry S., President of the United States, 1945–1952

Tsiang, T. F., Permanent Representative of the Republic of China at the United Nations; Ambassador to the United States from January 12, 1962

Tubby, Roger W., Assistant Secretary of State for Public Affairs, March 2, 1961–April 1, 1962

Tuch, Hans N., Deputy Assistant Director (Soviet Union and Eastern Europe), United States Information Agency, 1963

Turner, Bruce R., Under Secretary-General and Controller of the Budget of the United Nations

Tuthill, John W., Permanent Representative, Organization for Economic Cooperation and Development, October 4, 1961–October 22, 1962

Tyler, William R., Deputy Assistant Secretary of State for European Affairs, Department of State from May 1961; Assistant Secretary of State for European Affairs, August 20, 1962–May 18, 1965

Vaille, Charles., French Representative to the 18th Session of the UN Commission on Narcotic Drugs, 1963

Vaughn, David B., Under Secretary-General for General Services of the United Nations

Vedeler, Harold C., Director, Office of Eastern European Affairs, Bureau of European Affairs, Department of State

Vertes, I., Hungarian Representative to the 16th Session of the UN Commission on Narcotic Drugs, 1961

Wachuku, Jaja Anucha, Nigerian Foreign Minister

Wallner, Woodruff, Deputy Assistant Secretary of State for International Organization Affairs

Warren, George L., Adviser to the Deputy Under Secretary of State for Political Affairs on Refugee and Migration Affairs from May 1963; later Adviser to the Administrator, Bureau of Security and Consular Affairs

Washburn, Abbott, Acting Director, U.S. Information Agency, 1961

Waterman, Alan T., Director, National Science Foundation

Watters, Harry J., Member, Ad Hoc Committee on Space

Webb, James E., Administrator, National Aeronautics and Space Administration

Wellons, Alfred E., Officer in Charge, General Assembly and United Nations Organization Affairs, Office of United Nations Political Affairs, Bureau of International Organization Affairs, Department of State, July 1961–June 1963

Welsh, Edward C., Executive Secretary, National Aeronautics and Space Council

Westfall, Virginia C., Director, Office of International Administration, Bureau of International Organization Affairs, Department of State, from December 1962

Whitman, Walter G., Science Adviser, Department of State, until September 1962

Wiesner, Jerome B., Special Assistant to the President for Science and Technology; Chairman of the Ad Hoc Committee on Space

Wilcox, Francis O., Assistant Secretary of State for International Organization Affairs, July 28, 1955–January 20, 1961

Williams, G. Mennen, Assistant Secretary of State for African Affairs after January 30, 1961

Wilson, Donald M., Deputy Director, U.S. Information Agency

Wilson, Thomas W., Special Assistant to the Assistant Secretary of State for International Organization Affairs from April 1961

Yates, Gilbert E., Director, UN Division of Narcotic Drugs, until June 1963

Yates, Sidney R., U.S. Representative to the UN Trusteeship Council from February 1963

Yeh, George K. C., Chinese Ambassador to the United States until January 12, 1962

Yingling, Raymond T., Assistant Legal Adviser for Special Functional Problems, Department of State

Yost, Charles W., U.S. Deputy Representative at the United Nations

Zafrulla Khan, Sir Mohammed, Permanent Representative of Pakistan at the United Nations; President of the 17th Session of the UN General Assembly

Zolotas, Xenophon, Governor of the Bank of Greece

Zorin, Valerian A., Deputy Foreign Minister of the Soviet Union; Permanent Representative of the Soviet Union at the United Nations, 1962

Organization and Administration of Foreign Policy

White House and Interdepartmental Coordination

1. Editorial Note

Following the election of November 4, 1960, President-elect John F. Kennedy and his transition advisers focused among other things on questions involving the organization and administration of foreign policy, particularly proposals for modifying and streamlining the structure of the National Security Council apparatus as it had developed during the Eisenhower administration. Among principal transition advisers to the President-elect were Clark M. Clifford, a Washington attorney who had served as Special Counsel to President Truman, and Richard E. Neustadt, Professor of Public Law and Government at Columbia University. Clifford served as a channel of communication with the Eisenhower administration and maintained contact with General Wilton B. Persons, President Eisenhower's Assistant, from the time of their first meeting on November 14, 1960, through the weeks that followed. See Arthur M. Schlesinger, Jr., *A Thousand Days: John F. Kennedy in the White House* (Boston: Houghton Mifflin, 1965), pages 118–127, 209–210; and Bromley K. Smith, *Organizational History of the National Security Council During the Kennedy and Johnson Administrations* (Washington: National Security Council, 1988) pages 5–14.

Several transition memoranda Neustadt prepared for President-elect Kennedy dealt with aspects of the organization and administration of foreign policy. These included "Staffing the President-Elect," October 30, 1960; "Conversation with Richard Bissell about a 'Personal Assistant to the Commander-in-Chief-Elect'," November 25, 1960; "The National Security Council: First Steps," December 8, 1960; "Next Steps in Staffing the White House and Executive Office," December 9, 1960; and "Introducing McGeorge Bundy to General Persons," January 3, 1961. Copies of these memoranda are in the Kennedy Library, National Security Files, Departments and Agencies Series, Richard E. Neustadt.

On December 6 President-elect Kennedy met with President Eisenhower at the White House. They discussed various subjects, including the organization and operation of the White House staff, the National Security Council, and the Pentagon. Eisenhower urged the President-elect to avoid any reorganization until "he himself could become well acquainted with the problem." The full text of Eisenhower's account of the meeting is in the Eisenhower Library, Whitman File, Eisenhower Diaries. It is printed in *The White House Years: Waging Peace, 1956–1961*, pages 712–716. See also *Foreign Relations, 1958–1960*, volume III, page 493.

During the transition period the President-elect was influenced by the findings and recommendations of the Senate Subcommittee on National Policy Machinery of the Committee on Government Operations, chaired by Senator Henry M. Jackson of Washington. Senator Jackson had begun hearings on the national security system in 1959, and Neustadt had become a consultant to the subcommittee. The subcommittee's initial recommendations, first released during the transition period on November 22, 1960, largely coincided with Kennedy's views on streamlining the National Security Council mechanism. See Schlesinger, *A Thousand Days*, pages 209–210; Smith, *Organizational History*, pages 5–7. For the first published Jackson subcommittee hearings and reports from the 86th Congress, Second Session, and the 87th Congress, First Session, see *Organizing for National Security: Inquiry of the Subcommittee on National Policy Machinery of the Committee on Government Operations, United States Senate*; vol. 1, Hearings; vol. 2, Studies and Background Material; and vol. 3, Staff Reports and Recommendations (Washington, U.S. Government Printing Office, 1961).

On January 1, 1961, in announcing the appointment of McGeorge Bundy as his Special Assistant for National Security Affairs, Kennedy indicated that he had been impressed by the recommendations of the Jackson Subcommittee, and that these would provide a starting point for the task of reorganizing the operations of the National Security Council. The President-elect stated: "I intend to consolidate under Mr. Bundy's direction the present National Security Council secretariat, the staff and functions of the Operations Coordinating Board, and the continuing functions of a number of special projects staffs within the White House. I have asked Mr. Bundy to review with care existing staff organization and arrangements, and to simplify them wherever possible toward the end that we may have a single, small, but strongly organized staff unit to assist me in obtaining advice from, and coordinating operations of, the government agencies concerned with national security affairs."

"Mr. Bundy will serve as my personal assistant on these matters and as director of whatever staff we find is needed for the purpose. It will be part of his assignment to facilitate the work of the National

Security Council as a body advisory to the President. I intend to seek advice from the members of the Council, both collectively and individually, and it is my hope to use the National Security Council and its machinery more flexibly than in the past. I have been much impressed with the constructive criticism contained in the recent staff report by Senator Jackson's Subcommittee on National Policy Machinery. The Subcommittee's study provides a useful starting point for the work that Mr. Bundy will undertake in helping me to strengthen and to simplify the operations of the National Security Council." (Statement from the Press Office of Senator John F. Kennedy, Palm Beach, Florida, for release Sunday January 1, 1961; text in Henry M. Jackson, ed., *The National Security Council: Jackson Subcommittee Papers on Policy-Making at the Presidential Level* (New York: Praeger, 1965), pages 302–303.

Additional documentation on the reorganization of the National Security Council mechanism during the Kennedy administration is in *Foreign Relations*, 1961–1963, volume VIII. On aspects of the organization and administration of foreign policy in the Kennedy administration generally, see also the following works by participants: George W. Ball, *The Past Has Another Pattern: Memoirs* (New York: Norton, 1982); John Kenneth Galbraith, *Ambassador's Journal* (Boston: Houghton Mifflin, 1969); Roger Hilsman, *To Move a Nation* (New York: Doubleday, 1967); Walt W. Rostow, *View From the Seventh Floor* (New York: Harper & Row, 1964); Dean Rusk, as told to Richard Rusk, *As I Saw It* (New York: Norton, 1990); and Theodore C. Sorensen, *Kennedy* (New York: Harper & Row, 1965).

---

2.   Memorandum From Secretary of State Herter to the President's Assistant (Persons)[1]

Washington, January 16, 1961.

SUBJECT

Transition Arrangements

In connection with our efforts to make the transition process a smooth one, I met personally on several occasions with Mr. Rusk, following the

---

[1]   Source: Eisenhower Library, Whitman File, Presidential Transition Series. Confidential. Initialed by Persons. Another copy indicates that the memorandum was drafted by Walter J. Stoessel, Jr., Director of the Executive Secretariat of the Department of State, and by Herter. (Ibid., Herter Papers)

announcement on December 12 of his appointment, to discuss operations of the Department and to keep him currently informed on political problems, such as Cuba and Laos. These meetings took place on December 20, 1960, January 2, 3, 6, 7, 9 and 16, 1961.

Mr. Rusk designated Mr. George McGhee to serve as his representative to receive current briefings on the Lao situation. Pursuant to this designation, Mr. McGhee was briefed daily by our intelligence staff on Laos and was in regular contact with Mr. Merchant and our geographic bureau experts.

Both Mr. Rusk and Mr. Bowles were also briefed on State Department organization and procedures. They received unclassified briefing books on these subjects.

As soon as possible following their appointment and after ascertaining that security clearances had been obtained, we provided Mr. Rusk and Mr. Bowles with briefing books on policy matters. I enclose a list of the subjects covered in these books.[2] This list was previously furnished to you through Mr. Patterson.[3] The policy books covered current situations of interest around the world and did not include policy recommendations on any subjects.

Although Mr. Rusk did not attend staff meetings in the Department following his appointment as Secretary-designate, he received daily summaries of State Department cable traffic. Particular cables relating to post-inaugural problems and events were provided to Mr. Rusk and Mr. Bowles on a selective basis. Likewise, briefing papers on matters which would be of concern to the new Administration after January 20 were forwarded to Mr. Rusk from time to time after specific approval from my office.

Following Mr. G. Mennen Williams' designation as Assistant Secretary of State for African Affairs in the new Administration, Mr. Williams was given a general briefing on African matters by officers in the Bureau of African Affairs and was introduced to personnel in that Bureau.

All of the new appointees, together with such staffs as they brought with them, were given temporary office space in the Department of State and were provided with all necessary and appropriate administrative services.

C.A.H.

---

[2] Not printed. The attached list of subjects, entitled "Index—Policy Briefing Book," indicates that the attachments were classified Top Secret and included the following major headings (with subheadings under each): I. Africa; II. American Republics; III-IV. Europe; V. Far East; VI. Near East and South Asia; VII. United Nations; VIII. Economic; IX. Mutual Security Program; X. Disarmament, Atomic Energy, and Outer Space; XI. Military Facilities System; XII. Legislative; XIII. Information; XIV. Cultural; XV. Consular and Security; XVI. Fisheries; and XVII. Visits.

[3] Presumably Bradley H. Patterson, Jr., Assistant to the Secretary to the Cabinet.

3.   Memorandum for Record[1]

Washington, undated.

Wednesday, January 11, 1961—10:20 to 12:50 a.m.

In this meeting I had my first conversation with Mr. McGeorge Bundy, who has been named by the President-elect to be his Special Assistant for National Security Affairs, in connection with the transfer of responsibility of January 20, 1961. [Here follows brief discussion of personnel and procedural matters.]

I then told Mr. Bundy that General Persons, following a telephone call from Mr. Clark Clifford, had asked me to arrange for Mr. Bundy to talk with Mr. Lay, Mr. Harr and Mr. Bromley Smith. There ensued a discussion about Mr. Bundy's immediate commitments and it was ultimately agreed that he would talk with Mr. Smith on Thursday morning and Mr. Lay Thursday afternoon, inasmuch as Mr. Lay would be engaged in NSC business in the morning. Mr. Harr being out of town and the time of his return unknown to me, we made no plans for that conference.

Mr. Bundy indicated that beginning on Monday, January 16, he would be in Washington full time. I told him that I was prompted, with some hesitation to make a suggestion to him and that was that he might accompany me on Monday to the Armed Forces Staff College in Norfolk where I was to deliver a lecture. The purpose of the rather hesitant suggestion was not to involve him in the lecture business but to take advantage of the time afforded by the plane ride down and back for discussion. Mr. Bundy felt that in view of the fact that he would be in Washington all of next week, he could more profitably spend his time seeing other people in my absence. I took occasion at this point to say to him that I thought one of the more important functions of my office was to accept invitations to the various service colleges to lecture on the NSC and related matters, and I strongly urged him to seek to arrange his schedule so as to meet this worthwhile but also pleasant requirement during his encumbency.

---

[1] Source: Eisenhower Library, Whitman File, Presidential Transition Series. No classification marking. Drafted by President Eisenhower's Special Assistant for National Security Affairs, Gordon Gray, who sent the memorandum to Persons under cover of a January 17 note indicating that his notes of conversations with Bundy "have been hastily drafted and their literary quality is greatly inferior to their accuracy." In a separate memorandum for record, dated January 12, Bromley Smith, Executive Secretary of the Operations Coordinating Board, described a 2-hour briefing he provided Bundy on January 11 concerning the Board's operations. (Ibid.)

I then tried to make it clear to Mr. Bundy that our instructions were to be of every possible assistance to our successors. I said that I hoped that I would not in any way appear to be "lecturing" him and certainly my aim was not to tell him how to organize his own affairs. My whole motivation was to give him my philosophy about the functions of the office; to point out mistakes that we had made; and to make suggestions for whatever value they might be to him.

Our discussion then covered a wide range of topics which I now set forth not necessarily in the order of their discussion:

1. I made clear to him my judgment that he should resist any tendency to have any other individual seek to insert himself between the President and the Special Assistant.

2. I expressed the view to him that rather than having two Special Assistants to the President operating generally in the same area (for National Security Affairs and for Security Operations Coordination) it would be better to have one man with an extremely competent deputy (or deputies). I explained to him that there had been no difficulties between Mr. Harr and myself but that I felt that his job was really less than a full-time job and mine was more than a fulltime job and that much greater efficiency might have resulted had the structure been different. In any event, I suggested that if the job Mr. Harr has is retained, a better title should be found. I suggested also that if Mr. Bundy had such a deputy and if the decision were to retain the OCB the deputy could still be the Vice Chairman.

3. As to the Chairmanship of the OCB, I expressed my judgment as to the wisdom of the President's move in January in making the Special Assistant for National Security Affairs the chairman instead of retaining the State Department member as Chairman. I said I felt the change was an improvement both in theory and in practice for a variety of reasons, including the elimination of a situation in which a protagonist was also the "impartial chairman," and the more direct involvement of the President through his Special Assistant.

4. As to general procedures, I described for him the functioning of the NSC under President Eisenhower in considerable detail, including the conduct of meetings and types of papers going before the NSC. I also described in some detail the Planning Board process and the duties of the NSC staff.

5. I discussed briefly the relationships of the Office of the Special Assistant to the President for National Security Affairs to the office of the Staff Secretary to the President and suggested that that be pursued further in the 4 o'clock meeting with General Goodpaster and Mr. Dungan.

6. As to the internal security responsibilities of the Council, I described the responsibilities and the committee structure. Mr. Bundy had not been aware of this function of the Council.

7. In connection with the scope of Mr. Bundy's responsibilities, he had the impression that the President-elect would wish to look to him as his principal staff officer in all matters involving the national security and he asked what in my opinion this really involved beyond the NSC and its subordinate machinery and the CFEP. (He indicated that he expected to see Mr. Clarence Randall and I replied that I understood that General Persons was arranging for this appointment.) I indicated to Mr. Bundy that in my view the scope of such a responsibility would include not only an interest in and somehow a responsibility for the CFEP function, whether the CFEP were continued or eliminated. I also pointed out to him the situation with respect to the National Advisory Council indicating that the National Advisory Council was statutory and discussed with him some of the irritating difficulties that we had had in the past involving OCB and NAC responsibilities. I said further that he would have to interest himself in the international activities of the Department of Agriculture, the Department of Commerce and other agencies. I said that he would have to have a personal relationship with Dr. Kistiakowsky's successor and if this were not possible on a personal basis it would have to be arranged structurally, because of the inter-relationship between the interests of the two offices. (Mr. Bundy indicated to me that he knew who Dr. Kistiakowsky's successor would be and they would have no problem.) I said there were certain elements also in the Office of Civil and Defense Mobilization which would involve the interest of the Special Assistant. I expressed the hope to Mr. Bundy that the scope of his responsibilities would be as he had indicated subject always to one caveat which would run throughout everything I had to say to him. I wanted to make certain that he undertook those things he could physically do and that perhaps my notion of the job would be more than one man could handle. He acknowledged this difficulty and indicated his awareness that he would have to have some good assistants.

8. With respect to OCDM, I expressed my view that the whole complex needed a thorough-going reappraisal. In this connection he wished my view about continuing the Director of OCDM as a statutory member of the NSC. I pointed out to him the need for the integration of the resources point of view in the formulation of national policy. He wondered whether a President could not look to his Council of Economic Advisers for such a function. I pointed out to him that if he was thinking in terms of reducing the number of people in an NSC meeting the Chairman, CEA would be a body just as much as the Director of OCDM. He said he only wished to raise the question particularly since the Jackson Committee Staff Report had made the recommendation. I said this of course was something that the new President would have to decide. However, apart from this point, with a profession of some bias,

I expressed my opinions about the Jackson Committee Staff Study pointing out the process of selective quotations, etc. I said that there were many things in the Jackson Committee Staff Study that I thought simply could not be supported.

9. Mr. Bundy wished to return again to the question of the Director of OCDM. He asked whether it would not be possible to appoint an Acting Director who could serve while a reappraisal was going on and who as Acting Director would not be a statutory member of the Council. I suggested to him that before such a decision was made two points ought to be considered: (1) The old Federal Statute which casts doubt upon the legality of acts of an acting head of a department after the expiration of thirty days and (2) the wording of the Reorganization Plan which created OCDM. I said it was my recollection although I could not be sure that that reorganization plan did not permit the flexibility he had in mind, if the Acting Director were the Deputy Director.

10. As to relationships with the President, Mr. Bundy asked me my view as to daily briefings of the President. I said that I felt of course that this was a Presidential decision. One possibility would be having the Director of Central Intelligence do it although this would, as a practical matter, be inconsistent with the practice of having the DCI brief the Council every week which I thought was a very useful device. I then said to him that I had made a note several months ago to discuss with my successor "Intelligence briefings in the Council. I believe that these should be crisper and should be conducted by more junior officers with a special briefing competence." I acknowledged to Mr. Bundy that this would cause serious personal problems and I was not sure I would advise him to tackle it. It was simply a question I left with him.

11. We discussed the question of attendance at Council meetings. I acknowledged that I thought the greatest vulnerability of the operation as it had been in recent times was the number of people who customarily attend meetings and that this was one of the most difficult problems he would face. I expressed the view that the attendance under President Eisenhower had not inhibited discussion but that the battle would constantly be fought. I explained to him the device of special meetings which the President may choose to use on occasion involving only statutory members and advisers and only one or two people with a special competence of the subject at hand.

12. Mr. Bundy wished to know how we prepared agenda for Council meetings. I explained to him that the President had largely left it up to the Special Assistant with a request for Presidential direction as necessary. I also explained to him the practices as to the conduct of the meetings and the development of the Records of Actions and their dissemination in considerable detail.

13. Mr. Bundy wondered whether he would need a lawyer on his personal staff. I suggested to him that I had been most adequately served by the lawyers on the White House Staff and that my guess would be that he need not make arrangements for legal services.

14. We discussed office space. I expressed the view to him that it would be desirable that he maintain his office in the White House itself in view of the kind of responsibilities that the President-elect will place upon him. I felt that he should be at the end of "the buzzer."

15. Mr. Bundy indicated that his present thinking was that he would not proceed in the same manner as General Cutler had proceeded in 1953. That is to say, he now sees no need for an urgent and massive review of all policy papers inherited by the new Administration. Mr. Bundy ventured the opinion that our policies are largely dictated by external events and that he didn't anticipate that there would be any significant policy shifts. He felt that his time and the time of the various elements of the NSC should be spent getting ahead with the immediate and pressing problems. I suggested to Mr. Bundy that at least he would wish to review the Basic National Security Policy paper.

Wednesday, January 11, 1961 — 4 o'clock

Mr. Bundy and I joined Mr. Dungan and General Goodpaster in the Conference Room of the White House where we had a discussion lasting about an hour involving the roles of the Staff Secretary and the Special Assistant for National Security Affairs. General Goodpaster largely led the discussion describing the nature of his duties and the general responsibilities of the Special Assistant. He pointed out with great clarity the spectrum which at one end had the Staff Secretary functions and at the other end the work of the NSC. He then explained how in between there was a gray area in which the interest began to merge, overlap, and become confused. The ends of the spectrum were clear but the problem facing Mr. Bundy and Mr. Dungan was how to sort out their respective responsibilities in the gray area. It was agreed that such sorting out was the responsibility of the new people. The discussion was cordial and I think successful.

Wednesday, January 11, 1961 — 5 o'clock

Following our discussion with Mr. Dungan and General Goodpaster which ended at 5 o'clock, Mr. Bundy and I toured most of the first floor of the White House and then returned to my office where we talked for forty minutes. I said that I had wished to talk to him about the OCB and the burden of my discussion would be that he use his influence to avoid hasty decisions to abolish any of the machinery that had been established and evolved over the years. I confessed some personal bias for I said that I felt that my reaction to the suggestion that the OCB be abolished would be perhaps the same as his to the suggestion that now the College of Arts and Sciences at Harvard be abolished. In response Mr. Bundy laughed and replied that his immediate question would be, "What have I been doing for the last several years." I sought to describe the circumstances leading up to the creation of the old Psychological Strategy Board and pointed out its shortcomings. I said, however, that it had been an important first step leading to the establishment of the OCB, whose function and philosophy I described in some detail. I constantly reiterated that I was simply asking for avoidance of hasty decision and that the main point was that the functions assigned to the OCB were vital in Government and that it did not make sense to me to abolish the agency and then find it necessary to recreate it. This would be an unhappy waste of time and resources. I said even the suggestion that it might be abolished had an eroding effect on the structure especially in the lower echelons of the departments.

I said that I wished to reserve the minutia of procedures of operation for Mr. Bromley Smith's discussion with Mr. Bundy.

I then expressed the view that he might be alert to possible problems arising out of the appointment of Mr. Dillon as Secretary of the Treasury. I said that I thought this was a fine appointment. However, from Mr. Bundy's point of view there was a combination of factors to be considered. First, Mr. Dillon becomes the statutory Chairman of the National Advisory Council whose prerogative had been jealously guarded by the Treasury staff. Second, Mr. Dillon in his role as coordinator of mutual security had shown a disposition to be somewhat enamoured of his individual coordinating role. There had been occasions when the coordinating function of the administrator in the well-defined and somewhat narrow area of mutual security in the whole field of national and international security problems had come in conflict with the functions assigned to the OCB. I wondered whether Mr. Dillon would be eager to have a complete government-wide coordinating function. However, I simply pointed out these considerations for Mr. Bundy's reflection.

Finally, I repeated that my main notion was to avoid hasty decisions. The new Administration would of course want to make adjustments in the structure as best suited its requirements. Mr. Bundy assured me he came with no preconceived notions but expressed his gratitude for the warning flags I had put up.

[Here follow notes of a brief discussion of personnel and procedural matters on the afternoon of Thursday, January 12.]

Monday, January 16, 1961 — 3:45 to 4:45 p.m.

1. We discussed special clearances and Mr. Bundy said he would arrange for a briefing for January 17. I explained to Mr. Bundy the various reasons why I thought it important for him to be cleared now including the probable desirability of his controlling situation as far as the other White House Staff were concerned. In this connection I suggested to him that he would want to consider the question of whether he would like all of those who would regularly attend NSC meetings to have full clearances in order to avoid inadvertent disclosures which has happened in Council meetings on one or two occasions.

2. We discussed the desirability of the use of outside consultants and I explained to him some of the positive considerations including the occasional substantive contribution which can be made as well as the public relations aspects of the matter. In this connection I expressed my view about the reconstitution and elevation of the Science Advisory Committee in 1957 which had substantially eliminated the use of consultant groups which had been put together in the past such as the Technological Capabilities Panel, the Gaither Committee, etc. Mr. Bundy fully understood the problem and thought he would wish to make full use of the panels of the Science Advisory Committee. I pointed out to him that Dr. Kistiakowsky had more or less attended all NSC meetings and suggested that he would wish to consider whether he would want to extend the same privileges to Dr. Wiesner. I expressed views why this was desirable. Mr. Bundy felt that he wished to keep such people as the Science Adviser, the Director of the Bureau of the Budget, etc. well informed but he thought that their presence would be more meaningful if they came on particular occasions. I said if he pursued this course then he would probably wish to think of some briefing device for these individuals similar to the one we use now for the Planning Board so that they could have the full flavor of Council meetings.

3. I suggested the need for some machinery for the identification of private citizens who wished to contribute their time and energy which might involve something like a central registry at which national security agencies would have access and to which they would make known their requirements. In this connection I described the frustration of Mr. Gene E. Bradley, Editor of the *General Electric Defense Quarterly*.

4. I pointed out to Mr. Bundy that both Ambassador Lodge and Ambassador Burgess have standing invitations to attend the NSC meetings whenever they are in Washington. President Eisenhower had made this arrangement in order to enhance their prestige with their colleagues. I informed Mr. Bundy that Mr. Burgess particularly had taken this quite seriously. In view of the President-elect's intention to keep the attendance very small in NSC meetings, I suggested he would want to consider what

should be done with respect to the two new Ambassadors. Mr. Bundy felt this might constitute something of a problem.

5. I suggested that Mr. Bundy make certain that he or a designee of his arrange for continued participation in State–JCS meetings.

6. I described the procedures by which Mr. J. Edgar Hoover forwards reports to this office for the information of the President.

7. We again discussed the matter of "policy" vs. "operations." I expressed the view to Mr. Bundy that where there is not a very clear distinction, errors should be made on the side of including things in NSC meetings.

8. I pointed out to Mr. Bundy the real need for an improved meeting room for the Planning Board or whatever interagency groups he might use in staff support of the Council.

9. We discussed at quite considerable length, Mr. Bundy's notions about assuming the position of Executive Secretary. I pointed out to him some of the disabilities and ways in which he might overcome them. One was the administrative burden which I felt he could handle by delegation. Another was protecting his privileged position with the President, especially for Congressional purposes. I suggested to him that he could be both Executive Secretary and Special Assistant to the President. In the course of this conversation I urged him to be sympathetic with Mr. Lay's problems should he proceed with this plan. I said it was my view that it would be very unfair to ask Mr. Lay to take a cut in salary. Mr. Bundy expressed his understanding of the situation and assured me that in that respect Mr. Lay would be given the opportunity to find himself an equally good situation.

---

4. Memorandum From the President's Special Assistant for National Security Affairs (Bundy) to President Kennedy[1]

Washington, January 24, 1961.

SUBJECT

The Use of the National Security Council

Everyone who has written or talked about the NSC agrees that it should be what the President wants it to be; this is right. So the following

---

[1] Source: Kennedy Library, National Security Files, Departments and Agencies Series, Bundy Memoranda to the President, 1/61–2/61. No classification marking.

comments are entirely to stir your reactions. All we need for now is your decisions on opening steps—the Council can readily be shaped and reshaped to your taste as we learn from experience.

The Council has four elements: (1) its formal meetings under your chairmanship, (2) a Planning Board (of Assistant Secretaries), (3) an Operations Coordinating Board (of Under Secretaries), and (4) staff for the above. Numbers (2), (3), and (4) are, in my view, ripe for re-organization. They are too big, too formal, and too paperbound to do the immediate or the planning work you want. This reorganization will take a little while and its exact shape will depend, among other things, on what you do with (1) the Council itself.

My suggestion is that the Council can provide a regular and relatively formal place for free and frank discussion of whatever major issues of national security are ready for such treatment. I believe such discussion can do two things for you and one for your associates. For you it can (1) open a subject up so that you can see what its elements are and decide how you want it pursued; and (2) present the final arguments of those principally concerned when a policy proposal is ready for your decision. Both of these tasks can be performed in other ways; in emergency situations they must be. But the Council ought to be a good place for much of this work.

The special service the Council can render to your associates is a little subtler: it can give them confidence that they know what is cooking and what you want. The NSC, under Eisenhower, got too big; and we can and should cut back its attendance. But there remains a number of men whose self-confidence, as well as their ability to help you, can be strongly reinforced by participation in the work of the Council. Examples, quite different in their shape, are Vice President Johnson and Jerry Wiesner. So I think you will gain, at the start, by having reasonably regular meetings of NSC. The Eisenhower Administration used weekly meetings, but I suggest we begin with a fortnightly calendar, using special meetings of selected individuals as you may want them. Ken O'Donnell thinks Wednesday morning at 10:00 will be a good time.

Membership

The membership, by statute, includes:

1. President
2. Vice President
3. Secretary of State
4. Secretary of Defense
5. Director, OCDM

Two additional regular members, by standing invitation, going back to Truman, made a lot of trouble in the last Administration—in this one they will, I think, be valuable:

6. Secretary of the Treasury
7. Director of the Budget

The statutory "advisers", who have regularly attended in the past, are:

8. Director, CIA
9. Chairman, JCS (representing the Joint Chiefs as a group)

From the Presidential staff, customarily, there have been

10. The Science Adviser (nearly everything military is of major interest to him, and his separate counsel is important to you)
11. The Special Assistant for National Security Affairs
12. Goodpaster (tending the door and handling urgent messages silently—a wise and good man)
13., 14.? And in this Administration, you may want to add Sorensen? or Dungan? or Rostow?

From the NSC staff

15.? The Executive Secretary (Lay), The Deputy Executive Secretary (Boggs)
(I'd drop the Deputy at once, and the Executive Secretary-ship should presently be merged with me.)

A number of additional people like the Chairman of AEC, the Under Secretary of State, the Director of ICA, the Director of USIA, and various White House staff men, were usually included by the last Administration. I'm against this (unless you want it) except where the agenda calls for it. But there will be squawks—I've already had pressure from USIA's Wilson, for example, and he has a relatively good case. What about him? Stevenson? Bowles?

Agenda

Traditionally, the meetings have begun with a briefing by the Director of CIA. This can be as short or as long as you want. I have the impression that occasionally in the past these briefings have been quite long, and my suggestion is that at the beginning you may want to give clear instructions that they be limited to fifteen minutes, except where you have a particular topic that you would like discussed at greater length.

Beyond that, the agenda is quite free. My own suggestions for the first meeting are two—they are not the most urgent, but in some ways they are the ones most fitted for the present Council discussion.

The first is that we should discuss ways and means of bringing defense policy and its budgetary meaning closer together. Both McNamara and Bell have made it clear to me that in their judgment this problem is at the heart of effective control of our military posture; both of them think it is ripe for attack. They would both gain strength from a brief discussion in your presence which might lead to a clear direction that they should attack this problem and bring explicit proposals for its long-range handling to the Council promptly.

The second agenda item is quite different: it is the billion dollar defense of freedom fund which Dean Rusk mentioned yesterday. I would include the wider problem of the dollar and foreign trade and foreign aid if it were not already being quite urgently and immediately discussed in preparation for your coming messages. As it is, I think this one has certain special value, partly because it is a separable and urgent item, and partly—to be frank—because I think it would be a dandy one for assignment to Rostow and me for preparation. Any such fund should be plainly and clearly in the President's hands for a whole lot of reasons, and the staff work should be done by your people. We can get a preliminary paper for discussion at the first NSC meeting if you want.

Urgent Reviews of Existing Policy

There are a number of existing policy papers which raise questions that should be promptly reviewed. I am scouting these papers myself (mainly through Walt) and I suggest we ask Rusk and McNamara also to state the ones that they find most in need of attention. A whole lot of these papers are fairly useless exercises, I think; these can be ignored for now. But some are important because they really do guide the executive branch and especially the Pentagon; these we must review and get right where they are wrong.

Organization of NSC and its Various Boards

While this is your business, and mine for you, the opinion of NSC members may be useful, and accordingly, we might put this on the agenda for the first meeting—but only if you should be ready. I'll make a preliminary sketch of what I think you ought to want when we talk Tuesday. In general, I agree with Dick Neustadt's remarkable analysis.

A Separate Subject: Briefing

There are a large number of activities and intelligence estimates you need to get caught up on, and this work will take longer than a short preamble to NSC meetings. But there is a problem deriving from the different habits of your predecessor. He used the military briefing process—charts and speeches—and I think the habit of quite long expositions is widespread. Moreover, everyone will want to keep you as long as you can stand it and maybe longer. On the other hand, you ought to listen to a lot of these men to get an estimate of them as men. Would you like me to coordinate a set of briefing meetings—military, CIA, AEC, and State? And if so, how much time do you want to spend?

5. Letter From President Kennedy to Vice President Johnson[1]

Washington, January 28, 1961.

Dear Mr. Vice President:

Recognizing the need for a Vice President who is fully informed and adequately prepared with respect to domestic, foreign and military policies relating to the national security of the United States, and recognizing also the need for a closer working relationship between the President and Vice President in this vital area, I would like you to preside over meetings of the National Security Council in my absence and to maintain close liaison with the Council and all other departments and agencies affected with a national security interest.

In addition, I am hereby requesting you to review policies relating to the national security, consulting with me in order that I might have the full benefit of your endeavors and your judgment.

You will need, in fulfillment of this assignment, pertinent information concerning the policies and operations of the departments and agencies concerned with national security policies, including the Department of State, the Department of Defense, the Office of Civil and Defense Mobilization, the National Aeronautics and Space Administration, the Bureau of the Budget, and the Central Intelligence Agency.

I will expect the departments and agencies concerned to cooperate fully with you in providing information in order for you to carry out the responsibilities outlined above.

Sincerely,[2]

---

[1] Source: Kennedy Library, National Security Files, Departments and Agencies Series, National Security Council Organization and Administration, 2/1/61–5/4/61. No classification marking.

[2] Printed from an unsigned copy.

6.   Memorandum From the President's Special Assistant for
        National Security Affairs (Bundy) to the Under Secretary of
        State for Political Affairs (Merchant) and the Assistant
        Secretary of Defense for International Security Affairs
        (Nitze)[1]

Washington, January 30, 1961.

SUBJECT

A proposal for the NSC meeting of Wednesday, February 1, 1961

At the President's direction, the three of us have met and talked
about the problem of identifying crisis problems and arranging for
effective leadership in dealing with them here in Washington.[2] I think
we are agreed on the following general position:

The identification of such problems should be the responsibility of
all interested parts of the government. Insofar as such problems are in
the first instance political, special responsibility rests with the
Department of State, but there is every reason to expect alarm bells to
be rung by someone in CIA or Defense whenever there is a strong conviction in either place that we need to act promptly. Such alarm bells
can be rung in any one of a number of ways. In the most urgent cases
the President himself will wish to be directly informed, but if there
should be a regularly meeting group of senior officers of State,
Defense, CIA and the President's office, such a committee might well
be used for less urgent signals. And of course alarms may always be
rung directly by a Secretary or to him. It did not seem to us that it was
useful to establish a single tightly defined system here.

Where we do think that system is needed is in the assignment of
responsibility once a problem has been identified and marked for concerted action. Since we agree that the President and his Cabinet officers
will all want such problems identified before they get big and troublesome, if possible, we need a plan which will work for both small problems and big ones.

On the small ones, we believe it best that direct responsibility ordinarily be assigned to the Assistant Secretary of State of the region con-

---

[1] Source: Kennedy Library, National Security Files, Meetings and Memoranda Series,
NSC Meetings, 1961, No. 475. Confidential. Also on January 30 Bundy sent a memorandum to President Kennedy on the subject of: "Policies previously approved in NSC which
need review." The text is printed in *Foreign Relations*, 1961–1963, vol. VIII, Document 7.

[2] In a separate January 30 memorandum, Bundy outlined for a luncheon discussion
later that day with Merchant and Nitze the President's interest in the rapid identification
and effective executive management of crises. (Kennedy Library, National Security Files,
Bundy Memoranda to the President, 1/61–2/61)

cerned. He may wish to make the matter his own urgent business, or he may wish to assign it to a deputy, but in either case he should have for this problem the same kind of authority and responsibility that we propose for a different individual in particularly urgent and large-scale problems. To this special arrangement I now turn.

Our proposal is that in the case of an unusually urgent, difficult, and complex problem, it will be desirable to center responsibility in a single full-time officer under the Secretary of State. This officer might or might not be the Assistant Secretary for the region, but in any case he should be free of other responsibilities while he is handling this one. He should be the Chairman of an executive committee of senior officers of immediately interested agencies, but this executive committee should not be one in which everything is decided by vote, and still less a place in which unanimous concurrence is required for any action. It should be an instrument of cooperation and coordination but the man in charge should be the chairman and his decisions should stand unless they are successfully challenged through appropriate channels to the Secretary of State or the President. This officer would have authority to coordinate all actions in the field, and he should be responsible for continuous reporting of his progress or lack of progress, his needs and his assessments to the President, the Secretary of State, and other agency heads. He should be provided with explicit and continuous direction on the policy of the United States by the President and the Secretary.

Our discussions showed that an individual holding this kind of responsibility will have to be kept in close touch not only with other departments but with the whole range of political problems which will relate to his immediate task. What we do in Laos, for example, is plainly and deeply interdependent with problems of relations to our allies and the Soviet Union. Thus no task force commander can be given the illusion that he is free to go his own course.

But it should be possible to arrange a framework of continuous guidance which gives him a kind of ability to act which no committee system can provide.

One particular device seemed to us a useful one in helping such task force commanders: it is that there should be regular weekly meetings of senior officers of State, Defense, CIA, and the President's staff, to keep in touch on day-to-day operating matters. Such a committee might be the one thing to keep from the old OCB and it might be a natural and easy place of regular review, short of the top level, of your departmental efforts in support of a task force commander's work.

We did not give detailed attention in our discussion to the problem of coordination in the field, but I think we would all agree that the

Ambassador should be the senior responsible operating officer except in the most extraordinary circumstances.

McGeorge Bundy[3]

---

[3] Printed from a copy that bears this typed signature.

---

7.   **Memorandum From the President's Special Assistant for National Security Affairs (Bundy) to President Kennedy[1]**

Washington, January 31, 1961.

I think you may want to begin the meeting[2] with some description of the way you want NSC to run: here are some possible points:

The Council is *advisory*: it does *not* decide. (This is self-evident, but it has been overlooked in a lot of NSC papers which report that "the Council approved," or "the Council agreed.") *You* will decide—sometimes at the meeting, and sometimes in private after hearing the discussion.

Members should feel free to comment on problems outside their "agency" interest. It's not good to have only State speak to "politics" and only Defense speak to "military matters." You want free and general advice from these men (or you don't want them there).

Formal meetings of the Council are only part of its business; you will be meeting with all its members in other ways, and not all decisions or actions will go through this one agency. And the NSC staff (*your* staff, really) will have other jobs than preparing for the meetings—but this problem can wait for Agenda Item 4, on NSC organization.

Comment on the agenda (attached, annex A):[3] If you want, I can introduce each item with a line of comment—or, even better, you can do it yourself.

---

[1] Source: Kennedy Library, National Security Files, Bundy Memoranda to the President, 1/61–2/61. No classification marking.

[2] Reference is to the initial Kennedy administration meeting of the National Security Council, scheduled for February 1. The Record of Actions taken at this 475th NSC meeting is printed in *Foreign Relations*, 1961–1963, vol. VIII, Document 8.

[3] None of the annexes is printed.

1. *The briefing*, for fifteen minutes, will be handled by Allen Dulles, who will have one assistant (Amory) present only for this part of the meeting. This will be a general briefing and will go on longer only if you encourage questions or ask them yourself.

2. *Military Budgets and National Security Policy* will be discussed by Bell and McNamara. Bell will go first, on the problem as it now is, and McNamara will continue on what he and Bell mean to do about it. The essential elements here are that they intend to pull the budget process and the military plan into one process of judgment, directly under the Secretary of Defense. This will be new. It is *not* the same as the basic question of national policy that will come up in 3, below; it is the practical question of carrying policy out effectively and at the right cost, and it is enormously important. It should be regularly discussed at the highest level, and this is a way of starting.

3. *National Security Policies requiring Urgent Attention.* I have discussed this in a separate memo which you have read. (Annex B) The basic policy paper (5906/1)[4] is the one that needs to be replaced most urgently, and we need to say why, to the whole group, quite briefly. The essence of it is that this paper, with others which grow out of it, sets the basic policy on which military planning builds. This should be re-examined by any new administration, and there are particularly urgent reasons for doing it now.

4. *Organization and Procedures of the National Security Council.* This is really your private business, but there is a lot of curiosity around the government, and in a formal way the problem ought to come before NSC before we act. The essence of it is that the organization should reflect your style and methods, not President Eisenhower's. The jobs it can do for you are two: one is to help in presenting issues of policy, and the other is to keep in close touch with operations that you personally want to keep on top of. Both of these things were done, in theory, by a large, formal, paper-producing staff for President Eisenhower. I'm sure you don't want that, and what you do want is what I need to ask you before the meeting. I have ideas, but I think it will be easier to talk about them than write.

5. A new item—on *Effective Action in Crisis Areas.* This you put on the agenda yourself (Annex C), and I have alerted all concerned that you will want names of task force leaders at the meeting.

McG. B.[5]

---

[4] For text, see *Foreign Relations*, 1958–1960, vol. III, pp. 292–316. Documentation on the paper's revision is ibid., 1961–1963, volume VIII.

[5] Printed from a copy that bears these typed initials.

8.   **Editorial Note**

On February 18, 1961, President Kennedy issued Executive Order 10920 abolishing the Operations Coordinating Board. (26 *Federal Register* 1463) On February 19 the President issued a statement explaining how work formerly done by the OCB would be performed in other ways as part of the administration's program for strengthening the responsibility of individual departments. First, the Secretary of State and the Assistant Secretaries for regional bureaus, in consultation with other departments and agencies, would be the usual means of coordinating efforts with respect to a country or area. Second, to the extent the OCB, as a descendant of the former Psychological Strategy Board, was concerned with the impact of American actions on foreign opinion and with the American "image" abroad, this work would be done by the President, the Department of State, and the U.S. Information Agency. Third, to the extent the OCB was responsible for ensuring action at the President's direction, this function would continue by direct White House communication with the responsible agencies. For text of the President's statement, see *Public Papers of the Presidents of the United States: John F. Kennedy, 1961*, pages 104–105.

---

9.   **Memorandum From John Kenneth Galbraith to President Kennedy and Secretary of State Rusk**[1]

Washington, March 22, 1961.

SUBJECT

Fire Brigade Operations Abroad

I have been reflecting on a problem suggested by recent developments in Bolivia, Iran, Korea and prospectively in Jordan, Viet-Nam and elsewhere. This is the case of the country with a disintegrating economy which is the cause and consequence of a disintegrating government. The pattern is familiar. The budget is unbalanced, inflation is endemic. Stabilization efforts are creating industrial and social unrest—or would.

---

[1] Source: Kennedy Library, National Security Files, Departments and Agencies Series, Department of State—General, 3/6/61–3/31/61. No classification marking. Galbraith's appointment as Ambassador to India was announced on March 29.

American aid, though considerable, is insufficient—perhaps partially as a result of egregious misuse. Maladministration and corruption are general. Underneath is a nauseous social situation in which the landlords and politicians rape the poor with an energy which they apply to no other purpose. Without going into detail, I believe that foreign policy of the recent past including that on aid was peculiarly designed to nurture such developments.

We have also a certain uniformity in reaction when the position becomes dangerous. We send a high level mission. This is done partly because no one can think of anything else to do. But it also makes a measure of sense. It puts the immediate prestige of the United States behind essential social and economic reforms. It enables us to change past policy with grace. And the mission legitimizes the infusion of needed dollars hopefully with safeguards to insure less larcenous employment.

Since the situation is recurrent and widespread, and the remedy is much the same, I am persuaded that these operations should be arranged more thoughtfully than in the past. In the past, each has been an individual crisis: as in the case of the recent mission to Bolivia, an ad hoc group was hastily recruited and dispatched.

This is a sloppy and more than slightly dangerous procedure. We have here a rather intricate problem in economic and political diagnosis and therapy. Highly qualified economic knowledge is required of a very rare sort. There is no certainty that sufficiently talented and experienced people of requisite prestige can be assembled on short notice and there is a real chance that the wrong leader will do damage. It would be dubious policy for the Massachusetts General to recruit brain surgeons on a crisis basis whenever someone was brought in with a bad concussion.

Timing is also important. There are instances when conditions must get very bad before corrective action can be taken. But were this combination of economic and political therapy put on a more regular basis preventative action might more often be possible. Thus I am of the impression, based on intelligence from economists working there, that high level pressure on the Iranian government at the moment would avoid a larger outlay of money and a greater likelihood of disorder later on.

Accordingly I suggest that there be planning for these crises operations since, in fact, they will continue to be a normal aspect of our foreign policy. For the sake of being specific, I suggest that the President and the Secretary of State empanel a small group of men who would be properly qualified and permanently on call for emergency economic and political work abroad. The greatest consideration should be given to their selection for this is work of great subtlety and importance. Members should, with possible exceptions, be men already in the government. Their designation should not be publicized but the likelihood of such employment should be known to them. It should be recognized as an assignment of high distinction to take precedence on occasions of need over most regular activity. Some senior official, either in the Department of State or the White House, should be designated to keep in touch with the group. The members should be asked, within reason, to keep themselves informed on situations of potential concern and should have access to relevant cables and dispatches. They should, on occasion, be invited by the Secretary of State to meet for a review of situations of potential concern. Perhaps the group might be accorded some general designation such as "The President's Council on Economic and Political Policy."

Such men as Willard Wirtz of the Department of Labor, James Tobin of the Council of Economic Advisers, Edwin Martin of the Department of State, Arthur Schlesinger and Walt Rostow of the White House come to mind as combining the requisite economic and political sophistication but I cite them only by way of example.

---

10.   Memorandum From the Counselor of the Department of State and Chairman of the Policy Planning Council (McGhee) to the President's Special Assistant for National Security Affairs (Bundy)[1]

Washington, March 28, 1961.

SUBJECT

Future Responsibility for Activities Handled Formerly by OCB Functional Working Groups

The Department of State has already taken steps to carry forward the activities of those former OCB Working Groups which dealt with specific geographic regions or countries. Those steps are consistent with the statement which was made by the President upon issuing the Executive Order of February 18, 1961 which abolished the OCB. In certain instances where it may appear desirable or necessary to reestablish interagency working groups in connection with those activities this will be done under the Department's leadership.

---

[1] Source: Kennedy Library, National Security Files, Subject Series, Policy Planning, 2/11/61–5/61. Secret.

There were, in addition, twelve OCB Working Groups on subjects of a functional nature whose activities have as yet not been assigned as the continuing responsibility of any single department or agency.

Seven of those functional groups, each formerly chaired by a representative of the Department of State, concerned activities which were of primary concern to the Department and will continue to have significant foreign policy implications. They might well be dealt with in a manner similar to that which I understand has already been agreed to informally between yourself and Under Secretary Bowles for the activities of the former working groups on Antarctica and on Civil Aviation Policy Toward the Sino-Soviet Bloc, i.e., that the Department will assume leadership of the coordination and implementation of policies in those areas. Those seven groups were:

1. Working Group on Antarctica
2. Civil Aviation Policy Toward the Sino-Soviet Bloc
3. Cultural Presentations Committee
4. Ad Hoc Working Group on Foreign Disaster Relief Operations
5. Interdepartmental Escapee Committee, Escapees and Refugees
6. Working Group on Nuclear Energy Projects and Related Matters
7. Technical Panel on International Broadcasting

The activities of two of those functional groups, the one on Outer Space and the one on Security of Strategically Important Industrial Operations, appear not to require a specific assignment of responsibility for the future since the former is now the concern of the reactivated National Aeronautics and Space Council and the latter no longer requires special interdepartmental attention.

The three remaining former functional groups concerned subjects which are of principal interest to the other departments and agencies, i.e.:

1. The Exhibits Committee (USIA)
2. The Committee on People-to-People Program (USIA)
3. The Trade Fair Committee (Commerce)

The Department of State would be prepared, if you agree, to accept responsibility for the activities of the seven working groups enumerated in the third paragraph above and suggests that responsibility for the three working groups enumerated in the penultimate paragraph be assigned elsewhere as indicated.

George C. McGhee[2]

---

[2] Printed from a copy that bears this typed signature.

11.   **Memorandum From the President's Special Assistant for National Security Affairs (Bundy) to the Counselor of the Department of State and Chairman of the Policy Planning Council (McGhee)**[1]

Washington, March 30, 1961.

There follow several comments on the memorandum you sent me about the assignment of responsibility for activities formerly handled by OCB working groups.[2]

As you point out, the President clearly expressed in his February 18 statement his expectation that the Secretary of State would take the initiative for providing continuing coordination of U.S. actions with respect to a country or an area. Incidentally, I would appreciate receiving copies of completed papers which result from the work already begun by the State Department.

1. With respect to the functional assignments, the group that met with me on February 23 reached certain agreements that are in effect as far as I am concerned.[3]

2. With respect to Antarctica, the group agreed that:

"d. The Department of Defense will continue to be responsible for the logistics of U.S. activities in the Antarctic. Mr. Bowles will tell us when decisions have been reached on the way the State Department will provide policy guidance and insure coordination of all U.S. activities in the area."

I conclude from your memorandum that the decisions referred to have been reached.

3. With respect to civil aviation, the group agreed that:

"e. The State Department will assume responsibility for whatever coordination and policy guidance is required in the field of civil aviation, subject to further discussion at a later date."

This should be read in the context of the President's recent National Security Action Memorandum 32, dated March 21, 1961.[4]

4. With respect to trade fairs and exhibits, the group agreed that:

"a. USIA will assume responsibility for coordinating the planning and programming of all U.S. exhibits and trade fairs overseas."

---

[1] Source: Kennedy Library, National Security Files, Departments and Agencies Series, Operations Coordinating Board, 1/27/61–7/27/61. Secret.

[2] Document 10.

[3] No other record of this meeting has been found.

[4] Entitled "US–USSR Commercial Air Transport Agreement." (National Archives and Records Administration, RG 59, S/S–NSC Files: Lot 72 D 316, NSAM No. 32)

This also covers the question of what is to be done with the Cultural Presentations and Trade Fairs committees, which were created by action of the Director of the U.S. Information Agency. As you undoubtedly know, the administration of these two parts of the President's Special International Program is now under study by the Bureau of the Budget.

5. The OCB had no continuing concern with or working group on Foreign Disaster Relief Operations. The OCB had been used as a vehicle whereby the several agencies of the U.S. Government having an interest in these matters had developed a modus operandi. As to the future, the group agreed on February 23 that:

"f. The State Department will assume responsibility for insuring that appropriate guidelines are developed to cover emergency relief in cases of natural disasters overseas."

6. The work with respect to escapees and refugees is principally the responsibility of the State Department but there is an important segment of this activity which is of major interest to CIA.

7. The OCB Working Group on Nuclear Energy Projects and Related Matters was a catch-all group to which a wide variety of assignments was referred. I do not see how the work of this group can be devolved to any one agency of the government. The major agencies with legislative responsibility, i.e., State, Defense, AEC, NASA, as well as the President's Science Advisor, would be expected to take the initiative on matters within their jurisdiction.

8. The Technical Panel on International Broadcasting has been completely inactive and, in my opinion, need not be reactivated by any department—at least in its old form. The Director of the U.S. Information Agency is responsible for initiating such interdepartmental actions as may be needed in this field.

9. I agree with the view expressed concerning work formerly done by the group on Strategically Important Industrial Operations. OCDM has noted the abolition of this group.

10. With respect to Outer Space, the group agreed that:

"c. As soon as the Space Council is organized and functioning, decisions will be sought on the assignment of activities formerly carried on by the OCB in this area."

In view of the above, it does not appear to me that additional assignments to the State Department are required at this time, but I would appreciate your reaction.

McGeorge Bundy[5]

---

[5] Printed from a copy that bears this typed signature.

12.   **Memorandum From the President's Special Assistant for National Security Affairs (Bundy) to President Kennedy**[1]

Washington, April 4, 1961.

SUBJECT

Crisis Commanders in Washington

Over and over since January 20th we have talked of getting "task forces with individual responsible leaders" here in Washington for crisis situations. At the beginning, we thought we had task forces for Laos, the Congo and Cuba. We did get working groups with nobody in particular in charge, but we did not get clearly focused responsibility. The reason was that the Department of State was not quite ready, in each case, and this in turn was because of two factors: first, the senior State Department man was usually an Assistant Secretary with twelve other things on his mind, and second, these Assistant Secretaries, although men of good will, were not really prepared to take charge of the "military" and "intelligence" aspects—the Government was in the habit of "coordination" and out of the habit of the acceptance of individual executive leadership. Thus it has repeatedly been necessary to bring even small problems to you and still smaller ones to the White House staff, while more than once the ball has been dropped simply because no one person felt a continuing clear responsibility.

By contrast, in two areas where the crisis was less urgent, we have had effective leadership from the Department of State: one is the Latin American task force under Berle, and the other is the NATO task force under Acheson. In both cases, it is worth noting, your own staff have been energetically cued in to the working group—Goodwin with Berle, Rostow, Komer and I with Acheson. The Berle and Acheson groups were successful because Berle and Acheson took charge and had the stature to take charge.

We now very much need this kind of explicit assignment of authority in two particular areas: Viet-nam and Iran. The agreement upon this proposition is general throughout the government, but nothing is likely to happen unless you yourself, in agreement with the Secretary of State, designate individuals to do these two jobs. They should be in the State Department while they are in charge of the crisis, but they could come from anywhere in the government. Probably it would be best to begin with the State Department people. Walt and I suggest that Averell Harriman would be perfect for Iran, and perhaps George McGhee for

---

[1] Source: Kennedy Library, National Security Files, Bundy Memoranda to the President, 3/1/61–4/4/61. No classification marking.

Viet-nam. Averell is available, but George would have to be set free from his planning duties because Viet-nam is a long job. That would probably be a gain, because in all candor he is not a planner.

But the essential point is that the men involved should be sufficiently senior to take charge of the government as a whole, and to feel confident in acting directly for you and the Secretary. And they will have to be on these jobs full time.

McG. B.[2]

---

[2] Printed from a copy that bears these typed initials.

---

13. Memorandum From the President's Special Assistant for National Security Affairs (Bundy) to President Kennedy[1]

Washington, May 16, 1961.

SUBJECT

White House Organization

I'm giving this to Walt Rostow to give to you on the way back from Canada[2] because it can wait till then and because I hope you'll be in a good mood. We need some help from you so that we can serve you better, and incidentally prevent stories like the one from Oslo about chaos in the White House.

In the main that story and others like it are nonsense. Except for a brief period of disorder right after Cuba,[3] the White House under your direction since January has been a center of energy—and controlled energy—which has revived the Executive Branch. Don't take my word for it—take the word of all the old-timers who now fear that because of Cuba we may turn back to cautious inactivity.

Cuba was a bad mistake. But it was not a disgrace and there were reasons for it. If we set our critics on the left and right against each other

---

[1] Source: Kennedy Library, National Security Files, Bundy Memoranda to the President, 5/16–5/31/61. No classification marking.

[2] The President was in Canada May 16–18 for his first official visit outside the United States.

[3] Reference is to the abortive Bay of Pigs invasion of Cuba; see *Foreign Relations, 1961–1963*, volume X.

they would eat each other up, and we already know more about what went wrong and why than any of them. If the rules of the game allowed an explanation, we could give a good one—as you have been doing privately with great effect. Against our hopes and our responsibilities, Cuba is a nit-pick—it must not throw us off balance.

But we do have a problem of management; centrally it is a problem of your use of time and your use of staff. You have revived the government, which is an enormous gain, but in the process you have overstrained your own calendar, limited your chances for thought, and used your staff incompletely. You are altogether too valuable to go on this way; with a very modest change in your methods you can double your effectiveness and cut the strain on yourself in half. What follows is only one way of doing it—but it's worth some attention and represents, I think, a fair consensus of what a good many people would tell you—O'Donnell, Sorensen, Bell, R. Kennedy, Rusk, and Dungan.

First: you should set aside a real and regular time each day for national security discussion and action. This is not just a matter of intelligence briefing—though that is important and currently *not* well done by either Clifton or me (we can't get you to sit still, and we are not really professionals). It is at least as much a matter of taking time for reports of current action, review of problems awaiting solution, and planning of assignments that have a long-term meaning. The National Security Council, for example, really cannot work for you unless you authorize work schedules that do not get upset from day to day. Calling three meetings in five days is foolish—and putting them off for six weeks at a time is just as bad. Similarly, planning for a trip to Canada or a trip to Paris can be about three times as effective if you take part in it *ahead* of time, not just the morning before you leave. Or again, you cannot get what you need on a problem like test resumption if you don't take plenty of time to hear the arguments—and send back for more.

Truman and Eisenhower did their daily dozen in foreign affairs the first thing in the morning, and a couple of weeks ago you asked me to begin to meet you on this basis. I have succeeded in catching you on three mornings, for a total of about 8 minutes, and I conclude that this is not really how you like to begin the day. Moreover, 6 of the 8 minutes were given not to what I had for you but what you had for me from Marguerite Higgins, David Lawrence, Scotty Reston, and others. The newspapers are important, but not as an exercise in who leaked and why: against your powers and responsibilities, who the hell cares who told Maggie? But of course you must not stop reading the papers, and maybe another time of day would be better for daily business. After lunch? Tea? You name it. But you have to mean it, and it really has to be every day, with an equal alternate time when your schedule requires it.

The point about a regular meeting, at a reasonably fixed time, is that it can save you a lot of time and can redouble your influence—it can give your staff a coordinated sense of what you want and it can give everyone who needs it a time of day when they can reach you through an easy channel. It also gives you a way of keeping track of your own tremendous flow of ideas. Right now it is so hard to get to you with anything not urgent and immediate that about half of the papers and reports you personally ask for are never shown to you because by the time you are available you clearly have lost interest in them. If we put a little staff work on these and keep in close touch, we can be sure that *all* your questions are answered and that when you ask a big one the expert himself is brought in to recite.

Will you try it? Perhaps the best place for it would be the new Situation Room which we have just set up in the basement of the West Wing; the best time would be whatever you say. 9:30 without Maggie would be ideal—or even with Maggie—we could undertake to staff out all rough stones before you arrive. The operational business of action and plans would be my job, but I think we ought to have a professional for the intelligence briefing, and my personal suggestion is that you start with Bob Amory. He is really the Chief Intelligence Analyst of CIA, and before you decide they don't know their stuff you might try working with him—that part could be daily or three times a week, as you choose. Ted Clifton should be on hand with any business from the Joint Chiefs, and we could have anyone else you wanted.

Second—and much easier—if you can possibly manage it you must run closer to your schedule. When you start a big meeting half an hour late and let it go an hour overtime, you have not only disrupted the schedules of 30 men, but you have probably set 100 men under them to still greater trouble. This doesn't matter, except that it wastes executive energy, the most precious commodity you have brought to Washington. You should never forget that everyone who sees you *at all* is lucky—anyone who keeps you beyond the schedule is an imposition. The White House is a taut ship in terms of standards—but not in terms of schedules. By the same token—though it hurts to say it—you should close the back door to your office. Right now it is a great device for those of us who find it open—but it drives Ken O'Donnell crazy and it really makes it impossible for him or for anyone to protect you, so that recently you have had to take refuge *from your own office* in the little anteroom or in the garden. Possibly as a compromise you could let it be open only in the late afternoon and only for a specified list.

Third—there is the staffwork. Here we are making progress, but we need to be sure we are doing what you want; we can do much better for you than we have so far. For example: you deserve better protection from foreigners; you ought to get better briefing on their relevance; you should get more help on tough appointments like Assistant Secretary for Latin America (what's everyone's business is no one's business); and above all you are entitled to feel confident that (a) there is no part of government in the national security area that is not watched over closely by someone from you own staff, and (b) there is no major problem of policy that is not out where you can see it and give a proper stimulus to those who should be attacking it. Here the main duty is ours, and with your stimulus and leadership we'll do the job. If you'll agree to a daily meeting, I'll tell you how we can help you a whole lot more than we have yet succeeded in doing.

All this, if it is done right, will strengthen, not weaken, your Secretary of State, your Secretary of Defense, and your head of CIA. But most of all it should be useful to you.

McG. B.[4]

---

[4] Printed from a copy that bears these typed initials.

---

14. **Memorandum From Charles E. Johnson of the National Security Council Staff to the Professional Staff of the National Security Council**[1]

Washington, June 19, 1961.

SUBJECT

Operations Center of the Department of State

Attached is a description of the Operations Center recently established in the State Department under the direction of Mr. Achilles and Mr. Stutesman, his deputy. This is distributed as a matter of general information to the Staff, in view of the close working relationship that will be maintained between the National Security Council Staff and that of the Operations Center.

Charles E. Johnson[2]

---

[1] Source: Kennedy Library, National Security Files, Departments and Agencies Series, Department of State General, 6/17/61–6/20/61. No classification marking.

[2] Printed from a copy that bears this typed signature.

Attachment

OPERATIONS CENTER

In the Operations Center, with its interdepartmental staff, the Secretary has an instrument for following up government-wide action in the field of foreign affairs, for conducting informal interdepartmental reviews of emerging foreign policy problems, and for creating major interdepartmental Task Forces under his direction at an instant's notice.

I. Crises

S/O provides, on an around-the-clock basis, the secretariat, office and conference space and rapid communication facilities for the establishment and operation of as many as three major Task Forces at the same time.

Called into being by the Secretary, a Task Force gathers all pertinent facts bearing on a specific problem in the field of foreign affairs and prepares recommendations for action. The membership is drawn at appropriate levels from the Department and other agencies of the Government. The Chairman is usually the Assistant Secretary of the Geographic Bureau most directly concerned.

The Chairman and the substantive officers of the Task Force are given office space and officer and secretarial staff assistance in S/O. Intelligence and operational data regarding the problem under study flow on a 24-hour duty basis directly into S/O from the State Department Telegraph Branch, the intelligence community through INR, from the Defense Department and from other agencies as required.

Task Forces should be disbanded as soon as possible after the functions for which they are established have been fulfilled, subject to reconstitution if and when needed.

II. Potential Crises

As an emerging or potential crisis is identified, the Secretary may place it under special watch in S/O. In view of the fact that communications from the field, from other agencies and from the intelligence community are more rapid and complete to S/O than to a Geographic Bureau, it may be useful to detail an appropriate Geographic Bureau officer to S/O for the period of watch. This gives that substantive officer the full benefit of S/O facilities and removes him from the pressures of daily routine so that he can devote full time to the significant questions of the problem under study.

In effect, an interdepartmental Task Force in a minor key is thus established as the permanent Defense, CIA and USIA members of S/O work on an easy, continuing and informal basis with the Department officers concerned. This group, studying all alert signals and reviewing existing policies, establishes a foundation of interdepartmental understanding upon which a major Task Force can be built at an instant's notice.

III. Follow Up

Basic responsibility for the implementation of policies requiring interdepartmental coordination rests with the appropriate Assistant Secretaries under the coordinating supervision of the Deputy Under Secretary for Political Affairs. S/O assists the Deputy Under Secretary in the exercise of his responsibilities and follows up, at the Secretary's direction, any interdepartmental action in the field of foreign affairs whether it originated within the Department or in the National Security Council or in other inter-agency decision.

With a minimum of written reports and a maximum of informal consultation, S/O maintains a continuing review of programs and can identify at an early stage problems in the implementation of those programs which may require high level attention. Formal interdepartmental committee meetings or "progress reports" are called for only when essential.

S/O thus serves the Secretary by keeping a continuing review of government-wide action on certain programs. At the same time, S/O assists the Geographic Bureau desk officers by offering them a constant high level contact with Defense, CIA and USIA through the representatives of those agencies assigned to S/O.

IV. Watch

S/O has an officer (generally FSO-3 level), a clerk and a messenger-driver on duty at all times.

Other around-the-clock watch officers in the Department are: (1) the INR duty officer who monitors all intelligence reports; and (2) the Telegraph Branch Watch Officer who monitors all operational cables. They are under instruction to alert the S/O duty officer the instant any significant message appears regarding any problem being dealt with by S/O.

Thus, the S/O duty officer is constantly in touch with all major developments on those problems and is prepared to take the necessary action to deal promptly with any question or problem which may arise. Some questions he may be able to answer on the basis of his own knowledge of S/O activities and the briefing he received before going on duty. Other matters may require a search for information. In this connection, he is furnished with a daily revised list of telephone numbers where every S/O officer may be reached that evening or night. He will take counsel with the S/S duty officer in the office during the day or at home at night if an operational problem outside S/O jurisdiction should arise.

15. Editorial Note

A White House memorandum of June 22, 1961, prepared for President Kennedy, was entitled "Current Organization of the White House and NSC For Dealing With International Matters." The memorandum summarized efforts to date, indicating that "The President's staff is at present about two-thirds of the way toward a sound and durable organization for his work in international affairs. Since January a number of steps have been taken, and in the same period the President's concept of what he wants has developed somewhat. There is still unfinished business." The memorandum is printed in full in *Foreign Relations*, 1961–1963, volume VIII, Document 31.

16. Editorial Note

On September 4, 1961, McGeorge Bundy described the Kennedy administration's changes in and operation of the National Security Council in a letter to Senator Henry M. Jackson as Chairman of the Subcommittee on Policy Machinery of the Senate Committee on Government Operations. For text, see Jackson, ed. *National Security Council*, pages 275–279. In a subsequent letter to Jackson of January 28, 1965, Bundy stated: "In almost every particular, the principles and procedures set forth in the [September 4,] 1961 letter have governed the work of the Council under both President Kennedy and President Johnson." (Ibid., pages 279–280)

At the end of 1961, Bundy established a Standing Group of the National Security Council that was to meet weekly in the White House

Situation Room to "organize and monitor the work of the National Security Council and to take up such other matters as may be presented to the group by its members." This NSC Standing Group was to meet 15 times between January and August 1962. Its chairman was the Under Secretary of State for Political Affairs, and its members included the Deputy Secretary of Defense, the Director of Central Intelligence, and the President's Special Assistant for National Security Affairs. The Executive Secretary of the NSC would participate, as would representatives of other agencies in accordance with particular agenda items. After a lapse in meetings, Bundy revived the Standing Group in April 1963 under his chairmanship, first as the Plans and Operations Committee, then as the Standing Committee, and shortly as the NSC Standing Group, the original name. (Smith, *Organizational History of the National Security Council,* pages 51–53; see also Document 23)

President Kennedy, in his opening remarks at the 469th meeting of the National Security Council on January 18, 1962, described the role of the NSC with respect to Executive Branch departments and agencies. The meeting summary noted that "The President referred to the Council's responsibility for integrating the work of the Departments of State and Defense and the Central Intelligence Agency, with the participation of the Treasury Department and other agencies when matters of interest to them were being considered. He asked the members to cooperate in making the Council meetings useful, and ensuring that decisions arising out of the Council meetings were effectively carried out." See *Foreign Relations,* 1961–1963, volume VIII, Document 69.

17.   Memorandum by the Under Secretary of State (Bowles)[1]

Washington, October 31, 1961.

Foreign Policy and Operations Guidelines

As you may recall, the President on February 19, 1961, abolished the Operations Coordinating Board and stated:

. . . we will center responsibility for much of the Board's work in the Secretary of State.   He expects to rely particularly on the Assistant Secretaries in charge of regional bureaus, and they in turn will consult closely with other departments and agencies. This will be our ordinary rule for continuing coordination of our work in relation to a country or area.

Correspondingly it was agreed that country and regional policy papers formerly prepared by the NSC Planning Board would be prepared by the Department of State, though some of exceptional security importance might still be submitted to the NSC before dissemination.

Accordingly the Department of State has been developing a series of policy and operations Guidelines papers intended to replace both NSC and OCB country and regional papers. Our aim is to make them as useful as possible in the coordinated guidance of the national foreign effort. They are still in the experimental stage, and your suggestions for improving their usefulness would be most welcome.

Our regional Assistant Secretaries are responsible for the preparation of these papers. The procedure we have evolved so far includes consultation with other agencies at the working level while a paper is being drafted, referral to the field for comment by the chief or chiefs of mission concerned, after consultation with members of the country team, clearance at bureau level in the Department of State, referral to other agencies principally interested for formal comment; and (a) dissemination in final after any important differences have been resolved or (b) submission to the NSC if that is decided upon in a particular case. We plan to revise the papers once a year.

---

[1]   Source: National Archives and Records Administration, RG 59, S/S–NSC (Miscellaneous) Files: Lot 66 D 95, NSC Administrative, 1961. No classification marking. A handwritten notation on the memorandum indicates it was "Sent to all Cabinet heads (members)." In an October 31 covering note to Bundy, attached to another copy, Bowles wrote that the memorandum had been prepared for governmental departments and agencies to explain procedures for preparing papers to replace the former NSC and OCB regional and country papers. Bowles recommended that the President rescind papers in the former NSC series as papers in the new series appeared. Bowles would submit specific recommendations at the time papers were transmitted to the White House and sent for comment to interested agencies and departments. (Memorandum from Bowles to Bundy, "Preparation of Policy Guidelines Papers," October 31; Kennedy Library, National Security Files, Department of State, General, 10/16/61–10/31/61)

The first of these papers has reached the stage of referral for agency comment. These papers will be addressed to your office for this purpose unless you prefer otherwise. We would appreciate your helping us expedite the process.

Chester Bowles

---

18. Memorandum From Secretary of State Rusk to the Assistant Secretaries of State[1]

Washington, July 2, 1962.

SUBJECT

Systematic Planning for Crises

As a result of several meetings on the anticipation of crises, I am requesting a new procedure to strengthen our performance in this area.

While the exact shape and date of a particular crisis is virtually unpredictable, we can endeavor to isolate and act briskly to exploit moments of transient opportunity, observe trends and situations that are likely to produce crises, and systematically think out ahead of time the critical dimensions of the problems these crises will create. In the light of such thought we may generate lines of action which could prevent, mitigate, or even turn such situations to our advantage. A great deal of work within the Department is already addressed to these objectives.

A successful program to meet these objectives will require the closest cooperation among those who illuminate the alternatives available to us, those who make decisions, and those who carry them out. I want to insure that a greater portion of the energies of the desk officers, who are so often absorbed in the day's immediate problems, are directed toward steps we should be taking now in order to improve our posture in the future. The purpose of this program is to provide a systematic means for strengthening the contribution of the Policy Planning Council to the operating bureaus in this respect. The operating bureaus retain full discretion and responsibility for the implementation of recommendations emanating from the informal working groups organized under this program.

---

[1] Source: National Archives and Records Administration, RG 59, S/P Files: Lot 70 D 199, Planning, 1962. Confidential.

I am therefore requesting Mr. Rostow to consult with each of you in order to undertake the following program:

1. Arrangements for consultation on a regular and systematic basis, between designated officers of the Policy Planning Council and the operating bureaus to select an initial list of problems for anticipatory planning on a priority basis and to establish a regular procedure for identifying situations of opportunity.

2. Establishment of small, informal working groups under the leadership of the Policy Planning Council, including representation from the responsible bureaus, and the intelligence and planning community, to develop specific plans and time tables for action on each designated priority problem.

3. Presentation of reports and recommendations of the working groups to the Assistant Secretary of the responsible bureau for his consideration and such action as he finds appropriate.

Dean Rusk

---

19.   National Security Action Memorandum No. 173[1]

Washington, July 18, 1962.

TO

The Secretary of State
The Secretary of Defense
The Attorney General
The Chairman, Joint Chiefs of Staff
The Director of Central Intelligence
The Administrator, Agency for International Development
The Director, United States Information Agency
The Chairman, Special Group (Counterinsurgency)

SUBJECT

Interdepartmental Field Visits

I feel that there is a need for accelerating our programs for underdeveloped countries and for effecting a closer tie between the County Team planning in these areas and the Washington departments which

---

[1] Source: National Archives and Records Administration, RG 59, S/S–NSC Files: Lot 72 D 316, NSAM No. 173. Confidential. Regarding the implementation of NSAM No. 173, see Document 20.

participate in these programs. It would seem to me that the technique of interdepartmental team visits used last fall in South Viet-Nam and early this year in certain Latin American countries could be broadened and applied to this requirement.

To this end, I would like to have organized a program of field visits by senior interdepartmental teams, under State Department chairmanship, to a number of selected countries, with particular attention to Latin America. These teams would consult with the Ambassador, his staff and local officials, would review the Country Team plans, and would form a judgment as to their adequacy, their consistency with United States objectives, and the reliability of the intelligence upon which they are based. Upon return to Washington, the teams would submit appropriate recommendations to me, through the Secretary of State, for strengthening United States activities in the countries visited which, when approved, would receive the same kind of intensive implementation as that being accorded the current South Viet-Nam program.

I would like the Secretary of State, in consultation with the Special Group (Counterinsurgency) to initiate as a matter of urgency a program of visits of the kind outlined above.

John F. Kennedy

---

20.   Editorial Note

In response to the President's request of July 18, 1962, in National Security Action Memorandum No. 173 (Document 19) for the initiation of a program of Interdepartmental Field Visits by specially constituted teams, Secretary Rusk met later that day with General Maxwell D. Taylor, the President's Military Representative, and William H. Orrick, Jr., Deputy Under Secretary of State for Administration. Rusk subsequently assigned Orrick responsibility for developing a program of Interdepartmental Field Visits. In early August, Rusk discussed the matter again with Taylor and with Attorney General Robert F. Kennedy, and Rusk approved a paper dated August 7, drafted by Orrick, for discussion by the Special Group (Counter-Insurgency) at its August 9 meeting. These discussions are described in a memorandum from Orrick to Rusk, August 7. (National Archives and Records Administration, RG 59, S/S–NSC Files: Lot 72 D 316, NSAM No. 173)

The August 7 paper set forth the terms of reference and composition of the Interdepartmental Field teams. In consultation with the Ambassador in a given country and the members of his staff, as well as with local officials as appropriate, the teams would:

"(a) ascertain whether our country team plans are adequate to meet existing conditions, are consistent with our national interests and policy objectives, and are based upon reliable intelligence;

"(b) ascertain whether U.S. Government officials, under the leadership of the Ambassador, are pursuing the country team plans aggressively and effectively enough. For example, given the local situation, is there adequate contact with youth, labor, opposition and other outside-government groups as well as with Government circles;

"(c) ascertain whether the Ambassador is fulfilling his role as leader of the country team, is familiar with all country team programs, and is thoroughly aware of all policy directives from Washington to country team members;

"(d) ascertain the total image of the country team operation in the country under survey, including the standing of the Ambassador and the country team in the local community."

Each team was to submit a detailed report to the Secretary of State, who would then forward it to the President. Each team would be under State Department chairmanship and would not exceed in membership a total of four persons, excluding an Executive Assistant from the State Department. In addition to the Department of State, the Department of Defense, AID, USIA, CIA, and other agencies would be represented as appropriate to conditions in a given country. From time to time a public member might be added. Because of the immediate importance of relations with Latin America, it was recommended that the first team visit the Dominican Republic and Colombia as soon as possible, with a second team visiting Brazil and Argentina.

At a meeting later in August of the Special Group (CI) under the chairmanship of General Taylor, it was decided that the first team would visit Venezuela and Guatemala. (Letters from Rusk to John G. Bell, Ambassador to Guatemala, and from Rusk to C. Allan Stewart, Ambassador to Venezuela, both dated August 20; ibid.)

Under the provisions of NSAM No. 173, the Special Group (Counter-Insurgency) approved the creation of a joint survey team, headed by General William H. Draper, Jr., to visit Brazil and submit appropriate recommendations. The report of the Survey Team on Brazil to President Kennedy, dated November 3, 1962, is in *Foreign Relations, 1961–1963*, volume XII, Document 228.

An Interdepartmental Survey Group on Liberia and Tunisia was also formed by the Special Group (Counter-Insurgency) under the authority of NSAM No. 173. The report of this group to President Kennedy was dated April 19, 1963; the portion on Tunisia is printed ibid., volume XXI, Document 184. Additional documentation on the Survey Group on Liberia and Tunisia is in the National Archives and Records Administration, RG 59, S/S–NSC Files: Lot 72 D 316, NSAM No. 173.

---

21.   Memorandum by Director of Central Intelligence McCone[1]

Washington, November 16, 1962.

In discussions with General Eisenhower on a number of occasions during the past several months, he has raised the question of the adequacy of organization of the Executive Branch of the government as now constituted. Specifically General Eisenhower feels that

1. NSC meetings should be held regularly, at weekly intervals, and should be attended by designated members.

2. Benefit of such meetings is so that the President can hear the views of his principal advisors on all matters of interest expressed in the presence of one another, so that he, the President, will have the benefit of differing points of view on any particular problem expressed in the presence of one another and in his own presence.

3. Of particular importance in General Eisenhower's opinion is to have regular intelligence briefings at NSC meetings so that the President can benefit by conflicting evaluations or opinions of his principal advisors with respect to intelligence matters. Eisenhower feels very strongly that the circulation of intelligence reports fails to accomplish this specific objective.

4. The NSC, to function properly and adequately serve the President, must be supported by properly organized planning staffs.

---

[1] Source: Central Intelligence Agency, DCI (McCone) Files, Job 80–B01285A, DCI Memoranda for the Record, 9/24/62–12/31/62. Secret. This memorandum is referred to in a November 16 memorandum from Bundy to President Kennedy entitled "The National Security Council and Supporting Staff Organization." In his memorandum Bundy, apparently in response to remarks by former President Eisenhower, reviewed the NSC organizational changes put into effect by the new administration. Bundy advised President Kennedy that the reorganized system had always had "rather more organization than General Eisenhower probably recognizes" and that "much of General Eisenhower's criticism may be directed against phenomena which were more characteristic of our first few months than of your present operations." For text, see *Foreign Relations*, 1961–1963, vol. VIII, Document 108.

Eisenhower supports the concept that Operations Coordinating Board and the Planning Board have permanent, established organizations to prepare for NSC meetings and to insure decisions are properly carried out and he recognizes organizations of this type must be tailored to the desires of the President. In this connection Eisenhower feels that committees established for specific purposes are frequently not supported by staff and their work is not carefully coordinated with related problems which may be outside of the jurisdiction of the committee.

John A. McCone[2]

---

[2] Printed from a copy that bears this typed signature.

---

22. Memorandum From the Chairman of the Policy Planning Council (Rostow) to Secretary of State Rusk[1]

Washington, November 16, 1962.

SUBJECT

Status of Systematic Planning for Crises

On July 2, 1962, you issued an instruction to the Assistant Secretaries concerning the establishment of a new procedure to strengthen our performance in the anticipation of crises.

Pursuant to that instruction the geographic bureaus submitted lists of problems requiring anticipatory planning. From these lists S/P and the operating bureaus have distilled an initial list of priority problems and work has been instituted on these. In reviewing the problem of anticipating crises with the bureaus, it was noted that there are all manner of crises with which the bureaus are daily concerned and which are subject to intensive planning efforts. The priority list as finally prepared was limited to those crises which were not already upon us and which it appeared would not become acute until a time period a little farther off in the future. The initial priority list which follows was chosen on a selective basis with the idea of starting off modestly with just a few topics and doing these well:

---

[1] Source: National Archives and Records Administration, RG 59, S/P Files: Lot 70 D 199, Planning, 1962. Confidential.

AF

Ghana Succession Problem:

This was one of the priority problems selected as falling within the purview of your July 2, 1962, instruction. Work was already in a well advanced stage in AF and S/P when a White House request for a paper on this subject was received. A paper was promptly furnished the White House on September 29, 1962.

Southwest Africa (UNGA action to enforce respect for the mandate):

The work developed on this subject in AF was sent to USUN in the form of staff studies, a position paper, and telegrams. Additional work must await the outcome of UNGA debate.

Angola (reassessment of Angolan Nationalist leadership):

A paper on this problem is in an advanced stage in AF.

EUR

Succession Problem in the Iberian Peninsula:

The first draft of a post-Franco paper has been completed and is currently being circulated in the Department for comment. A first draft on a post-Salazar paper is scheduled for January 1.

De Gaulle Succession Problem:

Work has commenced in EUR on this problem. A first draft is expected by January 1.

FE

Indonesian Economic Crisis:

Pursuant to your instruction work on this problem had already begun when a National Security Action Memorandum was received requesting a program of emergency aid to Indonesia. A paper on this subject was prepared in FE, in consultation with S/P and other agencies, and sent to the President in the form of a memorandum from you dated October 10, 1962. A study of the long-range aspects of this problem is continuing in FE and S/P.

Second Bandung Conference:

Preliminary steps have been taken by FE in the form of circular telegrams and airgrams to feel the world-wide pulse on this subject and quietly discourage participation in this conference. A circular telegram to FE posts containing general guidance on this subject is nearing completion.

NEA

Arms Control Problem (Israel vs. Arab States):

S/P, in consultation with NEA, has nearly completed a first draft of a paper on this subject.

ARA

Due to the chronic crisis condition of the area, Assistant Secretary Martin and I agreed that it might be better to subsume crisis planning under the Strategic Studies in Latin America. Mr. Martin and I have requested your approval of this procedure in a separate memorandum concerning the Strategic Country Studies.

---

23.   Editorial Note

On January 18, 1963, the Senate Subcommittee on National Security Staffing and Operations chaired by Senator Henry M. Jackson issued a staff report entitled *Administration of National Security: Basic Issues* (Washington, 1963). The Senate had established the subcommittee in May 1962 as successor to the Subcommittee on National Policy Machinery. As the foreword to this report indicated, the subcommittee's purpose was to "review the administration of national security at home and in the field, and to make findings and recommendations for improvement where appropriate." The subcommittee was "concerned with the administration of national security—with getting good people into key foreign and defense posts and enabling them to do a job. It is not inquiring into the substance of policy." The report outlined basic issues on which the subcommittee would hold hearings during the present Congress. These issues included the President's problems in dealing with national security issues; dilemmas of administration; the President, the Secretary of State, and the problem of coordination; the Ambassador and the Country Team; Executive responsibility for administration; and communications.

In a memorandum to President Kennedy on April 2, Bundy referred to recent discussion of the need for strengthening interdepartmental planning and coordination of major national security issues. The Executive Committee of the NSC established during the Cuban Missile Crisis in October 1962 had been useful for major interdepartmental decisions, but was "not so good for lesser matters of coordination." Bundy proposed a new Standing Group of the NSC to be known as the Plans and Operations Committee. The Committee would be parallel to the NSC Executive Committee, but would not include the President, Vice President, Secretary of State, or Secretary of Defense. The new

Standing Group would meet weekly with Bundy as chairman; it would review ongoing interdepartmental programs and future planning problems and would be "used for the occasional discursive review of drastic alternatives to existing policies." The text of Bundy's memorandum, entitled "A Standing Committee of the National Security Council," is printed in *Foreign Relations*, 1961–1963, volume VIII, Document 131.

---

24.   Memorandum From the President's Special Assistant for National Security Affairs (Bundy) to the President's Special Counsel (Sorensen)[1]

Washington, March 8, 1963.

SUBJECT

Decisions in the White House

It is a great advantage for you not to know how much academic nonsense is written about "the decision-making process," and it is probably not sensible for me to try to add to what you know so well about the real life here. Nevertheless the subject is interesting even outside the world of academic jargon, and the following points occur to me:

1. The modes of Presidential decision are enormously varied: there is the legislative method, the press conference reply, the individual appointed, the candidate encouraged, the interview granted and refused, the news that is made or prevented, the effort at persuasion included or omitted, the speech delivered, and perhaps as important as any group of these together, the ceaseless process by which, if an administration is lively, recommendations and proposals are ground forward for consideration. What I think many people forget is that the entire Presidential existence is in this sense a process of decision.

2. Most big decisions have lots of history. In the most notable single case, the missile crisis, it appears as if the decision were made between Tuesday and Sunday. But the fact is that very important antecedent decisions were made at the end of August and in early September, and incorporated in Presidential statements of major significance. Earlier still, in the speeches which followed the Bay of Pigs and in a consistent set of com-

---

[1] Source: Kennedy Library, National Security Files, Bundy Chron File, March 1963. No classification marking.

ments on Cuba for more than a year thereafter, the President had laid down a line of policy which was plainly inconsistent with a strategic missile base in Cuba. Equally clearly he had laid down a line of conduct developed out of his conviction that invasion of Cuba by the U.S. Armed Forces, in the absence of a major change in the situation, would not be in the national interest. Carefully construed, the decisions of October 1962 are an outgrowth of a line of policy developed by the President in many different modes over a long period of time. (And one may say, by contrast, of the Bay of Pigs, that it grew out of an early history which was not of the President's making and had to be grafted on to a point of view which was incompletely shaped in his own mind by the time decision became necessary—and in addition he was hampered by all the difficulties and unfamiliarities and failings of men who did not know him or their own roles as perhaps they have been learning to do since.) I think the steel case[2] has quite a similar trail of preparation which was really governing in what was required of the President when the moment came, but you know much more about that than I.

3. At least in my experience there is always a lot of discussion of the relative roles of the WH Staff and of Cabinet officers and their Departments and Agencies. You know as much about this as I do; my own belief is that our best course as staff officers is to make it clear that we are operating within the framework of the President's own immediate responsibilities and are not trying to replace or blockade those who have major operational, statutory, and advisory responsibilities of their own.

4. The President's use of all arms for information and comment is as striking as his very good record in using only responsible officers for final advice and decision. This is familiar to you—but not to everyone else.

5. The President's larger policies: an open door to Moscow, an open door to all underdog Americans, an open door to intelligence and hope, honor to bravery, equal sense of past and future, gallantry to beauty, and pride in politics—these are colors of a permanent palette—reflected in the small as well as the large decisions, drawn from in a hundred ways.

6. The President relies heavily on others for all sorts of follow-up, and intercommunication, and preparation and recommendation. He also delegates, massively but selectively. But he is still probably the most personal President of modern times—doing more himself. You know the millions of examples.

McG. B.[3]

---

[2] Reference is to President Kennedy's successful effort in April 1962 to persuade the steel industry to rescind steel price increases.

[3] Printed from a copy that bears these typed initials.

25. Memorandum From the President's Special Assistant for National Security Affairs (Bundy) to President Kennedy[1]

Washington, April 12, 1963.

I have been very slow in sending this memorandum on long-range planning aspects, prepared in Walt Rostow's office and forwarded at the end of February by Dean Rusk.[2] The reason is that I just could not find a time when I thought you were likely to give it the attention they would like. But perhaps now you could have a quick look and agree to have a meeting with Walt and the Secretary and a very few others next week on these planning problems. My own guess is that what is needed for Walt is a real sense of your own interest and some sense on priorities, and beyond that we could probably organize the consideration of some of these long-range problems in the Standing Committee which you, Bobby and I have been discussing.

That Committee is now, incidentally, agreed around town and will begin operation next week. Its title will be "Standing Committee of the NSC" and we intend to have absolutely no publicity about it in order to avoid useless chatter about seizing the initiative from the State Department or restoring the OCB, or otherwise reorganizing ourselves in the spring of our discontent.

McG. B.[3]

---

[1] Source: Kennedy Library, National Security Files, Meetings and Memoranda Series, Standing Group Meetings General, 4/63–5/63. No classification marking. Another copy is ibid., Bundy Memoranda to the President, 3/63–4/63.

[2] Reference is to a February 28 memorandum from Rusk to the President, entitled "Critical Planning Tasks." (National Archives and Records Administration, RG 59, S/S–NSC Files: Lot 70 D 265, BSNP 1963) The memorandum, drafted in the Policy Planning Council, described the status of 32 basic national planning tasks (see *Foreign Relations, 1961–1963*, vol. VIII, Documents 70 and 83), 8 strategic studies on individual countries, all in Latin America and Africa, and 13 political contingency plans. The memorandum recommended that the President "meet soon with a few of your key advisers to review the state of national security planning and, especially, to isolate those planning tasks you personally regard as critical." For additional background, see ibid., Document 126.

[3] Printed from a copy that bears these typed initials.

26.   Editorial Note

On December 5, 1963, President Lyndon B. Johnson chaired the first National Security Council meeting of his administration. Because there was no Vice President, the President invited Representative Sam Rayburn of Texas to attend National Security Council meetings "from time to time as his schedule permitted." Rayburn was Johnson's successor in the event of the President's death in office. For an outline of remarks Bundy prepared for the President and the summary record of this 520th NSC meeting, see *Foreign Relations, 1961–1963*, volume VIII, Documents 149 and 150. See also Smith, *Organizational History of the National Security Council*, page 57.

Organization and Reorganization of the Department of State and Foreign Service

27. Memorandum From the Deputy Under Secretary of State for Administration (Jones) to Secretary of State Rusk[1]

Washington, February 14, 1961.

SUBJECT

Closing Marginal Posts

The attached list (Tab A) of marginal posts includes the five least important in each geographic area, as ranked last summer by the Regional Bureaus. The combined staff and total annual cost of these 25 posts is 233 positions and $1,876,500. SCA reviewed the list and expressed opposition to closing eight of them because of their importance to consular work; simultaneously SCA suggested seven others which might be considered for closing.

There seems little doubt that the 32 posts listed are those of least importance to the United States in the conduct of diplomatic relations and consular work. During the past few months consideration has been given to closing some or all of these posts. ARA announced the closing of Colon, Panama, in August, but because of local pressures, now plans to keep the post open on a limited basis. EUR is planning to close Aruba this month. No other definite action toward additional closings has been taken.

The decision to close any post is, in the final analysis, a political one. Political factors to be considered are: the reaction of national and local governments to what they may interpret as a loss of prestige; the current status of relations which may at a given moment focus greater attention on a post closing than objectively it warrants; inter-city rivalries and jealousies within a county where the United States maintains several consulates; adverse public relations which may result from inconveniences to those receiving services from a post; pressures from United States citizens resident or travelling in a locality because they like to maintain a close and tangible contact with home. These, and similar factors, can be assessed properly only by the Regional Bureaus.

We should not overlook the importance of the human factor involved. The workload at such posts is somewhat routine and unchal-

---

[1] Source: National Archives and Records Administration, RG 59, Management Staff Files: Lot 69 D 434, Miscellaneous Subject Files, 1960–1967, Marginal Consular Posts, 1961. No classification marking. Drafted by Paul G. Sinderson, Office of Budget (OB), and James G. Hoofnagle, Office of Budget and Finance (A/BF).

lenging. As a result the officers assigned tend to get in a rut and eventually lose their initiative. It seems to me that the human resources which can be recaptured and channeled into more urgent tasks are more important than the mere dollars involved.

I believe the need for review of marginal posts is urgent. You may wish to have Mr. Bowles take it up as a high priority, political item for discussion with the Assistant Secretaries involved.

Recommendation

That you ask Under Secretary Bowles to discuss the subject of closing marginal posts with the Assistant Secretaries of the Regional Bureaus and recommend the appropriate action.[2]

Tab A

DEPARTMENT OF STATE

List of Least Important Posts as Ranked by Regional Bureaus
(June, 1960)

ARA	American	Local	Total	Total Cost Annual Rate
Mexicali	3	2	5	$36,400
Antofagasta	2	3	5	29,000
Piedras Negras	2	3	5	26,800
Santos	1	3	4	17,600
Colon	2	2	4	25,000
	10	13	23	134,800
EUR				
Aruba	4	5	9	74,100
Antwerp	7	19	26	149,700
Trieste	9	9	18	119,300
St. John	2	7	9	62,200
Basel	3	5	8	57,500
	25	45	70	462,800

---

[2] Rusk initialed his approval. He sent a copy of this paper to Under Secretary Bowles on February 18, under cover of a memorandum that reads as follows: "I am enthusiastic about a good look at the possibility of closing some of our marginal consular posts in different parts of the world. The problem is somewhat like the organization of our county governments in the United States. Modern communication and ease of travel have greatly reduced the need for consulates which are too close together. Desk officers in geographic bureaus may be somewhat over sensitive about the short term political effect of closing a consulate. If we are too impressed by these considerations, we shall never get our house in order." (Ibid., Rusk Files: Lot 72 D 192, Chron File, February, 1961)

DEPARTMENT OF STATE

List of Least Important Posts as Ranked by Regional Bureaus
(June, 1960)

NEA	American	Local	Total	Total Cost Annual Rate
Alexandria	4	8	12	103,400
Iskenderun	3	6	9	75,400
Aleppo	5	8	13	104,500
Isfahan	3	7	10	90,200
Haifa	3	7	10	80,000
	18	36	54	453,500
FE				
Mandalay	3	6	9	50,900
Brisbane	4	3	7	35,600
Cebu	3	5	8	56,000
Hue	2	5	7	41,800
Adelaide	2	3	5	40,900
	14	22	36	225,200
AF				
Kaduna	4	6	10	52,800
Lourenco Marques	4	9	13	71,500
Capetown	7	7	14	120,700
Port Elizabeth	2	3	5	40,300
Durban	3	5	8	53,900
	20	30	50	339,200
PER costs	-	-	-	261,000
Total	87	146	233	1,876,500

Note: SCA opposes the closing of the following posts listed above because of their importance in consular work: Mexicali, Piedras Negras, Aruba, Trieste, St. John, Haifa, Capetown, and Durban.

SCA suggests the following posts not listed above might beconsidered for closing: Cork, Edinburgh, Manchester or Liverpool, Turin, La Havre, Southampton, Vera Cruz.

28. Memorandum From the President's Special Assistant for National Security Affairs (Bundy) to President Kennedy[1]

Washington, February 25, 1961.

The more I see of the developing pattern of responsibility in the Department of State, the more I am inclined to share the view of Dean Rusk and Chester Bowles that the key job over there will be the Deputy Under Secretary of State for Political Affairs. This has not been so in the past, but in the pattern which is now developing this officer will necessarily be a point of responsible action and coordination for many of the things in which State must take the lead, and must also work in close cooperation with the Defense Department and CIA. The man who fills this job will have to be an active and decisive person, quite different from the ordinary foreign service type.

[Here follow four paragraphs concerning personnel options.]

McG. B.[2]

---

[1] Source: Kennedy Library, National Security Files, Departments and Agencies Series, State Department, 2/21/61–3/5/61. No classification marking.

[2] Printed from a copy that bears these typed initials.

---

29. Editorial Note

Secretary of State Rusk, in a staff meeting on April 14, 1961, requested the Executive Secretary of the Department of State, Lucius D. Battle, to ask the Assistant Secretaries to submit brief papers on the long-range problems facing their respective bureaus. By May 5, nine bureaus had responded, and six others had not. (Note from Battle to Rusk, May 5; National Archives and Records Administration, RG 59, Central Files 1960–63, 110.10/4–1961) The responses included a report from Deputy Under Secretary for Administration Roger W. Jones, dated April 22; from Assistant Secretary for Administration William J. Crockett, dated May 4; from Assistant Secretary for Public Affairs Robert Tubby, dated May 5; from Assistant Secretary for European Affairs Foy D. Kohler, dated May 3; from Assistant Secretary for Near Eastern and South Asian Affairs Lewis

Jones, dated April 19; from Acting Assistant Secretary for Inter-American Affairs Wymberley DeR. Coerr, dated May 4; from Assistant Secretary for African Affairs G. Mennen Williams, dated May 4; and from the Director of the Bureau of Intelligence and Research, Roger Hilsman, dated May 3. Battle transmitted the reports to Rusk under cover of his May 5 note.

30. Memorandum From the Under Secretary of State (Bowles) to Secretary of State Rusk[1]

Washington, June 14, 1961.

SUBJECT

The Need to Improve the Administration of Foreign Policy

Our ability to create a more effective, more realistic, and more affirmative American foreign policy rests in large measure on the ability of the top echelon of the Department of State under the general direction of the President and in conjunction with other agencies to produce wise decisions.

It is equally dependent on greatly improved administrative State Department operations, reaching into every section and country desk in Washington and out to every overseas mission, that will assure that these decisions are carried out.

The following measures to achieve this greater effectiveness are either now being taken or are immediately contemplated.

I. *Improvement of our Operations here in Washington*

At a recent meeting in my office, I asked each bureau head personally to review the operations of each country desk and other working components within his bureau.

These studies are now being completed, and with the help of Roger Jones, Bill Crockett and Herman Pollack, I am holding meetings with each bureau head to discuss whatever personnel changes and adminis-

---

[1] Source: Kennedy Library, National Security Files, Departments and Agencies Series, State Department, 6/17/61–6/20/61. No classification marking. Bowles sent a copy of this memorandum to Bundy on June 19 with a note that reads as follows: "I thought you might be interested in seeing a copy of the memorandum I wrote Dean [Rusk] last week on improving the administration." (Ibid.)

trative changes are required to assure both the necessary experience and fresh perspective at all levels of each bureau.

We should avoid the appearance of a shake up, yet those who have been too long on a single assignment and who have become somewhat stale and fixed in their views should be switched to posts which will offer them a fresh challenge.

I am also making personal visits to each bureau. These visits include an hour or more of frank discussion with the thirty or forty top people dealing with the new administration's policies and specific problems which concern the particular bureau in carrying out these policies.

II. Improvement of our Operations Abroad

The letter from the President to all Ambassadors which went out two weeks ago establishes each Chief of Mission as responsible for the combined U.S. effort in the country to which he has been assigned and entrusts him with necessary working authority.[2] This action has had a most favorable reception.

To help assure a tactful and effective response to this letter, we are sending out a series of guidance letters to all mission chiefs. These letters will deal with the following subjects:

a. The broad role of the Ambassador as leader, coordinator, and administrator.

b. Methods of improving the reporting and policy guidance provided by each mission.

c. Techniques for establishing closer working relationships within the American official community.

d. Techniques for improving the impression created by American officials (and Americans generally) in each country.

e. Methods to insure closer contacts with the internal culture, institutions, and people.

The press of daily business makes it difficult for even the ablest of mission chiefs to give sufficient priority to programs which involve basic changes in working relations and habits.

To help assure the necessary thought and action, each Ambassador will be asked to write me a letter within one month of the receipt of these guidance memoranda outlining precisely what changes have occurred in his mission's operations as a result.

In this way we may persuade each Ambassador to focus personally on these fundamental operating questions. The response from each mission chief should also give us valuable insights into his understand-

---

[2] For text of this May 29 letter, as well as President Kennedy's covering memorandum to the heads of executive departments and agencies, see *American Foreign Policy: Current Documents, 1961*, pp. 1345–1347.

ing of his own mission. Further status reports will be asked for at periodic intervals.

As a second stage in the campaign to freshen up our operations abroad, I am planning to hold approximately nine regional Chiefs of Mission Conferences abroad between the end of July and the end of October.

These conferences, which will last for two or three days, will be somewhat larger than the usual Chiefs of Missions' Meetings. The Ambassador will be asked to bring with him his Administrative Officer, the AID Mission Director, the USIS Public Affairs Officer, and in some cases his Deputy.

I expect to take with me from Washington the appropriate Assistant Secretary for each region, Roger Jones, or one of his Deputies, and high level representatives from the new AID Agency and from USIA.

I shall personally attend each of these meetings. We will cover not only policy discussions but the practical problems involved in coordinating the activities of our various agencies abroad; personnel selection, training and management; improved reporting; and so forth.

I believe such meetings are essential to assure that the new emphasis and direction on foreign policy questions the President has approved carries through into action at all operating levels abroad.

We are now working on initial planning for the first three of these conferences. They have tentatively been scheduled for the period from July 25th through August 11th and will probably be held in Lagos, Beirut or Cairo and New Delhi. In September and October we will follow up with similar meetings in Latin America, East Asia and Europe.

We are also planning to lengthen the normal tour of duty at all posts to three years and in some cases longer. Although this will require legislation and considerable adjustment, it is essential if we are to develop knowledge of each country in greater depth, closer personal contacts and better language abilities.

I have also asked for a study of the reports now required of each Embassy and the extent to which the number, frequency and scope of these reports can be reduced. This is essential if we are to free our mission chiefs and their top associates for increased travel outside the national capital.

III. A Study of U.S. Personnel Overseas

In 1958 studies were completed by the old Operations Coordinating Board dealing with the broad range of questions resulting from the total U.S. presence abroad, military and civilian. The objective was to persuade the agencies now operating overseas to tighten up administrative practices, personnel selection, attitudes, etc.

The OCB made a number of thoughtful recommendations. Some of these have been carried out in the intervening period. In other instances, however, there appears to have been little improvement.

In any event, the time has come to review this report in light of our present operations, to bring its recommendations up to date, and to establish the procedures that will assure that they are carried out.

Because of the large number of military personnel and dependents now overseas, the Pentagon has a particularly important role to play. In this regard I have discussed procedures with Ros Gilpatric, and a preliminary meeting has been set up with Herman Pollack and Bill Bundy. Procedures will then be agreed upon to explore all questions involving living areas, PX's, general attitudes, preliminary training, indoctrination, and so forth.

Each regional Assistant Secretary will be asked to follow through with the Pentagon and other agencies which are involved in his geographic area.

Roger Jones had an excellent meeting with Elmer Staats and some of the Budget Bureau people here on June 8th. A number of the problems involved in reaffirming State's responsibility for asserting primary authority in the overall field of U.S. international activities were discussed at length.

Elmer Staats and the Budget Bureau are taking a most constructive and helpful approach to all these questions. A special liaison man is being brought in to assure the necessary follow through between the Bureau and State.

IV. *Foreign Military Personnel in the U.S.A.*

Another area of our overseas operations which we should consider most carefully is the thousands of military personnel from foreign countries who are brought each year to the United States under the Military Assistance Program for training by the U.S. military in the use of new weapons and techniques. (Ed Murrow tells me that the total budget for this effort is half as large as that of the entire USIA.)

These many contacts provide a ready-made opportunity to create a better understanding of our country, its beliefs, and policies.

In cooperation with Defense we are planning to reexamine the handling of these foreign nationals who are exposed during their stay in this country. Together, we shall then work out a program that will improve their general understanding of the United States, its people and its policies.

I am asking Phil Coombs to coordinate this effort.

V. *Reorganization of the Economic Aid Organization*

I am deeply impressed with the present aid program which has been prepared for Congress. In my opinion it deals most effectively with the objectives and requirements of foreign assistance.

However, as I read it, I was again conscious of the urgent need for a highly competent administrative operation to carry out the program. Criticisms of the past operations have often been overstated, but many are valid.

If we are going to get this program through Congress and if the program itself is to live up to the objectives set by the President, we must vastly improve the administrative set up and personnel.

Hank Labouisse and his staff are, of course, acutely conscious of this need. Yet, with their heavy load of Congressional contacts and day-to-day administrative problems, I cannot see how they can devote the necessary time to the immediate task of creating a new, highly competent organization with the necessary new faces.

I suggested to Hank Labouisse the possibility of bringing in (perhaps on a temporary basis) a high level administrator in public administration who would concentrate exclusively on the problem of personnel, organization, and assignments. I shall explore this possibility further.

In my opinion, it is also important to find more effective ways to use the talent in Labor, Agriculture, HEW and elsewhere in operations and planning overseas. It is essential that the State Department keep close control on policy questions. Yet, there are many highly expert people in these agencies with wide overseas experience whom we should learn how to use. At present many of them feel shut out.

I am having lunch with Orville Freeman today to discuss this question. I have already talked in general terms to Abe Ribicoff.

Cabinet members, themselves, with an interest in foreign affairs can play a most constructive role. It is our task to find an effective way to put their energies to work without disrupting or diffusing our normal operations.

This will give you an idea of the effort that is being made. Please give me any thoughts that may occur to you.

31.   **Memorandum Prepared in the Department of State**[1]

Washington, undated.

Summary of Major Improvements in State Department
Administrative Operations
January 20–July 20, 1961

(Source: Memorandum of July 20 from A—Mr. Crockett
to O—Mr. Jones)[2]

1. Internal Organization Changes

a. Development of integrated regional approach to aid programs through new *Agency for International Development* (AID).

b. Enlargement of *Disarmament Administration.*

c. Establishment of *Peace Corps.*

d. Grouping of bureaus with *politico-military-intelligence functions* under Deputy Under Secretary for Political Affairs for day-to-day operations.

e. Elevation of head of *cultural affairs* programs to Assistant Secretary rank.

f. New emphasis in *intelligence operations* on studies of current and emerging problems.

g. Creation of *Operations Center* for emergency, inter-departmental action.

h. Strengthening *long-range planning* by consolidating the positions of Counselor and Chairman of the Policy Planning Council.

i. Expansion of *Protocol Office* activities.

j. Assignment to *Director General of the Foreign Service* of responsibility for adequate support for ambassadors.

k. Increase in Department support for the *Export Expansion Program.*

l. Setting up of an *Office of Management* to focus responsibility on management problems.

m. *Abolishment of 109* inter- and intra departmental committees.

n. Improvement of internal communications through publication of the *Department of State News Letter.*

---

[1] Source: National Archives and Records Administration, RG 59, Central Files 1960–63, 110.10/7–2061. No classification marking. The memorandum does not indicate a date or drafting office; it was presumably prepared in the Bureau of Administration.

[2] Not found in Department of State files.

o. Beginning study on use of *automation* to expedite Departmental operations of various kinds.

2. Overseas Changes

a. Strengthening of concept of *unified U.S. foreign affairs activities abroad* under guidance of Ambassador.

b. *Combining of previously separate* post administrative services operations.

---

32.   Letter From the Under Secretary of State (Bowles) to U.S. Ambassadors[1]

Washington, July 8, 1961.

Dear Mr. Ambassador:

As you know from President Kennedy's recent letter to you, he is deeply interested in our operations, not only here in Washington but also abroad.

In order to strengthen our efforts here and to give improved support to our overseas operations, I have been taking a close look at the administrative structure of our Bureaus here in Washington, going over each Bureau in detail with its Assistant Secretary and our Administrative people.

We are also planning to hold a series of regional meetings of Chiefs of Missions throughout the world. The first of these meetings will be in Lagos, Nigeria, in late July, a second is scheduled for Nicosia, Cyprus, and the third for New Delhi. Additional meetings will be held later in Europe, Latin America and the Far East.

I plan to attend each of these meetings, and with me will be high officials from USIA, ICA, Defense and appropriate areas of the Depart-

---

[1] Source: National Archives and Records Administration, RG 59, Conference Files: Lot 65 D 366, ROCs Miscellaneous. Confidential. The letter is a master letter intended for separate transmission to each individual Ambassador. Attached are four additional memoranda, each addressed to "All Chiefs of Mission" and dated July 8: Memorandum No. 1, Leadership and Supervisory Responsibility of the Ambassador (Document 33); Memorandum No. 2, Foreign Service Reporting (not printed); Memorandum No. 3, Establishment of Close Relationship with People of Country of Assignment (not printed); and Memorandum No. 4, Impact of American Official Personnel on Local Community (not printed).

ment. It is my hope that you will be able to bring with you your chief advisers. You will shortly be receiving or may have already received specific details about these conferences.

In the meantime we thought it might be useful to send you some thoughts which we have put together here on various aspects of the problems we want to discuss in these conferences. The attached memoranda spell out in some detail the kinds of problems we feel you might profitably consider in advance of the meetings. They include suggestions and ideas which have proved useful in some of our Missions in achieving better integration of our activities and presenting a more positive impression to the people of the country in which we work.

Our purpose in sending them now is simply to elicit your reactions and suggestions. We will then discuss reactions from you and your colleagues in detail at our regional meetings. The memoranda will be the basis for much of our discussions.

Although the time is obviously very tight, I would appreciate getting at least some of your views before I leave Washington on July 24 for the first of these regional meetings. A preliminary reply by cable would be very helpful.

Let me add that these memoranda were written with considerable hesitation. The subjects touched upon are complex and often personal. We do not pretend to have all the answers. However, our embassy relations are so vital that I am sure you will agree that we must explore every practical way to improve our performance.

With my warmest regards,

Sincerely,

Chester Bowles[2]

---

[2] Printed from a copy that bears this typed signature.

33.   Memorandum From the Under Secretary of State (Bowles) to All Chiefs of Mission[1]

Washington, July 8, 1961.

LEADERSHIP AND SUPERVISORY RESPONSIBILITY
OF THE AMBASSADOR

Background

Before World War II the Ambassador's authority was seldom challenged by any other United States representative abroad. The limited responsibilities of the few representatives of other departments on his staff caused little difficulty.

After World War II this situation was dramatically changed by the United States new role of leadership and by the shrinking of the world through modern communications. Matters previously of domestic concern now impinged on foreign countries.

The immediate post-war years saw (1) the establishment abroad of numerous semiautonomous, strong special missions; (2) the retention and establishment of military bases and missions; and (3) the sending abroad of representatives by many Government departments and agencies.

The Ambassador during these years lacked the authority to supervise, direct or control these missions or representatives. By 1948 with the establishment of aid missions abroad largely independent of the Chief of the Diplomatic Mission, the Ambassador's authority had reached an all-time low.

The first important step to rectify this situation was the Clay Paper of February 1951, a memorandum of understanding between State, Defense, and ECA. It established the Country Team concept and was the first clear statement of the primary position of the Ambassador with regard to the personnel of other agencies.

From 1951 to 1961 the Ambassador's responsibility and authority were consolidated by a series of Executive Orders, Presidential letters and memoranda, and State Department instructions.

Key steps were Executive Order 10893 of November 8, 1960, the Presidential Memorandum of the same date, and the Department's

---

[1] Source: National Archives and Records Administration, RG 59, Conference Files: Lot 65 D 366, ROC's Miscellaneous. Confidential. The memorandum, designated "Memorandum No. 1," is attached to Document 32.

Circular Airgram No. 4334 of November 14, 1960. The President's letter to all Ambassadors of May 29, 1961 was the most recent step in this development.

Philosophy

An able Ambassador is in a position greatly to improve the tone for all American officials in his country of assignment. If he has the necessary tact and skill, he can be of great help to the representatives of other U.S. Government departments and agencies in carrying out their missions. It is his task to create a satisfactory, easy working relationship with them and to encourage and support their activities in a way that will enable the Country Team to work more effectively in furthering our national objectives.

It is particularly important that an Ambassador make the representatives of other departments and agencies feel that they are an integral part of his official family. There are a number of ways by which this can be accomplished:

(1) by making sure that they are fully informed concerning overall American objectives in the country;

(2) by making sure that they are fully informed of the current and longer-term problems and obstacles in attaining these objectives and of the means best calculated, in the Ambassador's judgment, to overcome these difficulties;

(3) by having the Ambassador use his position socially and officially to assist them in accomplishing their specific missions;

(4) by having members of the Country Team regularly attend the Ambassador's staff meetings and members of the Embassy's Political, Economic, and Administrative Sections attend staff meetings held by the USIA, AID and other Country Team members;

(5) by including these Team members regularly in the small dinners or luncheons given for high-ranking officials;

(6) by providing helpful advice and guidance while remaining sensitive to the danger and undesirability of interfering in the minutiae of their operational responsibilities;

(7) by ensuring that the Ambassador is always available to members of the Country Team;

(8) by ensuring that each group understands the functions and activities of the others;

(9) by making sure that representatives of other departments and agencies know that the Ambassador will welcome their suggestions on any matter; and

(10) by encouraging close working relationships among all personnel interested in similar fields.

Exercise of Ambassador's Decision-Making Authority

The President is the focal point in the United States Government where divergent interests are reconciled in the national interest.

The Ambassador, his personal representative, is best able to reconcile the divergent interests of the representatives of various departments and agencies in a foreign country. This is essential to prevent the export abroad of the perhaps inevitable bureaucratic conflicts of Washington.

An Ambassador and his Foreign Service staff do not and should not consider themselves as representing just the State Department. They represent and serve the entire United States Government.

The Ambassador is in a position to:

(1) ensure that all United States activities in a given country contribute to the achievement of United States foreign policy objectives;

(2) reconcile the special interests of the representatives of other Government departments and agencies with the national interest;

(3) coordinate all United States activities in a foreign country;

(4) identify in advance and forestall actions which in his judgment would adversely affect United States relations with the country concerned;

(5) ensure that all United States representatives fully understand United States objectives, speak with a common voice and are not played off one against the other by a foreign government; and

(6) provide advice, guidance, and leadership to assist the representatives of other departments and agencies in carrying out their responsibilities.

An imaginative, intelligent, and sympathetic exercise of leadership by an Ambassador should, in all but extremely rare instances, prevent situations from developing to a point where he must make a decision which will be appealed by the representative of another department or agency to higher authority in Washington.

The President's letter makes clear that the Ambassador's decision stands pending appeal, if any, to Washington. Similarly, circumstances which would make it necessary for him to request the departure of an individual should arise most infrequently.

When time is not an important factor, the Ambassador may wish to consult the Department by official-informal letter or "Eyes Only" telegram addressed to the Deputy Under Secretary for Administration prior to making a final decision affecting the activities of personnel of another department or agency.

New regulations will be issued soon setting forth the procedures to be followed by an Ambassador in obtaining the departure of a member of the Foreign Service.

Responsibility of Representatives of Other Departments and Agencies

The representatives of other Departments and agencies are responsible for keeping the Ambassador fully informed of their views and activities.

This should be understood to include giving the Ambassador any information which they send to their departments and agencies, whether orally or through informal communications channels. This is particularly important if such information should reflect any disagreement with the Ambassador's views

Conclusion

The Ambassador is the leader, the coordinator, and the supervisor of all official United States representatives in the country to which he is accredited. As such, he bears the responsibility for success or failure in achieving United States foreign policy objectives in his country of assignment.

---

34.   Letter From the Under Secretary of State (Bowles) to President Kennedy[1]

Washington, July 27, 1961.

Dear Mr. President:

I am enclosing a memorandum on the organization of the Department of State which I promised you before leaving Washington.[2]

In this memorandum I have tried to eliminate any references to my own emotions and commitments. However, I hope you will bear with me if I offer a few additional and highly personal comments on a situation that has been difficult for all of us.

When you asked me to accept the post of Under Secretary, I did so because I was convinced that a basic revitalization of the State Department both in Washington and in our overseas missions was long overdue and because I felt that I could help bring about the essential changes.

Much of my experience has been in administrative work. In the 1930's I organized a private business with more that a thousand employees. In the 1940's I reorganized a badly demoralized war-time agency with some 60,000 paid employees and 350,000 volunteers.

---

[1] Source: Kennedy Library, National Security Files, Departments and Agencies Series, State Department, 7/21/61–7/27/61. Personal and Private.

[2] Document 35, inexplicably dated one day later than the covering memorandum.

In India I reorganized not only our embassy but USIA and the foreign aid program which were then being greatly expanded and integrated into the embassy operation—exactly as we are doing with our overseas missions today.

In each case we brought in new people to head each bureau, men dedicated to the President's policies. And in each case there was a clear sense of purpose and high morale.

I do not make these comments as an expression of self-esteem. I do it simply because so much has been said about my alleged lack of interest in administration, and I would like to set the record straight.

The weak performance of some sections of the State Department has largely been due, in my opinion, to failure to introduce fresh faces where they are needed.

An additional weak point relates to the area of communications. Although no single individual possesses all the qualities desirable in the Secretary of State, I know of no one who possesses so high a percentage of them as Dean Rusk, nor anyone with whom I would prefer to work. For a variety of reasons, however, most of them the result of pressures, Dean, Adlai, and I have not worked together as closely as I believe we should.

Finally, I have been at fault in not maintaining close connections with the White House staff and you personally. My visit with you two weeks ago was the only direct exchange of views we have had since we had breakfast in your N Street home last November. If we had talked for no more than an hour a month, this situation would never have developed.

However, I was hesitant to take advantage of our former association or to infringe on the position which properly belongs to the Secretary, and so I held back.

As far as my own future is concerned, my strong preference is to continue where I am, with your support and that of Dean Rusk, so that we may bring about the changes in emphasis and direction which I believe to be needed in certain areas.

Once the right individuals have been selected and installed in the key bureaus where our principal difficulties lie, I would be in a position to divert a sizable amount of time to special policy problems in the Middle East, Southeast Asia, Northeast Brazil, and elsewhere. I would also have time for more travel and for the essential task of explaining your policies in key nations abroad.

If you prefer to have someone else tackle these organizational problems, I will be glad to reshuffle various assignments with George Ball. This should also enable me to attend to special policy problems, overseas missions, and the achievement of a better understanding of your policies in the United States.

If neither solution seems advisable to you and Dean, I will find myself in a most difficult position. I am deeply dedicated to your aims in foreign policy, and I have prepared myself in depth for many years to serve the Department of State. Yet in view of the totally false and malicious attacks on me, most of them from people with an equal disdain for all liberal-minded Democrats, I do not see how I could accept a down-graded role from my present position of Under Secretary and still appear to retain your confidence.

With my warmest regards,

Sincerely,

Chet Bowles

35.   Memorandum From the Under Secretary of State (Bowles) to President Kennedy[1]

Washington, July 28, 1961.

Before leaving Washington, I promised to send you a memorandum with my views on the organizational needs of the Department of State. Such a report can be valuable to you only if it is frank. My frankness, however, should not be interpreted as a criticism, direct or indirect, of any individual.

Nor should it suggest any lack of respect for the career service. Within the ranks of the Foreign Service and the Department are many of the nation's most able, experienced, and dedicated specialists in foreign policy.

We have extraordinary assets, for instance, in such people as Bob Woodward, Tommy Thompson, Charlie Yost at the United Nations, Fred Reinhardt in Rome, Ellis Briggs in Athens, Tyler Thompson as Director General of the Foreign Service, Ed Martin in the Bureau of Economic Affairs, and many others.

Generally speaking, however, your approach to foreign affairs is inadequately understood by many of the able career officers of the

---

[1] Source: Kennedy Library, National Security Files, Departments and Agencies Series, State Department, 7/21/61–7/27/61. Confidential. In a letter of July 23 to Adlai Stevenson, Permanent Representative to the United Nations, Bowles set forth a long and more personal discussion of much the same subject. (Princeton University, Seeley G. Mudd Library, Stevenson Papers, Public Policy Papers, Box 341, File 4)

Department who have attained senior rank in the last ten years. It is our task so to organize the various bureaus that the experience and skills of these men can be put to good use through a structure which assures you the kind of policies which you have been advocating for years. The key to such structure, in my opinion, lies in the appointment of bureau heads and deputies who clearly understand your foreign policy objectives, who believe these objectives are right, and who can work effectively as members of a team to achieve them.

Everyone knows that the performance of the Department of State in the first six months of the new Administration has been uneven.

In certain bureaus fresh ideas have begun to flow, morale is high, and there is a clear sense of purpose and direction. In others, there has been resistance to fresh thinking and a continuing attachment to the sterile assumptions and negative policies that we criticized so vigorously when we were out of office.

Let me emphasize that the difference to which I refer does not involve the efficiency of the bureaus' day-to-day operations, but rather their capacity to bring a fresh perspective to old situations, to sense the weakness or irrelevance of old positions, and to produce—or allow others to produce—the new policies which in some areas are so long overdue.

There are, I believe, two basic and interrelated reasons for the uneven performance of the bureaus: first, differences in leadership, and second, differences in the process of policy formation.

Where fresh blood that is keenly attuned to the New Frontier has been introduced, the performance by and large has been impressive. Where the outlook and personnel of the old Administration still prevail at the top of the bureau, we have been falling down.

Let me be specific.

In the up-graded and reorganized Bureau of Educational and Cultural Affairs, headed by Phil Coombs and two able new assistants, Joe Slater and Max Isenbergh, the substantive improvement since January has been spectacular.

In Protocol we also see a new sense of direction and increased effectiveness under the leadership of Angie Duke. These qualities have already produced concrete results in the life of the African and Asian diplomatic community and elsewhere.

Abe Chayes in the Legal Adviser's office, with a reinvigorated staff, has introduced a much more affirmative approach to a vitally important and previously negative area of operations.

This pattern has been repeated in the Bureau of Intelligence and Research under Roger Hilsman and Tom Hughes, who are demonstrating how raw intelligence, thoughtfully interpreted, can provide a much more effective tool in our policy making.

At the same time, George McGhee, as Counselor, has transformed the Policy Planning Council from an ineffective and negative instrument into a respected producer of new ideas and perspective.

In the administrative section we see similar changes for the better. Here Roger Jones, with the help of two able career people, Bill Crockett and Herman Pollack (who in recent years had seen their ideas frustrated and bypassed), has vastly improved administrative procedures in regard to our operations in Washington and also in the field.

The Bureau of Public Affairs under Roger Tubby, ably assisted by Carl Rowan, has developed new techniques to further public understanding of foreign policy. For the first time, for instance, local newsmen and radio and television commentators from all over the United States have been invited to Washington for successful briefings in depth.

Under Adlai Stevenson, our operation at the United Nations has also substantially improved. Here the credit belongs not only to Ambassador Stevenson and his able assistants in New York but also to the vigorous support they have received from the reorganized Bureau of International Organization Affairs under the leadership of Harlan Cleveland and Dick Gardner.

We are also making substantial progress in improving the effectiveness of our overseas mission. A letter from you in late May expanded and redefined the role of our ambassadors. This was followed by more specific guidance papers which spelled out ways in which our overseas operations could be strengthened. The success of this effort has been dramatically demonstrated in the meeting which I am now attending in Lagos.

In addition, the overseas service term for career officers is being lengthened, language standards raised, and sixteen Foreign Service Officers of ministerial or ambassadorial rank who in the past Administration would now be heading embassies have been retired so that younger, abler officers could be promoted.

Even the most casual study of State Department operations will, I believe, underscore this central point: Wherever people who understand the Kennedy policies and believe in them have been brought in to head bureaus or to occupy top deputy posts, our performance has been greatly improved. Where we have failed to introduce such individuals, our performance has been less satisfactory.

Let us consider, for instance, the operations of the five geographic bureaus. At present each Assistant Secretary is supported by two Deputy Assistant Secretaries. This means that fifteen top officers are running the core of the Department under the office of the Secretary. Yet only four of these fifteen individuals are Kennedy-oriented men brought in from outside the Department. Two of the four are Assistant Secretaries and two are Deputy Assistant Secretaries.

In the Bureau of European Affairs, Inter-American Affairs, and Far Eastern Affairs, almost no fresh blood has been introduced.

All three of these bureaus are headed by individuals of great integrity and experience. Their staff are experienced, loyal, and efficient on day-to-day operations. But because top leadership in these bureaus in our first six months has been much less sensitive to your views and priorities, there has been a tendency to cling to outworn assumptions, to resist new approaches, and to gloss over setbacks.

The apathy towards the need for a review of old policies and for fresh approaches, which is evident in varying degrees in each of these three bureaus, is dramatized by a comparison with the Bureau of African Affairs under Soapy Williams, with his two able assistants, Wayne Fredericks, and John Abernethy.

Although the personnel in the African Bureau is younger and by and large less experienced, morale is probably higher there than in any other part of the State Department. Moreover, there is a clear understanding within the bureau of the principles which were laid down in your campaign, in *The Strategy of Peace*, and in the Democratic platform.

This brings me to a second and closely related point: Where we have Assistant Secretaries and Deputy Assistant Secretaries who understand and believe in your views on foreign policy, guidance is easily applied from the top. Communications are natural and uninhibited. Fresh ideas and criticism are welcome. There is an atmosphere of purpose and dedication.

Where a new Kennedy-oriented leadership has been lacking, such top-side guidance is resisted and policy tends to flow from the bottom up. The papers start from the country desks and then move gradually up through the various interested bureaus and levels of authority. Where disagreements arise, meetings are held, compromises are struck, and the papers then continue on their way.

When they finally reach the Secretary and the Under Secretary, the ideas are often fully crystallized, and the entire apparatus which is responsible for their development goes all out in their defense.

As a result, the top officers who are responsible for the final decisions have little knowledge of the compromises which have been built into these papers on their way up through the bureaucratic machinery; nor are they necessarily in tune with these compromises; nor are they adequately aware of the possible alternatives which for reasons good or bad may have been discarded.

By the day the paper is finally presented, time is likely to be short, pressures against changes are well developed not only in the State Department but throughout the government, and an NSC meeting may be just around the corner.

In these circumstances the Secretary and Under Secretary have no alternative but to accept the paper largely unchanged or send it back and start all over.

Such a procedure would be workable only if the lower and middle levels of the Department were infused with the foreign policy views which you outlined in your book and in your speeches. With due credit to the scores of able and dedicated professionals who hold these positions, such understanding is now the exception rather than the rule.

A single example will emphasize the essential point. Early last February it was clearly apparent that Berlin and Germany would erupt as a major issue during the spring. This called for an urgent review of our situation in that area, an assessment of the new forces, and the creation of a new position which would enable the new President to move from the negative posture of the previous Administration and seize the initiative with the Soviets and with world opinion generally.

Yet our efforts to stimulate this review were hampered by the convictions of many key professionals within the Bureau that our old position was adequate and that no further action was needed.

Let me say with the greatest emphasis that these remarks are not intended as a personal criticism of any individual. The Bureau of European Affairs which I have used to illustrate my point is, in my opinion, the best *administered* bureau of the Department.

However, like the Inter-American and Far Eastern Bureaus, it has clung to old positions and resisted fresh approaches because its principal architects of policy and operations have not been emotionally and intellectually attuned to your criticism of old Eisenhower positions and to the new approaches which you had consistently advocated.

Although this situation is difficult and frustrating, it is not, in my opinion, difficult to correct. A few new people properly placed and vigorously supported in a relatively brief period introduce new depth, understanding, and vigor into U.S. foreign policy where it is needed most. In cooperation with the Secretary, Adlai Stevenson, and me, they could enable us to reverse the present policy-making procedure which in certain key areas now operates largely from the bottom up rather than from clearly established guidelines at the top.

When an old policy seems to be losing its relevance or when an emergency situation arises, the first discussions, I believe, should involve the Secretary, Adlai Stevenson, and myself, and the Assistant Secretary for the geographic bureau, in addition perhaps to Harlan Cleveland, Abe Chayes, and, in some cases, George McGhee and George Ball.

From such a discussion, alternative approaches are almost certain to emerge. The further development of one of them could be assigned to the geographic bureau, another to the Policy Planning Council, and a third perhaps to some outside group headed by Harlan Cleveland or Abe Chayes.

But this procedure should go beyond emergencies. Right now, for instance, there is urgent need for policy review in all the geographic bureaus and particularly in Europe, the Far East, the Middle East, and Southeast Asia. I believe that we need to create new NSC papers for at least a dozen geographic areas.

The guidelines of these papers should be outlined in advance by the Secretary, Stevenson, myself, and others who know what you want and would be in a position to contribute directly at the early stages of the full development process.

One final point which I have recently come to believe is of primary importance: The top officials of the Department can take control of policy formation only if they have able staff assistants with a "passion for anonymity" to help them.

These assistants should be in on the earliest policy discussions. They should then keep in close touch with the various task forces on a day-to-day basis so that they can inform the Secretary of progress on policy-making along the lines which have been agreed to.

Only in this way can the Secretary and Under Secretary be well and consistently aware that their ideas and your ideas are being developed as intended and also warned of emphasis change or deadlock or imperfections in the original proposals.

In no sense should this mechanism be viewed as a substitute for the Secretariat, which is an essential operation under the very able direction of Luke Battle, but rather as a supplementary operation which should also be directed by Luke. The Secretariat, as presently organized, lacks the personnel and authority to follow through on the policy-making process.

Most emphatically, I am not suggesting a reorganization but rather a revitalization of certain key bureaus of the Department. Although these bureaus are reasonably efficient in day-to-day operation, they are in large measure still emotionally tied to old policies which run counter to the commitments of the new Administration.

Instead of undermining the morale of the Department of State, the changes which I suggest will, I believe, give the Department a spirit and confidence which in some areas is now largely lacking.

36.   Editorial Note

In a memorandum to the President on July 28, 1961, Secretary of State Rusk set forth details for implementing a new system of foreign economic policy coordination. Rusk noted that the Council on Foreign Economic Policy had been abolished on March 12 and its functions transferred to the Secretary of State. In a letter to Congress of May 26 transmitting the foreign assistance bill, the President had indicated that he expected the Secretary of State to become the focal point of responsibility for coordination of foreign economic policy, and to choose appropriate mechanisms for carrying this out. Accordingly, Rusk now designated the Under Secretary of State for Economic Affairs to assume responsibility, under Rusk's direction, for interagency consultation and coordination of foreign economic policy. Rusk's memorandum of July 28 to the President is printed in *Foreign Relations*, 1961–1963, volume IX, Document 4.

---

37.   Memorandum From the President's Special Assistant (Schlesinger) to the President's Special Assistant for National Security Affairs (Bundy)[1]

Washington, August 11, 1961.

SUBJECT

Mr. Bowles's Memorandum of July 28[2]

1. I agree with the essential argument of the Bowles memorandum—that the State Department would be more effective as an instrument of government if more top officials believed vigorously in the purposes and objectives of the Administration. Old Frontier people cannot carry out New Frontier policies. Or rather I agree with this argument so far as it goes, while at the same time wishing to emphasize that, in

---

[1] Source: Kennedy Library, National Security Files, Departments and Agencies Series, State Department, 8/5/61–8/14/61. Secret.

[2] Document 35. A draft memorandum to President Kennedy from David E. Bell, Director of the Bureau of the Budget, dated August 9, also commented on Bowles' July 28 memorandum. (Kennedy Library, National Security Files, Departments and Agencies Series, State Department, 8/5/61–8/14/61)

my judgment, it only covers a part of the problem. If Mr. Bowles's concentration on personnel suggests that he thinks bringing in more New Frontiersmen will solve all the troubles of the State Department, I do *not* agree with this. The appointment of more able Kennedy outsiders will help create the conditions for solution; but the problems are deeper and more obstinate than the Bowles memorandum suggests.

2. My few months at the White House have convinced me that the traditional tripartite division of the national government into executive, legislative and judicial branches is inadequate. With a strong President, there are really *four* branches of government: the executive, the legislative, the judiciary and the Presidency. A President who advances new ideas and policies may well encounter as much resistance in the executive branch as in the Congress or the Supreme Court. I was academically aware of this from my excursions into the Roosevelt era; but I know much more vividly today how acute and deep-rooted the problem is of mobilizing the executive branch behind new programs and purposes.

3. This problem may be especially acute in the State Department because of the 'non-political' and 'élite' character of the Foreign Service.

The typical Foreign Service officer is well above the average in decency, intelligence and devotion. However, the typical Foreign Service officer also tends to be somewhat emasculated so far as policy commitment is concerned. One reason for this is that Foreign Service training has the effect of divesting the professional officer of strong views on substantive policy. It almost seems as if the Foreign Service receives a group of spirited young Americans at the age of 25 and transforms them in the next twenty years into a collection of eunuchs (or possibly my protracted exposure to ARA has distorted my judgment).

Why this process of emasculation?

(a) Foreign Service traditions derive from the time when America's role in the world was passive and spectatorial; consequently Foreign Service officers still tend to be reporters rather than operators.

(b) Foreign Service officers are regularly shifted from one country to another and from one job to another. This lack of continuity—Iceland one year, Tanganyika the next—discourages them from developing a very intense interest in policy issues. (In any case, they are taught that their job is to carry out the policy, however idiotic they may personally consider the policy to be.)

(c) It is no coincidence that the areas where the problem of learning a difficult language compels continuity—the Russia Service and the China Service—are precisely the areas where the Foreign Service professionals have been least emasculated and most independent and outspoken. But it was precisely these areas which suffered most heavily in the Dulles period. Dulles's punitive action against the men in the Foreign Service who were most conspicuously free and strong individuals (Bohlen, Kennan, Davies, Service, Thayer, etc.) proved to the rest of the Foreign Service what a mistake it was ever to go out on a limb. The Department is still suffering from the hangover of the Dulles period.

(d) The system of promotions within the Foreign Service further discourages policy initiative, because it is hard to propose new policies without seeming to criticize present ones. Junior officers may well hesitate to challenge Assistant Secretaries with power over their next assignments or, indeed, over their future careers.

Obviously the Foreign Service cannot consist of a collection of free-wheelers each pursuing his own foreign policy. But the factors listed above have exaggerated an inherent tendency toward caution to a dangerous point. And Foreign Service resistance to innovation is further reinforced—and often in a most unwholesome way—by the prevailing sense that the Foreign Service is an exclusive club which must jealously guard foreign policy from the meddling of naive and presumptuous amateurs.

4. How to overcome this built-in resistance to change? How to annex the State Department to the Kennedy Administration?

The answer begins, of course, with strong leadership at the top—of the sort which has enabled McNamara and Gilpatric to proceed so successfully in their reconquest of the Pentagon. Strong top leadership has been lacking in State.

It is also important, as Mr. Bowles suggests, to get able, Kennedy-oriented men in jobs of middle-level administrative responsibility. I believe that he is, in the main, right when he claims that the New Frontiersmen have done much more to revitalize our conduct of foreign affairs than the Foreign Service professionals. It is natural enough that this should be so. Men who were in tune with John Foster Dulles are not likely to come up with bold initiatives for the New Frontier. Probably too many such men are still in key jobs. In ARA, and no doubt elsewhere, some of the Foreign Service officers are out of sympathy with the Kennedy foreign policy. It would certainly help to get more men of the Ball–Cleveland–Coombs–Chayes–Williams order at the Assistant Secretarial level.

At the same time, there should be no crusade against Foreign Service officers. They have to do most of the work. Many of them will begin to adjust to the new dispensation. The best among them (Bohlen, Kennan, Thompson, Woodward, Gullion and others) enjoy the New Frontier and flourish in the new expansive atmosphere.

5. More important: new men are only part of the problem. The Bowles memorandum ignores a number of structural questions which

increase the Department's inherent tendencies toward inaction and postponement. Making policy in the State Department is like negotiating a hopelessly intricate obstacle course. One may recognize the need for interminable clearance and concurrence while at the same time wonder whether these things are not sometimes erected into excuses for doing as little as possible. The Bowles memorandum also ignores fundamental, long-run questions, like that of the training and philosophy of the Foreign Service.

In short, we require more Kennedy-oriented men in State, especially, as Bowles suggests, in ARA, FE and European Affairs. Why not develop a general pattern for the geographic areas of insider/outsider teams, one as Assistant Secretary, the other as Deputy? But we also require a hard and skeptical reexamination of the policy-making process within the Department. (This reexamination might also be carried out by insider/outsider teams; it cannot be entrusted to the Foreign Service alone—or to the Council on Foreign Relations alone!)

6. In the end, let us face the fact, only one man can exert the leadership to do the job. That is the Secretary of State.

Arthur Schlesinger, jr.

---

38.   Editorial Note

On August 14, 1961, George C. McGhee, Counselor of the Department of State and Chairman of the Policy Planning Council, circulated a draft paper entitled "Foreign Policy: Toward Clarity in Terms and Method," for discussion at a Policy Planning Council meeting to be held on August 17 at 9:15 a.m. (Memorandum from McGhee to Rusk, Bowles, Ball, Roger W. Jones, U. Alexis Johnson, Battle, Chayes, Hilsman, and the Assistant Secretaries of eight Bureaus of the Department of State; Kennedy Library, National Security Files, Subjects Series, Policy Planning 6/61–8/61)

The study was issued by the Policy Planning Council on September 11. (Ibid.) McGhee sent a copy to Bundy for his information on September 13, indicating in a covering note that the study had been discussed with the Secretary of State and the Bureau of the Budget. (Ibid.)

39. Memorandum From President Kennedy to Secretary of State Rusk[1]

Washington, August 16, 1961.

I would appreciate it if you would prepare a memorandum on the present assignment of responsibility within the Department of State. We discussed this at breakfast this morning, but I think if we could get it down on paper all concerned on the White House staff, as well as the State Department, would have a better idea of how they should conduct their responsibilities.

---

[1] Source: Kennedy Library, President's Office Files, JFK Memos to Departments and Agencies—State. No classification marking.

---

40. Memorandum From the Under Secretary of State (Bowles) to Secretary of State Rusk[1]

Washington, August 18, 1961.

SUBJECT

Regional Operations Conferences in Lagos, Nicosia and New Delhi

As you know from my preliminary reports on the Lagos and Nicosia meetings, these three conferences were extremely valuable from a number of points of view.

Our purpose, as you will recall, was twofold: to carry the Kennedy foreign policy message more effectively to our field personnel and to underscore the President's recent letter re-emphasizing Ambassadorial responsibility for all phases of our overseas operations.

The agenda and the formula of interagency participation which we followed turned out to be generally sound, although we had to revise

---

[1] Source: National Archives and Records Administration RG 59, Conference Files: Lot 65 D 366, ROC Lagos. Secret. Secretary Rusk transmitted a copy of the memorandum to President Kennedy under cover of a brief undated memorandum that stated in part: "I believe you will find it of interest. Reports from many quarters indicate that the conferences were highly successful." (Ibid.)

our schedule as we went along to allow more time for discussions of policy and less for operational matters.

We can make further improvements in the format of the meetings; one change should be to reduce slightly the overall number of people present since we were pressing the effective limit, particularly at Nicosia.

With these changes we can proceed with two meetings in Latin America in mid-October and one in the Far East in mid-November or early December with the assurance that they will be well worth the expenditure of time and funds.

Perhaps the major strength of these meetings was supplied by the interagency approach. The cross-fertilization of ideas among agencies produced some remarkable results.

The presence of the wives of the Mission Chiefs also proved to be an excellent idea. They were brought for the first time fully into the official family and made some real contributions to our discussions. We should include them in future conferences without reservation.

The region bureaus and the administrative bureau are hard at work trying to solve dozens and dozens of specific problems of policy, administration, and coordination raised in the meetings. I shall monitor their follow-up reports to make certain we get the maximum benefit out of the discussions.

There are, however, some overall conclusions both for our policy and for our techniques of operations which I would like to cite. These are areas which we should all be conscious of in the coming months, and where top level follow-up will be particularly important.

I. Operations

A. The principle of full ambassadorial responsibility outlined in the President's letter of late May met with unanimous enthusiasm at all our meetings. Other agency representatives from Washington and the field approached the principles with a great deal of good will and I am heartened by my conviction that we are enjoying the best inter-agency relationships with our Defense, USIA and ICA colleagues that Washington has seen for a long time.

Joint meetings of this type proved to be a tangible demonstration of the sort of mutual trust we so often talk about but have not always demonstrated in practice.

The Ambassadors all accepted our assurances eagerly but several went out of the way to stress the importance of full support from Washington when they exercise their overall executive responsibility in ticklish cases.

Fully integrated operations should be easiest to achieve in Africa where no large, well entrenched bureaucracies are already in existence but I feel confident the situation will be satisfactory in the Middle East and Asia as well.

B. There are three essential areas in which we must follow up carefully here to make sure our Ambassadors are able to carry out their increased responsibilities effectively.

1. In selecting future Ambassadors we must pay a great deal more attention to the breadth of their backgrounds, their sensitivity to political dynamics, and their degree of understanding of aid, defense and information programs: if they are to act as chief executives for these programs in the real sense their training must include some prior exposure to problems in these fields.

One of the Ambassador's most important responsibilities must be to fight the necessary battles with the other Washington agencies on behalf of his public affairs officer, his aid mission director, or his MAAG chief, just as he represents his State components to the regional bureau. Only if this sort of concrete support is demonstrated will our Ambassadors get the sort of wholehearted cooperation and loyalty from their other agency staff members.

This suggests that we should take a critical look at our present emphasis on specialization for younger Foreign Service officers. While the need for specialists is undoubtedly great, particularly language and area specialists, if Foreign Service officers are to be able realistically to aspire to ambassadorships they must at some stage in their careers get sufficiently exposed to other than traditional Department functions to fit them for the broad executive role we are assigning to our Ambassadors.

With this in mind, I intend to ask our personnel people to expand as rapidly as possible interchange of personnel between our Foreign Service, USIA and the aid program. Our exchange program with the Department of Defense, which is proving very successful, should also be stepped up accordingly.

2. While all agencies accept without reservation the new role of the Ambassador, there is some reluctance, particularly among the aid people, to include the Deputy Chief of Mission as the Ambassador's alter ego in that role. We are going to make clear to all our missions that the DCM no longer is to be considered merely the operating head of the traditional embassy sections, but that he must be the Ambassador's right hand and alter ego for executive direction of all agency programs.

We will also take steps to insure that our DCMs have sufficient rank, experience and ability to handle this sort of job satisfactorily.

We also were impressed that at large missions Ambassadors will need one or perhaps two personal staff assistants to assist them in coordination of all agency operations. Steps are being taken to provide for such positions wherever they are needed.

3. We must keep up the steady campaign initiated at these conferences to instill in all of our State personnel, and especially our administrative people, a philosophical acceptance of the "embassy family" concept. Bill Crockett is working vigorously at this in the administrative area and we must see that our regional bureaus absorb the spirit as rapidly as possible.

Only when our people really begin to think of their other agency colleagues as equals in the Embassy will we begin to achieve the real meaning of the President's letter. This will be slow in coming in some places. Our top people have the concept, but there are still many old wounds which must be closed and many bitter memories to be forgotten all over the world.

C. It was strikingly clear at all these conferences and particularly in Lagos that our administrative procedures are incredibly burdened with red tape.

Roger Jones and Bill Crockett are slashing it as rapidly as possible and are preaching to their own staffs the right doctrine. This is a doctrine of decentralizing Washington's administrative monopoly, reducing reports of all sorts, simplifying and clarifying regulations and relying on a test of common sense in their interpretation and, most important, trusting in the judgment of our Ambassadors and our administrative officers overseas.

One reaction common at all meetings was the desire for speed in making these major administrative changes, even if we make a few mistakes. I am asking Bill to move ahead with all possible dispatch, even at the risk of stepping on bureaucratic toes.

D. With a few exceptions we can be proud of our Ambassadors and their staffs in these areas. While it is unwise to conclude too much from brief observation in meetings, most of us from Washington came away with the impression that our personnel in Africa are an able and particularly dedicated group. Their morale is excellent in spite of the staggering administrative problems with which most of them are faced and they are well versed in the philosophy and policies of the Administration.

We had similar good impressions in New Delhi from our South Asian and Southeast Asian posts. I think we have about the right mixture in that area of career and noncareer Ambassadors. Man for man, that was the most impressive group of chiefs of mission with whom we met.

While several of our top career people, such as Ellis Briggs, Ray Hare, and Phil Bonsal, were outstanding at Nicosia, the group as a whole from North Africa and the Middle East were somewhat less impressive at that conference. However, I am convinced that the problem there is partly one of over-exposure to the area. Many Arab specialists have been concentrating too long without a change of scene on the immensely frustrating problems of that region.

I think this problem is another reason for taking a hard look at our current emphasis on specialization. While it is undoubtedly necessary to build a corps of well qualified specialists for language areas, such as the Arab world, we must make certain these officers serve frequently enough in other areas to bring fresh perspective and breadth of view to problems within their field of specialization. This concern may clash head-on with our current drive for longer tours of duty and fewer separate assignments in the course of an officer's career. I am asking our personnel people to suggest some ways in which we can accomplish both worthwhile objectives.

E. It is apparent that we have significant communications gaps between the Department and our field posts on policy. Meetings such as these short-cut many months of written communications and avoid cumulative misunderstanding.

In order to close this gap we must encourage more consultation in Washington by our top people from the field and more intra-regional travel, as well as periodic regional meetings. We found it was very helpful to have Ambassadors from two regional bureaus meeting together, as was the case in Nicosia and New Delhi.

Our bureau lines are often artificial and tend to make it more difficult to solve questions which affect a number of missions. Not only travel but our mechanical communications net must be greatly improved if we are to get maximum usefulness from our missions abroad. This will cost more money but it will be money very well spent.

F. While we all agree it is desirable to cut our staff where possible to eliminate waste and non-essential functions, we must be extremely careful to do so in ways which will really forward our policy objectives.

Our Foreign Service personnel abroad are working long hours and what fat there is overseas is more likely to be found in other agency programs. We must concentrate first on reducing unnecessary reporting requirements to free our people for more local travel and broader contact with people of their areas and then look at possible staff reductions.

I have instructed Phil Sprouse, of the Foreign Service Inspection Corps, to carry out an experimental inspection in Paris covering other agencies as well as State. If this is successful, we will set up joint inspection teams to allow us to look at the whole range of mission activities and make cuts where they are really meaningful.

G. I am increasingly led to believe from this trip that some redefinition of regional bureau lines is desirable. For example, the Arab states of North Africa share many common problems with those of the Near East and few with those of Africa south of the Sahara.

As another example, the problem of China weighs heavily in South Asia as well as Southeast and East Asia and it may be that closer organizational ties between our missions in South Asia and those to the east would assist us in evolving sound policies all around the Chinese periphery.

I intend to explore this problem in the coming weeks with the regional bureaus, Alex Johnson and George McGhee and will have some firm recommendations ready by October.

[Here follows section II, Policy, comprising 6 pages of discussion under the following headings: A. Berlin; B. Africa; C. Arab World; D. Communist China; E. India–Pakistan; F. AID; G. Nuclear Testing; H. Race Relations.]

---

41. National Security Action Memorandum No. 91[1]

Washington, September 6, 1961.

FOR

The Secretary of State
The Secretary of Defense
The Secretary of the Treasury
The Administrator, General Services Administration

SUBJECT

Expediting Publication of "Foreign Relations"

The effectiveness of democracy as a form of government depends on an informed and intelligent citizenry. Nowhere is the making of choices more important than in foreign affairs; nowhere does government have a more imperative duty to make available as swiftly as possible all the facts required for intelligent decision.

---

[1] Source: National Archives and Records Administration, RG 59, S/S–NSC Files: Lot 72 D 316, NSAM No. 91. No classification marking. In a February 23 memorandum to Bowles, Secretary Rusk had asked the Under Secretary to look into policy with respect to publication of the Department's official historical documentary series *Foreign Relations of the United States*. Rusk suggested that volumes be published in a regular and predictable chronological sequence to avoid overtones of politics or propaganda. He cited the previous administration's interest in publishing records on China for the period 1942–1949. Rusk felt that publishing basic papers after a 15-year interval might be suitable, "although there would be those who would argue that this is too short." (Ibid., Rusk Papers: Lot 72 D 192, Chron Files, February 1961)

As many of these facts as possible should be made public on a current basis. But, because of the inherent need for security in the current conduct of foreign affairs, it is obviously not possible to make full immediate disclosure of diplomatic papers. However, delay in such disclosure must be kept to a minimum.

It has long been a pride of our government that we have made the historical record of our diplomacy available more promptly than any other nation in the world. The Department of State has the responsibility within the Executive Branch for putting out this permanent record in the series "Foreign Relations of the United States." The discharge of this responsibility requires the active collaboration of all departments and agencies of our Government in the submission and clearance of papers necessary for the completeness of this record.

In recent years the publication of the "Foreign Relations" series has fallen farther and farther behind currency. The lag has now reached approximately twenty years. I regard this as unfortunate and undesirable. It is the policy of this Administration to unfold the historical record as fast and as fully as is consistent with national security and with friendly relations with foreign nations.

Accordingly I herewith request all departments, agencies and libraries of the Government to collaborate actively and fully with the Department of State in its efforts to prepare and publish the record of our diplomacy. In my view, any official should have a clear and precise case involving the national interest before seeking to withhold from publication documents or papers fifteen or more years old.[2]

John F. Kennedy[3]

---

[2] In a September 22 memorandum to President Kennedy, Acting Secretary Bowles expressed appreciation for the action taken in NSAM No. 91 requesting the collaboration of all departments, agencies, and libraries of the Government. Bowles noted that an official of the Treasury Department had already provided assurances of cooperation. (Ibid., S/S–NSC Files: Lot 72 D 316, NSAM 91)

[3] Printed from a copy that indicates the President signed the original.

42.   Paper Prepared in the Office of Management, Department of State[1]

Washington, September 11, 1961.

PROPOSED STUDY OF ASPECTS OF STATE DEPARTMENT STRUCTURE AND OPERATIONS

Problem—Over the past few years it appears that there has developed in the Department of State an organizational proliferation and operational complexity that has increased points of interest and work clearance, established what may be duplicate or overlapping functions and reviews, extended the line of command between the desk officer and policy-decision-making, diluted the authority and effectiveness of regional Assistant Secretaries and resulted in functional bureaus organized internally on a geographic basis and geographic bureaus organized and staffed to perform a complete array of functional responsibilities.

Also, in its inter-agency relationships, careful consideration needs to be given to State's effectiveness in providing foreign policy guidance and leadership to other agencies of Government and in meeting the needs of agencies that have a direct interest in the conduct of overseas activities.

Study Proposed—It is recommended that a study be made of:

(1) bureau organizational structure;
(2) functional and geographic bureau responsibilities;
(3) effectiveness of existing decentralization of Departmental staff functions such as public affairs and administrative services;
(4) Department's inter-agency relationships; and
(5) related management aspects.

Its purpose would be (a) to develop proposals for internal simplification and stream-lining of structure including reduction in operational layering, increased delegations of authority, elimination of any functional overlapping and duplicating work reviews, and reductions in personnel and other costs, and (b) to examine existing inter-departmental relationships and recommend measures for their improvement.

---

[1] Source: National Archives and Records Administration, RG 59, Management Staff Files: Lot 69 D 434, Miscellaneous Subject Files, 1960–1967, Humelsine Task Force. No classification marking. A covering memorandum of September 5 from Ralph Roberts, Deputy Assistant Secretary of State for Management, to Assistant Secretary Crockett, indicated that the proposed study of bureau organizational structure would be conducted by Carlisle H. Humelsine, President of Colonial Williamsburg, Inc. Humelsine had formerly served as Executive Secretary of the Department of State (1947–1950) and Deputy Under Secretary of State for Administration (1950–1952). Secretary Rusk was personally involved in planning for the study.

Staff Resources—On a temporary consulting basis, the services of two or three former officers of State who are knowledgeable regarding its operational needs, and who have demonstrated a competence in management. To these will be added, on a highly selective basis, such numbers of existing officers as may be necessary, with the support of the Office of Management, to accomplish the task within approximately 30 days.

Report—The study group will prepare and submit to the Secretary a report on its findings and recommendations. If in the course of its work, the group identifies organizational or management problems requiring further attention, its report should so indicate and recommend a course of action.

---

43. Memorandum From the President's Special Assistant for National Security Affairs (Bundy) to President Kennedy[1]

Washington, September 28, 1961.

SUBJECT

Washington News

[Here follow paragraph 1, which deals with the appointment of John McCone as Director of Central Intelligence; paragraph 2, concerning the defense budget for fiscal year 1963; and paragraph 3, dealing with the management of foreign aid. Paragraphs 1 and 3 are printed as Documents 91 and 75, respectively.]

4. Chester Bowles and I smoked a peace pipe this week. He is still wholly unclear about his relation to the Secretary and to the Department. With a man who had time to keep a close eye on him, I am now convinced that he could be an effective deputy for certain kinds of work. He really does have a sharp eye for personnel, and he understands better than the Secretary the need for executive energy in the geographical bureaus and other Assistant Secretaryships. The trouble is that he is constantly wanting to make policy, without even knowing, really, that this is what he is doing. And his policy is not on all fours with your own, and still less with Mr. Rusk's. I recommended to him

---

[1] Source: Kennedy Library, National Security Files, Bundy Memoranda to the President, 8/22/61–9/30/61. Secret.

that he have a wholly frank and clear-cut discussion with the Secretary, but I am not hopeful of the result. Rusk finds it hard to use a Deputy, and Bowles finds it even harder to be a No. 2.

Yet when we turned to talk of empty embassies and how to fill them, Bowles made good sense, and I think his recommendations are well worth your attention. Unless you are planning to keep him in the deep freeze, I suggest that you invite him in for a talk on this specific subject.

[Here follow paragraphs 5 and 6 concerning Syria and Berlin, respectively.]

McG. B[2]

---

[2] Printed from a copy that bears these typed initials.

---

44.   Memorandum From the Under Secretary of State (Bowles) to the President's Special Assistant (Dutton)[1]

Washington, October 6, 1961.

SUBJECT

Equal Employment Opportunity

As you know, the Secretary, Mennen Williams, and I, as well as other newcomers in the Department of State have always had strong views on the question of civil rights. I among others have been critical of the slow pace with which the Department has recruited qualified Negroes for responsible positions. Until we took office, however, we did not know just how bad the situation was.

As of February 28, 1961, of 3732 Foreign Service officers, 17 were Negroes, of 1140 Foreign Service Reserve officers, 3 were Negroes; and of 3527 Foreign Service Staff employees, 38 were Negroes. (The figure of 38 in the Staff corps is on the low side. It was not feasible to canvass each overseas post to determine the number of Negro Staff corps employees.) In the Department, of 4570 Civil Service employees, 1064

---

[1] Source: Kennedy Library, National Security Files, Departments and Agencies Series, State Department, General, 10/1/61–10/6/61. No classification marking. No response to this memorandum was found.

were Negroes but less than fifteen percent of that number were higher than grade GS-5, and none higher than grade GS-13.

Soon after entering the Department last winter we started a real campaign to speed up action in this field. While there is a great deal more to do at least we have made a good start.

A number of regulatory controls have been instituted or revised; Assistant Secretary Williams has been named Employment Policy Officer for the Department of State and the executive director of each bureau has been designated as an associate employment policy officer, each of whom is responsible not only for the processing of formal complaints of discrimination but for promoting compliance with the concept of fair employment within his jurisdiction; an instruction has gone to the field directing that no discrimination is to be permitted in employee recreational activities at overseas posts; and the field inspection team has been instructed to observe for evidence of compliance with the nondiscrimination policy. Moreover, the Deputy Assistant Secretaries of minority group background served this year on the examining panel for FSO-8 candidates. However, to effect a change in the aforementioned statistics, action of a more remedial nature must be instituted. This is being done.

On August 16, the Department held a day-long conference with top Negro leaders and representatives of national agencies to discuss steps that might be undertaken to achieve a more representative officer and staff corps and to assure better recruitment and utilization of Negro civil service employees. Secretary Rusk told the conferees "we are determined to do everything that we can to insure that discrimination is not practiced in the State Department." They, in turn, made nine recommendations to the Department.

Following are the recommendations of the conference, each with brief commentary on Departmental action to date:

1. Launch a campaign to make it known that qualified Negroes are wanted.

The conference of August 16 was the kick-off of such a campaign. Since that time, a communication has been sent to each participant asking that they send the names of any people they feel qualified for employment with the Department. In addition, application forms for the FSO-8 examination have been sent them with the request that they encourage Negro young people of their acquaintance to take the examination this year. The conferees were asked to talk up the fact that the Department is interested in finding qualified Negroes for service at home and abroad, and four of the conferees have been asked to serve on a liaison committee which is to meet periodically to assess the Department's progress. A meeting of this committee is planned for November.

2. *Appoint Negroes to "high level policy positions" in the Department so as to inspire bright Negro youngsters to train for work in the field of foreign affairs.*

The Department has this recommendation under consideration. When circumstances are appropriate, i.e. when suitable assignments occur for which we have qualified Negroes, the Department will not hesitate to make such appointments.

3. *Use Negroes as recruiters, both at predominantly Negro and at integrated colleges.*

The paucity of Negro officers in the senior grades both in the officer corps and in the Civil Service makes it difficult for the Department to meet this recommendation. The Foreign Service officers used in the college visitation program are Class 4 or higher while Civil Service employees, when used are at least grade GS-14. There are no Negro Civil Service employees at this grade level in the Department, and of four Foreign Service officers Class 4 or higher, all are currently serving in assignments overseas. One Negro Reserve officer is teaming with a white officer for a special recruitment trip to five of the larger metropolitan areas which, hopefully, will provide both some additional candidates for the examination this year and lay a base on which to build a better recruitment program in these cities among the Negro population over the next few years. Plans are presently underway to assign a Negro employee to clerical recruitment activities.

The number of predominantly Negro colleges to be visited in the college relations program has been increased this year. Whereas seventeen were visited last year, that number has been increased to twenty-six this year, making a net gain of nine. Moreover, the officers participating in the recruitment program have been supplied with a copy of the summary of the conference on equal employment opportunity and time was allotted during the recent briefing session to inform them of the Department's efforts to increase the representativeness of the Service.

4. *Immediately place more qualified Negroes in middle and high level posts by making Foreign Service Reserve appointments.*

On or about November 1, three new Negro employees are to enter on duty. All are being appointed as Reserve officers in the middle grades. One is to be assigned to the Bureau of Economic Affairs, one to the Bureau of Cultural and Educational Affairs in the Leaders and Specialists Division, and the third to the Office of Personnel. It is anticipated that as more of the conference participants begin to supply names of qualified applicants, other appointments will be made.

5. *Survey the great number of Negroes now clustered in the lower ranks so as to determine which, if any, are deserving of immediate promotion.*

Three steps are underway which should relieve the imbalance presently found in the distribution of Negro employees by grade. (1) The Office of Personnel is currently surveying job classifications in the Department to discover those in which there is a preponderance of Negroes. When this information is obtained efforts will be made to reduce the concentration. (2) A listing of Negro employees who have demonstrated potential for more responsible assignments is being prepared. This list of names will be judiciously used when vacancies occur for which these employees are qualified. (3) Every fourth promotion panel is being surveyed to determine the frequency with which Negroes appear on such panels. This will be continued over a six months period and a report will be prepared monthly detailing the type of panel, number of Negroes and the selection results. This activity in combination with the aggressive recruitment program underway should result in substantial change in Departmental employment within the next six months.

6. *Survey Negro Foreign Service Reserve appointees now working in State and such related agencies as the United States Information Agency and the International Cooperation Administration (ICA) to see if some merit lateral transfer into the Foreign Service.*

This effort is currently underway. Because of the highly specialized qualifications and skills of employees of these departments, it is not anticipated that many officers will be found possessing the broad background desirable for work in the Foreign Service. Neither does the Department have any assurance that any officers now employed by either of these agencies would be willing to forego their career status to accept employment with the Department of State. However, this effort will be pursued vigorously.

7. *Do not compromise with quality or make any special concessions of competence as a favor to Negroes, but the examination procedure ought to be investigated to determine whether it automatically excludes categories of persons who are potentially valuable Foreign Service officers.*

Dr. Kenneth Clark, one of the participants in the conference of August 16 and a Professor of Psychology at City College of New York has recently volunteered the services of a subcommittee of the Society for Psychological Study on Social Issues for the purpose of taking a hard look at the entrance examination to see if it places a handicap on applicants from culturally disadvantaged backgrounds. The Department has accepted this invitation and three officers of the Department will meet with the subcommittee this month.

8. *That predominantly Negro colleges be advised as to any special courses or curriculum materials that might better prepare students for Foreign Service careers.*

Dr. Jerome Holland, also a conference participant and a college president, is being asked to chair a committee whose objective will be to look into the problem of the long term supply of Negro candidates for the entrance examination. This committee is to be asked to develop a prospectus for such a program.

9. *That Negro youngsters be included in the summer student trainee program of the Department.*

Two Negro students out of twenty were included in the intern program this summer. If funds are available for this activity next summer, Negro students will continue to be included.

The Department is making every effort to find qualified Negro applicants for service overseas and in Washington. This program is of first priority and will continue to receive the personal attention of Mr. Herman Pollack, Deputy Assistant Secretary for Personnel.

There are attached for your information copies of news articles on the conference of August 16.[2]

Chester Bowles[3]

---

[2] Not found.

[3] Printed from a copy that bears this typed signature.

---

45. **Memorandum From Secretary of State Rusk to the Assistant Secretary of State for International Organization Affairs (Cleveland)[1]**

Washington, October 29, 1961.

SUBJECT

Delegation to International Conferences

I believe that our delegations to international conferences and meetings can be reduced in size and thereby be made more efficient and

---

[1] Source: National Archives and Records Administration, RG 59, Rusk Files: Lot 72 D 192, Chron File, October 1961. No classification marking. Drafted by Rusk.

less costly. The critical test should be the minimum number and roles of persons required to accomplish the particular U.S. objective at the conference or meeting. Our delegations should be looked upon as negotiating delegations, not as policy makers. It is not necessary for every agency, or every portion of the Department, which has or claims an interest in the subject matter, to have representatives on delegations.

I have myself initiated the same policy with respect to my own visits abroad. In requesting you to give rigorous scrutiny to the makeup of U.S. delegations, I am also assuring you of my full support, especially during the period when people will have to adjust themselves to the requirements of this policy.

Dean Rusk[2]

---

[2] Printed from a copy that bears this typed signature.

---

46.   Editorial Note

On November 15, 1961, Secretary of State Rusk and Secretary of Commerce Hodges signed a "Memorandum of Agreement between the Department of State and the Department of Commerce on International Commercial Activities." The agreement began with the following statement of objective:

"The President has directed the Executive Agencies to place maximum emphasis on enlarging the foreign commerce of the United States in seeking to maintain an over-all balance in our international payments. He has charged the Department of Commerce with the leadership within the Government to insure that a vigorous effort be made to expand trade, travel, and investment and 'to provide energetic leadership to American industry in a drive to develop export markets.' He has called upon the Departments of State and Commerce to proceed jointly to increase commercial representation and facilities abroad. And he has made it clear that Chiefs of Mission shall oversee and coordinate all such activities abroad.

"To provide effective leadership, the Department of Commerce is assuming primary responsibility and direction for foreign trade promotion activities at home and abroad, giving due consideration to interests of other agencies.

"The Departments of State and Commerce agree that the President's directive can best be carried out abroad by a single overseas service. To fulfill their respective responsibilities, the two Departments undertake to establish new arrangements for the purpose of providing optimum commercial services within the frame-work of a unified Foreign Service.

"To this end the Department of State agrees to develop, with the full participation of the Department of Commerce, a Commercial Specialist Program within the Foreign Service."

The agreement provided an opportunity for Foreign Service officers to elect commercial work as a career specialty and permitted advancement within this specialty to the highest levels in the Foreign Service. Personnel would be augmented by an enlarged number of appointments from the Department of Commerce and the business community, who, along with Foreign Service career specialists, would provide the expertise needed to assist American business in meeting the increasing competition for world markets.

In order to attract economic and commercial talent, the two Departments would establish joint recruitment teams to visit educational institutions granting graduate and undergraduate degrees in business administration or foreign trade, and the Department of State would make special provision in its written Foreign Service examinations for candidates with background and interest in commercial activities. A department of commercial affairs would be established in the Foreign Service Institute of the Department of State, chaired by a mutually acceptable nominee of the Department of Commerce. The chairman would develop a commercial training program and supervise its implementation and operation.

The Department of Commerce would normally initiate instructions to commercial specialists for carrying out their operational and reporting duties and responsibilities. Current instructions would be modified to provide increased emphasis on the promotion of trade, investment, and travel. Commercial specialists would be encouraged to travel more widely in their respective districts in order to develop market information which would be rapidly communicated to the American business community.

The Memorandum of Agreement, November 15, 1961, is in the National Archives and Records Administration, RG 59, Rusk Files: Lot 72 D 192, Miscellaneous Correspondence, Hodges, Luther. See also U.S. Department of Commerce, *Foreign Commerce Weekly*, April 21, 1962, page 1; Department of State *Bulletin*, April 30, 1962, pages 741–742. The text of the State–Commerce Agreement was transmitted to all posts in Circular Instruction CW 9672, June 4, 1962. (National Archives and Records Administration, RG 59, Central Files 1960–63, 120.201/6–462)

47.   Editorial Note

On November 26, 1961, the White House announced that Chester Bowles would become the President's Special Representative and Adviser on African, Asian, and Latin American Affairs, with particular emphasis on the problems of the new and developing countries. In this post, Bowles would "report directly to the President and Secretary of State on long-range planning and policy in this area, and on the improvement of our operation and representation in the countries involved. He will hold the rank of Ambassador, and also serve as an ex-officio member of the Policy Planning Council. He will continue to have an important role in explaining and promoting American foreign policy to key individuals and audiences both at home and abroad, and will from time to time undertake special missions for the President." (Memorandum of Understanding, November 27; Kennedy Library, National Security Files, Departments and Agencies Series, State Department, General, 11/20/61–11/30/61) For President Kennedy's remarks concerning Bowles at his news conference of November 29, and his remarks at the swearing in of Bowles as the President's Special Representative on December 12, see *Public Papers of the Presidents of the United States: John F. Kennedy, 1961*, pages 759 and 798.

Among other organizational changes in the Department of State, George Ball was to become Under Secretary of State; George McGhee would move from the Policy Planning Council to replace Ball as the second Under Secretary of State (but for Political rather than Economic Affairs); and W. Averell Harriman would become Assistant Secretary of State for Far Eastern Affairs. Leaving the White House for the State Department, Walt Rostow would become Counselor of the Department and Chairman of the Policy Planning Council; Fred Dutton would become Assistant Secretary of State for Congressional Relations, and Richard Goodwin would become a Deputy Assistant Secretary of State for Inter-American Affairs. On the State Department reorganization in the fall of 1961, see Schlesinger, *A Thousand Days*, pages 442–445; memorandum from Jones to Rusk, December 1, in the National Archives and Records Administration, RG 59, Central Files 1960–63, 110.10/12–161; also Department of State Foreign Affairs Manual Circular No. 44, Responsibilities of the Under Secretaries and Deputy Under Secretaries of State, December 15, 1961, in the Kennedy Library, National Security Files, Departments and Agencies Series, State Department, General, 12/61.

48.   Memorandum From the Executive Secretary of the Department of State (Battle) to the President's Special Assistant for National Security Affairs (Bundy)[1]

Washington, January 30, 1962.

SUBJECT

Duty Officers

You will recall that I mentioned to you several weeks ago the changes in the arrangements between the Executive Secretary's office and the Operations Center. I would like to confirm one or two points which I gather have caused some confusion.

We now have an integrated watch in the Department which is in the Operations Center. As part of this watch, the Reports Staff of the Executive Secretariat now functions on a 24-hour day rather than a 19 as previously constituted. The watch in the Operations Center is no longer a "sleeping" watch awakened as necessary but is now on a sit-up or stand-up basis on an 8-hour shift. This office can be reached on extension 4141-2.

Integrated into the watch is the duty officer in my own office who is here each night and over week-ends as long as needed. This is normally until about 11:00 p.m. on week nights and usually through the day Saturday and Sunday. When he leaves he turns over any pending problems to the Operations Center duty officer but remains on call at home in the event he is needed. For those matters involving the normal flow of paper, etc., you will probably wish to continue to talk with the duty officer in my office, extension 5381-2.

As I told you, the Operations Center follow-up unit and my follow-up unit have been merged but the nature and detail of follow-up will continue as previously. The follow-up unit is under Mr. Tom Rogers but Miss Moor on extension 6952 may be the most useful point of contact for your office.

I hope the foregoing is helpful. Please call me if there is any further information you feel is lacking.

N.A. Veliotes[2]

---

[1] Source: Kennedy Library, National Security Files, Departments and Agencies Series, State Department, General, 2/62. No classification marking. In a February 9 memorandum for heads of Bureaus in the Department of State, Battle described procedures for designating Bureau duty officers and stand-by officers in support of 24-hour coverage, coordinated through the Operations Center, to meet emergencies and other matters requiring immediate attention during non-working hours. (National Archives and Records Administration, RG 59, Central Files 1960–63, 110.10/2–962)

[2] Veliotes signed for Battle above Battle's typed signature.

49.   Paper Prepared in the Department of State[1]

Washington, February 8, 1962.

SPECIFIC ADMINISTRATIVE ACCOMPLISHMENTS DESIGNED
TO IMPROVE EFFICIENCY AND FOSTER ECONOMY
OF OPERATIONS

1. Strengthening of Ambassadorial performance through President's letter of May 29, 1961, and designation of the Director General of the Foreign Service as the focal point for assuring that Ambassadors are adequately oriented, informed and supported.

2. Elimination of 99 administrative reports from overseas posts.

3. The number of committees having Departmental participation was reduced from 339 to 144.

4. Abolition of Correspondence Review function.

5. Curtailment of newspaper clipping service.

6. Consolidation of Operations Center with Secretariat.

7. Reduction of Administrative personnel by more than 125 persons.

8. Review of Department's appraisal, inspection, and audit activities to improve the Department's capacity to evaluate overall performance of the Department, including overseas posts.

9. Reorganization of The Bureau of Research and Intelligence with reduction of 230 in employment.

10. Decentralization of operating authority on administrative matters to geographic bureaus and to the field.

11. Plans formulated for the establishment of a consolidated administrative service center at Lagos for 20 African posts, with particular attention to supply and medical problems of these posts.

12. Department's directive regarding the use of tourist class accommodations for air travel in the U.S. and over the North Atlantic except under unusual circumstances. (Savings of about $300,000 on North Atlantic travel had to be used for other high priority items.)

13. Decision to hold personnel at 1962 level—no increase overall in 1963, but some redistribution in authorized Bureau strengths.

14. Simplification of procedures for handling and processing security reports from other agencies.

---

[1] Source: National Archives and Records Administration, RG 59, Central Files 1960–63, 110.10/2–862. No classification marking. No drafting officer is indicated; the paper was presumably drafted in the Bureau of Administration.

15. Reduction from 15 to 11 Foreign Buildings offices overseas.

16. Improvement of payroll and bond programs with less people. (Bonds are now issued currently instead of one month behind date of last deduction.)

17. Elimination of special group for Communist economic activities.

18. Elimination of special officer for East-West Exchanges.

19. Abolition of special position to review and advise on security appeals.

20. Sharp curtailment of overhead position in Bureau of Security and Consular Affairs.

21. Curtailment of unnecessary Departmental inspections.

22. Extension of Paris Regional Finance Center to serve African posts to cut down African staff buildup.

---

50. Memorandum From Secretary of State Rusk to President Kennedy[1]

Washington, February 9, 1962.

There has been informal discussion with you of a meeting with policy officers of the Department down to the Desk level. This should include not only officers with responsibility for specific countries but also officers at comparable levels who have United Nations, economic, intelligence, administrative or other such responsibility. If you will set a time for the meeting, I shall call these officers together in the New Auditorium in the Department. I cannot think of any step which would be more useful from a morale standpoint and for increasing understanding of the spirit and objectives of the Administration.[2]

[1] Source: Kennedy Library, National Security Files, Departments and Agencies Series, Department of State, President's Talk to State Department, 3/30/62. Official Use Only.

[2] The President met with Department officers on March 30; see Document 52. Additional suggestions to the President concerning points he might raise in his meeting with Department officers were contained in a memorandum from Hilsman to the President, February 3, and in a memorandum from Battle to Bundy, March 23. (Both in the Kennedy Library, National Security Files, Departments and Agencies Series, Department of State, President's Talk to State Department, 3/30/62)

You might wish to talk about American responsibilities in a revolutionary world and the new concepts of diplomacy which this demands, our relationships with the advanced nations of the West in meeting these responsibilities, our attitude toward the Sino-Soviet bloc, and our role in such organizations as the United Nations, the Organization of American States, the General Agreement on Tariffs and Trade, etc.

Against this background, you could speak of the imaginativeness, forcefulness, and leadership which is expected of all officials of the Department. I think it would be useful to say that we expect Desk officers to make decisions and to exercise initiative and leadership in relations abroad and within the United States Government. For this they need a broad understanding of the philosophy and purposes of our foreign policy, and they must be expert without being parochial. These officers especially need to understand that this Administration recognizes the authority and responsibility of the Department in foreign affairs and has consciously given the duty of executive leadership to its Ambassadors and the Assistant Secretaries of State. This calls for a new consciousness on the part of Desk-level officers of the role of other agencies in foreign affairs, the closest relations with them, and a sensitivity to all factors—social, economic, political, military, commercial, administrative, intelligence and public information. It requires a broad knowledge of all the resources and mechanisms of the American Government.

Special mention might usefully be made of a need for taking into account problems of public relations and Congressional relations in making policy, although action in these problems will generally fall on the "political level" of the Administration.

Having said what is expected of them, there will be need for a word of assurance of support and confidence for these officers and for their colleagues in the Department and the Foreign Service. They would be glad to be assured again of the Administration's determination to defend them against political abuse and to promote careers on the basis of merit.

These officers will know of your own great interest in foreign affairs and welcome it. I doubt that any other President has come to know as many officers of the Department of State, of all ranks, as have you. A main impression which I think the meeting should leave is of your reliance on team effort between career and non-career officers to assist you in the creation and execution of policy and of our joint responsibility to keep you informed of facts and judgments about current developments.

Dean Rusk

51.   Memorandum From the Assistant Secretary of State for Administration (Crockett) to the Deputy Under Secretary of State for Administration (Jones)[1]

Washington, March 22, 1962.

SUBJECT

Bureau of the Budget Report on *State Department Organization for Foreign Economic Affairs*

Attached is a preliminary analysis of the Report by the Bureau of the Budget Study Team on *State Department Organization for Foreign Economic Affairs*.[2] The analysis is intended to be no more than a starting point for intensive consideration of the aspects of the Report. Consideration will be most effective if undertaken with the active participation of the new Assistant Secretary for Economic Affairs, when he is named.[3]

In particular his concepts of the total goals and purpose of E, of E's relationships to the regional bureaus and other parts of the Department, and of the internal organization of E may give new insights into the problem of how we may improve our organization for foreign economic activities.

The Department, it should be noted, has been active during the period since the Bureau of the Budget team completed its examination. The Secretary's reorganization of last December began establishment of a sound organizational pattern aimed at clarifying lines of authority and achieving more effective coordination of functional responsibilities. This constituted an important step upon which future changes should be predicated. We have also made some changes that anticipated the Budget Bureau's recommendations. For example, the Department has integrated in AID, economic development responsibilities previously assigned to E. More recently, the Under Secretary has directed that the Foreign Economic Advisory Staff be moved from his immediate office to E.

In addition, current steps to establish back-to-back space arrangements for related functions in the geographic bureaus for Latin American activities suggest directions in which the over-all structure of

---

[1] Source: National Archives and Records Administration, RG 59, Management Staff Files: Lot 69 D 434, Miscellaneous Subject Files, 1960–1967, State Department Organization for Foreign Economic Affairs, 1962. No classification marking. Drafted by Gladys P. Rogers in the Office of Management (OM) on March 21.

[2] Dated March 1962; attached but not printed.

[3] G. Griffith Johnson was appointed Assistant Secretary of State for Economic Affairs on May 12, succeeding Edwin M. Martin.

the Department may develop. Whether these arrangements are limited to physical location or eventually become organizational in nature, their intent is clearly to improve coordination in carrying out inter-related functions affecting the political, economic and other content of United States foreign affairs.

We are, thus, in the process of feeling our way along certain paths. Our readiness and ability to clarify the ultimate direction these paths will take, will in large measure determine the effectiveness of the use we make of this study.

---

52. Editorial Note

On the morning of March 30, 1962, President Kennedy visited the Department of State for a scheduled off-the-record meeting with Department officials down to the level of desk officer. The meeting was held in the Department's new auditorium. In introducing the President, Secretary of State Rusk noted that "there has been no other President who could look around this room, in which are gathered the policy officers of the Department of State, and see as many officers whom he has known personally, and with whom he has worked intimately and directly on a great many complex and important questions in the conduct of our foreign relations, and that is deeply appreciated."

President Kennedy began his remarks by indicating his and the country's dependence on the experience and counsel of the Department of State and the Foreign Service. "I know that those of you who work in the Foreign Service frequently feel beleaguered and surrounded, dealing not only with those who are our adversaries abroad, but also with those who are our most difficult friends, and here in the United States with those who fail to understand the complexities of foreign policy. I recognize, therefore, that you may sometimes get tired of reading magazine articles on what's wrong with the State Department. You may occasionally wonder whether the long work that you do, with your willingness to serve here and abroad, is fully understood by the people of this country. I'm sure it is not and I'm sure it never will be in its entirety. We have had such a long tradition of isolation that to be thrust suddenly upon the world scene as a leading power requires a change in thinking which is bound to cause serious misunderstandings among our people about those who conduct our foreign policy.

"In addition, our foreign relations are so complicated and so difficult and so sophisticated and so sensitive that it is impossible—except for those very few who live with these problems—to be fully aware of the subtle distinctions of policy. How could the average American be expected to understand the reasons why we help Yugoslavia and try to isolate Cuba, or why we recognize and carry on intensive dialogues with the Soviet Union and isolate China, or why we assist a dictatorship in Spain while we preach the doctrine of freedom and democracy in Latin America, why we insist as a matter of policy on a coalition government in Laos (even though coalition governments have not always had happy results, in our experience) while on the other hand we become more and more involved in sustaining the government of nearby Viet-Nam. These are all difficult and complicated and sensitive decisions upon which we may or may not be right, but which in any case require a good deal of understanding. So I do not think you should ever expect that they will be fully understood, and therefore you must carry on your struggle with a recognition that you are serving the interests of your country, and that it is the responsibility of those of us who hold public positions to attempt to explain those problems as best we can."

The President then referred to "a tendency in this country—this is particularly true of our press, and I think it's probably true also of our Foreign Service, from the cables that we read—to be overly sensitive to hostility abroad. . . . I do sometimes feel that as a country, as a people, as a service, as an executive, and as a Congress, we are too responsive to the pressures which those who are associated with us bring to bear upon us—pressures of disapproval which cause us to be constantly reexamining our own policies to see how we can bring them into line with one country after another. I think we probably should be tougher and try to pursue our own style with a little more vigor and direction."

The President referred to a statement once made by former British Prime Minister Winston Churchill. "He said that the secret of the survival of the British Empire was that they never trusted the judgment of the man on the spot. I never understood that until recently, but I do think we have a tendency to oversympathize with the problems of the country to which we are accredited—those of us who may be serving abroad. . . . We want to be sure that we have very disinterested and hard-boiled judgment by the people who are there because we depend upon those people to give us guidance in our policy, but if what we get constantly represents not merely a report of the viewpoint of the other country, but an endorsement of that viewpoint, then those of you who sit at the desks and must make a judgment—and coordinate our policy with the desks of other countries and other regions—will find yourselves with an almost impossible job."

The President called for maintaining "the utmost discretion so that we can have a good deal of ease and fluidity in carrying on our negotiations abroad." Turning to another point, "if I have one real criticism, it is that I think we move too slowly. I know the difficulties of coordinating policy and making judgments on sensitive matters, but I do think we have to move with more speed . . . more vigor here. We depend completely on the Department. . . . You have to coordinate the policy within the Department and within the various agencies, but I do think that you should attempt in every way possible to speed your work up, and to make sure that committees and inter-departmental groups do not permit a smothering of your initiative on which so much depends."

The President referred to the important work of Ambassadors and Foreign Service officers on the spot at crucial moments. "It is a remarkable fact that the most interesting offices—the areas which place the greatest responsibility upon an Ambassador—are not the traditional ones of Western Europe, but Latin America, Africa, and Asia. These areas I think give the greatest opportunity to a Foreign Service officer to render direct and really unique service. . . . Thirty years ago it seemed that the great days of Ambassadors of the nineteenth [century] were over because of the cable. Now suddenly we have a new period where Ambassadors can play a most significant role."

President Kennedy then took questions from the floor on several subjects, including the possibility of increased communication with Communist China, the Department's relationships with Congress and with other agencies, and Presidential broadcasts on foreign policy to the American people. ("Draft for President's Revision," Transcript of the President's Remarks, prepared by Bundy; Kennedy Library, National Security Files, Departments and Agencies Series, Department of State, President's Talk to State Department, 3/30/62; an unedited draft transcript is ibid.)

A covering memorandum of April 4 from Bundy to Deputy Executive Secretary Brubeck transmitted Bundy's draft with the following comment:

"Here is a draft which I cleaned up over the week end for the President's consideration. His current feeling is that the paper should not have further circulation. If it is to be circulated, some of the informal comments will have to come out—and if they come out, what is left is a bit dull.

"On the other hand, I am sure he will be glad to know the Department's views on this matter. If, for example, the Department thinks that a summary, omitting the bracketed passages, would be useful to Ambassadors, I think the President might well be willing to have it circulated." A handwritten notation by Bundy reads: "This should *not* be copied or duplicated over there, in any way, without President's further consent—or circulated except to men you *yourself* choose." (Ibid.)

53. Memorandum From the Ambassador to Yugoslavia (Kennan) to President Kennedy[1]

Washington, undated.

I offer the following observations for whatever they are worth, in connection with your questions about the Foreign Service:[2]

(1) There is not just one thing wrong with the State Department and Foreign Service, but many things.

(2) There is no sudden and drastic action that could taken to remedy these ills. Both organizations are the victims of many past mistakes, and particularly of erratic and misguided treatment on the part of a long succession of masters. A good professional organization is like a tree: you can affect its growth but only by long, patient and constant action. What the Foreign Service needs, in particular is fifteen years of consistent treatment along sound lines of personnel selection and advancement.

(3) The quality of the Foreign Service is today surprisingly good—much better than one would have a right to expect, in the light of the treatment the organization has received in recent years. The Department, too, contains hundreds of first rate men; but they are all embraced in a system too cumbersome to be fully manageable—in a machine so over-elaborate that the bulk of its energy is consumed by its own internal friction.

(4) So far as I know nobody inspects the Department of State. Our missions abroad (the civilian component, that is) are the objects of at least four inspection systems today. Whether it would be better if there

---

[1] Source: Kennedy Library, National Security Files, Departments and Agencies Series, State Department, General, 5/26/62–5/31/62. Confidential.

[2] Kennan's memorandum was one of several documents assembled by Bundy to aid the President in preparing remarks at a luncheon to be held by the American Foreign Service Association in Washington at the end of May. In a May 29 covering memorandum to the President, Bundy wrote in part: "The more I look at this, the more I doubt that you should make a speech about the Foreign Service as such. It would not stay off the record, and I am impressed by what George Kennan said to me yesterday: the Foreign Service is like a badly trained horse—if you try to punish him, you will only make him worse. So I would vote for a modified version of your January remarks to the NSC, with perhaps just a few informal comments on the fact that the State Department has the role of leadership if only it will grasp it. On this you could well refer back to Acheson." (Kennedy Library, National Security Files, Bundy Chron Files, Staff Memos 5/21/62–5/31/62)

President Kennedy delivered his off-the-record remarks before a luncheon meeting of the American Foreign Service Association at the Sheraton-Park Hotel in Washington on May 31. An edited transcript was forwarded by Woodruff Wallner, Chairman, Editorial Board, *Foreign Service Journal,* under cover of a June 18 letter to Bundy. (Ibid., Departments and Agencies Series, Department of State, General, 6/1/62–6/18/61) For the published version, see "The Great Period of the Foreign Service," *Foreign Service Journal,* July 1962, pp. 28–29.

were a single unified system, I do not know. The regular Foreign Service Inspection Corps is about to be taken over by an excellent man: Norris Haselton. I think he should be given support and a chance to show what he can do. It would be very inadvisable, in my opinion, to try to set up an inspection corps composed of, or headed by, outsiders who have had no experience in the Service. What is needed here are experienced competent, and conscientious Foreign Service Officers. One of the great troubles is that the Department does not like to assign its ablest officers for this work; when it does so, it leaves them there for too short a time, and yanks them out whenever it wants them for something else. The work of the Inspection Corps should be up-graded, the men should be kept in it for longer periods; arrangements should be made so that their home life would not be inordinately disrupted by this sort of work, as it now unfortunately tends to be.

(5) I do not profess to be an expert on the administrative problems of the Department. I feel fairly confident that there are far too many people and too many layers of authority. I suspect the Department needs a more rigid system of designation of respectability [*responsibility?*], with a view to getting away from the evils of the "clearance" system and committee rule. With fullest sympathy for the Secretary of State in the face of the demands made upon him for commitment of his personal time to travel and negotiation and attendance at conferences, I would submit that if the Department of State is to work more smoothly, it must have on duty at all times a full-time boss armed with authority to resolve promptly any and all questions within the competence of the institution.

(6) The Foreign Service officers with whom you meet on Thursday are by and large the victims, not the authors, of the inadequacies of the present system. Many of them are excellent and deeply devoted public servants. They will have heard something of your questions and anxieties about the Service. They will know that these are generally justified. Nevertheless, there will be some nervousness about your attitude toward them.

It seems to me that the best thing that you could do would be to indicate your awareness of the seriousness and recalcitrance of the administrative problems with which the Department and Foreign Service are beset; to remind them of the brevity of the time that has been available for the correction of these various evils or inadequacies by the present administration, and to assure them that this problem will have serious and continued attention of yourself and the Secretary of State. It could be pointed out that whereas there is a science of administration and management that has been worked out for mechanical processes such as the work of men at machines, where the relation of function to human effort can be statistically measured and defined, there is no such science for the work of bodies whose task in essentially analytical and advisory, such as the Department of State. The objective to be sought might well be defined, it seems to me, as the avoidance of the two extremes of (1) an apparatus so bloated and over-elaborate that it loses all the advantages of intimacy, flexibility and smartness of operation, and (2) such drastic and brutal curtailment as to involve injustice to those who are dropped and an inordinate burden on those who are retained. There must be a reasonable middle ground between these two extremes. The problem is to find it. The United States already has a Foreign Service second to none other in many respects. But it is spotty in quality, diffuse, inadequately coordinated, shaken by too many past changes of policy, uncertain as to what is expected of it and what can be expected. These deficiencies cannot be cured over night. But with time, patience, and imaginative insight they *can* be cured, and they will be.

George F. Kennan[3]

---

[3] Printed from a copy that bears this typed signature.

---

54.   **Memorandum From the Deputy Assistant Secretary of State for Management (Roberts) to the Executive Secretary of the Department of State (Brubeck)**[1]

Washington, May 10, 1962.

Bill—

With regard to the Budget Bureau study of our organization for foreign economic affairs[2]—

1. We have already acted affirmatively on some matters which the study recommends. For example—

—we have abolished the Office of Under Secretary for Economic Affairs, and have thus eliminated a basic premise on which some of the Budget Bureau's recommendations were formulated.

---

[1] Source: National Archives and Records Administration, RG 59, Central Files 1960–63, 110.10/5–1062. No classification marking. Gladys P. Rogers (OM) is shown as the drafting officer on another copy of this memorandum. (Ibid., Management Staff Files: Lot 69 D 434, Miscellaneous Subject Files, 1960–1967, State Department Organization for Foreign Economic Affairs, 1962)

[2] See Document 51.

—we have integrated in AID the bulk of E's economic development functions.

—we have, in effect, transferred the Foreign Economic Advisory Staff to E. (The formal announcement will be made when Griffith Johnson has an opportunity to determine the reporting channel to him which he considers most useful.)

—we have arranged to include an economic option in future foreign service examinations.

2. Most of the other changes recommended for *immediate adoption* concern the internal organization of E. Griffith Johnson could not appropriately take actions along this line until he is sworn in. He must have time to familiarize himself with E before he can react usefully to the proposals. He has read the report and is considering it.

3. In addition, the study included certain recommendations "contingent upon other structural changes in the Department." As the study itself indicates these cannot be acted on immediately. They involve organizational choices which can be made only when AID is more settled and the alternative concepts of what a regional bureau should be are fully explored.

Ralph

---

55.   **Memorandum From the President's Special Representative (Bowles) to President Kennedy**[1]

Washington, May 25, 1962.

SUBJECT

Recommendations for Strengthening the Foreign Service

Summary and Recommendations:

Some progress has been made in streamlining and modernizing our operational techniques of dealing with the problems of foreign policy. Two key obstacles stand in the way of further movement:

1. There is no single focal point in Washington comparable to the Ambassador abroad where full responsibility for all U.S. programs and operations in a given country is lodged. The result is often delay in decision making and diffusion of responsibility.

---

[1] Source: Kennedy Library, National Security Files, Departments and Agencies Series, Department of State, General, 5/18/62–5/25/62. Limited Official Use.

2. Although the antiquated Foreign Service personnel system is being gradually improved, much remains to be done if we are to make the Service a more effective instrument of Presidential policy.

Therefore I suggest the following actions:

1. That you and the Secretary agree on the need to give a higher priority to improving the effectiveness of the Department and the Foreign Service, and that the Secretary communicate this priority on your behalf to the Department.

2. That you seek legislation to establish five regional Under Secretaries of State with full legal authority to supervise all U.S. Government programs in their regions on your behalf and that of the Secretary.

3. That the individual selected to fill Roger Jones' position in the Department be given a mandate to carry out a series of specific changes in the Foreign Service personnel system within a maximum of six months. A few examples of the changes which I recommend are:

a. Grant "temporary rank" at higher grade for the duration of specific assignments, thus permitting a more flexible system of assignments for outstanding younger officers;

b. Speed up the promotion of outstanding young officers by eliminating any "time-in-grade" requirement for promotion and instructing Promotion Boards to use liberally their existing authority to make double promotions;

c. Detail one or two members of the White House staff to serve in rotation on promotion boards for the top FSO classes; also obtain the services of outstanding private citizens and representatives of other agencies to serve along with high caliber Foreign Service Officers on these promotion boards;

d. Increase the rate of "selection out" of marginal officers and obtain legislative authority to permit officers to retire after 20 years of service regardless of their age, with the Secretary's permission;

e. Reorganize the Foreign Service Institute as an expanded National Academy of Foreign Affairs to meet the training needs of all government agencies operating abroad;

f. Assign a far greater number of qualified FSO's to tours of duty with AID, Defense, USIA, and the Peace Corps, as well as a number of officers from those agencies to tours of duty with State;

g. Reorganize the Foreign Service Inspection Corps into interagency teams to evaluate the effectiveness of our total programs abroad;

h. Provide increased career incentives for cultural, administrative, economists and other types of specialists;

i. Reshape the Career Development program in the State Department to make certain that the top 25% of the FSO's are better trained for command positions.

[Here follow 12 pages of discussion.]

---

56.   Memorandum From President Kennedy to Secretary of State Rusk[1]

Washington, June 19, 1962.

I was concerned when I read a newspaper report on costs of Embassy residences. Of course, I believe that the residence of an American Ambassador should reflect credit on him and his country. On the other hand, I feel that excessive expenditures for such a residence will make us look ridiculous in the eyes of the people in the countries concerned.

Knowing the type of house that $300,000 will buy in the United States, it is difficult for me to see the need for Ambassadors' residences in that price range in such places as Senegal, Cyprus, and Seoul, unless there are unusual factors involved. I believe that Embassy residences should present an image of dignity and charm without being ostentatious or luxurious. Careful thought should be given, and possibly some re-examination of plans made, to assure that they reflect the proper impression of our Ambassadors and of our country.

---

[1] Source: Kennedy Library, President's Office Files, JFK Memos to Departments and Agencies, State. No classification marking.

**57.   Memorandum From Secretary of State Rusk to the Deputy
Under Secretary of State for Administration (Orrick)[1]**

Washington, August 27, 1962.

This is a personal observation on your memorandum of August 20
about the recruitment of junior Foreign Service officers.[2] It should not
be taken as policy guidance.

The arguments submitted in behalf of an increased stress on graduate study or equivalent work experience have been used before. But I
recall that about eight years ago we shifted emphasis from graduate
studies to the "fresh B.A.". We must have had what we thought were
good reasons at that time.

My guess is that this is one of those arguments which swings like a
pendulum. Other instances: geographic versus functional organization,
or college faculty arguments about letter or number grades.

I would not want to be quoted on this but there are one or two
strong arguments in favor of recruiting younger people that I draw out
of my experience. My impression is that graduate school experience
tends to snuff out the "gleam in the eye" of many young people who finish college with a real spirit about making a contribution in some worthwhile undertaking. My guess is that, in graduate schools, they get closer to marriage and closer to jobs in this country; it might even be that in
most graduate schools a "gleam in the eye" is a sign of naivete. Further,
I have seen relatively few courses (and I have seen a great many) which
give a highly intelligent young person much more than he could get out
of reading some good books in a fraction of the time and cost. Finally, I
am not very sure that what the professors say will be very relevant to the
problems young people will encounter in the Foreign Service.

However, my only suggestion at this time is that you get somebody
to dig out the policy consideration which threw the emphasis upon
undergraduate work some years ago and then we can talk about it.

Incidentally, I do feel strongly that FSOs, after entering the Service,
should be evaluated and promoted on the basis of work performed in
the Service and the graduate degrees should bear no relevance *after
entry*. The principal reason for this is that graduate degrees come a dime
a dozen and high quality work comes from often unlikely places.

Dean Rusk[3]

---

[1] Source: National Archives and Records Administration, RG 59, Rusk Files: Lot 72
D 192, Miscellaneous Correspondence–O. Personal and Confidential. Drafted by Rusk.

[2] Not found in Department of State files.

[3] Printed from a copy that bears this typed signature.

58.   Memorandum From Secretary of State Rusk to President
          Kennedy[1]

Washington, December 19, 1962.

SUBJECT

"Personnel for the New Diplomacy"—Report of the Committee on Foreign Affairs
Personnel

Because of your deep interest in a foreign affairs staff which can meet
our demanding international requirements now and in the foreseeable
future, I think you will find the enclosed report highly significant.[2]

"Personnel for the New Diplomacy" is the result of more than a
year's work by the Committee on Foreign Affairs Personnel, a group of
knowledgeable private citizens whose chairman was Governor Herter.
The Committee operated independently of the Department, financially
and otherwise. It was sponsored by the Carnegie Endowment for
International Peace.

The report and its recommendations have been studied by our
experts who share my view that the report is impressive and that it will
be extremely useful to us in upgrading the whole area of foreign affairs
personnel. We welcome unqualifiedly the majority of the recommendations. Especially welcome is the proposal for a single foreign affairs personnel system instead of the dual foreign service and civil service systems with which we now work. Equally helpful are the recommendations directed to greater compatibility of personnel policies and practices between State, United States Information Agency, and Agency for
International Development.

The Department is proceeding promptly to act on the report and in
so doing to provide a coordinated approach with the other two agencies
most concerned, the Agency for International Development and the
United States Information Agency.

Dean Rusk[3]

---

[1]   Source: Kennedy Library, National Security Files, Departments and Agencies
Series, Department of State, General, 12/16/62–12/31/62. No classification marking.

[2]   Not attached. The Committee on Foreign Affairs Personnel was established in late
1961 under the auspices of the Carnegie Endowment for International Peace and chaired
by former Secretary of State Christian A. Herter. The Committee's report was published
in December 1962 as *Report of the Committee on Foreign Affairs Personnel—Personnel for the
New Diplomacy* (Washington: Carnegie Endowment for International Peace, 1962), 161
pages. Excerpts from the report are printed in *American Foreign Policy: Current Documents,
1962*, pp. 1545–1553.

[3]   Printed from a copy that indicates Rusk signed the original.

59. Letter From Secretary of State Rusk to the Director of the Bureau of the Budget (Bell)[1]

Washington, December 21, 1962.

Dear Mr. Bell:

I understand that the Department of Commerce has submitted to your Bureau for consideration a draft legislative proposal for the establishment of a separate foreign commercial service.

I have reviewed a copy of the draft proposal and am opposed to it or any similar action that would remove the commercial function overseas from the Foreign Service.

My objection is based on the following principal considerations:

1. The ultimate test—that of getting the job done most efficiently and effectively at our overseas posts—is best met by keeping economic and commercial work integrated; splitting these inter-related functions into separate services would only create problems and wasteful duplication.

2. Virtually all of our Ambassadors favor an integrated economic-commercial operation for both substantive and administrative reasons. Objection is predicated on knowledge of present circumstances and past unsatisfactory experience under a separate service.

3. The existing State–Commerce Agreement gives Commerce full participation and indeed a primary role in all commercial matters. The Agreement has been operative only eight months.[2] Given a reasonable chance, the Commercial Specialist Program can accomplish within a unified service all that a separate service could accomplish, without the inefficiencies and problems inherent in a new and parallel service abroad.

4. Appropriation history, including experience on 1963 budget proposals, strongly suggests that the overseas commercial program would fare no better if it were budgeted for under a separate service.

5. The Commerce proposal is incompatible with recommendations contained in the Herter Committee report on which we plan to move forward vigorously.

It would seem much more positive and fruitful to me for State, Commerce and the Bureau of the Budget to pull together to strengthen—not weaken—our total effort to attain our commercial goals within

---

[1] Source: National Archives and Records Administration, RG 59, Central Files 1960–63, ORG 4–COMM. No classification marking.

[2] See Document 46.

our foreign policy and balance of payments objectives. If the State–Commerce arrangements need revision for this purpose, I suggest that this be done within the framework of the Agreement.

Sincerely yours,

Dean Rusk[3]

---

[3] Printed from a copy that bears this typed signature.

---

60. Memorandum by the President's Special Assistant for National Security Affairs (Bundy)[1]

Washington, January 25, 1963.

A Framework for Executive Operations in the State Department

This memorandum concerns itself with the organization of the operation of the Department of State at the level just under the Secretary and the Under Secretary. It proceeds from the premise that the two top men in the Department will necessarily be preoccupied with whatever

---

[1] Source: Kennedy Library, National Security Files, Departments and Agencies Series, State Department, General, 1/25/63–1/31/63. Confidential. A covering memorandum from Bundy, also dated January 25, marked Personal and Private, is addressed to Attorney General Robert F. Kennedy, Chairman of the Joint Chiefs of Staff General Maxwell D. Taylor, and the President's Special Assistant, Ralph A. Dungan. It reads as follows: "I attach a brief outline of the framework we discussed this morning. I have removed all names from the memorandum, but this paper is designed with the notion that the man I have described as the Political Under Secretary would be Averell Harriman, and his Deputy for Operations would be Bill Orrick. I think our framework makes good sense even without these individuals, and I am sure that in any discussions we may have with others—except the President—we do not want names mentioned at this stage. This is a first draft, and it is circulated in the hope that you may be willing to comment before the weekend so that I can polish it up for Monday."

A March 5 memorandum from Bundy to Harriman, also attached to Bundy's covering memorandum, reads as follows: "The attached memorandum had the approval of the President, the Secretary and the Under Secretary a month ago, and as far as I know it still does. Of course, now its working out will depend more on you than on anyone else, however exalted, but in talking it over with quite a number of disinterested people, I found a good deal of support for this concept, and I send it along in the thought that it may be helpful in giving you the background of your job as others think about it. I would be delighted to have a chance to talk about this at any time, especially with respect to interdepartmental and White House coordination. The one thing that seems clear to me is that you will not be unemployed, whatever may have been the case with others."

are the most pressing and immediate diplomatic and political questions of each day—at the moment, for example, the Secretary is testifying on Cuba, and the Under Secretary is dealing with de Gaulle and Europe. Their Congressional, diplomatic, and expeditionary responsibilities make it certain that neither the Secretary nor the Under Secretary can be the day-to-day operating executive of the Department of State.

It is still clearer that neither of these two officers can take immediate responsibility for the Department's task of ensuring leadership and coordination of interdepartmental responsibilities both in Washington and in the field.

These executive responsibilities should be centered in the offices now described as the Under Secretary for Political Affairs, the Deputy Under Secretary for Administration, and the Deputy Under Secretary for Political Affairs.

The Under Secretary for Political Affairs, as third-ranking officer in the Department, should have the responsibility for ensuring that the Department's business is getting done. This means that where problems are not being handled directly by the Secretary and Under Secretary, he should have senior responsibility himself. It means that when problems are or should be in the hands of his superiors, he should know about it and ensure that there are no loose ends. He should be available to make necessary policy decisions for Assistant Secretaries in all bureaus; he should be responsible for ensuring that all necessary machinery for interdepartmental coordination is established; he should be in the closest touch with the White House staff so as to ensure that the special interests and concerns of the President are being met; he should be responsible for meshing the administration of the Department with its operational needs. By the same token this officer should stay out of most external diplomatic efforts; he should avoid travel; he should not be responsible for Congressional testimony, wherever this can be avoided; he should, in short, be an operating executive officer for his two interchangeable senior commanders.

This is an enormous job, and the man who does it will need powerful help. In particular, he should have the direct support of the two Deputy Under Secretaries who now report directly to the Under Secretary. If this were done, the Deputy Under Secretary for Administration should be responsible not only for the administration of the Department, but for ensuring that the operational responsibilities of the Department are met. This would imply supervisory concern for interdepartmental committees and task forces, to ensure that they are properly organized and manned, and effective in meeting their responsibilities. It would imply immediate responsibility for the connection of administration with operational needs. It would imply a general responsibility, on the organizational and operational side, for executing the desires of the three top officers; in that sense this officer should be thought of as Deputy Under Secretary for Operations.

The Deputy Under Secretary for Political Affairs would be responsible, as he is now, for such political judgments, and their execution, as, were delegated to him by his superiors. Where the Deputy Under Secretary for Administration would be expected to take policy guidance on his operational responsibilities from the Political Under Secretary, the Deputy Under Secretary for Political Affairs must be an officer with a responsibility for substantial independent political judgment.

As an alternative, which in certain circumstances might be even more satisfactory, the responsibility for operations and executive follow-up might be assigned directly to an Under Secretary for Operations, who would then be the fourth ranking officer of the Department and who would add these responsibilities to those now held by the Deputy Under Secretary for Administration. In such an arrangement this new Under Secretary would need to understand very clearly the importance of the closest cooperation with the Under Secretary for Political Affairs, as that officer is described above; it would be important to rank him after the Political Under Secretary and to put their two offices next to each other if possible.

Finally, it should be noted that the Political Under Secretary would be expected to maintain the most intimate and immediate day-to-day contact with the Administrator of AID, since a very large proportion of his work would involve effective coordination with that agency.

---

61. Letter From Secretary of Commerce Hodges to Secretary of State Rusk[1]

Washington, February 5, 1963.

Dear Dean:

As you know, we have submitted for consideration by State and the Budget Bureau legislation for a separate commercial service. I am advised that your Department is wholly opposed to the separation of the services,[2] but I think it desirable to set before you the reasons why we think such a move is required.

---

[1] Source: National Archives and Records Administration, RG 59, Central Files 1960–63, ORG 4–COMM. No classification marking.

[2] See Document 59.

First, so long as there is rotation among various functional assignments for Foreign Service Officers, the kind of competence and familiarity with problems, procedures, and people that is required in commercial work cannot be developed.

Second, the present institutional arrangements at foreign posts place the commercial officer under an economic officer who frequently has no appreciation of the requirements of the Department of Commerce and, worse, sometimes has an antipathy towards commercial work. I have actual illustrations from personal experience.

Third, the fact that commercial officers know who keep their personnel files and who acts on their promotion makes them cautious in initiating actions which would more actively represent American business overseas.

Fourth, the fact that funds for commercial work must compete not only with all other activities in State but also area by area (since each bureau in State I understand sets its own priorities) and the fact that changes in work assignments may be made at the posts without our notification, much less permission, means that we do not know what resources are in fact available to us and we cannot move quickly to meet changing commercial situations. For example, we have been unable even to get into the field to explain our present programs and needs and the working of the State–Commerce Agreement because of State's unwillingness to allocate funds for commercial officers conferences during calendar 1962.

Fifth, serious problems have arisen in London, Frankfurt, and Tokyo concerning the authority over the Trade Centers we have established there. The lack of preparation of many commercial officers for this type of work makes undesirable an arrangement whereby they are overseers or in authority over the Centers.

Sixth, partly for lack of funds in the FY 1963 budget but also for continued lack of interest within the State Department, there have been few personnel added who can make market and industrial analyses and do promotional work. Nor is there an adequate training and retraining program for existing officers and locals.

As you know, there are times when radical change is necessary and I believe that this is one of those times. The low standing of commercial work in the Foreign Service is too ingrained and the present personnel are too unfamiliar with the type of actions needed to permit an evolutionary process to succeed in the short time available.

While I recognize that such a move as we propose appears to run counter to the Herter report, there was recognition in the report that special conditions merit separate treatment. I would agree that in no event should the Ambassador's responsibility be reduced. He must of necessity control activities at his post.

I am sending copies of this letter to Kermit Gordon and Myer Feldman for their information and consideration.

Sincerely,

Luther

---

62.   **Memorandum by the Assistant Secretary of State for Congressional Relations (Dutton)**[1]

Washington, February 28, 1963.

With the press almost daily anticipating "another shake up in the State Department," I want to offer a few unsolicited comments as one of those cast here in the last shake up.

1. *Tinkering with the Department in a few places will have negligible effect at best . . . and could even result in a worse, not better, situation.*

If the White House wants to use one of the high positions here, as George McGhee's, to get sort of another special assistant to the President, as for global troubleshooting, that can be justified for its own sake. But it will not have any significant effect to strengthen the competence, creativeness or responsiveness of the State Department. Rather, another of the principal officials supposed to help give executive direction to this intricate organization will have been taken away much of the time for tasks elsewhere.

If the Department is largely to be written off during this Administration (and an arguable case can be made for that), then the top slots should be skimmed off; and the rest of the organization will drift off into limbo for the most part. But in that event the decision

---

[1] Source: Kennedy Library, National Security Files, Departments and Agencies Series, State Department, 3/7/63–3/31/63. No classification marking. Attached is a brief covering memorandum from Dutton to Bundy, March 5, which reads: "Mac: I hope the Harriman appointment (which is really excellent) will not be the lone move made to strengthen this Department. About a week ago I put together the attached memo and send it along only to try to provoke further improvements in depth in this place. Fred Dutton. P. S.: I sent a copy of this to Dungan in relation to his personnel work." The appointment of W. Averell Harriman as Under Secretary of State for Political Affairs was effective April 4, 1963.

should deliberately be made that this place is to be recast as just a research and representational agency; and primary responsibility for conceiving and proposing policy in depth, as well as making final decisions on it, will be vested in the executive offices. I realize that much of the initiative for pulling together even the rough strands of policy has already had to be taken up by the White House; but the question presented by taking away another key Departmental official is whether the present level of executive prodding and coordination in the Department is to be allowed to drop even lower, and how much is the White House able and willing to take up the additional slack resulting from that.

Personally, I would guess that the world is too various, the international tempo too fast and the White House already too burdened with pressing domestic as well as foreign concerns to take on this more detailed function. But it seems to be an inescapable consequence of tinkering with a few appointments here without undertaking at the same time to strengthen the Department in a basic and comprehensive way.

2. *State's troubles are principally institutional, not individual personalities; and the White House must accept a considerable part of the responsibility for these institutional difficulties getting worse, not better, in the last two years.*

The key officials and the overwhelming bulk of the foreign service are dedicated, competent individuals. But the Department does not come close to adding up to the sum of its parts.

Some of the Department's difficulties obviously result from the incredibly complex and mercurial problems with which it works. But some of its deficiencies are also the historical and contemporary consequence of the foreign service, which is really quite a "remote society" from the rest of this country and most of the rough tough elements in the world, being allowed to direct, instead of being directed in, the political institution for which its members work. Even John Foster Dulles, who usually ignored the career service, left it independent of direction; and it ran the State Department while he ran Eisenhower.

The need for pioneering insights, vigorous executive initiative and incisive political skills in our foreign policy apparatus is not likely to be met in the present set up very often. Most career officials place too high an emphasis on job security to get caught outside the worn ruts that already exist here; they generally seek to protect themselves against changing tides in Washington and wherever else they are assigned in the world. They are forever mindful, for instance, (and understandably) of some in their ranks who expressed critical opinions of Chiang Kai Shek in the 1940s and paid a high personal and family price. The dilemma of having to report on the Batista–Castro "facts" of the 1950s is a more recent example that is cited.

The basic caution here is aggravated by the usual tendency toward conformity in a career service, the natural by-product, in fact, of almost any closed system. The domination of promotion boards and personnel channels by career people helps make the group even more inbred. Finally, even as to its strong points the system is intellectual, analytical, tentative—but not very creative, intuitive or politically perceptive. As one of the Department's best friends on the Hill, Hubert Humphrey, said recently in a moment of exasperation, "The goddam place is rational, maybe, iffy at best." In the same vein I sometimes wonder why everyone so uncritically takes the reports of career officers on the politics of the Congo, Laos or Italy when they obviously are so lacking in understanding about American politics, which exist in an environment whose assumptions and conditions they really must know far more about.

I believe the White House must accept a considerable share of responsibility for the present shortcomings of the Department. And that does not flow just from the overall responsibility for operation of the executive branch. The truth of the matter is that some of the key people in our Administration started out with a feeling the foreign service had to be made up to for what happened in the McCarthy and Dulles periods, as though even more recognition and free reign would somehow cause it to be more competent and responsive.

Far worse, merit appointments have increasingly been considered to be synonymous with career appointments—and the result, has been some senior foreign service mediocrities going up to the Senate for confirmation as Presidential appointees. Below that level, career officials have moved in mass into exempt positions that at least theoretically exist to allow changing Administrations flexibility and the opportunity for its own people to give direction in depth in a Department already 99% foreign service and civil service. Personnel offices have been left totally made up of career officials. The overall result, as several FSOs have told me, is that the Department is now even more in the grip of the foreign service than when Loy Henderson presided on the inside instead of in absentia from the Metropolitan Club.

Finally, practically every statement issued to Department personnel from the executive offices has been solicitious and reassuring of the foreign service even while the White House has privately been most frustrated over the quality of the work here. This is a strange and unfortunate contradiction for a supposedly tough and objective Administration. I urge that a little frank talk, direct and to the point, will be a healthy tonic with many career people more interested in just keeping, than compulsively trying to make something of, their jobs.

Personally, I have a great admiration for Secretary Rusk. He has to hold together and lead the disparate factors here. The White House, however, needs to provide the external executive influence to prevail over the inevitable internal institutional forces at work here.

In brief, instead of just railing against the State Department, I believe the White House needs to reassert itself here in major appointments, personnel channels and occasional commands.

3. *Some constructive steps that should at least be considered are these:*

a. *Strengthen in Depth:* Even while retaining the present conduct of foreign policy in the White House (and I would think a President in these times generally must be his own Secretary of State, as the press expresses this situation), I urge the Department be strengthened in depth internally and not just a few higher up changes be made, as the rumored Harriman shift.

b. *Executive Officer:* A high official should be designated to provide full-time, specific executive direction of the State Department under the supervision of the Secretary, who is already heavily occupied directly with the President, attending to his Congressional meetings and public and diplomatic obligations, and occasionally having to travel to conferences abroad. Ball is similarly preoccupied; and apparently McGhee's slot is going to be similarly used. Either one of those, or a special assistant to the Secretary, or another position, needs to be given real authority to prod the policy machinery to define problems promptly, pull together study groups early in developing situations, break substantive bottlenecks, and keep providing the Secretary and White House with timely recommendations.

Personally I strongly urge that the task not be assigned to the Deputy Under Secretary for Administration. Executive direction of the policy-making channels is needed—this is a substantive, creative, program-oriented task that should be kept separate from cut and dried administrative attitudes and channels. A second reason for not using the Deputy Under Secretary for Administration is that however frustrating the policy bureaus are here, they are historically and at present far more responsive than the administrative sector of the Department. The Deputy Under Secretary for Administration and Assistant Secretary Crockett, who is really quite effective in his present office, are needed full time to improve the administrative channels.

A third reason is that the Deputy Under Secretary's operation historically and now operates primarily through personnel offices dominated by career officials—in fact, it is the target of most of their lobbying. Increasing the authority of this office in the Department (as the Herter Committee recommends) will only tighten the hold of the institutional interests and influences that are the source of most of the Department's deficiencies.

For a "substantive executive officer" for the Department I suggest someone like Bill Bundy or Ken Hansen, assistant director of the Budget

Bureau, as possibilities. International subsidiaries of large U.S. corporate structures should be able to yield other possibilities with executive competence and relevant general background.

c. *Personnel Office*: Competent new personnel should be pumped into the Department in depth. This can most effectively be achieved by placing an exempt person from the President's own staff in charge of the Department's personnel office. I suggest Dan Fenn for this appointment. Even if it is not Dan, I personally think that obtaining control of the personnel office with a competent, exempt individual completely identified with this Administration is the most important single step that can be taken to reinvigorate the Department over the long haul ahead.

d. *Major Appointments*: Whenever a career ambassador or other major nomination is proposed by the Department, someone on the White House staff (as Ralph Dungan) or in the Budget Bureau, should prepare for the President's consideration, along with the name proposed by the Department, at least one qualified outsider. This will assure that the stream of career recommendations from the Department is measured against specific competent individuals from private life—and that this Administration actually is encouraging merit appointments, not just career appointments.

e. *Special Emissaries:* Besides measuring career possibilities for ambassadorial slots against able individuals from private life, the same should be done with the major special assignments that come up from time to time, as recently with Merchant and Bunker. I find it difficult to reconcile the White House's frustration over the State Department with the persistence with which it turns so often to career diplomats that are almost stereotypes of everything for which State is pilloried. Personally I think the criticism is fairly sound—but it is evidently neglected when personnel appointments are made. Surely a country with the size and vigor of ours can turn up competent, experienced, vigorous, new-style representatives from public life, business, the bar and universities for missions abroad.

f. *Schedule C:* Far more exempt positions in the Department on Schedule C should be filled by genuinely qualified, noncareer individuals, not foreign service people who want the special pay and status but will not accept noncareer risks, responsibilities and attitudes. As a rule of thumb, after a six month grace period, no more than 10 to 15% of these exempt positions should be filled with career personnel.

g. *Middle Level Positions:* If, as mentioned in the press, Harriman is to be moved up in the Department (and he is really a breath of fresh air here: direct, tough, no-nonsense), I hope that the other assistant secretaryships will also be looked at with a critical eye and any strengthening done in one major move. I would hope that at least eventually several of the President's noncareer ambassadors who have proved themselves as really outstanding in the last two years might be brought back to invigorate the Department.

---

63. Letter From Secretary of State Rusk to Secretary of Commerce Hodges[1]

Washington, March 2, 1963.

Dear Luther:

Thank you for your comments in your letter of February 5 on the case for a separate commercial service.[2] My views were conveyed to David Bell by letter dated December 21.[3] I had instructed that a copy be sent to you simultaneously and I am sorry this was not done.

Without question, we both agree our goal is the most encompassing and adequate commercial service possible within the framework of our foreign policy. I still feel that the State–Commerce Agreement is the vehicle to accomplish this task. The problem, simply stated, is getting it into motion.

What I think we must do is give this Agreement the effort and application it warrants, in spite of the inherent difficulties. I understand that within the past month Assistant Secretaries Behrman and Crockett renewed their work on the Agreement. I have asked Assistant Secretary Crockett to make a determined effort to put its provisions into full operation and to attempt to resolve promptly problems arising in this connection. I hope you can give similar guidance in Commerce, and that we can move quickly in the proper direction.

With warm regards,

Sincerely,

Dean[4]

---

[1] Source: National Archives and Records Administration, RG 59, Central Files 1960–63, ORG 4–COMM. No classification marking. Drafted by Herman Pollack, Deputy Assistant Secretary of State for Personnel, on February 15; earlier versions of the February 15 draft are ibid.

[2] Document 61.

[3] Document 59.

[4] Printed from a copy that indicates Secretary Rusk signed the original.

64.   Report Prepared in the Office of Management[1]

Washington, March 6, 1963.

ORGANIZING FOR ACTION IN THE REGIONAL BUREAUS[2]

Successive attempts to meet complex country problems with complex organizational answers have relegated the country desk officer to a role bearing remote resemblance to his traditional purpose. What he does today—with a few notable exceptions—is serve as a contact point for overseas posts, prepare first drafts and initial recommendations, store information, and try to keep abreast of the activities of colleagues at his own level in other agencies. What he does *not* do is provide leadership in policy-formulation, coordination or decision-making.

Nor has the diminution of the country desk officer's role produced compensating improvements in the policy-making and action capacity of the regional bureaus. At the top the bureau structure is complicated and confusing; at the bottom it is rigid and wasteful of manpower resources. In between, a series of layers compound reviews. Responsibility for action—to be taken or consciously postponed—is so widely shared below the Assistant Secretary that accountability is uncertain.

The basic premise of the country officer has not become invalid by reason of being ignored. There is greater need than ever for expert, knowledgeable officers to be held responsible and accountable for achieving a unified approach to United States relations with other countries; to give clear foreign policy direction to other departments and agencies; to act promptly on matters which have not been reserved for decision at higher levels. What has changed is the nature of demands for country leadership, the level of ability country officers must bring to their tasks and the depth of support they must be given.

This report recommends measures to make possible a return to the original country officer concept—but in an environment which responds to today's needs. It proposes fundamental changes in existing bureau structure, and a new title for the country officer so that there may be no mistake as to the role he should play.

The country officer, if these recommendations are endorsed, will become a Principal Policy Officer[3] whose value is acknowledged as

---

[1] Source: National Archives and Records Administration, RG 59, Management Staff Files: Lot 69 D 434, Miscellaneous Subject Files, 1960–1967, Interagency Administrative Matters. No classification marking.

[2] A subtitle on the title page of the report reads: "A Study of the Country Desk Officer."

[3] Other titles considered included Principal Officer, Policy Director, Policy Coordinator, Deputy for (name of country, or countries), and Foreign Affairs Executive. [Footnote in the source text.]

comparable to that of a chief of mission. He will report directly to the Assistant Secretary and be authorized to act for the Assistant Secretary on matters concerning his assigned country or countries. His staff support will be organized to meet his needs rather than any predetermined pattern.

Above the Principal Policy Officer the action capacity of the regional bureau will be strengthened by providing the Assistant Secretary with an alter ego deputy and by confining all other officers to true staff roles.

These proposals are no more ambitious than the urgency of the problem warrants. Despite recognition of the Department's perennial shortage of senior officers combining substantive and executive skills, it is recommended that these proposals be fully implemented within a period of one year.

Summary of Recommendations

1. Concentrate the leadership and action responsibilities of the desk officer in a new position of Principal Policy Officer.

2. Locate the Principal Policy Officer immediately under the Assistant Secretary.

3. Assign to the Principal Policy Officer responsibility for one country or a group of countries depending on the nature and complexity of country problems.

4. Give to each Principal Policy Officer the freedom to organize and use staff to meet his needs as he sees them.

5. Initiate a one-year program for phasing into the Principal Policy Officer concept as rapidly as officers with demonstrated executive and leadership ability are available for such assignments.

6. Designate in each bureau one alter ego Deputy Assistant Secretary.

7. Restrict functional advisers, and all other officers outside the direct chain of command, to advisory and liaison roles and reduce the number of those at the bureau level as the Principal Policy Officer concept is phased into the bureau organizations.

[Here follows the remainder of the report.]

65. Memorandum for the Record[1]

Washington, March 13, 1963.

SUBJECT

Division of Seventh Floor Responsibilities

Messrs. Ball, Harriman, and Alex Johnson met for lunch on March 13 to discuss this subject.

The following topics were covered:

1. *Fish.* After an extended discussion by Alex Johnson to the desirability of Governor Harriman taking over this problem, it was decided that the handling of this matter would be analyzed further. Governor Harriman and Mr. Johnson will talk about it and then talk further with the Secretary as to who should have primary responsibility for this activity.

2. *Labor.* It was agreed that Governor Harriman will take over the labor problem. (This will necessitate a change in the FAM Circular #44.)

3. *Bill Jorden and Psychological Warfare.* Mr. Johnson recounted at some length the background of the initiation of this operation, citing the interest of the Attorney General in this activity. It was agreed that a decision on the disposition of this activity would be deferred until Governor Harriman had had a chance to talk with Bill Jorden and acquaint himself further with the nature of this operation.

4. *Timberlake and Soviet Counter Strategy.* The historical background of this operation (first under Dillon, then Ball, and then transferred in part to INR) was recounted by Mr. Johnson. The Governor agreed that he would look at it further before making a final decision as to what to do with this operation. Both Messrs. Ball and Johnson, however, suggested that it should be liquidated.

5. *Special Group–CI.* Governor Harriman indicated that Mac Bundy had urged that he take over this particular activity. Mr. Johnson said that he would be glad to have the Governor undertake this operation. Before a final decision was reached, however, it was agreed that Messrs. Johnson and Harriman would talk about this between themselves and then with Mac Bundy.

6. *Under Secretary's Committee on Foreign Economic Policy.* While this was not a specific item for discussion, it was mentioned in connection with the examination of the problem with Bill Jorden and psychological warfare that Governor Harriman might broaden out this Committee to

---

[1] Source: National Archives and Records Administration, RG 59, Central Files 1960–63, ORG 10. Official Use Only; Limited Distribution. Drafted by Springsteen. Copies were sent to Brubeck (S/S), Sullivan (FE), and Hackler (G).

include other agencies and use it as a forum for acquainting them with the Department's operations and what they might do to assist the Department. Specific mention was made of including the Department of Justice on the Committee.

7. *Outer Space.* It was agreed that Alex Johnson would handle both the peaceful and the military aspects of Outer Space, but that Governor Harriman would represent the Secretary on the Vice President's Space Council. All matters relating to space would come to Governor Harriman through Mr. Johnson.

8. *Science.* There was very little discussion of this subject. It was agreed that the Science Office under Dr. Rollefson was a functional unit (much like the Legal Adviser's Office) and that it was not necessary to make it the particular responsibility of any one individual.

9. *Disarmament.* Mr. Johnson explained that his office did the staff work on this while the Under Secretary for Political Affairs sat on the Deputies Committee of the Committee of Principals. Mr. Johnson also stressed, however, that the Secretary looked primarily not to the Department, but to ACDA, for briefing on this particular subject. While it was suggested that Alex Johnson might take over this particular function it was agreed that Governor Harriman would take a look into it before a final decision on this subject is made.

10. *Civil Aviation.* Governor Harriman said that he understood that there was a problem here vis-à-vis Jeeb Halaby. He asked who handled it now in the Department. He was informed that Phil Trezise was the man who was on top of the aviation problem on a day-to-day basis. The Governor indicated that he would talk with Mr. Trezise about this matter in order to acquaint himself with it.

66.   Letter From the Assistant Secretary of State for
        Administration (Crockett) to the Director of the Bureau of
        the Budget (Gordon)[1]

Washington, October 1, 1963.

Dear Kermit:

I would like to explore with you plans for implementing the Secretary's agreement to cooperate with the Bureau of the Budget in controlling the overseas activities of the U.S. government agencies. We have given this subject considerable thought during the past few weeks and have reached the following tentative conclusions which might serve as a basis for future discussion:

1. *Need for a control mechanism*—One of the most critical problems confronting us is the absence of an effective mechanism for controlling the activities of U.S. agencies conducted abroad. This gap is apparent both with respect to the approval of new activities and the systematic review of existing activities.

While it is true that we usually hear about the establishment of new offices overseas, there is no formal requirement for review and approval of the initiation of an activity or the establishment of an office. Our involvement ordinarily arises from such things as conferring diplomatic rank and privileges, furnishing office space, or arranging for passports and visas. This is not a satisfactory situation from a control standpoint because we seldom learn of a proposal until it is too far down the line for us to do much about it.

The situation in the case of the on-going activities is even more difficult. It is true the President's letter of May 29, 1961 to the Chiefs of Missions states that all agencies are expected to keep the Chief of Mission informed of their activities. The letter also indicates that the President has instructed all heads of departments and agencies of this responsibility. However, neither of these instructions has been fully implemented. The Ambassador's review of the activities of the major foreign affairs agencies takes the form of approving their annual programming and budget documents. Information concerning the activities of other agencies is much too sporadic and inconsistent to be useful for control purposes.

The situation in Washington is even more difficult. To my knowledge there is no instruction requiring agencies to keep the Department

---

[1] Source: National Archives and Records Administration, RG 59, Management Staff Files: Lot 69 D 434, Miscellaneous Subject Files, Interagency Relationship, Bureau of Budget Circular. No classification marking. A copy was sent to Ralph Roberts.

regularly informed of their overseas activities. The situation in the field is such that we see little profit in attempting to get the Ambassador to furnish us with this kind of information on a systematic basis.

Thus far, we have been considering merely the availability of pertinent data upon which to base a control mechanism. There is also the question of the authority for controlling the actions of other agencies. I am not sure that this authority exists short of the President—that is, I doubt if the Secretary could either prevent another agency head from undertaking an activity or control the level at which such an activity is to be carried on. Furthermore, my interpretation of the President's letter does not grant the Ambassador final authority to veto proposed activities or to set levels for existing activities.

All of this convinces us that meaningful control of overseas activities will necessitate either an elaboration of existing rules and regulations or the promulgation of new regulations. On balance, we favor the first alternative and believe that some elaboration of the President's legislative and budget procedures could best provide the necessary handles for controlling the overseas activities of the various departments and agencies.

2. *Nature of State participation*—We have experienced considerable difficulty in the past in determining the criteria by which we can judge the propriety of agencies' proposals for establishing programs and offices overseas. Attitudes within the Department vary from those like former Ambassador Briggs, who believe that overseas representation should be limited to employees of the State Department, to those who for purely parochial reasons actually join with other agencies in promoting requests for new offices and programs. We are now attempting to develop a consistent policy. One thing is clear—our ability to make meaningful judgments varies with the type and purpose of the program or project we are called upon to review. A case that recently came to our attention, and upon which I will communicate with you further in the near future, illustrates the point. In this case, our Ambassador to Lebanon reports that he was visited by representative of the Navy Department with a view to establishing a management group composed of three GS 18's, whose mission would be to investigate the capabilities of the Lebanese to conduct unspecified research for the Navy. Ambassador Meyer in his cable to us makes three points: (a) visiting Congressmen have been critical of the number of Americans in Lebanon; (b) the Congressmen have threatened to block construction of proposed new Embassy building until the number of Americans is substantially reduced; and (c) Meyer has no problem (other then a and b) with the activity proposed by the Navy. This is the kind of a case which is most difficult for us to resolve. First, it is apparent that additional U.S.

presence is not inimical to our interests in Lebanon and may actually be advantageous in terms of US-Lebanese relations. Second, we have no expertise in evaluating the desirability of the research activities involved. Third, the type of activity is obviously beyond State's ability to perform. As a result, unless we adopt the Briggs' philosophy, which I personally believe to be completely untenable in today's world, or unless we are to hide behind the balance of payments argument, which I really think is more in your arena than ours, we have no basis for taking a position.

I could also cite other examples such as the authorization of a Secret Service employee in Paris to assist Interpol in investigating counterfeiting, and the celebrated case of the FAA European regional office, which I believe illustrate the same point—namely, the difficulty this Department has in making appropriate value judgments on programs that are essentially outside of the stream of foreign affairs.

We can, of course, make much more meaningful evaluations of the need for those activities which contribute directly to the achievement of our foreign policy objectives. But even here the relationships that have been established between the State Department and the various agencies charged with carrying out those programs—AID, CIA, USIA, the Department of Defense, ACDA, the Peace Corps—make it difficult for us to actually control the level or composition of annual operating programs.

3. *Proposed budget circular on international activities*—We have reviewed the October 16, 1961 draft circular[2] in accordance with your request. With some minor reservations, I believe it would fill the need outlined in the foregoing paragraphs. I would be pleased to have members of my staff join in discussions with your people in an effort to resolve our reservations.

4. *Actions in connection with the 1965 budget*—We will be happy to participate in any way we can in reviewing agency estimates for overseas activities. The nature and scope of our participation will of course depend upon the information and data made available to us. If you believe, as I do, that the draft circular reflects the right approach in the long run, I would suggest that to the extent possible we use it as the basis for our effort this year. In any event, we would like to get information on any programs or activities that you would like us to comment on in sufficient time to permit our obtaining field comments.

Once again, let me emphasize the Secretary's interest and concern with the increasing complexity of U.S. operations abroad. I believe the course of action outlined above would go a long way toward resolving

---

[2] Not printed. (Ibid.)

what up until now has been an exceedingly chaotic situation. I will be pleased to discuss this matter further with you or with members of your staff at your convenience.

Sincerely yours,

Bill[3]

---

[3] Printed from a copy that indicates that Crockett signed the original.

---

67. Memorandum From the Deputy Assistant Secretary of State for Management (Roberts) to the Assistant Secretary of State for Administration (Porter)[1]

Washington, November 5, 1963.

SUBJECT

Budget Bureau Study on "State Department Organization for Foreign Economic Affairs"

1. Attached is a copy of the study referred to Thursday by Ken Hansen. Also attached are analyses (Tab A)[2] made by OM when the study was first received, and later when the Budget Bureau called Bill Brubeck on the status of action. Because AID is concerned in the larger area covered by the report, Dave Bell's transmittal letter (as Budget Bureau Director) may also be of interest (Tab B).[3]

2. The study had three focuses: internal E organization; general Department arrangements for strengthening economic expertise and distributing it throughout the regional bureaus; and the over-all organization of the Department (including AID) for foreign economic functions.

3. In the first two areas the Department has moved some distance, although we have not had occasion to make an evaluation in depth (nor

---

[1] Source: National Archives and Records Administration, RG 59, Management Staff Files: Lot 69 D 434, Miscellaneous Subject Files, 1960–1967, State Department Organization for Foreign Economic Affairs, 1962. No classification marking. A handwritten notation on the memorandum by Roberts reads: "P.S. Please return attached when it has served your needs. RSR."

[2] Not printed; see Document 51.

[3] Not attached.

do I recommend one immediately). By the time the report was released a number of lesser organizational rearrangements had been completed or agreed to and PER had begun to concentrate more on the need for economists. About six weeks later Griff Johnson became Assistant Secretary for Economic Affairs (Ed Martin had already moved from E when the report came out). Since then there has been a serious and, I understand, successful effort to bring into E some first-rate economic specialists.

4. No change has, however, been made in E's status within the Department by upgrading its head to Deputy Under Secretary. Neither have the larger organizational relationships between the AID Director, E and the rest of the Department been altered. When current developments in the AID program become somewhat clearer, we might well seek another reading from the Secretary or Mr. Ball on this. I should welcome an opportunity to discuss this with you.

Ralph S. Roberts

68.   Letter From the Assistant Secretary of State for Congressional Relations (Dutton) to Senator J. William Fulbright[1]

Washington, November 20, 1963.

Dear Senator Fulbright:

In my letter to you of June 26, 1963,[2] I informed you that the Department was considering the closing of 14 consulates throughout the world and changing the status of five other posts.

The following posts have now been closed:

Salzburg, Austria	Haifa, Israel
Santos, Brazil	Venice, Italy
Edmonton, Canada	Penang, Malaysia
Manchester, England	Basel, Switzerland
Le Havre, France	Cardiff, Wales
Cork, Ireland	Sarajevo, Yugoslavia

[1] Source: National Archives and Records Administration, RG 59, Central Files 1960–63, ORG 8. No classification marking. Drafted by Sinderson of the Office of Budget (OB) on November 14 and cleared in draft by Ribble (EUR), Spector (ARA), Egert (NEA), and Jones (FE).

[2] Not printed. (Ibid.)

The Consulate General at Geneva has been closed and the consular work transferred to Bern. Arrangements have been made for the United States Mission at Geneva to perform urgent diplomatic visa services. The consulates at Tangier, Morocco, and Yokohama, Japan, have been made branch offices of our Embassies in these two countries. These offices will continue to perform consular functions. The consulate at Mandalay, Burma, has been reduced in size and its functions limited to political reporting and protective services to American citizens in the area.

Because of the adverse reaction of the foreign governments and other factors, the Department reconsidered the plan to close the consulates at Windsor, Canada and Turin, Italy. These offices will remain open. The citizens of Piedras Negras, Mexico and Eagle Pass, Texas, requested the Department to reconsider the plan to close the consulate at Piedras Negras. This office will remain open for the indefinite future. Further study will be made of United States representation and the requirement for consular services in all of Mexico, including the border posts.

In the case of Basel, the municipal government and certain American business interests there objected strenuously to the closing of the consulate. The Department, therefore, has undertaken a new and detailed study of the situation to ascertain if there is in fact a commercial reason for maintaining the post.

The Department has concluded action resulting from the survey of consular establishments. No further actions are contemplated at this time. The Department will keep you informed of future developments affecting the status of our posts abroad in the normal manner.

Sincerely yours,

Frederick G. Dutton[3]

---

[3] Printed from a copy that bears this typed signature.

New Programs and Agencies

69.   Editorial Note

"Studies of Executive branch organization" was an agenda item discussed by the National Security Council at its meeting of February 1, 1961. Following this discussion President Kennedy approved, among other items, NSC Action No. 2399–c, which "Noted the President's view that the foreign assistance program must be reorganized before presentation to the Congress; and that the Director, Bureau of the Budget, was planning to submit such a reorganization along with the new foreign aid program." (National Archives and Records Administration, RG 59, S/S–NSC (Miscellaneous) Files: Lot 66 D 95, Records of Action by the National Security Council) This assignment was confirmed in National Security Action Memorandum (NSAM) No. 6, February 3, 1961, from Bundy to David E. Bell, Director of the Bureau of the Budget. (Ibid., S/S–NSC Files: Lot 72 D 316, NSAM No. 6)

On March 22, in a special message to Congress on foreign assistance, President Kennedy discussed, among other things, a proposed reorganization of foreign aid programs that would integrate into a single agency all the Washington and field operations of the International Cooperation Administration, Development Loan Fund, Food-for-Peace, Export-Import Bank, and the Peace Corps. Field work would be under the direction of a single mission chief in each country who would report to the Ambassador. "Similarly, central direction and final responsibility in Washington will be fixed in an Administrator of a single agency—reporting directly to the Secretary of State and the President." (*Public Papers of the Presidents of the United States: John F. Kennedy, 1961*, pages 203–212)

On May 26 President Kennedy sent identical letters to the President of the Senate and to the Speaker of the House of Representatives describing major features of a draft bill on foreign aid he was forwarding to Congress. The bill assigned overall responsibility and authority for the formulation and execution of foreign development aid programs to a single entity—the Agency for International Development (AID)—within the Department of State. It would replace the International Cooperation Administration and the Development Loan Fund, which were to be abolished. The new agency would be headed by an Administrator of Under Secretary rank who would report directly to the Secretary of State and the President. For text of President Kennedy's letter, see ibid., pages 407–411. The draft bill became S. 1983, which Senator J. William Fulbright introduced for the administration on May

31. For text of the bill, see *International Development and Security: Hearings Before the Committee on Foreign Relations, United States Senate, Eighty-seventh Congress, First Session*, Part 1, pages 1–25. Hearings on the bill in the Senate and House of Representatives were held from May 31 to July 6. For text of these hearings, see ibid., Parts 1–2, and *The International Development and Security Act: Hearings Before the Committee on Foreign Affairs, House of Representatives, Eighty-seventh Congress, First Session*, Parts 1–3. Testimony in closed session of the Senate Foreign Relations Committee has been published in *Executive Sessions of the Senate Foreign Relations Committee (Historical Series), Eighty-seventh Congress, First Session, 1961*, volume XIII.

For additional documentation concerning reorganization of the foreign assistance program, see *Foreign Relations, 1961–1963*, volume IX, Documents 84–177.

---

70.   Editorial Note

On March 1, 1961, President Kennedy signed Executive Order 10924, which provided for the establishment of a Peace Corps on a temporary pilot basis. (26 *Federal Register* 1789) Under the authority of this Executive Order, the Peace Corps was initially established as an agency within the Department of State, with R. Sargent Shriver, Jr., as Director. (Department of State Delegation of Authority 85–11, March 3, 1961, in 26 *Federal Register* 2196) In September 1961 the Peace Corps began operating under the authority of the Peace Corps Act of September 22, 1961; see Document 73.

In a message to Congress, also on March 1, the President recommended "the establishment of a permanent Peace Corps—a pool of trained American men and women sent overseas by the U.S. Government or through private organizations and institutions to help foreign countries meet their urgent need for skilled manpower.

"The temporary Peace Corps will be a source of information and experience to aid us in formulating more effective plans for a permanent organization. In addition, by starting the Peace Corps now we will be able to begin training young men and women for overseas duty this summer with the objective of placing them in overseas positions by late fall. This temporary Peace Corps is being established under existing authority in the Mutual Security Act and will be located in the

Department of State. Its initial expenses will be paid from appropriations currently available for our foreign aid program."

The President pointed out that the Peace Corps would "differ from existing assistance programs in that its members will supplement technical advisers by offering the specific skills needed by developing nations if they are to put technical advice to work. They will help provide the skilled manpower necessary to carry out the development projects planned by the host governments, acting at a working level and serving at great personal sacrifice. There is little doubt that the number of those who wish to serve will be far greater than our capacity to absorb them." (*Public Papers of the Presidents of the United States: John F. Kennedy, 1961,* pages 143–146)

On May 30, in identical letters to the President of the Senate, Lyndon B. Johnson, and the Speaker of the House of Representatives, Sam Rayburn, President Kennedy transmitted proposed legislation to authorize the establishment of a Peace Corps in fiscal year 1962, as he had recommended in his message of March 1. The President stated that "enactment of this legislation will provide authority for the recruitment, training, and service overseas of American men and women whose skills and knowledge can contribute in a most valuable and practical way to the achievement of social and economic development goals of developing countries."

The President noted that projects had already been announced for Tanganyika, Colombia, and the Philippines, and others would be announced soon. Over 8,500 Peace Corps Volunteer Questionnaires had been returned. The President asked Congress to authorize $40 million for the program for fiscal year 1962. This was intended to enable the Peace Corps to have between 500 and 1,000 volunteers abroad by the end of 1961, 2,700 abroad or in training by June 1962, and provide for summer 1962 training of volunteers expected to be enrolled in June 1962. The President noted that he had "requested the Secretary of State to establish arrangements to assure that Peace Corps activities are consistent and compatible with country development assistance plans. These arrangements will assure that the Peace Corps and the Agency for International Development programs are brought into close relationship, while at the same time preserving the separate identity and unique role of the Peace Corps." (Ibid., pages 418–419)

71.   Letter From the Director of the Peace Corps (Shriver) to
       Secretary of State Rusk[1]

Washington, June 26, 1961.

Dear Mr. Secretary:

We shall certainly keep in mind your recommendations that we
start from the talent available rather than from the requests sent to us
from foreign countries in establishing what we will, or will not undertake as Peace Corps enterprises in the future. I want to reassure you,
however, that we have not undertaken any final commitments to send
people abroad unless we were morally certain that we had the people
available to do the work.

I have just returned from visiting our first group of Peace Corps
Volunteers who are assembled at Rutgers University for a 2-month
training period. They are a most inspiring group of men. Everybody
connected with CARE, which is cooperating with us in this particular
enterprise, is enthusiastic about the selectees. I think you would be, too,
if you had a chance to visit New Brunswick to see them. I feel confident
that we can maintain the same high standards in the other programs.

You said you would be glad to talk to Senator Fulbright about the
amount of money being asked for the Peace Corps and the numbers of
persons we propose to involve in the Peace Corps program this year, if
he asked you. May I respectfully suggest that it would be very helpful
if you could find it possible in some appropriate way to take the initiative in this matter. I think it would be helpful if Senator Fulbright realized that our proposal had the support of the administration as a whole,
especially the Secretary of State. Moreover, I think it would be a
tragedy if, in response to the President's call for a Peace Corps, we on
the executive side responded with a program any smaller than the one
we have proposed.

Sincerely yours,

Sarge

---

[1] Source: National Archives and Records Administration, RG 59, Central Files
1960–63, 800.00–PC/6–2651. No classification marking.

72.   Editorial Note

On September 4, 1961, President Kennedy signed into law the Foreign Assistance Act of 1961 (P.L. 87–1985; 75 Stat. 424; see Document 69). On October 3 Fowler Hamilton was sworn in as Administrator of the new Agency for International Development (AID).   The Foreign Assistance Act of 1961 had specified that a new agency was to replace the International Cooperation Administration and the Development Loan Fund within 60 days after the law was enacted. Executive Order 10973 specified the terms of establishment for the Agency for International Development.   Department of State Delegation of Authority No. 104, November 3, 1961, conferred specific responsibilities on the new agency. (26 *Federal Register* 10608)

73.   Editorial Note

On September 22, 1961, President Kennedy signed the Peace Corps Act. (P.L. 87–293; 75 Stat. 612) For text of the President's remarks on this occasion, see *Public Papers of the Presidents of the United States: John F. Kennedy, 1961,* pages 614–615.   The Act formalized the authority and purpose of the activities of the Peace Corps, which included the placement abroad of volunteer men and women of the United States in newly developing nations of the world to help fill needs for critical manpower.   Peace Corps volunteers, carefully selected and trained, were to serve for periods of 2 years teaching, building, or working in the communities to which they were sent.   They would serve local institutions and live with the people they were helping.   Volunteers could also be used to support existing economic assistance programs of the United States, the United Nations, or other international organizations.

The Peace Corps would provide skilled manpower to newly developing nations through several different channels of operation, as follows: 1) arrangements with private voluntary agencies to carry out Peace Corps-type programs; 2) arrangements with colleges, universities, or other educational institutions; 3) programs of other U.S. Government agencies; 4) programs of the United Nations and other international agencies; 5) directly administered Peace Corps programs with host countries.

R. Sargent Shriver, Jr., as Director of the Peace Corps, was responsible to the Secretary of State for all activities of the agency. He was assisted by a Deputy Director and an Executive Secretariat. The operating components of the Peace Corps included an Office of Program Development and Operations; Office of Public Affairs; Office of Peace Corps Volunteers; Office of Management; Office of Planning and Evaluation; General Counsel; Division of Contracts and Logistics; Division of Public Information; Division of Private Organizations; Division of University Relations; and Division of Research.

Documentation on the establishment, organization, and operations of the Peace Corps is in the National Archives and Records Administration, RG 490, Records of the Peace Corps; and in the Peace Corps Historical Collection, maintained by the Peace Corps, Reference, Research, and Distribution Division, Washington, D.C.

---

74.   **Editorial Note**

On September 26, 1961, President Kennedy signed H.R. 9118, creating the U.S. Arms Control and Disarmament Agency (ACDA). As enacted, H.R. 9118 was Public Law 87–297. (85 Stat. 631) The new agency was to be responsible for the conduct, support, and coordination of research for arms control and disarmament policy formulation; the preparation and management of participation in international negotiations in the arms control and disarmament field; the dissemination and coordination of public information concerning arms control and disarmament; and the preparation for, operation of, or, as appropriate, direction of U.S. participation in such international control systems as might under treaty arrangements become part of U.S. arms control and disarmament activities.

The agency was to be headed by a Director, appointed by the President with the advice and consent of the Senate. The Director was also to function as the principal Adviser to the President and Secretary of State on arms control and disarmament matters and, under the direction of the Secretary, have primary responsibility within the government for such matters. The Agency's program responsibilities would be primarily discharged through four bureaus: International Relations Bureau, Weapons Evaluation and Control Bureau, Science and Technology Bureau, and Economics Bureau.

At the signing ceremony in New York City on September 26, the President emphasized the importance the United States placed on arms control and disarmament in its foreign policy. The ultimate goal was a "world free from war and free from the dangers and burdens of armaments in which the use of force is subordinated to the rule of law and in which international adjustments to a changing world are achieved peacefully. It is a complex and difficult task to reconcile through negotiation the many security interests of all nations to achieve disarmament, but the establishment of this agency will provide new and better tools for this effort." The President announced that William C. Foster, who had been a consultant to John J. McCloy, the President's Adviser on Disarmament, would be Director of the new agency. (*Public Papers of the Presidents of the United States: John F. Kennedy, 1961*, pages 626–627)

Transferred to the new agency was the former U.S. Disarmament Administration, which had been established within the Department of State on September 9, 1960. (Department of State Circular No. 370, October 12, 1960; copy in Eisenhower Library, President's Office Files, ACDA) During the course of 1961, there had been considerable discussion concerning the location and functions of a new disarmament agency. Presidential transition adviser Richard E. Neustadt in a memorandum to Rusk on January 2, 1961, indicated that President-elect Kennedy had a "'superficial preference' for locating the work of policy development and attendant research on 'disarmament' or 'arms control' in the Executive Office of the President, rather than in the Department of State." In a memorandum of January 4 to Kennedy, Neustadt stated his own view "that an Executive Office unit should be avoided if possible and that a try should be made with an autonomous unit under the Secretary of State but with access to you insofar as you want it. McCloy's presence makes this easier to work than might otherwise be the case." (Kennedy Library, National Security Files, Staff Memos, Richard E. Neustadt, 10/60–11/63)

In a letter of January 27 appointing McCloy as his Adviser on Disarmament, Kennedy asked McCloy to make recommendations concerning the organization of the U.S. Disarmament Administration and related activities. (*Foreign Relations, 1961–1963*, volume VII, Document 2) After studying the question, McCloy concluded that the agency should be established by statute "at an authoritative level in the Government with the exceptionally broad competence, functions and resources required to work on the problems of arms control and disarmament, including the conduct of the research so essential to progress in this field. I was also of the opinion that those conducting this research should be in the same organization as those charged with actually carrying out negotiations in the field and that the organization should be subject to the direction of the Secretary of State, although distinct from the Department of State. The Director of the new Agency would have to deal with and coordinate the activities of many other agencies of government which have direct access to the President. The Director, therefore, should serve as the principal adviser to the President in the disarmament field, with direct access to the President upon notification to the Secretary of State."

McCloy prepared a draft bill to establish the proposed new agency and transmitted it to the President under cover of a letter of May 9. After a government-wide clearance process, McCloy sent a slightly revised draft bill to the President on June 23. The President transmitted this draft bill to Congress by letter of June 29. In the Senate it was introduced by Senator Hubert H. Humphrey as S. 2180. About 70 other similar or identical bills were introduced in the House of Representatives, many of them calling for the proposed entity to be named the "Peace Agency." (Letter from McCloy to Kennedy, May 9 and June 23, 1961, and related documents; National Archives and Records Administration, RG 383, ACDA/DD Files: FRC 77 A 17, Chron File, April–June 1961; draft letter from McCloy to President, September 29, 1961, ibid., July–September 1961)

---

75.   Memorandum From the President's Special Assistant for National Security Afffairs (Bundy) to President Kennedy[1]

Washington, September 28, 1961.

SUBJECT

Washington News

[Here follow paragraph 1, dealing with the appointment of John McCone as Director of Central Intelligence, printed as Document 91; and paragraph 2, dealing with the military budget for Fiscal Year 1963.]

3. There is an important management decision brewing in the foreign aid field. Dave Bell has been working on the executive order to put the new legislation into effect, and he is coming up against the key question of assignment of responsibility, within the Department of State, for coordination of military and economic assistance. Formally, this must go down through the Secretary of State, but the operating question is which of his subordinates will do the job for him, since no Secretary can find the time for this type of judgment—and, in any event, this is not Dean Rusk's major interest. Bell and I and our respective

---

[1] Source: Kennedy Library, National Security Files, Bundy Memoranda to the President, 8/22/61–9/30/61. Secret.

experts are inclined to press hard for delegation of authority here to Fowler Hamilton. In this case he would act as the Secretary's agent and not simply as the Director of the AID agency, and he would have to show the kind of wider judgment that is implied in balancing political, military, and economic considerations. But of the available senior men in the Department, he seems the best qualified. And, in particular, this seems a better answer than the one the Secretary may prefer—which is to have the coordination managed directly from his office by a relatively junior special assistant acting in the name of the Secretary. An arrangement of this sort simply would not stick, and the result would be that issues would always be pressed beyond the Department to the White House. Big issues are bound to come to you, but day-to-day matters really should be settled by a man who has the seniority to make decisions stick. The Pentagon is happy to entrust this to Hamilton. Dave Bell is going to try to sell this solution to the Secretary of State, but if he fails, you are likely to find the issue on your desk next week.

[Here follow paragraph 4, concerning Chester Bowles, printed as Document 43; paragraph 5, dealing with Syria; and paragraph 6, dealing with Berlin.]

McG. B.[2]

---

[2] Printed from a copy that bears these typed initials.

---

76.   Letter From Secretary of State Rusk to President Johnson[1]

Washington, December 3, 1963.

Dear Mr. President:

I welcome and will give full personal support to your memorandum of November 30 about thrift and frugality in Government.[2] I should like to emphasize the importance of a single policy throughout the Executive Departments on matters of personnel. Unless such poli-

---

[1] Source: National Archives and Records Administration, RG 59, Rusk Files: Lot 72 D 192, White House Correspondence, 12/63–6/18/64. No classification marking. Lyndon Johnson became President after President Kennedy's assassination on November 22, 1963.

[2] President Johnson's "Memorandum on the Management of the Executive Branch," November 30, 1963, is printed in *Public Papers of the Presidents of the United States: Lyndon B. Johnson, 1963–64*, pp. 15–16.

cies are pursued diligently and systematically across the board, those who achieve the desired result in prudence and economy would face morale problems arising from a sense of inequity or lack of confidence in their immediate leader's dedication to the interests of their own Departments.

It would be my suggestion that you make it clear to all of the Executive Departments that you expect them to hold the line on numbers of personnel except (a) where there is a clear and almost mathematical relationship between the numbers of persons required and the necessary services to be rendered, and (b) where new programs have been specifically approved by the Congress and require additional personnel.

As one who served in the Department of State in the 1940's and has now returned to it after a decade, I have been tremendously impressed by the way in which the Department has measured up to rapidly increasing responsibilities without a comparable increase in personnel. This means a gratifying increase in productivity in ways that are difficult to measure.

Respectfully yours,

Dean Rusk[3]

---

[3] Printed from a copy that bears this typed signature.

---

77.   Editorial Note

Secretary of State Rusk testified on December 11, 1963, before the Senate Subcommittee on National Security Staffing and Operations, chaired by Senator Henry M. Jackson. In a broad statement, Rusk discussed a variety of issues concerning the staffing and operations of national security policy. He discussed the scope of foreign affairs; the role of Congress and Executive-Legislative relations; the respective roles of Desk Officers, Assistant Secretaries, and Ambassadors; the role of intelligence; and problems of coordination and administration. For text of his testimony, see *Administration of National Security: Hearing Before the Subcommittee on National Security Staffing and Operations of the Committee on Government Operations, United States Senate, Eighty-eighth Congress, First Session,* December 11, 1963, Part 6.

Intelligence

78.   Editorial Note

In the fall of 1959, the Bureau of the Budget proposed, and President Eisenhower approved, a study of the intelligence agencies. The Joint Study Group on the Foreign Intelligence Activities of the United States Government was chaired by Lyman B. Kirkpatrick, Jr., Inspector General of the Central Intelligence Agency. Other members were Lieutenant General (Ret.) Graves Erskine, Special Assistant to the Secretary of Defense; Allan Evans, Deputy Director of the Bureau of Intelligence and Research, Department of State; James Lay, Executive Secretary of the National Security Council; Robert Macy of the Bureau of the Budget; J. Patrick Coyne, Executive Secretary of the President's Board of Consultants on Foreign Intelligence Activities; and Brigadier General Jesmond Balmer, Assistant to the Director of Central Intelligence for Interagency Coordination. The Group submitted its 141-page report on the deadline date, December 15, 1960. (Eisenhower Library, White House Office Files, Project Clean Up, 1960)

The National Security Council addressed the report of the Joint Study Group in the waning days of the Eisenhower administration, at its meetings of January 5, 12, and 18, 1961. For the memoranda of discussion at the January 5 and 12 meetings, see Documents 80 and 84. The NSC approved most of the 43 recommendations in the report on January 18. (Memorandum of Discussion at the NSC meeting of January 18; Eisenhower Library, Whitman File, NSC Records)

The Kennedy administration subsequently adopted many of the Joint Study Group's recommendations. One of the most far-reaching was the need for modernizing and streamlining the military intelligence system, which led to the creation of the Defense Intelligence Agency in August 1961 (see Document 89).

79. Memorandum of Meeting With President Eisenhower[1]

Washington, January 3, 1961, 2:35 p.m.

ALSO PRESENT

General Goodpaster

[Here follows discussion of the manned space flight program.]

2. I then said that General Goodpaster and I wished to discuss in general terms the Intelligence Study Group report and procedures to be followed from this point on.[2] I reported that the Committee of Principals had met in the morning and that it was apparent that whereas there was agreement with respect to a great many of the recommendations, there were some which would be in controversy, particularly recommendations with respect to reorganization within Defense, in the USIB and the role of the DCI. There then followed a discussion between the President, General Goodpaster, and myself about the report but centering particularly on the main policy question of whether the President wished to take action with respect to any of the recommendations before he leaves office and particularly as to whether he would wish immediately to give authority to the Secretary of Defense to begin to take steps within the Defense Department. The President indicated that as a matter of policy he would wish to move in those areas where it was wise. Therefore he approved the following guidelines.

(1) The NSC in its meeting on January 5 should consider any recommendations of the Secretary of Defense with respect to amendment of the NSCID's as might affect Defense responsibilities.
(2) The Committee of Principals should identify those recommendations with respect to which there is no disagreement with an indication as to those which should be put into effect immediately and those which would be better to pass along to the new Administration.
(3) An identification of those recommendations with respect to which there is disagreement with the understanding that a smaller group would meet with the President to advise him as to the areas in which he should move notwithstanding dissenting viewpoints.
(4) Identification of those issues which were important but which should not be acted upon in this Administration. (The President had in mind any recommendation with respect to which the JCS were completely opposed feeling that their support was needed to accomplish the purposes of the recommendations.)

---

[1] Source: Eisenhower Library, Records of the Special Assistant for National Security Affairs, Meetings of the President. No classification marking. Prepared by Gordon Gray on January 4.

[2] See Document 78.

I explained to the President that this process was in train, the principals having agreed substantially upon this procedure at their meeting and that we expected to be in a position to deal with this matter in the NSC meeting of January 12.

At this point I departed the President's office and General Goodpaster remained to take up other matters with the President.

Gordon Gray
Special Assistant to the President

---

80. Memorandum of Discussion at the 473d Meeting of the National Security Council[1]

Washington, January 5, 1961.

[Here follows a paragraph listing the participants at the meeting.]

There follows a summary of the discussion at the Meeting and the main points taken.

1. National Security Council Intelligence Directives

Mr. Gray said he wished to bring up first a matter which was not on the formal agenda. The Joint Study Group on Foreign Intelligence Activities, composed of representatives of the Director of Central Intelligence, the Secretaries of State and Defense, the Director, Bureau of the Budget, and the Special Assistant to the President for National Security Affairs had submitted its report and was now preparing a list of recommendations on which the Principals had agreed, as well as a list of recommendations which had not been concurred in.[2] A question had arisen whether a revision of the NSCID's would be necessary as their provisions affect the authority of the Secretary of Defense in the intelligence field. At the present time, the NSCID's refer to the Military Services, not to the Secretary of Defense. The suggestion had been made that the Secretary of Defense be given authority by amendment of the NSCID's to proceed with reorganization of military intelligence within the Department of Defense.

---

[1] Source: Eisenhower Library, Whitman File, NSC Records. Top Secret; Eyes Only. The meeting took place from 9 to 10:40 a.m. (Ibid., President's Daily Appointment Book)

[2] See Document 78.

Secretary Gates said this matter would affect the next Secretary of Defense. The first issue involved in the report of the Joint Study Group was the one Mr. Gray had mentioned, namely, the question of amending the NSCID's. Another issue, however, was also involved, namely membership on the U.S. Intelligence Board. The report by the Joint Study Group recommended that the Secretary of Defense and the Joint Chiefs of Staff rather than the Military Services be represented on the USIB. Secretary Gates was in favor of this recommendation but understood the Military Services were opposed. Mr. Dulles said he was also opposed to this recommendation. Secretary Gates said this matter affected the NSCID's since the organization of the USIB was covered in the NSCID's.

The President said he had been told that about $1.4 billion was being spent for the intelligence function in the Department of Defense. He believed we were not good administrators if we could not perform this function at less expense. He also believed that we were not doing everything that could be done to implement the concept of integrated strategic planning unless military intelligence could be placed under the Joint Chiefs of Staff. He was unable to understand why the antiquated system of separate intelligence organizations for each Military Service was retained.

Mr. Dulles pointed out that the Military Services at the present time had the personnel, the competence, and the background in intelligence. Until this situation was changed, he would rather deal with representatives of the Military Services, who know intelligence, than with the representative of the Secretary of Defense, who would not have the experience, the personnel, and the background judgment required. When organizational changes were made so that the representative of the Secretary of Defense had competent collectors and analysts working for him, then Mr. Dulles would not disagree with the recommendation for a change in the membership of the USIB, but at present, he repeated, the change suggested would merely result in putting on USIB representatives with inadequate intelligence support.

The President believed that the Services should collect battlefield intelligence but did not see the necessity for strategic intelligence in the Services. He wondered what intelligence officers in the Services could do to get information from the center of the USSR and correlate it with intelligence on the rest of the world. He said when he supported the establishment of the Central Intelligence Agency in 1947, he did it on the basis that the function of strategic intelligence should be in CIA and that duplication should be eliminated. General Lemnitzer felt that the acquisition of technical intelligence, e.g. information about enemy nuclear submarines, required officials who know nuclear submarines.

The Services would be very much concerned if they were not represented on USIB. The President believed that the information referred to by General Lemnitzer was battlefield intelligence, whereas the discovery of the shipyards where nuclear submarines are being constructed was the business of CIA. He did not see why four intelligence services should attempt to find out where the submarines were made. He believed it was the function of CIA to acquire strategic intelligence. General Lemnitzer believed that each Military Service was working on a different intelligence target.

Mr. Gray pointed out that a substantive discussion of the material in the Joint Study Group report seemed to be underway. The President said that perhaps the membership of USIB could not be changed at once but that a different type of intelligence board could be organized once military intelligence within the Department of Defense was re-organized. Secretary Gates did not agree that the membership of USIB could not be changed immediately. A Defense representative on the Board could do his homework in the Pentagon and bring the Defense position to the Board in the same way a Defense representative on the Planning Board reports the Defense position. The President felt that changes in the membership of USIB must be correlated with changes in the military intelligence organization. Mr. Gates said that thus far intelligence has not been affected by reorganization of the Department of Defense. Mr. Dulles said when changes were made in the organization of military intelligence, there would be a reason for changing the membership of USIB, since there would then be one high-ranking official who knows intelligence representing the Department of Defense. The President said that there would in any case remain the need for technical intelligence gathered in connection with the normal deployment of forces.

Mr. Dulles said the figure of $2 billion had been mentioned occasionally as the sum spent by this government on intelligence activities. He wished to point out, however, that this figure included support of the radar station at Thule, support of SAMOS, etc., all of which were really early warning functions.

The President said he had read a summary of the report by the Joint Study Group. He felt that up to now we had not accomplished all it was possible to accomplish in integrating all our intelligence activities. Secretary Gates said there was no review in the Department of Defense of intelligence requirements. General Lemnitzer said the JCS agreed on the need for Defense review of intelligence requirements.

Secretary Gates believed the policy question before the Council now was, how far would this Administration wish to go in reorganizing intelligence during its last two weeks in office. The President said he felt a directive on agreed matters could be issued and that he could pass on to his successor his views on other intelligence questions. Mr. Dulles said he would like to see the matter of the pictorial center worked out soon.

The President then remarked that soon after Pearl Harbor, he was engaged in an operation which required him to have certain information which he was unable to obtain from the Navy, i.e. the strength the Navy had left in the Pacific. The President also noted that the U.S. fought the first year of the war in Europe entirely on the basis of British intelligence. Subsequently, each Military Service developed its own intelligence organization. He thought this situation made little sense in managerial terms. He had suffered an eight-year defeat on this question but would leave a legacy of ashes for his successor.

Mr. Gray said language would be prepared to permit agreed recommendations from the report of the Joint Study Group to be put into effect.

The President pointed out that in military history a single man usually dominates the intelligence service of a country at any given time. He felt that a strong central position with respect to intelligence was necessary. The Joint Chiefs of Staff should not be required to consult individually each of the Services, as well as CIA, in formulating their strategic plans; they should have their own intelligence service.

The National Security Council:

a. Discussed the question raised by the Secretary of Defense as to revising the National Security Council Intelligence Directives in the light of the recommendations relating to the military intelligence organization within the Department of Defense and to the membership of the U.S. Intelligence Board, submitted on December 15, 1960, by a Joint Study Group on Foreign Intelligence Activities, composed of representatives of the Director of Central Intelligence, the Secretaries of State and Defense, the Director, Bureau of the Budget, and the Special Assistant to the President for National Security Affairs.

b. Agreed that the Secretary of Defense should submit his recommendations for appropriate revisions in the NSCID's directive to the authority of the Secretary of Defense over the military intelligence organization within the Department of Defense in consonance with the Defense Reorganization Act of 1958.

c. Noted that the recommendations of the Secretary of Defense pursuant to b above, together with the views of the Principals of the Joint Study Group regarding the Group's report which are being consolidated by the Director of Central Intelligence, would be considered at the next NSC meeting on January 12, 1961.

Note: The actions in b and c above, as approved by the President, subsequently transmitted of the Secretary of Defense and the Director of Central Intelligence.

[Here follows discussion of the remaining agenda items.]

---

81.   Memorandum of Conference With President Eisenhower[1]

Washington, January 5, 1961.

OTHERS PRESENT

> General Hull, General Doolittle, Admiral Conolly, Messrs. Lovett, Ryerson, Baker, Darden, Coyne, Gordon Gray, General Goodpaster

General Hull made an oral report to the President from a text which he said he would send to me.[2] The President said he not only agreed with the observations of the group, he agreed so strongly he might have written them himself. He said he hoped that the new administration would continue a board such as this one, but was loath to make a suggestion since this might prove "counter productive."

Regarding intelligence organization in Defense, he said he favored the recommendation outlined by General Hull. As a second solution, however, he would center all intelligence about foreign military matters in the JCS with a strategic intelligence group concerned with broader matters, feeding in worldwide intelligence, in the CIA.

The President said he will endorse the Board's recommendation and will give it to Mr. Gates with a request that he pass it on to his successor in the new administration. He repeated that he wants to avoid any fatherly or professorial manner toward his successor. General Hull commented that the report had been prepared so that it could be provided to the new administration.

Governor Darden said he was convinced from the work he had done with the Board that reorganization would result in substantial savings in the intelligence field (or at any rate, better use of the resources now being made available). Mr. Lovett said he agreed but thought the resources should go toward better use. Admiral Conolly supported this

---

[1] Source: Eisenhower Library, Records of the Special Assistant for National Security Affairs. Secret. Prepared by Andrew Goodpaster on January 7. This meeting was held immediately after the NSC meeting; see Document 80.

[2] Document 82.

judgment, stating that organization is now the root cause of excess costs, and that better organization can bring better efficiency.

G.

Brigadier General, USA

---

82.   Report From the Chairman of the President's Board of Consultants on Foreign Intelligence Activities (Hull) to President Elsenhower[1]

Washington, January 5, 1961.

Mr. President:

I.

We appreciate the opportunity of again reporting to you on the continuing review of the U.S. foreign intelligence effort which we have been making pursuant to your Executive Order (#10656) of February 6, 1956.[2]

Since we have all submitted our resignations to you, and because this will be our last meeting with you as members of your Foreign Intelligence Board, we propose this morning to give you a brief accounting of stewardship, as well as a few impressions concerning the present status and future trends of the U.S. foreign intelligence effort.

If agreeable to you, we will limit our briefing to a few of the more significant aspects of our association with, and our views concerning, the foreign intelligence effort.

II.

Since you created the Board five years ago, we have held 18 full-scale meetings covering a total of 31 working days. In between these meetings continuity in the work of the Board has been provided by the Board's

---

[1] Source: Eisenhower Library, Records of the Special Assistant for National Security Affairs.   Top Secret.   Following the creation of the President's Foreign Intelligence Advisory Board to replace the Board of Consultants on May 4 (see Document 87), a copy of this report was transmitted to Bundy for President Kennedy under cover of a May 18 memorandum from J. Patrick Coyne. (Eisenhower Library, Records of the Special Assistant for National Security Affairs)

[2] Executive Order 10656, signed by President Eisenhower on Februgy 6, 1956, established the Board of Consultants on Foreign Intelligence Activities. (21 *Federal Register* 859)

Executive Officer (on detail from the NSC staff) who has worked on a full-time basis in furtherance of the business of this Board. Additionally, in between these meetings individual members of the Board and the Board's Executive Officer have made periodic on-the-scene reviews of the foreign intelligence activities of the Central Intelligence Agency, the Departments of State and Defense, the Joint Chiefs of Staff, the Unified and Specified Commands, the Army, the Navy, the Air Force, the National Security Agency and its three supporting cryptologic services. These reviews have been made at the Seat of Government, elsewhere in the Continental United States, and in a great many countries in Europe, Asia, the Middle East, Africa and South America. In addition, at varying times, review has been made in all those locations of selected major cold war activities conducted by CIA's Clandestine Services.

In the past 5 years we have made 7 written and 6 oral reports to you, consisting of 37 major recommendations covering the most significant phases of the foreign intelligence and covert action business. From time to time, on subjects of lesser importance we have made observations and recommendations directly to member agencies of the Intelligence Community.

Of the 33 recommendations approved by you, action has been completed on 15. The remaining 18 are in varying stages of consideration or implementation by the agencies concerned. (We will comment on these pending matters later in this briefing)

At your direction 9 of the 18 pending recommendations have been made the subject of specific, continuing review by this Board and/or the subject of future reports (annual, semiannual, etc.) to the President and to the President's Foreign Intelligence Board (if there is to be such Board in the future).

III.
Manpower and Dollar Costs

As you appreciate, our foreign intelligence effort is a very large one when measured in terms of manpower and money. As of June, 1960, an estimated [3 lines of source text not declassified]. As of December, 1960 the cost of the effort was estimated to range between [less than 1 line of source text not declassified] a large fraction of these dollars going to the procurement of the very expensive intelligence hardware involved.

IV.
Recommendations Pertaining to Coordination, Integration, Reduction of Duplication, and Strong Centralized Direction of the Foreign Intelligence Effort

To reduce undesirable duplication and to improve coordination, integration, direction and control of the entire foreign intelligence effort (including the manpower, dollars and related assets just referred to), we proposed and you approved 16 recommendations in this area. Among the noteworthy actions which resulted were: (a) the abolition of three committees, and the establishment of a single forum, the United States Intelligence Board (USIB) which is now utilized on a regular basis (at least weekly) by the heads of all intelligence agencies for the collective consideration of important foreign intelligence matters; and (b) a re-examination of all National Security Council Intelligence Directives (NSCIDs) leading to the issuance of revised NSCIDs (reduced in number from 17 to 7) which clarified the basic duties and responsibilities of the member agencies of the Intelligence Community and which placed increased emphasis on several critical aspects of foreign intelligence organization and activities.

While we recognize that these results are noteworthy, we are of the view that there is still considerable room for improvement in the coordination, integration, direction and control of the intelligence effort.

We believe that, in the months ahead, consideration should be given to: (1) further revising pertinent NSCIDs to reflect the increasing intelligence role of the Joint Chiefs of Staff under the Department of Defense Reorganization Act of 1958; and (2) reducing ultimately the size of the USIB membership to provide the Director of Central Intelligence with a more efficient mechanism to assist him in carrying out his mission of coordinating all foreign intelligence activities. (At present USIB is composed of 6 Defense agencies [OSO, J-2, NSA, G-2, ONI, A-2], 2 civilian agencies [State, CIA] extensively engaged in foreign intelligence, and 2 additional civilian agencies [AEC, FBI] which are engaged in the foreign intelligence effort in only a marginal way.)[3]

In addition to our recommendations on USIB and the revised NSCIDs, we have made some 14 other recommendations (40% of all our recommendations) pertaining to coordination, integration, reduction of duplication and strong centralized direction of the foreign intelligence effort. Because we consider this to be one of the most significant problem areas confronting the Community, and since this problem is tied inextricably to the role of the Director of Central Intelligence, we next address ourselves to that subject.

V.

The Role of the Director of Central Intelligence

We are pleased that the unique capabilities of the present Director will continue to be utilized by the next administration, thereby providing continuity in this important area. However, we continue to be concerned by the great burden of work involved in the assignment to one

---

[3] Brackets in the source text.

individual of the two-fold responsibility of serving simultaneously as administrator of the Central Intelligence Agency, a large and complex organization, and as Director of Central Intelligence with responsibility for coordinating all foreign intelligence activities of the ten agencies comprising the Intelligence Community. We believe that the present incumbent has made progress in the direction of increased integration of the total Community effort, but that this progress has not proceeded with sufficient speed, because he has been preoccupied in the main with commanding the work of the CIA. Further, we believe that his effectiveness as Director of Central Intelligence is impaired somewhat by the feeling on the part of several member agencies of the Intelligence Community that he is "both umpire and pitcher" in that he is, at the same time, the coordinator of the entire Intelligence Community and the head of an operating agency which in many quarters is looked upon as a competing element of that Community.

We do not believe that this situation would be materially improved by the recommendation of the Joint Study Group (Recommendation #29) that the DCI establish a coordinating staff to assist him in carrying out his duties as coordinator of all intelligence activities. Rather, we believe that the situation would be bettered substantially if the DCI would divest himself voluntarily of many of the functions he currently performs in his capacity as Head of CIA and by assigning such duties elsewhere within CIA. To accomplish this purpose we again recommend that he be provided with a Chief of Staff or Executive Director to act for him, together with the Deputy Director, in the management of the CIA, thereby relieving him to perform the even more important duty of coordinating, integrating and directing all U.S. foreign intelligence activities.

After a reasonable trial period, if this course of action does not accomplish its intended goal, serious consideration should be given to complete separation of the DCI from the CIA.

VI.

Recommendations Pertaining to Signals Intelligence and the Management of the National Security Agency

We have made 8 recommendations on various aspects of the COMINT–ELINT business. Significant actions which have resulted in this area include the following: (a) the issuance of a new NSCID (No. 6) calling for the fusion of COMINT and ELINT activities under the Director, NSA; (b) a detailed study and constructive proposals to the NSC by Dr. Baker and his associates [2-1/2 *lines of source text not declassified*] and (c) periodic assessment and guidance by the Office of the Secretary of Defense with respect to NSA's plans, programs, and allocation of resources.

Although there has been some improvement in the fusion of COMINT and ELINT, we feel that it has been too slow and that much more can be done to improve their coordination by: (a) requiring positive operational and technical control of COMINT and by the Director, NSA, rather than the practice of yielding to individual service claims, and (b) actually combining COMINT and ELINT planning in USIB, rather than present handling of this in separate committees of USIB.

VII.
Recommendations Pertaining to the Strategic Warning Process

You have approved the four recommendations we have made on the vital matter of strategic warning. We are pleased to report that, as a result of your action, highly commendable progress has been made by the Department of Defense in perfecting the CRITICCOMM System to assure rapid transmission to Washington of critical intelligence data.

Apart from the *communicating* aspects of this matter, however, we continue to have misgivings as to whether USIB's Watch Committee and its National Indications Center are organized, supported and operated in such manner as to (a) assure timely receipt, *processing and evaluation* of *all* available information pertaining to strategic warning, and (b) assure timely transmission to higher authority of significant information bearing on the early warning problem.

In the Intelligence Community we believe that there is no subject more deserving of continuing attention, if the President and the National Security Council are to place reliance on USIB's Watch Committee and its National Indications Center to supply them with timely, strategic warning of enemy attack. Accordingly, we would urge that the DCI and USIB reexamine the current organization and functions of the Watch Committee and, particularly, its National Indications Center, to assure that both are properly organized and supported in such a way as to carry out their vital mission in the most effective manner possible.

VIII.
Recommendations Pertaining to CIA's Covert Action Programs

You have approved the 4 recommendations we made on various aspects of CIA's covert action programs. As a result, we are pleased to report that at present the Special NSC 5412/2 Group appears to be better organized and to be functioning with greater effectiveness than was the case in earlier times.[4] However, we continue to have concern

---

[4] The NSC 5412/2 Special Group was established pursuant to the issuance of NSC 5412/2, December 28, 1955, to review and approve covert action programs initiated by the CIA. See William M. Leary, ed., *The Central Intelligence Agency: History and Documents* (The University of Alabama Press, 1984), pp. 63, 146–149.

as to whether the Clandestine Services of CIA are sufficiently well organized and managed to carry out covert action programs. Further, we have been unable to conclude that, on balance, all of the covert action programs undertaken by CIA up to this time have been worth the risk or the great expenditure of manpower, money and other resources involved. In addition, we believe that CIA's concentration on political, psychological and related covert action activities have tended to detract substantially from the execution of its primary intelligence gathering mission. We suggest, accordingly, that there should be a total reassessment of our covert action policies and programs and that the Head of CIA should devote continuing attention to improving the organization and management of CIA's Clandestine Services.

IX.

The Joint Study Group Report

We have reviewed the recommendations recently submitted by the Joint Study Group (established to study the organization and management of the foreign intelligence effort). We believe the report is an excellent one and that it is deserving of most careful study by USIB and the responsible agency heads concerned.[5]

Except for Recommendations #29 and 30 and the additional recommendations which pertain to the intelligence element of the JCS, we concur generally in the recommendations of the Group. We have previously expressed our views on #29 (dealing with the coordinating role of the DCI).

As to Recommendation #30 (which calls for a very substantial reduction in the membership of the USIB, we would make the following observations. Military intelligence should be brought into conformity with the Defense Reorganization Act of 1958, as recommended by the Group. However, the recommended reduction in USIB should not occur until the J-2 element of the JCS develops the vitality, experience and capability which are prerequisite to a meaningful fulfillment of the recommendation. Army, Navy, and Air Force Intelligence should not be removed from USIB until the J-2 (JCS) and the Secretary of Defense's Office of Special Operations are capable of serving as effective substitutes.

As to the recommendations pertaining to the intelligence element of the JCS we do not believe that the JCS, with its present composition and activities, can provide intelligence direction of the sort proposed by the Joint Study Group.

---

[5] See Document 78.

X.
Summary

By way of summation, we would like to express the following convictions based on our 5-year Board activity: (a) the Intelligence Community has made substantial progress in several significant areas and is more productive than at any time in the past; (b) we foresee no reduction in the vital role which intelligence must play in support of the Nation's security, or in the cost of an intelligence program adequate to meet the ever increasing threats to our national security; (c) we will continue to experience serious intelligence deficiencies due to rigorous Soviet bloc security measures, but these can be overcome in large measure if our Nation is prepared to meet the challenge and the costs involved; and (d) we feel that maximum utilization must be made of scientific and technological know-how because positive intelligence and counterintelligence will rely increasingly on sophisticated scientific techniques.

Finally, we refrain from commenting concerning the desirability or need in the future for a Presidential Board of Consultants on Foreign Intelligence. We feel that you are in a much better position than we to assess the value of an activity of this sort.

However, we would urge a recommendation to your successor that, if he does not find the need for such a Board, a staff officer of the NSC be assigned full-time responsibility to maintain a continuing review of these subjects and to report periodically thereon to him. Until a decision is made on the aforementioned matters, we suggest that, as an interim arrangement, it be recommended to your successor that our present Executive Officer be continued on detail from the NSC staff to provide necessary continuity with respect to the handling of the variety of previously mentioned matters which, at your direction, are scheduled to be the subjects of future reports by the Intelligence Community.

XI.

Finally, Mr. President, the other members of the Board and I appreciate the trust and confidence you reposed in us by appointing us to this Board, and we wish to record our pleasure at being permitted to serve you.

John E. Hull[6]
Chairman of the Board

---

[6] Printed from a copy that bears this typed signature.

83.   Memorandum From Director of Central Intelligence Dulles
        to the President's Special Assistant for National Security
        Affairs (Gray)[1]

Washington, January 9, 1961.

SUBJECT

    Sixth Report to the President by the President's Board of Consultants on Foreign
    Intelligence Activities dated May 24, 1960 (Recommendation on "Organization and
    Management of CIA's Clandestine Services")[2]

REFERENCE

    Memorandum for Director of Central Intelligence, same subject, from Mr. Gordon
    Gray, dated December 16, 1960[3]

1. In compliance with your request I submit the following self-contained compilation of my previous reports on the various steps which have been taken in response to the two recommendations made by the Board on October 30, 1958 and May 24, 1960. As you requested, the following compilation is so arranged as to identify those actions which were taken or considered in connection with the Third Report of the Board as distinguished from actions which were taken or considered in connection with the Sixth Report of the Board.[4]

2. The Third Report to the President by the President's Board of Consultants on Foreign Intelligence Activities, dated October 30, 1958 and presented to the President on December 16, 1958 contained the following recommendation:

"The present mission of the Plans Group of the CIA be reviewed with consideration given to relieving that Group of, and placing elsewhere in the Agency, the responsibilities (1) for the review of (i.e., reporting on and evaluating) the Political, Psychological and Para-Military operations of the Agency, and (2) for the formulation of the intelligence estimates and recommendations upon which the plans for such operations are based."

3. The text of the report of December 16, 1958 to the President explained some of the reasoning of the Board resulting in this recommendation. This report referred to "some of the virtually autonomous functions assigned to this Group", and states, "From evidence we have seen, it is our feeling that within this frame of reference, the Plans Group (for the Agency) may be incapable of making objective

---

[1] Source: Eisenhower Library, Records of the Special Assistant for National Security Affairs. Secret.

[2] The report is not printed.

[3] Not printed.

[4] The Board's Third Report is not printed.

appraisals of its own intelligence information as well as of its own operations when it is involved in Cold War activities which are the subjects of its own reports. We are concerned about the implications of this not only because of possible impacts on the programs of the Agency but, more importantly, because of the influences which may be brought to bear on foreign policy determinations which, in large measure, may be based upon Agency reporting."

4. The Board of Consultants may have felt that there was a greater degree of autonomy or independence possessed by the Deputy Director for Plans (Plans Group) than actually existed. Final responsibility and authority for all activities of the Clandestine Services rest with me as Director of the Central Intelligence Agency. It is a fact that the DD/P may take action on behalf of the Director, but in the case of operations under NSC 5412 only after the necessary policy guidance has been obtained from the 5412 Committee.

5. It is particularly important to note that before CIA Cold War (5412) activities are initiated all available intelligence, including National Intelligence Estimates, which are produced by the Intelligence Community, is taken into account. Further, while it is true that in covert operations a major source of information on the accomplishments of the project may be clandestine, we analyze all available information from all sources to guard against subjectivity or self-serving reports.

6. The present Deputy Director (Plans) assumed his position on January 1, 1959, shortly after the Third Report was submitted to the President. He at once undertook a complete review of the mission and organization of the Clandestine Services. In concert with this the Inspector General of the Agency was engaged in reviewing the overall organization of the Clandestine Services. As a further measure I initiated a Program for Greater Efficiency within the Agency as a whole in order to ensure a continuing effort to improve its organization and methods of operation. This program and other aspects of the Board's Third Report were discussed at the meeting of the Board on July 17, 1959. As a result of these several reviews a number of organizational changes were made and many others were considered but rejected for various valid reasons. The main objective of these changes was to improve the efficiency of the Clandestine Services. A new Assistant Deputy Director (Plans) for Psychological and Paramilitary Operations was appointed to assist the DD/P in the operational direction of activities in these functional fields. An Operational Services grouping was created, combining and centralizing the direction of several elements which perform functions of common concern to all the Operating Divisions and Staffs. The Inspection and Review Staff, DD/P was abolished and the Inspector General of CIA made solely responsible for the comprehensive review of the activities and operations of the Clandestine Services, reporting directly to me.

7. The planning system within the Clandestine Services was revised so that a greater distinction is made between operational planning directives and budgetary estimates. The revised system calls for an initial DD/P operational plan containing guidance and direction for the operating divisions and staffs for the forthcoming fiscal year. From this the divisions and staffs can prepare their more detailed Operational Programs which go forward for review and approval by the Project Review Committee which reports directly to me. The budget and fiscal requirements are generated as a by-product of these Operational Programs. Finally, Related Mission Directives, also based on the Operational Plan and Programs and the particular situation in the area concerned, set forth more precise and realistic objectives and tasks for each field station.

8. In addition to the above these reviews of the mission and organization of the Clandestine Services highlighted the following aspects of its work which merited further attention and study and on which action has been or is being taken:

a. the Agency's responsibility for the coordination of U.S. clandestine activities abroad
b. delegation of more authority to the field
c. increased emphasis on scientific and technical collection methods and systems
d. refinements in what we are reporting and how we are reporting it
e. greater reliance on over-all country programs in the control and management of our operations as opposed to reliance on individual projects
f. [2 lines of source text not declassified]
g. more emphasis on political action in underdeveloped areas
h. development of our capability for "covert limited warfare"
i. increased records mechanization.

In this major effort to improve the organization of the CS but most especially the methods and procedures—the way business is transacted—the DD/P and his Staff have kept in mind the recommendation of the Board quoted above. Several of the changes made are responsive to this recommendation.

9. The second part of the Board's recommendation was concerned with the location of responsibility for the formulation of intelligence estimates and of recommendations upon which plans for operations are based. It suggested that such responsibility not be located in that portion of the Agency which is responsible for planning operations.

10. The problem of insuring the provision of a valid and unbiased intelligence base for operational planning purposes has been given much consideration within CIA during the development of the Clandestine Services planning cycle. The Board's concern, I feel, has been met by the procedures described below.

11. Planning for Psychological, Political and Paramilitary operations is not based on intelligence provided solely by the DD/P. The primary source of intelligence for planning purposes is the Office of National Estimates (ONE). Present DD/P procedures provide for the use of ONE guidance throughout the entire planning cycle. The Clandestine Services General Plan, DD/P's basic planning document, derives from current NIE's the contingencies against which clandestine activities must be directed. Moreover, specific projects are tested against pertinent NIE's or, if a current or relevant NIE is not available or time is sufficiently urgent to make a coordinated NIE impossible, an ONE estimative memorandum is obtained.

12. There are further independent checks of PP/PM projects internally within CIA. Such projects are generally reviewed by the Project Review Committee which is presided over by the Director or Deputy Director of CIA and is widely representative of the Agency as a whole, including the Deputy Director for Intelligence, the Deputy Director for Support, and the Inspector General.

13. Significant PP/PM projects having political import and involving substantial expenditures receive a thorough review and concurrence by the Department of State and by the 5412 group, before final approval by the Director. Such concurrence is sought on the basis of relevant intelligence available to the Agency as a whole. While PP/PM projects may be recommended by the DD/P, action thereon in all significant cases is not possible until internal and external procedures, as described above have been satisfied. Thus action is not taken on intelligence or recommendations from the DD/P alone.

14. The Sixth Report to the President by the President's Board of Consultants on Foreign Intelligence Activities, dated May 24, 1960, included the following comments and recommendation:

"Organization and Management of CIA's Clandestine Services
"Based upon an exchange of correspondence between the National Security Council and this Board in November, 1959, we have continued to follow developments relating to needed improvements in the organization and management of CIA's Clandestine Services. Although a few significant changes have been made in this area in recent months, we believe that a way can be found to organize these Services along more simplified and efficient lines. While we appreciate that the missions assigned to the Clandestine Services are complex, we are hopeful that, through the continuing studies being made by CIA's Deputy Director/Plans, these Services will be organized in such manner as to eliminate unnecessary duplication of effort and achieve increased effectiveness."

15. I concurred with these comments of the Board and reaffirmed that the continuing studies being made by the DD/P of the organization of the Clandestine Services and the methods and procedures employed

in carrying out the mission of the CS had as principal objectives the elimination of unnecessary duplication and the achievement of increased effectiveness. As noted by the Board and as reported above in this paper significant changes in the organization and management of the CS were made. [2 *lines of source text not declassified*]

[1 *page of source text not declassified*]

Through these organizational changes, revision and simplification of certain basic procedures, and clarification of the functions and responsibilities of both staff and line components we made progress toward our objectives. It is important to realize that this is a continuing process and one which must be carried out on a progressive basis with the least possible disruption of current activities.

16. The CS accomplishes its mission through components responsible for a prescribed geographical area and through other components responsible for a prescribed function without geographical limitations. This approach is required because of the complexity of the tasks and broad interests of the CS. Under these arrangements it is inevitable that some duplication exists but it should not be inferred that all such duplication is unnecessary. We make every effort to reduce duplication to that which is unavoidable if we are to assure that all our responsibilities are discharged in a competent and secure manner.

17. The roles of the Special Staffs recently have been further clarified and delimited with the objective of eliminating duplication and relieving the staffs of the responsibility for any activity which can properly be performed in the operating divisions. I am satisfied that the Special Staffs have unique and important functions of common concern and world-wide application, that cannot be accomplished in the operating divisions. It is of course essential that these functions are carefully identified and that all officers of the CS clearly understand precisely which activities are the responsibility of the Special Staffs. To accomplish this the Deputy Director (Plans) is now revising the functional statements of the Staffs which will concentrate on their four basic functions, viz.:

   a. Services of common concern such as liaison with other agencies and with other components of CIA, screening of requirements, and certain specialized activities [3 *lines of source text not declassified*].
   b. Support activities including certain forms of research, the promulgation of doctrine, development of new ideas and the provision of expert advice and guidance in the several functional fields.
   c. Developing plans for and assisting in the coordination of functional programs involving activities in two or more geographic areas.
   d. Participating in the evaluation of the production and accomplishment of the CS.

18. As an additional measure to prevent possible duplication the Deputy Director (Plans) further modified the staff organization in the area divisions to eliminate separate Foreign Intelligence, Counter Intelligence and Covert Action sections. These divisions now have centralized operations staffs.

19. [*10 lines of source text not declassified*]

20. In order to make the most effective use of our resources in the performance of certain important functions the Deputy Director (Plans) is developing standing operating procedures which will be followed for specific activities. Planning, for example, will be a joint endeavor of the Projects and Programs Group, the Special Staffs, and the Operating Divisions under the general supervision and guidance of the Senior Planning Officer. This planning community will insure that the talents of appropriate officers and the capabilities of all interested components of the CS are brought to bear on specific problems. Similarly, appropriate operating procedures will delineate the capabilities of properly qualified officers and components in the research and evaluation functions. This is an economical way to do the job since it will permit effective planning, research, evaluation, etc. without requiring a number of small units formally established for these functions.

21. The Deputy Director (Plans) believes the changes he has made in the past two years in the organization structure and the way of doing business in the CS have corrected deficiencies and that the situation in this regard is now satisfactory. I concur in this belief. This does not imply that we have achieved such perfection in these important matters that no future modifications will be desirable. We may require further adjustments to meet new situations. We must strive progressively to improve our methods and simplify our structure where feasible. To meet these requirements the Deputy Director (Plans) will continue to study the organization and procedures of the Clandestine Services and take such action as may be required to contribute to our goal of greater efficiency in the Clandestine Services.

Allen W. Dulles

84.   Memorandum of Discussion at the 474th Meeting of the
        National Security Council[1]

Washington, January 12, 1961.

[Here follows a paragraph listing the participants at the meeting.]

There follows a summary of the discussion at the Meeting and the main points taken.

[Here follows discussion of agenda items 1–3.]

4. *Foreign Intelligence Activities* (NSC Action No. 2367; Memo for NSC from Executive Secretary, same subject, dated January 9, 1961, Special Limited Distribution Only)[2]

Mr. Gray introduced this subject to the Council. (A copy of Mr. Gray's Briefing Note is filed in the Minutes of the Meeting and another copy is attached to this Memorandum.)[3]

After indicating that the 43 recommendations of the report of the Joint Study Group on Foreign Intelligence Activities and the recommendations by the Department of Defense for revision of the National Security Council Intelligence Directives (NSCIDs) were before the Council,[4] Mr. Gray turned to the recommendations of the Joint Study Group in the order in which they appeared in the January 9 memorandum of the Director of Central Intelligence on the subject.

The first category of recommendations consisted of those, 28 in number, on which all of the Principals of the Joint Study Group were in agreement. The Council concurred in these 28 recommendations.

Mr. Gray then turned to the second category; namely, 7 recommendations on which the Principals were in substantial agreement with the exception of dissents or reservations on each such recommendation by single agency head (See Paragraph 5 of the Briefing Note). Recommendations 21, 22 and 23 called for the establishment of a central requirements facility by the U.S. Intelligence Board (USIB). Defense felt that these recommendations should be given further study. Secretary Gates said he had not had time to thrash this matter out with the Joint Chiefs of Staff. He felt that he would personally be able to agree to

---

[1] Source: Eisenhower Library, Whitman File, NSC Records. Top Secret; Eyes Only. Prepared on January 13.

[2] Regarding NSC Action No. 2367, see Document 80. The Executive Secretary's January 9 memorandum presumably transmitted Allen Dulles' January 9 memorandum (Document 83) to the NSC.

[3] Not printed.

[4] See Documents 78 and 82. The Department of Defense recommendations have not been further identified.

Recommendation 21 at least, but the JCS felt that a problem was involved concerning the general relation of military influence to operational intelligence. General Lemnitzer said the JCS were not so much in disagreement with the objectives of the recommendation as they were inclined to feel the need for further study in the field. He added that problems as to where the central requirements facility might be located, etc. had been raised. Secretary Gates said the purpose of the recommendation was to remedy the present situation in which intelligence requirements can be issued without being checked in a central clearing house to see whether someone else has the same requirements. Mr. Dulles noted that a great volume of requirements were issued. The President wondered why the JCS objected to this recommendation. He felt finding out the exact requirements in intelligence was the road to efficiency. Secretary Gates said the JCS had lumped Recommendations 21, 22 and 23 together. He believed their dissent was a matter of the details rather than the philosophy. Mr. Dulles suggested that the three recommendations be accepted in principle and referred to the USIB for implementation and consultation with Defense and the JCS. Secretary Gates endorsed this proposal and the Council adopted it.

Mr. Gray then turned to Recommendation 24 which would place on U.S. Mission Chiefs overseas the responsibility for coordinating all overt and clandestine intelligence requirements in their area. Mr. Gray said he suggested granting an exception in instances where State and CIA agreed that the Chief of Mission should not exercise this responsibility. Mr. Dulles said Mr. Gray's exception was acceptable to him. The President agreed.

Mr. Gray then suggested that Recommendation 31 be passed over until Recommendation 29 was taken up. Mr. Gray then turned to Recommendation 34 which would require that military agencies intelligence instructions to components of unified commands be transmitted through the JCS. Mr. Dulles said he concurred in this recommendation, subject to the proviso that it did not include NSA communications to the service cryptographic agencies in the field. General Lemnitzer said this recommendation involved a problem because of the vast volume of requirements in the technical intelligence field. The JCS were not organized for transmission of this vast volume of requirements. He felt there must be some middle ground; perhaps broad operational requirements as distinct from technical requirements could be transmitted through the JCS. The President pointed out that the recommendation referred to "instructions". Mr. Dulles suggested that the recommendation be amended to indicate that instructions be transmitted through the JCS or as the JCS may direct. General Lemnitzer and Secretary Gates and the President agreed with Mr. Dulles' suggestion.

Mr. Gray next took up Recommendation 37 which would continue the responsibility of CIA stations abroad to coordinate clandestine activities but would relieve CIA case officers of the authority to veto proposed clandestine operations of another agency. Mr. Dulles said he believed this recommendation unnecessary and distinguished between the final decision to approve and the final decision to veto. He said if a military service wishes to appeal the veto of a CIA case officer, the matter could be decided in Washington by the Director of Central Intelligence and the Chief of the Military Intelligence Service. He pointed out also that if a field commander considers an operation essential to the security of his command, he can go ahead with the operation pending Washington's decision regardless of the objection of the CIA case officer in the field. General Lemnitzer said the JCS agreed with this recommendation. Mr. Dulles said he had no further objection to the recommendation.

Mr. Gray then turned to a category of recommendations, two in number, on which there is disagreement but with respect to which the DCI recommends a decision at this time. The first recommendation in this category was No. 16 which called for the issuance of a new NSCID No. 8 establishing a National Photographic Intelligence Center.[5] Mr. Gray pointed out that the Secretary of Defense and the DCI were in disagreement on this recommendation, each feeling that his agency should have responsibility for administering the proposed Center. General Lemnitzer believed the Center should operate under the general direction of the Defense Department because the vast amount of the in-put would be produced by the Military Services. Moreover, the Military Services would be required to provide training for and would be the principal customers of the Center, which would be especially important in time of war. He recognized the need of other agencies for photographic intelligence and such intelligence would be made available. He gave assurance that the Center would not be removed from Washington if it were placed under the Department of Defense. Vast quantities of photographic intelligence were now being acquired. No photographic center was available at the present time and the Joint Chiefs of Staff wished to avoid duplicate centers. The Chiefs feel that the center could most effectively be operated by the Department of Defense with the participation of CIA. Secretary Gates added that Mr. Dulles had agreed that the Center should be operated by Defense in time of war but he (Mr. Gates) felt the need of continuity in the quick transition from peace to war which might occur in the future. This problem was not one of intelligence interpretation but was one of management. Every user agency could interpret the intelligence. Secretary Gates added that the existing Center would have to be expanded in the near future.

---

[5] National Security Council Intelligence Directive (NSCID) Nos. 1–14 are printed in *Foreign Relations, 1945–1950, Emergence of the Intelligence Establishment,* Documents 422–435.

Mr. Dulles said some misinterpretation appeared to exist on this subject. The present photographic Center was a joint enterprise consisting of 140 CIA officials, 100 Army officers, and a small but competent Navy contingent of 10 and 7–15 Air Force officers. The Center had been a joint operation for five years and had handled mostly U-2 photography under the management of CIA. The President asked whether the Defense suggestion was that the Center be under J-2. General Lemnitzer replied, no, under the Department of Defense. Secretary Gates added, directly under the Secretary of Defense just as NSA is. The President thought the three Military Services should not be separately involved in this Center. Since the basic danger to be detected by the Center is military, he believed it would be satisfactory for the military to give central direction to the operation.

Mr. Dulles said the information obtained through this Center was chiefly military only in the targeting field. Photographic intelligence had tremendous political significance and was a matter of common concern to the Washington agencies. The matter was one which fell within the field CIA was established to coordinate. In its five years of operation the Center had developed a group of career officials who intended to make photographic intelligence their life work. If the Center were placed in the hands of the military, rotation of personnel would be the principle followed, if past practice is any guide. The President felt rotation would be fatal to an operation of this kind. Secretary Gates said that if the Center were placed under Defense, a career staff would be retained and developed. Mr Dulles said abandonment of rotation was a new idea for the military. He added that the Center had been operated for five years without a leak. Preliminary analysis of photography is made by the Center and information is then disseminated to user agencies. Some of this information is vital to the Department of State. Mr. Dulles felt it would be very damaging to morale to disrupt this going concern at the present time. The President said he would like to inquire into the time element. While some of the information coming from the Center might be vital to the Department of State, he wondered whether it was not the military rather than the State Department which had an instant need for the information. Mr. Dulles said the information developed by the Center was important to the military but was also important to other agencies such as State because of its effect on policy. The President said the information was important but need not reach State as soon as it reached the military. The information might be needed in a matter of seconds by the military.

Secretary Gates said the Center would be considerably expanded in the future and the operation would be different from the U-2 operation. The President believed that the Center must be operated by an expert career staff. This was a question of management which, perhaps, should be studied before being decided so quickly. If he had to decide at the present time, however, he would say, since the present Center is doing well, let it alone except for its enlargement. He understood that the Department of Defense and the JCS had no complaints about the operation of the Center.

Mr. Stans said one difficulty was that the Air Force was establishing its own Center. Secretary Herter said he understood that the film was processed by the Air Force before it went to the Center. Mr. Dulles said this understanding was erroneous. The film is developed by a private company, which has the greatest competence in this field. This company has been developing this film for five years in the greatest secrecy. The film goes to a special branch of the company and is then flown to Washington. The Air Force gets the film at the same time as the Center.

The President said there should be only one Center and that no Service should establish a separate center. Matters of this kind were placed under CIA by the National Security Act because of their common usefulness. Secretary Gates said Mr. Stans was correct in his statement that the Air Force intended to have its own center. When great masses of photographic data were involved, there was a question of what should be looked at first and how soon. Mr. Gray said he felt the discussion was getting on to very sensitive grounds. The issue was whether there should be a single center or not. The President said there must be a single photographic center. Since CIA was the principal user and collector, he believed the center should be under CIA management as a principle of organization even though the time element still bothered him.

On being called on by the President, Dr. Kistiakowsky said that the existing photographic Center under CIA provided copies of its material without delay to all Services which concentrated on tactical intelligence. The Center does not retain the matter until it makes an exhaustive analysis; it passes it on immediately. Dr. Kistiakowsky felt the existing Center was a revolution in photographic techniques. In a year we would be able to obtain as much information from photographs taken 200 miles above the earth as we were able to get from our best reconnaissance plane in World War II. Operation of the Center required expertise. CIA had taken the lead in managing and developing this Center in the past. Dr. Kistiakowsky felt it would result in delay and loss of progress to disturb the Center at the present time. From the technical point of view, he would much prefer an expansion of the present Center to a transfer of the Center away from CIA management.

Mr. Stans raised the possibility of joint CIA/DOD management. The President said he disliked divided responsibility. He believed Defense had not shown any unhappiness with the existing Center.

While he knew how important the time element was, he believed the present Center should be kept under CIA management and expanded. The DOD should state its requirements for photographic intelligence. There should be a single center and no Service should be allowed to set up its own center. Mr. Dulles pointed out that the draft NSCID No. 8 provided that the Director of the Center would be chosen by agreement between the DCI and the Secretary of Defense.

Mr. Gray then turned to Recommendation 29 which would provide the DCI with a Coordinating Staff. The sole dissent on this recommendation was that of the Secretary of Defense who feels that the DCI should be separated from the CIA without further delay. Mr. Gray also mentioned the views of the Hull Board on this matter (bottom of Page 3 of the Briefing Note). Secretary Gates said the Defense view mentioned by Mr. Gray was the view of the Defense representative on the Joint Study Group. He (Mr. Gates) did not feel that he should comment on the organization of CIA; accordingly, he would take no strong position on this recommendation. The President believed the Defense Department should be interested in getting the best administration possible in this field and therefore should take a position. Secretary Gates said the Department of Defense had taken a position favoring the separation of the DCI from CIA. The President said he had believed for some time that the structure of our intelligence organization was faulty. He thought the Services should confine themselves to gathering combat intelligence while strategic military intelligence should be collected by an organization under J-2. He was convinced that better intelligence would be obtained by a centralized intelligence organization. Such an organization, however, needed to be streamlined.

Mr. Dulles said a great deal had been accomplished in the intelligence field over the past ten years. He believed coordination and cooperation was now better than it had ever been. He noted that no country had succeeded in achieving complete intelligence coordination, not even the U.K. and certainly not Germany under Hitler. Mr. Dulles vas compelled to dissent from the Hull Board proposals because they were illegal until the law is changed. The DCI was responsible under the law for intelligence coordination and he could not delegate that responsibility. A body floating in thin air could not be created for the purpose of intelligence coordination until the statutes were amended. He doubted that such a body could accomplish coordination even if the law were amended to permit it to try. The President said he was convinced that some streamlining of our intelligence organization was needed. The streamlining probably should have been undertaken three years ago rather than at the last minute. Mr. Gray said the recommendation of the Joint Study Group was for a Coordinating Staff under the DCI. If the Secretary of Defense did not wish to press the proposal for a complete separation of the DCI from CIA, then a first step could be taken by adopting the Joint Study Group recommendation. Mr. Dulles said he concurred in the Joint Study Group recommendation. General Lemnitzer said the JCS agreed with the Secretary of Defense; they felt a separation of the DCI from CIA was to be preferred. Mr. Dulles said the objective of the Defense Department would be accomplished to a considerable extent by adopting the Joint Study Group proposal, particularly if Defense would assign a top-level official with real authority to the Coordinating Staff. Mr. Gray said the recommendation was not intended to fix intelligence organization for all time but would be a step forward.

Mr. Gray then proposed that the Council turn back to Recommendation 31 which would establish a management group under USIB. The President wondered whether the Coordinating Staff would not have to manage. Mr. Gray referred to the complicated committee structure under USIB but said no committee was charged with management problems. The Joint Study Group felt the need for a group which would deal with management matters. The DCI had suggested that this function be performed by the Coordinating Staff called for in Recommendation 29, which had just been discussed. The President wondered whether there was a difference between intelligence coordination and management. He felt that two separate bodies might clash. Mr. Dulles pointed out that he proposed a single group, namely, the Coordinating Staff. Secretary Herter suggested that the Coordinating Staff under the DCI be charged with management problems for six months after which the matter could be reviewed.

Secretary Gates referred to a new coordinating board which would be responsible for intelligence planning and estimating. Mr. Dulles felt that Secretary Gates was confusing two things, the membership of USIB and the recommendation of the Joint Study Group for a management group. Secretary Gates said he favored a change in the membership of USIB. He believed Defense, not the Services, should be represented on USIB and that the Defense representative should have a Defense position in the same way he has a Defense position when he comes to an NSC meeting. Mr. Dulles said that as soon as the necessary intelligence reorganization took place in the Pentagon, he would concur in a reorganization of USIB but not before.

Mr. Gray asked whether the Council agreed to give the Coordinating Staff referred to in Recommendation 29 the management function. The Council, including the President, indicated that it did agree with this proposal.

The President said the job of streamlining intelligence had not yet been seriously tackled. He had received a body blow when he learned that USIB consisted of ten people. Mr. Gray asked whether the

Secretary of Defense wished to speak further on the membership of the USIB. Secretary Gates said he had recommended a change in USIB membership and he believed this change could be made at the present time. Accordingly, he had submitted proposed amendments to the NSCID's. The President asked why Defense could not effect the necessary reorganization without the blessing of the Council. Secretary Gates replied that the NSCID's had been adopted by the Council. The President said that the Council was only advisory to the President and that he (the President) as Commander-in-Chief looked to the Secretary of Defense to effect proper organization of intelligence in the Pentagon. The President added, however, that until intelligence in the Pentagon was reorganized, Defense would have to go along with the idea of changing the membership of USIB in phase with changes in Defense. Secretary Gates said he believed the changes he had proposed would force the Department of Defense to do its homework in intelligence. Mr. Dulles said if the Secretary of Defense wanted to assume the task of coordinating Army, Navy, and Air Force views on such a subject as missiles, he would be delighted. He felt, however, that such coordination would consume a great deal of the time of the Secretary of Defense. He believed he had more time than the Secretary of Defense to attempt this coordination. Secretary Gates said that USIB with Army, Navy, Air Force, DOD, and JCS representatives was a discussion board. No Defense position and no ironing out of Service positions was possible. The whole Defense position was turned over to USIB by default. The President said we were groping toward improvement in our intelligence organization. However, he wondered where the Services obtained the information which Mr. Dulles found so important. He did not believe the Services could find out how many missiles the Soviets have. Mr. Dulles said a distorted estimate would result if it were not for all the Services. For example, the Army had a great deal of experience in the amount of factory floor space required for the building for particular numbers of missiles. An acceptance of an Air Force point of view without regard to this Army experience would result in distortion. The President said he was talking about the views of the Secretary of Defense. He believed technical and tactical intelligence should be in the hands of the Services but broad strategic matters were different. He felt a better definition of the responsibility of each Service as to collection was needed, after which coordination should be less difficult. He believed military strategic intelligence should be centralized in Defense or JCS. General Lemnitzer said intelligence was different from other matters since intelligence estimates were based on a wide variety of information. He pointed out that the proposal by the Secretary of Defense would result in two Defense representatives on USIB, one from the Office of the Secretary of Defense and one from J-2. These two Defense representatives might have a difference of opinion. Moreover, the Secretary of Defense did not have an intelligence staff to help him resolve differences of view. Secretary Gates said he did a great deal of homework on NSC papers before a Council meeting. He believed it should be part of his job to spend time also in resolving intelligence differences. The President said he could not agree more. His inclination would be to put Pentagon intelligence under the JCS and let the latter send one man, not two, to USIB. Secretary Gates said his recommendation involved setting up one intelligence organization in the Pentagon. The President said that nevertheless, the present system, even it if worked creakingly at present, could not be radically changed until the necessary people were trained. The President, therefore, felt that the language in the Joint Study Group recommendations as to phasing was correct with respect to the membership of USIB. He hoped, however, that the phasing would not require eight years.

Mr. Gray turned next to another category of recommendations, six in number, on which there were differences of view among the Principals and on which the DCI recommends deferral of action. The first recommendations in this category were Nos. 1, 2 and 35 which would require a reorganization of intelligence within Defense and in field commands, with particular reference to the role of the Joint Staff and the unified commands in relation to military intelligence services. The Secretary of Defense approves these recommendations in principle but feels that Recommendation 35 should be deferred until experience is gathered in implementing Recommendations 1 and 2. The DCI objects to Recommendation 1(b)(2), which would require the JCS to coordinate intelligence views within Defense. Secretary Gates said this was a matter of internal directives within the Department of Defense and was related to the discussion just concluded. He felt the matter should be deferred.

The President said he was impressed by Recommendations 1 and 2 but felt that Recommendation 35 should be deferred. Mr. Gray then referred specifically to Recommendation 1 (b)(2). Mr. Stans said that there was no need for three military medical services, three military procurement services, or three military intelligence services. He believed a single military intelligence service should be achieved ultimately and the sooner the better. The President thought this matter would be settled by the reorganization of military intelligence which the Secretary of Defense would undertake. However, he thought intelligence direction by the JCS would have to be phased; such direction could not be accomplished until the intelligence organization in the Pentagon was changed. Secretary Gates said the amendments he had proposed to the NSCID's would permit a reorganization of intelligence in the Pentagon.

At this point Mr. Gray asked the Council to consider the amendments to the NSCID's proposed by the Deputy Secretary of Defense. Mr. Gray explained these proposed amendments.

In connection with NSCID 3, Mr. Stans noted that the Secretary of Defense proposed that Defense undertake the collection of economic information pertinent to the Department of Defense. Mr. Stans thought it would be possible to interpret this provision as including almost any type of information; accordingly, he felt the provision should be eliminated or limited. The President said that Military Attachés would inevitably collect some economic information. If an attempt were made to put intelligence in rigid compartments, some information would be lost. He was ready to admit that the primary responsibility for economic intelligence rested with State and CIA, but he believed the Military Services could not be denied the right to get any information they could obtain. Secretary Gates said his proposal merely updated the language of the existing NSCID, which permitted the three Services to collect economic intelligence. General Lemnitzer pointed out that the Military had to gather certain types of economic intelligence; for example, in order to evaluate Soviet missile capabilities, it was necessary to analyze the floor space of factories. Mr. McCone thought it would be unwise to exclude the Military from economic intelligence activities. Mr. Stans said Budget officials feared that each Military Service would attempt to collect all the economic information it was possible to collect. Mr. Gray pointed out that if the Defense proposals were adopted, Mr. Stans would need to deal only with the Secretary of Defense, rather than the three Services, in attempting to keep intelligence collection within bounds. The President said we should be content with the progress represented by the Defense amendments to NSCID 3. Mr. Stans suggested that the word "directly" be inserted in the provision under discussion so that Defense would collect "economic information directly pertinent to the Department of Defense." Mr. Gates said he would not argue over an adverb and the President approved Mr. Stans' suggestion.

In connection with NSCID 5, the President saw no reason to object to designating the Secretary of Defense as the agent with whom the DCI would negotiate coordination of espionage and clandestine counterintelligence activities in active theaters of war. He felt, however, that while the JCS should not be held responsible, the Secretary of Defense should lean on them for advice in this field.

Secretary Herter said that the Defense proposals for amendment to NSCID 6 were worded in such a way as to exclude the Department of State, the FBI, and AEC from COMINT and ELINT activities. In response to a question from the President, he indicated that State negotiated international agreements for ELINT stations, for example. Secretary Herter suggested that NSCID 6 might be amended simply by indicating that "only the Secretary of Defense shall exercise or delegate this authority within the Department of Defense." Mr. Dulles concurred in Secretary Herter's suggestion.

Mr. Gray then reverted to the two remaining Joint Study Group recommendations. He said that Recommendation 5 would have military intelligence agencies develop a capability for war-time clandestine intelligence collection, to be carried out under coordination of the DCI. The President said he could speak with the authority of a former theater commander in time of war in saying that the theater commander could not be responsible to anyone but the Joint Chiefs of Staff. Secretary Herter believed Recommendation 5 required further study. The President said that rather than providing for coordination by the DCI, the recommendation might say that the DCI would be kept completely informed. Mr. Dulles pointed out that Recommendation 5 referred to peace-time, not war-time. The President said he was inclined to agree with Recommendation 5, on the understanding that it applied to peace-time activities only. He did not wish to see developed the theory that a theater commander could be interfered with in time of war.

Mr. Gray then noted that Recommendation 18 would have the DCI focus the attention of the intelligence community on counter-intelligence and the security of overseas personnel and installations with periodic reports to USIB. Secretary Herter said this matter was under intense study at the present time. He believed it would be premature to take action on this recommendation until study and research had been completed. The President said the report referred to in Recommendation 18 could be made through channels. Secretary Herter noted that State Department officials did not wish State Department research activities in this field curtailed as a result of a directive for a joint operation. Mr. Dulles said he hoped some action would be taken on Recommendation 18. He believed coordination was important in this field. The recommendation was not meant to upset the research and study already under way. Mr. Gray suggested that the agencies concerned should make periodic reports to the agency heads.

The President said he hoped this Administration would recommend to the new Administration that the Hull Board be kept in existence. Mr. Dulles concurred. The President added that in his view, the recommendation for continuance of the Hull Board should be made to the new Administration by the DCI and the Secretary of Defense rather than by him (the President) in view of the apparent tendency of the incoming Administration to downgrade the record of the outgoing Administration. Mr. Gray said that in a conversation with his successor, Mr. McGeorge Bundy, he had formed the impression that Mr. Bundy agreed that the Hull Board should be retained. Mr. Bundy's only question about the Board seemed to be concerned with its relationship to the President. The President said a great many relationships which had been working satisfactorily for a long time were now being questioned by people new to the job.

The National Security Council:

a. Discussed the views of the Principals of the Joint Study Group regarding the Group's report, as consolidated by the Director of Central Intelligence (transmitted by the reference memorandum of January 9, 1961); and took the following actions with regard to the recommendations of the Joint Study Group:

(1) Concurred in Recommendations Nos. 3, 4, 6, 7, 8, 9, 10, 11, 12, 13, 14, 15, 17, 19, 20, 25, 26, 27, 28, 29, 32, 33, 36, 37, 38, 39, 40, 41, 42 and 43.

(2) Concurred in Recommendations Nos. 1, 2 and 30, provided that:

(a) Implementation of Recommendations Nos. 1 and 2 should take place after study by the Joint Chiefs of Staff and in a manner to be established by the Secretary of Defense.

(b) The implementation of Recommendations Nos. 1, 2 and 30 with respect to the organization and functions of the USIB should be taken in phase with the carrying out of the related internal adjustments within the intelligence components of the Department of Defense.

(3) Concurred in Recommendation No. 5, with the understanding that this recommendation did not modify the arrangements in this field under wartime conditions.

(4) Concurred in Recommendation No. 16 and approved draft NSCID No. 8 as submitted, with the provision that the National Photographic Intelligence Center (NPIC) should be under the Central Intelligence Agency; and noted the President's statement that there should be no other center duplicating the functions of the NPIC, and that the military services and other departments and agencies should state clearly to the NPIC their particular requirements.

(5) Concurred in Recommendation No. 18, subject to the deletion of the words "and assign responsibility for periodic reports to the United States Intelligence Board" and the addition of the words "and the agencies concerned should make periodic reports to their agency heads."

(6) Concurred in principle with Recommendations Nos. 21, 22 and 23, and referred them to the USIB for implementation in consultation with the Secretary of Defense and the Joint Chiefs of Staff.

(7) Concurred in Recommendation No. 24, subject to the addition of the words "except in situations with respect to which the Secretary of State and the Director of Central Intelligence may agree do not warrant such allocation of responsibility."

(8) Agreed that, in lieu of establishing the management group proposed in Recommendation No. 31, the functions recommended for that group should be performed by the coordination staff proposed in Recommendation No. 29.

(9) Concurred in Recommendation No. 34 subject to the addition of the words "or as the Joint Chiefs of Staff may direct, subject to the understanding that National Security Agency communications to service cryptologic agencies in the field are excepted from the provisions of this recommendation."

(10) Deferred action on Recommendation No. 35.

b. Discussed the recommendations of the Deputy Secretary of Defense (transmitted by the reference memorandum of January 9, 1961), and adopted the following amendments to National Security Council Intelligence Directives:

(1) *NSCID No. 1, paragraph 4-a, 3rd sentence*: Delete the words "with intelligence production responsibilities."

(2) *NSCID No. 2. paragraph 3*: Delete this paragraph and substitute the following:

"3. The Department of Defense shall have primary responsibility for, and shall perform as a service of common concern, the collection of military intelligence information. Owing to the importance of scientific and technical intelligence to the Department of Defense and the military services, this collection responsibility shall include scientific and technical, as well as economic, information directly pertinent to Department of Defense missions."

(3) *NSCID No. 3, subparagraph 7-b*: Delete this subparagraph and substitute the following:

"b. The Department of Defense shall produce military intelligence. This production shall include scientific, technical and economic intelligence directly pertinent to the missions of the various components of the Department of Defense."

(4) *NSCID No. 5, subparagraphs 8-a, -b and -c*: Substitute the words "Secretary of Defense" for the words "Joint Chiefs of Staff".

(5) *NSCID No. 6, paragraph 2*: Add the following words: "except that only the Secretary of Defense shall exercise or delegate this authority within the Department of Defense."

c. Noted the President's conviction that further streamlining of the entire foreign intelligence organization still needs to be accomplished.

Note: The action in a above, as approved by the President, subsequently transmitted to the Director of Central Intelligence, the Secretary of State and the Secretary of Defense for appropriate implementation.

The amendments in b above, as approved by the President, subsequently incorporated in revised NSCID's.

85.   Briefing Paper by A. Russell Ash of the National Security
        Council Staff[1]

Washington, January 13, 1961.

BRIEF FOR DISCUSSION WITH THE PRESIDENT

SUBJECT

  Sixth Report to the President by the President's Board of Consultants on Foreign
  Intelligence Activities dated May 24, 1960 (Recommendation on "Organization and
  Management of CIA's Clandestine Services")

1. In memorandum of December 16, 1960, Mr. Gordon Gray requested the DCI to furnish a self-contained, current compilation of actions which have been taken to implement two Hull Board recommendations made in 1958 and 1960 (and subsequently approved by the President) which called for improved organization and management of CIA's Clandestine Services. The DCI's response is set forth in his memorandum dated 1/9/61 (attached).[2]

2. *The first recommendation* was made in a report of the Hull Board dated October 30, 1958. The Board noted that the CIA's Plans Group was responsible for supervising, administering and reviewing the clandestine activities of CIA, including covert foreign intelligence activities and Cold War operations—and the Board questioned whether the Plans Group was capable of making objective appraisals of its own intelligence information and its own operations, when it is involved in Cold War activities which are the subject of its own reports. The Hull Board was concerned about this not only because of possible impacts on the programs of the CIA, but because of the influences which might be brought to bear on foreign policy determinations which, in large measure, may be based on CIA reporting. Accordingly, the Board proposed a review of the CIA's Plans Group and that consideration be given to placing elsewhere in CIA the following responsibilities of the Plans Group: (1) the responsibility for reporting on and evaluating Political, Psychological and Para-Military operations, and (2) the responsibility for the formulation of intelligence estimates and recommendations upon which the plans for such operations are based.

3. *In the second recommendation,* made on 5/24/60, the Board noted that some changes had been made toward improving the organization and management of CIA's Clandestine Services, but the Board felt that a way could be found to organize them along more simplified and effi-

---

[1] Source: Eisenhower Library, Records of the Special Assistant for National Security Affairs. Secret.

[2] Document 83.

cient lines so as to avoid unnecessary duplication of effort and to achieve increased effectiveness.

4. *The DCI's Response*: In his report dated 1/9/61, the DCI refers to corrective actions and indicates reasons why the responsibilities of the Plans Group are not placed elsewhere in CIA as suggested by the Board. Highlights of the DCI's report include the following:

(1) The Hull Board may have felt that the Plans Group possessed a greater degree of autonomy and independence than actually existed.

(2) Although the Deputy DCI for Plans may take action for the DCI, operations under NSC 5412 are conducted only after the necessary policy guidance has been obtained from the 5412 Committee.

(3) Before Cold War (5412) activities are initiated, all available intelligence, including National Intelligence Estimates produced by the Intelligence Community, are taken into account—and while it is true that in covert operations a major source of information on the accomplishments of a project may be clandestine, CIA analyzes *all* available information from all sources to guard against subjectivity and self-serving reports.

(4) In 1959 the Deputy DCI for Plans reviewed the mission and organization of the Clandestine Services, in concert with a review by the Inspector General of CIA, and the DCI initiated a Program for Greater Efficiency within CIA as a whole.

(5) A number of organizational changes were made with respect to the Clandestine Services, including the appointment of a new Assistant Deputy DCI for Plans; an Operational Services grouping was created to combine and centralize certain elements.

(6) The Inspector General of CIA was made solely responsible for the comprehensive review of the activities and operations of Clandestine Services, reporting directly to the DCI.

(7) Operational Programs go to a Project Review Committee which reports directly to the DCI, and Mission Directives set forth objectives for the field stations.

(8) Action has been or is being taken with regard to such aspects of the Clandestine Services as coordination of activities abroad, delegation of more authority to the field, more emphasis on political action in underdeveloped areas, increased records mechanization, etc.

(9) The DCI has reaffirmed that continuing studies by the Deputy DCI for Plans of the organization, methods and procedures of the Clandestine Services be directed toward elimination of unnecessary duplication and the achievement of increased effectiveness—objectives which were set forth in the Hull Board's recommendations. As a result, CIA has made such organizational changes as the establishment of a Division to direct and coordinate sensitive air operations, and the pending revision of functional statements of responsibilities of the Special Staffs.

(10) Other organizational steps have been taken to promote efficiency, as detailed in the DCI's report.

(11) As previously indicated, the DCI feels that steps have been taken to meet the Hull Board's concern over the problem of insuring a valid and unbiased intelligence base for operational planning purposes in the Clandestine Services. The DCI points to procedures calling for guidance from the Office of National Estimates throughout the planning cycle, and the use of current NIE's in deriving contingencies against which clandestine activities are to be directed. The DCI refers to further independent checks on Psychological, Political and Para-Military projects in CIA, including review by components of CIA as a whole. The DCI also refers to the fact that such projects which have political import and involve substantial expenditures receive thorough review by State and by the 5412 Group before final approval by the DCI.

(12) Finally, the DCI concurs in the belief of the Deputy DCI for Plans that changes made in the past two years in the organization and procedures of the Clandestine Services have corrected deficiencies, and that the situation is now satisfactory. The DCI recognizes that future modifications may be desirable, and he asserts that the Deputy DCI for Plans will continue to study the organization and procedures of the Clandestine Services and take such action as is required to contribute toward greater efficiency.

5. *Observation*: The organizational changes and procedures which have been made, or are contemplated, in CIA's Clandestine Services should continue to be periodically reassessed to insure that the objectives of the two Hull Board recommendations are being met in this critical area of Foreign Intelligence activities. Whether or not there is to be a continuation of the kind of scrutiny which has heretofore been afforded these matters by the President's Board of Consultants on Foreign Intelligence Activities, it would seem desirable that the DCI be asked by the President at this time to maintain a continuing review of CIA's Clandestine Services.

6. Accordingly, it is recommended that the President be briefed on the highlights of the DCI's memorandum dated 1/9/61, and that the President approve an action along the following lines:

The President (a) noted the memorandum dated January 9, 1961 to the Special Assistant to the President for National Security Affairs from the Director of Central Intelligence, on the status of implementation of recommendations made by the President's Board of Consultants on Foreign Intelligence Activities on October 30, 1958, and May 24, 1960, concerning the CIA's Plans Group and the organization and management of CIA's Clandestine Services, and (b) requested that the Director of Central Intelligence continue to review the action being taken with a view to meeting the objectives of the recommendations, and as the basis for the submission of a further progress report at an appropriate time.

86.   Memorandum of Meeting With President Eisenhower[1]

Washington, January 18, 1961, 2:40 p.m.

Mr. Allen W. Dulles and General Goodpaster were present for Item 1.

1. I indicated to the President that the purpose of the meeting was to discuss precisely what he felt he required in the way of records with respect to 5412 actions taken during his Administration. Mr. Dulles then explained to the President the status of the records which has varied from time to time during the Administration. After some discussion, the President gave Mr. Dulles instructions which Mr. Dulles indicated were clear and with which he would comply.

Mr. Dulles reported to the President that Admiral Jerauld Wright had joined the CIA Board of Estimates. At this point Mr. Dulles and General Goodpaster withdrew.

2. I took up with the President three Hull Board Reports. The first was the Sixth Report to the President by the President's Board of Consultants on Foreign Intelligence Activities dated May 24, 1960[2] (Recommendation on "Status of CIA Station Chiefs in [*less than 1 line of source text not declassified*]"). I reported to the President that I had monitored negotiations between Dulles and Mr. Loy Henderson over a period of time on this subject. The President wondered why CIA people in the field wished to get more visibility through more status. I pointed out to the President that this recommendation involved station chiefs and that there were many human and personal relationships involved. I recommended to the President that on his behalf I would request the Department of State and the Director of CIA to continue their joint efforts in connection with the subject. He agreed. (A briefing note is attached.)[3]

3. Next was the Sixth Report to the President by the President's Board of Consultants on Foreign Intelligence Activities dated May 24, 1960 (Recommendation on "Organization and Management of CIA's Clandestine Services"). I reminded the President that many times he had addressed himself to this general problem. He said that he had long since concurred in principle with the various recommendations of the Hull Board on this subject. However, as long as Mr. Dulles was the

---

[1] Source: Eisenhower Library, Records of the Special Assistant for National Security Affairs, Memoranda of Meetings with the President, January 1961. Secret. Drafted by Gray on January 19.

[2] Not printed.

[3] Dated January 17; not attached. A copy is in the Eisenhower Library, White House Office Files, Project Clean Up, Meetings with the President.

DCI he had to hold him responsible and would not order him to take organizational steps which the DCI resisted. The President approved my recommendation that the record show that the President noted the memorandum and requested that the DCI continue to review the action being taken with a view to meeting the objectives of the recommendations and as the basis for submission of a further progress report at an appropriate time (briefing note attached).[4]

4. Next was the Seventh Report to the President by the President's Board of Consultants on Foreign Intelligence Activities dated October 4, 1960 (Recommendation on "Duplication (Publications)"). I conveyed to the President the substance of the attached briefing note and recommended that the action show that he had noted the memorandum and requested that the DCI (a) continue to follow the progress made by the member agencies of the intelligence community in implementing the recommendation and (b) submit a report thereon as of June 1.[5]

5. I then took up with the President the Record of Actions of the NSC meeting of 12 January.[6] As to paragraph 4 a (1) in the draft record it seemed necessary to add a new 4 a (2) on the basis of various comments from the agencies concerned. I pointed out to him that the AEC questioned whether any decision was made on Recommendation #30. Upon examining Recommendation #30 the President recalled that he had clearly decided that it should be approved inasmuch as it called for changes in the USIB in phase with reorganization actions taken in Defense. Next I pointed out that Defense and JCS wanted the record to show that implementation of Recommendations #1 and 2 should take place after study by the JCS and in a manner to be established by the Secretary of Defense. The President approved this qualification. I then pointed out to the President that the DCI wished to have the records show that the decision to implement Recommendations No. 1, 2, and 30 with respect to the organization and functions of the USIB should not be taken prior to the carrying out of the related internal adjustments within the Department of Defense. The President felt that he would not wish to delay decision on this matter and thought the record should show that these recommendations with respect to the organization and functions of the USIB should be taken in phase with the carrying out of the related internal adjustments.

With respect to paragraph 4 a (8) I indicated to the President that Defense and JCS would like to provide that the carrying out of Recommendation #29—that is to say, establishing a coordinating staff

[4] Document 85.

[5] The Seventh Report is not printed. Ash's January 6 briefing paper on this recommendation is in the Eisenhower Library, Records of the Special Assistant for National Security Affairs.

[6] See Document 84.

under the DCI—would only be on the basis of a six months' trial after which the matter would be reconsidered. I reported to the President that the CIA objected on the ground that with this provision the staff would never have a chance to demonstrate its worth. The President agreed that approval of the recommendation should not be on a six months' trial.

As to paragraph 5 b (2) of the draft record of actions, I pointed out to him that despite the confusing brackets, OCDM and HHFA were in agreement as to how the paragraph should be worded and he authorized me to record it in accordance with the agreement. I also pointed out to him that in paragraph 5 b (4), OCDM and Budget had reached agreement and I would make the record reflect that agreement.

As to paragraph 5 c, I pointed out that the BOB preferred language noting the President's statement that the Congress should be asked to consider the desirability of requiring that all new housing construction include fall-out shelters. I said to the President that I had a question about the constitutionality of such legislation and recommended that he approve language which would note the President's statement that legislation should be sought as appropriate to support the principle that all new housing include fall-out shelters. I pointed out that this would include State as well as federal legislation and could be applicable to public and also private housing. The President approved this language.

6. I then took up various NSC matters which had been dealt with by other members of the Council by vote slip in accordance with the attached briefing note. The President approved each of the 12 items, No. 11 being subject to the concurrence of the Secretary of State, which has not yet been obtained.

Gordon Gray[7]
Special Assistant to the President

---

[7] Printed from a copy that bears this typed signature.

---

87. Editorial Note

Executive Order 10938, May 4, 1961, established the President's Foreign Intelligence Advisory Board (PFIAB) in the wake of the failed Bay of Pigs invasion of Cuba and increased attention to the role and activities of the intelligence community. The proposed order was prepared in the Bureau of the Budget from a draft submitted by the Special

Assistant to the President for National Security Affairs and was forwarded to President Kennedy by Attorney General Robert Kennedy on April 27. A May 4 White House press release announced the issuance of the new executive order and listed the members of the President's Foreign Intelligence Advisory Board as follows: Chairman Dr. James R. Killian, Jr., of the Massachusetts Institute of Technology; Dr. William O. Baker, Vice President of Research of Bell Laboratories; Lieutenant General (ret.) James H. Doolittle; Dr. William L. Langer, professor of history at Harvard University; former Under Secretary of State Robert D. Murphy; and General Maxwell D. Taylor (ret.). J. Patrick Coyne, Executive Secretary of the President's Board of Consultants on Foreign Intelligence Activities, PFIAB's predecessor, continued to serve as Executive Secretary. Documentation is in the Kennedy Library, White House Central Subject Files, FG 732 (Executive), President's Foreign Intelligence Advisory Board, Box 205.

The text of Executive Order 10938 signed by President Kennedy reads as follows:

"By virtue of the authority vested in me as President of the United States, it is ordered as follows:

"Section 1. There is hereby established the President's Foreign Intelligence Advisory Board. The function of the Board shall be to advise the President with respect to the objectives and conduct of the foreign intelligence and related activities of the United States which are required in the interests of foreign policy and national defense and security.

"Sec. 2. In the performance of its advisory duties, the Board shall conduct a continuing review and assessment of all functions of the Central Intelligence Agency, and of other executive departments and agencies having such or similar responsibilities in the foreign-intelligence and related fields, and shall report thereon to the President each six months or more frequently as deemed appropriate. The Director of Central Intelligence and the heads of other departments and agencies concerned shall make available to the Board any information with respect to foreign intelligence matters which the Board may require for the purpose of carrying out its responsibilities to the President. The information so supplied to the Board shall be afforded requisite security protection as prescribed by the provisions of applicable laws and regulations.

"Sec. 3. Members of the Board shall be appointed from among qualified persons outside the Government and shall receive such compensation and allowances, consonant with law, as may be prescribed hereafter. Such compensation and allowances and any other expenses arising in connection with the work of the Board shall be paid from the appropriation appearing under the heading 'Special Projects' in title I of the General Government Matters Appropriation Act, 1961, 74 Stat. 473, and, to the extent permitted by law, from any corresponding appropriation which may be made for subsequent years. Such payments shall be made without regard to the provisions of section 3681 of the Revised Statutes and section 9 of the act of March 4, 1909, 35 Stat. 1027 (31 U.S.C. 672 and 673).

"Sec. 4. Executive Order No. 10656 of February 6, 1956, is hereby revoked." (26 *Federal Register* 3951)

According to Clark Clifford, who was one of the original members of PFIAB and its Chairman from April 1963 until the beginning of 1968, PFIAB met for the first time on May 15, 1961, under Killian's chairmanship. Thereafter PFIAB met regularly during President Kennedy's administration, holding 25 meetings between May and November 1961 and presenting to the President 170 formal recommendations, of which the President approved 125, rejected 2, and deferred action on the remainder. Clifford recalled that 85 of the 125 approved recommendations were implemented. President Kennedy met at length with the PFIAB on at least 12 occasions. Clifford's account of his service on PFIAB under President Kennedy emphasizes the President's objective of seeking a Board membership of diverse backgrounds and expertise. Clifford recalled that for him the two most valuable members of PFIAB were scientists Dr. Edwin Land, inventor of the Polaroid Land camera, and Dr. William Baker, who brought to the PFIAB the most recent scientific knowledge and discoveries bearing on the technical acquisition of intelligence information. (*Counsel to the President: A Memoir*, New York: Random House, 1991, pages 350 ff.)

The editors of this volume researched the historical records of PFIAB for the purpose of documenting the Board's main lines of activity and its major recommendations to the President. PFIAB subsequently suspended the research access for Department of State historians for security reasons, and at PFIAB's request the Department's Office of the Historian returned to PFIAB all copies of documents obtained from PFIAB files, before declassification of any of those records was approved by PFIAB.

Documentation on the President's Board of Consultants on Foreign Intelligence Activities established by President Eisenhower's Executive Order No. 10656, February 6, 1956, is scheduled for publication in a volume of the *Foreign Relations* series documenting the development of the intelligence community beginning in 1950 through 1955.

88.   Telegram From Director of Central Intelligence Dulles to All
        Chiefs of Station[1]

Washington, August 10, 1961.

DIR 05454. Rybat.

1. President Kennedy's letter to Ambassadors of 29 May 1961,[2] affirms their responsibility "to oversee and coordinate" all programs or activities of the United States in their particular areas, whether of the diplomatic mission or of other US agencies. Further, he made clear he expects Ambassadors to be fully informed of these programs or activities.

2. As you are aware you have always carried the responsibility for reviewing with the Ambassador covert action matters growing out of our responsibilities under the 5412 directive of the National Security Council. Furthermore, most of you have arrived at relationships with Ambassadors in the past which have made you conscious of the need to keep the Ambassador informed so that he may judge the political risks inherent in any activity, whether deriving from "5412" or developed in pursuit of our statutory responsibility in the field of espionage and clandestine counterintelligence. However, the feeling had developed over the past few years within diplomatic missions around the world that Ambassadors are not sufficiently well informed properly to protect them in their responsibility as the principal United States officers in their respective areas who bear the brunt of any covert or clandestine activity that inadvertently becomes known to and represents a serious affront to the local government.

3. Where espionage and clandestine counterintelligence are concerned we have always been aware of the possible political risks inherent in our activities. This is the reason for the language of NSCID 5, paragraph 6, which states Ambassadors will be kept "appropriately informed."[3] However, it is clear today that many Chiefs of Mission feel that our officers' interpretation of this phrase has not produced sufficient information.

4. Therefore, you will take steps to insure that the Ambassador is informed of your espionage and clandestine counterintelligence programs in addition to your covert action projects. With relation to these operations, he should be made sufficiently aware of them so that, in his

---

[1] Source: Central Intelligence Agency, DCI (Dulles) Files, Dispatch and Book Dispatch, 1963, Box 6, Folder 11. Top Secret. Drafted by W. Lloyd George of the Deputy Directorate of Plans, Central Intelligence Agency.

[2] See footnote 2, Document 30.

[3] National Security Council Intelligence Directive No. 5/2, September 15, 1958. See footnote 5, Document 84.

capacity as principal officer responsible for the United States position in the country to which he is accredited, he is enabled to make an informed judgment as to the political risks involved.

5. In advising him of your various programs, you should pay particular attention to clarifying in his mind their general nature, scope, and purpose. Review with him, for example, the categories of covert action such as psychological warfare, black and gray propaganda, political action and economic action in pursuit of approved 5412 programs. Present your clandestine intelligence activities in categories such as scientific, political, technical, economic and military information objectives carried on against approved requirements, through working relationships with local intelligence and security services and through independent activities. Review your clandestine counterintelligence objectives to acquire knowledge of all other intelligence organizations and membership, to manipulate some members of these to a U.S. advantage, to obtain information by counterintelligence activities, as well as espionage, about all Communist Parties and to counter their objectives through local services and independent activities, and to develop higher capability through training the so-called friendly services.

6. In many of your activities there are involved sensitive source identities and sensitive techniques, which it is desired that you safeguard. The Ambassador at times will feel he needs to know these and, in some instances, has a right to know. Judgment with respect to these, however, may have to be made ultimately in Washington. If you are in doubt about passing these ultimate details, the matter should be referred to Washington where decision will be made after consultation between the Director of Central Intelligence and Chief ODACID as to whether you should give the Ambassador these details.

7. There will be occasions when an objectively discussed problem will result in an honest difference of opinion between you and your Ambassador regarding whether an operation should be carried on. President Kennedy's letter makes clear that you have your own channels of communication and may use them to refer your problem to higher levels here. While the Ambassador also has his own channels to Washington, he will normally expect you to convey his views on such matters via your channels.

8. You should consider this instruction to be of interim nature, pending review of the 1957 agreement between this Headquarters and ODACID (STACIA).[4]

9. ODACID has seen and concurs with this message and is requesting all its chiefs of missions and certain principal officers to confer with you regarding it. They may, of course, see it.

---

[4] Not found.

89.   Letter From the Deputy Secretary of Defense (Gilpatric) to
       President Kennedy[1]

Washington, August 21, 1961.

Dear Mr. President:

To determine how the Department of Defense could best implement the approved recommendations of the Joint Study Group Report
on Foreign Intelligence Activities of the United States Government
applicable to the Department, I initiated an intensive analysis of the
organization and management of Defense intelligence activities last
January. This analyis is continuing in specialized areas of Defense intelligence activities with participation by all major components of the
Department, and where appropriate, by other organizations in the
national intelligence community.

The major product of the first six months of study has been the creation of the Defense Intelligence Agency, or DIA, which will be activated on October 1, 1961, and whose first Director, Lieutenant General
Joseph F. Carroll, USAF, was appointed on August 12, 1961.[2]

Fundamental to the decision to establish this new Defense Agency
was the conclusion that only through the establishment of such an organization could the majority of the Joint Study Group recommendations
applicable to the Department be most effectively achieved.
Furthermore, we concluded that only through a DIA would the over-all
capacity of the Department of Defense to collect, produce, and disseminate military intelligence information be greatly strengthened and
greater unity of effort achieved among all components of the
Department in the development of military intelligence information.

In determining the specific intelligence functions which will be
directly controlled by DIA, we were guided by the Joint Study Group

---

[1]   Source: Kennedy Library, National Security Files, Departments and Agencies
Series, Department of Defense, Defense Intelligence Agency, 1961. Top Secret. A copy
was sent to Bundy.

[2]   The Defense Intelligence Agency (DIA) was established as an agency of the
Department of Defense by DOD Directive 5105.21, August 1, under provisions of the
National Security Act of 1947, as amended, to operate under the direction, authority, and
control of the Secretary of Defense. The chain of command ran from the Secretary of
Defense, through the Joint Chiefs of Staff to the Director. Under its Director, the Defense
Intelligence Agency was responsible for: (a) The organization, direction, management,
and control of all Department of Defense intelligence resources assigned to or included
within the DIA; (b) Review and coordination of those Department of Defense intelligence
functions retained by or assigned to the military departments; (c) Supervision of the execution of all approved plans, programs, policies, and procedures for intelligence functions
not assigned to DIA; (d) Obtaining the maximum economy and efficiency in the allocation and management of Department of Defense intelligence resources. A copy of
Department of Defense Directive 5105.21, August 1, 1961, is ibid.

recommendations. Similarly, the Joint Study Group recommendations were carefully considered in ascertaining what intelligence functions should be retained in the military departments but made subject to DIA's supervision (as distinguished from DIA's direct control).

The Defense Intelligence Agency will also achieve a more efficient allocation and management of Defense intelligence resources as it becomes operational. The assumption of specific intelligence functions by DIA, however, will be on a graduated basis with each step carefully planned and executed so as not to degrade any existing Defense intelligence capability. It probably will take at least two years for the DIA to become fully operational.

One of the principal recommendations of the Joint Study Group was that the intelligence functions of the Department be brought into consonance with the Defense Reorganization Act of 1958. The integration of Defense intelligence activities under DIA will, we belive, obtain this objective. Through the establishment of DIA the Department of Defense will be able to provide better intelligence support not only to you but also to the national intelligence community as a whole.

With the exception of those Joint Study Group recommendations applicable to the activities of the National Security Agency, I have specifically charged General Carroll with the expeditious implementation of all Joint Study Group recommendations falling within the functional responsibilities of his new Agency and with monitoring all other recommendations applicable to the Department. Furthermore, I have directed General Carroll to develop all activation plans necessary for the establishment of DIA.

A far reaching reorganization of the National Security Agency (NSA) was approved by me and is now being put into effect. This will facilitate accomplishment of the Joint Study Group recommendations relating to that Agency, in particular those which strengthen the control of the Director, NSA, over Defense ELINT and cryptologic resources. Detailed steps to implement these recommendations are now being examined by the Director, NSA.

Implementation of those Joint Study Group recommendations jointly applicable to the Department of Defense and to other organizations in the national intelligence community must await completion of studies now under way, and, in some cases, the activation of DIA.

Finally, for certain specific intelligence problems incident not only to the establishment of DIA but also to full implementation of all Joint Study Group recommendations applicable to the Department, I have appointed one of my civilian staff advisors to prepare within 90 days recommendations thereon and to monitor for me, on a continuing basis, the establishment of DIA.

For your information, I am enclosing three attachments to this report. The first is the Department of Defense Directive establishing DIA, and the second and third are memoranda detailing procedures and assigning responsibilities for implementing the reorganization of Defense intelligence activities.[3]

As the Defense Intelligence Agency becomes operational, I shall keep the Director of Central Intelligence and your Foreign Intelligence Advisory Board continually abreast of the status of implementation of DIA and of all approved Joint Study Group recommendations.

Sincerely,

Roswell Gilpatric[4]

---

[3] Not attached. Regarding the first attachment, see footnote 2 above. The other attachments were not found.

[4] Printed from a copy that bears this stamped signature and an indication that Gilpatric signed the original.

---

90.   **Letter From the Deputy Secretary of Defense (Gilpatric) to Director of Central Intelligence Dulles**[1]

Washington, September 6, 1961.

RE

Management of the National Reconnaissance Program

Dear Mr. Dulles:

This letter confirms our agreement with respect to the setting up of a National Reconnaissance Program (NRP), and the arrangements for dealing both with the management and operation of this program and the handling of the intelligence product of the program on a covert basis.

1. The NRP will consist of all satellite and overflight reconnaissance projects whether overt or covert. It will include all photographic projects for intelligence, geodesy and mapping purposes, and electronic signal collection projects for electronic signal intelligence and communications intelligence resulting therefrom.

---

[1] Source: National Reconnaissance Office, P&A/PR Library/104–1/DOP. Top Secret; Special Handling. An attached chart entitled "Single Management for National Reconnaissance Program" is not printed.

186 Foreign Relations, 1961–1963, Volume XXV

2. There will be established on a covert basis a National Reconnaissance Office to manage this program. This office will be under the direction of the Under Secretary of the Air Force and the Deputy Director (Plans) of the Central Intelligence Agency acting jointly. It will include a small special staff whose personnel will be drawn from the Department of Defense and the Central Intelligence Agency. This office will have direct control over all elements of the total program.

3. Decisions of the National Reconnaissance Office will be implemented and its management of the National Reconnaissance Program made effective: within the Department of Defense, by the exercise of the authority delegated to the Under Secretary of the Air Force; within the Central Intelligence Agency, by the Deputy Director (Plans) in the performance of his presently assigned duties. The Under Secretary of the Air Force will be designated Special Assistant for Reconnaissance to the Secretary of Defense and delegated full authority by me in this area.

4. Within the Department of Defense, the Department of the Air Force will be the operational agency for management and conduct of the NRP, and will conduct this program through use of streamlined special management procedures involving direct control from the office of the Secretary of the Air Force to Reconnaissance System Project Directors in the field, without intervening reviews or approvals. The management and conduct of individual projects or elements thereof requiring special covert arrangements may be assigned to the Central Intelligence Agency as the operational agency.

5. A Technical Advisory Group for the National Reconnaissance Office will be established.

6. A uniform security control system will be established for the total program by the National Reconnaissance Office. Products from the various programs will be available to all users as designated by the United States Intelligence Board.

7. The National Reconnaissance Office will be directly responsive to, and only to, the photographic and electronic signal collection requirements and priorities as established by the United States Intelligence Board.

8. The National Reconnaissance Office will develop suitable cover plans and public information plans, in conjunction with the Assistant Secretary of Defense, Public Affairs, to reduce potential political vulnerability of these programs. In regard to satellite systems, it will be necessary to apply the revised public information policy to other nonsensitive satellite projects in order to insure maximum protection.

9. The Directors of the National Reconnaissance Office will establish detailed working procedures to insure that the particular talents, experience and capabilities within the Department of Defense and the

Central Intelligence Agency are fully and most effectively utilized in this program.

10. Management control of the field operations of various elements of the program will be exercised directly, in the case of the Department of Defense, from the Under Secretary of the Air Force to the designated project officers for each program and, in the case of the Central Intelligence Agency, from the Deputy Director (Plans) to appropriate elements of the Central Intelligence Agency. Major program elements and operations of the National Reconnaissance Office will be reviewed on a regular basis and as special circumstances require by the Special Group under NSC 5412.

If the foregoing is in accord with your understanding of our agreement, I would appreciate it if you would kindly sign and return the enclosed copy of this letter.

Roswell L. Gilpatric

CONCUR:

C.P. Cabell, General, USAF[2]
Acting Director
Central Intelligence Agency

---

[2] Printed from a copy that bears these typed signatures and an indication that both Gilpatric and Cabell signed the original. Despite Cabell's concurrence, the letter did not address differing objectives and fundamental disagreements between CIA and the Air Force over the entire satellite reconnaissance program. In particular, the Air Force did not want to relinquish control over what it regarded as one of its primary missions. On July 24 Under Secretary of the Air Force Joseph V. Charyk had sent a memorandum to Secretary of Defense McNamara, which forwarded drafts of two CIA–Defense memoranda of understanding with differing solutions to the problem of management of the National Reconnaissance Program. Solution B, which was prepared by Deputy Secretary of Defense Vance, placed the entire responsibility for the program in the Department of Defense. (National Reconnaissance Office, NRO Office of Policy Files) The memorandum and its attachments are available on the Internet, National Security Archive (www.gwu.edu/~nsarchiv), Electronic Briefing Book No. 35, "The NRO Declassified," Documents 1–4. For a summary of this issue, see Gerald K. Haines, *NRO: The National Reconnaissance Office, Its Origins, Creation, and Early Years* (Washington, National Reconnaissance Office, 1997), pp. 19–22. Although the letter of September 6 laid the groundwork for the National Reconnaissance Program Agreement signed by McCone and Gilpatric on May 2, 1962 (ibid., pp. 21–22), the NSC 5412/2 Group and the 303 Committee recommended against a co-directorship concept, and the agreement never went into effect. Charyk was named the first Director of the National Reconnaissance Office in September 1961, serving until March 1963. Additional documentation on this issue is scheduled for publication in *Foreign Relations, 1964–1968*, volumes X and XXXIII.

91. Memorandum From the President's Special Assistant for National Security Affairs (Bundy) to President Kennedy[1]

Washington, September 28, 1961.

SUBJECT

Washington News

1. The McCone appointment is the big news here.[2] I, for one, under-estimated the strength of the opposition in the second and third levels of CIA and State. It appears that most of the people involved in intelligence estimates on atomic energy matters thought McCone was highly prejudiced. He also had a reputation, in these circles, as an "operator" whose loyalty to Administration policy was doubtful. So there is a significant problem in working out a pattern of strong cooperation and support for him.

Less important in the long run, but more urgent at the moment, is the unrest in the President's Board of Consultants on Foreign Intelligence.[3] Killian has made noises about resigning, and indicates that he thinks one or two other members of the Board may also withdraw. In part this is because they feel they were not consulted, but more deeply it arises from the fact that several of them—Killian, Gray, and Baker—have had sharp disagreements with McCone in the past. General Taylor has talked to Bobby about this and probably is trying to calm Killian down. I am planning to have a talk with Allen Dulles about it with the same purpose in mind, and I think I can also do something with Baker and the scientific community generally. I have also talked to Joe Alsop, and I think we will got a helpful column from him, aimed in part at this same problem. He thinks it is the best possible appointment and says he will try to say so in terms calculated to encourage sensible scientists and bureaucrats. (I have some doubt whether he will succeed—Joe's feeling is that anyone who is against McCone is a proven follower of twaddley, and I doubt his ability to be gentle with people whom he views in this light—unfortunately his diagnosis is wrong, and some very good men are disquieted.)

[Here follow paragraphs 2–6 concerning other subjects. Paragraph 2 deals with the defense budget. Paragraph 3, concerning foreign aid legislation, is printed as Document 75; paragraph 4, concerning Chester

---

[1] Source: Kennedy Library, National Security Files, Bundy Memoranda to the President, 8/22/61–9/30/61. Secret.

[2] President Kennedy appointed John A. McCone to the position of Director of Central Intelligence on September 27.

[3] The former President's Board of Consultants for Foreign Intelligence Activities was replaced on May 4 by the President's Foreign Intelligence Advisory Board; see Document 87.

Bowles, is printed as Document 43. Paragraphs 5 and 6 deal with Syria
and Berlin, respectively.]

McG. B.[4]

---

[4] Printed from a copy that bears these typed initials.

---

92. Paper Prepared in the Department of Defense[1]

Washington, undated.

PLAN FOR THE ACTIVATION OF THE DEFENSE
INTELLIGENCE AGENCY

I. General

To accomplish the objectives for the Defense Intelligence Agency
(DIA) as specified by the Secretary of Defense, this plan provides for the
initiation of action in all areas which are clearly the responsibility of the
Director, DIA. The plan is aimed at achieving:

a. The full integration of intelligence resources and functions
assigned to the control of the Director, DIA, on a graduated basis;

b. Immediate assumption of planning, coordinating and management responsibilities of all Department of Defense intelligence activities
within the purview of the Director, DIA, to achieve maximum economy
and efficiency.

Full recognition is given to the necessity to avoid disruption or
degradation of these vital intelligence efforts.

In order to preserve the continuity of operations throughout the
consolidation process, the plan provides for the taking over and utilization of existing facilities, functions and resources of an individual military department and/or the Joint Staff, wherever feasible. Following
this, related activities, resources and functions of the other departments
and the Joint Staff are integrated into these facilities under the operational control of the Director, DIA. Initially, this will result in some

---

[1] Source: Kennedy Library, National Security Files, Departments and Agencies
Series, Department of Defense, Defense Intelligence Agency, 1961. Secret. The paper is
undated, but a typed notation on the cover page indicates that the plan was approved by
the Secretary of Defense on September 29. Annexes A through G are not printed.

imbalances in Service representation within DIA in each facility so utilized. This is considered necessary in the interests of continuity. However, the governing policy will be to achieve to the highest practicable degree, an optimum balance of personnel representation from the three military departments. This will be accomplished in accordance with DIA personnel policies aimed at the maintenance of the highest possible quality and security criteria.

As the DIA assumes full operational stature, the Director, DIA, will absorb many of the intelligence responsibilities now exercised by the intelligence chiefs of the military Services, as well as the responsibilities for substantive intelligence matters now exercised by the J-2, Joint Staff. Thus, the Director, DIA, will become the principal staff advisor to the Joint Chiefs of Staff for substantive intelligence matters, and, acting through the Joint Chiefs of Staff, the principal staff assistant to the Secretary of Defense for both substantive intelligence and managerial matters within his areas of assigned responsibility.

The DIA will be a balanced organization designed to support the major echelons of the military operational chain-of-command, the military departments, non-DOD agencies and international treaty organizations, in peace and war, without requiring major organizational readjustments after the onset of hostilities.

Coordination of all intelligence activities and responsibilities remaining with the military departments will be effected by the Director, DIA, supported by the operating elements of the DIA in their respective areas of responsibility, and by the headquarters staff. This arrangement will ensure the efficient allocation of intelligence resources and the effective management of all DOD intelligence efforts. The Military Intelligence Board (Annex A) will be established to advise and assist the Director, DIA, in the exercise of his responsibilities.

II. Organizational Stucture

A. Operations (Annex B)

The DIA will arrive at a fully operational status through an evolutionary process. The plan provides for the rapid strengthening of DOD capabilities in the fields of collection, production and dissemination through the establishment of:

1. *A Directorate for Acquisition (Annex C)*

This Directorate, which will be charged with DIA functions and responsibilities in the fields of intelligence requirements and collection will be further sub-divided as follows:

a. *The DIA Requirements Office* which will establish the DOD Central Requirements Registry. This Office will also be charged with the examination and validation of all DOD intelligence requirements, the assignment of collection priorities, the designation of collection resources, and the restatement of requirements where necessary to ensure their responsiveness to the needs of all consumers of military intelligence.

b. *The DIA Collection Management Office* which will maintain a complete and current inventory of all collection resources to include their capabilities, limitations, equipments and operations. This Office will levy validated requirements on appropriate collection agencies and resources, monitor collection responses thereto, and evaluate collection efforts to determine reliability, efficiency and cost factors involved. In addition this Office will stimulate intelligence collection effort through creative planning and the exploitation of scientific and technological developments in their application to intelligence collection activities.

2. *A Directorate for Processing* which will be charged with the principal substantive intelligence functions and responsibilities of the DIA, and which will directly control and coordinate the production, estimating and current intelligence/indications elements of the DIA. This grouping is essential to the maintenance of a close and continuous interrelationship among these elements, as well as to provide for a similar working relationship with the estimates and production elements of the military Services. This will ensure the full utilization of Service production and estimates capabilities and the incorporation of their inputs into intelligence produced by the DIA. In order to accomplish its mission, the Directorate for Processing will be divided into the following elements:

a. *The DIA Current Intelligence/Indications Center (Annex D)*
This organization will provide for a single, integrated DOD Current Intelligence/Indications Center designed to meet the needs of the Secretary of Defense and his principal staff assistants, the Joint Chiefs of Staff, the military departments, and the commanders of the unified and specified commands and their component commands. In addition, this Center will provide current intelligence/indications support to the President and other senior governmental officials and agencies on a 24-hour basis. It will maintain close working relationships with the production and estimates elements of the DIA and the Services.

b. *DIA Estimates Office (Annex E)* which will provide all DOD intelligence estimates and contributions to National Intelligence Estimates and the United States Intelligence Board (USIB), and which will assume the estimative responsibilities now charged to the J-2, Joint Staff.

c. *The DIA Production Center* (Annex F) which will, through a time-phased schedule, and in consonance with the concept provided herein, integrate DOD intelligence production as required to discharge the functions and responsibilities assigned to the Director, DIA.

B. *Headquarters Establishment, DIA (Annex G)*

The headquarters establishment of the DIA will provide adequate administrative support to the headquarters and supervision over the administration of the entire organization, and will assist the Director, DIA, in the exercise of his planning, programming, management and supervisory responsibilities for the overall DOD intelligence effort. This organizational structure will provide for maximum efficiency of operation with minimum requirement for revision during the evolutionary development of the DIA. The headquarters organization will provide the structure for all the elements which will be required in the headquarters when the DIA becomes fully operational.

1. Initially, the manning of the headquarters requires assignment of approximately 125 people, including both professional and administrative support personnel. This level of manning should be provided for as early as practicable after 1 October 1961, but in any event, no later than 31 October 1961.

2. During the period ending 1 July 1962, the headquarters complement will increase to a maximum of 250 personnel. This increase reflects the development of a full capability within the headquarters staff to discharge the responsibilities presently assigned.

C. Management Responsibilities

The major elements of the staff will be responsible for management functions as follows:

1. The Assistant Chief of Staff, Administration, will provide for headquarters administrative support and security and will be responsible for the initiation and conduct of an integrated personnel program for the career development of defense intelligence personnel. This office will manage the personnel activities of the headquarters, DIA, and will coordinate a Defense Intelligence Personnel Program for both civilian and military personnel. The Defense Intelligence Personnel Program will be initiated on 1 July 1962.

2. The Assistant Chief of Staff for Plans, Policies and Programs will initiate short and mid-range planning immediately upon activation. The Office of the Assistant Chief of Staff, Plans, Policy and Programs will be responsible for the development of an aggressive program for the improvement of defense intelligence activities under the cognizance of the Director, DIA. Long range plans for defense intelligence operations and activities will be developed and will serve as the basis for evaluation and possible consolidation of the intelligence programs of the Services. In the development of long range plans and of programs, full cognizance will be taken of probable resource availability for future requirements based on scientific and technological forecasts.

3. The Assistant Chief of Staff for Intelligence Support Systems will be responsible for the development of intelligence R&D requirements, for coordination of intelligence research and development, for liaison with all defense research, development and testing organizations having related interests or programs. He will also be responsible for the implementation of systems management in intelligence major project

areas as directed. In addition, this office will be responsible for the integration of intelligence plans and programs for automation and automatic data processing to ensure that they complement each other and those of non-DOD intelligence agencies to the maximum extent practicable.

4. The Assistant Chief of Staff, Comptroller, will provide financial management and direction for obtaining effective utilization of Department of Defense intelligence resources. This office will review and evaluate budget estimates for all intelligence activities assigned or subject to review and coordination by the Director, DIA, and prepare and submit a consolidated budget for DOD intelligence activities together with recommendations pertaining thereto; and will participate in the administration of the consolidated budget. This office will conduct management engineering studies and review and analysis of programs to ensure maximum economy and efficiency. Statistical services, reports control and design, and other internal management services will be provided as directed.

5. The Inspector General will perform normal inspection functions within the internal DIA organization and for all agencies, installations and facilities assigned to the operational control of the Director, DIA. His inspection function will emphasize manner of performance, quality evaluation and operational readiness. In addition, he will perfom such duties as relate to the monitoring, coordinating, and supervisory responsibilities of the Director, DIA, as the Director, DIA, requires.

---

93. **Memorandum From the President's Special Assistant for National Security Affairs (Bundy) to Director of Central Intelligence-designate McCone**

Washington, November 28, 1961.

[Source: Kennedy Library, National Security Files, Departments and Agencies Series, Central Intelligence Agency, General, 9/61–11/61. Top Secret. 4 pages of source text not declassified.]

94.   Memorandum From Secretary of State Rusk to the Deputy Under Secretary of State for Political Affairs (Johnson)[1]

Washington, December 9, 1961.

Please follow up on this:

1. CIA now provides certain support to private organizations of an educational or philanthropic nature.

2. These covert funds become the subject of common gossip, or knowledge, both here and abroad.

3. Covert funds draw suspicion upon the organizations concerned and, indeed, may bar them from entry into certain countries.

4. Covert funds scare away funds from other sources which do not wish to become involved with CIA-type activities or purposes.

5. In most cases, there is no need to conceal that funds are being provided by the U.S. Government. (See marked portions of attached.)[2]

6. Every effort should be made to move from covert to overt support in many of these cases. This might involve inter-agency transfers of funds from CIA to overt agencies such as AID or CU in the Department.

7. What can be done about this in connection with such organizations as (a) Asia Foundation, (b) African student activities and (c) possibly others?

Dean Rusk[3]

---

[1] Source: National Archives and Records Administration, RG 59, Rusk Files: Lot 72 D 192, Chron Files, December 1961. Secret (Special Handling).

[2] Not printed.

[3] Printed from a copy that bears this typed signature.

95.   Memorandum for the File[1]

Washington, December 27, 1961.

SUBJECT

Discussion with Attorney General Robert Kennedy, 2:45 P.M., 27 December 1961

[Here follows numbered paragraph 1 concerning an unidentified defector.]

2. McCone outlined in suitable detail the current thinking on changes in organization of the Agency,[2] naming principally the reorganization of USIB; DCI as Chairman representing the President, not the Agency; DDCI as a member of USIB and the spokesman for the Agency; the FBI and NSA remaining as members; DIA to be the sole representative of the Department of Defense and members representing intelligence arms of Army, Navy, Air Force, JCS would drop off of the Board and the AEC member would be an ad hoc member to be called when matters of importance to AEC were up for consideration.

DCI would direct policy of the Agency and exercise extensive coordinating and supervising responsibility over the community. Arrangements would be made for the more thorough distribution of evaluated intelligence to interested government officials.

Deputy DCI would be the Chief Executive Officer of the Agency operating under policy guidance of the DCI. DDP would be divided into two divisions—one to cover conventional types of clandestine intelligence, the other scientific clandestine intelligence, each section to be headed by a Deputy Director. There would be some rearrangements of the functions of the DDI to insure proper dissemination of

---

[1] Source: Central Intelligence Agency, DCI (McCone) Files, Job 80–B01285A, Memoranda for the Record, 11/29/61–4/5/62. Secret; Eyes Only. Drafted by McCone.

[2] In an earlier meeting with Attorney General Kennedy on November 29, McCone discussed several organizational questions relating to the intelligence community. McCone's memorandum for the record includes the following two paragraphs on this subject:

"(6) [Kennedy] expressed agreement that DCI should exercise coordinating control and direct activities of the entire Intelligence Community, and operations of the Agency should be assigned to Deputy Director. Discussed, but made no comment, on possible legislation to create two distinct posts.

"(7) McCone outlined his views on problem, including establishment Deputy Director as Agency general manager, have Deputy Director represent Agency on USIB so that Chairman would not represent Agency's case in disputes before the Board, attach the Office of Coordination to the DCI, and possibly attach the National Board of Estimates to the DCI. Kennedy made no specific comments but indicated general approval." (Ibid.)

information estimates, etc., to USIB and the interested government agencies.[3]

3. With respect to personnel, McCone advised that General Cabell had submitted his resignation effective January 31st and that he would soon propose a name, or list of names, to the President as the new DDCI. McCone generally advocated promotion from within for means of securing continuity and raising the morale of the Agency and stated he had found many men of very great competence in the Agency to choose from. Alternatively, McCone pointed out that in view of his personal circumstances, the President may wish to appoint a man of greater public recognition than anyone presently in the Agency and that if this was the case, McCone would have at least one name to propose (certain names were discussed). Mr. Kennedy generally favored promotion from within as he, too, realized there was an important morale factor within the Agency which must be given consideration.

McCone advised that he intended to discuss this and other matters with the President in Palm Beach on Wednesday, January 3rd.

4. McCone then expressed the view that he had observed that both in the Eisenhower administration and this administration intelligence which was disseminated was not "getting through" and being used for both short-term and long-term policy planning. He gave as examples Syria, Tshombe–Adoula meeting, the Laotian situation, etc. McCone said that he felt the basic purpose in establishing the Agency was to provide a facility for placing current, evaluated intelligence in the hands of policy-makers, including the President, but that this Agency's role had through the years been subordinated to operational activities. Mr. McCone said this had to be changed.

[Here follows paragraph 5 concerning General Edward G. Lansdale.]

John A. McCone[4]

---

[3] When McCone took up his duties as Director of Central Intelligence on November 29, he asked the CIA Inspector General, Lyman B. Kirkpatrick, to head a study of his role as Director of Central Intelligence, his relationship to the White House and other agencies, and the organization of CIA and the intelligence community. The President's statement of January 16, 1962 (Document 99), was a result of the study. Subsequently McCone launched a reorganization of the CIA that called for the CIA Comptroller reporting directly to the Director of Central Intelligence and the creation of the positions of Deputy Director of Science and Technology and Executive Director. The Executive Director became the number three position in the CIA, responsible for internal management of the agency. In 1963 the positions of Executive Director and Comptroller were combined.

[4] Printed from a copy that bears this typed signature.

96. Memorandum From Director of Central Intelligence McCone to President Kennedy[1]

Washington, January 7, 1962.

SUBJECT

Reorganization of the United States Intelligence Board

The Secretary of Defense and I have agreed that with the creation of the Defense Intelligence Agency and the assignment thereto of the responsibility for the integration of defense intelligence resources and functions, a change in the composition of the United States Intelligence Board is desirable.

At the present time the United States Intelligence Board is composed of eleven representatives (the Director of Central Intelligence as Chairman, six from the Department of Defense, one each from the Department of State, the Central Intelligence Agency, the Atomic Energy Commission, and the Federal Bureau of Investigation). When I assumed the Chairmanship of the United States Intelligence Board I advised the Board that as the Government's principal foreign intelligence officer I would represent you, and that the Deputy Director of Central Intelligence would become a member and represent the Central Intelligence Agency. The Board accepted this change.

Accordingly I recommend and the Secretary of Defense concurs that Defense representation be reduced to two (the Director, Defense Intelligence Agency and the Director, National Security Agency). I also recommend with the concurrence of the Atomic Energy Commission, that the Commission membership be on an ad hoc rather than a full-time basis since the Atomic Energy Commission participation is required only infrequently, when matters within its cognizance are discussed.

If these recommendations are approved, the reconstituted United States Intelligence Board would consist of: Director of Central Intelligence, Chairman; State Department, Defense Department,

---

[1] Source: Central Intelligence Agency, DCI (McCone) Files, Job 80–B01285A, Meetings with the President, 12/1/61–6/30/62. No classification marking. In a short covering memorandum to the President, also dated January 7, McCone wrote: "In accordance with our discussion concerning the role of the Director of Central Intelligence as the principal intelligence officer of the Government and the coordination of the work of the various intelligence agencies, I have reviewed pertinent recommendations of your Foreign Intelligence Advisory Board, particularly as they related to the responsibilities of my position. Based thereon I recommend that you approve the enclosed draft directive, which I believe will accomplish the objectives you have in mind. I believe further that the substance of the directive is not inconsistent with applicable recommendations of your Foreign Intelligence Advisory Board. I enclose also for your approval a memorandum proposing a reorganization of the United States Intelligence Board."

National Security Agency, Central Intelligence Agency and Federal Bureau of Investigation, members.

In limiting the regular membership of the United States Intelligence Board as recommended above, it would be our view that substantive dissents (including those of the military intelligence services) should continue to be reflected in estimates and other findings and decisions of the United States Intelligence Board.

This proposed reorganization of the United States Intelligence Board does not envisage limiting the composition of the United States Intelligence Board subcommittees to member agencies. The United States Intelligence Board subcommittee structure will be re-examined following your consideration of this memorandum to assure that membership includes representatives of all agencies with significant interests in the various intelligence fields.

John A. McCone[2]

---

[2] Printed from a copy that bears this typed signature. An approval line at the end of the memorandum is blank.

---

97. Memorandum of Discussion[1]

Washington, January 7, 1962.

MEMORANDUM OF DISCUSSION BETWEEN PRESIDENT
KENNEDY AND DCI ON SUNDAY, JANUARY 7, 5:30 to 7:15 p.m.,
AT THE WHITE HOUSE RESIDENCE

Note: Mr. Earman is to have this memorandum read by DDCI, DDP, and DDI, and appropriate actions taken immediately.

1. Agenda Item 2. McCone discussed the memorandum on the reorganization of USIB (copy attached)[2] and advised the President that in view of JCS objections, which had been consistently stated for the past year, McCone now concluded that USIB would remain as is (except for DDCI's membership) for a few months allowing DIA to complete orga-

---

[1] Source: Central Intelligence Agency, DCI (McCone) Files, Job 80–B01285A, Meetings with the President, 12/1/61–6/30/62. Secret; Eyes Only. Drafted by McCone on January 9. In a handwritten notation on the memorandum, Earman noted that Bissell and Amory had read it.

[2] Document 96.

nization and assume responsibilities. McCone emphasized this did not change the ultimate conclusion that USIB should be organized in accordance with NSC and President Eisenhower's and President Kennedy's decisions. The President stated that Lemnitzer would like to meet with President protesting this decision. McCone suggests no further discussions for several months. The President agreed. *Action: This matter will be held in abeyance; however, subject to be placed on agenda next USIB meeting for oral discussion by McCone and indication that NSC will ultimately be implemented.*[3]

2. McCone submitted proposed memorandum from the President to interested agencies concerning DCI responsibility. Copy attached. McCone also submitted SecState's letter advising President the letter was to be returned to Mr. Rusk.[4] (President read Rusk letter with obvious amusement.) The President read memorandum and approved subject to staff review and asked memorandum be submitted to Mr. McGeorge Bundy promptly. *Note:* Bundy requested memorandum on January 8th, however, when Rusk's letter returned to SecState he had requested memorandum be returned to him for review and either modification or submission of revised letter. This must be completed by January 9. *Action: Mr. Earman should secure letter or revised memorandum from SecState on January 9, review again with Kirkpatrick and Coyne and Schuyler, to be sure memorandum conforms with recommendations of Killian Board and then submit memorandum to Mr. Bundy for immediate implementation.*[3]

[Here follow paragraphs 3–12, dealing with other subjects.]

John A. McCone[5]

---

[3] A marginal notation by Earman reads "Done."

[4] For the memorandum, see Document 99. The Secretary's letter was not found.

[5] Printed from a copy that bears this typed signature.

98. Memorandum of Discussion[1]

Washington, January 8, 1962.

MEMORANDUM OF DISCUSSION WITH THE JOINT CHIEFS AT
11:00 O'CLOCK ON MONDAY, JANUARY 8, 1962

After a preliminary exchange of amenities, McCone stated that there were two problems.

(a) The reorganization of USIB.

General Lemnitzer gave a very articulate and persuasive argument as to why this should not be done. McCone responded by stating that it was a decision of the NSC, President Eisenhower and President Kennedy, and would ultimately be implemented. However, it was agreed, without changing the principle, that date of implementation would be postponed for a few months pending the completion of organization of DIA and permitting a few months for the operation of this agency. It was obvious that the Chiefs are very much opposed to removing the Service intelligence officers from the USIB, and probably will protest this move for reasons which have been expressed many times. The Chiefs have a unanimous paper on their position.[2]

(b) Selection of a Deputy DCI.

The Chiefs made strong argument that this must be a military man and McCone agreed that he was perfectly willing to add a high level officer providing a man of great competence and experience was proposed. McCone explained the plan of reorganization of the office, the fact that Deputy DCI would have much greater responsibility than heretofore and therefore it would not be satisfactory to him to accept anyone except the most competent and experienced officer with some intelligence background, and great administrative ability and scientific knowledge. A list of candidates had been prepared by the Chiefs and submitted to Secretary McNamara for transmission to the DCI. They expected to receive this list today.

The Chiefs then invited occasional meetings with the DCI and this was agreed.

JAM

---

[1] Source: Central Intelligence Agency, DCI (McCone) Files, Job 80–B01285A, Memoranda for the Record, 11/29/61–4/5/62. Secret. Drafted by McCone on January 9.

[2] Not further identified.

99.   Memorandum From President Kennedy to Director of
        Central Intelligence McCone[1]

Washington, January 16, 1962.

In carrying out your newly assigned duties as Director of Central
Intelligence it is my wish that you serve as the Goverment's principal foreign intelligence officer, and as such that you undertake, as an integral
part of your responsibility, the coordination and effective guidance of the
total United States foreign intelligence effort. As the Goverment's principal intelligence officer, you will assure the proper coordination, correla-
tion, and evaluation of intelligence from all sources and its prompt dissemination to me and to other recipients as appropriate. In fulfillment of
these tasks I shall expect you to work closely with the heads of all departments and agencies having responsibilities in the foreign intelligence field.

In coordinating and guiding the total intelligence effort, you will
serve as Chairman of the United States Intelligence Board, with a view to
assuring the efficient and effective operation of the Board and its associated bodies. In this connection I note with approval that you have designated your deputy to serve as a member of the Board, thereby bringing to
the Board's deliberations the relevant facts and judgments of the Central
Intelligence Agency.

As directed by the President and the National Security Council, you
will establish with the advice and assistance of the United States
Intelligence Board the necessary policies and procedures to assure adequate coordination of foreign intelligence activities at all levels.

With the heads of the Departments and Agencies concerned you will
maintain a continuing review of the programs and activities of all U.S.
agencies engaged in foreign intelligence activities with a view to assuring
efficiency and effectiveness and to avoiding undesirable duplication.

As head of the Central Intelligence Agency, while you will continue to
have over-all responsibility for the Agency, I shall expect you to delegate
to your principal deputy, as you may deem necessary, so much of the
direction of the detailed operation of the Agency as may be required to
permit you to carry out your primary task as Director of Central
Intelligence.

It is my wish that you keep me advised from time to time as to your
progress in the implementation of this directive and as to any recommendations you may have which would facilitate the accomplishment of these
objectives.

John F. Kennedy

---

[1] Source: Johnson Library, National Security File, Subject File, PFIAB. No classification marking. Copies were sent to the Secretary of State, Secretary of Defense, Attorney
General, and Chairman of the Atomic Energy Commission.

100.   Memorandum for the Record[1]

Washington, April 7, 1962.

SUBJECT

Discussion with McGeorge Bundy

After briefly reviewing the organizational changes in CIA, including the series of appointments which have been made and the discussion of the selection of a Deputy for Intelligence Community affairs, I questioned Mr. Bundy concerning the procedure being followed by CIA to currently inform the President and the members of NSC on intelligence matters. I expressed concern because of my statutory responsibility to report to the NSC, pointing out that since the NSC seldom met, and when it did meet it was for the purpose of discussing specific problems, and it appeared to me that the regular NSC meetings were not practical. Therefore an alternate procedure must be developed.

Mr. Bundy stated as follows:

1. The morning briefings of himself, General Taylor, General Clifton and others are very satisfactory.

2. The President is generally informed on intelligence matters though he seems to get his information from a variety of sources and Mr. Bundy was not clear who all of them were.

3. At the moment it seemed impractical to count on regular NSC meetings as the President was not disposed to such arrangements.

4. He asked that I insist on meeting with the President not less than once a week for the purpose of making an intelligence report and that I keep a record of such discussions. He asked that I make a point of doing this and that I charge one of my assistants with arranging weekly meetings.

5. He asked whether a record existed of all prior meetings with the President and that I review my files and complete them.

6. Mr. Bundy observed that the Secretary of State and the Secretary of Defense were well informed through their respective intelligence facilities and the "Check List" and he suggested that I arrange to brief the Vice President, the Attorney General, and the Secretary of the Treasury and the Director, Office of Emergency Planning, at least every two weeks. Bundy thought this could be done by a briefing officer or by me personally if time permitted.

The arrangements as outlined in Item 4. above will be the responsibility of Mr. Earman and Item 6. above, the responsibility of Mr. Earman

---

[1] Source: Central Intelligence Agency, DCI (McCone) Files, Job 80–B01285A, DCI Memoranda for the Record, 4/7/62–8/21/62. Secret; Eyes Only. Drafted by McCone.

to arrange appointments. Mr. Sheldon to prepare the briefings. I would appreciate any comments DDCI may have on the above.

John A. McCone[2]

---

[2] Printed from a copy that bears this typed signature.

---

101. Editorial Note

On July 23, 1962, Director of the National Reconnaissance Office Joseph V. Charyk sent a memorandum to NRO Program Directors and the Director of the NRO Staff setting forth the "Organization and Functions of the NRO." The memorandum established the basic organization of the NRO, described the functions of the elements, and outlined the concept and operation. After a discussion of the sensitivity of the NRO mission and the necessity for concealing the organization behind "plausible, overt" names, the memorandum described the responsibilities of the directors of the three elements: "Director, Program A being responsible for NRP satellite effort conducted by the NRO through utilization of Department of the Air Force resources, and the Director, Program B being responsible for NRP effort conducted by the NRO through utilization of Central Intelligence Agency resources. A Director, Program C is being established to be responsible for NRP effort conducted by the NRO through utilization of Naval Research Laboratory resources." The NRO Staff was responsible for assisting the Director, coordination and liaison with the U.S. Intelligence Board and the principal consumers of the intelligence collected, and overall management and monitoring of projects and staff. (National Reconnaissance Office, NRO Office of Policy Files) Charyk's memorandum, along with organization charts of the National Reconnaissance Office and the NRO Staff, is available on the Internet, National Security Archive (www.gwu.edu/~nsarchiv), Electronic Briefing Book No. 35, "The NRO Declassified," Document 6.

102.   Memorandum From the Director of the Bureau of Intelligence
        and Research (Hilsman) and the Deputy Director for Plans,
        Central Intelligence Agency (Miller) to the President's Special
        Assistant for National Security Affairs (Bundy)

Washington, August 1, 1962.

[Source: Kennedy Library, National Security Files, Departments
and Agencies Series, Central Intelligence Agency, General, 5/62–12/62.
Secret. 4 pages of source text not declassified.]

103.   Letter From Director of Central Intelligence McCone to
        Gordon Gray[1]

Washington, August 23, 1962.

Dear Gordon:

Just a note to tell you how delighted I am that we will work together on
the problem you and I have been discussing, immediately upon my return
from a trip of great personal importance, which I am starting on today.[2]

I have discussed our telephone conversation with General Carter
and Walter Elder, and Walter will arrange appropriate office accommodations for you and secretarial service. Also, there are several recent
studies and reports having to do with community coordination, which
I feel it might be constructive for you to peruse.

I can appreciate, and feel it completely acceptable, that your work
be done on a consultative basis under a consulting contract with a per
diem remuneration, and in so doing would involve no official appointment, nor will it involve a resignation or a leave from your other activities, including the President's Board. Of course this will be with the
full understanding that your work is being undertaken at my initiative,

---

[1] Source: Eisenhower Library, Gordon Gray Papers. No classification marking.

[2] Gray and McCone had agreed in a telephone conversation on August 21 that Gray
would assist McCone in "examining and developing the manner in which the coordination and guidance responsibility given to him as DCI by the President can best be discharged." Gray would also assist and advise McCone in selecting his Deputy for
Coordination. (Memorandum for the file of a telephone conversation with John McCone,
August 21; ibid.) In a subsequent telephone conversation, Gray explained the arrangement to McGeorge Bundy, who expressed "pleasure" and also informed Gray that he had
cleared the matter with the President. (Memorandum for the file of a telephone conversation with McGeorge Bundy, August 21; ibid.)

and involves my responsibility in fulfilling the President's directive to me, which was made after his review of a great number of recommendations of the President's Board.[3]

To reiterate the objectives of this exercise, it is my feeling that the Deputy Director for Coordination is, and will be, a most important and effective post. However, if it is filled, as it has been in the past, without careful exploration of the manner in which the office is to function, and a thorough understanding with the secretaries of the departments involved, principally State and Defense, as well as the Chairman of the Joint Chiefs of Staff, the effort will fail. However, I believe, as I have told you, because of your broad experience and the respect you command throughout government, you can approach the problem in a way that will command support of all involved rather than indifference, and from your effort there will evolve "terms of reference" for the office which will endure.

I feel this will be brought about best by seizing upon specific problems of an inter-service nature, dealing with them, resolving them, and by so doing establish a pattern which could apply to all future problems. In addition, Gordon, there is the question of selection of the man who will fill the job on a permanent basis. I am sure you will be of great assistance to me in this regard.

I will return on September 24th. You will have been back about ten days by then, and hence I believe the timing will be such that we can move forward aggressively.

With warm personal regards.

Sincerely

John

---

[3] In his telephone conversation with McCone, Gray had agreed that his actions undertaken on behalf of the DCI would be separate from those undertaken as a member of PFIAB, nor would he participate in Board consideration of matters specifically relating to his assistance to McCone. Bundy, in a September 18 letter to PFIAB Chairman Killian, commented that "any work that Gordon may do in this job would not limit the President's own freedom of judgment, and I myself am really unable to see why individual advisory assignments of this kind do not fit right in with the concept of the President's Board and its role in helping him with the broad issues of the intelligence community." (Ibid.) Gray recalled in 1974 that other PFIAB members felt that his position with McCone constituted a conflict of interest with his membership on PFIAB and that Gray should resign from the Board. Gray also recalled that McCone did not plan to stay permanently in the CIA and hoped that Gray would succeed him. (Memorandum from Gray to Wheaton B. Byers, December 10, 1974; ibid.)

104.   Memorandum of Conversation[1]

Washington, September 26, 1962, 4:30 p.m.

Memorandum of Conversation with Mr. Robert S. Amory, Chief,
  International Division, Bureau of the Budget, 4:30 P.M., 26 Sept.

1. The first part of the discussion concerned itself with the role of the Bureau of the Budget (BOB) in respect to coordination and guidance. While Mr. Amory did not claim any responsibility for "policy" he nevertheless asserted a keen interest in "management." He indicated that BOB intended to be much more active with regard to the intelligence community in general than has been the case in the past. He referred to some reorganization which had taken place in the BOB which had made his office the focal point for foreign intelligence matters with the exception of certain military functions.

2. I asked whether he could speak on behalf of the BOB with respect to the role of the DCI in "coordination and guidance matters." Mr. Amory replied that he could speak not only for himself but could also repeat Mr. Bell's often asserted views. He said that they took very seriously the President's Directive to the DCI and supported it fully, including the aspect of a "Chief Intelligence Officer" for the Government.

3. Mr. Amory went on to say that in the last eight or nine months he and others in BOB had been very much concerned at the lack of movement in respect to coordination. He said he had felt that there had been a good deal of fanfare earlier this year about a more positive role for the DCI but that results had been disappointing. He acknowledged that the DCI had been faced with a number of things which had necessarily complicated and delayed certain actions. He expressed the hope that Mr. McCone as DCI would pursue a different approach than his predecessor in respect to devoting an excessive amount of his time to operating details of CIA. I reminded him of the delegations to General Carter.

4. I asked Mr. Amory whether if he or any others in the BOB at any time believed that the DCI was not performing his proper role, it would not be appropriate for such feeling to be communicated to the DCI. Mr. Amory agreed that this was a necessary course and indicated that this process exists largely through the staff. I then pressed him for specifics with respect to his allegation about lack of movement. He said that one example he had in mind was the failure to act in USIB with respect to the elimination of service members and the complete substitution there-

---

    [1] Source: Eisenhower Library, Gordon Gray Papers. Secret. Prepared by Gordon Gray on September 27.

for of the Director of DIA. He spoke in detail of postponements and indicated that his grapevine led him to believe that a new postponement was about to take place. He pointed out the budgetary implications in terms of personnel. He said that it was alleged that General Carroll could not properly represent Defense until he had sufficient competent personnel which would come from the services. On the other hand the services are not willing to give up personnel supporting them in their respective memberships on USIB. He left me with the impression that budget projections for 1964 did not reflect a firm decision to proceed with the personnel transfers.

5. I asked Mr. Amory whether he was concerned about the relationships between the DCI, the Secretary of Defense and Mr. Rubel with respect to NSA affairs. Mr. Amory adverted to the familiar conflict between departmental and national intelligence requirements and between military and other general requirements. [9 lines of source text not declassified]

6. I then asked him what he conceived to be the role of the DCI in respect to these matters including projections of large increases in NSA personnel and budget. He acknowledged that the DCI has no command function but asserted that it was a DCI responsibility to make certain of the proper allocation of resources. As to NSA, Mr. Amory believes that Mr. Rubel has made great strides from the management point of view. I pointed out to him that by Mr. Rubel's own statement, he was devoting no more than ten to fifteen percent of his own time to NSA matters which I felt was quite inadequate. Mr. Amory agreed that it was inadequate.

7. When I pressed Mr. Amory further about how he felt the DCI could exercise his responsibility in this area especially in the light of the fact that the DIA has no real relationship to NSA, he only could suggest a close working relationship between Mr. Rubel and his associates on the one hand and Mr. Cline, Mr. Sheldon and perhaps others on the other hand.

8. Mr. Amory indicated that in his area he was responsible for about eight billion dollars expended in the foreign field. He said that it was his view as well as the view of Mr. Bell, Mr. Sorensen, Professor Schlesinger and others of the New Frontier in the White House that [less than 1 line of source text not declassified] was an excessive proportion of this overseas expenditure. He said further that there was a determination that the proportionate amount spent on intelligence would have to be reduced. [3 lines of source text not declassified] In the discussion on this point he made several cost comparisons which reflected his impression that the intelligence effort was receiving a disproportionate allocation of resources. I pointed out to Mr. Amory that he was trying to equate things which could not be equated and that I questioned this approach.

9. I sought to bring the conversation back to specific roles. I posed as an example the possibility that the technical services of the army might be performing estimating and production chores which were in duplication of other efforts in the community. I asked Mr. Amory whether the budget process was not perhaps the best vehicle for detecting and eliminating such unnecessary duplication. He replied it was very difficult to identify people in the military with the size of the establishment and its budget and with only about 50 people in the BOB concerning themselves with the Defense Department.

10. In closing the conversation I again repeated that it would be only fair for him and his associates to report to the DCI any failures or omissions which they felt they had detected. I said I felt there had been enough general talk about failure of coordination and unless allegations in this regard were made on the basis of specific instances, general talk only complicated the problems of the DCI. Mr. Amory did not take issue with this point of view.

G.G.

105.   Memorandum of Discussion[1]

Washington, November 17, 1962.

MEMORANDUM OF DISCUSSION BETWEEN PRESIDENT
KENNEDY AND GENERAL EISENHOWER AND McCONE AT
McCONE'S RESIDENCE ON SATURDAY, NOVEMBER 17th,
FROM 9:00 UNTIL 10:10 A.M.

[Here follow six paragraphs of discussion concerning the situation in Cuba and Western Europe, particularly Berlin. Portions dealing with the Cuban situation are printed in *Foreign Relations, 1961–1963*, volume XI, Document 189. A paragraph concerning Western Europe and Berlin is not printed.]

The meeting then turned to discussion of organization and Eisenhower reviewed at some length his concept of how the NSC must be supported by a Planning Board who are studying and reporting on the situation in each critical country or critical area and in addition the principals must meet frequently to discuss special acute situations. He recalled how

---

[1]   Source: Central Intelligence Agency, DCI (McCone) Files, Job 80–B01285A, Meetings with the President, 7/1/62–12/31/62. Secret; Eyes Only. Prepared by McCone.

studies were made by the Planning Board on all areas, that these served as broad guidelines for policy makers. In addition he recalled how he would meet with his principals on particularly acute situations such as Lebanon, Guatemala, Quemoy, Matsu, etc., and that these meetings would be held frequently, in some instances as often as once a day for several days, and that policies would develop from such meetings. The President seemed to concur that he should have more staff support; he expressed great pleasure at the functioning of the Executive Committee and the desire to have the Executive Committee established as a permanent organization, to meet once a week, to review special situations and to hear intelligence reports. There seemed to be no disagreement between the two men concerning the need for different type of organization than now exists. Eisenhower readily volunteered that any plan of organization must be tailored and must meet the particular desires of the man in charge and that a pattern acceptable to him may not necessarily meet President Kennedy's needs.

The meeting was cordial and constructive. Both President Kennedy and General Eisenhower expressed their appreciation to me and their desire to continue communication one with the other in about the same form and in the manner of this meeting.

John A. McCone[2]

[Here follows an added paragraph on Cuba, dated November 19, 1962.]

---

[2] Printed from a copy that bears this typed signature.

---

106. Memorandum for the Record[1]

Washington, January 10, 1963.

SUBJECT

Meeting between DCI and Mr. Bundy in Bundy's office at 4:30 p. m. on January 10th

1. Mr. Bundy spoke of the concern regarding friction between CIA and Defense which apparently had been reported to him, and possibly to the President, by McNamara and Gilpatric. McCone responded that, in his opinion, the friction arose from two sources. One, DIA in establishing its areas of activities was giving substantial indication (at the

---

[1] Source: Central Intelligence Agency, DCI (McCone) Files, Job 80–B01285A, DCI Memoranda for the Record, 1/1/63–2/9/63. Secret; Eyes Only. Drafted by McCone on January 11.

working level) of a desire to duplicate rather than utilize CIA facilities. This tendency had been noted by General Carter and was a reason for many strong positions taken by General Carter in defense of this Agency. However, DCI noted that he believed all such controversies involving General Carter were, in the final analysis, amicably settled. Two, problems with Dr. Scoville, which to a certain extent were attributable to Scoville's personality. Underlying these arguments was the constant desire of Defense and Air Force to pre-empt entirely all reconnaissance. Bundy volunteered that this would not be acceptable because history had indicated that Air Force reconnaissance [*1-1/2 lines of source text not declassified*] would be placed on a lower priority to operational Air Force programs and this would be undesirable.

Action: Despite the pros and cons of the various arguments, it is essential that both CIA and Defense adopt policies and understanding which will avoid so far as possible controversy and jurisdictional disputes. DCI should discuss this whole subject very frankly with Secretary McNamara.

2. McCone stated to Bundy that he felt that he must have a stronger voice in reconnaissance than now exists or was contemplated in the defunct NRO arrangement.[2] He pointed out that the actions of SAC in connection with Cuba demonstrated the point that a military unit will, if left to its own devices, place operational requirements on a higher priority than intelligence-gathering during peace time. McCone stated and Bundy agreed that CIA and not SAC was responsible for both the U-2 and Discoverer, as well as Oxcart. I pointed out that Air Force efforts in satellite photography had failed completely and this was agreed to by Bundy. McCone stated that he would discuss this matter frankly with McNamara but that he would not continue to be responsible for intelligence unless he, and through him CIA, was the final authority on reconnaissance operations, [*less than 1 line of source text not declassified*]. Overt operations during a war are in preparation for military action and should very logically be a military responsibility.

3. McCone outlined his views on the reorganization of USIB and the manner in which the national resources such as NRO, AFTAC and NSA should be handled by a full-time Assistant Secretary of Defense. The alternative would be a new Deputy Director of Intelligence to handle these particular operations; however this seemed impractical in view of the very large amount of support required in the Defense Department.

[Here follow paragraph 4 dealing with Cuba, paragraph 5 concerning Chinese Communist nuclear capabilities, and paragraph 6

---

[2] See footnote 2, Document 90.

briefly indicating that Cuba and the Chinese Communist nuclear threat were issues of high importance.]

John A. McCone[3]

---

[3] Printed from a copy that bears this typed signature.

---

107. Editorial Note

On February 4, 1963, James R. Killian, Jr., Chairman of the President's Foreign Intelligence Advisory Board (PFIAB), sent President Kennedy a report based on the Board's survey of intelligence coverage, assessment, and reporting by U.S. intelligence agencies prior to the Cuban missile crisis in the fall of 1962. The report was based on PFIAB's review of intelligence on the Soviet military buildup in Cuba during the months preceding the President's report to the nation on October 22, 1962, on the Soviet establishment of offensive missile sites in Cuba. The February 4 PFIAB report was signed for the Board by Killian as Chairman, and included the names of the other Board members, William O. Baker, Clark Clifford, James Doolittle, Gordon Gray, Edwin H. Land, William L. Langer, Robert D. Murphy, and Frank Pace, Jr. Killian transmitted the report under cover of a shorter separate memorandum to President Kennedy, also dated February 4, 1963. The texts of the report and covering memorandum are in Central Intelligence Agency, DCI (McCone) Files, Job 80–B01285A, and also printed in *CIA Documents on the Cuban Missile Crisis, 1962*, pages 361–371. Documentation on the crisis is in *Foreign Relations, 1961–1963*, volume XI.

The PFIAB report noted by way of introduction that the Board's review "sought to determine whether there were lessons to be learned from an objective appraisal of the strengths and weaknesses of the U.S. foreign intelligence experience as disclosed by the Cuba experience. We directed particular attention to those areas of the intelligence process which are concerned with such matters as (1) the acquisition of intelligence, (2) the analysis of intelligence, and (3) the production and dissemination of intelligence reports and estimates in support of national policy formulation and operational requirements."

The report discussed the U-2 reconnaissance overflights of Cuba from October 14, 1962, onward that provided photographic evidence the Soviet Union had begun to establish a strategic missile complex in Cuba. The report noted that "the definitive photographic evidence obtained as a result of the October 14 and subsequent overflights of Cuba were promptly processed and submitted to the President in time for decisive action before the Soviet MRBM and IRBM systems became fully operational. Beginning with the President's initial receipt of this crucial intelligence there was an effective performance on the part of the U.S. intelligence community in providing the President and his top policy advisers promptly with the coordinated intelligence necessary to enable our Government to respond effectively to the offensive missile threat in Cuba."

With respect to the period prior to October 14, 1962, the report concluded that "our foreign intelligence effort should have been more effective in (1) obtaining adequate and timely intelligence as to the nature and scope of the Soviet military build-up as it developed over a period of months, and (2) exploiting the available intelligence as a basis for estimating Soviet and Cuban plans and intentions."

On the subject of intelligence acquisition, the report found that "clandestine agent coverage within Cuba was inadequate," and that "full use was not made of aerial photographic surveillance, particularly during September and October when the influx of Soviet military personnel and armaments had reached major proportions." With respect to aerial photographic surveillance of Cuba, the report found that "the President granted authorization for all U-2 flights which were recommended to him by his policy advisers on the Special Group having responsibility for such matters." But until October 3, "it appears that there was a failure on the part of the intelligence community as a whole to propose to the Special Group U-2 reconnaissance missions on a scale commensurate with the nature and intensity of the Soviet activity in Cuba."

With respect to the issue of intelligence analysis, the report found a "need for improvement of the processes used in making national intelligence estimates and the processes used in making current intelligence analysis, and also in the techniques for relating these two functions." The report noted that "the President and policy-advisory officials were ill served by the Special National Intelligence Estimate issued by the intelligence community on September 19, on 'The Military Buildup in Cuba.'" This Estimate "pointed away from the likelihood of the establishment of Soviet nuclear missile systems in Cuba."

The report found that "in the analysis of intelligence indicators and in the production of current intelligence reports, the intelligence community failed to get across to key Government officials the most accurate possible picture of what the Soviets might be up to in Cuba, during the months preceding October 14." The report further stated: "We believe that the near-total intelligence surprise experienced by the United States with respect to the introduction and deployment of Soviet strategic missiles in Cuba resulted in large part from a malfunction of the analytic process by which intelligence indicators are assessed and reported. This malfunction diminished the effectiveness of policy advisers, national intelligence estimators, and civilian and military officers having command responsibilities." The report continued: " We believe that the manner in which intelligence indicators were handled in the Cuba situation may well be the most serious flaw in our intelligence system, and one which, if uncorrected, could lead to the gravest consequences."

In its review of the intelligence reporting process, the Board found that "limitations which were placed on the publication and dissemination of reports and information concerning the situation in Cuba were either misinterpreted or misapplied. This inhibited the flow of significant data." With respect to the subject of emergency planning, the Board noted that the Cuban missile crisis "points up the need for advance planning to ensure that our human and material intelligence resources are sufficient, and are adequately organized, to meet the demands of an emergency such as that which confronted our Government in this instance."

On February 23, 1963, Director of Central Intelligence John A. McCone sent a memorandum to President Kennedy commenting on the PFIAB report of February 4. McCone indicated that in appearances before the Board on November 7, December 9, and December 28, 1962, he had stated that "there was an understandable reluctance or timidity in programming U-2 overflights over Cuba after we had discovered the presence of surface-to-air missile installations. This caution was understandable not only because of the extremely severe criticism of 'U-2 incidents'" dating from the downing of a U-2 aircraft piloted by Francis Gary Powers over the Soviet Union on May 1, 1960 (see *Foreign Relations*, 1958–1960, volume X, Part 1), and the more recent loss of a Chinese Nationalist-piloted U-2 over Sakhalin on September 9, 1962 (see ibid., 1961–1963, volume XXII, Document 154).

McCone noted that "for two years the intelligence community had been surfeited with reports of 'missiles in Cuba,' all of which proved to be incorrect prior to those which we received on or about September 20." McCone stated: "I continue to feel that the intelligence community performed well. I have examined this performance personally and in depth, and incidentally with a critical eye. As you know, my own views differed from those of the community. I believe that the conclusions reached from my study made for the Board at your request reflect a more reasonable judgment of the performance of the intelligence community in the six months' period prior to the October crisis." McCone attached his conclusions, which read in full as follows:

"1. Although the intelligence community's inquiry into its actions during the Cuban crisis revealed certain areas where shortcomings existed and where improvements should be made in various areas of intelligence collection and processing, the intelligence community operated extensively and well in connection with Cuba. Every major weapons system introduced into Cuba by the Soviets was detected, identified, and reported (with respect to numbers, location and operational characteristics) before any one of these systems attained an operational capability.

"2. A relatively short period of time ensued between the introduction of strategic weapons into Cuba, particularly strategic missiles, and the commencement of the flow, although meager, of tangible reports of their presence; detection of their possible presence and targeting of the suspect areas of their location was accomplished in a compressed time frame; and the intelligence cycle did move with extraordinary rapidity through the stages of collection, analysis, targeting for verification, and positive identification.

"3. The very substantial effort directed toward Cuba was originated by an earlier concern with the situation in Cuba and the effort, already well under way, contributed to the detection and analysis of the Soviet build-up.

"4. Information was disseminated and used.

"5. Aerial photography was very effective and our best means of establishing hard intelligence.

"6. The procedures adopted in September delayed photographic intelligence, but this delay was not critical, because photography obtained prior to about 17 October would not have been sufficient to warrant action of a type which would require support from Western Hemisphere [or?] NATO allies.

"7. Agent reports helped materially; however, none giving significant information on offensive missiles reached the intelligence community or policy-makers until after mid-September. When received, they were used in directing aerial photography.

"8. Some restrictions were placed on dissemination of information, but there is no indication that these restrictions necessarily affected analytical work or actions of policy-makers.

"9. The 19 September estimate, while indicating the improbability that the Soviet Union would place MRBM's and IRBM's in Cuba, did state that 'this contingency must be examined carefully, even though it would run counter to current Soviet policy'; the estimators in preparing the 19 September estimate gave great weight to the philosophical argument concerning Soviet intentions and thus did not fully weigh the many indicators.

"10. The estimate of 19 October on probable Soviet reactions was correct."

The Report from McCone to Kennedy, February 28, 1963, is in the Central Intelligence Agency, DCI (McCone) Files, Job 80–B01285A; it is also printed in *CIA Documents on the Cuban Missile Crisis, 1962*, pages 373–376.

108. Editorial Note

On March 13, 1963, Director of Central Intelligence John McCone and Deputy Secretary of Defense Roswell Gilpatric signed an agreement on the "Management of the National Reconnaissance Program," which designated the Secretary of Defense as the Executive Agent for the NRP. In order to carry out his responsibilities, the Secretary of Defense would "establish as a separate operating agency of the Department of Defense a National Reconnaissance Office under the direction, authority and control of the Secretary of Defense." The agreement strengthened the authority of the Director of the National Reconnaissance Office who would report directly to the Secretary of Defense and would be responsible for the "management of all aspects of the NRP," including developing all projects for intelligence collection by "collection systems exclusive of normal peripheral operations, responding "directly and solely" to the requirements and priorities of the U.S. Intelligence Board, scheduling all overflight missions, processing initial imagery and producing and delivering intelligence to users, planning and conducting research and development of future NRP projects, and directing and managing all funds made available for the NRP. The NRO Director was also given authority to assign all project tasks to appropriate elements of the Central Intelligence Agency and the Department of Defense. (National Reconnaissance Office, NRO Office of Policy Files) The text of the agreement is available on the Internet, National Security Archive (www.gwu.edu/~nsarchiv), Electronic Briefing Book No. 35, "The NRO Declassified," Document 7.

The agreement superseded the agreement of May 2, 1962; see footnote 2, Document 90. In March 1963 Brockway McMillan succeeded Joseph Charyk as Director of the National Reconnaissance Office.

109. Editorial Note

On March 25, 1963, at 12:15 p.m., Director of Central Intelligence McCone met with President Kennedy and raised a number of issues. A memorandum of conversation prepared by Bundy, who was also present, includes the following item:

"The Director reported he was very dissatisfied with the reports of the Killian Board [i.e., the President's Foreign Intelligence Advisory Board, of which Killian was Chairman]. He felt that these reports and recommendations very often covered proposals or policy which he himself had earlier described to the Killian Board so that in a sense they provide a misleading record which might leak and be very damaging to the CIA. The President replied that he thought the Board's record of discretion was excellent, that any report would be filed with the answer of the Director or the affected agency, and that he thought that in this area the advice of an independent group of observers was invaluable. He thought it best that the Board should continue. He told the Director that Dr. Killian had asked for relief, and it was agreed that we should see what happens under new leadership before making any changes." (Memorandum of conversation with the President, March 25; Kennedy Library, National Security Files, Bundy Memoranda to President, 3/63–4/63)

McCone's record of this conversation included the following: "The President advised McCone in confidence that Dr. Killian had submitted his resignation as Chairman of the Advisory Board for health reasons and this resignation would be accepted as soon as a replacement could be found. The President suggested, and Bundy later reaffirmed, that the recommendations should be answered by the DCI and he should feel free to point out in his answers that there are subjects upon which the Board made recommendations, which had been discussed with the Board, and the DCI in these discussions had indicated actions which the intelligence community, CIA and DCI had initiated." In a note, McCone wrote: "Bundy later asked DCI for recommendations. McCone suggested that when the change takes place, terms of reference for the Board should be reviewed and perhaps modified so that the Board could constructively assist the intelligence community and the entire intelligence portion of the Government as they had in the past, but would not assume quite as much operational responsibility as they had in the past." (Central Intelligence Agency, DCI (McCone) Files, Job 80–B01285A, Meetings with the President, 1/1/63–3/31/63)

110. Memorandum for the Record[1]

Washington, July 11, 1963.

SUBJECT

Discussion with Secretary McNamara, 11 July, 5:00 p. m.

1. The content of my letter of July 10th[2] on the subject of the budget was discussed in considerable detail. It was agreed that I, as DCI, should have access to the Defense intelligence budgets. SecDef plans to prepare for all intelligence budgets by function, setting forth cost and manpower requirements similar to that of the CCP study. This will be true for NRO, which is now nearing completion, for General Carroll's DIA, and the classical Service intelligence operations, and for certain other particular activities. All of these are in preparation at the present time, and will be completed by Fall. The guidelines for the preparation of budgets have been established and there will be ample opportunity for review.

2. I confirmed that such a procedure would meet my needs, but that it was essential that I assure myself and the President that existing resources in all Agencies are being used to the maximum, that there is minimum duplication, that there are no visible gaps, and that the intelligence community is operating efficiently and effectively. McNamara agreed. I particularly raised the question of utilization of CIA resources and special skills. McNamara agreed that these should not be duplicated by DIA, but that DIA should make maximum utilization of such skills.

3. I raised the question of LeMay's desire to take over all aerial reconnaissance. McNamara indicated that this would not be advisable; he would not approve it; he had so told LeMay that as far as he was concerned this issue was dead. He said he thought NRO was operating more effectively now, and he hoped there would be a continual close-working arrangement between Fubini, McMillan and the CIA staff.

4. I raised the question of the control of detection and analysis of Soviet missile and space activity, referring particularly to Dr. Wheelon's plan for Mistic. McNamara asked that Dr. Wheelon review this organizational plan with Fubini, as McNamara felt the idea had great merit, although he was not familiar with the details.

---

[1] Source: Central Intelligence Agency, DCI (McCone) Files, Job 80–B01285A, DCI Memoranda for the Record, 6/5–7/20/63. Secret; Eyes Only. Drafted by McCone on July 12.

[2] In his letter of July 10 to McNamara, attached but not printed, McCone described discussions with the Director of the Bureau of the Budget concerning the extent to which McCone as Director of Central Intelligence (as contrasted with Director of the Central Intelligence Agency) was involved in the planning, preparation, and review of budgets, programs, and personnel requirements of the intelligence community. The letter set forth a brief agenda of issues for discussion at the July 11 meeting with McNamara.

5. McNamara had not been brought into the discussion of membership of GMAIC. He had no comment, except to say that he felt there were far too many people involved in all decision-making processes. He did not see why NASA necessarily had to be brought into the intelligence processes merely to make their facilities available, that the disciplines in NASA existed elsewhere, and in general he had some reservations about the plan merely because he thought that too many people were involved in all Government policy-making processes. He pointed out that the number of people who had injected themselves into the test ban discussions really had no right to a voice with respect to policy. I would expect McNamara would support Carroll's objection to NASA's membership on GMAIC.

6. Reference the supplying of NATO with information on Soviet capabilities as outlined in the 11 July memorandum of Elder's and the June 14th memorandum of USIB,[3] McNamara could not recall how this question arose, and asked that we discuss it further later, with General Carroll, and if the issue still was unresolved, further discussion could take place.

7. [1 paragraph (12 lines of source text) not declassified]

---

[3] The July 11 memorandum is attached but not printed; the June 14 memorandum was not found.

---

111.   Memorandum From Director of Central Intelligence
         McCone to the Deputy Director of Central Intelligence
         (Carter)[1]

Washington, October 21, 1963.

1. The National Security Act charges the Central Intelligence Agency with the responsibility to correlate and evaluate intelligence relating to national security and to provide appropriate dissemination of such intelligence within the Government, using where appropriate existing agencies and facilities. The law further provides that departments and other agencies of government shall continue to correlate and disseminate departmental intelligence. Under existing Priority National Intelligence Objectives intelligence relating to threat of attack on the United States is considered the highest priority.

---

[1] Source: Central Intellence Agency, DCI (McCone) Files, Job 80-B01285A, DCI Memoranda, 3/1/62–4/30/65. Top Secret.

2. Hence, the proper handling of intelligence relating to Soviet missile and space firings is of the utmost importance. The analysis of all raw intelligence of Soviet activities and operations gathered from all sources and the reporting and dissemination of these analyses in a timely and comprehensive manner is a responsibility of the Central Intelligence Agency. It is my observation that CIA through its Office of Scientific Intelligence, and USIB through the Guided Missiles and Astronautics Intelligence Committee are not satisfactorily organized for this task, despite the fact that the efforts of both organizations have produced a very considerable number of very valuable analyses and reports on Soviet missile and space activities through the years.

3. This memorandum therefore will confirm my previous instructions to you to create, within the resources of the Central Intelligence Agency an organization for the complete analysis of all data on Soviet missile and space firings. This organization should be established as a unit within the DD/S&T which in my opinion has the advanced technical capability required as a focal point for this effort. Naturally this Foreign Missile and Space Analysis Center would not only be satisfactorily equipped with specialists of appropriate background and training, but will likewise utilize the best of our national capabilities, both private and governmental, in accomplishing the sophisticated technical analyses required to exploit on a timely basis the extensive collection activities now in being under the direction of various Services and agencies, most of which are being augmented.

4. The group you will establish within the DD/S&T under this directive should bring together all of the technical intelligence data for joint analysis, should work in close coordination with GMAIC and report its results to the USIB through GMAIC.

5. Likewise this analytical group should work closely with the agencies who now collect raw intelligence data and process and analyze their data independently.

6. It is assumed that the analytical group established under this directive through its study of all collection resources and the raw intelligence produced by them will develop judgments as to how our resources might be improved or more effectively directed. When and if such views are developed, I would appreciate them being brought to the attention of USIB immediately so that appropriate instructions can be issued for the implementation of such recommendations.

John A. McCone[2]

---

[2] Printed from a copy that indicates McCone signed the original.

112. Memorandum for the Record[1]

Washington, November 28, 1963.

SUBJECT

Discussion with President Johnson, 28 November 1963, 10:00 a.m.

[Here follows paragraph 1 concerning Ambassador Henry Cabot Lodge and developments in Vietnam.]

2. The President then stated that he had the greatest confidence in me personally. He recalled the background for our relationship through the years and also the fact that on several important issues which have come up since my assuming the position of DCI that he had forced me to express myself on policy and noted that he approved of the positions I took on various matters. He said that he felt my work in intelligence was of greatest importance, but he did not wish me to confine myself to this role. He said that he had observed that I had rather carefully avoided expressing myself on policy or suggesting courses of action and he suggested that it might be for interdepartmental reasons that I would wish to continue to do this in meetings (which he felt was a mistake), but nevertheless he invited and would welcome my coming to him from time to time with suggestions of courses of action on policy matters which, in my opinion, were wise even though they were not consistent with advice he was receiving from responsible people. He said he was not satisfied with the advice he was getting from many quarters and he noted that in issues such as nuclear testing, the disarmament test ban, discussions on Cuba and South Vietnam that he, McCloy and I had always been very close together, with Dillon for the most part conforming to our views, but more often than not these views differed in degree from those of a great many others who are in the Administration. In this context he did not mention Mr. Bundy, however, on other occasions he had expressed confidence in Bundy.

3. I received the definite impression from this discussion that the President would move rather rapidly on the role of advisers and some of his Cabinet members as he is not at all happy with a great many of them. I think the same might be expected of some of his ambassadors.

---

[1] Source: Central Intelligence Agency, DCI (McCone) Files, Job 80–B01285A, Meetings with the President, 11/23/63–12/31/63. Top Secret; Eyes Only; No Distribution. Drafted by McCone on November 29.

113.   Memorandum for the Record[1]

Washington, December 7, 1963.

SUBJECT

Discussion with the President on Saturday, December 7th, 12:00 for about one half hour

1. The President confirmed that he thought I should go to Saigon to meet McNamara, that he wished our new Chief of Station to be in place by that time, that he wished to meet the Chief of Station personally before he went to Saigon and again expressed apprehension over the situation in South Vietnam.

2. Reviewed with the President, modified, and apparently approved draft of a cable to Ambassador Lodge on the above subject.

3. I reviewed briefly my discussion with Robert Kennedy on Saturday morning, details of which are covered in another memorandum.

4. Reviewed my practice of briefing General Eisenhower. The President asked that I continue and he expressed the greatest of confidence in and friendship for General Eisenhower.

5. Discussed the organizational plan for the Alliance for Progress which was submitted in a memorandum last week. The President said that Robert Anderson flatly refused the President's personal appeal. He said he was turning towards placing Ambassador Thomas Mann as an Undersecretary of State for Latin American affairs, responsible not only for the Alliance for Progress but for all Latin American activities.

6. I told the President that I was dissatisfied with the "image" of the DCI. It has been created because Allen Dulles and also a number of men in the Administration had built up the operational side of the Agency and had not emphasized the activities of CIA and DCI which were first and carefully outlined in the law and were most important. I said the result of this had been that the DCI was now considered strictly a "cloak and dagger" operator and that this image had developed to a point that my contribution to him and to the Department was impaired, travel is difficult, visiting foreign countries is practically an impossibility all to the end neither the DCI nor the Agency were serving the President as effectively as they could in view of the vast resources of talent existing in CIA. In saying this I did not diminish the very great importance of the operational side as well as the technical side but indicated that our real contribution was to take all intelligence,

---

[1] Source: Central Intelligence Agency, DCI (McCone) Files, Job 80–B01285A, Meetings with the President, 11/23/63–12/31/63. Secret; Eyes Only. Drafted by McCone on December 9.

including clandestine and technical intelligence, and meld it into a proper and thoughtful analysis estimate of any given situation. The President agreed and asked that I prepare a memorandum of a few paragraphs which he could use from time to time in talking with the press or in press conferences or even in speeches.[2]

_____

[2] See Document 115.

_____

114.　　Memorandum From Director of Central Intelligence McCone to President Johnson[1]

Washington, December 21, 1963.

SUBJECT

Proposed Reorganization of the United States Intelligence Board

In recent consultation with Secretary McNamara regarding measures which should be taken in the intelligence community to achieve your goal of good management and economical administration in government,[2] we have concluded that the management of the foreign intelligence activities of the Department of Defense would be very greatly simplified if you would approve a reorganization of the United States Intelligence Board.

The Board, essentially in its present role of advising and assisting you as its Chairman in coordinating and guiding the total intelligence effort, was established in 1958 with the approval of the President under directives of the National Security Council. As approved by the President, the composition of the Intelligence Board currently consists of the Director of Central Intelligence as Chairman; the Deputy Director of Central Intelligence representing the Central Intelligence Agency; the intelligence chiefs of the Department of State, Defense Intelligence Agency, Army, Navy, Air Force and National Security Agency; together with representatives of the Atomic Energy Commission and the Federal Bureau of Investigation.

Since the Defense Intelligence Agency (DIA) was created in 1961 to coordinate and supervise all intelligence functions in the Department of Defense (except those under the National Security Agency), it has been

_____

[1] Source: Central Intelligence Agency, Job 80–B01676R, Reorganization of USIB. No classification marking.

[2] McCone sent a letter on the same subject to McNamara on December 12. (Ibid.)

contemplated that the intelligence chiefs of the Army, Navy and Air Force would be removed from membership on the U.S. Intelligence Board at such time as the Director, DIA, has sufficient authority and resources to represent all the military services. Secretary McNamara and I believe that this change in membership on the Intelligence Board is now warranted in the interest of better management and more effective administration.

To put this reorganization into effect, I recommend that you approve the following membership on the United States Intelligence Board to become effective 1 January 1964:

> Director of Central Intelligence, Chairman
> Deputy Director of Central Intelligence
> Director of Intelligence and Research, Department of State
> Director, Defense Intelligence Agency
> Director, National Security Agency
> A representative of the Atomic Energy Commission
> A representative of the Federal Bureau of Investigation

Subject to your approval of this recommendation, I will institute action to effect such changes in existing directives as are necessary to implement this reorganization.

John A. McCone[3]

---

[3] Printed from a copy that indicates McCone signed the original.

---

115.   Memorandum for the Record[1]

LBJ Ranch, Texas, December 27, 1963.

SUBJECT

> Discussions with President Johnson at the Johnson Ranch on Friday, December 27th

1. I arrived at the ranch by Jet Star from Seattle, arriving at midnight on Thursday, December 26th. I stayed in a guest room at President Johnson's residence. President Johnson and I ate breakfast alone the following morning and then with Pierre Salinger took a long walk. Following the discussion two memoranda were prepared by me for the President's subsequent use. Memorandum marked #1 was to be

---

[1] Source: Central Intelligence Agency, DCI (McCone) Files, Job 80–B01285A, Meetings with the President, 11/23/63–12/31/63. Top Secret; Eyes Only. Drafted by McCone on December 29.

used by him in discussing our meeting later in the day when he met with a large number of the press. Memorandum #2 was for discussion with Secretary Rusk and others and for subsequent release to the press.[2]

2. At breakfast the President immediately brought up his desire to "change the image of the DCI" from a cloak and dagger role to the role of an adviser to the President on world situations derived from intelligence sources which were of importance to the President in reaching policy decisions. For this reason he intended to call upon me for a great many activities which would be different from those of the past. As an example, he wished me to return to California to meet with President Eisenhower to discuss with him certain aspects of the world situation and also the particular actions which President Johnson [*Eisenhower?*] had taken in the interest of government economy.

3. I responded that this was very much in line with my thinking. I was willing to do anything that he desired. I then produced the Truman article and the Starnes article[3] and explained to him that a statement of this type by President Truman would do great damage, that it would be used by many columnists who enjoyed criticizing CIA, that the Truman article and later editorials such as the Starnes article would undoubtedly be introduced into the *Congressional Record* by such critics of CIA as Senator Eugene McCarthy and would be used in an attempt to bring about legislation creating a joint committee on intelligence (Watchdog Committee). The President said that he had read the Truman article, that he thought it was a mistake and that he would do all that he could to arrest any such impressions concerning CIA's activities.

[Here follow paragraphs 4–15, dealing with various unrelated subjects, including Cyprus, Yemen, South Vietnam, the Soviet Union, Communist China, and Cuba.]

There are a number of items which I had intended to discuss with the President, but time ran out. They were:

1. The general scope of activity of CIA, most particularly in the areas of DDP. However, I am satisfied, after discussing the Truman article with the President, that he is in complete accord with our covert operations, including political action and paramilitary activities. However, he wishes to emphasize the correlating, estimating and reporting functions (i.e., DDI) in order to minimize the "cloak and dagger" aspects of CIA and the DCI.

2. I intended to suggest to the President that CIA be represented in his inter-departmental organization to examine foreign aid, or alternatively that we have an adviser or consultant sit with the committee. I would like the staff to give some consideration to this idea and give me

---

[2] The two memoranda are attached but not printed.

[3] Not further identified.

their views upon my return. Frankly, I feel that our Stations have sources that can provide independent evaluations of certain aid programs and make suggestions which would be exceedingly valuable. However, there is some question as to whether we should become involved, either by direct participation or as consultants in this field.

[Here follow five additional paragraphs dealing with unrelated subjects.]

Information Policy

116.   U.S. Information Agency Background Paper[1]

Washington, undated.

THE "PRESTIGE POLLS" ISSUE

The mission of the U. S. Information Agency is to inform and influence peoples abroad.

If we are ignorant of public opinion abroad, we have to shoot in the dark.

With these two facts in mind, the Office of Research and Analysis has sought to refine the assessments of popular opinions and attitudes.

We know that an accurate measure of the opinions of a people cannot be obtained by diplomatic reporting, press analysis, or other traditional research methods. These methods measure opinions of special groups and measure the opinions subjectively.

Public opinion polls or surveys can, however, measure objectively the opinions of a whole population.

This is not to say that we need only the public opinion polls. Although increasingly precise, survey data cannot be taken as the last word but must be weighed along with all other types of evidence to produce a comprehensive assessment.

As our reports concerning world public opinion measurements grew more comprehensive and more incisive, the demand for more and more pointed reports followed. Since those reports were expected to remain within the executive family of the government in order to help guide government programs, we had no trepidation about calling the shots as we saw them. Objective analysis, we felt, provided the only justification for the exercise.

Unfortunately, these reports got caught in the domestic political line of fire. Now there is some thought that to avoid future difficulties, we might discontinue these surveys. Several factors discount this easy solution.

---

[1] Source: Washington National Records Center, RG 306, USIA Files: FRC 68 A 1415, FOIA/Classified Folder. Confidential. Attached to a memorandum from Oren Stevens of USIA's Office of Research and Analysis to USIA Director-designate Edward R. Murrow, February 1, 1961, when Murrow and the rest of USIA were turning their attention to the proper scope, utility, and classification of their foreign opinion analytical products.

1) Our difficulties highlight a major governmental problem, the "security" system. At the root of this problem is the difficulty of deciding, under heavy pressure, precisely which facts and conclusions can be made public or must be kept within the governmental family. Once a decision is made that a report is a security matter, it should remain secure. If it doesn't remain secure, this is the fault of the security system.

2) Public opinion surveys conducted by USIA are an essential part of the intelligence-gathering mechanism of the U.S. Government. All government intelligence estimates, including public opinion assessments, have to be made on the assumption that the resultant product is for government guidance rather than for public print. If USIA surveys were taken out of this intelligence complex and released to the public, the picture would be incomplete and could be distorted.

3) The USIA survey mechanism has been made available by former Director Allen to other departments and agencies of the government to collect facts of particular interest to them. Through arrangements with the Bureau of the Budget, other users can reimburse the Agency. This arrangement means that more comprehensive surveys can be run with proportionately less cost to the cooperating agencies. The first such survey is being made in seven countries in Latin America and it will provide data for a specific National Intelligence Estimate on the situation in that crucial area.

4) President Kennedy has committed himself to fully and frankly inform the American people. He has implied not that a particular report or series of reports must be automatically released or discontinued but he and his authorized spokesmen will, after considering all the evidence, report to the people through public pronouncements.

A more comprehensive research program is possible now for several reasons. Research techniques have improved considerably in recent years. Coincident with this development the Agency has established a survey research mechanism which extends to all parts of the world. Moreover, this mechanism has gained enough experience to move ahead with confidence.

A comprehensive research program cannot confirm or revolutionize the information program in a single year. A build-up is necessary. In three years, however, a comprehensive research program could go a long way toward guiding, supplying, and evaluating the information program.

This program can enable us to know more about the basic aspirations of the people we are trying to reach. It can give us concrete indicators of the current climate of opinion. With this basic knowledge, it can determine the target "influentials" we have to work through and it can tell us the most effective communications channels to use. Finally the program of the future will provide more facts, objective facts, for evaluation of Agency programs and products.

Most USIA surveys are omnibus surveys. In addition to public opinion questions, they include questions on communications habits (how they learn and from what media), on reaction to specific USIA programs and products, and other incidental information.

The new frontiers around the world are immense. Rather than reduce any intelligence-gathering mechanism, we should seize and exploit all techniques for learning more, particularly in the field of human relations.

USIA has proved the survey technique. It should be brought to full flower.

---

117.   Memorandum From the Director of the Office of Research and Analysis, U.S. Information Agency (Stephens) to the Acting Director of the U.S. Information Agency (Washburn)[1]

Washington, February 2, 1961.

SUBJECT

Your Draft Memorandum on "Overseas Opinion Studies"

Yours was a noble and much appreciated effort to defend our public opinion studies.[2] Unfortunately, everybody in this office who has had to deal with these problems for several years feels that neither of your alternatives is the answer to our difficulties.

We have striven for several years to classify our reports as low as possible and have succeeded in producing more and more unclassified reports, particularly in connection with Communist propaganda. But it would be extremely difficult if not impossible to try to "sanitize" many of the most essential reports we produce. Trying to keep two sets of books creates more problems than it solves.

---

[1] Source: Washington National Records Center, RG 306, USIA Files: FRC 68 A 1415, FOIA/Classified Folder. Confidential. Drafted by Stephens. Copies were sent to Donald M. Wilson (I), James J. Halsema (IOP), G. Lewis Schmidt (IOA), and Henry Loomis (IBS).

[2] Reference is to a January 31 draft memorandum to the Secretary of State, which analyzed the USIA's opinion surveys. It recommended that either edited versions of the surveys or only the polling figures be made public. (Ibid.)

We have also carefully considered the possibility of releasing only the figures in public opinion polls. But this also creates more problems than it solves. The bare figures can lead to gross misinterpretation and if we try to produce even a few brief paragraphs of interpretation, we are still releasing an official governmental interpretation.

I think we have to maintain the position that our public opinion estimates are in the same category as all of the other intelligence estimates of the intelligence community, and that the administration, to fulfill its commitment to fully and frankly inform the American people, should utilize the information it gets from all intelligence data—not just the necessarily fragmentary and ephemeral insights of a particular poll, useful as it may be—to inform the people through public preannouncements. I don't think the administration can ever give in completely to the "right to know" crusade of the Fourth Estate which implies that all governmental documents should be subject to public scrutiny.

This IRI stand does not mean that this public opinion data can never be published. Following the precedent established by the State Department in its publication of the historic record of our foreign relations, we can make this material available after its sensitivity ends, and after the interest centers on the data itself rather than its relation to some other issue. We can also release certain data to certain research organizations for unattributed use, and it might also be used on appropriate occasions in testimony before Congressional committees.

For a fuller exposition of our views on the subject, I call to your attention the memorandum and the attachment, the "Prestige Polls" issue, which I sent to Mr. Murrow, Mr. Wilson and to you yesterday.

Also there are several inaccuracies in your memorandum. For example, the first sentence is an overstatement. Given funds we could in fact make surveys in almost all countries around the world, outside the Curtain, exept in a few countries where the political situation is in turmoil. In the last paragraph the third survey that you mentioned is a 7-nation study in Latin America rather than a 16-nation study. However, the number was limited to 7 only because of the fund limitation.

118. Memorandum From the Director-Designate of the U.S. Information Agency (Murrow) to President Kennedy[1]

Washington, February 7, 1961.

We propose to discontinue the use of foreign public opinion polls as such because (1) we do not want to give the impression abroad or at home that U.S. foreign policy is determined on a "popularity" basis, and (2) we question their value in view of the time lag between taking the polls and using them as a basis for action.

USIA's need is for political intelligence, based primarily on CIA reports and field interviews with political, business, labor, educational and other opinion leaders and only secondarily on public opinion sampling. To protect our sources, and assure their continuing usefulness, these Preoccupation Analyses would be classified and not made public.

Edward R. Murrow[2]

Approved[3]
Disapproved

---

[1] Source: Washington National Records Center, RG 306, USIA Files: FRC 69 A 6135, 1/1, Director's Staff Meeting Notes/61. No classification marking. Drafted by Thomas C. Sorensen on February 7.

[2] Printed from a copy that bears this typed signature.

[3] Although neither option is checked, the Director's staff meeting notes of February 13 indicate that the memorandum did go to the White House. (Washington National Records Center, RG 306, USIA Files: FRC 69 A 6135, 1/1, Director's Staff Meeting Notes/61)

---

119. Memorandum by the Under Secretary of State (Bowles)[1]

Washington, March 3, 1961.

MEMORANDUM TO

USIA—Mr. Edward R. Murrow
P—Mr. Roger W. Tubby
CU—Mr. Philip M. Coombs
C—Mr. George C. McGhee

---

[1] Source: Washington National Records Center, RG 306, USIA Files: FRC 64 A 853, 5/5, Directors Chrons, March '61. Confidential. Copies were sent to McGeorge Bundy and USIA Deputy Director Donald M. Wilson.

I have already spoken with Roger Tubby and with Ed Murrow at the Thursday Luncheon[2] of the crying need to improve public understanding of the US abroad. It seems to me we must review quickly the question of how we wish to portray ourselves, our society, our policies, and the motivations behind our major programs and consider how to correct many existing impressions abroad of American life and purpose. New techniques and procedures should be devised for improving our public relations efforts covering not only what we say but how we say it. The Thursday Luncheon was in agreement as to the importance of going ahead with this project with Ed Murrow taking the lead.[3] I would appreciate it, therefore, if you together would give it your early attention and keep me informed.

CB

---

[2] March 2; no record of this meeting, one in a series of regular meetings among Bowles, Murrow, and others in the U.S. foreign policy community, has been found.

[3] Murrow spoke to Bowles at a luncheon meeting on March 8 about the USIA's "need to know" and his agency's need to be included in the distribution of high-level correspondence within the administration. (Memorandum from Murrow to Bowles, March 8; Washington National Records Center, RG 306, USIA Files: FRC 64 A 853, 5/5, Directors Chrons, March '61)

---

120. Draft Letter From President Kennedy to the Director-Designate of the U.S. Information Agency (Murrow)[1]

Washington, undated.

Dear Ed,

This is to confirm our several conversations regarding the role of USIA and its relationship to me and the State Department.

---

[1] Source: Kennedy Library, National Security Files, Departments and Agencies Series, USIA, Box 290. No classification marking. According to a handwritten notation, the letter was drafted by Thomas C. Sorensen on March 10. No record has been found of the President signing a letter resembling this draft, but according to an attached March 10 memorandum from Murrow to McGeorge Bundy, this draft reflected at least the intentions of the White House at that time. It was sent in response to a written request by Bundy which, Murrow wrote, grew out of Bundy's earlier discussions with Deputy Director Wilson.

1. Organizationally, there is no change. USIA as presently constituted remains an independent agency, reporting directly to me. I have
charged the State Department with the responsibility of providing policy guidance to you and other agencies dealing in foreign affairs.

2. The State Department will continue to direct the Exchange-of-
Persons and Cultural Presentations programs. Overseas, USIA will
continue to operate these programs under the direction of the Chief of
Mission. On matters dealing with these programs your Public Affairs
Officers and their Cultural Affairs staffs should report directly to the
State Department through State channels. You and Assistant Secretary
Coombs, and your respective staffs, must work together closely and
harmoniously so this joint enterprise may have maximum effectiveness.

3. I consider you one of my principal advisors, with a special concern and competence in assessing the psychological factors dealing
with foreign affairs.[2] As such, I want you to participate when appropriate in the development of foreign policies and programs.

Sincerely,

John F. Kennedy[3]

---

[2] Bundy revised this sentence; before his changes, the sentence read: "I consider you
my principal advisor on psychological factors dealing with foreign affairs."

[3] Printed from a copy that bears this typed signature.

---

121. Memorandum From the Director of the U.S. Information Agency (Murrow) to U.S. Information Agency Staff[1]

Washington, April 22, 1961.

If USIA is to have maximum effectiveness as the psychological
instrument of U.S. foreign policy, our media output must be more
responsive to policy direction and emphasis, and faster and more flexible than heretofore. This requires the closest coordination of all media
efforts. I have asked IOP to undertake this responsibility and have
appointed Mr. Edgar D. Brooke, a senior Career Foreign Service Officer,

---

[1] Source: Kennedy Library, National Security Files, Departments and Agencies
Series, USIA, Box 290. No classification marking. Two copies of this memorandum were
provided to McGeorge Bundy under cover of a memorandum from Frederic Bundy of
USIA, April 27. (Ibid.)

as Director of Media Content. He reports directly to the Deputy Director of Policy and Plans.

Specifically, our purposes are:

1. To define the themes which media should convey and the subjects they should cover in their world-wide output, and to establish priorities among them.

2. To synthesize Area requirements for media output to best meet overall field needs.

3. To organize detailed programming of media efforts on behalf of priority themes to assure desired emphasis and appropriate division of responsibility.

4. To assure policy control of media output through continuing review.

Procedures:

1. *Themes and Subjects*

a. IOP, in consultation with the Areas, shall develop a definitive list of themes to be conveyed and subjects to be covered in world-wide output, and shall recommend to the Director which themes and subjects should be given priority.

b. IOP, working with the Areas and IRI, shall keep abreast of U.S. policy developments, field needs, and attitudes of key audiences, and shall revise the Agency's themes, subjects and priorities accordingly.

c. IOP shall provide the media with these approved lists of priority themes and subjects, and policy guidance on their handling

2. *Planning and Programming*

a. The media shall periodically provide IOP with their plans for production and acquisition of major items for world-wide use. ("Major items" shall be defined by IOP in consultation with the media.) IOP shall continuously review these plans to assure conformity with current national policy and Agency priorities.

b. IOP shall organize joint planning by the media to assure that world-wide output supports priority themes and that there is appropriate division of responsibility among the media for each theme.

3. *Policy Control*

a. In production of major items, the media shall provide drafts, scripts, or rough-cuts to IOP for policy review in time to permit changes if necessary.

b. IOP shall spot-check other output to assure conformity with policy.

4. *Applicability*

a. These procedures shall apply primarily to media output intended for more than one Area. Present procedures for servicing individual posts and for guidance covering output for a single geographic area are not altered by this memorandum.

b. The present fast news guidance procedures are not altered by this memorandum.

There is no intention to interpose a barrier between media chiefs and my deputies and myself. Rather, we seek to insure that all media are used with maximum effectiveness and that they are consistently and immediately responsive to policy decisions by the Government and program decisions of this Agency.

In this effort I ask your unstinting cooperation.

Edward R. Murrow

---

122.   Paper Prepared in the U.S. Information Agency[1]

Washington, undated.

AREAS OF CONFLICT

1. In programming, the principal problem caused by the existence of several U.S. broadcasting stations each with a different mission is that overseas listeners cannot always be certain to which they are listening. There have been many reports in recent years, from our embassies, refugees, and other sources, that many listeners in the USSR and the satellites frequently are unable to distinguish between VOA and RFE–RL. All three are known to be U.S.-supported so it is understandable that these listeners often do not attempt to make a distinction. The credibility—or lack thereof—of one U.S. radio tends to rub off on the others. This is also true, but to a lesser extent, with respect to VOA and VUNC broadcasts to Korea and the Chinese mainland. AFRTS broadcasts also are confused in some countries with VOA English transmissions. It can be argued, of course, that it is desirable to have more than one U.S. radio available to listeners, each designed for a different segment of the audience.

---

[1] Source: Kennedy Library, Arthur M. Schlesinger Papers, White House Subject Files, Classified Subject File, USIA, Box 48. Secret; Eyes Only. An attached covering memorandum from Murrow, dated May 8, transmitted this paper to Walt Rostow at the White House. It reads in part: "It seemed to me best to try to outline the magnitude of the problem we face in attempting to coordinate or consolidate United States radio efforts. This is our effort to do so. As you will observe, the paper is stripped of technicalities and I fear the alternatives are none of them satisfactory."

2. In the case of AFRTS there is a possibility that the relatively large-scale use of frequencies and filling of the airwaves with a foreign language causes people to resent the presence of U.S. troops. Such broadcasting undoubtedly makes the presence of the troops more visible to a larger section of the population. This can be both good and bad. These issues are somewhat similar to those raised by the ostentatiousness of PX's.

3. Frequency Usage. Frequencies for international broadcasting are becoming an increasingly more difficult resource to obtain. Particularly in the high frequency spectrum, the outlook is very bleak because of the fact that the total amount of useful spectrum space is decreasing considerably while at the same time new broadcasting services are increasing. VOA could use part of the spectrum space now used by RFE and RL. From the standpoint of delivering a U.S. message to the world, their use of these frequencies is inefficient since their targets are limited to only a few countries. Their use of the frequencies makes them unusable by others over a much wider geographical area; in addition since RFE and RL are always jammed even neighboring frequencies are interfered with.

The operation of AFRTS stations overseas also adds to the frequency problem. In Germany for example, AFN uses several powerful 100 KW transmitters on several desirable medium wave frequencies. These frequencies would be very valuable to VOA, for example, which has only one mediumwave frequency for its relay station in Munich. The German stations also would like very much to have use of one or more of these frequencies and may some day demand them back. Possibly we would be better off by arranging for VOA to have one of these frequencies and the Germans the rest . . . before we are forced to give them all back. U.S. willingness to give up one or more of these frequencies now night even be used as the "Quid" for extending or enlarging our VOA agreement with the German government.

The use of frequencies for AFRTS, particularly those with high power, becomes increasingly difficult to justify to international conferences working on frequency availability.

4. Interference. Because of the band crowding which is greatly increased by the large RFE and RL use of frequencies, there is considerably less than desirable separation between stations. Because of this, RFE and RL cause interference to VOA transmissions. VOA could utilize the same number of transmitters and frequencies without this detrimental effect because it has a much wider target area and could therefore plan the frequency usage so as not to cause itself this interference.

5. Jamming. RFE and RL attract a great deal of jamming, much of which spills over and jams VOA programs which are not otherwise jammed. Permanent jammers can be set up efficiently on RFE and RL frequencies to cover their limited target area. VOA usage of a frequency to widely separated areas makes the problem of jamming much more

difficult since many more jammers are required to work on a given number of transmitters and frequencies.

Every time we bring up the subject of Communist jamming (either at the International Telecommunications Union, the United Nations or directly with the Russians), they counter-challenge by accusing the United States of broadcasting "evil propaganda broadcasts." While we have always pointed out that the Voice of America broadcasts do not fall into the category they describe, they immediately make reference to the broadcasts of RL and RFE. We claim to have no control over the broacasts of RFE and RL, but this is not believed by many countries of the world. Up until now, our attempts to condemn Communist jamming have always ended in a stalemate. We attack the Russians for jamming us and they counter-attack by claiming that we are directing broadcasts of an inflammatory nature to them (and the broadcasts they usually refer to are RL and RFE).

In 1950 the UNGA condemned both sides by stating that both jamming and inflammatory propaganda broadcasts should cease. It is very difficult for us to take a strong position against jamming on the one hand and defend the broadcasts of RL and RFE on the other.

6. International Conferences. The existence of RFE and RL are becoming more embarrassing to handle at international conferences concerning broadcasting and telecommunications regulation. It is obvious to a great many of the members of these conferences that these two radio operations are U.S. government supported, and yet explanation of the need for these operations is very difficult for anyone to give. In conferences dealing with the problems of frequency shortage, interference, attempts to find useful spectrum for the new and developing countries, etc., explanation of these operations, which use such big chunks of the bands, is difficult, and results in weakening the U.S. position, since it leaves the impression of something in which the U.S. is deeply involved but is not willing to admit or explain.

7. Host Agreements. Another way in which RFE and RL cause some difficulty to VOA is in the matter of agreements with host governments. RFE and RL are able to make agreements of a type which would not be permitted for VOA, because they do not have the same restrictions on expenditures or other terms. This makes it difficult for VOA to obtain satisfactory agreements wherever the host is familiar with the RFE or RL arrangements.

8. AFRTS Use of VOA Facilities. VOA provides AFRTS with transmission facilities for the broadcast of AFRTS programs from the U.S. to overseas locations and, in one instance, for relay of the programs abroad. The service to AFRTS amounts to 79:45 transmitter hours daily—or 9% of VOA transmitter usage—and is absorbed in the VOA budget with no reimbursement from AFRTS.

If prorated as a part of the overall VOA network costs, the value of the AFRTS transmissions would be approximately $386,000 annually. However, the savings to VOA if the AFRTS utilization of our facilities should be terminated would be only about $85,000. Obviously separate AFRTS transmitting facilities would be more expensive.

In addition to the daily AFRTS schedule, VOA facilities are furnished to AFRTS on an ad hoc basis for the coverage of special events, mainly sports. We comply with AFRTS requests for facilities on such occasions whenever it is possible to do so without serious harm to our own operations.

Since our facilities do not now provide the flexibility we require for our own purposes, the carrying of AFRTS affects our program decisions, limiting the diversity of our programs.

It should be mentioned that VOA and AFRTS work together to some extent in the program area. The degree of cooperation varies from area to area, depending upon the need and the personnel involved.

---

123. Memorandum From Secretary of State Rusk and the Director of the U.S. Information Agency (Murrow) to President Kennedy[1]

Washington, June 8, 1961.

SUBJECT

An Effective Countertheme to "Peaceful Coexistence"

In the period since early 1956 the Soviets have transformed the concept and phrase, "peaceful coexistence," into a useful political tool by assiduous and continuous propagation at all levels of the government and party apparatus. They have gained abroad a substantial measure of acceptance of this concept as a legitimate objective, not only of their foreign policy but of other countries. It appears as such in repeated joint communiqués of the Soviet Union and other countries and all too

---

[1] Source: Washington National Records Center, RG 306, USIA Files: FRC 68 A 1415, Policy and Plans—Nuclear Testing/61. Official Use Only. According to a memorandum from Frederic O. Bundy, this memorandum did not go directly to the President, but was intercepted by Arthur Schlesinger, Jr., who then forwarded it to McGeorge Bundy under cover of a June 19 memorandum. (Ibid.) Schlesinger's memorandum is printed as Document 124.

frequently in the speeches and conversations of leading political figures, particularly but not exclusively, from the uncommitted countries.

We have attempted to combat it by pointing out both the hypocrisy and true meaning of its major tenets and by indicating that it is nothing more than a Soviet rationalization for using every measure of struggle against the free world except nuclear warfare. Toward this end we have made occasional public speeches and have instructed our posts abroad to disseminate our views of it. This has been manifestly inadequate. In the field of propaganda one simply can not beat something with nothing.

We have needed a single, simple countertheme if we are to do the job. After a long study of the possible alternatives, we have concluded that "peaceful world community" is the most effective phrase we can find. Although this phrase seems to embody the essence of our basic foreign objectives, we recognize that neither it nor any other single phrase will magically accomplish our purposes. If, however, we devote the same degree of attention and effort to it that the Soviets give to "peaceful coexistence," we should be able to invest it with meaningful content, achieve an increasing measure of understanding of the difference between our and the Soviet concept and have some success in associating other countries with our view. "Peaceful world community" also helps us in our efforts to emphasize that "general and complete disarmament" is not an end in itself but an important component of a larger aim. John McCloy quite independently used the exact phrase for that purpose in his conversation with Gromyko. USIA is instructing all its media to employ the term whenever it is appropriate.

If you approve of this phrase and of its employment in the manner indicated, we will give some thought as to how it can be most auspiciously launched.

Dean Rusk

Edward R. Murrow

124.   Memorandum From the President's Special Assistant
         (Schlesinger) to the President's Special Assistant for
         National Security Affairs (Bundy)[1]

Washington, June 19, 1961.

SUBJECT

The Rusk–Murrow Memorandum on "An Effective Countertheme to 'Peaceful Coexistence'"

The attached memorandum for the President from Dean Rusk and Ed Murrow proposes that we attempt to combat the Soviet propaganda emphasis on "peaceful coexistence" by developing the countertheme of "peaceful world community."[2] USIA has apparently already instructed its people to employ the term whenever it is appropriate.[3] I am not convinced by this memorandum; and, before it is taken up with the President, I would welcome your views on the matter.

Obviously a new propaganda phrase is not going to solve our problems. In any case, I doubt whether this phrase is the right one for the simple reason that it does *not* do what it is supposed to do—that is, it does not establish an "understanding of the difference between our and the Soviet concept." The heart of that difference, I would have thought, lies in the question of human dignity and freedom—and this is not immediately suggested by the proposed phrase. If one were to ask Khrushchev whether he was against a "peaceful world community," he would of course reply—and truthfully in his terms—that this is exactly what he is working day and night to bring about. "Peaceful world community" and "peaceful coexistence" do not constitute a meaningful antithesis.

I am informed also by Roger Tubby and Philip Stern of State that the phrase "peaceful world community" presents tricky problems in translation. In many languages, it will come out, when translated, very close to "peaceful coexistence." In Russian, I understand, the words for "peaceful" and "world" are identical, which would make our proposed slogan very clumsy indeed (*mirnoye mirnoye obschchestvo*). Also "community" is hard to render; in many languages, it will come out as "village" or, if transliterated, will be hard to distinguish from "communism."

---

[1] Source: Washington National Records Center, RG 306, USIA Files: FRC 68 A 1415, Policy and Plans—Nuclear Testing/61. No classification marking.

[2] Document 123.

[3] In a memorandum of April 18, Murrow notified Under Secretary of State Bowles of USIA's intention "to employ the term 'peaceful world community' in all media whenever appropriate." (Washington National Records Center, RG 306, USIA Files: FRC 68 A 1415, Policy and Plans—General, Jan–Jun 61)

I share the Tubby–Stern view that "world of free choice" would be a preferable phrase. "World of free choice" suggests an immediate antithesis: the pluralistic world vs. the monolithic world. The phrase implies human dignity, political freedom, self help, cultural independence, etc. It should strike a particularly responsive chord in the underdeveloped world where nations and individuals probably care much more at the moment about freedom for national self-assertion than about a peaceful world community. Since free choice is one thing the Communists can't bear and always eradicate at the first opportunity, Khrushchev would be much harder put to claim that he too wanted a world of free choice. Moreover, the phrase apparently presents no very serious translation problems.

Let me quote from Dean Rusk's eloquent statement on May 31 before the Senate Foreign Relations Committee, "We seek, above all, a world of free choice in which a great diversity of nations, each faithful to its own traditions and its own genius, will learn to respect the ground rules of human survival. We do not wish to make the world over in our own image—and we will not accept that the world be made over in the image of any society or dogmatic creed. Against the world of coercion, we affirm the world of choice. We believe that the revolution of human liberty will never come to an end."[4] This seems to me to be the main point.

Arthur Schlesinger, jr.

---

[4] For full text of Secretary Rusk's May 31 statement, see Department of State *Bulletin*, June 19, 1961, pp. 947–955.

---

125. Memorandum From the Director of the U.S. Information Agency (Murrow) to the Under Secretary of State (Bowles)[1]

Washington, June 24, 1961.

SUBJECT

The Nuclear Test Ban Issue

At your request my colleagues and I have undertaken careful study of the impact of the nuclear test ban issue. We have drawn on suggestions by the Disarmament Administration, Ambassador Galbraith and Mr. Chayes.

---

[1] Source: Washington National Records Center, RG 306, USIA Files: FRC 68 A 1415, Govt. Agencies, DOD/61. Secret. Drafted on June 24 by Thomas C. Sorensen and J. O. Hanson.

We believe this issue is a key, conceivably *the* key, to our Cold War posture in the coming year. Unless we persuade our allies and the uncommitted nations of the rightness of our course in this respect, we stand in grave danger of losing their support on other issues, notably Berlin.

Whether we decide to resume testing or not, world opinion must be persuaded that:

1. The United States has done everything in its power to obtain a treaty banning nuclear testing.
2. The Soviet Union does not want a test-ban treaty and thus has not negotiated in good faith.
3. If and when the United States resumes testing, it is because the irreducible minimum security needs of the free world including the neutrals require it.

To achieve these psychological objectives, it is essential we begin now on a massive, three-phase information effort. Abroad, this is a highly emotional issue. As Ambassador Galbraith said in his memorandum to the President: "A resumption of testing would cause us the gravest difficulties in Asia, Africa and elsewhere . . . The issue between ourselves and the Soviets at Geneva are abstract and poorly understood . . . If we are the first to test that will be the one noticeable and noticed thing. Those who are unfriendly to us will have a field day on an issue where they can arouse a great deal of popular passion."

Our task, then, is to meet this emotional issue with the patient repetition of reasonable arguments cast in emotional terms. We have six months—the time it will take the military to prepare significant weapons tests. Specifically we propose:

Phase One:

1. Ambassador Dean returns to Geneva. If he does not, our stated willingness to go the "last mile" to obtain a treaty will not be credible in the eyes of the world.
2. The President makes a major "peace" speech in which he reviews U.S. and free world efforts toward disarmament since 1945, making the test-ban treaty the symbol of these efforts. He calls on the Soviets to put the world's fears at rest.
3. A few hours before the President delivers this address, our Ambassadors call on the heads of government to whom they are accredited and give them copies of his message. Our Chiefs of Mission use the occasion to brief the foreign leaders on the US–UK draft treaty, and our position in general, in greater detail than the President does in his speech.
4. Dean flies from Geneva to certain "neutral" capitals (e.g., Delhi, Cairo, Djakarta) to assist in briefing foreign leaders. Certain U.S. scientists are employed to brief their counterparts abroad.

5. USIA undertakes a massive information campaign to stimulate interest in and support for our position among world opinion leaders. *Themes*: U.S. determination to reach agreement, contrasted with Soviet intransigeance—e.g. insistence on Troika and refusal to accept reasonable inspection. Importance of test-ban treaty as first step toward disarmament; without the former, the latter is unobtainable. If peace is to be preserved, the Soviets must give up some of their irrational secrecy which is unworthy of a modern nation. What are they hiding, secret nuclear tests?

6. CIA covertly: (a) Launches a signature campaign by indigenous groups appealing to the Soviets to sign the US–UK draft treaty; (b) plants rumors in the foreign press that earthquakes, TNT explosions, etc., in the USSR may actually be secret nuclear tests.

7. Get one or more neutral nations to introduce a resolution at next autumn's U.N. General Assembly session calling on the atomic powers to sign a workable test-ban treaty with adequate controls. Stevenson and staff tirelessly press our case in the corridors.

Phase Two:

1. If the President determines that free world security absolutely requires resumption of testing should we fail to obtain a treaty from the Soviets (and this is a big *if*), preparations should be as secret and low-key as possible so as not to hurt the credibility of our agreement-seeking posture. There should not be a White House announcement; when the story leaks, the AEC confirms we are making contingency preparations pending a decision.

2. If our information campaign, our pressure on world leaders and efforts at the U.N. fail to budge the Soviets, the President and Mr. Macmillan make a final, solemn public plea to Khrushchev. Again, our Ambassadors in the field personally brief heads of government on this appeal.

3. USIA obtains widest possible dissemination and discussion of the Kennedy–Macmillan appeal. *Themes*: Free world security and survival requires either an effective test ban or resumption of testing. The Soviets may now be testing in secret. The Chinese may be behind Soviet intransigeance.

Phase Three (assuming a decision to resume testing):

1. If Khrushchev remains adamant, the President and Macmillan simultaneously announce their decision to resume testing, emphasizing that it is being done solely because free world security absolutely requires it. The history of our efforts is reviewed. The two leaders make it clear that we will not test in the atmosphere, and thus there will be no fallout.

2. The President and Macmillan write personal letters to all heads of government, for delivery by our Ambassadors just before the US–UK announcement, disclosing their decision and repeating the reasons for it.

3. The President, Mr. Rusk and Ambassador Stevenson—in carefully-spaced statements to keep our position before the public over a period of weeks—restate that position. USIA obtains widest possible dissemination of these statements.

4. Foreign correspondents and observers, including Soviets, are invited to witness the tests so that the public may be reassured about our no-fallout safety precautions. Worldwide scientific opinion is mobilized in support of this contention.

5. Shortly after weapons tests (but only *after*, because security is the only valid reason for resuming testing), we carry out tests for peaceful uses of nuclear power—AEC's "Project Plowshare." USIA gives widest possible dissemination to this project which seeks to utilize atomic power for digging harbors, generating electricity, extracting oil, etc.

6. After our first tests, the President reaffirms the U.S. desire for a test-ban treaty and invites the Soviets to resume negotiations.

Edward R. Murrow[2]

---

[2] Printed from a copy that bears this typed signature.

---

126.   National Security Action Memorandum No. 61[1]

Washington, July 14, 1961.

MEMORANDUM FOR

Secretary of State
Director, U.S. Information Agency

SUBJECT

An Effective Countertheme to "Peaceful Coexistence"

The President completely endorses the effort to combat the Soviet propaganda trap contained in the phrase "peaceful coexistence" by the use of symbolic language that expresses our view of the nature of the conflict in which we are engaged. The statements by the Secretary

---

[1] Source: Washington National Records Center, RG 306, USIA Files: FRC 68 A 1415, Policy and Plans—Nuclear Testing/61. Official Use Only.

of State before the Senate Foreign Relations Committee and, more recently, at the Press Club,[2] have provided the language we need to do the job. He has expressed the conflict as being between the "world of free choice and free cooperation" and "the world of coercion."

The President has requested that immediate steps be taken to give this formulation the widespread currency and usage that would make it an effective countertheme to the Soviet formula. It is requested that the facilities available to the Department of State and the U.S. Information Agency be employed in this effort.[3] This request is also being passed along to the appropriate members of the White House Staff for action.

McGeorge Bundy[4]

---

[2] Regarding Secretary Rusk's statement before the Senate Foreign Relations Committee, see footnote 4, Document 124. For text of his address to the National Press Club on July 10, see Department of State *Bulletin*, July 31, 1961, pp. 175–178.

[3] In a July 18 memorandum to Murrow, Sorensen reported on the President's endorsement of the phrase "World of Free Choice" and indicated that instructions to "all offices in Washington" and the field on the phraseology were carried in "News Policy Note" (No. 114–61, July 13) and "Infoguide" (No. 62–1, July 17). (Washington National Records Center, RG 306, USIA Files: FRC 68 A 1415, Policy and Plans—Nuclear Testing/61)

[4] Printed from a copy that bears this typed signature.

---

127. Memorandum From the Director of the U.S. Information Agency (Murrow) to the Director for Policy and Plans, U.S. Information Agency (Sorensen)[1]

Washington, July 19, 1961.

Please get the word around the Agency that we are to drop from our lexicon the words "under-developed countries," "undeveloped countries," "backward countries," and any similar terms.

As substitutes, IRI reports that the words which translate the best in all languages and are positive in their connotations are "developing countries" and "modernizing countries."

---

[1] Source: Washington National Records Center, RG 306, USIA Files: FRC 68 A 1415, Policy and Plans—General/61. No classification marking. Drafted by C. R. Payne of the Office of the Director. Copies were sent to Schlesinger, Bundy, and Rostow at the White House and to Assistant Secretary of State Tubby later the same day under cover of a memorandum from Murrow and Rostow. (Ibid.)

"Emerging countries" is not considered to be good,[2] and the use of "new" before "developing" and "modernizing" is confusing in translation in most languages.

When your shop has time, I would like to have an updated "Guidance on Preferred Terminology" prepared which would propose positive words to be used as substitutes for such terms as "East-West," "Cold War," "pro-West," "pro-American country" and many others which are misleading, inaccurate and not in our best interests. All new suggestions should be checked out for a worldwide translatability.

Edward R. Murrow[3]

---

[2] In a July 7 memorandum to Payne, IRI Director Stevens wrote: "'Emerging countries' is not considered so good. The 'emerging' has some of the connotations of the old colonialism and is more political than 'developing' and 'modernizing' which have a more economic meaning." (Ibid.)

[3] Printed from a copy that bears this typed signature.

---

128. National Security Action Memorandum No. 63[1]

Washington, July 24, 1961.

TO

The Secretary of State
The Secretary of Defense
Director, U.S. Information Agency
Director of Central Intelligence

SUBJECT

Policy Guidance and Preemption of U.S. Government-Controlled Broadcasting

After consultation with the heads of Departments and agencies concerned, the President has approved the following:

1. The Department of State shall provide foreign policy guidance to all international radio broadcasting and television stations controlled by U.S. Government agencies. This includes stations of the Armed

---

[1] Source: Kennedy Library, Arthur M. Schlesinger Papers, White House Subject Files, Classified Subject File, USIA, Box 48. Top Secret. Copies were sent to the Chairman of the Joint Chiefs of Staff, the Secretaries of the armed services, and to the President's Special Counsel, Military Representative, and Military Aide. Copies were also passed to Arthur Schlesinger, Evelyn Lincoln, McGeorge Bundy, and Bromley Smith/Charles E. Johnson.

Forces Radio and Television Service and the Voice of the United Nations Command in Korea, operated by the Department of Defense, and those stations [*less than 1 line of source text not declassified*] influenced or financed by the Central Intelligence Agency.

2. This guidance shall be relayed through the U.S. Information Agency, which will provide supplemental information policy guidance as required. The Director, U.S. Information Agency shall establish appropriate procedures for conveying guidance.

3. The Director, U.S. Information Agency is authorized to preempt time on any of these radio and television stations for special programs when he deems it to be in the national interest. The Director, U.S. Information Agency shall establish appropriate procedures for arranging for such special programs.

4. Every effort shall be made to avoid public awareness of the relationship between the various ostensibly non-governmental broadcasting stations and the U.S. Government.

McGeorge Bundy[2]

---

[2] Printed from a copy that bears this typed signature.

---

129. Memorandum From the Director of the U.S. Information Agency (Murrow) to the Heads of all U.S. Information Agency Elements and All U.S. Information Service Posts[1]

Washington, July 24, 1961.

SUBJECT

Special Program Emphasis

Until further notice, Washington media and field posts will focus attention on, and give special emphasis to, persuading our audiences that:

1. Despite Soviet intransigeance, the United States is doing everything in its power to obtain a treaty banning nuclear testing, the first, vital step toward general disarmament. (Test Ban)

2. Soviet efforts to abrogate their agreements and deprive West Berliners of their freedom threaten the security and freedom of people

---

[1] Source: Washington National Records Center, RG 306, USIA Files: FRC 68 A 1415, Office of the Director—Circular Letters/61. Official Use Only. Drafted by Edgar D. Brooke.

everywhere. Under no circumstances, therefore, will the U.S. abandon Free Berlin. (Berlin)

3. An effective United Nations which has sufficient authority to act in crisis situations is indispensable to the security of small nations. Knowing this, the Soviets are seeking to paralyze the U.N. Secretariat with an unworkable "troika" arrangement. (United Nations)

4. The Sino-Soviet Bloc, despite lip-service support to emerging nationalism, is implacably opposed to independent nationalist movements and genuine neutrality. Man's best hope is in "a world of free choice" such as sought by the U.S., not a "world of coercion" as favored by the Communists. (Free Choice)

5. Modernization of newly-developing nations can best be achieved through democratic, pragmatic political and economic development consistent with the traditions, character and aspirations of a people. (Modernization)

These areas of emphasis are not intended to supplant all other Agency output. We simply are seeking to focus adequate media and field attention for a period of time on subjects currently of overriding importance. I have been specifically charged by the President with the task of undertaking major efforts on items (1) and (2).

The duration of these efforts will vary. There cannot be universal and equal emphasis, either by all media or in all countries. I will expect IOP (in the person of Mr. Brooke, Director of Media Content), working with the Area offices and the media, to develop appropriate emphasis and application of these efforts in the various countries in which we operate, along the lines set forth in my memorandum to the Staff of April 22.[2] IOP will provide detailed policy guidances to the media and to the field in support of these efforts.

I ask your full cooperation and support.

---

[2] Document 121.

130. Memorandum From the Director of the U.S. Information Agency (Murrow) to President Kennedy[1]

Washington, August 31, 1961.

SUBJECT

Considerations Regarding Nuclear Testing

1. What is now to be tested is not so much nuclear devices as the will of free men to remain free.

2. Those who today urge you to resume testing immediately will tomorrow contend that the decision to do so was merely another belated reaction to Soviet action.

3. What is required is *time*. We can within weeks achieve the position of the last best hope of freedom, sanity and survival. This can be done not only by the exposure of Soviet duplicity, but also by playing heavily upon the fears of hazards to health and future generations.

4. No further public statements should be made during the Belgrade Conference. Our people there should be instructed to say quietly that our arsenal is adequate to any demands that may be made upon it and that the President is considering the advisability of giving Khrushchev one final chance to draw back.

5. There should be no indication of consultation with our allies lest this be interpreted as a sign of vacillation or indecision.

6. Steps should be taken to bring the question before the U. N. General Assembly, where in the course of a roaring debate the Russians can be hoist on a troicka of their own making, Berlin, colonialism and nuclear testing.

7. I have heard no arguments from the military or scientific community to indicate a delay of a few weeks in the resumption of testing would endanger the national security. This time, if properly employed, can be used to isolate the Communist Bloc, frighten the satellites and the uncommitted, pretty well destroy the *Ban the Bomb* movement in Britain, and might even induce sanity into the SANE nuclear policy group in this country.

8. During this interval, special effort should be made to arrange for an Administration spokesman to appear on television and radio, not to make statements of policy but rather to explain why precipitate action is unnecessary and unwise and why this country should not, by the immediate imitation of Soviet tactics, throw away this opportunity to consolidate its leadership of the non-communist world.

Edward R. Murrow[2]

---

[1] Source: Kennedy Library, National Security Files, Subjects Series, Nuclear Testing, Box 799. Confidential.

[2] Printed from a copy that bears this typed signature.

131.   Memorandum From the Director of the Research and
        Reference Service, U.S. Information Agency (Stephens) to
        the Director of the U.S. Information Agency (Murrow)

Washington, October 30, 1961.

[Source: Washington National Records Center, RG 306, USIA Files:
FRC 68 A 1415, FOIA/Classified Folder. Confidential. 2 pages of source
text not declassified.]

---

132.   Memorandum From the Director of the U.S. Information
        Agency (Murrow) to the President's Special Assistant for
        National Security Affairs (Bundy)[1]

Washington, November 1, 1961.

Ambassador Tuthill, our permanent representative to the OECD,
has come up with a proposal which I believe will have great impact not
only among the Western European countries but more particularly in
the uncommitted countries of the world. It is an idea which I believe
will interest the President.

As you know, the OECD will hold its first meeting on the
Ministerial level in Paris on November 16–17. This will give Western
European nations the opportunity to review the economic success they
have achieved over the last 12 years as a result of the cooperative efforts
symbolized by the OEEC, the Marshall Plan, the Common Market, Steel
and Coal Community, the European Payments Union, etc. In summarizing these achievements, it can be shown that the economic vitality of
the West is far greater under our capitalistic system than any like
achievements which can be boasted by the Soviet bloc.

The second part of this proposal, which I find even more important,
is that the representatives of the OECD nations would outline a vigorous economic plan for the future. They should set goals for the next five

---

[1] Source: Kennedy Library, National Security Files, Departments and Agencies
Series, USIA, Box 290. A handwritten note on the memorandum by Bromley Smith reads:
"Kaysen's views attached." Another handwritten note by Bundy reads: "I told him on
phone OK." The memorandum was passed to Bundy under cover of a November 2 memorandum from Kaysen. (Ibid.)

or ten years not only for their own countries but also for the aid in the development and economic progress of the less favored nations of the world.[2] Details of this plan are contained in the telegram from Ambassador Tuthill which I attach to this memorandum.[3]

The time is short for obtaining the approval of all the nations involved in this plan but I think it can be done if Ambassador Tuthill is given the go ahead signal right away. He has in his hands in Paris all the necessary elements. USIA would of course be prepared to bring this story to all parts of the world as soon as the Ministerial conference had approved the plan.

Edward R. Murrow

---

[2] Kaysen's November 2 memorandum included the following comments regarding economic goals: "Murrow is right; it would be an excellent idea to get something agreed on this. . . . The general line we [the Council of Economic Advisers, including participation by officials from the Departments of State and Treasury and Kaysen] have discussed is to set growth goals in absolute terms for the whole OECD community by the end of the decade. The numbers involved are something on the order of 50% increase in the combined gross product of the whole area by 1970." Such an agreement was reached at the OECD's opening Ministerial meeting.

[3] Cedto 295 from Paris, October 27. (Kennedy Library, National Security Files, Departments and Agencies Series, Department of State, 11/1/61–11/5/61) For additional information on this OECD Ministerial Meeting, see *Foreign Relations, 1961–1963*, vol. IX, Document 127.

---

133. Memorandum From the Director of the U.S. Information Agency (Murrow) to President Kennedy[1]

Washington, December 5, 1961.

Weekly Report:

1. *Izvestia* moved your interview[2] to the last two pages in the second of its two editions. (The first edition is primarily for street sales; subscribers get the second, which is believed to be the larger in circulation.) Khrushchev's Novosibirsk speech of November 26 on agriculture occupied practically all of pages one, two and three in the second edition.

---

[1] Source: Kennedy Library, National Security Files, Departments and Agencies Series, USIA, Box 290. No classification marking.

[2] For the transcript of this interview on November 25, see *Public Papers of the Presidents of the United States: John F. Kennedy, 1961*, pp. 741–752.

The interview may have been read by as many as 40 million people. On a story of this great interest, *Izvestia* is credited with up to ten readers per copy, or roughly one out of every five citizens of the USSR.

Our experts do not believe the "debate" character of the exchange, widely commented on here, detracted from the intense interest with which readers searched your words for clues to the question of war or peace.

You may now wish to consider doing the same thing from time to time for other countries such as Poland where the American view does not get through adequately.

2. Outside the Communist Bloc, editorial comment on your *Izvestia* interview was largely favorable, with most editorials stressing the significance of an uncensored presentation of U.S. policies. Some European media credited the Soviets with a sincere effort to present the U.S. view. A number of Near and Far East papers strongly approved both the granting of the interview and the content; *Asahi* of Japan suggested an exchange of such interviews with Communist China. Three French papers, however, expressed concern over the development of bi-lateral relationships. A Cuban radio commentator charged you with lies, hypocrisy and a variety of other evils.

3. A tough *Pravda* editorial and a TASS dispatch on December 1 may signal intensification of the Soviet propaganda drive to keep Austria out of the Common Market. *Pravda* said flatly that Austrian participation would violate neutrality, and TASS equated the Market with NATO. Preliminary Austrian reaction was firm and cool, with officials taking the position that Austria must be the judge of its own neutrality.

4. The construction of our new shortwave transmitting complex near Greenville, N.C., is proceeding well, with all phases on schedule. I inspected the work last week, and was well satisfied with both the design and progress in construction. The Greenville facility will give us a capacity of 4,800 kilowatts, on eighteen transmitters, as compared with a present east-coast capacity of 1,385 kilowatts. It will provide a greatly improved signal to Africa, the Middle East, South America and Europe for direct shortwave, relay and emergency communications. The entire installation will be operational at the end of 1962.

5. More than half the British public (52 per cent) supports admission of Communist China to the United Nations, according to a Gallup survey made available to USIA. Another Gallup survey showed 42 per cent of the British people favoring representation of both Communist China and Nationalist China, 11 per cent opposed to both, 9 per cent for Nationalist China only, 9 per cent for Red China only, and 29 per cent without an opinion.

6. The Scandinavian press continues uneasy over Soviet pressures on Finland, after temporary relief over what appeared to be a solution.

The conviction now is widespread throughout Scandinavia and Western Europe generally that this is only the first in a series of moves aimed at Finland.

7. Communist Bloc distribution of books and periodicals in Africa has increased markedly in 1961, according to a year-end USIA research report.[3] The countries well-penetrated include Cameroun, Ghana, Guinea, Mali, Morocco, Nigeria, Senegal, Somali Republic and Zanzibar.

8. I am leaving for Paris Thursday evening for three days of discussions with my British, French and German opposite numbers in the continuing effort to harmonize our activities. I expect to be back on December 13, after a brief stop in London.

Edward R. Murrow[4]

---

[3] At a news conference on March 23, President Kennedy was queried about Soviet and Chinese Communist publication of "3 to 4 million books a year," and sending many of them to "noncommitted" nations. In comparison, the USIA's book delivery paled in what the questioner termed a "book gap" that would perhaps "present a tremendous obstacle to our winning the minds of the uncommitted peoples." The President responded: "Well, I agree that both the Chinese Communists and the Russians have poured large sums of money into subsidizing cheap book publications which have poured into many sections of the world and is a matter of concern. I think the point is excellent. Mr. Murrow has been considering what we could do in an expanded way in this area. There are areas where they've also made a greater effort, radio broadcasts to Africa and so on as well as exchanges. So that we have the whole problem, of which books is a part, in this struggle between freedom and control." (Ibid., p. 219)

In a weekly report from Murrow to President Kennedy, August 27, two related items were presented: "6. The Soviet Union spent an estimated $10,000,000 on propaganda in India last year, according to a USIS-New Delhi study. The tab for paid advertising alone ran to one million dollars. Our own budget for India was $4,900,000 in the last fiscal year, a rate that can only be supported because of the supply of local currency available under P.L. 480. 7. The volume of orders for books and pamphlets on Communist China, produced by USIA's special China Reporting Program in Hong Kong, doubled during the last fiscal year. In FY 1962, USIS posts ordered 140,000 for distribution in their respective countries; last year it was 287,000." (Kennedy Library, Arthur M. Schlesinger Papers, White House Subject Files, Classified Subject File, USIA, Box 48)

[4] Printed from a copy that bears this typed signature.

134.   Editorial Note

At a Director's staff meeting in January 1962, Acting USIA Director Wilson corroborated press reports that Murrow was in Paris "with Pierre Salinger for a meeting with the Soviet press officer Karmalov concerning exchanges in television and other communications media with the USSR." (Washington National Records Center, RG 306, USIA Files: FRC 88 A 18, 1/1, Director's Staff Meetings/61) Henry Loomis, USIA's "media head" for broadcasting, had broached the idea of a television exchange at a USIA Director's staff meeting on March 6, 1961. He then reported that the "Soviets at last have indicated their willingness to proceed with the radio-TV exchanges provided for in the US-USSR exchange agreement." The Soviets wished to send a team to the United States in order to develop arrangements for the exchange, and Loomis felt it best for the United States to do likewise to "prevent being short-changed." (Ibid.) The exchange agreement for 1960–1961 was signed in Moscow on November 21, 1959, and entered into force on January 1, 1960. (10 UST 1934)

On February 20, 1962, Charles Bohlen, Special Assistant to the Secretary of State, sent a telegram on behalf of Secretary Rusk to George F. Kennan, Ambassador to Yugoslavia, expressing President Kennedy's request for Kennan's input on the Kennedy–Khrushchev television exchange, for which draft texts were supposed to be exchanged on March 8. (Telegram 878 to Belgrade, February 20; Kennedy Library, National Security Files, Country Files, USSR, TV Exchange, 3/8/62, Box 190) Kennan responded on February 23 that the exchange's "main target will be the Soviet people" and that the President should not consider this a suitable occasion for direct personal sole-mizing [sic] with Khrushchev" but use it "to correct by skillful indirection certain impressions Soviet propagandists have endeavored to build up: namely, that we are militaristic, wedded to Cold War, averse to peaceful coexistence, animated by imperialistic designs on others and uninterested in any constructive collaborative trend on international life." (Telegram 3991 from Paris, February 23; ibid.)

In a February 21 memorandum to his brother Ted at the White House, Tom Sorensen indicated that the President would "have the same advantages in his TV appearance with Khrushchev that he had in the Nixon debates: obvious sincerity, obvious ability, obvious youth and vigor." The memorandum continued: "Questions and comments directed to Russian-speaking guides at our recent exhibits in the USSR provide a useful insight into the Soviet public's concerns and misconceptions about the U.S. and its policies. Based on this experience and the advice of our demonologists, we recommend that the President emphasize" the U.S. desire for peace, its stance on Berlin and disarmament and nuclear testing, and the "welfare base of [its] free enterprise (or mixed economy) system." (Washington National Records Center, RG 306, USIA Files: FRC 68 A 4933, Government Agencies, White House/62)

On the same day, Ambassador Thompson sent a telegram to Secretary Rusk, indicating that as a result of his understanding from Salinger that "Cold War themes are barred," he felt that the "target should be average Soviet citizen" for which the "problem uppermost. . . is peace. . . . Therefore suggest plus for disarmament might be one of the main themes." (Telegram 2255 from Moscow, February 21; Kennedy Library, National Security Files, Country Files, USSR, TV Exchange 3/8/62, Box 190)

In the wake of President Kennedy's announcement of the resumption of nuclear testing on March 2, the Soviets cancelled their plans to proceed with the exchange. In response to McGeorge Bundy's inquiry as to whether the cancellation represented any personal slight by Khrushchev against the President, Charles Bohlen wrote on March 9, one day after the planned exchange: "The Soviets undoubtedly feel it would be quite incompatible at a time when Soviet propaganda was denouncing the President's speech as 'aggressive' or 'atomic blackmail' to have" the exchange. He continued that no affront could have been meant by Khrushchev in his cancellation of the event since the event was at no point official and, therefore, nothing was ever publicly retracted; the only public knowledge of the event was in the United States as a result of leaks. Bohlen also pointed to Khrushchev's desire to "bring about a Summit in Geneva," a goal not consonant with "rebuff[ing] the President." Because of these factors, Bohlen viewed the Soviets' cancellation not as petty but "quite sensible." (Ibid.)

Hans Tuch, a USIA specialist in Soviet affairs, reported to Murrow on February 27, 1963, nearly a year later, that at the conclusion of the 1962–1963 U.S.-USSR Exchange Agreement's mid-term discussions, the USIA "expressed complete dissatisfaction with Soviet performance but received no particular encouragement that they will do better." (Washington National Records Center, RG 306, USIA Files: FRC 72 A 5121, Field—Soviet Bloc/63) The exchange agreement was signed in Washington on March 8, 1962, and entered into force the same day. For text, see *American Foreign Policy: Current Documents, 1962*, pages 726–740.

135.   **Memorandum From the Director of the U.S. Information Agency (Murrow) to All U.S. Information Agency Media Heads**[1]

Washington, April 24, 1962.

SUBJECT

Attribution of USIA Media Materials

Receptivity to USIA media output is nearly always greater when the output is not attributed to the Agency or the U. S. Government. I have therefore instructed our field posts not to carry USIA attribution on pamphlets, motion pictures, television shows and other media products (but excluding periodicals) except when local custom or law dictates otherwise. This rule henceforth shall also apply to media materials produced in Washington.

The posts were asked to consider attribution to credible local groups when appropriate and feasible. In Washington, you should consider attribution to appropriate U. S. groups, when feasible and useful, in the production of media materials.

An exception to this rule would be those instances when we want to make it clear that we are presenting the official viewpoint of the U. S. Government.

We must continue to distinguish between "unattributed" and "unattributable." Our materials may be "unattributed" but never "unattributable." We are willing to acknowledge, if questioned, the origin of any Agency product. My point is that we should not publicize, emphasize or otherwise call attention to the USIA-origin of our output except when necessary. Our job is not to advertise the Agency or any element thereof but to influence foreign public attitudes in furtherance of U. S. objectives.

This directive supersedes all previous instructions and guidances on this subject.

Edward R. Murrow

[1] Source: Washington National Records Center, RG 306, USIA Files: FRC 68 A 4933, Policy and Plans—General (IOP)/62. Confidential.

136.   Memorandum From the Under Secretary of State for
         Political Affairs (McGhee) to the Director of the U.S.
         Information Agency (Murrow)[1]

Washington, May 15, 1962.

SUBJECT

Psychological-Political Program

The purpose of our meeting on May 23[2] is to provide you with a
status report on the psychological-political program which you helped
launch as a member of the President's ad hoc committee on this problem. I have asked Mr. William J. Jorden of my office to report to us on
what is being done and what is planned in this area. He has been
assigned primary responsibility for developing, coordinating and conducting programs in the psychological-political field.

He will discuss the organizational forms he has developed to carry
out this function. He will also describe programs now underway or
soon to be launched. Among others, these will include:

1) The positive "image" of the United States—the effort to explain
to our own people and to the rest of the world what we are for, and why;
to counter the impression that we know better what we oppose than
what we favor; to correct the distorted image of America that has developed in many parts of the world as a result of misinformation and
Communist propaganda.

2) The failures of the Soviet bloc—to expose for all to see the weaknesses and failures of the communist system; to counter the "wave of
the future" propaganda line; to reveal the flaws of communist theory
and Soviet practice.

A number of sub-themes fall in this broad category:

a) The Sino-Soviet split—to expose the facts of increasing dissen-
sion within the Bloc; to stimulate broad discussion of the theoretical and
practical problems that bedevil the Bloc and divide Moscow and
Peking; the strike at the fiction of "monolithic unity" in the Communist
world.

b) Bloc agriculture—to reveal in detail the story of the huge and
continuing failure of the communist system to produce enough food for
its people; to destroy the fiction that collectivization provides the best
pattern for less developed countries in facing their agricultural problems.

---

[1] Source: Washington National Records Center, RG 306, USIA Files: FRC 68 A 4933,
FOIA. Confidential.

[2] Typed notes on the memorandum indicate that the meeting took place on May 29
at 2:30 p.m., and that Deputy Director Wilson attended instead of Murrow.

Countering short-range moves by the Communists, such as:

a) The Helsinki Youth Festival
b) The Accra Peace Assembly
c) The Moscow Conference on Peace and Disarmament

3) Future developments which we can begin now to counter or minimize, such as:

a) achievement of a nuclear capability by the Chinese Communists
b) claims or demonstrations of an anti-missile or anti-satellite capability by the Soviets

4) Promoting the flow of information to our posts abroad and, through them, to our friends and other governments and individuals.

5) Extending the breadth and depth of our contacts abroad with non-governmental groups and individuals—intellectuals, youth, labor unions, political oppositionists, etc.

Any ideas or suggestion you may have on these or other possible activities in the psychological-political field will be welcome.

George C. McGhee

---

137. Letter From Secretary of State Rusk to the Director of the U.S. Information Agency (Murrow)[1]

Washington, July 11, 1962.

Dear Ed:

In a memorandum dated June 23 the President directed that a procedure be developed to guarantee coordination of economic and military aid agreements with foreign policy objectives before announcement of major aid actions.[2] Attached for your information, along with a copy of the President's directive, is a copy of my reply dated July 11 describing steps being taken to ensure the necessary coordination.[3]

I would appreciate your cooperation and assistance in seeing that the actions of our respective departments and agencies fully meet the

---

[1] Source: Washington National Records Center, RG 306, USIA Files: FRC 68 A 4933, Policy and Plans—Genl. (IOP)/62. Confidential.

[2] For text, see *Foreign Relations*, 1961–1963, vol. IX, Document 145.

[3] For text, see ibid., Document 148.

requirements which the President has set forth. Compliance with the President's wishes will require close cooperation between appropriate members of your staff and Assistant Secretaries of the geographic bureaus of the Department of State to whom I have assigned full responsibility in this important area. I propose therefore that members of your staff who are responsible for actions of this character which have foreign policy implications consult, when and as appropriate, with the Assistant Secretaries of this department in order to effect coordination.

If you have further thoughts on this problem, I would be glad to hear from you or to discuss it with you.[4]

Sincerely,

Dean

---

[4] In a July 16 letter, Murrow replied: "I have advised my policy people and the Assistant Directors of the Agency who head area offices of the contents of your letter to me of July 11, the memorandum addressed to you by the President of June 23 and your reply to him of July 11. I believe my principal officers have been working in close cooperation with the Assistant Secretaries in situations of the sort outlined, but I have asked them to be especially alert to the importance of the fullest coordination." Murrow's reply is attached to Rusk's letter.

---

138.   Memorandum of Meeting[1]

Washington, August 15, 1962.

SUBJECT

Operation of the New Soviet Branch

The Director called media directors and others concerned to discuss with them his concept of how the new IAB should function.[2]

He stated that it should become the best body of expertise on Soviet affairs in this town. It should perform useful coordination between our own branches within and other elements outside the Agency. It should as well examine what we are doing and not doing.[3]

---

[1] Source: Washington National Records Center, RG 306, USIA Files: FRC 68 A 4933, Field—Soviet Bloc (IAB)/62. No classification marking. A handwritten notation at the top of the page reads: "To: Reed Harris."

[2] No other record of this meeting has been found.

[3] In a memorandum to Murrow, July 9, 1963, Leslie Brady noted that "July 1 marked the first full year of IAS." He went on to gauge the merits of his branch in accordance with Murrow's hopes expressed at the outset of Evans' memorandum: "now, we are in a

As an example, there are African students studying in Russia that call at our Embassy. They are a receptive target for information, and could be particularly useful in their travels to other European capitals and returning home. ERM suggested that if a plan could be devised in about a week specifying what to do and how much it would cost he could probably obtain money for it. But to do so he would need specifics.

Each Director was advised to stir up his own people and to get going with ideas on subjects and projects.

From his luncheon with the Russian Ambassador, ERM said the one subject that seemed most on Dobrynin's mind was American publicity about anti-Semitism in Russia. With this as a lead perhaps we could do an *Ameryka* magazine article on Jews in the United States or a VOA series on Jews in Latin America. This was the kind of idea ERM had in mind.

Loomis mentioned a need for personnel trained in VOA languages of broadcast. He suggested establishing a personnel plan so that language speakers could have an Agency-wide career. General concurrence.

The Director mentioned to Schmidt that he would like to see personnel with Russian background posted to Latin America, the Far East, etc. Schmidt replied it was already being done to some extent.

There was general concurrence on a need to look at personnel policies for people with language capabilities so as to attract them, develop them, and keep them.

Loomis suggested that *Problems of Communism*, now written for a free world audience and one of the Agency's best products, might be done in another edition aimed at Communist audiences.

Chinese relationships regarding Russia might also be exploited much more in media output.

ERM stressed the need to attempt the unorthodox. He mentioned his Dobrynin conversation in which the Ambassador said that *Ameryka* and *USSR* need more self-criticism. Murrow said he immediately offered to swap editors for one issue. Dobrynin was noncommittal. The

position to advise colleagues in USIA, other Government agencies, and private organizations as to how their activities might directly or indirectly influence public opinion in that part of the world. And more and more often we are consulted by such individuals and such institutions." (Washington National Records Center, RG 306, USIA Files: FRC 72 A 5121, Field—Soviet Bloc/63) Murrow responded in a July 26 memorandum to Brady: "the creation of IAS wasn't a mistake. You and your boys are to be congratulated on the shakedown here. It is always difficult to carve out a new division, but you have done it gracefully and effectively without creating undue friction. As I told you at the outset, it is my hope that you will develop in IAS the best body of expertise on current affairs in the Bloc countries to be found anywhere in Washington. I venture the opinion that today's signing of the limited nuclear test ban in Moscow will not put you and your colleagues out of business!" (Ibid.)

Director commented that the idea may be good or bad but it was unorthodox and he wanted to encourage more such unorthodoxy.

It was suggested that if the bureaucracy could be relaxed to obtain funds we could have a person or persons travel for long periods of time in Bloc countries, writing articles, cutting tapes, etc. To continue this for a long period we would, however, need an overcomplement of language speakers.

Paid vacations in Russian resort areas were mentioned. An officer on salary would spend time in resorts such as Sochi and in doing so contact a wide range of Russians.

Tom Tuch's interest rose.

Russian tourists coming to the United States could be contacted and be interviewed. They are more official than tourists of other nations, and hence worth the effort of contact.

It was suggested that we could investigate Russian society, observe how well they are developing, and speculate what they might develop into. This entails telling them things about themselves which they do not know.

The necessity of cooperation with other Western European nations was mentioned.

Loomis described the dual mission of Project Larry in Liberia: we are to be both the Voice of America and the Voice of Africa. He observed that we might extend a similar mission to our Bloc broadcasts: become both the Voice of America and the Voice of Communism. This would entail relating matters such as what goes on in other Communist parties, who controls Cuba, who is on top in African Communism, etc. The Russian people have only one source of information; this would seek to give them an alternative.

The need for government coordination on visiting dignitaries was mentioned. When Udall goes to Russia with Robert Frost, or Newton Minow is approached for a television exchange with Russia, they should seek a briefing first either at USIA or State.

It was suggested that Dobrynin himself might be induced to do a VOA report to his people.

Murrow closed the meeting by observing that in a week or three he would like to see some plans and "unorthodoxy".

Robert Mayer Evans[4]

---

[4] Printed from a copy that bears this typed signature.

139. Memorandum From the Director of the U.S. Information Agency to Attorney General Kennedy[1]

Washington, August 22, 1962.

SUBJECT

Youth Programs and Problems in 92 Countries

To tackle our problems with youth abroad, we felt it was necessary to know what is specifically "bugging them" on the country-by-country basis; what, if anything, USIA is doing about it; and what more, if anything, we can do about it.

We now have returns on a questionnaire designed to give the answers from 92 countries (out of the 101 where USIA operates), which are summarized in the attached report.[2] The findings confirm some of our previous conclusions, but also gave us some surprises. Example (on page 2): Intellectual restrictions imposed by the government do not seem to be a major source of frustration among youth, as many of us had previously believed.

The world-wide conclusions give some valuable information. We are using it and the individual country returns to recast our programs to meet insofar as possible the specific needs now identified. I shall give you some specifics in a few weeks.

Edward R. Murrow[3]

---

[1] Source: Washington National Records Center, RG 306, USIA Files: FRC 68 A 4933, Policy and Plans—Genl. (IOP)/62. Official Use Only.

[2] Entitled "Youth and Students," not printed.

[3] Printed from a copy that bears this typed signature.

140. Memorandum From the Director of the U.S. Information Agency (Murrow) to the Executive Secretary of the National Security Council (Smith)[1]

Washington, September 26, 1962.

REFERENCE

Your Memorandum of August 9, 1962[2]

We appreciate the opportunity to re-do the statement of the mission of the U.S. Information Agency. Our proposed restatement, a substitute for NSC 165/1–10/24/53, is attached.[3]

I agree it would be desirable if the President issued it, rather than making it a National Security Council document.

We do not think it necessary for part of the statement to be unclassified, as was the case in 1953.[4] We no longer need a statement to hang on the wall; rather we desire a realistic, meaningful definition of the Agency's mission for internal use within the Government.

Edward R. Murrow

---

[1] Source: Kennedy Library, National Security Files, Departments and Agencies Series, USIA, Box 94F. Top Secret.

[2] In this memorandum to Murrow, Bromley Smith extended the opportunity to "re-do" the existing 1953 NSC directive establishing the U.S. Information Agency "in light of the agency's current mission," a reference to the various extensions and clarifications of that mission that had occurred since President Kennedy's inauguration. The opportunity came to Murrow as part of the overall "effort to rescind, reaffirm or revise National Security Council policies" then underway. (Ibid.)

[3] The proposed restatement, which is marked Confidential, is not attached, but a copy is ibid., Box 290. Text of NSC 165/1 is in *Foreign Relations*, 1952–1954, vol. II, pp. 1753–1754.

[4] Murrow believed that the unclassified nature of the earlier mission statement could not be repeated in the new statement because doing so would preclude an accurate description of the USIA's expanded national security role. However, the U.S. Information Agency later believed that the inability to point publicly to any statement would be as much a hindrance as an incomplete statement, and eventually favored the issuance of a partially unclassified statement. See footnote 3, Document 144.

**141.   Letter From the Director of the U.S. Information Agency
(Murrow) to the Assistant Secretary of Defense for Public
Affairs (Sylvester)[1]**

Washington, November 30, 1962.

Dear Arthur:

Don Wilson is out of the country, and I am replying to your letter of
November 16 on Defense Department accreditation of USIA representatives.[2]

I am surprised at your equation of USIA representatives with commercial news media correspondents, particularly since you well understand the use of news and public affairs as "weapons" of diplomacy and
power. It would be more accurate to equate our representatives with
uniformed and civilian staff of the Defense Department who work with
the commercial media people.

USIA representatives are government officials, not "correspondents" as the meaning is applied to representatives of the *Washington Post*
or CBS. We are not in the news business as such, but in the business of
furthering U.S. objectives through information activities abroad. The
importance of our activities in supporting the national interest was reemphasized in the Cuban affair.

We seek Defense Department accreditation and authorization for
travel on military carriers only when successful carrying out of our mission requires us to do so. I hope, therefore, that you will not treat us "on
the same basis as a non-government newsmen" but on the basis of our
common desire to further the government's interests. This to me means
taking care of our needs (along with yours) first, not last.

Sincerely,

Edward R. Murrow[3]

---

[1] Source: Washington National Records Center, RG 306, USIA Files: FRC 68 A 4933,
Government Agencies—DoD/1962. No classification marking. Drafted by Tom Sorensen
on November 30.

[2] This letter contained the message: "Recent increase in the number of requests for
Defense Department accreditation suggests there may be some misunderstanding on this
subject.... We will continue to do this but not on the basis of blanket accreditation of your
correspondents any more than any other group." (Ibid.)

[3] Printed from a copy that bears this typed signature.

142. **Letter From the Assistant Secretary of Defense for Public Affairs (Sylvester) to the Director of the U.S. Information Agency (Murrow)**[1]

Washington, December 5, 1962.

Dear Ed:

Your letter of November 30,[2] has delivered me into the "hands of your enemies," friendly ones that is, in my shop.

They have argued from the outset exactly as you do, that USIA representatives are not "correspondents" in the sense that representatives of the *Washington Post* or CBS are, to use your own examples. They agree wholeheartedly with you, and always have, that USIA men are not in the news business but are in the business, as you say, "of furthering United States objectives through information activities abroad."

Under these standards they are not entitled to the accreditation, which you had wanted them to have. As you well know, accreditation intended for commercial newsmen cannot be extended to government employees except in the lenient formula I devised for your people.

If you want me to rule that USIA representatives are not to be equated with the non-government news media representatives for the purpose of accreditation that will make you a hero among my staff. It will confirm their conviction I was wrong all along and they will happily dis-accredit USIA men.

What I have been trying to do is make life easier for the USIA reporters with whom I have worked abroad and for whom I have great admiration. Because of that, I have insisted they be accredited, a policy I will change if you desire.

Ever sincerely,

Arthur

---

[1] Source: Washington National Records Center, RG 306, USIA Files: FRC 68 A 4933, Government Agencies—DoD/1962. No classification marking.

[2] Document 141.

143.   Memorandum From the Director of the U.S. Information Agency (Murrow) to the President's Press Secretary (Salinger)[1]

Washington, December 19, 1962.

SUBJECT

President's "Year-Ender" Briefing

We understand that the President again this year will brief selected correspondents on a background basis, covering events of the past 12 months. Following is a run-down of USIA's year for the President's possible use:

In 1962, the U.S. Information Agency made significant contributions in support of U.S. policies in the Cuban crisis, on the U.S. resumption of nuclear testing, the Berlin issue, and the challenge of space.

U.S. policies and actions in the Cuban affair, and the evidence on which they were based, were more thoroughly documented for foreign audiences everywhere in the world than any other issue in peacetime history.

This was accomplished by the heaviest possible use of all media and concentration by our posts abroad on local placement and face-to-face persuasion. It included round-the-clock broadcasting in Spanish to Cuba and Latin America, the first use of commercial U.S. stations to supplement our own transmitters, and the first tactical employment of a USIA air-transportable 50-kilowatt transmitter. We massed 52 transmitters to penetrate Soviet jamming and successfully tell the people facts on Cuba which they got from their own media much later or not at all.

The success of the Cuban campaign was due in large measure to our direct participation in the NSC Executive Committee.

USIA generated wide understanding of and support for our need to resume nuclear testing, and opposition abroad was surprisingly mild when the new tests were announced.

Continuing intense coverage of space events and the world exhibition tour of the Glenn capsule did much to improve our position in the space race.

We continued to develop support for our position on Berlin, one of five priority issues of U.S. foreign policy. The others, which we gave heavy, all-media emphasis throughout the year are a world of free choice vs. a world of coercion, a strong United Nations executive, safe-

---

[1] Source: Washington National Records Center, RG 306, USIA Files: FRC 68 A 4933, Govt. Agencies—White House Oct.–Dec. 1962. No classification marking. Drafted by Anderson and Sorensen on December 18.

guarded disarmament, and modernization of developing nations as a means of evolution in freedom.

There were these other important developments during the year:

USIA's basic build-up in Africa and Latin America was nearly completed. In Africa we now have posts in 33 of the 35 independent countries, including a substantial program in Algeria. In Latin America we increased our missions from 35 to 45 major cities, and we now have 29 student affairs officers and nine labor information officers at work there.

The first half of the 4,500-kilowatt Greenville, North Carolina, shortwave transmitter complex went on the air.

USIA films had such a marked increase in quality that popular and Congressional demand caused us to make two of them (on Mrs. Kennedy's trip to India and Pakistan) available for showing to the American people.

The number of people being taught English by USIA in classrooms reached a quarter of a million. "Let's Learn English," a series of 130 television teaching films, has been placed in 33 countries on 55 stations with an audience of 80 million. Audience response is typified in Austria, where 10,000 copies of the textbook were sold out the day after the series began, and in Japan where 60,000 copies of the final examination were distributed.

About 430 U.S. corporations are distributing USIA materials on important foreign policy issues to their 8,000 representatives abroad, almost all of them Americans, on a continuing basis.

For the first time in history, USIA has enjoyed a consistently good domestic press.

Among our remaining problems:

We have not yet succeeded in finally negotiating rights for broadcasting sites in the Eastern or Western Mediterranean, the Philippines, and Thailand—but are hopeful of success.

We have not been able to mount a fully adequate book program in Latin America because of the loss of an anticipated supplemental appropriation, although our book translation and publishing program there is double what it was a year ago.

Edward R. Murrow[2]

---

[2] Printed from a copy that bears this typed signature.

144.   **Memorandum From President Kennedy to the Director of the U.S. Information Agency (Murrow)**[1]

Washington, January 25, 1963.

The mission of the United States Information Agency is to help achieve United States foreign policy objectives by (a) influencing public attitudes in other nations, and (b) advising the President, his representatives abroad, and the various departments and agencies on the implications of foreign opinion for present and contemplated United States policies, programs and official statements.

The influencing of attitudes is to be carried out by overt use of the various techniques of communication—personal contact, radio broadcasting, libraries, book publication and distribution, press, motion pictures, television, exhibits, English-language instruction, and others. In so doing, the Agency shall be guided by the following:

1. Individual country programs should specifically and directly support country and regional objectives determined by the President and set forth in official policy pronouncements, both classified and unclassified.

2. Agency activities should (a) encourage constructive public support abroad for the goal of a "peaceful world community of free and independent states, free to choose their own future and their own system so long as it does not threaten the freedom of others;" (b) identify the United States as a strong, democratic, dynamic nation qualified for its leadership of world efforts toward this goal, and (c) unmask and counter hostile attempts to distort or frustrate the objectives and policies of the United States. These activities should emphasize the ways in which United States policies harmonize with those of other peoples and governments, and those aspects of American life and culture which facilitate sympathetic understanding of United States policies.

The advisory function is to be carried out at various levels in Washington, and within the Country Team at United States diplomatic missions abroad. While the Director of the United States Information Agency shall take the initiative in offering counsel when he deems it advisable, the various departments and agencies should seek such counsel when considering policies and programs which may substantially affect or be affected by foreign opinion. Consultation with the United States Information Agency is essential when programs affecting communications media in other countries are contemplated.

---

[1] Source: Kennedy Library, National Security Files, Departments and Agencies Series, USIA, Box 290. Confidential. Murrow submitted this restatement of the USIA's mission to the NSC on September 26; see Document 140.

United States Information Agency staffs abroad, acting under the supervision of the Chiefs of Mission, are responsible for the conduct of overt public information, public relations and cultural activities—i.e. those activities intended to inform or influence foreign public opinion—for agencies of the United States Government except for Commands of the Department of Defense.[2]

Where considered advisable, and except for direct international broadcasts by the Voice of America, the United States Information Agency is authorized to communicate with other peoples without attribution to the United States Government on matters for which attribution could be assured by the Government if necessary. The United States Information Agency shall, when appropriate, coordinate such activities with the Central Intelligence Agency.[3]

John Kennedy[4]

---

[2] In an October 25 memorandum to Bromley Smith, the Chief of the Bureau of the Budget's International Division, Robert Amory, Jr., commented negatively on this paragraph of the draft statement submitted to NSC on September 26: "we do not believe USIA has legal authority to carry out all public information activities of other agencies abroad, e.g., Peace Corps, HEW, Commerce, AEC, etc." The paragraph, however, was not changed.

[3] President Kennedy signed an unclassified version of this memorandum on February 25 for public dissemination that omitted the last paragraph on CIA coordination. (Department of State, USIA Historical Collection, Agency History/63) In a May 25 memorandum to Bromley Smith, Tom Sorensen requested that the January 25 statement be declassified except the last paragraph, which should remain confidential in order that the USIA have a single statement with more force. McGeorge Bundy replied affirmatively in a June 17 memorandum to Sorensen. (Both in the Kennedy Library, National Security Files, Departments and Agencies Series, USIA, Box 290)

[4] Printed from a copy that indicates President Kennedy signed the original.

145. **Memorandum From the Director of the U.S. Information Agency (Murrow) to Secretary of State Rusk**[1]

Washington, February 5, 1963.

Until such time as the Administration shall have formulated new policies in regard to the problems created by de Gaulle's current actions and attitudes toward the Common Market and the Atlantic Alliance, USIA plans to operate from the following position as suggested by Ambassador Bohlen's telegram 3098 of February 3,[2] namely:

a) To move steadily ahead with the promoting of the Atlantic Alliance, the establishment of a NATO nuclear force, and the reduction of trade barriers, without attempting to push France into any of these projects, but also without closing the door to her participation in whatever degree she desires;

b) To exploit French fears of being isolated by offering our friends knowledge of programs which they will find more in their long-term interest than French proposals;

c) To support the efforts of European countries to consolidate their strength through the Common Market; and

d) To refrain from harsh or discourteous attitudes toward France and maintain toward her a position of persuasive dignity. The French though sometimes volatile in the extreme are basically a people to whom logic has great appeal.

Edward R. Murrow[3]

---

[1] Source: Washington National Records Center, RG 306, USIA Files: FRC 72 A 5121, Field—Europe/63. Confidential.

[2] Not printed. (National Archives and Records Administration, RG 59, Central Files 1960–63, POL FR–US)

[3] Printed from a copy that bears this typed signature.

146.   Memorandum From the Director of the U.S. Information
        Agency (Murrow) to the Deputy Directors and the Deputy
        Assistant Directors of the U.S. Information Agency[1]

Washington, February 28, 1963.

SUBJECT

USIA Policies on Handling of Public Opinion Poll Data

Effective immediately, we will observe the following policies with respect to the handling of foreign public opinion polls sponsored by this Agency.

A. *Availability Outside the Executive Branch*

1. Foreign public opinion polls bearing the classification "Confidential" and the contracts under which such polls were taken will, upon request by the Chairman of the appropriate Committees or Subcommittees of the Congress, be made available to the requesting Chairman and the ranking Minority Member of such Committees or Subcommittees. This availability will be made with the understanding that the material furnished will not appear in the records of the Committees or Subcommittees nor in any way be made public.

2. Polls bearing the classification "Confidential" will be declassified automatically two years after their completion unless at that time the interests of national security require them to remain classified. The declassified polls will be available upon request of Members of Congress or the press.

3. Polls bearing the designation "Official Use Only" will, upon request by the Chairman of the appropriate Committees or Subcommittees of the Congress, be made available to the Members of such Committees or Subcommittees. This availability will be made with the understanding that the material furnished will not appear in the records of the Committees or Subcommittees nor in any way be made public. One year from the completion of these polls, they will be available upon request of Members of Congress or the press.

4. Poll results will be declassified at monthly intervals upon authorization of the Director, and will be made available to the Congress and the press according to the above formula on request.

---

[1] Source: Department of State, USIA Historical Collection, DF: Murrow–IRS Archives. No classification marking. The memorandum was addressed to: Donald M. Wilson (Deputy Director), Tom Sorensen (Deputy Director for Policy and Plans), Oren M. Stephens (Director of the Office of Research and Reference), Lowell Bennett (Director of the Office of Public Information), Edward V. Roberts (Assistant Director, Africa), Morrill Cody (Assistant Director, Europe), W. Kenneth Bunce (Assistant Director, Far East), Hewson A. Ryan (Assistant Director, Latin America), William B. King (Assistant Director, Near East and South Asia), and Leslie S. Brady (Assistant Director, Soviet Union and Eastern Europe).

5. Since USIA lacks authority to disseminate classified material originating in other agencies of Government, documents in which such classified material is integrated with our polls will not be made available. The polls contained in such documents will be isolated from the other classified material and treated in accordance with points 1–4 above.

B. Determination of National Security Interest

1. Thirty days before the scheduled declassification of "Confidential" poll data, the Deputy Director (Policy and Plans) and the Director of the Information Research Service (IRS) shall recommend to the Director of the Agency what portion of the data if any shall remain classified in the interests of national security, as per A. 2. above. The decision to retain security classification on any poll data shall be made by the Director or, in his absence, the Acting Director.

2. Normally, security classification will be retained only when one or more of the following circumstances prevail: (a) Release of poll results would embarrass the host country, and such embarrassment would be detrimental to U.S. relations with that country; (b) release of poll results would identify and embarrass the polling organization, making it difficult or impossible for it or other local polling organizations to conduct further surveys for USIA; (c) release of poll results would embarrass a third country, and such embarrassment would be detrimental to that country's relations with the U.S. or its relations with the country in which the poll was taken.

3. Poll results involving the popularity of the United States or that of any U.S. political figure shall not, in the absence of circumstances listed in paragraph B. 2., be construed as involving national security and therefore will be declassified as per the formula in section A. above.

C. Policy Clearance of Questionnaires

IRS shall submit to the Office of Policy (IOP) for prior policy clearance all questions to be included in polls financed or sponsored, in whole or part, by the Agency.

Edward R. Murrow

147.   **Memorandum From the Deputy Director of the U.S. Information Agency (Wilson) to the President's Special Assistant for National Security Affairs (Bundy)**[1]

Washington, March 7, 1963.

Here are some additional USIA surveys from Western Europe.

You have already received the surveys entitled "Some Current Public Trends in Western Europe" and "West European Opinion Trends on U.S. and Soviet Strength". The ones enclosed differ in that the returns from Italy have been included.[2]

Donald M. Wilson

Attachment

CURRENT WEST EUROPEAN PUBLIC OPINION ON SOME DISARMAMENT ISSUES

Trend in Support For General and Complete Disarmament

Support for whatever is understood by "general and complete" disarmament has increased in Western Europe over the past year and a half, and now ranges from a majority level in Great Britain to the order of 86 percent in Italy.

---

[1] Source: Kennedy Library, National Security Files, Departments and Agencies Series, USIA, Box 290. Confidential.

[2] Attached are several surveys of public opinion in Western Europe prepared by the Survey Research Division, Research and Reference Service, USIA. Despite USIA's avowed policy, many of the questions in the surveys continued to focus on "prestige" issues such as whether, in the respondent's opinion, the United States or the Soviet Union was ahead economically or militarily. In addition to the one printed below, the other titles were: "West European Opinion Trends on U.S. and Soviet Strength" (February 1963), "The Sino-Soviet Conflict Through Western European Eyes" (March 1963), "West European Assessment of the Outcome of the Cuban Crisis" (March 1963), and "Current West European Public Opinion about NATO and Nuclear Issues" (March 1963).

Table 1. "What are your feelings in general about disarmament? Are you for general and complete disarmament throughout the world, for some partial limitation on arms, or for no limitation on arms?"

| | Great Britain | | West Germany | | France | | Italy | |
	Jun/Jul '61	Feb. '63	Jun/Jul '61	Feb. '63	Jun/Jul '61	Feb. '63	Jun/Jul '61	Feb. '63
No. of cases	(633)	(400)	(572)	(600)	(659)	(633)	(600)	(400)
General and complete disarmament	43%	57%	70%	72%	73%	80%	73%	86%
Some partial limitation	35	31	18	15	15	13	7	10
No limitation	13	6	4	3	3	2	3	*
Qualified answer	2	1	2	*	3	1	1	*
No opinion	7	5	6	10	6	4	16	4
	100%	100%	100%	100%	100%	100%	100%	100%

*Asterisks indicate less than half of one per cent.

Would General and Complete Disarmament Require an International Police Force?

The strongly predominant opinion among those in favor of general and complete disarmament is that such a state of affairs would require some sort of international organization with its own police force.

Table 2. "Do you think that general and complete disarmament would or would not require an international organization with its own policy force?"

Would require	45%	48%	52%	52%
Would not	6	9	12	14
No opinion	6	15	16	20
	57%	72%	80%	86%

Support For Nuclear Disarmament

On the more specific issue of nuclear disarmament support rises to overwhelming levels in the countries surveyed.

Table 3. "What about nuclear disarmament? Would you favor or not favor the abolition of nuclear weapons throughout the world?"

	Great Britain Feb. '63	West Germany Feb. '63	France Feb. '63	Italy Feb. '63
No. of cases	(400)	(600)	(633)	(400)
Favor	70%	87%	94%	96%
Not favor	11	2	2	1
No opinion	19	11	4	3
	100%	100%	100%	100%

That sentiment in favor of the abolition of nuclear weapons is rather intense is suggested by returns available from three countries on whether or not nuclear weapons should be banned, if thereby the Western military forces were left weaker than communist forces. In France a majority, or near majority, is for a nuclear ban even if the West is left weaker as a consequence. Another 23 per cent are undecided rather than opposed.

In Great Britain and in Italy there appears to be more opposition than support for a nuclear ban that would leave the West militarily weaker than communist forces. But only minorities are explicitly opposed, which means that the majority in these countries are either for a nuclear ban under such circumstances or are undecided.

Table 4. "Assuming that banning nuclear weapons would leave the Western military forces weaker than the Communist forces, would you be for such a ban or against it?"

For ban	25%		52%	33%
Against ban if West left weaker	39	Not Avail-	25	38
No opinion	36	able	23	29
	100%		100%	100%

Is Nuclear Disarmament Possible?

The widespread sentiment in favor of nuclear disarmament is not accompanied by equally general feeling that such a course is possible.

While optimism holds an edge it does not attain a majority level in any of the countries surveyed, and except in France, is almost matched by the extent of pessimistic views.

Table 5. "Do you think it will be possible or not possible to abolish nuclear weapons throughout the world?"

	Great Britain Feb. '63	West Germany Feb. '63	France Feb. '63	Italy Feb. '63
No. of cases	(400)	(600)	(633)	(400)
Possible	48%	47%	47%	46%
Not possible	41	43	32	38
No opinion	11	10	21	16
	100%	100%	100%	100%

Any pessimism, however, on the possibility of attaining nuclear disarmament would appear to be tempered by a widespread feeling that the countries of the world will get together before any general nuclear war on some way to avoid such a happening.

Table 6. "All things considered, do you believe that a general nuclear war is inevitable some time in the future, or do you believe that the countries of the world will get together in time on some way to avoid such a happening?"

Nuclear war inevitable	9%	11%	5%	5%
Will be avoided	74	72	85	82
No opinion	17	17	10	13
	100%	100%	100%	100%

Support For Verification in a Nuclear Test Ban

Despite the widespread desire for nuclear disarmament, evident in the preceding indications, the prevailing opinion in all four countries surveyed is that the U.S. should continue to insist upon adequate inspection as a part of any agreement to ban nuclear tests. The trend indication, where the same question has been employed, is that support for inspection has increased somewhat since earlier measurements in mid 1962.

The table below is somewhat complicated by the fact that an updated question version was substituted during the course of the study in time for the entire sampling in West Germany and Italy and part of the sampling in France. Results on the revised question, it will be noted, parallel indications from the earlier wording in indicating predominant support for inspection.

Initial Version

Table 7. "A main reason why there has been as yet no U.S.–Soviet agreement to ban nuclear tests is that the U.S. wants checking by international inspectors on each other's soil, and the Soviet Union opposes this because they say it will lead to spying.

"Should the U.S. enter an agreement with U.S.S.R. to stop testing without such inspection, or should the U.S. continue to insist upon such inspection as part of any agreement?"

	Great Britain		West Germany		France		Italy	
	June '62	Feb. '63	June '62	Feb. '63	June '62	Feb. '63	June '62	Feb. '63
No. of cases	(647)	(400)	(620)		(615)	(223)	(672)	
Should enter agreement	23%	20%	27%	Not asked	45%	12%	25%	Not asked
Should insist on inspection	54	67	51		40	18	42	
No opinion	23	13	22		15	5	33	
	100%	100%	100%		100%	35%	100	

Updated Version

"Now on this card we find two people expressing different views about banning nuclear tests. (CARD)

Mr. A. says: 'The U.S. should enter into an immediate agreement with the Soviet Union to ban nuclear testing even if the Soviets will not permit as much checking in both countries as the U.S. requests in order to verify that the agreement is kept.'

Mr. B. says: 'The U.S. should not enter into an agreement with the Soviet Union to ban nuclear tests unless the Soviets agree to as much checking in both countries as the U.S. feels necessary to verify that the agreement is kept.'

"Do you agree more with Mr. A or more with Mr. B?"

	Great Britain		West Germany		France		Italy	
	June '62	Feb. '63	June '62	Feb. '63	June '62	Feb. '63	June '62	Feb. '63
No. of cases				(600)		(410)		(400)
Mr. A	Not asked	Not asked		30%	Not asked	16%	Not asked	26%
Mr. B				47		38		47
Qualified answer				1		1		2
No opinion				22		10		25
				100%		65%		100%

How Hard Are the U.S. and the U.S.S.R. Working To
Reach a Disarmament Agreement?

Currently the majority feeling, except in France, is that the U.S. is working at least fairly hard to try to obtain an agreement with the U.S.S.R. on some degree of disarmament. In France opinions divide on this score, with as many as feel otherwise holding that the U.S. is not working very hard or not at all.

In contrast, in all four countries the viewpoint prevails that the Soviet Union is not working as hard as it might to achieve a disarmament agreement.

Since almost all in each of the countries surveyed favor at least partial arms limitation, these figures can be taken as approximate indications of comparative satisfaction with current U.S. and Soviet disarmament efforts.

Table 8. "In your opinion, how hard is the U.S. working to obtain an agreement with the Soviet Union on some degree of disarmament? Very hard, fairly hard, not very hard, or not at all?"

	Great Britain Feb. '63'	West Germany Feb. '63	France Feb. '63	Italy Feb. '63
No. of cases	(400)	(600)	(633)	(400)
Very hard	29%)	29%)	11%)	33%)
Fairly hard	34) 63	33) 62	28) 39	34) 67
Not very hard	22)	20)	27)	11)
Not at all	6) 28	2) 22	14) 41	2) 13
No opinion	9	16	20	20
	100%	100%	100%	100%
Not Favorable	35	40	-2	54

Table 9. "And how about the Soviet Union. In your opinion, how hard is the Soviet Union working to obtain an agreement with the U.S. on some degree of disarmament? Very hard, fairly hard, not very hard, or not at all?"

	Great Britain	West Germany	France	Italy
Very hard	8%)	1%)	6%)	9%)
Fairly hard	27) 35	7) 8	17) 23	25) 34
Not very hard	36)	38)	32)	35)
Not at all	14) 50	36) 74	24) 56	9) 44
No opinion	15	18	21	22
	100%	100%	100%	100%
Net favorable	-15	-66	-33	-10

Support For Some Degree of Disarmament in Europe

Specific inquiries about disarmament thinking were concluded in the present survey by a query designed to illuminate the extent of general receptivity to proposals for disarmament in Europe. The results indicate a majority disposition in all four countries surveyed to be favorable toward an agreement between the Western Powers and the Soviet bloc providing for some degree of disarmament in Europe. This state of opinion tends to suggest, of course, that proposals for a nuclear free zone in Europe fall on fertile soil in the Western countries principally concerned.

Table 10. "Would you approve or disapprove of an agreement between the Western Powers and the Soviet Union and its European allies providing for some degree of disarmament in Europe?"

	Great Britain Feb. '63	West Germany Feb. '63	France Feb. '63	Italy Feb. '63
No. of cases	(400)	(600)	(633)	(400)
Approve	64%	62%	72%	60%
Disapprove	9	18	7	14
No opinion	27	20	21	26
	100%	100%	100%	100%

---

148.   **Memorandum From the Director of the U.S. Information Agency (Murrow) to the Administrator of the Agency for International Development (Bell)[1]**

Washington, April 23, 1963.

SUBJECT

The Bokaro Steel Plant

Construction of a steel plant at Bokaro either serves the U.S. national interest or it does not. My understanding is that it does, not only in

---

[1] Source: Washington National Records Center, RG 306, USIA Files: FRC 72 A 5121, Field—Near East/63. Official Use Only. Drafted by Tom Sorensen. Copies were sent to McGeorge Bundy, Chester Bowles, and W. H. Weathersby.

narrow economic terms but also for political and propaganda purposes as well.

Therefore I strongly endorse Ambassador Galbraith's warning (New Delhi telegram 4009, April 17) that we not throw the baby out with the bath water by applying the Clay Report formula here.[2]

All things being equal, we favor aid to private rather than public enterprise. But all things are not equal here.

Ambassador Galbraith has accurately described the consequences for us in India if we accept the Clay dictum. I want to warn of the consequences elsewhere.

We will fuel Communist propaganda fires in Asia, Africa and Latin America. We will undermine our posture of seeking a world of free choice as against a world of coercion. Worst of all, we will make mockery of the goal set for the U.S. by the President in his first State of the Union message—"a peaceful world community of free and independent states, free to choose their own future and their own system so long as it does not threaten the freedom of others."

Edward R. Murrow[3]

---

[2] In telegram 4009 from New Delhi, Ambassador Galbraith recommended U.S. support for a state-supported enterprise in India as a means of demonstrating a commitment to political pluralism. (National Archives and Records Administration, RG 59, Central Files 1960–63, AID (US) INDIA) Regarding the Committee To Strengthen the Security of the Free World (Clay Committee), see *Foreign Relations*, 1961–1963, vol. IX, Documents 158, 160, 164, and 166.

[3] Printed from a copy that bears this typed signature.

149. Memorandum From the Acting Director of the U.S. Information Agency (Wilson) to President Kennedy[1]

Washington, May 9, 1963.

SUBJECT

Public Opinion in Italy Prior to the Elections

Two factors in Italian public opinion may have contributed to the Communist gain of about 1,000,000 votes in the recent national elections.

Before the election Italians increasingly regarded the Soviet Union as moderate and reasonable in its policies, according to a public opinion survey conducted for USIA in Italy.

In addition, there was a pre-election increase in the number of Italians who said it is possible to be a good Communist and a good Catholic at the same time, according to an independent survey by a Gallup affiliate.

Those two public opinion factors were present at a time when Italian esteem for the United States and its leadership was at a new high.

1. General Reactions to the U.S.

The USIA survey, made in February, 1963, did not find any rise in anti-American sentiment. On the contrary, a substantial number of trend indices showed the U.S. and its leadership has rarely ranked higher in Italy. General esteem for the U.S. continued to rise from its 1960 levels and in February reached a new peak.

Favorable reactions to "what the American Government has been doing in international affairs recently" moved in precisely the same way. The belief that the U.S. was doing all it should do to prevent war; confidence in American leadership of the West; belief in the credibility of American statements—all these were at the highest levels in three years. There was the feeling—shared by a new high of two out of three—that American and Italian basic interests were in harmony. Finally, Italian neutralism, predominant in 1960, fell to a minority posi-

---

[1] Source: Washington National Records Center, RG 306, USIA Files: FRC 72 A 5121, Field—Europe/63. Confidential. Drafted in USIA/IRS on May 8. In a May 25 memorandum to Stephens (whose office bore the major responsibility for the Communist-related polling requested in this memorandum) Murrow wrote: "I have just read the memorandum to the President on public opinion in Italy prior to the elections. It is a first-class job. Pray convey congratulations to all hands concerned." (Ibid.) The President requested on June 11 more thorough USIA polling results on Communist influence in Europe, including complete tables from the agency's "worldwide survey." (Ibid.)

tion as it was overtaken by those who preferred their nation to side with the U.S. against the U.S.S.R.

2. General Reactions to the Soviet Union

Fewer Italians than in 1960 found any commonality of national interest with the Soviet Union: general esteem for the U.S.S.R. and the credibility of Russian statements remained as low as ever.

However, net favorable reaction to Soviet international actions showed a sharp increase, from a net figure of -10 in June, 1962, to a +14 in February, 1963. The reasons given for such favorable reactions were nearly all couched in terms of Russian "moderation" and "reasonableness" in the Cuban crisis. In terms of Soviet efforts to prevent war, the net index rose from -15 to +7 between June, 1962, and February, 1963.

Therefore, relative to its previous standing, the Soviet Union was quite favorably regarded in Italy at the time of the survey.

3. Estimates of American and Soviet Strength

It is doubtful whether Italian voters' estimates of American and Soviet strength were involved in their voting behavior. On the eve of the elections, the U.S. was in a relatively strong and improved position. Militarily, the U.S. was, for the first time, given a slight edge by Italian public opinion in nuclear weapons and—more important—a substantial edge in total military strength. In economic strength the U.S. was seen ahead by huge majorities and in scientific development as no worse than even. Only in space did the Soviet lead continue to be substantial. Finally, in terms of the wave of the future, the U.S. was expected to be the eventual winner of a quarter-century of "peaceful competition"—a sharp increase from 1960.

4. NATO and Nuclear Weapons

Reactions to NATO were, if anything, complacent. Consciousness of the organization was low and among those aware of NATO's existence, the predominant view was that it was in a good enough condition, was strong enough, and that both Italy and the U.S. were contributing their share. Few appeared to favor either national or exclusively "European" nuclear forces. The predominant view was for reliance on American nuclear forces or some sort of all-NATO, jointly-controlled organization.

It was on the issue of nuclear war in general (not necessarily in a NATO framework) that Italians displayed the greatest sensitivity—a widespread emotion common to adherents of all political parties. Nearly nine out of ten opposed the tactical use of nuclear weapons against enemy soldiers attacking Western Europe with conventional weapons; a majority would still disapprove even if the alternative were being over-run. Two-thirds indicate they did not believe that nuclear warfare could be kept tactical and expressed the opinion that it would spread to attacks on cities. Three out of four saw no hope of personal survival of a nuclear war. On the optimistic side, by a slight margin, Italians felt that neither side would use nuclear weapons; and as many as two out of three were confident that the U.S. would not be rash in using nuclear weapons.

5. Issues of Disarmament

Closely linked to sensitivity to nuclear issues are Italian reactions to disarmament. In principle, nearly 100 per cent wanted world-wide disarmament—just about all desiring it to be "general and complete." A clear majority favored an agreement with the Soviet Union to provide some degree of disarmament on the European continent. There was also a predominant feeling that American nuclear bases near the Soviet Union should be dismantled—presumably in some instances meaning those in Italy as well as those in Turkey. About one in ten voluntarily mentioned Italian bases though they were not brought into the question.

The huge figure of 96 per cent favored abolition of nuclear weapons throughout the world; as many as one in three felt so strongly that they favored the idea even if it meant leaving the West weaker than the Communist forces. At the same time, only about half the population believed that such a ban was possible. Despite this reaction to nuclear weapons, the very high proportion of 82 per cent believed that, in fact, nuclear war would somehow be avoided and was not inevitable.

With the feeling in favor of nuclear disarmament went the desire to ban nuclear testing; but here the predominance of opinion took a skeptical view and considered that effective inspection—"as much checking in both countries as the U.S. feels necessary"—was a prerequisite.

On the whole issue of disarmament, two Italians out of three gave the U.S. credit for working to reach an agreement; but as many as one out of three—and most of these neither Communist nor left-wing socialist sympathizers—reacted favorably to Soviet efforts.

6. Common Market Issues

On current issues related to the Common Market, Italian opinion appeared to be lined up with the American position and against either the Soviet line or Gaullist nationalism. Two out of three wanted Britain in the organization, and substantial pluralities desired to see the Market extended to include various other nations. Proponents of "independence" from the U.S. were far outweighed by those wanting to work for an integrated Europe "in close partnership with the U.S."

7. The Outcome of the Cuban Crisis and Revised Opinions of Soviet Russia

A major outcome of the Cuban crisis, other than American gains, appears to have been an increase in the number of Italians attributing such qualities as "moderation" and "reasonableness" to the Soviet Government. As cited above, as many as 30 per cent reacted favorably to "what the Soviet Union has been doing in international affairs recently," compared to only 16 per cent reacting negatively. Most of this favorable group—comprising all segments of Italian political affiliation—went on to praise Soviet moderation and reasonableness in the Cuban crisis. When the question was asked directly in terms of Cuba, from 10 to 22 per cent of the parties ranging from the Center-left to the Liberals reported that their views of the Soviet Union had changed for the better. The reasons for this favorable change was nearly always given in terms of Soviet moderation and willingness to avoid war. Indeed, the proportion of those expressing improved opinions of the U.S.S.R. was just as high as the proportion expressing more favorable views of the U.S. Again, when the question was asked directly, public opinion was just as inclined to credit Soviet moderation as U.S. military strength for the outcome—an outcome which nearly all aware of the crisis felt had decreased the chance of nuclear war in the future.

Thus the gains of the U.S.—general acceptance of its need to act unilaterally and improvement of its already high general esteem and military image—to some degree appear to have been offset by the increased acceptance of the Soviet image as moderate and reasonable. The original Soviet provocation appears in the net to have been swallowed up by its subsequent behavior.

8. The Soviet Union and Europe

Although the P.C.I., like most local Communist parties, has of necessity stressed its independence, patriotism and indigenous quality, it has undoubtedly repelled a considerable number of possible sympathizers because of its connection with Moscow. Stressing its independence on the one hand, and on the other concentrating on improving the image of the Soviet Union so that the connection will be less damaging, have been permanent necessities for the P.C.I. Certain events of the past year and their reflection in Italian public opinion appear to have worked effectively for the Italian party's propagandists.

We have noted the favorable reactions of all segments of the Italian population—ranging from a tenth to a third and higher—to the Soviet posture of moderation in the field of international relations. Another reinforcement of this view can be noted in Italian reactions to the Sino-

Soviet conflict—a conflict which to a considerable degree tends to put Soviet Communism into the position of being a reasonable, moderate, conservative, almost pacific force as compared with the Chinese extremists. This conflict appears to have had particular impact among the non-Communist forces in Italy. Thus P.C.I. adherents are most likely to deny that relations between the Soviet Union and Communist China are bad, while adherents of the other parties—no less on the right than on the left—predominantly hold that relations have deteriorated. Again, it is the non-Communists who are most hopeful that eventually the Soviet Union "will think of herself as a European state and seek friendship with the West in order to oppose Communist China." The P.C.I. sympathizers widely deny this possibility.

Such feelings on the part of large segments of the population provide a psychological atmosphere in which the Italian Communist party can operate effectively. The P.C.I. always has been among the most "reasonable" and "legal" in Europe.

9. Communism and Catholicism

The findings of an independent survey casts light on the effect of recent tentative contacts between the Kremlin and the Vatican. The study was made by the Gallup affiliate, DOXA, at about the same time as the USIA survey. It asked Italians: "Can you be, at the same time, a good Communist (enrolled in the P.C.I.) and a good Catholic?"

The results—only partially available—reveal that among right-wing socialists (P.S.D.I.) those answering "Yes, one can be a good Communist and a good Catholic at the same time" rose from 9 per cent in 1953 to 21 per cent in 1963; among Christian Democrats the rise was from 5 per cent to 16 per cent. For the nation as a whole, the "yes" response rose from 21 per cent to 23 per cent. In terms of the voting population, this 7 per cent switch would in itself amount to between two and two and a half million votes. It should also be noted that the question was posed in the extreme terms of being "enrolled in the P.C.I.". Merely voting on occasion for specific P.C.I. candidates, for any number of reasons, would be felt by many to be considerably lesser offense—particularly if the voting were rationalized as merely being a protest against the government or against the rise of 12 per cent last year in the cost of living.

A follow-up study of the elections is underway.

Donald M. Wilson[2]

---

[2] Printed from a copy that bears this typed signature.

150.   Memorandum From the Acting Director of the U.S.
        Information Agency (Wilson) to President Kennedy[1]

Washington, July 9, 1963.

SUBJECT

Reactions to Your European Trip

Here is a summary of media reaction to your trip to Europe.

Western Europe:

Western European media were almost unanimous that the visit was an overwhelming personal and psychological success but a limited political success.

You were widely viewed as projecting the image of a spirited and determined leader whose personal warmth and dynamism had previously been underestimated. The themes developed in your speeches most widely acclaimed were: Western unity, your categorical pledges to stand by our European allies, the promotion of peace, and your efforts to find better relations with the East. Comments on counteracting Gaullist policies and the quest for a multilateral nuclear force were divided and more critical. In only a few instances did commentators judge the trip an unqualified success.

The Visit to Germany:

Following the official welcome at Wahn Airport, the crescendo of popular and press acclaim rose rapidly. Even strongly Gaullist papers conceded that your reception by the Germans surpassed that of de Gaulle.

Prior to your visit, *Die Welt* of Hamburg had pictured you as "a political manager without passion, an engineer or a manufacturer of power." Subsequent to the Berlin visit, it wrote: "This was a Kennedy we had not seen before. His former coolness gave way to passion and to an unconditional personal commitment for this city."

A number of papers credited the visit with changing your views on Germany. The independent *Kölner Stadt-Anzeiger* said "if Kennedy ever

---

[1] Source: Washington National Records Center, RG 306, USIA Files: FRC 72 A 5121, Government Agencies: White House, Jul–Dec/63. No classification marking. In a July 3 memorandum to President Kennedy, Murrow noted that the U.S. Information Agency was making a special survey in France of the President's trip to Europe. (Ibid.) President Kennedy's Personal Secretary Evelyn Lincoln replied in a July 5 note to Murrow that the President wanted "a commentary on his entire trip." (Ibid.) This memorandum is the apparent result. A research report, "Western European Reaction to President Kennedy's Trip," is attached but not printed.

had reservations vis-à-vis the Germans—and there are indications that this was the case—his Berlin visit has certainly lessened them."

Your statements on European unity drew support from Scandinavia to Italy, but were also widely interpreted as directed in part against de Gaulle. Many papers found a positive aspect in this approach, crediting you with "opening the way (to European integration) which de Gaulle has barred, (something) which no European politician has been able to do since the break in Brussels" (*Berlinske Tidende*, conservative, Copenhagen).

Several German papers appeared uneasy at the prospect of an ultimate choice between the U.S. and France, and tried to ride the fence. The Social-Democratic *Neue Rhein Zeitung* of Cologne wrote: "Kennedy will not hesitate to make political capital out of his new friendship with the Germans, but he also will not overtax this friendship to the disadvantage of our solidarity with France."

French papers were less outspoken on this issue. *Le Figaro*'s comment that West Germany needed both American and French friendship and "could not choose between the two" was representative.

The Western European press was as one in praise of your renewed pledges to defend our allies, including some French papers. The anti-Gaullist *Depeche du Midi* of Toulouse, one of the most influential provincial papers, spoke of the "categoric manner" in which the U.S. assured the security of Europe and that its contribution was both "necessary and sufficient."

Berlin:

The Social-Democratic *Neue Rhein Ruhr Zeitung* of Essen summed up the views of many papers when it wrote "nobody in the White House, nobody in Germany had expected the President to identify himself so unreservedly and so courageously with the cause of Berlin and with the German cause as he did in his address at the Schöneberg city hall. Never before has a foreign statesman identified himself with the German cause in this form, on such a stage and so convincingly."

A sour note was sounded by the hyper-Gaullist *Paris Presse* which complained that your pronouncements in Berlin might have gone beyond assuring Europeans of U.S. determination to stand by its pledges and that "the U.S. President is now accountable for the enthusiasm he aroused."

Your statements on relations with the Iron Curtain countries were generally supported. The left-center *Frankfurter Rundschau* said, for example, "Mr. Kennedy's great peace offensive nourished our hopes for a rapprochement with the young progressive forces in the East."

Ireland:

In Europe generally, your visit to Ireland was seen as a "sentimental journey" and a "homecoming" without political implications. Within Ireland, no event in modern times has received such detailed press, photographic, and TV coverage. There is still no consensus about the political significance of the visit, but there has been speculation about Ireland's role in world events and relationships with NATO.

Great Britain:

Papers of all political colorations welcomed you for what was described by the pro-Labor *Daily Mirror* as "a hustling working visit."

The majority of papers welcomed the decision to delay the multilateral force. The conservative *Daily Telegraph* said, "Mr. Macmillan convinced the President of the strength of British misgivings and the American plan . . . is unlikely to reemerge in its present form." Among the minority of papers still favoring the force, the conservative *Daily Mail* expressed the hope that mixed-crew surface fleet with Polaris missiles would ultimately be accepted "because the advantages are much greater than the objections."

Papers elsewhere construed the postponement of the multilateral force as a victory for Macmillan, particularly in France. Said the Gaullist mouthpiece *La Nation*: "Reality will prevail."

A number of papers interpreted the decision on the multilateral force as a move to improve chances for a nuclear test ban with the Soviets.

Italy:

Italian editorialists were embarrassed by the relatively small crowds which greeted you in Rome, but following your appearance and speech in Naples papers from Socialist to Right supported your views with enthusiasm.

Conservative *Corriere Della Sera* wrote that de Gaulle's concept is designed to "isolate Europe," but that you, Segni, and Leone were agreed on the necessity of "European unity within the framework of the interdependence of Europe and the U.S."

Christian-Democratic *Gazetta del Popolo* said that your trip ended "with the solemn reaffirmation of a pledge of united effort . . . The special atmosphere created around this welcome American guest confirms the existence of the deep and vital roots of the Alliance, which the Italian people want as a guarantee and token of freedom, and which Italy now reaffirms, not only as a guarantee of security but as a new pledge and a hope of progress and peace."

Socialist *Avanti* gave heavy and generally friendly coverage to your visit, emphasizing the "peaceful" line. You have a "bag of ideas which deserve close consideration," *Avanti* commented.

A complete report on Western European reactions is attached.

Latin America:

Papers gave heavy coverage to the early part of the trip and to the audience with Pope Paul VI. Major dailies in Mexico, Peru, Argentina, and Chile had editorials supporting your objectives, particularly strengthening the Atlantic Alliance. The only non-communist negative reaction received was from *La Prensa* of Mexico City, which said that "not only North American . . . but also our own Mexican cities will be destroyed (in a third World War) and no one can dispose of our destiny so carelessly as the President of the United States seems to do." The editorial recommended a protest to the United Nations and censure by it of you.

Africa:

African media gave the trip moderate coverage, but there was little editorial comment. Radio Accra and other stations reported favorably on your remarks in Bonn welcoming African unity efforts. But Radio Accra also reported a statement by Malcolm X criticizing you for talking of freedom in Europe while "millions of Afro-Americans are denied freedom in the United States." The Tunisian Neo-Destour daily *L'Action* spoke highly of your "courage, frankness, and determination in defining the new trends of (your) strategy" and of your decision-making capability, "a clear-cut end to the indecision of (your) predecessors."

Near East and South Asia:

There was extensive news coverage and limited editorial comment, except in India and Pakistan. Editorialists in these two countries dwelt heavily on the reference in the communiqué from Britain to military aid for India, the Indians largely favorably, the Pakistani critically.

Several papers in the Near East reported that your trip had failed to change de Gaulle's policy, and criticized you for not visiting France.

Far East:

News coverage was moderate. Japanese commentators were inclined to agree that you had allayed German fears over West Berlin, and also interpreted the journey as an effort to form a unified base for negotiations with the Soviets. Comments in Viet-Nam were similar.

The Taipei press supported your efforts for Western unity, but, typically, called for a greater U.S. effort in Asia with the comment that "the root of the international communist evil is in Asia and not in Europe."

Communist Bloc:

Soviet output on your trip was relatively mild in tone and low in volume, never exceeding more than two per cent of total radio comment. Among the propaganda themes were Western disunity, failure of the multilateral force, the alleged discrepancy between your American University and German speeches, and the opportunity your visit provided for "revanchist" leaders to fan "the slanderous campaign against East Germany." Moscow concluded that you were "evaded" in Italy, "approved only in principle" in Britain, and "warmly received" by the revanchists in Bonn.

Peking was harshly critical, picturing the tour as a "cunning diplomatic move with evil designs." A New China News Agency report of June 27 said you had made "five provocative and aggressive speeches . . . unscrupulously slandering the socialist system and expressing U.S. determination to . . . subvert the German Democratic Republic and other East European socialist countries." A Red Chinese labor official asked: "How can this satan incarnate be viewed as an envoy of the people?"

Cuban media interpreted the trip as an effort to gain approval for U.S. "aggressive policies" and adjudged it a complete failure.

Donald M. Wilson[2]

---

[2] Printed from a copy that bears this typed signature.

---

151. Memorandum From the Director of the U.S. Information Agency (Murrow) to President Kennedy[1]

Washington, July 29, 1963.

I understand that you have expressed interest in United States participation in the 1963 Moscow International Film Festival and in the selection of the American film entry "The Great Escape."

"The Great Escape" was selected by the Hollywood Guilds Festival Committee, which is comprised of members appointed by the presidents

---

[1] Source: Washington National Records Center, RG 306, USIA Files: FRC 72 A 5121, Film Festivals/63. No classification marking. Drafted by Reed Harris on July 26. A copy was sent to Anthony Guarco, Deputy Director of the Motion Picture Service.

of the Directors Guild of America, the Screen Actors Guild, the Screen Producers Guild and the Writers Guild of America. The need to increase and augment the prestige of the United States and of the American film art at international motion picture events was immediately apparent when I took over as Director of this Agency. It seemed obvious that a qualified body of experts of the motion picture industry itself, in cooperation with the government, was required to meet this objective effectively. Thus, this Festival Committee was formed at the instigation of George Stevens, Jr., Director of the Motion Picture Service of the Agency, and has made the selection of the official American film entries to all major festivals since the spring of 1962. Where political considerations obtain, as is the case with the Moscow Film Festival, the Committee consults with the government on the appropriateness of any motion picture as an official entry. Present members of the Committee are: Willis Goldbeck, Gene Kelly, Richard Widmark, John Houseman, Walter Mirisch, Ernest Lehman, Allen Rivkin, Joseph C. Youngerman, and Fred Zinnemann, Chairman.

The Committee considered a number of motion pictures in the process of selecting the official United States entry in the Moscow Film Festival, including the film "How the West Was Won." Almost up to the time of the Festival entry deadline, the Committee did not feel that it had found just the right film for this event. When "The Great Escape" was offered for consideration, however, Committee members were unanimous in selecting it as the official Festival entry.

Upon receipt of the Committee's nomination, the Agency made arrangements for review of the film by government officers in the Department of State and USIA. Those who saw the film felt that in addition to its technical and cinematographic excellence, it dramatically illustrated the precept that whatever the conditions, the human spirit will strive to remain free. They also noted, as did the Russians, that it gave counterpoint to the image of Nazi Germany military leadership set forth in present Communist propaganda.

Officials of the Soviet Embassy also saw the film. They thought the treatment given the Nazi prisoner of war camp and Nazi military leadership not understandable within Russian experience with the Nazis, but interposed no objection to the film's entry in the Moscow Festival.

The American Embassy at Moscow has since reported that the Soviet publications *Pravda*, *Izvestiya* and *Trud* praised "The Great Escape" for the performance of its cast (Steve McQueen received the award for best actor), and have otherwise acclaimed the excellence of the picture. They have been caused, however, to rise in the defense of their own anti-German propaganda.

Mr. Stevens was accredited as the Chairman of the United States Delegation to the Moscow Festival. He is expected to return to duty in the Agency very shortly, and I look forward to receiving his personal comments on the effectiveness of United States participation in the Festival. I shall, of course, be happy to report to you more fully the substance of his observations as well as to supply you with a copy of the written report of the Delegation.

Edward R. Murrow[2]

---

[2] Printed from a copy that bears this typed signature.

---

152.   Memorandum for the Record[1]

Washington, September 9, 1963.

SUBJECT

Discussion of U.S.–Russian Press Problems

PARTICIPANTS

Mr. Pierre Salinger, The White House
Mr. Donald Wilson, USIA
Mr. Llewellyn E. Thompson, S/AL
Mr. Richard Davis, EUR
Mr. Robert Manning, P

Problems involving accreditation of American correspondents to USSR and Soviet correspondents to the United States were raised in the hope of achieving an agreed package proposal for presentation to the Soviet authorities.

Two types of problems are at issue:

1. Involving the desire of Novosti, the Soviet propaganda agency to be permitted to operate in Washington and the possible desire of USIA to establish more extensive operation in USSR.

2. The desire of the *Los Angeles Times* and *Chicago Tribune* to establish news bureaus in Moscow and the Soviet counter request for permission to open bureaus in Los Angeles and Chicago.

It was the sense of the meeting that the Novosti–USIA problem should be dealt with separately from that of bona-fide correspondents. Mr. Wilson agreed to discuss with his USIA colleagues the nature of

---

[1] Source: Washington National Records Center, RG 306, USIA Files: FRC 72 A 5121. Field—Sov. Bloc/63. No classification marking.

possible USIA requests as quid pro quo for the granting of permission for Novosti to operate in this country. Ambassador Thompson had serious doubts that USIA would be able to get from the Russians permission to operate an open reading room or permission to engage in other activities of the sort that USIA pursues in other countries.

On the matter of the request of *Los Angeles Times–Chicago Tribune*, it was pointed out that the Russians have already been told that we would not open Los Angeles and Chicago to Soviet correspondents as quid pro quo for admission of these two American newspapers to Moscow. Instead the Russians were offered two more accreditations for correspondents in Washington in return for the *Los Angeles Times* and *Chicago Tribune* accreditations to Moscow. There has been no Soviet response to this proposal and it was the opinion of Mr. Thompson that there would be no such response until the Russians received our answer to their Novosti request.

As a means of breaking the deadlock and liberalizing news policies in both countries, Mr. Salinger suggested a package proposal along the following lines:

U.S. would admit two more Soviet correspondents to Washington or New York and would open Los Angeles and Chicago for the establishment of one bureau each representing Tass or some other bona-fide Soviet news operation. In return the Soviet Union would accredit two more correspondents to Moscow (*Los Angeles Times* and the *Chicago Tribune*) and would open Leningrad and Kiev to one bureau each for some American news organization or newspaper.

It was agreed that Mr. Salinger would informally explore with the AP and UP whether each might be interested in establishing a bureau in Leningrad or Kiev.

The meeting agreed that the package proposal was a worthwhile proposition to put to Soviet authorities. It was also agreed to solicit the opinion and guidance of Ambassador Foy Kohler after his imminent return to Washington for consultation.

Informally there was a brief discussion of the advisability of a meeting between top Soviet authorities dealing with news matters and a group made up of Mr. Salinger, Mr. Manning and Mr. Murrow at some future date, both to discuss the bulk package proposal and perhaps also to take up other grievances and restrictions affecting the work of newsmen in the two countries.

153.   Memorandum From the Director of the U.S. Information
        Agency (Murrow) to the Under Secretary of State for
        Political Affairs (Harriman)[1]

Washington, September 18, 1963.

From all indications, Hungary has been adopting changes in the direction of moderation and pragmatism which reflect the interests of the Hungarian people. This tends to make Hungary at present more receptive to Western influence and opens up new opportunities for us. In the light of this development, I should like to suggest that this is a propitious time to modify our policy with regard to a cultural and informational program directed toward that country.

It is our belief that a careful advance in cultural and informational offerings now might further current policy objectives in Eastern Europe in general and in Hungary in particular. If Hungarians are as eager to receive manifestations of the Western world as they seem, such presentations, offered in measured doses, might well represent for them additional incentive to move even more rapidly away from the rigid positions of the past. It would naturally be well to proceed step by step, taking advantage of what appear to be major opportunities, but with watchful consideration for the reaction of articulate minority groups here at home.

We believe a telling program of cultural and informational activity could be directed at the following "target audiences" in Hungary: professional people, managers and technocrats, party and government officials, the intelligentsia, youth and student leaders—those who mold public opinion and influence policy and action. The welcome, but woefully meager, informal activities carried on to date through various private American organizations have been too restricted to touch them more than a little. Only activities of potentially greater impact can have much influence. Without much formalization—we are thinking neither of a publicized effort on our part nor of a cultural agreement with Hungary—we recommend such moves as sending one of our traveling exhibits; distributing at an appropriate time a simple Cultural Bulletin (similar to those we already disseminate in the Soviet Union, in Poland, Romania, and Bulgaria); facilitating the visits of performing artists or athletes; encouraging representative American writers, artists or educators to include Hungary in their planned itineraries.

---

[1] Source: Washington National Records Center, RG 306, USIA Files: FRC 72 A 5121, Field—Sov. Bloc/63. Confidential. Drafted by Leslie Brady and Hans Tuch on September 17. Copies were sent to Donald Wilson, Thomas C. Sorensen, Harold C. Vedeler (EUR/EE), Frank G. Siscoe (EUR/SES), and Chargé Owen T. Jones and Leon A. Shelnutt at the Legation in Budapest.

For reasons obviously its own, the Hungarian regime seems willing to accept such advances now. We propose therefore that we take advantage of the opportunities while they are offered, under the belief that once a start is made, Hungarian authorities will be under pressure to permit still more. If that is true, then perhaps cultural and information exchange itself will come to represent a bit of extra leverage for the attainment of other things we want from Hungary.

Edward R. Murrow[2]

---

[2] Printed from a copy that bears this typed signature.

---

154. Memorandum From the Assistant Director (Soviet Union and Eastern Europe) of the U.S. Information Agency (Brady) to the Director (Murrow)[1]

Washington, September 25, 1963.

SUBJECT

Direction of Policy Concerning Hungary

I look forward to giving you an oral account of the meeting this afternoon in Secretary Harriman's office. Suffice it to say here that the memorandum over your signature had the full effect for which we hoped.[2]

Net result was a three-point request from Secretary Harriman:

(1) that we get on with an expanded program in Eastern Europe in general and in Hungary in particular, since there would seem to be an entirely new situation developing as the result of the Tito–Khrushchev meeting, which Harriman believes will tempt other political leaders in Eastern Europe to demonstrate that they too can sell a few points to Chairman Nickie;

(2) that the Department send a letter to each of the East European posts asking whether they have any suggestions as to how fast and in what directions we might present a broadened program to people in their countries; and

---

[1] Source: Washington National Records Center, RG 306, USIA Files: FRC 72 A 5121, Field—Sov. Bloc/63. Confidential.

[2] A typed note on this memorandum indicates that Murrow discussed the meeting with Brady on September 26. For Murrow's memorandum, see Document 153.

(3) that USIA come up with any specific ideas for an expanded program in Hungary and in the other satellites in the months ahead.

Can't ask for much better than that. I have put Carl Sharek immediately to the task of drawing up specific suggestions for Hungary, together with a schedule covering the next couple of years. I shall submit it to you, if you agree, for transmittal to Secretary Harriman the same way we transmitted the original memorandum.

LSB

---

155. **Memorandum From the Assistant Director (Soviet Union and Eastern Europe) of the U.S. Information Agency (Brady) to the Director (Murrow)**[1]

Washington, September 26, 1963.

SUBJECT

Selling Wheat to the USSR

As the press is fully informing us, the Russians are buying wheat. They will apparently get it where they can. Their purchases may or may not include us, depending upon whether we make up our minds to sell and how soon.

Without going into ramifications of the problem which are not of our direct responsibility, and strictly from the psychological viewpoint, IAS believes it would be in the interest of our foreign policy objectives to sell wheat, and other farm commodities, to the USSR and the Communist states of Eastern Europe in return for hard cash.[2]

Here are the points in our reasoning:

1. Selling wheat to the Soviet Union is consonant with our policy to encourage in that country an improvement in a peaceful consumer economy satisfying the desires and aspirations of Soviet citizens for a better daily life.

---

[1] Source: Washington National Records Center, RG 306, USIA Files: FRC 72 A 5121, Field—Soviet Bloc/63. Confidential.

[2] Brady's thinking was shared by the Department of State and withstood detractors at an NSC meeting on October 1, leading President Kennedy to announce on October 9 the sale of 4 million metric tons of wheat to the Soviet Union. For a summary record of the October 1 meeting, see *Foreign Relations*, 1961–1963, vol. V, Document 359.

2. Such sales would demonstrate that we are sincerely interested in trade of non-strategic and peaceful commodities as another step in the lessening of tensions.

3. A decision to sell would be tangible indication of humanitarian interest on the part of the American people, considerate of the welfare of the Russian people.

4. It would bear witness to the productive superiority of U.S. agriculture, demonstrating without any "embroidering" on our part who is outdistancing whom, in spite of Khrushchev's repeated braggadocio about "catching up and overtaking" us.

5. It would have a psychological impact on the Soviet people as they found themselves even to this extent dependent upon us, and it would condition them for further economic dependence, of one sort or another, in the future, should matters develop in that direction.

6. It would encourage Soviet authorities, and the Soviet people under them, to think still more often of positive relations with the U.S., and less often of any possibilities in the direction of Communist China. This might in its own way help their quarrel along a bit.

7. It would improve our surplus agricultural products situation, and along with that our balance of payments situation.

LSB

---

156. Memorandum From the Office of Public Information of the U.S. Information Agency to Agency Employees[1]

Washington, October 28, 1963.

SUBJECT

Some Changes in USIA since March, 1961

Since the appointment of Edward R. Murrow as Director, in March, 1961, a number of far-reaching changes have been effected in the policies, operations, procedures and output of the U.S. Information Agency. Inventoried below are some of the more significant of these changes. This listing is for the information of USIA employees who, engrossed in

---

[1] Source: Department of State, USIA Historical Collection, Agency History/63. No classification marking. No drafting information appears on the memorandum.

their own segment of the Agency operation, may like to know of changes and developments in other areas.

The role of the Director and his senior officers in the formulation of foreign policy has been greatly strengthened. No longer is USIA handed a policy and told to make the best of it. The Agency's counsel is now sought whenever national policies with foreign implications are being formulated. The Director participates actively in all meetings of the National Security Council and its executive committee. His key officers consult daily with their counterparts in the White House, the Department of State and other federal departments and agencies. President Kennedy's January 25, 1963 statement of mission for USIA charged the Agency with the responsibility for "advising the President, his representatives abroad, and the various departments and agencies on the implications of foreign opinion for present and contemplated United States policies, programs and official statements."[2] That statement is very much an operational fact.

A revamping of functions has taken place in the Agency's Office of Policy to meet the problems and opportunities of the changing times. The country planning mechanism was overhauled to streamline and sharpen the functioning of USIS as an integral component of the overseas country teams. A media coordinator has been assigned to ensure that the many instruments of communication used by USIA are synchronized both in content and in timing. A long range planning officer has also been assigned to provide guidelines for other than immediate policy and media objectives to be reached in five to 10 years. A youth and student affairs officer plans and promotes activities and output directed to these critically important audiences. Another officer has been assigned to ensure the inclusion of overseas research findings in the Agency's policies and programming.

Field Posts

At overseas posts paper work has been subordinated to leg work. The volume of reporting from the field to headquarters has been reduced by about 20% to permit a corresponding increase of field officers' time in furthering programs and policies. Remaining reporting procedures have been simplified and streamlined.

Length of overseas tours, except in critical hardship posts, has been extended 50% from two to three years and a policy is followed whereby key officers often return to the same post for a second tour. This permits better use of officers who thus have greater time to develop contacts and know the problems.

---

[2] Document 144.

Regional specialization for foreign service officers has been made the rule. No longer are officers assigned from one area to another throughout their careers, thus acquiring a smattering of expertise in one area only to be assigned away from it for the next tour. To the extent possible, they now spend the bulk of their overseas careers in a single cultural or ethnic region.

The diffusion of effort and output that characterized USIA during the first years of its existence is ended. No longer is the Agency's mission "to tell America's story abroad"; no longer does USIA scatter its fire indiscriminately to all segments of all populations. "Targeting", always an ideal, is now a reality. Audiences are carefully selected—together with the techniques of reaching them and the contents of the message—to achieve maximum influence leading to political action. All USIA media function in synchronization: if the theme is Free Choice, and the peg is Berlin, each medium devises a message best communicated through its instrument. The messages are carefully related each to the other and each supports the other. This results in a multiplied opinion impact.

A much greater awareness of the function of USIS has spread among senior U.S. operating officials in the 106 countries abroad where the Agency now has posts. Chiefs of mission now know that the public affairs officer and his staff have a dual responsibility: (1) to advise the mission on the psychological implications in the country of U.S. policies, plans and actions and (2) to serve as the information, cultural and psychological link between the mission and the people of the host country.

Since the spring of 1961 the Agency has increasingly emphasized operations in Africa and Latin America and because of these priorities has had to curtail somewhat its operations in Western Europe where normal communications with the U.S. are relatively full and open. The Agency has opened 12 new mission posts and eight branch posts in Africa in this period; 11 new branch posts in Latin America; two mission posts and one branch post in the Far East; one mission post and two branch posts in the Near East; in Western Europe, USIA closed four branch posts and opened one new one.

To assist the African area in its tasks of organizing many new posts, the Agency has conducted in Africa a series of training workshops for local employees. These have covered subjects such as office practices, maintenance and operation of motion picture projectors, the establishment and operation of a library, techniques of handling small exhibits, and the servicing of multilith presses.

The Agency has become increasingly effective in acting as a catalyst in producing the maximum favorable impression overseas out of the travels abroad of prominent American Government officials, and others.   USIS posts thoroughly prepared for trips such as President Kennedy's to Latin America and Europe, Mrs. Kennedy's visit to India and Pakistan, and Vice President Johnson's travel to the Near East and Scandinavia. All the media in Washington did their advance work, too. During the trips, foreign service officers facilitated coverage by commercial media and also covered the events themselves. Films, special editions of magazines and pamphlets help to broaden, and make more lasting, the impact of such visits.

A Foreign Correspondents' Center was opened in New York City to help some 500 journalists who usually live in the U.S. to cover America and the United Nations. The Center arranged briefings by prominent American officials and others. It also facilitates visits outside New York. A documentation center is another service.

Greatly increased Agency-wide attention is being paid to key youth, student and labor groups abroad. For details see 20th Semi-Annual Report to Congress, pages 18–21 and 28–35.

Voice of America

In February, 1963 the short wave power of the Voice of America was doubled. A giant new transmitter complex—nearly five million watts, equal to the broadcast power of 96 of the top U.S. commercial radio stations—was completed at Greenville, North Carolina. This complex gives USIA a far better signal to Latin America, Europe and Africa.

Four highly versatile air-transportable transmitters have been constructed and put into operation. Three are near Monrovia. They provide an interim signal to Africa south of the Sahara until a large permanent transmitter complex of 1.6 million watts is completed in March, 1964. The fourth, on Marathon Key off Florida, beams medium wave broadcasts to Cuba.

Improvements in VOA's short wave broadcast service include: consolidation of Chinese-language casts by eliminating Amoy and Cantonese and concentrating on Mandarin, the principal language on the mainland and on Formosa; inauguration of Portuguese broadcasts to Brazil; increase of Spanish broadcasts to Latin America from one hour to nine hours daily; inauguration of dictation-speed newscasts in Spanish and Portuguese to facilitate wider diffusion by the printed word; considerable increase in the number of (stringer) correspondents reporting to VOA.

Other VOA construction advances: (1) the first of six new transmitters at Woofferton, England—increasing VOA power there fivefold to 1.25 million watts—goes on the air shortly; (2) relay facilities aboard Coast Guard Cutter, *Courier*, are being land-based on Island of Rhodes where the Near East Arabic services are being concentrated; (3) agreements for relay-transmitter installations were made with Greece and the Philippines; (4) relay facilities in the U.S., at Bethany, Ohio, and Delano and Dixon, California are being modernized; (5) new antennas have been built for RIAS, the Agency's station in West Berlin, with a resulting five-fold increase in power at night for broadcasts that blanket East Germany.   Meanwhile, obsolescent relay transmitters at Brentwood, Long Island, Schenectady, New York, and Wayne, New Jersey, were retired from service.

The volume of VOA short wave broadcasting has increased nearly 30% since January, 1961: from 617'45" to 796'15" hours weekly.

The volume of placement on overseas medium wave transmitters of VOA-produced tapes has increased more than 150% since January, 1961: from 5,457 to 14,000 hours weekly.   Some 5,500 radio stations in the free world, both commercial and government-owned, carry such VOA taped programs.

Twice the Voice of America has massed its transmitters to deliver to listeners behind the Iron Curtain an electronic Sunday punch consisting of vital information which Communist governments had been denying their people.   The first: November 5, 1961, employing 52 transmitters, 4.3 million watts and 80 frequencies during an eight-hour period.   It told the Russian people of world-wide revulsion because the Soviets had callously broken the atomic testing moratorium and resumed atmospheric tests.   The second: October 25, 1962, employing the same strength and number of frequencies as the year previous, to broadcast the full story of the crisis confrontation over Cuba.   In both cases, monitoring and the reports of correspondents in the USSR confirmed that, despite intensive jamming efforts, the broadcasts got through to an immense audience.

Motion Picture Service

Sixty-seven films have been completed since March, 1961.   Thirty-six of these are documentary, and 31 are major films on the visits of foreign dignitaries and other topical subjects.   Among the more important films have been:

"United in Progress", two reels in color, based upon the participation of President Kennedy in the Costa Rican conference of Central American chiefs of state;

"A Philosopher's Journey", two reels in color, on the visit of the President of India to the United States, symbolizing the friendship between the two nations;

"Invitation to India" and "Invitation to Pakistan", both in color, depicted Mrs. Kennedy's visit in 1962 to those countries;

"The Farmer and I", two reels in color, shows the life and labor of an American farmer;

"China and the Far East", two reels, black and white, is one of a number of anti-Communist films;

"Escape to Freedom", three reels, black and white, shows the drama and the tragedy of the flight of refugees from Communist lands;

"School at Rincon Santo", "Evil Wind Out" and "Letter from Colombia" were produced to support the Alliance for Progress. Each is one reel, black and white.

"The Five Cities of June", three reels in color, depicts five significant events in June, 1963.

Since March, 1961 sixty-six films have been acquired from non-Agency sources at little or no cost. For its "packets" of films of specialized subjects, IMS acquired 1,173 prints, and 801 more prints are on loan for field use. It is estimated that acquisition activities during FY 1963 saved IMS $501,097. Sources for these films were several organizations, societies and associations, hospitals, doctors and institutions, trade unions, government agencies, foundations, museums and private industry. Among the more outstanding films acquired were: "Agriculture USA", "Project Telstar" and "The John Glenn Story."

The Agency is now placing special emphasis on one-reel documentaries because this type of picture is relatively easy to place in public theaters, whereas lengthy films are rarely accepted by theaters. Strong evidence of the success of this operation is the report from USIS Santiago. The report concerns "Horizons", the news magazine for Latin America. Recently USIA adopted the policy of issuing "Horizons" as two separate one-reel productions per month instead of a single two-reel production. USIS Santiago reported that 10 first run theaters accepted prints of the single reel version of "Horizons", whereas only five of these theaters would accept the two-reel issues. The audience for the two-reel version was 50,400, whereas the two 10-minute issues were placed in a total of 18 principal theaters in Santiago and were seen by 132,500.

With the cooperation of the American Science Film Association, USIA has sponsored, organized and coordinated American Science Film Forums in many countries. These traveling forums show selected American science films, accompanied by lectures, discussions and seminars under the leadership of outstanding American scientists. Their purpose is to emphasize U.S. pre-eminence in science; the relationship of science to human progress; and to demonstrate the application of films to research, education and the popularizing of scientific knowledge.

The U.S. Government and the American film industry participation in major international film festivals has been greatly strengthened. George Stevens served as Chairman of the American delegations to the festivals at Cannes and Venice in 1962; in 1963 he was chairman of the

American delegations to the Moscow and Venice festivals and a member of the delegation to the Berlin festival. Because of the reluctance of the Motion Picture Association of America to select U.S. entertainment feature films for the 1962 Cannes film festival, the Hollywood Guilds Festival Committee was established upon the recommendation of USIA.

Opinion Research

To fulfill its advisory function and to tailor output, USIA must know continuously and quickly what people abroad think about U.S. foreign policy actions and statements, along with their reaction to other major happenings. In recognition of this, reporting of such reactions has been expanded and speeded.

During the October 1962 Cuban crisis, for example, reports on global reaction were prepared twice a day, then daily, then intermittently as required. An over-all assessment of the situation was prepared later when there was time for adequate evaluation. Similar reports were issued on many subjects including the Sino-India border conflict and the Buddhist protests in South Viet-Nam.

Public opinion studies overseas have been enlarged in scope and depth to examine long-term values and aspirations as well as current views. In 1963 the Agency's Survey Research Division conducted its first world-wide public opinion study designed to measure attitudes on a global basis. Surveys also are used to study target groups that USIA is attempting to influence, to investigate channels and methods of communication and to examine the effectiveness of specific Agency programs. There has been a substantial increase in field commissioned research projects, including pre-testing of media materials and studies to determine the impact of particular programs. An effort is being made to study the attitudes of emerging peoples. This work has been expanded considerably in the past two years with an accumulation of invaluable information.

The Agency's research staff has stimulated applicable study by independent American scholars, foundations and universities. Survey findings now are being exchanged through information centers established at several universities.

A special projects research division was established in January, 1962 to cultivate fields of private research by offering suggestions, encouragement and limited financial backing. Additional resources have been utilized when research objectives converged with those of USIA and other government agencies. The values and aspirations of developing peoples, the clash of ideologies and political semantics have been the chief fields of exploration under this program. Research findings are being used to help tailor Agency information output.

Communist propaganda reporting and analysis now is handled on a daily basis. An early morning briefing from the overnight files informs key Agency officials on the latest Communist propaganda lines. Soviet and Cuba specialists prepare daily reports summarizing the foreign and domestic output from Moscow and Havana. Interviews with refugees and travelers from Communist countries have been utilized to probe public opinion in nations closed to us. By this method the Agency has acquired some indications of popular attitudes and communications habits in the Communist orbit.

The Agency's research library has introduced an automatic punch-card system of procurement, which reduced overtime and cut out hundreds of man hours spent annually in typing and filing. New equipment has speeded the transmission of materials between the library's several branches and has made file materials more readily available to operating services. Two new library branches were opened. One is the Foreign Correspondents' Center, a reference and circulating library near the United Nations headquarters in New York. The other is a limited collection selected for the particular benefit of Agency trainees.

Private Cooperation

During the past two years, American business and individuals have given the Agency a considerable volume of materials, otherwise unobtainable because of budget limitations, which were essential in overseas posts for initiating and welding a relationship with priority audience groups. Examples:

About half of all donated books are now carried overseas free by several major steamship lines; in the past two years some 800,000 books were shipped this way. At no charge, U.S. truckers are also moving impressive quantities of books and other materials from points of donation to the Agency's Brooklyn and Washington warehouses where they are screened and shipped.

Last Spring the U.S. Post Office Department agreed to give the Agency all books received in its 14 dead letter centers—100,000 to 150,000 annually. Most are new books, delivered by the Post Office to the USIA warehouse in Washington at no cost to the Agency. Some 150 wives of Agency officers have volunteered a half-day or more a week to sort and pack them. Supervised by a professional librarian, they so far have selected about 60,000 volumes for USIS use overseas. These include new high-quality reference works, texts, publications suitable for special presentations, as well as fine groups of American fiction, both hard and paper backed.

USIA's cooperative effort with American industry to inform U.S. businessmen stationed abroad on critical issues of American foreign policy now enters its third successful year. Over 8,000 such business-men receive from their home office briefing material supplied by the Agency to 441 international companies. The most recent was on the Nuclear Test Ban Treaty; it reached recipients while international inter-est in the treaty was at its peak.

For the past year the Agency has operated an editorial exchange program with company and professional association publications that circulate overseas. USIA provides those publications with feature and policy materials for background, and which also suggest articles that will help to convey U.S. objectives to overseas readers. More than a mil-lion people are reached by the 67 American private publications now receiving such Agency material. In exchange, the Agency obtains, with-out cost, industrial and association material of value to Agency editors and writers. Additionally, a hundred exceptionally high quality publi-cations, showing the achievements of American business, science and technology, are now received monthly or quarterly for distribution to USIS libraries.

The increasing need for sports equipment abroad led to the creation of an International Sports Kit Project in cooperation with the People-to-People Sports Committee. Begun in September 1962, the project result-ed in requests for more than 12,700 Sports Kits from USIS posts in 86 countries. During the first year U.S. organizations and individuals donated 250 Sports Kits valued at $7,000 for distribution by USIS posts in 50 countries. Recent promotional efforts are expected to result in a significant increase in the giving of Sports Kits. Within a price range of from $12 to $64, the six kits provide equipment for boxing, baseball, softball, volleyball, soccer and basketball.

Emphasis in the donated books and magazine program has shifted from used to new material. Most of the 800,000 donated books shipped overseas by the Agency last year were new. In addition, the Book-of-the-Month Club has donated full subscriptions to 700 foreign libraries recommended by USIS posts. To avoid duplication and achieve greater effectiveness, a joint USIA–Peace Corps Donated Book Pool has been established to solicit book donations and to fill Peace Corps Volunteer and USIS book needs. While the magazine newsstand program contin-ues at the 2,000,000 annual new magazine level, greater stress has been placed on technical and professional journals such as medical journals or the *Scientific American*.

Agency officers and executives of American companies with inter-national operations have been meeting to delineate areas of mutual interest. These discussions, with over 150 companies, have served two purposes: first, to encourage these industries to identify their overseas activities with the economic and social development of the countries where they are operating, and second, to explore the possibilities of cooperation abroad between industry and Agency representatives. In this connection, USIS Public Affairs Officers are now visiting the home offices of companies with substantial operations in the countries where these officers are stationed.

Just over a year old, and now managed by a private non-profit corporation, the "Books USA" program allows Americans to purchase packets of 10 selected paperback books, at $4.00, for distribution abroad by USIS and the Peace Corps. This project, which requires no appropriated funds, takes advantage of the "at cost" basis on which many paperback publishers are prepared to make good books available, and it allows USIA control of distribution and presentation according to current target priorities.

Three automobiles, each towing a fully equipped travel trailer, have been made available to Agency foreign service officers for refamiliarization trips during their home leave in the United States. All costs, including gas, oil and insurance are borne by the Wally Byam Foundation. Twelve USIS officers and their families this year were able to benefit from this opportunity to reacquaint themselves with the grass roots life of the country for which they are spokesmen overseas on their next assignment.

Training

The Agency has expanded the training program for junior officers to include the eight week, basic officers course at State's Foreign Service Institute. USIA officers thus receive essentially the same basic preparation as do junior diplomats. At the same time, USIA has the opportunity of indoctrinating future ambassadors in the role of the Agency. This is done through professional contributions to the curriculum and by the presence and actions of Agency junior officers participating in the courses.

The Agency has also increased its participation in the mid-career course from four or five officers a year to 20 or 25. With USIA assistance the course of instruction has been completely revised. Slightly over half of the Foreign Service Officers of this Agency are in grades R-5 and R-4. Training opportunities, other than language, for officers at this level are limited. For this reason USIA attaches great significance to the mid-career officers course and hopes to increase its participation in the future.

Substantial changes have been made in the training and placement of junior officers. In addition to the basic officers course, language training is heavily emphasized. Approximately 70% of the Agency's junior officer trainees now receive six months of language instruction before leaving for the field. Of these, 50% are trained in languages other than French, German and Spanish. Every junior officer now gets a basic course in the language of his training post; previously, European languages were stressed. A junior officer is now assigned to his training post or area for at least one tour of duty following his ten-month training period, unless there are overriding reasons to the contrary. This is completely contrary to previous policy. USIA has encouraged the Foreign Service Institute to develop a series of short courses (six months or less) in the so-called "hard" languages. Many USIA junior officers achieve phenomenal results from these intensive studies and, when followed by living in the country for three years, they develop a high degree of proficiency.

USIA has organized a number of special seminars and institutes for the domestic establishment of the Agency. These have covered such topics as youth and student affairs, international labor, U.S. efforts and accomplishments in space and the special seminar on problems of developing areas. Approximately 1,200 employees of the Agency have benefited from the program; for many it has been their first formal Agency training.

The USIA Intern Program for young graduates of university cinematography schools was inaugurated in October, 1962. Those selected, five in number, have done graduate work in films, have made films of their own and have worked closely with skilled professionals. They work for a year in the Agency on motion picture projects and receive special technical training and general instruction during those activities in preparation for assignment overseas. A new group of five interns will be inducted very soon.

The Printed Word and Pix

During the past two and one-half years, the Press and Publications Service has developed new directions in both the nature of its output and its operational methods. In content, the major change has been in the emphasis on five major themes, which are the framework for the bulk of the service's output. The main effort has been to create Press and Publications material designed to emphasize the sources of strength on which U.S. foreign policy is based. Simultaneously, material not linked to America has been diminished.

Direction of IPS visual output has been concentrated in one operating branch with a direct line of responsibility to the director of IPS. Previously, it was diffused. A Run of Paper color service has been initiated to provide overseas publications with color separations on thematic subjects, which greatly reduces reproduction costs and increases use.

Picture service on chief-of-state visitors has been speeded. The old presentations albums that took a minimum of two months to produce have been replaced with prestige leather portfolios presented to the visitor before he leaves the United States to return home.

In graphics, the True Tales continuity strip is now being offered the field in jumbo size suitable for display and presentation. All regular cartoon continuity strips are now being produced in Spanish as well as English.

A series of cartoon-type booklets was devised to carry the Alliance for Progress and anti-Castro messages to the mass audience in Central and South America. Each booklet depicts actual happenings in color-drawing sequences. They have been extremely effective, making necessary large volume reprints. Twenty titles have been published. Nearly 20 million copies have been printed and distributed.

In order to improve the Agency's still picture output and keep abreast of technical developments, the Agency's photo laboratory was modernized. The lab's capacity for speedily turning out large quantities of copy negatives was greatly increased by the purchase of a continuous film processor. A Log-E-Tronics Unit, the first step toward electronic production of multiple prints was installed.

The IPS newsroom was reorganized as follows: Coverage, formerly the sole responsibility of a press coverage desk, was divided between the Washington desk and the telegraph desk. For the first time, a copy desk was created, to edit not only newsroom copy but also that of the features section and the visual materials branch. A news editor was added to supervise these desks. Several experienced newsmen were added to these desks (for example, a former associate editor of the *Saturday Evening Post*, an assistant city editor of the Louisville *Times*, a Sunday editor of the Corpus Christi *Caller Times*). An additional reporter has been assigned to the IPS UN Bureau. Coverage-in-depth, as opposed to straight top of the news coverage, has increased, with the production of a markedly greater number of backgrounders, situation pieces and interpretive stories.

The volume of IPS content has been tightened materially, but the Wireless Files have been expanded, largely in Africa. In March, 1961, 91 posts were equipped for direct Wireless File reception, of which only 18 were in Africa. In 1962, receiving equipment for 15 new African posts was put into operation and a separate African regional file was inaugurated. It started as a four-hour English transmission and now is six hours in English and French to 30 countries. Jamaica, British Guiana, Malaya, the Dominican Republic and Guayaquil also started getting the Wireless File. Altogether, 111 posts now receive it.

IPS pamphlet output has sharpened its political accent while reducing quantity which conforms with the Agency's role as the psychological arm of the Government in implementing foreign policy. Consequently, much of the material once presented as Americana is no longer used, except when it is essential as a means of suggesting a method for action in other countries. Examples of this closer keying to major current objectives were when the nuclear test ban treaty was under negotiation. IPS quickly issued a number of pamphlets in support; when Berlin was the hot issue, graphic pamphlets were produced. Heavier emphasis on graphics resulted in a picture pamphlet on Castro's betrayal of the Cuban people. Currently a comprehensive documentation of the Sino-Soviet split is being prepared.

In IPS mail features, science output has doubled, with space developments by far the biggest subject, but with increases also in subjects such as medicine, scientific applications in industry and similar subjects of great interest abroad, particularly in underdeveloped areas. Overseas rights have been acquired for material produced under domestic commercial contracts with the Astronauts. The volume of material on Civil Rights also has doubled in the past two years.

The number of IPS special packets, on such subjects as "The U.S. Trade Expansion Program", "Thirty Years of U.S. Social and Economic Progress", and "New Products and Processes in U.S. Industries", has increased sharply. Much more is being done to explain how the Democratic form of government assists and benefits its citizens. For example, a series called "How the U.S. Government Helps the People" has been running more than two years, and has developed more than 30 byliners by heads of various Federal Agencies outlining functions directly benefitting the citizen and the community. The effort to explain America within a mutual frame of reference is being carried out in the series, "Profile of an American", which has included a school teacher, doctor, farmer, steel worker and editor, among others.

In magazine reprints, a special service has been established to increase the number and variety of articles with intellectual appeal, for use in USIS-produced scholarly magazines. This in turn has led to servicing of more articles on public affairs by such government policy-makers as Arthur Schlesinger, Jr., and Walt Whitman Rostow.

Special materials output by IPS has devoted increasing attention to the international effects of Communism. For example, an exhaustive series of articles was produced on Communist infiltration of free nations, covering most of the world's non-Communist nations. More is being done on the Communist economic offensive to show how trade and aid are used to promote purely political goals. The volume of background articles on the Sino-Soviet split has increased, and they point out that the dispute is primarily ideological and that the goals of world conquest remain unchanged.

The Africa Branch of IPS completed its second year of operation last month. It now serves 33 countries through 47 USIS posts. Thirty of them have radio telephone and telegraph equipment to receive the daily bilingual file. A small French staff provides French versions of both Wireless File and mail materials. From its beginning, the Branch has carried a heavy load in supplying copy on African visitors and other U.S. African firsts, and has played a leading role in telling a frank but constructive and continuous story of race relations in this country.

In September, 1963, secure teletype circuits were put into service between the State and Agency wire rooms and USIA assumed the responsibility for its own terminal processing. Reproduction workloads were sharply reduced and delivery times, both in and out, greatly improved.

A Regional Service Center was established in Mexico City in March, 1962. It was staffed with editorial specialists directing their efforts to selected audiences of labor, students, and self-help phases of the Alliance for Progress. Their end products are in the form most suitable for the transmitting media— finished printed material, lithographic negatives for local printed reproduction and manuscripts of material designed for placement in local magazines, newspapers, radio and television stations. Two other overseas Centers, at Beirut and Manila, sharpened their operations by increasing services while reducing costs. Services to using posts were increased and unit costs reduced. Meanwhile, a survey of press requirements for West Africa was made and the new posts were provided with minimum equipment for producing printed materials.

Exhibitions

Exhibits prepared initially for showing in the USSR under US-USSR Cultural Exchange Agreements and later shown in other East European countries:

"Plastics USA" (5,000 sq. ft.): Shown for three weeks each in Kiev, Moscow and Tbilisi, between May and September, 1961, to audiences totalling 375,000 people. Exhibited in Rumania at Bucharest and Cluj; at Posnan (as part of an International Trade Fair) and Warsaw, Poland; and in Zagreb, Yugoslavia (again as part of an International Trade Fair)—between March and September of 1962—to an additional audience of 1,590,000.

"Transportation USA" (7,000 sq. ft.): Displayed in Volgograd and Kharkov between October 24 and December 27, 1961 to a total audience of 172,000. Shown again in Belgrade and Ljubljana between May and October of 1962, to an additional audience of 390,000.

"Medicine USA" (7,000 sq. ft.): Shown in Moscow, Kiev, and Leningrad for three weeks in each city, between March and July, 1962—to a total audience of 206,954. It was displayed in Zagreb and Belgrade in April and May to an additional 202,600 persons. This exhibit also formed the U.S. representation at Izmir (Turkey) International Fair in August, 1963, attracting there a quarter of a million visitors.

"Technical Books USA" (7,000 books and reference materials): Shown in Moscow, Leningrad and Kiev between January 23 and June 11, 1963—three weeks in each city—to 140,423 visitors.

"U.S. Astronaut Orbits the Earth": This exhibit consisted of seven unmounted panels printed in color. Two thousand copies were prepared and shipped to posts all over the world well in advance of John Glenn's orbital flight. The posts made them ready for display as soon as word of Glenn's safe landing on February 20, 1962, was received, and many posts have continued to display them on appropriate occasions.

"Friendship Seven Mercury Capsule": in which John Glenn made his orbital flight. The capsule was made available by NASA, transported by the Air Force and toured under USIA auspices to 23 countries between April and August of 1962. Standing-in-line and attendance records were broken by the Friendship Seven all along the way.

"U.S. Progress in Space Sciences": A 30-panel free-standing exhibit with seven models. Eleven sets have been distributed to all areas. Among the places where this exhibit has been shown with success to date (usually in combination with other Agency-supplied exhibits and models) are Rome and Sao Paulo in international affairs, Tokyo and four cities in Portugal.

"Graphic Arts USA" opened in Alma Ata in early October and was an immediate smash hit.

Book Publication and Distribution

Fiscal Year 1963 was the most productive year in the history of the Agency's book publishing program. One thousand two hundred and two editions totalling 10,850,000 copies were published in 36 languages.

The Agency's Latin American Book Translation Program was expanded dramatically during the last two years, increasing from contracting of 64 editions in Spanish and Portuguese totalling 541,000 copies in fiscal year 1961 to contracting of 332 editions totalling over 3,500,000 copies in fiscal year 1963. To insure that these vastly increased quantities of books reach Latin American readers, a campaign to encourage vigorous commercial promotion and sale of these books has been developed throughout the area.

With the emergence of some 16 Sub-Saharan French-speaking colonies and dependencies into independence, low-priced American book translations into French became an important concern of the Agency. By July, 1963, over one million copies of more than a hundred titles were available in French to African readers at the equivalent of 20 cents a copy.

Since the spring of 1961, over a million copies of some 200 American textbooks have been translated into 18 languages and published and placed in schools and universities in 17 countries under the PL-480 Textbook Programs.

The Low-Priced Book Program in English has produced 3,085,921 paperbacks since March, 1961, and has sold 1,830,294. Reflecting improved distribution and promotion during the past two years, sales represented almost 50% of the total sold since the program began seven years ago.

The criteria by which the eligibility of informational materials for Informational Media Guaranty coverage is determined were substantially revised in September 1961. Eligibility is now limited to those materials which make a positive contribution in support of U. S policy objectives and reflect favorably on the United States. The limited IMG resources are now allocated on a priority basis to assure that certain basic needs are met. For example, in fiscal year 1963, $350,000 in IMG contracts were issued for English-teaching materials. The bilateral agreement with Pakistan was amended to remove restrictions on the use of rupees acquired under the IMG program. A bilateral agreement was negotiated with the Republic of Guinea. Two new country programs were started (Korea and Afghanistan) and three other programs were phased out (Burma, Israel and the Philippines).

The Agency identified as of potential usefulness, and reviewed in relation to Agency objectives, over 10% of the books issued by the American publishing industry (18,000 titles published in 1961; 22,000 in 1962).

As a field service based on ICS book reviews, the Agency recommended about 3,000 titles a year to USIS posts for special consideration in ordering books. Blue Books have also been compiled and distributed to all USIS posts. These annuals combine, cumulate and list in an orderly fashion all the books recommended to USIS posts by various elements of ICS.

The Agency compiled and issued periodic subject bibliographies and special lists of books to assist USIS officers in obtaining useful materials. Of particular importance were book lists on modernization, labor, history, periodicals, a series entitled Focus U.S.A., and shorter lists on areas of particular Agency emphasis.

Books were selected to accompany the increasing quantity and range of Agency-sponsored exhibits. These varied from large book collections shown in Iron Curtain countries, to a model American book store for presentation in the Middle East, and to smaller book displays which accompany exhibits travelling throughout the Free World.

The Agency's American Studies Program came of age with the publication of "The United States of America, A Syllabus of American Studies." This "Syllabus", along with complementary material on the University of Pennsylvania certificate program, is helping to promote the growth of American Studies at many posts around the world. By September, 1963, 63 posts had requested 1,883 sets of the Syllabus for presentation to university libraries, education officials and professors.

"Restatement of Purposes and Technique of Agency's Cultural Packets" was published in July, 1961. In it the cultural operations division announced the continued production of ghost-written lectures on those aspects of American society, culture, history and government of interest to overseas audiences, and of importance to the Agency's over-all program.

Nineteen new information centers have been opened on the African continent for an area total of 54. Two additional regional librarians have been appointed: one for Dakar and former French West Africa, one for Brazzaville and former French Equatorial Africa. This brings the total number of librarians in Africa to six.

Collection of books in French have been increased considerably for French-speaking countries with the institution and growth of the "Nouveaux Horizons" series of low cost books in French for Africa. Over 100 titles in this series are now on USIS Library shelves in Africa.

Television

The Agency has steadily increased its production of television programs to meet the immense need and interest overseas. In Fiscal Year 1963, slightly more than 113 hours of programs on film and tape were produced compared with 101 hours in 1962. In 1963, 22 new positions were added in the Television Service to improve the production, quality and capacity: 10 positions in production, six on the technical staff, four in programming, and two in administration. These additions, and the Agency acquiring its own production equipment, have resulted in quality programs at costs lower than commercial stations.

New TV studios, nearing completion, will permit USIA to more than double the volume of in-house productions. The new facilities will enable USIA to do language adaptations, dubbing, editing, original programming and transfer of programs from tape to kinescopes. They also will make it possible to record audio and video direct transmissions from any of the three networks via the leased circuits, to transmit audio and video to 1776 Pennsylvania Avenue for direct screening and produce programs in three scanning standards. The equipment can handle many technical jobs that formerly had to be done under contract.

Agency productions and acquisitions have been placed on more than 40 new stations world-wide since mid-1961.

A series of 13 programs, entitled "World Americana", was recently produced especially for the Japanese national television network. These programs described significant and interesting aspects of American life—leisure time, the American housewife, American youth, an American university and other subjects. Another targeted TV series, entitled "Personal Report", was inaugurated for Nigeria, using a Nigerian student in Washington as the commentator. This series projected selected aspects of the American scene to a Nigerian audience in terms comprehensible to them. Twelve programs have been produced to date. In 1962 a series entitled "Washington Reports" was started for Japan. This bi-weekly program features a Japanese correspondent reporting on various current events of interest to Japan. Still another series aimed for the Far East is "Washington Newsletter", a monthly series of reports to Thailand on events of interest in the United States.

In Fiscal 1963 a series of 13 half-hour Spanish-language programs, entitled "The Experts Answer", was inaugurated for Latin America. In this series, Latin American newspaper correspondents question an American expert in the fields of government, labor, industry, science and the performing arts. This series has been sent to 19 Latin American countries for placement.

A 15-minute weekly public affairs type of TV show in Spanish and Portuguese, "Panorama Panamericano", begun in 1961, has been improved and streamlined. Today it is carried in 19 Latin American countries.

Two special film programs on the Alliance for Progress were produced in Fiscal 1963. "Report from Colombia", commemorating the first anniversary of the Alliance for Progress, was sent to 17 Latin American countries; and "Report from Venezuela", on the subject of land reform, was distributed to 19 countries in Latin America for television and film showings. Recent films dealing with Castro have included "Focus: Cuba", "Cuba—A World Verdict", "The Lost Apple", "Castro and Cuba", among others, were produced and distributed world-wide for both TV and motion picture showings.

Television correspondents from the United Kingdom, France, Germany, Sweden, Holland and Italy are getting increased help from USIA in producing programs on the United States. Notable among these was a one-hour program produced in early 1961 by British Independent Television on the Kennedy administration, entitled "The New Americans". It featured interviews of top New Frontier officials and the President himself. The following year the same network returned to produce, with USIA assistance, a one-hour program on the United States entitled "State of the Union".

Other cooperative programs in which USIA has recently helped foreign television networks and stations include: two one-hour programs entitled "Science International" with the BBC; a program on the U.S. space effort entitled "Destination Moon"; a series to consist eventually of 13 programs on the United States by the French National television; six programs on the United States by Finnish television; a one-hour program on integration produced by Italian television; a series of 13 programs on science with Belgian television; a film documentary on the history of the American Negro by French National TV; a program on the space communities of Cape Canaveral and Houston by Italian TV; three shows on the U.S. space program for the new second German television network.

English Teaching

Another major achievement has been the Agency's "Let's Learn English" series which is or has been telecast in 37 countries to an audience of millions around the world. Because of the phenomenal popularity of the programs a second set called "Let's Speak English" has been produced and a third is planned for production in the near future.

"Science Reports", a television series comprising two 15-minute program segments per month and featuring achievements in science and technology in the U.S., is currently telecast in 52 countries around the world.

The first two volumes of a six-book English Teaching textbook series were produced under contract with the National Council of Teachers of English and the McGraw-Hill Publishing Company. A new English teaching quarterly, "The English Teaching Forum", is aimed at the overseas teacher of English. Articles include both linguistic theory and practical classroom problems.

Because of the limited number of professionally trained linguists available, the Agency has initiated a program whereby selected, outstanding teachers of English with broad Agency experience are sent to a university to undertake special studies in linguistics and the teaching of English as a foreign language. A professional training program has also been instituted for English teachers and binational center administrative personnel prior to departure for overseas posts.

Personnel Utilization

The Agency has made significant progress in the more effective utilization of women officers. One woman has risen to the FSR-1 level, the highest career grade in USIA; another is the country public affairs officer for Chile; a third opened and operated a country program in Africa and is the only Agency officer to achieve a working proficiency in

Swahili. Another woman has become the Agency's deputy budget officer; the editor-in-chief of "America Illustrated" is a woman, and three women officers have attained the GS-15 level.

Since the spring of 1961, the Agency has made strides in developing fuller utilization of minority personnel and in according them rank commensurate with their skills. Since that date, the number of Negro officers of GS-12 or higher rank in the domestic service, for example, has increased from one to seven. The number of Negro officers in the foreign service has about doubled from the 1960 figure of two dozen. Three country public affairs officers are Negroes. About 10% of all foreign service officers of rank equal to GS-12 or above are Negroes.

USIA officers are participating in Washington seminars on the "Problems of Developing Countries", examining techniques and materials that assist emergent countries to develop viable political structures resistant to Communist and other hostile attempts to subvert and weaken them. These seminars bring together some of the most skilled and experienced U.S. and foreign personalities in the field.

USIA officers also actively participate in both the Inter-Departmental Committee and the faculty responsible for the Country Team Seminar on Problems of Development and Internal Security. USIA normally enrolls 12 senior officers in each of the six sessions of this seminar and has one officer assigned full time to the faculty. USIA also has a liaison officer attached to the faculty of the Army Special Warfare School at Fort Bragg.

The quality and quantity of candidates for positions in the Agency's domestic and foreign services have increased sharply during the past 30 months.

General knowledgeability in the United States about USIA purposes and operations has also increased sharply; domestic press attention to the Agency, as one index, has increased in volume by some 2,000%, virtually all of it favorable.

157.   Memorandum From the Assistant Director (Soviet Union
        and Eastern Europe) of the U.S. Information Agency (Brady)
        to the Director (Murrow)[1]

Washington, October 1, 1963.

SUBJECT

Clichés That Should Be Discarded

As you know, we have led a rather long, and particularly success-ful, campaign against certain clichés that are no longer useful to American best interests. IAS dropped "Soviet Bloc" in its title, as more embarrassing than pertinent. VOA no longer refers to the "Communist bloc" or the "bloc countries." We think the trend is conducive to better listenership.

Current developments are leading others in the Government to thinking along the same general line. Yesterday morning Bill Tyler told me he had raised the question with Foy Kohler at the UNGA, specifi-cally as concerns use of the term "satellites," with reference to Eastern European countries. Bill feels we are in no way advancing our objec-tives at this juncture by continuing to employ this designation, which he thinks must be galling to every true patriot in the area. I fully agree.

He asked me whether I would bring the matter to your attention, as a psychological factor of some importance. His hope would be that you might raise the point at an early NSC meeting, so that not only the Voice and other USIA media would stop using the pejorative term, but major speech writers, document drafters, and official reporters as well. He believes a decision at NSC level would get observance as would noth-ing else.

Matter of fact, State itself is one of the chief offenders—as witness the attached Airgram (CA–3272, September 23, 1963),[2] which violates what we are opposing in just about every form.

Here are six expressions which we think it best to avoid, in our own interest, under current circumstances; they are more misleading than helpful:

Communist bloc }
Soviet bloc   } use instead Soviet Union and Eastern Europe
bloc countries   }

---

[1] Source: Washington National Records Center, RG 306, USIA Files: FRC 72 A 5121, Field—Soviet Bloc/63. Secret.

[2] Not attached. A copy is in the National Archives and Records Administration, RG 59, Central Files 1960–63, POL COMBLOC–FWORLD.

satellites   } use instead Eastern Europe, or
Communist countries   }Eastern European countries
Communist-dominated countries }

Continued use of such terms is not only psychologically unsound, in view of current goals—it also makes us look ignorant of the evolution we believe is taking place in that area of the world.

LSB

---

158.   Memorandum From the Acting Director of the U.S. Information Agency (Wilson) to President Johnson[1]

Washington, November 25, 1963.

SUBJECT

USIA Coverage of President Kennedy's Death and Your Assumption of the Presidency

USIA is using all media to describe your accession to the Presidency and to document the orderly transfer of power following President Kennedy's death.

Since 2:00 p.m. Friday, the Voice of America has been broadcasting a special program around the clock to all parts of the world. This coverage will continue through your address to a joint session of the Congress on Wednesday.

Our Wireless File, a teletype service to 108 posts in 101 countries, has carried full accounts, including biographies of you and the late President. News photos, including a 17-picture biography of you, were rushed out by air.

We are transmitting the text of a brief pamphlet on you to all posts for immediate translation and distribution.

Extensive newsreel coverage, for both theater and TV use, is being air-shipped daily.

A 15-minute TV biography of you is almost completed, and will be air-shipped to countries having TV by Tuesday.

A full half-hour TV documentary of your rise to the Presidency will be completed and shipped within 10 days.

---

[1] Source: Johnson Library, Office Files of Bill D. Moyers, Box 55. No classification marking.

Two motion picture documentaries in color, one featuring the life work of President Kennedy and the other on your life and assumption of the Presidency, are to be completed within 30 days.

A six panel photographic exhibit an your career is in preparation for shipment to all posts by air on Friday.

Donald M. Wilson[2]

---

[2] Printed from a copy that bears this typed signature.

---

159. Memorandum From the Director of the U.S. Information Agency (Murrow) to Agency Heads of Elements and Public Affairs Officers Worldwide[1]

Washington, December 20, 1963.

It is essential that we help maintain a high level of foreign confidence in the continuity of American Government and policy under President Johnson and in our nation as the leader of the Free World. The President already has done much to assure the world. He has reaffirmed in several ways and in the most specific manner possible his commitment to the continuation of President Kennedy's foreign policy—a policy which he helped shape and carry out.

For some time I have been considering the priorities for Agency output, first issued July 24, 1961.[2] They have not changed substantially, which reflects in still one more way the continuity of U.S. policy. There have been enough shifts in emphasis, however, to warrant a restatement of these priorities.

There has been and is some confusion as to what these priorities represent and what proportion of our output should be devoted to them. The Agency's function, stated by the President in a directive of January 25, 1963,[3] is to "help achieve United States foreign policy objectives." There are, of course, differences among these objectives: some are world-wide in scope, others limited in geographic applicability; some are capable of achievement in a limited time, others will be with

---

[1] Source: Department of State, USIA Historical Collection, Agency History/63. Limited Official Use.

[2] Document 128.

[3] Document 144.

us for the foreseeable future. These goals are spelled out specifically in our Country Plans, which continue to be the basis of our operations in the field and support activities in Washington.

The diversity of our objectives around the world requires a wide variety of approaches, techniques, and activities. It also requires that we define our priorities, and co-ordinate our activities in support of them.

The attached priority subjects are those which I consider most urgent at the present time and which should be given full and persuasive treatment in all Media before other subjects are tackled.

The relative efforts in behalf of any of the five priorities will, as in the past, vary with the unfolding of events, the nature of the medium, and the situation in individual countries.

The responsibility for co-ordinating Media output on the priority and other subjects will continue to rest with the Assistant Deputy Director (Media Content).

E.R. Murrow

Attachment

While providing a broad range of materials required to support a diversity of objectives in Country Plans, until further notice Agency media will focus attention on, and give priority to:

THE PURSUIT OF PEACE

The United States has no more urgent task than the pursuit of peace. In the words of President Johnson, "We will be unceasing in the search for peace; resourceful in our pursuit of areas of agreement even with those with whom we differ." We believe this search for an attainable and honorable peace should be based on a gradual evolution in human institutions and on a series of concrete actions and effective agreements (such as the limited nuclear test ban) leading to general and complete disarmament. The United States will continue to encourage the settlement of international issues by peaceful means rather than force.

STRENGTH AND RELIABILITY

The United States, matured and tested under the responsibilities of free world leadership, will maintain its strength in all fields to protect its own freedom and to aid in the defense of other free nations against threats to their independence and institutions. The United States can and will keep its commitments to its allies and to other countries.

FREE CHOICE

The United States believes in a peaceful world community of free and independent states, free to choose their own future, free to build and change their own systems so long as they do not threaten the freedom of others. We believe in the dignity of the individual, and will continue to help other nations in their efforts to modernize their societies, to resist coercion, and to construct and maintain free institutions.

RULE OF LAW

The fundamental commitment of the United States is to freedom of the individual, of the community, and of the nation under law. This commitment is the hallmark which distinguishes societies of free men from societies where rule is based on privilege and force. Historically, the rule of law was a commitment of the people of the United States to themselves; today it is the cornerstone of both our domestic and international policies. We will continue to work toward perfecting the rule of law at home and encourage its extension to and among all nations.

UNITED NATIONS

The United States will continue its full support of the United Nations, seeking in concert with other countries to strengthen the UN's peacekeeping machinery. It will also continue to support UN functions which assist all free nations, large and small, to maintain their independence and to move toward political, economic, and social justice.

[Here follow examples of talking points corresponding to these priorities.]

United Nations

160. **Telegram From the Mission to the United Nations to the Department of State**[1]

New York, February 2, 1961, 2 p.m.

2078. Subject: 16th GA Presidency. Plimsoll (Australia) asked us whether we would like to see Slim (Tunisia) as next GA Pres. He said Slim just returned from Tunis with indication he be FonMin and with Govt Tunisia approval his candidacy.

Plimsoll reported several conversations with U Thant (Burma) who said to be Slim supporter. Thant wrote Ali Sastroamidjojo (Indonesia) (who is planning become serious ASAF candidate) seeking to discourage him from running. Thant claimed according to Plimsoll, he was urging others to write Ali in same sense. Thant said he had found surprising number Asians whom he would have expected be Ali supporters to feel Indonesia not right country to provide next GA Pres, that it should be African. In fact only UAR and Morocco seemed opposed to Slim, and are hoping urge Sudan FonMin to run.

Plimsoll said Thant leaving for Burma early next week and suggested if USG favored Slim it be important get word to Thant before he leaves. Opportunity act on Deptel 1346[2] not yet presented itself. Hope be able do so during SC mtg Thurs morning.

Stevenson

---

[1] Source: National Archives and Records Administration, RG 59, Central Files 1960–63, 320/2–261. Confidential.

[2] In telegram 1346 to USUN, January 26, the Department of State authorized USUN to discuss informally with Mongi Slim a report that Tunisia would put forward his candidacy for President of the 16th General Assembly. (Ibid., 320/12–1560)

161.   Telegram From the Mission to the United Nations to the
        Department of State[1]

New York, February 2, 1961, 6 p.m.

2084. 16th GA Presidency. Deptel 1346.[2] Stevenson met with Slim
(Tunisia) during translation in SC this morning. He told him of high
regard in which US holds him and his talents and expressed hope that
these would be at service GA as presiding officer 16th Session which
will mark moment of great crises and need for UN. This would be tribute both personally, to his country, and to continent of Africa. Stevenson
added hope that Slim might make announcement his candidacy as early
as possible and appropriate.

Slim replied by expressing gratitude for confidence shown and
indicated his definite intention to run. He said his candidacy would be
on behalf of all of Africa and for that reason he intended announce it as
soon as he had been able ascertain backing of Africans was available.
He therefore felt it not possible make announcement before resumed
session commenced, at which time he would actively pursue his goal.

In response to Stevenson's question Slim said he felt confident he
would be able obtain support from all of Africans. He mentioned having heard of possibility Ali (Indonesia) had been considering running,
but he thought it doubtful Asia would be entitled to consideration for
Presidency when Africans had for so long been denied it. We noted
report that several Asians seeking discourage Ali from running which
would confirm his feeling about candidacy of African state being entitled consideration this year.

Stevenson

---

[1] Source: National Archives and Records Administration, RG 59, Central Files
1960–63, 320/2–261. Confidential.

[2] See footnote 2, Document 160.

162.   Telegram From the Mission to the United Nations to the
         Department of State[1]

New York, February 8, 1961, 8 p.m.

2131. Resumed 15th GA. Yesterday Korean observer Liem urgently queried USUN concerning rumor heard from Afghan and Japan Dels to effect resumed session would only consider those items which were absolutely necessary, as result of which items such as Korean one would not be taken up. We assured Koreans so far USUN concerned we not aware any intention not to take up various important items such as disarmament, Congo, Korea, and others at resumed session.

Today we learned from other quarters this rumor gaining some credence. At lunch today Schurmann (Netherlands) spoke favorably of it to Yost. Matsch (Austria) sought sound us out as to whether US support proposal of this kind. Plaja (Italy) called on us to inquire as to possibilities in this regard. Jha (India) said he liked idea avoiding discussion disarmament now.

Subject also came up in US-UK discussion Congo this afternoon. UKDel had done study on items remaining for consideration at resumed session which were musts from British point of view. Copy this list being sent separately. Basically it refers to Comite 4 and 5 items, Congo, TC composition and ECOSOC items in plenary and raises problem of disarmament.

In discussion with UK it was agreed everything hinges upon whether agreement with Soviets possible and desirable, whereby disarmament could be shelved until 16th regular session. Would seem be highly undesirable to shorten resumed session only to pave way for special session on disarmament as Khrushchev has demanded.

This afternoon we asked GA Pres Boland (Ireland) whether he aware current status pressure on this subject. He unaware this precise rumor, but recalled at time Soviet release RB-47 fliers,[2] question of Soviets dropping U-2 item and obtaining deletion Hungary and Tibet bruited. Unofficial suggestions to this effect from Eastern European countries were then made to him but no formal approach made.

Stevenson

---

[1] Source: National Archives and Records Administration, RG 59, Central Files 1960–63, 320/2–861. Confidential.

[2] Documentation on the release of the crew of the U.S. Air Force RB-47 aircraft shot down by the Soviet Air Force on July 1, 1960, is in *Foreign Relations*, 1958–1960, vol. X, Part 1, pp. 540 ff.

163.   Memorandum of Conversation[1]

Washington, February 27, 1961.

SUBJECT

Candidacy of Ali Sastroamidjojo for Presidency of the 16th General Assembly

PARTICIPANTS

Mr. Nugroho, Chargé d'Affaires ad interim, Indonesian Embassy
FE:SPA—Mr. James D. Bell
FE:SPA—Mr. Robert S. Lindquist

Mr. Nugroho presented a Note in which the Government of Indonesia proposes Dr. Ali Sastroamidjojo as candidate for the presidency of the 16th General Assembly The Note states that the support of the United States would be deeply appreciated.[2]

Mr. Nugroho said that Ali's candidacy is partially an outgrowth of a previous Indonesian withdrawal in favor of Mexico in connection with the Disarmament Commission, and what he believes to have to have been at that time an understanding that this future candidacy of Dr. Ali's would receive certain Latin American support. He said also that the backing of the Arab states for Ali's candidacy may be affected by Mongi Slim's possible candidacy but nevertheless Indonesia is seeking Arab support. Mr. Nugroho believes that substantial Afro-Asian support can be lined up for Ali.

---

[1]   Source: National Archives and Records Administration, RG 59, Central Files 1960–63, 320/2–2761. Confidential. Drafted by Lindquist on February 28.

[2]   Text of the February 15 note is Enclosure No. 1 to despatch 866 from USUN, February 20. (Ibid., 320/2–2061) The Indonesian Government formally confirmed Sastroamidjojo's candidacy for President of the General Assembly on June 5. (Note from the Indonesian Representative to the United Nations, June 5, Enclosure No. 1 to despatch 1336 from USUN, June 23; ibid., 320/6–2361)

164. **Memorandum From the Assistant Secretary of State for International Organization Affairs (Cleveland) to Secretary of State Rusk[1]**

Washington, March 20, 1961.

SUBJECT

Presidency of the 16th General Assembly

Discussion:

The Tunisian Foreign Secretary has written you announcing the candidacy of Ambassador Mongi Slim for President of the 16th General Assembly and expressing the hope that his candidacy will have our support (Tab C).[2]

You will recall that Ambassador Stevenson, on your authorization (Tab D), spoke to Slim on February 2 to encourage him to put forward his candidacy (Tab E). According to the attached uncleared memorandum of conversation, the President on February 6 assured him of "U.S. backing" (Tab F).

The only other announced candidate is Dr. Ali Sastroamidjojo of Indonesia (Tab G). While there are no indications that his candidacy has so far received any widespread support, his election would be in the interest neither of the orderly conduct of the Assembly's business nor the attainment of United States objectives at the session.

Against this background, a prompt commitment to support Slim's candidacy appears desirable. The last five Assembly Presidents have been from the Far East, the Commonwealth, the Middle East, Latin America and Western Europe, respectively. Only Africa and Eastern Europe among the geographic regions have never held the Presidency. If the Slim candidacy gains widespread support early, this should serve to discourage the Soviet bloc from putting forward a candidate and might persuade Sastroamidjojo to withdraw. At the same time, it is recognized that any United States campaign on behalf of the Slim candidacy is likely to prove counterproductive.

Recommendation:

That you sign the attached letter to the Tunisian Foreign Secretary (Tab A) and approve the attached instruction to USUN (Tab B).

---

[1] Source: National Archives and Records Administration, RG 59, Central Files 1960–63, 320/3–1761. Confidential. Drafted by Virginia F. Hartley (IO/UNP) on March 17; concurred in by Donald Dumont (AF), William H. Sullivan (FE), George N. Monsma (ARA), James M. Ludlow (NEA), and Larry C. Williamson (EUR).

[2] Tabs A–F are not printed.

165.   Telegram From the Department of State to the Legation in
        Hungary[1]

Washington, April 6, 1961, 6:48 p.m.

269. Zorin announced in Political Committee April 5 USSR would
not press U-2, RB-47 complaint against US and suggested states concerned take steps clear agenda of Hungary and Tibet. Yost welcomed
Zorin's statement re U-2 and RB-47 case but observed Hungary and
Tibet not in same category. Later, spokesman USDel informed press US
not prepared drop Hungary and Tibet.

Rusk

---

[1] Source: National Archives and Records Administration, RG 59, Central Files
1960–63, 320/4–661. Official Use Only. Drafted by Edward J. Trost (EUR/EE), cleared by
Michael Newlin (IO/UNP), and approved by Robert M. McKisson.

---

166.   Memorandum From the Assistant Secretary of State for
        International Organization Affairs (Cleveland) to Secretary
        of State Rusk and the Under Secretary of State (Bowles)[1]

Washington, April 12, 1961.

SUBJECT

    United States Position on "Package" Membership Proposal Including Mauritania
    and Outer Mongolia

The Brazzaville Group, who are the sponsors of the draft resolution
before the General Assembly on the admission of Mauritania to the UN,
have accepted the Soviet amendments to their resolution to include,
and give priority in the resolution to, Outer Mongolia, and have
requested that the U.S. agree to this "package" in order that another
Soviet veto of Mauritania in the Security Council may be avoided. The
French, who have agreed to support the Group on this matter, have

---

[1] Source: National Archives and Records Administration, RG 59, Central Files
1960–63, 303.702/4–1261. Confidential. Drafted on April 12 by Virginia F. Hartley. The
date is handwritten on the memorandum. An attached draft memorandum from
Cleveland and Deputy Assistant Secretary of State for European Affairs William R. Tyler,
on the question of negotiations with the Outer Mongolians, dated July 20, is not printed.

informed us that the admission of Mauritania constitutes the "number one objective" of the Group under the instructions given them by their respective chiefs of state, and the Group have made clear that they will insist upon consideration of this matter at the resumed session. In this situation, the draft resolution with the Soviet amendments is practically certain of adoption despite strong Moroccan opposition to the admission of Mauritania and regardless of the U.S. position. A somewhat similar resolution, strongly and actively opposed by the U.S., was defeated in 1957, when the Assembly composition was much more favorable, by a vote of only 33 to 37 with 10 abstentions.[2] There is general agreement that the U.S. should vote against the Soviet amendments and abstain on the resolution as a whole if the amendments are adopted.

The pending draft resolution with the Soviet amendments would do no more than find Mauritania and Outer Mongolia qualified for UN membership and endorse their admission, with a request to the Security Council that it take note of this finding. In view of our recent decision to undertake negotiations looking toward recognition of Outer Mongolia, it would obviously be highly preferable if Security Council consideration of this request could be deferred until just before the 16th General Assembly. However, if the resolution is adopted by the Assembly, an African request for immediate Security Council consideration of this matter is likely so that the Assembly can act to admit Mauritania (and Outer Mongolia) before it adjourns, and is practically certain when the Security Council acts on Sierre Leone's application following its independence on April 27. Ceylon is President of the Council in April and is most unlikely to resist an African request for an immediate Council meeting. While Chile is Security Council President in May, pressure from Sierre Leone for early consideration of its application, which the UK would almost have to support, would make postponement for any length of time extremely difficult.

There are two courses open: (1) the U.S. could abstain or join China in voting against the admission of Outer Mongolia in the Security Council and attempt to organize a sufficient number of negative votes and abstentions so that the negative votes of U.S. and China do not constitute a veto, as the U.S. did in 1957 and last December; or (2) the U.S. could abstain as it did on the package proposal including Outer

---

[2] The 12th Session of the UN General Assembly had considered a series of draft resolutions concerning the admission of the Republic of Korea, Vietnam, and the Mongolian People's Republic as members. On October 17, 1957, the General Assembly rejected draft resolution A/PC/C.17, introduced by India and Indonesia, that called for the relevant records and proposals regarding all three applicants to be re-submitted to the Security Council for further consideration (on September 9 the Soviet Union had vetoed the admission of the Republic of Korea and Vietnam, while a Soviet draft resolution to admit the Mongolian People's Republic was defeated by a vote of 5 to 2, with 4 abstentions). (*Yearbook of the United Nations, 1961*)

Mongolia in 1955, which was vetoed by the Chinese, and try to persuade the Chinese also to forego use of their veto. (If the GRC were to agree, this course would result in admission of both Outer Mongolia and Mauritania.)

Arguments in favor of the first course are:

1) It would put the U.S. in a much better bargaining position in its negotiations on the recognition of Outer Mongolia;

2) It would permit us to approach the Chinese in the broader context of our negotiations on the Chinese representation issue, in which we contemplate urging that both the U.S. and the GRC agree to forego use of their veto on membership;

3) It would not risk a Chinese veto of the "package" proposal, with the serious damage to the over-all position of the GRC in the UN that would result from such a veto, and particularly among the Africans;

4) It would not have the implications for the GRC's status that adoption of a more flexible position on the Outer Mongolia question by the U.S. (and the GRC) at this particular juncture would have;

5) It would avoid a "back to the wall" reaction from the GRC just when we are trying to negotiate the representation issue;

6) It could give us a strong bargaining point with the Africans in obtaining their support of whatever handling is decided on with respect to the Chinese representation at the 16th General Assembly.

Arguments against the first course are:

1) It would almost certainly result in a Soviet veto of Mauritania for which the Africans would blame us;

2) The U.S. rejection of their approach would be strongly resented by the Africans, particularly as we could not explain our basic dilemma to them, and would be seriously prejudicial to our efforts to make them more responsive to U.S. influence;

3) It would probably result in such a reaction against the GRC as to reduce its support among African states, although the reaction would probably be less severe than in the event of a GRC veto under the second alternative;

4) It is far from certain that we could organize the necessary number of negative votes and abstentions in the Security Council to avoid the U.S. and Chinese veto which would be the "kiss of death" for the GRC in the UN. (There are five certain votes on the Council in favor of the "package": USSR, France, UAR, Ceylon, Liberia; whether in the face of French-African agreement on the "package" and GA endorsement of it, the UK, Turkey, Chile and/or Ecuador could be persuaded to abstain is far from certain.) If we were to vote against, and this were also to be a veto, this would be contrary to established U.S. policy.

5) It is questionable whether the active U.S. opposition to acceptance of the "package," which would be required not only in the Security Council but also in the GA to assure a substantial number of at least abstentions on the resolution there, is consistent with the decision to open negotiations on the recognition of Outer Mongolia, since we would not be in a position to explain that our opposition is essentially tactical and temporary.

The second course, which is that reflected in the attached telegram,[3] avoids, in my opinion, these disadvantages and has the following advantages:

1) It would result in the admission of Mauritania;

2) It would go far to meet the request of the Brazzaville Group;

3) It would not be too unpalatable to Morocco;

4) It would undoubtedly be warmly received by the great majority of UN members;

5) It would avoid a complete reversal of our previous position on Outer Mongolia pending the outcome of the projected negotiations;

6) If the GRC agrees to forego the use of the veto, this course would avoid focussing the resentment of the Africans on the GRC at this critical time. It is, however, by no means certain the GRC would agree, whatever pressure exerted, to join us in an abstention. Its veto in 1955 came despite U.S. representations at the highest levels urging that it forego use of its veto in its own self-interest. If the GRC were to veto, the consequences in terms of loss of African support for its position in the U.N. would be extremely serious.

The disadvantages in this course are the obverse of the advantages in the first course and relate exclusively to our policies with respect to the GRC and Outer Mongolia.

We have been informed by USUN that Ambassador Stevenson has agreed to meet with the Brazzaville Group before the end of the week to give them our answer and there is a possibility that the Africans may raise their draft resolution at the next plenary, scheduled for April 13.

---

[3] Not found.

167. Circular Telegram From the Department of State to Certain Posts[1]

Washington, April 14, 1961, 10:30 p.m.

1583. I. Following is US position re admission Mauritania and Outer Mongolia to UN:

1. We should urge the Africans to insist that the "package" be split, pointing out that in our opinion Mauritania will get such an overwhelming vote in the General Assembly that it will be most difficult for the USSR to veto its application in the Security Council if the Africans maintain pressure on them. The Africans must realize that it is with the USSR not the US that the ultimate decision on the admission of Mauritania lies. It is the Soviet Union that has vetoed Mauritania.

2. We support the admission of Mauritania now as we have in the past and hope splitting the package will lead to its admission.

3. We will be prepared to support and even co-sponsor the admission of Outer Mongolia when we have had an opportunity to determine whether it in fact has the attributes of an independent state. The new administration has been reviewing this question with a view to initiating conversations at an early date.

4. If asked as to the meaning of this statement you should indicate that:

(a) we are beginning discussions with our friends immediately; and
(b) our review will include the question of the willingness and ability of Outer Mongolia to send and receive diplomatic missions and carry on normal diplomatic, consular, commercial and cultural relations with other countries.

5. The Chinese, UK and French Delegations should also be informed of our position immediately.

II. In light above Dept believes USGADel should, if tactical situation GA remains unchanged:

1. vote against Soviet amendments;
2. vote for 11-power draft if not amended;
3. if Soviet amendments adopted, arrange for para-by-para vote on amended resolution and vote against first Soviet preambular paragraph and first Soviet operative paragraph; vote for paragraphs remaining as

---

[1] Source: National Archives and Records Administration, RG 59, Central Files 1960–63, 303/4–1461. Confidential; Priority. Drafted by Virginia F. Hartley; cleared in AF and EUR, and by George N. Monsma (ARA), James M. Ludlow (NEA), and William F. Sullivan (FE); and approved by Assistant Secretary Cleveland. Sent to USUN and repeated to Paris, London, Taipei, Abidjan, Dakar, Yaounde, Rabat, Tokyo, Moscow, Ankara, Quito, Santiago, Lome, and Tananarive.

they originally appeared in 11-power draft; and abstain on third operative paragraph as amended and on resolution as whole.

4. make explanatory statement along lines I (points 1–4) above.

Should also be pointed out Soviet efforts make admission one applicant contingent on admission another contrary UN Charter under 1948 advisory opinion ICJ. However, since US does not wish appear oppose admission Mauritania or disposed thwart will majority UN members on membership issue, it will abstain on 11-power draft resolution if Soviet amendments carried. For same reasons, US will endeavor prevent linking of admission Mauritania and Outer Mongolia in SC, will continue support admission Mauritania but cannot at this time support admission of Outer Mongolia.

III. USGADel should immediately consult with Chinese Del pointing out question admission Mauritania and Outer Mongolia could be raised SC before resumed session adjourns on basis GA action and in any event likely be raised when Sierra Leone application considered shortly after its independence on April 27. Our view best way prevent favorable SC action on Outer Mongolian application at this time is to organize sufficient number abstentions so that recommendation its admission fails to receive necessary seven votes, and we intend proceed accordingly. We would therefore urge Chinese Del obtain authorization Taipei join us in abstaining on "package" proposal in GA and SC since negative vote by GRC would only serve alienate such support as GRC now enjoys among new African members, particularly Brazzaville Group.

IV. USGADel should also urgently seek agreement other SC members likely be responsive our approach this matter (particularly UK, Turkey, Chile and Ecuador) to abstain in both GA and SC vote on "package" proposal.

Rusk

168. Telegram From the Department of State to the Mission to the United Nations[1]

Washington, April 21, 1961, 12:06 a.m.

2090. Re urtel 2944.[2] Confirming telecons today, Mission authorized agree GA recess on schedule April 21.

While we very much wanted complete debate on Korea, Hungary and Tibet, we recognize that extending session would likely encounter strong opposition. We doubt seriously we could muster two-thirds majority to reconsider earlier decision to adjourn April 21 and moreover it is clear that extending session would open the gates to numerous pressures to prolong session indefinitely. Moreover, in context atmosphere engendered by Cuban and UNRWA debates in particular, we think drawing session out unlikely be productive from our viewpoint even if we could do so. As far as African item is concerned, as long as Africans themselves are not distressed by failing conclude consideration this item, and particularly since they have insisted in injecting unacceptable elements on target dates into res on our item, we prepared see this wind up without res.

Main additional action Dept eager to see taken not covered by urtel is Political Committee decision on seating North Korean representatives. We believe North Korean response to Committee's condition on seating their representatives clearly unsatisfactory and that it would be desirable, especially from viewpoint domestic ROK problems, to have Committee take decision that North Korean response is unacceptable and they are not to be seated. This also confirms Department's position you should seek "no decision" on Hungarian credentials.

Rusk

---

[1] Source: National Archives and Records Administration, RG 59, Central Files 1960–63, 320/4–2061. Confidential. Repeated to Seoul. Drafted on April 20 by William B. Buffum (IO/UNP); cleared by Olcott Deming and Henry J. Tasca (AF), Harlan M. Cleveland (IO), William H. Sullivan (FE), and Edward T. Long (EUR); and approved by Woodruff Wallner (IO).

[2] Telegram 2944 from USUN, April 20, described a meeting that Dean and Deputy Representative Charles W. Yost had with General Assembly President Frederick H. Boland, Secretary-General Dag Hammarskjöld, and Under Secretary Andrew W. Cordier on April 20. Boland pointed out that all items on the agenda could not be covered before the General Assembly's scheduled adjournment. He proposed that a group of neutral countries might introduce a resolution that would defer consideration of certain specified issues (Korea, outer space, the second conference on the peaceful use of atomic energy, a vacancy in the investment committee, the Czech item, the Romanian item, Tibet, Hungary, and Africa) until the 16th General Assembly. (Ibid., 320/4–2061)

169.   Memorandum From the Assistant Secretary of State for
        International Organization Affairs (Cleveland) to Secretary
        of State Rusk[1]

Washington, May 2, 1961.

SUBJECT

Toward a Strategy for the United States in the United Nations

Now that the Resumed Session of the United Nations General
Assembly has adjourned, it is none too early to be planning for the
General Assembly session in the fall, and more generally for the future
of the United Nations. In this memorandum I will suggest a *widespread
program of consultation* with governments on UN matters.

I

Before coming to recommendations on procedure, I think it would
be useful to set forth some facts of life about the UN.

1. As we all know, the growing importance of the UN combined
with rigid application of the one country–one vote principle, makes for
increasing difficulty in mobilizing a two-thirds majority in the
Assembly for sensible and moderate programs and policies. The presence of "swirling majorities" in the Assembly in turn tends to raise the
emotional temperature of the atmosphere in debates in the smaller
councils, notably in the Security Council and the Trusteeship Council,
but to some extent in the Economic and Social Council as well.

2. However, the Resumed Session did demonstrate that it remains
possible, even in a General Assembly of 99 members with 25 African states
in attendance, to keep action (as differentiated from talk) under control.
Despite our well-publicized difficulties in New York during the last few
weeks, there was literally no (repeat no) action item which was able to get
a two-thirds majority in the General Assembly over our active opposition.
The Arab bloc could not sell its proposal for Alien Property Custodian in
Palestine. The Mexican resolution on Cuba fell far short of a two-thirds
vote. The provisions in the Indian resolution calling for Belgian withdrawal from the Congo within 21 days and the threat of sanctions were
not approved. Even the demand for economic sanctions against the Union
of South Africa because of its apartheid policy was not accepted.

3. On the other hand, a two-thirds vote was put together, with
much sweat and sleeplessness, for acceptable resolutions on (a) the
Cuban situation, (b) financing the Congo operation, (c) reaffirming the

---

[1] Source: Kennedy Library, National Security Files, Subjects Series, United Nations
(General), 1/61–7/61, Box 310. Confidential.

UN role in the Congo, (d) exhortations to the Portuguese on Angola and to the Belgians on Ruanda Urundi, (e) approving and implementing the plebiscite to split the Cameroun trust territory, (f) a Credentials Committee report recommending that the Assembly take "no decision" on Hungarian credentials, and (g) several non-controversial items, including the US-USSR resolution deferring General Assembly discussion of disarmament.

4. Thus in the actual event, the less constructive proposals were defeated and the most necessary actions taken. It must of course be recognized that the absence of economic and social items on the agenda of the Resumed Session, the decision to defer the disarmament debate, and the deadline set for adjournment contributed to this result. The Assembly did not consider certain questions on which we have the greatest difficulty mustering either a blocking third or a two-thirds majority. While no agreement was reached on a "bob-tailed" session, this was in fact what we got.

5. The picture is by no means of swirling majorities under the leadership of the Soviet Union defeating the US at every turn. The US is not—yet at least—being defeated at every turn; and the swirling majorities are far from being subject to Soviet leadership. Indeed, the Soviets do not operate in such a way as to exercise the leadership they could in this forum, since they take a relatively extreme position on nearly every issue, often change their positions suddenly in the later stages of debate, and have not yet learned to use their financial influence in the UN. (They could jeopardize the Congo operation far more by participating in its financing and then threatening to withdraw than by boycotting the agreed assessment from the outset.)

6. In the midst of all these stirring parliamentary events, highly significant executive operations are going on outside of the Assembly debates. The UN Emergency Force continues to sit on the Gaza Strip. The mediation machinery in the Middle East survives the April 20 Israeli parade in Jerusalem. By far the most important of all, the UN executive has been building its Congo force back up to nearly 20,000 again, in spite of earlier defections. Also during this period, the UN is managing a sufficient show of firmness to convince the central Congolese Government that the best way to get rid of the UN in the long run is to cooperate with it in the short run. At the same time, unnoticed and unsung, the UN Congo staff is conducting in the technical, economic and financial fields one of the world's largest civilian advisory operations.

7. In spite of all the talk about the devastating effects of the Soviet attack on the Secretary General, that estimable executive clearly won the 1960–61 round in what will doubtless be a continuing fight.

Khrushchev came in like a lion with his proposal last fall for a tripartite Secretary General; Gromyko ascertained in March that in its present form this proposal was strictly no sale; and Zorin was duly instructed to go out like a lamb.

The predicted timidity of the Secretariat, as a result of the Soviet attack, has materialized among subordinates to some extent, but is not much in evidence in the Secretary General's office. Mr. Hammarskjold is currently working out a new "UN presence" in connection with the difficulties between Cambodia and South Vietnam. And some of the countries most concerned with avoiding trouble in West New Guinea are, in consultation with Mr. Hammarskjold, putting together a proposal for a new UN operation—a trusteeship over that disputed territory.

II

These are lessons that can be derived from past experience. If we look now to the future of the United Nations, some additional facts of life are discernible.

8. There is hardly a major subject in international politics which does not have a United Nations angle, presently or prospectively. To put the same thought another way, nearly every major matter handled by every Foreign Office in the world had to be handled both in bilateral diplomatic channels and in the multilateral channels of international organization.

9. Every United Nations matter (thus, by the definition I have just suggested, nearly every major matter of foreign policy) is sooner or later subjected to the full glare of international publicity. The United Nations has become a world news center rivaling and, on some subjects, upstaging the traditional news centers of London and Washington.

10. The United Nations and other international organizations are developing and can much further develop a capacity to take executive action on behalf of the world community as a whole. The unnoticed lesson of the events of the past few weeks is the great potential importance to our national interest of these international operations. The Kennedy Administration inherited three prime trouble spots: the Congo, Laos, and Cuba. It is not without meaning that of these three, we have had to move backwards or sideways on Cuba and Laos, where either no international field operation has been developed (Cuba) or the UN operation was inadequate for the task (Laos). In the Congo the presence of a field operation maintained by an international organization has enabled us to move forward (by fits and starts, to be sure) precisely because the world community can "intervene in the name of non-intervention" while a single nation, however powerful, cannot. The development of

the United Nations operational capability should now be a central target of American foreign policy.

11. It will be important, as we go along, not to confuse actions and operations with the rhetoric and symbolism of public debates. We have to be able to operate at the level of symbolism as well as the level of reality; but in order to do so successfully it is important not to confuse the one with the other. At the symbolic level, for example, we can assume that the imprecision of resolutions and the extremism of rhetorical hyperbole will continue to increase as the square of the membership in the General Assembly—and can afford to be a good deal more relaxed about it if we have learned to apply our dignity and our power effectively in support of UN operations.

12. For the new nations and their even newer representatives, the discussions in the General Assembly and the smaller United Nations Councils and Commissions, including the regional commissions and the Specialized Agencies, have a very important role to play as a global training ground for responsibility. The development of voting blocs in the Assembly is deplored by some people; yet they are not only inevitable in so large a body but also potentially a force for more responsible actions by individual delegates. During the Cuban debate, the Nigerian delegate proposed to amend the Latin American resolution in an unfriendly way; he was brought to his senses by a Latin American threat to prevent a two-thirds majority for a resolution on the Cameroun issue that was favorable to the Nigerian point of view. The immersion of excitable diplomats in practical politics of this kind has its educational value.

As we work through the final years of the colonial era, for example, the primary problems facing the new nations will not be those associated with generating opposition to the "colonialists" or speeding the day of self-determination for their non-self-governing brothers. The primary problem for the leaders of these nations—in different ways in Africa, Asia and Latin America—is how to govern their own societies effectively and by the consent, whether or not expressed in traditional forms, of their own people. The task of institution building for social and economic development; the invention of appropriate forms of public communication and political leadership; the recruitment and training of internal security forces at once politically loyal and militarily effective; the reconciliation of a mystique of nationalism with the hard facts of international interdependence—these are the big items on the agenda for the national leaders of the less-developed parts of the world. It will be important for us, and for others of the "more developed nations", to find ways of making sure that these leaders and their successors are continually reminded of the obligations of public responsibility, which are not only (in the words of the

Charter) "to promote social progress and better standards of life" but to do so "in larger freedom," protecting "fundamental human rights" and "the dignity and worth of the human person", and "to practice tolerance and live in peace with one another as good neighbors."

III

If the United Nations is to be made more effectively operational, if the symbolic debates are to be used to put pressure on the newer and more revolutionary governments as well as on the older and more democratic ones, if the United Nations is to fulfill its mission as a training ground for public responsibility, then there will have to be some changes made in the way we have traditionally operated in the United Nations. Most of them are obvious from this rehearsal of "the facts of life"; and some are already contemplated or under way in New York.

For example:

1. The United States Mission in New York, taken as a whole, needs to be on a day to day first-name relationship with about 600 key individuals in 98 national delegations. The subject matter of this relationship cannot and should not be limited to tactics on particular issues that may arise in the United Nations; it should instead be a process of continual consultation across the whole range of shared concerns about foreign policy. This requirement raises important problems about recruitment of staff, and the assignment of political officers from the Department at peak periods; it also makes the question of quarters allowances and representational funds in New York an important matter of United States foreign policy.

2. The requirements of the situation argue for a strong United States delegation to the United Nations General Assembly, with a minimum number of delegates (preferably none) who are there for show rather than for hard diplomatic work. The delegation should be of the highest professional caliber.

3. We also require urgently a modernization of our communications system with New York. When quick instructions are required in New York, we are having to send them over an ordinary, open telephone line. We are looking into ways to assure instantaneous and secure transmission to New York so that the long telegraphic delays are avoided as well as open telephone calls.

4. The planning of our work in the Department and in New York should provide for careful advance preparation through diplomatic channels (and on some issues in the public prints as well) on each item of each General Assembly agenda—and major items in the Councils, too.

5. The United States Embassy in each UN country needs to be generally familiar with United States thinking on the United Nations angles

to all major questions of foreign policy—*not* only those which happen to be of concern in that particular country or region. Thus the United States Ambassador in Baghdad should be briefed on any change in thinking on Korea; the United States Ambassador to Japan should know what we intend to do about the African item; the United States Ambassador in Buenos Aires should be brought up to date on the Palestine Refugee problem; and so on around the circle.

6. We should arrange full and frequent discussions between responsible officers of the Department and of USUN with the Foreign Office people in key countries, particularly those officials who formulate instructions to their delegates in New York. This can partly be done by embassies on the basis of instructions from the Department; but there is much that can be accomplished in informal views across the whole range of United Nations affairs. You and I have already discussed plans for visits on my part to some of the European capitals for this purpose; later it may be useful to cover key bases in other parts of the world.

We surely have the courage and leadership to organize to do this job right not only in New York but in Washington and in every diplomatic post overseas. Whether the Congressional support for a first-rate effort will be forthcoming cannot be predicted; but the Congress has normally responded when the full weight of Presidential leadership has been publicly placed behind a major foreign policy push. In agreement with Ambassador Stevenson, I will shortly be making further detailed proposals to improve our technique and our capacity for effective "parliamentary diplomacy".

Beyond repairing the repairable deficiencies in technique, our preparations need to cover a detailed assessment of the situation surrounding each item now or likely to be on the agenda of the XVI session of the General Assembly, now scheduled to begin September 19, 1961, at the United Nations in New York. Here again detailed analyses and recommendations are in preparation at USUN and in the Department. They will be presented for your review as they are ready, in an effort to avoid the last-minute pile-up of United Nations policy questions and to emphasize the strategic rather than the merely tactical issues involved.

There are, however, three overriding questions on which it is necessary to develop a general sense of direction, as they affect nearly all the more specific items on the United Nations agenda. These three questions are:

—The financing and management of an operational United Nations.
—The Secretary-General and "tripartitism".
—The issue of Chinese Communist representation in the United Nations.

IV

Financing and Management of Operations

I have referred earlier to the symbolism which the UN represents—a parliament of peoples from the nations of the world replete with rhetoric and resolutions which at times appear to counter the aims of American foreign policy—and to the need for making a distinction between undisciplined parliamentarianism and the responsibility of executive operations. I venture to predict that the coming months will require, perhaps more so than in previous years, serious deliberations by this Government whether or not to use the UN as an "executive agent" in areas experiencing political, economic or social upheaval. If it should be determined that the UN will be so employed then we must do some rethinking about its managerial capacity.

Because of the one country–one vote principle the political debates which may rage around the UN presence in troubled areas of the world are inevitable. Inevitably, criticism will be heaped upon whatever agent—be it this Government, a consortium of countries or the UN—is employed to maintain peace and security. But this principle and criticism should not be allowed to throttle the tools required for the task.

Peace and security is a responsibility of every nation, but our foreign aid effort is testimony to the fact that every nation does not have the wherewithal to meet the cost of attaining these goals. These nations are also members of the UN. And here, many countries are finding it impossible to meet the costs of UN peace and security operations based on the prevailing assessment scale.

To continue this system will pit against each new proposal for an operating function three groups of delegates—those, like the Soviets, who are opposed to the development of operating functions at all; those who think that the particular operation proposed might adversely affect their national interest; and those who believe the proposed operation will be too expensive for their treasuries.

The last category of countries is able to meet less costly obligations such as those supporting the UN Special Fund, the Expanded Technical Assistance Program and certain refugee activities. They are in fact, willing to delegate action to the governing bodies directing such activities. Thus, it appears to us that these precedents might be applied to emergency operations. To be sure, such operations have political implications far greater than UN technical assistance or refugee relief, and the General Assembly would continue to remain the forum for the airing of views on these questions.

But a large share of the financing burden of peace and security operations must inevitably fall on UN members with a capacity to pay.

If there are a number of such operations, the burden probably will fall on the same members. The membership as a whole is probably willing to contribute moderate amounts annually toward peace and security (say $18–20 million), but some other provision has to be made for the bulk of the expense of an operation such as the Congo.

We are considering presently a number of alternative means of financing, including a plan which would provide for loans to a UN emergency fund with initial capital to come from the capital exporting countries and with repayments to be made by all UN members over a number of years. Any such arrangement should, following a determination that emergency action must be taken, be accompanied by a delegation of authority from the General Assembly to a consortium of nations making the major contributions to the operation both in cash and in kind. This consortium would then support and advise the United Nations executive in carrying out the operation. As long as the one member–one vote principle prevails, it is unlikely that the Assembly would be willing to delegate outright the political control of such an operation to a consortium group. It might, however, be willing to give such a group, in recognition of its contribution, a greater voice, perhaps in an advisory capacity, in the management of the operation. Without such a delegation of authority it is doubtful that continuing financial support of the major contributing powers could be expected and maintained.

In the absence of some such arrangement it is feared that the peace and security efforts of the UN will take on a quixotic character whose weakness adds to the strategy of the Sino Soviet Bloc, receives the derision of a de Gaulle, and causes erosion of United States support.

The Secretary General and "Tripartitism"

Another major question of strategy arises from the Soviet attack on both the Office of Secretary General and on the Secretary General personally. Dag Hammarskjold's present term of office expires in the spring of 1963. The question of what happens after that will be on the agenda of the 17th General Assembly, convening in September 1962 since Article 97 of the Charter provides that the Secretary General shall be appointed by the General Assembly on the recommendation of the Security Council. This question will therefore presumably be under active consideration during the summer of 1962, hardly a year from now.

The first General Assembly, in its appointment of the first Secretary General, followed the recommendation of the United Nations Preparatory Commission that he be appointed for a five-year term. (The Commission also recommended that the Security General be eligible for reappointment for a further five years.) When in 1950 Trygve Lie's term was about to expire, the Security Council, meeting in closed session, was unable to reach a recommendation because of lack of unanimity among the permanent members. (The USSR vetoed the reappointment of Lie because of his strong support of the United Nations action in Korea and the United States let it be known that it was prepared to veto anyone other than Lie.) The General Assembly then adopted by a show of hands vote of 46 to 6 (Soviet bloc), with 8 abstentions, a resolution in which the Assembly simply "decides that the present Secretary General shall be continued in office for a period of three years." The legality of the action was challenged by the Soviet bloc and certain other members. It was justified on the grounds that the Assembly having set the term of office could extend it and that it was essential to insure the uninterrupted exercise of the functions vested by the Charter in the Office of Secretary General.

Trygve Lie, whom the USSR refused to recognize as Secretary General after the extension of his term, submitted his resignation in November 1952. In April 1953, acting on the recommendation of the Security Council, the General Assembly appointed Dag Hammarskjold and decided that "the terms of appointment of the second Secretary General shall be the same as those of the first Secretary General" (i.c., a five-year term). In 1957, Hammarskjold was reappointed by unanimous vote in both the Council and the Assembly, later deciding the "terms of appointment . . . . during his second term of office shall be the same as during his first term."

Khrushchev, in his address to the General Assembly on September 23, 1960, proposed replacement of the Secretary General by a "collective, effective body of the United Nations comprising three persons, each of whom would represent a certain group of states" (i.e., "colonialist," "socialist", and "neutralist"). This proposal followed the forced withdrawal of Soviet bloc personnel from the Congo and endorsement of the Secretary General's role there by the Fourth Emergency Special Session of the General Assembly after a Soviet veto in the Security Council. Khrushchev enlarged upon his proposal in the Assembly on October 3, stating not only that "we" do not and cannot trust Mr. Hammarskjold but also that "any other Secretary General will also fail objectively to represent the interests of the three different groups of states." Soviet spokesmen subsequently explicitly extended this tripartite concept beyond the Office of the Secretary General to include the Secretariat, the Security Council, and the Economic and Social Council and its functional commissions and have raised it in other international meetings, such as the current Nuclear Test Ban talks and the recent Conference on Diplomatic Privileges and Immunities.

On February 14, 1961, the USSR issued an official statement on the situation in the Congo, denouncing the Secretary General and declaring that "the Soviet Government will not maintain any relations with

Hammarskjold and will not recognize him as an official of the United Nations." The Soviet bloc has since refused to have any official communication with the Secretary General. The response among the UN membership generally has, however, been so negative that the USSR did not really make an issue of the Secretary General at the resumed General Assembly. A Guinean proposal to delete in the Congo resolution a request to the Secretary General to take executive action was defeated 83 to 11, with 5 abstentions. While the USSR will undoubtedly continue to press its tripartite proposal and to attack Hammarskjold personally, the focus of this attack so far as the Office of the Secretary General is concerned is likely to shift to the Under Secretary level, where it has a better chance of obtaining some Afro-Asian support.

Unless there is a change in the Soviet attitude toward Hammarskjold, his reappointment is probably not feasible. Should the USSR decide to push its triumvirate proposal, the Soviet veto would probably preclude agreement on any successor and in any event, great-power agreement on a successor sympathetic to the West is highly unlikely. In these circumstances there appear to be five alternatives:

1) Persuade Hammarskjold to allow himself to be "continued" in office by Assembly action as Lie was. Since Hammarskjold is already being given the "silent treatment" by the USSR, he may be hard to convince but it might be done if he believed the future of the United Nations was at stake.

2) Persuade the General Assembly to designate some other Secretariat official as Acting Secretary General pending great-power agreement on a successor. This would require planning, since it was tacitly agreed at the San Francisco conference that the Secretary General would not be a national of one of the five permanent members of the Security Council and all the Under Secretaries General are great-power nationals. It is also unlikely that an Acting Secretary General from one of the great powers would be acceptable to the General Assembly.

3) As the price for the USSR's abandoning its "triumvirate" proposal, agree to some "neutral" acceptable to the USSR. However competent such an individual, this would inevitably mean a downgrading of the Secretary General's role in the Organization. He could not be expected to act without a Soviet blessing and the USSR would undoubtedly withhold its blessing if there were any chance his actions could thwart Soviet designs.

4) Accept a "neutral" as Secretary General with administrative responsibility for the Secretariat and for the conduct of UN sessions but place the responsibility for UN operations in the hands of semi-autonomous individuals or committees. This solution raises a serious question of how such an individual or group would be designated,

since 1) the Charter vests the power of appointment in the Secretary General, 2) a neutral Secretary General could not be counted on to designate either an individual susceptible to Western influence or a group in which the Western influence would predominate, and 3) the composition of any committee designated by some other UN organ, given the present membership of the UN, is much more likely to approach the Soviet tripartite concept than to be Western in its orientation. Similarly an individual appointed by a UN organ is much more likely to be "neutral" than Western in sympathies. Moreover, unless there is one strong head of the Secretariat, it is not likely to be administered effectively; various organs and sub organs operating more or less autonomously are likely to result in more disparate, uncoordinated action within the UN system.

5) Accept the Soviet tripartite concept at Under Secretary level in exchange for Soviet acceptance of a Western-oriented Secretary General. This alternative probably would appeal to some Afro-Asians but is almost certain to hamstring the Secretary General and to be reflected throughout the Secretariat, thus undermining the Organization's capacity for executive and operational action.

Chinese Representation

The many opportunities to develop the United Nations as an executive operation depend for their fulfillment on our not allowing the United Nations to be blown apart on the issue of Chinese Communist representation. For ten years now this issue has been an ubiquitous element of discord in the United Nations and almost all other important international bodies. While the Chinese Communist behavior has been abominable, the United States rightly or wrongly bears a large measure of the onus for failure to solve the Chinese representation question. This attitude is to be found not only among those who are opposed to the moratorium resolution, but also among those who support it at our request. It has limited the exploitation of the full powers of the United Nations and has inhibited the orderly development of some important activities and programs.

The China issue has debilitated the vigor of the United Nations and frustrated its natural development and evolution as its membership increased and the scope of its responsibilities and programs expanded in number, depth and type. The Communist bloc has utilized this issue not only to provoke acrimonious debate but to cynically exploit it as an excuse to prevent the adoption of action desired by the majority. Solutions to such problems as the enlargement of the Security Council and the Economic and Social Council, and consideration of such problems as Charter review have been frustrated by the Soviet bloc on the excuse that China is not properly represented.

This problem, like an unhealing wound, has required considerable effort to maintain the position of the Republic of China. The United States has had to spend an inordinate amount of effort and good will to insure that the composition of the United Nations Councils, Credentials and other committees and subordinate bodies and the instructions given to them were consistent with its position on this question. Pressure and hard bargaining have also been necessary to insure that resolutions, invitations, treaties, conventions and other diplomatic documents were drafted with the view to preventing the Chinese Communists from being included. Many (including some of our friends in the United Nations) believe that disarmament agreement would be facilitated if the United States would alter its position on the question of Chinese representation.

United States objectives and interests in the United Nations require that the onus for the continuing failure to resolve the issue be shifted to the Communists. This means new tactics must be evolved that permit the United States to remain faithful to its commitments to the Republic of China; that assure the continuing membership of the GRC in the United Nations; that GRC can accept (or at least not oppose); that the majority of the United Nations finds reasonable, and that keep the Chinese Communists out of the United Nations as long as they persist in defying the principles of the United Nations Charter.

Consultations

As we develop and refine our policies on various issues of concern in a United Nations context, we will want to carry on a more intensive program of consultation with other countries. This program of augmented consultation that I am suggesting would provide for a stepped-up exchange of views on four levels.

1. *The Department: General.* IO and interested geographic bureaus will continue to discuss with representatives of foreign governments in Washington the continuing problems of the United Nations. It is important that these consultations take place early in the consideration before policy has hardened. Many nations maintain ambassadors in Washington who double in brass as United Nations Representatives. Similarly most of the embassies on Washington have at least one person responsible for keeping current with the Department on United Nations matters. It is important that we give these traditional diplomatic exchanges a new dynamism by keeping the flow of information meaningful, mutual and current. Furthermore, it is desirable that consultations be frequent across the board and not confined to the more aggressive of our allies.

2. *The Department: IO.* I believe it is particularly desirable at this time to send people from IO to consult with policy making officials concerned with United Nations affairs in various world capitals. We need

to do more in the way of exploratory exchanges rather than converting people to "our" firmly determined policy. In our redoubled efforts to reach the uncommitted countries, particularly in Africa, as well as to strengthen the ties that exist with our allies, it would be helpful to have policy making officials in various countries consult directly with officers in IO who have an intimate knowledge of the particular problem. I hope to do some of this on the trip that I will take this summer along the lines that I have already discussed with you. It is no reflection on the hard-working Foreign Service generalist not to expect him to know in detail the involvements of United Nations problems as complicated as the Congo problem, Palestine Refugees, etc. But by the same token it is important that the Foreign Office of a small African country which has to instruct its delegation on these matters should understand them clearly. Furthermore, on such field trips our IO officers can contribute to a fuller understanding of UN matters by our own Foreign Service Officers.

3. *USUN.* Our Permanent Mission to the United Nations maintains daily contact with the representatives of ninety-nine countries. This daily contact becomes much more intensive during the General Assembly. It is important that these foreign United Nations Representatives not feel that our contact with them is motivated solely by a desire to obtain information or support. Much can be done between General Assemblies in developing a fuller understanding of United States policy, but this has to be a part of skillful diplomacy involving the creating of a firmly based rapport. The staff in New York is being strengthened so that our liaison will be more continuous, regular and effective. We are also seeking housing allowance so that able Foreign Service Officers can afford to serve in New York.

The need for this rapport is complicated further by the fact that during voting periods in the various committees of the United Nations, our permanent staff buttressed by Departmental support often has to move with great speed. An additional facet of this consultation at the United Nations would be the exploration of pre-General Assembly conferences with groups of our allies and provision of educational trips throughout the United States at our expense for newer UN delegations at various levels to increase their understanding of the United States.

4. *U.S. Foreign Service—the Capitals.* On numerous occasions it is necessary "to go to the capitals" to enlist support for the United States position on a particular issue. When this happens U.S. policy implementation is dependent on the skill of our Foreign Service. No matter how skillful our Foreign Service is, if the particular officer does not understand, for example, the involvement of the concept of a property custodian in the complex welter of the Palestine Refugee problem, he can be of only limited help if this is the issue that is being decided. This means that we must

improve our continuing flow of current information to the field, possibly by a special reports officer for field dissemination or by circulating more widely in the field the unclassified daily summary which comes to the Department from USUN. Trips to the field by USUN officers should be encouraged as should a more regular UN briefing for all political officers en-route from Washington to the field. IO has attempted in previous years to implement the field's understanding by circular airgrams to the field detailing our preliminary thinking on U.S. policy on the various items to be considered by the General Assembly—these circulars are sent out a month or so before each General Assembly.

You would not expect such a memo as this to contain pat answers to all (or any) questions pending in the United Nations. It is instead an attempt to inventory the strategic questions to which we have to address ourselves between now and September, all the while dealing from day to day with the tactical crises of the moment. With your permission and encouragement, I would like to make this memorandum (and any first reactions which you and the Under Secretary may have at this stage) the basis for some intensive discussions with Ambassador Stevenson and his associates in New York, and with my colleagues in other Bureaus of the Department here in Washington. I would moreover propose to use this memorandum to generate some correspondence with a number of our Ambassadors abroad, on United States strategy in the United Nations.

---

170. Memorandum From the Regional Planning Adviser in the Bureau of Far Eastern Affairs (Jenkins) to the Assistant Secretary of State for Far Eastern Affairs (McConaughy)[1]

Washington, June 1, 1961.

SUBJECT

Secretary's Policy Planning Meeting this morning Concerning the United Nations

The Secretary was not present. Mr Bowles took the chair and requested Harlan Cleveland to kick off. Harlan mentioned some of the lessons we had learned from UN affairs in recent years and expressed the opinion that it was probably a good thing that the originally envi-

---

[1] Source: National Archives and Records Administration, RG 59, Central Files 1960–63, 310/1–661. Confidential. Copies were sent to Deputy Assistant Secretary of State for Economic Affairs Avery F. Peterson, all Advisers, and Officer Directors.

sioned "peace force" in being under UN auspices had not materialized. He believed that in conditions as varying as Korea, Lebanon and the Congo no permanent force could be tailored to handle such a broad spectrum of demands on it. At the same time, the conscience of the world community would no longer accept military intervention on the part of individual nations. For the most part the days when the flag could be run up and one's forces cross borders have passed. The communists found this out ten years ago in Korea. The British and French found it out five years ago at Suez. We found it out a few weeks ago (Cuba), except that we did not run up the flag. He felt that across the spectrum of matters in which the UN was engaged, its greatest service could be at the intervention end of the spectrum and that bilateral arrangements would for the foreseeable future cluster more at the aid end of this spectrum. In between are a great many activities to be handled, partly by the UN and partly through other means.

One of his most interesting points was made in connection with our passing quite rapidly at this time out of the colonial era. He thought that once attention of the underprivileged nations could be directed from major attention to the colonial issue, it was most likely to settle next upon human rights issues. He said that in other areas of UN activity we have to a considerable extent passed beyond the purely forum stage and become operational—with varying degrees of success. He believed that willy nilly the UN was going to have to become operational in the human rights area. He believed that it would be in the United States interest to be in the vanguard of the inevitable on this count and that we should plan forthrightly accordingly. (I hope we can encourage him and perhaps S/P to come forth with some tangible planning on this.) We tend to forget how near we are to the post-colonial period, and we must plan how to lead the Afro-Asians in matters of their next major attention so that trends will be more in accordance with United States interests and traditional beliefs.

He also spoke of the difficult problem of financing operational matters in the UN. He said we had to find a means of avoiding situations whereby every action is dependent upon everyone's willingness to pay. He pointed out that in instances where the communists do not approve of action they will not support it financially. In the present stage of French disenchantment with the UN they, too, are unlikely to be willing to support many of its activities consonant with their ability to do so. The poorer nations are unable to do so. The combination of all of these is equivalent to more than a blocking third in the UN. He did not offer a solution to this one.

George McGhee said he was struck by the pessimism shown at Oslo with regard to the future of the UN. He said if we should be faced at some point with a choice between our NATO alliance or our support of the UN, it would be an exceedingly difficult choice for us. While not supporting the Portuguese view of their own colonial problem, he said they at least serve to flag some coming dangers. In their words we had for some time been "appeasing" the new nations of the world by handing over colonies. When they are all gone they will surely turn to other matters related to privileges of the "have" nations and the self-appointedly "superior" races. At this time they will use their growing influence in this world body to turn to such problems as Berlin, oil monopolies and military bases.

George said that while the problem of overt aggression may be in general solved now, the problem of indirect aggression certainly was not. Harlan Cleveland said that there was some promise even in this regard, however, in the Congo lesson in recent developments.

Mr. Bowles said that he thought the discussion so far had been overly pessimistic. He said a decade ago the communists had six revolutions going on in Asia and the only one they won was the Indo-China one, where Asians were fighting the white man. The British of course were associated with the suppression of the Malayan rebellion, but the point is that because of their history of preparing their colonies for independence and then in fact granting that independence, they were believed by the Malayans. This was certainly not true with respect to the French. He continued by saying that we have a number of advantages over the Soviets:

1) We do not want to take over the world, and the world does not want to be taken over.

2) We can use the tremendous forces associated with nationalism if we have the courage and intelligence to do so.

3) With all the predicted dangers inherent in the UN of a rapidly changing character, it is still likely to continue to be more in our interest than in that of the communists (Khrushchev can take small comfort from what he got out of the last session of the UN).

4) We must recognize that both the United States and the Soviets will become less powerful percentage wise in the world which is so rapidly evolving. This will definitely be bad for the Soviets but it need not be so bad for us considering the sort of world we not only can live with but would like to help bring about.

5) The days when we ran the UN are over, but this is not necessarily bad unless we indicate that we consider it to be so.

He said in general he was optimistic about the UN of the future. For one thing, he had always felt that if you couldn't solve a certain problem, it was often helpful to attempt to get the problem hopelessly confused. He said we were pretty good at that and the UN could help us in it.

Allan Evans feared that the "have nots" would, as they turn from the colonial issue, enter an era of "soaking the rich" and that we were likely to become more acutely conscious as time went on that we whites were the distinct minority in the world. He wondered whether the UN, in so far as it must lend itself to be a vehicle for the underprivileged and pigmented to get back at the privileged and white, was in our over-all interest after all. Several expressed opinions that it definitely was, provided we acted maturely ourselves. In this part of the discussion it was pointed out that even though the UN acted as a catalyst in the formation of blocs, without the UN powerful forces at work in the contemporary world would doubtless form regional associations which might give even more trouble if they were not part of a global council.

Harlan Cleveland advanced the interesting thesis that regional approach to security, while seeming to make all the sense in the world and did to a limited extent, was not proving to be what we had expected of it. Somehow nations are much readier to contribute forces to the solution of problems far from their boundaries than they are near home. India, for instance, has contributed a brigade in Africa but we would be fortunate indeed to get a couple of companies from India in any action which might eventuate with respect to Laos, even though the fate of Laos is of more immediate concern to India. We, too, in recent years with a notable exception or two have not felt free to engage our forces in Latin America. It seems that today security is best served by considerable cross-breeding.

One member (whom I did not know) expressed the view that while attempting to understand the rather widespread disillusionment with the UN characteristic of our European friends, we must resolutely carry on with our own belief in the UN despite their attempts to deflect us. Time, he felt, would prove that such a course would in the long run be very much in the interest of our European friends as well as in ours and that of the whole world community.

Considerable discussion was held concerning the mechanics of keeping our officers in the field adequately educated with regard to UN matters in other than their immediate areas so that they could in turn educate their hosts and solicit views from them. The opinion was expressed that we would do well to do more soliciting and less arm-twisting.

The meeting ended with the observation that perhaps the best advertisement of the virtues of the UN with regard to our interests lay in the fact that the Soviets did not like the UN and were doing everything in their power to make it ineffective.

171.   Telegram From the Mission to the United Nations to the Department of State[1]

New York, June 1, 1961, 7 p.m.

3227. 16th GA. We have reviewed political items before 16th GA on which decisions are needed. Fol are, in our opinion, most important:

1. Elections and slates: (A) LA candidate not yet in field for SC; we working on this with Argentina and propose raise question with Betancourt in Caracas; (B) we have had no response from Dept re desirability active campaign for Philippines in SC; (C) no word yet received from Canada or whether it interested in Comite I.

2. Disarmament: Must await decisions on nuclear testing (see USUN 3200[2] for our comments) and results of disarmament discussions.

3. Hungary: Since Dept prefers Boland not approach Hungarians in New York (Deptel 2358–USUN 18419)[3] we are awaiting Dept's decision re alternative initiative.

4. Korea: Coup in Korea creates exceedingly difficult situation for us in GA, both on seating of del and on substance of issue. Having put invitations to dels at 15th GA on basis acceptance UN competence it important new ROK govt again explicitly accept UN competence. Also appears necessary to us that we have new policy on Korean issue for this fall. We felt this before coup, which makes it even more imperative. Present policy created restlessness even among 16 and if, as is likely, neutrals such as India seek raise new elements there will be considerable support, probably including French Africans. We not certain what elements would be best or feasible in new approach, but if be able offer some kind of conf or meeting on our terms good vote might be expected. Possibility of avoiding Korean item entirely at 16th GA should also be considered. We note Seoul's 1686[4] comments ROK probably would not wish have issue come up this year. In light fact 15th GA referred issue to 16th session and it therefore on provisional agenda, this may not be easy course. However, if ROK requested further postponement of issue it might be possible.

5. African item: We believe it might be best if African item could be referred to Second Comite with view to avoiding more readily question of target dates, which will be one of first items in Comite IV. Suggest we

---

[1] Source: National Archives and Records Administration, RG 59, Central Files 1960–63, 230/6–161. Secret; Priority.

[2] Dated May 26. (Ibid., 397.561–GE/5–2661)

[3] Dated May 26. (Ibid., 764.00/5–2651)

[4] Dated May 29. (Ibid., 325.95/5–2961)

be authorized explore this with selected African dels. Also believe postponement item gives opportunity for modifications in economic portion of draft res and suggest Dept examine it with view to making res more meaningful. If African dels not willing refer item to Comite II believe we must be at least as forthcoming on concept target dates as we were finally prepared to be at 15th GA and that we should tell UK this soon.

6. "Troika" Secretary General: Consideration by Assembly of top-level structure of Secretariat will be required as result report of comite of eight experts to review Secretariat's organization. Sov drive for three-headed SYG will undoubtedly collapse of its own weight, but will produce counter proposals which may be even more difficult. One such proposal put forward last year by Nehru and Nkrumah and supported by certain members of expert comite will undoubtedly be for three Deputy SYGs—one from Sov Bloc, one Western, and one "neutral." Suggest we be instructed tell SYG we as much opposed to "troika" at deputy level as at SYG level and to ascertain his views. We will withhold recommendations until we have studied report of comite of experts and have had SYG's reaction to it.

7. Mauritania: What we do on Mauritania and Outer Mongolia in SC will vitally affect our relations with French-speaking Africans for entire GA. Approach being made Moscow per Deptel 2088 will materially assist us in this connection. If approach results in establishment of relations and admission of Outer Mongolia to UN, we should be authorized discuss this with French African states before public announcement is made in order to parley this change into maximum support from them on other issues in GA such as ChiRep, Korea and disarmament. If Outer Mongolian reply is not negative we should also be authorized discuss it with French Africans before public knowledge so that we can shift much blame as possible to USSR if Mauritania again vetoed. Suggest also Dept now request British delay application of Sierra Leone in SC until situation with Outer Mongolia clarified.

8. South Africa: Our observations re policy on South Africa conveyed in USUN 3102.[5] Dept's comments requested.

9. UNRWA: We see little alternative to extending UNRWA for another period. Given other problems we likely to face it would be politically dangerous to alienate Arabs to point which termination UNRWA would cause; we believe it highly important decision on UNRWA be made in light entire GA picture. Key issue likely revolve around length of UNRWA extension. Property rights custodian and/or repatriation also likely be raised by Arabs as major political contention. If material progress made through PCC Special Rep or otherwise on

---

[5] Dated May 12. (Ibid., 870X.411/5-1261)

repatriation-resettlement issue, we may find it possible make policy advance over simple UNRWA continuation, i.e., generate some movement toward repatriation and resettlement.

10. Budget: Finding solution of critical cash problem of UN and financing of ONUC and UNEF will certainly be of crucial importance to future of UN. In our view, best approach probably is through establishment of peace and security fund; our preliminary thoughts re one possible solution pouched OIA/Westfall. In effort reduce magnitude of problem, suggest Dept review need for continuation UNEF at present level. As Dept undoubtedly aware, Secretariat giving serious consideration possibility reducing magnitude and, accordingly, cost of ONUC operation by end 1961.

11. Angola: Momentum of this item grows steadily and at 16th GA Angola could easily become one of two or three major issues. We will therefore need have worked out our policy objectives and next steps to be taken well before GA. In fact by then we may already have given definitive shape to our position under pressure of SC meetings. Assuming Portuguese fail take effective reform measures policy decisions will be (A) whether West should try deal with Angola problem primarily outside UN, with the UN action held to minimum; (B) if primarily in UN, what kind of practical arrangements can be set up to provide effective but orderly steps toward self-determination on basis which will get GA support. Present Portuguese policy certain to produce continued pressures for even stronger UN reses.

12. Procedures: We have discussed with UKDel desirability initiating steps to improve UN procedure. Campbell (UK) tells us there some hesitation about this in UKDel but he believes they will soon start consultations with other Commonwealth members on cosponsorship of item. If they get balanced cosponsorship they probably will go ahead but otherwise are not likely put item on this fall.

13. Outer space: Whether or not Sovs participate in work of outer space comite this summer, this field will be ripe by time of GA for US initiative designed reduce Sov prestige and put US efforts and objectives in favorable light before world public opinion. USUN developing ideas which we will forward.

14. Tibet: So far as we know decision has not yet been reached whether or not US will encourage Malaya, Thailand, and possibly Ireland, to resume their initiative for inscription this item at 16th GA. If Hungarian item dropped, subsequent dropping of Tibet item would seem equate it in eyes of many Afro-Asians as "cold war" item which had been maintained purely at US insistence. We therefore suggest prompt consultations with Malaya and Thailand to see if, without US prodding, they plan request inscription. (GA decision at end 15th ses-

sion unclear about what done with Hungary and Tibet items but presumption is they were not transferred to 16th GA.)

15. Future of TC: Unless it clear early in GA future we wish TC have, debate likely be disorganized with decision contrary US interests. With departure from Council Belgium 1962, TC again be out-of-balance with but nine members and influence on GA be considerably diminished. Choices before us seem be (A) do nothing and allow influence TC wither; (B) amend Charter to provide larger membership; (C) provide for elected or appointed members of subcomite of Council under Rule 66 of procedures (Australian proposal), or find other means strengthen TC. We believe (C) offers most promise finding some satisfactory solution, pending conditions favorable to Charter amendment.

16. Comite on Info, renewal and terms: All-out effort will be made extend comite life indefinitely until all territories self-governing, and to revise terms reference enable hearing petitioners, full discussion of political development, including target dates for individual territories, and, generally, give to Comite on Info powers provided TC. UK has said it would not participate in comite on this basis. In any event question essentially one of competence (i.e., whether GA competent dictate to member states in absence specific provision Charter) and ties in with issue of target dates.

17. Southwest Africa: GA will have decide what is next step take to bring about change in South African policies. Comite SWA will by then have reported unable enter SWA despite terms GA res. It possible we will be faced with res which could seek revoke mandate and impose UN trusteeship or one which would request imposition sanctions against Union. Both discussed 15th GA without res and probable both will be proposed formally. Main problem for US is find something positive to support rather than simple opposition to extremist res.

18. Initiatives in UN: This GA, like last year's, most likely be negative in nature from US point of view. Chief points of our concern likely be ChiRep, "troika" proposal, budget, Council elections. On other items we will be making little, if any real progress, and on East-West items we will continue be in weak position. (Nature disarmament discussion unpredictable now.) We and UKDel believe we must do something to overcome this negative appearance of GA (which may continue into future also), and must look for initiatives.

(A) If we can make proposal for billion dollar economic program (USUN 3152)[6] this would provide dramatic initiative this fall.

---

[6] Telegram 3152 from USUN May 19, referred to a proposed "Plan To Establish and Activate a UN Development Authority." (Ibid.)

(B) We also suggest proposals for African program be firmed up to point where we can make concrete offers of support for large-scale new African project, perhaps willingness put large amount into African development banks if established. African item now suffers from lack firmness of our part either (1) on what we wish see done or (2) on what we willing put into it. With advances on these positions, which we could put forward as response to African sentiment at 15th GA, we could again capture initiative and African imagination on this item.

(C) We should also make most in UN of program to use surplus food to assist food-deficient peoples through UN system.

(D) Another initiative which we believe US could take, and on which we should seek cosponsorship of other friendly dels, is something on concept of "open world." Low key but substantial and extended efforts to propagate this concept both in UN and elsewhere would in our opinion be of substantial benefit to Western world. It represents what we stand for as contrasted to what Sovs stand for. Phrase "open world" is succinct and descriptive enough to capture world imagination as earlier concept such as "Iron Curtain" and we should be able put sufficient substance into basis US (and Western) national policy on such issues to make it something Russians will ultimately have to come to terms with. Current Russian hesitation on inspection systems, which is becoming better known to world opinion, will make them more vulnerable to sustained program on our part to promote this concept.

Stevenson

---

172.   **Letter From the Deputy Assistant Secretary of State for International Organization Affairs (Wallner) to the Assistant Secretary of State for International Organization Affairs (Cleveland)**[1]

Washington, June 30, 1961.

Dear Harlan:

In the interstices of Adlai Stevenson's reporting to the authorities, the Congress and the press on his South American tour, we got a certain amount of IO business done with him. I am enclosing for your information

---

[1] Source: Kennedy Library, Cleveland Papers, China, Box 16. Secret. Cleveland was in Paris.

(Tab A) a copy of his notes on his meeting with the President June 26.[2] We are following up on these various aspects, and I shall confine the rest of this letter to Chinese Representation.

After we received your report from Ottawa removing hopes of the Canadians' carrying the ball for us on the successor state business, we wrote a memorandum to the Secretary (Tab B) urging him to ask the President to initiate congressional consultations and to authorize us to start our diplomatic campaign. Alex Johnson threw some cold water on this but passed it along with the suggestion that perhaps the Australians, after all, might be a good stalking horse. Three days later on the basis of some other reports from the field, we reiterated the urgency of getting a decision on our recommendations (Tab C).

As far as I know, the Secretary didn't act on these memoranda. He did, however, answer questions on the general subject in executive session before the Senate Foreign Relations Committee (Tab D). (This testimony, I am told too emphatically to believe, will not be published and is being held very close.) He also discussed the alternatives in rather frank terms with the Japanese Foreign Minister. Freddie Kuh got wind of this from a member of Ikeda's Delegation and wrote a story in the *Sun Times* implying that we had decided in favor of the successor state approach. Three days later, on June 24, Bill Jorden re-wrote Kuh's story from Mt. Olympus, and it appeared in the same issue of the *Times* that announced his (Jorden's) appointment as a member of the Policy Planning Staff. I enclose the clipping as Tab E. To this Linc White merely stated that our policy remained in favor of keeping Taipei in the UN and Peiping out of the UN and that no decision had been made as to our parliamentary tactics at the GA. We have stuck to this story pretty much and it is now our official line, although the Secretary did embroider a bit on it in Chicago this week (Tab F).

Adlai Stevenson's return on June 22 marked renewal of our activities here to get things off dead center. He talked to both the Secretary and the President and thought he had general agreement to proceed. Just before he left for New York, the Secretary summoned Chet Bowles, Alex Johnson, Walter McConaughy and me, and laid down the rule that it was too dangerous for us, at least, until after the aid bill was passed, to proclaim that our policy was to keep Peiping out of the UN and at the same time peddle, like a Parisian postcard dealer, a resolution which in fact invited them to become members as the successor state approach does. He rejected our arguments against the dangers of waiting until September. In fact he has given me quite a hard time in discussions of this subject both in staff meetings and in private meetings. Tab G contains Pete Thacher's uncleared and unofficial summary of the June 27 meeting.

---

[2] None of the tabs is printed here. The portion of Stevenson's memorandum on the question of Chinese representation is printed in *Foreign Relations*, 1961–1963, vol. XXII, Document 34.

I informed Adlai Stevenson of this decision just before he left for New York, and Chet Bowles also talked to him about it, and AES was quite disturbed. IO and USUN are rather like field generals who ask for four divisions and ammunition for a forty-eight-hour barrage prior to the assault, and are told by Headquarters that they can have two divisions and a twenty-four-hour barrage, but are damned-well expected to achieve their objectives anyway. Headquarters in this case is moved by other considerations, i.e. the administration is faced with two parliamentary situations. One, right here and now on Capitol Hill relating to the aid bill, and another, in New York in September. The immediate one is now dominant, and there is well-justified fear that if we talk too much the joint resolution on China may well be strengthened and tacked on as an amendment to the aid bill.

I need not review for you all the counter-arguments that AES and we have made. I just do not believe that we can maintain the freeze on public debate of the question until September. On the other hand, we certainly must be careful not to provoke such a debate by our own actions, and we shall be sending you a telegram to this effect as guidance in your discussions at the Quai and before the NATO Council. The purpose of what may seem an unusually dull letter with a great many enclosures is to give you as full background as possible on developments here and to urge you to play Chi Rep in very low key in your NAC meeting. I think they have borne out the very wise conclusion which you and Doc Matthews came to in Vienna and which you mentioned to me on the telephone.

If I may burden you with one more angle, I enclose as Tab H, Harry Luce's reply to the President. This provoked the latter to ask AES to see Cabot Lodge in New York. The conversation has taken place, and we understand informally that Lodge remained unimpressed, although we have not yet seen a record of the conversation. We hear that Lodge recommended that the moratorium be pursued, and that he believes it can be won if the US is willing to make a public statement that we will be in favor of admission of Red China at such time as it changes its attitude and policy. In this connection please see paragraph two of New York's 3456,[3] which I am pouching to Paris for your attention.

Sincerely yours,

Woodie

---

[3] In the second item of this telegram, Stevenson noted that the United States would seek continuance of the moratorium for another year. "If this failed, then we might have consider pressing for delaying res which recommended Chicoms adherence principles UN Charter as prerequisite for admission." The telegram reported that French Permanent Representative Armand Berard said that a formula had to be devised that would allow the Brazzaville Group of francophone African counties to vote positively. He believed that this would be possible if "three Western powers" could adopt a joint policy on Chinese representation. (National Archives and Records Administration, RG 59, Central Files 1960–63, 303/6–2961)

P.S. As if you didn't have enough to read, I enclose the text of AES's remarks on his South American trip before the National Press Club.[4]

---

[4] For text of Stevenson's address to the National Press Club on June 26, see Department of State *Bulletin*, July 24, 1961, pp. 139–144.

---

173. Memorandum From the President's Special Assistant for National Security Affairs (Bundy) to Secretary of State Rusk[1]

Washington, July 13, 1961.

The President has more than once mentioned his concern over general planning for the UN session this fall. He is eager to have time to look at the major issues ahead of time, in the hope that we may have a well worked out U.S. position on as many as possible, always recognizing that in a forum of this sort unexpected and urgent questions are sure to arise.

While many of the questions at issue have interdepartmental ramifications, the orchestration of a UN session is peculiarly a task for the Department of State. May I therefore ask if you will make recommendations to the President with respect to the ways and means of working out our basic UN position? One thing which I venture to suggest is that you and the President and Ambassador Stevenson may wish to have a long and careful discussion of these matters at some stage which follows after preliminary planning and analysis, but before the hardening of expert positions.

McGeorge Bundy[2]

---

[1] Source: Kennedy Library, National Security Files, Subjects Series, United Nations, (General), Box 310, 1/61–7/61. Confidential.

[2] Printed from a copy that bears this typed signature.

174. Memorandum Prepared in the Bureau of International Organization Affairs for President Kennedy[1]

Washington, undated.

SUBJECT

United States Strategy at the Sixteenth General Assembly

I.

On September 19, 1961, nearly every major issue of American foreign policy will be before the Sixteenth General Assembly of the United Nations.

This would be largely true even if we did not want it that way. It is all the more true because we have deliberately decided, on some very important matters, that the United Nations must be the central forum in which to pursue our objectives.

Our philosophy is well expressed in statements by the President and the Secretary of State: it is to protect and develop the "world of free choice and free cooperation", and undermine and subvert by freedom's contagion "the world of coercion."

II.

United States strategy at the Sixteenth General Assembly derives from these three imperatives about the United Nations:

1. The United Nations is the only loom on which the western world and the Southern Hemisphere can "weave the fabric of common interests" so wide and so strong that it can some day contain—and then suffocate—the East-West struggle.

2. The Soviet Union wants a United Nations with a capacity limited to *debate;* the majority outside the communist bloc wants a United Nations able to *act.* Common interests are woven together through actions, not words.

3. If the United Nations is to build its capacity to act, there is no substitute for United States leadership.

Our strategy at the General Assembly is thus to exercise United States leadership with the objective of expanding the United Nations'

---

[1] Source: Kennedy Library, National Security Files, Subjects Series, United Nations (General), 1/61–7/61, Box 310. Secret—Confidential Without Tab C. Drafted by Cleveland and Thomas W. Wilson (IO) and Joseph J. Sisco (IO/UNP) on July 24. A July 24 covering memorandum from Cleveland to Secretary Rusk forwarded this memorandum and its attachments to the Secretary. A handwritten note on the covering memorandum reads: "For Tuesday luncheon meeting."

capacity to act in ways that will bind together the non-communist world; contain the communists if they want to play, and get along nicely without them if they don't; and prove to the last dogmatist the proposition that "those who would not be coerced" will not, in fact, be coerced.

This is an objective which would be embraced by every member outside the Soviet bloc. It is not just the symbolic stuff of which ringing preambles are made; it is an objective pursued in actions—actions by operational international organizations. Provided the leadership is there, the fundamental condition is favorable and the objective realistic—because the United Nations Charter and the constitutions of other major international organizations are vivid expressions of the philosophy of "free choice and free cooperation." Thus a willingness to lead is a prior decision—transcending by far the importance of the specific initiatives selected on which that leadership makes itself known.

"Leadership" of course does not usually—or even often—mean the insistent noisiness of the pitch man. What is involved is something more subtle and more effective: an activist attitude and a sense of direction, a willingness to be caught in the middle, because the middle is where power has to be exercised.

III.

The General Assembly increasingly mirrors the international climate; reflects the total policies of nations, particularly of the United States and the USSR; and provides the institutional framework within which the members pursue their respective national interests on the greatest issues of the times.

That the Sixteenth Session will meet in a climate of crisis hardly makes it unique. In 1950 it was Korea; in 1956 it was Suez and Hungary; in 1958 it was Lebanon; and last year it was the Congo. But if tension is not new to the United Nations it is likely to be unusually high this year. For Berlin, whether or not it is formally on the agenda, will provide a principal backdrop for the Assembly.

Along with this impending threat to peace and security will be the lack of progress toward resumption of disarmament negotiations and the impasse at Geneva on the cessation of nuclear weapons tests. Great pressure may be expected from the smaller powers, and particularly from the uncommitted, for reinvigorated efforts on these matters. We ourselves have already decided the United Nations is the best educational forum in which to state our case and build international support for it.

There will be strong pressure at least for full debate on Chinese representation. This and related items will be used by the Communists to attack our entire position in the Far East, the SEATO alliance, the offshore islands, and our policy in Korea and in Laos. They will press these issues because on them they find members of the Atlantic community dangerously at odds with each other. With the exception of Tibet, we are defending, not pressing forward in East Asia.

As in several past Assemblies, there will be "colonialism" in its various guises, including the questions of Angola, Algeria, New Guinea and target dates will be a predominant problem. As in the case of China policy, the "colonialism" issue lends itself to exploitation by the USSR because the free world can sometimes be split apart on questions about which political leaders feel strongly.

There will be a number of issues relating to the needs of the less developed areas for economic and technical aid; the dominant theme will again be the demand for a capital fund directly under United Nations auspices. One way of turning this recurrent demand toward a useful and flexible system, and also achieving a better relationship between our bilateral aid and our multilateral contributions, is outlined in one of the proposed Presidential initiatives in Tab A.[2]

There will finally be the crisis of the United Nations itself—epitomized by the facts that success is not yet assured in the Congo; that the office of the Secretary General is sustained but not yet secure against "Troika;" that ways must be found to put United Nations finances on a more stable basis; that the Councils and the United Nations Secretariat must soon reflect the changed composition of the Organization. Overhanging the whole Assembly will be a question not yet on the agenda: what to do next year to prepare for the end of Mr. Hammarskjold's term as Secretary-General in April 1963.

IV.

Beyond the issues of global concern are the nasty, embarrassing regional conflicts—each embarrassing to a special group of countries of which the United States is (because of its power not its wisdom) nearly always a member. Most of these issues are now outside of Europe, though the Alto Adige dispute is troublesome. The "German question", including Berlin, is regional in geography but global in its inter-action on all other issues.

The China problem will be doubly difficult in the United Nations this year. West New Guinea is a regional conflict for which both the Dutch and Indonesians see some advantage in throwing into the United Nations—with very different ends in view. Farther north in the Pacific area, Okinawa could become an ugly symbol and the development of the United States trust territory has suddenly come to critical notice as,

---

[2] Memorandum to the Secretary of State, "U.S. Initiatives in the Forthcoming U.N. General Assembly"; not printed.

near the end of the colonial era, the United States is revealed to every-body's surprise as among the last of the colonial powers.

On the Asian continent, the Laotian civil war is already deeply pen-etrated by major-nation power on both sides; the United Nations "pres-ence" there is on vacation but it could still become at a later stage the middleman in the process of building in Laos something resembling a national government. There is a United Nations political presence in Cambodia too—with a refugee hat on. The actuality of indirect aggres-sion in South Vietnam may require a more direct application of the "conscience of the world community" before we get through.

The United Nations has been "seized of" Kashmir, that stickiest leftover of the partition of British India, for more than a decade. We may be due for another seizure on that front this year. On the other side of Pakistan, the Afghans are showing signs of pressing again the ancient claim of nationhood for "Pushtoonistan."

In the Middle East, the temporary calm has been maintained part-ly by the presence of the United Nations—a sometime political repre-sentative in Amman, the United Nations Truce Supervisory Organization, a massive relief program for a million Palestine refugees, and a 5,000-man United Nations Emergency Force in the Gaza Strip. But the storm is gathering, sparked by Egyptian and Iraqi ambitions, the prickly defensiveness of Israel, and the endless running sore of the Palestine refugees. The United Nations relief agency for the refugees is up in this year's Assembly for abolition or continuation; in the resulting debate the refugees may be almost forgotten in the political clamor.

In North Africa, the Bizerte affair will still be on everybody's mind—and still on the United Nations' agenda, at least through the involvement of the Secretary General as mediator. Bizerte, in turn, may bring Algeria back into the United Nations, as a sign that hopes for a bilateral settlement are slimmer than ever. These two cases, plus the French boycott of UNEF and the Congo operation, raise a special problem for the West: how to use the United Nations effectively in situations where France has to be involved, if DeGaulle maintains his simple policy: "Je n'aime pas l'ONU."

South of the Sahara, the opera bouffe of Congolese politics and the difficulty of maintaining under United Nations auspices a large and com-plex nation-building operation will continue to interact; the Congo may once again be a major issue in the Assembly. Angola, apartheid in South Africa, and the status of Southwest Africa will doubtless be debated again in an atmosphere enflamed by the colonial reluctance of the Portuguese and the continued intransigence of the South African nationalists. The issue of "target dates" for independence will be with us again; on this one, the British and we are concerting a new line. And just under the surface, the Secretary General is extending his capacity to act a political adviser and technical consultant to new nations on a wide range of matters on their agenda of nationhood: in Togo a Special Representative of the United Nations regularly commutes from Geneva to talk to Olympio; in Somalia an informal political adviser operates from a base as resident representative of the Technical Assistance Board; in Tanganyika, the Secretary General has just completed arrangements with Nyerere to provide a similar service. The independence of Ruanda-Urundi is being arranged now by a United Nations Commission set up at the Fifteenth Assembly; some continuing United Nations concern for internal security and governmental institution-building is inevitable after the formal grant of independence, scheduled for next year. (Soon, perhaps—hopefully not too soon—the role of the United Nations in the internal development of new nations will be defined further in General Assembly debate. Meanwhile the United Nations crops up in many parts of the newly-developing world, because there is so often no bilateral alternative.)

In Latin America the United Nations presence has been less apparent, and from the United States point of view less useful, than in other parts of the world. Where international cooperation turns out to be feasible, the inter-American system has been used; debates in the United Nations, notably in the last couple of years on Cuba, have symbolized holes in the inter-American system. But with the penetration of Soviet power into the Hemisphere, an unnoticed rule of international politics may once again be evident: when it comes to tackling substantial security problems, the weaker nations are least courageous in applying their power to nearby situations, most courageous in applying it far away. To deal with Cuba, we may eventually need a vehicle (the United Nations?) with which to apply collective power from outside as well as inside the Hemisphere.

V.

Mr. Khrushchev said on July 10 that the Soviet Union would not accept any decisions of the United Nations which the Soviets consider contrary to their interests and that he would use force to oppose such decisions if necessary. This new law in unilateralism would indicate that the general Soviet posture will be one of bellicosity rather than accommodation in the Sixteenth General Assembly.

The Soviets are likely to have three principal objectives: (a) to project an image of the Soviet Union in favor of disarmament and to place the onus on the United States for failure to achieve progress in this crucial field; (b) to exploit the colonial question by every means, using as a basis the Soviet declaration of last year supporting the immediate independence of all colonies; and (c) to press its "Troika" concept across the board in a stepped-up effort to paralyze the Secretariat and to insure against any United Nations action anywhere except on Soviet terms. In this connection it is not unlikely that the Soviet Union will pursue its proposal to move United Nations Headquarters out of this country. A more detailed exposition of expected Soviet positions in the United Nations General Assembly is contained in the attached report (Tab C).[3] A similar report received by the State Department a year ago proved to be an impressively accurate forecast of Soviet policy in the United Nations during the Fifteenth General Assembly.

Judging from past experience, the reaction of many of the uncommitted countries of Asia and Africa to the Soviet-created tension will be to urge the West to compromise. At the same time, the United States is in a good position on the test ban issue and should develop the wit to acquire the initiative on general disarmament; the Soviet attack on the United Nations itself is extremely unpopular; and the colonial issue is about to burn itself out. Thus *if* the United States, both inside and outside the United Nations, takes specific constructive initiatives and generally displays speed, flexibility and self-confidence, Soviet hostility in the United Nations can mightily assist in "weaving the fabric of common interests" between the western world and the southern hemisphere which "by reaching beyond the cold war, may determine its outcome."

VI.

There is a truism regarding the 100-nation United Nations which is as significant today as it was in the 51, 60 and 82-nation Organization: there is no substitute for United States leadership. We can still mobilize required majorities, and we can prevent adoption of unacceptable proposals; but to do so we have to keep everlastingly at it. The luxury of sitting out every second dance is not for the leaders. The United States is still the number one power in the United Nations when it wants to be. Too often in past years, it hasn't wanted to be enough to be fully effective.

In more specific terms our aims at the coming Assembly should be:

(a) to adopt a posture of evident reason and firmness on political and security issues, such as Berlin and disarmament, which affect our vital interests;

(b) to press for the further strengthening of the executive capacity of the United Nations;

(c) to mobilize the moderate elements in the Assembly on colonial and other issues to deflect the initiatives of the Soviet bloc and other extremists;

(d) to offset the defensive United States position on certain issues by taking constructive initiatives of our own including a Western disarmament plan, a new U.N. program for outer space, a program for the development of the United Nations capacity to act for peace and security, and a United Nations Development Authority;

---

[3] Not printed.

(e) to exploit Soviet vulnerabilities on issues where this is possible, such as the test cessation talks, the Congo, U.N. financing, Tibet, Hungary, Soviet unwillingness to cooperate in the United Nations Outer Space Committee, and the enlargement of the Councils;

(f) to dramatize in speeches throughout the Assembly committees the advantages of open society versus closed society;

(g) To lay firmer groundwork for retention of the one Secretary General principle, to promote discreetly the idea of extending Dag Hammarskjold for another term and to bolster support for retaining the United Nations in the United States; and

(h) to press for more orderly procedures in the Assembly as a means of expediting constructive business and of recovering from the shambles made of such procedures by Khrushchev's shoe pounding and other efforts to degrade an Assembly that must operate in a civilized manner if it is to serve effectively as a school for political responsibility.

VII.

To carry out the strategy outlined in this memorandum, the United States effort at the United Nations needs to have certain special characteristics.

First, the President should be represented by a fully professional Delegation. On present plans, previously discussed in Washington by Ambassador Stevenson, the members of the Delegation will substantially meet this test; in future Assemblies the criterion of experience might be given even more weight than has, in the nature of things, been possible this year. Assignment of the delegates will also be important; for example, the strongest possible delegate should be assigned to the Fifth Committee which will deal with both the financing of the United Nations and with the politically explosive question of reorganizing the Secretariat.

Second, we should assign at least two key officers, the best tacticians we have, to deal full time with the Chinese representation question.

Third, we must step up our liaison activities during the Assembly; we made some progress at the Resumed Session in this regard. Parties and receptions must be systematically covered. African delegates must be helped with their housing problems and protected from discriminatory practices. Liaison officers from the Department's regional Bureaus who are assigned to the Delegation must remain full time; there should be no "split terms". Moreover, liaison officers should be sought who have had previous experience with the Delegation.

Fourth, the United States should engage its full prestige only on issues which are really important to us. We can distinguish in resolutions between the less essential symbolism of language and reality of substance. We will have to temper our sense of legal exactitude with a politician's feel for useful ambiguity.

Fifth, we should be procedurally alert, to counter or at least protest strongly and consistently any unparliamentary practices within all seven committees of the Assembly and its plenary body. The Delegation was too lax on this during the first part of the Fifteenth Session. We must apply a firm hand on this if the Assembly is to be restored as a properly functioning parliamentary body. Unparliamentary behavior serves Soviet interests in the General Assembly.

Sixth, we should lead and encourage the "fire brigade" group of moderates (Norway, Canada, Tunisia, Japan, Argentina) to develop proposals before the Soviets do, to move first and effectively and therefore channel constructively the action of the Assembly; otherwise the extremists take over and we are confronted with issues that force us to choose between holding our nose and holding our allies.

VIII.

There will be about eighty items on the agenda of the Sixteenth General Assembly. Of these, about twenty are key to us or confront us with particularly delicate decisions.

The three principal initiatives we have in mind, on which Presidential decisions would be required, are detailed in Tab A; the United States position on disarmament, which is in effect a fourth initiative, will presumably have been unveiled a few weeks before the General Assembly in the United Nations Disarmament Commission.

Commentaries on the main predictable items are contained in Tab B.[4]

---

[4] Entitled "Predictable Major Issues at the 16th General Assembly"; not printed.

175. **Memorandum From the Assistant Secretary of State for International Organization Affairs (Cleveland) to the President's Special Assistant for National Security Affairs (Bundy)**[1]

Washington, July 28, 1961.

SUBJECT

When Not to Use the U.N.

At lunch on Tuesday you asked if I thought there were any problems which should *not* be taken to U.N. You were called to the telephone before there was an opportunity for more than a general reply. It was a good question and deserves a more complete answer.[2]

There are obviously certain situations in which it is clearly in the United States interest that a problem be taken to the Security Council or the General Assembly. There are other situations in which a country, or group of countries, decides to take a question to the U.N.—and where such a move is either clearly in the U.S. interest or where it would be against our interest to oppose it with sufficient strength to defeat it.

I hope it will not surprise you if I agree that there are situations, in which it is so clear that a question could be handled better outside the U.N. that the U.S. should firmly chart that course! There are many good illustrations in the last category, of which the Antarctica Treaty and the bulk of our economic aid are two.

I don't know that it would be useful to attempt any definitive guidelines. But one can project four general types of situations in which it would be in the U.S. interest to take a question to the U.N.

a. If a crisis arose in which it was urgent that one or more U.N. members be reminded emphatically (and publicly) of their obligations under the U.N. Charter—and it appeared that sufficient support was available to do this.
b. If a crisis had arisen, or was impending, in which it appeared that a U.N. observer, policing or military operation was both a desirable and a possible way forward. In this respect we should not underestimate the extent to which certain types of U.N. field operations serve as a "school for political responsibility" for the newer countries that provide contingents. This has been the case in the Congo.
c. If the U.S. needed to muster international support for a particular political or economic approach to a question and was convinced this could

---

[1] Source: Kennedy Library, National Security Files, Subjects Series, United Nations (General), 1/61–7/61, Box 310. Confidential. Drafted by Cleveland and Elmore Jackson (IO). Copies were sent to Secretary Rusk, Under Secretary Ball, Deputy Under Secretary for Political Affairs Johnson, and Policy Planning Council Chairman McGhee.

[2] Bundy wrote "Noted" in the margin next to this paragraph.

be done most effectively through the U.N. Operating through a large number of bilateral channels can sometimes be equally (or more) cumbersome.

d. If an operational program was being projected in which there was a genuine need of cooperation from a majority of the U.N. membership.

All of this raises the question as to whether once U.N. gets in on something, it ever gets out. There are some good examples:

1. In 1946 the U.N. Security Council was instrumental in getting the Soviet troops out of northern Iran.
2. During the period 1947 to 1949 the U.N. got a Dutch-Indonesian cease-fire in Indonesia, and carried through to a political settlement.
3. Between 1946–1949, a U.N. commission helped bring guerrilla activity in Northern Greece to a close.
4. In 1958 during the Lebanon crisis the U.N. went into Lebanon with a 640 member Observer Group. The operation was terminated successfully in December of that year.

We could use some more examples of U.N. getting out of a situation with the problem having been "solved". (We are working right now on a device for dropping the Hungary item.) But in some of the places where U.N. is conducting a holding, or containment, operation (UNEF in the Middle East) it is costing the U.S. much less, financially and politically, than would be the case in any program which the U.S. could maintain by itself or in combination with its formal allies.

Even with the natural "deformation professionelle" of my present job, I would not hold that the UN should get into everything; indeed, I have frequently written nasty things about people whose one preoccupation in foreign policy discussions is to complain that "the U.N. is being bypassed."

What I would say is this:

(a) In every major diplomatic problem these days, including every so-called "country problem", there is a bilateral aspect and a multilateral aspect. We should therefore be tooled up to handle, on each issue, both the bilateral diplomatic operations and the multilateral diplomatic operations. On Cuba the UN aspects were not in the advance planning at all; but on Berlin, Laos, disarmament, and of course the Congo, the UN angle has been thoroughly explored well ahead of time. Sometimes contingency planning on the U.N. aspects turns out to be a dry hole; it has been so far on Laos. But it's always a *potential* gusher—and on occasion it gushes very suddenly, as it did in the current case of Bizerte.

(b) Because there is potentially a UN angle to every major subject, we have a serious problem of rationing the load we place on the Organization. Up to a point, loading more onto the U.N. helps enhance its capacity to act. Beyond that point, overloading can be dangerous if it makes the machinery creak too badly or exposes the U.N. executive to too many different kinds of political attack at one time.

176.   Confidential Report of the Chairman of the U.S. Delegation
to the Economic and Social Council of the United Nations
(Klutznick)[1]

Geneva, August 4, 1961.

I—INTRODUCTION

The 32nd Session of the Economic and Social Council was the first summer session attended by a United States delegation under the Kennedy Administration. It is appropriate under these circumstances to analyze the internal arrangements as well as the agenda and relationships within the Council itself. The character of the participation by the United States reflected a change of approach in two principal respects:

First, an effort was made to induce high-level attendance from our government. This was achieved by the presence of the Chief of the Mission to the United Nations, Ambassador Adlai E. Stevenson, Assistant Secretary of State for International Organization Affairs, Mr. Harlan Cleveland, and one of the members of the President's Council of Economic Advisers, Mr. Kermit Gordon. More will be said about their contributions elsewhere in this report.

Secondly, an attempt was made to include certain representatives on Commissions in attendance during portions of the session of the Council. Since our Representative on the Human Rights Commission, Mrs. Marietta P. Tree and our Representative on the Social Commission, Mrs. Jane W. Dick, were both scheduled to be in Europe in any event, we imposed upon them to join the Delegation during the anticipated periods when items which they had handled before their Commissions respectively were in Committee or Plenary.

We believe this practice has substantial merit for the future. It undoubtedly added to the quality of the United States representation and interventions. It also afforded important personalities an opportunity to get some of the flavor of the ECOSOC forums. This two-way transference should provide a precedent for the future. It certainly enhanced the US performance at the 32nd Session.

As a newcomer to the summer session, and to Geneva in that connection, it is difficult to evaluate the relative significance of this session. By and large the atmosphere was calm. The initiatives were very few,

---

[1]   Source: Kennedy Library, National Security Files, Departments and Agencies Series, Department of State, 8/1/61–8/4/61, Box 284. Confidential. The 32d session of ECOSOC was held in Geneva July 5–August 4. The report was transmitted under cover of a letter of August 4 from Klutznick in Geneva to Assistant Secretary of State Cleveland.

and most of them arose from proposals previously or currently undertaken by the United States. A key member of the Secretariat openly stated that unless the US undertook something the Council remained passive. A noticeable tendency not to expand or to enter new areas prevailed among friends and foes. This may be due in some measure to a watchful, waiting attitude with regard to the UN organization altogether.

At the 32nd Session the United States Delegation urged throughout the importance of a balanced concept of economic and social development. This began with an extraordinary speech by Ambassador Stevenson on the World Economic Situation, and the point was made time and time again that the end of all economic work is social betterment. This view was expressed in some detail by Kermit Gordon in his speech on commodity problems. Here he emphasized that the basic test in approaching the solution of price problems was to determine whether or not that solution provided some relief for the problems of the many in the commodity producing countries. Assistant Secretary Cleveland called upon the Technical Assistance Committee to find ways to strengthen its work in the less developed countries, making the point that the search for the many for a better life demanded a better use of our resources. Needless to say, this same theme was expressed in the United States Representative's speech on the World Social Situation as well as in submitting the volunteer personnel proposal to the Technical Assistance Committee.

A similar tone was struck by the Deputy Representative in the analysis of the problems of coordination. Throughout, the United States kept pounding away on the theme that we faced a new day and a new challenge, as well as a new opportunity. In the World Social Situation speech it was suggested that perhaps a general debate on the world economic situation and the world social situation should be combined, and the two reports should be coordinated.

In this report only certain selected items will be discussed, including certain administrative and procedural questions. The general report will reflect in greater detail all other developments.

II—ECONOMIC

The economic phase of the 32nd Session was literally in low gear. Ambassador Stevenson's opening address on the World Economic Situation was followed by a number of speeches that concentrated primarily on domestic economic situations rather than the global scene. When the Economic Committee went into session there was no general economic debate either. The net result was that the world-wide economic situation came in for limited attention.

Most of the items that were discussed excited very little attention or difference of opinion. We have already commented on the discussions on international commodity problems. This was the kind of problem which, of course, brought out some spirited discussion since there were vital national interests involved.

When the US initiated the discussion on the use of food surpluses there was surprisingly little interest in pursuing the subject to a conclusion. Actually, we were unable to secure sponsors for a resolution which was ultimately adopted with some changes. There was reluctance on the part of some member states to get involved in the possibility of being required to contribute any cash to a $100 million fund. The whole concept of surplus food as a means for economic development, which seems so exciting to some of us, found a few followers, but no great enthusiasm.

[Here follow Sections III–XVI.]

XVII—CONCLUSION

The most common complaint heard on all sides at Geneva concerned the decline in stature of ECOSOC itself. There is a great danger that when enough people begin to believe something it can accelerate that something into becoming a reality. The real trouble is not in the meetings of ECOSOC, even though they seem to labor so painfully to produce so little. The very character of the work and the nature of an international conference makes this somewhat inevitable. But, even producing bricks instead of houses can be a satisfying experience if the direction is right and the plan is clear. It is doubtless the lack of direction and the absence of a real over-all plan with regard to ECOSOC that constitutes the greatest present peril.

In this connection there are at least two deficiencies that must be cured. One is the size of ECOSOC. I realize all of the problems about expansion, but until this happens there will continue to exist a large body of opinion that considers ECOSOC unrepresentative and ineffectual.

Secondly, the major powers, or even the major power, our own, must put more trust in the multilateral economic and social programs. There is a sense of drifting in the absence of such an evidence of progress. The Soviet has no interest in this multilateral process. Our immediate friends are distressed about trusting it or paying for it. Therefore, unless and until we demonstrate a greater belief in multilateral economic and social programs, ECOSOC must decline.

This meeting demonstrated a great interest in improving the coordinating processes through ECOSOC. There is a certain amount of maturing in the Council's attitude toward these problems. The United States has played a very important role in bringing this about. But, coordination in and of itself is hardly a stimulating goal. What is worse, interest in coordination can only be related to the intensity and importance of substantive programs that need coordination. Consequently, our government is destined by events to reach a virtually unilateral conclusion that may determine the character and stature of ECOSOC. This is an awesome responsibility viewed against its potential.

Philip M. Klutznick[2]

---

[2] Printed from a copy that bears this typed signature.

---

177.   Notes on Discussions[1]

Hyannis Port, August 5, 1961.

SUBJECT

U.S. Strategy in the 16th General Assembly

PARTICIPANTS

The President
Ambassador Adlai E. Stevenson
Arthur Schlesinger, Jr., Special Assistant to the President
Harlan Cleveland, Assistant Secretary of State

The two discussions, one in the middle of the day and one late in the afternoon, were based on the background papers transmitted to the President by the Acting Secretary of State on Friday, August 4,[2] and particularly on two of these:

1. U.S. Initiatives in the 16th General Assembly, and
2. Tab B: Predictable Major Issues in the 16th General Assembly of the United Nations.

The general plan of action proposed in these papers was to prepare now for a possible Presidential speech to the General Assembly during the General Debate. The theme of this speech, which would be echoed in many other statements made in the course of the Assembly, would be the United States interest in the building of international institutions. One subhead under this theme would be an outline of the new U.S. disarmament plan and other sub-heads might be the building of a more effective administrative and financial arrangement for a UN action in the peace-

---

[1] Source: Kennedy Library, Arthur M. Schlesinger Papers, UN Speeches, 8/2/61–8/11/61, Box WH22. Confidential. Prepared by Harlan Cleveland.

[2] See Document 174 and footnotes 2 and 4 thereto.

and-security field; a further specification of U.S. international space policy, following the statements made by the President in his Inaugural
Address and in his policy statement of July24;[3] and an initiative in the
field of economic development of the less-developed countries.

The President indicated that an opening initiative at the General
Assembly in this general field was appropriate. He deferred a decision
on whether he would himself come up to the Assembly during the first
few days of the session; he agreed with the staff recommendation that
we should do our planning in such a way as to avoid encouraging other
Chiefs of Government and Chiefs of State to heighten by their presence
the sense of excitement and the opportunities for direct policy conflicts.
The staff work on the General Assembly initiatives will therefore proceed on the working assumption that either Secretary Rusk or
Ambassador Stevenson will make the opening speech in the General
Debate, with the possibility left open that the President might later
decide to make it himself.

The President has designated Arthur Schlesinger, Jr., as the person
on the White House staff to keep in touch with all the planning for the
General Assembly.

In the following summary report, the *Action* Office is listed after the
pertinent paragraph.

Disarmament

The presently contemplated procedure was outlined for the President:

1. Bilaterals (Ambassador Stevenson complained about their pro-
longation).
2. A section of the Presidential speech devoted to disarmament.
3. Follow-up speech by Secretary Rusk or Ambassador Stevenson.
4. Ambassador Stevenson thinks there should, in the meantime, be
public reference to the U.S. interest in disarmament.
5. Negotiations transferred to the Disarmament Commission.

Possible "polemicists" to represent the United States in the Disarmament Commission were discussed, but no conclusion was reached.

On substance, the President questions whether the United States
will really give power to a UN dominated by less-developed countries.
Stage III is too subject to description as "World Government", Mr.
Schlesinger thought.

Ambassador Stevenson thinks it is very important for the United
States to be for disarmament in a very positive way. We must take the
initiative on this and put the Soviets on the defensive.

---

[3] See *Public Papers of the Presidents of the United States: John F. Kennedy, 1961*, pp. 1–3
and 529–531.

Mr. Schlesinger and Mr. Cleveland argued these two points of view are readily reconcilable: an attractive vision of Utopia must be featured, but it must not be confused with practical next steps or be regarded as related in some way to next year's Defense budget.

The President said he knew little about the background of previous disarmament negotiations; he wanted to get Ambassador Stevenson's views, and also the Pentagon's, on the McCloy draft of July 28, 1961.[4] He (a) stressed the importance of the "open society" theme, (b) thought we had a big advantage over the Soviets in any debate or negotiation because we can really take a tough inspection system, and (c) was interested in staff opinion that disarmament is a big issue in domestic politics of a good many other countries, but didn't think it was much of an issue here. Ambassador Stevenson demurred, based on the experience of using the disarmament issue as a major theme in political campaigns.

In a discussion of the *Nuclear Test Ban Treaty* as a related matter, the United States agenda item and the probable Indian item were also touched on. Mr. Schlesinger suggested we take up Ambassador Thompson's proposal to make a big thing of banning "fall-out tests" (which are readily detectable) by a UNGA resolution—presumably after having beaten down an uninspected ban on underground tests as well.

Action: Ambassador Stevenson is to review the McCloy document, say what he thinks should be done in the UN on disarmament, and recommend the best tactics for doing it. The White House will also solicit Defense Department comments.

Action: USUN, D

2. Peace and Security

Mr. Cleveland described the Peace and Security proposal, related it to the Joint Chiefs of Staff paper[5] and the Congo operation. The President said it was all right to develop it as an initiative, with proper interdepartmental consultation.

3. Outer Space

Mr. Cleveland described this proposal, and indicated objections raised to it. The President raised the following questions: Can we follow through (analogy with President Eisenhower's Atoms-for-Peace and African projects)? On meteorological satellites, can we protect against the Soviets using the UN to criticize satellite picture-taking as high-level espionage? In gen-

---

[4] Presumably a reference to McCloy's proposal for a conclusion to U.S.-Soviet discussions and the convening of the UN Disarmament Commission.

[5] Not further identified.

eral, can we protect military uses? The President said it was okay to develop the proposal in interdepartmental discussions by floating our paper.

Action: IO, S/AE

4. UN Development Authority

Mr. Cleveland described the general ideas of UNDA. Ambassador Stevenson stressed the importance, and indicated his acceptance of change from proposal for $1 billion of additive aid money. The President said to work up a proposal on this.

Action: S/B with IO and ICA.

Related Matter—U.S. Item on Africa

Mr. Cleveland described the status of this item (including target dates). The President doesn't want to carry forward in this form, picking up and making good on an Eisenhower initiative. Ambassador Stevenson thought we should somehow challenge the Russians to join in the development of Africa through multilateral channels.

Mr. Cleveland suggested that we try to get out of the "Africa item" with a simple resolution declaring the development of Africa to be a good thing, and calling on all the nations to help. Also perhaps an exhortation to plan self-help and mutual help. Then we could develop the capacity of the Economic Commission for Europe to help in planning and pre-investment activities, using the strength of the Special Fund–UNDA for the purpose. We might then unilaterally earmark some money for projects receiving the UN's seal of approval through the participation in their development of the E.C.A. and, where they exist, the UN resident representatives in Africa.

Ambassador Stevenson indicated he would like to study the whole question of the Africa item further before making firm recommendations on how to handle it in the 16th General Assembly.

Action: USUN

Chinese Representation

Ascertain by intensive consultations (in New York and through diplomatic channels at government level around the world) what proposition can command a majority vote in the General Assembly.

Action: IO

Including an explicit arrangement with the French Africans as to their affirmative action on ChiRep if we are able to get Mauritania's membership application past the Soviet veto in the Security Council.

Action: USUN

Proposition to be floated will include two elements for a start:

a. the procedural proposition that ejecting the Chinese Nationalists or seating the Chicoms requires a two-thirds General Assembly vote as an "important" matter. (Watch out for pitfall of two-thirds requirement for *acceptance* of GRC credentials.)

b. the procedural step of establishing a committee of the Assembly to study Chinese representation in the context of proposals for enlarging the Councils. (Composition of such a committee would, of course, be highly important, and should reflect the relative strength in the General Assembly of the Peking recognizers (33) and the Taipei recognizers (49).)

Ambassador Stevenson gave his opinion that these propositions would not be sufficient, and that something like the successor state idea should not be in the picture.

The President said he realized the committee or any other means of postponement might only lead in time—next year, perhaps—to a Two-China proposal or even to Chicom admission in some form. But he wanted to avoid taking any major step along this road this year. He also was determined that the United States was not to be defeated on this issue in the United Nations. Based on discussions with Chen Chang this past week, the President fears that Chiang Kai-shek may be in what Mr. Schlesinger called a "gotterdammerung" mood, ready to pull the house down on himself—and on us in the process. Nevertheless, we had to keep on trying to persuade him that in the interest of protecting his UN seat (a national interest of the U.S. as well as of the GRC) some tactical adjustments would be required as we went along. One notable adjustment is the non-use of the GRC veto on the admission of Outer Mongolia.

The President wants to send a letter to Chiang this next week on this matter. Chiang's friends in this country, notably Roy Howard and Henry Luce, should also be enlisted in this effort of persuasion.

Action: FE

Other Issues in the United Nations

An item-by-item run-through of Tab B in the documentation ("Predictable Major Issues in the 16th General Assembly of the United Nations") produced these Presidential reactions that should be taken into account in preparing for the 16th General Assembly:

Security Council Election. The President asked whether anything needed to be done to get Guatemala to step aside in favor of a more widely acceptable LA candidate; he was informed that at present the danger of Cuba and Guatemala being the only candidates had been greatly reduced by the emergence of Venezuela with strong support from the LAs.

Committee Chairmanships. The President was informed that Roa (Cuba) was a candidate for Chairman of Committee Two (Economic Affairs), with the apparent support of Brazil and Mexico. He thought we should discuss the matter seriously with Mexico in view of Brazil's commitment, and our own, to sensible progress in international economic development.

Action: IO

Membership. While no decision was recommended at this stage on just how to vote when the Mongolia–Mauretania issue comes up in the Security Council, the President did not exclude the option of voting for the Mongolia application if we could be assured that as a consequence the French Africans would stand with us on Chinese representation.

Angola and *Apartheid in South Africa.* The President thought it served our purposes well to vote for criticisms of repressive policies, but thought the application of sanctions in such cases was unrealistic, improbable, and probably ineffective. The possibility was noted that another Congo-type operation might be required if Angola blows up in the near future.

The Congo. The President indicated his gratification at the turn of events in the Congo.

Algeria. We will presumably resist efforts to drag the Algerian issue back into the United Nations as long as there are any possibilities of achieving a settlement through direct French-FLN negotiations.

Tibet. Ambassador Stevenson expressed the opinion that the legal grounds for objection to China's action in taking over the administration of Tibet were relatively weak.

Korea. Ambassador Stevenson described the device used in the Resumed Session to frustrate the proposal that the North Koreans be heard by insisting they would then be bound by whatever action was taken by the UN. The President asked whether there was any thought of making South Korea a member of the UN, and was advised that to do so would spark an offsetting application from North Korea. To admit North Korea too would fly in the face of a long history of UN exhortations to bring about a unified Korea, and would also create a dangerous precedent for Germany and Berlin.

Vietnam. The President indicated his question on South Korea was provoked by considering whether South Vietnam could not be brought into the UN actions (some form of "presence" was mentioned in the discussion) that might help meet the actuality of large-scale indirect aggression in South Vietnam.

Hungary. During the day it developed that three of the President's sisters were planning a trip to Poland and Yugoslavia that might include a short visit to Hungary. In view of the present plans for a trip to Hungary by Frederick Boland of Ireland to try to clear up the "Hungarian item", and the involvement in the problem of the issue of religious prisoners, a question was raised about the inclusion of Hungary in the itinerary. A State Department opinion on the mater is requested.[6]

Target Dates for Self-determination. The President expressed a lively interest in the Interior Department's plans for speeding up the development of United States dependencies and the U.S. Trust Territory in the Pacific. He was informed that State, Interior and Defense were considering together how best to bring the issue of self-determination to a head, and asked to be informed soon of the Departments' conclusions in this regard.

Berlin

In a discussion of the UN aspects of the Berlin problem, the President asked Ambassador Stevenson to give some thought to the idea that a UN-supervised referendum might be held in West Berlin—a suggestion which had been canvassed with the Secretary before he left for Paris. The first reaction of Ambassador Stevenson was that such a referendum might better be proposed for the whole of Berlin including the Eastern Zone. (Signal to this discussion is in Secto 18, August 7, 1961.)[7]

Action: GER, IO, and USUN.

The President gave Ambassador Stevenson his copy of the latest report on Berlin strategy by Mr. Dean Acheson,[8] and asked him to study it and give the President his considered reaction.

Action: USUN

Mr. Cleveland said the Acheson memorandum reflected to some extent the suggestions in an IO memo which had been discussed in Ambassador Stevenson's absence with Ambassador Yost and other members of the USUN staff; however, the timing of "going to the UN" on Berlin is still subject to some discussion within the Department.

---

[6] Referred to S/S–Mr. Battle for action, August 7, 1961. [Footnote in the source text.]

[7] Not printed. (National Archives and Records Administration, RG 59, Central Files 1960–63, 762.00/8–761)

[8] See *Foreign Relations,* 1961–1963, vol. XIV, Document 89.

178.   Paper Prepared in the Bureau of International Organization
Affairs[1]

Washington, August 15, 1961.

Outer Mongolia and the Votes of African States in the
United Nations General Assembly

If Outer Mongolia is not admitted to the United Nations the
African states could mobilize at least eleven votes (French African or
Brazzaville group) or possibly as many as twenty votes (Monrovia
group) against the Chinese Nationalists and, depending on the circumstances, against the United States. This group of votes could
prove decisive on the Chinese representation issue and others of major
importance to us.

The key issue for the French African states is whether Mauritania is
admitted to the United Nations. African states generally, and the French
African states in particular, have made it quite clear that their voting on
Chinese representation and other issues would be affected by what happens to the application of Mauritania. Since the Soviet Union has
declared that it will veto the application of Mauritania if Outer
Mongolia is not admitted, the issue depends, in the eyes of the French
Africans, on what happens in the case of Outer Mongolia. Their reaction
will be almost equally adverse, so far as the GRC is concerned, whether
Outer Mongolia's admission to the United Nations is blocked by a veto
or by abstentions.

The evidence for this analysis, based on reports from many sources
over several months is quite impressive. The more important reports
are summarized below.

(1) In May, our Embassy at Dakar reported that the twelve states of
the African-Malagasy union had taken advantage of the Monrovia conference to discuss the admission of Mauritania to the UN. These states
reportedly agreed that if Mauritania's admission is blocked, whether by
veto or abstentions, they would "retaliate by breaking relations with the
Chinese Nationalists. In addition, the eleven states members of the UN
would at the next regular session vote for expulsion of Nationalist
China and the admission of Red China." These states expressed the

---

[1] Source: National Archives and Records Administration, RG 59, Central Files
1960–63, 303/8–1561. Confidential. Drafted by Alfred E. Wellons and Virginia F. Hartley,
and cleared by LaRue R. Lutkins (FE), William B. Buffum (UNP), Jesse MacKnight and
Donald Dumont (AF), and Woodruff Wallner (IO). A covering memorandum to
McGeorge Bundy, also dated August 15, signed by William H. Brubeck for Lucius D.
Battle, noted that Bundy's office had requested the study by telephone the night before.

hope that the United States would convince the Chinese Nationalists to abstain instead of using the veto (Dakar tel 783, May 24).[2]

(2) In June, Liberia, on behalf of the participants in the Monrovia Conference, circulated a letter to UN members stating that the group "looks with concern" on any attempt to prohibit the membership of Mauritania in the UN by exercise of the veto or by linking its admittance to other issues. The letter called on the Security Council, in the name of twenty independent African states, to approve the membership of Mauritania. (USUN tel 3324, June 14)[3]

(3) In July, USUN reported its belief that the French Africans will in fact carry out their threat to take reprisals against both the US and the GRC on issues important to us in the next GA and that they will do so "whether Soviet veto of Mauritania is engendered by GRC veto of Outer Mongolia or by defeat latter through abstentions organized by US. We therefore risk losing substantial bloc of votes not only on Chirep but on series of other issues of great importance to US if we do not proceed as planned with endorsement Outer Mongolia." (USUN tel 214 July 25)[4]

(4) On August 4, USUN reported that the Mauritanian representative (Lokman) said that Soviet representatives in New York are telling the French Africans they will veto all new membership applications if China goes through with its threat to veto Outer Mongolia. The Mauritanian representative said the French Africans had decided to retaliate at the 16th General Assembly by voting against China on the representation issue. (USUN tel 346, August 4)[5]

(5) President Senghor of Senegal told Attorney General Kennedy on August 6 that the Brazzaville states would work for the admission of Communist China to the UN if Nationalist China blocked the admission of Mauritania by vetoing the admission of Outer Mongolia. (Embassy Abidjan tel 95, August 8)[6]

(6) Our Embassy at Paris reported on August 14 a French official said that if the Chinese Nationalists use the veto and Mauritania was thereby excluded, the Chinese Nationalists "would of course be finished in Africa and at the UN so far as African support on the Chinese Communist issue is concerned." (Paris tel 805, August 14)[7]

In the last session of the General Assembly a key group of African states, including several French African states, demonstrated they are

---

[2] Not printed. (Ibid., 303/5–2461)
[3] Not printed. (Ibid., 303/6–1461)
[4] Not printed. (Ibid., 303/7–2561)
[5] Not printed. (Ibid., 303/8–461)
[6] Not printed. (Ibid., 303/8–961)
[7] Not printed. (Ibid., 303/8–1461)

disposed, when they consider their interests are thwarted, to react sharply and negatively on matters of grave importance to the United States. A good example was the group's reaction to the US abstention on the Northern Cameroon plebiscite issue and our negative reaction to the concept of target dates for independence for colonial areas. When we did not take their side, these African states had no hesitation in voting against the US, or abstaining, at one vital point in consideration of the Cuban issue. (Defeat on April 21, 1961 of operative para I of draft resolution submitted by seven Latin American states at US request.)

179.   Telegram From the Department of State to the Embassy in the Republic of China[1]

Washington, August 15, 1961, 10:08 p.m.

117. You should seek appointment with President Chiang soonest and personally deliver following message from President Kennedy. You should point out Security Council consideration of Outer Mongolia and Mauritanian applications will probably take place during week of August 21.

"Dear Mr. President:

Now that Vice President Chen has returned to Taiwan I want to express my keen appreciation for your having sent so distinguished, able and trusted a representative to consult with me.[2] My associates and I profited greatly from his clear presentation of the views of your Government on matter of common concern.

As I am sure the Vice President has reported to you, our talks were marked by cordiality and frankness. While agreement was not reached on all points, the talks showed our agreement on fundamental objectives and demonstrated the vital importance both our countries attach to maintaining and strengthening our traditional friendship. In this regard I was particularly heartened by Vice President Chen's assur-

---

[1]   Source: National Archives and Records Administration, RG 59, Central Files 1960–63, 303/8–1561. Secret; Niact. Drafted by Lutkins; cleared by Robert W. Rinden (CA), Wallner, William O. Anderson (EUR/SOV), Jesse MacKnight (AF), McGeorge Bundy, and William H. Brubeck (S/S); and approved by Assistant Secretary McConaughy (FE).

[2]   Vice President Chen Cheng of the Republic of China visited Washington July 31–August 3. For accounts of his meeting with President Kennedy and senior U.S. officials, see Foreign Relations, 1961–1963, vol. XXII, Documents 45–47.

ances that the GRC would never create any difficulties for the U.S. in its effort to meet the Communist challenge and that the overriding consideration motivating your Government in its relationship with the U.S. is its desire not to add to U.S. difficulties or see U.S. prestige suffer.

The joint communiqué issued by Vice President Chen and me following our discussions pointed out our mutual awareness of the worldwide nature of the Communist threat and of the belligerency and hostility displayed by the Communists in areas such as Berlin, Laos, Korea and Viet-Nam.[3] I am sure you will agree with me that the increasingly grave nature of the Communist challenge makes it imperative for all of us in the free world to maintain our solidarity and not allow the forces of Communism to divide and thereby undermine our joint strength.

In the international struggle between the free world and Communism, the United Nations is also a major battlefield. Whatever our appraisal of the strengths and weaknesses of the UN, we must recognize that it is a powerful force on a wide range of issues. The United States fully shares the strong views expressed by Vice President Chen on the importance to the GRC of not turning the UN battlefield over to the Communists. Moreover, as I explained to the Vice President, the prestige of the United States is deeply committed to preserving the GRC's membership in the UN and keeping the Peiping regime out. For ten successive years the United States has led the fight to prevent the entry of the Chinese Communists against increasingly serious opposition. Now, at what may well be a critical moment in this fight, we more than ever need to concert our efforts in this common cause.

In our discussion of the difficult problem of Chinese representation in the United Nations, Secretary Rusk and I outlined to the Vice President our proposed tactics to realize our common objective of preserving the GRC's position in the UN and keeping the Peiping regime out. I am gratified that the general outline of our proposed approach is acceptable to your Government. It remains, in the weeks before the opening of the next session of the General Assembly, for our staffs in Washington and Taipei and our Missions in New York to work together on a close basis to translate this general approach into detailed tactical plans to meet a wide range of possible parliamentary situations.

Our present tactical plan is, I am confident, the most promising that can be devised in the circumstances. I would not be frank with you, however, if I did not emphasize that there is a very grave danger we would not be able to muster majority support for it if your Government should invoke the veto to block Outer Mongolia's admission to the UN. Our most

---

[3] For text of the joint communiqué, see *Public Papers of the Presidents of the United States: John F. Kennedy, 1961*, pp. 545–546.

careful study of the situation clearly indicates that, if Mauritania is denied entry to the UN as a result of such action, most if not all of the French African states will, however illogically and unjustly, retaliate by voting against the GRC on the Chinese representation issue. In this eventuality we fear that despite our best efforts the GRC would be unseated and subsequently replaced by the Chinese Communists.

Vice President Chen's treatment of this subject and, more explicitly, your observations to Ambassador Drumright on July 1[4] indicate that you are aware of these possible consequences of a veto of Outer Mongolia and are prepared to accept them rather than alter your position. The record on this issue, both in 1955 and in recent months, makes clear that you consider fundamental GRC interests to be involved.

I fully appreciate the importance of this matter to the GRC. I must stress, however, that the problem is not one that affects only the GRC. It involves no less deeply and inescapably the position and prestige of the U.S., especially at a time when the mounting Berlin crisis poses a mortal threat to the free world. The GRC may consider that in certain circumstances it would prefer to leave the UN rather than to yield on a point of major importance to it. But before taking an action that could lead to such a situation, I urge you, Mr. President, to consider carefully not only the GRC's interests but also those of the U.S. As I emphasized to Vice President Chen, it would be extremely inimical to U.S. interests if the Chinese Communists should gain admission to the UN. We would remain in the UN with a continuing heavy responsibility for leadership of its free world members. But our capabilities for exercising this leadership would be seriously impaired by defeat on the Chinese representation issue. My advisers warn, moreover, of the likelihood that French African wrath over a veto of Outer Mongolia will be felt during the next General Assembly session not only on the Chinese representation question but on various other issues important to the U.S. In this regard it is pertinent that the French Africans, and indeed many other states, will wrongly hold the U.S. responsible for such GRC action in view of the close relationship between our two countries.

In explaining, both publicly and in private talks with the U.S., why it feels obliged to prevent Outer Mongolia's admission to the UN, the GRC has advanced several cogent arguments which I would like now to consider. It has stated that, in the first place, this is a matter of basic principle, that you and we should not for the sake of expediency submit to Soviet blackmail tactics and acquiesce in what amounts to a violation of the UN

---

[4] Regarding the meeting between President Chiang and Ambassador Drumright, in which the President said that the Republic of China would withdraw from the United Nations rather than accept a "two Chinas" arrangement, see *Foreign Relations, 1961–1963*, vol. XXII, Document 39.

Charter. The U.S. fully shares the GRC's repugnance for any action that allows the Soviets to get away with bare-faced blackmail. It also recognizes that there is a real question whether the Outer Mongolian regime possesses the qualifications for UN membership as provided in the Charter. Nonetheless, the cold, hard fact is that the French African states have accepted the Soviet linking of the Mauritanian and Outer Mongolian applications as a matter of practical power politics and have made the GRC and U.S. vote on the Outer Mongolian application the touchstone of their subsequent vote on Chinese representation. Our two countries are thus confronted with a situation in which we must choose the lesser of two evils. We must recognize that in order to attain our overriding objective of preventing admission of Communist China to the UN we will have to exercise tactical flexibility on the lesser consideration of Outer Mongolia's admission.

It has also been argued that admission of Outer Mongolia would seriously impair the UN's integrity and effectiveness and greatly enhance Communist prestige. No doubt admission would represent a tactical victory for the Soviets. But it seems to me inescapable that the adverse effects would be nothing compared to those that would flow from the GRC's departure from the UN and its replacement by the Chinese Communists, if GRC veto of Outer Mongolia should cause us to lose our voting majority on this larger issue. Moreover, once the GRC lost its seat, Outer Mongolia's admission could be expected to follow shortly in any case.

Finally, Vice President Chen and others have emphasized how difficult politically it would be for your Government to justify to the Chinese people and your representative bodies a reversal of your announced position on this issue. I am aware of the views expressed by the Standing Committee of the Kuomintang, by the five Yuans, and by your press and, as a practical politician, appreciate the problem that you face. Knowing, however, your long record as a statesman and the Chinese people's deep and abiding faith in your leadership, I am confident of your ability to explain to them the need for flexible tactics on the lesser issue of Outer Mongolia's admission to the UN in order to safeguard the GRC's international position and thereby to fulfill your national mission of thwarting the designs of the mainland Communist regime.

I also feel it necessary to emphasize the potential significance of the GRC's action on this issue in terms of its own security interests. GRC loss of its UN seat would impair the ability of the U.S. to muster support in the free world for military action in defense of the GRC should such action ever be required. U.S. support of the security of the GRC should not, moreover, be conceived of in purely military terms. Political, diplomatic and economic measures are also essential. Free world support for such measures may be extremely difficult to obtain in a situation in which the sympathies of a large part of the free world would probably have been lost, and the GRC's own juridical position undercut, by its attitude toward the UN. Its departure from the UN would inevitably lead to increasing isolation of the GRC as one country after another switched its recognition to Communist China. The problem of maintaining solid support for the GRC in the face of Chinese Communist pressures would become increasingly difficult. There would be a real danger of the U.S. itself becoming more and more isolated on this question. The GRC must not ignore the serious damage to its own security or that to U.S. interests which could result from its refusal, regardless of the cost, to maintain its UN position.

In your meeting with Ambassador Drumright on July 1 you stated that you would regard U.S. action to establish relations with Outer Mongolia and to support its admission to the UN as "incompatible with the consideration due a close ally." In this regard, you will recognize, I am sure, that our interests as well as yours are at stake. In the present instance the U.S., as I made clear to Vice President Chen, has deferred to the GRC's view and suspended our negotiations with Outer Mongolia for recognition. We are prepared to defer them indefinitely if the GRC will refrain from vetoing Outer Mongolia's application for UN membership.

Because the success of our efforts on the crucial Chinese representation issue is likely to be jeopardized if the Outer Mongolian application for UN membership fails, the U.S. considers it of the greatest importance that the GRC right of veto not be exercised. Assuming that the GRC agrees not to veto, the U.S. will abstain on the vote. While we cannot undertake to organize other abstentions, and recognize that Outer Mongolia will probably be admitted to the UN, we regard this as the minimum concession we both must make because of the larger issues involved.

For more than a decade the concerted action of the GRC and the U.S. has thwarted Communist divisive tactics on the Chinese representation issue. In the UN the position of the GRC has been maintained and the Chinese Communists have been excluded. At this crucial time for our two countries, and for the entire free world, in the struggle against the forces of international communism, it would be an unprecedented tragedy if we were now to find ourselves in disarray—and Communist stratagems to divide us were at last to succeed. We must, therefore, stand together—as we have in so many past dangers—so that victory may again be ours.

With great respect,

Sincerely, John F. Kennedy"

Rusk

180.   Memorandum of Conversation[1]

Washington, August 24, 1961.

SUBJECT

China Representation and Outer Mongolia

PARTICIPANTS

Dr. George K. C. Yeh, Ambassador, Chinese Embassy

Mr. Walter P. McConaughy, Assistant Secretary for Far Eastern Affairs

Mr. Woodruff Wallner, Acting Assistant Secretary for International Organization Affairs

Miss Louise McNutt, Acting United Nations Adviser

Mr. Robert W. Rinden, Acting Director for Chinese Affairs

The Ambassador called at Mr. McConaughy's request.

Mr. McConaughy said that we wished to work closely with the GRC in some "politicking" with the French African states on China representation, but that for this to be successful the GRC would have to abstain on Outer Mongolia. We were hopeful that we could make some headway with the Africans on China representation not only at the forthcoming UNGA session but on other occasions. We would tell them that a concession to Soviet blackmail was involved and that we could not make such a concession every time.

The Ambassador said that he suspected that his government was having difficulty in making up its mind. No one can say how the African countries, especially the former French colonies, will vote on China representation even if the GRC refrained from vetoing Outer Mongolia. If there was a rough estimate on how the African states would vote, it would be helpful. If the GRC gave up something it would want something in return.

Mr. Wallner said that we want to be able to ask the African states: what is it worth to you to have Mauritania get in the United Nations as a result of GRC absention? However, if we go to them now with this proposition and it turns out later that the GRC is not willing to abstain then the African states will be in an angry mood.

The Ambassador remarked that in his conversation August 22 at the White House with Mr. Bundy, the latter had stressed that President Kennedy's recent letter to President Chiang represented the President's views—as well, of course, as those of the State Department and the United States Government.[2]

---

[1]   Source: National Archives and Records Administration, RG 59, Central Files 1960–63, 303/8–2461. Secret. Drafted by Rinden.

[2]   Regarding Bundy's meeting with Yeh, see Foreign Relations, 1961–1963, vol. XXII, Document 55. For President Kennedy's letter, see Document 179.

Mr. McConaughy said that we didn't want to take the slightest chance of there being any misunderstanding on this point and added that the President had gone over every word of the letter and had shared in drafting it. It represented the considered judgment of the President.

The Ambassador said that he had wired Taipei an account of his conversation with Mr. Bundy and so there should be no misunderstanding on this point.

The Ambassador said that, with respect to developing support in the United Nations for the important question (Article 18) tactic and also for a committee to study China representation, enlargement of ECOSOC, et cetera, his government had asked for his views on the committee and had inquired if the United States had full confidence regarding the composition of the committee. The committee's composition was very important, his authorities felt.

Mr. Wallner said that, as the terms of reference of the committee had not yet been determined, it was not possible now to say what the composition of the committee should be. The committee might look at China representation plus United Nations membership qualifications and the composition of the Councils. We were in the stage of testing this idea, for enlargement of Councils was a controversial question. It was appetizing to the Africans and Asians but unappetizing to the Latin Americans, who were over-represented and afraid of losing something.

The Ambassador observed that in 1960 nine African countries pledged, in writing, their support for the GRC but at the last minute they all reneged and only two of them had the courtesy to inform the GRC of their change in position.

Mr. Wallner said that last year the African states were inexperienced in the workings of the United Nations; this year he hoped they would be better organized and better mannered.

In reply to the Ambassador's query as to how Sierra Leone might be affected, Mr. Wallner said that it depends on what the Russians do. They might say that no one gets into the United Nations until Outer Mongolia does. The French might say that no one gets into the United Nations until Mauritania does. It is not clear what may happen. Mr. Wallner said that the Security Council meeting on membership may be held early next week, possibly on August 28, owing to British pressure on behalf of the Sierra Leone and Kuwait applications.

The Ambassador said that if the GRC should decide not to veto Outer Mongolia, we ought to get the British and the French to put as much pressure as they can on the African countries to go along with us on China representation.

Mr. Wallner said that the French might wish to be helpful but he didn't know how much influence they had. He noted that the French had used a great deal of whatever influence they might have in seeking support on the Bizerte issue.

On the Outer Mongolia issue, the Ambassador said that the GRC Cabinet had asked Foreign Minister Shen for an estimate of how much support at the United Nations the GRC would get if it did not refrain from a veto on Outer Mongolia.

Mr. Wallner said it was clear that the African votes would be lost if the GRC used its veto. All 14 votes of the Brazzaville group would be lost and, with the loss of the Monrovia group's votes, as many as 20 votes would be gone.

The Ambassador said that, in view of the unhappy experience of 1960, his Foreign Minister asked if the United States would be able to get a firmer pledge this year from the Africans.

Mr. Wallner thought we might have better luck this year, but there was always the possibility that the Africans might change their views.

Mr. McConaughy said that we must break out of this vicious circle, for we can't succeed in our efforts vis-à-vis the African states if we work on a hypothetical basis.

Mr. Wallner added that, if we could say to the African states that there is some flexibility in the GRC position, we would be in a horse-trading position.

The Ambassador replied that he and Ambassador T. F. Tsiang had both stressed to Taipei the need for some flexibility so that we could sound out the African states. He hoped within a few days to have a reply from Taipei.

Mr. Wallner said that as early as August 28 there may be a Security Council meeting on membership as the British are being pressed by Sierra Leone and Kuwait. There is not much time for us to probe the Africans' reaction. Unless we have a favorable reply very soon from Taipei, we may lose the chance to capitalize on the GRC's restraint on Outer Mongolia.

The Ambassador said that the decision was not being taken by President Chiang alone. There was strong opposition in some quarters in Taiwan to a GRC abstention on Outer Mongolia and the matter had been referred to the Executive Yuan (Cabinet). Other Yuans had also been consulted. In any event, the GRC was fully informed and a substantive reply to President Kennedy's letter might be expected in the next few days.

181. Circular Telegram From the Department of State to Certain Posts[1]

Washington, August 31, 1961, 8:36 p.m.

365. ChiRep—Outer Mongolia. FYI only: GRC has responded negatively to high level US effort persuade them not veto Outer Mongolia's admission UN.[2] Every indication is that Chinese will veto Outer Mongolia when SC meets, probably early September, and that Soviets will then veto Mauritanian application. Further complication is French threat to veto Sierra Leone and Kuwait if Mauritania not admitted.

In New York Stevenson told French representative Berard that most recent reports from Taipei indicate Chiang determined to veto Outer Mongolia. Berard said he certain that French Africans would retaliate by voting against West on Chirep issue, including "important question" proposal. If OM not vetoed and Mauritania admitted Berard believed all Brazza group except Senegal would go along with US on this question. Berard doubted that French Africans would support US on important question issue if US voted for OM rather than abstain in face GRC veto; but Berard said he would sound out French Africans on this point.

USUN reported yesterday that Lokman (Mauritania) says it now clear to Brazza group from public statements coming from Taiwan that China will veto OM membership, thereby bringing about Soviet veto Mauritania. Lokman says reaction Brazza group UN representatives has been to "unanimously recommend to the Govts. to decide at Tananarive Conference" (Sept 6–12) to retaliate AGAINST China by voting against them on Chirep. USUN also reported French suggested Brazzaville group might consider alternative of not having Mauritanian application brought up at next SC meeting, in hope this will put group in better bargaining position.

Information this tel should be closely held. Total situation now being reviewed and further instructions will follow. End FYI.

Rusk

---

[1] Source: National Archives and Records Administration, RG 59, Central Files, 1960–63, 303/8–3161. Confidential; Priority. Drafted by Alfred E. Wellons, cleared by Virginia F. Hartley, William B. Buffum, and Gene F. Caprio (IO/UNP), Louise McNutt (FE), George L. Rueckert (EUR), Robert W. Rinden (CA), and Jesse MacKnight (AF); and approved by Wallner. Sent to Abidjan, Addis Ababa, Bangui, Benghazi, Brazzaville, Cotonou, Dakar, Fort Lamy, Freetown, Lagos, Leopoldville, Lome, Libreville, London, Mogadiscio, Monrovia, Niamey, Ouagadougou, Paris, Pretoria, Taipei, Tananarive, Tripoli, Tunis, Yaounde, and USUN.

[2] On August 25 Vice President and Prime Minister Chen Cheng, Deputy Prime Minister Wang Yun-wa, and Foreign Minister Shen Chang-huan reaffirmed the Republic of China's opposition to admitting Outer Mongolia to the United Nations. (Ibid., 303/8–2561)

182. **Memorandum From the Assistant Secretary of State for International Organization Affairs (Cleveland) to Acting Secretary of State Bowles**[1]

Washington, September 18, 1961.

SUBJECT

Situation Created by the Death of Hammarskjold[2]

1. There is no provision for an Acting Secretary-General nor has the Secretary-General ever formally designated anyone as "Acting" in his absence. There is no order of precedence among the Under Secretaries-General, of which there are 13. The nationalities of these 13 are: U.S.—3 (Cordier, Bunch, Vaughn), India—1 (Narasimhan), U.K.—1 (Hamilton), USSR—1 (Arkadev), France—1 (deSeynes), China—1 (Hoo), Yugoslavia—1 (Protitch), Brazil—1 (de Sa), Panama—1 (Huertamatte), New Zealand—1 (Turner), Greece—1 (Stavropoulos). (Tab A)[3] There has been a general understanding since the San Francisco Conference in 1945 that no national of one of the permanent members of the Security Council should serve as Secretary-General.

2. In this situation, it is proposed that the General Assembly tomorrow postpone all business except for (a) the election of the President of the 16th Session and (b) the adoption of a resolution requesting Mr. Mongi Slim (Tunisia), who is expected then to be the Assembly's President, to undertake pending the appointment of Mr. Hammarskjold's successor, the functions of his Office. (Tab B)[4] Such action is within the powers of the Assembly. This procedure was developed in consultation with the Secretary and Ambassador Stevenson. The British are in agreement and the resolution will be introduced by Ireland. Mr. Slim, of all those previously mentioned as pos-

---

[1] Source: Kennedy Library, National Security Files, Subjects Series, United Nations (General), 9/61, Box 310. Secret. Drafted by Virginia F. Hartley on September 18, and concurred in by Leonard C. Meeker (L).

[2] Regarding the death of Secretary-General Hammarskjöld in a plane crash near Ndola, Northern Rhodesia, on September 17, see *Foreign Relations*, 1961–1963, vol. XX, Document 116.

[3] The tabs are not printed. The titles of the 13 Under Secretaries-General were: Executive Assistant and General Assembly Affairs (Cordier), Special Political Affairs (Bunche), and General Services (Vaughn); Special Political Affairs (Narasimhan); Director of Personnel (Hamilton); Political and Secrity Council Affairs (Arkadev); ECOSOC Affairs (de Seynes); Conference Services (Hoo); Trusteeship Affairs (Protich); Public Information (de Sa); Commissioner for Technical Assistance (Huertematte); Controller of the Budget (Turner); and Legal Counsel (Stavropoulos).

[4] The draft resolution reads: "The General Assembly: *Records* with sorrow the tragic death of Secretary-General Dag Hammarskjöld in the service of the United Nations; *Decides* to invite M. Mongi Slim, President of the Sixteenth Regular Session of the General Assembly, to undertake provisionally the functions of Secretary-General pending the appointment of a Secretary-General."

sible successors to Mr. Hammarskjold when his term expires in 1963, is by far the most acceptable from the United States standpoint (Tab C).

3. It would obviously be impossible in fact for one man to perform all of the duties of Assembly President and also of Secretary-General. However, the Assembly's rules of procedure provide for the election of 13 vice presidents and that the President, whenever he is unable to preside, "shall appoint one of the Vice Presidents to take his place." So far as can be determined at this juncture before the elections are held Wednesday, the Vice Presidents will be: the five permanent members of the Security Council, Costa Rica, Mexico, Ghana, Niger, Cyprus, Netherlands, Greece, and an East European. Again, under the general understanding at the San Francisco Conference, it is unlikely that one of the five permanent members would be asked to serve.

---

183.   Editorial Note

On September 20, 1961, Mongi Slim of Tunisia was elected President of the 16th Session of the General Assembly by a vote of 96 to 0, with 1 abstention. For text of his address to the General Assembly after his election, see *American Foreign Policy: Current Documents, 1961*, pages 124–126. The next day Assistant Secretary of State for African Affairs G. Mennen Williams sent a message to Slim that read: "Congratulations. The best man got the job. May God go with you every step of the way." (Telegram 638 to USUN, September 21; National Archives and Records Administration, RG 59, Central Files 1960–63, 320/9–2161)

184.   Memorandum From the Under Secretary of State for
        Economic Affairs (Ball) to President Kennedy[1]

Washington, September 21, 1961.

SUBJECT

   The Problem of a Successor to Secretary-General Hammarskjold

The optimum solution to the situation created by the death of Secretary-General Dag Hammarskjold would be the regular appointment, under Article 97 of the United Nations Charter, of a successor by the General Assembly upon the recommendation of the Security Council. This will not be possible since the USSR, which has a veto in the Council, has announced that it will agree to no one as Secretary-General, not even Mr. Arkadev, the principal Soviet official in the United Nations Secretariat.

At the other end of the spectrum of possibilities, it might develop that no affirmative action would be taken by either the Security Council or the General Assembly to provide for proper discharge of the Secretary-General's functions. In this situation, the United Nations Secretariat and the United Nations operations in the Congo as well as the United Nations Emergency Force would be without an effective directing head. In practical terms, if this did not lead to disintegration of the United Nations, it would produce a de facto troika arrangement.

Between these extremes lie other possibilities with varying degrees of acceptability. Our delegation in New York has been instructed to seek adoption of a General Assembly resolution which would invest a single competent individual with the functions of Secretary-General provisionally until a new Secretary-General is regularly appointed by the Assembly upon recommendation of the Security Council. We are satisfied of the legal validity of this procedure within the United Nations constitutional structure. In this connection, it is reported that Ambassador Boland, of Ireland, and his neutral group have agreed on the following principles:

   (1) A single individual should be named;
   (2) He should be able to discharge on a provisional basis the functions of Secretary-General;
   (3) The designation of the individual should be made promptly and by the General Assembly alone; and
   (4) This should be done despite Soviet opposition.

Another and clearly less satisfactory possibility would be a General Assembly resolution inviting a named individual "to assume for the time being the direction of the Secretariat". This formula has been advanced by

---

[1] Source: Kennedy Library, National Security Files, Subjects Series, United Nations (General), 9/61, Box 310. Confidential. A handwritten notation on the memorandum reads: "Taken frm 9/23 week-end book."

Ambassador Boland as an alternative. Such a formula would appear to omit from the individual's mandate the Charter functions of the Secretary-General other than his capacity as chief administrative officer and also the functions of the Secretary-General under a number of Security Council and General Assembly resolutions dealing with such important matters as the Congo. The formula would be improved to some extent by the addition, as proposed by our delegation in New York, of the words "with the functions set forth in Chapter XV of the Charter". The obvious ambiguities remaining if this kind of language were to be adopted would be ameliorated if Ambassador Boland and other delegates were to state, in explanation of the proposed resolution before the General Assembly, that it was designed to give the named individuals all the functions of the Secretary-General on an interim basis.

We have asked the United States Mission in New York to make as firm a stand as possible, in the complex and difficult tactical situation that prevails there, in favor of language which would invest the person who is provisionally appointed with all the functions and powers he needs—which is to say the functions and powers that Dag Hammarskjold had. We are in hourly touch with the negotiations as they proceed and will check in with you when they reach the point when a final judgment about the United States position can be formulated.

George W. Ball

185.   National Security Action Memorandum No. 101[1]

Washington, October 6, 1961.

TO

The Secretary of State

SUBJECT

Follow-Up on the President's Speech to the United Nations General Assembly on September 25, 1961[2]

It will be appreciated if arrangements are made to ensure that the actions being taken within the government to implement the President's speech are brought to the attention of all parts of the government affected thereby, and are currently reported to the White House. It is understood that certain steps along this line have already been initiated. However, the following specific list identifying the items in which the President is interested in having continuing follow-up is furnished you for your guidance in coordinating the interdepartmental aspects of and in reporting on these items.

ITEMS IN THE SPEECH FOR SPECIAL IMPLEMENTATION
AND REPORTING

A. In Relation to the UN

1. "Selection of an outstanding civil servant to carry forward the responsibilities of Secretary General." (Page 2, paragraph 2)

2. "The prompt review and revision of the composition of United Nations bodies." (Page 2, paragraph 5)

3. Earmarking for all member nations "special peace-keeping units in their armed forces—to be on call of the United Nations—to be specially trained and quickly available—and with advance provision for financial and logistic support." (Page 5, paragraph 2-V)

4. Suggest "a series of steps to improve the United Nations' machinery for the peaceful settlement of disputes—for on-the-spot fact-

---

[1] Source: National Archives and Records Administration, RG 59, S/S–NSC Files: Lot 72 D 316, NSAM No. 101. No classification marking. Copies were sent to the Secretaries of Defense and the Treasury; the Directors of Central Intelligence, USIA, and ACDA; the Administrators of AID and NASA; the Chairman of AEC; the Executive Secretary of the National Aeronautics and Space Council; and the President's Special Assistant for Science and Technology. An attached covering memorandum from Executive Secretary Lucius D. Battle to Secretary Rusk, October 10, asked IO to report to the White House on activities to be undertaken in the UN context.

[2] For text of President Kennedy's speech to the UN General Assembly, see *Public Papers of the Presidents of the United States: John F. Kennedy, 1961*, pp. 616–626.

finding, mediation and adjudication—for extending the rule of international law." (Page 5, paragraph 3-V)

5. "Debate colonialism in full—and apply the principle of free choice and the practice of free plebiscites in every corner of the globe." (Page 7, paragraph 1)

B. *In Relation to Arms Control and Disarmament*

1. A new statement of newly agreed principles for negotiation (relating to "general and complete disarmament"). (Page 3, paragraph 2)

2. "Challenge the Soviet Union, not to an arms race, but to a peace race—to advance together step by step, stage by stage, until general and complete disarmament has been achieved. We invite them now to go beyond agreement in principle to reach agreement on actual plans." (Page 3, paragraph 3)

3. "Program to be presented to this Assembly—for general and complete disarmament under effective international control." (Page 3, paragraph 4)

4. "I therefore propose, on the basis of this Plan, that disarmament negotiations resume promptly, and continue without interruption until an entire program for general and complete disarmament has not only been agreed but has been actually achieved." (Page 4, paragraph 3)

5. A "treaty assuring the end of nuclear tests of all kinds, in every environment, under workable controls. The United States and the United Kingdom have proposed such a treaty that is both reasonable, effective and ready for signature. We are still prepared to sign that treaty today." (Page 4, paragraph 1-IV)

C. *In Relation to Outer Space*

"We shall urge proposals extending the United Nations Charter to the limits of man's exploration in the Universe, reserving outer space for peaceful use, prohibiting weapons of mass destruction in space or on celestial bodies, and opening the mysteries and benefits of space to every nation. We shall further propose cooperative efforts between all nations in weather prediction and eventually in weather control. We shall propose, finally, a global system of communications satellites linking the whole world in telegraph and telephone and radio and television." (Page 6, paragraph 1)

D. *In Relation to Economic Growth*

"Propose designating this decade of the 1960s as the United Nations Decade of Development. The United Nations' existing efforts in promoting economic growth can be expanded and coordinated. Regional surveys and training institutes can now pool the talents of many. New research, technical assistance and pilot projects can unlock the wealth of less developed lands and untapped waters. And development can become a cooperative and not a competitive enterprise—to enable all nations, however diverse in their systems and beliefs, to become in fact as well as in law free and equal nations." (Page 6, paragraph 3)

ITEMS ON WHICH FOLLOW-UP AND REPORTING WILL
CONTINUE THROUGH ESTABLISHED CHANNELS

A. *In Relation to the War in Southeast Asia*

B. *In Relation to the Crisis over Germany and Berlin*

McGeorge Bundy

---

186. Memorandum From Secretary of State Rusk to President Kennedy[1]

Washington, October 18, 1961.

SUBJECT

Follow-up on Your Address to the United Nations General Assembly—United Nations Aspects

Your address to the United Nations General Assembly on September 25, 1961 contained several specific proposals for action by the General Assembly, action in which you indicated the intention of the United States to play a major role. A brief status report on each of these proposals is set forth below, with a reference to National Security Action Memorandum (NSAM) No. 101[2] included in parentheses after the heading of each proposal. Wherever possible an estimate as to the timing of General Assembly action has been included. However, the General Assembly has not yet established a firm order of priority of

---

[1] Source: Kennedy Library, National Security Files, Meetings and Memoranda Series, NSAM 101, Follow-up, Box 332. Confidential.

[2] Document 185.

consideration of items nor begun action on any of the substantive items on the agenda, making timing difficult to assess accurately at this time.

I. Successor for Secretary General Hammarskjold (Item A.1 of NSAM 101)

The United States has been holding intensive consultations with a "middle group" of United Nations delegates from key Latin American, African, Asian and European countries in an effort to work out an acceptable formula for appointing a single successor to Dag Hammarskjold who would have the full powers of the Secretary General under Chapter XV of the United Nations Charter. There has been tentative agreement with this group on a formula whereby the successor would select a group of Under Secretaries from the principal geographic regions to assist and advise him. The details of this formula, to which the Soviet reaction has thus far been negative, are still being discussed with the "middle group" in an effort to obtain firmer agreement and more precise definitions of the relationship between the Under Secretaries and the Secretary General. U Thant of Burma appears to enjoy the broadest support for the post of Secretary General.

II. Review and Revision of the Composition of United Nations Bodies (Item A.2 of NSAM 101)

In connection with the handling of the Chinese representation issue at the 16th General Assembly, the United States has been consulting widely on the desirability of establishing a committee of the General Assembly to examine not only the Chinese representation question but also the broader problems of criteria for UN membership and the composition of the Security Council and ECOSOC. Reactions to this proposal have been mixed. Our consultations are continuing.

III. Strengthening the Peace Keeping Capacity of the United Nations (Items A.3 and 4 of NSAM 101)

The Departments of State and Defense are studying specific means whereby the peace-keeping capability of the United Nations can be strengthened. Particular questions presently being studied are those relating to: (1), the use of United States military assistance funds for United Nations military training programs (2), the development of a United Nations military training center; and (3), the future policy and command control of United Nations forces.

The United States Delegation to the General Assembly will make a major speech as part of the First Committee debate on ways to strengthen the peace-keeping machinery of the United Nations. Several delegations have responded favorably in their general debate statements to your proposal for ear-marking forces for possible use by the United Nations.

Our Delegation is presently consulting in New York with a number of key "friendly delegations" (including the United Kingdom) and the United Nations Secretariat with a view to determining both the specific resolutions which will be required and the feasibility of submitting these resolutions at this session of the General Assembly. The process of consultation will include the convening of an unofficial caucus of a number of delegations in early November for a series of informal discussions on the specific proposals which we will have developed by that time. Subsequent action will depend in large measure on the results of this caucus.

IV. Problem of Colonialism (Item A.5 of NSAM 101)

There are two items on the agenda of the Plenary dealing with colonialism, one proposed by the USSR on the implementation of last year's declaration on colonialism and one which carried over from the United States item on independence for Africa at the last session. Our Delegation in New York is negotiating with the United Kingdom and Australian delegations to develop a draft resolution which would be submitted under the Soviet Item. Our hope is that we can develop a resolution acceptable to us and the moderate Afro-Asians which would forestall the extreme resolution which the Soviets can be expected to introduce. We have received from the United Kingdom Delegation the text of a Nigerian draft resolution, moderate in tone and with a ten-year terminal target date for independence of African territories, which Nigerian Foreign Minister Wachuku hopes to introduce when the "United States Item" is considered. He also intends to request priority for the United States Item over the Soviet Item. The United Kingdom Delegation has received authorization to advise Wachuku it will vote for the operative paragraphs of his draft resolution, and we intend to take similar action. We cannot predict at this stage when the debates on colonialism will begin.

V. United States Disarmament Plan and the Problem of Nuclear Testing
    (Item B of NSAM 101)

1. *Nuclear Test Ban Treaty*—On September 28, 1961 the United States and the United Kingdom submitted to the General Assembly a resolution (Tab A) calling for the renewal of US-UK-USSR efforts to conclude at the earliest possible time a treaty on the cessation of all nuclear weapons tests in all environments under inspection, with control machinery adequate to ensure compliance with its terms.[3] The draft res-

---

[3] Not printed. An amended version of this draft resolution was approved by the UN General Assembly on November 8 as Resolution 1649 (XVI), by a vote of 71 to 11, with 15 abstentions.

olution sets forth the basis on which negotiations should be conducted, calls on the negotiating states to report to the Disarmament Commission by March 1, 1962, and calls on all states to adhere to the treaty once it is concluded. We hope that our item on nuclear testing will be discussed simultaneously with the Indian item on testing as the first item on the agenda of the First Committee, which should begin its work about October 16. We also hope that our resolution will be acted on before an Indian resolution, although this is doubtful in view of the strong emotional sentiment for an indefinite uncontrolled moratorium on all nuclear testing which we expect will be called for in the Indian resolution. Such an indefinite, uncontrolled moratorium is unacceptable to us. We expect that Ambassador Stevenson will soon make a statement reaffirming our readiness to negotiate a test ban treaty.

2. *Disarmament*—On September 25, 1961 our Delegation in New York, in conformity with the remarks made in your speech to the Assembly, had the United States Declaration on Disarmament circulated. This was done in order that the General Assembly might consider this document as a guide for the negotiation of a program for general and complete disarmament in a peaceful world. As a practical matter it will not be possible to present this declaration as a resolution to be formally approved by the General Assembly. It will serve an extremely useful purpose in educating the Assembly regarding our position. Also, it will help to divert the Assembly's attention from Soviet sloganeering and to focus instead on the practical problems posed by a comprehensive disarmament program. We are considering presenting to the Assembly a resolution which would (1) refer to the agreement on general principles reached with the Soviet Union and (2) recommend that the Disarmament Commission appoint a subcommittee comprised of Argentina, Brazil, Bulgaria, Canada, Czechoslovakia, France, India, Italy, Japan, Mexico, Nigeria, Pakistan, Poland, Rumania, Sweden, Tunisia, UAR, UK, USSR, and the US, to undertake as a matter of urgency the negotiation of a disarmament agreement which would serve as a basis for world wide agreement among nations on general and complete disarmament under effective international control.

VI. *United States Program for Peaceful Uses of Outer Space* (Item C of NSAM 101)

We have developed and cleared with appropriate Agencies proposals for submission at the 16th General Assembly which embody the points you made regarding outer space. The point concerning prohibition of weapons of mass destruction in space or on celestial bodies is contained in the United States Declaration on Disarmament introduced at the General Assembly on September 25th. In addition, we are consulting with selected delegations at the United Nations to seek support for a resolution concerning the other points you made regarding outer space (Tab B)[4] when the outer space item comes up for discussion in Committee I—probably not before the latter part of November. We plan to submit and seek maximum support for this resolution.

VII. United States Plan for United Nations Decade of Development[5] (Item D of NSAM 101)

Subsequent to your speech, the Department has revised and cleared with appropriate Government agencies a detailed position paper on the United States initiative for strengthening the capacity of the United Nations to act in the fields of economic and social development (Tab C).[6] Our representative made a major speech which was very well received on October 6 in Committee II in which he outlined our proposal for a UN Decade of Development. Consultations have been held at the General Assembly with friendly delegations and within the framework of the OECD in Paris and in London. Reactions have, on the whole, been positive.

Our present concept is that the Secretariat of the United Nations in cooperation with the Managing Director of the Special Fund (Paul Hoffman) would prepare and submit before the close of the present General Assembly detailed plans and recommendations for the organization and implementation of the UN Development Decade. Mr. Hoffman supports our proposals and stands prepared to act accordingly. We plan soon to introduce a resolution in Committee II embodying our objectives and assigning a particularly important role to the Special Fund.

Dean Rusk

---

[4] Not printed. On December 26 the UN General Assembly unanimously adopted an amended version as Resolution 1721 B (XVI) on international cooperation in the peaceful uses of outer space.

[5] Item VII is also printed in Foreign Relations, 1961–1963, vol. IX, Document 191.

[6] Tab C, a position paper entitled "United States Economic and Social Initiatives at the 16th Session of the General Assembly—Organization of United Nations Development Decade," September 19, is not printed.

187. Telegram From the Mission to the United Nations to the Department of State[1]

New York, October 18, 1961, 10 p.m.

1251. SYG.

1. Stevenson met with Dean (UK), Berard (France), Nielsen (Norway), and Boland (Ireland) this morning to discuss further tactics. Conclusion of mtg was that in further conversation with Zorin Stevenson should take position we favored returning to appointment of single SYG without qualifications but that we were still willing to accept five if Sovs insisted.

It was also agreed we should stand solidly against any procedures which would have effect of tying SYG's hands and prejudicing future elections.

It was further agreed that, as last resort, seven Under Secretaries might be contemplated if all other issues were settled satisfactorily but that this was not time to discuss such possibility outside this restricted group. Dean said UK instructions allowed him to accept this. Berard said his did not but he seemed to think he might get such instructions if necessary.

2. Stevenson saw Zorin at Zorin's request following First Comite mtg in afternoon. Stevenson read to him from talking paper (pouched UNP) which took position agreed upon in morning mtg, laying stress on reverting to appointment of unencumbered SYG.

3. Zorin expressed regret we were going back to initial US position, stated he must think this serious development over and report results to govt. Although Zorin tried to sound threatening we got definite impression he was preparing to accept agreement with five Under Secretaries (including Western Europe), with SYG's statement to be made after election in GA only, with no reference to any such statement in SC or GA reses, but with some kind of "consensus" statement by Pres of GA after declaration of new SYG. Estimate of Europeans that USSR was becoming extremely anxious to settle issue quickly seemed borne out.

4. Zorin asked the fol questions, "so that he could report to gov accurately":

(A) Did we agree to temporary SYG being appointed through SC by agreement with USSR. Stevenson replied we were anxious to reach

---

[1] Source: National Archives and Records Administration, RG 59, Central Files 1960–63, 310/10–1861. Confidential; Priority; Limited Distribution.

agreement with USSR and had been trying to do so for month. We did not agree that SC action on interim appointment was necessary but in effort to conciliate Sovs were willing to go there first;

(B) Did we agree that new SYG should make statement which should be coordinated among ourselves about intentions regarding his future work and that this declaration should be made after his appointment both in SC and GA; Stevenson replied that we agreed he should make declaration in GA after his election. Final wording of statement would have to be his;

(C) Did we agree that after SYG had made his declaration Preses of SC and GA would make statements that SYG's proposals were endorsed in some way by consensus of members? Stevenson replied we did not agree to statement in SC but only to statement in GA after his election. Idea of statement by presiding officer was new and his first reaction was that it was as objectionable as statement by SYG before his election because only reasonable interpretation was that body would have some right to endorse or reserve its position on SYG's statement. Zorin subsequently returned to same issue in context only of action by GA. He suggested GA Pres could express greeting to SYG and state that he took it there was a general approval by GA of SYG's statement; wording of this was something US and Sovs could agree to. Stevenson said US could not speak for what Pres of GA might do and Yost added we would be worried about any implication through such statement that GA approval was required. Zorin replied that no decision by GA was intended. Stevenson suggested that it might be all right for Pres of GA to welcome SYG and express "his" approval of SYG's intentions. Zorin suggested he add "and takes this to be general opinion of GA". Conversation broke off at this point by discussion of other problems and was not resumed.

(D) Zorin said he understood we objected to six or seven but were agreeable to four to which Western Europeans objected. Stevenson replied there was no agreement to four so there was no point discussing this issue. Zorin asked why we objected to EE but did not press us to add one.

(E) In attempt to pin down contents of declaration new SYG would make, Zorin then asked several questions about our attitude toward Sov version thereof. He asked whether we agreed to designation of "acting SYG." Stevenson said we preferred regular appointment but would accept this. Yost added our main point on declaration was related to "spirit of mutual understanding" in contrast to "basis," but we hardly thought it was worthwhile refining declaration until basic points of numbers of Under Secretaries and timing of declaration had been decided. We would not then have much trouble on language.

(F) Zorin asked whether we would object to SYG mentioning who Under Secretaries would be in his declaration. Stevenson said if this was satisfactory with candidate it would be satisfactory with us. Exact language was up to him. All we could do was suggest the number and that he consult in a spirit of mutual understanding and that we should make statement after his GA election.

(G) In summary, Stevenson repeated, we and others would prefer SYG appointment with full authority and without any specific mention of advisers. He thought both US and USSR understood U Thant intended to consult his principal Under Secretaries in a spirit of mutual understanding and that we knew his intentions. He also thought we could both trust him to carry out his understandings with us. This was therefore best course. On other hand, we could also agree to election of U Thant followed by statement in which he would indicate his intention to have selection of advisers who would come from the five principal geographical areas and with whom he would consult in a spirit of mutual understanding.

Stevenson

---

188. **Memorandum From the Assistant Attorney General (Katzenbach) to the President's Special Assistant for National Security Affairs (Bundy)[1]**

Washington, October 20, 1961.

RE

Appointment of successor to Secretary-General Hammarskjold

While it is difficult to judge from newspaper accounts the exact status of negotiations to appoint a successor to Secretary-General Hammerskjold, it seems to me that we may be approaching the moment when it is desirable to put some pressure on the Russians through the threat of action by the General Assembly. Herewith is one procedure in that connection, which may avoid some of the difficulties of too abrupt or final action. It has the advantages of putting pressure on the Soviet Union for a reasonable settlement without forcing the more timid neutrals to take a position in direct contravention to that of the Soviet Union.

---

[1] Source: Kennedy Library, National Security Files, Subjects Series, United Nations (General), 10/61–11/61, Box 310. No classification marking.

Under Article 101(1) of the Charter the Assembly can make regulations with respect to the staff to be appointed by the Secretary-General. Pursuant to this Article, regulations approved in 1946 (which I believe are still in effect) provide that "there shall always be one Assistant Secretary-General designated by the Secretary-General to deputize for him when he is absent or unable to perform his duties. . . ." I understand that Mr. Hammarskjold made no such designation prior to his last trip to Africa. If this is correct, I believe that the General Assembly could designate one of the existing Under Secretaries to deputize for the deceased Secretary-General. There should be little doubt that it has the authority to make a quasi-ministerial designation in lieu of the Secretary-General's doing so. In fact, in view of the 1946 precedent where the General Assembly authorized the Executive Secretary of the Preparatory Commission to carry out the duties of Secretary-General pending appointment of the Secretary-General, and the later action of the General Assembly extending Trygve Lie's term for three years upon the failure of the Security Council to agree on a successor, I have little doubt that it could designate a person who is now Under Secretary to act in this capacity. I am aware that there is disagreement among some members of the UN that the authority goes so far, although I understand this to be the United States position with respect to the powers of the General Assembly.

My suggestion is that, rather than requesting the General Assembly to deputize an existing member of the Secretariat or appoint a person to perform the duties of the Secretary-General, we now request the General Assembly merely to amend the existing regulation expressly to provide that upon the death of the Secretary-General, coupled with his failure to have deputized an Under Secretary, the General Assembly will act in his stead either by so deputizing or by naming a person to exercise the powers of the Secretary-General.

The introduction of a resolution framed in this way should strengthen the bargaining position of the United States in the current negotiations and would have the advantage of gaining support from all those who favor the power of the General Assembly generally but who might be opposed to any specific nominee or specific proposal or who hesitates to cross the Soviet Union directly.

If some countries question the legal authority of the General Assembly to take even this action, I should think this is one matter on which we could willingly accept the views of the International Court of Justice in an Advisory Opinion. The only difficulty I foresee here is one of delay. But even assuming some delay, the proposal would have the merit of positive action with the possibility of definitive resolution of a recurring problem. I have little doubt as to the conclusion which the court, as presently composed, would come to, but this judgment, of course, should be checked with those more familiar with the court than I.

In connection with the foregoing, I might add that press accounts of the current negotiations have generally not emphasized sufficiently the extent to which the position of the United States is consistent with the present provisions of the Charter, and the position of the Soviet Union is inconsistent with Articles 100 and 101 which proscribe the independence of the Secretariat from political guidance by countries. As you undoubtedly know, proposals similar to those now being put forward by Soviet Russia were put forward by Russia and by other countries at the time the Charter was being discussed in San Francisco and were rejected. Those familiar with the UN are undoubtedly aware of this, but it seems to me that some publicity to this effect might be desirable.

Nicholas deB. Katzenbach[2]

---

[2] Printed from a copy that bears this typed signature.

---

189. Telegram From the Department of State to the Mission to the United Nations[1]

Washington, October 25, 1961, 10:36 a.m.

1012. Re SYG.

1. Mission should see Zorin Wednesday[2] and inform him that US cannot accept either four or seven Under Secretaries but remains prepared accept five from principal geographic regions. Furthermore US prepared to see addition East European among present 14 Under Secretaries though not among inner five.

2. At same time, Mission should seek clarify following points:

a) Is Zorin definitely prepared drop "to decide in agreement, or in other words" (which unacceptable to us) and accept reference to "in spirit of mutual understanding" only?

---

[1] Source: National Archives and Records Administration, RG 59, Central Files 1960–63, 310/10–2561. Confidential; Priority; Limit Distribution. Drafted by Virginia F. Hartley and Joseph J. Sisco, cleared by William H. Luers (SOV), and approved by Cleveland.

[2] November 1.

b) As indicated in Deptel 966[3] Dept has reservations about any statement by GA President. If any statement to be made there must be agreement on text. US cannot accept any formulation that would tend undermine independence SYG and would want assurances from Slim his normal remarks on appointment new SYG would not in any way be phrased to imply GA consensus or endorsement of SYG's plans required.

c) US continues see difficulties from constitutional standpoint of any SC action in case appointment interim or acting SYG, since in our view this matter should be handled by GA exclusively. If USSR desires formal SC recommendation, US continues prefer he be named SYG. However if USSR considers interim nature of appointment overriding consideration, US prepared see SC members meet together informally without agenda and reach agreement on action in GA to present candidate.

We realize that such informal get together SC members may not fulfill what Soviets have in mind re SC meeting. If formal SC meeting is necessary then fuzzing formulation of agenda item, i.e., "to fill unexpired term of SYG caused by Hammarskjold's death" may help blur whether SC has been seized of permanent as against interim appointment and at least avoid SC taking jurisdiction over question of term of appointment. You authorized to discuss this also with USSR if they insist on formal SC meeting.

d) With respect five Under Secretaries, US believes SYG could avoid naming both areas and individuals in his statement of intentions, and believes naming individuals concerned highly preferable. We understand from Pederson–Sisco telecon Soviets indicated one or other acceptable.

3. In view current Soviet campaign with LAs and others to build support for seven Under Secretaries, Dept believes USUN should undertake active "corridor" campaign behalf our position in favor five Under Secretaries.

4. Further contingency instructions now under review but would prefer await word from you on developments next day or two as you pursue above line.

Rusk

---

[3] Telegram 966 to USUN, October 19, reads in part: "Dept. considers Soviet proposal for statement by presiding officer SC or GA either approving statement intentions or expressing consensus of SC or GA to this effect has serious implications for independence SYG and should therefore be rejected." (National Archives and Records Administration, RG 59, Central Files 1960–63, 310/10–1961)

190.   Memorandum From the Assistant Secretary of State for
        International Organization Affairs (Cleveland) to Secretary
        of State Rusk[1]

Washington, October 25, 1961.

SUBJECT

Appointment of a Secretary General

1. After our talk yesterday on the problem of replacing
Hammarskjold, we have analyzed the various avenues open to us. For
the time being, the best course seemed to be a holding operation which
essentially would have USUN restate our previous position, and an
instruction in this sense was sent this morning. (A copy of the instruction is attached (Tab A)).[2]

In view of the complexity of the problem, and since we did not give
USUN the authority which they requested to acquiesce in the naming of
seven Under Secretaries as special advisors to the new Secretary
General, I would like in this memorandum to explain the major ingre-
dients of the problem which set the framework for this instruction.

2. The points of disagreement with the USSR, or at least those
points which require further classification, fall into the following major
categories:

(a) Number of Under Secretaries

Zorin has stood fast on the Soviet position that there should be
either four Under Secretaries (USSR, U.S., Afro-Asian and Latin
American) or seven, adding one Western European, one Afro-Asian and
one Eastern European to the foregoing. We oppose the first formula
because it does not provide representation for Western Europe, one of
the most important groups in the Assembly, and the latter because it
gives a disproportionate amount of representation to the Communists
in the "inner group" around the SYG. Moreover, by accepting the addition of an "Eastern European", there is a greater flavor of political representation—as opposed to geographic—than we would like to see. At
the same time, this distinction is admittedly fuzzy, and most of our best
friends have taken this aspect of the problem less seriously than we.
(The UK Delegate in New York has contingency instructions that would
permit him to agree to seven Under Secretaries, but not to four.)

---

[1] Source: National Archives and Records Administration, RG 59, Central Files
1960–63, 310/10–2561. Confidential. Drafted by William B. Buffum and cleared by
Kellermann (EUR) and Van Heuven (L/UNA).

[2] Telegram 1012 to USUN, Document 189.

Thus the main difference between us and the USSR has tended to focus more and more on the question of numbers. The most relevant recent cables are attached (Tab B).[3]

(b) The nature of the statement to be made by the next Secretary-General

In our last meeting with the USSR, Zorin said the Secretary General should state he would have a group of principal advisers at the Under Secretary level with whom he would work in close collaboration and consultation in an effort "to decide in agreement, or in other words in a spirit of mutual understanding with them the important questions concerning discharging the functions imposed on the Secretary General by the Charter." We find the words "to decide in agreement" unacceptable, and USUN believes the Soviets will drop this phrase.

(c) Timing and Circumstances of SYG Statement

The Soviets have abandoned their demand that the new SYG should make a statement of his intentions in the Security Council or in the General Assembly before his election and have accepted our view that any statement must come after the GA election. However, they have added a new requirement that the GA President should make an approving statement after hearing the statement of the SYG referring "to general opinion of the General Assembly" in this connection. It is clearly the Soviet intent to seek by this approach to establish the principle that the SYG should organize his office and operate on the basis of a consensus of opinion in the General Assembly. I believe this demand should be resisted since it would derogate from the authority of the SYG as specified in the Charter.

(d) Title of New SYG

The Soviets have consistently sought to designate the new appointee as "interim SYG" whereas we have always preferred that the qualification "interim" not be added to his title. However, we are both agreed that a satisfactory term for the new man would be until April 1963 when Hammarskjold's term was scheduled to expire. The Soviets would prefer to have the maximum amount of formal SC action taken in connection with the appointment of the new man, including the fixing of his term of office. That would seem to give the Council jurisdiction over the length of the appointee's term. In the holding cable we have just sent out, we suggested that if the USSR desires a formal recommendation by the Council, the individual should be named as "Secretary General" (not "interim SYG") and that if the USSR sticks on the interim nature of the appointment, the Security Council members

---

[3] Not further identified.

should just meet informally, without an agenda, to reach agreement on the action to be taken in the Assembly.

3. Now that fairly extensive negotiations with the USSR have been held, with a definite narrowing of differences, there is increasing pressure among UN members for a solution based on US-Soviet agreement. This leads me to conclude that, whereas early in the game we might have proceeded in the General Assembly without Soviet agreement to name an interim SYG, we have now reached the point of no return as far as this possibility is concerned.

I frankly suspect that in the last analysis, if the Soviets agree to our other demands but stand fast on seven Under Secretaries, there will be irresistible sentiment in favor of this formula. However, since our agreement is important, I feel we should try to drive as hard a bargain as we can. Although a solution of the problem is indeed urgent, particularly because of the Congo situation, I believe we can afford the investment of two or three more days to try and get as many of these points ironed out as we can.

---

191.   Memorandum From the Executive Secretary of the Department of State (Battle) to the President's Special Assistant for National Security Affairs (Bundy)[1]

Washington, November 2, 1961.

SUBJECT

Attached Statement by U Thant

I am attaching for your information a copy of a statement which was given to Ambassador Stevenson on a confidential basis.

It is a statement which U Thant would make after he had been appointed Acting Secretary-General by the Assembly. You will note that the statement is a very good one from our point of view since no mention is made of either five or seven Under-Secretaries and it is clear that this is a matter for the Acting Secretary-General himself to decide.

I understand that copies of the attached letter have been given by U Thant to the UK, France, and USSR. The USSR apparently has been

---

[1] Source: Kennedy Library, National Security Files, Subjects Series, United Nations (General), 10/61–11/61, Box 310. Top Secret; Eyes Only.

pressing U Thant to make changes in it, and in particular to include reference to seven Under-Secretaries, but U Thant has indicated that it is not subject to negotiation or change.

MH Manfull[2]

Attachment

1. It is my intention to invite a limited number of persons who are at present Under Secretaries, or to be appointed as Under Secretaries, to act as my principal advisers on important questions pertaining to the performance of functions entrusted to the Secretary General by the UN Charter.

2. In extending this invitation, I am fully conscious of the importance of securing the highest standards of efficiency, competence and integrity, and with due regard to the importance of as wide a geographic basis as possible, as laid down in Article 101 of the Charter. I intend to include among these advisers Dr. Ralph J. Bunche and Georgy Arkadev.

3. It is also my intention to work together with these parties in close cooperation and consultation in a spirit of mutual understanding. I am sure that they will seek to work with me in the same manner. Of course this whole arrangement is without prejudice to such future organizational changes as experience may reveal to be necessary.[3]

---

[2] Manfull signed for Battle above Battle's typed signature.

[3] U Thant was appointed Acting Secretary-General of the United Nations on November 3 in Resolution 1640 (XVI), adopted unanimously. For text of the resolution, as well as Thant's, Adlai Stevenson's, and Valerian Zorin's remarks on the appointment, see *American Foreign Policy: Current Documents, 1961,* pages 82–86.

192.   Memorandum From Secretary of State Rusk to President Kennedy[1]

Washington, November 11, 1961.

SUBJECT

Financing United Nations Peace and Security Operations

The financing of United Nations peace and security operations has become increasingly acute since the Congo operation began. The UN has unpaid bills of nearly $100 million, all reserves will be exhausted in a few months, and spending authority for Congo and UNEF (Emergency Force in Palestine) expires December 31, 1961.

Soviet bloc nations, France, Belgium, China, many Latin American countries, and others are seriously in arrears. Some do not have the revenues to pay, some argue on principle that the permanent Security Council members should pay the bill, others refuse to pay to show disapproval of the operations. (See Tab A for key financial facts.)[2]

Funding of these operations to date has been by a combination of assessed and voluntary contributions. The U.S. payments were 47.5% of the total this year. Because we paid more than our usual UN share (32.5%), 79 smaller nations least able to pay were given rebates up to 80%.

The cost of the Congo operation is running $10 million and UNEF about $1.7 million per month. This General Assembly must take action if current Congo and UNEF operations are to continue. (See Tab B for additional details of funding.)

Course of Action

It might well be advantageous from the United States point of view for UN forces to be placed in other world areas, especially where indirect aggression occurs. Financial uncertainty or haggling over costs and assessments could abort necessary action. We therefore propose to use the "honeymoon period" of the new Secretary General to persuade him to present a plan both to solve the immediate cash problem and to get a little ahead of the game on peace and security operations through 1963. This plan would include three major steps:

1. Finance the immediate need to June 30, 1962, by pushing through a special scale of contributions somewhat like the present one. Ambassador Stevenson believes this may be possible for this short period. To make

---

[1] Source: Kennedy Library, National Security Files, Subjects Series, Congo. Confidential.

[2] None of the tabs is printed.

another "every member canvass" work, the U.S. would have to pay about 50% of the bill. Smaller nations' contributions would have to be rebated by about 90%. But even this will not be popular with most other nations.

2. Submit to the International Court of Justice for an advisory opinion the question whether Member States are legally required to pay peace-and-security assessments that are already past due. We expect a favorable opinion. In that event the Latin Americans, France and even the Soviets might find it politically easier to back down and pay arrearages.

3. Undertake by negotiation to secure the agreement of 15 or 20 key States to a one-time UN Peace and Security Bond issue. $200 million would be required. With 25 year repayments at 2% interest, about $10 million would be required annually to pay principal and interest. We should press for repayment by all members as a part of the regular UN budget based on the regular assessment scale. The United States might have to buy $100 million of the bond issue.

(Tab C is a staff paper which supplies additional facts on the UN financial crisis and on this proposal.)

Merits of this Approach

1. It could take care of the cash crisis for as much as two years. This would be a year longer than the UN has ever been able to look ahead.

2. It maintains principle of collective responsibility.

3. It brings the prospective annual repayment cost within capability of members.

4. It provides Secretary General with a new basis for collection of unpaid assessments.

5. It provides non-paying States with a "face-saving" device if they want to start paying again.

6. It avoids a U.S. contribution so large that propagandists could characterize Congo as a "U.S. operation."

7. It provides an initial approach and gives us time to work out more permanent arrangements. Our objective will be to devise an even longer range approach to financing UN peace and security efforts, perhaps by establishment of a special fund for this purpose.

U.S. Steps

1. Ambassador Stevenson and Ambassador Klutznick in New York are starting to discuss the whole UN financial problem with the new Secretary General to get him to act in a timely fashion.

2. Ambassador Stevenson would discuss this approach with a few friendly States. The Secretary General would discuss with the Soviets and other financially recalcitrant States.

3. The State Department will take soundings with Congressional leaders on the whole proposed strategy. If the proposal should go through at this session of the General Assembly, Congress would be asked rather early in its 1962 session to authorize purchase by the U.S. of $100 million of the UN bond issue. Other Member States would purchase the balance.

Concurrences

This whole range of ideas has been under review for several months. The Bureau of the Budget (Mr. Staats) and Treasury (Mr. Leddy) concur in the approach and in holding the exploratory discussions outlined above and spelled out in greater detail in Tab C. We all realize there are numerous problems associated with it, not the least of which is shortness of time; the General Assembly should really act before the end of the year. We are therefore asking Ambassador Stevenson to go ahead with consultations within this framework.

We believe the program has a fair chance of success. But our judgment on that will be better after we have had a chance to consult some of our European friends and some of the key members of Congress.

Dean Rusk[3]

---

[3] Printed from a copy that bears this stamped signature.

193.   Memorandum From the Assistant Secretary of State for
        International Organization Affairs (Cleveland) to Secretary
        of State[1]

Washington, December 20, 1961.

SUBJECT

Highlights of the Sixteenth Session of the General Assembly

1. From the point of view of the United States interests, a United
Nations General Assembly can be divided into two parts:

a. Constructive things we were trying to get done through the
United Nations—notably by building up the UN executive.

b. Destructive moves and propagandistic debates in which our
objective is to limit the damage to United States interests and UN executive functions.

2. The President's speech on September 25, 1961, proposed four major
institution-building moves. On all of them there has been real progress:

a. A new Secretary-General has been appointed, and his Office has
been maintained unimpaired.

b. Disarmament talks have been got under way again, with the
important addition to the scenery of a major emphasis on building
international peace-keeping machinery in parallel with the dismantling
of war-making capacity.

c. At President Kennedy's suggestion, the UN has taken on a whole
new function, to develop and supervise an international Outer Space
program.

d. The UN Decade of Development has been proclaimed and some
of the first contemplated steps—a UN-FAO Food for Peace Program
and a 1962 Conference on Science and Technology for the Less
Developed Areas—have been taken.

e. Financing the UN, which was not stressed in the President's
speech but is essential to the development of its executive function, has
also been advanced. By appropriation of adequate funds to carry the
Organization through next June, plus a UN bond issue to raise the necessary cash to pay off its deficit, are both in prospect.

---

[1] Source: Kennedy Library, National Security Files, Subjects Series, United Nations
(General), 12/61 Box 310. Confidential. A December 22 covering memorandum from
Cleveland to Rusk also transmitted a "Detailed Summary of Actions at the 16th GA." Both
summaries were sent to the President by Rusk on December 23 and by Arthur Schlesinger,
Jr., on December 26. Rusk wrote that the summaries "clearly indicate that the UN is nei-
ther dead nor out of control and that on the matters that count the influence of the United
States still prevails in the enlarged Assembly despite the one nation–one vote principle."
Schlesinger noted that although the United States did better than expected on China representation and colonialism, nuclear issues were becoming "the successor to colonialism
in emotional content in the Assembly." (Kennedy Library, National Security Files, Subjects
Series, United Nations (General), 1/62–2/62, Box 311)

3. With the notable exceptions of the Goa affair and some of the nuclear issues, the destructive potential of this Assembly was not realized. For example:

a. The Chinese Communists were farther away from admission at the end of the Assembly than they were at its beginning.

b. In debating and developing resolutions on the emotional Colonialism issue, the prevailing sentiment in the Afro-Asian group was surprisingly moderate and, indeed, often was uninterested. The Colonialism debate was the least well-attended of any of the major items on the agenda. The thorny issue of "target dates" for independence, which the British and we thought would be our major difficulty in this field, was successfully by-passed altogether.

c. On the nuclear issues, the Soviets got their comeuppance on the 50 Megaton bomb, and we did well in the propaganda battle over the nuclear tests negotiations. However, we had great difficulty with some of the subsidiary issues of great interest to the smaller countries—notably the African nuclear free zone and the various proposals to prevent the proliferation of nuclear weapons beyond the present nuclear powers. This issue is the successor to colonialism in emotional content in the Assembly and deserves more systematic thought than the U.S. has given it. A Committee for this has now been organized, under the Chairmanship of William C. Foster.

4. Attached is a brief statement which you or the President might want to use as a comment on the ending of the General Assembly session tomorrow or the next day.[2]

---

[2] Not printed. The draft speech was entitled: "The Many Lives and Deaths of the United Nations." It observed that at the end of the 16th General Assembly, the integrity of the Secretariat had been preserved, unanimous agreement had been reached on a forum and principles for disarmament talks and on peaceful uses of outer space, a resolution had been adopted on a Decade of Development, the "important question" formula had prevented the expulsion of the Republic of China, moderate resolutions had been passed on decolonization, and peacekeeping missions in the Middle East and the Congo had continued.

194. Memorandum From Secretary of State Rusk to President
Kennedy[1]

Washington, January 18, 1962.

SUBJECT

$200,000,000 Bond Issue

1. *Origins of Bond Proposal.* About mid-October Ambassador
Stevenson and the Department became convinced that the financial crisis in the United Nations was prospectively so bad, and there was so little support for continuing the financing of the Middle East (UNEF) and
Congo (UNOC) from special assessments, that a new means of financing these Peace and Security Operations was needed. United Nations
unpaid obligations, including borrowing, were estimated to total about
$110,000,000 by December 31. Unpaid assessments by that date (Soviet
bloc, France, Belgium, and the smaller, less-developed nations) totaled
about $80 million. Against this background, a plan had to be found on
which a majority of members could agree which would prevent a financial stalemate and produce the cash necessary to continue these peace-
keeping operations.

The United States conceived the idea of getting General Assembly
backing (a) to secure an advisory opinion from the International Court
of Justice to put pressure on the recalcitrant nations to pay their arrearages and (b) to authorize the Secretary General to sell United Nations
bonds. The outline of a plan was thrashed out in meetings between the
State Department, the Treasury Department, and the Bureau of the
Budget.

The UN bond issue was to finance the UNEF and UNOC operations for the eighteen months—July 1, 1962 to December 31, 1963. It was
considered a gamble that even this could be agreed on, but it was hoped
that this different plan utilizing U Thant's "honeymoon period" as
Secretary General might work and provide the needed breathing space
for these peace-keeping operations free from financial crisis. After
Budget and Treasury clearances, I authorized Ambassador Stevenson to
canvass the matter with the UN, my memorandum to you dated
November 11, 1961[2] explained fully the reasoning behind the proposal.

---

[1] Source: Kennedy Library, National Security Files, Subjects Series, United Nations
(General), 1/62–2/62, Box 311. Confidential. The date is handwritten. Another handwrit-
ten note indicates that the original went to the President and a copy to Schlesinger. A
January 18 covering memorandum from the Executive Secretariat to Schlesinger through
Bundy, noted that since Rusk had not read the memorandum on the UN bond issue, it was
essential that the President should at least "scan" it before his meeting with U Thant.

[2] Document 192.

U Thant did in fact decide to make the UN's financial problem his first order of business. In a remarkable series of interviews with every delegation, concentrated in six successful evenings, the Secretary General became convinced that the plan might work.

(From the beginning it was recognized that to succeed, this had to be a U Thant initiative. We advised no one of the United States role. It was inevitable that some newspaper comment would trace the original idea back to Washington. But it would be a mistake for us to do other than attribute it to U Thant, who developed and refined the plan in consultation with the United States and other major contributors. If the U.S. origin were to show through too clearly, it might seriously prejudice U Thant's sale of bonds to some of the other governments.)

The first contacts with Congress on this matter were made *after* the Secretary General's proposals had been introduced into Committee Five but before the General Assembly had acted on them. About ten members of the House and Senate Foreign Affairs and Relations and of the Appropriations Committees, and their key Clerks, were reached in person or by telephone. Contacts included Congressmen Zablocki, Fascell, Judd and Rooney and Senators Fulbright, Saltonstall, and Wiley. We had, of course, informed members of Congress in our hearings last year that we were exploring ways and means to put UN finances on a sounder basis. Additionally, Congressman Burleson of Texas and Congresswoman Church of Illinois were members of the U.S. Delegation to the current session of the General Assembly and the proposal was discussed with them.

2. *What happens if the bond issue does not pass Congress?* The Assembly adopted the UN bond plan by an overwhelming majority, with our affirmative support and vote, and over Soviet objections. If Congress fails to take favorable action, the political repercussions at the United Nations would be serious. It is known at the UN that while this was a U Thant initiative, the United States was active in the development of the plan. Our standing in the UN will have been undermined and there would undoubtedly be a loss of confidence by U Thant in us, for this would constitute the Executive's inability to deliver on a proposal and move which we encouraged U Thant to make. It would tend to demoralize the UN leadership in connection with the Congo operation, and the potential ability of the UN to take on another Congo in the future would have been seriously weakened—both politically and financially.

In these circumstances, in order that we continue to achieve our objectives in connection with both the UNEF and Congo operations, we would have to seek other means to keep these peace and security operations going. One such probability would be to request a special General Assembly with a view to having it authorize new financing beyond June 30, 1962. This would be in the same form as in the past, namely a special scale of assessments. The cost would likely be to the United States more than 47% of the total which we have heretofore paid if the UNEF and Congo operations are to continue on their present basis. Another possibility would be a direct U.S. loan to the UN to tide it over until next fall at which time the Assembly would have to consider the whole question of financial solvency.

3. *Size of Special UN Levies.* The UN budget for peace-and-security operations in the Congo (UNOC) and the Middle East (UNEF), is running about $140 million per year. In 1961, UNEF cost about $19 million of which the U.S. paid $7.9 million. The actual amounts paid so far for 1961 for the Congo operation were $47.5 million for a $100 million budget for the first ten months of that year.

If financing of these operations were to be continued on the same basis, the 1962 U.S. costs would total for the Congo, $56.4 million and for the Middle East, $8.9 million.

4. *Actions Being Taken by the Department with Congress.* It is clear that we will have a difficult job in the Congress, particularly on the House side. We are canvassing carefully individual members of the Senate and House Foreign Relations Committees with a view to convincing them that it is in the national interest of the U.S. to support fully the UN bond issue. There have already been about twenty-five such individual discussions and there are many more to come. As a supplement and a corollary to these discussions with key Congressmen, the Department has prepared a detailed summary describing the purposes of the UN bond issue and giving both the political and financial reasons why it is in our national interest to participate. These summaries are being made available to members of Congress and their staffs. Over a period of the next few weeks we intend to broaden out our background discussions with individual members of Congress with a view to getting key members to come out publicly in favor of the proposal. Moreover, a number of Congressmen are receiving a good deal of correspondence from their respective constituents, and the Department is providing the necessary material to respond to such correspondence.

We have prepared a Presidential Message to Congress which will be forwarded to the White House this week. In capsule form, this message reiterates both the political and financial reasons for the UN bond proposal and emphasizes in particular that the peace-keeping operations of the UN—in the Middle East and in the Congo—are serving the national interest of the United States.

5. *The Loss of Voting Privileges.* The General Assembly voted to ask the International Court of Justice at The Hague for an advisory opinion to settle the question of whether past and future assessments for peace

and security operations are mandatory obligations on governments under the UN Charter. U Thant has now transmitted the request to the International Court of Justice for the advisory opinion on debt payment. Presentations to the Court are scheduled to begin February 20. (The US will make a submission and oral agreements.) An opinion, which supports such assessments, would establish that such costs are to be considered as part of the regular expenses. This concept of collective responsibility for peace-and-security operations in the UN urgently needs to be reestablished. Armed with this opinion, the Secretary General, plus the concert of nations, may be able to persuade the recalcitrants to pay up.

6. *Steps taken to get other nations to subscribe.* The following steps have been taken to get other countries to fully subscribe the bond issue:

U Thant wrote a letter (January 5) to each member state urging them to buy bonds promptly.[3] He intends to follow this up with personal solicitations by himself and his staff.

President Eugene Black (IBRD) has written letters to the finance ministers in most nations of the world urging the purchase of bonds. In addition, Black is contacting the Germans and the Swiss to get them to buy bonds.

The Department has cabled our diplomatic posts and asked our Ambassadors to stress the importance the United States attaches to subscription of the full $200,000,000 promptly. In our recent conversations with the British we urged that they buy a generous share. Mr. Ball urged the Canadians last Friday to increase their Bond purchases over their announced intention to buy $6.24 million.[4] We will follow up with other nations on a selective basis.

The US Delegation announced, when it supported the bond issue proposal, that we have always stood ready to pay peace-and-security costs on a pay-as-you-go basis.

In summary, the technical case for the Bond Issue rests on three points: (a) the urgent need for cash by the United Nations; (b) the inability of smaller, less-developed nations to pay these heavy costs on a pay-as-you-go basis, and (c) the need for somewhat longer-range financing to remove the financial crisis from the difficult political problems of the Congo operation. The proposed Bond Issue would meet these requirements *and* reduce our United States contribution from 47-1/2 percent to 32 percent.

But essentially the case for our participation in the financing of the UN rests on broader political grounds. We cannot put a dollar sign on peace. For sixteen years the UN has served the national interest of the U.S. This has been particularly the case in its two principal peace-keeping operations—in

---

[3] Not found.

[4] Not further identified.

the Middle East and in the Congo. Soviet opposition to UN peace-keeping operations attests to their effectiveness. A stronger executive capacity to act means a stronger UN to serve our interests—and the reality of the matter is that this cannot be accomplished without firm financing.

Dean Rusk[5]

---

[5] Printed from a copy that bears this typed signature.

---

195. Memorandum From the President's Special Assistant (Schlesinger) to President Kennedy[1]

Washington, January 19, 1962.

SUBJECT

Conversation with U Thant

The attached somewhat bland memorandum from State will probably not tell you a great deal that you do not already know.[2]

A couple of additional points:

1. *West New Guinea.* It is the view of Harriman and of the White House staff that we can most effectively stop an Indonesian invasion of West New Guinea by indicating to the Indonesians that they are going to get West New Guinea in the long run anyway, and that the one thing which would fatally prejudice their case would be an act of aggression. The logic of this view would be for you to suggest that U Thant point out to the Indonesians that military action is the one sure way of jeopardizing something which must otherwise fall into their waiting arms. I must add, though, that the Secretary of State seems to dissent from this proposed line of action.

2. *US Attitudes toward UN.* I think it is fair to say that there is an impending crisis of confidence in American attitudes toward the UN. The new apprehensions, which you yourself, of course, do not share, rise in great part from the flow of new small nations into the UN, from the expec-

---

[1] Source: Kennedy Library, National Security Files, Subjects Series, United Nations (General), 1/62–2/62, Box 311. No classification marking.

[2] Not printed. The January 18 memorandum outlined topics for discussion with Acting Secretary-General Thant. The President held a luncheon meeting with Thant on January 19 between 1:05 and 3:10 p.m. in Suite 42A of the Waldorf Astoria Hotel during a visit to New York.

tation that this will continue for some time to come, and from the supposed consequence that the General Assembly will be dominated in the future by untried people from young and unsophisticated countries. The crisis has been foreshadowed in the tendency on the part of thoughtful pro-UN figures (Fulbright, McCloy) to propose the limiting of the US commitment to the UN as well as in the primitive "Get the UN out of the US and the US out of the UN" pitch of the John Birchers. Some of this will come to a head in the debate in the Congress over the bond issue.

You yourself have, of course, a steady confidence in the UN and in the purpose and capacity of the new nations to support the organization and live responsibly by the Charter. However, both the general situation and the bond issue debate suggest the need for moderate actions and tempers on the part of the new nations during the resumed session of the General Assembly. The most hopeful aspect, from the viewpoint of preserving US confidence in the UN, is the emergence of a reasoned and responsible group of statesmen from the new countries (among whom U Thant himself, of course, is a prominent figure).

3. *UN Future.* There is some speculation that U Thant finds the job burdensome, that he prefers to have more time for his own thought and work, and that he may therefore get out at the end of his present term. You might want to express sympathy for the sacrifices he has made in taking the job but add (if you are impressed by him) that he is playing a role of unique importance and that we hope that he plans to stay on. You might want to add that we are all interested in his long-term views about the future of the UN, and that you hope an opportunity will arise when you and he and Governor Stevenson can set aside present problems and try to figure out where the UN should be in, say, 1972 and 1987.

Arthur Schlesinger, jr.

196.   Memorandum From the Executive Secretary of the
        Department of State (Battle) to the President's Special
        Assistant for National Security Affairs (Bundy)[1]

Washington, February 7, 1962.

SUBJECT

Support for the UN Bond Issue

As you requested of Mr. Wallner on behalf of the President, here is an outline of State Department activities designed to arouse public support for the UN bond issue. They are designed to make use of existing private organizations to supplement the major effort going into Congressional testimony and constant liaison with key members of the Congress.

The United States Committee for the United Nations, under the Chairmanship of Robert Benjamin, is circulating material to 20,000 community leaders suggesting letters to Congress; offering supplies of the President's message[2] and other materials to 136 member organizations; and planning spot announcements for local radio stations.

The American Association for the United Nations has distributed copies of the President's message, an editorial by Norman Cousins, and a Fact Sheet to 10,000 small town dailies and weeklies; sent a similar packet to all AAUN chapters with suggestions for local campaigns of support; and sent a background piece on the Congo, tied to the bond issue, to both local chapters and the 10,000 newspapers. In response to a letter from the AAUN, former President Truman will hold a press conference in Kansas City, probably the week after next, to announce his support of UN bonds. Funds are being sought for newspaper ads.

A briefing session has been held in Washington for officials of twenty-three national organizations representing labor, professional, farm, veterans, womens', educational, church, and student constituencies. Some have started alerting their members through mailings, house organ articles and other means, and others are expected to do so. Some of these organizations are urging local chapter members to call on Congressmen home for Lincoln and Jackson Day events.

Regional briefing sessions, held by the Department of State in Chicago and Minneapolis last week, including a presentation of the case for the bond issue.

---

[1] Source: Kennedy Library, National Security Files, Subjects Series, United Nations (General), 1/62–2/62, Box 311. Official Use Only.

[2] For text of the President's message to Congress on January 30 transmitting a bill for the purchase of UN bonds, see Public Papers of the Presidents of the United States: John F. Kennedy, 1962, pp. 81–82.

Copy for newspaper ads, hopefully to be sponsored by a group of businessmen, is under preparation. State will consult with Ralph Dungan re financing and sponsorship.

USUN is working with NGOs in New York and Ambassador Klutznick briefed a group of New York businessmen last week. Governor Stevenson's television program last Sunday was devoted to the bond issue.

Personal calls have been made on a number of organizations, including the Committee for Economic Development, the U.S. Council of the International Chamber of Commerce, and the U.S. Chamber of Commerce, seeking support from the organizations, their executive committees, or their officers.

It is clear from efforts to date that the principal problem lies with the business community. It is indicative that in private sessions, the Foreign Relations Committee of the U.S. Chamber of Commerce approved unanimously the UN bond issue, but the Government Operations Committee unanimously disapproved, thus throwing the issue to the Board of Directors, which meets in April.

You also asked about the possibility of an announcement of purchase of UN bonds by Germany during the course of Congressional hearings. The Secretary discussed this with the German Ambassador last Friday prior to his return to Bonn yesterday.[3] He strongly urged a maximum pledge to purchase UN bonds and a prompt public announcement in the interests of Germany, of the United Nations, and of the Administration's effort to secure Congressional authorization. An informal aide-mémoire along these lines was presented to the German Ambassador.[4] Mr. Eugene Black previously urged the head of the Central Bank to support German subscription to the bonds. The Department will continue to press for favorable German action, but it is uncertain at this time what success we shall have. A complicating factor is Chancellor Adenauer's desire not to appear at cross purpose with General DeGaulle at this time.

MH Manfull[5]

---

[3] Not further identified.

[4] Not found.

[5] Manfull signed for Battle above Battle's typed signature.

197.   Memorandum From the Assistant Secretary of State for
        International Organization Affairs (Cleveland) to Secretary
        of State Rusk[1]

Washington, March 8, 1962.

SUBJECT

    Resumed Session of the 16th General Assembly

Time magazine recently described the 16th General Assembly as "the sensible 16th". In the assessment that I sent to you on December 20, I noted that real progress had been made at the first part of the session.

The resumed session, which with one exception was confined to colonial issues, did nothing to upset this favorable balance and in fact made it even more favorable. With solid Latin American support (except for Cuba itself), the Assembly refused, despite strenuous Soviet bloc efforts to the contrary, to take any action even of an anodyne nature on Cuba's charges against the United States. The greater moderation on colonial issues that had marked the first part of the session continued to prevail during the resumed session. Moderate resolutions on Angola and Ruanda Urundi were adopted by overwhelming majorities, and Soviet efforts on behalf of more extreme positions, particularly in the case of Ruanda Urundi, were not appreciated by the Afro-Asians. As we hoped, no resolution was adopted on British Guiana. Only in the case of Southern Rhodesia was action taken that we fear may aggravate rather than ameliorate the problem.

A more detailed account of the Assembly's action on the five items considered at its resumed session is attached.[2]

---

[1] Source: National Archives and Records Administration, RG 59, Central Files 1960–63, 320/3–862. Confidential. Drafted by Virginia F. Hartley on March 8.

[2] Not printed. The topics discussed in the "Résumé of Resumed Session" were General Assembly actions concerning Angola, Cuba, Ruanda-Urundi, Southern Rhodesia, and British Guiana.

198.   Telegram From the Department of State to the Mission to the United Nations[1]

Washington, March 23, 1962, 9:46 p.m.

2458. Subject: Definition of Aggression Committee. Refs: USUN 3009, 3115.[2] Dept adheres long established conviction that definition of aggression would not aid UN in maintaining peace and that further efforts arrive at definition be undesirable and unproductive. UN Charter contemplates determination of aggression be based on political evaluation by competent UN organ of all circumstances pertinent to incident in question, rather than automatic application or a priori formula. Pursuant this conception, San Francisco Conference specifically declined include definition of aggression in Charter.

Definition of aggression considered by GA at fifth, sixth, seventh, ninth, eleventh, and twelfth sessions. Also considered by ILC at its third session, and by special committees appointed by GA in 1953 and 1956. Fact that these efforts did not result in agreement on definition indicates futility of further efforts. Dept. accordingly hopes Committee will adjourn without recommending further consideration definition by aggression in GA.

Pursuant GA res 1181(XII),[3] committee composed of states members General Committee of most recent GA. Mission should consult with those delegations along foregoing lines in effort secure agreement committee should not recommend further consideration definition of aggression in GA.

In past, committee before adjourning fixed date for further meetings. If possible, Dept prefers omission this step. Instead, committee

---

[1] Source: National Archives and Records Administration, RG 59, Central Files 1960–63, 320/3–1462. Official Use Only. Drafted by Leonard C. Meeker and Ernest L. Kerley (L) on March 23, cleared by Joseph J. Sisco and Stephen M. Schwebel (L/UNA), and approved by Woodruff Wallner (IO).

[2] In these telegrams from USUN, the Mission observed that the Representatives of Australia, the Netherlands, and Italy had inquired about U.S. views on a General Assembly committee meeting, tentatively set for early April, on the question of defining aggression. (Ibid., 320/3–862 and 320/3–1962)

[3] Resolution 1181 (XII), approved by the UN General Assembly on November 29, 1957, asked the Secretary-General to request the views of member states, particularly new ones, on the question of defining aggression. Replies were to be referred to a committee composed of member states whose representatives had served on the General Committee at the most recent regular General Assembly session. The Committee was to study the replies to determine when it would be appropriate for the General Assembly to consider the question of defining aggression, and would report to the Secretary-General. Proponents of the resolution hoped that the subject could be placed on the General Assembly's provisional agenda no later than the 14th session.

should adjourn with understanding it might meet in future at such time as majority its members deem fruitful. Thus necessity meetings at fixed intervals would be avoided.

Mission requested ascertain who will represent members in comittee. FYI. Dept considers high level representation would lend undesirable importance to question, and does not contemplate high level US representation unless necessitated by representation other committee members. End FYI.

Ball

---

199. **Memorandum From the Director of the Office of United Nations Political and Security Affairs (Sisco) to the Assistant Secretary of State for International Organization Affairs (Cleveland)**[1]

Washington, April 6, 1962.

SUBJECT

Chinese Representation, US–UK Differences Over

As you know, a problem has arisen with the British over the handling of the Chinese representation issue in subsidiary United Nations organs and specialized agencies. Ambassador Bruce and more recently the Secretary have discussed this question with Lord Home. The latter is said to have evinced a more flexible attitude than some of his subordinates who are taking a narrow legalistic line on Chinese representation that accords with the UK policy of admitting Red China to the United Nations. Nevertheless, there is no evidence that Lord Home's views have prevailed. On the contrary, a telephone call to me from British Embassy Counselor R.J.D. Ledward on March 26, 1962, would seem to indicate that the working levels of the Foreign Office (particularly its Far Eastern Department) are still intent on forcing a showdown on the substance of Chinese representation similar to that which took

---

[1] Source: National Archives and Records Administration, RG 59, Central Files 1960–63, 310.2/4–662. Confidential. Drafted by Bertus H. Wabeke (IO/UNP). A handwritten note by Sisco to Cleveland reads: "H.C. You wanted to talk to Secr. on this before doing it. I think it ought to be done *here* not London because both you and Ormsby Gore are experts. JS."

place in the General Assembly in December 1961, in all those bodies which they consider "competent" to discuss and decide such issues.

According to Ledward's latest instructions the British now include in their category of "competent" bodies: the General Assembly, the Security Council, the Trusteeship Council, the ECOSOC, the IAEA, the deliberative bodies of the ILO, FAO, UNESCO, UPU, WHO, WMO, ICAO, the Board of Governors of the IBRD and the IMF and the Administrative Council and Plenipotentiary Conference of ITU. In discussing the matter with me on February 26, 1962, Ledward made it clear that if a "moratorium" proposal were introduced in any of these bodies, the United Kingdom delegation would be instructed to vote against it.

We strongly oppose reopening the debate on the substance of the Chinese representation issue in subsidiary United Nations organs and specialized agencies for reasons which are obvious. Since most of these bodies, however, are indeed "competent" in a strictly legal sense to debate and vote on the issue of Chinese representation, an "out of order" formula is not applicable and would not be honored. In order to avoid an open clash with the British therefore, it is essential that we obtain their agreement to or tolerance of some modification of our old "moratorium" formula.

In view of the conciliatory attitude displayed by Lord Home in his talks with Ambassador Bruce and the Secretary, the time appears to have come to resume our discussions with the British with a view toward developing a mutually acceptable formula whereby we can dispose of the Chinese representation issue in so-called "competent" lower United Nations bodies by procedural means. In particular we should press the British for consideration of the formula outlined in paragraph 5 of Department's telegram 4671 to London. (Tab A)[2]

To obtain agreement with the British on some such concrete formula has become a matter of urgency, for the Chinese representation issue is likely to arise in meetings of the following so-called "competent" United Nations bodies between now and the opening of the 17th General Assembly in September: ITU, 17th Session of the Administrative Council, May 5; WHO, 15th Assembly, May 8; Trusteeship Council, 29th Session, May 31; ILO Conference, 46th Session, June 6; ICAO, 14th Assembly, August 28. In addition the 7th General Conference of IAEA and the 12th General Conference of UNESCO are scheduled to meet concurrently with

---

[2] Not printed. This paragraph suggested that when the question of Chinese representation was raised in a UN organ or specialized agency, a motion or resolution should be presented that would: (a) recall General Assembly debate and action during the 16th Regular Session (which declared the matter an "important question"), (b) recall Resolution 396 (V) (which recommended that other UN organs and specialized agencies should take into account the General Assembly's position on the question of representation), and (c) in an operative paragraph, decide not to consider any proposal to change China's representation. (Ibid., 303/2–2662)

the 17th Session of the General Assembly in September/October and November of this year.

It was agreed between the Secretary and Lord Home in Geneva that the problems raised by the official British position on the admission of Red China to "competent associated UN organizations" should be discussed further "in Washington". I therefore suggest that at an early opportunity you call in the British Ambassador and discuss with him the specific formula for the handling of the Chinese representation issue in subsidiary United Nations bodies contained in paragraph 5 of Department's telegram 4671 to London, in the light of the recent general exchanges with Lord Home on this subject. You should invite his Government's reactions to this proposal and emphasize the desirability of obtaining early agreement on some such procedure in order to avoid unnecessary contretemps from arising between our Governments over this vexatious issue in the upcoming meetings of the agencies listed above.

---

200. Telegram From the Department of State to the Embassy in the United Kingdom[1]

Washington, April 19, 1962, 8:42 p.m.

5613. Assistant Secretary Cleveland invited UK Ambassador April 19 to discuss problem Chinese Representation in UN subsidiary organs. Cleveland recalled in conversation with Ambassador Bruce and Secretary, Lord Home had given impression he desired be helpful in connection this problem, saying it was not UK policy admit Chinese Communists to UN by back door. We agree with UK that legally a number of UN subsidiary bodies are competent determine own membership. However, given UN decision last fall and GA Resolution 396 (V)[2]

---

[1] Source: National Archives and Records Administration, RG 59, Central Files 1960–63, 303/4–1962. Confidential. Drafted by William B. Buffum; cleared by William H. Sullivan, Milton C. Rewinkel, Ernest L. Kerley, and Warren E. Slater; and approved by Assistant Secretary Cleveland. Repeated to USUN.

[2] General Assembly Resolution 396 (V), adopted on December 14, 1950, recommended in cases when more than one authority claimed to be the government of a member state that "the question should be considered in the light of the purposes and principles of the Charter and the circumstances of each case," the General Assembly (or the Interim Committee if the General Assembly was not in session) should consider the question, and the attitude adopted by the General Assembly (or the Interim Committee) should be taken into account by other organs and specialized agencies.

recommending that attitude adopted by General Assembly on membership be taken into account in other UN organs, we believe good case can be made for avoiding issue in subsidiary bodies. We anxious find formula which would avoid public display basic US-UK differences over substance Chinese Representation. With series of meetings of competent bodies scheduled begin next month, we consider it urgent that attempts be made reconcile our positions on this in near future. Cleveland stressed domestic problem which would be created in US if substantive differences with UK on this issue, which arouses such passions here, repeatedly exposed to public view in half-dozen upcoming meetings of subsidiary UN bodies. He pointed out only reason why this did not cause greater difficulties last fall was fact US position sustained by sizeable margin.

Cleveland then handed Ambassador two alternative versions procedural resolutions which we thought should serve as acceptable basis for approach to problem and said he hoped UK would find it possible accept one of these. Text follows:

I. a) a preambular paragraph recalling GA resolution 396 (V);
b) a preambular para recalling the action which the GA took at its 16th session on December 15, 1961;
c) possibly a preambular para declaring that any action at this time by the body in question to change the representation of China would be inconsistent with the above recommendations and decisions of the General Assembly;
d) an operative paragraph whereby the international body in question would decide not to consider at this session any proposal to change the representation of China.
II. a) a preambular paragraph recalling GA resolution 396 (V);
b) a preambular para recalling the action which the GA took at its 16th session on December 15, 1961;
c) an operative para whereby the international body in question would decide to refrain from taking action inconsistent with the above-mentioned recommendations and decisions of the GA.

Ambassador said UK has no desire whatever to see Chinese Communists seated in these bodies, but must act, and perhaps speak, in subsidiary bodies in manner consistent with position taken in GA. He recalled UK had voted against Resolution 396 (V). However, Cleveland pointed out this res had been adopted by overwhelming majority and did constitute clear recommendation to all governments by General Assembly. Ormsby-Gore said he did not know if UK would consider itself inhibited from voting for resolution containing reference to it. He thought this would be easier in any event if such reference contained in preambular paragraph rather than in operative paragraph reaffirming resolution. Ormsby-Gore stressed UK anxious not cause more trouble than necessary, but said correspondence between UK-UN and FonOff had not yet resulted in agreement as to how approach problem. He speculated possibly UK might decide simply remain silent when and if question arose and then abstain on resolution. He said however if either of foregoing formulae could be accepted by UK easiest combination for them would probably be (a), (b) and (d) of first alternative, omitting (c) in order avoid establishing general principles and limiting action in effect to year-by-year moratorium.

Rusk

201. Airgram From the Mission to the United Nations to the Department of State[1]

A-273   New York, April 19, 1962.

SUBJECT

    GA Voting

    1. In resumed session GA several factors emerged on votes of importance to us which require close attention inasmuch as similar issues and similar voting problems can be anticipated in future. Specifically, successful outcome in blocking undesirable aspects of colonial issues having wide Afro-Asian and Communist support (e.g. mention of Comite of 17 in Angola res and call for Belgian troop withdrawal in Ruanda-Urundi) as well as on Cuban issue was achieved as result alignment in our support of: (a) Solid WE and LA backing. This included WE "moderates" such as Norway, Canada, Ireland, Austria and Sweden, whose support came with unusual ease this spring and WE states with grievances against us such as Portugal, South Africa and Belgium; it also included more difficult LAs such as Brazil, Mexico, Chile, Ecuador; (b) Backing by US allies in Asia (e.g. Pakistan, Thailand, Japan, China, Philippines, Iran) and by Malaya; (c) Abstention by French-African states and to some extent by friendliest Middle East countries (Cyprus, Lebanon and Jordan).

    Chief factor assuring largest number these votes in UN appears to be our military and political alliances. Hard core of our supporters comes from NATO, OAS, CENTO and SEATO, and it is our mutual overall political and military commitments which seem to be primary factor in their

[1] Source: National Archives and Records Administration, RG 59, Central Files 1960–63, 320/4–1962. Confidential. Drafted by Richard F. Pedersen on April 18, cleared by Robert O. Blake and Charles P. Noyes, and approved by Zachary P. Geaneas.

voting on specific issues. Second important factor in maintaining our voting position in UN is developing shift of "moderate" Western countries toward support of our positions even in face of neutral opposition. Third important factor is fact French-Africans have so far been able maintain their moderate position. Our voting problem, as usual, is to continue to attract the "liberals" in this group while not losing the "conservatives".

2. While there was some voting improvement, as indicated above, there was also some deterioration. English-speaking Africans such as Nigeria, Sierra Leone, Ethiopia and sometimes Tanganyika tended to vote with Belgrade Group, if not for the most extreme proposals, nevertheless for proposals we opposed—for example for the Mongolian Resolution re Cuba in Plenary, and on second operative paragraph of Cuban Resolution in Committee—more often than they tended to abstain with French-Africans. Similarly Tunisia tended regularly to vote with this group, while a year ago it was more conservative. Saudi Arabia, which by any normal standards might be expected to be no more unhelpful than Lebanon and Jordan, continued to vote and take debate and corridor lines (primarily because of Shukairy and Baroody) similar to those of UAR and Iraq.

3. Both Boland (Ireland) and Algard (Norway) have asked us if we noted change in voting and attitude of "moderate" Europeans. They added this was deliberate policy on their part to help keep UN actions moderate and to combat "take it or leave it" tendency among some Afro-Asians when they have agreed on text of resolution among themselves. Boland told us he had himself witnessed decline of League due to disenchantment of major powers. Substantial European disenchantment with UN had already set in; radical Afro-Asians likely to produce even more of this; role of "moderates" in circumstances was to restrain radicals more than to press colonial powers (which was their main concern in last few years). Both Boland and Algard also said advance in US policy on colonial matters was key factor that made such attitude on their part possible. Because US policy helped keep pressures on our allies to come up-to-date on colonial matters, European moderates could keep pressures on Afro-Asian radicals not to go too fast. In particular they felt it was necessary to have something (especially from US) they could all be for rather than just to be against other proposals, and that we were now doing this.

4. Difficult to analyze exactly what we should do in light above voting situation. Suggest, however, we should give close attention to following:

a. *Measures to assure continued and better support from liberal Europeans, LAs, and modern Afro-Asians*

(1) We must maintain forward-looking policy on colonial questions. In particular we must examine issues before UN constantly with view to US initiatives or to actions we can support and which can be expected to

block or dull more extreme proposals. Early planning by Department is vital if we are to achieve this. Such policy is also essential to assure support of more liberal pro-West elements not only in Africa and Asia but also in Latin America and Western Europe.

(2) We must make major effort keep as close as possible to French-speaking Africans. They now possess balance of votes in Assembly. Their votes can determine who is elected GA President; their votes can determine whether GRC or Communist China has majority in GA; their votes are essential to give us two-thirds majority on issues in which Casablanca–Belgrade powers are willing to vote in conjunction with Communists against our desires; their votes could be either psychologically helpful or damaging even on issues where they do not determine outcome. Inasmuch as we will constantly be seeking their support we must be prepared to give them something in return, for example to support them actively for membership on UN bodies and to support them on some of their resolutions and amendments even if we not entirely happy with them. Conversely we should be prepared to caution them against positions which are hopeless and which will make them look bad among Afro-Asians generally even if some of our friends (including the French) sometimes object. (At the same time it is probably not desirable to talk to other dels, especially French-Africans, about how much importance we attach to their role.)

b. *Measures to attract further support among Afro-Asians*

(1) We need to make effort to break-up voting alignment of Arabs. Arabs now tend to follow UAR line, which sometimes puts them against us and almost never with us. They vote en bloc more consistently than any other group in UN except Soviet bloc. We now sometimes pull Lebanon and Jordan from this group; however they are always uncomfortable because it isolates them from the other Arabs. If Saudi Arabia and Libya could be persuaded at govt level to shift their voting pattern more in direction of Lebanon and Jordan than in UAR direction we might be able produce better Arab voting balance by making it easier for all of them to split away from UAR–Iraq line more often. It would be helpful to our voting situation in UN, in other words, if Arabs could be split into a "Casablanca" group including UAR, Morocco, Yemen and Iraq, and another group of Lebanon, Jordan, Saudi Arabia, and possibly Libya (possibly together with Tunisia). Key to such development is to seek to shift basic instructions to dels from Saudi and Libyan Govts. Their basic instructions now seem to be to vote in harmony with Arab group or majority thereof. Most frequently this results either in UAR-Iraqi domination of group or in following their lead when Lebanon and Jordan differ. If their govts could be persuaded to instruct their dels instead to vote in harmony with Lebanon and Jordan (and possibly Tunisia) we might have real gain. This would have to be done in capitals and might not be successful.

(2) We should also begin systematic campaign of persuasion here and in capitals to get more frequent votes for our positions from "middle group" (Nigeria, Sierra Leone, Tanganyika, Liberia) of English-speaking Africans. Dept may wish pay particular attention to this group in field approaches.

c. *Measures to hold support of our allies*

(1) We need to bring LAs into our GA and general UN planning on ground floor and insist Europeans consult with them on same basis. Once LA voting bloc cracks seriously here we will have profound voting problems. Their support more crucial than ever and we need to give them greater and earlier attention. (See USUN 3402 for specific recommendations.)

(2) While not modifying our policies on colonial questions we also should maintain in UN best possible general relations with Portugal, Union of South Africa, Belgium and Spain in order to assure them that our differences on specific issues do not reflect general relations and to assure their positive voting support to maximum extent on broad-range UN issues.

(3) We must give firm support to our allies in Afro-Asian world (Philippines, Thailand, Iran, Pakistan, in particular) expecially when they seek elections to UN bodies. These are Afro-Asian countries whose votes we count on, and get, on questions crucial to us. In doing this they risk being "ostracized" by neutralists, especially on elections. If we allow them to be badly defeated in such elections they will react in other UN votes, moving toward the protective coloration of "abstention", and we will see further deterioration of voting support such as we have already seen in Ethiopia, Liberia, Tunisia, and to some extent Jordan. Where we are not prepared to support them, we should seek to persuade them not to run or to withdraw.

Stevenson

202. **Memorandum From the President's Special Assistant (Schlesinger) to the Representative to the United Nations (Stevenson)**[1]

Washington, May 1, 1962.

SUBJECT

Keeping Abreast of the United Nations

The problem is to keep the President informed about impending UN problems so that he will know well in advance when the hard ones come along.

To do this effectively will probably require more in the way of direct USUN-White House communication than we have attempted in the past. Obviously neither of us wishes to bypass IO, but I am sure that Harlan will understand the President's desire for direct briefing. You will no doubt want to send Harlan copies of any reports that you may make directly to the President.

I would suggest the following procedure:

1) that every Monday you send the President a preview of the agonies of the week—either a short memorandum; or, if you prefer, tell them to me over the phone, and I will pass them on.

2) that, when a major issue of policy or strategy is under consideration, you plan to come to Washington and talk the matter out with the President or other interested officials.

3) that you prepare occasional memoranda on long-run problems of acute UN interest, like your recent memorandum on the Azores question (possible subjects: Communist pressure for increased representation in the Secretariat; the new stage of the China representation issue; etc.).

4) that, when you send memoranda requiring follow-up to the White House, you send me copies so that I can do something about them.

Arthur Schlesinger, jr.[2]

---

[1] Source: Kennedy Library, National Security Files, Subjects Series, United Nations (General), 3/62–5/62, Box 311. Confidential. A copy was sent to McGeorge Bundy.

[2] Printed from a copy that bears this typed signature.

203.   Memorandum From the President's Special Assistant (Schlesinger) to President Kennedy[1]

Washington, May 2, 1962.

SUBJECT

Meeting between the President and Ambassador Stevenson, May 2

The President and the Ambassador discussed the following subjects:

1. *The Azores.* The President said that in the nature of things the two issues—Azores and Angola—cannot be separated because Portugal will not permit them to be separated. The Ambassador said that, since the Azores were important not only to American security but to NATO as a whole, he felt that more of an effort should be made to seek the cooperation of the NATO countries, as well as Brazil, in bringing pressure on Portugal. He reported that he had talked to Macmillan along these lines, that Macmillan had said that Britain would be glad to cooperate to this end, and that Sir Patrick Dean was ready to do anything he could.

The Acheson memorandum was discussed.[2] With regard to Acheson's recommendation that the US not participate in drafting any more resolutions on Angola, the Ambassador said that American participation was essential in order to moderate the resolution; without American participation, any resolution on Angola would be much more extreme. Acheson's recommendation that aid to Angolan nationalists be stopped was not discussed.

Action: Schlesinger to get a precise statement of Ambassador Stevenson's views as to how he recommends that we proceed.

2. *Congo.* The President explained why he thought the negotiations concerting US and UK policy toward the Congo should take place in London. The Ambassador agreed and indicated the USUN interest in the instructions to be sent to Ambassador Bruce. *Action:* the President said that State's instructions should be cleared with the Ambassador before they are sent.

3. *Registration of Space Vehicles.* The Ambassador explained the problem—i.e., the unwillingness in Washington to register temporary space vehicles (those which go up for a short time and then come down). The

---

[1] Source: Kennedy Library, National Security Files, Subjects Series, United Nations (General), 3/62–5/62, Box 311. No classification marking. Copies were sent to McGeorge Bundy and Assistant Secretary Cleveland.

[2] The April 25 memorandum, prepared by former Secretary of State Dean Acheson at Secretary Rusk's request, urged that the United States make a determined effort to create a more favorable climate for renewal of the Azores Base Agreement, which was due to expire at the end of 1962. (Ibid., Cleveland Papers, Azores, 4/62–6/62)

President said that he did not understand why they should not be registered, since it was not necessary to report the content of the vehicle. *Action:* the President said that he would personally check into the matter and let the Ambassador know.

4. *Lake Tiberias.* The Ambassador said that he thought it would be a great mistake to send the proposed Lake Tiberias note to the Israeli Government. While he felt that we would come out on the Israeli side on the question, he argued that the present draft would throw away valuable bargaining power, and that we should stipulate certain conditions before we accept the Israeli position. *Action:* the President asked that the Ambassador get together with Mike Feldman and see whether they could agree on anything.

Stevenson and Feldman subsequently agreed that it would be a mistake to send any note at this time. When the Israeli representative to the UN returns to New York in about two weeks, Feldman will go to New York and he and Stevenson will explore the matter together.

5. *Kashmir.* The Ambassador said that USUN planned to take no initiative in working on the resolution.

6. *Chinese Representation.* The Ambassador said that the Brazzaville group has indicated that it does not feel obligated to support the US position in the next General Assembly. The President said that in due course there should be a meeting on the Chirep issue.

7. *UN Bonds.* The President and the Ambassador agreed in expressing skepticism as to whether Francis Plimpton would be the most effective man to help on the Hill when the bond issue goes before the House. *Action:* Schlesinger to call Dutton and find out why Plimpton was chosen for this assignment and whether it might not be better to use somebody else.

Arthur Schlesinger, jr.[3]

---

[3] Printed from a copy that bears this typed signature.

204.   Telegram From the Department of State to the Mission in
        Geneva[1]

Washington, May 8, 1962, 7:22 p.m.

1687. Following mutually acceptable formula has been worked out
ad referendum with British Embassy Counselor Ledward as procedural means to meet possible hostile proposals to unseat GRC representatives and seat ChiComs in subsidiary and associated UN bodies which
British consider competent decide question of membership and representation:

The Assembly,

Recalling the recommendation of the Fifth General Assembly of the
United Nations on Dec 14, 1950, that "the attitude adopted by the
General Assembly" regarding the representation of a Member State
"should be taken into account in other organs of the United Nations and
in the specialized agencies";

Recalling the action which the Sixteenth General Assembly of the
United Nations took on December 15, 1961 regarding the representation
of China;

Decides to take no action on any proposal to change the representation of China at this Session.

FYI. Ledward expressed personal opinion that UK would be able
vote for above formula in most so-called "competent" bodies provided
UK could make oral statements expressing certain reservations.
Ledward indicated, however, that for undisclosed reasons, in certain
instances UK may abstain instead of vote for. End FYI.

For Geneva: US Del to WHO should advise British colleagues that if
and when British cabinet approves above formula, US will use it instead
of formula contained in US position paper should Chirep issue be
raised in WHO Assembly in form proposal unseat GRC rep and seat
ChiComs.

For London: Please press, as necessary for HMG confirmation this formula, which we hope will be forthcoming before issue arises in WHO
Assembly. Geneva should be informed immediately of UK decision.

Ball

---

[1] Source: National Archives and Records Administration, RG 59, Central Files
1960–63, 303/5–862. Confidential; Niact. Drafted by Bertus H. Wabeke on May 8; cleared
by Joseph J. Sisco, Stephen M. Schwebel, William H. Sullivan, and Alf E. Bergesen; and
approved by Woodruff Wallner. Also sent to London and repeated to USUN and Taipei.

205. **Letter From the British Ambassador (Ormsby Gore) to the Assistant Secretary of State for International Organization Affairs (Cleveland)[1]**

Washington, May 21, 1962.

Dear Harlan,

I feel that I owe you an apology for not giving you a reply sooner to the proposals which you put to me on April 19 about Chinese representation in subsidiary organisations of the United Nations.[2] The matter has, as you will know, been under discussion between the Foreign Secretary and the Secretary of State on two separate occasions and a revised formula was put to us on May 8.[3] This read as follows:—

[Here follows the text of the formula identical to the text in Document 204.]

The above would be on the understanding that:—

(a) some other delegation raised the question in the form of a Motion. I gather that you would not yourselves do so and as you know we ourselves could not undertake to table or sponsor such a resolution;

(b) we would be free to make a statement in clarification of our position on the lines taken by our delegate at the General Assembly.

I am now authorised to say that our delegations in "competent" bodies will be instructed in these circumstances to vote in favour of a resolution such as that given above. You will, I am sure, understand that this does not reflect any change in our basic attitude to Chinese representation as a whole and that my Government will wish to reconsider the position after the next General Assembly.

Yours sincerely

David Ormsby Gore

---

[1] Source: National Archives and Records Administration, RG 59, Central Files 1960–63, 310.2/5–2162. Confidential. The salutation and complimentary close are handwritten.

[2] See Document 200.

[3] See Document 204.

206.   Memorandum From the Assistant Secretary of State for
         International Organization Affairs (Cleveland) to the Director
         of the Arms Control and Disarmament Agency (Foster)[1]

Washington, May 24, 1962.

SUBJECT

Present United States Efforts to Improve the Peacekeeping Capabilities of the UN

The development of UN's peacekeeping machinery is an integral
part of the U.S. disarmament program. It is also an important objective
in United States efforts to strengthen, over the near term, the peace-
keeping ability of the United Nations.

In moving from the administration of the United Nations
Emergency Force in the Middle East (UNEF) to the administration of
the UN force in the Congo (UNOC), the UN moved into an area of operational magnitude which placed major new strains on the organization.
We have reviewed with the USUN, the Military Advisors Staff to the
UN Secretary General, Ambassador Gullion and the Department of
Defense the means through which the administration of the UN Congo
operation would be improved. In particular we have looked at the need
for strengthened command and policy control, for better logistic planning, and for officer training progress. We have also reviewed the
Middle Eastern and Congo experience to see what it could tell us about
more general moves for improving UN's military and policing capabilities.

Our conclusions are set forth in the attached paper (Tab A) entitled
"The Development of the Military and Policing Capabilities of the
United Nations".[2] The paper was cleared throughout the Department of
State, with ACDA, and with the Department of Defense, and was given
to the British in February. The UK has informed us that they have
requested their Imperial Defense College for a similar paper. We anticipate that these two papers will be taken up in bilateral talks with the
British to be held probably during the last week in June or the first week
in July. Most of the proposals would not require new General Assembly
action. It might be advisable for implementation of some of the suggestions to await the election of a UN Secretary General at the 17th
Assembly.

I would call your attention particularly to the following proposals:

---

[1]   Source: National Archives and Records Administration, RG 59, IO Files: Lot 67 D
378, Peace and Security, 1962. Confidential. Drafted by Elmore Jackson on May 17.
[2]   Not found.

1. The Ear-Marking and Training of National Forces for Use by the United Nations

In response to President Kennedy's address to the United Nations on September 25, 1961, Norway, Sweden and Denmark informed the Acting Secretary General that they had ear-marked forces and equipment for UN military operations, in line with an earlier request of Mr. Hammarskjold in May 1961.

2. Officer Training Programs

Before his death Mr. Hammarskjold had approved a limited officer training program to be carried on in New York and in the field. The program was to be funded out of the current budgets of UNEF and UNOC. We understand that U Thant has now re-approved this training program. We expect it to be put into operation following the appointment of a UN Secretary General to a full five-year term at the 17th Session of the General Assembly.

3. Preparation of Manuals

The UN Secretary General's staff has begun an assessment of UN's experience in the Middle East and the Congo, with a view to manuals being prepared which could be used in an officer training program and in military colleges of member countries. (See proposal Tab A, page 6)

4. A UN Officer Training College

Our proposals recommend that the U.S., in cooperation with the UN Secretary General, explore the possibility of the UN establishing an officer training college—patterned in general on the NATO Defense College. Such an institution might be located at UN headquarters, or in a neutral country such as Sweden or Switzerland. It would be staffed in part by senior officers who have had field command and headquarters experience with the United Nations.

5. Policy Control Over UN Forces

We are giving earnest attention to means of strengthening policy control over UN policing operations (See Tab A, page 8). One idea which is receiving special attention is that each UN field policing operation might be under the advisory or policy direction of a consortia composed of these countries contributing the principal military, logistic, and financial support to the particular operation. These considerations are, of course, closely related to the more general ones concerned with future patterns of financing UN's peacekeeping operations—beyond the bond issue.

UN's work in peaceful settlement is a second major area in which it is important for new moves to be made in strengthening United Nations capabilities. We are now preparing specific proposals for discussion with the British in the bilateral conversations to be held in the early summer. I attach a memorandum (Tab B), prepared in IO, making preliminary suggestions.[3] While the memo proposes certain specific measures which could be taken to strengthen UN's peaceful settlement facilities, it places an emphasis (and I think an appropriate one) on the necessity for creating both a new world-wide political interest in UN operations in this area and a new general political atmosphere. I will be very interested to have your reactions to the suggestions which the memo sets forth.

As we move forward on these short-term possibilities, and as ACDA moves forward in outlining the longer-term ones, it is important that we keep in close relationship. Our proposals need to reflect ACDA's long-term goals. I am sure you will want your projections to reflect the progress we are able to make over the near term.

In this respect, I think you will be interested in seeing a copy of a memo prepared recently by INR at our request, entitled "Soviet Attitudes Toward Development of Military and Policing Capabilities of the United Nations". It is a direct commentary on the basic paper from which Tab A (a sanitized version) was prepared for the US-UK talks.

---

[3] Not found.

---

207. Memorandum From the Assistant Secretary of State for International Organization Affairs (Cleveland) to Secretary of State Rusk[1]

Washington, June 5, 1962.

SUBJECT

Notes on Adlai Stevenson Visit, June 5

Ambassador Stevenson spent June 5 in staff discussions here in the Department, and had a visit with the President at the White House. The following notes will indicate the main questions discussed:

1. General Assembly Delegation.

Six of the positions in the General Assembly Delegation are pretty well set: the five "regulars" at USUN (Stevenson, Plimpton, Yost, Klutznick, Bingham) and Marietta Tree. Three problems remain:

---

[1] Source: Kennedy Library, National Security Files, Subjects Series, United Nations (General), 6/62, Box 311. Secret.

a. A man to handle disarmament; further consultation with Mr. Foster and Ambassador Dean will be necessary.

b. Appointment of a Negro member of the Delegation, staying as far as possible within the concept of a "fully professional" Delegation.

c. Senator Fulbright is considering whether Senators Gore and Carlson could be the two Senators this year; he is also considering whether they should be billed as Congressional advisers or as members of the Delegation as such.

Governor Stevenson will write to George Meany and Walter Reuther to ask whether they can serve as Senior Advisers. He will discuss with Mrs. Roosevelt whether she would like to be a Senior Adviser this year. Other people who would be shown in the Senior Adviser category would be Mrs. Gladys Tillott and Mrs. Jane Dick. The rotation among the three women commissioners appears to be satisfactory to the White House.

2. National Security Council.

The President has asked Governor Stevenson to plan to make a one-hour presentation to the National Security Council some time on the UN considerations in national security policy. Governor Stevenson has asked us to develop an outline of such a presentation.

3. West New Guinea.

Governor Stevenson talked to U Thant, who had been in touch with the Indonesians but has not been asked by the Indonesians to confirm the Dutch acceptance of satisfactory ground rules for the resumption of negotiations. (A cable is going out to Djakarta to get the Indonesians to ask U Thant if they need more assurance than the United States has already given them.) U Thant is clear that there should be a brief further period of discussion between the Netherlands and Indonesia under Ambassador Bunker's auspices. Once an agenda is agreed on, U Thant will designate somebody to sit in on the last stage on behalf of the UN Secretariat.

4. Relationships with France.

Governor Stevenson had a most interesting farewell discussion with Berard, who is being assigned as French Ambassador to Rome. The memorandum of conversation is being sent to you separately.[2] I told Governor Stevenson what I knew of your first discussion with Ambassador Alphand. Governor Stevenson thought it might be useful to discuss relations with France directly with President de Gaulle; an

---

[2] Attached. [Handwritten footnote in the source text. The memorandum of conversation was not attached and has not been found.]

opportunity for this might be the invitation to visit de Gaulle which he believes may be forthcoming when he (Governor Stevenson) is in Europe this summer for the ECOSOC meeting.

5. Kashmir and Ruanda-Urundi.

Governor Stevenson had a very brief opportunity to bring the President up-to-date on the status of the Kashmir question in the Security Council, and the prospects for Ruanda-Urundi in the General Assembly.

6. Southern Rhodesia.

There is an urgent need to decide how far we will be going to oppose inscription of a Southern Rhodesia item on the agenda of the resumed General Assembly. The matter will probably come up at the General Committee on Friday morning, June 8th. The Department will await USUN's assessment of the voting situation, before trying to decide whether to campaign against inscription by making representations at government level to key members of the General Committee. On this subject, the President particularly asked whether we were planning to support the British, and Governor Stevenson said we were. If we decide not to oppose inscription, on the ground that we would lose on it, and thereby lose influence in the subsequent resolution, we may want to inform the President of the revised thinking on this subject.

7. President's Visit to Mexico.

Governor Stevenson is developing a memorandum for the President in connection with his visit to Mexico. We have made available to Governor Stevenson a copy of the present draft of the "scope paper", and will receive his draft for the President in due course.

8. UN Bond Hearings.

Governor Stevenson expressed to the President his concern, and ours, about the delay in the consideration by the House Foreign Affairs Committee of the UN loan legislation. Fred Dutton will follow up with Larry O'Brien to see whether more steam can be generated for earlier House consideration of the matter. The danger is that if the loan legislation is not passed reasonably soon, some of the opponents or lukewarm supporters will begin to suggest that the whole question be reconsidered in the upcoming General Assembly rather than acted on by the Congress at this time.

9. UN Future Financing.

We discussed with Governor Stevenson the varying proposals for the financing of the peace and security operations of the UN. It does not appear that, with as many unknowns as are still in the picture, we can now settle on a definitive answer to the question, "after the bond issue what?" However, we will need a line of policy and conversation for use in the Congressional hearings and consultations with other governments; this can be framed in terms of alternatives. A paper along these lines will be developed in IO after taking into account New York's 3897 of June 4.

10. Secretariat Personnel.

USUN has developed a memorandum on the Soviet attempt to enlarge its representation in the Secretariat, a copy of which will be sent to you separately. We are actively discussing this question here, as it appears to be the next major Soviet attack on the UN executive establishment after the failure of the Troika proposal. A draft letter answering questions from Senator Eastland on this subject was checked out with Governor Stevenson, and discussed by him with some of the White House staff. We are all agreed that there is no reason to be protective of the UN in this matter; the best way to protect the international civil service concept is to campaign publicly for it now and during the General Assembly. Frank discussion of the matter with interested members of Congress would fit in with this strategy.

11. Israel.

A considerable part of Governor Stevenson's session with the President was devoted to a discussion of policy towards Israel, on the basis of a draft letter to Prime Minister Ben Gurion, which had been drafted by Mike Feldman. Governor Stevenson is not clear that any letter is required. If there is a letter he believes it should:

a. Applaud Ambassador Harmon's declaration to Governor Stevenson that Israel now intended to stop using the retaliatory raid as an instrument of policy;
b. Express the hope that Israel will cooperate closely with the UN peacekeeping machinery in the area; and
c. Look forward to completion of the project for diverting Jordan waters and express the U.S. understanding that Israel will act within the limitations of the Johnston Plan.

12. Next Steps with the UN on Peacekeeping.

We discussed how best to develop the UN's peacekeeping capability, on the basis of the line of policy set forth in the planning paper, agreed with the Department of Defense and ACDA, entitled "The Development of the Military and Policing Capabilities of the UN". We emphasized that no legislative action by the UN was contemplated at this stage, but a number of useful steps could be taken by informal action within the UN Secretariat. While U Thant is unlikely to move vigorously on this front prior to his own election to a full five-year term as Secretary General,

Governor Stevenson thought it would be useful to have a session with U Thant and some of his chief advisers, for which he would want me to come to New York and at which we could indicate the kinds of steps that might reasonably be taken to plan for a more proficient discharge of the peacekeeping assignments laid on the UN Secretariat from time to time by the Security Council or the General Assembly.

---

208. Memorandum of Conversation[1]

Washington, June 11, 1962.

SUBJECT

    Tour d'Horizon

PARTICIPANTS

    Mr. Georgi M. Kornienko—Counselor USSR
    Mr. Joseph J. Sisco—Director UNP

At Mr. Kornienko's request I had lunch with him today at the Hay-Adams. The following principal points emerged during our luncheon conversation.

1. *Ruanda-Urundi.* Mr. Kornienko took the initiative in raising the question of General Assembly consideration of Ruanda-Urundi. He was particularly interested in the question of the continuing presence of Belgian troops. I indicated that our objective is to support independence of Ruanda and Burundi on July 1 under conditions which would give reasonable assurance that stability will be maintained. After Mr. Kornienko stressed the need to assure that Belgian presence was not an indefinite one, I pointed out to him that it was important that the USSR distinguish between symbolism and reality on this matter. I said that I understood why for propaganda reasons the Soviet Union might wish to stress in the Assembly the need for early Belgian withdrawal. However, I pointed out that the USSR has an interest in not creating conditions which might bring about another Congo-like situation in the heart of Africa. Mr. Kornienko said there was no need for a direct confrontation between the US and USSR on Ruanda-Urundi.

---

[1] Source: National Archives and Records Administration, RG 59, Central Files 1960–63, 611.61/7–1962. Limited Official Use. Drafted by Sisco on June 13. Assistant Secretary Cleveland referred this memorandum to Secretary Rusk under cover of a July 19 memorandum. (Ibid.)

2. *17th GA.* Mr. Kornienko indicated an interest in how we viewed the coming 17th General Assembly. He was particularly interested in knowing whether the US intended to make any formal proposal looking towards the establishment of a UN Peace Force or the strengthening of the UN peace-keeping machinery. I limited myself to indicating that these matters were under consideration and that no definite decisions had been taken. I did reiterate our continuing interest in strengthening the peaceful settlement procedures of the UN as indicated in a number of speeches given recently by Ambassador Stevenson and Department spokesmen.

3. *SYG.* In response to my statement that the question of the election of a Secretary-General would arise this fall, Mr. Kornienko said that "Mr. Thant had not fulfilled the hopes they had regarding him." Mr. Kornienko cited in particular Thant's failure to meet regularly with his "cabinet of under-secretaries." Mr. Kornienko affirmed that one of the purposes of receiving Thant in Moscow in August is to give Mr. Khrushchev the opportunity to have a personal look at the Acting Secretary-General.

4. *UN Financing.* I pointed out that a key issue this fall will be the question of UN financing. Assuming a favorable Court decision indicating that peace-keeping expenses would be mandatory obligations on the part of the members of the UN, I asked Mr. Kornienko what the USSR position would be. Mr. Kornienko was non-committal, saying that the USSR would not wish to indicate in advance what peace-keeping operations it would support. He indicated USSR willingness to support peace-keeping operations decided upon by the UN "in accordance with the Charter." He expressed dissatisfaction with the UN operation in the Congo. He held out very little hope that the Russians would support putting UN finances on a more firm footing.

5. *Disarmament.* I asked whether he felt that disarmament would be considered at the fall session. Mr. Kornienko said historically the USSR has always felt that the Assembly should consider disarmament each year. However, he indicated that whether they would favor a discussion at the Assembly would depend on whether any progress was being made in Geneva. I asked whether this would not also depend on whether or not the USSR had resumed testing by that time. Mr. Kornienko smiled and said "Yes it would" and that if they resumed testing by that time they would be less anxious for a discussion in the Assembly, but that we would be more favorable to such a debate.

6. *Hungary.* Mr. Kornienko expressed the hope that we would not once again press the Hungarian issue at the GA this fall since it was only an irritant to US-USSR relations. I pointed out that Hungary, after so many years, had yet to fulfill any of the objectives of the innumerable UN resolutions adopted on this matter and that its complete disregard

of the UN resolutions made it difficult for this question to be removed from the agenda.

7. *Laos.* Mr. Kornienko had received, as we had, the report of the provisional agreement on the new Laotian Government under Souvanna Phouma. He limited himself to saying that the USSR was cooperating with the US to achieve a neutral Laos. He also contended, though mildly, that Communist China shares these objectives.

8. *Geneva Conference.* Mr. Kornienko said that the American press had made much too much of the Soviet reversal on the war propaganda resolution. He said it was just a case of second thoughts on their part. He then went on to say that it would have been foolish for an agreement to have been achieved on this matter between the US and USSR while "the US was putting troops into Thailand." He said the climate was not propitious for such an agreement.

9. *Walter Lippmann.* I asked Mr. Kornienko if he had any observations regarding the Lippmann telecast last week and Lippmann's writings that the balance of force had changed in favor of the West over the past year and a half. Mr. Kornienko did not understand on what basis Lippmann was making this evaluation. He said such an evaluation could be dangerous if it led the American people to think that the US has overwhelming strength and therefore could take greater risks in its diplomatic dealings with the USSR. I indicated to Mr. Kornienko that we realize that this was no time for rash action on the part of any of the principal powers. I expressed the hope that the USSR would avoid incautious action in Berlin. Mr. Kornienko said he wished to stress that the USSR cannot "put on ice" the Berlin question indefinitely. The situation is risky and dangerous, and that while the matter can be kept on ice for a while, the dangers and risks increase if the situation continues. He reaffirmed the desirability of continuing the talks.

10. *Stevenson–Zorin Talks.* The luncheon concluded with Mr. Kornienko commenting "as a personal suggestion" the desirability of Stevenson and Zorin having full discussions before the opening of the 17th General Assembly so that some of the key items could be discussed beforehand.

Joseph J. Sisco[2]

---

[2] Printed from a copy that bears this typed signature.

209.   Telegram From the Mission to the United Nations to the Department of State[1]

New York, June 21, 1962, 7 p.m.

4078. Statements by SYG UN to Advisory Comite on Administrative and Budgetary Questions (ACABQ).

U Thant made fol statements to ACABQ in closed mtg today.

1. At next GA he intends propose increase in working capital fund to $40–$45 million.

2. UN will have explore new sources of revenue to help finance peace-keeping operations. (However, Turner and Vaughn/UN informed ACABQ they saw no prospects increasing UN income substantially from sources other than governmental contributions. By substantially they meant in excess of $1 million.)

3. He informed by number of govts they withholding decision purchase UN bonds until after affirmative opinion of ICJ.

4. He intends review ONUC financial situation and future of ONUC operation with Congo Advisory Comite in July and decide then what recommendations make to SC re future of ONUC operation. He believes cost of ONUC operation can be substantially reduced in second half 1962.

5. He has made clear to all parties interested in Ruanda-Urundi, including sponsors of Afro-Asian res, that any UN mil personnel going to R-U would have their activities limited to advice, instruction, and observation. Accordingly, he anticipated that UN expenses in connection with R-U would not be sizeable.

6. In response to question of Sokirkin (USSR), he stated he had no present intention submitting report to 17th GA on recommendations of Comite of 8 (Comite of Experts on review of activities and organization of Secretariat).

7. Said UN will not incur any cost in connection with controversy between Indonesia and Netherlands re New Guinea since two govts concerned had indicated they would share all costs.

Plimpton

---

[1] Source: National Archives and Records Administration, RG 59, Central Files 1960–63, 321.5/6–2162. Limited Official Use.

210.   **Letter From the Assistant Secretary of State for International Organization Affairs (Cleveland) to the Representative to the United Nations (Stevenson)**[1]

Washington, June 22, 1962.

SUBJECT

The NSC Meeting on the UN

Dear Adlai:

You have in New York two excellent pieces of briefing material, both of which are in Dick Pederson's hands. One is a series of talking points drafted here as a result of your request to me. A clean copy of this draft is attached. The other is an excellent outline drafted by Dick Pederson, entitled "U.S. Policy as Seen from New York".[2]

In this letter I am making some additional suggestions, that have to do with the kind of presentation which would, it seems to me, best serve the purpose of the NSC meeting itself.

1. First, as to the general theme. The most important impression for you to leave on your audience Tuesday,[3] it seems to me, is that *you think of the UN as an instrument of U.S. policy.*

It is a *complicated* instrument, of course, because it is also an instrument of the foreign policy of 103 other countries. But we are not without resources and skill to get our way where it matters.

It is also a *limited* instrument: if we want to defend Europe, the UN is largely irrelevant and NATO is essential. If we want to relate ourselves to the less-developed countries of Asia, Africa and Latin America, the UN is essential and NATO is irrelevant.

It is an *important* instrument, not only because it generates a great deal of the world's political noise, but because it now has the *capacity to act:* The UN system spends $502.3 million a year, $311.5 million of which is U.S. contributions to various programs and projects. The UN employs 33,494 civilians and has 22,600 troops in the field. It has successfully intervened in eight peacekeeping situations (Greece, Indonesia, Kashmir, Korea, Suez Crisis, Lebanon, Laos, and the Congo), and has operated as the "third man" in a very large number of international disputes (current examples: Ellsworth Bunker on West New Guinea, Joseph Johnson on Palestine Refugees).

---

[1] Source: Kennedy Library, Cleveland Papers, NSC Meeting—Gov. Stevenson, June 26, 1962, Box 20. Confidential. A June 22 covering memorandum from Cleveland forwarded the letter and Tabs A and B to Acting Secretary Ball, with copies to Under Secretary for Political Affairs McGhee, ACDA Director Foster, and McGeorge Bundy.

[2] Tabs A and B, neither printed.

[3] June 26.

2. It is essential to make a clear distinction between what is symbolic and what is real in the UN. The General Assembly session we are just winding up contains one excellent example of each. The General Assembly has been (a) deciding the future of Ruanda-Urundi, making important executive decisions that will really affect the lives of five million Rwandans and Burundis; and it has also been (b) holding a big public protest rally on the situation in Southern Rhodesia, for which the GA has no responsibility. It is notable that the delegates are a good deal soberer on Rwanda-Urundi than they are on Southern Rhodesia.

On this point, you might use an analogy: There is a difference, in Congress, between a joint resolution on freeing the captive nations of Europe, and an executive decision to move the Marines into Eastern Europe during the Hungary revolt—which was carefully not done by the administration and not recommended to the Congress.

Throughout the field of UN affairs, it is essential to keep clearly in mind this distinction between what is talk and what is action. The newspapers do not make this distinction, most of the time—witness recent commentaries by Tom Hamilton in *The Times* and Roscoe Drummond in the *Herald-Tribune*. But most of the UN delegates make this distinction pretty clearly and it behooves responsible Americans to be clear about it.

3. I would strongly recommend that the classified nature of this discussion be exploited by regular use of incidents to illustrate general points. What I mean is that you should tell stories and name names that could not be told and named in public to help bring your points to life. Examples of the kind of thing I have in mind are:

—reference to some African or Asian who performed as a demigod but sobered up when given the chairmanship of a committee or some other responsible task (Miss Brooks? Or hasn't she sobered up enough to be a good example?)

—or perhaps of the embarrassment caused to other delegations from new countries when one of their members behaves irresponsibly (Jaja Wachuku?).

—an actual incident supporting the point that the eight neutralists at Geneva have been educated and impressed by our performance at the Geneva Disarmament Conference. (We will try to provide one.)

—perhaps a story or two to make the point that we have some pretty good pipelines into other delegations and into international caucuses—i.e., that we have a reasonably good intelligence system in New York.

—perhaps the now-it-can-be-told story about the behind-the-scenes negotiations leading to the election of U Thant. (I have in mind here the thought that in the National Security Council you are in a position to blow our horn on some quiet diplomatic victories which we cannot claim out loud.)

—perhaps a reference to the frustrations inherent in the business due to the fact that we frequently cannot take credit for what we've done because we have to exercise leadership without appearing to lead, much less to dominate.

4. It is entirely clear that no great power, and probably no minor power either, is going to violate what it regards as its own security interests to bow to majority of the UN or even to the principles of its Charter. Khrushchev has said this in so many words. We have not, but only because we have had no need to. The differences between the U. S. and Soviet performances in the United Nations reflect the fact that UN stands for a kind of world diametrically opposed to the Soviet vision of a Communist one-world; that the U.S. normally can agree with the majority of the members and the Soviet Union normally cannot agree with the majority; and that the Charter of the UN is an accurate projection of our own basic documents on the international plane and is anathema to the Soviet Union.

5. The UN is a politico-parliamentary mechanism which operates according to procedures which are familiar to us and unfamiliar to the Soviet Union, which partly accounts for why we do as well there as we do. Personally, I am much less impressed with the Russians now than I was when I took over this job a year and a half ago. In diplomatic maneuvering they seem to me to be rigid and often clumsy; sometimes they seem not to do their homework adequately, and often they operate against their own long-range interests (as in boycotting the Security Council in 1950 and boycotting the operation—thereby excluding themselves from any influence in it or over it—in the Congo).

6. Building the UN is the world's toughest, most complex, most delicate, most advanced task of institution building in the world. It is only seized of disputes after other forums and tactics have been exhausted. But the stake is no less than a future system of world order in which the U.S. can find long-term security in the post-colonial age of atoms and outer space. In a small way, we are learning some of the essential operational lessons that would make it possible to organize a world order if we can ever get anywhere in the disarmament negotiations.

Warmest regards,

Sincerely,

Harlan Cleveland[4]

---

[4] Printed from a copy that bears this typed signature.

211.　Summary Record of the 500th Meeting of the National Security Council[1]

Washington, June 26, 1962, 10:30 a.m.

Ambassador Stevenson read the attached paper, as marked.[2]

In response to a request by the President, Ambassador Stevenson discussed in general the major issues which will arise in the 17th General Assembly of the UN, which begins September 19th. He predicted a long and different session which would deal with some 90 issues. Among the problems which will have to be faced are:

a. The Latin American caucus is breaking up. We can no longer count on their voting as a body. Dissidents are Brazil, Mexico, Bolivia and Chile. The major cause of the breakup is differences over Cuba.

b. The African vote is increasing in strength, but the problem which this creates is not much worse than we faced last year.

c. The colonial issue will become more difficult this year because the areas under discussion now are the white settler areas involving the UK and Portugal.

The President complimented Ambassador Stevenson on his presentation and suggested that a transcript of his remarks be circulated to the Council members. He asked Ambassador Stevenson to discuss the problems of Chinese Representation.

Ambassador Stevenson replied that if the Chinese Communists continue the strident tone of their public statements, and if Sino-Soviet differences remain the same, the representation issue will be less difficult this year than last. He said that Chiang's invasion statements were laughed at in New York and asked how we could control such statements in order to avoid the embarrassment which they cause us. In his view, the Chinese Communist buildup was provoked in part by the fear of invasion, but it might be related to local unrest on the mainland. He predicted that a Soviet resolution on Chinese representation would be soundly defeated, but he anticipated serious trouble for us if the Russians asked only for the admission of the Chinese Communists and not for the expulsion of the Chinese Nationalists.

In response to the President's question as to how he should answer press queries with respect to our policy toward Quemoy and Matsu,

---

[1] Source: Kennedy Library, National Security Files, Meeting and Memoranda Series, NSC Meetings, 1962, No. 500, 6/26/62, Box 313. Confidential. No drafting information appears on the document. Another record of this meeting, prepared by McCone, is in the Central Intelligence Agency, DCI (McCone) Files, Job 80–B01285A, SCI Meetings with the President, Box 6.

[2] Not found.

Ambassador Stevenson said any answer would be difficult prior to the receipt of a report from Ambassador Kirk. He wondered whether Chiang was losing control of his government, and he felt that we should make clear that the U.S. would not support an invasion of the mainland. He admitted that he would like to say we are leaving the islands, but he fully recognizes that we cannot so state. He felt that all that could be said was that the U.S. supports its treaty commitment to defend Formosa, and that this commitment does not involve support of a mainland invasion.

The President commented on the number of troublesome problems which are dealt with in the UN. He expressed his desire to be certain that the White House is closely coordinated with the UN Mission in New York and asked whether the White House was receiving adequate intelligence material from the UN Mission.

Ambassador Stevenson said the Mission was filing thousands of words of intelligence daily to Washington. There is nothing wrong with the reporting, but he believed that if there were more officers assigned to the Mission, it would be possible to do more interpretive reporting, which he felt would be of great value to Washington. He indicated that the Mission's relations with the Department of Defense were satisfactory and cited the long service of Admiral Wellborn on the UN Military Staff Committee. His link on disarmament matters is William Foster. He felt that the tie to State Department could be improved. He acknowledged that there were some inadequacies in information furnished and he promised to pay more attention to improving this situation. He felt that more information to the White House could be provided and he felt that direct reporting could be handled by summaries of Mission actions.

In response to a question by Mr. Bundy about the debate on outer space in the UN, Ambassador Stevenson predicted that there will be a sizeable amount of emotional discussion of ways of avoiding the use of outer space for military purposes. He said we now lead in the use of space for peaceful purposes, but we are criticized for proposing high altitude nuclear tests. He referred to public statements indicating that we are moving toward the military use of outer space and suggested that such statements should be related to the President's speech last fall.

Mr. Bundy said we did have a military program in space, but this is a peaceful program. He said that many people think that any military program is a violation of the principles stated by the President in his speech. He said we need to do a considerable amount of educational work in order to make clear that military uses of outer space were peaceful uses and not a contradiction of the President's policy.

Ambassador Stevenson agreed and suggested that a group be formed to undertake this educational work. He suggested that we make our views clear to the British.

Mr. Cleveland said there was considerable confusion on this subject. He noted that we do not say that space was to be reserved for peaceful uses only. He then said many had not accepted the analogy of outer space being the same as the use of the high seas by military ships on peaceful missions.

Mr. Bundy referred to the questions of weapons of mass destruction in outer space and the problem of inspecting outer space.

Ambassador Stevenson said that we did not contemplate the use of force in space, but we must continue to discuss the weapons problem in outer space in the Geneva disarmament talks. He hoped that it would be possible to keep this subject from being discussed by the General Assembly.

Mr. Foster said we could keep the actual negotiations on the subject in Geneva, even though the Geneva talks were recessed, but we could not prevent speeches from being made at the UN.

Ambassador Stevenson resumed his discussion of General Assembly problems:

a. Nuclear testing, ban-the-bomb resolutions, and efforts to prevent the proliferation of nuclear weapons.
b. Colonialism.
c. Denuclearized shots. (The President's view was that if the countries in a proposed zone agree to denuclearization, we cannot vote against their action.)
d. Palestine. (The work of Joseph Johnson on the refugee problem would be helpful this session.)
e. Election of a Secretary General. (U Thant may accept again. His views may be clearer after he visits Moscow in July.)
f. Integrity of the UN Secretariat. (Soviet attacks will continue. The Africans are trying to use population figures as the criteria for representation on commissions in UN business.)
g. Long-term UN financing. (The importance of the bond issue is clear.)
h. The decade of development.
i. World trade. (The Common Market is viewed with concern by some UN members, as was expressed in the conference of 30 non-aligned states in Cairo. The USSR proposal for a world trade conference may also be troublesome.)
j. Cold war items. (These items are becoming unpopular and the question arises as to whether we should continue to press them. The main one, Hungary, is difficult because we do not know how to abandon the issue. The effort last year to resolve the problem by having the Secretary General visit Hungary at the time the Hungarians granted amnesty to their political prisoners did not work out. The Tibet issue is one that we are not pushing. The Korea issue is ours, but we may attempt to keep it out of discussion this session.)
k. Finance problems. (U Thant is deeply concerned about the immediate financial situation. He is cutting costs of the military in the Congo, but he fears that if the Congo situation is not resolved promptly, mili-

tary units will be withdrawn and some states now committed to buy UN bonds will not fulfill their pledges.)

There followed a discussion of current plans to bring agreement in the Congo. The President made clear his view that we must move in concert with the British and the Belgians and that the U.S. should make no commitment to use force in the Congo until there had been further discussion of any such proposal at the White House.

The President concluded the meeting by again expressing his appreciation to Ambassador Stevenson. He mentioned again that the closest possible liaison should be maintained among State, Defense, the White House and the UN Mission in New York.

---

212.   Memorandum From the Assistant Secretary of State for European Affairs (Kohler) to the Assistant Secretary of State for International Organization Affairs (Cleveland)[1]

Washington, July 3, 1962.

SUBJECT

Intimations of Soviet Desire for Bilateral Discussion of 17th General Assembly

I found the memorandum of conversation between Joe Sisco and the Soviet Counselor of Embassy of June 11 interesting indeed.[2] However, considering the general Soviet tactic at this time of suggesting quiet talks with the U.S. on a number of different issues, I am not surprised by the "personal suggestion" of Kornienko that a Stevenson–Zorin discussion would be desirable.

As a quick reaction it is my feeling that: (1) We not take the initiative in proposing such talks but respond should Zorin or some other responsible Soviet official repeat Kornienko's "personal suggestion." (2) Considering the number of issues in which both the USSR and the U.S. have an active interest at the time, I can understand that there are some possible agenda items which the USSR might wish to treat with caution

---

[1] Source: National Archives and Records Administration, RG 59, Central Files 1960–63, 616.61/7–362. Limited Official Use. Drafted by William O. Anderson on July 2. Cleveland forwarded a copy to Secretary Rusk under cover of a July 19 memorandum. (Ibid., 611.61/7–1962)

[2] Document 208.

for its own reasons. Thus, a convergence of interests between us is possible at least in a limited sense. Over-all, however, my judgment is substantially the same as that which you expressed in your letter of June 25 to Ambassador Stevenson: i.e., "While this probably would not be productive of very much agreement, it might be a useful exercise."[3]

Assuming that the Secretary does go to Geneva for the purpose of signing the Laotian agreements approximately the third week of July, and if there is indeed a serious Soviet intent to arrange a discussion of General Assembly matters, Gromyko would have an opportunity to suggest it at that time. In any event, the actual discussions, if they develop, probably should be centered in New York where Ambassador Stevenson and his staff have the details at their fingertips.

I would assume that, should such talks take place, appropriate steps would be taken to keep our allies fully informed.

---

[3] This letter has not been found.

---

213. Memorandum From Acting Secretary of State Ball to President Kennedy[1]

Washington, July 20, 1962.

SUBJECT

U Thant Visit to Washington

While talking with U Thant, Acting Secretary General of the United Nations, in April Assistant Secretary Cleveland expressed the hope that he would come to Washington for a visit during the summer. Subsequently U Thant indicated to Governor Stevenson that he would like to come to Washington but would expect a formal invitation from Governor Stevenson.

I believe it would be desirable for you to receive him in Washington for a brief visit early in September before the General Assembly opens for the following reasons:

1. U Thant has already visited several European capitals, including London, Dublin, Oslo and Paris, this summer and plans to visit

---

[1] Source: National Archives and Records Administration, RG 59, Central Files 1960–63, 310/7–2162. Confidential. Drafted by Alfred E. Wellons on July 20 (retyped in S/S on July 21); cleared by Francis E. Meloy, Jr., Samuel L. King, Cleveland, and Sisco. An attached biographical sketch of U Thant is not printed.

Moscow, Warsaw, Prague and Vienna from August 24 through September 4, 1962. A visit to Washington would be an appropriate and desirable conclusion to his tours of major European capitals.

2. A Thant visit would permit a useful exchange of views with him both on his European trips and on the forthcoming session of his General Assembly.

3. No Secretary General of the United Nations has visited the White House since May, 1953 (Hammarskjold).[2]

Receiving U Thant would demonstrate your continued personal interest in the United Nations as well as your satisfaction with the role he has played as Acting Secretary General. U Thant may be elected this fall to the full five year term of Secretary General of the United Nations which begins in April, 1963, although he has not yet admitted that he is even a contender for that position. From our point of view, Thant has done a good job so far and it would be difficult to find a better man who could be elected Secretary General at this juncture of world affairs.

I therefore recommend that you issue an invitation for U Thant to visit Washington, preferably on September 10 or 11, 1962. I also recommend that you host a small luncheon for Thant during his visit to Washington and that you agree to meet with him for about one hour beginning at 4:00 p.m. on the day of his visit.

George W. Ball[3]

---

[2] This meeting with President Eisenhower took place on May 8, 1953.

[3] Printed from a copy that indicates that Ball signed the original.

214.   Memorandum From the Executive Secretary of the
         Department of State (Brubeck) to the President's Special
         Assistant for National Security Affairs (Bundy)[1]

Washington, July 26, 1962.

SUBJECT

The Candidacy of Sir Zafrulla Khan (Pakistan) for President of the Seventeenth
General Assembly

There are two announced candidates for President of the
Seventeenth General Assembly—Sir Zafrulla Khan and Dr. G. P.
Malalasekera, Representatives, respectively, of Pakistan and Ceylon to
the United Nations. This year is generally recognized as an "Asian
year" since the last Assembly President from this area was Prince Wan
of Thailand in 1956. The Zafrulla candidacy appears to have attracted
substantial support and has the quiet endorsement of the Secretary
General. So far as we are aware, the Malalasekera candidacy is supported only by the Soviet bloc and India.

Malalasekera formally announced his candidacy on May 3. At that
time both Zafrulla and Okasaki, the Japanese United Nations
Representative, had indicated their interest in the presidency to our
Mission in New York and had been told that either would be acceptable
to us. Okasaki, in fact, informed our United Nations Mission that he
was a candidate on April 26 but he has never circulated a formal
announcement, as is customary. We avoided taking any position in
favor of one against the other in view of our close relations with both
Pakistan and Japan. The situation was made more delicate by the fact
that Zafrulla (and the Pakistan Government) have held us primarily
responsible for Zafrulla's failure to be reelected to the International
Court of Justice last year, when we supported the Japanese candidate
and not Zafrulla. Okasaki made it clear that he did not wish to enter
into an open contest with Zafrulla and has not pressed his candidacy
since Zafrulla formally announced his candidacy on May 11.

We have so far given no formal commitment of support to Zafrulla,
not wishing to do so until the Security Council's consideration of

---

[1] Source: Kennedy Library, National Security Files, Subjects Series, United Nations
(General), 7/62–8/62, Box 311. Confidential. A July 26 covering note to Brubeck from Sam
Belk reads: "The attached memorandum was prepared at my request following our chat
on Tuesday. One minor point not mentioned in the memorandum was that Malalasekera,
the Ceylonese candidate, was once Ambassador to Moscow and has the reputation of having a disposition very much like Krishna Menon's. In view of the difficulties US-Indian
relations have encountered over the past year and chronically bad Indian-Pak relations, I
think we should expect Menon to make every effort to whip the Assembly into a frenzy
in an attempt to keep Zafrulla from being elected."

Kashmir had been concluded and the Indian aid issue was out of the way. However, this has been a matter of timing rather than of substance. Malalasekera would not make an acceptable General Assembly President, not only because of his Government's radical neutrality but because he, personally, is widely regarded as both incompetent and unreliable. It appears very unlikely that Okasaki would advance his candidacy so long as Zafrulla is a candidate and, in any event, our United Nations Mission believes it is too late for him to make an effective campaign.

Our Embassy in New Delhi is concerned that open United States support of Zafrulla's candidacy may exacerbate United States-Indian relations because of current Indian-Pakistan tensions, Zafrulla's role in the Kashmir debate in the Security Council, and the possibility that the Kashmir issue will be brought to the General Assembly. We believe it highly unlikely that Pakistan would bring Kashmir to the General Assembly. However, were we to have any indication that Pakistan might do so, we would indicate our opposition. The Pakistan United Nations Delegation has recommended to Karachi against this and believes the Government will accept its recommendation. We agree with this estimate on the basis of the clear self interest of both Pakistan, and Zafrulla personally, in not having this issue raised at the Seventeenth General Assembly.

We have authorized our United Nations Mission to give a formal commitment of support to Zafrulla next week after having made clear to him our views of the handling of the Chinese representation issue at the Seventeenth General Assembly. Pakistan did not support us on this issue at the Sixteenth General Assembly and current Pakistan-Chinese Communist exchanges are not reassuring. However, we would expect Zafrulla as a reputable jurist to be an impartial presiding officer and we believe our position on the handling of the Chinese representation issue at the Seventeenth Session to be well founded from the legal standpoint. We are not in a position to exact a quid pro quo from him since Malalasekera provides no alternative. We should, however, make completely clear to Zafrulla our unshakeable determination not to be defeated on this issue.

We do not propose to seek assurances from him with respect to Kashmir since we believe it most unlikely Pakistan would seriously consider raising this issue at the forthcoming session and we do not wish to waste our bargaining power. We do, however, intend to point out that an active United States campaign on behalf of Zafrulla might well prove counterproductive by provoking an organized Indian campaign against him. We will of course, as is our usual custom, make known our support of him when asked and in the course of our normal pre-Assembly consultations. Since the vote is by secret ballot, without nominations or discussion, it is not our custom to make any public announcement of how the United States will vote.

C. K. Johnson[2]

---

[2] Johnson signed for Brubeck above Brubeck's typed signature.

---

215. Circular Telegram From the Department of State to Certain Posts[1]

Washington, August 10, 1962, 7:14 p.m.

227. Subject: Acceptance by 17th UNGA of ICJ Advisory Opinion on UN Expenses. Embassy should approach FonOff at highest appropriate level with objective of assuring its support of acceptance by 17th UNGA of ICJ Advisory Opinion on Certain Expenses of the UN. The following points may be useful in your presentation.

1. ICJ Advisory Opinion of 20 July authoritatively resolves in the affirmative legal question of whether UN assessments for Congo and UNEF are "expenses of the Organization" within the meaning of Article 17(2) of the Charter. Consequence is that all Members are legally bound to pay outstanding UNEF and ONUC assessments. ICJ decision by vote 9–5. Two of dissents were not on substance decision, but on ability of Court to deal with question; accordingly, decision actually 9–3 with 2 "abstentions."

2. While there have been differences of view among some UN Members on binding character of UNEF and ONUC assessments, USG trusts addressee Govt unites with it in adherence to rule of law in world affairs and importance of strengthening role of law in UN.

3. Just as in a contentious case, so in advisory opinion ICJ has declared the law. As report of 6th Committee UNGA noted, "the authoritative nature of the advisory opinion should be taken for granted" (A/1101, p. 200).

4. UNGA has unfailingly accepted or acted upon all past advisory opinions (nine). 17th UNGA inevitably will be confronted with question

---

[1] Source: National Archives and Records Administration, RG 59, Central Files 1960–63, 320/8–1062. Confidential. Drafted by Stephen M. Schwebel on August 7; cleared by George N. Monsma, Jesse MacKnight, Richard Friedman, James M. Ludlow, Wilbur H. Ziehl, William B. Buffum, Louise McNutt, and Abram Chayes; and approved by Schwebel. Sent to all posts except those in the Soviet bloc, Paris, Cairo, and Mexico City.

of action in respect to *Expenses* opinion, which already appears as item on provisional agenda. USG assumes 17th UNGA will accept *Expenses* opinion, by resolution noting or approving it. USG attaches highest importance to such acceptance. While it trusts opinion will be accepted as matter of course, USG prepared if necessary to exert its most earnest efforts to insure acceptance. Failure to accept Court's opinion would gravely damage prestige and potential of international law, standing of ICJ, integrity of UN, and responsibility of UN membership.

5. Accordingly, USG hopes addressee Govt will support acceptance of *Expenses* opinion by 17th UNGA, and would appreciate assurance to that effect.

6. Action by UNGA in accordance with *Expenses* opinion has great importance for US public opinion. President and Dept have publicly committed USG to acceptance and enforcement by UN of *Expenses* opinion.

7. FYI. In connection with enforcement, US Congress and public much concerned with large amount arrears on Congo and UNEF accounts. Prompt payment of all or part of arrears would have significant and immediate effect on reversing growing dissatisfaction here with UN Members considered by Congressional and public opinion to be "financially irresponsible." This would also facilitate US purchase $100 million bonds from UN. End FYI.

For all addressee posts except Addis Ababa, Abidjan, Ankara, Athens, Bangkok, Bangui, Brussels, Canberra, Caracas, Colombo, Copenhagen, Dakar, Dublin, Hague, Helsinki, Karachi, Kuala Lumpur, Lagos, Leopoldville, Libreville, Lome, London, Luxembourg, Manila, Monrovia, New Delhi, Nicosia, Oslo, Ottawa, Phnom Penh, Quito, Rangoon, Reykjavik, Stockholm, Tokyo, Tunis, Wellington, Yaounde:

If opportunity arises and in your judgment raising question will not prejudice objective of securing support for acceptance of Court's opinion, you may suggest that some prompt payment on addressee Govt's arrears would be highly desirable.

For Athens, Brussels, Caracas and Manila:

Seek opportunity to state that payment by addressee Govt of its arrears now would mitigate UN financial crisis and, in view of its influential position in UN, assist effort of SYG to collect other arrears, facilitate US purchase of UN bonds, and constitute important and concrete support of ICJ opinion. To maximize effect on other Members thereby promoting fiscal responsibility so urgently needed if UN is to survive as important force for world order, public announcement by Govt that payment is being made in response to Court opinion highly desirable. Announcement might state that Court has "settled any question of mandatory character of expenses" for UNEF and Congo which is occasion for Govt making these payments.

For Addis Ababa and Lome:

Seek opportunity to state, if in your judgment raising question not prejudicial to US interests, that payment by addressee Govt of its arrears now would, in view of its influential position, assist effort of SYG to collect other arrears, mitigate UN financial crisis, facilitate US purchase of UN bonds, and constitute important and concrete support of ICJ opinion. To maximize effect on other members thereby promoting fiscal responsibility so urgently needed if UN is to survive as important force for world order, public announcement by Govt that payment is being made in response to Court opinion highly desirable. Announcement might state that Court has "settled any question of mandatory character of expenses" for UNEF and Congo which is occasion for Govt making these payments.

8. *For La Paz, Guatemala and Asuncion:* Foregoing should be correlated with Embassy's action pursuant to Depttel sent to La Paz 60, Guatemala 15 and Asuncion 20.[2]

9. *For WE posts and Canberra, Ottawa and Wellington:* Stavropoulos (UN Legal Under Secretary) and Dept for tactical reasons disposed to seek allocation of item on ICJ opinion directly to Plenary rather than Fifth Committee or other GA Committee. Inquire view FonOff.

10. Report reactions, rpt info USUN.

11. *For French Speaking Posts:* French text this cable follows.[3]

Rusk

---

[2] This telegram, dated July 23, advised these Embassies that, according to the ICJ advisory opinion of July 20, assessments levied for UNEF and UNOC were "expenses of the Organization" within the meaning of Article 17 of the UN Charter, and should be counted toward a country's arrears under Article 19. (Ibid., 312/7–2362)

[3] Not found.

216.   Memorandum From Acting Secretary of State Ball to President Kennedy[1]

Washington, August 16, 1962.

SUBJECT

The Seventeenth General Assembly

You have called a meeting for 4:00 p.m., on Tuesday, August 21, to consider United States strategy at the 17th Session of the General Assembly. I am attaching a strategy paper which has been fully considered throughout the Department, with Ambassador Stevenson and his staff, and with the Secretary.[2]

Last year our objective was to get certain activities started or restarted in the United Nations: to begin disarmament talks on a new basis, to get the United Nations and some of its constituent agencies into the outer space business, and to put more vigor into economic and social activities under a UN Decade of Development.

This year, the Organization needs a breathing spell in which to consolidate its strength, get its finances in order, and improve its executive capacity for peacekeeping and nation-building. In general, we believe the United States should not try to add significant new tasks to its load this fall, except a new emphasis on the development and use of peaceful settlement procedures under the United Nations. The successful conclusion of the ticklish negotiations over West New Guinea helps re-emphasize the importance of the "third man" in international politics.

Nearly every element of United States foreign policy enters into planning for a General Assembly. But in our meeting on Tuesday, I suggest we focus on the following issues on which we need a clear signal from you as a basis for the wide consultations on many subjects which will be undertaken between now and September 18 in New York and with Foreign Offices all over the world:

1. Peaceful Settlement and Development.

The themes of the opening United States speech in the general debate should be (a) the further development under the United Nations of the machinery of pacific settlement, and (b) the opportunities for growing prosperity as the more advanced nations work with the less-developed nations in a broad United Nations framework which makes

---

[1] Source: Kennedy Library, National Security Files, Subjects Series, United Nations (General), 7/62–8/62, Box 311. Confidential. Forwarded to Bundy under a covering note from Deputy Executive Secretary Brubeck, also dated August 16.

[2] This 22-page paper is not printed.

possible a relationship of equality and mutual respect between stronger and weaker members of the international economy.

United Nations resources for "quiet diplomacy" need to be developed as a real alternative to acrimonious public debate. The strategy paper includes suggestions for reforms in General Assembly procedures, the use of rapporteurs, establishment of a United Nations institute in this field, and the development of international law.

2. United Nations Finances.

The General Assembly will have to face up to the question, "After the Bond Issue, What?". Presumably we want to expand the regular budget to take care of as much of the peacekeeping expense as possible. Beyond a rise in the regular budget, there is a fork in the road: one road leads to a special scale in which the United States would probably have to pay 44% or so; the other is to finance each United Nations peace-and-security operation by special voluntary contributions from a smaller number of countries which would, however, have more explicit control over the operations to which they are contributing. We need to make a political judgment, in consultation with the Congress, which of these roads best serves the United States national interest.

3. Disarmament and Nuclear Issues.

Our objective should be to keep the Geneva discussions alive and use them to prevent irresponsible exhortations from being passed as resolutions in the General Assembly. We will want to make clear that we don't want other nations to develop national nuclear capabilities, but clearly leave the door ajar to a multilateral NATO nuclear deterrent. We should support any moves by other countries (for example, the Africans) to pass self-denying ordinances against nuclear weapons in their zones. And, we should press in the General Assembly for a nuclear test ban along the lines we finally decide to recommend in Geneva, resisting again (as we did last year) any uninspected moratorium. (In addition to the comprehensive test ban, ACDA is considering a recommendation to revive the atmospheric test ban idea in some form.)

4. Outer Space.

The fact that the Soviets put two men in space last week changes the political atmosphere without changing the basic problem. Our objective in the United Nations should be to push along the arrangements for wide cooperation in the use of space for weather services and weather research, and for communications. One United Nations "operation" can probably be started, an international rocket sounding facility near the geomagnetic equator, probably in India.

Defense of our space program will also be high on the agenda. A clear pronouncement on our part as to the peaceful motivations of our military space program will be essential.

5. *Colonial Issues.*

We will face a series of dilemmas with mounting pressures from the Africans and Asians for rapid solutions to the most complicated "hard core" colonial problems, including not only those created by South Africa and Portugal policies, but a growing attention to British decolonization plans, particularly in the Federation.

One troublesome issue is the irresponsible way in which the Committee of 17 has developed; we would like to consider with you the advantages and the disadvantages of forcing the Soviets off the Committee of 17 by getting off the Committee ourselves.

We will face this year, for the first time in a serious way, the question of sanctions by the General Assembly to express its dissatisfaction with policies of colonial powers. The sanctions issue may arise in various forms requiring on our part various types of response. In the foreseeable cases, we should vigorously oppose sanctions as a way of dealing with Portuguese colonial policy and South African race policy; if the sanctions issue is brought up in connection with Katanga, it is not quite so clear that we would want to rule out United Nations legislation on the subject.

6. *Congo.*[3]

If, as is not improbable, the present "Course of Action" fails to produce a reconciliation between Leopoldville and Elisabethville, we will have to work out some other way of disengaging the United Nations from its peacekeeping responsibility in the Congo before the United Nations runs out of Bond money, energy, and will to cope with the problem.

7. *UNRWA.*

The United Nations Relief and Works Agency comes up for extension this year. Our bet will presumably be on the Johnson proposals. We will need to protect them from diversionary resolutions from both sides; but we should avoid the appearance of opposition to direct negotiations between Israel and the Arab states whenever in the future that becomes possible.

8. *Hungary.*

The Hungary item has become very unpopular in the General Assembly because of its repetitive character and its status as a "Cold

---

[3] In the margin next to this item, Bundy wrote, "G. Ball."

War" issue. On the other hand, it is an important issue to some of the nationality groups in this country. The problem is to make clear our continuing opposition to Communist oppression in Hungary while eliminating the item as a hardy perennial on the General Assembly agenda.

9. Berlin.

Berlin is not on the General Assembly agenda. Khrushchev may decide to use the 17th General Assembly to present the Soviet case either before or after a "Peace Treaty" with East Germany. We have developed a separate contingency paper on this topic.[4]

Ambassador Stevenson will be in Washington August 21 for the meeting in your offices on these matters.

George W. Ball[5]

---

[4] In the margin, Bundy wrote: "Paper not at hand."

[5] Printed from a copy that bears this stamped signature.

---

217. Memorandum of Conversation[1]

Washington, August 21, 1962.

SUBJECT

United States Strategy at the 17th General Assembly

PARTICIPANTS

The President
The Secretary
Harlan Cleveland—IO
Ambassador Stevenson
Arthur Schlesinger
Joseph J. Sisco—UNP

The following principal points emerged from the discussion with the President on US strategy in the United Nations at the 17th General Assembly.

---

[1] Source: Kennedy Library, National Security Files, Subjects Series, United Nations (General), 7/62–8/62, Box 311. Confidential. Drafted by Sisco and approved in S on August 27 and in the White House on August 29. Transmitted to Bundy under cover of an August 31 memorandum.

1. Presence of the President at the UNGA.

The President felt we could not advise U Thant to oppose Khrushchev's attendance at the General Assembly. He agreed U Thant might be asked to indicate to Khrushchev that if he decides to come to the General Assembly it might be for only a few days. While the President thought it was probably inevitable that other chiefs of state and government would want to attend if Khrushchev came to the Assembly, he agreed that U Thant might also be advised to tell Khrushchev it would be desirable not to make this matter a big show and that he should not encourage attendance of Tito, Nasser, Castro, etc. As to the President's plans, the matter would be kept open pending U Thant's return from Moscow. Governor Stevenson felt the President, without a lot of the build-up of last year, should come to the General Assembly, make a temperate, moderate speech, and that this would help maintain public confidence in the United Nations in this country. The Secretary felt that the President's attendance again, and on more or less a regular yearly basis, might be resented by other delegations. He thought that if Khrushchev does not come then perhaps the President might go to the General Assembly and meet the delegates at a reception or possibly go up later in the session to make a major speech on disarmament. The President felt that if Khrushchev comes to the Assembly in the latter part of September he himself should go at the beginning of the session and speak before Khrushchev. If Khrushchev does not come to the General Assembly, the President is reserving judgment as to his attendance. In general, he was disinclined to go to the Assembly just twelve months after his last appearance. While leaving open whether he would attend in the absence of a Khrushchev appearance, the President asked that a possible draft speech be prepared for him so that he could make a determination on whether something worthwhile could be said. As to what might be included in such a speech, the Secretary suggested one section should be devoted to the settlement of disputes, citing in particular the role played by the United States on both the Laotian and West New Guinea issues. The Secretary felt also that some of the suggestions contained in the strategy paper[2] for strengthening the UN in the peaceful settlement field might be incorporated in the speech. Governor Stevenson said emphasis in the speech should be given to economic and social programs, trade, the Common Market and that this general area might provide one of several useful themes. Governor Stevenson also felt the speech should include a section on disarmament. In addition, he felt a strong pitch should be made in favor of responsible and moderate action on the part of the General Assembly as a way of increasing public confidence in the United Nations in this country.

---

[2] See Document 216 and footnote 2 thereto.

2. Visits of Chiefs of State and Governments.

The President asked that a memorandum be prepared for him suggesting the ways in which such visits should be handled. Should they be invited to Washington? Should the President see them in New York?

3. UN Finances.

Mr. Cleveland posed the question, "After the bond issue, what?" He said that there were two possibilities: a special scale in which the United States would probably have to pay 44% or so; the other is to finance each UN peace and security operation by special voluntary contributions. The President felt it was easier to get money from Congress to support peace-keeping operations in specific crises than to get it to agree on the specific percentage contribution the United States would make for all peace-keeping operations. He agreed preliminary consultations could be undertaken with members of Congress and with delegations at the United Nations on the question of long term financing. However, such consultations would be undertaken on the assumption there would be no formal Assembly action until late in the session or at a special session in the spring of next year.

4. General Assembly Delegation.

The President reviewed the delegation list and found it satisfactory. The formal papers nominating the members of the delegation will be sent to the President for approval in the next few days.

5. Colonial Questions.

The President agrees we should oppose sanctions as a way for the Assembly to deal with Portuguese colonial policy and the South African questions. He also agrees we should attempt to get the Soviets off the Committee of 17 on the assumption that we would also do the same. The Secretary reported we had made no progress in our negotiations with the Portuguese on the Azores base and that they have linked this question with the United States position in the United Nations on colonial questions. The Secretary said we want to make a strong effort to get the Azores base negotiations completed before the General Assembly gets involved in a number of the Portuguese colonial questions. The President agreed we should see how far we can get with the Portuguese on this matter, although he was not disposed to make concessions on the colonial issues if the Portuguese were not going to make any movement towards moderation and were going to use the base negotiations as a means of exerting pressure on us.

6. Hungary.

The President was interested in having this item come up late in the session. He hoped any procedure to keep this question under review, while at the same time eliminating it as a formal item on the agenda in the future, could be justified as a more effective way to deal with this matter now than in the past.

7. Outer Space.

The President agreed we should make a vigorous defense of various aspects of US space programs on which we anticipate Soviet attacks. He agreed with the Secretary's suggestion that the State Department, in consultation with the other interested departments, be asked to develop the lines of our response in speeches in the General Assembly on the four areas which the Soviets will attack: our alleged plans to "militarize" outer space; our alleged "contamination" of space through nuclear testing and project West Ford; our reconnaissance satellite program; and our alleged plan to achieve "US private monopolies" of space communications. The President agreed also we should try to secure Assembly approval for constructive measures of international space cooperation.

8. Berlin.

The President agreed with the Secretary we could not now determine whether Berlin would be brought to the United Nations and/or whether we should take an initiative ourselves if it appeared the Russians were about to do so. The Secretary reported contingency discussions were in train among the Four Powers on this question.

**218.   Telegram From the Department of State to the Mission to
the United Nations[1]**

Washington, August 24, 1962, 6:57 p.m.

456. Ref: Your 561, 562.[2] Subject: ICJ Opinion. Dept is firmly of view
ICJ opinion must be accepted by 17th GA and expects broad support for
res to this effect. We will not agree to postponement this action to 18th
GA.

Reftel does not make clear whether LA's contemplate payment in
installments would apply to entire amount of indebtedness due to UN, or
whether such mode of payment be applicable merely to arrearages in
excess of amount equal to or exceeding contributions due for preceding
two full years. Even after ICJ opinion holding UNEF and ONUC expenditures are "expenses of the Organization" within meaning Art. 17, it is not
anticipated arrears of Members will lead to loss of voting rights at 17th
GA. Further, the amounts by which Members are likely to exceed the Art.
19 limit in 1963—and therefore must pay to avoid loss of vote—will be
small enough so no installment payments plan required or advisable for
those excess amounts. Unless unexpected 17th GA financing resolutions
adopted, USSR and those with like arrearage situation will have until
January 1964 to pay relatively small arrears before Art. 19 becomes operative. Real problem is to get additional payments or arrears within Art. 19
limit in order to pay UN debts and improve UN cash position. As USUN
knows, important US objective (once ICJ opinion adopted) is to assist and
ensure arrears collection by SYG.

Dept believes it extremely undesirable consider special scale of
assessments "in conjunction with" consideration ICJ opinion. Past
UNEF and ONUC expenditures have already been assessed and ICJ
rendered opinion under these circumstances. For GA to reconsider
assessments already made would set plainly awkward and unworkable
precedent and would make sound financial planning impossible. As to
future scale of assessments, USUN aware US problems in proposing or
agreeing with special scale without full, prior, specific Congressional
consultation. Any special scale should be considered on its own merits
in any event, and should in no way be tied to GA acceptance ICJ opinion.

Ball

---

[1] Source: National Archives and Records Administration, RG 59, Central Files
1960–63, 320/8–2362. Confidential. Drafted by Van Heuven, Herbert Reis, and Wilbur H.
Ziehl; cleared by Sisco; and approved by Ernest Kerley.

[2] Both dated August 23. (Ibid.)

219. Research Memorandum Prepared in the Bureau of Intelligence and Research[1]

RSB–148   Washington, August 27, 1962.

SUBJECT

  Soviet Tactics on Some Major Issues at the 17th UN General Assembly

This memorandum assessing probable Soviet tactics at the forthcoming UN General Assembly was prepared in response to a request from Mr. Harlan Cleveland.

Abstract

Without attempting to exhaust the list of more than one hundred items on the General Assembly's agenda, this paper singles out those subjects on which Soviet initiatives or responses will be of particular concern for US policy.

We note the possibility of a Soviet initiative on Berlin in the UN and of Khrushchev's heading the Soviet delegation. The Soviets will almost certainly give major emphasis to a series of disarmament questions and attempt to make up for the relatively poor showing of their delegation at the Geneva talks.

The space exploit of Nikolayev and Popovich in addition to contributing a note of self-confidence to Moscow's foreign policy generally may foreshadow more pointed Soviet attacks on US space programs at the General Assembly. The Soviets will doubtless continue to exploit issues on which they can pose as the leaders of anti-colonialism and may attempt to present their proposal for an international trade conference as a means for underdeveloped countries to reply to the threat posed by the EEC.

I. GENERAL CONSIDERATIONS

Looking forward to the 17th session of the UN General Assembly, the Soviets do not expect the Assembly to endorse completely the Soviet line on any major issue before the UN. However, the Soviets probably do hope to use the forthcoming Assembly session to enhance their ability to influence neutralist opinion while at the same time attacking and if possible embarrassing the West on a number of issues.

UN Finances. The July 20 decision of the International Court of Justice (ICJ) affirming the legality of expenditures for peace-keeping operations carried out on the Assembly's initiative was a major setback for Soviet UN policy. The Soviets had taken the unprecedented step of

---

[1] Source: Kennedy Library, National Security Files, Subjects Series, United Nations (General), 7/62–8/62, Box 311. Secret. Sent from Roger Hilsman (INR) to Secretary Rusk.

participating in oral argument before the ICJ in their effort to stave off the decision. While Moscow may possibly hope to avoid either paying its arrears for peace-keeping expenses outside of the regular annual budgets or suffering the loss of its voting rights (the Soviets may reckon that the number of countries in arrears would make immediate imposition of the sanction envisaged by article 19 of the Charter politically impractical), the USSR nevertheless will probably wish to recoup the loss to its prestige occasioned by the ICJ decision by skillfully exploiting other issues before the General Assembly.

II. SPECIFIC ISSUES

1. Berlin and Germany

It is possible that the Soviet Union will bring the question of Berlin and Germany before the UN General Assembly this year. Humiliated when the German question was last debated at the UN a decade ago, the Soviets have been chary of opening up a debate of which they might easily lose control. However, in recent years Moscow appears to have been giving increasingly serious consideration to raising the issue before the UN, and this year Khrushchev, personally, appears to have been engaged in policy discussions on such an initiative.

The Soviet Union probably has no hope that the General Assembly would rubber-stamp the USSR's position on Berlin and Germany, but Moscow may now hope that the General Assembly—many of whose members have little interest in what appears to them to be a purely European problem—would tend to seek a "compromise" resolution which would be more damaging to the Western than to the Soviet position.

The Soviets might pose the question in terms of a Western threat to the peace in hopes of ultimately securing a "compromise" resolution enjoining both sides from the use of force in the Berlin dispute. The Soviet Union would hope that such a resolution would help to inhibit a vigorous Western response to unilateral changes in the local situation which the Soviet Union and the GDR might impose either in preparation for or by way of implementing a separate peace treaty. The Soviet Union might also believe that the UN General Assembly would be a favorable forum in which to plead the bloc's case for a free-city. The USSR might calculate that proposals to turn West Berlin into a free-city under UN auspices can be made to appear natural and reasonable to many members of the Assembly (if not to the two-thirds majority needed to carry a resolution), even though such proposals would seriously undermine Western rights. By appearing to make concessions by providing for continued US, UK and French troop presence as UN forces, Moscow might hope to make it difficult or even impossible for the West to reject the Soviet proposal and to maintain its position that Western presence in Berlin is not a negotiable question.

For the moment the Soviets do not appear to have decided yet whether or not to raise the Berlin issue at the 17th General Assembly.

If the Soviets decide to take a major initiative on Berlin at the UN, Khrushchev very probably would attend in order to present it in person. Khrushchev may decide to come in order to lend maximum dignity to Soviet participation, even if there is no Soviet move on Berlin. There have been hints and rumors that Khrushchev may be coming to the 17th General Assembly at some time during its deliberations, but at the present time there is no firm basis for predicting that he will attend.

2. Disarmament

Unless there is a dramatic move on Berlin, disarmament will probably be the central issue at the UN General Assembly, and Moscow apparently hopes to exploit the UN as a favorable forum to recover from its relatively poor showing at the Geneva disarmament conference.

From Moscow's point of view, the General Assembly, where disarmament debate is necessarily limited to generalizations, is a better forum than the disarmament conference, where the discussion gets down to details, for the Soviet Union's propagandistic approach to disarmament issues. While Soviet diplomats have indicated that the USSR will not risk another rebuff by the neutrals by repeating its June proposals for a prolonged recess in the disarmament conference with its reconvening in New York rather than Geneva, the possibility cannot be excluded that the Soviets will again seek to reconvene the conference in New York where it is likely to be overshadowed by other UN business.

General and Complete Disarmament. Moscow's principal objective will be to develop the image that it sincerely desires disarmament while the West is frustrating the will of world opinion by dragging its feet in disarmament negotiations. The Soviet Union will probably use its now standard propaganda line alleging US aggressive intentions (e.g., quoting out of context a remark attributed to President Kennedy in the Alsop article in the March 31 *Saturday Evening Post* to prove that the US administration advocates preventive war and citing the remark in Defense Secretary McNamara's June 16 speech about attacking military rather than civilian targets as an effort to sell the American people on the desirability of nuclear war) in order to lend the appearance of substance to their argument that US demands for controls are in reality schemes to develop espionage agencies on Soviet territory.

Moscow will probably continue to argue that the US plan is deficient because it prolongs the danger of nuclear war by not providing for the elimination of delivery vehicles in Stage I, because its provisions on transition from stage to stage (despite US willingness to forego having a veto over transition), do not guarantee that the disarmament process—once begun—will be carried through to completion, because failure to provide for abolition of foreign bases would give the US a strategic advantage and because the peace-keeping arrangements envisaged by the US would both throttle the national liberation movement and violate the UN Charter.

On the other hand the Soviets will attempt to create the impression that they are earnestly seeking disarmament by emphasizing the concessions they have made at Geneva where the USSR has accepted the US figures for Stage I reductions in conventional arms and has said that it was prepared to accept a five-year rather than a four-year overall time period for general and complete disarmament.

The Soviets will also use amendment of their draft treaty to include measures for the prevention of war by accident or miscalculation (exchanges of military missions and establishment of rapid communications among heads of governments and the UN Secretary General) as "evidence" of their effort to meet the US halfway. At the same time the Soviet Union can use its proposal to provide in the treaty on a general and complete disarmament for a ban on combined military maneuvers of two or more states as a vehicle for attacking NATO maneuvers such as last year's Checkmate exercises which were alleged to be "provocative." Moscow may well use other standing propaganda arguments—for example, anecdotes in the press about false US alerts resulting from communication failures and radar errors, the unreliability of the American rockets used for lifting nuclear weapons to be tested in space, charges that US planes have buzzed Soviet ships and examples of neurosis among US military personnel—in order to create the impression that "irresponsible" practices of the US military create a threat to the peace of the world.

To the present the Soviets remain firmly opposed to the American plan for zonal inspection, arguing that it would jeopardize Soviet military secrecy before the disarmament process had gone far enough to protect the Soviet Union from the possibility of attack by the West. However, the Soviet Union appeared earlier this year to have considered the idea of introducing some form of statistical sampling into its control proposals and a bloc delegation in Geneva has spoken of a modified zonal plan. The Soviet Union has long been vulnerable on the control issue, and the possibility of a move to enhance the Soviet position cannot be excluded.

The Soviets appear to have considered—and a Polish diplomat recently mentioned once more—the possibility of a separate agreement on the first stage of disarmament, and there exists the possibility of such a Soviet move at the UN General Assembly.

Test Ban. Clearly the Soviets do not wish to pay a high price (in terms of control) for a test ban, and it is problematical whether they have any interest at all in reaching a test-ban agreement. The USSR does not in any case expect to negotiate such an agreement at the UN, and Moscow's objective in discussing the test-ban issue at the General Assembly will be to make the West bear as large a share as possible of the opprobrium for the continuation of nuclear weapons testing. The Soviets appear to believe that their position on this question has improved over last year when the USSR was guilty of ending the de facto moratorium.

The Soviet Union can be expected to continue their rejection of the latest US proposal to consider scaling down control requirements on the basis of new scientific data resulting from the Vela test series if the USSR would agree to recognize in principle the need for on-site inspection. Moscow can be expected to hold to its position that the US proposal is not a significant concession since the US insists on the need for obligatory inspection. The USSR will probably continue to argue that national means of detection are adequate to police a test ban, and that on-site inspection is not necessary.

Moscow will continue to claim that the Soviet Union and not the United States has genuinely accepted and correctly interpreted the compromise memorandum (of April 16, 1962) of the 8 unaligned members of the Geneva disarmament conference. The Indian delegate at Geneva, Arthur Lall, has been informally circulating a draft treaty on testing—based on the memorandum—which supports the Soviet contention that inspection would be voluntary and not compulsory; Moscow at the General Assembly would welcome such a treaty—whether put forward by the eight or by India alone—as "proof" that the USSR and not the US was responsive to neutral opinion on nuclear testing.

Because the USSR claims that national means of detection are adequate to monitor observance of a test ban, the Soviet Union is free to support any appeals for an uncontrolled moratorium on testing. In supporting such a proposal, Moscow might well link its endorsement of a moratorium with a demand for Western recognition of the USSR's claim that because the US began nuclear testing the Soviet Union has the "right" to be the last country to carry out nuclear weapons tests.

Moscow is likely to respond to any proposals for a ban on tests in the atmosphere by calling—as it has in the past—for the end of tests in all environments.

Soviet propaganda has made much of US nuclear weapons tests in space, and Moscow will probably seek—either in the context of debate on disarmament or outer space—to stigmatize these US tests.

Non-dissemination. In discussing non-dissemination of nuclear weapons at the forthcoming General Assembly, the Soviet Union will apparently make a point of attacking potential creation of a NATO nuclear force.

Heretofore, Moscow has in two previous sessions voted in favor of the Irish resolution which referred to transfer of control over nuclear weapons, and left aside the question of arrangements within alliances. Moscow has publicly broached the issue by including a specific provision against transfer of nuclear weapons to alliances in its draft treaty on general and complete disarmament tabled at the opening of the Geneva disarmament talks. The Soviets will probably demand that a UN resolution contain a similar provision and may hope to win neutral support for its position, thus forcing the West to vote against a widely supported disarmament resolution.

In future negotiations the Soviet Union may be persuaded that it must either accept the creation of a NATO force or be faced with the prospect of an independent West German nuclear force. If Moscow becomes convinced that such a choice cannot be put off, and, further, if it is assured that creation of a NATO force would not in fact be a step toward an independent West German force, it may well sign a non-transfer agreement worded along the lines of the Irish resolution, i.e., one which would permit creation of a NATO nuclear force. For the present Moscow does not appear to be prepared to accept a NATO force, and will probably use the General Assembly debate to press its case against NATO and play upon anti-German prejudices by charging that NATO arrangements are a forerunner of nuclear weapons for the West German army.[2]

While the Soviet Union may have an interest in using the non-dissemination issue as a justification for not granting further nuclear assistance to the Chinese Communists, this appears to be a purely secondary consideration. Soviet delegates are hardly likely to discuss Communist China in debates on non-transfer, but the bloc delegates may not be above mentioning the CPR to lend emphasis to the importance of non-dissemination in lobbying for support of the Soviet position.

Presumably, the Soviet Union shares with the US a desire to prevent the emergence of other potential Nth countries, not members of either Eastern or Western alliances. However, this consideration does not appear to have actively motivated Soviet policy makers in dealing with this issue. Moscow will almost certainly avoid statements which might offend potential non bloc Nth countries (excepting Israel).

Denuclearization

The Soviets will almost certainly raise or support initiatives for the creation of nuclear-free zones as well as proposals along the lines of last year's Swedish resolution for the creation of a "club" of countries which

---

[2] Alternatively, the USSR appears to be prepared to sign a nontransfer arrangement which singles out the FRG and GDR, but makes no mention of alliance, in effect trading off an explicit anti-NATO provision for an agreement likely to undermine NATO by discrimination against the Federal Republic. [Footnote in the source text.]

pledge neither to develop their own nuclear forces nor to allow foreign powers to station nuclear weapons on their territory. The bloc may attempt to revive the Polish proposal of 1960 for a freeze on foreign bases together with a ban on transfer of nuclear weapons.

Non-use

This year the Soviet Union will almost certainly support proposals for a ban on the use (or first use) of nuclear weapons. While statements in Soviet journals about the inevitability of escalation of local wars and Khrushchev's remark to Sulzberger last September that someone who signed such an agreement in good faith would in the exigency of war be proved a liar show that the Soviets have no illusions about the effect of such a declaratory agreement. Moscow has long advocated such a ban as a means of detracting from the credibility of the Western nuclear deterrent. This year Moscow's advocacy of such a ban will probably be used as a backdrop for further propaganda exploitation of the Soviet distortion of the Alsop article in the March 31 *Saturday Evening Post.*

Moscow may also raise the issue of a ban on the use of other weapons of mass destruction, i.e. chemical and bacteriological weapons. Soviet propaganda has already commented upon the use of defoliants in South Vietnam and in several instances has described them as causing injury to persons and as an attempt to produce famine by destroying crops. The recent death of a British scientist who had been working on bacteriological agents—an event duly recorded by TASS—affords another point of departure for a possible Soviet attack on alleged Western preparations for aggressive war.

3. Space

The Soviets will approach the UN General Assembly discussion of outer space matters with its prestige greatly enhanced by the recent exploits of Nikolayev and Popovich. They can be expected to use the occasion to glorify Soviet scientific achievements, to project the image of Soviet peaceful intentions and willingness to cooperate with other countries and to set forth once more Soviet criticisms of American space programs. Moscow does not appear to have added very much to its repertoire of propaganda arguments since the meetings of the UN Outer Space Subcommittees in Geneva last summer. However, it appears likely that the Soviets will state their case in sharper terms at the General Assembly this autumn. While using a harsher tone in its criticisms of the US, Moscow will probably continue to exercise a measure of restraint to avoid jeopardizing its public posture of seeking more active cooperation with the free world in this field, to minimize the risk of spoiling prospects for agreements with the US on possible joint projects and to avoid statements which might embarrass Soviet programs for use of space for military purposes.

Reconnaissance Satellites. Most principal interest in attacking US space efforts would appear to be to inhibit (or make as politically costly as possible) US development of reconnaissance satellites. Until last year Moscow gave little publicity to the subject of reconnaissance satellites, apparently because it was reluctant to make a public display of Soviet impotence. However, this inhibition appears to be diminishing as the Soviet Union develops a reputation for being well on the way to early acquisition of an anti-satellite capability. Along with the voicing of Soviet anti-missile claims (with the implication of a possible anti-satellite missile) there has been more frequent references in Soviet propaganda to the need for a ban on espionage satellites. Soviet success in putting Vostok III into orbit close to Vostok IV has produced widespread press speculation that Soviet capability for shooting down reconnaissance satellites and provides a favorable context for a Soviet political attack on the US.

In addition to demanding a ban on spies in the sky, the Soviets may attempt to embarrass the US by demanding that it register with the UN data on all satellite launches. The Soviet news agency, TASS, has made a point of meticulously reporting announcements of launchings of US satellites whose purpose is not announced and the USSR may use these as a talking point in attempting to embarrass the US. However, in demanding registration of data the USSR will almost certainly wish to include some limitations in order to avoid undertaking (even by implication) an obligation to reveal certain information about its own space efforts

US Militarism in Outer Space. The enhancement of the USSR reputation for military prowess in space resulting from twin manned satellites will also make it possible for the Soviets to denounce American military space programs from a position of apparent strength. Soviet media have been increasingly picking up and exploiting articles in the US press on use of space for military purposes, and the Soviets may attempt to accuse the US of attempting to launch an arms race in outer space.

At the Geneva disarmament conference the Soviets reacted coolly to suggestions that disarmament in space be considered as a topic for separate measures of disarmament. And while the Soviets will doubtless remain opposed to arrangements entailing control over rocket launchings outside the context of general and complete disarmament, pejorative references in Soviet propaganda to American schemes for bombardment satellites suggest that Moscow may be considering a proposal for a declaratory ban on stationing nuclear weapons in orbit.

Moscow will probably renew its charges that the US programs have contaminated outer space, referring in particular to the West Ford project for putting a large number of copper needles into orbit and to US nuclear tests which leave radioactive fallout in space.

In discussing communications satellites the Soviets will probably again advocate a ban on the use of satellites for the transmission of war propaganda and may reiterate the bloc's argument that capitalistic private business not be allowed to operate in space.

4. Anti-Imperialism

Soviet long-range ambitions in the UN appear to be predicated upon the hope that the USSR may with time gain sufficient influence over non-aligned members to assure the Soviet Union of the one-third vote necessary to block resolutions detrimental to Soviet interests while affording the Soviet Union an increasingly great opportunity to shape resolutions aimed against the West. Obviously, the colonial issues occupy a key place in Moscow's attempt to win over neutralist sentiment and to direct it into anti-Western channels.

Committee of 17. The Soviets appear to have been gratified by the work of the 17-member committee established last year to oversee implementation of the UN declaration on granting independence to colonial countries. Gratified by the anti-Western bent of many of the Committee's decisions, the Soviets appear to be developing ambitions for enhancing the committee's importance and the Soviet role in it.

The USSR will very likely resist strongly any attempt to deprive it of its seat, and may attempt to secure greater Asian and African representation. In addition a Soviet official in New York has indicated that the Soviet Union is preparing to propose some form of enlarged program of work for the committee; Moscow may argue that the committee should deal directly with governments rather than report to the General Assembly and might propose that it undertake visits to nonself governing territories.

The Soviets may hope that the committee—a promising new institution from the Soviet point of view—can ultimately become the principal UN organ in the field of colonialism to the detriment of the present role of the more conservative Trusteeship Council and Fourth Committee of the General Assembly.

Policy lines. Little change is to be expected in the now standard Soviet approach to issues to which it can give an anti-imperialistic cast. Moscow will doubtless avail itself of opportunities to embarrass Western colonial powers, and probably believes Portugal to be the most vulnerable of them. The Soviet Union will welcome, and attempt to claim credit for, the "liberation" of West Irian. The Soviets will probably urge greater vigor in dealing with Katangan separatism in the hope of later similarly claiming credit for the reunification of the Congo. The USSR can be expected to welcome discussion by the General Assembly—either in general debate or as a separate agenda item—of Cuban charges of American aggressiveness both as an opportunity to embarrass the US and as a means of creating an impediment to any potential US move against the Castro regime.

Soviet Colonialism. The Soviet delegation would probably prefer to avoid discussion of Soviet imperialism, and will doubtless react sharply to any mention of the subject. Moscow probably believes that, because most of the former colonies regard Soviet affairs as remote and are preoccupied with their own problems, the best Soviet rebuttal is to brand the Western charge a "cold-war" tactic and a stratagem to absolve the West from its guilt.

5. World Trade Conference

The Soviet Union will probably carry its fight against the Common Market to the General Assembly this autumn and attempt to brand the EEC as an imperialist device for discriminating against the less developed countries.

On May 30 Khrushchev publicly called for a world trade conference and a resolution endorsing such a conference was passed at the ECOSOC meeting in July.

In light of the Cairo conference's resolution endorsing the idea of a trade conference (though it made no reference to the USSR) and the favorable reaction of the underdeveloped countries to the resolution on a possible trade conference at the General Assembly last year, the Soviet Union may hope to capture leadership of a popular cause and use the international-trade-conference issue in attacking the EEC.

6. Korea

The Soviet Union by demanding inscription on the Assembly agenda of an item on the withdrawal of US forces from South Korea has indicated that it hopes to take the offensive on the Korean issue this year. If the Soviet Union can focus the debate on the presence of US troops, it may hope to popularize arguments which mutatis mutandi can support the Soviet case for withdrawal of US troops from foreign bases as a disarmament measure, for withdrawal of Western forces from Berlin and for withdrawal of US forces from other areas including South Vietnam.

Moscow's ability to manipulate successfully the Korean issue at the Assembly, and possibly to effect changes in the composition of UNCURK favorable to it, is seriously circumscribed by Soviet and North Korean unwillingness to take a cooperative attitude toward the UN and their rejection of a UN role in Korea.

7. Secretary General

Moscow almost certainly hopes eventually to replace the single Secretary General with a "troika" or some other arrangement which will afford the Soviets an effective veto over UN executive actions. The Soviet Union, must, however, take into account the climate of opinion in the UN; the Soviets probably do not expect to secure early adoption—presumably including amendment of the UN Charter—of their "troika" proposal. Moscow must realize that prolonged obstruction of the question of filling the Secretary General's office will be counterproductive; the Soviet Union would bear the onus for not cooperating with the UN.

In the immediate future Moscow will probably avoid committing itself either to support U Thant's election to a regular term or to oppose him. The Soviets would apparently wish to put U Thant in the position of having to seek Soviet favor (perhaps by not exercising his authority in applying Article 19 of the Charter to deprive the Soviet Union of its vote because it is now in arrears in its contribution to the UN). At the same time they would retain their freedom of action while assessing the parliamentary situation in order to determine what Soviet proposals for downgrading the status of the Secretary General (increasing authority of his deputies, for example) might stand a chance of being accepted by the Assembly.

8. UN Financing

The Soviet Union will probably resist efforts to carry out the July 20 decision of the International Court of Justice. But, if Moscow expects that it may be defeated on a resolution on this subject, it may hope that the General Assembly will not recommend and the SYG will not take immediate action under Article 19 to take voting rights from members who are in arrears.

9. Chinese Representation

The Soviet bloc will doubtless again go on record as favoring a change in Chinese representation, both for the purpose of making a friendly gesture toward Communist China and in order to avoid making a show of intra-bloc differences at the UN. But, the Soviets are probably comforted by the calculation that their efforts are not likely to succeed, for while Moscow may be constrained to fight for Communist China's claims, it probably has little desire to see the Chinese Communists become members of the UN.

If demands for Chinese participation in disarmament agreements are raised—Indian delegate Lall has begun referring to the need to have all militarily significant powers participate from the very first stage—the Soviet Union will probably repeat its disavowal of being empowered to negotiate for the Chinese which was voiced by Gromyko at the Supreme Soviet last April 24.

10. Charter Revision

The USSR will probably continue to oppose proposals for charter revision on the ground that new arrangements cannot be made until after the Chinese Communists take their rightful seat.

11. General Assembly Procedures

Moscow thus far has shown little interest in improving General Assembly procedures, and the USSR does not appear to regard the subject as particularly important.

---

220.   Memorandum From the Assistant Secretary of State for International Organization Affairs (Cleveland) to Secretary of State Rusk[1]

Washington, August 29, 1962.

SUBJECT

Enlargement of the Security Council

Discussion

Following your discussion with the Nigerian Foreign Minister you asked that the legal people take a new look to see if there is any way of enlarging the Security Council without amending the Charter. Their conclusion is negative and the alternatives short of full membership they suggest as possibilities are not promising (Tab A).[2]

In this situation and given the history of our efforts to enlarge the Council (also described in Tab A) the only solution to the problem created by the Afro-Asian demand for greater opportunities of representation seems to lie in 1) continued pressure on the USSR to permit enlargement and 2) pending enlargement, an adjustment in the geographic allocation of elective seats on the Council. As you will recall, the Nigerian Foreign Minister made it clear that he would seek to pre-empt for Africa at the

---

[1] Source: National Archives and Records Administration, RG 59, Central Files 1960–63, 330/8–2962. Confidential. Drafted by Virginia F. Hartley on August 8 and concurred in by C. Vaughn Ferguson, Abram Chayes, Richard Friedman, George N. Monsma, James M. Ludlow, and William H. Sullivan.

[2] The memorandum, drafted in IO/UNP and L/UNA on July 31, is not printed.

forthcoming General Assembly either the West European seat or one of the Latin American seats. Neither would be in the United States interest. He has also evidenced some interest in seeking enlargement of the Council (Tab B).[3] In view of his insistence at the 15th General Assembly on coupling immediate reallocation of existing seats with enlargement, however, it is not clear that he is now prepared to concentrate on enlargement to the exclusion of reallocation.

The readjustment that would do the least damage to the Western position in the Council, provide a seat each for black Africa, the Middle East, and Asia, and maintain the maximum pressure on the USSR would be to shift the Commonwealth seat to Africa and the East European seat to Asia. The difficulties in this proposal are 1) that the Afro-Asians have been reluctant to put pressure on the USSR by depriving Eastern Europe of its seat and 2) that the British have been reluctant to let the Commonwealth seat go. However it appears from my recent consultations in London that they may now be prepared to consider this possibility. A decision to make this concession might be used to persuade the Afro-Asians that Eastern Europe should also be denied its seat so long as the USSR blocks enlargement. This plan could, however, not be put into effect until the 18th General Assembly when elections will be held to fill both the Commonwealth seat and the seat originally allocated to Eastern Europe.

Adoption of this plan would in no way preclude our support of any efforts by Wachuku or others directed toward enlargement, which continues to present the only really satisfactory solution of the problem. The prospects for success of any such efforts, however, do not appear sufficiently good for us to rely upon them exclusively to head off the Afro-Asian drive for reallocation at the expense of Western Europe and/or Latin America.

Recommendation[4]

1. That we promptly resume our consultations with the British on this matter and if they are responsive, extend these consultations to other friendly states with a view to a) reaching agreement on the scheme for reallocation outlined above, or some variant thereof, which could be put to friendly African and Asian delegations early in the 17th General Assembly and b) persuading the Afro-Asians thereby not to try to "raid" either the WE or LA seat at the 17th session.

2. That we continue to encourage and support any efforts by the Nigerian Foreign Minister or others directed toward a reasonable increase in the number of non-permanent members on the Security Council.

---

[3] Telegram 175 from Lagos, August 6; not printed.

[4] Secretary Rusk initialed his approval of both recommendations.

221.   Circular Airgram From the Department of State to Certain Posts[1]

CA–2368   Washington, August 30, 1962, 8:02 p.m.

SUBJECT

Committee of 17 in the Seventeenth United Nations General Assembly

REF

Department Circular Telegram 328[2]

At the Seventeenth General Assembly the United States expects to lay considerable stress on the need for responsible and moderate action by the GA, particularly on colonial questions. For example, it is expected that the major speech by the United States at the opening of the Assembly will stress this theme. As part of this overall approach, we, and hopefully others, shall also make a major effort to reconstitute the Committee of 17 in the hopes that it will act more moderately and responsibly than in the past year.

The United States continues to favor the achievement of self-determination by dependent peoples throughout the world, and we believe that the United Nations has a vital role to play in the process of decolonization. Moreover, we recognize and sympathize with the strong feelings against colonialism held particularly by the Afro-Asians and Latin Americans. However, we believe that the United Nations Committee of 17, the committee established by the Sixteenth General Assembly to oversee the implementation of the Colonialism Declaration, has often demonstrated an unjustified doctrinaire extremism and impracticality in its proceedings and recommendations. This attitude is, in large part, due to the presence of the USSR on the Committee and its patent attempts to use the Committee as a "cold war" instrument with which to belabor the West, in general, and specifically, to link the United States with European colonial powers pursuing what the Soviets, for propaganda purposes, describe as "aggressive and repressive colonial policies." With the USSR consistently pressing for the most extreme "anti-colonial" positions in the Committee, most of the other members, with the exception of Australia, Italy, the United Kingdom, and the United States, are usually reluctant to lag behind the Soviets' propaganda posi-

---

[1] Source: National Archives and Records Administration, RG 59, Central Files 1960–63, 320/8–3062. Confidential. Drafted by James B. Parker; cleared by Jesse MacKnight, Captain Rosse E. Freeman, Joseph J. Sisco, George N. Monsma, Louise McNutt, Herbert Reis, and James M. Ludlow; and approved by Assistant Secretary Cleveland.

[2] Dated August 24. (Ibid., 320/8–2462)

tion lest they appear to be "soft on colonialism." This has appeared especially the case with the Afro-Asians. Unfortunately, the Latin American members of the Committee have tended to be unwilling to take a stand contrary to that of the Afro-Asians while admitting privately the impracticality and questionable legality of some Committee action. We fear other Latin Americans may follow this tendency. The result has been the passage of a number of irresponsible resolutions with unworkable recommendations.

The Department believes that, in the interest of having the United Nations' contribution toward ending colonialism progress on a sound basis, an intensive effort is justified to moderate and improve the Committee's future performance and behavior by ridding it of the USSR. While we continue to support the Committee's objectives and purpose, we believe that the United States, together with the USSR, should be replaced, considering this to be the best method of minimizing the "cold war" issue in the Committee's colonialism debates. The elimination of the USSR from the Committee of 17 might best be achieved through a broader reconstitution by the General Assembly of the Committee's membership (this would not rule out the continued membership of such present members as Australia and the United Kingdom).

The Department accordingly believes that an intensive effort should be made as soon as possible to gain support for this measure among UN delegations in New York and in key capitals. While the Department is opposed to United States withdrawal from the Committee if the USSR retains its membership, this should not be revealed to foreign governments, except the United Kingdom, since knowledge of this might undermine our main goal of getting rid of the Soviets.

Addressee Action Posts, unless they perceive overriding objections, are requested to take up this matter on an urgent basis and at an appropriately high level with the respective governments to which accredited. Embassy London should inform the Foreign Office of these démarches and urge the UK Government to make similar approaches.

USUN should also discuss this matter with United Nations delegations representing both Action Post and Info Post member states, except the USSR and Ethiopia. (The démarche to Ethiopia should be made exclusively in Addis Ababa.) Info Post countries include those whose UN delegations in New York tend to have the major voice in the fixing of their governments' positions on this issue. In the case of such countries, we believe, the démarches should be made exclusively in New York. As the support of the Africans, Asians and Latin Americans is of utmost importance if our effort is to succeed at the Seventeenth General Assembly, the approaches made in these countries, and with their

United Nations delegations, will be of particular importance. The approaches should be made verbally.

Action Posts are requested to report Foreign Offices' reactions telegraphically, with messages repeated to USUN. The Department would appreciate receiving any comments Embassy Moscow cares to make on this matter.

Action Posts' presentations should include the following six points, and Posts may draw on the background information contained in Annex I to this Airgram and the examples given in Annexes II and III[3] to the extent considered necessary. Citation of the examples contained in Annexes II and III will obviously have to be tailored according to the country or delegation being approached.

Points to be Made to Foreign Governments and UN Delegations

1. The United States will continue its policy of encouraging and contributing to practical actions which should result in the achievement of self-determination by dependent peoples as soon as possible. We support the principles contained in the United Nations' Colonialism Declaration, particularly the principle that "All peoples have the right to self-determination; by virtue of that right they freely determine their political status and freely pursue their economic, social and cultural development." The traditional United States position on colonialism was summed up by President Kennedy speaking before the General Assembly last fall when he said: "My country favors a world of free and equal states . . . Within the limits of our responsibility in such matters, my country intends to be a participant, and not merely an observer, in the peaceful expeditious movement of nations from the status of colonies to the partnership of equals." We continue to believe that the United Nations can play a vital and constructive role in the liquidation of colonialism.

2. In line with the above, the United States supported the establishment of the Committee of 17 and agreed to serve on it. We continue to believe that the Committee can make an important contribution toward the decolonization process. While we have differed with the majority of its members in some of their recommendations and the procedures they have employed, we are prepared to cooperate with the Committee whether we are members or not.

3. Up to now, however, the Committee's record has been clouded by the Soviets' exploiting it for propaganda purposes. Their participation in it has not been for the legitimate purpose of contributing to the

---

[3] None of the annexes is printed. Annex I is entitled "Background"; Annex II is entitled "Examples of Soviet 'Cold War' Tactics in the Committee of 17"; Annex III is entitled "Examples of Unwise Action Taken by Majority of Committee of 17."

orderly termination of colonialism, but rather to exploit the Committee of 17 as a "cold war" forum. While posing as the most ardent champion of dependent peoples, the Soviets have attempted to lump the United States with European colonial powers allegedly following "aggressive and repressive policies." We do not believe that it is in the interests of countries sincerely desirous of contributing to colonialism's demise for them to provide a forum for such "cold war" propaganda exercises against the United States when the record of concrete US assistance in the United Nations and elsewhere to dependent peoples gives the lie to such false propaganda.

4. In order for the Committee of 17 to fulfill its potential constructively and to avoid, if possible, further "cold war" maneuvers, we believe that the USSR should be replaced on the Committee and ask the governments being approached to support this measure when the future of the Committee of 17 is being discussed in the Seventeenth General Assembly. We have no wish to see the Committee used for "cold war" purposes and are also prepared to withdraw in the interests of improving the Committee's work.

5. In addition to replacing the USSR and the United States, we believe further changes in the Committee's membership might be desirable so as to give countries which have not yet had a chance to serve the opportunity of making their contribution to the work of this important body. The Committee's membership should be equitably balanced geographically, and it should continue to include member states which have recently become independent as well as some member states which administer colonial territories. FYI. Posts should avoid entering into a more detailed discussion about the future membership of the Committee. End FYI.

6. (Posts have discretion in presenting the following points.) We believe that the Committee of 17 can be made a more effective instrument in the decolonization process if it begins to proceed on a more responsible and realistic basis to consider the actual problems faced by an Administrating Authority in advancing individual territories toward self-determination. The practice of unrestrainedly criticizing all Administering Authorities and the adoption of impractical and intemperate resolutions have the following negative results:

(a) Extremism and lack of realism in the United Nations on the colonial question, as well as other issues, tend to undermine the effectiveness of the General Assembly—the only body in which all member states have an equal voice. Intemperate debate and the lack of realism in resolutions may very well create a situation in which Administering Authorities, instead of heeding the United Nations, will come increasingly to look upon it as a forum for oratory only, thereby diminishing the authority and effectiveness of the United Nations in colonial matters.

(b) In the United States, the country on which so many crucial UN operations depend for political and especially financial support, the passage of unrealistic resolutions, drafted more for their anticipated propaganda impact than for their contribution to a solution of colonial problems, tends to make important segments of American public opinion, and consequently Congressional opinion, question United States support for the United Nations and its operations. Therefore, the extent of our future cooperation with the Committee of 17 may well depend on the degree of realism and responsibility which that body displays.

(c) The adoption of extreme and unworkable measures tends to undercut United States efforts to influence colonial powers to adopt policies regarding their dependent territories in line with the wishes of the world community as expressed in the United Nations. Such measures also tend to strengthen the hands of the more conservative elements in countries administering colonial areas, often encourage negative approaches to solutions of problems and thereby impede the achievement of the goals we and other opponents of colonialism support.

Rusk

---

222. Telegram From the Department of State to the Mission to the United Nations[1]

Washington, September 6, 1962, 9:27 p.m.

1341. Security Council.

1. Dept has been giving intensive consideration problem created by Soviet blocking of SC enlargement. As Mission aware original geographic allocation non-permanent seats makes no provision for Asian other than Commonwealth members and entirely inadequate provision for Africa given large number new African members. While we have had limited success in using seat originally allocated Eastern Europe to provide some opportunities representation non-Commonwealth Asian members, situation in which there only one seat available for entire Middle East–African

---

[1] Source: National Archives and Records Administration, RG 59, Central Files 1960–63, 330/9–662. Confidential. Drafted by Hartley, cleared by Monsma, MacKnight, Sisco, Richard Friedman, McNutt, Ernest L. Kerley, and James M. Ludlow; and approved by Assistant Secretary Cleveland. Repeated to London.

area, with 40 members, cannot in Dept's view continue indefinitely and can only lead increasing threat to retention LA and WE seats, which of major importance to Western voting position on SC. While situation mitigated slightly by existence Commonwealth seat, this not regarded as any solution by non-Commonwealth African and Asian members.

2. Given present and potential size UN, enlargement SC presents only really satisfactory solution problem, and Dept believes US should continue strongly support any efforts by Africans or others directed toward reasonable increase number non-permanent SC seats. However prospects early success any such efforts do not appear sufficiently good permit us continue rely exclusively on enlargement to head off Afro-Asian drive for reallocation existing seats at expense WE and LA. Mission will recall this drive gained substantial momentum at 15th GA under leadership Wachuku (Nigeria) and there every indication, as Mission aware, he intends pursue same tack at forthcoming session.

3. Dept has given some thought to possibility providing additional opportunities non-voting participation in work SC through some form of "regional" or "associate" representation under Article 31 of Charter. Any such arrangement however would probably be regarded by new members as unacceptable in that it would give them "second class" status and is therefore unlikely deter them from seeking election to regular seat.

4. Dept has therefore concluded it necessary explore possibility agreement on some acceptable readjustment in present allocation of seats. Ideal solution which would involve least damage Western voting position in SC; provide seat each for Africa (excluding Arab States), Middle East (including African Arabs), and Asia; and maintain maximum pressure on USSR permit enlargement, would be shift of Commonwealth seat to Africa and EE seat to Asia. Principal difficulties this proposal are a) reluctance UK and other Commonwealth members relinquish Commonwealth seat; b) reluctance LAs and some WEs depart "gentlemen's agreement" in interest preservation own seats under original allocation; and c) reluctance many A-As put pressure on USSR by depriving Eastern Europe of seat.

5. Dept recognized these difficulties present formidable obstacle obtaining any general agreement (exclusive Soviet bloc) to such reallocation. However, British appeared recognize this as possibility when Cleveland broached matter in London recently. Old Commonwealth members, while likely oppose surrender Commonwealth seat in first instance as Australians have already indicated they do, might be persuaded on grounds they stand better chance election SC if eligible WE seat (as in General Committee) than if eligible Commonwealth seat given present UN membership and lack other seats for Asia and Africa. Incorporation old Commonwealth with WEs would also serve buttress latter's claim to seat. New Commonwealth members might be persuaded

relinquish exclusive claim to seat in interest relations their African and Asian neighbors.

6. Dept would hope WEs and LAs could be persuaded recognize that best hope preserving WE and LA seats in present situation lies in shifting two seats to A-As, that accommodation A-As should not be made at cost West exclusively, and that best means exerting pressure on USSR permit enlargement is to deprive Eastern Europe opportunity representation pending enlargement. Finally Dept would hope sufficient number A-As might be persuaded agree deprive Eastern Europe of seat in interest obtaining two seats for themselves to make plan workable.

7. Mission should therefore urgently consult with British along above lines so that if they at all responsive they might undertake discuss matter at Commonwealth meeting next week. Depending on outcome these preliminary consultations, Dept would then have in mind extending consultations to other friendly WE and LA delegations with view reaching agreement on this scheme of reallocation, or some acceptable variant thereof, which could if this appears tactically advisable be put to friendly African and Asian delegations early at the 17th General Assembly in effort forestall A-A "raid" on WE or LA seat during forthcoming session. Plan of course could not be put into effect until 18th GA when Commonwealth and "floating" seats must be filled.

8. Dept recognizes launching this proposal now could prove prejudicial Norway's current effort obtain Soviet bloc support its election this GA session. If in Mission's view and that UK Del this constitutes overriding consideration, further consultations could be delayed until it possible assess more accurately progress Norwegian candidacy and strength expected A-A drive to "raid" Western seat.

Rusk

---

223.   Telegram From the Mission to the United Nations to the Department of State[1]

New York, September 12, 1962, 8 p.m.

743. Reelection SYG. SYG told me he loath be candidate for reelection and preferred not commit himself re his availability until it clearer that

[1] Source: National Archives and Records Administration, RG 59, Central Files 1960–63, 310/9–1262. Secret; Limit Distribution.

problem of Congo would be resolved satisfactorily. He foresaw possibility of period of real difficulty ahead in Congo leading to further strain being placed on already over-burdened UN financial condition and consequent forced disengagement of UN from Congo. At same time, however, he understood difficulties with which UN would be faced if he appeared be unwilling accept reelection.

In any event, he planned await Gromyko's arrival and some disclosure of Sov attitude towards his reelection. He thought he might not be able obtain such indication before approximately Oct first. If Sovs prepared support him unconditionally, his reelection could proceed immediately. On other hand, if Sovs imposed unacceptable conditions, situation would become more difficult. In meantime, he has dissuaded AsAfs from publicly proposing his name. He hoped for early disposition this matter, agreeing with us that otherwise whole GA would be clouded and positive action on other matters be difficult to achieve.

SYG indicated US position supporting his reelection was well known. He thought it preferable if he not appear to be US candidate and therefore suggested we should remain inactive with respect his candidacy. He made no reference to length of his term of office.

Foregoing jibes with report Dean (UK) gave us confidentially yesterday. Dean said he had had long talk with U Thant regarding his reelection. SYG indicated he not anxious be reelected both for personal reasons and because he foresaw period of real difficulty ahead. He recognized, however, that there is no other candidate and in interests of UN he was prepared to stand for reelection. At same time, he indicated that full five year term was too long a commitment and was leaning towards three year term. He implied that possibly Russians would come forward with such suggestion, believing for their own reasons that five year commitment under present circumstances was too long. We agreed with Dean that it be mistake for either UK or US give any indication we prepared consider reduction in present five year term of SYG. Term fixed by GA and in any case could not be changed by SC. It would be mistake for it to be shortened at will of any candidate for office and even worse mistake for it to be shortened at insistence of Sovs. Dean suggested that as possible fall-back, if necessary, we might come to rest on pre-dating of SYG's election so that five year term would start on date of Thant's election as acting SYG of year ago. This would in effect give him three and half year term. It was agreed we would consider this as possibility but in interim should resist any such suggestion at this stage.

During conversation with Mission officer, Natarajan (former SYG of Indian UN Del, now employed in Secretariat) believed that while Sovs had no alternative to voting for reelection of U Thant due to latter's ASAF support, they would attempt nevertheless to limit his term and his power. Natarajan said just prior to SYG's trip to Moscow, he (Natarajan) had been approached by three different individuals (one a member of Sov Del, another a member of Rumanian Del and a third a Sov national in Secretariat) who asked him what Indian Govt reaction would be to proposal for reelecting U Thant for only a two to three year period rather than for five years and to continue his status of Acting SYG for that period. Natarajan said he told questioners that in his opinion India would support U Thant for full five year term as SYG. Natarajan said, however, that he had reason to believe Sovs would continue their efforts in this regard and would therefore attempt delay action on election in hope of achieving their objective.

Narasimhan (SYG's Chef de Cabinet) also told us today Secretariat had received hints from Eastern Europeans that Sov bloc might support U Thant for three year term. Narasimhan strongly opposed to this, believing that five year term should be maintained. We of course strongly supported this position.

Stevenson

224. Memorandum of Conversation[1]

Washington, September 13, 1962, 4:15 p.m.

SUBJECT

Tour d'Horizon—UN Matters

PARTICIPANTS

U Thant—Acting Secretary General of UN
Philip Dean—Director, UN Information Center
Mr. Ball, Under Secretary (in part)
Mr. McGhee, Under Secretary for Political Affairs
Governor Stevenson, US Representative to UN
Governor Harriman, FE
Governor Williams, AF
Mr. Cleveland, IO
Mr. Talbot, NEA
Mr. Wallner, IO
Mr. Godley, AFC
Mr. Sisco, UNP

---

[1] Source: National Archives and Records Administration, RG 59, IO Files: Lot 64 D 191, Woodruff Wallner Subject Files, U Thant Visit, September 13, 1962. Confidential. Drafted by Sisco and approved in M and U on September 18.

After Mr. McGhee welcomed the Acting Secretary General, the following principal points emerged from the conversation:

1. *Palestine Refugees.* Mr. Talbot outlined our approach to the Johnson Mission, emphasizing in particular that what was being sought was *acquiescence* of the parties and not necessarily approval. (From Thant's reaction it was clear he had not previously understood this point.) Thant, who was obviously fully familiar with recent developments, said he did not intend to express a public view on this matter at this stage, particularly since the principal parties concerned had not yet reacted. However, if at a later stage an expression of his support would be helpful he would give this sympathetic consideration.

After agreeing generally with the views expressed by Mr. Talbot regarding the Johnson Plan and the steps envisaged, Thant said he thought it would be difficult to go ahead if one of the parties should disagree. Mr. McGhee stressed we cannot let this problem drift since it would become even more difficult in the future. Mr. Cleveland said there is increasing unwillingness in this country to continue the "UNRWA retail operation" indefinitely and that if the Johnson Plan does not work we will have to look to ways and means to have the host governments undertake responsibilities for the refugees.

2. *West New Guinea.* After Mr. McGhee complimented U Thant on the role he played in bringing about a settlement of the West New Guinea issue, the Secretary General in turn said modestly that a settlement would not have been possible without the vigorous support of the United States. He paid special tribute to Ambassador Bunker. In response to Governor Harriman's inquiry, U Thant said Indonesia has suggested a Mexican, Osorio-Tafall, who has been heading up the UN Technical Assistance program in Cairo, as the UN Administrator in West New Guinea. U Thant is now awaiting the Netherlands' response on whether Osorio-Tafall is acceptable.

3. *Thai-Cambodian Question.* After Governor Harriman outlined our views on the Thai-Cambodia question, U Thant reviewed his conversations with the Thais and Cambodians in New York. After receiving the Thai request for sending either a representative or team to investigate the facts, the Secretary General communicated this request to the Cambodians on September 6. He received a favorable Cambodian reply last Sunday (Sept. 10), but they have suggested that the UN role not be limited to Thai-Cambodia but also include South Viet Nam. U Thant said this placed him in a delicate position since South Viet Nam is not a member of the United Nations.

U Thant reported Sihanouk prefers a Burmese as a UN representative in the area and the Secretary General has discussed two possible Burmese diplomats with Ambassador Barrington, Burma's UN Permanent Representative in New York. The Secretary General expects to get the

Burmese Foreign Minister's reaction this coming weekend, and assuming an affirmative reply from the Burmese Government, he intends to send a UN representative to the area as soon as possible, probably by the end of this month. He will also send a UN staff official along with him. If the UN presence is limited to a UN representative or so, the Secretary General intends to defray the costs out of the present UN budget. If, however, a UN Commission is sent, the Secretary General intends asking the two governments to pay the costs equally. When the Secretary General indicated that he was thinking of sending a UN representative for a period of 3–6 months, Governor Harriman asked that he keep the period of time open since it would probably be necessary for such a presence to remain for an extended period. Governor Harriman also pointed out the difficulties which would be involved if South Viet Nam were included within the area of responsibility. He expressed the hope Thant could convince Sihanouk to go ahead with a UN presence dealing with the Thai-Cambodian area and to defer its possible extension to South Viet Nam.

4. *Laos*. Governor Harriman sketched briefly our present thinking on Laos, including the "growing pains" which the agreement is experiencing and explaining why more of a UN presence has not been possible to date. He expressed the hope that the UN Representative in Laos could act with more vigor. Thant informed us he intends to replace the present representative with an individual who could be expected to act more vigorously and decisively. U Thant agreed with Governor Harriman that the UN presence can have a salutary effect, although he felt Souvanna Phouma has certain obsessions and suspicions which will have to be dispelled. According to Thant, Souvanna Phouma sees the UN role limited to technical assistance. Thant said it would take sometime to breakdown some of the adverse psychological factors prevalent in the present situation.

5. *Congo*. Mr. Ball joined the group as the conversation turned to the Congo and asked the Secretary General to give his present assessment of the situation.

Thant gave a detailed interpretation of the events of the last 48 hours in the Katanga in which he maintained strongly that Tshombe had contrived the incident in which two Katangese were killed for the purpose of influencing the Congress on the UN bond issue. U Thant placed great emphasis on the need for the British to apply pressure on Welensky. U Thant is convinced that Welensky is in an excellent position to influence Tshombe and that the British in turn can contribute greatly by exercising influence on Welensky.

Thant said he was thinking in terms of about 30 day period (Oct. 10) in which the reconciliation plan should be put into effect. He detailed the steps taken by the UN experts in consulting with the various provinces on the Constitution, indicating a much more optimistic time schedule than our own as to how long it would take to achieve changes and complete the ratification process in the provinces. He said UN experts have consulted all provincial parliamentary leaders, including the Katanga (we do not have confirmation of this and are making further inquiry). He predicted the main problem would be where the residual powers reside; Adoula wants them to be maintained in the Central Government, whereas Tshombe wants them in the provinces. U Thant predicts we will know within a short time whether the reconciliation plan will work, the first test being whether the Katangese cooperate with the various commissions.

Once again Thant returned to the need for the British to get Welensky to influence Tshombe. In response to U Thant's inquiry, Mr. Ball informed him that Mr. Streulens' visa has expired and under our procedures it would be necessary for him to reapply if and when he left the country.

The conversation concluded with Mr. Ball and others emphasizing in particular the importance of full consultations with the Katangese on the question of the constitution.

---

225.   Memorandum of Conversation[1]

SecDel/MC/59   New York, September 29, 1962, 5 p.m.

SECRETARY'S DELEGATION TO THE SEVENTEENTH SESSION OF
THE UNITED NATIONS GENERAL ASSEMBLY
New York, September, 1962

PARTICIPANTS

US	Foreign
Secretary Rusk	Foreign Minister Jaja Wachuku of Nigeria
Mr. Richard Sanger, USDel	H.E. Chief S.O. Adebo, Permanent
Mr. Robert Oakley, USDel	Representative of Nigeria to United Nations

SUBJECT

An African Seat on the Security Council, and the Election of U Thant

Foreign Minister Wachuku of Nigeria then said that the African States were conscious of the fact that in spite of their number they did not have a seat on the Security Council. Other bodies of the UN have

---

[1] Source: National Archives and Records Administration, RG 59, Conference Files: Lot 65 D 533, UNGA No. 17. Confidential. Approved in S on October 3. The meeting was held at the Waldorf-Astoria Hotel.

recently been enlarged by geographical area and it was the intention of the Africans to raise this matter and try to get two more non-permanent seats added to the Security Council, both of which would be allocated to Africa.

The Secretary said that the US would support the idea of expanding the size of the Security Council and wondered if "someone else" could go to Gromyko and talk to him about this matter, asking him to abandon the Soviet position on Communist Chinese representation for this one question and permit enlargement.

Wachuku said that he personally would like to talk to Gromyko and explain to him that while other parts of the world such as Latin America, Europe and the Middle East, are represented on the Security Council, Africa, with the largest single membership in the General Assembly, is without a vote there.

When Mr. Oakley suggested that there is in fact an African seat on the Security Council at present the Foreign Minister said that neither he nor his African colleagues saw things that way. Morocco and the other North African states were not considered to be African for this purpose due to their membership in the Arab League.

Secretary Rusk then said that in spite of the possibility that the Russians would again bring forward the idea of a troika the United States hoped U Thant would be elected for a full term. He did not think the Russians would push the troika idea hard at this session, but he felt Russia might agree to keep U Thant on only as Acting Secretary General. The first choice of the United States in this matter was to have U Thant become Secretary General for a full term with the approval of the Security Council. If the Russians should block this the General Assembly could vote to have U Thant stay on as Acting Secretary General for a full five-year term in order to keep the machinery of the Secretariat running.

Wachuku replied that what counted was the man, and the work he did, rather than his title. It was essential, however, that the man be able to carry out freely his responsibilities under the Charter and that he be appointed for a full term.

226.   Memorandum of Conversation[1]

Washington, October 2, 1962.

SUBJECT

Meeting with The President—United Nations Matters

PARTICIPANTS

The President
Ambassador Adlai E. Stevenson, U.S. Representative to the United Nations
Assistant Secretary Harlan Cleveland

1. General Assembly.

Governor Stevenson reported on a relatively quiet and orderly beginning of the General Assembly, with Zafrulla Khan proving to be an admirable Chairman. He said there seemed to be a widespread awareness by Assembly members of a political season in the United States, and predicted that major excitement would be withheld until after the U.S. Congressional elections.

2. Cuba.

The President of Cuba, Dorticos, will speak in the Assembly next week. Governor Stevenson said he was tentatively planning to speak under the Right of Reply Assembly procedures. The President warmly commended Governor Stevenson on his quick reply to the Gromyko speech last week, and suggested that this time, in addition to the U.S. reply, a Latin American be recruited to chime in if possible.

3. Southern Rhodesia.

The President commented that at the Sunday, September 30 luncheon with Lord Home,[2] the British did not indicate any inclination to take any new steps, but wanted to hold things still until after the spring elections, because they thought that would best serve the purpose of keeping Whitehead in power. Governor Stevenson and Mr. Cleveland discussed the desire of most members of the General Assembly for assurance that the British would not leave Southern Rhodesia to become an independent country until the franchise had been broadened to include many more Africans. Governor Stevenson said he had suggested to Lord Home a simple statement which the British might make,

---

[1]   Source: Kennedy Library, National Security Files, Subjects Series, United Nations (General), 9/62–10/62, Box 311. Confidential. Drafted by Assistant Secretary Cleveland.

[2]   Not further identified.

giving this assurance in a way that should not upset the political prospects of Whitehead in Southern Rhodesia.

4. Nuclear Testing.

After some discussion of the arrangements for the debate on nuclear testing, the President indicated he thought it would be appropriate for Governor Stevenson to make the opening U.S. speech in Committee I on that subject; the presumption is that Arthur Dean will make a major speech on Disarmament, and will of course handle the day to day debate on both of these, and related subjects, in Committee I.

5. Johnson Plan.[3]

A discussion of the present state of the Johnson Plan produced ready agreement that the present purpose of the exercise, from our point of view, is to keep the matter open until November, and meanwhile to discuss with the Israelis some of the specific problems involved, including the point they have raised on the ceiling of the number of Arab refugees who would be repatriated to Israel.

Governor Stevenson expressed the hope that what would be kept open would be the substance of the Johnson proposals, and not merely the manner in which they might be buried. In the course of the discussion, Mr. Cleveland described the essence of the Israeli position as an unwillingness to make a side arrangement with us on a ceiling (for example, one refugee being repatriated for every nine resettled outside of Israel) if this crucial part of the arrangement was not known and at least acquiesced in by the Arab states concerned.

In this connection, Governor Stevenson reported on a conversation yesterday with Foreign Minister Fawzi of the UAR, who had seemed prepared to discuss the matter of a ceiling on repatriation but was anxious to discuss two other questions:

a. the number of refugees who would be accepted by Israel, and
b. some indication of how they would be treated when they went to Israel.

Governor Stevenson reported that the Israeli Delegation in New York seemed to be recruiting co-sponsors for the "Brazzaville Resolution" calling for direct negotiations between Israel and its Arab neighbors. The President expressed his understanding that the Israelis had undertaken not to introduce it. Mr. Feldman, who joined the meeting for a few minutes at this point, said the Israelis had assured him that they would not introduce it unless there was a major change in the sit-

---

[3] Documentation on the Johnson Plan is in *Foreign Relations*, 1961–1963, volumes XVII and XVIII.

uation. An illustration of a major change would be if the U.S. decided to support a pro-Arab resolution such as the Arab Custodianship Proposal or the reconstitution of the Palestine Conciliation Commission (PCC). The President asked Mr. Feldman to convey to the Israelis his (the President's) understanding that they were not going to introduce the resolution and the President's desire that they let him know if this understanding was, or turned out to be, incorrect.

6. *Hungary.*

Governor Stevenson reported that the vote on inscription of the Hungary item had gone rather badly; the item had been inscribed, but with a considerably smaller vote than in previous years. He thought there was some possibility of negotiations with the Hungarians on amnesty for political prisoners, but that the vote might stiffen their resistance again.

7. *Congo.*

Governor Stevenson said that Foreign Minister Spaak of Belgium is about to go back to Brussels and consider with his government whether they should now move to a decision to consult with Union Miniere that revenues would be paid only to the Central Government and that in the event of Tshombe's resistance to reconciliation, the mines would be shut down. He thought that Spaak might add withdrawal of Belgian technicians to the agenda of possible measures. He commented that Ambassador MacArthur believes that there is only a fifty-fifty chance they could take such measures in the present state of Belgian politics. The consequence of failure in the Congo, Governor Stevenson said, would be extremely serious. Adoula would fall and his successor would be far less satisfactory from our point of view. There would be pressure in the UN, particularly from the Africans, for some kind of military action against Tshombe. If the U.S. refused to go along with such action, it would be like breaking faith with the United Nations action and its own Congo policy. The prospect of U Thant's reelection or indeed his willingness to run for reelection would be dimmed. And on the ground in the Congo, there would be a break-up of the Congo, continuous civil war, and a golden opportunity for the Soviets.

Governor Stevenson mentioned the idea of Wachuku and possible other African moderates' coming in as conciliators, but referred to it as a last resort after the West's and the UN's efforts to bring the situation to a head had seemed doomed to failure.

The President hoped the Belgians would be willing to use as much influence as they have, but did not indicate what the U.S. policy would be in the event of failure of the present efforts toward reconciliation. He indicated he would await a report from Under Secretary McGhee, particularly on his trip to Elisabethville this week.

The President asked Mr. Cleveland to secure from the Defense Department an up-to-date appraisal of the military balances in the Congo, taking into account the latest information available on the apparent build-up of both ground troops and air capability on the part of Katangese forces.

---

227. Circular Airgram From the Department of State to All Posts[1]

CA–3524 Washington, October 3, 1962, 10:15 a.m.

[Here follows a paragraph explaining that the purpose of the paper was to "provide useful background on the complexities of what will continue to be a troublesome problem for the United States in future General Assemblies."]

SECURITY COUNCIL ELECTIONS

Procedure

Three members are elected to the Security Council annually for a term of two years. Security Council elections are by secret ballot without nominations or discussion. Members customarily announce their candidacies but voting is in no way restricted to announced candidates. United Nations members simply write the names of their three choices on a single ballot. Any country receiving a two-thirds vote (74 on the basis of 109 members and barring invalid ballots and absences) is elected. If all three members are not elected on the first ballot, this is followed by two "restricted" ballots limited, as the results of the first ballot may require, to the two, four, or, conceivably, six members having received the highest vote short of two-thirds on the first ballot. If the necessary number of elections do not result from those two ballots, there is another "unrestricted" ballot, followed if necessary by two more "restricted" ballots and so on ad infinitum until three members are elected. If the election deadlocks, as it has on occasion, a split-term compromise, arranged privately but announced and endorsed publicly, may be necessary to achieve the requisite two-thirds vote.

---

[1] Source: National Archives and Records Administration, RG 59, Central Files 1960–63, 320/10–362. Confidential. Drafted by Virginia F. Hartley on September 24; cleared by John N. Washburn, Louise McNutt, George N. Monsma, James M. Ludlow, Richard Friedman, and Jesse MacKnight; and approved by Woodruff Wallner.

Precedents

At the first General Assembly in 1946, it was agreed that the six elective seats on the Council would be allocated geographically as follows: 2 seats for Latin America, 1 seat for Western Europe, 1 seat for the Commonwealth, 1 seat for the Middle East and Africa, and 1 seat for Eastern Europe. This was an equitable distribution at that time when there were only three African members—Egypt, Ethiopia and Liberia—besides the Union of South Africa (eligible for the Commonwealth seat) and only one Asian member—the Philippines—besides China (a permanent SC member) and India (eligible for the Commonwealth seat). Until recently, despite the expanding UN membership, this pattern has continued to enjoy very substantial support, primarily because each area saw in it the best means of protecting its own seats under the original allocation. United States efforts since 1955 to use the seat originally allocated to Eastern Europe to provide for Africa and Asia have, therefore, been only partially successful. This seat was split between the Philippines and Yugoslavia in 1956–57, occupied by Japan in 1958–59, split between Poland and Turkey in 1960–61, and split between Rumania and the Philippines in 1962–63. The only other departure from the "gentlemen's agreement" of 1946 was in 1960 in the case of the West European seat, when Liberia contested the Portuguese candidacy and Portugal eventually withdrew as part of a compromise reached between the West Europeans and the Africans splitting the term between Ireland and Liberia.

Present Status of Candidacies

Chile, Ireland, and the UAR leave the Council at the end of this year. Brazil is the LA choice to succeed Chile; Norway is the WE choice to succeed Ireland; Morocco is the Arab League choice to succeed the UAR. This latter seat, however, is not an Arab League seat but, as noted above, a Middle East-African seat; and Afghanistan, Iran, Ethiopia, Mauritania, and Nigeria from this general area have also all announced candidacies. Ethiopia has now withdrawn its candidacy. Reports indicate that the UAM states at their recent meeting decided to withdraw the Mauritanian candidacy. Nigeria has specifically stated that it is a candidate for any of the three seats to be filled. The Nigerian Foreign Minister, Wachuku, and other Africans argue that Latin America, with two of the six elective seats on the Council, and Western Europe, with Britain and France permanent SC members, are both overrepresented on the Council in terms of the present UN membership. Reports from the recent UAM meeting also indicate that in deciding to withdraw the Mauritanian candidacy those states further decided to seek to reach agreement in New York on a single Monrovia group candidate, with Nigeria the most likely choice. If this agreement is reached, there will be four serious contestants for the three seats to be filled this year. There is no indication that the Afghanistan or Iranian candidacies have attracted any substantial support.

[Here follows a section on the relative strength of the candidates.]

Possible Outcomes

On the basis of the above analysis:

1. Norway could be elected on the first ballot if it gets the Soviet bloc vote or if it gets a sufficient number of neutralist and/or Monrovia group votes.

2. If, however, the Monrovia group makes a concerted attack on the WE seat and therefore votes as a bloc for Morocco, and the Soviet bloc and the neutralists support this attack by voting for the Monrovia candidate instead of Norway, the end result is likely to be a split-term between Norway and the Monrovia group.

3. If, on the other hand, the Latin Americans split as between Morocco and the Monrovia candidate and the Monrovia powers either vote as a group for Norway or split as between Morocco and Norway, the end result could be a split term between Morocco and the Monrovia candidate, depending on how the splits were divided.

4. Morocco could be elected on the first ballot if it gets either all the Latin American or all the Monrovia group votes or a substantial number of both.

Alternatives for the United States

In order to protect the Western voting position on the Security Council, the primary US objective in this selection is to preserve intact the LA and WE seats to be filled, without seriously jeopardizing UAM support of our position on other Assembly issues and with as little damage as possible to our relations with Morocco and the other Arabs and with Iran. If the WE seat, which appears the most vulnerable, is again split, a split-term tradition for this seat will be well on the way to becoming established as it has been for the seat originally allocated to Eastern Europe.

We have taken no position among the various Middle East and African candidates. Iran would undoubtedly be the most helpful on the Council but its candidacy appears to have little chance of success. In the United Nations context, we see nothing to be gained by a vote for Morocco, which has one of the poorest voting records in the General Assembly from our standpoint. Moreover, with Ghana already on the Council, our vote for another Casablanca power against a Monrovia power is certain to be deeply resented by the Monrovia group, whose voting record generally is more favorable to us than that of the Casablanca group and which includes the UAM on whose support we depend heavily on certain vital issues in the Assembly such as Chinese representation. Moreover, a United States vote for Morocco would not appear to have any value in obtaining additional votes for Norway. However, we have acquiesced tacitly in Norway's deal with Morocco, i.e., 15 WE votes for Morocco in return for 15 Arab votes for Norway, and we are therefore not in a position to undertake any active campaign either against the Moroccan candidacy or in support of any rival candidate.

In this situation, we would appear to have the choice of either voting for Iran as an ally in the absence of any Middle East-African agreement on a single candidate (if the Iranian candidacy is maintained) or voting for the Monrovia group candidate (if it is clear that the group's objective is not the WE seat and that our vote for the Monrovia candidate would in no way prejudice Norway's chances). The situation is in fact so delicate that we may wish to keep our vote secret. In any event we are not in a position to make any decision until the intentions of the Monrovia group and trend of developments in New York are clearer.

Tactics

Unless it is clear that any Monrovia group drive is directed toward the Middle East-African seat and not the WE seat, it will be to our advantage to have the elections held as early in the session as possible, thus giving the Monrovia group as little time as possible to organize a drive against the WE seat. Liberia's successful drive in 1960 was greatly assisted by two facts—1) that Portugal was the WE candidate, and 2) that the elections were held very late in the session.

We will also be in a better position to try to ward off an African drive against the WE seat if we can assure the Africans that there will be one elective seat available for Africa south of the Sahara next year and thereafter. The African drive for a seat this year is more emotional than reasonable since with Ghana already on the Council, Africa south of the Sahara is assured of representation in 1963 whoever succeeds the UAR and with the Philippines succeeding Rumania, the Afro-Asians will hold half of the elective seats on the Council next year, which is roughly equivalent to the proportion they represent of the total United Nations membership.

At the same time, we are sympathetic with the aspirations of the Africans for a designated seat of their own and we have under consideration some scheme of reallocation next year. One possibility would be to try to shift the Commonwealth seat to Africa. Given the present composition of the Commonwealth, the loss of this seat would do less damage to the Western voting position on the Security Council than the loss of the WE or an LA seat. As part of this plan we would also have to try to shift the original East European seat to Asia. In the absence of such a shift and with the Commonwealth seat allocated to Africa, Asian members would have no chance of representation except through the permanent SC membership of China.

Enlargement

Charter amendment is necessary to increase the size of any UN Council and amendments do not become effective until ratified by two-thirds of the members including the five permanent members of the SC. The enlargement question first came before the Assembly in 1956 and was debated at every session thereafter through 1960. While there was generally support for enlargement throughout this period, any Assembly action was discouraged by the consistent Soviet position, reiterated as recently as September 5 of this year, that it would not ratify any amendment of the Charter in the absence of the Chinese Communists. In 1960 it was decided to put the Soviets to the test by Assembly resolutions amending the Charter to increase the number of non-permanent seats on the Security Council and the number of seats on the Economic and Social Council. These resolutions failed of adoption in committee (majority vote) after they had been amended on a Nigerian initiative to provide for the immediate reallocation of existing seats. Nigerian Foreign Minister Wachuku said that to "bring up the question of amending the Charter was simply a delaying tactic".

The United States continues strongly to support reasonable enlargement of the Councils to accommodate the new members. The extent to which the Russians have succeeded in focusing attention on the Chinese representation issue rather than on enlargement has operated to the disadvantage of the United States. In this situation any United States initiative on enlargement is likely to be regarded as insincere by the Africans. For example, the Ghanaian representative in the 1960 debate equated the United States and USSR position, pointing out that while both supported enlargement "they made it impossible for reasons of national policy". This of course is a distortion of the facts. It is the USSR, not we, which is making conditions. We have consistently reiterated this in our discussions of the Russian position. However retention of the African support we now have for our position on the Chinese representation issue is crucial to the successful maintenance of this position in the General Assembly. There is a danger that the Africans, to whom the issue of equitable representation in the Council is of greater importance than the question of who represents China in the UN, may reach the conclusion that the quickest and least costly way of obtaining more seats on the Council, would be to pull the rug out from under us on Chinese representation.

The Department wishes to emphasize that the foregoing is particularly sensitive background material. It is of course obvious that we do not wish to indicate in any way that we are even contemplating that the Africans might make such a move.

Rusk

228.   Editorial Note

On October 17, 1962, Brazil and Norway were elected as non-permanent members of the Security Council for 1963, receiving 91 and 85 votes respectively. A second ballot, restricted to Morocco and Nigeria, resulted in Morocco's election by 73 votes to 35. (Memorandum from Woodruff Wallner to Secretary Rusk, October 17; National Archives and Records Administration, RG 59, Central Files 1960–63, 330/10–1762)

229.   Telegram From the Mission to the United Nations to the Department of State[1]

New York, October 19, 1962, 11 a.m.

1355. Re-election SYG. Stevenson discussed with SYG yesterday his intentions concerning re-election.

SYG said that, despite indications Sovs might seek have him once more named Acting SYG and limit his term to two or three years, he intended make clear he would serve only as full SYG and that principle five year term must be preserved. On other hand he admitted prospect five more years after Apr 1963 unwelcome to him on personal grounds and he would accept as maximum compromise five years from Nov 1961 when he was first elected, perhaps extended two more months so that close his term would not fall in midst GA

---

[1] Source: National Archives and Records Administration, RG 59, Central Files 1960–63, 310/10–1962. Confidential; Limit Distribution.

sessions. To Stevenson's suggestion he might take full five year term from Apr 1963 and, if he so desired for personal reasons, resign after three years, Bunche, who was present, argued it would be impossible for SYG to resign before end his term without "walking out on the world."

Thant also said he is being urged by many Afro-Asian friends to permit presentation his candidacy in near future and many, including even Yugos, urging he not make this dependent on Congo developments. He is therefore inclined authorize action as soon as UAR replaces Sovs in chair Nov 1.

SYG also said he has told Bunche his final decision on candidacy will be affected by whether or not latter also agrees to stay on.

Comment: We urged Thant to move forward rapidly lest developments after mid-Nov complicate UN situation. While we would prefer full five year term from Apr 1963, we consider five years from Nov 1961 acceptable in view his strong personal preferences. Unless Sovs prove unexpectedly difficult, we would expect, in light strong GA sentiment, they would accept this "compromise" and election might be carried through rapidly by mid-Nov.

Stevenson

230.   Information Memorandum From the Assistant Secretary of
        State for International Organization Affairs (Cleveland) to
        the Under Secretary of State for Political Affairs (McGhee)[1]

Washington, October 31, 1962.

SUBJECT

   Analysis of the General Assembly Vote on Chinese Representation

On October 30, 1962, the General Assembly defeated the Soviet
draft resolution which would have replaced the Republic of China in
the UN by the Chinese Communist regime. The vote was 42 in favor, 56
against, with 12 abstentions. (A detailed voting list is attached.)[2] The
vote on a similar draft last year was 37 to 48 with 19 abstentions.

The big gain for our position this year consisted of winning the
affirmative votes of the seven UAM states which abstained in 1961
(Central African Republic, Chad, Congo (Brazzaville), Dahomey, Ivory
Coast, Niger, and Upper Volta). The defection of Laos was to be expected; on the other hand the defections of Malaya and Tunisia are disappointing. (Malaya moved from a negative vote on the Soviet draft to
abstention, while Tunisia shifted from abstention to an affirmative
vote.)

Of the six new members who voted, Jamaica and Rwanda voted in
our favor; Algeria, Burundi and Uganda supported the Soviets; and
Trinidad abstained.

---

   [1] Source: National Archives and Records Administration, RG 59, Central Files
1960–63, 303/10–3162. Official Use Only. Drafted by William B. Buffum on October 30 and
cleared by Sisco.
   [2] Not printed. The draft resolution is UN doc. A/L.395, October 18.

231. Airgram From the Mission to the United Nations to the Department of State[1]

A–923   New York, December 5, 1962.

SUBJECT

    Private Meeting of SC to Recommend the Appointment of a Secretary General

The UN Security Council held its 1026th meeting at 11:00 Friday, November 30. Since no official records are kept of private SC meetings, the following is transmitted for information and Department records.

The President of the Council for November, Mahmoud Riad of the UAR declared that under Rule 48 of the SC Provisional Rules of Procedure the meeting would be held in private and that the requirement for consecutive translation would be dispensed with.

After exchanging compliments with Amb Zorin on the latter's conduct as October's SC President (this being the first—and only—meeting in November), Riad ascertained that there was no objection to the adoption of the agenda. He then called attention to the draft resolution sponsored by Chile, Ghana, Ireland, Romania, United Arab Republic, Venezuela which reads as follows: "The Security Council, having considered the question of the appointment of the Secretary General of the United Nations, in accordance with Article 97 of the Charter, recommends to the General Assembly to appoint U Thant as Secretary General of the United Nations for a term expiring on November 3, 1966." There followed a lengthy dissertation on the parliamentary situation with regard to the election of Secretaries General. Riad noted that the Council was acting under Article 97 of the Charter, the text of which he read. He then cited the General Assembly Resolution deciding to fix the term of the Secretary General at five years and the resolution of November 3, 1961 appointing U Thant Acting Secretary General to fill out the unexpired term of the late Dag Hammarskjold extending until April 10, 1963.

The import of Riad's remarks was to convey the idea that the power to deal with the term of office of the Secretary General resided in the General Assembly.

Having completed his introductory remarks Riad then called on the members in the order in which they had inscribed starting with Ghana,

---

[1] Source: National Archives and Records Administration, RG 59, Central Files 1960–63, 330/12–562. Limited Official Use. Drafted by Franklin L. Mewshaw and cleared by Richard F. Pedersen.

Venezuela and Chile all of whom made pro forma speeches in favor of Thant's election.

The next speaker was Professor Haseganu of Romania who observed, among other things, that the entire structure of the United Nations must in due course reflect the major transformations which had taken place in the world over the past 17 years and specifically that the Secretariat must in time give full recognition to the "principle of equal representation" among the three groups of states in the world. Meanwhile Professor Haseganu assured the Council that Romania had only the highest regard for U Thant and would vote in favor of the draft resolution.

Mr. Tadgh O'Sullivan of Ireland then spoke in place of Ambassador Boland who was, O'Sullivan said somewhat unconvincingly, absent because he thought the meeting would be held in the afternoon.

Ambassador Stevenson spoke next. The text of his speech is appended as an annex.[2]

Ambassador Seydoux then spoke followed by Sir Patrick Dean of the UK who loyally associated himself with the reservation entered by Ambassador Stevenson as to the propriety of the SC expressing itself on the question of the term of office of the Secretary General. Sir Patrick said, ". . . while the Security Council may wish to recommend a specific term it is for the General Assembly to determine the length of that term."

The next speaker was Ambassador Zorin of the USSR who recalled turgidly the well-known Soviet position on the proper constitution of the organs of the UN, as stated by Chairman Khrushchev at the 15th GA and by other Soviet speakers thereafter. To leave no one in any doubt as to his drift, Zorin stated that the USSR favored entrusting the direction of the Secretariat to three individuals. He said the USSR would continue to strive for the arrangement as being the only one consonant with reality. But in the meantime, the USSR was prepared to support the election of U Thant, taking into account the good job he had done in the preceding year, and especially the "positive action" he had taken to meet the "dangerous crisis in the Carribbean." Thant, Zorin said, had demonstrated his ability, in this and other crises, to take into account the legitimate interests of the main groups of states. Hence, the USSR had been prepared to support Thant's election to a full five year term but was willing to support the draft resolution which recommended a shorter term.

Ambassador Liu of China then spoke followed by President Riad of the UAR who praised Thant in glowing terms including more than perfunctory references to the UAR's friendship with Thant's homeland, Burma.

---

[2] Not printed.

The meeting ended with an elaborate and lengthy minuet wherein Riad requested the Under Secretary Kiselev of the USSR, first to read the draft communiqué. This Kiselev did in fluent, Cairo-accented English. The communiqué was then solemnly assented to by the Council. At Riad's request Kiselev then read for the Council's approval the text of a letter notifying GA President Zafrulla Khan of the Council's action. The Council assented and Riad signed. Finally came a letter to U Thant, read by Kiselev, assented to by the Council and signed by Riad.

The meeting ended at around 12:15 p.m.

Stevenson

232. Memorandum From Secretary of State Rusk to President Kennedy[1]

Washington, undated.

SUBJECT

The 17th General Assembly: A Summary Round-Up

I.

The 17th General Assembly shaped up rather better than we predicted in the Strategy Paper which formed the basis for the United States Delegation's marching orders. Our main objectives for this session were achieved. We avoided predicted trouble in the debates on nuclear issues and outer space. We successfully walked the tightrope on such ticklish matters as Palestine Refugees, Angola, and Population policies. We had predicted trouble on colonialism in the form of extreme resolutions on Portugal and South Africa which were adopted over our opposition. Above all, we succeeded in strengthening the Organization's capacity to act in several significant ways.

We hope that part of the reasons for this outcome was the major effort we put into advanced planning both in Washington and in New York; the thorough consultations we had in Europe and elsewhere on specific issues ahead of time; the three intensive months of first-rate politicking and

---

[1] Source: Kennedy Library, National Security Files, Subjects Series, United Nations (General), 9/52–12/62, Box 311. Confidential. Transmitted to Bundy under a December 26 covering memorandum from Assistant Secretary Cleveland.

advocacy by an outstandingly professional delegation in New York; and the speed with which both the White House and the Department were prepared to consider and decide the major policy issues on which Ambassador Stevenson required guidance from Washington.

But perhaps the most important reason for the good results in this Assembly, from the United States point of view, was the effect inside the General Assembly of two external events: the Cuban crisis and the invasion of India. To be realistic, the 17th General Assembly must be described in terms of the impact of these two concurrent peace-and-security crises. This much at least can be said:

—The normal Soviet stridency was muted. The Soviet Delegation was in some disarray; it seemed to go back to Moscow more frequently than before for instructions on small points. This was particularly noticeable on the nuclear issues and in the outer space debate.

—The damage which the Cuban missiles did to the credibility of Soviet statements was pervasive. By contrast, it helped to increase confidence in the words, and the actions, of the United States.

—The Latin American caucus, confused and leaderless before the Assembly got under way, coalesced into a more effective political grouping after the demonstration of unanimity in the OAS vote on Cuba. This was particularly notable on issues like Disarmament and Nuclear Testing where the security of the free world was more obviously at stake. The Latin American consensus fell apart, however, on some colonial issues.

—The Western Europeans were much more active this year than last, and much more successful in getting their way—except on some colonial matters. This was quite directly the result of our working, bilaterally and through the North Atlantic Council, to energize our European allies on General Assembly matters.

—There was sharp shift in the sub-surface attitude of the Indian Delegation. Where, as on Chinese Representation, a cultural lag resulted in a neutral Indian vote, the Delegation's lack of enthusiasm for its own role was evident. India voted with us on Hungary and Korea for the first time.

—The dramatic demonstration, in Cuba, that aerial photographs could contribute to maintaining world peace took the fire out of the predicted Donnybrook Fair over observation satellites during the Outer Space debate.

—The Assembly was somewhat more willing to stand up and be counted on the "anti-Communist" issues. The Soviet position on Korea took an exceptional drubbing. And there were more references to Soviet colonialism and imperialism, with fewer Communist rebuttals and less neutralist yawning, than in recent years.

—The neutrals were busily engaged in agonizing reappraisals of their own policies. The outcome is unclear, but the reassessment will doubtless reinforce the central place which the United Nations occupies in protecting the interests of the world's smaller and weaker nations.

Thus while events in the Cuban sunshine and the Himalayan mists never reached the agenda of the General Assembly, the drama of that Security Council confrontation and the spectacle of the world's leading neutrals appealing for Western military aid was deeply felt on all the major items of parliamentary diplomacy this season.

II.

Our Strategy Paper emphasized that we should look upon the 17th General Assembly as a period of consolidation as distinguished from a platform of new initiatives—that we should concentrate on strengthening existing machinery for nation-building, peaceful settlement, and peacekeeping.

Much of this machinery, of course, goes on without requiring Assembly action from year to year except to finance it. United Nations Technical Assistance activity was carried on in 109 countries; the expanding Special Fund (of which Paul Hoffman was reelected Managing Director by this General Assembly) touched 88 countries; and the effort to make sense out of the Specialized Agencies' work, country by country, has now placed a coordinating UN technical aid "presence" in more than 50 countries; many of these UN representatives also serve in practice as informal political advisers to new governments trying to decide how to use what kinds of external aid.

The several United Nations peacekeeping operations have continued—without much attention from the Assembly—in the Congo, the Middle East, Korea, and Kashmir. The idea of a UN presence to help resolve secondary security threats continues to spread—the UN's executive attention has been engaged this year in the West New Guinea transfer, and in the Thailand–Cambodia dispute; the Secretary General may also be asked to supervise the disengagement of the UAR and Saudi Arabia from Yemen. And the 17th General Assembly extended the concept of a UN presence to British-protected Oman and South Africa's mandated territory of South West Africa.

In strengthening the United Nations machinery, the high-light actions were these:

—The unopposed election of U Thant for a full term, with an eloquent silence about the Troika, except for a plaintive "history will prove us right" from the Soviets.

—The consequent assurance that there will be no radical upset in staffing patterns in the Secretariat.

—The World Court's opinion on UN peacekeeping expenses in the Congo and the Middle East was accepted by an overwhelming majority (76–17–8) in spite of French and Soviet opposition.

—Unanimous approval of steps toward a UN Institute to train international operators, conciliators, and peacekeepers.

—An increase (from $25 million to $40 million) in the UN's Working Capital Fund.

III.

On disarmament, nuclear testing, and outer space, United States objectives were fully achieved and the 17th General Assembly behaved in a noticeably more restrained manner than the 16th Assembly did.

The *disarmament* debate was referred back to Geneva, where we wanted it.

On *nuclear testing,* one resolution clearly endorsed the US–UK comprehensive test ban proposal. The other, which started out as an uninspected ban, was amended to make it acceptably ambiguous; we even got in a reference to verification.

On *outer space,* the Assembly pushed along the cooperative arrangements in scientific research, meteorology, and communications. The Soviets started with a proposal for "general principles" of space law, but was discouraged from pressing the matter when we came up with our own set of "principles".

IV.

Colonialism is the only area in which we emerged with a spattering of egg on the face. We had to vote against an extreme resolution on *apartheid* (because it called for sanctions) and another extreme resolution on Angola (because it called, in effect, for ejecting Portugal from NATO). Our effort to get a United Nations rapporteur for the *Portuguese territories* brought the Portuguese a little farther than they had intended to go—but not far enough to satisfy the dominant opinion among the Africans.

The continuing fireworks between the Africans and the colonial powers, focusing more and more in the Decolonization Committee (formerly the Committee of 17, now 24), will continue to present our most difficult UN dilemmas. We may soon need to face the question whether we should get into the middle of each colonial question at the committee stage.

But outcroppings of moderation about the unfinished business of decolonization were also in evidence. We were able to help get a relatively mild resolution on *South West Africa* (which proposes a UN presence there), and we succeeded again in eliminating from the annual omnibus resolution against colonialism a dangerous section calling for target dates to be set for each territory not yet free.

The General Assembly continued to make quite a distinction between South Africans and the Portuguese as unregenerate, and the British who are regarded as trying, though not hard enough, to get on with the decolonization process. We abstained on two resolutions about *Southern Rhodesia,* which urged the UK to do what it was unwilling (and now, with Whitehead's surprising defeat will be unable) to do.

As the number, if not the intensity, of colonial issues declines, the Soviet empire stands out more and more prominently on the horizon. Last year our long and careful statement on Soviet colonialism was well received but not widely echoed. This year during the debates on colonialism, some ten delegations made a point of referring to the dependent status of Soviet satellites, and to the subject peoples inside the Soviet Union itself.

V.

The Chinese Representation vote came out even better than last year, with no challenge to the "important question" issue.

The Soviet move to seat a representative of North Korea during the debate on the Korean item was resoundingly defeated. Our resolution reaffirming the United States position on Korean unification attracted 55 votes, against the 45 with which it was passed last year.

The Hungarian item was kept on the UN's action agenda in a way that should be both more popular and more effective. The Secretary General will not try to achieve at least an amnesty for the 1956 Freedom Fighters.

VI.

Under the general umbrella of the Decade of Development, the United Nations in 1962:

—Joined with the FAO in the World Food Program;
—Completed plans for the UN Conference in Geneva in February, on the application of science and technology for the benefit of less developed areas;
—Called a world trade conference for 1964 that will present major political dangers and also opportunities for the Atlantic nations;
—Started building regional economic development institutes in Latin America, Africa, and Asia;
—Struggled with the population dilemma by formally recognizing its importance but voting against UN technical aid for population control;
—Completed the UN Convention on Marriage; and

—Passed a remarkably good declaration on "Sovereignty Over Natural Resources" which affirms the importance and the legal rights of private investors in the less developed countries.

A detailed summary of the main issues in the 17th General Assembly is appended for your information.[2]

Dean Rusk[3]

---

[2] Not printed.

[3] Printed from a copy that bears this typed signature.

---

233.   Memorandum Prepared in the Department of State[1]

Washington, undated.

MEMORANDUM ON UN FINANCING

1. A Special Session of the United Nations General Assembly will convene in May or June to consider the problem of financing UN peace and security operations beyond June 30, 1963. In the meantime, starting at the end of January, a twenty-one member working group including the United States will begin meeting to produce a financing proposal to be put before the Assembly. The purpose of this memorandum is to review briefly UN financial developments over the past year and to indicate the present thinking of the Administration as to how the United States should seek to influence the working group's proposal and the Assembly's action on this matter.

2. When U Thant was elected in the fall of 1961 to serve out the unexpired term of Dag Hammarskjold, he turned at once to an interim solution of the financial crisis of the United Nations, caused by non-payments of assessments for peace-keeping operations in the Middle East and the Congo. Such non-payments now amount to about $100 million. After consultation by the Secretary-General with the World Bank and the U.S. and other delegations it was proposed that the General Assembly:

---

[1] Source: Kennedy Library, National Security Files, Subjects Series, United Nations (General), 1/63–4/63, Box 311. Official Use Only. Transmitted from the State Department Executive Secretary to McGeorge Bundy under a January 21 covering memorandum. According to the covering memorandum, Secretary Rusk had approved the memorandum on UN financing and asked for the opinions of Bundy and the President prior to consultations with Congressional leaders. A handwritten note by Bundy on the covering memorandum reads: "P[resident] approves."

a) assess all members for the cost of the peace-keeping missions in the Middle East and Congo for the first six months of 1962.

b) request an advisory opinion from the International Court of Justice as to whether the assessments for the Middle East and the Congo operations were legally binding on members.

c) authorize a $200 million issue of UN Bonds, repayable out of regular budget assessments, to provide stopgap funds until more durable arrangements could be made.

3. These things were done. The six-month assessment was passed by the Sixteenth General Assembly—using as a basis the regular administrative budget scale, modified by substantial reductions for the poorer countries and supplemented by voluntary contributions from the U.S. and, as to the Middle East, the UK. The World Court rendered a favorable advisory opinion, and the 17th General Assembly accepted the opinion by a vote of 76 to 17 with 8 abstentions. As of January 9, 1963 about $148 million of bonds have been sold or pledged, including presumed U.S. matching of pledges already made by others.

4. Meanwhile additional steps are being taken to put UN finances on a better basis. The Secretary-General has secured the services of Mr. Eugene Black as financial adviser to the United Nations; an energetic campaign to collect arrearages, based on the World Court opinion, is getting underway; and the UN Working Capital Fund has been increased by the General Assembly from $25 to $40 million.

5. Thus bankruptcy has been at least temporarily averted; the peace-keeping missions in the Middle East and Congo have been maintained; the legality of the assessments for these operations has been affirmed; delinquent members are now confronted with Article 19 of the Charter, which provides that any member with arrearages totalling more than the last two years' assessments loses the right to vote; and the twenty-one member working group has been established to grapple with the problem of financing further peace-keeping costs.

6. The regular UN scale of assessments was developed for meeting administrative expenses: the present U.S. percentage is 32.02%. The majority of UN members have taken the position that this regular scale should not be applied to the costs of substantial peace-and-security operations like those in the Middle East and the Congo. They contend that the regular scale was intended to apply only to the ordinary budget, that its application to peace and security operations of this magnitude is inconsistent with the primary peace-keeping responsibility of the five permanent members of the Security Council under the UN Charter (particularly in operations where all troops are furnished by smaller nations) and with relative capacities to pay. Besides, they believe, it would impose too heavy a financial burden on the smaller members, particularly the developing nations.

7. In financing any international operation there are two main alternatives: to levy an assessment on all countries, or to depend on voluntary contributions from some countries. During the past few years, peace and security operations have in practice been financed by a combination of these methods. The Administration and the Congress have already determined that they do not wish to continue this past practice.

8. If the remaining peace and security expenses in the Middle East and the Congo were to be financed only by voluntary contributions, our judgement is that the United States would probably have to pay considerably more than half of the total amounts required. If these costs are to be met by assessment, the experience of the past five years has shown that it is not politically feasible to get a two-thirds vote of the General Assembly for meeting them according to the regular administrative scale. Consequently a special scale for these peace and security operations (or different special scales for each of them) would have to be developed, which would put a relatively smaller load on the smaller and poorer countries and a relatively larger load on the financially stronger countries.

9. Since we cannot predict the nature of any future peacekeeping operation, it would not be desirable to establish ahead of time a peace and security scale for unknown contingencies. Some operations might be of sufficient interest to the United Nations as to justify a somewhat higher share, others might be regarded by the United Nations as not justified unless they could be financed on the regular budget scale. The United Nations should, therefore, oppose any general decision to establish a peace and security assessment scale for all purposes, but should participate in developing special scales for meeting the necessary costs of the Middle East and Congo operations for the coming year or so.

10. After months of consultations with experts in and out of the government, therefore, we are inclined to work for a program which:

a—encourages, whenever special circumstances make it possible, the financing of peace-keeping operations primarily by the nations most directly concerned (for example, the cost of the West New Guinea operation is being split between The Netherlands and Indonesia);

b—continues, as at present, to finance minor peacekeeping operations through the Regular Budget at the regular scale (as is now done for armistice supervision teams in Kashmir, Korea, and the Middle East);

c—adopts no "peace-and-security scale" for more than a year or so in advance, and makes no advance financial decisions about future costs of unknown peacekeeping operations;

d—maintains for the Middle East and the Congo the principle of collective financial responsibility of all UN members (this means a general assessment against all states rather than a resort to voluntary contributions);

e—assigns to small and developing states smaller shares of the costs of such operations than they pay under the regular scale (this means a "special" scale in which the major powers are assessed more than in the regular scale); and

f—gives a greater voice—in view of their greater contributions—to the larger contributors as to the establishment of any special peace-and-security scales in the future (which means a new mechanism such as the peace-and-security financing committee described below).

11. Specifically, the United States would be prepared to work with the other members of the United Nations in meeting Middle East and Congo costs after July 1, 1963, through a program that would combine these two elements:

a. Special scales of assessment for the Middle East and Congo operations which provide somewhat larger percentages for the U.S., other major powers, and those which can afford it; and provide smaller percentages for the developing countries. (Such increased assessments on the U.S., above the present 33-1/3% Congressional limitation, should be considered in light of (i) the cost to the U.S., in dollars and in American lives, if the U.S. were required to conduct, directly, similar operations in its own interest; and (ii) the capacity to pay and special responsibilities of the stronger UN members).

b. The establishment of a new peace-and-security financing committee of the GA, in which larger contributors would have relatively stronger representation than in the GA. This Committee would be established by a new rule of procedure of the GA, which would give it the sole authority to recommend to the GA special scales of assessments for peacekeeping operations, and provide that no such special scale can be established by the GA without the committee's concurrence.

234. Telegram From the Mission to the United Nations to the Department of State[1]

New York, February 1, 1963, 11 a.m.

2937. Policy. Possible SC problems.

1. As we have indicated in previous tels we may find ourselves in unusually difficult situation in SC this year on colonial issues.

2. Balance voting in SC on such questions is obviously different than on questions in which US has direct political interest, as LAs,

[1] Source: National Archives and Records Administration, RG 59, Central Files 1960–63, UN 3 SC. Confidential; Priority.

Norway, China and Philippines will all be reluctant to oppose African initiatives or to see SC sessions on colonial questions end without any action. China would find it particularly difficult avoid voting for reses desired by French-Africans. Not inconceivable therefore that we could find ourselves in position where, under Moroccan-Ghanaian sponsorship, these issues would come to SC and reses be put through with 7 votes which we did not like at all but which many of our friends would support and we would not voting against (veto).

3. Way to meet this is to develop policies for SC action which we could support and which could either be put forward by us or be floated through friendly small powers. Such policies would unquestionably have to go beyond positions which South Africans or Portuguese would accept and possibly also somewhat beyond what UK or French (or even we) would prefer. But this might be opportunity make SC function at its best through eliminating extremism among African demands while inducing some movement from administering authorities.

4. Hope therefore Dept can give early attention to steps we could advocate on main colonial questions which we likely to face in SC.

5. In terms GA reses these questions are specifically Angola and apartheid, with possibility also of sessions on other "Portuguese territories" or on issues which may be referred from Comite of 24. Pertinent sections of reses read as fol:

Angola: SC is requested "to take appropriate measures, including sanctions" to secure Portugal's "compliance" with pertinent reses.

Apartheid: SC is requested "to take appropriate measures, including sanctions" to secure South Africa's compliance with pertinent reses and "if necessary, to consider action under Art 6 (expulsion)." Special Comite on South Africa also requested to report to SC as appropriate on South African "racial policies."

Portuguese Territories: SC requested, in case Portugal refuses to comply with pertinent reses, "to take all appropriate measures" to secure "compliance of Portugal with obligations as member state."

Comite of 24: Requested to apprise SC of any developments which may threaten international peace and security.

6. UKDel also very much concerned with this problem and raised it with respect to apartheid on their own initiative in our talks yesterday. They already realize that unless UK policy can go at least as far as recommendations for arms embargo they will be in real difficulty. They are therefore anxious for close consultation with us on this whole SC problem.

Stevenson

235.   **Letter From the Representative to the United Nations (Stevenson) to Secretary of State Rusk**[1]

New York, February 5, 1963.

Dear Dean,

As you may have noticed from some of our recent telegrams, the Secretary-General and some of his senior staff officers, particularly Ralph Bunche, are becoming increasingly sensitive about any appearance that their actions are dictated or unduly influenced by the United States. The Secretary-General has as you know proved remarkably cooperative and has been willing to accept our counsel to a degree which none of us could have predicted when he was first elected. His guiding principles and main objectives are close to ours and I am confident he will continue his cooperation providing we do not embarrass him by revealing how close it is. As you well know he must, as the world's principal international civil servant, maintain a public posture of impartiality and, to the extent he may have felt he has been publicly exposed as cooperating too intimately with the United States, he may come to feel he has either to reduce that cooperation or to balance it by actions more pleasing to the Soviet bloc.

Unfortunately a number of cases have recently occurred in which we have either taken up with other Governments or revealed to the press matters of UN concern on which we assumed his cooperation would be forthcoming but about which he either had not yet been consulted or had not reached a decision.

For example, in a number of our diplomatic consultations concerning the Congo, concerning the Bunker mediation on West New Guinea, concerning a UN Representative to Thailand–Cambodia and, most recently, concerning Yemen, the Department has on occasion moved rapidly ahead before he was aware of or had approved our plans. As a result he had been asked from time to time by other Delegations about plans which are supposedly his but about which he is only vaguely aware and which are in actual fact our plans for him. This is understandably embarrassing to him.

Similarly, press statements and background briefings in Washington or elsewhere have sometimes revealed prematurely the

---

[1] Source: Kennedy Library, National Security Files, Subjects Series, United Nations (General), 1/63–4/63, Box 311. Personal and Confidential. An attached memorandum from Schlesinger to Bundy, February 9, reads: "I attach a copy of a letter from Governor Stevenson to the Secretary of State discussing an issue which is causing certain problems in our relationship with U Thant."

Secretary-General's plans or our plans for cooperation with him in ways which have not only been embarrassing but have occasionally resulted in his abandoning a course we favored which he had intended to pursue. There were several such cases in the closing stage of the Katanga affair, at least one in connection with Yemen, and most recently a statement by the Cleveland Mission in Leopoldville which gave Bunche the mistaken impression the Mission was injecting itself between UNOC and UNNY.

The problem is not really one of substance, since the Secretary-General has generally approved and appreciated what we have been doing and has been more than willing to cooperate if given time and appropriate diplomatic cover. I suggest, therefore, that we refrain, despite the urgency of a particular problem, from negotiating a solution with other Governments before the Secretary-General has approved our proposed solution and requested our cooperation. In the second place we must exercise extreme caution in public statements (including backgrounding) on matters on which we are working in cooperation with the UN, and particularly on matters in which we have asked the Secretary-General to play a leading role.

Above all we must avoid the natural temptation to let it be known that a projected future action or a successful past action by the Secretary-General was really our idea in the first place. A few more such revelations will, I fear, make him shy away from future U.S. assignments for him no matter how sensible and desirable they may be.

It would be most helpful to me if you could at some point review this problem with the senior officers in the Department and ask them to pass the word down through the ranks. I am sure the main difficulty arises from the fact that it is not always appreciated how circumspect we have to be about our close relationship with an international official of the stature and responsibility of the Secretary-General.

Sincerely,

Adlai E. Stevenson[2]

---

[2] Printed from a copy that bears this typed signature.

236.   Telegram From the Mission to the United Nations to the
        Department of State[1]

New York, February 7, 1963, 7 p.m.

2985. Deptel 2084.[2] Working Group of 21 re financing UN peace-keeping operations.

Mtg held this morning with Reps of UK, Canada, Netherlands, Australia, Japan, and Italy. Plimpton outlined major points of US position contained in memo of Jan 21, 1963,[3] and asked for reactions.

All reps of above-mentioned states said they were without instructions and would have refer Plimpton's remarks to govts before indicating official reactions. However, personal reactions summarized as fol:

1. There appeared be general doubt we could secure complete acceptance of concept of ad hoc approach to future financing of peacekeeping operations. Barton (Canada) indicated his govt felt rather strongly there should be decision now which would govern future operations. However, from discussion, appeared likely we could convince states represented go along with this approach, at least for present.

2. Several reps indicated we must have better definition of states entitled to lower percentages in special scale than that used in past. We indicated we recognized this problem and hoped be able solve it.

3. There appeared be general acceptance of idea that special scale be treated in segments with under-developed countries receiving smaller percentage assessments as total cost of operations increased.

4. There was no stated objection to our view that all states represented at mtg must expect increased assessment percentages in any special scale. However, several reps, particularly those of Canada, UK, and Australia, pointed to fact that their govts considered they were already overassessed in regular scale of assessments because of US ceiling. They indicated that they would have to know specific percentage increases which we contemplated for them before committing themselves to acceptance of increase.

---

[1] Source: National Archives and Records Administration, RG 59, Central Files 1960–63, UN 10. Confidential.

[2] In telegram 2084 to USUN, the Department authorized the Mission to "consult with friendly governments represented on Working Group of 21 to learn reaction to major points of U.S. position as outlined in memorandum on UN financing dated January 21, 1963." Priority was given to obtaining the views of the United Kingdom, Sweden, the Netherlands, and Australia. The Mission was instructed that it did not need to be specific about the percentage to which the United States might agree. (Ibid.)

[3] Document 233.

5. Doubts were expressed as to possibility of our success in securing acceptance of comite on financing of major peace and security operations. Barton said he believed Canadian Govt would be strongly opposed to including on comite states such as USSR and France, which had significant arrears.

6. Appeared to be majority view there was little hope we could secure acceptance of position that $10 million of expenses for each of existing UN operations be financed on basis regular scale of assessments in 1963. Consensus seemed be that, while we should try for this result, we could not realistically hope to finance on regular scale more than a total of $10 million; that is, $5 million per operation.

Reps present extremely anxious have firmer and more detailed statement US position so that common view can be introduced into Working Group as soon as possible. Other reps had fear, which we share, that it dangerous permit Working Group proceed very much longer with only extreme views of China and LA's serving as basis for discussion.

Stevenson

---

237. **Telegram From the Department of State to the Mission to the United Nations**[1]

Washington, February 14, 1963, 4:07 p.m.

2147. For Plimpton. Revised draft instructions.

Consultation with number of Congressional leaders, several friendly governments and further consideration within Executive Branch, lead to following conclusions and instructions which should govern USUN on UN financing issue under consideration in Committee of Twenty-One:

UN Congo and Middle East operations continue to serve national interest of U.S. and our financial support must be continued even in face of opposition by communist bloc members, certain non-communist powers, and financial incapacity or limited sense of responsibility of

---

[1] Source: National Archives and Records Administration, RG 59, Central Files 1960–63, UN 10. Confidential; Priority; Limit Distribution. Drafted by Woodruff Wallner and Wilbur H. Ziehl and cleared and approved by Frank Hefner.

certain less developed governments. Support for this assistance will be on increase as favorable developments continue in Congo and size and cost of UN Congo forces are reduced.

However, measure of support for our financial assistance for Middle East and Congo operations, particularly in Congressional arena, will also be influenced by extent to which our negotiations successfully

(a) enable substantial reductions from level of 47-1/2% (assessed and voluntary contributions) to a maximum contribution of less than 40% for U.S.,

(b) eliminate system whereby our voluntary contributions have, in effect, provided reductions to smaller countries—including communist countries,

(c) provide for increased contributions over regular budget scale for other major powers, including USSR,

(d) establish ad hoc "peace and security scale or scales," to apply not beyond 1964 and only for existing operations, and

(e) provide for a control mechanism which affords greater voice to the U.S. in UN financing of large scale peace-keeping operations.

USUN is urged support general criteria which recognize: that whenever special circumstances make such financing possible, peace-keeping operations shall be financed primarily by the nations most directly concerned (for example, the present split in costs for West New Guinea between the Netherlands and Indonesia); that minor peace-keeping operation shall, as at present, be financed through the regular budget at the regular scale (as is now done for armistice supervision teams in Kashmir, Korea, and the Middle East), and the collective financial responsibility of all UN members for approved operations.

Ideally, U.S. contribution based on regular UN scale, should be used as basis for supporting UN peace-keeping operations. Dept. fully aware of conditions that will not enable achievement this objective. USUN should, however, stress our strong views this position in view all other U.S. contributions to international organization, magnitude our foreign assistance and support regional defense arrangements.

Mission should seek to secure acceptance of principle that a minimum amount for Congo and Middle East operations should be financed at regular budget scale rates. Dept. believes this minimum should be set at $10 million for each operation.

Basic point of departure for amounts above $10 million per operation should be effective rates which experience has shown to be maximum which could be assessed, by nation, in 1962 for Congo and Middle East. (For example, 1962 Afghanistan regular budget rate was 0.05%. Effective assessment peace-keeping rate was 0.01%.)

Remaining unassessed percentage (after above computations) to be distributed over UN membership based on criteria which assures that costs are shared as widely as possible among major contributors and holds the U.S. percentage of total costs as close to 32.02% as possible. In no event should U.S. cost reach 40% of total cost.

USUN should urge 21-Committee to ask SYG for forecast soonest of budget requirements, separately for Congo and Middle East, for periods July thru December, 1963; January–June 1964; and July–December, 1964. Magnitude believed partial key to construction of special scale.

Every effort shall be made to provide a control mechanism which affords greater voice to the U.S. in the financing of large-scale peace-keeping operations. (A small Committee, preferably of 15 nations or less, seems preferable.)

P.L. 87–731 (bond authorization legislation),[2] especially sections 1, 4, and 5 contain guidance and prohibitions and are to be considered a part of these instructions. They should be strictly construed. Similarly the law restricting budget commitments to 33-1/3% must be carefully observed by USUN in its negotiations and public statements.

USUN shall urge the inclusion of a strong section in 21-Committee's report on the need for immediate, effective emphasis on collection of back debts and 1963 assessments. Consider also whether a formal recommendation from the Committee for a "Finance Minister" is advisable.

USUN authorized use own discretion in discussing these instructions in advance with friendly nations and reporting reactions prior unveiling position in 21-Committee.

Rusk

---

[2] An Act to promote the foreign policy of the United States by authorizing a loan to the United Nations and the appropriation of funds therefor, signed into law on October 2, 1962. (76 Stat. 695)

238.   Memorandum From the Assistant Secretary of State for
        Congressional Relations (Dutton) to the Assistant Secretary
        of State for International Organization Affairs (Cleveland)[1]

Washington, February 21, 1963.

I want to express genuine concern over several points in cable
#3065 from Ambassador Plimpton to the Department on February 18
concerning UN financing.[2]

1. The proposal that we provide for the Congo operation in excess
of our 33% financial contribution through "goods and services" is not a
legitimate alternative unless authority can be cited for providing the
goods and services. I would appreciate any information you have on
legal authorization for that course.

2. Congress should be consulted before U.S. representatives even
privately urge the Committee of 21 to adopt such an approach, regardless of whether we reserve our right later to oppose it. You will recall
that much of the Congressional suspicion over the UN loan proposal
stemmed from the belief that the U.S. had launched the idea in New
York before consulting with principal members of the Foreign Relations
Committee in Washington. This consideration is wholly apart from the
damage I would think would be done in the UN if we "steer a group
toward a solution" and then find out Congress won't go for it.

3. I must take strong exception to the statement that "special scale
may be imposed on us over our objection." Congress is in no mood this
year to have the UN impose anything on the U.S.

4. Congress will not likely agree to even the 33% levy if Cuba, Albania
and others get their contribution decreased, as proposed in the cable. I
realize that we should not allow communist policy to determine whether
or not we will support the UN—but that is exactly the psychological situation confronted on the Hill this year. If there is a reduction in the assessments for Cuba, Albania, etc. I anticipate an amendment will be offered on
the House floor to reduce our contribution by the same percentage.

5. I find the talk under paragraph #2 in the cable about a voluntary
U.S. contribution to make up for any deficiency caused by non-payment

---

[1] Source: Kennedy Library, Cleveland Papers, UN Financing 1963, #2, Box 19. No
classification marking. The memorandum bears a handwritten note reading: "H. Here we
go again. W."
[2] In telegram 3065 from USUN, Ambassador Plimpton noted that there were three
alternatives: a special scale (possibly involving U.S. contributions in goods and services),
a combination of regular scale and voluntary contributions, or drastic reduction or elimination of UN peacekeeping operations if special financing were not forthcoming.
(National Archives and Records Administration, RG 59, Central Files 1960–63, UN 10–4)

by communist bloc as unrealistic at best. The cable indicates that there is considerable sentiment in the UN to reduce the level of the UN Congo forces. Exactly the same sentiment prevails in the U.S. Congress.

Fred

---

239. Telegram From the Mission to the United Nations to the Department of State[1]

New York, February 21, 1963, 7 p.m.

3102. Department pass O'Brien at White House. Working Group of 21. We are informed Dept is considering instructing USDel take position in Working Group that US Govt will not contribute in excess of 33-1/3 per cent—whether by assessed or voluntary contribution—to cost of ONUC and UNEF for second half of 1963.

We fully understand that such position would be desirable in light of general Congressional attitude towards unsatisfactory UN financial situation and past reliance of that organization on what are thought excessive contributions from US. We appreciate that this attitude has been aggravated by such factors as continued failure majority UN members pay their arrears despite GA acceptance of ICJ opinion, failure of UN members fully to subscribe UN bond issue, Special Fund project in Cuba, and UNESCO pamphlet.

Despite this Congressional attitude, we find it difficult relate insistence on 33-1/3 per cent limitation on such US contributions to vital US interest in UN operations in Middle East and Congo. This vital interest was clearly expressed in Cleveland's memo of Jan 21 to Secy concerning UN financing.[2] This memo pointed out that in "the real world of international politics . . . there will doubtless be cases where the US interest would call for US support beyond its 'fair share'—despite the cost in dollars and damage to the principle of collective responsibility." It indicated that there was "compelling rationale for . . . recognizing that, for other major operations (those not financed by countries directly concerned), we can use UN for peace-

---

[1] Source: National Archives and Records Administration, RG 59, Central Files 1960–63, UN 10. Secret; Limited Distribution. Passed to the White House at 11:05 p.m.

[2] Document 233.

keeping (in larger operations) only if we are prepared to pay more than one-third of cost."

We agree completely with foregoing statements. Accordingly, we have very grave doubts about wisdom of position Dept now considering if US really desires continuation of ONUC and UNEF operations in second half of 1963. Further, in our view, such position likely adversely affect rather than improve UN financial position.

Our reasoning is as follows:

1. US is one of rather small minority of UN member states interested in continuing ONUC and UNEF operations at anything like their present levels. Indeed, there is undoubtedly absolute majority of states which believe it would be better for organization discontinue both operations immediately. We realize that it difficult for US Govt accept this assessment of situation because of its belief that these operations have been extremely important to US and vital to UN itself if its peace-keeping ability were to be maintained. Nevertheless, we are convinced that our assessment is sound and that sizeable majority of members would prefer have UN spend its available funds on economic assistance rather than use them for UNEF and ONUC. Certainly this is and always has been position of all LA states.

2. It is for foregoing reason that it has been necessary, in effect, for US to "buy" votes for Congo and UNEF financing reses over years. There has simply not been any possibility of securing two-thirds majority for assessment on basis of regular scale of assessments of any sizeable amount of money for two UN military operations. As result, US has made substantial voluntary contributions in order secure necessary two-thirds by ensuring reduction of assessment percentages of many states. Fact that US alone made such voluntary cash contributions in case of ONUC, despite our efforts to convince others to contribute, is clear evidence of fact that few, if any, of major powers consider operation to be as important as we did.

3. It has been largely because of US willingness to make these very large contributions for ONUC that this govt has been able call tune. By and large, Congo operation has been run by SYG exactly as we wished, and other countries (except Sov bloc) have been prepared accept this in silence so long as they were not required pay large amounts for operation. It cannot be expected that this acquiescence in US domination of Congo operation can continue if we now take position that we have no greater responsibility for financing costs of this operation than we have for financing regular budget.

4. If we now insist that all costs of ONUC and UNEF for second half of 1963 ($50–60 million) be financed on basis of regular scale of assessments, it will mean that we are requesting less-developed countries to

contribute at five times rate at which they have contributed for last two years. There is absolutely no possibility of securing two-thirds votes in Assembly on this basis.

5. It has been proposed that only portion of UNEF and ONUC costs be assessed on basis of regular scale and that balance be secured by voluntary contributions with US share of voluntary contributions being at 33-1/3 per cent. First of all, on this basis it unlikely that more than total of $10 million, if that, could be assessed on basis of regular scale: balance would have be raised by voluntary contributions. Even assuming, which we believe impossible, that $30 million could be assessed on basis of regular scale, there is no chance securing necessary $30 million balance from voluntary contributions from other govts if US can offer no more than $10 million. Most members, including particularly other potential contributors, namely, Commonwealth and Western Europe, simply do not accept proposition that US fair share is only 33-1/3 per-cent. It important that we face up to this fact when making our calculations. This proposal is in our view highly unlikely to produce desired results, and if we stood on it we must be prepared to see UNEF and ONUC soon brought to halt.

6. Apart from causing wind-up of ONUC and UNEF, proposed US position is likely worsen UN financial situation and our ability to deal with it. It will antagonize less-developed countries, and make it less likely they will pay arrears and less likely they will support US in applying Art 19 when it becomes applicable in 1964 to USSR. It will antagonize other major powers, who, as mentioned above, simply do not accept proposition that US share of UN peace-keeping operations should be no more than 33-1/3 percent. Certainly these countries will not be encouraged to buy additional UN bonds.

7. In our view, UN financial situation today is better than it was year ago and is likely improve if we take constructive action in Working Group, and if we avoid kind of action described above. In considering failure of UN sell entire $200 million bond issue, we must recognize that any real chance of selling entire issue was almost surely lost as result of long delay on part of US Govt in deciding that it would purchase UN bonds. Failure sell entire issue should not be taken as indication of lack of responsibility on part of other UN members, particularly when it is noted that fifty-eight countries have made purchases or pledges and that number of these are buying bonds in relatively greater amounts than is US. With respect to arrears, we must recall that Assembly accepted advisory opinion of ICJ only on Dec 19, 1962, and that we cannot reasonably expect that govts which were awaiting this event could take necessary legislative action to commence payment of arrears by this date. As matter of fact, however, Greece, which had made no payment

on UNEF and ONUC since 1957, has not paid up all its arrears totalling almost $300,000. Further, all LA govts, which until last Assembly had refused make payments for ONUC and UNEF, have now announced publicly they will pay their arrears. In our view, this is real progress, and indeed as much progress as we could hope for at this stage. We do not think that we should now jeopardize further progress by taking position which cannot be accepted by countries in arrears and will in fact antagonize them.

8. We must recognize that major cause of financial predicament of UN today is amount of arrears owed by Communist bloc, China, and France. Vast majority of UN members consider that they are in no position contribute to solution of these arrears problems until they are called upon to vote on application of Art 19 of Charter to countries in arrears. They believe that only US is possibly in position at this time to deal with countries in question and bring about payment of arrears owed by them. We cannot see how position Dept now considering can favorably affect this situation.

9. Finally, in our opinion there is reasonable possibility of securing in Working Group majority support for financing formula which will be more palatable to Congress than that used in past, in that it will reduce US percentage significantly below past 45–49 per cent and will provide that other major contributors come along with us in paying either by assessments or by voluntary contributions an amount in excess of regular budget percentages. We believe this can be worked out either on basis of regular scale of assessments or on basis of assessed plus voluntary contributions.

10. In our view it is important that we choose immediately which of these courses to follow. It would be most difficult to negotiate two alternative proposals either of which might be satisfactory to us. It would be unwise to expend heavy energies now to work out satisfactory formula for special scale including committee, etc., and be faced with possible necessity within two or three months of attempting to scrap it if it then appeared it would run into Congressional difficulties. We would much prefer to choose now even though choice were to give up special scale for present. This would provide best chance of preventing adoption of special scale calling for US assessment of over 33-1/3 percent and would permit US to focus Working Group's attention in next two or three weeks on constructive proposal along lines previous financing patterns.

11. Suggest that our course of action in Working Group be as fol:

That we make strong statement along lines of draft submitted Dept, indicating our serious dissatisfaction with present financial situation of UN and attitudes of members; that we indicate that as long as this situation continues US will not be in mood to be particularly forthcoming supporting future UN peace-keeping operations and that in particular we are unable to accept for 1963 special scale of assessments in which US percentage is in excess of 33-1/3 percent; that we indicate we would like to see UN work its way out of its difficulties and are prepared to work in cooperation with others towards constructive solution of immediate problem of providing finances for UNEF and ONUC during last six months 1963; that we are prepared to support our normal percentage of such costs but that our willingness to go further than this will depend on present conditions being substantially improved; that subject to this condition being fulfilled we would be prepared to negotiate assessment res for costs of ONUC and UNEF for second half of 1963 along general lines of past reses which combine assessments with voluntary contributions but with certain modifications as fol:

(A) That for last six months 1963 all UNEF expense (estimated $10 million) and first $10 million of ONUC (estimated $40–$50 million) be assessed on basis regular scale of assessments;

(B) That assessment percentages for less developed countries beyond initial amount assessed on regular scale should be at least 50 percent of those in regular scale rather than 20 percent as in assessment res for ONUC in 1961. We would base this argument on fact that costs to be financed in 1963 are less than half of those which had to be financed in 1961;

(C) That US will consider making voluntary contribution (subject to Congressional approval) towards deficit resulting from assessment of less than 100 per cent of costs, provided burden is shared by other larger countries, and it does not increase total US percentage above, say, 38 percent of total costs.

12. Given (A) strong pressure in Working Group for special scale of assessments and (B) our need secure voluntary contributions from other "developed" states, it occurs to us that fol "compromise" might be possible. Instead of having GA merely appeal in general terms as in past for voluntary contributions to fill gap resulting from assessment of less than 100 percent of costs, GA might recommend that, or invite, the 15–20 developed member states, which are assessed significant percentages, to make voluntary contributions sufficient bring their total contribution to certain specific percentages which would be above regular scale percentages. For example, GA might invite US make voluntary contribution sufficient to bring its total percentage to 38 percent. Thus, GA res would specify percentages totaling 100 percent, but contributions in excess of regular scale percentage would be voluntary. This approach would avoid our 33-1/3 percent limitation problem and at same time be more likely bring contributions from such countries as Canada and Australia which have found difficulty in past in responding to general appeal for voluntary contributions.

13. Crucial element in our thinking is need to have respectable negotiating position which can attract support of our friends from beginning. We must be able to hold out hope that US will be prepared to contribute more than 33-1/3 percent of total costs if we are to exert any real leadership toward constructive results.

Stevenson

---

240.   Telegram From the Mission to the United Nations to the Department of State[1]

New York, February 22, 1963, 4 p.m.

3120. United Nations Financial Situation.

Plimpton spent forty-five minutes with Secretary General describing very serious concern of Congress and executive branch of US Govt at lack of improvement in UN financial situation and necessity for immediate steps to be taken in attempt to bring about improvement. He gave SYG up-to-date figures as to arrears and bond purchases, pointing out lamentable number of countries which have not paid anything for peace keeping operations or subscribed for bonds.

Plimpton pointed out that in his consultations with Congressional leaders re US contribution to UN peacekeeping operations, he found acute awareness of failure by many member states to pay arrears or purchase bonds. Question being asked why US should do far more than its fair share in supporting UN if institution itself not making determined efforts to put its house in order and if its members, particularly the uncommitted states to whom the UN should be far more important than it is to the US, are not doing their share. Many members of Congress doubt wisdom of US continuing to contribute at anything like past level for UN operations in Middle East and Congo. As result of this Congressional attitude, US was finding it extremely difficult to take a position in Working Group of 21 on question of how peacekeeping operations should be financed. It appeared almost certain that US could not accept a mandatory assessment in excess of 33-1/3 percent.

---

[1] Source: National Archives and Records Administration, RG 59, Central Files 1960–63, UN 10. Limited Official Use.

Plimpton then pointed out importance of Secretary General taking personal interest in this matter and giving it very highest priority. He argued that while Secretary General could probably do little directly with the Communist countries and France, he could take strong lead, particularly with the UN-committed countries, to develop an atmosphere which would emphasize necessity that all countries support the UN financially, evidence GA's intent to apply Art. 19 of the Charter to the Communist countries and France when appropriate, and pressure them through feeling of diplomatic isolation. He should use Eugene Black as much as possible to induce the smaller countries to commence to pay their arrears and to make bond purchases. It was vitally important that some signs of progress be evident within the next month or two.

The Secretary General said that he was in full agreement with the US attitude on this matter and assured Plimpton he would give his personal attention to it. He pointed out, however, that the primary cause of most of the arrears was political and not the failure to press governments for payment.

Turner (UN), described discussion which had already taken place between Black and Secretariat officials (previously reported to Department).[2]

Secretary General closed by saying that he would have a further discussion with Black February 28, and would report to Plimpton the following week what action was being taken.

Stevenson

---

[2] Not further identified.

241. **Memorandum From the Assistant Secretary of State for Congressional Relations (Dutton) to the Assistant Secretary of State for International Organization Affairs (Cleveland)[1]**

Washington, March 1, 1963.

The proposed cable to Plimpton on financing UN peacekeeping operations[2] is generally excellent—but I have several minor objections:

1. The language near the top of page 2 that "our national interest would cause us not to favor abrupt phasing out of UN Congo operation" is irrelevant to the limited purpose of this first cable and prejudges a matter that deserves far more attention. Before Congress would approve any voluntary contribution or other special UN support in excess of 33-1/3%, key members would closely examine the Department as to whether a sharp reduction of UN forces in the Congo had been undertaken promptly on removal of Tshombe from the picture there. There is a strong possibility that we will be charged with deceit (and with some foundation for it) if we now try to keep UN forces there for a half year or more in order to supplement the local army or "do nation rebuilding" after going to Congress for funds for a year and a half allegedly to get Katanga re-integrated. Many in Congress will say the Department keeps changing its grounds for asking for these funds and this will be the third time we have shifted the basis of the UN being in the Congo.

USUN reports have said practically all UN members want the organization's forces there quickly phased out. The Secretary over three weeks ago[3] seemed to me to have indicated in a direct statement that a sharp reduction could be made in a month or so and a further drop to no more than a third of the present forces by early summer. For the present cable to say that no reduction is intended now (or perhaps for even six months) creates a record and confirms a policy that will cause vigorous Congressional objections that could impede if not checkmate later appropriations above 33-1/3%. At the least, the reference on page 2 should be deleted. Far better, the proposed policy behind the statement should be examined and that has not been done for key members of Congress as yet.

2. Reference to "whatever formula" near the bottom of page 2 seems to me to be extraneous and could be construed as an instruction to allow

---

[1] Source: Kennedy Library, Cleveland Papers, UN Financing 1963, #2, Box 19. No classification marking.

[2] Not found.

[3] Woodie was present. I believe you were abroad. [Handwritten footnote in the source text.]

far more discretion to negotiators than I think should be left open. Our maneuverability with Congress is not potentially that open-ended.

3. In order to keep the record straight, I think it would be useful for Plimpton to have specifically stated at this stage (even though it would not come up in negotiations for the present) that even if voluntary contributions are made above 33-1/3%, Congress would almost certainly attach at least two conditions to them. Only damage would be done by Plimpton negotiating or USUN agreeing to a compromise which could not be gotten through Congress because it failed to raise two limitations that would almost certainly be imposed by the legislative branch in the domestic environment that will exist here for at least the next year and a half. Those two conditions are following:

(a) That the contributions by small nations will have to be raised so that the U.S. would not, by any construction, be making up for amounts that Cuba and Albania should pay. Regardless of the strength of the small nations in the UN, no Congressman that is up for election in 1964 is going to to on record as providing contributions that allow Cuba and Albania to contribute less than their share of the regular UN budget for the Congo operation.

(b) Any voluntary contribution by the US to make up a deficit will be put on a matching basis with increased commitment from other large nations so as to be sure that any Congo deficit is actually met in full and there is not a second round when we would go back to Congress to ask for more money. In brief the matching formula imposed in the loan measure would almost certainly become a standard part of special U.S. contributions provided by Congress hereafter.

Fred

---

242.   Memorandum From the Assistant Secretary of State for Congressional Relations (Dutton) to the Assistant Secretary of State for International Organization Affairs (Cleveland)[1]

Washington, March 5, 1963.

I want to comment briefly on incoming telegram #2383 from USUN concerning the meeting of the Working Group of 21 in New York yes-

---

[1] Source: Kennedy Library, Cleveland Papers, UN Financing 1963, #2, Box 19. No classification marking.

terday.[2] The telegram indicates we are still not effectively communicating the adamancy of Congress on this problem and the fairly intractable problem we have. We still need to get across to Plimpton the urgency of our situation before his Wednesday meeting.

The following points in the telegram are particularly bothersome:

1. The next to last paragraph indicates little recognition of the importance of cutting the ONUC forces and overhead within the next several months.
2. The scale charges for the smaller countries cannot be reduced under any circumstances without payments by us in excess of 32.02% appearing to help Cuba and Albania, at least in some small amount.
3. I do not see how Plimpton can hold open the possibility of a voluntary contribution until we have gotten a Presidential decision and undertaken Congressional consultation.

Looking beyond tomorrow's meeting, we should have a prompt report on how much in military supplies the Defense Department can advance to the UN Congo forces and the President could then direct the Pentagon to write off. After we know the dollar value of that, we will know whether we can permanently stand fast at 32.02%, have to go to 38%, or will have to hit some figure in between.

A staff member of the Foreign Relations Committee told us today that the Secretary will shortly receive a letter from Fulbright indicating the Senate at this session will not agree to any contribution in excess of the 32.02%. We will be on the lookout for this letter.

Fred

---

[2] Reference should be to telegram 3211 from USUN, March 4. (National Archives and Records Administration, RG 59, Central Files 1960–63, UN 10–4)

243. Circular Telegram From the Department of State to Certain Posts[1]

Washington, March 5, 1963, 8:22 p.m.

1517. Re: Working Group of 21 on Financing UN Peacekeeping Operations.[2]

You requested approach Government to which accredited at high level and advise that U.S. plans make speech in Working Group of 21 on March 6 along following lines:

Begin speech summary:

Since 1957 when UNEF began, UN been unable find single solution peacekeeping financing satisfactory to all.

Believe current session Working Group must—because of time and impossibility of knowing nature of future—limit future financing discussion to Congo and Middle East operations.

Solution must be found by Working Group by March 31 and by GA by June 30 or face necessity discontinuance operations.

Strong case can be made for financing entire cost present operations at regular budget rates:

(a) rates broadly based on capacity to pay
(b) U.S. in past had no assistance through voluntary contributions of other members on Congo operation
(c) U.S. has 33-1/3% legal limit for assessed contributions
(d) 32.02% U.S. assessment rate is more than twice second largest contributor (USSR)
(e) U.S. contributions to entire UN family of agencies was 47% of budgets in 1962, both assessed and voluntary
(f) U.S. has paid (when voluntary contributions included) 44–49% of Congo and Middle East costs since 1947
(g) U.S. cannot agree that "token" or "symbolic" contributions from developing countries will meet the need this year: nothing token about keeping the peace.

Lack of demonstrated financial support by other members creates great difficulty for U.S. continuing contributions above 32.02%:

---

[1] Source: National Archives and Records Administration, RG 59, Central Files 1960–63, UN 10. Confidential. Drafted by Wilbur H. Ziehl on March 5; cleared by W. Paul O'Neill, William H. Sullivan, George N. Monsma, James M. Ludlow, and Richard Friedman; and approved by Woodruff Wallner. Sent to Buenos Aires, Canberra, Cairo, The Hague, Karachi, Lagos, London, Mexico City, Moscow, New Delhi, Ottawa, Paris, Rio de Janeiro, Rome, Sofia, Stockholm, Tokyo, Taipei, and Yaounde, and repeated to USUN.

[2] In telegram 3130 from USUN, February 25, Stevenson urgently requested instructions from the Department concerning the U.S. position in the Working Group of 21. (Ibid., UN 10–4)

(a) Only 52 countries have paid regular budget in full for 1962; UNEF, only 41; Congo, only 32

(b) Total arrears $121 million

(c) Only $74 million of $200 million bond issue subscribed by other nations than U.S. (and $14.3 million of this by non-UN members).

Conclusion: U.S. will assist other members in formulation of cost-sharing proposals to solve financial peacekeeping difficulties, but not in position at this time to accept mandatory assessments in excess regular budget percentage. Contribution of even a little more by U.S. through voluntary contributions dependent on whether vast majority of membership has the will to give financial support absolutely essential to survival. *End speech summary.*

FYI. Fuller details of U.S. position and support desired Gov'ts expected follow shortly to all non-Bloc posts. Background facts sent all diplomatic posts circular airgram 9150, Feb. 26.[3] Present instruction intended give short advance notice to member Gov'ts Working Group of 21 of position U.S. plans take in Plimpton speech March 6 before closed meeting Working Group. Advance notice to capitals Working Group members believed necessary because importance continued financing these peacekeeping operations. Realize some UN missions may report inadequately, if at all. End FYI.

This message being sent U.S. diplomatic posts all Working Group countries: Argentina, Australia, Brazil, Bulgaria, Cameroun, Canada, China, France, India, Italy, Japan, Mexico, Netherlands, Nigeria, Pakistan, Sweden, USSR, UAR, UK. (Mongolia and U.S. other two Working Group members.)

Parliamentary situation in Working Group is that Group is expected come up with solution to future financing of peacekeeping operations, especially UNEF and Congo, by March 31 looking to Special Session of General Assembly in May to deal solely with peacekeeping financing problems. Little progress has been made. Developing nations are urging reductions in assessments for peacekeeping (similar to those they received in the past) through special scale of assessments which would (a) reduce their assessments by 80% or more from regular budget scale and (b) assess U.S. and others they consider able pay higher percentages to make up difference. Friendly nations that more able pay favor combination of assessing portion of budget on regular scale for all nations and either (a) assessing balance on special scale with reductions for developing nations, or (b) making up balance through voluntary contributions from wealthier states. U.S. position stresses reasons why entire budget should be financed on regular scale. USSR, Bulgaria, and

---

[3] Not printed. (Ibid.)

Mongolia so far refuse agree or sponsor any method meeting these costs in which they pay any amount. France, although full member, sitting as observer.

FYI. Strong position being taken by U.S. in line with public opinion as to contribution U.S. should make and legal limit on mandatory assessment Executive Branch can accept of 33-1/3%. Only slight hint being given to Working Group at this time that if the member states put their house in order by paying past assessments U.S. might request authority to make additional voluntary contributions above regular budget percentage. U.S. position expected to shake Working Group and hope result will be more businesslike approach and recognition that financial support of peacekeeping collective responsibility of membership. End FYI.

For Ambassadors Moscow and Sofia: Approach Government at your discretion.

For USUN: Use discretion in advising delegations members of Working Group of general outlines Plimpton speech before delivery.

Rusk

---

244.   Telegram From the Mission to the United Nations to the Department of State[1]

New York, March 6, 1963, 8 p.m.

3236. Financing UN Peace-keeping Operations.

Stevenson and Plimpton called on U Thant yesterday and informed him of US statement to be given in Working Group of 21 today, outlining US position, and reasons therefor.

U Thant limited his reaction to statement he understood reasons for US position. Said his present intention cut Congo forces to 6,000 by July 1 and continue them at that level for balance of year should result in expenditure $5 million per month for July 1–Dec 31 period. Did not believe this figure could be reduced despite force reduction because of need retain at least eight fighter aircraft and transport equipment and

---

[1] Source: National Archives and Records Administration, RG 59, Central Files 1960–63, UN 10–4. Confidential.

because of high-level of civilian air costs (now $2 million per month). Said some fighter aircraft must be retained because of threat of former Katanga aircraft now in Angola and since only 25 per cent of Katanga gendarmerie had surrendered weapons. Said he saw little chance reducing UNEF cost unless character of operation changed or units of force drawn only from countries charging smaller amounts in reimbursable costs. He doubted political wisdom of changing "geographical distribution" in force units.

Turner argued that maintenance of UNEF at present level had little financial impact and that main problem was ONUC. He questioned whether USG could face possibility of financing ONUC even at $30 million level if US maintained its newly announced position re financing. He pointed to projected "net deficit" figures of $127 million at June 30, 1963, and $130–$150 million at Dec 31, 1963, unless extraordinary developments occurred and asked what US thought SYG should do when faced with these circumstances. He also made point that US was perhaps overstating lack of voluntary cooperation among member states in connection with ONUC and UNEF if it overlooked fact that the many countries furnishing troops were making voluntary contributions of services of these men and paying their salaries. He believed this element had never been taken fully into account when calculating cost-sharing for these peacekeeping operations.

At suggestion Narasimhan, it was agreed that SYG would immediately organize arrears-collection campaign in addition to efforts of Eugene Black, which would probably involve sending some senior staff members to various Finance Ministries in attempt collect arrears. Said he would report further re this within next week or two and hoped that some substantial results could be achieved by May.

(In separate conversation of Plimpton with Black, latter said he commencing writing of letters to Finance Ministers and planned visit some major capitals in attempt collect arrears.)

Stevenson

245. Memorandum From the Executive Secretary of the Department of State (Brubeck) to the President's Special Assistant for National Security Affairs (Bundy)[1]

Washington, March 7, 1963.

SUBJECT

Meeting with William Benton

William Benton is calling at the White House Saturday, March 9, 1963 at 12 noon to discuss with the President his nomination as United States Member of the UNESCO Executive Board.

In connection with this meeting, there are a few points about our policy towards UNESCO which the Department believes it would be useful for the President to emphasize to Mr. Benton and which he should understand in taking the Executive Board position. Additional background information on UNESCO is attached.[2]

The Department has recently been following a hard-hitting, critical but constructive policy vis-à-vis UNESCO in an attempt to make the Organization more efficient and effective. We have been endeavoring to suggest to UNESCO that it achieve a clearer direction of effort by curtailing activities of marginal and questionable value, so that the Organization may achieve an increasing capability to deal with the more urgent needs of the developing nations. In this regard, we have stressed that UNESCO, along with the other Specialized Agencies of the United Nations, should redirect its program so as to make its maximum contribution to the UN Development Decade; and that, in this connection, it should concentrate its efforts on educational development in the context of over-all economic and social development.

While UNESCO has the potential for making a tremendous contribution to educational development, it must be realized that, even in this field, there are serious limitations on the magnitude of the tasks it can assume—limitations imposed not only by the capacity of the Organization but by the unwillingness of Member States to increase their contributions to UNESCO in any appreciable degree. Most of the large contributors—the United Kingdom, France, West Germany, and the Soviet Union—will undoubtedly continue to channel most of their assistance to under-developed countries through their own bilateral programs; and the United States cannot be in the position of contributing more than its fair share of the Organization's budget. In addition,

---

[1] Source: Kennedy Library, National Security Files, Subjects Series, United Nations (General), 1/63–4/63, Box 311. No classification marking.

[2] This background paper is not printed.

we feel that UNESCO has not achieved the high operating standards of some of the other Specialized Agencies, particularly with regard to its management and the efficient implementation of its programs.

As you are aware, UNESCO is not a particularly popular organization in the United States. Much of the criticism directed against it is based on misconceptions. On the other hand, there is some criticism of it which is legitimate, as for example the recent outcry over the publication by UNESCO of a booklet on "Equality of Rights between Races and Nationalities in the USSR," a publication used by its Soviet authors for political purposes and blatant Soviet and anti-Western propaganda.

Senator Frank Church's Subcommittee of the Senate Foreign Relations Committee held a session on the UNESCO booklet early this week at which Assistant Secretary Battle was called to testify. The Subcommittee was reassured by Mr. Battle's statement that the U.S. is doing its utmost to discourage publication by UNESCO of documents of this sort and that the Department is trying to effect basic reforms in UNESCO. The Subcommittee was critical of UNESCO's activity, seriously questioned the usefulness of some of it, and indicated that it would continue to keep a close eye on the Organization.

As indicated above, the Department believes it important that Mr. Benton, in assuming his new duties, be aware of the critical but constructive approach the U.S. is taking in UNESCO and that he be sympathetic toward it.

Robert Kent[3]

---

[3] Kent signed for Brubeck above Brubeck's typed signature.

246. Memorandum From the Representative to the United Nations (Stevenson) to Secretary of State Rusk[1]

New York, March 7, 1963.

SUBJECT

Financing UN Peace-keeping Operations

1. The first steps have now been taken in our current efforts to improve the financial condition of the UN. Ambassador Plimpton has made a strong statement to the Working Group and the Department has sent out a series of circular telegrams to the non-Communist capitals urging that Member States agree that the regular budget scale percentages be used for assessing the Middle East and Congo expenses for the last 6 months of 1963.[2] It will now be necessary to wait for reactions to these approaches before we will be in a position to assess where we are and exactly what course we should take.

2. The purpose of this memorandum is to explore with you now the basic alternatives that lie before us and their relative advantages and disadvantages so that as we receive the replies from various capitals we will have an agreed basis for making our final choice.

3. Let me clear away immediately a number of points on which I think we are all agreed. Our objective is to obtain by June 30 a General Assembly resolution which finances the UNEF and ONUC operations for the last 6 months of 1963 on a reduced basis but not so far reduced as seriously to damage any political interests of the United States. We have decided and said to the Working Group that for this year we will oppose the use for this purpose of a compulsory special scale of assessments which would carry the United States beyond the present regular scale of 32.02% of the total cost (or the Congressional limitation of 33 1/3%). We have left open the possibility of other means of raising these funds, including some combination of compulsory assessments and voluntary contributions. We have so indicated to the Working Group, but have said that the United States is not prepared to make any commitment with regard to a voluntary contribution unless there is improvement in the UN financial situation and unless we are joined by

---

[1] Source: Kennedy Library, National Security Files, Subjects Series, United Nations (General), 1/63–4/63, Box 311. Confidential. An attached paper on "regular" and "aggregate" percentages contributed to the United Nations by certain states is not printed. Ambassador Stevenson forwarded a copy of this memorandum and one on the future of NATO under cover of a memorandum to the President on March 9. (Ibid.) An attached and undated note by Bundy reads: "Mr. President: the UN financing part of this is damn complex and can wait. The NATO part is an interesting anti-Acheson statement. McG. B."

[2] See Document 243.

a sizeable number of other countries for sizeable amounts. We are all agreed that the total contribution by the United States should not exceed 38%—needless to say, no indication of this figure has been given to the Working Group.

4. The problem that causes us concern is that under our present instructions we see no practical alternatives available to us at the end of the road which will enable us to attain our basic objective. There are only three means, as we see it, of obtaining the necessary funds. In our view two of these will almost certainly turn out to be impractical and the third may be barred by our present instructions.

5. The first means is to utilize the regular scale of assessment for the full cost of the operation. The second means is to use the regular scale of assessments to the maximum extent possible and to rely on voluntary contributions for the remainder. The third means is to utilize some form of the three-bite approach which involves utilizing the regular scale up to the maximum extent possible, then the regular scale with certain reductions for smaller states, and finally the larger states voluntarily contributing the shortfall caused by the reduction to the smaller states. An alternative three-bite approach would be to provide that the short-fall be funded out of the UN's Miscellaneous Income which is running around $6 million per year.

6. We have been assuming that the total costs we are dealing with here will probably amount to $50 million for UNEF ($10 million) and ONUC ($40 million) during the last half of this year. This may be reduced and to the extent that it can be the problem will be eased.

The Regular Scale Alone

7. Our view has been and remains that it will not be possible to raise this much money on the regular scale of assessments. We may be wrong; the returns from the capitals will soon tell us. If we are right, we must fall back on either the second or the third alternative. If we are right that the first alternative is not practical, the reason will be that, as some 6 years' experience has shown, the small states are not willing to be assessed for these large peace-keeping expenses under the regular scale of assessments. In other words, they will be insisting, as they have in the past, on adjustments making their part of the burden relatively smaller than under the regular scale, which necessarily means that the larger countries would pay a proportionately larger portion of the burden.

The Regular Scale Plus Voluntary Contributions

8. The regular scale would be applied to the maximum amount possible and voluntary contributions would be solicited for the balance. For

example, $10 million would be assessed on the regular scale; assuming that the smaller states are willing to pay at the rate of, say, 50% of the regular scale as to the $40 million balance (this is optimistic), do not assess the $40 million balance at 50% of the regular scale but assess 50% of the balance, namely $20 million, under the regular scale, leaving a $20 million balloon for voluntary contributions. These are the difficulties:

(a) This approach was tried in 1957 and discarded as unsatisfactory.

(b) The small countries want percentage relief rather than dollar relief, since only the former openly recognizes the principle that they should pay a lesser share of large peacekeeping operations.

(c) The larger countries are unwilling to make the large voluntary contributions involved.

(d) The Communists, French and other non-volunteers are not assessed as to the $20 million balloon and get off completely Scot free as to that part of the cost.

(e) If *all* the $20 million balloon is to be raised, the United States would have to put up, say, 80% of it, which would bring the U.S. total contribution to some 51% of the $50 million total, and it is extremely doubtful whether the balance could be obtained from others.

(f) If the U.S. contribution is to be limited to 38% of the $50 million total, this would mean it could only contribute $9,400,000 of the $20 million balloon, and, assuming (optimistically) that others would contribute as much as 25% of the U.S.'s contribution, there would be an unassessed and irretrievable shortfall of some $8,250,000 which could never be recovered from anyone. The operations would have to be cut down accordingly.

Finally, we do not think this formula could obtain the necessary 2/3rd vote in the General Assembly.

9. The only advantage that has been put forward in support of this formula is that it does not *in form* provide a "reduction" to the small states which the larger states make up. It is true that it does not, but it is also true that in *substance* it does: the smaller states pay *less* of the total than the regular scale would provide for, and some of the larger pay *more*. Furthermore, the price of avoiding the form of "reductions" is to give the same percentage reduction to all other member states, including the large Communist countries and France, and therefore either to leave a very substantial unassessed and irretrievable shortfall or to make it necessary for the United States, if the operation is to be funded, to pay much more than 38% of the total cost.

10. It would appear to us that the disadvantages from the point of view of the United States would far outweigh the advantages. We therefore wonder whether the Congress is really concerned with form rather than substance and whether it would not be wiser to explain the situation to them fully and try to persuade them to our view rather than take

a disadvantageous position because it is on the surface consistent with their views.

The Three-Bite Approach

11. This involves assessing an initial amount, as large as possible, on the regular scale and assessing the balance on the regular scale except that the percentages of the smaller countries are lowered. The balance is provided by voluntary contributions. Thus, of a $50 million total cost, $10 million might be assessed on the regular scale and the 18.47% aggregate regular scale percentages of the smaller states reduced, as to the $40 million balance, by 50% to 9.24%. This would produce a shortfall of $3,692,000, which would be met by voluntary contributions by the U.S. and other friendly developed states. Assuming that the U.S. put up 80% of the shortfall, its total contribution, assessed and voluntary, would be 35.5% of the $50 million total.

12. This is obviously much cheaper for the United States than the second alternative, and, indeed, seems to us the only means by which we can obtain the desired results within the 38% limitation.

13. It is, of course, similar to the approach used last year, which involved a "reduction" to Albania, Cuba, etc., and resulted in Congressional criticism. However, in that case the *entire* shortfall was taken up by the United States; we believe it possible, as regards the last 6 months of 1963, to get a sizeable number of other States to join in voluntary contributions to take care of a shortfall of this size.

14. The three-bite approach has made some headway in the Working Group. It is being carefully considered by some of our important friends, including the Australians and the Canadians. We think it might be possible to negotiate some such solution before the end of June within the 38% limitation. My feeling is therefore that we should concentrate our attention on the construction of a formula along the lines of the three-bite approach which would present the least difficulties to Congressional opinion. We have suggested several devices for this purpose.

15. The first would be to provide that voluntary contributions can be made in goods or services acceptable to the Secretary General. The United States could provide such goods and services and the President could waive reimbursement therefor under the Participation Act, in case it were decided that it would be inadvisable to ask for a Congressional appropriation of more than 32.02%. (This point is discussed in the last paragraph of our telegram 3130.)[3]

16. The second would be to ensure that other states make substantial voluntary contributions, which would differentiate the formula

---

[3] See footnote 2, Document 243.

from that criticized by Congress last summer—where the United States made up for *all* of the reductions. This could be done by prior agreement between the developed states or by the United States making its contribution on a matching basis.

17. A third possibility would be to provide that no reduction would be afforded to any state which has refused as a matter of principle to pay its peace-keeping assessments. Such a provision, if it could be put through, might well eliminate Congressional criticism, as no reduction would go to any Communist countries. However, it would cause serious difficulties as regards the Arab States, who have refused to contribute to UNEF.

18. It would, of course, be possible to arrange that the three-bite approach be presented to the world without the use of the word "reductions" appearing in any texts. There are many ways this could be done, and they should be fully explored, but the fact of the matter is that no formula has any chance of acceptance by the General Assembly which does not in fact provide relief to the smaller states and add correspondingly to the burdens of the larger states.

19. As things stand, our instructions, although they envisage the possibility of the United States going up to 38% and contemplate our entering into consultations with the Working Group, preclude the "reductions" which alone, we think, would make it possible for us to negotiate the financing of these peace-keeping operations on a U.S. 38% basis.

The Alternative Three-Bite Approach

20. The alternative three-bite approach is the same as the above, except that the shortfall resulting from lower assessments for underdeveloped countries would be financed from the miscellaneous income of the UN for 1964, which should amount to more than $6,000,000.

This approach would appear to have the advantages of avoiding voluntary contributions and of assuring the full collection of the shortfall. It is true that by reducing the miscellaneous income of the UN it would add to the dollar amount assessed against the United States as well as all other members in 1964. This method of dealing with a subject matter distasteful to the United States would be similar to that used for many years in dealing with the tax reimbursement of US nationals employed by the UN and in paying the awards made in 1953–54 by the Administrative Tribunal to the US nationals dismissed from the Secretariat. In both cases miscellaneous income of the UN has been used for these purposes without objection by the United States.

It appears possible on the basis of hasty calculations that this method could be used in connection with UNEF and Congo financing resolutions at the May Special Session of the General Assembly (and repeated at the Regular Session in the fall if these operations are to be continued into next year). The present level of miscellaneous income would appear to be sufficient for this purpose but it could perhaps be supplemented by having the UN issue a special series of UN stamps commemorating its peace-keeping operations.

21. Finally, let me share my concern that we are permitting ourselves to get bogged down in technicalities so that neither the Administration nor the Congress is able to take a clear view of our national interests in relation to the UN. We will, after all, have an annual financial problem in connection with the UN. We do need in the long pull to carry Congress with us in our broad view of those national interests. This broad view should, it seems clear to me, include the idea that the US should not allow the opposition of the Communist states or the inferior sense of responsibilities of others to stand in the way of our using the UN for such peace-keeping operations as we determine are in our national interest. This undoubtedly will mean, as it has in the past, that we will be called upon to pay more than one-third of the cost of these operations. It would, in my opinion, be a shame if through lack of real leadership with the Congress we allow ourselves to get permanently boxed in so that our true national interests cannot be served.

---

247. **Memorandum From the Executive Secretary of the Department of State (Brubeck) to the President's Special Assistant for National Security Affairs (Bundy)[1]**

Washington, March 18, 1963.

SUBJECT

U.S. Participation in the UN Committee of 24

The following memorandum provides information concerning the current meetings of the UN Committee on Decolonization.

General Assembly Resolution 1810 (XVII) (enclosed)[2] enlarged the Special Committee on the Implementation of the Colonialism

---

[1] Source: Kennedy Library, National Security Files, Subjects Series, United Nations (General), 1/63–4/63, Box 311. Confidential.

[2] Not printed. Resolution 1810 (XVII) was adopted by the General Assembly on December 17, 1962, by a vote of 101 to 0, with 4 abstentions.

548 Foreign Relations, 1961–1963, Volume XXV

Declaration from 17 to 24 members and requested it "to seek the most suitable ways and means for the speedy and total application of the Declaration to all territories which have not yet attained independence." A list of members is enclosed.[3]

At the 17th General Assembly the United States voted for Resolution 1810 (XVII) after defeating an attempt to have the Committee's mandate include the setting of target dates for the achievement of independence by the remaining dependent territories.

Our objectives are to have the Committee: (a) Operate by consensus rather than by voting; (b) Make factually accurate and politically realistic recommendations which we will be able to support; (c) Foster cooperation between the UN and Administering Authorities; and (d) Eliminate the Cold War from the Committee. In corridor conversations we have let it be known that we reached our decision to serve on the Committee again only after serious soul-searching and that our participation will be kept under review pending the actual operations of the expanded Committee. We should be prepared to take a walk if the Committee degenerates into a sounding board for the Soviet bloc, Mali, Iraq, Tanganyika and others who place a higher value on strident anti-colonial propaganda than they do on serious and constructive initiatives.

When votes are taken on what we consider to be unrealistic proposals, the prospective voting lineup is even more unfavorable than the one we faced last year. We must anticipate lopsided votes on the order of: 19 (Afro-Asians, Latin Americans and Soviet bloc)–5. On some of the more extreme proposals we will try to induce the three Latin Americans to abstain if they cannot vote with us. In view of the Committee's composition, we shall, so far as possible, concentrate on moderate and constructive policies rather than expand political capital in trying to increase the minority in which we will find ourselves on a number of issues.

The Committee held its first meeting on February 20 and to date has displayed unusual moderation. Coulibaly of Mali was elected Chairman and we succeeded in having a Western power, Uruguay, elected as first Vice-Chairman over Soviet objections. Cambodia was elected second Vice-Chairman. Syria was re-elected rapporteur. What promised to be a donnybrook if the Afro-Asian majority attempted to draw up a definitive list of all remaining dependent territories has not yet developed. This highly contentious issue, which might have involved Okinawa and might have obliged us to press for inclusion of

---

[3] Not printed. The members were: Australia, Bulgaria, Cambodia, Chile, Denmark, Ethiopia, India, Iran, Iraq, Italy, Ivory Coast, Madagascar, Mali, Poland, Sierra Leone, the Soviet Union, Syria, Tanganyika, Tunisia, the United Kingdom, the United States, Uruguay, and Venezuela. All but Bulgaria, Chile, Denmark, Iran, Iraq, Ivory Coast, and Sierra Leone had belonged to the Committee of 17.

certain Soviet non-self-governing territories, has thus far been avoided when the Committee adopted a practical work program approach.

In another display of initial moderation, the Committee decided to operate on the basis of consensus as much as possible. The Committee's current and prospective work program is as follows:

Portuguese Territories. As requested by the 17th Assembly, the Committee has decided to give priority to Portugal's African territories. Although the Soviets advocated going directly to the Security Council, Mali and other Afro-Asian Members have shown interest in reviving our rapporteur proposal which they rejected last fall. Chances are slender that some kind of UN role, e.g. a variation of our rapporteur proposal at the 17th General Assembly or a mission by the Secretary-General or his representative, can be developed in which Portugal and the Committee of 24 would acquiesce. We will nevertheless make an effort in this direction in order to keep it from an extreme tack. Portugal has declined an invitation to participate in the Committee's discussions of Portuguese Territories and has told us it cannot cooperate to any degree with the Committee, although it has left the door open for informal contact. Portugal has stated that it would be willing to have the rapporteur proposal reintroduced in the General Assembly.

If some form of Portuguese-UN cooperation cannot be worked out in the near future, we face the probability of a Security Council meeting where the African Members (Ghana, Morocco) might seek enforcement action including diplomatic and economic sanctions. In the absence of renewed large-scale violence in Angola, there is little prospect that seven affirmative votes could be mustered for such proposals. Should fighting erupt in the territories, the pressures for some kind of action in the Council (including a UN presence) would be considerably greater. We also face Security Council meetings on apartheid, inside or outside of South West Africa, particularly if large-scale violence develops.

Southern Rhodesia. The Secretary-General is awaiting a substantive reply to his letter of February 28 to the UK in which he offered to play a good offices role among the various elements concerned with Southern Rhodesia as requested by the resolution adopted by the 17th General Assembly. The UK appears to favor the Secretary-General's involvement; however, given Winston Field's overall approach and his antipathy toward African appeals to the UN, we should not be optimistic that his attitude will be favorable. Together with the UK we should counsel moderation in and outside of the Committee and should point out the dangers of creating a situation in which Southern Rhodesia would declare its independence.

South West Africa. We and the UK have urged the South African Government to cooperate with the resolution adopted at the 17th

General Assembly to the extent of admitting some kind of UN executive presence into South West Africa. While South Africa will not permit the establishment of a political UN presence, we hope that it will agree to a resident UN technical assistance mission prior to the Committee's consideration of this item.

Spanish Territories. Since the Committee of 17 did not have time to take up Spanish Territories, we believe the Committee of 24 will wish to consider them. We hope that a spirit of cooperation will evolve between Spain and the Committee. Spain has recognized its Charter obligations to submit information on its territories to the Committee on Information from Non-Self-Governing Territories. While the Spanish Government has accepted the principle of self-determination and has instituted vigorous economic and social development programs for its territories, this problem remains a highly controversial and sensitive one within the Government. US policies in Africa are viewed with suspicion in Spain and in any discussions with the Spanish in the Committee of 24 context we must realize that our motives may be misconstrued. The likelihood that discussions of the future of the Spanish territories would bring out competing claims for them among various African countries may reduce resolutions of the Committee to vague generalities.

British Guiana. Developments will depend on what use if any Jagan believes he can make of the Committee of 24. Burnham appeared as a petitioner on March 7 and made a favorable impression, especially on the African members. Burnham clearly and succinctly made his case for a plebiscite on the question of proportional representation.

US Territories. In spite of the lobbying of the Pro Independencia group in New York we believe that we can prevent Committee of 24 consideration of Puerto Rico on the ground that the Assembly has already recognized its present form of self-government. If the Committee wishes to consider some US territories, we plan to steer it in the direction of the Virgin Islands, Samoa, and Guam.

Grant G. Hilliker[4]

---

[4] Hilliker signed for Brubeck above Brubeck's typed signature.

248.   Letter From the Representative to the United Nations (Stevenson) to Secretary of State Rusk[1]

New York, March 20, 1963.

Dear Dean,

I appreciated very much your bringing to the attention of your staff my letter of February 5 which concerned our relations with the Secretary-General.[2] This is a matter which I continue to think is of central importance for our effectiveness with the Secretary-General. I am afraid we are in a comparable situation now on the Yemen negotiations.

On the Department's instructions and with considerable difficulty we finally persuaded the Secretary-General to assume the major role in resolving the United Arab Republic–Saudi Arabia disagreement problem. He also accepted our suggestion of using an American (Bunche) to do the job but politely refused to use Bunker, despite our repeated suggestions, because he preferred to have the mediator in the UN family. He and Bunche had just gotten started when—with only a few hours notice to him—we sent Bunker out ourselves. We assured him, however, that Bunker was essentially concerned with our bilateral relations with Saudi Arabia and that we wanted the United Nations to do the main job. However Bunker was in fact instructed to present to Faisal a concrete and detailed disengagement proposal, which he did with his usual skill and effectiveness. After Bunker's return to the U.S. we dispatched him to Jidda a second time—again with only a few hours notice to the Secretary-General—when difficulties arose over Faisal's invitation to Bunche. We are moreover now engaged in trying to persuade a reluctant Nasser (who has already conferred with Bunche on this subject) to receive Bunker and in fact would appear to be endeavoring to negotiate a whole disengagement process ourselves under a supposed UN umbrella which U Thant has in fact never offered us.

I realize of course the reasons for the most urgent handling of this problem and also recognize that the UN, in its initial attempt to do so, has not been as brisk or as skillful as we had hoped. Whether it will, because of Nasser's attitude, prove the better instrument for resolving this problem, remains to be seen. What I wish to bring to your attention is the inappropriateness and indeed impracticality of in effect pulling and pushing the Secretary-General in and out of a problem. Not only will this jeopardize his effectiveness, and perhaps ours as well, in deal-

---

[1] Source: Kennedy Library, National Security Files, Subjects Series, United Nations (General), 1/63–4/63, Box 311. Secret. Copies were sent to Cleveland and Schlesinger.

[2] Document 235.

ing with that particular problem, but he is certain to be sufficiently annoyed so that he will be extremely reluctant and perhaps unwilling when next we seek his intervention on a matter in which we find it most difficult for us to act ourselves. I believe that we should follow the general principle, once we have asked the Secretary-General to take on a role of this kind, of allowing him to carry it out with only discreet advice and assistance on our part, unless and until he and we agree his efforts require a U.S. supplement or substitute.

I realize you are very much aware of this general problem but wish to bring to your attention this latest example which shows once again how easy it is for us, in our zeal to get a job done, to cause serious and perhaps lasting damage in our relations with the Secretary-General.

Sincerely yours,

Adlai E. Stevenson[3]

---

[3] Printed from a copy that bears this typed signature.

---

249. Telegram From the Department of State to the Mission to the United Nations[1]

Washington, March 21, 1963, 8:28 p.m.

2412. We are concerned at reports reaching us indirectly that Secretary General and some members of his inner cabinet are becoming discouraged at prospects of obtaining sufficient financing operations in Congo and are inclined to blame us for failure Working Group 21 to produce funding formula.

You should make early occasion review frankly with Secretary General our overall objectives, which we believe to be identical with and in support of his own (i.e., to enable the Organization to carry out effectively existing peace-and-security operations) and the tactics we are pursuing to this end in Working Group and in capitals. We believe that these tactics which are calculated to create a crisis atmosphere are most likely to achieve these common objectives.

---

[1] Source: National Archives and Records Administration, RG 59, Central Files 1960–63, UN 10–4. Confidential. Drafted by Frank K. Hefner and Woodruff Wallner on March 21 and approved by Wallner.

He should understand that the hard line we are pursuing on the assessment scale and unprecedently wide-spread and intense diplomatic efforts we are making in almost 90 capitals are an indispensable prerequisite to continuance of U.S. contributions at satisfactory level. Doubts about proportion of our contribution will continue to exist as long as large number UN members continue press for sizable reductions in contributions, fall further in arrears and evidence no real signs of collective responsibility. We continue believe our two-pronged diplomatic campaign in Working Group and in capitals will achieve objectives common to ourselves and SYG. We believe our actions, together with efforts of Secretary General, will produce positive results in coming weeks.

Rusk

---

250. Circular Telegram From the Department of State to Certain Posts[1]

Washington, April 9, 1963, 7:45 p.m.

1740. Ref: Purchase of UN Bonds by New Members. Depcirtel 1526,[2] CA-9150.[3]

The United Nations financial condition continues to be difficult because many members have not paid their Congo and UNEF assessments and because only 59 members have subscribed $148.7 million in bonds, leaving over $50 million yet to be pledged. The country to which you accredited, being a new member of UN, has not as yet been assessed for any UN costs.

If the new members could make even token purchases (range $10–$25 thousand) this would jump the number countries participating into the mid-60s. You can point out importance of UN to newer and less developed countries. A token bond purchase would tangibly demonstrate interest and value they attach to their membership.

---

[1] Source: National Archives and Records Administration, RG 59, Central Files 1960–63, UN 10–4. Confidential. Drafted by A. K. Lampert and Wilbur H. Ziehl, cleared by George N. Monsma and W. Paul O'Neill, and approved by Frank K. Hefner. Sent to Algiers, Kampala, Kigali, Kingston, Port of Spain, and Usumbura, and repeated to USUN.

[2] Circular telegram 1526 requested posts to approach their governments within 2 weeks to encourage purchases of UN bonds. (Ibid.)

[3] See footnote 3, Document 243.

To be effective, pledges should be made by May 14 when Special Session begins. Even though increasing the number of bond subscribers is important, further approach is in your discretion and should be weighed in view your total efforts with govt you accredited on UN financing efforts.

Ball

---

251.   Department of State Memorandum[1]

Washington, April 11, 1963.

SPECIAL SESSION OF THE GENERAL ASSEMBLY ON FINANCES

We are developing our strategy for the upcoming Special Session of the General Assembly on finances which opens on May 14. Our objective will be to get the Assembly to adopt a financial plan, satisfactory to us, which will defray the costs of the peacekeeping operations in the Congo and the Middle East for the last half of calendar year 1963. Our recommendations to this end will be forwarded to you sometime next week at which time the replies being received to our circular will have been evaluated as to support for our position that these costs should be financed at the regular budget assessment rates. We will also know more clearly what other governments plan to do to pay arrearages and buy more bonds.

As a corollary to the foregoing, we will also wish to make every effort to assure that the principles of Article 19 are applied in accordance with the Charter if our present efforts fail to get such delinquents (Argentina, Bolivia, China, Haiti, Honduras, Paraguay and United Arab Republic) to make enough of a payment to avoid the Charter sanction. Guatemala has just paid up; Cuba and Hungary are also delinquent, but we are making no approaches to either. Indeed, there may be advantage in having one or two less contentious cases come up now to set the precedent—both procedurally and substantively—in the Assembly and thereby help to reinforce our position for the future when the tougher cases (USSR, France) come within the range of Article 19.

---

[1] Source: Kennedy Library, Cleveland Papers, UN Financing 1963, #2, Box 19. Confidential. An April 13 covering memorandum from Brubeck to Bundy indicates that Cleveland drafted the memorandum.

There are also a number of organizational and substantive political questions on which our planning is proceeding.

1. United States Delegation

From a practical point of view, there is no doubt that our regular staff at USUN under Ambassador Stevenson, with some augmentation from the Department, can readily handle the Special Session. The key question is whether we should ask Senators Gore and Allott to join the Delegation for the duration of the Session. We see real political advantage if the Senators could be prevailed upon to participate, even on a limited basis. We will need all the Congressional support we can get in the future and their participation with the Delegation should be helpful in this regard. They may well feel that the demands on Capitol Hill preclude their participation with the Delegation. Moreover, Senator Allott might have a reservation about serving if our position allows for any cost-sharing plan other than the regular scale. I believe they should nevertheless be given the opportunity to "turn down" the offer. Assuming you agree with this approach, I would like to discuss this initially with Ambassador Stevenson, and, if he agrees, subsequently with Senator Fulbright before approaching Senators Gore and Allott. I should also like to explore as an alternative the possibility of asking two members of the Senate and House Foreign Relations and Appropriations Committees respectively as "special advisers" to the Delegation. This would be of symbolic importance and offer possibilities for education of key Congressional representatives.

2. Slates at Special Session

We have normally followed the practice of seeking to have the Assembly at any of its Special Sessions organize itself in the most expeditious and non-contentious manner. To this end, the practice has developed of electing the same officers at a Special Session as served in the previous regular session. This would mean re-electing Zafrulla Khan as President and the other officers who served last fall. Where the individuals themselves are not present, as may be the case in some instances, the chiefs of their delegations would serve. Moreover, we should seek to have the same Credentials Committee appointed as served at the Seventeenth Session (Canada, El Salvador, Greece, Guinea, Indonesia, Mexico, Nigeria, USSR, and United States).

3. Chinese Representation

We do not expect the Soviets to raise the Chinese representation issue in any formal way, but we will be prepared with the appropriate tactics to cope with it should it arise. We would hope the Credentials

Committee might meet very late in the Session and send forward a perfunctory report which would be adopted in plenary without debate.

4. *Hungarian Credentials*

We will, of course, be confronted with a major decision regarding the question of Hungarian credentials. As you know, we are reasonably satisfied that the amnesty announced by the Hungarians is bona fide and that this represents a constructive step on their part. We also continue to believe it would be symbolically important for the Secretary-General to agree to visit Hungary some time before the opening of the Special Session. This would be interpreted as an additional step on the part of the Hungarians to accommodate themselves to United Nations opinion.

While it does not appear that the Secretary-General will be able to fit such a trip into his schedule prior to the Special Session on finances, we hope he can at least announce some time in May his intention to visit Hungary during the month of July.

The amnesty is likely to be broadly interpreted in the world as a reasonable step on the part of the Hungarians, and we can expect a further erosion of support for our position if we decide to pursue once again the "no decision" procedure at the coming Special Session. In view of the delicate considerations involved in this question—both domestic and international—it will be necessary, should we decide not to pursue the "no decision" procedure, to undertake appropriate consultation with a very few interested Congressional members and key opinion leaders among the Hungarian refugee groups in this country. I do not believe a change in our policy on Hungarian credentials will have a major impact on public opinion at home, but, nevertheless, we need to prepare the ground and our tactics carefully. In general, our feeling is that such a change should be played in the lowest possible key and that our consultations here and at the General Assembly should not have the effect of magnifying the change.

5. *Kuwait*

Kuwait has indicated it wishes to become a member of the United Nations at the earliest possible moment, and the way now seems clear since the USSR has apparently dropped its past opposition. We can expect, therefore, that a Security Council meeting will be held in early May to recommend approval of Kuwait's application and that the Assembly will admit Kuwait, probably before getting substantive consideration of the item on finances. This can be done very easily under the rules, and we do not expect any major difficulties on this question.

6. Southern Rhodesia

As you know, a subcommittee of the Committee of 24 is expected to visit London April 22 to discuss current developments on Southern Rhodesia. We can expect pressure to increase on the United Kingdom to state categorically its unwillingness to grant independence to Southern Rhodesia as Prime Minister Field has requested. In these circumstances, we are likely to be confronted with a major campaign by the Africans and the Asians to add the Southern Rhodesian item to the agenda of the Special Session. While we will wish to forward specific recommendations in light of the results of the consultations between the United Kingdom and the subcommittee of the Committee of 24, our present tentative assessment is that, even though a two-thirds vote is required, we would probably have great difficulty preventing the inscription of this item. The United Kingdom will probably agree with our assessment that the prime focus of our efforts should be to channel the substantive consideration of the Southern Rhodesian question toward as moderate an outcome as possible rather than to expend considerable prestige on the procedural question of inscription, where the odds are very much against our winning. This, of course, does not represent any final assessment on our part, and we will wish to consult fully and closely with the United Kingdom should there be a move to add Southern Rhodesia to the Special Session's agenda.

7. Congo

There is also the possibility of a move to add the Congo item at the Special Session. The Secretary-General, who has expressed serious reservations regarding a possible United Nations administrative umbrella over the Congolese military training program, thinks that it might be desirable to have the Special Session of the General Assembly consider this matter. He is looking for ways to absolve the Secretary-General from the requirement in General Assembly Resolution 1474 that military assistance in the Congo be given only at the request of the United Nations through the Secretary-General. He believes a resolution could be adopted which would empower the Adoula government to enter into bilateral arrangements for ANC retraining. We believe consideration by the Special General Assembly would only serve to delay the start of ANC retraining and open a needless debate on the whole Congo question which would not serve our objectives. Moreover, no such resolution of the Assembly is needed since we believe the Congolese government has the sovereign right to ask whomever it pleases to assist it in training its own forces. We are, therefore, seeking to discourage the Secretary-General from pursuing this course of action.[2]

---

[2] At the end of the memorandum is the handwritten heading, "Portuguese territories . . .".

252. Memorandum From Secretary of State Rusk to President Kennedy[1]

Washington, April 17, 1963.

SUBJECT

Presidency of the Eighteenth General Assembly

In response to your inquiry concerning the presidency of the next General Assembly, it is correct that, in accordance with the tradition of regional rotation, it is generally accepted that this year's president will be a Latin American.

The Venezuelan United Nations Delegation has announced the candidacy of Sosa Rodriguez, head of the Venezuelan Delegation, for president of the Eighteenth General Assembly. Sosa claims the support of nine other Latin American Delegations and appears to have the inside track. Guatemala has put forward the candidacy of Flores Avendaño, and Benites of Ecuador apparently has a latent interest. The Brazilians have recently made informal approaches to certain Latin American Delegations in New York to explore the chances of launching ex-President Kubitschek as a candidate. There are unconfirmed rumors that the USSR may be behind this move.

It is not surprising that Kubitschek may be interested in the presidency of the General Assembly. Kubitschek wants to become President of Brazil again and running for the General Assembly's top office would be helpful to his campaign. However, never in the history of the United Nations has the Assembly elected an individual as president who has not had considerable previous U.N. experience and who is not widely known to other Delegates.

It is normal practice, in the selection of Latin American candidates for U.N. posts, for the Latin Americans, jealous of their prerogatives, to agree among themselves to endorse a single candidate who is then normally accepted by the United States and the rest of the members.

In this case, because of the possible emergence of Kubitschek and because Sosa seems over-confident and is not yet actively campaigning, we are seeking discreetly to stimulate Sosa to greater activity and to encourage the Latin American countries to reach early agreement. We

---

[1] Source: Kennedy Library, National Security Files, Subjects Series, United Nations (General), 1/63–4/63, Box 311. Confidential. An attached memorandum from the President to Assistant Secretary of State for Inter-American Affairs Edwin M. Martin, April 9, reads: "It is my understanding that a Latin American may be considered for President of the General Assembly in the next session and the Soviets may support a Brazilian. What is our strategy on that?"

feel it would be counter-productive, however, for the United States to undertake an active campaign for him at this time. Ambassador Stevenson, with whom we have discussed this matter, agrees with this approach.

DR

---

253. Paper Prepared in the Department of State[1]

Washington, April 29, 1963.

SUGGESTED COMMENTS BY THE PRESIDENT TO CONGRESSIONAL LEADERS ON FINANCING THE UNITED NATIONS

Background:

1. Sales of the UN Bonds will just about cover the Middle East and Congo peacekeeping operations for the twelve months from July 1962 to June 1963.

2. The UN's deficit is still fluctuating around $100 million. The arrears owed on the Middle East and Congo operations are also about $100 million, of which two-thirds is owed by the Soviet bloc. (The other big debtors are France, the Republic of China, Belgium, and the Arab States.)

3. There is no provision for financing peacekeeping costs after July 1, 1963.

4. The UNEF must continue to sit on the lid in the Middle East which is more dangerously explosive right now than at any time since Suez—witness the precarious state of Yemen and Jordan and the recent coups in Syria and Iraq.

5. The Congo Force will be down from 19,000 troops last December to under 7,500 by July 1. We do not yet know whether some part of this Force will need to be maintained in the Congo in 1964; but the

---

[1] Source: Kennedy Library, National Security Files, Subjects Series, United Nations (General), 1/63–4/63, Box 311. Confidential. Drafted by Cleveland on April 29 and sent to the President under cover of a memorandum from Acting Secretary Ball on the same date. Ball indicated that the "talking paper" was to be used by the President in discussions with Congressional leaders, and that a longer position paper on UN financing, dated April 27, had already been sent to him. That paper is ibid.

Congolese National Army is not nearly well enough trained and disciplined to risk eliminating the Congo Force now.

The Special General Assembly

6. A Special General Assembly of the UN has been called for May 14th, to consider UN financing. Unless we take the lead, the small countries will try to put through a new assessment scale for peacekeeping under which we would be obligated to pay more than forty percent of the cost of any future peacekeeping force.

7. We have been opposing, and will continue to oppose

(a) any general arrangement for the financing of peacekeeping that would apply to unknown future operations.
(b) a "special scale" for peacekeeping by which the United States would be *assessed* at more than our Regular Budget percentage (32.02%).

8. The President is instructing the State Department and the United States Delegation to take the lead in developing a common position among the main Free World contributors. The framework for this position would be a modified version of an earlier British proposal, which has come to be called "Three-bite" approach.

(a) *Bite one* would finance a minimum amount on the Regular Budget scale of assessments.
(b) *Bite two* would assess the developed countries in the Regular Budget scale, but assess the less-developed countries at a lower rate— perhaps fifty percent of their Regular Budget share.
(c) *Bite three* would cover the resulting shortfall through small voluntary contributions from the developed countries.

9. We will try to make some arrangement whereby those countries (like Cuba) which are unwilling to pay on principle, or which failed to pay on time, would not get the benefit of the lower rate in bite two. Thus Cuba and Outer Mongolia, among the Soviet Bloc countries now considered as "less developed" in UN terminology, could be disqualified, and we would hope *not* to be in the position of helping reduce assessments for communist countries.

What the United States Would Pay

10. The total amount of money we are trying to raise in this somewhat complicated manner is around $40 million for July–December 1963. On this basis, we would need about $12.8 million to cover our thirty-two percent, plus a voluntary contribution in the range of one to one-and-a-half million dollars. (FYI. On the basis of these figures, our share of the total, would come out to just under thirty-six percent. However, it is not recommended that the matter be discussed in terms of percentages.)

11. The assessed amount would be funded in the usual way by a supplemental appropriation request, after the bargain is struck in the Special General Assembly next month.

12. The small voluntary contribution could be met under existing authority by Presidential Waiver of the cost of airlift services which the United States provides the United Nations for UNEF and the Congo. While we would of course make perfectly clear to Congress what the whole arrangement entails, the Congress would not need to vote the amount above our regularly assessed share.

Article 19 — The "Loss of Vote Provision"

13. The only section the Charter provides for nonpayment of dues is Article 19 which says a country will lose its vote in the General Assembly "if the amount of its arrears equals or exceeds the amount of the contributions due from it for the preceding two full years."

14. Lumping regular peacekeeping dues together (which is the way the Article 19 liability is figured), there were until recently ten countries to which this sanction would have been applied this next General Assembly. It now seems that all ten of these countries will pay enough to get within the two-year rule, before the Assembly meets two weeks from now. Two of the ten countries are Cuba and Hungary; whether they pay or not will be some indication of Soviet willingness to face a loss of vote under Article 19.

15. The Soviets are continuing their financial boycott of both UNEF and the Congo operation. If they fail to pay current assessments and nine million dollars more they will be subject to an automatic loss of vote in the General Assembly next year. We intend to campaign vigorously to make sure we have the necessary majority to deprive the Soviet Union of its vote if it continues its financial boycott of the UN. If they are faced with certain defeat on this issue, the Soviets would probably find a way to wriggle off the hook on which they have placed themselves. The alternative would be for them to leave the UN.

USUN will be consulting with other governments during the next couple of weeks. At the same time, the State Department will explain the present position to key members of the Foreign Relations, Foreign Affairs, and Appropriations Committees in both Houses of Congress.

Our bargaining position in the UN will be weakened by an outbreak of public debate on this subject in Congress during the next couple of weeks. We would hope the Leadership can help us create the conditions for striking a bargain in the General Assembly which *both* gets these two important operations (UNEF and Congo) financed for the rest of the year *and* does it at the very minimum cost to the United States.

254. Circular Telegram From the Department of State to Certain Posts[1]

Washington, May 10, 1963, 5:15 p.m.

1931. Ref: Dept. Cirtel 1526; CA–9150.[2]

1. Special Session of UN General Assembly which begins May 14 must act on resolutions concerning future financing of UN peace and security operations.

2. In reftel Ambassadors were requested to approach non-Soviet Bloc governments at highest level to determine whether governments would support U.S. view that peacekeeping costs for UN Congo and Middle East operations for the last six months of 1963 should be at regular assessment rates, i.e., without reductions in rates levied against less developed countries which rates applied up through June 1962. Since June 1962 no assessments have been levied and UNEF and UNOC costs are being financed from the proceeds from UN bonds. U.S. view was based on fact it difficult to justify continued high level of U.S. financial support—47% of UNEF and UNOC costs and 50% of UN bond issue—while majority UN members owe substantial overdue amounts on their reduced peacekeeping assessments. Tangible demonstration by UN membership of collective financial responsibility required to demonstrate realization that each member has stake in peace and security of world and in UN role in international affairs.

3. U.S. view as contained reftel has been modified because of responses by governments, the outcome of the Working Group of 21, and subsequent consideration within U.S. government.

4. Responses indicate your efforts have produced fuller consideration of UN financing by governments; that many countries have promised to pay arrears within next several months. Therefore, as indicated paragraph 14 reftel it may be possible for U.S. to contribute above 32.02%. We now negotiating in N.Y. financial formula which may include some form of voluntary contributions by U.S. and other developed countries along lines of suggestion originated by U.K.

5. U.S. position currently includes these principal elements:

(a) That the UNEF force in the Middle East must be continued because of the dangerous continuing situation in that area, and that the

---

[1] Source: National Archives and Records Administration, RG 59, Central Files 1960–63, UN 10–4. Confidential. Drafted by Wilbur H. Ziehl and Virginia C. Westfall; cleared by Richard Friedman, George N. Monsma, Herbert Reis, W. Paul O'Neill, Louise McNutt, and James M. Ludlow; and approved by Assistant Secretary Cleveland. Sent to 99 posts.

[2] See footnote 2, Document 250, and footnote 3, Document 243.

Congo force, to be greatly reduced by July 1, must be continued until the Congolese national army can be trained to take over the job.

(b) Current estimated budget for last half 1963 for the Middle East operation is $9.5 million and for the Congo operation is $33 million.

(c) We oppose any financial arrangement that would apply to unknown future peacekeeping operations. We also oppose any "special scale" of mandatory assessments for peacekeeping by which U.S. rate would be higher than our regular budget percentage of 32.02.

6. British suggestion on "three bite" approach is as follows:

Bite one would finance an initial amount entirely on regular scale of assessments, U.S. and others being liable for regular shares of an amount which we hope will be ten million dollars per operation.

Under *bite two*, the remaining cost would be assessed but rate would be different. For the developed countries the regular scale would be used for bite two. For the less developed countries the rate would be one-half their regular rates. Less developed countries would not be eligible for this special rate in bite two unless they indicate willingness to pay their assessments for these peacekeeping operations.

Bite three would cover the shortfall resulting from bite two and would be financed from voluntary contributions from a substantial number of developed members, or possibly by the use of UN miscellaneous income.

Our support for three bite approach is subject to certain conditions to be negotiated during the Special Session GA. However, essence includes U.S. voluntary pledge provided: (a) most other members are in fact contributing to the cost of peacekeeping operations; (b) a substantial number other developed countries also make voluntary contributions to cover shortfall; and (c) it is agreed voluntary contributions may be made "in kind" by supplying goods and services needed for peacekeeping purposes.

7. Arrears situation remains much as reported to you in reftel. Of present total of 100 million dollars peacekeeping arrears the Soviet Bloc owes $62.6 million. However, almost one-third of members have made payments on arrears this year, including payments or promises of sufficient amounts to avoid loss of vote under Article 19 UN Charter by ten countries. It is of continuing importance that member nations demonstrate through payment of their arrears the necessary spirit of collective financial responsibility indicated by some in their payments referred to above or indicated by their promise to pay in response to your earlier approach.

Another way to demonstrate that each member considers it has a stake in peace and security of the world and in UN role in international affairs is to purchase UN bonds. At present only 59 countries have purchased or pledged, and despite U.S. dollar for dollar matching of purchases, $51 million of the authorization still has not been subscribed.

Even token purchases by the less developed countries, say in the range of $10,000 each would have a salutary effect on the financial health of the Organization and increase the sense of financial responsibility to the UN of those making the purchases.

8. The above information concerning the modification of U.S. position from that set forth in Cirtel 1526 is provided principally for your information. As appropriate, you are encouraged to pass this information on to appropriate government officials. Solid support for our revised position is necessary in the GA Special Session (financing resolutions require 2/3rds vote), if the financing impasse on peacekeeping operations is to be satisfactorily resolved, and if the UN is to receive the financial resources it needs to carry on these peacekeeping tasks in Middle East and Congo. Such additional efforts as in your judgment will help to accomplish these purposes with govt. you accredited should be undertaken to support our negotiating efforts at Special Session.

Rusk

---

255.   Paper Prepared in the Department of State[1]

Washington, undated.

FIRST SESSION OF THE COMMITTEE OF 24
(February 20–May 10, 1963)

On balance the results of the first session of the Committee of 24 were not as unsatisfactory from our viewpoint as we had anticipated. In our opinion, the following factors in combination produced this relatively favorable outcome:

(1) The Afro-Asian members of the Committee seemed to have been genuinely concerned at the possibility the United States might refuse to serve on the Committee if it indulged in extreme and irresponsible conduct;

---

[1] Source: Kennedy Library, National Security Files, Subjects Series, United Nations (General), 5/63–7/63, Box 311. Confidential. Transmitted under a May 16 covering memorandum from Brubeck to Bundy. Another covering memorandum from Sam Belk of the National Security Council to Bundy, May 17, reads: "The attached memorandum represents, I think, a very good run-down of the activities of the Committee of 24 over an almost three-month period. You and Arthur will know best whether the President should see it. I think he should, but then I find the Committee far more interesting than most."

(2) At least some of the Afro-Asian members had become disillusioned with the fruitless process of passing resolutions that had no chance of implementation;

(3) On certain issues, e.g., South West Africa and Southern Rhodesia, the United States was able to go at least part of the way toward meeting the Afro-Asian position;

(4) Our Representatives at the United Nations, headed by Ambassador Yates, engaged in some very successful lobbying on individual issues;

(5) The Soviet Union, probably engrossed in a basic re-evaluation of its policies following the Cuban debacle, played a relatively more restrained role in the Committee and sounded cold war themes less frequently and less virulently than heretofore;

(6) The African members of the Committee presumably anticipated that a definitive anti-colonialist program would be coordinated and enunciated at the Addis Ababa conference and they therefore did not wish to act prematurely on the big issues of sanctions and expulsions.

It is very likely that the outcomes of the Addis Ababa Conference, particularly of its summit phase beginning on May 23, will determine if and in what manner the colonial items are raised either in the Special Session of the General Assembly or in the Security Council during June when the Presidency is held by Ghana. As in the past, colonial and racial incidents on the African continent would also serve to precipitate these issues rapidly into the forums of the United Nations.

When the Committee of 24 concluded its first session May 10, it had discussed the Portuguese territories, Southern Rhodesia, Aden, South West Africa and Malta. When it reconvenes on June 10, the Committee plans to begin with North Borneo, Brunei, Sarawak, Fiji, and British Guiana, as well as considering, whenever the members so choose, the report of the Sub-Committee on Southern Rhodesia.

The following is a brief summary of the outcome of the Committee's deliberations on the issues it discussed during its first session:

Portuguese Territories

As reported in our memorandum to you of April 12,[2] the Committee of 24 adopted by a vote of 19–0–5 (Australia, Denmark, Italy, the United Kingdom and the United States) a resolution condemning Portugal's attitude and drawing the Security Council's attention to the situation with a view to the Council's "taking appropriate measures, including sanctions, . . . to secure compliance by Portugal of the relevant

---

[2] Not printed. (Ibid.)

566 Foreign Relations, 1961–1963, Volume XXV

resolutions of the General Assembly and of the Security Council." As a result of this resolution, it is quite likely that the issue of the Portuguese territories, including the sanctions question, will face us in the Security Council in June. We are continuing our efforts to induce the Portuguese to adopt a more positive posture on these matters.

Southern Rhodesia

Pursuant to the Committee's resolution of April 8, its Sub-Committee (Mali, Uruguay, Syria, Tunisia, Sierra Leone and Tanganyika) held discussions in London between April 22 and 24 with R. A. Butler, Duncan Sandys, and Lord Home. The Sub-Committee was generally impressed by the British desire to improve the situation in Southern Rhodesia but was "depressed" that the British would not intervene militarily if the white minority government in Southern Rhodesia declared its independence. The Sub-Committee's report recommended that the full Committee should consider additional ways and means of dealing with the situation including (a) consideration of Southern Rhodesia at "a special session of the General Assembly"; (b) drawing the Security Council's attention to the deteriorating situation; (c) requesting the Secretary General to continue to lend his good offices. The United Kingdom has withheld granting Prime Minister Field the independence he has sought for Southern Rhodesia, and we continue to support the British efforts towards early broadening of the franchise.

Aden

On May 3, the Committee adopted a resolution by a vote of 18 in favor and 5 (Australia, Denmark, Italy, UK and US) against (Sierra Leone was absent) which, among other provisions, called for the sending of a Sub-Committee to visit the Aden Territories "to ascertain the views of the population . . . and hold talks with the administering authority." Australia, Denmark, Italy and the US (with the approval of the UK) had tabled a resolution which demonstrated their support for self-determination and independence and recommended that the people be given an early opportunity freely to decide their future. This resolution, however, was not pressed to a vote following meddlesome attempts by the Soviets to amend it.

On May 10, the Aden Sub-Committee was named (Cambodia as Chairman, Iraq, Madagascar, Venezuela, and Yugoslavia). At that time, the Chairman of the Committee of 24 announced his intention of sending a letter to the UK asking the British Government to reconsider its previously announced decision not to cooperate with the Sub-Committee. We do not believe that this letter will cause the British to change their position, nor do we believe this non-African item has sufficient pressure behind it to reach a larger UN forum before fall. We support the UK position.

South West Africa

Although in Committee debates the US and the UK were subjected to oft-repeated charges that they were "doing nothing" to persuade South Africa to change its policy regarding apartheid and South West Africa, both the US and UK resisted the temptation to describe their parallel confidential diplomatic efforts vis-à-vis the South Africans because public indication at this time might undermine our future efforts to this end. Committee of 24 consideration of this item was characterized by Afro-Asian difficulty in reaching agreement on a draft resolution which would have had the effect of abrogating the mandate and calling on the UN to take over the administration of the territory by force, if necessary. Eventually, with our help, a much more moderate resolution along the lines of previous GA resolutions was tabled, and on May 10 it received the affirmative votes of 23 members of the Committee with only the UK abstaining. It requested the Secretary General to continue his efforts to establish "an effective UN presence" in the territory and drew the Security Council's attention to the situation there.

Malta

The Committee on May 10 concluded desultory debate on Malta with the unanimous adoption of a very moderate and non-controversial resolution which noted the UK intention "to consider favorably Malta's request for independence", and invited the UK to hold a conference with the Maltese to that end. We did not speak in the Committee on the subject of Malta because of the absence of any US policy objectives which would have been served thereby.

256.   **Memorandum From the Principal Deputy Assistant Secretary of State for International Organization Affairs (Wallner) to the President's Special Assistant (Schlesinger)**[1]

Washington, undated.

SUBJECT

United Nations Financing

The compromise "package" of resolutions of UN financing sailed through both the 5th Committee and the General Assembly with overwhelming majorities. On the 7 resolutions the favorable votes ranged from a high of 95 to a low of 79. But more significant, the negative votes did not exceed 12; the Soviet Bloc, Cuba, and France. The key vote was on the Principles resolution, 92–11–3 (with 5 absences).

The resolutions covered general principles for the sharing of future peacekeeping operations involving heavy expenditures; the appropriation of $9.5 million and $33.0 million, respectively, for financing the Middle East and Congo operations from January through December 1963; an appeal stressing the essentiality of payment of all the peacekeeping arrears as soon as possible; the extension to December 31, 1963 of the time during which the remainder of $200 million bond authorization can be sold; a request to the Secretary-General to study the "desirability and feasibility" of establishing a peace fund; and the continuation of the Working Group of 21 to study and report in 1964 on equitable sharing of costs among members, other sources of financing, and securing "widest possible agreement among member states on financing." (The last quote is aimed at getting the United States, Russia and France to get together on a way out of the financing dilemma.)

Our insistence that no general agreement should be adopted that would apply to unknown future operations and our opposition to a "special scale" for peacekeeping by which the United States would be *assessed* at more than our regular budget percentage were successful (this time). The two resolutions providing funds for the Middle East and Congo operations assess the developed countries at 100% and the "economically less developed countries" at an overall percentage of 52%, of their regular scale rates. (Our hope to assess the LDC's at 50% was slightly bettered: they had been paying 20% under previous financing schemes.) The U.S. assessed contributions, at 32.02%, will be $13.6

---

[1] Source: Kennedy Library, National Security Files, Subjects Series, United Nations (General), 5/62–7/63, Box 311. Confidential. Transmitted under cover of a July 3 memorandum from Acting Executive Secretary Richard S. Little to Bundy.

million: for UNEF, $3. million and for the Congo, $10.6 million. A supplemental appropriation request for State's regular budget will be submitted soon.

The total "shortfall" due to the lesser assessments of LDC's will be about $3.7 million. 17 Western developed countries (includes U.S., subject to its constitutional processes) have agreed to make up this shortfall through voluntary contributions based on their regular percentage scale relationships. This is especially heartening since only the U.S. and the U.K. (in a minor amount) made voluntary contributions last year. The U.S. voluntary contribution share will be about $2. million. Whether this amount should be contributed in airlift and other services under authority of the United Nations Participation Act—and reimbursement from the UN waived under Presidential determination that it is in the national interest—or whether we should face the Congress directly with an appropriation request as a part of AID Chapter 3 funds must be determined within the next several weeks.

We also managed to find a way which we believe will avoid the accusation that U.S. voluntary contributions are being used to give reductions to communist countries, such as Cuba. The resolutions provided that the voluntary contributions of the developed countries can only be used to match proportionally *contributions actually paid in* for these assessments by the less developed countries by December 31, 1965. Because the Satellites refuse to pay, Western funds cannot be used to offset their reductions. Any unused voluntary contributions revert to the donor members.

Although the results of the Special Session of the General Assembly are gratifying, agreement has been reached on UN financing for only six months. Many of the same questions, in varying degrees of urgency, will have to be faced again at the General Assembly this fall, in financing UN peacekeeping operations for 1964.

Woodruff Wallner[2]

---

[2] Printed from a copy that indicates Wallner signed the original.

257. Circular Airgram From the Department of State to All Posts[1]

CA–166   Washington, July 3, 1963, 5:04 p.m.

SUBJECT

    Security Council Election at 18th General Assembly

There are at this time four candidates—Bolivia, Czechoslovakia, Ivory Coast, and Malaya—for election at 18th GA to fill three SC seats currently occupied by Ghana, Philippines, and Venezuela. Both Malaya and the Ivory Coast have said they are candidates to succeed Ghana in what has been traditionally the Commonwealth seat, although we hope they will decide to drop their specification about which seat they want. (This is important. Otherwise they will compete with each other, leaving Czechoslovakia uncontested for the Philippine seat.) According to Malayans, they have endorsement of the old Commonwealth, Ghana, Nigeria, and several other Asian and African countries, while the Ivory Coast candidacy has UAM endorsement and reportedly that of a substantial number of other African countries. There are, so far as Dept aware, no other African or Asian SC candidacies on horizon.

UN Charter stipulates that in electing non-permanent members SC "due regard" should be paid to their contribution to the maintenance of international peace and security and other purposes of Charter and also to "equitable geographical distribution". The original geographic allocation of SC seats provided such equitable distribution in terms original membership. In terms of present membership it fails to do so, making no separate provision for either Asian or African representation.

Only real solution to this problem lies in enlargement SC, which however, USSR prevents by its position it will ratify no amendments UN Charter until Chinese Communists seated in UN. In this situation U.S. has taken position since 1955 that seat originally allocated Eastern Europe should be considered "floating" pending enlargement. While this approach has not been entirely successful, it has provided some opportunity for Asian representation outside Commonwealth members; Philippines twice and Turkey once have held "floating seat" for term split with Eastern Europe and Japan occupied "floating seat" for full term. With the large increase since 1960 in number of African UN members further adjustment obviously required if legitimate African as well as Asian demands for greater opportunity representation on SC to

---

[1] Source: National Archives and Records Administration, RG 59, Central Files 1960–63, UN 8 SC. Confidential. Drafted by Virginia F. Hartley on July 2; cleared by Curtis Strong, George N. Monsma, Joseph J. Sisco, Richard Friedman, Louise McNutt, and James M. Ludlow; and approved by Woodruff Wallner.

be met. A second seat can, however, only be made available at expense of free world and therefore presents delicate political problem. Moreover, further political problem of protecting Western voting position on SC is also involved, since loss of WE or LA seat to A-As would undermine this position.

In circumstances, Dept believes best device is now to think in terms of an "African" and an "Asian" seat, using "floating seat" and "Commonwealth seat" for this purpose, at same time seeking to preserve concept that one of non-permanent members continues to be from Commonwealth. Adoption of this concept would give Africa, the Middle East (under original allocation), and Asia each one SC seat, thus providing the A-As as a whole with three out of the six non-permanent seats on SC, and thereby meeting the Charter criterion of equitable geographic distribution since the A-As constitute roughly one half UN membership. Adoption of this concept would also be consistent with the precedent set by the 12th GA resolution allocating geographically GA vice presidencies and committee chairmanships. Finally, adoption of this concept would have least adverse effect on over-all composition SC from Western standpoint since Commonwealth now very largely comprised newly independent countries, most of them in Africa or Asia.

If matter SC elections raised by FonOff or on first appropriate occasion Embassy should therefore make clear to FonOff, unless it perceives serious objections, U.S. believes A-As should continue hold three of six non-permanent SC seats as they do now (Ghana, Morocco, Philippines) commensurate with their number in UN. Dept also believes both Asia and Africa south of Sahara, as well as Middle East, should continue be represented on SC. Therefore, while U.S. has so far given no formal commitment of support to any candidates for election SC at 18th GA, Dept expects vote for an Asian and an African candidate to succeed Philippines and Ghana, respectively, and to vote for LA to succeed Venezuela. On basis present candidacies this would mean Malaya and Ivory Coast, both of which US would be happy see on SC. U.S. also expects vote for an LA to succeed Venezuela. Malaya in Asian seat would also represent Commonwealth.

Dept hopes other friendly UN members will reach same conclusion. Not only does Dept believe this only equitable solution problem created by Soviet prevention enlargement SC but also that denial seat to Eastern Europe is concrete means of maintaining pressure on USSR to permit enlargement.

If possibility shifting one of two LA seats on SC to Africa is raised, Embassy should make clear that in U.S. view remedy of one injustice by another offers no solution. LAs originally proposed and have since consistently supported enlargement SC to provide great opportunities for representation of new UN membership and USSR alone prevents success of this LA initiative. In these circumstances, U.S. would hope free world nations would not permit situation to arise in which regional groups within free world bicker among themselves over possibility raiding LA seat, and thus jeopardize success one of their candidacies to advantage Soviet bloc.

Embassy should also make clear U.S. not prepared see "floating" seat go back to Eastern Europe until USSR permits enlargement SC.

For LA Posts: You should indicate FonOff Dept assumes LAs will wish make every effort protect their SC seat in view possible development African drive, apparently led by Ghana, gain SC seat at expense LA. Dept believes LAs would be well advised promptly agree support both African and Asian candidates, once situation with respect these candidacies sufficiently clarified, in return for assurances of support of LA candidate. Dept recognizes some defections among A-As probably inevitable but sees no real threat LA candidacy even if Soviet bloc fails support, so long as no concerted drive for LA seat develops among A-As.

For AF Posts: FYI. Success formula described above depends not only on minimization bickering over particular seat to be filled but also on avoidance rival candidacies within region. You should point this out as appropriate and report any indication of AF candidacies other than that mentioned first paragraph. End FYI.

For Abidjan: Embassy may wish draw particular attention FonOff desirability its not continuing specify seat for which it candidate.

For London: As Embassy will recall, need provide for African representation SC and possible shift of Commonwealth seat to meet this need has been discussed both with FonOff and UK Del in New York. UK has never given any definitive response our approaches this subject. It is USUN's impression insistence on response most likely produce negative one but that British prepared, so long as formal concurrence not requested, acquiesce in solution described first full paragraph on page 2 above.

Rusk

258.   Memorandum From the Deputy Legal Adviser of the
         Department of State (Meeker) to the Assistant Secretary of
         State for International Organization Affairs (Cleveland)[1]

Washington, July 16, 1963.

SUBJECT

    Portugal and South Africa in United Nations Bodies

While I went along with Nat McKitterick's proposal to delete the specific reference to Articles 55 and 56 of the Charter in the formula on South Africa's participation in the Economic Commission for South Africa, I continue to feel that the question of South Africa's conformity with Charter obligations remains a highly relevant one.[2] We do not want to take the position that, when a United Nations Member's policies reach a certain level of unpopularity, that Member's further participation can simply be declared incompatible and the Member in effect excluded. The significant thing about the South African situation is that its highly "unpopular" policies of racial discrimination and apartheid constitute a systematic violation of solemn obligations laid down in the UN Charter. This affords a far firmer ground for an "incompatibility" formula than a set of national policies which are merely highly distasteful to a majority of the UN membership.

I agree with you that "klieg light diplomacy" of exposing through the UN what is in fact going on in the different countries of the world is a powerful means of inducing better conduct on the part of governments. One of the weaknesses of the Human Rights Commission has been its theoretical inability to consider actual situations in particular countries, and the restriction of its activities to the realm of the abstract. In effect, the General Assembly and even the Security Council have come to fill this vacuum in the more egregious instances.

I would favor putting this function on a more regular and organized basis, as a means of promoting effectuation of the Charter's obligations on human rights. This could prove more practical and effective than the prolonged effort expended on human rights covenants which may never be completed and which, if completed, may never be widely ratified as treaties. The Human Rights Commission could be given new terms of reference so that it could consider actual situations—making findings, measuring government performance against Charter standards, and proposing recommendations for action where this

---

[1] Source: Kennedy Library, Cleveland Papers, Human Rights, Box 19. No classification marking.

[2] McKitterick's July 9 memorandum to Wallner is not printed. (Ibid.)

appeared useful. I believe we ought to give serious thought to a proposal of this kind as a means of making the Human Rights Commission a more meaningful agency for forwarding the purposes and obligations of the Charter.

---

259.   Message from Foreign Secretary Lord Home to Secretary of State Rusk[1]

London, July 29, 1963.

I have sent you my official reply to your proposal for a "moderate" Resolution on Portugal and Angola but it only hints at what I want to say for your and the President's ear.[2]

2. Time and again you face us with situations in which you ask us to vote for Resolutions which will undermine any chance we have to keep the pace of independence for our remaining colonial territories under reasonable control. Time and again you beg us on bended knee to prevent British Guiana from achieving independence within the foreseeable future, but everywhere else you make it almost impossible for us to maintain control. I do not seem to be able to persuade your people that you cannot have it both ways.

3. If we have to vote for a Resolution which insists on the employment of a highly placed United Nations personage who will go to colonial territories with instructions which clearly contemplate that he will confer with the members of the opposition parties, our policy of bringing independence by orderly processes would be completely undermined.

4. If you set store, as you obviously do, by our maintaining control of the situation in British Guiana, we cannot obviously allow a United Nations personage to consult with Dr. Jagan.

5. If we are to bring Southern Rhodesia to the point of adjusting their franchise and accepting a programme whereby the African majority will control the government machine within a reasonable time, the

---

[1]   Source: National Archives and Records Administration, RG 59, Presidential Correspondence: Lot 66 D 204, UK Officials and Rusk, Box 181. Top Secret. A July 29 covering memo from Denis A. Greenhill of the British Embassy to Secretary Rusk indicated that the attached message was for his and the President's eyes only.

[2]   Document 260.

very last thing we would do would be to introduce the United Nations. It would immediately close the ranks against any such plan and make Rab's aims unobtainable.

6. I do beg you to help us in this matter and not to corner us and face us with a dilemma whether to veto, because we cannot wish upon Portugal what we could not accept for ourselves, thereby getting the Africans steamed up about us again in Southern Rhodesia and the High Commission territories; or whether rather ingloriously to abstain and then see action taken under a Resolution for which we have voted solely because we did not like being parted from our friends and find ourselves the next victims and unable to stand up for ourselves because we have set a precedent.

7. I have sent certain suggestions in my "open" message and I do hope they can be adopted. The Prime Minister and I feel very strongly about this and I hope you can instruct your Delegation in New York to take account of our difficulties.

8. Without your help we will be bound to chuck in our hand in our remaining Colonies and you cannot, I know, want that. I look forward to talking about this soon. Meanwhile, forgive this straight talking.

H.[3]

---

[3] Printed from a copy that bears this typed initial.

---

260.   Message From Foreign Secretary Lord Home to Secretary of State Rusk[1]

London, July 29, 1963.

I am still very worried about the wording of paragraph 3 of the American draft Resolution about the Portuguese Territories. I realise that your delegation has made an effort to help us by altering somewhat the reference to the functions of the eminent person designated by the Secretary-General, but the latest wording, as we see it, would still make it absolutely impossible for us to resist a demand that a United Nations

---

[1]   Source: National Archives and Records Administration, RG 59, Presidential Correspondence: Lot 66 D 204, UK Officials and Rusk, Box 181. Confidential. A covering memorandom from Denis A. Greenhill of the British Embassy, dated July 29, is not printed. For the reactions of President Kennedy and other senior U.S. officials to this letter, see *Foreign Relations*, 1961–1963, vol. XXI, Document 370.

Mission should visit territories such as Southern Rhodesia and British Guiana. The words which give us difficulty are "to visit the territories and to take such other steps as may help to bring about the attainment of self-determination." We would go along with amended wording which read "to conduct such other consultations as may be appropriate to attain the elimination of the causes of international friction, etc."

I am very anxious that we should be able to associate ourselves with your moderate resolution which has a number of valuable features in it; and I should be very unhappy if we found ourselves separated from working closely with your delegation by the difficulty over the words I have concluded. Do you think you could possibly see your way to getting these words omitted and those I have suggested substituted? Alternatively, if this is out of the question, I should like you to know that we would be prepared to go along with your resolution as it stands provided your delegation makes it clear in the debate that their interpretation of these words is that the action taken in operative paragraph 3 will be taken in consultation with the Portuguese.

---

261.   Telegram From the Department of State to the Mission to the United Nations[1]

Washington, August 13, 1963, 7:22 p.m.

422. Committee of 24.

1. Pursuant to US-UK talks held by Cleveland in London we have (a) weighed pros and cons our continued participation in work of Cmte and (b) desirability of making effort with key members prior to Sept 5 meeting to induce greater moderation.

2. Re (a), Cmte's 1963 record thus far exhibits both moderation and lack of realism. Initial consensus to approach Portugal for talks with Cmte representatives without preconditions was model of how we believe Cmte should act. GOP sharp rebuff triggered res drawing situation to attention SC. In our view, Cmte acted with moderation in cases of SWA and Malta but acted unwisely re Aden, Fiji, High Commission

---

[1] Source: National Archives and Records Administration, RG 59, Central Files 1960–63, POL 10 UN. Confidential. Drafted by Michael H. Newlin on August 12; cleared by Henry J. Tasca, Richard Friedman, and William B. Buffum; and approved by Richard Gardner. Also sent to Pretoria and repeated to London.

Territories, British Guiana. To date, Cmte's officers have resisted pressures take up Puerto Rica. Because Cmte now scheduled consider US Trust Territory Pacific Island and can be expected take up other US territories in next six months, Dept inclined believe over-all US interests best served by remaining on Cmte for the time being in order have possibility explaining and, if need be, defending our record in person. Since we suspect UK anxious to have us remain for their own reasons, we should be careful not to give UK impression our decision firm but rather that it "knife edge" similar to UK position described Cleveland (London's 144) and subject to constant review.

3. Re (b), we should where not counter-productive seek to convey to key Afro-Asians our sincere conviction that remaining "hard core" colonial problems not susceptible to doctrinaire approach of immediate independence in every instance. US dedication to principles 1514 (XV) requires no proof. We earnestly desire assist remaining two per cent of world's population living in dependent territories to achieve self-government or independence as rapidly as possible without precipitating serious new dangers for such populations. Certain actions of Cmte have come close to falling into latter category. Unrealistic res calling for early independence SR at this delicate stage of negotiations on colony's future ran risk of provoking what Cmte and UN most wishes avoid— independent SR under white supremacist govt. Similar indiscriminate action re High Commission Territories risked provoking their incorporation into South Africa. Worst example of Cmte's 1963 session was its call for immediate independence Fiji with almost total disregard for complicated internal political situation and effect Cmtc's action would have thereon. We have all too often heard otherwise responsible Cmte members explain privately that, while they recognize important differences between territories considered, once others raise demand for unqualified immediate independence they unable do anything but support simplistic approach. US hopes more responsible trend in Cmte will prevail and that greater discrimination and leadership will be shown by responsible members Afro-Asian group, enabling Cmte play constructive role in decolonization process. If less responsible trend should prevail, we see real danger Cmte's actions could damage rather than further cause of decolonization, and could cause us reassess our attitude towards Cmte.

4. Would appreciate addressee's comments and suggestions soonest re approach along lines para 3 to: non-bloc Cmte members except LA's and Cambodia. We would not plan approach LA's since ASAFs are key to possible future moderation. After comments received we will, as Cleveland promised FonOff, consult UK.

Rusk

262.   Letter From the Representative to the United Nations (Stevenson) to President Kennedy[1]

New York, August 19, 1963.

Dear Mr. President:

I understand you want my views as to whether you should attend the General Assembly.

Yes, I think you should because:

1. The United States must stay in the forefront of the "peace" issue, and this would be a good occasion and forum to carry forward the American University speech.

2. The Assembly would afford an opportunity to make our desire for further détente and disarmament emphatic and sincere.

3. A more affirmative and hopeful posture about the Test Ban Treaty breakthrough will be desirable after all the deflating talk during the ratification process.[2]

4. You could give some balance to an Assembly that will be largely an "African session", by demonstrating that anti-colonialism is not the only problem the world faces.

5. The Assembly would afford an opportunity to reaffirm emphatically our policy on colonialism, self-determination and human rights, and perhaps temper the next assault by the Africans and Soviets.

6. With so many African and other Heads of State coming to the Assembly, it might be misinterpreted if you did not come.

7. I think Khrushchev will come to exploit the "peace" and "end colonialism" issues to strengthen his position in the dispute with China. If you should then decide to come, it would look like "me too."

8. It would be helpful in the Congress and the country to reaffirm the U.S. commitment to the United Nations and the building of international organizations for peace and progress. The Assembly would be a good time to do it after the Test Ban Treaty which grew out of the U.N. Committee of 17, the U.N. Congo operation, which is now popular even in England and Belgium, the U.N. settlements in New Guinea, Yemen, and now Malaysia.

---

[1] Source: Kennedy Library, National Security Files, Subjects Series, United Nations (General), 8/63, Box 311. Confidential. A covering memorandum from Benjamin Read to Bundy, also dated August 19, indicated that the text of the letter had been received telegraphically from Stevenson that afternoon.

[2] On July 25 representatives of the United States, the United Kingdom, and the Soviet Union initialed a treaty prohibiting nuclear weapons tests in the atmosphere, outer space, and under water.

9. A good speech can be built on developments since your last appearance in 1961, successful U.N. peacekeeping, the test ban and further steps to peace, other fields of East-West cooperation large and small, "openness" as an ingredient of cooperation, human rights and change, etc.

But, there may also be reasons for not coming that should be considered:

1. While they may come anyway, I think your decision to come would insure the attendance of Macmillan and Khrushchev (and Nasser, Tito, etc.)—Macmillan for domestic political advantage and Khrushchev for the reasons mentioned above. An informal "Summit" meeting would logically follow. But, as I wrote you in July, I think periodic and more casual Summit meetings at U.N. sessions would actually be better than the occasional over-dramatized meeting.

2. While there are plenty of good generalities and atmospherics for a speech, the "hard content" might be modest, depending on how much you could say at that point on next steps in disarmament and détente. Of course, East-West cooperation in space, medicine, communications, cultural exchanges and other fields of research could be dealt with but there may not be enough new programmatic content for a Presidential speech.

3. It is unlikely that an "African Assembly" can be diverted from colonialism, human rights and the problems of Southern Africa. Any frailties or omissions in your speech in this area would be conspicuous. I think, by the way, that we must promptly formulate our own policy on these questions and not risk being dragged along reluctantly, thereby losing influence and friends on both sides.

4. With the Congress still in session and the program so far behind schedule, there may be domestic reasons why public attention should not be diverted by a full dress affair and your presence at the General Assembly.

An alternative to a comprehensive Presidential speech in the general debate might be a ceremony for the registration of the Test Ban Treaty with yourself, Khrushchev, Macmillan and U Thant making brief speeches, as suggested in my letter of July 29, a copy of which is attached.[3] To arrange this would require some initiative on our part with Khrushchev and Macmillan, and I doubt if we could be sure that Khrushchev would restrain himself.

I think it would be well to have a general strategy conference about the Assembly, including the question of your appearance, the speech and the timing of the announcement.

Sincerely yours,

Adlai E. Stevenson[4]

---

[3] Not printed.

[4] Printed from a copy that bears this typed signature.

263. Position Paper Prepared in the Bureau of International Organization Affairs[1]

Washington, undated.

UNITED STATES STRATEGY AT THE 18TH GENERAL ASSEMBLY

Summary

Two themes are likely to dominate the 18th United Nations General Assembly:

1) Colonialism and racial discrimination; and
2) the opportunities for international cooperation opened up by the limited test ban agreement.

The African members, strengthened by the presence of a number of Heads of State and increasingly disturbed by the lack of progress in the Portuguese territories and the apartheid policy of South Africa, will use the Assembly to press African issues hard.

At the same time, the conclusion of the limited test ban agreement seems likely to stimulate interest in "next steps" in the disarmament field and perhaps other aspects of East-West cooperation. The "cold war" between the USSR and China will have some effect in the Assembly, and there are signs that the Soviets are perhaps reassessing certain aspects of their attitude toward the United Nations in this light.

The need to avoid complete preoccupation with African issues and to build on the limited test ban lead us to conclude that we should probe systematically for next steps to new agreements on the basis of mutual national interest; that we should seek to engage the USSR in an increasingly complex network of cooperative undertakings based on mutual interest; and that the UN has a role to play in both the probing operation and the engagement process, if the latter is in the cards.

We hope it may be possible to focus proportionately less attention on African issues and to use the Assembly to increase the incentives to the Soviet leaders to live at peace with us. To do this will require broad-

---

[1] Source: Kennedy Library, National Security Files, Subjects Series, United Nations (General), 9/1/63–9/8/63, Box 311. Confidential. Only the summary is printed; the entire position paper comprises 33 pages. A covering memorandum to President Kennedy from Secretary Rusk, August 30, indicates that a meeting to discuss U.S. strategy at the 18th General Assembly was scheduled for September 9. A second covering memorandum from Belk to Bundy called the paper "exhaustive and exhausting." Belk suggested that the President read "(1) the 4-page summary; (2) skip Part One: the Political Climate; (3) proceed to the Table of Contents of Part II and select whatever further subjects he may find of interest for more detailed reading."

ening the focus of the Assembly at the outset, to which end we recommend a major address to the Assembly by the President, picking up from the American University speech and stressing the great common interests of man, both in relation to his environment and to his fellow man. Such broadening can be accomplished only if there is some visible crack in the almost total impasse over self-determination in the Portuguese territories and apartheid in South Africa.

There follows a review of the major problems at the 18th Assembly, including where possible preliminary policy recommendations respecting the United States position.

1. African Issues

The key African issues are the Portuguese territories, apartheid in South Africa, and perhaps Southern Rhodesia. Unless the United States is prepared to lend some support to African demands for more far-reaching measures against Portugal and South Africa, we risk being accused in the Assembly of frustrating the anti-colonialist crusade. The Africans will also threaten to bargain their votes on non-African issues of importance to us (e.g. Chinese representation) against United States support on African issues. To minimize U.S. losses, we shall probably have to go beyond our past positions in the absence of significant movement by Portugal or South Africa. We must also be prepared to deal with a possible African walk-out or other disruptive parliamentary tactics directed against the presence of Portugal and South Africa in the Assembly. The United States should frankly tell the Africans that the future not only of the UN but of all international institutions is threatened by such conduct and urge, publicly if necessary, that orderly procedures be followed. By thus standing firmly for peaceful change, we shall inevitably be cast in the role of honest broker between extreme positions, pleasing no one entirely, hopefully alienating no one totally.

2. Human Rights Issues

The Assembly will be dealing with a report of the Secretary General on the action of UN members to eliminate racial and religious discrimination and with a Draft Declaration on the Elimination of all Forms of Racial Discrimination. This will sharpen the Assembly's focus on racial issues. With UN interest increasingly turned to the problem of implementing respect for human rights we are considering the possible establishment of some new institution in the field of human rights which could investigate and report on how Members are fulfilling their Charter obligations on human rights. We think this would, among other advantages, spotlight human rights problems in closed societies and help broaden attention beyond racial issues.

3. Disarmament and Nuclear Issues

The conclusion of the "hot line" with the Soviets and the limited test ban agreement should have a favorable impact on the debate and create momentum for further progress. We expect full discussion of disarmament questions. The Assembly will certainly endorse the test ban agreement and call on all States to adhere. It may also repeat its call for agreement on an underground test ban with effective verification. Our general objective should be to encourage further negotiations in the ENDC or through bilateral or limited multilateral channels on collateral measures (e.g. surprise attack) and further negotiations on general and complete disarmament. We hope to be able to refer specific issues such as those related to prohibition and dissemination of nuclear weapons to the ENDC for detailed consideration.

4. Outer Space

The United States should be prepared to take the initiative to put new energy into UN outer space activities and to reach agreement in areas that will promote the peaceful use and exploration of outer space. We may wish to make specific proposals for new cooperative projects and to move forward with our plans for a Declaration of General Principles regarding the legal aspects of outer space by the UNGA.

5. Other Important Issues

We expect to be able to achieve our objectives on two East-West issues, Chinese representation and Korea, on the same basis as in the past. This means maintaining the seating of the Republic of China and reaffirming the aim of Korean unification through free elections under UN supervision.

The questions of Hungary and Tibet are not now on the agenda. We do not anticipate further discussion of the Hungarian question. In the absence of some new major reason for its inscription, we should probably take no initiative on Tibet.

The only Near Eastern issue certain to arise is the problem of the Palestine refugees, on which prospects for progress remain poor. We hope heated debate can be avoided. No major action is required since at the 17th General Assembly UNRWA was extended for two years.

6. Future of United Nations Operation in the Congo

The continuation of the UN military operation in the Congo is likely to be considered. Although the Secretary General now seems disposed to recommend its closing out by the end of this year, we believe it would be useful to continue the operation another six months. We have been actively discussing UNOC's future with key UN Members.

especially the Africans, to ascertain whether there is broad support for continuation and whether necessary financial arrangements can be made. We estimate the cost at about $8–9 million, which would have to be assessed by an appropriate financing resolution in the General Assembly.

7. UN Peacekeeping

To strengthen the UN's military capabilities, we will continue our efforts (1) to obtain a modest increase in the Secretary General's military staff; (2) to encourage the earmarking of national forces for UN peacekeeping service; and (3) to set the stage for the training of officer personnel for UN service. Bearing in mind the broad objective of strengthening UN peacekeeping institutions we should support the establishment of a United Nations Institute which would train personnel for service with the UN system or with UN-related functions in their own country; conduct operations research designed to enhance the UN's effectiveness; and engage senior citizens of UN members as faculty, lecturers or part-time fellows who could be used by the Secretary General for special missions.

8. UN Financing

The arrearages of the Soviet bloc members will not bring them within the provisions of Article 19 until January 1, 1964. The question of the application of Article 19 is not on the agenda, but interest has been shown in the idea of referring to the International Court of Justice the question of the automatic application of Article 19 to Members who are now more than two years in arrears. If there is general sentiment in favor of resort to the Court, we should agree. If the ICJ decides the question in favor of automaticity, this should strengthen our position in an eventual showdown.

9. Other

The final two sections describe economic, trade and development matters and the prospects for elections to the Security Council, Economic and Social Council and International Court of Justice, as well as for officers of the General Assembly.

[Here follows the remainder of the paper.]

264.   Memorandum From William H. Brubeck of the National Security Council Staff to President Kennedy[1]

Washington, September 6, 1963.

1. You are meeting Monday afternoon[2] with State and Ambassador Stevenson to survey the UN General Assembly that begins September 17. The session is for general discussion and guidance, not firm decisions. The gist of State Department views is contained in a 4-page summary (Tab II) in the attached briefing book.[3]

2. There are presently apparent no crucial issues or overriding subjects for the GA—e.g., Chinese representation will probably not be a serious issue, unless it gets tied in to bargaining over African problems.

3. In addition to the South Viet Nam Buddhist issue, the biggest item will probably be another round on African issues with several African heads of states present; under last month's Security Council's resolutions the Secretary General will report back the end of October on South Africa and Portuguese Africa so we will automatically be caught in these dilemmas again in both the Security Council and the GA. It is too early to say yet what we can do about those.

4. The only important question for your decision on Monday is your own possible appearance and speech in New York (a State Department draft of a proposed speech is attached).[4] The Department would propose to tie your appearance to UN interest in further peaceful initiatives following the Test Ban Treaty; you will have to consider whether you want to use the UN at this time as a place to say anything important on this subject. Although the State Department argues that your appearance might deflect some emphasis from African topics, it seems more likely that the South African and Portuguese issues would be just as strenuous and difficult in any event.

5. State may particularly ask your views on several other points, such as—(a) the Hungarian issue which will not be on the GA Agenda unless there are some particular domestic reasons for reviving it at this time; (b) a possible proposal for a "UN Commissioner on Human Rights" (Tab IV, page 7)[5] on the general proposition that our human rights problems are already an international open book and that such a

---

[1] Source: Kennedy Library, National Security Files, Subjects Series, United Nations (General), 9/1/63–9/8/63, Box 311. Confidential.

[2] September 9.

[3] Not attached. See Document 263.

[4] Not found. See Document 267.

[5] Not found.

Commissioner might help to illuminate comparably the human rights problems of some of our critics abroad.

William H. Brubeck[6]

---

[6] Printed from a copy that bears this typed signature.

---

265. Memorandum From the Assistant Secretary of State for International Organization Affairs (Cleveland) to Secretary of State Rusk[1]

Washington, September 7, 1963.

SUBJECT

Subjects for Discussion with the President on September 9 Relating to the 18th General Assembly

In our meeting with the President on September 9, there are a number of points I believe it would be useful for you to highlight. We do not yet need to ask the President to make specific decisions on individual issues, except the very important question whether he will address the General Assembly. However, a number of policy questions covered in the Strategy Paper for the Eighteenth General Assembly should be brought to his attention because of their political ramifications with a view to having the President provide us with any further guidance. Accordingly, I recommend that in addition to discussing the possibility of a Presidential statement to the General Assembly, you touch on the following points:

1. *Congo.* The Secretary-General expressed the view that if UNOC is to be retained beyond December 31, the minimum viable level is 6,000 men, which would cost $30 million. We have pressed for his agreement at the 3,000-man level, which our JCS believes feasible, at a cost of about $10 million. We have suggested a compromise to the Secretary-General under which there would be 6,000 troops in the Congo on January 1, 1964, but they would be phased down to 3,000 by March 30, looking

---

[1] Source: National Archives and Records Administration, RG 59, Central Files 1960–63, UN 3 GA. Confidential. Drafted by Joseph J. Sisco and William B. Buffum on September 7. Copies were sent to Ball, W. Averell Harriman, U. Alexis Johnson, Abram Chayes, Phillips Talbot, G. Mennen Williams, William R. Tyler, Roger Hilsman, Jr., William C. Foster, and Edwin M. Martin. A notation on the memorandum indicates that the Secretary saw it.

toward their total withdrawal by June 30. We estimate the cost at $15 million. We would have to mobilize a two-thirds majority of the General Assembly for the necessary financing (hopefully on the basis of the formula adopted at the Fourth Special Session). It may be possible to get such support in the Assembly if, as now seems possible, U Thant's report does not recommend against it. The critical decision will be whether the United States should take an initiative early in the General Assembly session to this end. More consultations with key U.N. members are required. We will also want to consult with selected members of Congress, especially on the Appropriations Committee, if we decide to pursue this course in the General Assembly.

2. *Enlargement of Councils.* The question of enlargement of United Nations councils is assuming increasing importance to the new members, especially in Africa. There are indications that the U.S.S.R. may be prepared to support or take an initiative on enlargement of the Economic and Social Council and possibly of the Security Council (unlinking this from the Chinese representation question). We must measure the pressures and determine whether we should take any lead in securing enlargement of the Councils. We should not abandon our announced position that the new members are entitled to greater representation. However, our recent experiences in the Security Council require us realistically to admit that we would be in a less favorable position in an enlarged Security Council. There may be a major decision for the President to take on this question during the course of the Assembly. Any Charter amendment would require ratification in accordance with our Constitutional processes, including Senate advice and consent.

3. *Chinese Representation.* We expect to be able to mobilize the necessary support to maintain our position on Chinese representation. However, if the Soviets should decide to relax their position and opt for a "two China" solution (there is one unconfirmed report to this effect) we will face serious difficulties in the Assembly. The President should be made aware of this possibility even though it is remote.

4. *"Cold War" Issues.*

(a) *Korea.* We expect to be able to maintain our position on the Korean unification item, but the amount of support will be affected by whether and how the October elections are held.

(b) *Hungary.* For the first time since 1956 there is no Hungarian item on the provisional agenda, and we do not anticipate taking an initiative. Support would not be forthcoming in view of the general amnesty and the Secretary-General's trip. We will need to decide during the Assembly whether to express again a reservation on the Hungarian credentials as we did at the Fourth Special General Assembly. In view of the past keen Congressional interest, we can expect some domestic fall-out.

(c) *Tibet.* India now is willing to have the Tibetan item inscribed and would support a resolution limited to human rights. There is an even chance therefore that two or three countries may again ask Assembly consideration.

5. *Colonial Issues.* We cannot assess the full dimensions of the Portuguese territories question until we know the outcome of Mr. Ball's efforts in Lisbon.

In the case of South Africa, we must expect to be pressed again to take far-reaching sanctions, including suspension or expulsion.

We will be pressed again by the United Kingdom to help it on Southern Rhodesia.

Consideration of these items is likely to stimulate strong emotions and possibly staged walkouts. We will be required to take a strong stand in favor of orderly procedures.

6. *Human Rights.* We will be pressed to take a vigorous stand against religious persecution in South Vietnam.

On a broader scale, given increasing preoccupation of the world community with the human rights questions, we will need to decide whether to encourage the United Nations to intensify its activity in this area. One possibility would be the establishment of a U.N. Commissioner for Human Rights.

7. *Reference of Article 19 Question to ICJ.* The question of applying Article 19 to the Communist bloc for non-payment of dues will not arise directly. However, we can expect a sharp division in the Assembly on whether Article 19 has automatic application. While holding firmly to the view of automaticity, we will probably be pressed for a decision to refer this question to the Court. Our initial estimate is that we could accept a properly framed question to the Court, though we will wish to make a final decision on the matter in light of developments.

8. *Disarmament and Nuclear Issues.* In general, we will seek to remand most of the disarmament and nuclear issues to the 18-nation Disarmament Commission. In addition, we will have to (a) counter pressures from third countries, including Canada, for more far-reaching measures than we would like; (b) oppose any unpoliced moratorium; (c) face a final decision on whether to support the Brazilian proposal for a denuclearized Latin American zone. Finally, the presence of Gromyko and other foreign ministers will offer further opportunity for quiet probes.

266. Memorandum of Conversation[1]

Washington, September 9, 1963, 11:30 a.m.

SUBJECT

Strategy at the 18th General Assembly

PARTICIPANTS

The White House—The President
                   Mr. Bundy
                   Mr. Schlesinger
                   Mr. Sorensen (in part)

The Department—The Secretary
                   Ambassador Stevenson
                   Mr. Ball
                   Mr. Harriman
                   Mr. Cleveland, IO
                   Mr. Sisco, UNP
                   Amb. Thompson, S/AL

The question of the President's possible attendance at the General Assembly is discussed in a separate memorandum.[2] The Secretary indicated that the enlargement of the Councils and the question of the Congo were two important issues before the Assembly.

1. *Enlargement of the Security Council and the Economic and Social Council.*

The Secretary asked Mr. Cleveland to outline briefly the question of the enlargement of UN Councils. Mr. Cleveland said there were indications that the USSR may be prepared to support or take an initiative on enlargement of the Economic and Social Council and possibly the Security Council by unlinking the latter from the Chinese representation question. Mr. Cleveland pointed out that we have come out publicly in favor of enlargement, but we must recognize that, bearing in mind recent difficulties, we would be in a weaker position in an enlarged Security Council. He pointed out also that any Charter amendment would require ratification in accordance with our Constitutional process, including the Senate's advice and consent. He indicated also that ratification requires a two-thirds vote of the UN membership, including all the permanent members of the Security Council. Ambassador Stevenson indicated the strong inter-

---

[1] Source: Kennedy Library, National Security Files, Subjects Series, United Nations (General), 9/9/63–9/30/63, Box 311. Confidential. Drafted by Sisco. Approved in S on September 12 and in the White House on September 13.

[2] Document 267.

est of the Africans in this matter and expressed the fear of possible defection of the Africans on the Chinese representation question if we are not able to adopt forthcoming positions on such questions as enlargement of the Councils, the Portuguese territories, apartheid and other similar issues. The President decided that we should restate our public position in favor of enlargement of the Councils, but that we should not push the Security Council proposal, leaving the initiative to others.

2. Extension of UNOC.

Ambassador Stevenson outlined the difficulties we are encountering with Secretary-General Thant regarding retention of UNOC for six months beyond the end of this year. The President suggested that he might write to four or five African Prime Ministers. Ambassador Stevenson suggested deferring this matter until he has had a further opportunity for discussion with key Africans, including the Nigerians. The President agreed. He also agreed we should include an appropriate reference in favor of an extension of UNOC in the United States speech before the Assembly.

The President asked whether an OAU Force is not a viable substitute. Mr. Cleveland pointed out that, while such a force might be helpful in the Congo, there is danger that it might be used in other places in Africa, i.e., Angola and Mozambique. Mr. Ball likewise agreed. The President thought we might talk to the Portuguese on this matter with a view to seeing whether they would be willing to talk to the French. He thought the Portuguese might tell the French that the alternative to UNOC extension is an OAU Force which, in turn, carries risks for Portugal in Angola.

3. United States Speech in the General Assembly.

It was decided that the following additions would be made to the United States speech: (a) a stronger section on the significance of the test ban designed to offset some of the negative thinking that has been projected as part of the ratification process; (b) a paragraph or so indicating our support for continuation of the Congo operation; (c) a reference to the trade negotiations and the World Trade Conference scheduled in early 1964; (d) references to the hard issues, including Laos, Viet-Nam, Berlin and Cuba; (e) material on enlargement of the Councils; (f) reference to the Buddhist issue in Viet-Nam; and (g) strengthening the "Man's Mastery over Environment" section based on suggestions made by the President's Advisory Committee. Ambassador Stevenson was asked to provide the President with suggestions on the above material.

4. Submarines for South Africa.

The question of supplying South Africa with three submarines was discussed inconclusively after the Secretary raised the question. The President felt the question was primarily one of balancing the foreign exchange advantage (one hundred million dollars) against the anger which it might cause among the Africans. Ambassador Stevenson felt that, from the point of view of our position in the United Nations, it would be better not to provide the submarines, but he realized there were other considerations that must be weighed in making a decision on this matter. The President said we would need to discuss this matter further at a later date. Moreover, no decision was taken regarding the sending of a technical mission to South Africa.

5. Chinese Representation.

After Ambassador Stevenson outlined the difficulties confronting us if the Soviets should decide to relax their position and opt for a two-China solution, the President said we should do what is necessary to keep Red China out and to maintain our position.

6. Hungary.

The Secretary said there did not appear to be much concern domestically over this question. The President took note of the fact that no item will be submitted this year. The question of whether the United States should state a reservation in the Credentials Committee, as it did at the Fourth Special Session, was left open.

7. Human Rights.

There was a very brief reference to the human rights questions as the meeting was breaking up. The President said that this matter could be decided in the context of what to include in the United States speech.

267.   Memorandum of Conversation[1]

Washington, September 9, 1963.

SUBJECT

The President's Attendance at the General Assembly

PARTICIPANTS

The White House—The President
                Mr. Bundy
                Mr. Schlesinger
                Mr. Sorensen (in part)

The Department—The Secretary
                Ambassador Stevenson
                Mr. Ball
                Mr. Harriman
                Mr. Cleveland, IO
                Mr. Sisco, UNP

After a brief discussion of the pros and cons, the President decided that he would attend the Assembly and asked Ambassador Stevenson to arrange with the Secretariat to speak the first thing on Friday morning, September 20. The President felt that his presence at the Assembly would give him an opportunity to put the test ban treaty in perspective and to dispel doubts in the world that may have arisen as a result of the debate within our country over ratification. At the Secretary's suggestion it was agreed that the President's attendance at the General Assembly would be announced on Monday, September 16, and that this late announcement would help to avoid stimulating a huge attendance of high-level leaders at the Assembly. The President asked Ambassador Stevenson to provide Arthur Schlesinger and Ted Sorensen with any further substantive thoughts he might have for additional material for inclusion in the President's speech.[2]

---

[1] Source: Kennedy Library, National Security Files, Subjects Series, United Nations (General), 9/9/63–9/30/63, Box 311. Secret; Limit Distribution. Drafted by Sisco. Another copy of the memorandum gives the time of the meeting as 11:30 a.m. (Ibid.)

[2] President Kennedy addressed the UN General Assembly at 11 a.m. on September 20. For text of his speech, see *Public Papers of the Presidents of the United States: John F. Kennedy, 1963*, pp. 693–698, or *American Foreign Policy: Current Documents, 1963*, pp. 106–113.

268. Telegram From the Department of State to Secretary of State Rusk in New York[1]

Washington, September 26, 1963, 10 p.m.

Tosec 70. Subject: Talk with Gromyko re UN Financing. Ref: Talking Paper—Gromyko, 18th GA–P/7, 7th Para, 9-16-63.[2] Problem of UN financing likely lead to open confrontation with Soviets at first session of GA in 1964 when perforce Article 19 will be involved unless Sovs have made payment of back UN peacekeeping assessments totaling about $6 million and are fully up to date on regular budget assessments. If there is resumed or special session this confrontation could take place early in 1964. We therefore believe it important in view of impact that will have on US-Soviet relations to alert Gromyko to this prospect. Following are suggested talking points:

We hope USSR is giving most serious attention to settling its financial accounts with UN. USSR is aware of our position on application of Article 19. While this essentially matter between USSR and UN, unless issue satisfactorily resolved, it could affect prospect for long-range cooperation between us both inside and outside UN framework.

At this stage important thing is to remove the specter of such confrontation by having the Soviets settle all or most of their arrearages so that Article 19 is not brought into play. We do not want to advise Soviets on how to go about this. We do note that other countries that share USSR reservations have nevertheless paid assessments on some peacekeeping operations (e.g., France and Morocco on UNEF).

Dept assumes you will not want to discuss this issue in first go-around beyond such general exhortation and assertion of our seriousness in this matter. However, in event you find it useful to pursue matter further at future meetings, following additional talking points may prove useful in event they seem to be looking for way out.

Assuming UNOC phased out by mid-1964 could not Soviets consider paying some or all of their Congo arrears in 1964—if necessary

---

[1] Source: National Archives and Records Administration, RG 59, Central Files 1960–63, UN 10–4. Confidential. Drafted by Nathan A. Pelcovits (IO/UNP) on September 25; cleared by William B. Buffum, Virginia C. Westfall, Richard H. Davis, George S. Springsteen, Walter H. Lubkeman, and Ernest L. Kerley; and approved by Cleveland. Repeated to Moscow.

[2] Not printed.

"under protest"—based on fact or expectation that UNOC terminated but that they want to help UN clear up its financial problem. Or Soviets might offer to make voluntary contribution in settlement of assessed arrears. (We not sure whether UN could accept such substitution under regulations now in force, but if USSR even made probe of feasibility of such substitution this would show readiness consider settlement).

Soviets might consider paying UNEF arrears (about $14 million) as voluntary act without explicitly recognizing assessment as obligatory. (Though Soviets oppose assessments because UNEF not authorized by SC, they are aware that states concerned have accepted UNEF as useful peacekeeping operation.)

We also hope Soviets will tacitly drop their earlier insistence on withholding part of their assessment on regular budget which goes to servicing of bonds and paying for special missions (UNTSO, Field Service, etc). Organization's operational capacity would be seriously impaired if members attempt to pick and choose among budgetary items they will support.

Ball

269. Telegram From the Mission to the United Nations to the Department of State[1]

New York, September 28, 1963, 2 p.m.

1042. UN Scale of Assessments.

Fedorenko (USSR) called me out of plenary today to discuss UN scale of assessments and handed me an unofficial Sov memo as fols:

Begin Verbatim Text

"In his address to the plenary meeting of the United Nations General Assembly on 20 September the President of the United States John F. Kennedy expressed the opinion that 'it is high time that many disputes on the agenda of this Assembly were taken off the debating schedule and placed on the negotiating table.'

---

[1] Source: Kennedy Library, National Security Files, Subjects Series, United Nations (General), 10/63–11/63, Box 311. Confidential; Verbatim Text. A handwritten note from Bundy to Belk reads: "Sam: Is there some hope in this? McG B."

The scale of assessments for sharing expenses of the United Nations is one of the highly disputed and unsettled question on which there exist substantial differences between the positions of the United States and the USSR and on which heated discussion had taken place at a number of General Assembly sessions. Further aggravation of differences of opinion on this question would affect most adversely the development of cooperation of states within the framework of the United Nations and could threaten the whole financial basis of this organisation.

The divergencies on the scale of assessments have resulted from the wrong approach to assessing the contributions of the USSR and other socialist countries, on the one hand, and of the United States and other Western powers, on the other hand. The bias of this approach is due to the failure to take into account, contrary to the decision of the 1st General Assembly session, such an important criterion set by the 1st session as comparative income per head of population. This failure was due to fixing the ceiling of 30 per cent for the United States assessment. Although it was intended to use this ceiling only when normal conditions prevail in the world, in practice this ceiling is wrongfully used already now.

Besides while determining the scale of assessments such important criteria as opportunities of individual members for acquiring foreign currency and temporary dislocation of the national economy as a result of World War II had not been taken into account.

The first of these criteria is of paramount importance for the USSR and other socialist countries whose foreign trade is still being subjected to barriers established mainly by the United States.

The second criterion is still of some importance for assessing the contributions of the USSR and a number of other countries, which is proved, for example, by the fact that according to the 1957 census the number of women in the Soviet Union exceeds by 20 million the number of men. These data reflect most important and grave consequences of war which still greatly influence many aspects of life in our country. It is as a result of World War II that the Soviet Union still bears enormous expenditure on pensions to the veterans of war and their families, as well as big expenditure on medical service for both the military and civilian personnel—veterans of war whose health had been undermined during the war.

As a result of these wrong attitudes there exists such an abnormal situation when the assessments of the United States and other Western countries are substantially reduced with every passing year while the assessments of the USSR and other socialist countries increase, as is shown by the following table.

Assessments for United Nations Budget

	1947	1963	1963 (percentage of 1947)
USA	39.88	32.02	80.3 percent
Great Britain	11.98	7.58	63.2 percent
France	6.00	5.94	99.0 percent
USSR	7.40	17.47	236.0 percent
Poland	0.95	1.28	134.7 percent
Czechoslovakia	0.90	1.17	130.0 percent

Replying to a reporter's question Mr. Adali Stevenson, United States Representative to the United Nations, said on 21 May 1961 with reference to the United States assessment that based on the ability to pay, the United States assessment for the United Nations regular budget is smaller than it should be. He said he believed that the figures of total national output indicated that the United States should pay 38.5 per cent instead of 32 per cent.

A year later, on the 27th of June 1962 Mr. Stevenson, replying to a question concerning the assessments of the United States for the United Nations budget, stated in the Committee on Foreign Affairs of the House of Representatives of the United States Congress, 'that, based on ability to pay, the United States should pay something like 44 or 45 per cent of the UN assessments'.

The Soviet Union regards as most unsatisfactory the present situation in regard to the scale of assessments to the United Nations budget, and believes that the USSR assessment was established on a wrong and unjust basis.

Not only socialist countries but many other members of the United Nations object against the failure to observe the above mentioned criteria adopted by the 1st Session of the General Assembly and particularly against fixing the ceiling for the United States assessment.

To avoid the aggravation of the situation during the consideration at this and future sessions of the General Assembly of the scale of assessments for the United Nations budget, including the question of the ceiling for the United States, which could have certain effect on the general political atmosphere, the Soviet Union is prepared to seek ways of settling this question on the basis of the proposal to freeze the existing scale of assessments for the United Nations budget for the period of ten years." *End Verbatim Text.*

I attempted find out what exactly meant by last para. Fedorenko explained that they wanted discuss with us bilaterally possibly changes in scale of assessments, taking present scale as basis for discussion, and then fix scale agreed upon for 10 years.

Stevenson

270.   Memorandum of Conversation[1]

SecDel/MC/97   New York, October 2, 1963, noon.

SECRETARY'S DELEGATION TO THE EIGHTEENTH SESSION OF
THE UNITED NATIONS GENERAL ASSEMBLY
New York, September 1963

SUBJECT

   Nigerian Foreign Minister's call on the Secretary

ITEM OF DISCUSSION

   Enlargement of UN Councils

PARTICIPANTS

   The Secretary   Mr. Jaju Anucha Wachuku—Foreign Minister
   Ambassador Stevenson   Mr. E. Anyaoku—First Secretary at Nigerian Del to UN
   Mr. Dickinson   Mr. A. O. Nnorom—Private Secretary to Minister
   Mr. Dean (reporter)

The Secretary asked whether there is any possibility of enlarging
the Security Council and ECOSOC without thereby raising the question
of Chinese representation. The Nigerian Foreign Minister replied that
on the basis of his conversation with Mr. Gromyko, he concludes there
has been no change in the Soviet position. According to Wachuku,
Gromyko feels that the Eastern European seat in the Security Council
"really isn't of much use to them" since it has only rarely been occupied
by a Communist country. If there is no support for revising the UN
Charter, Wachuku continued, the Africans are determined to try for
enlargement of certain organizations in order to give Africa fair representation. Hence the amendment of the Charter proposed by the
Africans might be limited to this specific point.

The Secretary then asked whether all African nations would support the Ivory Coast's candidacy in the Security Council. Wachuku did
not think so because the Ivory Coast is seeking the Commonwealth seat
and Nigeria is already committed to supporting Malaysia for this seat.
The Secretary pointed out that if the Ivory Coast is elected to the
Security Council, it would give Africa two seats inasmuch as Morocco
is already a member. Wachuku indicated that this approach is not
acceptable to the Africans because they are interested in the principle of
clearly setting aside a certain number of seats as African seats. He

---

[1] Source: National Archives and Records Administration, RG 59, Conference Files: Lot 66 D 110, 18th U.N. General Assembly. Confidential. Drafted by John Gunther Dean on October 4 and approved in S on October 4. The meeting was held at USUN. The memorandum is Part 1 of 4.

stressed that the Africans don't want to "raid" seats allotted to other geographic or political areas, nor do the Africans want to be forced to lobby for seats in every General Assembly. The Africans feel they deserve seats on a strictly geographic basis. Referring to his speech before the General Assembly, he repeated that Nigeria does not want Latin America to lose its seats.

Mr. Dickinson suggested that voting for Malaysia does not automatically force Nigeria to support Czechoslovakia. Since Nigeria can vote for three candidates, it would be able to vote for Bolivia and the Ivory Coast in addition to Malaysia.

In determining which countries to support for the Security Council seats, ideological differences among Africans will also play a role, said Wachuku. Furthermore it is not certain that all UAM states will vote for the Ivory Coast and that petty rivalry among UAM members may lead to some defections.

The Nigerian Minister said that Guinea had asked the Special Political Committee to give priority to the question of enlargement of the UN Councils. On the basis of the outcome of this debate and what is said at that time, the Africans will determine their position on who to support for the Security Council. Wachuku also said that he had emphasized to Gromyko that the question of enlargement should not be linked to the question of Chinese representation in the UN.

271. Memorandum of Conversation[1]

SecDel/MC/98   New York, October 2, 1963, noon.

SECRETARY'S DELEGATION TO THE EIGHTEENTH SESSION
OF THE UNITED NATIONS GENERAL ASSEMBLY
New York, September 1963

SUBJECT

Nigerian Foreign Minister's Call on the Secretary

ITEM OF DISCUSSION

Chinese Representation

PARTICIPANTS

[Here follows the same list of participants as Document 270.]

Wachuku stressed that there is no question of expelling Nationalist China from the UN, but he was equally determined that Continental China should be admitted to the UN. As for which one of the two Chinas should obtain the seat on the Security Council, Wachuku suggested that the Asians may wish to decide this question.

The Secretary expressed the opinion that the Chinese communists would not accept admission to the UN under these circumstances. He then pointed to a number of acts by the Chinese communists which would indicate that they have not renounced their policy of aggression. He cited the Moscow–Peking debate in which the Peking regime reasserted its view that war remains an instrument of foreign policy. He mentioned Peking's decision not to sign the test ban treaty and pointed out how China has blocked agreement on the Geneva Accords dealing with Indo-China. While listing examples of ChiComs aggressive policy, he also mentioned that there appears to be some kind of a review going on within China which may determine its future foreign policy. Therefore, it is important that no encouragement be given at this time to those who advocate a hard line. The Secretary added that it may be of some significance that it was Albania and not the Soviet Union which introduced the motion on Chinese representation this year.

The Nigerian Minister stated that there is no evidence that Continental China would not live up to its obligations which it would have to assume by becoming a member of the United Nations. Unless

---

[1] Source: National Archives and Records Administration, RG 59, Conference Files: Lot 66 D 110, 18th U.N. General Assembly. Confidential. Drafted by John Gunther Dean on October 4 and approved in S on October 4. The meeting was held at USUN. The memorandum is Part 2 of 4.

China accepts the principles embodied in the UN Charter, it would be in the same position as South Africa and then would become the object of the same types of pressures from member states as presently experienced by South Africa. Wachuku expressed the opinion that China would also not wish to alienate its supporters by violating the UN Charter.

Ambassador Stevenson asked whether Continental China might be admitted under the two China policy? Wachuku replied that it was his intention to introduce an amendment asking for the admission of China "provided they apply for it." He added that he doubts Continental China would accept under these conditions. Nevertheless, he believes that this tactic would smoke out China's real intentions.

Ambassador Stevenson injected that it would indeed be a very significant day if China would apply for membership and also renounce its claim on Taiwan.

Wachuku explained that if Continental China would apply for membership, this in itself would imply renunciation of its claim to Taipei and disavowal of aggression as an instrument of Chinese policy. Mr. Dickinson pointed out that the real question is whether China should be admitted before its views have been fully tested or afterwards when Chinese membership may disrupt the UN. To this, Wachuku replied that Chinese membership in the UN could have no worse effect than Soviet membership.

Ambassador Stevenson queried whether this was a propitious moment to advance a two-China policy especially since the question of Chinese representation is scheduled for discussion on October 11. Wachuku replied that the best thing that can be done now is "to call China's bluff which would take the wind out of China's sails." He claimed that at the present time the onus of keeping Continental China out of the UN is clearly on the United States. The tactics he is advocating would change this. He stressed again that neither Nigeria nor the other Africans want to expel Taipei. The Chinese Nationalists have proven themselves to be good and loyal members of the United Nations. Also, Nationalist China has the veto to prevent its own expulsion.

The Secretary suggested that events in Continental China may make it desirable to postpone the discussion of Chinese representation in the United Nations beyond the presently scheduled date. Mr. Dickinson asked whether the Nigerian Minister had thought of the adverse effect increased support for Chinese admission would have on small Southeast Asian countries which have been pursuing an anti-communist policy. If China were admitted, Wachuku replied, it would become subject to UN pressures and the UN certainly has means at its disposal to deal with China if it interfered in the internal affairs of another country.

The Secretary said that China is not bent on building a peaceful world. Its decision not to sign the test ban treaty is merely an example of this. If China ever became a nuclear power, it would create major problems for the world. Wachuku replied that Chinese membership in the UN would also solve some of the problem. Once China comes into the United Nations it would have to behave like any other peace-loving nation. He repeated again that "no harm would be done to the UN or anybody else if an amendment is brought forward to bring in China."

Ambassador Stevenson asked whether China's refusal to sign the test ban treaty should not affect its admission to the UN. Wachuku replied that it is easier to control China from within the UN than from without. Ambassador Stevenson pointed out that were China to be admitted at this point, after its refusal to sign the test ban treaty, it would be tantamount to rewarding China for its aggressive policies.

The Secretary said that he would have a clearer picture of the problem once he knew what is presently going on in Peking. He promised to keep in touch with the Nigerian Government on this important question.

---

272. Telegram From the Mission to the United Nations to the Department of State[1]

New York, October 7, 1963, 7 p.m.

1200. Soviet Views re UN Financial and Administrative Problems.

Roshchin (USSR) stated to Mission officer that USSR considers that Fifth Comite agenda at current session contains three difficult and important problems: (1) financing of peace-keeping operations, (2) regular scale of assessments (report of Comite on Contributions), and (3) personnel item.

---

[1] Source: National Archives and Records Administration, RG 59, Central Files 1960–63, UN 10–4. Limited Official Use.

Roshchin said that scale of assessments issue could be removed if US agreed to freeze scale for ten years in accordance with memo handed by Fedorenko (USSR) to Stevenson.[2] He felt confident that Comite Five would accept such freeze if US and USSR concurred.

Although making no specific proposals re other matters, Roshchin stated several times that US and USSR Dels should sit down and discuss all difficult questions presently in Comite Five. Re financing peacekeeping operations, he added it was unthinkable that USSR should be forced pay $60 million in so-called arrears for financing operations which had been dealt with in violation of Charter. He appeared more defensive on this point than at any time in past, and his manner indicated Soviets now feel their position more difficult re this issue.

When Mission officer expressed surprise that USSR Del considered personnel item to be difficult one, Roshchin said Soviets still very unhappy about fact they had absolutely no influence within Secretariat and that Secretariat decisions constantly made without any consideration being given to Soviet views.

Stevenson

---

2 See Document 269.

273.   Memorandum of Conversation[1]

Washington, October 13, 1963, 10 a.m.

SUBJECT

Chinese Representation

PARTICIPANTS

United States:
The President
Under Secretary of State George W. Ball
Assistant Secretary of State for African Affairs G. Mennen Williams
Ambassador to Mauritania Philip W. Kaiser
Officer-in-Charge of Mauritania Converse Hettinger
Deputy Chief of Protocol William J. Tonesk
Protocol Officer Jay Rutherfurd
Interpreter Alec G. Toumayan

Mauritania:
President Moktar Ould Daddah
Foreign Minister Sidi Mohamed Deyine
Director of the President's Cabinet Abdoul Aziz Sall
Chargé d'Affaires a.i. in Washington Mohamed Nassim Kochman
Aide-de-Camp to the President Lieutenant Mohamed Sidina Sidya

President Kennedy then raised the Chinese representation issue, stressing that it would be a serious mistake to admit to the United Nations a country committed to a policy of war. It would be particularly unfortunate to do this at the expense of the Republic of China, a founding member of the organization, which has some equity in the matter. While the situation may change in time and Communist China may abandon its present policy of attempting to communize the world by war, Communist China's admission to the United Nations at this time would do very serious injury to United States efforts to prevent communist takeovers all around the rim of Asia, where the United States is heavily involved. Commenting that he was aware that President Moktar, in his recent UNGA speech, spoke of the desirability of admitting all nations to the UN, President Kennedy stated that he felt strongly there should be some recognition of a country's peaceful intent before it is invited to join the UN.

President Moktar recalled Mauritania's friendly relations with the Republic of China since his country's accession to independence, and noted that the Republic of China maintains an Embassy in Nouakchott.

---

[1]   Source: National Archives and Records Administration, RG 59, President's Memoranda of Conversation: Lot 66 D 149, October–November 1963. Confidential. Drafted by Hettinger on October 31 and approved by the White House on November 5. The memorandum is Part V of VI.

At the same time, if there is a country in Africa which cannot be accused of being communist, it is certainly Mauritania. On the question of China, however, Mauritania has its own point of view. Mauritania is for universality as are the United Nations. When President Moktar referred to the admission of all independent states to the UN, he meant those which fulfill all conditions of the Charter. When a country fulfills all these obligations, it should be permitted to enter the organization; when not, it should be left out. For Mauritania, the principle of universality has arisen very naturally after the model provided by the UN. The Republic of China is a founding member of the UN and should not be expelled. As for Communist China, Mauritania's point of view is not based on very precise information, since Mauritania does not have all the information available to the U.S. Nevertheless, Mauritania thinks that if Communist China accepts all conditions of the Charter, it should be admitted to the UN. In an organization where the majority of people are reasonable, Communist China would be influenced by the other members and rendered less dangerous than if left to itself. The evolution of Soviet policy suggests the correctness of this view, and the Western decision to negotiate with the USSR has proven successful in that the Soviets have ended by accepting the dialogue. In conclusion, President Moktar said Mauritania, as an African state, intends to respect OAU solidarity, and his country's position is that of the majority of reasonable African states.

President Kennedy replied that the United States is militarily committed by treaty to the defense of a number of free countries right under the belly of Communist China. Under the circumstances, and in view of the recent history of Soviet-Chinese relations, it would be a serious blow to both the United States and the UN to admit to the latter this year a country which is committed to nuclear war. While respecting the Mauritanian view, the President emphasized that the admission of Communist China to the United Nations at this time would have a disastrous effect in the United States. It would, moreover, be awkward, at the very time we are trying to do something about Portugal and South Africa, to admit to the UN a country whose policy, judging from its dialectic, is war. Perhaps, in due time, the situation will change: Communist China may abandon its war policy, and a two-China solution may prove possible.

The discussion then turned to United States-Mauritanian relations.

274.   **Memorandum From the Assistant Secretary of State for International Organization Affairs (Cleveland) to Secretary of State Rusk**[1]

Washington, October 21, 1963.

SUBJECT

Analysis of General Assembly Vote on Chinese Representation October 21, 1963

The General Assembly rejected an Albanian resolution to expel the representatives of the GRC and to replace them with Chicom representatives by a vote of 41 in favor, 57 opposed and 12 abstentions. The vote in 1962 was 42 in favor, 56 opposed and 12 abstentions. Ethiopia, which normally supports the Chicoms though it recognizes neither the GRC nor the Chicoms, was absent. Kuwait, the only new UN member this year, abstained. As in 1962, the proposal to eject the GRC and seat the Chicoms was rejected by an absolute majority.

Of 110 countries that voted on this issue in 1962, only six (not counting Ethiopia) changed their position. Of these changes, four were in our favor and only two were to our disadvantage. Yemen, whose support for us in 1962 was entirely fortuitous, reverted to support of the Chicoms. Mauritania, alone of the UAM states, defected and abstained instead of voting against as it did in 1961 and 1962. On the positive side, Sierra Leone, which in 1961 and 1962 had voted in favor of comparable Soviet proposals, abstained. Typical abstainers like Cyprus and Togo changed to outright rejection of the Albanian proposal. And Malaya, which last year wandered off the reservation toward abstention, this time returned to the fold and voted against as in 1961.

The question of "Two Chinas" never arose. Wachuku was out of town and never even made a statement. Tunisia asked for a separate vote on the two operative paragraphs of the Albanian resolution, but dropped this request at the behest of Algeria.

---

[1] Source: National Archives and Records Administration, RG 59, Central Files 1960–63, UN 6 CHICOM. No classification marking. Drafted by Bertus H. Wabeke (IO/UNP) on October 21 and concurred in by Sisco. A notation indicates that the Secretary saw the memorandum.

275.   Telegram From the Department of State to the Mission to the United Nations[1]

Washington, October 22, 1963, 8:32 p.m.

1143. Exploratory Talks with Sov Del re UN Financing.

We are continuing our appraisal of strategy we should follow in exploring with Soviets possibility of reaching understanding on UN financing. Points raised by USUN in very thoughtful papers we had from you earlier this month and in comments to Cleveland in last week's discussion of draft three-point package have raised number of questions on which further deliberation required before we are ready to wrap up strategy paper. We are, in particular, reassessing way in which we could reach understanding with Soviets and others on how larger contributors could be given larger voice in future peacekeeping operations without impairing potential of UN to act in face of Soviet obstruction. Under circumstances it would be premature for you to engage in discussion with Soviets on points of substance even in preliminary manner.

Dept would therefore want you to use occasion of Thursday lunch to set framework for later discussions and to probe Soviet readiness to discuss regular scale in broader context of regularizing arrangements for UN financing, including satisfactory settlement of arrears. Using arguments familiar to you, following would appear to be reasonable and useful line to take:

1. Question of holding line on regular scale cannot be treated in isolated manner. Given U.S. and USSR responsibilities as big powers, such question must be considered in context of two related aspects of UN financing, settlement of arrears and financing of future peacekeeping.

2. We believe that such three-fold framework for exploratory discussion has a chance of proving fruitful since problems interrelated. We have common interest in (a) achieving equitable and stable scale for regular budget; (b) clearing away underbrush of old debts through satisfactory Soviet settlement of its arrears so as to avoid confrontation on Article 19, and (c) harmonizing our views on the handling and financing of future peacekeeping operations so that larger contributors have voice commensurate with their responsibilities. FYI. In this connection, we must assure that any understanding on future arrangements does

[1] Source: National Archives and Records Administration, RG 59, Central Files 1960–63, UN 10–4. Confidential. Drafted by Nathan A. Pelcovits on October 22; cleared by Sisco, John C. Guthrie, Richard N. Gardner, Louis E. Frechtling, and Richard H. Davis; and approved by Sisco. Repeated to Moscow.

not impair our capacity to get UN to act if USSR unwilling to do so. We could not agree to any arrangement which would give USSR this kind of veto. End FYI.

3. We do not have fixed views or position on these but believe they offer promising framework for future discussions. We would welcome Soviet views on whether this appears to them reasonable and useful way to approach discussions. We are open to suggestions, but want to make it clear from outset that we would not regard separate and isolated discussion on freezing regular scale as holding hopeful prospect. In particular, settlement of arrears is sine qua non of any accommodation on holding regular scale to more or less present level.

Rusk

276. **Memorandum From Samuel E. Belk of the National Security Council Staff to the President's Special Assistant for National Security Affairs (Bundy)**[1]

Washington, October 23, 1963.

SUBJECT

The Upcoming Talks with the Russians on UN Financing

A memorandum from the Secretary to the President on the U.S. strategy on the over-all problem of financing, including bilateral talks with the USSR, is being prepared, but it is long overdue. I am, therefore, passing along the following as a means of keeping you abreast of the Soviet side of the problem since we must soon be clear as to what our position is before the bilateral talks with the Soviet Union begin (as yet unscheduled).

The Soviet position has not greatly changed since they first suggested in an unofficial memorandum on September 28 that bilateral talks should begin between the U.S. and the USSR on the matter of freezing the existing scale of assessments for ten years. The U.S. is quite amenable to such discussions, but we also have insisted on discussing the matter of settling arrearages in order to avoid confrontation with the USSR on the application [of] Article 19 in the 19th GA. We also would

---

[1] Source: Kennedy Library, National Security Files, Subjects Series, United Nations (General), 10/63–11/63, Box 311. Confidential. A copy was sent to Schlesinger.

like to discuss the matter of future peace-keeping operations (the U.S., and certainly the Soviet Union, would like to protect the political interests of the big powers against the possibility that the small powers would—because of their numerical superiority—be in a position to direct future peace-keeping operations).

On all three aspects of the problem—regular assessments, payment of arrearages and future peace-keeping operations—our own interests, to some degree, are shared by the USSR. They are the three topics the Department now plans, with the President's approval, to instruct Stevenson to explore with the Russians.

The most worrisome aspect of the problem is how to find a way to avoid a confrontation with the Russians on the application of Article 19. As you probably know, Soviet spokesmen in New York and elsewhere have stated categorically they will confine themselves to discussion only of freezing the present scale of assessments and that they will not discuss their arrearages in peace-keeping operations (we would, of course, have to discuss arrearages before we could properly discuss future peace-keeping operations).

There is no question that we potentially face a most serious problem in the 19th GA if the Russians remain adamant about payment of their arrearages. There has developed a large body of opinion in the UN which will not go along with the ICJ interpretation of Article 19 if it means denying the USSR its GA vote. This opinion is especially apparent among the Afro-Asians and the Latin American states, although it is too early to predict how much of this opinion would be translated into voting strength. The best one can say is that we are not sure we can muster a two-thirds vote on this Important Question. Some countries believe the precedent of denying a GA vote to a member state might one day be used against them; others insist that denial of the USSR's vote would "destroy" the UN.

The Russians thus far have been very cavalier about the matter. They do not appear to believe the GA will throw them out and, even if it did, one member of the Soviet delegation has noted that at least the Soviet Union will continue to have a vote in the Security Council. The Russians base their present approach on their long-standing argument that peace-keeping operations fall under the Security Council as provided by Chapter VII of the Charter which provides that, "The Security Council shall determine the existence of any threat to the peace, breach of the peace, or act of aggression and shall make recommendations, or decide what measures shall be taken in accordance with Articles 41 and 42 [also in Chapter VII][2] to maintain or restore international peace and security."

---

[2] Brackets in the source text.

As you know, the matter of peace-keeping operations came under the GA by the passage in 1950 of the "Uniting for Peace" resolution which authorizes the GA to act when the SC is paralyzed by the veto. The U.S., which then had a dependable, solid majority in the GA, pushed this resolution through, and it has been used as an umbrella for Korea, UNEF, and UNOC. The Russians have consistently insisted (along with the French) that the GA acted illegally in giving itself powers which the Charter had delegated to another UN body.

Despite the foregoing, there is good reason to believe the Russians are more concerned about their posture on financing than they have been in the past. It would appear that, as a minimum, they are seeking a clarification of their position and, in order to do so, they apparently consider themselves in a position to enter into hard bargaining.

It may be that the Russians would find a way to make the minimum payment necessary to get past Article 19 in exchange for U.S. agreement to freeze the present scale of assessments—a formula not wholly unpalatable to the U.S. or the USSR. Another course the Russians might choose would be to make a minimum payment on UNOC (there is a SC resolution empowering the UN to act in the Congo) under protest, based on an understanding that the operation will terminate on June 30, 1964, and as a gesture to help the UN out of its financial difficulties. Another alternative would be the payment of their arrears of $14 million for the UNEF operation as a voluntary—not an obligatory—gesture; thereby not compromising in principle. Any one of these three approaches might be satisfactory; especially as the day of reckoning draws nearer. Actually, in order for the USSR to avoid an impasse on Article 19 in a totally regular way, a relatively small sum is involved—about $6 million on either UNEF or UNOC plus their assessment on the regular budget (which they always pay).[3]

The Department will recommend—and I think rightly so—that we should allow the Russians to have no illusions about our seriousness to see Article 19 applied, but we should also make it abundantly clear that we have no desire to deprive them of their GA vote. We should strongly impress upon them the value we attach to having all members— especially great powers—retain their votes in the GA.

The next step in the exercise is to take the Secretary's proposals for over-all strategy on UN financing to the President—hopefully by the end of the week. After that, as USUN explores the problem with the Russians, we will be in a better position to judge the size of the problem we face and what kind of compromises, if any, we may have to make.

SEB

---

[3] The words "Actually" and "in a totally regular way" have been added by hand.

277.   Telegram From the Department of State to the Mission to
        the United Nations[1]

Washington, November 8, 1963, 7:44 p.m.

1364. Re Enlargement Councils. Dept in general agreement positions and tactics recommended Urtels 1442 and 1457.[2] Dept's specific comments follow:

1. In general, we should maintain our public posture in favor of enlargement of both Councils. There are obvious advantages to us of approach by stages, concentrating on ECOSOC in first instance in order to test Soviet intentions before getting into details of a much more complex nature of Security Council enlargement. Best results from our point of view would be to have reasonable enlargement of ECOSOC but for Security Council remain as it is. Our hope is that division of forces on question of Security Council enlargement will be such as to result in impasse. We know you are fully aware that any enlargement of Security Council less likely to be favorable to us than with present composition. Moreover, Security Council enlargement would raise difficult questions for us in ratification process which not case with respect ECOSOC.

While our bargaining power should not be over-estimated in light of strong feeling that has developed over the years in favor enlargement both Councils, and our public position in favor of enlargement, we would hope it would be possible for USGADel to use as appropriate leverage we have in direction of amendments acceptable to us; no Charter amendment is possible without our agreement.

We realize fully that it may not be possible to focus action on ECOSOC enlargement alone. Therefore, following is supplementary guidance as it relates to possible Security Council enlargement.

2. It of major importance we hold any SC enlargement to 2 in order protect US interests in Council. In this connection Dept fully

---

[1] Source: National Archives and Records Administration, RG 59, Central Files 1960–63, UN 8 SC. Confidential. Drafted by Hartley on November 8; cleared by Nathaniel McKitterick, John P. Walsh, William B. Buffum, George N. Monsma, Curtis C. Strong, Louise McNutt, Abram Chayes, Cleveland, and William C. Burdett; and approved by Sisco.

[2] In telegrams 1442 and 1457 from USUN, both dated October 17, Stevenson reported on consultations with the French and British Delegations concerning enlargement of UN councils. The British would support an increase of two seats in the Security Council in the hope that a seat could always be held by a Commonwealth member. Should the Security Council be enlarged, the French had been instructed to seek an increase in the majority necessary for passage of a resolution from seven to nine. (Ibid., UN 8 SC)

concurs line taken with LAs (Urtel 1811)[3] with respect importance coordination WE and LA positions, and encouraged both WEs and LAs apparently prepared agree on 2 (Urtels 1654, 1866).[4]

3. Dept prefers voting majority of 8 with increase of 2. While voting majority of 9 would make it easier defeat proposals in SC, it would at same time make it more difficult obtain necessary majority for Western proposals. Nine would therefore not appear desirable and is unnecessary from viewpoint protecting our interests since our position already protected by veto if situation sufficiently serious from standpoint US interests to warrant its use.

4. Dept agrees that the 2 additional seats should be allocated Asia and Africa, respectively, with "floating" seat reverting Eastern Europe. History our efforts deprive Eastern Europe seat originally allocated to it makes it clear any effort continue do so in enlarged Council would encounter stiff opposition and seriously prejudice chance, if any, Soviet ratification, thereby leaving us open charges bad faith. Moreover it obviously causes fewer political complications for US to accept formula permitting Eastern Europe retain seat it has either held or shared (with one exception) since 1946 than to seek amendment Charter to give Eastern Europe seat de novo.

5. Dept shares your doubts it will prove practical retain both Commonwealth and 2 LA seats. Recent SC elections would appear already to have seriously undermined concept Commonwealth seat and Dept would expect Africans to insist on two seats so long as LAs hold two, even though argument can be made that with Commonwealth seat they would in fact have one plus seats, since Commonwealth seat would for most part be shared between Asia Africa.

6. If Commonwealth seat goes to Africans and Council enlarged by 2, over-all geographic distribution including 5 permanent members would be as follows: Asia—2, Middle East—1, Africa—2, Latin America—2, Eastern Europe—(including USSR) 2, Western Europe—3, and U.S. Any allocation less favorable our position would raise serious problems for US ratification.

---

[3] In telegram 1811 from USUN, November 1, Stevenson reported that the Latin American delegations had agreed to support enlargement of the Security Council, ECOSOC, and the General Committee. (Ibid.)

[4] In telegram 1654 from USUN, October 28, Plimpton reported that the Western delegations agreed to adding two seats to the Security Council, six to ECOSOC, and "a small increase in General Comite." Whether eight or nine votes should constitute a majority and preservation of the Commonwealth seat were still at issue. Telegram 1866 from USUN, November 5, reported that the Latin American caucus agreed to support enlargement of the councils, to oppose redistribution of seats, and to seek cooperation with other groups on a formula for expansion that could command a two-thirds vote. (Both ibid.)

7. Dept also shares your doubts A-As (or EEs) will be satisfied with "understanding" rather than resolution with respect allocation since it clear from experience under "gentlemen's agreement" such understandings unlikely remain firm.

8. We, of course, would like to avoid resolution on across-the-board reallocation non-permanent SC seats entirely, but realize this may not be possible. Dept inclined believe any resolution allocating seats likely be considered procedural as in nature amendment GA rules of procedure and therefore difficult avoid even if LAs and WEs stand firmly together.

9. Re ECOSOC, Dept agrees we should hold line at increase of 6 and believes you should seek encourage LAs join forces with WEs in maintaining this position. With respect allocation these additional seats, Dept would hope see WEs regain seat lost in 1961, 2 seats go to Asia, 1 seat to Middle East and 2 seats to Africa. Dept believes 4 seats for Africa sufficient (2 additional plus 2 it now has) and that 2 additional seats Asia desirable in order permit India and Japan serve more frequently than they can now hope to. With respect return seat lost by GRC in 1960, Dept recognizes this may not prove feasible but believes question should be discussed GRC Del before final decision reached on this point. Re resolution now pending Committee II to enlarge committees of ECOSOC, Dept prepared consider this as interim step to Council enlargement if debate in SPC is concluded without action.

10. Re General Committee, Dept believes plan outlined Urtel 1442 about as much as we can hope for and agrees we should be as flexible as possible with respect its size and geographic allocation in order bolster our position with respect SC and ECOSOC. At same time Dept would hope see increase in number of vice-presidencies held to 2 on grounds GC should not become too unwieldy in size.

Rusk

278.   Telegram From the Department of State to the Mission to the United Nations[1]

Washington, November 13, 1963, 4:43 p.m.

1402. Ref: Deptel 1143, USUN 1665.[2] Talks With Sov Del re UN Financing.

In further assessment draft strategy paper you discussed with Cleveland in mid-October, we conclude it would be premature and unprofitable to attempt at this time to reach harmonization of views with Sovs on handling and financing future peacekeeping operations in context your current talks. We believe workable device for giving bigger voice to larger contributors—such as GA financial screening out or opting out provision—is not simply technical matter but is intertwined with (a) policy decision on politically acceptable US share of costlier peacekeeping operations, which necessarily involves Congressional support and (b) safeguards to ensure we do not impair UN capacity to act in face of Soviet opposition. This complex issue must be separated out for intensive planning between us over next few months so that we can take sound and approved position into Working Group discussions. Meanwhile we see no objection (and some merit as suggested below) to your indicating to Sovs on informal basis that we are giving attention to long-range problem of financing and management of future peacekeeping operations in preparation for deliberations of Working Group, taking into account special problems of large contributors.

Under circumstances we would plan to do separate longer-range paper geared to key policy decision on financing and managing future peacekeeping, and limit what follows to strategy in more immediate context of current talks. In place of three-fold framework outlined in Deptel 1143 you should be guided by following considerations in pursuing talks, adapting tactics as necessary.

---

[1]   Source: National Archives and Records Administration, RG 59, Central Files 1960–63, UN 10–4. Confidential. Drafted by Pelcovits on November 7; cleared by Sisco, Burdett, Captain Freeman, Leonard C. Meeker, Virginia C. Westfall, Richard N. Gardner, Ernest L. Kerley, John C. Guthrie, and William B. Buffum; and approved by Assistant Secretary Cleveland. Also pouched to Moscow, Geneva, and Paris.

[2]   Telegram 1143 is Document 275. Telegram 1665 from USUN, October 28, described a luncheon meeting on October 24 between four members of the U.S. Delegation and four members of the Soviet Delegation. During the luncheon, the Soviets insisted that their country's assessment scale should be frozen or reduced because it had not recovered from the devastation of World War II and because of its difficulty in obtaining foreign currency. At a later reception, Roshchin said that the Soviet Union would agree to a freeze on regular assessments and to removal of "operational programs" from the budget. Payment of any arrears for ONUC or UNEF was "absolutely excluded." (National Archives and Records Administration, RG 59, Central Files 1960–63, UN 10–4)

1. New turn reported in USUN 1930 and 1943[3] (re proposal for short resolution on 1964 scale of assessments which would list only changes and not publish entire scale) suggests that Sovs may be backing away from freeze idea for time being. We are inclined to doubt that Sovs have dropped idea entirely, and we propose following strategy on assumption they will want to continue talks before end of GA or early next year.

2. You should therefore continue to be receptive to Sov desire resume talks. Our main objective is to achieve satisfactory solution of arrears so as to avoid or at least delay beyond 1964 threatened hassle on Article 19. Despite negative attitude of SovDel reported urtel 1665 (which to be expected at this early stage) we must insist on tie-in between arrears settlement and our receptivity to discuss freeze on regular scale. Without indication of Soviet readiness to clear up arrears issue, we would see no prospect of mutually acceptable outcome on regular scale freeze. This linkage is not to be regarded by Sovs as capricious or artificial on our part, nor is it simply advanced by us as bargaining counter. Sovs should be aware of following considerations: a) we would find difficulty justifying to American people and Congress standstill on regular scale (instead of expected reduction in our share and sizeable increase in Sov share) while Sovs and others continue resist obligation to pay for previously-assessed fair shares for UN operations; b) in same vein we could not argue convincingly for new, higher peacekeeping scale while arrears for past peacekeeping operations remain unsettled; c) other members whose proportionate share of regular budget will be higher if regular scale is frozen can be more readily persuaded to acquiesce in freeze if it is combined with settlement of arrears.

3. At same time you should indicate to Sovs that with solution of problem of old debts we would be in better position to turn our attention to long-range problem of financing and management of future peacekeeping operations, taking into account special problems of larger contributors. On this point too early to discuss particulars but Dept giving close study this problem in developing US position on questions that will come before Working Group next spring. (Unofficially, as illustration one possibility, you might speculate that in event special scale adopted for costly peacekeeping operations, arrangements might be established so that bigger contributors would have larger voice in determining when such special scale would be applied.)

4. In addition to holding out carrot of favorable attitude on our part to their freeze proposal, we believe that despite Sov intransigence you should adopt following course: (a) reiterate that overwhelming GA acceptance of ICJ ruling on peacekeeping assessments removes any doubt as to legal and political validation of their obligation to pay UNEF and UNOC assessments; (b) reiterate, using familiar arguments,

---

[3] Neither printed. (Both ibid.)

that terms of Article 19 make it clear that loss of vote is automatic; (c) continue to assert as you did in last go-round that US position on application Article 19 remains unchanged; and (d) enlist support appropriate third countries in pressing Sovs to clear up arrears problem.

5. Dept believes politically-important third countries could play useful role in urging Sovs to settle arrearage problem. We would like your views on embarking on such corridor talking campaign with third countries in such way as to ensure its getting back to Sovs. Countries such as India, UAR, Nigeria, Brazil occur to us but you are in better position to judge. Our arguments would be: arrears must be settled if UN to go forward in orderly and businesslike manner; underbrush of old debts must be cleared away if we are to make progress on future peacekeeping formula in Working Group next spring; settlement of arrears is not US-USSR issue but involves delinquent behavior on part certain members with which entire UN membership must be concerned.

6. Initial sessions should thus concentrate so far as possible on question of arrears to probe area of give on this matter. You should of course make it clear that we will not make issue of means by which debts are paid, nor do we insist on open confession of sins. We would assume that Sovs could work out acceptable formula with UN Secretariat which would allow them to pay up without appearing to compromise on principle. For example, they could make minimum payment on UNOC, perhaps initially for period in 1960 when UNOC operated under SC reses they endorsed authorizing SYG provide GOC with military assistance and, in addition, for later period when Thant became SYG, and in expectation that operation would wind up by mid-1964. They could advertise payment as act of grace to help out UN in financial difficulties, thus avoiding endorsement Congo operation. They could pay UNEF arrears ($14 million) as "voluntary" act while continuing deny that assessment obligatory. Of course you should not leave impression that any partial payments could be regarded as full discharge of their legal assessments.

7. If Sovs give satisfactory indication that they are moving to resolve arrears issue, you could move on to discussion of substance their proposal for freeze on regular scale. We assume that meanwhile your preliminary "technical" talks would have gone long way in exposing spuriousness of their statistics and arguments re fairness of scale. In substantive discussion of regular scale you should complete refutation their arguments so that whatever accommodation we may reach does not in any way imply acceptance of Sov premise re fairness of scale. Whatever validity there is to Sov plea for more favored treatment has already been cranked into criteria used by Contributions Cmte in determining capacity to pay, and there is no justification for favoring Sovs at expense of rest of membership.

8. We would in any case consider freeze for ten years as unrealistic and unjustifiable in terms of balance of interests of all members. If we were to entertain concept of freeze it would be for next three-year round and would be on two grounds: (1) that arrears had been settled; (b) that stabilization of assessments for this period would be in general interest of UN. It would provide time for Organization to digest effects of recent budget and program increases; take account of effect on UN program and operations of rapid influx of poor members whose demands on organization not offset by contributions; and give UN time to wrestle with problem of achieving viable formula for financing future costly peacekeeping operations. In addition, we would want assurance that any freeze formula would provide some net reduction for US share by taking account of receipts from any new members who will pay their share of regular budget within 100 percent scale. Applying this principle to eight new members now outside scale, our proportionate payment comes out at about 31.90.

9. FYI. You are aware that freezing scale would not be without advantage to us quite apart from arrears settlement. Ceiling principle has become increasingly contentious. While we have been inching our way to GA-approved 30% ceiling, we would not want risk reopening debate on ceiling principle, and it may eventually become desirable for us to acquiesce in maintaining roughly our present share during next 3 year assessment period. On balance, however, we would not find freeze of all shares on regular scale, including Sov share, to our net advantage and it becomes politically palatable only if combined with solution on arrears. End FYI.

10. Dept assumes above strategy would be effective if Sov desire for freeze is important objective. If not, it is unlikely in our estimation that Sovs would back down on arrears this early, if at all. Dept would appreciate early assessment from USUN and Embassy Moscow on how strongly Soviets desire freeze. We would also be interested in probing Sov intentions re future peacekeeping operations. What importance do you attach to Solodovnikov's repeated remark that USSR cannot be expected pay arrears if it not have single technician in Congo operation or in Civops Congo? Is this search for face-saver or does it presage Soviet desire to get directly involved in future peacekeeping acts? If latter, what in your estimation are implications for US policy?

11. Dept believes that whether or not you make headway in achieving kind of deal we have in mind, process of exploration with Sovs will be beneficial to us in preparing our policy on financing and management of future peacekeeping operations. It is thus very timely apart from hopefully successful outcome of immediate issue.

Rusk

279. Telegram From the Mission to the United Nations to the Department of State[1]

New York, November 13, 1963, 7:15 p.m.

2032. Deptels 1045, 1143;[2] USUN's 1295,[3] 1449,[4] 1665,[5] 1771.[6] Meeting With Sov Del on UN Financial Problems.

Expected technical meeting on USSR ability to pay and why it believes it over assessed on UN regular scale of contributions held Nov. 12: Solodovnikov (USSR) and Ziehl (USDel). Little new learned, but USSR arguments included:

1. USSR dollar contributions to UN and specialized agencies $25 million per year which too large an amount for USSR to pay. SovDel believes Supreme Soviet may refuse pay increased percentage if voted, because too difficult secure foreign exchange. When queried about magnitude total foreign trade and fact USSR refuses publish balance of payments information, Solodovnikov replied he realized this puts USSR in difficult position and he feels his government wrong in not making these data available to show real USSR problem. In response to line of argument "You can't have your cake and eat it," Solodovnikov again repeated this is real problem for USSR and his govt's position on not publishing balance of payments figures makes SovDel's position difficult.

2. Principal argument, that UN scale is based national income figures while accumulated wealth is the significant real factor was that little new wealth accumulated USSR during World War II, and war destroyed much existing wealth. Rates of growth on national income not appropriate measure until real wealth restored. In other words, much Soviet economic growth and capital accumulation still required to re-establish USSR wealth. When asked whether Western European countries did not have similar problems and the relationship their scale rates to scale rates of Soviets, Solodovnikov replied situation is not analogous, but would not elaborate. (It appeared to DelOff that Solodovnikov's heart not in this argument.)

---

[1] Source: National Archives and Records Administration, RG 59, Central Files 1960–63, UN 10–4. Confidential.

[2] Neither printed. (Both ibid.)

[3] Not printed. (Ibid., POL 7 UAR)

[4] Not printed. (Ibid., UN 10–4)

[5] See footnote 2, Document 278.

[6] Not printed. (National Archives and Records Administration, RG 59, Central Files 1960–63, REF 5 UNRWA)

3. Veterans benefits and excess women in labor force lumped together by Solodovnikov, who alleged USSR veteran benefits very high, but stated he did not know magnitude, and that excess of women very high, but he not know numbers. Factual basis had been laid by DelOff that in 1959 disparity between able bodied males and females in USSR was just over 4 million. It hard to reconcile these figures with 20 million excess women figures and relate this figure (often used by USSR) to significant economic arguments bearing on the scale of assessments. Solodovnikov, while insisting this a significant item, supplied no answer except to say that the figures DelOff quoted must deal with USSR as a whole, whereas there were serious imbalances in parts of the Soviet Union. These imbalances had required large expenditures, for example, to create factories for the sole employment of males in areas where 95 percent of the remaining population were women. The arguments advanced were never tied up with their effect on the USSR ability to pay or the fairness of its scale of assessments.

In closing discussion, Solodovnikov stressed personal belief that USSR and US must find ways to cooperate more fully in the UN. He stated he realized many nations, including the Africans, beginning resent this display of cooperation, but it important to world peace. His final (emotional) comment was that all the Russians who had met US military during the wars liked them, and there was a great reserve of friendship for the US.

Solodovnikov also stated he had been on two weeks emergency leave to see his sick wife last summer; hoped to go home for a month and half this summer and "maybe stay there." He stated no one knew about this desire, but that he hoped "to get back to the institute" where he could make a further contribution to economics and international relations. Also stated he planned go to Washington after this GA and hoped see Bowman, US national on Contributions Committee.

Stevenson

280. Telegram From the Mission to the United Nations to the Department of State[1]

New York, November 20, 1963, 7 p.m.

2170. Talks with SovDel re UN Financing. Ref: Deptel 1143 and USUN 1665, 1999.[2]

USUN agrees questions of financing and managing future peace-keeping operations in manner more fully in accord with interests of larger contributors is intertwined with US policy decision on accept-ance special scale. As pointed out USUN 1999, subject: UNEF financing 1964, it will be difficult negotiate acceptable UNEF financing res early December, unless US prepared during UNEF negotiations indicate it likely be willing agree some version special scale when Working Group 21 meets. Currently expected Working Group begin meeting about Feb 1. USDel concerned unless Congressional soundings already undertak-en or can be taken promptly, USDel be very difficult position not only during UNEF financing negotiations in two weeks, but also when Working Group meets. Time and difficulty of both consulting Congress and getting Executive Branch clearance within month of Jan recognized by all.

USUN also concurs safeguards necessary so US capacity to act not impaired. But little time remains for dealing with Soviets exclusively. Several members Working Group 21 have already indicated they believe Working Group mandate to work out methods financing peace-keeping operations involving heavy expenditures likely be "only chance" to bring USSR back into fold for past arrears and for future par-ticipation in time avoid necessity Article 19 showdown.

With respect your suggestion USDel indicate to Sovs on informal basis we giving attention to long-range problem of financing and man-agement of future peacekeeping operations in preparation for delibera-tion of Working Group, taking into account special problems of large contributors, USDel so far finds little interest by Sovs in this approach, except repeated statements financing must be in Security Council with veto. Therefore, believed imperative US position on acceptable perime-ters control mechanism for large contributors be available soonest. Restating to Sovs that with solution of problem of old debts, we be in better position to turn to long range financing and management prob-lem considered highly unlikely be productive. In any case we need deci-

---

[1] Source: National Archives and Records Administration, RG 59, Central Files 1960–63, POL 27–4 UN. Confidential.

[2] None printed. (All ibid.)

sion soon on these questions within Executive Branch so that necessary govt position can be prepared before Working Group meetings.

With respect freezing scale assessments, SovDel appears have dropped freeze idea for present. Tactical situation is that unless Sovs bring this before current GA—only logical item being scale of assessment discussion which began Fifth Committee this week—possibility security freeze becomes increasingly difficult. Best bet work out freeze would have been instructions from this GA to Committee on Contributions, before it meets next June, to take freeze action on the scale. Without instructions, Committee on Contributions will have no alternative but to apply present criteria to development revised scale. (It appears such revision would increase USSR percentage substantially and give reductions to many members.) To reverse such Contributions Committee recommendations once made, would be uphill battle even if Sovs throw in sponge next fall and pay arrears. The appeal of reduced contributions for the many LDCs which be so entitled next year be very difficult LCDs resist. Admittedly, major attack next fall on US ceiling— if USSR not press freeze—might appeal many LDCs as way of getting double reductions. USDel will, of course, continue probe Sovs on their ideas on freeze and future intentions.

With respect role of politically important third countries in urging Sovs to settle arrearage problem, we will continue talking third countries but at this stage mainly to bring our information on their opinions up to date. Most these countries appear be waiting for opportunity for negotiations in Working Group 21. Problems likely be created if India, UAR, Nigeria and Brazil go off on their own until US position on financing and managing is shored up. Encouraging these countries take independent lead on settlement arrears might well start snowballing of proposals inimical to US interest.

With respect Solodovnikov repeated remark USSR cannot be expected pay arrears if it not have single technician in Congo operation or Civops Congo, best present appraisal this complaint rather proforma. Only usefulness might be inclusion in policy guideline for USDel on US attitude inclusion USSR technicians in future operations. USDel willing explore importance USSR attaches to technician for Civops Congo, if Dept believes it advisable. USDel present view is further mentioning or pressing this point better left to USSR.

In summary, USUN intends keep door open for further talks regarding UN financing and plans be receptive further meetings, preferably during present GA, but (1) unless developments in current scale of assessment debate (which began Nov 20) are other than expected, or (2) Dept furnishes further guidelines on financing and management aspects of future peacekeeping operations, any future talks expected only result in keeping channels open and not in development much new information useful in formulating our position.

Within several days USUN expects submit memo to Dept on analysis of possible opting out procedures. Believe personal talks between Dept and USUN personnel also advisable this and other management phases of US needed position.

Stevenson

---

281. Memorandum From the Assistant Secretary of State for International Organization Affairs (Cleveland) to Secretary of State Rusk[1]

Washington, November 26, 1963.

SUBJECT

President Johnson on the UN

The following indications are available as to President Johnson's policy on UN affairs:

1. Ambassador Stevenson was invited to meet with President Johnson yesterday afternoon, before the reception in the State Department building. In the course of the 15 or 20 minute talk, the President confirmed his desire to carry on the policy of President Kennedy in the field of international cooperation on outer space matters. (This is also confirmed by the fact that the paragraphs from Ambassador Stevenson's prospective UN speech on outer space cooperation, which you sent over to the White House for clearance, have been returned with changes that do not affect the main thrust of our recommendation.)

The President had had some homework done on his own previous utterances on international cooperation in outer space, and gave Ambassador Stevenson marked copies of his previous speeches, drawing attention to passages with strong remarks on the subject. A selection of these excerpts, to which the President drew specific attention, is attached at Tab A.[2]

---

[1] Source: Kennedy Library, Cleveland Papers, President Johnson Transition, Box 20. Confidential. Drafted by Cleveland on November 26.

[2] Tabs A and B are not printed.

2. Ambassador Stevenson also discussed with the President the line he intended to take in the short speech he is making this afternoon in the General Assembly, answering on behalf of the U.S. the dozen or more eulogies that will be given in the General Assembly by representatives from other nations. Ambassador Stevenson told the President that it would be useful to put some words in his (the President's) mouth, in reassuring the Assembly about U.S. policy toward the United Nations. The President said that whatever Ambassador Stevenson said along that line would be alright with him, but to make it strong.

3. At the reception, the President spent 3 or 4 minutes with Secretary-General U Thant; Ambassador Stevenson and I were present. The Secretary-General led off by saying that he had followed with some interest President Johnson's personal public statements on the UN, and it seemed clear that his interest in and support of the UN was strong. President Johnson replied that his support of the United Nations was "total". He went on to say something very much like the following: "It would be hard to be a more vigorous and effective supporter of the UN than President Kennedy was, but if I can manage it, that's what I will be".[3]

After the President's talk with Ambassador Stevenson following the Cabinet meeting Saturday, November 23, the President directed his office to make available to us some quotations from previous speeches about the UN. These quotations are attached at Tab B.

Harlan Cleveland[4]

---

[3] This paragraph was derived from Cleveland's November 25 memorandum of this conversation. According to Cleveland's record, President Johnson also mentioned at the end of their talk that he wanted to have U Thant to Washington for lunch sometime soon. (Kennedy Library, Cleveland Papers, President Johnson Transition, Box 20)

[4] Printed from a copy that bears this typed signature.

282. Memorandum From the Assistant Secretary of State for International Organization Affairs (Cleveland) to Secretary of State Rusk[1]

Washington, November 27, 1963.

SUBJECT

Current Issues Before the United Nations

On Tuesday President Johnson, through Ambassador Stevenson, reaffirmed support for "every practical move to add to the capacity of the UN to keep the peace and aid new nations to reach the stage of self-sustaining growth."

Our ability to achieve the above will depend principally on what happens in regard to the following:

1. Whether the Soviet Union will insist upon provoking a constitutional crisis by maintaining its "financial veto" on peacekeeping operations although threatened with loss of its vote under Article 19.

2. Whether emotionalism over the hard-core remnants of colonialism, plus the racial issues in Africa, will present us with the hard choice of backing mandatory sanctions against South Africa and Portugal or losing the support of Africans on issues vital to us.

3. Whether the majority in the General Assembly—now speaking for the underdeveloped "south"—will insist upon new institutions, programs, or actions in the economic and social areas which are unacceptable to the United States and the other members from the industrialized "north".

The issues which we face in the United Nations fall under five headings:

I. The Development of the UN's Peacekeeping Capacity

Much of the growth of UN's peacekeeping capacity has been achieved despite obstruction from the USSR and its associated countries. On the whole these countries have looked upon the UN as an instrument for "conference diplomacy". But despite Soviet vetoes in the Security Council and despite Soviet efforts to impose a troika over the office of the Secretary-General, the UN has steadily moved forward in strengthening its executive and peacekeeping operations.

The Soviets have shown some signs of reconsidering their hard line of attempting to prevent the development of the UN's operational

---

[1] Source: National Archives and Records Administration, RG 59, Central Files 1960–63, UN 3–1. Confidential.

capacity. If there is a change of tactics and they begin participating more actively in the executive side of the UN's work, the opportunities this opens up will be matched by increased difficulties for the United States—for the Soviet policy of boycotting and complaining from the sidelines in the UN has enabled the U.S. and some of its Western allies to build an organization responsive to Western leadership, embracing in our interests the universal symbolism of a global organization. The Soviet attempts to share this leadership in UN operations from day-to-day could require substantial changes in our own tactics—just as things would have been far different if the Soviets had decided to participate in, say, the Marshall Plan or the UN Congo operation in the past.

The Crisis in Peacekeeping Financing. The most urgent problem which will face the United Nations during the next few months concerns the financing of peacekeeping operations. Last year, the General Assembly accepted an Advisory Opinion of the International Court holding that assessments for peacekeeping operations were binding upon all the members. This brings arrearages in the payment of such assessments within the provisions of Article 19 of the Charter. Under this Article if the Soviets fail to pay approximately $14 million of their arrears on the UN peacekeeping operations in the Middle East and the Congo, they would lose their vote at the first meeting of the General Assembly held in 1964. A direct confrontation in the UN on this issue would mean a major constitutional crisis. The Soviets maintain that the loss of vote is not automatic but would require, contrary to the express wording of Article 19, a 2/3 vote of the General Assembly.

Some hints have been dropped to both UN and US officials by Soviet diplomats in New York that a US-USSR agreement with regard to the future financing of peacekeeping operations might be helpful in resolving the arrearage question. Before entering into any serious discussion with the Soviet Union on this matter, the United States (with Congressional support) should be clear as to whether or not we ourselves can accept an assessment scale for peacekeeping operations which would put our assessment in the 37 to 38% range. Secondly, we will need to be clear as to whether any new measures are required to protect the US against future General Assembly assessments for peacekeeping operations of which we might not approve. It is possible that there should be some new screening mechanism through which all special UN peacekeeping financing measures should pass before being laid before the full UN membership in the Fifth Committee. Staff work is underway on both of these issues at the present time and policy decisions will need to be made early in the new year.

The question of arrearages is not a matter for the UN alone. It has arisen in the Organization of American States (OAS), in an even more acute form. Here there is no loss of vote provision and the US pays at an assessed rate of 66%.

Continuation of Present Peacekeeping Operations. The UN Emergency Force (UNEF) continues its effective work on the Israel-Egyptian border. The UN Congo Force (UNOC) has been continued until July 1, 1964. The UN Observation Group (UNYOM) in Yemen has been extended until January 4. UN Observers continue to police the cease-fire line in Kashmir.

Norway, Denmark, Sweden, Finland, the Netherlands and Canada have earmarked military units for UN service. It is anticipated that informal discussions between these countries and the UN Secretary-General on the training of officer and unit personnel will take place soon after the conclusion of the 18th General Assembly.

II. Colonialism and Human Rights

The decolonization process has now come firmly against the hard-core racial issues in the southern third of Africa. The African countries are beginning more seriously to relate our support or lack of support of their policies in this struggle to other issues in the United Nations (Chinese representation and loss of vote for USSR) which are of major importance.

Apartheid in South Africa. In the Security Council debate on apartheid, which began on November 27, the United States may be faced on a racial issue with the choice of casting its first veto or permitting a resolution to be adopted providing for punitive sanctions against South Africa. We are seeking to sidetrack extreme proposals, including a provision in a resolution calling for an oil embargo. Venezuela's vote is likely to be key and an approach to President Bentancourt of Venezuela will be necessary.

Southwest Africa. Also looming on the horizon is the question of South Africa's attempt to incorporate the mandated territory of Southwest Africa into the Republic and to extend to it South Africa's apartheid policies. The question of Southwest Africa is clearly an international one and poses the sanctions problem in a very different context.

Portuguese Territories. The Security Council will also consider the Portuguese territories question. Our objective is to utilize the Council to promote a resumption of quiet talks between Portugal and the Africans. Council consideration will bring to the fore again the role and relative importance in our overall strategy of the military base in the Azores. The debate will also highlight afresh the apparent Portuguese division of American military assistance for use in the Portuguese territories.

Captain Galvao. The United States may be confronted within the next two weeks with another difficult conflict of obligations. Captain Galvao is opposed to Salazar's policies on the Portuguese territories; he achieved fame by hijacking the Portuguese liner *Santa Maria* early in 1961. Galvao has now been invited (by an Afro-Asian majority) to appear before the UN General Assembly's Fourth Committee.

Under the UN Headquarters Agreement the U.S. is required to admit him so that he may appear before the Committee. At the same time, the United States has an extradition treaty with Portugal, the terms of which would make him subject to arrest for a hearing on his extradition—once he sets foot on U.S. territory. The Portuguese have said they will exercise their rights under the treaty. We are asking the Portuguese not to exercise their rights under the treaty. If they do, we will need to decide whether to arrange Galvao's visit so as to avoid his being arrested.

Human Rights. The growing power of the Afro-Asian nations in the United Nations has resulted in pressure for the Declaration on Racial Discrimination to be followed by a Convention on Racial Discrimination. This convention would be drawn up early in the new year by the UN Human Rights Commission and would be presented to the next General Assembly. While it is difficult in the present setting to oppose such a convention, the U.S. is exploring ways in which the UN's operational capacity can be increased for defusing certain human rights questions through quiet fact-finding, and in which other human rights questions can be handled in a less political way through being considered in the context of the world-wide development of human rights. This may involve giving the UN Human Rights Commission, or a rapporteur responsible to it, more freedom of initiative. It was decided last week to withhold a U.S. proposal along these lines, in order not to confuse further the domestic debate on civil rights legislation.

III. The Rich Countries and the Poor Countries

With the entry of so many former colonies into independence and UN membership, the confrontation of the world's impoverished "south" and the industrialized "north" is reflected in several issues of major concern at the United Nations.

UN Conference on Trade and Development. Ever since World War II, the United States has relied on GATT as a primary instrument for dealing with trade and tariff questions. Now the less-developed countries are moving to try to create a new mechanism in which they could have a predominant voice. In response to a decision at the Seventeenth Session of the General Assembly, the United Nations beginning on March 25 will hold a Conference on Trade and Development (UNCTAD). The conference is expected to last for approximately three months. The less-developed countries, led by Brazil, the UAR, Yugoslavia, India and Nigeria, have indicated they expect a new set of UN institutions to emerge from this conference—with effective powers to review, and if possible to change, existing international arrangements governing trade relationships.

The ability of the Western nations, led in this case by the United States, to preserve the status of GATT, while providing within existing UN framework a better opportunity to conduct trade discussions and debates, will be crucial both for the evolution of GATT and the future usefulness of the UN as an instrument in the trade field.

Initiatives at the 18th General Assembly. In his speech at the opening of the Eighteenth General Assembly, President Kennedy proposed the establishment of a World Health Communications Center under the World Health Organization (WHO), to warn of epidemics and the adverse effects of certain drugs, and the establishment of regional research centers which would advance medical knowledge and provide for the training of scientists and doctors in less-developed regions. Meanwhile the French have proposed the establishment of a World Cancer Research Unit under WHO to which nations would contribute up to 1/2 of 1 percent of their budgets. These several initiatives will be discussed in detail early in the new year by the Executive Board and plenary meetings of WHO.

IV. Cooperation in Outer Space

The United Nations has under way a vigorous program of international cooperation in the peaceful uses of outer space. A Declaration of Legal Principles is expected to be approved at this Assembly, followed by the drafting of international agreements on liability for space vehicle accidents and the return of astronauts and equipment which land in other than the launching countries. Measures will be taken under the UN's aegis to strengthen scientific cooperation as, for example, in the endorsement by the UN of a sounding rocket facility in India open to space experiments by all members. The World Meteorological Organization will be implementing plans already approved to establish a world weather watch, using satellites as well as ground facilities, to bring improved weather forecasts and increased knowledge in the atmospheric sciences. Finally, following the successful agreements reached by the International Telecommunications Union on the allocation of radio frequencies for space communications, the U.S. and other countries will be negotiating an international agreement establishing a new organization for the ownership and management of a global communications satellite system.

V. Institutional Questions

It is not surprising that an institutional structure developed for an initial United Nations membership of 51 is proving inadequate for a membership of 111.

An Increase in the Membership of the Security Council and the Economic and Social Council. The United States for several years has been on record publicly in favor of an increase of the Security Council to 13 from its present membership of 11 and an increase of the Economic and Social Council to 24 from its membership of 18. We are being pressed by the new nations to broaden their representation on the UN Councils, and would like to bring them in rather than redistribute seats at the expense of Europe and Latin America. We are concentrating in the first instance on the enlargement of the Economic and Social Council which does not raise a number of delicate issues which arise in connection with the Security Council. In the past the enlargement of the Security Council has been blocked by the Soviet Union since it has linked this question with Chinese representation. This has helped us maintain the present favorable composition of the Security Council without any appreciable adverse criticism being directed at us. There are indications that the Soviets may unlink the enlargement question from the Chinese representation issue. We will continue to indicate our willingness to support a modest increase of two on the Security Council. A resolution incorporating one or both of such proposed Charter amendments may pass this session of the Assembly. Any Charter amendments will be subject to ratification.

Improving the Operation of the UN Agencies. For the past year there has been underway a U.S. program designed to improve the staffing, the effective administration and the financial management of UN agencies. The Department has had the assistance of an *Advisory Committee on International Organizations,* composed of leading persons who have held important posts either in the UN or the U.S. Government. Two reports have been issued. The first is entitled "Staffing International Organizations." The second is entitled "The Technical Cooperation Programs of the United Nations System". The third report, just being published, deals with financial management of the UN agencies.

The principal proposal made in the technical assistance report was for the merger of the United Nations Special Fund and the Expanded Technical Assistance into a single UN Development Administration. This proposal will be taken up by a UN committee early in the new year. The third report on financial management deals, inter alia, with the problems of effective controls on the budgets of the UN Specialized Agencies. This is a problem which has also been of concern to Congress. The Foreign Assistance Act currently before Congress includes a Senate amendment which would place a dollar limit on the annual contribution of the U.S. to the Food and Agriculture Organization (FAO). While the elimination of this amendment may be possible, it points to the timeliness of the type of initiative already underway in the Department of State.

Economic Aid to Cuba. During the consideration of the AID authorization, the House approved, but the Senate did not insert, an amendment to prevent voluntary contributions to any international organization providing assistance to Cuba. It is thus clear that the United States
must have a defensible position on economic assistance to Cuba by UN
bodies. This issue could arise in January in connection with the programs of UNICEF or the UN Special Fund. In general, the U.S. continues to oppose economic assistance to Cuba.

Date for the Next Session of the General Assembly. In the election year
of 1956, the opening of the General Assembly was delayed until after
the United States election. This coming year, UN Headquarters in New
York will be undergoing substantial interior reconstruction in order to
accommodate the larger membership. In view of the delicate issues likely to arise next fall (Article 19 and Chinese representation), there may be
considerable advantage in promoting quietly a delay in the opening
date of the 19th General Assembly to November 1964.[2]

---

[2] A proposal for a delay was transmitted in telegram 1530 to USUN, November 27.
(Ibid., UN 3 GA)

---

283.   Telegram From the Mission to the United Nations to the Department of State[1]

New York, November 27, 1963, 7:30 p.m.

2245. Enlargement of Councils.

1. From number of sources in all groups we get impression there
now enough support pass res for increase of two in SC and six in
ECOSOC. All LAs and Eurs lined up. Asians held what is as far as we
can determine first Asian group meeting today to discuss increase.
Natwar Singh (India) informs us his del and as far as he knows other
Asian dels all ready to support two and six formula as long as one seat
set aside for Asia. Essafi (Tunisia) and Ben Hima (Morocco) report
Africans have decided accept two and six formula as long as two seats
set aside for Africa. Tunisia and Algeria wish to qualify for African seat
while Morocco hopes maintain Middle East seat which would run from
Morocco to Iran; on latter point, Ben Hima says Morocco will not insist.

---

[1] Source: National Archives and Records Administration, RG 59, Central Files
1960–63, UN 8 SC. Confidential.

2. Moves for larger increases in Council do not appear have much chance of success. Campbell (UK) says Dean told Canadian, Australian, and New Zealand Ambs last night that although UK would of course consider their proposal for increase of four in SC, he doubted strongly London would agree to this proposal since UK convinced West problems become more difficult with every increase. Mission Off again spoke with Canadian, New Zealand, and Australian Dels, showing them our calculations whereby each increase adds to our problems in SC. We see no sign today that as yet old Commonwealth waging major battle for their proposal. Quaison-Sackey (Ghana) quite separately has told us he desires see increase of three in SC with extra seat going to Commonwealth. However, he not sanguine about prospects for his proposal.

3. So far, Sov Bloc Dels keeping very quiet on enlargement except to pass word Communist China being consulted on increase.

4. Principal problem remaining seems to be whether and how to record distribution of SC seats following increase. Brazilians are shying away from recording distribution in formal res and thereby are making other dels wonder whether they have double play in mind. After talking to Correa da Costa (Brazil), we are convinced they have just not thought problem through. We suggested to them it essential work out means of recording distribution at same time res negotiated.

5. SPC has adjourned until Mon[2] PM in order give time for groups to work out agreement.

Plimpton

---

[2] December 2.

284. **Telegram From the Mission to the United Nations to the Department of State**[1]

New York, November 29, 1963, 9:15 p.m.

2291. Opening Date of 19th Session. Deptel 1530.[2]

We, also, have been concerned with possible unfortunate effects of opening 19th Session shortly before US elections. Some days ago Stevenson inquired of Dean (UK) whether UK would be prepared to take lead in proposing later opening date. Dean has told us he expects to be able give reply Dec 2.

In meantime, pursuant reftel Yost raised question informally with Bunche, to whom advantages of delay did not have to be explained. We emphasized, however, fact that capital improvement program would constitute excellent reason. Bunche was entirely sympathetic but did not feel SYG could take initiative in proposing delay. He believed some delegation or delegations other than US could do so and that in that case SYG could concur, noting that extra time would be very useful in assuring completion building program.

Subsequently, at SC luncheon today Bunche mentioned matter to SYG in Yost's presence. SYG said that he had already been giving serious consideration to this matter since he recognized serious disadvantages of having Article 19 confrontation while US election campaign in progress. He was, therefore, also sympathetic but not sure building program could be cited as reason for delay, since he had been assured work could be completed in August. Bunche and we pointed out that construction people rarely complete a job as soon as they expect. (Some days ago Vaughan told Yost he expected to complete work before GA opening but any unforeseen interruption or delay could make this impossible.) SYG concluded by saying he would give further consideration to problem.

Incidentally, in course of conversation, SYG inquired whether US is still determined to push Article 19 issue. Yost replied that our views on financial responsibility UN members, our interpretation of Charter, and our political commitments to US Congress make it certain that we shall do so unless in meantime Sovs find some means of making sufficient payment on arrears so that Article 19 would no longer apply to them. Naturally, we hope the latter will occur. SYG remarked that he had had some indication from Poles that they might follow "Yugoslav formula,"

---

[1] Source: National Archives and Records Administration, RG 59, IO/UNP Files: Lot 71 D 504, UNGA Position Papers, 1953–1967, Timing of GA Sessions. Confidential.

[2] See footnote 2, Document 282.

i.e., make payments for Congo operations after Nov 1961. However, he had no such indication from Sovs and is deeply concerned with problem and its possible repercussions.

Plimpton

---

285. Memorandum of Conversation[1]

Washington, December 4, 1963, noon.

SUBJECT

United Nations Affairs

PARTICIPANTS

Canadian Side
Paul Martin, Secretary of State for External Affairs
Hedard Robichaud, Minister of Fisheries
Marcel Cadieux, Deputy Under Secretary of State for External Affairs
Charles S. A. Ritchie, Canadian Ambassador
H. Basil Robinson, Minister, Canadian Embassy

U.S. Side
The Secretary
William R. Tyler, Assistant Secretary, EUR
Willis C. Armstrong, Director, BNA

Mr. Martin said that he was very much concerned over the proposal for the expansion of the Security Council of the United Nations and the possible loss of the Commonwealth seat. He said the British had reacted as had the United States to the Canadian proposal for four new seats.[2] He knew why the United States wanted two, but such action would be very prejudicial to Australia, New Zealand and Canada. The Secretary said he had not supposed that the Commonwealth seat would be lost if two seats were added. Mr. Martin said he did not see how this could be avoided, since the Africans and Asians would wipe out any

---

[1] Source: National Archives and Records Administration, RG 59, Central Files 1960–63, UN. Limited Official Use. Drafted by Armstrong and approved in S on December 13. The meeting was held in the Secretary's office. The memorandum is Part 4 of 8.

[2] On November 27 the Australian, Canadian, and New Zealand Ambassadors discussed with Cleveland the Canadian plan, which called for enlargement of the Security Council by four in order to preserve the retention of the Commonwealth seat. (Telegram 1548 to USUN, November 28; ibid., UN 8 SC)

possibility of the older Commonwealth being elected. If there were four seats added, the chance would be better, because seats could be given to the Africans and Asians. Canada had already told the United Kingdom it could not agree on the proposal for two additional seats. Canada has been thinking of a resolution in the UN, but realizes that the resolution might not pass, and would be subject in any event to a Soviet veto.

The Secretary questioned again the thought that the Commonwealth seat was lost if only two were added, because of the number of African and Asian countries now in the Commonwealth. Mr. Martin agreed that there were many Asian and African Commonwealth members, but pointed out that the older Commonwealth countries would be at a serious disadvantage. He said that a study had been done in Ottawa which indicated that if two seats were added, the chances of Canada being elected were approximately once in 23 years. The same problem would come up with ECOSOC, despite Canada's importance in the world economy. The Secretary raised a question as to the present distribution of seats, and it was noted that Malaysia and Ghana are now in such seats, but Ambassador Ritchie remarked that Ghana regards its seat as a regional African one. The Secretary wondered whether Ghana obtained its seat with Commonwealth support and the Canadians conceded that this had been so. The Secretary said he would look into the matter to consider the impact on the Commonwealth seat of an addition of two seats in the Security Council.

The Secretary wondered about Mr. Martin's possible reaction to a Japanese regiment available for UN purposes. Mr. Martin said he welcomed the decisions of the Nordic and the Dutch and he thought a Japanese regiment a good idea. The Secretary said it was important to get African and Asian countries in a position of contributing to UN military forces, and he had also thought about Nigeria. Mr. Martin said that he had talked to the Nordics about having a meeting of military people in Ottawa next spring, to review the problem. He certainly could see no objection to having a Japanese unit, but perhaps people like the Indians or the Filipinos might wonder about it. The Secretary said he was conscious of this possibility, and he emphasized we had not talked to the Japanese about the matter.

286.   Telegram From the Mission to the United Nations to the Department of State[1]

New York, December 10, 1963, 8:45 p.m.

2436. Enlargement of Councils.

1. Federenko (USSR) dropped bombshell today in SPC when he told Comite Sovs would take tough line against enlargement of councils because of opposition of Chinese Communists (ourtel 2427).[2] Previously Sovs had indicated they expected take relatively soft line towards enlargement. Hostile reaction of Africans was immediate; Bindzi (Cameroon) proposed delay of mtg in SPC until Thurs[3] PM. Diallo (Guinea) suggested GA remain in session until enlargement question settled. Under circumstances, all previous bets off on what action will be taken by SPC.

2. SC enlargement: LA draft of increase by two tabled with two year ratification period but without annex until question of ECOSOC distribution agreed upon. Knowing that ASAFs pushing hard for increase of 4 in SC, our liaison officers told Africans and Asians quietly but bluntly that US not in position to support this larger increase. Result was that Asians pulled back from insisting on larger increase, for moment at least. Hakim (Lebanon) tells us Arabs continue oppose larger increase and that those Africans who desire 13 member council will insist on right to vote for LA res. At this state it impossible predict what effect Sov position will have on question of SC enlargement.

3. ECOSOC enlargement: With breakdown apparent Eur–LA agreement on ECOSOC distribution, returning one seat to Eurs, Eurs immediately began talking in terms of increase of 7 or 9; this had auxiliary advantage from UK viewpoint of providing greater support for Commonwealth position on ECOSOC. Eurs proposed formulas for increase of 7 or 9 to LAs and once they got agreement from latter, both LAs and Eurs proposed formulas to Tarazi (Syria) as pres of ASAF caucus. Meanwhile, Malhotra (Nepal) reports Asians have also separately nearly reached agreement on 27 man ECOSOC. In Eur and LA formulation distribution would be as follows: LA—4-1/2, 4 perm members, WE—3-1/2, ASAFs—12, EE—2, Others—1. Asian formula would provide LAs 4, 4 perm members, ASAFs 13, WEs 3, EE 2, plus one floating seat to be divided among various groups on still undecided basis.

---

[1]   Source: National Archives and Records Administration, RG 59, Central Files 1960–63, UN 8 SC. Confidential. Repeated to London.

[2]   Dated December 10. (Ibid.)

[3]   December 12.

Proposal for 25 members in ECOSOC came from Netherlands which suggested that of 7 new seats, 6 would go to ASAFs and one to WE.

4. Since we got wind of Eur proposal, and after checking with Dept, we told number of leading Eurs and LAs that US strongly committed internally at this point to limiting increase in ECOSOC to 6 and that all we could do was take their proposal under consideration. We also indicated clearing new position might indeed be time consuming. Our recommendations follow.

5. General Comite: Only new development re GC was Sov statement in favor of amending GC res to provide for annual rotation of GA Presidency in following order: Africa, Eastern Eur, Middle East, Western Eur, LA. We have indicated to number of dels that we strongly opposed to taking decision which would impose rigid schedule of elections for GA Presidency. On other hand Cambridge (UK) showed us tel from London which instructed UK to support formula for deciding GA Presidency. They instructed support amendment to provide for succession to GA Presidency over 10 year period during which EE would hold post only once. Instructions also called for formula which would insure Eur would get GA Presidency in 1964 or 1965. British Emb Wash instructed consult closely with Dept prior to making their position public while UKUN instructed consult with old Commonwealth on point.

Stevenson

---

287. Telegram From the Mission to the United Nations to the Department of State[1]

New York, December 11, 1963, 1:50 p.m.

2446. Opening Date 19th GA. Ourtel 2349.[2]

SYG told Yost yesterday that, following Stevenson approach reported reftel, he had decided to assist in delaying opening 19th GA until after US elections.

---

[1] Source: National Archives and Records Administration, RG 59, IO/UNP Files: Lot 71 D 504, UNGA Position Papers, 1953–1967, Timing of GA Session. Confidential; Limited Distribution.

[2] In telegram 2349 from USUN, December 4, Stevenson reported that he discussed postponing the opening date of the 19th General Assembly session until after the U.S. Presidential elections with Secretary-General Thant. Thant was described as "receptive but not enthusiastic," and willing to consider using the remodelling of the conference chambers at the UN Headquarters as a pretext if the United States felt strongly about the issue. (Ibid.)

He said he had asked his administrative staff to prepare report for circulation end this month to effect that UN building reconstruction probably will not be completed before sometime in Oct. On basis this report SYG would circularize UN members and propose postponing opening GA until second week Nov.

SYG added blandly he had already talked this matter over informally with Sovs, pointing out disadvantages to all concerned of involving Article 19 question in US elections. According SYG, Sovs had agreed informally that delay in opening GA would be advisable, though of course their formal reaction would only come in response to SYG's proposed circular.

Plimpton

---

288.   **Telegram From the Mission to the United Nations to the Department of State[1]**

New York, December 13, 1963, 8:30 p.m.

2496. Enlargement of Councils.

1. After hectic all-day palaver, ASAFs tonight introduced and decided to press to vote reses for 15 seat SC (majority of 9, non-perm seats distributed as follows; 5 ASAF, 2 LA, 2 Eur and others, 1 EE) and 27 seat ECOSOC (8 of 9 additional seats to go to ASAF's with other additional seat to rotate between LAs and EURs). It appears there blocking third made up of LAs, Eurs, and EEs, on both ASAF reses but we suspect some of these negative votes may cave under ASAF pressure. Czechs and Poles also introduced amendments to ASAF res in Gen Comite for rotation of GA Presidency. Our vote count shows defeat this amendment small margin but again we fear bandwagon psychology.

2. SC: LAs and WEs remained firm for 13 seat SC and against 15 seat SC, although Italy (because of fear of ASAF retaliation) and Netherlands (because they believe 15 is better number) wobbly. We fear there may be bolt. Decision if ASAFs press vote on 15 seat SC res taken against judgment majority Asian countries, according Kaya (Japan), and most Asians therefore refrained from cosponsoring res as they do not favor pressing it to vote against clear opposition of perm SC members.

---

[1] Source: National Archives and Records Administration, RG 59, Central Files 1960–63, UN 8 SC. Confidential; Priority.

3. ECOSOC: ASAFs did not pick up offer made to them by LAs in morning to vote for their res provided LAs specifically assigned 4-1/2 seats in new Council plus 2 comite chairmanships in General Comite. Instead ASAFs appeared, again on African impetus, ready to press their res to vote without agreements other groups.

4. Gen Comite: Czech amendment provides for rotating GA Presidency as follows: Africa, Asia, EE, LA, ME, WE and others. ASAF meeting decided to ask sponsors to replace ME category and rotate that place between Africa and Asia. Sponsors reportedly agreed. ASAFs did not take group position on amendment but only Liberia and Cameroon spoke against rotation concept. LAs almost equally divided between negative vote and abstentions. Third amendment to ASAF res may be submitted by LAs calling for one more VP, to be LA, and removing, at Venezuelan request, according Bueno (Brazil) words "and Caribbean states" from LA category named in ASAF res. Starey (Australia) feels Canadian, NZ, and Australian amendment to Gen Comite might be withdrawn as it has called attention to Commonwealth problem and good effect might be lost if it were voted down.

5. On possibility that ASAFs may withdraw their SC and ECOSOC reses before Plenary if blocking third demonstrated in SPC, we plan speak against their draft reses as well as against GA Presidency rotation amendment at 10:30 SPC mtg Dec 14.

6. Sovs had speech prepared ready to give at Dec 13 afternoon session refuting ChiCom attack on Federenko statement.

Stevenson

289.   Memorandum From Acting Secretary of State Ball to President Johnson[1]

Washington, December 13, 1963.

SUBJECT

The Current Session of the United Nations General Assembly

You will be meeting with a number of Delegation heads on Tuesday at the United Nations. The following information may be helpful to you in your discussions.

In general, the current 18th Session of the General Assembly has achieved results quite satisfactory to the United States. The highlights are:

1. Organizational:

a. A friendly Latin American (Sosa-Rodriguez of Venezuela) was elected President.

b. Bolivia and the Ivory Coast, whom we supported, were elected to full terms on the Security Council. We also supported Malaysia but it finally had to decide to split the two-year term with Czechoslovakia.

2. On Disarmament:

a. The partial test ban treaty and the direct line between Moscow and Washington were endorsed;

b. A historic resolution calling on all States not to station or place in outer space any objects carrying nuclear weapons or weapons of mass destruction was approved by acclamation; and

c. A resolution on a Latin American nuclear free zone was adopted consonant with our interests since it left the matter to members of the region for further study.

3. Outer Space:

The Assembly called for expanded and strengthened cooperation in the exploration of Outer Space and defined legal principles that should govern our astronauts and the traffic of our space vehicles.

---

[1] Source: National Archives and Records Administration, RG 59, Central Files 1960–63, UN 3 GA. Confidential. Drafted by Sisco on December 12. An attached memorandum from Cleveland, also December 12, recommended that Acting Secretary Ball sign the memorandum to the President. Ball approved it on December 13.

4. On East-West Issues:

a. The U.S. position in favor of unified Korean independence on the basis of free elections was again maintained by virtually the same vote as last year; and

b. Our position on Chinese representation was again sustained, this time by a slightly wider margin than the previous Assembly.

5. Colonial Issues:

Even though we could not support two African resolutions on Southern Rhodesia appealing against transfer of powers to the white minority groups, and a resolution on South West Africa calling for an oil embargo against South Africa, the results on colonial issues were better than expected.

The Security Council met twice during the General Assembly and adopted resolutions which did not go beyond our arms embargo policies in relation to South Africa and Portugal, and avoided mandatory sanctions and proposals for expulsion from the United Nations. Both resolutions were relatively moderate and designed to stimulate a dialogue between the respective parties.

6. Racial Discrimination:

After a difficult negotiation, we were able to support the universal Declaration Against all Forms of Racial Discrimination, making clear our intention to carry out its terms in accordance with our constitutional processes.

7. Peacekeeping Operations:

The Assembly carried forward the peacekeeping operations in the Congo and the Middle East based on a financial formula in which the U.S. contribution is only 37 percent.

Suggested Points To Make:

During the reception, there will be opportunity only for simple greetings. However, at the luncheon you will have an opportunity to discuss with the Secretary General, the Soviet Representative to the UN (Federenko) and other key Delegates some of the principal issues and problems facing the United Nations. While Ambassador Stevenson intends to take up a number of these matters with you in more detail, we would suggest the following points might be made:

1. Strong Peacekeeping Capacity.

You might indicate our continuing strong support for the United Nations and in particular that its peacekeeping capacity should be strengthened. We do not believe in a United Nations limited to a debating society. Its utility depends on its capacity to act effectively in peace and security crises.

2. Need to Solve the Financial Problem.

The USSR must find a way to pay its UN arrearages, otherwise the United States will have no alternative but to press for a denial of vote to the Soviet Union when this matter arises in 1964. (This point can be made generally and in particular to the USSR. To the French Delegate [Seydoux],[2] you might "express the hope" that France will find a way in the near future to pay its own back UN bills.)

3. Disarmament: We will press for further agreements at Geneva.

The Assembly this past fall has given a shot in the arm to future disarmament discussions. It has referred these matters to the Geneva Conference where the United States will continue to press for further agreement.

4. Moderation on Colonial Issues:

On Colonial issues, we are confronted with the remaining hard-core white settler problems in southern Africa. The United States will continue its efforts on the side of moderation and peaceful change. This can be achieved best by quiet talks rather than playing the gallery.

5. Yemen:

We hope the Secretary General will keep his representative (Spinelli) in Yemen next year to help work out a solution of the problem.

George W. Ball[3]

---

[2] Brackets in the source text.

[3] Printed from a copy that indicates Ball signed the original.

290. Telegram From the Mission to the United Nations to the Department of State[1]

New York, December 16, 1963, 10:15 p.m.

2515. SPC—Enlargement of Councils.

1. SPC Dec 16 voted three reses: 15 seat SC (96–11–4), 27 seat ECOSOC (95–11–4), and 25 seat Gen Comite. On SC and ECOSOC negative votes were all from France, Sov bloc and Cuba. Albania voted in favor. US, UK (together with SAG and Portugal) abstained on SC and ECOSOC reses. China favored SC res but did not participate in vote on ECOSOC, having alluded to Quaison-Sackey's (Ghana) reference to ECOSOC seats of "four permanent members of SC." France opposed both reses, explaining regret at SPC haste, referring to "problem of majority in SC," and noting that it had expected abstain but had just received instructions to oppose (suggesting a decision by De Gaulle).

2. Wide agreement on SC and ECOSOC reses developed after it became apparent at LA group in morning that ASAFs could not bring sufficient number LAs along with their reses to obtain two-thirds majority. However, when ASAFs conceded to LAs one additional ECOSOC seat, 1 additional Gen Comite VP, and commitment not to raid on LA seat in SC next year if enlargement reses not ratified, entire LA group came along. WEs followed quickly obtaining one of additional nine seats in ECOSOC for themselves. Final agreement expressed in form of ASAF amendments to LA reses. Quaison-Sackey explained that after ECOSOC increased by nine (7 ASAFs, 1 LA, 1 WE) breakdown of 27 would be: 4 perms, 2 EEs, 4 WEs and others, 5 LAs, 12 ASAFs, of which 7 would be Africans, 5 Asians. In SC breakdown, 5 perms, 2 LAs, 1 EE, 2 WE and others, 5 ASAFs; there will be 3 Africans, 2 Asians, he said.

3. Gen Cmite res had separate vote on Polish-Czech amendment, as altered by Nigerian wording which had one opponent, Bindzi (Cameroon) and eleven scattered abstentions. Pres GA and 17 VPs on 25 man Gen Comite now will have following distribution: 7 ASAFs, 3 LAs, 1 EEs, 2 WEs and others, 5 perms, while Comite chairmen will be 3 ASAFs, 1 WE, 1 EE, 1 LA, 1 alternating between WE and LA.

Stevenson

---

[1] Source: National Archives and Records Administration, RG 59, Central Files 1960–63, UN 8 SC. Confidential.

291. **Information Memorandum From the Assistant Secretary of State for International Organization Affairs (Cleveland) to Secretary of State Rusk**[1]

Washington, December 19, 1963.

SUBJECT

Briefing of Congress on Enlargement of UN Councils

As a follow up to our breakfast meeting with members of the Senate Foreign Relations Committee, I asked for a meeting with the Committee on December 16 to pursue the question of enlarging UN Councils since it then appeared that resolutions amending the UN Charter to expand the Security Council and ECOSOC would be brought to a vote that day. Although this hearing was worked out on very short notice, I believe we can consider that a reasonable spectrum of Senate opinion was consulted since those attending included Senators Fulbright, Hickenlooper, Sparkman, Aiken, Mundt, and Lausche.

The atmosphere in the Committee was good. While there are clearly many apprehensions about the implications of the increased UN membership for the US power position in the Organization, I had the feeling that everyone present felt this was a problem which we all, as Americans, find thrust upon us and that the Executive Branch and the Congress have a common interest in finding a way to deal with this problem so as to protect vital US interests.

Two major concerns were manifested in the questions asked. The first was whether an increase in the Security Council would result in a substantial dilution of our authority there. I explained that if we had our "druthers," there would be no enlargement, but added that in view of the increased membership and the pressure for greater representation, there will almost certainly be a raid on seats of our friends in the present Council if some sort of an expansion is not forthcoming; thus we would do better to acquiesce in enlargement rather than fight it. Senator Fulbright quickly put his finger on the answer to this by volunteering "It wouldn't be good politics to oppose it."

There was a certain malaise about the possibility that the distribution of seats in an enlarged Council could be changed again by Assembly vote even though the distribution provided for in the current

[1] Source: National Archives and Records Administration, RG 59, Central Files 1960–63, UN 8. No classification marking. Drafted by Cleveland and Buffum on December 19. Copies were sent to Under Secretary Ball, Governor Harriman, U. Alexis Johnson, Abram Chayes, and Frederick G. Dutton. The memorandum bears a notation indicating that Secretary Rusk saw it.

resolutions might not hurt us too much. The tenor of these comments would seem to indicate a preference that the distribution of seats should be actually written into the Charter so that it could not be revised without further Charter amendment. In intimating this, however, I do not think that the Senators present balanced out in their own minds the relative advantage that this would give us against the political disadvantage that some of them might have in voting for a formal Charter amendment which assigns a full-time seat to Eastern Europe.

The second consideration which emerged was that any talk of enlargement of the United Nations will revive a discussion over the one-nation, one-vote principle in the General Assembly. Critical remarks were made concerning a country the size of Zanzibar now joining. There was considerable interest in what the ultimate size of the United Nations is expected to be, and I reported our estimate as 125–130. It clearly sticks in the craw (even of a Senator from South Dakota who has the same vote as a Senator from New York) that the one-half million Zanzibaris should have a vote equivalent to the nearly two hundred million Americans. I agreed that this is a problem we are all concerned with and took the occasion to float in a very tentative manner the possibility of developing something like a special screening committee to approve special scales of assessment for peacekeeping operations. This appeared to strike a responsive chord.

As far as policy on US ratification of the Charter amendments is concerned, I weighted the scale in favor of no submission to the Senate in the absence of a change on the part of the Soviet Union. However, I left a crack in the door in case we should find it desirable to do so. The situation is still too confused in the aftermath of the recent vote to know how other permanent members will proceed, including France, the United Kingdom and China. (France voted against both resolutions, the United Kingdom abstained on both, and China voted favorably on the Security Council resolution. China abstained on the ECOSOC resolution since it does not reinstate China's membership on ECOSOC.) Therefore, I do not believe we need to cross this bridge just yet.

I will send you separately an analysis of the enlargement problem which we will give to Fred Dutton for distribution to interested members of Congress.

Human Rights

292.   **Letter From the Representative to the UN Commission on Human Rights (Tree) to Secretary of State Rusk[1]**

New York, April 17, 1961.

Dear Mr. Secretary:

I appreciated the opportunity of serving as the United States Representative to the seventeenth session of the United Nations Commission on Human Rights which met in New York February 20 to March 17, 1961. Enclosed is my report on this session.[2]

As stated in this report, the work of the Commission proceeded satisfactorily from the standpoint of United States policy interests. Since decisions taken by the Commission were consistent with the position papers provided by the Department of State, we voted for the decisions adopted by the Commission. I believe we were able to achieve our goals in large measure because of the flexibility provided by the position papers with the emphasis placed on broad policy objectives rather than the details and tactics involved.

I would like to add a few personal-political notes to my report. The Human Rights Commission has several built-in advantages for international cooperation. As there are only 18 nations on the Human Rights Commission a group identity soon emerges. Also all nations must seem to be vigorously for human rights, which is another binding force. For instance, we had three unanimous votes in this session. Mr. Morosov, the Russian Delegate, agreed to do a Russian dance on the rostrum for a fourth unanimous vote. Alas, this never came to pass, but on the other votes the Soviet bloc abstained and did not vote against Human Rights principles which the US did support.

At this session I think we got some added marks for sincerity and social concern. For instance, India, Pakistan and Afghanistan put forward a World Freedom from Prejudice Year. As I happened to know some groups in the United States which were working towards the same thing nationally in 1963, we gave this proposal strong support, and stuck by them through thick and thin for which they were grateful

---

[1] Source: National Archives and Records Administration, RG 59, Central Files 1960–63, 341.7/4–1761. Official Use Only.

[2] Not printed.

and slightly surprised, as our European friends lacked enthusiasm for this idea.

On the item of anti-semitism, we supported the French to keep the word "Anti-Semitism" in the title of a resolution. The Moslem group (Iraq, Afghanistan and Pakistan) in order to eliminate this word had been voting previously with the Russians in order to get a quid pro quo on this point. The Russians must have encouraged them in this bargain. However, when the moment came to vote the Communist bloc voted (with us) to retain the word, thus letting down their Moslem colleagues to their obvious chagrin. It was interesting to me that the Soviet bloc would break with the Moslems and apparent obligations to keep a good propaganda face. Incidentally, the Russians did not enjoy my referring to anti-semitic outrages in Russia recorded in a UN document by B'nai Brith.

Perhaps the most important change in the other nations' attitude toward us was brought about first by Mrs. Roosevelt (who came to visit the Commission). She suggested that the US Government might be reconsidering its view on the ratification of conventions on the basis of individual merit. The Communist bloc had to pretend they were delighted, but were obviously dismayed as it deprived them of their biggest stick against us and loosened a spurious bond with the other nations. I cannot exaggerate the good effect of this news and sincerely hope that we will be able to reconsider this policy of ratification. A change would result in a participation and influence that we have not had in the Commission for eight years.

Our delegation took the initiative on a number of major items considered in the Commission. As a result of this initiative, the three Soviet bloc members of the Commission were isolated on several issues. The enclosed report points out that Poland, the Ukrainian SSR and the USSR abstained on three major resolutions adopted—those on advisory services in the field of human rights, periodic reports on human rights, and studies of freedom from arbitrary arrest, detention and exile and the right of arrested persons to communicate with legal counsel and others. The members of the Commission repeatedly rejected efforts of the Soviet bloc countries to delete references to the Secretary General in resolutions adopted.

I believe we maintained excellent working relations with our colleagues on the Commission from five Western European countries, three Latin American countries and six Asian countries. In the case of a particularly difficult resolution on periodic reporting on human rights, we obtained five co-sponsors as a result of considerable personal negotiations, the five co-sponsors being Afghanistan, Austria, France, India and Panama. In the case of the resolution on the expansion of information media, the delegations of Pakistan and the Philippines co-sponsored with us. Venezuela co-sponsored an amendment with us to provide for the study of the right of arrested persons to communicate with legal counsel and with others, and to request the preparation of draft principles on freedom from arbitrary arrest, detention and exile.

In view of the constructive work done by the Commission at this session, I am particularly pleased to have participated in its activities.

Sincerely,

Marietta Tree

---

293. Position Paper Prepared in the Bureau of International Organization Affairs[1]

SD/A/C.3/242   Washington, September 1, 1961.

DRAFT INTERNATIONAL COVENANTS ON HUMAN RIGHTS

The Problem

The Commission on Human Rights worked on the drafting of the proposed Covenants on Human Rights from 1947 to 1954. The original draft of a single Covenant was divided by the Commission in 1952, in accordance with a decision of the General Assembly, into two draft Covenants, one on Civil and Political Rights and the other on Economic, Social and Cultural Rights. The Commission at its spring 1954 session completed the initial drafting of the two texts, which were then forwarded through the Economic and Social Council to the General Assembly. There was a general debate on this item at the ninth (1954) session of the Third Committee of the General Assembly. The draft Covenants were then circulated to Governments and the specialized agencies for comment. The Third Committee of the General Assembly at its tenth (1955) session adopted a revised Preamble and Article 1 of the two draft Covenants and decided not to vote on Part II until the substantive articles in Part III of the two draft Covenants were adopted. The Third Committee of the General Assembly at its eleventh (1956–57)

[1] Source: National Archives and Records Administration, RG 59, IO/UNP Files: Lot 71 D 504, U.N General Assembly Position Papers, 1953–1967, 16th and 18th UNGA Position Papers, 3rd Committee, 16th GA (1961). Official Use Only. Prepared for the 16th Regular Session of the UN General Assembly.

session agreed to discuss first the substantive articles of the draft Covenant on Economic, Social and Cultural Rights and then the substantive articles of the other draft Covenant. The Third Committee at that session revised Articles 6 to 13 of the draft Covenant on Economic, Social and Cultural Rights. At its twelfth (1957) session, the Third Committee revised Articles 14 to 16 of the draft Covenant on Economic, Social and Cultural Rights thus completing the consideration of the substantive articles of that draft Covenant. The Third Committee also revised Article 6 of the draft Covenant on Civil and Political Rights. At its thirteenth (1958) session, the Third Committee revised Articles 7 to 11 of the draft Covenant on Civil and Political Rights; at the fourteenth (1959) session, the Third Committee revised Articles 12 to 14 of this draft Covenant; and at the fifteenth (1960) session, the Third Committee revised Articles 15 to 18 of this draft Covenant. Since the Third Committee was unable to complete the examination of the draft Covenants, the General Assembly decided to continue the consideration of the draft Covenants at its sixteenth (1961) session. See UN document A/4789 dated June 30, 1961 on the current situation relating to the draft Covenants in the Third Committee.

United States Position

1. The U.S. Delegation should participate in the drafting of the Covenants on Human Rights in order that they will be in the best possible language and as consistent as possible with United States constitutional safeguards. Attached as Annex is general guidance to the United States Delegation in the consideration of the remaining substantive Articles 19 to 26 of the draft Covenant on Civil and Political Rights and the possible consideration of new articles on property and asylum.[2] It is not expected that the Third Committee will go beyond the consideration of these articles. If the Delegation finds that additional articles will be considered, the Delegation should consult the Department. As explained in UN document A/4789, following the consideration of substantive Articles 19 to 26, the Third Committee will take up the general provisions (Part II of each Covenant), the measures of implementation (Parts IV and V of the Covenant on Civil and Political Rights and Part IV of the Covenant on Economic, Social and Cultural Rights) and the final clauses (Part VI of the Covenant on Civil and Political Rights and Part V of the Covenant on Economic, Social and Cultural Rights).

2. In the event there is a proposal to call a plenipotentiary conference to complete the draft Covenants on Human Rights the U.S. Delegation should make known U. S. opposition to the proposal. U. S. opposition to such a proposal rests on several reasons: (a) if the

---

[2] Not printed.

Covenants are to continue to be considered they should be discussed in the Third Committee which has already considered them for some time, (b) the considerable expense involved in having such a conference, and (c) if such a conference is held in New York, it is likely to be attended by permanent representatives of Member States rather than experts. If strong sentiment develops, however, for calling such a conference, the Delegation should request further instructions from the Department. If it appears likely that a proposal for a plenipotentiary conference will be approved, the Delegation should make every effort to ensure that the conference is limited to States Members of the United Nations and of the specialized agencies.

3. In the event it is proposed that the Third Committee continue to meet (after the other work of the General Assembly is completed), the U. S. Delegation should make known U. S. opposition to the proposal. It is the U. S. view that items should be considered and completed within regular sessions rather than having individual items extend the meeting time of any particular Committee of the General Assembly. If strong sentiment develops for doing so, the Delegation should request further instructions from the Department.

---

294.   Letter From the Representative to the UN Commission on Human Rights (Tree) to Secretary of State Rusk[1]

New York, May 14, 1962.

Dear Mr. Secretary:

It is with pleasure that I submit to you the attached report of the 18th session of the Commission on Human Rights.[2] I take the liberty of adding some personal comments regarding this session.

Periodic Reports on Human Rights. Although the Human Rights Commission in its 18th session deferred a good many agenda items to

---

[1] Source: National Archives and Records Administration, RG 59, Central Files 1960–63, 341.7/5–1462. Official Use Only; Official–Informal.

[2] Dated April 16, not printed. Assistant Secretary Cleveland acknowledged Tree's report in a May 24 letter in which he expressed encouragement at the growing involvement of non-governmental organizations in human rights affairs, and expressed concern at the accumulating workload of the Commission and the slowness of action in the General Assembly. (Ibid.)

the Economic and Social Council and to next year's session, one great decision was taken following United States' initiative. In the words of John Humphrey, Chief of the Human Rights Division of the UN, this was "the most revolutionary step ever made in the history of the Human Rights Commission". In a resolution concerning Periodic Reports on Human Rights, we introduced an amendment providing for a "verifying presence" or check on the reports of Member States. Nongovernmental organizations in consultative status will now be invited to "submit comments and observations of an objective character on the situation in the field of human rights to assist the Commission. . . ."

At first there was considerable opposition to our initiative stemming from the bloc countries (USSR, Ukraine, Poland), from India and, surprisingly, the Philippines. But after a good deal of parliamentary maneuvering our amendment was adopted with no negative votes. The NGO's were even more surprised by our success and have been sending in congratulations ever since.

My fear is that this amendment might be struck out in the next session of the Economic and Social Council, but we have begun to lobby for it already. Our position is that there is nothing in the US concerning human rights that is not known both at home and abroad due to the "verifying presence" of our free press, and, while other nations have condemned us for our lack of perfection, they have been less than candid about their own deficiencies. This amendment may stir up a hornets' nest, but ought to result in more honest reporting and progress in human rights throughout the world. As W. H. Auden says,

> "True democracy begins with free discussion of our sins
> In this alone we are all the same
> All are so weak that none dares claim,
> 'I have the right to govern,' or
> 'Behold in me the moral law,'
> And all real unity commences
> In consciousness of differences."

I am confident that the NGO's will not press their new privileges too hard to begin with.

Draft Principles of Religious Freedom. The Human Rights Commission devoted many days of hard work to the draft principles on religious freedom and produced an agreement on only five preambular paragraphs, because of the wide and frequently wild differences between those Member States where organized religion has considerable political status and others where organized religion and the state are separated. I am afraid that many years will pass before these draft principles are finally completed in the UN. After discussion with the Pope, I am told, Ex-Ambassador Amadeo of Argentina introduced a vast number of amendments which, inter alia, proposed to delete all references to atheism and divorce, and provided for protection of an established church where one exists, as well as introducing metaphysical concepts, etc. I learned from his successor after he had resigned following President Frondizi's fall, that these amendments stem very largely from his own convictions and not necessarily from his Government. We wonder if they will be offered again next year by the Argentine Government. The Afghan (Moslem) delegate strongly supported the Argentine amendments, but the other Moslem states (Pakistan, Turkey, Lebanon) did not follow as enthusiastically.

National Advisory Committees on Human Rights. Judging from the interest evoked in the Commission by the US report on its national advisory committees on human rights (national and state Civil Rights Committees as well as the hundreds of NGO's devoted to human rights) and the comparative lack of government and voluntary committees on human rights in all other countries, the US can afford to be proud. For it is probably the foremost nation in honestly facing its human rights problems and then trying to solve them with the variety of methods at its disposal. Perhaps our Government and citizens could profitably elucidate this point at home and abroad—especially for the benefit of African and Asian states who have not faced up to similar problems in discrimination.

The Human Rights Commission's Vote for Membership on the Sub-commission on Prevention of Discrimination and Protection of Minorities. It may be significant that the US candidate (Mr. Morris Abram) received the unanimous vote of the 21 nations on the Commission for election to this Sub-commission. The next candidates (Poland, USSR, Italy, France, Chile) received only 19 and the United Kingdom 18 votes.

Advisory Services in the Field of Human Rights. As a program for fellowships in the field of human rights was initiated by the US (with 21 co-sponsors), and passed by the 16th General Assembly, we are pleased that several US citizens of distinction and experience in human rights work have submitted applications through the State Department for these fellowships.

Relations with USSR in the Human Rights Commission, 18th Session. Ambassador Morozov, the regular delegate to the Human Rights Commission, appeared only rarely during the session to shoot off a few salvos about colonialism and racial discrimination in the US by implication. His alternate, Mr. Ostrovski, was a young man who seemed rather to concentrate on the issues at hand and showed a willingness to be constructive and cooperative, generally speaking. He and his pretty wife came to all social gatherings of the Commission and were agreeable and gay. My adviser, Martin van Heuven, and myself decided to go to him informally about our concern, and that of many NGO's, regarding religious persecution of the Jews in the USSR. We felt, without much hope, it might help to improve religious rights of the Soviet Jews to ask him to relay our aide-mémoire on the subject to his Foreign Office. We have learned that denunciations in open meeting result in long retaliatory speeches and no action.

One afternoon in informal conversation, Marten van Heuven asked Mr. Ostrovski about the recent ban in the USSR on the production of Matzoh bread which is eaten during Passover. Ostrovski said that if we had mentioned this ban in public meeting he had a long speech prepared in riposte, but since we had talked to him privately, he would relay our concern to the Foreign Office. The facts were, said he, that Matzoh flour was available to all in the USSR, and anyone could bake it at home or have it baked at a private bakery. (This would not conform to Jewish ritual.) We informed some of the NGO's of this conversation, and alas, the story in garbled version appeared prominently in all the New York papers.

When next I approached Ostrovski with a short aide-mémoire about general discrimination against Jewish religious freedom in the USSR, repeating that we thought it more helpful to approach him privately, he replied that he couldn't listen to me as the newspaper articles had "embarrassed" him. I expressed my regret that the articles had appeared and pointed out that if we had been responsible for them they would have been accurate. He refused my aide-mémoire saying he had "trusted" Mr. van Heuven, but the articles were published and now he could not discuss discrimination against the Jews with me further. I told him politely that I was not interested in his reactions but hoped he would transmit my message to the Foreign Office. Then I asked if it would be less embarrassing for him if I gave the aide-mémoire to his superior Mr. Morozov. He evaded my question.

Evidently the Soviet Mission to the UN is not too well coordinated because on two occasions Ambassador Morozov made speeches in the Human Rights Commission which were the opposite of speeches by Mr. Ostrovski on the same subject only a few minutes before. I told Mr. Ostrovski that we did not point this out publicly to save him from embarrassment and problems with his superior.

Sincerely yours,

Marietta Tree

295.   **Memorandum From the Deputy Director of the Office of International Economic and Social Affairs, Bureau of International Organization Affairs (Rossow) to the Deputy Assistant Secretary of State for International Organization Affairs (Gardner)[1]**

Washington, November 20, 1962.

SUBJECT

> Human Rights Conventions (in addition to Marriage Convention) which might be considered for ratification (texts attached)[2]

1. Supplementary Convention on Slavery. 39 parties to date, including Soviets.

The Department of Justice is preparing a commentary on this Convention which we hope to have within the week. Article 2 calls for specification of a minimum age for marriage, but in this context such provision might be covered by the 13th Amendment.

The United States is already a party to the Slavery Convention of 1926 and to a protocol making the UN its depository. A copy of the 1926 Convention is attached to the text of the Supplementary Convention, along with pertinent provisions in US Constitution and law.

2. Genocide. 72 parties to date, including Soviets.

This is already before the Senate; it was forwarded by President Truman in 1949. The matter of ratification was reconsidered thoroughly in the Department last Spring, and the White House concurred in the decision not to press for action in the 87th Congress.

Attached to the text are (a) the letter of transmission, (b) the legislative history of consideration in the Senate Foreign Relations Committee in 1950, and (c) Mr. Dutton's memo to Mr. Chayes, June 19, 1962, on the current situation.

3. Political Rights of Women (a) Inter-American and (b) UN Convention.

(a) The Inter-American Convention on the Granting of Political Rights to Women is also before the Senate, on the basis of President Truman's transmission in January 1949. No hearings have been held. This Convention falls wholly within our Federal Constitution; it covers

---

[1] Source: National Archives and Records Administration, RG 59, IO Files: Lot 67 D 378, Human Rights. Official Use Only. Drafted by Rachel C. Nason (IO/OES). Copies were sent to Eleanor C. McDowell (L/T) and Martin H.A. Van Heuven (L/UNA).

[2] Not printed.

the right to vote and "to be elected to national office", but does not apply to state office or to appointive office. As of last count, 13 LA's had ratified, several more are in process. Women now vote throughout the Americas.

(b) The UN Convention on Political Rights for Women, adopted in 1952, with the U.S. voting for. This includes appointive and all elective office, as well as suffrage. Article 3 refers to "public functions". Some of the parties have made reservations to Article 3 excepting military service from the requirement for equality for women. If the U.S. became a party, we would probably have to reserve on military and also on jury service.

36 parties to date, including Soviets.

4. ILO Convention on Freedom of Association.

The Department of Labor is now reviewing this Convention. It is already before the Senate, transmitted by President Truman in 1949. The Federal-State provision of the ILO Constitution would not apply to this Convention.

5. UN Convention on Nationality of Married Women. 27 parties to date, including Soviets.

This Convention falls within US law and practice; it is actually narrower than the Inter-American Convention on Nationality of Women to which the US became a party in 1934. Both texts are attached.

296. Memorandum of Conversation[1]

Washington, April 21, 1963.

SUBJECT

Fifteenth Anniversary of Universal Declaration of Human Rights

PARTICIPANTS

Mrs. Tree, USRep UN Commission on Human Rights
Mrs. Nason, OES

I saw Mrs. Tree in response to her request for information on developments on her suggestion for a Presidentially appointed Committee to promote appropriate observance of the 15th Anniversary of the Universal Declaration of Human Rights. She had proposed such a committee before her departure in March for the 1963 Session of the Human Rights Commission in Geneva.

I explained that further thinking seemed to be needed on the function of such a committee. The U.S. National Commission for UNESCO had regularly promoted observance of Human Rights Week in the U.S. and had already developed active contacts with the public schools, many private organizations and information media. It would be important to enhance and strengthen these regular procedures rather than develop a new channel which would appear to bypass them.

Mrs. Tree said she had not realized the full scope of the regular activities when she had made her first suggestion. However, she thought there should be some special effort in connection with the 15th Anniversary, in line with the UN suggestions and our own leadership for this purpose. She also thought it would be very useful to provide some opportunity for the President to endorse Human Rights Week celebrations. She noted that the President had not thus far taken personal leadership except through the proclamation of Human Rights Week.

I agreed that there had been long term interest in obtaining participation by the President in Human Rights Day ceremonies. However, we had not thus far worked out what form would be useful.

Mrs. Tree thought that a committee might wish to develop its own plans and suggestions and that there would be no point in anticipating their decisions to any great extent. Her own interest was in some public pronouncement by the President—such as reading his proclamation as a broadcast, commenting on the importance of the day in a press conference, possibly bestowing a citation for human rights work well done

---

[1] Source: National Archives and Records Administration, RG 59, Central Files 1960–63, SOC 14 ECOSOC. Unclassified. Drafted by Nason on April 22.

or some similar action. Mrs. Tree thought a committee might also give thought to proper display of the text of the Universal Declaration in connection with United States Archives as well as at the United Nations. The importance of the Declaration is greatly increased by the large number of new countries coming into the UN and making use of the Declaration in their constitutions and legislation. Since the Universal Declaration has become the symbol of the inherent and inalienable nature of human rights, we should make certain that it is constantly kept in the forefront of public attention.

Mrs. Tree asked whether the U.S. National Commission for UNESCO might not wish to join in recommending appointment of a Presidential Committee to give special attention to the 15th Anniversary from the policy as well as the promotion point of view. I said I thought this might be possible since the National Commission would be having its annual meeting this week. I agreed to report her interest to Mr. Minnich, the Director of the Commission Secretariat.[2]

Mrs. Tree also thought she would like to talk personally with Mr. Gardner of IO and appropriate officers in CU to expedite prompt selection of a committee. We reviewed the roster of the present commission and former members. Among these were Archibald MacLeish who had helped draft the Preamble of the Universal Declaration in 1948 and Luther Evans, former Director General of UNESCO and Librarian of Congress, who has long experience in display and archive work. Mrs. Tree felt certain there should be some plan by which a Presidential Committee could strengthen the long term objectives of the UNESCO National Commission as well as the short term interests of the 15th Anniversary.

---

[2] Mr. Minnich later disagreed; he thought any Committee should be appointed by and from the Commission, with some additional members possibly designated by the White House. [Footnote in the source text.]

297.   **Letter From the Assistant Secretary of State for International Organization Affairs (Cleveland) to the Representative to the UN Commission on Human Rights (Tree)[1]**

Washington, June 25, 1963.

Dear Marietta:

Thank you very much for your reports on the 19th Session of the Human Rights Commission. I have been asked to acknowledge also your submission to the Secretary. We appreciate your comments on the issues at stake, and especially on the political setting in which they were considered.

We are, of course, gratified that the draft declaration on the elimination of all forms of racial discrimination could be adopted in a reasonably satisfactory form. The draft Declaration will undoubtedly be a major item in the General Assembly next fall, and we should plan accordingly. As always, we are grateful for your careful presentation of United States positions in the Commission and your thoughtful constructive recommendations for further work.

I also have your letter recommending that the United States send an observer to the UN seminar on The Rights of the Child in Warsaw.[2] I agree with you that the United States should have an observer there and I hope very much that you can carry through your plan to attend. We are looking into the possibilities regarding John Means.

It looks more and more as if this next General Assembly will be a kind of Human Rights Assembly, what with the impact of our own domestic situation, the Portuguese and South African racial issues, and your own draft Declaration on Racial Discrimination. I recently gave a speech in Chicago on the *Pacem in Terris* encyclical. A copy is enclosed.[3]

Meanwhile, just so you are not wholly deprived of reading matter, I'm sending along a little essay on the Hot Springs Conference of

---

[1] Source: National Archives and Records Administration, RG 59, Central Files 1960–63, SOC 14 ECOSOC. Limited Official Use. Drafted by Nason on June 10 and retyped on June 20. Cleared by Robert Rossow, Jr. (IO/OES), Richard N. Gardner (IO), John N. Washburn (L/UNA), and Marian Stilson (OIC).

[2] Not found.

[3] Not printed. For text of Cleveland's speech, see Department of State *Bulletin*, July 8, 1963, pp. 38–43.

twenty years ago, which has a couple of passages I think you may find amusing.[4]

Warmest regards,

Sincerely,

Harlan Cleveland[5]

---

[4] Not printed.
[5] Printed from a copy that bears this typed signature.

---

298.   Memorandum From the Director of Special Protocol Services (Sanjuan) to Secretary of State Rusk[1]

Washington, July 8, 1963.

SUBJECT

Future status of special diplomatic service

For the last few weeks the creation of a Special Assistant for Human Rights in the Secretariat has been discussed confidentially and otherwise throughout the Department, in the local press and in a magazine of national circulation (Tab A).[2] The inference is drawn by the press that a policy advisor is to replace a front line operation.

A Special Assistant for Human Rights is needed. I imagine such a person could stimulate proper consideration by overseas posts for the civil rights program of this Administration; could advise on how much attention to give the human rights aspects of our policy towards Portugal and South Africa; could report on the treatment of Africans in the Sino-Soviet Bloc, the religious question in South Viet-Nam, our human rights posture at the U.N., and matters within the Department which concern human rights.

The operation which I direct should maintain close contact with such a Special Assistant for Human Rights—if that is the name—just as we maintain close relations now with the Bureau of African Affairs, for example. But to place Special Protocol Services under someone dealing exclusively with human rights is to destroy a good deal of our effec-

---

[1] Source: National Archives and Records Administration, RG 59, Central Files 1960–63, ORG 8. No classification marking.
[2] Neither Tab A nor Tab B was found.

tiveness. Not only have we claimed up to now that we cater to all the needs of all the diplomats, but we do in fact—and we also protect the interests of many Americans with legitimate complaints against diplomats. These cases can involve Africans, Asians, Europeans or our hemispheric neighbors. Many of the problems which we try to solve do not have a thing to do with human rights. In certain instances our relationship is and should be much closer to the Legal Advisor's office than to any other area in the Department.

Incidents involving racial discrimination, which affect diplomats or other visitors, naturally enter into this broad context. But Africans and Asians now come to us with their many problems without feeling that they alone have all the troubles since we also help European and other diplomats besides the Afro-Asians.

The functions of Special Protocol have very little to do with the substance of Protocol, as Mr. Duke has pointed out numerous times (Tab B). To a certain degree ours are functions which have grown out of the recent diplomatic explosion and the resulting need to assist many small embassies whose staffs are here mostly to observe rather than to transact much business. I believe Special Protocol should be separated from Protocol and placed directly under the Under Secretary (U) as a small office with a unique function. I believe the name should be changed to Office of Special Diplomatic and Visitor Services. Ours is a line function.

I respectfully submit these considerations for your scrutiny without meaning in any way to belittle the need you may have for a Special Assistant for Human Rights.

299. Memorandum From the Chief of the Economic and Social Affairs Section of the Mission to the United Nations (Finger) to the Representative to the United Nations (Stevenson)[1]

New York, July 16, 1963.

SUBJECT

18th GA—Human Rights

Mr. McKitterick (OES) has told me that Harlan Cleveland is eager to have a "klieg light" approach by the United States to human rights at the 18th GA.

In giving some very preliminary thought to this question, the following occur to me:

1. Open Societies. You are familiar with this proposal elaborated a few years ago but never presented as a package. I think it might be time to take another look at this idea in the light of new developments.

2. Emphasis on the right of independent organizations. This is clearly a fundamental difference between a totalitarian and a free society. The very existence of organizations like CORE and the NAACP, not to mention the Communist Party of the USA and the John Birch Society, testify to the deep-rooted nature of this right in the United States. Its denial to African students in Bulgaria precipitated the serious incidents which developed there. This is a concept which should appeal to the Africans and Asians; it is not an issue bearing a cold war label. Indeed, the right of independent organizations, whether of trade unions or of political groups, has often been a key element in the attainment of independence around the world.

3. Declaration on Freedom of Information. The United States launched this proposal at ECOSOC four years ago. A declaration has been approved by ECOSOC, but the Third Committee of the General Assembly has not yet acted upon it. According to a decision of the Third Committee last fall, freedom of information is to get priority treatment at the forthcoming session.

It seems to me that emphasis on the foregoing aspects of human rights would put the spotlight on areas in which the United States is relatively strong and the Soviets relatively weak. Obviously we would make no attempt to evade the question of racial equality—on the contrary, I assume we would continue to meet it by full and frank exposi-

---

[1] Source: Kennedy Library, Cleveland Papers, Human Rights, Box 19. Confidential. Copies were sent to Charles W. Yost (USUN), Jonathan B. Bingham (USUN), and Nathaniel McKitterick (IO/OES). An attached handwritten note by Stevenson reads: "Mr. Cleveland—Could we discuss this? AES."

tion—but I think there is a certain tactical advantage in emphasizing general principles in areas where we are strong.

Thank you very much for your letter of July 10.[2] I am glad that my draft made a modest contribution to your speech at ECOSOC which, by all accounts, was most successful.

---

[2] Not found.

---

300. Editorial Note

On July 22, 1963, President Kennedy forwarded three human rights conventions to the Senate for advice and consent to their ratification. The conventions were: the Supplementary Convention on the Abolition of Slavery, the Slave Trade and Institutions and Practices Similar to Slavery (18 UST 3201), ILO Convention No. 105, concerning the Abolition of Forced Labor (320 UNTS 291), and the United Nations Convention on the Political Rights of Women (27 UST 1909). For text of the President's message to the Senate, see *Public Papers of the Presidents of the United States: John F. Kennedy, 1963,* page 586.

---

301. Memorandum From the Director of the Office of United Nations Political Affairs (Sisco) to the Deputy Assistant Secretary of State for International Organization Affairs (Gardner)[1]

Washington, September 4, 1963.

SUBJECT

Proposal for a United Nations Commissioner for Human Rights

I am concerned about the proposal in the Strategy Paper (which is elaborated in the Bilder–Nason memorandum defining terms of refer-

---

[1] Source: National Archives and Records Administration, RG 59, Central Files 1960–63, SOC 14 ECOSOC. Limited Official Use. Drafted by Nathan A. Pelcovits. A note on the memorandum indicates it was not sent.

ence) to establish a United Nations Commissioner on Human Rights "to investigate and report to the General Assembly on how the members of the United Nations are fulfilling their obligations under Articles 55 and 56 of the Charter." The arguments against the proposal contained in L/UNA's lineup of pros and cons and in Finger's memorandum of August 29, strike me as well taken. In addition, I should like to point out a number of other serious political risks inherent in the proposal. Moreover, I see no reason to incur these risks, since I believe that we can derive the same political advantages by following the alternative course of strengthening the executive arm of the United Nations to take action in specific human rights situations, rather than establishing new United Nations machinery.

I.

A permanent United Nations Commissioner, armed with a staff and a roving mandate as "watchdog" for the General Assembly, would be tempted to encroach on politically sensitive areas and to compound the problems that we have faced in the General Assembly and the Committee of 24 on racial issues. The natural ambition of such a man will be to take on juicy political issues which promise a harvest of publicity and of favorable notices from the Afro-Asian majority in the United Nations. The Commissioner's authority to initiate investigations and engage in "fact finding" wholly at his discretion, which is the essence of the proposal, is particularly open to abuse. He will tend to interpret his mandate in the broadest manner, and to intervene in domestic human rights situations by making studies and issuing reports with the imprimatur of the United Nations. We might find ourselves faced with the kind of free-wheeling and grandstanding operation that has characterized the Committee of 24.

Moreover, pressures on the United Nations Commissioner from the Afro-Asian majority and from many of the lobbies will tend to direct his attention to human rights problems in our societies rather than in those of the bloc or the Afro-Asians. Apartheid, the treatment of Buddhists in South Vietnam, the denial of political rights in the Republic of Korea are obvious areas in which the United Nations Commissioner and his staff would be persuaded to intervene.

What is to keep him out of Puerto Rico? Denied a hearing before the Committee of 24 will not the Puerto Rican petitioners be likely to appeal to the human rights commissioner? Technically we could not oppose this on the same ground that we have used to keep the Puerto Rican nationalists out of the colonialism committee, namely that the Puerto Ricans have chosen self-determination in the form of association. What is to prevent the commissioner from hearing the petitioners and issuing a report on United States compliance with Articles 55 and 56 in Puerto Rico?

Or, for that matter, what is to prevent the United Nations Commissioner from undertaking an investigation of the United States racial situation next time the headlines flaunt an incident in Birmingham or Cambridge or Chicago? Even if we succeeded in blocking such moves—as we probably could—the anti-UN lobby in the United States would have a field day every time an African leader called on the Commissioner to intervene in the United States racial situation.

But, would not this risk be counterbalanced by the political gains we could hope to get when the commissioner acted to spotlight human rights violations in the bloc? I doubt it. Certainly we can expect our citizenry to press the commissioner to investigate, for example, violations of human rights by the GDR authorities at the Berlin wall and the mistreatment of religious minorities in the USSR. The initial impact of a Soviet refusal to let the investigators in will be damaging in Moscow. But the more lasting effect will be the diversion of frustration into resentment against the Administration and the Department for failing to "force" the United Nations to do something about human rights violations in the bloc. Powerless to act in the closed societies the United Nations Commissioner will naturally want to earn his keep and maintain his self-respect by busying himself where he can—in the open societies of the West.

II.

I believe the same objective envisaged in the proposal for a United Nations Commissioner could be achieved by adapting and strengthening existing United Nations machinery. Any scheme to be workable and politically acceptable to us must contain two elements that are missing from the Commissioner proposal. First, the system must be so designed as to selectively employ investigating and reporting mechanisms in specific instances. Second, the investigating and reporting activities of any United Nations representative must flow from the authority of the Secretary-General, acting either under his implicit constitutional authority or on the basis of an explicit mandate from the General Assembly or the Security Council. What we certainly do not want is the establishment of another autonomous United Nations institution armed with a broad fishing license from the General Assembly. Instead what appears to be called for is the adaptation to the human rights field of the kind of machinery and administrative style that is invoked when the Secretary-General assumes peacemaking or plebiscitory assignments on behalf of the United Nations.

Our preference should therefore be for strengthening the resources and broadening the options open to the Secretary-General, so that he can select and adapt the instrumentalities that suit particular cases.

Such a system has proved politically and administratively sound in the past, and would put us in a much better position to exercise some influence on the Secretary-General's choice of representatives and procedures. The Secretary-General should be able to call both on his staff and on neutral and experienced diplomats outside his own establishment to accomplish this task.

I would therefore suggest that in place of a United Nations Commissioner, we consider taking the initiative, on an appropriate occasion during the 18th General Assembly discussion of human rights, in proposing that the United Nations executive capacity to act in the human rights field be strengthened in the following way:

a. To enable the Secretary-General to take on broader functions in the field of human rights, expand the staff of the Under Secretary for Social and Economic Affairs by the addition of experts who could advise the Secretary-General on problems arising in connection with both advisory and investigative activities of the United Nations.
b. Include in the staff personnel who would be available to the Secretary-General to undertake investigations and make reports on all human rights problems with which the Secretary-General is charged.
c. Request and authorize the Secretary-General to set up a panel of distinguished world figures, with the appropriate academic, judicial and administrative experience and background in various fields of human rights, so that they would be available to him for assignment as his special representatives as occasion requires.

Thus, one could envisage the Secretary-General at the request of interested members and with the approval of the South Vietnamese government naming a special representative to visit South Vietnam to observe and report on the treatment of Buddhists, thus deflecting a premature call for General Assembly consideration. In the Berlin situation, to take another example, we might want to involve the United Nations in the human rights aspects without engaging the United Nations in the basic political issues of Berlin. We could consider the possibility on an appropriate occasion of a General Assembly request to the Secretary-General to send a special representative to Berlin to report on the humanitarian aspects.

Many other instances will come to mind. The main point is that we can expect in the future that the functions of the United Nations in human rights matters will be expanded, and that they will be broadly interpreted to include racial situations with political dimensions. We should encourage the Secretary-General's involvement, rather than that of another General Assembly committee or commissioner both of which are likely to cause us more political trouble than recourse to the tested facilities of the Secretary-General. Our effort should therefore be directed toward broadening the responsibilities of the Secretary-General and giving him the staff and facilities to do the job. Such a staff would work with the human rights commission and supplement its activities, particularly in studies and reporting. But when the staff undertakes human rights assignments with political aspects—and this would definitely include any investigative activities—it would be administratively controlled by the Secretary-General who would accept political responsibility for its work.

302.　Memorandum From the Special Assistant to the Assistant Secretary of State for International Organization Affairs (Wilson) to the Assistant Secretary (Cleveland)[1]

Washington, September 27, 1963.

SUBJECT

Civil Disobedience and the UN

I suspect we should be pretty cautious for the time being on human rights issues in the UN and particularly about drawing analogies between peaceful change and orderly procedures at home and within the UN context.

As I read it, the Southern whites know what they're doing: the resistance in Alabama, the rising toughness of the cops, the failure to carry out the agreement in Birmingham, and the general delaying tactics on the Hill are designed to force the Negroes to move into more militant action. There now appears to be a good chance it will work.

I am told that Martin Luther King is on the verge of endorsing civil disobedience. If this happens, it could split the Negro movement wide open. Roy Wilkins, Whitney Young, and the other good moderates could be swept aside by the Farmers, Baldwins, Rustins and worse. In the process, the white liberals could be driven out of the movement.

Then all the Eastlands and Thurmonds would have to do is discover that the Student Non-Violent Coordinating Committee has been penetrated by communists (which already could be the case).

If, in fact, the militants get control, and if the government is forced to turn against the major Negro organizations over the issue of civil disobedience—meaning cops carrying Negroes off airport runways and so

---

[1] Source: Kennedy Library, Cleveland Papers, Racial Discrimination File, Box 19. Confidential.

on—our job of selling orderly procedures and democratic institutions to bring about peaceful change will hardly be facilitated in the UN.

This is only to suggest that perhaps we'd better play by ear. It may also be that we should keep in closer touch with Justice.

303. Draft Memorandum From the Bureau of International Organization Affairs to President Kennedy[1]

Washington, undated.

PROPOSAL FOR A UN RAPPORTEUR ON HUMAN RIGHTS

In line with your statement before the General Assembly, I believe the United States should take the initiative during the current session in proposing more effective human rights machinery in the United Nations in the form of a permanent UN Rapporteur on Human Rights.

At the present time, the United Nations has no effective way of considering current human rights problems in a world-wide context. This is due primarily to the absence of up-to-date information. The Human Rights Commission receives various reports, but these are summaries of official documents, usually bland and incomplete, and already some months old by the time the UN can process them. No objective analysis of current happenings is available, with the result that the General Assembly debates "hot issues", such as apartheid, without the benefit of previous consideration in the Commission or the restraint and balance which might be imposed by an overall presentation of progress and problems in the human rights field.

---

[1] Source: National Archives and Records Administration, RG 59, Central Files 1960–63, SOC 14 ECOSOC. No classification marking. Drafted on November 4 by Rachel C. Nason. This memorandum formed Tab A of a package sent under cover of a memorandum to the Secretary by Assistant Secretary Cleveland on November 13. In the memorandum, Cleveland suggested that "a low-key proposal, in limited terms, for a United Nations Rapporteur on Human Rights" would be a suitable follow-up to President Kennedy's address to the UN General Assembly on September 20, during which he called for new initiatives to promote human rights. For text of the President's speech, see *Public Papers of the Presidents of the United States: John F. Kennedy, 1963,* pp. 693–698.

The package also included Tab B, a background paper; Tab C, a statement by Legal Adviser Chayes, with concurrence by Assistant Secretary Dutton (see footnote 2, Document 304); and Tab D, Cleveland's comments on Chayes' statement (Document 304).

Various suggestions have been advanced to deal with violations of human rights, including a UN Court similar to the European Court of Human Rights, a UN Committee to hold hearings and assess blame, and even a UN Attorney-General with power to call governments to account. We have rejected these suggestions because we do not believe the United States should be made subject in any way to the judgments of an outside body. Moreover, the need is to stimulate responsible—and if necessary remedial—action at the domestic level through the influence of an informed public opinion. We believe the most effective way of meeting this need will be by establishing a permanent Rapporteur on Human Rights in the UN, who can provide an annual report on the current status of human rights and be available for consultation with the Human Rights Commission.

The Rapporteur would be an elder statesman who would merit recognition as an independent expert. For his report he would draw on outside sources as well as government reports, but he would hold no hearings and make no on-the-spot investigations. He would work under the general direction of the Human Rights Commission. His statement would provide a basis for regular discussion, and should broaden awareness and concern throughout the UN beyond the present preoccupation with race problems in South Africa and the United States.

In addition, the Rapporteur could be available to the Secretary General for advice on human rights aspects of UN activities in economic and social development, and for good offices in response to requests from Member States.

Action Requested

It is recommended that the U.S. Delegation in the General Assembly be authorized to consult with other Delegations regarding the above-described rapporteur, with a view to support and possible co-sponsorship.

304. Memorandum From the Assistant Secretary of State for International Organization Affairs (Cleveland) to Secretary of State Rusk[1]

Washington, undated.

SUBJECT

Human Rights Initiative in the General Assembly—Proposal for a Permanent Rapporteur on Human Rights

Attached herewith is my memorandum proposing a permanent UN rapporteur on human rights in follow-up of the President's speech in the General Assembly.[2]

You recall that we discussed some of the elements in this proposal with you during preparation of his speech last September.

Also attached is a memorandum to you from Mr. Chayes expressing some doubts. Mr. Dutton has associated himself with this statement.[3]

I believe the doubts expressed by Mr. Chayes are met in large measure in my underlying statement. However, I would like to comment on certain specific points:

1. We have several defenses against the rapporteur being pressed into making investigations of U.S. racial problems. In the first place, he would work under the direction of the Human Rights Commission, the composition of which is relatively favorable from the western point of view. Moreover, most members of the Commission—and indeed of the UN generally—will be reluctant to establish precedents or give the rapporteur authority which might be turned against them at some later time.

2. The existence of a human rights rapporteur will provide no additional opportunity for US negro leaders to make use of the UN system to expose grievances. The rapporteur would not receive complaints or petitions; he would not hold hearings or conduct independent investi-

---

[1] Source: National Archives and Records Administration, RG 59, Central Files 1960–63, SOC 14 ECOSOC. No classification marking. Drafted on November 12 by Rachel C. Nason and retyped on November 13. This memorandum formed Tab D of a package sent to the Secretary by Cleveland on November 13; see footnote 1, Document 303.

[2] Document 303.

[3] In his November 8 memorandum Chayes had no serious objection to the proposed UN Human Rights Rapporteur, but was "dubious about it." Should the Rapporteur become involved with "racial incidents in the United States," his activities would be injurious to both U.S. public support for the United Nations and to "satisfactory resolution of our own civil rights problems." Only marginal benefits were likely, if, as proponents claimed, a Rapporteur would provide perspective to U.S. problems by emphasizing human rights violations elsewhere. Dutton wrote, "I concur" on Chayes' memorandum.

gations. Our race situation is already known to all through our public press; on occasion agitators have circularized all UN Delegations in New York with negro housing and other complaints. The rapporteur should help protect us against sensational charges.

The UN receives thousands of letters each year from individuals or groups alleging human rights violations. These are made available to the Human Rights Commission for information (usually without the signature to safeguard the writer), but the Commission does not discuss or take action on the basis of these communications. The Rapporteur would have similar access. Negro leaders can add to the total of these communications if they wish, and the Rapporteur could report on their substance in his discretion. However, if the matter were of importance, he would have access to similar information in the public press, and would find it easier to make use of a public source.

So far as the General Assembly and other UN bodies are concerned, any Delegation is free to propose an agenda item on any subject, including a race problem. This situation would not be changed one way or the other by the existence of a human rights rapporteur, but the objective nature of his reports should discourage efforts to embarrass the United States on race grounds.

3. While it is true that racial matters will continue to be a "hot issue" in the United Nations, there is no reason why we should not take steps to enlarge the scope of human rights considerations. Indeed, Mr. Chayes concedes this in suggesting possible advantage "through more aggressive use of the Human Rights Commission . . .". For the United States to benefit by such use, it seems to us essential that the Commission be equipped with up-to-date and objective information.

4. Our proposal at this time is to ask the General Assembly to establish the rapporteur post in principle, leaving detailed implementation to the Economic and Social Council next summer. Selection of the rapporteur, on the nomination of the Secretary General, would require confirmation by the General Assembly next fall. The rapporteur would accordingly not be able to take any action which could influence civil rights legislation now pending in Congress.

As for the effect of introduction of the proposal in the General Assembly, we expect to keep this in low key and to move only in association with a number of co-sponsors.

305.   Letter From the Assistant Secretary of State for International Organization Affairs (Cleveland) to the Assistant Attorney General for Civil Rights (Marshall)[1]

Washington, November 16, 1963.

Dear Burke:

As you know, the Secretary of State has invited you to a meeting in his office at 3:00 on Monday, November 18th, to discuss a proposal for a permanent Human Rights Rapporteur in the United Nations system.

The essence of the issue is whether we ought to take this step during this General Assembly (that is, in early December), to carry out the indication in the President's UN speech that the United States Delegation would have proposals to make in this area.

The Secretary is particularly anxious to consider the relationship between the substance and timing of this proposal and the Federal Government's domestic civil rights program, including the legislation now pending on the Hill.

Perhaps the best preparation for this meeting would be our internal documentation on the matter, which includes our original proposal as agreed with Governor Stevenson and embodied in a draft Memorandum to the President, a supplementary memorandum by Abe Chayes expressing some doubts, and a brief rebuttal thereto.

With warmest regards,

Sincerely,

Harlan Cleveland[2]

---

[1] Source: Kennedy Library, Cleveland Papers, Human Rights, Box 19. Limited Official Use. An attached note reads: "Re 3:00 meeting today in Secretary's office: Secretary and Attorney General have been in touch on the telephone and Secretary has decided not to press ahead with the rapporteur proposal for the time being in view of the judgement that it would make considerable difficulties on the domestic civil rights front and that those considerations must be considered as overriding at this time. Since the question at issue has been settled for this season, the Secretary has called off the meeting he was to have in his office at 3:00 today. Attorney General; Burke Marshall; Sorensen; Chayes and HC."

[2] Printed from a copy that bears this typed signature.

306.   Editorial Note

On November 20, 1963, the UN General Assembly adopted unanimously Resolution 1904 (XVIII), a Declaration on the Elimination of All Forms of Racial Discrimination. For text of the resolution, see *American Foreign Policy: Current Documents, 1963,* pages 152–156. Extracts from the text of Ambassador Stevenson's address to the General Assembly after the resolution's adoption are printed in *U.S. Participation in the UN, 1963,* pages 250–251.

Following approval of the declaration, the General Assembly unanimously adopted Resolution 1906 (XVIII) urging "absolute priority" for preparation of a draft convention on the elimination of racial discrimination, to be ready for the 19th session of the General Assembly in the fall of 1964. (UN Document A/1555)

---

307.   Memorandum From the Administrator of the Bureau of Security and Consular Affairs (Schwartz) to the Assistant Secretary of State for International Organization Affairs (Cleveland)[1]

Washington, December 11, 1963.

SUBJECT

Comments on "Resolution on Freedom to Travel"

Reference is made to a request from your office for brief comments on the Resolution on Freedom to Travel adopted and submitted by the United States Section of the Women's International League for Peace and Freedom.[2]

There is attached a statement which sets forth our comments and views on this Resolution. It has been cleared with the Bureau of Far Eastern Affairs and the Bureau of Inter-American Affairs.

---

[1] Source: National Archives and Records Administration, RG 59, Central Files 1960–63, SOC 14. No classification marking.

[2] When the National Board of the Women's International League for Peace and Freedom met in Philadelphia on October 25–27, it called for an "immediate end to the arbitrary withholding of passports by the Passport Office of the State Department and to the practice of withdrawing passports as a penalty for travel to certain countries." Copies of the resolution were sent under cover of letters from the National Board to the President, the Secretary of State, and the Director of the Passport Office on November 1. (Ibid.)

Attachment

FREEDOM TO TRAVEL

The Department is in complete agreement with and follows the guarantee contained in the Universal Declaration of Human Rights that "everyone has the right to leave any country, including his own, and to return to his country." It is also our view that restriction on travel is an inroad and a hindrance to the free exchange of information upon which our domestic society depends. It follows, therefore, that restrictions on the travel of our citizens to certain countries or areas abroad should be and are imposed only when such travel constitutes a serious threat to our foreign policy or other national interest.

The designation from time to time of certain countries or areas of the world as forbidden to United States citizens who desire to travel there falls within the power to conduct foreign affairs. The decision to restrict is in and of itself a foreign policy determination and every citizen should do his part to aid in the implementation of this policy.

It is axiomatic that the conduct of foreign affairs necessarily involves flexible measures and policies which must be reviewed and adjusted to meet changing conditions. The Department has under constant review the countries or areas which are restricted to U.S. travellers and makes changes in the designations when warranted.

The policy of restricting travel of U.S. citizens to certain designated countries or areas does not mean that no U.S. citizens can travel to those areas. Specially validated passports have been and are being issued to travellers when the travel is regarded as being in the best interests of the United States. In the implementation of our foreign policy and especially in relation to Communist China, an arrangement exists whereby news-gathering agencies with a demonstrated interest in reporting foreign news have designated news representatives who are authorized to travel to Communist China. With the exception of two rather atypical cases, the Peiping regime has refused visas to all American correspondents to enter that area. Family members of United States citizens imprisoned in Communist China have also been issued passports valid for travel to Communist China, and usually are permitted to enter.

In the case of Cuba, the important current reason for closely controlling travel to Cuba is that the United States and other governments of this Hemisphere are engaged in a cooperative effort to isolate Cuba in order to limit the Castro regime's ability to promote subversion in other countries and to prevent the consolidation of communism in Cuba. The Castro regime is bringing Latin American trainees to Cuba, instructing them in subversive techniques, including guerrilla warfare, and returning them to their countries to initiate or support subversive movements.

Legitimate newsmen and other news media personnel have been issued specially validated passports to enable them to observe the Cuban scene and keep the American public informed on the true situation there. Also, American Red Cross personnel and others travelling for humanitarian reasons have been granted passports validated for travel to Cuba. It should be noted, however, that the Castro regime, through its control of visas, determines which persons may enter Cuba. In many instances persons who have passports validated for travel to Cuba have had their visas refused or long delayed because the Castro regime did not want them to enter Cuba,

The Department desires to emphasize to the National Board of the Women's International League for Peace and Freedom that the decision to place such restrictions on travel is a supplementary phase in the conduct of foreign affairs and that it will contribute to our ultimate objectives of world peace and stability, reduction of tensions, and resistance to Communism.

Refugees

308. Telegram From the Mission in Geneva to the Department of
State[1]

Geneva, February 21, 1961, 5 p.m.

930. Deptel 1305.[2] Schnyder welcomed US interest in question of
Deputy, had intended even before our intervention to discuss matter
with US authorities before taking any actual steps. He expects be in
Washington soon after middle of March to consult on this and other
matters with Dept officials concerned.

Schnyder said he has tried to conceive of structure of his office in
terms of present and future activities, which are rather different from
those undertaken to meet "classic" European refugee problems. He
cited Algerian refugees as type of situation that seems likely command
more of UNHCR's attention than situation which 1951 Convention was
designed to meet.[3] His preliminary thinking therefore was that Afro-
Asians should have stronger representation on staff. One approach
might be to appoint Afro-Asian as consultant and see how he worked
out (implying that if successful he would become Deputy).

Schnyder asked if we had any individual in mind. We said we did
not know. He said and repeated twice that he would be very interested
in Dept's reaction to his ideas, which he stressed were "preliminary."

In view of lack of urgency with which Schnyder considering problem and prospect of his visiting Dept in March, we refrained from
putting forward counter-arguments during this interview. Would
appreciate guidance for further talks. Our impression was that in spite
of Schnyder's rationale for Afro-Asian candidate he would be disposed
to make his final decision on basis of ability of individual candidate
rather than his nationality.

Although not touched on in this conversation, it is obvious that
Schnyder is well aware of personnel problems facing any new adminis-

---

[1] Source: National Archives and Records Administration, RG 59, Central Files
1960–63, 324.8411/2–2161. Official Use Only.

[2] In telegram 1305 to Geneva, February 15, the Department suggested that the
Mission should discuss with Schnyder whether he agreed that the next Deputy UNHCR
should be an American. (Ibid., 324.8411/2–1561)

[3] Reference is to the Convention Relating to the Status of Refugees of July 28, 1951.
(189 UNTS 150)

tration and concomitant political pressure for finding positions. This awareness may well be contributive to Schnyder's preference for going slowly. In any event, I suggest we seek between now and time of Schnyder's Washington visit outstanding candidate with background, experience, and other qualifications which will be impressive to Schnyder.

Martin

---

309.   Memorandum of Conversation[1]

Washington, March 14, 1961.

SUBJECT

Rumored Appointment of New Deputy High Commissioner for Refugees

PARTICIPANTS

M. Claude Lebel, Minister Counselor, French Embassy
M. Pierre Pelen, Counselor, French Embassy
Mr. Wallner, Deputy Assist. Secretary   IO
Mr. Otis Mulliken, Deputy Director OES
Mr. Buffum—UNP
Mr. MacDonald—WE

Mr. Lebel wondered if we had heard of a plan to appoint an Afro-Asian as Deputy High Comissioner for Refugees. He thought this would be a very poor idea. Article 1 of the Convention on Refugees limited the Commisson's jurisdiction to pre-1951 refugees, and in addition, he pointed out, Europe and the United States were responsible for some three-fourths of the Commission's expenditures. He thought that the appointment of an Afro-Asian could mean a much more vigorous policy on Algerian refugees in Tunisia and Morocco, which would be the worst sort of development now from France's point of view.

Mr. Mulliken said that we first heard of this plan from Mr. Schnyder, the High Comissioner. Upon hearing reports that he was thinking of appointing a deputy, we had approached him to say that we might be interested in suggesting some Americans for the post, especially since an American had held it previously. Mr. Schnyder then said

[1] Source: National Archives and Records Administration, RG 59, Central Files 1960–63, 324.8411/3–1461. Confidential. Drafted by John W. MacDonald, Jr.

he was thinking of an Afro-Asian. Since that time, we have even heard unconfirmed reports that Schneider was thinking of offering the post to the Aga Khan.

This was a totally new idea to Mr. Lebel, for whom the Aga Khan was "a special kind of Afro-Asian". However, he wondered if the Aga Khan would accept. Mr. Lebel asked if Mr. Schnyder could appoint a deputy on his own. Mr. Mulliken replied that he could, but added he would be most surprised if Mr. Schnyder would do so without prior consultation.

Mr. Lebel asked if we could name the Americans we were thinking of suggesting to Schnyder—and especially if we had decided on a candidate. He said that the French would certainly be prepared to support our candidate, if we had one. Mr. Mulliken said that we had not yet decided on a candidate, but would inform the French if and when we do.

---

310.   Memorandum From the Director of the Office of International Administration, Bureau of International Organization Affairs (Westfall) to the Assistant Secretary (Cleveland)[1]

Washington, March 31, 1961.

SUBJECT

Deputy UN High Commissioner for Refugees

Mr. Schnyder, UN High Commissioner for Refugees, will be in Washington for 3 days beginning April 11. A briefing paper will be sent to you prior to that date. One item which Mr. Schnyder will wish to discuss with you is the appointment of a Deputy High Commissioner. The following information is being sent to you now in order to provide time for such consultation and discussion as you deem necessary.

Background

James Morgan Reed (U.S.) was Deputy UNHCR from 1951 until his resignation to become President of Wilmington College (Ohio) on October 1, 1960. Since Dr. Auguste Lindt (Swiss), who was the UNHCR at that time, was about to resign to become Swiss Ambassador to the

---

[1] Source: National Archives and Records Administration, RG 59, Central Files 1960–63, 324.8411/3–3161. No classification marking. Drafted by Elmer M. Falk (IO/OIA).

U.S., he took no action to fill the vacancy. Felix Schnyder (Switzerland) was elected by the 15th General Assembly to serve as UNHCR from February 1, 1961 to December 31, 1963, which is the terminal date for the present UNHCR mandate.

Recent Developments

Since assuming office on February 2, 1961, Mr. Schnyder has been considering the appointment of a Deputy. Through our Resident Delegation in Geneva he was recently advised of our interest in having qualified Americans at reasonably high levels in all international organizations, and that we are interested in having a U.S. national appointed to the "traditionally" American post of Deputy UNHCR. He was also told of our willingness to recommend a candidate or candidates for the position if this was agreeable to him. His reply was to "welcome U.S. interest" and to indicate that he planned to discuss the matter when he came to Washington. Mr. Schnyder stated that he is trying to conceive of the structure of his office in terms of present and future activities which he sees as being rather different from those undertaken to meet "classic" European refugee problems. His preliminary thinking is that Afro-Asians should have stronger representation on the staff. He suggested that one approach might be to appoint an Afro-Asian as consultant and see how he worked out. The implication was that if successful he would become Deputy.

Miss Aline Cohn, U.S. Representative of the UNHCR, has reported informally her understanding that Mr. Schnyder has already "offered" the Deputy position to Prince Sadruddin Khan (Iran). If Prince Khan "accepts" Miss Cohn thought it would be very difficult for Mr. Schnyder not to make him a formal offer. For obvious reasons, Miss Cohn does not want to be quoted on this although she has spoken to Prince Khan and believes her information to be correct.

In view of the above developments no attempt has been made to "select" a well qualified American to present to Mr. Schnyder as a candidate for Deputy UNHCR. The Department has, however, assembled a list of candidates for the position, some on the basis of direct application and others based on recommendations. Other qualified candidates could be found among our foreign service and departmental staff.

For your information, Mr. Roger Jones in a conversation with Mr. George Warren, Sr. expressed the opinion that the U.S. should make a strong effort to have Mr. Schnyder appoint an American as his Deputy.

Recommendation

1. That you discuss the matter of the Deputy position with Mr. Jones before your meeting with Mr. Schnyder at 4 p.m. on April 12. In

your conversation with Mr. Jones you might indicate that the extent to which we can "push" for an American as Deputy UNHCR will depend upon developments during your meeting with Mr. Schnyder.

2. If Mr. Schnyder is committed to Prince Khan it would not appear to be in the U.S. interest to pressure Mr. Schnyder to appoint an American. (You will recall that you met Prince Khan at the Blair House Luncheon for Dr. Veronese. Prince Khan is "western" in his orientation and would be acceptable to us if we could not arrange for the appointment of an American.)

---

311. Despatch From the Mission in Geneva to the Department of State[1]

No. 213 Geneva, April 6, 1961.

REF

Department's Airgram G–190 rptd USUN New York G–74[2]

SUBJECT

Possible Shift in Emphasis in Program of UNHCR

Summary

Neither the U.S. Mission nor U.S. delegations have encouraged enlarging the scope of the United Nations High Commissioner for Refugees (UNHCR) program or indicated any possibility of an increase in U.S. assistance to refugees outside of Europe.

Although the sentence, contained in Geneva Despatch 175[3] and referred to in the referenced airgram concerning statements by U.S. spokesmen in support of a shift in emphasis in the program of the

---

[1] Source: National Archives and Records Administration, RG 59, Central Files 1960–63, 324.8411/4–661. Official Use Only; Air Priority.

[2] Airgram G–190 reads in part: "Department concerned over apparent misunderstanding its position on future UNHCR programs. Ref despatch refers to US statements made to the Executive Committee of the UNHCR and elsewhere to effect US favors shift in emphasis of UNHCR program away from refugee problem involving European refugees and in direction refugee problem outside Europe. It commented this would appear support greater participation by Afro-Asian governments in the activities of the UNHCR program." (Ibid., 324.8411/2–2161)

[3] Not printed. (Ibid., 324.8411/2–1561)

UNHCR away from problems involving European refugees, may exaggerate or over-simplify the situation, the record of U.S. public statements including that of Mr. McCollum before the House Appropriations Committee, Mr. Hanes before ICEM Council (December 1960) and even the text of the Presidential letter to Dr. Lindt, the outgoing High Commissioner, appears at least consistent with such a shift in emphasis if not actually calling for it. Moreover, the lack of U.S. opposition to the trend apparent in recent years toward broadening the UNHCR responsibility through special UNGA resolutions, would appear to encourage such a shift in emphasis as the problem of European refugees is reduced to manageable proportions.

It is clear from several indications, including the UNHCR press release 638, dated February 1, 1961,[4] that Mr. Schnyder envisages a liberal interpretation of the operative paragraph of UNGA Resolution 1499 (XV)[5] and contemplates a shift of emphasis to refugee groups on other continents.

The Mission questions the wisdom of opposing this development in the face of historic trend. However, if the Department believes the opposition desirable, it is recommended that the U.S. position be made clear to Dr. Schnyder when he visits Washington and that it be incorporated in the position papers for the U.S. Delegation to the 5th Session of the UNHCR Executive Committee.

This despatch has been prepared in four parts. The first part contains a general discussion of the issue raised by the Department's Airgram, namely, whether the U.S. has encouraged a shift in the emphasis of the High Commissioner's program from Europe to other areas. The second part comprises quotations from statements made by U.S. spokesmen and from other public documents on or relating to this subject. Part three presents the High Commissioner's attitude, together with developments within the High Commissioner's Executive Committee and elsewhere which support his position. Part four is the Mission's recommendation for clarification of U.S. policy on this subject.

I. General Discussion

At no time has the U.S. Mission or its representatives or, to the Mission's knowledge, the U.S. Delegations concerned, referred to any

---

[4] Not found.

[5] Resolution 1499 (XV) approved the annual report of the UN High Commissioner for Refugees. It was adopted by the General Assembly on December 5, 1960, by a vote of 66–0, with 10 abstentions. Section (d) invited member states to continue to devote attention to unsolved refugee problems "by continuing to consult with the High Commissioner in respect of measures of assistance to groups of refugees who do not come within the competence of the United Nations." (*Yearbook of the United Nations, 1960*, p. 368)

possibility of an increase in U.S. assistance to refugees in non-European countries. Moreover, consistent with Department policy, the Mission has opposed the expansion of UNHCR operational activities in connection with Algerian refugees and has refrained from offering any encouragement to the UNHCR to enlarge the geographic or functional scope of his activities.

Although the statement contained in Geneva Despatch No. 175, and referred to in the 1st paragraph of Department Airgram G–190 regarding the effect of U.S. statements may, in fact, amount to an exaggeration or at least an over-simplification, the statement is not basically inconsistent with what has actually transpired. In brief, although there has been no resounding endorsement by U.S. spokesmen of a formal shift of emphasis in the UNHCR responsibilities, the question has not been entirely skirted and there has been no U.S. rebuttal to statements of encouragement in this direction by representatives of some other governments and of influential voluntary agencies. It is difficult for the U.S., in its position of leadership, to avoid the appearance of supporting a premise of this nature short of actually opposing it.

Moreover, the carefully worded statements of U.S. representatives on this subject have seldom sounded altogether neutral or undecided on this point. Indeed, within the context of current trends and world developments, U.S. statements can hardly be considered as inconsistent with a shift in emphasis to meet these trends and developments.

To say the least, it has been only natural that the election and installation of the new U.S. Administration has encouraged UNHCR representatives, among others, to look to their own "new frontiers" where their services can be put to good or better use. The nomination of a new UNHCR who takes over as the program for Europe is well in progress toward liquidation has furthered this trend. The absence of forceful U.S. opposition has perhaps not formally encouraged this tendency but also has not resulted in its discouragement.

It is believed that the trend of world events in recent months has moved this matter well along to the point where a further formal expansion of the UNHCR's role in global refugee affairs may be difficult to avoid.

In one view it may be seen that the trend toward wider responsibility for the UNHCR has been developing for several years. With the termination of the UNREF program in 1958 the U.N. General Assembly approved Resolution 1166 (XII) which, among other things, contained provision for the UNHCR to undertake new refugee situations as they arise. Resolution 1167 (XII) appealed for assistance to Chinese refugees in Hong Kong and authorized the UNHCR to use his "good offices" in this connection. General Assembly action in behalf of refugees from Algeria and more recently in the form of GA 1499 (XV) are further steps in this direction. The sending by the UNHCR of a representative to Cambodia is another instance of events pointing toward wider UNHCR responsibilities. In extension of this trend it would seem logical to assume that the U.N. will call upon the UNHCR increasingly as new, unforeseen refugee problems arise as a result of political events in Africa and elsewhere.

The Mission assumes that the Department's concern, expressed in G–190, stems from a desire to avoid financial commitment rather than from opposition to this trend. However, should the Department wish to oppose this trend, a clear U.S. position should be developed as quickly as possible, and the U.S. delegation to the forthcoming Fifth Session of the Executive Committee of the High Commissioner's Program beginning May 25, should be prepared to make this position known to all.

II. U.S. Statements on the Future of the UNHCR's Functions

As to various U.S. statements made to the Executive Committee of the UNHCR and elsewhere in the past, there are quoted below several statements which doubtless have been interpreted as indicating a willingness to see the work of the UNHCR (and also of ICEM) not only continued but perhaps shifted, at least geographically, outside Europe:

A. The formal justification material presented to the House of Representatives' Subcommittee of the Committee on Appropriations in March, 1960 (and published in the volume of Committee Hearings in 1960) contained the following passage respecting the UNHCR program proposed for Fiscal Year 1961:

"In the past several years through the UNHCR program and through the efforts of the cooperating voluntary agencies and of ICEM and USEP much progress has been made in reducing the refugee problem, particularly in Europe. Nevertheless, events of the same period make it clear that refugees, as the product of international and nationalistic tensions, will continue to be an international problem. Therefore, U.S. assistance to refugees through the UNHCR must be anticipated as an annual program. Although the prospective cost of such programs in the years ahead will depend entirely upon the dimensions of the future refugee problem, every effort will be made to reduce the area of international assistance by stimulating greater acceptance of responsibility by asylum countries, thereby reducing the scope of the UNHCR program and the U.S. contributions thereto."[6]

---

[6] *Mutual Security Appropriations for 1961 (and Related Agencies): Hearing Before the Subcommittee of the Committee on Appropriations, House of Representatives, Eighty-Sixth Congress, Second Session, Subcommittee on Foreign Operations Appropriations, Part 1* (Washington, 1960), p. 658.

In explaining the Department's view that the UNHCR must be anticipated as an "annual program," Mr. Robert S. McCollum, Deputy Administrator of SCA, said before the House Subcommittee, "I think the High Commissioner's program in the concept of the legal protection work must continue. This goes back many years, even back to League of Nations days; that as situations such as Algerian or Tibetan refugees arise, there will be need for international cooperation. We are not referring here to what ordinarily we refer to as the old caseload, which, as I mentioned, we hope to close out this year; at the end of this year. What we are anticipating, which has been true for the last 15 years, that something new occurs almost every year or every other year, such as the ones I mentioned, the Hungarian crisis, Algerians, Tibetans, which we think the U.N. as an organization would have a part in."[7]

B. The text of President Eisenhower's letter to Dr. Lindt, signed October 4, 1960, stated, inter alia, "You can, I believe, take proper pride in two major achievements. Your efforts to gain acceptance by more governments of the principles governing asylum and the protection of the legal status of refugees now stand as beacons of hope and security to countless thousands who are still striving to adjust to a new life in a new country. Of hardly less importance, your efforts to secure a greater world consciousness of the tragic material plight still suffered by many refugees has resulted in a remarkable increase in aid for these victims of oppression and political strife, and in substantial progress toward permanent solutions which we have all witnessed."[8]

Comment. This letter was read to the High Commissioner during the Fourth Session of the Executive Committee of the UNHCR Program. It is noticeably lacking in references to the mandate limitations and in any phrases indicating an official U.S. concern to restrict the High Commissioner's functions or future role. On the contrary, the praise for the UNHCR's "efforts to secure a greater world consciousness" almost endorses the notion of a global role for the UNHCR. Moreover, connecting this function with "the tragic material plight still suffered by many refugees" indicates a relaxation of the attitude frequently expressed by U.S. spokesmen, namely, that the UNHCR's future function should be primarily in the field of legal protection.

C. At the Fourth Session of the Executive Committee of the High Commissioner's Program, October 1960, Mr. Richard R. Brown, Chief of the U.S. Delegation, is quoted as being "sure that everyone concerned with refugees must be extremely pleased with the results of World Refugee Year. The seed had been sown abundantly during the first part

---

[7] Ibid., p. 666.

[8] For full text, see Department of State *Bulletin,* November 7, 1960, p. 732.

of the year, and the harvest was now being reaped. What was, perhaps, even more important, the world had awoken to its responsibilities towards refugees, and had at last come to regard them as human beings above everything. It was heartening to learn that World Refugee Year had done the refugees themselves much good psychologically. In addition, it had made it possible to help groups of refugees, in the Far East and in Africa, for whom the High Commissioner's Office had hitherto not been able to do much. That great effort must be continued."

D. Report from the Thirteenth Session of the ICEM Council Meeting December 6, 1960, at 10:30 a.m. at the Palais des Nations, Geneva.

"Mr. Hanes, United States of America, expressed his gratitude to the Director-in-Charge of the Office of the United Nations High Commissioner for Refugees for his statement made at the 120th meeting. A superficial review might give the impression that the refugee problem had been practically solved; whereas just after the war there were eight million displaced persons in Europe, there were currently only about one hundred thousand in need of assistance.

"*Nevertheless, in other areas, such as Africa, the Middle and Far East, there are several million refugees for whom the solution which had proved effective in Europe, namely immigration, was not always suitable.* (Italics inserted.) Besides, the one hundred thousand refugees in Europe required urgent help from ICEM not only for humanitarian and moral reasons, but also because, with the regular arrival in Western Europe of refugees from the Eastern countries, the problem would probably become a permanent one. The Committee's operations in the migration field as well as the steps taken on behalf of refugees by the United States and the Office of the High Commissioner were inseparable; governments had well defined responsibilities regarding the problem as a whole.

"It might be feared that in the United States the enthusiasm raised by World Refugee Year would be followed by a period of relative apathy during which it would prove increasingly difficult for instance to find sponsors for refugees. The efforts which for the past ten years had led to such remarkable success must nevertheless be continued."

III. The New U.N. High Commissioner for Refugees Already Looks Beyond Europe for Principal UNHCR Tasks of the Future

The new High Commissioner, Felix Schnyder, assumed his duties on February 1. Although he has not made controversial statements or given positive indications concerning his future functions, it is already apparent that he and his staff are inclined to interpret liberally his responsibilities both under his mandate and under certain U.N. General Assembly resolutions passed since 1957 which have broadened his orig-

inal functions. Moreover, with most of the specific program and material assistance tasks assigned the UNHCR in Europe nearing a successful completion, the new High Commissioner and his chief aides are
almost inevitably turning their eyes and their interest beyond Europe to
the numerous refugee problems of Asia and Africa, seeking a basis for
offering the assistance of the UNHCR and his office in helping alleviate
these problems.

The very human desire to project the functions of the agency beyond
its hitherto prescribed tasks has been whetted by the experience of World
Refugee Year and by a growing awareness not only that large-scale
refugee problems exist already in areas outside Europe but also that forces
of change active now in the less developed continents bid fair to aggravate
and even multiply these problems. The attitude of the new UNHCR was
foreshadowed in the statement on World Refugee Year made by Dr. Lindt
at the Fourth Meeting of the Executive Committee of the High
Commissioner's Program last October, that there are "many indications—
particularly the manner in which the national committees have decided to
distribute the sums they have collected—that the refugee problem is tending to move from Europe to other continents." Dr. Lindt agreed then with
the Swedish representative that the Executive Committee would be wise
to examine the possible effects of that tendency on the High
Commissioner's program at its next session, when the full results of World
Refugee Year would be known.

In mid-January even before Mr. Schnyder took up his post, he
expressed a distinct willingness to view his future functions as global,
making particular reference to Asia and Africa. Speaking in New York
to members of a special U.S. mission assigned to review the U.S. assistance to refugee programs in the Far East and South Asia, he said that,
"although the (U.N.) mandate was useful in Europe, it had much less
relevance to Asian conditions. He thought that in Asia the important
thing was for the UNHCR to give practical help in the form of funds
and immigration opportunities. And that . . . two (UN General
Assembly) resolutions . . . gave him ample scope within which to operate. He considered it his function to focus world attention on specific
refugee problems and to encourage governments to contribute. There
had been little response to the resolution of 1957 on Chinese in Hong
Kong, but quite a large response during World Refugee Year. *Given the
increased Afro-Asian representation in the U.N., he thought that the refugee
problem of these areas would receive increasing attention."* (Italics inserted.)

Members of his staff have been hardly less subtle on the same subject.

Further evidence that the new High Commissioner considers a shift
in emphasis as ordained may be found in his press release No. Ref. 638,
dated February 1, 1961, in which he noted "a shift in emphasis to

groups in other continents." In reply to the Department's query regarding the degree of liberality in which he will interpret the GA Res. 1499 (XV), this same press release states in its final paragraph as follows:

"The High Commissioner said that in his opinion the 'good offices' concept was elastic enough to permit him, when asked, to bring effective aid to nearly any group of refugees provided there was sufficient interest and support on the part of the international community."

There is no doubt that the UNHCR and members of his staff have received encouragement to adopt a more liberal and expanded view of the High Commissioner's functions, directly and indirectly from some governments and directly from representatives of certain international voluntary agencies, including American agencies, which have begun themselves to shift more and more of their staff and programming efforts to areas outside Europe.

At the Fourth Session of the Executive Committee of the UNHCR Program, October 1960, "the representative of Belgium stated that as the problems of refugees of European origin seemed to be in the course of being solved, equal attention should from now on be given to the considerable number of refugees in other parts of the world and particularly in Asia and Africa, where their plight remained a source of concern. The Belgian delegation hoped that in the course of the present session of the General Assembly the United Nations would clearly indicate their formal wish that the efforts of UNHCR should in the first place be directed towards assistance to these refugees. Some representatives supported the suggestion made by the representative of Belgium. Other representatives, while recognizing the needs of refugees in other parts of the world, felt that due consideration should still be given to outstanding refugee problems and in particular to that of the camp population."

Representatives of the Holy See and Norway heartily endorsed the view of the Belgian delegate. The representative of Sweden "agreed that in the near future the refugee programme would have to be reconsidered and given a new direction, but he did not believe that the matter was ripe for consideration at the present session. The camp clearance programme was running late, and if efforts were diverted from it those who had made generous contributions to enable the camps to be quickly cleared would be disappointed. The Executive Committee would be in a better position to make up its mind after the end of the year—for example, at its Spring session in 1961. All members of the Committee were agreed that there should be no discrimination on grounds of race or nationality; but the problem with which the Committee was faced at that moment was, in his opinion, mainly psychological, and not one of principle."

Also, at the Fourth Session of the Executive Committee of the High Commissioner's Program, on October 14, 1960, Mr. Jean Chenard, a

United States citizen speaking on behalf of the Standing Conference of Voluntary Agencies Working for Refugees, stated, inter alia, that "It is hoped that opportunity will be found for a full-scale debate on the Chinese refugee problem during the next Session of the Executive Committee of the High Commissioner's Program. However, the warning is not out of place here that the High Commissioner will not be able to *initiate* programs for the Chinese refugees, unless Resolution No. 1167 of the UN General Assembly passed in November 1957, is radically altered. That was the Resolution which recommended that the High Commissioner should 'lend his good office for the arrangement of contributions.' Not at all the same things as starting up programs.

"We are grateful for the intervention during this Session of the distinguished representatives of the Holy See, Belgium and Norway, concerning assistance to refugees in Asia and Africa. In these fields too the voluntary agencies are already carrying on programs of feeding, housing, integration and emigration assistance."

Another specific example of encouragement for the UNHCR came at the meeting last December of the Standing Council of Voluntary Agencies in Geneva, when a spokesman for the voluntary agency Jami'at al Islam, an international group with headquarters in the U.S., urged that both the UNHCR and ICEM be authorized and equipped to provide more services to refugees in Asia and Africa, most of whom he described as being practically excluded, at present, from receiving direct benefits from these international organizations. Similar views have been expressed, perhaps less vehemently but nonetheless earnestly, by representatives of the larger voluntary agencies, including NCWC and WCC. The International Conference for World Refugee Year (ICWRY), which convened in Geneva in January 1961, called for several forms of enlarged activity by the UNHCR in behalf of refugees in and from Asia and Africa: (1) to investigate the condition of Algerians in Europe; (2) to include within the UNHCR mandate Tibetan refugees in India and Nepal and Chinese refugees in Hong Kong; and (3) to send a competent fact-finding mission under UNHCR or other appropriate auspices to ascertain the present condition of Chinese refugees in India, Nepal, Burma, Thailand, Laos, Vietnam, Pakistan, Indonesia, and Macao.

IV. Conclusion and Recommendations

Regardless of whether or not U.S. statements have had the effect of encouraging a shift in the emphasis of the UNHCR program away from the European refugees and in the direction of refugee problems outside of Europe, it seems clear that such a shift is imminent if not already in motion. To this Mission the alternative to supporting such a shift appears questionable and, indeed, rather belated. After supporting a series of General Assembly Resolutions assigning additional and diverse responsibilities to the UNHCR; after a series of public statements, if not actually in support of, at least not inconsistent with such development; and in an era in which the concept of collective action through the U.N. has acquired increased importance, it might appear detrimental to U.S. leadership to oppose what could be regarded as a historic trend.

Unless the Department is determined to oppose what might be termed the "new frontier" for the UNHCR program, it may not be necessary to adopt any special attitude or position with respect to it at this time. The U.S. can "go along" with developments and reserve its right to lend support to the extent desired to any aspect of the new program that appears to be in the U.S. interest. (The Mission assumes this is the thinking reflected in the referenced airgram.) Although somewhat at odds with the principle of U.S. leadership, this may be the more attractive policy in view of budget and related problems. Moreover, it would be generally consistent with the spirit of UNGA Resolution 1166 (XII).

On the other hand, should the Department be determined to oppose the shift in emphasis, it would appear highly desirable to make this position clear to the UNHCR during his forthcoming visit to the U.S. and of even greater importance to reflect this attitude clearly in the position papers prepared for the U.S. delegation to the Fifth Session of the Executive Committee of the High Commissioner's Program.

For the Ambassador:

Charles H. Owsley
Deputy United States Representative
to International Organizations

312.   Memorandum of Conversation[1]

Washington, April 13, 1961.

SUBJECT

>   Courtesy Visit by Ambassador Felix Schnyder, United Nations High Commissioner
>   for Refugees

PARTICIPANTS

>   Under Secretary for Economic Affairs—George W. Ball
>   Ambassador Felix Schnyder
>   Miss Arlene Cohn, Representative of the High Commissioner in the U.S.
>   Deputy Assistant Secretary Richard N. Gardner
>   Otis E. Mulliken, IO:OES

Ambassador Schnyder expressed appreciation for the assistance that the United States had rendered to the activities of his Office. He indicated that he thought there might well be a shift in the traditional activities of his Office, which had previously been concerned primarily with European refugee problems, to a concern with non-European refugees, as for example those in Cambodia. He indicated that, as a first principle of operating policy, he thought there should be a definite terminal date for all projects carried out by his Office, such as closing refugee camps. He described his views on increasing international cooperation over refugees, such as the increasing willingness of countries of first asylum to accept refugees.

In his general presentation, Ambassador Schnyder referred to the activities of his Office relating to Algerian refugees and, in response to questions by Mr. Ball, gave a brief description of the scope and character of these activities.

Ambassador Schnyder made no requests for any policy decisions or policy guidance and no commitments of any kind were made to him.

---

[1] Source: National Archives and Records Administration, RG 59, Central Files 1960–63, 324.8411/4–1361. Unclassified. Drafted by Mulliken and approved in the Office of the Under Secretary of State for Economic Affairs on April 20.

### 313.	Instruction From the Department of State to the Mission in Geneva[1]

A–191	Washington, April 24, 1961.

SUBJECT

> Possible Shift in Emphasis in Program of the United Nations High Commissioner for Refugees

The Department appreciates the Mission's excellent despatch which discusses the role the United States may be expected to play in support of the continuing activities of the office of the United Nations High Commissioner for Refugees (UNHCR).[2]

The Department believes that the image of United States policy in this connection created by statements of various United States officials quoted in the reference despatch is essentially correct in that it is a reflection of United States awareness of the existence of refugee problems outside Europe, of its interest in seeking solution to those problems, and of United States support of the principle of international responsibility for refugee problems. However, the Mission should discourage any interpretation of these statements as indicating automatic increases in United States support for refuges outside of Europe. Pending review of these problems as called for in the report of the Department's Task Force on Refugees the Department has desired in prepared public statements of policy only to give recognition to the fact that the problem of older refugees in Europe is nearing solution and, consistent with traditional United States refugee policy, to call attention to the fundamental responsibility of asylum countries for refugees in their territory.

The Department has recently prepared a statement of the Executive Branch position on the continuation of the UNHCR as follows:

"The United States recognizes the principle of asylum for those fleeing from persecution and supports this principle through its own and international programs to assist Free World countries in maintaining liberal policies of asylum and in developing facilities and procedures therefor. It is in the United States interest to continue to join with other countries in accepting international responsibility for refugee problems in the Free World.

---

[1] Source: National Archives and Records Administration, RG 59, Central Files 1960–63, 324.8411/4–2461. Official Use Only. Drafted by Robert F. Lent (SCA/ORM) on April 24, cleared by Elmer M. Falk (OIA), and approved by Richard R. Brown (SCA/ORM).

[2] Document 311.

"To achieve specific national political and other interests, the United States Escapee Program (USEP) assists new anti-Communist escapees from Soviet bloc countries and from Yugoslavia, and certain escapees from Communist China or the Asian satellites. United States assistance to other refugees, exclusive of Palestine Arab refugees, is generally provided through the programs of the United Nations High Commissioner for Refugees and through the Intergovernmental Committee for European Migration.

"The UNHCR material assistance program was begun in 1955 with the objective of providing permanent solutions for the older groups of Soviet bloc refugees. It has been United States policy progressively to reduce its contributions toward the solution of this problem and where feasible to leave the burden of the residual problem on the countries of asylum. Consistent with progress achieved in the solution of this problem in Europe the Department has regularly reduced its requests to Congress for funds for this purpose. The United States has announced that it is unlikely that it would contribute substantially after 1961 to the solution of the residual European problem in those countries now able to bear the burden themselves.

"The United States also contributes to support UNHCR action in connection with other refugee problems which have arisen since 1955. One such program initiated in 1957 for the re-establishment of Hungarian revolt refugees in the Free World is now virtually completed. Other programs of assistance to Jewish refugees in Europe from the United Arab Republic and to Algerian refugees in Morocco and Tunisia continue. The eventual solution of the Algerian refugee problem is dependent on a basic political solution to the over-all Algerian problem, and the reduction of the refugee problem meanwhile is beyond the control of the United States and the UNHCR. Therefore, United States contributions to the UNHCR for the purpose of providing care and maintenance pending a basic political solution will be required. The level of such assistance should remain relatively constant from year to year, but may possibly increase slightly as the refugee population is augmented by natural increase. Such United States assistance serves vital United States policy objectives by demonstrating United States sympathy and concern for the refugees and the people generally in North Africa.

"In addition to these current programs the UNHCR may become seized of other problems of new refugees falling within his mandate in consequence of the continuing interplay of dynamic political and social forces. Such situations may arise out of the unsettled conditions in Africa south of the Sahara, or in other areas of the world.

"In appraising new refugee emergencies or in reviewing current refugee programs, the United States will determine on the basis of its interests whether United States assistance should be provided or continued and, if so, will decide in the light of existing circumstances whether to arrange for the provision of such aid as may be required through the United States Escapee Program, through bilateral arrangements with the countries of asylum or through an international agency such as the UNHCR. In making this determination, the Department will take into account the advantages from the standpoint of achieving United States objectives which might accrue from providing assistance through USEP or through bilateral arrangements, and will also take into account political and cost advantages which may be gained from providing United States assistance through internationally supported organizations. The channeling of United States aid through the UNHCR, to which the normal contribution does not exceed 33-1/3 percent, offers patent cost advantages."

Within the context of this policy the United States would not oppose increasing UNHCR attention to refugee problems outside of Europe particularly within the framework of the good offices resolutions. United States support of General Assembly resolutions 1166 (XII), 1167 (XII), 1388 (XIV), 1389 (XIV), 1499 (XV), 1500 (XV), 1501 (XV), 1502 (XV) which deal inter alia with new refugee situations and the good offices function of the UNHCR is consistent with this policy. In considering the extent of its support of any UNHCR new activities which might be proposed the United States will weigh carefully its national political and security interests against the availability of resources as is the case with regard to continuing escapee and refugee programs including those of the UNHCR.

During recent conversations in the Department the High Commissioner indicated that his basic approach to the activities of his Office will be to seek, where possible, to avoid the development or creation of problems. He feels that the identification or recognition of certain refugee situations needlessly creates problems which then must be solved. As an example he cited Algerian refugees in Europe. Certain agencies claim that these Algerians are in fact refugees, as the Algerians in Morocco and Tunisia and as those escapees from Communist-dominated countries, and that they are in need of the protection of the UNHCR. It is the High Commissioner's view that these refugees are for the most part employed and in satisfactory condition, and that action on his part to recognize them as being within his mandate would merely create a problem and not help the refugees. He further indicated that the involvement of his Office in any refugee situations would follow, among other things, a cautious approach to the government of the country involved and recognition and agreement by that government that UNHCR action on behalf of refugees on its territory would be in the interest of that government. The High Commissioner is also cognizant of the necessity of consulting with members of the Executive Committee in connection with the provision of assistance to new groups of refugees. The UNHCR stated that he was not planning to bring additional groups of refugees within his mandate. If he felt that a given group of refugees should be helped through his Office he would plan to serve as a catalytic agent in obtaining the material support required. This he felt he could do under existing authority of the good offices resolutions.

The Department is in agreement with these views of the High Commissioner on the future work of his Office. It appears, however, that they differ somewhat in emphasis from the attitude reported in the reference despatch that "the new High Commissioner and his chief aides are almost inevitably turning their eyes and their interest beyond Europe to the numerous refugee problems of Asia and Africa, seeking a basis for offering the assistance of the UNHCR and his Office in helping alleviate these problems." The Department would appreciate receiving comments from the Mission on the possible divergency of views as between the High Commissioner and his chief aides.

The Department's views on the future of the UNHCR set forth above will be reflected in position papers to be prepared for the United States delegation to the 5th Session of the Executive Committee. The Department would welcome the Mission's comments on these views and any suggestions the Mission may wish to make with regard to the position to be taken by the United States on the agenda items for the forthcoming session.

Rusk

314.   Report of the U.S. Delegation to the Fifth Session of the Executive Committee of the UN High Commissioner's Program for Refugees[1]

Washington, July 14, 1961.

[Here follow the first six sections of the report: 1. Background of the Conference, 2. Agenda as Adopted, 3. Participation, 4. United States Delegation, 5. Organization of the Conference, and 6. Work of the Committee.]

---

[1] Source: National Archives and Records Administration, RG 59, Central Files 1960–63, 324.8411/7–1461. No classification marking. The Executive Committee met in Geneva May 25–31. Richard R. Brown led the U.S. Delegation; Edward J. Rowell and Edward W. Lawrence prepared the report.

7. Working of the Conference

A copy of the report (with appendices) of the Fifth Session of the Executive Committee of the High Commissioner's Programme (A/AC.96/127) appears as enclosure 3.[2]

The Committee:

(1) Noted the progress and financial reports and statements of the High Commissioner for Refugees dealing with the various programs under his jurisdiction, including the regular annual program and the former UNREF program as of December 31, 1960 (A/AC.96/110 and A/AC.96/111); the program for new Hungarian refugees (A/AC.96/112); the assistance program for refugees from Algeria in Morocco and Tunisia (A/AC.96/113 and Addendum 1); the Far Eastern program (A/AC.96/117); and the program of the World Refugee Year (A/AC.96/121);

(2) Noted the provisional financial statements for the year 1960 (A/AC.96/114 and A/AC.96/118);

(3) Recommended that the UNHCR continue his efforts to raise funds for assistance to refugees from both governmental and non-governmental sources (A/AC.96/115);

(4) Noted the progress made and agreed with the recommendations put forward by the Mental Health Advisor with respect to assistance to refugees in the "special cases" category (A/AC.96/116 and Addendum 1);

(5) Reviewed and endorsed the High Commissioner's proposals for additions to and modifications in his regular programs for the balance of 1961, including the projects for legal assistance and the country clearance program for Italy (A/AC.96/110 and A/AC.96/120 and Addendum 1);

(6) Approved provisional fund allocations by country for the regular program for 1962 (A/AC.96/124);

(7) Noted a report on housing for refugees and agreed that the High Commissioner should continue to study this program (A/AC.96/128);

(8) Noted and approved conclusions reached by the UNHCR regarding the financing of transport of refugees to the effect that, with full regard to the long standing division of financial responsibility between UNHCR and ICEM, his office would not hesitate to take immediate action to avoid a situation where refugees could not be resettled owing to lack of transport funds and would continue to support where needed the Director of ICEM in his requests for additional contributions from governmental and other sources (A/AC.96/126);

[2] Not printed.

(9) Discussed and agreed to consider further, at a later date, the related questions of the future responsibilities of the UNHCR and the assistance to be rendered to refugees in various areas under the United Nations Resolutions pertaining to the use of the High Commissioner's good offices to deal with emergency problems. In this latter connection the Committee noted the developments to date with respect to the particular problems of Chinese refugees in Hong Kong and Macau and refugees in Cambodia.

(10) Examined and agreed to a proposal by the UNHCR that, in the future, major questions would be considered at a main session of the Executive Committee to be held in the Spring. Consideration of a related proposal for the establishment of a preparatory sub-committee of the Executive Committee was deferred to a subsequent session.

The reports presented by the High Commissioner indicated that funds now available were sufficient to insure that the problem of "old" refugees in camps in Europe could be liquidated by the end of 1961 or early in 1962 without additional international support. In connection with the problem of non-settled out-of-camp refugees areas which appear to require continued international attention relate in the main to handicapped persons. It is the intention of the High Commissioner to press for international assistance also in connection with the completion of certain so-called "country clearance programs" where the economic circumstances of the host countries would make for undue delay in the alleviation of the refugee problems.

From a policy point of view, the major item under consideration was that of the future role of the High Commissioner in facing new refugee problems, particularly those of refugees who do not fall within his mandate. There was evidence of considerable divergence of opinion on this important subject. The representative of Canada, for instance, questioned whether the Executive Commitee, under the Economic and Social Council Resolution XXV, was competent to consider problems of assistance to refugees outside of the mandate of the UNHCR. No formal decisions were reached and this subject will be discussed further at future sessions of the Committee. However, it was clear from the debate that, in connection with problems of refugees not within the mandate, there is general agreement for the cautious exercise by the High Commissioner of his good offices in their behalf.

Several delegations also questioned the propriety of the use of the High Commissioner of his emergency fund for assistance in emergency problems of refugees outside his mandate. After considerable discussion during which the U.S. Representative favored liberal discretionary usage of the fund, the majority opinion seemed to support judicious use of the emergency funds by the High Commissioner for new refugee problems on a provisional basis even where the status of these new refugees might be doubtful in terms of his mandate.

It was the view of the High Commissioner that the Resolution of the 13th and subsequent General Assemblies expanding the scope of his interest in refugees did not carry with them the legal authority to expend funds in behalf of such refugees without prior authorization from the appropriate organ of the United Nations. Certainly, further searching consideration of all aspects of the future activities of the High Commissioner with respect to emergent problems can be anticipated in future sessions of the Executive Committee as opinion is far from solidified to date.

With respect to the future work of the Executive Committee, it was agreed that the major session would be held in the Spring and that the Fall session would be shorter in duration and essentially limited to a review of progress. In taking this decision, it was recognized that special problems might arise between the Spring and Fall sittings of the Executive Committee and in support of the U.S. Delegation's contention, it was agreed that the projected arrangement should not prejudice the review of such problems by the Executive Committee at its Fall Sitting.

Other than brief mention by the High Commissioner within the context of an address on his good offices responsibility, the problem of the refugees from Angola in the Congo did not arise for discussion although it was the subject of numerous informal conversations between individual delegations and with the High Commissioner. Discussions were also held by the UNHCR with a representative of the Portuguese Red Cross who acted as Observer for Portugal to the Session, and it was the High Commissioner's opinion, shared by many, that open discussion of the subject in the Session would create difficulties of a political nature without advancing the humanitarian cause of assistance to the refugees.

Some friction developed between the delegations of China and the U.K. over the question of a resolution the Chinese Delegation had intended to introduce at the Session. Relating to the future activities of the UNHCR, the draft resolution called upon the High Commissioner to take the initiative in discussing refugee problems with the authorities or governments concerned with a view to determining whether the problems in question were of a nature to warrant the exercise of the good offices or other responsibilities of the High Commissioner in their behalf. Considering that it was designed primarily to bring about greater international, and hence Chinese Government, participation in the alleviation of the Chinese refugee problem in Hong Kong, the U.K. Delegation was opposed to the resolution. After discussing the text of the draft resolution privately with several delegations, including the

United States, the Chinese Delegation was persuaded by the UNHCR staff and by the U.K. Delegation to withhold the resolution with the apparent understanding on the part of the Chinese Delegate that he could submit the text of the resolution to the Committee in the form of a speech. When he attempted to do so the U.K. Delegate challenged this move as being "out of order" on the grounds that a delegation could not submit a resolution in such form. The chair ruled in favor of the point of order and a compromise was eventually reached whereby the Chinese Delegate alluded to the proposed resolution in his speech and the text of the draft resolution was circulated by the secretariat.

8. Future Meetings

The next meeting of the Executive Committee was provisionally scheduled for the second half of October 1961, with the proviso that it should not conflict with the Meeting of the Executive Board of the Intergovernmental Committee for European Migration.

9. Conclusions

The work of the Committee was expeditiously handled and no conclusions were reached that were not in accord with the instructions to the United States Representative. The U.S. Delegation was particularly gratified both with the manner in which Mr. Salvesen, the Chairman, performed his functions and with the work of the Secretariat.

---

315. Memorandum From John Harter of the Office of International Economic and Social Affairs, Bureau of International Organization Affairs to the Director of the Office (Kotschnig)[1]

Washington, October 18, 1961.

SUBJECT

UNHCR Report at ECOSOC

I was interested in the comments in the Official Use Only Report of the Chairman of the United States Delegation to the 32nd Session of ECOSOC on the UNHCR Report.

---

[1] Source: National Archives and Records Administration, RG 59, Central Files 1960–63, 324.8411/10–1861. No classification marking. A copy was sent to Frank Hefner (OIA).

I know that as the heat of the Berlin Crisis[2] grows hotter it is considered less and less in good taste to say anything that agrees with anything that any Russian officials say. However, I was interested that "in the course of the debate on the UNHCR report the U.S.S.R. and Bulgarian Delegations stressed that the virtual conclusion of the European refugee problem clearly indicated that the need for the Office of the UNHCR was drawing to an end and that measures should be taken to liquidate the Office and most of its functions over the next eighteen months. They argued that the functions of legal assistance and good offices could be carried on by other branches of the United Nations Secretariat."

This is exactly what quite a number of us around the Department feel. Particularly after attending the 15th General Assembly when the UNHCR Annual Report was debated, I came to be quite concerned that the continued existence of an Office like the UNHCR Office, created particularly for European problems, becomes increasingly anomalous in an expanding United Nations. It seems more and more unjustifiable that the United States Government continues to prop this office—one of the most costly of the United Nations programs. During the year and a half I was officially concerned with these matters, I found a wide range of criticism of our traditional stand on refugee programs throughout the Department—especially in EUR, FE, NEA, and M/OP. Their only defense appears to be among "refugee experts," such as those in ORM and those in the voluntary agencies which operate under contract with our refugee programs and in close harmony with ORM, and a sprinkling of Congressmen whose constituents include heavy representation of certain minority groups and who erroneously believe ORM legitimately represents the considered view of "the Department." Such people have been so closely identified with European refugee groups since the end of World War II that they have difficulty grasping current global perspectives. Especially under these circumstances I was disappointed to see that we said in ECOSOC that it was clear "it might be necessary to continue" the UNHCR Office "for some time to come." His mandate is now due to expire in 1963, and I believe it would be a serious mistake to continue it in its present form beyond that date.

I would suggest these views be considered in the preparation and approval of future Position Papers relating to UNHCR.

---

[2] A handwritten note reads: "written when it *was* growing hotter."

316. Editorial Note

On February 1, 1962, the Office of the UN High Commissioner for Refugees announced that Prince Sadruddin Aga Khan was appointed as Deputy UN High Commissioner for Refugees. (Telegram 750 from Geneva, February 1, 1962; National Archives and Records Administration, RG 59, Central Files 1960–63, 324.8411/2–162)

---

317. Telegram From the Department of State to the Mission in Geneva[1]

Washington, March 27, 1962, 5:39 p.m.

1411. Your A–151.[2] Re UNHCR proposed 1963 regular program the Department: (a) considers UNHCR should plan finance annual program of projects for which he can assure same year initiation and intensive action toward implementation. Thus US considers his budget should be submitted on year to year basis as refugee problem may dictate. In any event US will consider its contributions on year to year basis. (b) Mission should call UNHCR attention to continuing US belief that solution of remaining refugee problems in countries with flourishing economies should be primarily responsibility of host government with minimal contributions from international resources. This particularly applicable in cases of refugees fully employed and integrated except for provision adequate housing. US would wish impact its contribution directed toward solution problem in less flourishing countries.

Re continuing program primarily Europe Department in accord legal assistance activities. Department would wish more specific and detailed information re program content other items before commenting.

---

[1] Source: National Archives and Records Administration, RG 59, Central Files 1960–63, 324.8411/3–662. Official Use Only. Drafted by Elmer M. Falk, Laurence A. Dawson, and Robert F. Lent on March 27; cleared by Falk in substance; and approved by Richard R. Brown (SCA/ORM).

[2] In airgram A–151, March 6, the Mission in Geneva reported that Schnyder had requested Mission officials' and the Department's opinion concerning his proposal to seek approximately $7.6 million for UNHCR programs during 1963. (Ibid., 324.8411/3–662)

As UNHCR aware US contributions must be made on basis extant problems. Thus US unable contribute to "open fund account" but would not oppose creation such account if other governments desire contribute to it. US considers preferable emergency fund continue be used for good office's purpose as in past. Also considers that expenditures for housing unless on emergency basis should not be made from emergency fund but should be covered within regular program.

US over-all contribution to 1963 programs unlikely exceed 1962 level.

Falk will discuss administrative grant-in-aid with Schnyder during ICEM meeting.

Ball

318. **Report of the U.S. Delegation to the Seventh Session of the Executive Committee of the UN High Commissioner's Program for Refugees**[1]

Geneva, July 10, 1962.

[Here follow the first six sections: 1, Background of the Conference; 2, Agenda as Adopted; 3, Participation; 4, United States Delegation; 5, Organization of Conference; and 6, Work of the Committee.]

Working of the Conference

In general the Seventh Session of the Executive Committee of the United Nations High Commissioner for Refugees was concerned with receiving a current status report on the work of the Office of the High Commissioner and on progress made in the implementation of previously agreed programs and projects. These involved no basic difficulties for either the United States or most of the other governments present.

While the United States Government was in a position to support the various findings of the Committee it also had the opportunity to

---

[1] Source: National Archives and Records Administration, RG 59, Central Files 1960–63, 324.8411/7–1062. Unclassified. This regular semi-annual meeting of the Executive Committee was held in Geneva May 14–22. Richard R. Brown led the U.S. Delegation.

express certain views of the United States Government. These were as follows:

That the United States assumed that in the funding of the $5.4 million target program for the final aid projects for "old" refugees, the High Commissioner will not only utilize all of his present resources which may appropriately be devoted to this purpose but will also obtain substantial contributions from private voluntary sources and maximum matching assistance from governments of asylum countries. Without these assumptions a target program of $5.4 million would be too high. Several other governments also observed that the sum of $5.4 million appeared to be rather high as contrasted with the estimate of $700,000 for the new refugee groups, and stressed the importance of supporting contributions, recommending that the High Commissioner use all the uncommitted balances at his disposal.

The Committee's discussion of the $700,000 "open fund" to be used in connection with "good offices" programs was closely linked to its discussion of two other subjects. These were the use of the High Commissioner's emergency fund including loan repayments in excess of the authorized $500,000 ceiling of that fund and the proposal to utilize these loan repayments for a special housing project in France and for other similar projects.

In accordance with its instructions, the U.S. Delegation advised the Committee and the High Commissioner that while the U.S. fully approved of the continuation by the UNHCR of the exercise of his good offices to meet newly developing refugee problems the U.S. would not contribute to an "open fund" for this purpose.

The U.S. Delegation further set forth the U.S. position that the resources of the emergency fund, including loan repayments in excess of the ceiling of that fund, should be utilized for financing programs undertaken through the "good offices" function or other program requirements as approved by the Committee. The U.S. Delegation opposed the use of these loan repayments for such purposes as the proposed special housing project in France, maintaining that such projects should be considered by the Committee on the same basis as the rest of the material assistance programs for European refugees for which contributions are being requested from governments.

Following a rather prolonged discussion of these related matters, the Committee (1) decided in approving the allocations of the High Commissioner's program for 1963 to take into account the reservations expressed on establishing open funds, (2) expressed its interest in the suggestion for housing loans but asked the High Commissioner to consider other means for financing this suggestion, and (3) took no action with respect of the use to be made of the loan payments in excess of the $500,000 ceiling of the emergency fund.

During the debate on program allocations for 1963 (Document A/AC.96/162) the U.S. Delegate had the opportunity to commend the High Commissioner for giving high priority to the problem of camp clearance and to note with gratification that the High Commissioner hoped to have sufficient funds to complete this operation. He also noted that due importance had been given to the resettlement of the residual group. However, the thought was expressed by the U.S. Delegate that the UNHCR should use all the funds in its possession to implement the projects due for completion in 1962 instead of carrying over outstanding balances from one year to another.

In connection with the item on international protection, the United States representative reasserted the basic U.S. position which places emphasis on the importance of this permanent function of the UNHCR, particularly as the programs for material assistance are coming to an end.

Discussion of the item on assistance to refugees from Algeria in Morocco and Tunisia afforded an opportunity to point out that the U.S. had maintained a major interest in this program; that since the beginning of the program in 1958, the U.S. had contributed $13,922,750 in various commodities (including the cost of transportation) for the feeding of these refugees; that the U.S. had twice contributed tents and tenting material for their shelter; that up until the end of 1961 the U.S. had contributed an amount of $1,753,375 in cash to the UNHCR for the administration of the program and for the purchase of required items not contributed in kind through other governments and agencies participating in the program; that for 1962, the U.S. has continued its contribution of food and in addition has contributed $600,000 in cash for administration; that since this program may at long last be reaching a satisfactory conclusion, and as the full amount of the $600,000 contributed for this year may not be needed for administration of the relief program, the U.S. has suggested that the UNHCR use these funds for the repatriation program now underway; that in addition to the cash contribution, the U.S. has agreed to contribute food to the League of Red Cross Societies for the feeding of refugees being repatriated in the amounts of 9,000 metric tons wheat, 750 MT flour, 300 MT edible oil, 300 MT beans, and 150 MT dried milk; that in response to an urgent appeal for shelter for the refugees being repatriated, the U.S. has agreed to provide a total of 10,000 tents; that these tents together with the cost of tent poles, ropes, and tent stakes, which must be purchased by the U.S., will amount in total value to a contribution of $800,000; that, in addition, the U.S. has undertaken to provide transportation of these tents to North Africa. In concluding, the U.S. Delegate congratulated the UNHCR and the League of Red Cross Societies on the excellent job being done and all the governments which had contributed to this program.

In the course of the discussion of the Progress Report on UNHCR Regular Programmes for 1959, 1960, and 1961, and on the former UNREF Program, the Delegate from Yugoslavia gave a somewhat lengthy statement in which he expressed appreciation for the work done by the High Commissioner in clearing camps and assisting refugees outside of camps; reviewed the work done by his country in assisting refugees; recalled the joint efforts of the UNHCR, and the Governments of Belgium, France, and the United States begun in 1961 which had made it possible to clear Camp Gerovo; and appealed to the Executive Committee to take steps to include Yugoslavia in the 1963 program of assistance in connection with the integration of refugees in his country. In response the U.S. Delegation emphasized its satisfaction over the final closure of Camp Gerovo and extended congratulations to the High Commissioner, the Government of Yugoslavia and particularly the Government of Belgium which had accepted the great majority of the refugees moved from Gerovo. The U.S. Delegation further stated that the Government of Italy had also provided a haven for some of these refugees, that the Government of France is now undertaking a share of the balance of the refugees formerly in Gerovo, adding that the U.S. Government has participated financially with the UNHCR in the placement of the refugees in Belgium and France.

During the discussion on new refugee situations the Delegate from the Republic of China, noting the recent large influx of Chinese refugees from the mainland into Hong Kong, drew attention to the fact that these refugees were being turned back by the Hong Kong authorities and asked the Committee to give the matter close attention in order to find means of assisting the Hong Kong authorities to solve this problem. The Delegate from the United Kingdom was not prepared to discuss the present situation and merely outlined the Hong Kong Government's policy of immigration control which has been in effect since 1956, as well as restating the problems which faced the Hong Kong authorities with the ever increasing population there. With the tacit agreement of the Committee no particular action was recommended. However, after the close of the official Session, the Delegate from the Republic of China informed the delegations to the Session of a five point program that his Government was prepared to undertake on behalf of these refugees as contained in the final report of the Session. The Delegate from the United Kingdom simply stated at this point that the problem of Chinese refugees would be brought to the attention of his government.

Also during the discussion on New Regugee Situations and following the statements made by the Delegates from the Republic of

China and the United Kingdom, the Observer for Portugal announced that a plan for the assistance of Chinese refugees in Macau had been submitted to the High Commissioner and circulated to the members of the Committee. The plan provides in particular for the construction of a reception center, housing, schools, and industrial premises designed to accommodate some 30,000 refugees. While the Committee members were not prepared to discuss this plan during the Session, at the close of the Session the U.S. Delegate endorsed the action taken by the High Commissioner under his good offices function to encourage contributions towards the establishment of Chinese refugees in Macau, and the Delegate from Belgium stated that the Belgian Government had earmarked part of its 1961 contribution to the UNHCR to be used for the Portuguese Government's project in Macau.

8. Future Meetings

The next meeting of the Executive Committee was provisionally scheduled for the last week in October or first part of November 1962.

9. Conclusions

The work of the Committee was expeditiously handled and no conclusions were reached that were not in accord with the instructions to the United States Representative.

---

319.   Letter From the UN High Commissioner for Refugees (Schnyder) to the Assistant Secretary of State for International Organization Affairs (Cleveland)[1]

Geneva, July 20, 1962.

Dear Mr. Cleveland,

It was a particular pleasure for me to meet with you last Saturday[2] and I want to thank you very much for the warm and encouraging interest you have, again on this occasion, shown for the problems of my Office.

---

[1] Source: National Archives and Records Administration, RG 59, Central Files 1960–63, 324.8411/7–2062. Personal.

[2] Schnyder met with Cleveland on July 14.

The possibility to speak with you about these problems was highly welcome just now, shortly before the Economic and Social Council and then the General Assembly will discuss the question of the future of my Office and at a time when its work in new refugee situations is beginning to consolidate itself and when, finally, strong efforts should be made to finish its major aid projects for "old" refugees within the mandate.

As promised, you will find in the annex a note describing various aspects of the latter problem.[3]

I am convinced that, if we want to complete this task, we must concentrate on it now in the most effective way. This is a challenging but certainly also a realistic aim. Otherwise the work of my Office, as it is now organised, would soon risk becoming somewhat futile.

However, the financial responsibilities with which I am confronted are heavy. The cost of completing the programme for "old" mandate refugees in 1962 and 1963 will total 10.4 million dollars of which 5 million dollars is the target for 1962 and 5.4 million dollars for 1963. In addition, for 1963 my Executive Committee has approved an amount of 1.4 million dollars to meet the needs for new refugee situations throughout the world and to provide for continuing complementary aid activities primarily in Europe. It is already apparent that there will be a shortfall of some 2 million dollars in contributions toward the 1962 regular programmes of 5 million dollars. Assuming governmental contributions for 1963 do not exceed the 1962 level there will be a shortfall of 4 million dollars in the amount required toward the completion of the major aid program which, added to the 1.4 million dollars for new situations and continuing activities in 1963, will make our total unmet needs almost 6 million dollars.

In view of this serious situation I feel it is my responsibility to make an earnest appeal to governments to renew their efforts to provide the necessary funds to carry out those programmes. I shall concentrate my efforts on countries in Europe and I have good hopes that it will be possible to stimulate among them a significant new movement of solidarity. I am also determined to take advantage of some rather promising other sources of income. But it is very evident that, without substantial help from the United States, I shall not be able to fulfil my task, or even to find the European countries ready and confident enough for the act of generosity required from them.

My Office, and indeed the entire international community, is ever aware and appreciative of the leadership and generosity of the Government of the United States over the years in the cause of refugees. Since the establishment of UNRRA immediately after the Second World War, and continuing through the implementation of the programmes of

---

[3] Annex not printed.

the International Refugee Organisation and more recently the Office of the United Nations High Commissioner for Refugees, your Government has been in the front rank of nations who have stimulated the conscience and inspired the efforts of the entire international community on behalf of refugees.

I feel that such an international humanitarian undertaking will ultimately and largely be judged by the way it will be brought to its completion. Countries which have carried and are still carrying the heavy load of that enterprise should therefore be interested in making an appropriate final effort to guarantee the success of this undertaking while, at the same time, highlighting what has been achieved by their earlier sacrifices, amounting literally to hundreds of millions of dollars.

Making such an effort would not only give them this satisfaction but also allow them, later on, to reduce very substantially the contributions to the regular programme of my Office.

Under the given circumstances, I would like to suggest that the United States Government may consider a level of contribution, regarded as justified in relationship to the Programme of complementary assistance of my Office for which it is expected to spend 1.4 million dollars for 1963 (and approximately the same during the following years).

Furthermore, it would be particularly helpful if the United States Government could envisage an appropriate contribution towards meeting the still uncovered financial requirements of my Office under its regular programme for 1962 and 1963, for the latter as far as the last major aid projects are concerned.

I do in no way wish to anticipate the conclusions which the American authorities may finally draw from these facts. But, reading these personal lines, you will perhaps forgive me or even find it useful if, looking on the question in a purely practical way, I give you an estimate of a final contribution with which the United States Government could effectively play its part to make sure that the last major aid projects for "old" mandate-refugees can be properly implemented. Having in mind the requirements of this task, amounting to 10.4 million dollars minus 3 million dollars already contributed, and a possible matching percentage of 33%, I think that a United States participation to the extent of 2 million dollars would well serve the purpose, it being understood that my Office would have to search for any additional (especially private) source of income available to finance the remaining difference. Such a one time United States contribution could hardly be considered unreasonably high if compared with contributions pledged by the United States Government during the last years:

1960—$1,650,000.
1961—$1,300,000.
1962—$1,200,000.

However, what has affected the financial position of the regular programme of my Office in 1961 and 1962 was the fact that 500,000. dollars and 600,000. dollars respectively were earmarked for the entirely separate and self-sustained action in favour of Algerian refugees.

I do not know what kind of budgetary problems could arise in this context. I would only like to point out that the final contribution towards major aid projects should, if possible, be paid or at least pledged early in 1963 so that the work of my Office, implementing these projects, will not be delayed (to the detriment of the refugees as well as of the United Nations budget and of the governments who have to finance it).

I would be most grateful to you for further sympathetic consideration of this matter. When, in this respect, any contacts with the European governments will have led to more tangible results, I shall not fail to inform you.[4]

With kindest regards,

Sincerely yours,

Felix Schnyder

---

[4] On August 6 Cleveland replied to Schnyder in a letter which concluded: "While the United States endorses your program, in view of the economic recovery in Europe to which you make reference, it will be difficult for us to justify increasing our contribution to your regular program for 1963. Contributions which may be made to programs supported by your good offices function will depend upon developments which cannot fully be foreseen at present. As you know we are providing extensive support through other channels to meet refugee needs in other parts of the world, including Cuban refugees in our own country. The requirements which you outline will be carefully reviewed in light of these overall needs in determining the extent of refugee assistance which we will be able to provide through your office." (National Archives and Records Administration, RG 59, Central Files 1960–63, 324.8411/7–2062)

320. Airgram From the Mission in Geneva to the Department of State[1]

A–104   Geneva, August 31, 1962.

SUBJECT

   Continuation of United Nations High Commissioner for Refugees

   Officers of this Mission have been advised by representatives of the UNHCR that the Canadian Ambassador in Geneva, Mr. S.F. Rae, has expressed the desire of his government to sponsor a resolution in the General Assembly supporting the continuation of the Office of the UNHCR for five years. The Canadian Ambassador added that Canada hoped to have the resolution co-sponsored on a wide geographic representation. He mentioned Congo (Leopoldville), Tunisia, or Morocco, a Scandinavian country and another British Commonwealth government as desirable co-sponsors. He did not name but seeks Asiatic co-sponsorship as well. Although the Mission has no copy of this Canadian draft it is endeavoring to obtain one.

   According to Mr. Jamieson, the UNHCR is concerned about the text of the Canadian resolution which in addition to being extremely legalistic, commends the High Commissioner on his assistance in many politically controversial problems, i.e., Angolian refugees in Congo, Algerian refugees, and Chinese refugees in Hong Kong and Macau. The UNHCR feels that such a resolution would antagonize many countries with whom he has good relations.

   The High Commissioner reportedly does not wish to be placed in a position of drafting or dictating his own resolution in the General Assembly. Accordingly, he is reluctant to advise Canadian Ambassador of the problems involved in the Canadian draft although he may do so if necessary.

   Despite this reluctance one staff officer of UNHCR has prepared an informal draft of a resolution which reportedly has the UNHCR's blessing. The text of this draft appears at the end of this airgram.

   Mr. Jamieson was unable to suggest why the Canadian Government has particular interest in sponsoring the UNHCR resolution unless it was to counterbalance Canadian decision recently communicated to the Director of the Intergovernmental Committee for European Migration (ICEM) of Canada's intention to withdraw from that organization.

---

[1] Source: National Archives and Records Administration, RG 59, Central Files 1960–63, 324.8411/8–3162. Limited Official Use. Drafted by E.W. Lawrence (RMA). Repeated to USUN and Ottawa.

UNHCR staff officials also expressed grave concern over a report that the U.S. may be planning to recommend that the composition and method of selection of the UNHCR Executive Committee be placed on a rotating basis similar to that utilized in the UNICEF Committee. Allegedly this concept would envisage the election of some governments for three years, some for two years and others for one year.

The Mission has not been advised by the Department that any such change in the composition or method of selection of the UNHCR Executive Committee is under consideration within the Department and Mission officers informed the UNHCR representatives to this effect.

Comment: Without knowledge of the validity of the report cited by the UNHCR representatives, the Mission considers that a rotation plan for the membership of the Executive Committee would be extremely ill advised for the following reasons:

1. The Executive Committee has been, is, and should be, composed essentially of countries sufficiently sophisticated, affluent and benign to interest themselves in participating in the program to the extent of contributing money to aid refugees. With very few exceptions, all such countries are already members of the Committee. Although it might be possible to rotate some of the recipient nations, the removal of any of the contributing nations would probably mean the loss of that nation's contribution for the period it was off the Committee.

2. Despite the political implications inherent in all refugee problems, the Executive Committee and the UNHCR have been remarkably able to avoid involvement in political controversy in the several years of their existence. The rotation of membership, particularly with some one-year members, would mean raising the question of membership each year with the result that membership or denial of membership would inevitably acquire a much more political complexion. The rotation system would appear, by its very nature, to plunge the UNHCR, or at least his Executive Committee, into the type of political controversy the avoidance of which probably has contributed substantially to whatever success his program has enjoyed to date.

3. The UNHCR program in some of its aspects is so complex that a government elected for only one year would have difficulty learning what it was all about before its year was up.

4. The fact that UNICEF Executive Committee has a rotating membership doesn't appear to have any particular application to the situation of the UNHCR. After all, there is nothing very controversial or political about assistance to children while refugee problems are created by political developments.

The draft resolution prepared by Mr. Jacques Colmar and approved unofficially by the UNHCR follows:

DRAFT RESOLUTION

The General Assembly,

Having considered the report of the United Nations High Commissioner for Refugees and having heard his statement,

Noting with appreciation the progress achieved by the High Commissioner in carrying out his task both in the field of international protection and in the search for permanent solution through voluntary repatriation, integration in the countries of asylum or resettlement in another country,

Satisfied with the way in which the High Commissioner has been able to adapt his action to the needs of new groups of refugees, while keeping within the limits prescribed by his statute and by the good offices resolutions,

Considering that only by sustained humanitarian action on the part of an organisation such as the Office of the High Commissioner is it likely that concrete, constructive and, where possible, final solutions to the problems of refugees will be achieved, and the extension and the deterioration of these problems, in so far as they continue to exist, will be prevented,

Taking into account resolution 1165 (XII) of 26 November 1957 in which it decided to review no later than at its seventeenth session the arrangements for the High Commissioner's Office with a view to determining whether the Office should be further continued beyond 31 December 1963,

Decides to continue the Office of the United Nations High Commissioner for Refugees as from 1 January 1964 and to review no later than at its 22nd session the arrangements for the Office.

Tubby

321.   Telegram From the Mission to the United Nations to the
        Department of State[1]

New York, November 13, 1962, 4 p.m.

1756. Verbatim Text. For: Bell (OES). Third Committee—UNHCR.

Heroux (Canada) presented Mission following draft resolution regarding UNHCR mandate continuation agreed on with 12 co-sponsors (Algeria, Morocco, Norway, Denmark, Colombia, Malaya, Tanganyika, Netherlands, Italy, Sweden, Congo (Lime), Iran):

"The General Assembly,

Noting the report of the United Nations High Commissioner for Refugees,

Recalling its resolution 1165 (XII) of November 1957, in which it was decided to review, not later than at its 17th Session, the arrangements for the Office of the United Nations High Commissioner for refugees with a view to determining whether the Office should be continued beyond 31 December 1963,

Convinced of the continuing need for international action on behalf of refugees,

Considering the valuable work which has been performed by the Office of the High Commissioner in providing international protection for refugees and in promoting permanent solutions for their problems, with the joint participation of governments, international organizations and voluntary agencies;

Commending the High Commissioner for the efforts he has made in finding satisfactory solutions for refugee problems affecting groups of refugees within his mandate and those for whom he lends his Good Offices,

1. Decides to continue the Office of the United Nations High Commissioner for refugees for a further period of five years from 1 January 1964;

2. Requests the High Commissioner to continue to report to the Executive Committee of the High Commissioner's programme, and to abide by the directions which the Committee gives him with regards to refugee situations;[2]

3. Invites member states of the United Nations and the specialized agencies to lend support to the High Commissioner's programme;

---

[1] Source: National Archives and Records Administration, RG 59, Central Files 1960–63, 324.8411 / 11–1362. Confidential. Repeated to Geneva and Ottawa.

[2] The final text of this paragraph reads: "Requests the United Nations High Commissioner for Refugees to continue . . .".

4. Decides to review, not later than at its 22nd Session, the arrangements for the Office of the High Commissioner with a view to determining whether the Office should be continued beyond December, 1968."[3]

Although all USG objections have not been met, Mission convinced serious attempt made to accommodate US position. Draft resolution to be tabled November 14 PM. Request authority to support text without reservations.

Stevenson

[3] The final text of this paragraph reads: ". . . whether the Office should be continued beyond 31 December, 1968." The draft resolution was approved by the UN General Assembly as Resolution 1783 (XVII) of December 7, by a vote of 99 to 0, with 1 abstention.

322.   Report of the U.S. Delegation to the Eighth Session of the Executive Committee of the UN High Commissioner's Program for Refugees[1]

Geneva, December 17, 1962.

[Here follow Section 1, Background of the Conference; Section 2, Agenda as Adopted; Section 3, Participation; Section 4, United States Delegation; Section 5, Organization of the Conference, and Section 6, Work of the Committee.]

7. Working of the Conference

A copy of the report (with apendices) of the Eighth Session of the Executive Committee of the High Commissioner's Program (Document A/AC.96/185) appears as enclosure 3.[2]

In general the Eighth Session of the Executive Committee of the United Nations High Commissioner for Refugees was concerned with receiving a current status report on the work of the Office of the High Commissioner and on progress made in the implementation of previously agreed programs and projects. The Executive Committee also was concerned with the approval of specific projects proposed by the

[1] Source: National Archives and Records Administration, RG 59, Central Files 1960–63, 324.8411/12–1762. Unclassified. Margaret Wiesender and Edward W. Lawrence prepared the report; James T. Devine led the U.S. Delegation.

[2] Not printed.

High Commissioner within the framework of previously agreed programs.

While the United States Delegation was in a position to support the various findings of the Committee, it also had the opportunity to express certain views of the United States Government.

In commenting on the High Commissioner's opening statement, the U.S. Delegate noted that the financial situation seemed to have changed appreciably in the last few months and that a detailed and up-to-date statement reflecting the changes would be useful. Later in discussing the program for the completion of major aid projects, the High Commissioner recapitulated the status of financial contributions and explained that in July the 1962 program showed a shortfall of $2 million. At that date, a total shortfall of $6 million in the financing of the 1962 and 1963 programs taken together, was to be expected. Since then, there was reason to believe that the shortfall might be reduced as much as $1,500,000 with the result that the total target for the balance of 1962 and for 1963 stands at roughly $.5 million.

In accordance with its instructions, the U.S. Delegation supported a motion to note the document on the completion of major aid projects and congratulated the High Commissioner on the fact that progress by the end of 1961 and continuing into 1962 made it possible for his office to plan the comprehensive final effort toward the solution of the problem of "old" refugees.

With regard to the Far Eastern operation, the U.S. Delegation noted that its completion by the end of 1963 depends upon the movement of 2,000 European refugees from Mainland China in 1962 and 2,200 in 1963. However, by the end of July, according to the High Comissioner's report, only 506 had been moved with 172 moved in August, and a further 469 in September. The U.S. Delegation set forth its position that even considering this tremendously increased rate of movement in August and September, there was no assurance that this program could be brought to completion by the end of 1963. Therefore, should the $300,000 for the 1963 program be insufficient for completion of the operation, further activity could be funded under the current program for complimentary assistance.

Further, during the discussion on major aid programs, the U.S. Delegation expressed the concurrence of the U.S. Government in the High Commissioner's proposed allocation of $150,000 for settlement of approximately 200 mandate refugees in Latin America in 1963. It also took the opportunity to concur in the High Commissioner's statement in the Document, that requirements of this kind in Latin America which would develop during the coming year would be met to some extent under the program for complementary assistance.

During the debate on current programs for complementary assistance, the U.S. Delegation had the opportunity to congratulate the High Commissioner on the correct manner in which he has handled the problem of the Rwanda refugees, by taking care of their most urgent needs until they are able to support themselves without prejudice to their eventual return to their homes. It expressed the U.S. Government's opinion that this operation, which has contributed significantly to the stability of the area is a good example of the role the High Comissioner can play in stimulating action and funding under the General Assembly "Good Offices" Resolution. It also noted with interest that plans were being studied together with the Government of Tanganyika and the Government of the Congo to move an additional 25,000 refugees from Burundi into those countries at the request of the Government of Burundi and together with several other members of the Committee, gave support to the High Comissioner's action in this connection.

In accordance with its instructions the U.S. Delegation gave U.S. Government support to the High Commissioner's proposal to allocate $50,000 to assist voluntary agencies in helping extremely needy cases (20,000 to 30,000 persons), in Latin America, including refugees from Cuba.

The Agenda item which brought the most extended discussion was that dealing with housing for refugees as it related in particular to the establishment of a housing loan fund for refugees living in France. It had been proposed at the Seventh Session, that sums arising out of the repayments of loans granted under UNREF and UNHCR projects in so far as they exceeded the $500,000 ceiling fixed for the Emergency Fund, be used for this purpose. The U.S. Delegation, with the U.K. Delegation in strong support, maintained the U.S. position in opposition to this plan as expressed at the previous session. In dealing with the question at this present session, the U.S. Delegation commented on the financial aspects of the proposed scheme rather than on the merits of the project itself. The U.S. Delegation stated that if the Executive Committee was convinced that the urgency of the project justified the use of the already limited UNHCR resources, the U.S. Government would prefer that it be financed as part of the so called "regular program" rather than by the allocation of sums derived from loan repayments which would create an undesirable precedent bringing with it requests for similar financing of additional special programs of this nature.

Although the viewpoint of the U.S. and U.K. Delegations was not sustained by the majority of the Committee, the expression of this viewpoint was instrumental in the Committee's decision to have the matter reviewed again at its next Executive Session. On the basis of a proposal made by the Swedish Representative and a compromise text proposed by the Turkish Representative, the Committee decided by 19 votes to none, with the U.S. and the U.K. Delegations abstaining, to authorize the High Commissioner to:

(a) Sign with the French Government, an agreement of principle concerning the form which the scheme should take, its implementation being dependent on the availability of the necessary funds, and
(b) Use, for the implementation of the said scheme, up to the amount of $100,000 the sum arising out of the repayment of loans made under projects UNREF and UNHCR regular programs in so far as the repayments in question were not required to maintain the Emergency Fund at its ceiling of $500,000, on the understanding that this decision would not prejudice the subsequent policy decisions which the Committee would be called upon to make.

At the conclusion of the discussion on assistance to Algerian refugees, the Committee paid tribute to the United States, along with the French and other Governments, for its support and assistance to these refugees.

8. Future Meetings

The next meeting of the Executive Committee was provisionally scheduled for the last week in April or first week in May, 1963.

9. Conclusions

The work of the Committee was expeditiously handled and with exception of the Committee's decision to approve financial support of the French housing scheme while reserving the decision until the next session as to whether this would be part of the regular program, no conclusions were reached that were not in accord with the instructions to the United States Representative. The U.S. Delegation was particularly gratified both with the manner in which Lady Tweedsmuir, the Chairman, performed her functions and with the work of the Secretariat. The U.S. Delegation joined with other Delegations in congratulating Lady Tweedsmuir on her excellent Chairmanship.

323.   **Memorandum From the Director of the Office of International Administration, Bureau of International Organization Affairs (Hefner) to the Assistant Secretary of State for International Organization Affairs (Cleveland)**[1]

Washington, January 11, 1963.

SUBJECT

UN High Commissioner for Refugees

You will recall Mr. Gardner's note of December 28 on the above subject.[2] In discussion of the matter with Mr. Abba Schwartz so as to determine the position our Government will take, we should keep the following thoughts in mind:

1. Mr. Schnyder might not have performed his duties as UN High Commissioner in a most dynamic way, but he appears to have carried out his mandate and his "good offices" in a creditable manner. As you know, the U.S. Government has sought a rather limited area of responsibility for the organization. There appears to be a consensus here that Mr. Schnyder has performed in a satisfactory manner and if we continue to take a rather restrictive view of the functions of the office, it may be to our advantage to propose another term for him. This conclusion would probably not incur too much opposition from other Member Governments.

2. If we decide that we cannot support the incumbent for another term, we should then determine whether a U.S. national should be supported or a national of another government. In my opinion, there are a number of other international organizations of more importance which calls for our efforts to secure appointments of Americans.

3. Should we decide to support the national of another country, we ought to keep in mind the limited terms of reference we have consistently supported for this organization. If we continue to follow this line we should make certain that we do not support a national who would tend to extend the Charter of the UN High Commissioner beyond that which presently governs.

---

[1] Source: National Archives and Records Administration, RG 59, IO Files: Lot 67 D 378, Refugees. Official Use Only. Drafted by Lewis M. Lind and Frank K. Hefner (IO/OIA). Copies were sent to Elmer M. Falk and John C. Sauls.

[2] Not found.

324. Editorial Note

On November 6, 1963, Secretary-General U Thant proposed that Felix Schnyder's term of office as High Commissioner for Refugees be extended for 2 years, from January 1, 1964, to December 31, 1965. On November 27 the General Assembly decided, by acclamation, to extend Schnyder's term. (National Archives and Records Administration, RG 59, Central Files 1960–63, REF 3 UN, and *Yearbook of the United Nations, 1963*, page 367)

325. Report of the U.S. Delegation to the Tenth Session of the Executive Committee of the UN High Commissioner's Program for Refugees[1]

Geneva, December 11, 1963.

[Here follow Section I, Background of the Conference; Section II, Agenda as Adopted; Section III, Participation; Section IV, United States Delegation; Section V, Organization of the Conference; and Section VI, Work of the Committee.]

The Executive Committee sat as a committee of the whole throughout the proceedings without resort to sub-committees, working parties or other similar arrangements.

VII. Working of the Conference

The report of the Tenth Session of the Executive Committee of the High Commissioner's Program (Document A/AC.96/214) is the official report of the meeting and can be referred to as appropriate. Brief comments on the main items of discussion follow.

In general, the Executive Committee at its Tenth Session was concerned with receiving a report on the last phases of the work of the Office of the High Commissioner as it dealt with the Major Aid

---

[1] Source: National Archives and Records Administration, RG 59, Central Files 1960–63, REF 3 UN. No classification marking. The meeting was held in Geneva September 30–October 8. Stanislaus B. Milus prepared the report; Elmer M. Falk led the U.S. Delegation. Two enclosures were attached but are not printed. The first outlined the agenda of the meeting, the second was a list of participants.

Programs on behalf of the residual group of European Refugees and more specifically in assessing the new direction the UNHCR would follow in meeting new refugee problems which have arisen in other parts of the world.

The Executive Committee also was concerned with the budget proposal being presented by the UNHCR to meet the programs envisaged for CY 1964.

In commenting on the High Commissioner's opening statement the U.S. Representative congratulated the High Commissioner on the work done in the past and noted that the work of his office had been done with a minimum of guidance from the Executive Committee. He stated, however, the desire of his Government that the Executive Committee assume a more active role in giving guidance and direction to the UNHCR program and not merely serve as a "rubber stamp." He expressed the view that the Executive Committee should carefully analyze and evaluate the manner in which the old program was being brought to a close and should assess with more precision what the new programs were to be and in particular the financial arrangements for their implementation. He indicated his Government's reservations toward the financing of the future program as outlined by the UNHCR. The Committee subsequently agreed to defer action on the UNHCR proposal for the future financing of his program.

In concurring with the expression of the Committee in noting with satisfaction document A/AC.96/205 dealing with the Resettlement of Refugees, the U.S. Representative drew the Committee's attention to the immigration record of the U.S. Government. He said that most of the 190 million inhabitants of the United States were immigrants or the offspring of immigrants. He pointed out that recently the United States had given asylum to 200,000 Cuban refugees; that 8,000 Chinese from Hong Kong had already been resettled within U.S. borders; and that the United States had authorized the immigration of 500 difficult cases of whom 350 had already been settled, including many "Jensen" cases. He said that paragraph 21 of the report put the basic principles of resettlement in the right order and agreed that the vital role of the countries of first asylum should be given first consideration. The report, he concluded, gave reason for satisfaction and he was encouraged to note that many countries were prepared to do even more than they had already done. The United States was continuing its direct program of immigration, which was needed in addition to the international program.

In his observations concerning document A/AC.96/206 (Corr. 1 and 2) the U.S. Representative congratulated the mental health adviser on the excellent work he had done. He expressed the desire that at some ensuing session the Committee would be furnished with a detailed final report on the subject, showing the areas in which operations had been cancelled out with the relevant expenditures and results. He agreed that the work should be continued in the field but expressed the hope that the High Commissioner would be able to arrange for the countries concerned to finance and handle such assistance themselves. He expressly drew attention to paragraph 6 of document A/AC.96/209 which in brief expressed the objective that the asylum countries "having been helped to solve serious old problems, should, as far as their present economic conditions allow, be expected to assume the main burden of smaller, currrent and new problems."

In referring to the Administrative Expenditure document (A/AC.96/212) the U.S. Representative noted that his delegation was prepared to support the administrative exependiture for 1964 as proposed in the document. He said that the position of the UNHCR was unique among international organizations in that its administrative budget was included within the United Nations overall budget which meant that the Advisory Committee on Administrative and Budgetary Questions (ACABQ), the Fifth Committee and the General Assembly had ultimate authority in establishing the amount and details of the High Commissioner's operation. Since this budget had already been established in the printed budget of the UN (A/5505) after being reviewed by the ACABQ, he thought it rather late for the Executive Committee to discuss it. He suggested that it endorse what had been done by thought that the members of the Executive Committee, who were more intimately connected than anyone with the operation of the UNHCR programs, should be more closely informed about the development of the administrative budget in the future before it reached the stage of publication. The Executive Committee in noting this document expressed a need for more information in the future on the administrative expenditures of the Office of the High Commisisoner.

Commenting on Section III of document A/AC.96/R.2, *Grant-in-Aid*, the U.S. Representative proposed in respect to 1964, and without prejudice to the principle involved and to the Committee's decisions on the amount of grant-in-aid in future years, to adopt the figure of $350,000 as grant-in-aid for 1964, this amount to be financed by means of interest on investments and savings in the programs. After considerable discussion this proposal was adoped by the Committee.

In commenting on document A/AC.96/213 dealing with the program for 1964, the U.S. Representative expressed continued support for the legal and political protection activities of the UNHCR. He then stated that the French Representative had rightly pointed out that the 1964 program consisted of two broad groups of projects: first, reasonably well justified projects amounting to $1.5 to $1.6 million; and secondly, projects amounting to about $1 million for which firm justification had not been presented. The U.S. Representative said that his Government would be prepared to support the projects in the first group but could not support projects in the second group in the absence of adequate justification. The Committee finally took note of the estimated financial target of $2.6 million submitted by the UNHCR but only approved specific projects amounting to $1,583,000. The UNHCR was authorized to submit additional projects during 1964 for the consideration of the Committee.

Future Meetings

The next meeting of the Executive Committee was provisionally scheduled to open in June 1964.

Conclusions

The work of the Committee was expeditiously handled and the U.S. Delegation was gratified with the manner in which Mr. Alacam, the Chairman, performed his functions and especially with the active participation and interest of many delegations in considering the 1964 UNHCR budget proposal. It was felt that a good start had been made in having the Committee assume its proper responsibility rather than merely act as a "rubber stamp." This feeling was shared by many delegations and hopefully will lead to more careful review of UNHCR projects by member governments in connection with future sessions of the Executive Committee.

Narcotics

326. Instructions From Secretary of State Rusk to the U.S. Representative to the UN Conference for the Adoption of a Single Convention on Narcotic Drugs (Anslinger)[1]

Washington, January 19, 1961.

Sir:

The following instructions will guide you in your capacity as United States Representative to the United Nations Conference for the Adoption of a Single Convention on Narcotic Drugs to be convened at New York, New York, on January 24, 1961. I shall appreciate your communicating these instructions to the other members of the delegation.

The conference at New York will be an official inter-governmental conference called to adopt a single convention on narcotic drugs, to replace the existing multilateral treaties in the field. A position paper has been prepared on specific items of the agenda and on the principal issues expected to arise. This paper, which is enclosed, constitutes a part of your instructions.[2]

It will be noted that the enclosed position paper bears an administrative control designation. Even after the substance of this paper has been made known to the conference in the presentation of the position of this Government, there may remain in it material that should not be revealed. For this reason the position paper is to be protected in accordance with its administrative control designation even after the United States position has been made public.

In the absence of specific authorization from the Department, no representative of the United States may offer or subscribe to any written or oral statement that might be construed to commit this Government to a definite course of action requiring specific approval by the President or the Congress or that might involve an obligation to expend governmental funds not previously appropriated and allocated.

---

[1] Source: National Archives and Records Administration, RG 59, Central Files 1960–63, 341.9/1–1961. Official Use Only. Anslinger was Commissioner of Narcotics in the Department of the Treasury. The instructions were drafted on January 18 by Chester G. Dunham (IO/OIC) and cleared and approved by Assistant Secretary of State for International Organization Affairs Francis O. Wilcox.

[2] Not found.

Your delegation has been officially accredited to this conference and is accordingly attending in an official capacity for the United States Government. Any statement made for the delegation or by its members will be interpreted as the official views of the Government and not the views of individual members or of organizations or groups with which they are affiliated. The delegation accordingly must act as a unit. You are responsible for maintaining necessary conformity within the delegation, and in the event of a division among the members of the delegation, your decision shall be final and binding.

If prompted to express opinions on United States policies or programs not germane to the conference, delegation members should be especially mindful to be cautious in their remarks and to identify them as personal.

As head of the delegation you are responsible for its organization and the specific assignment of work to each member. If because of absence, disability, or any other reason you should become unable to discharge your duties, you may delegate your authority for as long as necessary to another member of the delegation of appropriate rank.

Upon reaching New York, you should report promptly to the United States Mission to the United Nations in order that the United States Representative to the United Nations may be informed of your arrival. You should look to the Mission for any official assistance required during the conference. Substantive matters affecting foreign policy not covered by your instructions should be discussed with the Mission and, if appropriate, referred to the Department without delay.

Funds have been made available to the delegation for the official entertainment of foreign delegates and officials of the conference secretariat, and the Mission has been authorized to expend these funds at your discretion. The amount approved was determined on the basis of experience with similar meetings and an appraisal of any special circumstances concerning this meeting. You are responsible for ensuring that representation activities are carefully planned and that expenditures do not exceed the amount authorized unless prior approval has been received from the Department.

Upon the successful negotiation and conclusion of an instrument concerning narcotic drugs, the Department will recommend to the President that he issue full power to sign the instrument on behalf of the United States of America. When the document has been issued, indicating that the President has invested you with full power to sign in the name of the United States the instrument agreed upon at the conference, it will be transmitted to you. Signature of the instrument for the United States will be only by you and such other person or persons as may be designated in the Presidential document. It is to be understood that signature will not commit the United States to the terms of the instrument until the stipulated requirements for bringing it into force have been fulfilled and until such action as may be required by this Government has been taken to make the instrument effective for the United States. If it should be deemed necessary or advisable during the conference to sign the instrument subject to a specific reservation or understanding, inscribed together with the signature, instructions for this purpose should be sought. The document should be deposited with the conference authorities at such time as you deem appropriate. If its use is not required, the document will be returned by you to the Department of State. Aside from the instrument itself, you are authorized to sign other statements of findings reached as a result of the labors of the meeting, provided they are within the terms of these instructions and are in the form of final acts, resolutions, recommendations, or the like, and not in the form of a further treaty or other binding international agreement.

During the course of the meeting the Department will appreciate being kept fully informed of all significant developments. The reporting facilities of the Mission are available to you for this purpose.

Within thirty days after the close of the meeting, you are requested to submit a report covering the work of the delegation and the final actions taken. This report, which will become a part of the permanent records of the United States Government, should follow as closely as possible the enclosed guide entitled "Reports Required of United States Delegations to International Conferences" (IC/7).[3] You are also requested to submit a separate classified report covering the subjects mentioned in the above guide under the heading "Classified Report of the United States Delegation." Reports should be addressed to the Secretary of State and marked for the attention of the Office of International Conferences. In addition, you should assure that four complete sets of all official conference documents and United States Delegation documents are assembled and sent to the Department marked for the attention of the Office of International Conferences.

The Department of State is pleased that you will again head a United States Delegation to an international conference concerned with the problem of narcotic drugs and its confident that you will effectively represent the interests of this Government at this important meeting.

Very truly yours,

For the Secretary of State:

Francis O. Wilcox[4]
Assistant Secretary

---

[3] Not found.

[4] Printed from a copy that indicates Wilcox signed the original.

327. Memorandum From the Deputy Director of the Office of International Economic and Social Affairs, Bureau of International Organization Affairs (Mulliken) to the Deputy Assistant Secretary of State for International Organization Affairs (Gardner)[1]

Washington, April 10, 1961.

SUBJECT

Meeting of the Interdepartmental Committee on Narcotics—Friday, April 7

A meeting of the Interdepartmental Committee on Narcotics was held at the White House from 2:30 p.m. to 5:00 p.m. Friday, April 7. Mr. Flues, Assistant Secretary of the Treasury, served as Chairman and there were representatives present from the Department of Health, Education and Welfare, the Department of Defense, the Department of Justice, the White House Staff, and the Bureaus of Narcotics and of Customs. The Department of State was represented by Mr. Gardner of IO, Mr. Bevans of L/T, and Mr. Mulliken of OES.

The announced purpose of the meeting was to provide for the Committee being briefed by Mr. Anslinger, Commissioner of Narcotics, on the recent negotiation of a Single Convention on Narcotic Drugs and to consider Mr. Anslinger's recommendations that the U.S. signature to the Single Convention be held in abeyance until such time as the indications are that the 1953 Protocol will definitely not come into force.[2]

Mr. Anslinger gave an account of the development of the Single Convention and pointed to what he considered its weakness in that it did not provide a closed list of countries which could export opium. He referred to the 1953 Protocol, which contained such a list, and argued that the U.S. should continue its efforts to secure the ratification of the 1953 Protocol prior to considering signing the Single Convention. Mr. Bevans of L/T and Mr. Gardner of IO presented the arguments that the Single Treaty was on balance a satisfactory instrument and should be signed, especially since the U.S. had taken the lead in the ten years of negotiations leading up to the formulation of the Single Convention. It was further pointed out that the 1953 Protocol had been in existence for eight years and had not yet been ratified in such a manner as to bring it into effect and the prospects of appropriate ratification in the near future were not promising.

[1] Source: National Archives and Records Administration, RG 59, Central Files 1960–63, 341.9/4–1061. No classification marking. Drafted by Otis E. Mulliken (IO/OES).

[2] Reference is to the Single Convention on Narcotic Drugs, done at New York on March 30, 1961 (18 UST 1407), and to the Protocol for Limiting and Regulating the Cultivation of the Poppy Plant, the Production of, International and Wholesale Trade in, and Use of Opium, done at New York on June 23, 1953 (14 UST 10).

Most of the discussion took place between the representatives of the Department of State and the Department of the Treasury, with the other members of the Committee asking questions for clarification.

During Mr. Anslinger's presentation, he referred to the fact that Mr. Flues was going to be attending a meeting of the Commission on Narcotic Drugs in Geneva in the near future and that he could easily proceed to Ankara, Turkey to persuade the Turkish Goverment to ratify the 1953 Protocol. The ratification by Turkey would put the Protocol into effect. The general sentiment of the Committee was that this might be done without necessary prejudice to the signing of the Single Convention and that the delay involved was not significant.

The Committee agreed that the Department of State would decide whether there were any overriding objections to approaching the Turkish Government on this matter.

Subsequent to this decision, the Committee would meet again to decide whether the U.S. negotiating position with respect to the Turkish Government would be strengthened if the U.S. had signed the Single Convention.

It was also agreed that before a decision on signing the Single Convention was taken there would be a consultation with Congressional leaders, but there was no agreement as to how this consultation should be arranged.

Mr. White of the White House Staff requested the Department of State and the Department of the Treasury to provide Committee members in writing with the argumentation which had been advanced in favor of and in opposition to the signing of the Single Convention.

There then took place a discussion as to whether there should be a White House Conference on Narcotics. The President during the campaign had promised that he would call such a conference. Officials concerned with narcotics problems have been skeptical as to the value of such a conference. At the same time, the domestic political ramifications of the problem have been recognized. It was decided to set up a subcommittee under the chairmanship of the representative from the Attorney General's office. The Department of State was requested to provide a representative.

328.   Report of the U.S. Delegation to the Sixteenth Session of the UN Commission on Narcotic Drugs[1]

Washington, May 23, 1961.

[Here follow Section 1, Background of the Conference; Section 2, Agenda for Conference; Section 3, Participation in Conference; Section 4, United States Delegation; and Section 5, Organization of the Conference.]

6. Work of the Committee.

The Committee on Illicit Traffic reviewed the illicit narcotic traffic for the year 1960. The work of the Committee was guided by summaries on illicit transactions and seizures, by annual report documents, by discussion of international investigations, and by special documents prepared for study by the Committee.

The representative of the United States on this Committee presented documented cases showing international cooperation in tracing the source of the narcotic contraband, and obtained endorsement of strict enforcement procedures for presentation to the Commission.

7. Work of the Conference.

The Commission adopted two resolutions presented by the United States Delegation, as follows:

a. *Abuse of Drugs (Drug Addiction)*

The Commission on Narcotic Drugs,

(1) *Declares* that one of the most effective methods of treatment for narcotic addiction is civil commitment in a hospital institution having a drug-free atmosphere;
(2) *Urges* Member Governments having a serious drug addiction problem, and the economic means to do so, to provide such facilities.

b. *Illicit Traffic*

(1) *Recognizing* the urgent need for increasingly effective narcotic enforcement procedures, for close co-operation between governments with prompt exchange of information, and for strong national legislation including adequate narcotic penalty provisions,

(2) *Realizing* that too great a disparity in penalties awarded in different countries to convicted traffickers and smugglers of narcotics prej-

---

[1] Source: National Archives and Records Administration, RG 59, Central Files 1960–63, 341.9/5–2361. No classification marking. Assistant Secretary of the Treasury A. Gilmore Flues headed the U.S. Delegation.

udices international efforts to counter illicit traffic in cocaine, opium, morphine, heroin and cannabis in many areas of the world,

(3) *Considering* that in countries having a serious problem of illicit narcotic traffic sustained programs of strict enforcement which would ensure the arrest of narcotic traffickers and the certainty that on conviction they would be confined for substantial minimum periods without any provisional release, in accordance with the constitution of any country concerned,

(a) *Recommends* that Governments having a serious problem of illicit traffic in narcotics take necessary measures for close co-operation and for prompt exchange of information and to ensure imposition of adequate sentences against such unlawful narcotic traffickers.

The Commission adopted a resolution presented by the United Kingdom calling for a study and ratification of the Single Convention on Narcotic Drugs, as follows:

(c) *The Single Convention on Narcotic Drugs*

The Commission on Narcotic Drugs recommends to the Economic and Social Council the adoption of the following draft resolution:

The Economic and Social Council,

(1) *Noting with satisfaction* that the Plenipotentiary Conference called under the terms of its resolution 689 J (XXVI) for the adoption of a single convention on narcotic drugs has adopted such a treaty,

(2) *Considering* that this Convention when in force will in particular codify the multilateral treaty law in this field and simplify the international control machinery,

(3) *Desirous* that the international society of States should benefit from these new provisions as soon as may be possible; *desirous* also that the transitional period of simultaneous existence of the old and new treaty system should be shortened to the greatest possible extent, and

(4) *Noting* that under the terms of the new Convention the ratification and accession of forty States will be necessary for its coming into force,

(a) *Invites* all Members of the United Nations and all non-member States which are Parties to the Statute of the International Court of Justice or members of a specialized agency of the United Nations, to study as expeditiously as possible the Single Convention on Narcotic Drugs, 1961, opened for signature at United Nations Headquarters in New York on 30 March 1961, with a view to signing and ratifying, or acceding to, the Convention, as the case may be.

8. Future Meetings.

The United States Delegation was able to obtain a postponement until the 17th session of debate on a resolution sponsored by Turkey,

United Arab Republic, and Yugoslavia concerning international control of barbiturates. The resolution proposed is as follows:

Control of Barbiturates

The Commission,

Recalling resolutions VI and VII adopted by the Commission on Narcotic Drugs at its twelfth session,

Considering the social danger and the danger to public health arising from the abuse of barbiturates, as reported by the World Health Organization,

Recommends

a. that governments should take appropriate measures to place the production, distribution and use of such drugs under strict control;

b. that the competent organs of the United Nations and the World Health Organization should examine the necessity and the possibility of adopting adequate measures for the international control of such drugs.

9. Conclusions.

At the opening of the Sixteenth Session of the Commission on Narcotic Drugs, the following statements were made with reference to the Question of the Representation of China. The statements of the USSR, Hungary, and Yugoslavia were apparently political instructions. Statements of this nature are usually made at the beginning of each meeting of the Commission.

QUESTION OF THE REPRESENTATION OF CHINA

Mrs. Vassilieva (Union of Soviet Socialist Republics) expressed regret that the People's Republic of China, a country which occupied nearly one-quarter of the total land area of the globe and had a population of more than 600 million inhabitants, was not represented on the Commission.

Mr. Liang (China) found it regrettable that the representative of the USSR had once again raised a political issue in a functional Commission. The General Assembly at its fifteenth session had rejected proposals to discuss the question of the representation of China and it was out of place for a body such as the Commission to touch upon it.

Mr. Vertes (Hungary) deplored the fact that China was unable to participate in the campaign against narcotic drugs. The possibilities of increased international co-operation in that field were hampered by the fact that the Central People's Government of the People's Republic of China was not represented on the Commission.

Mr. Flues (United States of America) regretted that the representative of the USSR had raised the question of China's representation. The

Commission on Narcotic Drugs, like other functional commissions, had repeatedly refused to consider the issue on the grounds that it was not competent to do so.

Mr. Nikolic (Yugoslavia) urged that the Chinese seat on the Commission should be occupied by a representative of the Central People's Government of the People's Republic of China.

The Chairman said that the views expressed would be noted in the summary record of the meeting.

The USSR, Hungary, Yugoslavia, India, and the United Kingdom abstained in the vote on the United States sponsored resolution for civil commitment of narcotic addicts. The United Kingdom, explaining its abstention, stated its own narcotic addiction problem was minor.

Twelve delegations, including the USSR, Hungary, India, Yugoslavia, joined the United States Delegation in voting for strict enforcement of narcotic laws, including minimum mandatory penalty laws for traffickers.

Turkey abstained, its representative stating that his country believed strict controls should be applied in all countries rather than in only those countries having a serious narcotic problem, as stated in the resolution.

The United Kingdom resolution on the Single Convention on Narcotic Drugs was adopted with 12 votes for, and 3 abstentions, they being the USSR, Yugoslavia, and Hungary.

The United States proposal to postpone debate on barbiturate control until the 17th session was adopted by 8 votes for (United States, United Kingdom, Canada, Mexico, Iran, Netherlands, Peru, and China), 2 against (India and Hungary), and 5 abstentions (USSR, Yugoslavia, Hungary, United Arab Republic, and France).

Generally, Soviet Bloc action during the session was at a minimum. The United States was able to maintain leadership and substantial support throughout the session. The support of the Canadian delegate as Chairman and a close working relationship with the United Kingdom delegate were strong factors. Among the observers, representatives of Thailand, Greece, Burma, Iran, Ghana, and Brazil were particularly strong in their interest and support of the United States Delegation.

The two resolutions adopted under the sponsorship of the United States Delegation represent important forward steps in repressing and correcting narcotic addiction and traffic. The delay on the resolution concerning barbiturates was obtained to prevent the adoption of a resolution concerning drugs which are not significantly found in the illicit traffic, and which more appropriately should be subjected to strict national control rather than international control.

The United States is a recognized leader in narcotics control, both licit and illicit, throughout the world. It has vigorously encouraged and assisted every effort toward better controls wherever and whenever narcotics problems exist. The resolutions sponsored by the United States Delegation and adopted by the Commission are significant milestones along the road toward effective narcotics control, and as expressions of world opinion speaking through such an expert body as the Commission represents must have a definite impact on the programs and procedures for narcotic control within the several countries. As such steps as civil commitment of narcotic addicts for treatment in a drug-free environment, closer cooperation between governments, more prompt and comprehensive interchange of information, and minimum mandatory sentences for illicit traffickers, become accepted procedures, enforcement authorities the world over will look confidently toward achieving their control objectives, while people everywhere will benefit from an alleviation of the narcotic addiction curse.

---

329.   **Paper Prepared by the Head of the Narcotics Division of the United Nations (Yates)[1]**

Geneva, undated.

1. The criticism of the Single Convention made by the U.S. at the Narcotics Commission session was that illicit production would be greater under the Single Convention than under the existing conventions (E/CN.7/SR.466).[2]

---

[1] Source: National Archives and Records Administration, RG 59, IO Files: Lot 67 D 378, Deputy Assistant Secretary Richard N. Gardner Files, 1961–65, Opium. No classification marking. In a July 7 covering letter to Deputy Assistant Secretary Gardner, Walter Kotschnig, Deputy U.S. Representative to the Economic and Social Council, noted that he had asked Yates for summary arguments in favor of ratification of the Single Convention by the United States. He had concluded that "from where I sit it is absolutely plain to me that we ought to ratify the Single Convention both because it will make for better rather than for weaker controls, and because it would be disastrous if two systems of control were set up if the 1953 Protocol should be ratified by a sufficient number of countries." He urged Gardner not to attribute the paper to Yates.

[2] U.S. Representative A. Gilmore Flues commented that the United States was concerned that the Single Convention, by allowing additional countries to cultivate and export opium, would facilitate an increase in illicit opium production. (United Nations, Economic and Social Council, *Commission on Narcotic Drugs, 16th Session, Summary Record of the 466th Meeting, Held at the Palais des Nations, Geneva, Monday, 1 May, 1961 at 10:30 a.m.,* p. 3)

2. First, as regards *licit* production, since surplus licit production tends to find its way into illicit channels. Under the existing conventions there is no international obligation *at all* to limit production of opium, *or* to control the process of cultivation and production, if production takes place, by a Government monopoly, *or* against exporting opium.

3. Under the Single Convention, on the other hand,

(a) new producers for export would have to notify the Board, up to 5 tons, and get the permission of the Council over 5 tons (Article 24);

(b) *all* countries producing opium, for internal consumption or for export, would have to set up a strict internal Government monopoly on the lines of the Indian system (Article 23);

(c) subject to the transitional provisions (Article 49), which apply *only* to countries in which opium smoking or opium eating is at present traditional and legal, and which have a limited life, *all* countries would be under an obligation to limit the cultivation, production and consumption of opium to medical and scientific purposes (Article 4).

4. Comment as regards Article 24. It is quite true that the limitation provisions, either as regards more or less than 5 tons, do not provide for any specific limits and are not worth much in themselves: except that they do provide for advance notice of *intention* to export by new exporters—which, if any country did develop this intention, could be a valuable provision, since it would enable the matter to be discussed in advance and considerations such as those below to be pointed out.

But the fact is that, during the U.N. period, for commercial and social reasons, *even though* there has been no limitation on producing opium for export, countries have in fact been giving up such production—Iran and Afghanistan in particular.

The licit market for opium amounts to something between 800 and 900 tons a year. There is not enough money in this—900 tons at $20 a kilo—$18 million as a rough estimate—to make it worth while for more than a very few big producers. The cost of administering a highly-policed Government monopoly (Article 23) emphasizes this situation. In fact, India and Turkey have a dominating position in this market in the Western world, with well-established connexions with purchasers, and new producers would be likely to burn their fingers. (Burma for instance which had ideas of this kind appears to have given them up.)

Again, the largetst proportion of the opium in licit trade is used to produce codeine. As soon as a fully acceptable synthetic replacement for codeine comes into wide clinical use—several have already been marketed with partial success—the long-term outlook for opium will be further affected.

5. *Illicit opium.* The Single Convention maintains and does not weaken the obligations of Governments as regards fighting the illicit

traffic. For those countries which are constitutionally able to accept the 1936 Convention, that convention will continue, while in Articles 35 and 36 the Single Convention provides more general obligations which should be acceptable to all Governments—many of whom are not now bound by any such obligations—and not only to the limited group of the 1936 Convention.

The U.S. spokesman stated in the Commission that U.S. experts estimated that under the existing conventions the illicit production amounted to 3,070 tons and that under the Single Convention it would be 5,575 tons. Others in the Commission were simply not able to follow this argument (E/CN.7/SR.466).[3]

There is nothing in the Single Convention to encourage either the licit or illicit production of opium, and much to control licit production and to stop leaks therefrom. It is difficult to see how any valid estimates can be made for a hypothetical future. Are the U.S. prepared to name publicly even one country in which illicit production will go up as a result of the Single Convention? The main factor in the increase or decrease in illicit opium in the future must be the relative effort which the Governments concerned put into the policy of limitation and suppression.

Attention is drawn in this connexion to para. 234 of the Commission report (E/3512) in which a short account is given of the frank views expressed by a group of administrators from South-East Asia regarding the admittedly high production of illicit opium in that region. This passage indicates the sort of effort that is required, over and above any type of action that can be expressed in treaty form, if headway is to be made as regards indigenous opium production in such regions.

6. *1953 Protocol and the Single Convention.* The 1953 Protocol would come into force if ratified by one further producing country of the following 7: Bulgaria, Greece, India, Iran, Turkey, USSR, Yugoslavia; India and Iran having already ratified, and Iran's ratification being valid for this purpose even though it is in fact no longer a producer of opium.

7. The 1953 Protocol applies to opium only, not to other narcotics, and its provisions are considerably different from, and more elaborate in a number of respects than, those of the Single Convention.

8. Article 44 of the Single Convention provides that, as from its coming into force, the Single Convention will replace, as between the parties to it, the older conventions, including the 1953 Protocol if that Protocol should by then have come into force.

---

[3] Flues' statement is ibid.

9. The effect of the 1953 Protocol coming into effect before the Single Convention would therefore be very confusing. It would introduce a new regime for opium—and one which a number of producers have said they regard as unacceptable—for a period which would not be known in advance. This regime would then be superseded within a relatively short time by that of the Single Convention. The process would be burdensome and confusing both for producing and importing countries and for the international organs, especially the Board.

10. The time it will take for the Single Convention to be ratified can of course only be guessed. It requires ratification by 40 Governments, but without any limitations to their being producers, manufacturers, etc. 43 countries signed the Convention at the close of the conference. There are more than 100 countries entitled to ratify it, and it is thought that there are considerably more than 40 who are quite willing to ratify it.

11. The disadvantages also of two international regimes, adhered to by different groups of countries, i.e. one under the Single Convention, and one under the old conventions plus the 1953 Protocol, continuing for an extended period of time *after* the Single Convention comes into force need no underlining.

---

330.   Telegram From the Embassy in Turkey to the Department of State[1]

Ankara, July 15, 1961, noon.

63. Pass Treasury. Reference: Deptel 21.[2] After briefing by Ambassador per reftel Flues accompanied by Cusack Narcotics/Rome and Embassy officer during three-day Ankara visit conferred with Minister Agriculture Tosun and Minister Commerce/Acting Minister Foreign Office Baydur, Minister Interior Zeytinoglu, Minister Finance Kurdas and Assistant Secretary General Foreign Office Hayta along lines reftel.

---

[1] Source: National Archives and Records Administration, RG 59, Central Files 1960–63, 341.9/7–1561. Official Use Only. Repeated to Athens and Rome.

[2] Telegram 21 notified the Embassies in Ankara and Athens that Assistant Secretary Flues planned to visit Ankara and Athens to "explore in general terms implications of ratification by these two countries of [the 1953 Opium] Protocol." Flues was to inform Turkish and Greek officials that the United States had not decided whether to ratify the Single Convention. (Ibid., 341.9/7–761)

Suggested in general terms desirability GOT reexamining implications ratification 1953 protocol particularly in terms provisions governing opium production/export in the several previous treaties in light
provisions included Single Convention. Importance to Turkey as one of
authorized producing countries of adequate international control legislation reemphasized as well as importance to US. Very receptive attitude evinced by Ministers Commerce, Agriculture, Finance, Interior.

Hayta interested, sympathetic but said frankly re-look unlikely
change GOT position on 1953 protocol which developed by technical
experts. This connection also conferred M. Ozkul, Turkell UN Narcotics
Commission and top Turkish Technical Adviser International Narcotic
Affairs now on leave as member constituent assembly. His views well
known Department and Treasury. Has been committed to Turkish non-
ratification 1953 protocol for past eight years and talk indicated he
unlikely change views. Hayta however promised take new look at
Turkish position on 1953 protocol as well as Single Convention. He
agreed persuasiveness previous GOT objections to protocol might be
lessened by deficiencies controls in Single Convention to point where
advantages ratifying protocol might prevail. Hayta stressed, Flues
agreed talk pertained usefulness re-look, not substantive discussion
GOT position. All Ministers voiced thanks usefulness conversations as
contribution to GOT study. Especial support for re-study/discussion
GOT position given by Kurdas who took initiative stress broad
social/economic aspects favoring strictest control this critical field.

Hare

---

331.   **Telegram From the Embassy in Greece to the Department of
        State[1]**

Athens, July 17, 1961, 7 p.m.

97. Reference: Department telegram 24.[2]

1. Assistant Secretary Flues of Treasury and Cusack arrived Athens
July 13 for two-day visit. After meeting with Chargé d'Affaires, Flues

---

[1] Source: National Archives and Records Administration, RG 59, Central Files
1960–63, 341.9/7–1761. Official Use Only. Repeated to Ankara and Rome.

[2] Not printed. (Ibid., 341.9/7–1661)

and Cusack, accompanied by Embassy officer and USOM public safety advisor, called on following: Deputy Interior Minister Kalantzis and staff; Director Customs Research and Investigation, Ministry Finance; Foreign Office Director General Palamas; Foreign Office Deputy Director Economic Affairs; and Bank of Greece Governor Zolotas (courtesy call).

2. Flues reviewed with Greek officials present and pending international narcotics controls, pointing out weaknesses "Single Convention" and advantages 1953 Narcotics Protocol. He suggested Greeks re-study their position and give serious thought to ratification 1953 Protocol, which would bring it into effect. This would provide reasonably satisfactory control system pending efforts US and others to modify and strengthen "Single Convention."

3. Greek officials expressed appreciation for presentations by Flues and Cusack, some indicating they previously unaware implications of ratification 1953 Protocol. Palamas said GOG would undertake re-examination its position in light of points raised by Flues. Both Palamas and Foreign Office Deputy of Economic Affairs commented they not aware any technical objections to ratification 1953 Protocol, but Greece would have to take into acount Turkish views this subject. Lalantzis showed lively interest in Flues' remarks. Ministry Finance officials said concerned only with the technical aspects of control which would re-study. They asked Flues if competent US narcotics control officer could be detailed Greece for a few months to help reorganize narcotics contraband controls. Flues offered look into this and give answer.

4. Flues remarked on departing Greece that his discussions here very useful and that he intended follow up by forwarding memoranda on this subject for use by GOG officials in position re-study.

Bennett

332.   Letter From the President of Eli Lilly and Company (Beesley) to the Commissioner of the Bureau of Narcotics, Department of the Treasury (Anslinger)[1]

Indianapolis, July 26, 1961.

Dear Commissioner Anslinger:

As a producer of narcotics and a company much concerned with public health and proper control over the manufacture and distribution of narcotics, we have studied carefully the Single Convention on Narcotic Drugs of 1961, which was adopted March 25, 1961, by a Plenipotentiary Conference convened by the United Nations. We should like to express to you our views in relation to this document.

It is our considered judgment, after thorough analysis of the Single Convention, that it radically departs from the initial purpose of codifying the existing treaties and of supplementing these treaties with such additional measures as were required to attain more effective international control. In our opinion, this Convention, on the contrary, would substantially relax existing controls in opposition to the public interest.

In this presentation of our views, we shall not attempt to enumerate the many inadequate provisions of the Single Convention but shall comment on some of its principal weaknesses.

In general, it is quite evident that the reservations by which individual nations may depart from the general requirements for transitional periods lasting for as long as twenty-five years seriously weaken the force and control of the treaty. In effect, these reservations practically negate international control of the use of narcotics.

Perhaps even more serious is the threat to world health posed by the relaxation of production and export controls over opium. So-called "new countries" may, under the Convention, export 5 tons of opium annually without international control or sanction.

While the Convention provides for establishment of a Narcotics Control Board, it also permits signers to void the right of the board to

1. establish estimates for a country which has failed to file its annual estimate reports [Article 12, Sections 2 and 3][2]

---

[1] Source: National Archives and Records Administration, RG 59, Central Files 1960–63, 341.9/7–2661. No classification marking. In a covering letter to Secretary Rusk, Beesley wrote that, in his company's opinion, the Single Convention did not provide adequate international controls over the production and distribution of addicting drugs and should not be signed or ratified by the United States. Otis E. Mulliken, Acting Director of the Office of International Economic and Social Affairs, acknowledged Beesley's letter on August 7. (Ibid.)

[2] All brackets in the source text.

2. examine statistical returns to determine whether a party has complied with the provisions of the Convention [Article 13]

3. ask for explanations from a government it believes is not abiding by the provisions of the Convention [Article 14, Section 1(A)]

4. call upon such government to adopt remedial measures [Article 14, Section 1(B)]

5. call the attention of the parties, the Commission of Narcotics, and the Economic and Social Council of the United Nations to a government's failure to adopt recommended remedial measures [Article 14, Section 1(C)]

6. recommend imports and exports be stopped until compliance is achieved [Article 14, Section 2].

In short, the Narcotics Control Board would not have the authority needed to control parties unwilling to honor the intent of the Convention. Many of its rulings could be ignored and flouted with impunity.

Under the Single Convention, parties may also elect to export drugs to another country in excess of the established import quotas for that country. They may also elect to void the final determination by the International Court of Justice of any dispute relating to the interpretation or application of the Convention.

It is obvious that these provisions emasculate the Convention as an effective tool for international control of addicting drugs.

Only one more nation is needed to bring the 1953 Protocol into force. In view of the fact that this Protocol, together with existing treaties would provide far more effective international machinery for proper control of the production and distribution of addicting drugs, we believe that it would be very much against the public interest for the United States to sign and ratify the Single Convention.

We should welcome an opportunity to discuss this matter in greater detail with you or others in government who are concerned with the tremendously important problem of adequate international control of addicting drugs.

Sincerely,

Eugene N. Beesley[3]

---

[3] Printed from a copy that bears this typed signature.

333.   Memorandum of Conversation[1]

Washington, October 18, 1961.

SUBJECT

Single Convention on Narcotic Drugs, 1961

PARTICIPANTS

Mr. Mehmet Baydar, First Secretary, Embassy of the Republic of Turkey
Mr. Charles I. Bevans, Assistant Legal Adviser for Treaty Affairs
Miss Sylvia E. Nilsen, L/T
Miss Helen Dougherty, OES

Mr. Baydar came in at 10:30 this morning by appointment to discuss the above-mentioned subject.

Mr. Baydar explained that his Government was seriously considering ratifying the Single Convention, but wished to have the views of other governments before reaching a decision. He stated that he was unfamiliar with the narcotics treaties, and that someone in the Embassy had given him a short briefing on the 1948[2] and 1953 Protocols and the Single Convention.

I informed him that the United States Government had not yet reached a position regarding the Single Convention; that the Convention was not signed on behalf of the United States during the period it was opened for signature because no position was reached during that time. I pointed out to him that among the matters requiring further consideration by this Government was the omission from the Single Convention of a closed list of export-producing countries. It was pointed out that under the terms of the Single Convention any country could export up to 5 tons of opium which it produced, provided it first notified the International Narcotics Control Board and indicated the names of the countries it expected to export such opium to and the controls in force as required by the Single Convention. Under the 1953 Protocol only the 7 named export-producing countries would be permitted to export opium. It was pointed out that at the present time any country is free to produce opium and to export it so far as the narcotics conventions in force are concerned. In the course of the discussion it was brought out that thirty-nine States have ratified the 1953

---

[1] Source: National Archives and Records Administration, RG 59, Central Files 1960–63, 341.9/10–1861. No classification marking. Drafted by Bevans.

[2] Reference is to the Protocol Bringing Under International Control Drugs Outside the Scope of the Convention of July 13, 1931, for Limiting the Manufacture and Regulating the Distribution of Narcotic Drugs, as Amended by the Protocol Signed on December 11, 1946; done at Paris on November 19, 1948 (2 UST 1629).

Protocol but that among the States which had not ratified were the United Kingdom, the USSR, and the African States.

I pointed out to him also that we were giving serious consideration to the reservations permitted with respect to certain articles but that we were very much gratified to see that the States which took advantage of those reservations at the time of signature did not do so to the full extent permitted but limited the effect of the reservations to their relations with countries not permitted to participate in the Convention.

I told Mr. Baydar that we would keep him informed of any position reached by this Government with respect to the Single Convention.

---

334. Telegram From the Department of State to the Mission to the United Nations[1]

Washington, December 6, 1961, 9:20 p.m.

1456. Re your 1774.[2] U.S. position on Single Convention on Narcotic Drugs 1961 not yet determined. Two U.S. representatives to whom reference was made were probably Assistant Secretary Flues of Treasury and Mr. James Reed of Justice who recently visited a number of countries on Treasury business. In course of discussion of Treasury business they also exchanged views and comments on the Single Convention with the representatives of the other governments. Both men however stressed that the views expressed at this time were those of Treasury and Justice and not agreed U.S. Government views which have not yet been formulated.

Rusk

---

[1] Source: National Archives and Records Administration, RG 59, Central Files 1960–63, 341.9/11–2461. Official Use Only. Drafted by Mulliken and Flues, cleared by Bevans and Gardner, and approved by Assistant Secretary Cleveland.

[2] In telegram 1774 from USUN, November 24, Stevenson informed the Department that Secretary-General Thant had been told that two U.S. representatives had been trying to persuade governments to adhere to the 1953 Protocol rather than to the Single Convention. Thant asked if this was current U.S. policy. (Ibid., 341.9/11–2461)

335.   Memorandum of Conversation[1]

Washington, January 25, 1962.

SUBJECT

Single Convention on Narcotic Drugs, 1961

PARTICIPANTS

Mr. A. Gilmore Flues, former Assistant Secretary of the Treasury
Mr. James A. Reed, Assistant Secretary of the Treasury
IO—Mr. Cleveland
L/T—Mr. Bevans
OES—Miss Dougherty

Mr. Flues' call on Mr. Cleveland today was purportedly for the purpose of introducing Mr. Flues' successor, Mr. Reed.

After introductions, however, Mr. Reed stated that they would like to discuss this Government's position regarding the Single Convention on Narcotic Drugs, 1961. Mr. Flues stated that he would be remaining on at Treasury as a Consultant to see several matters through, including that of the Single Convention.

Mr. Flues summed up Treasury's position regarding the Convention. He felt that the 1953 Protocol contained provisions more acceptable to Treasury, and asked if the Department would consider again asking the Greek and Turkish Governments whether it is their intention to ratify the 1953 Protocol, which needs ratification by only one of them to bring it into force. He stated that the Greek official with whom he had discussed the subject on his previous trip,[2] had since been deceased, and that he felt his successor was inclined to look a little more encouragingly at the subject.

Mr. Cleveland stated that the subject of narcotics control was the responsibility of the Treasury Department, and that it was not the position of the State Department to ask Treasury to accept a treaty under which they felt they could not operate. He asked whether, if certain provisions were included in the Single Convention, Treasury would be satisfied with it, to which both Mr. Flues and Mr. Reed answered yes. Mr. Flues thought that perhaps another conference might be held and the Single Convention amended to include these provisions. Mr. Cleveland stated that, if Treasury considered the Single Convention unacceptable, we would not only not seek ratification of it, but we would circularize other governments advising that we did not plan to

---

[1] Source: National Archives and Records Administration, RG 59, Central Files 1960–63, 345.2/1–2562. Official Use Only. Drafted by Helen E. Dougherty.

[2] Regarding Flues' visit to Greece in July 1961, see Document 331.

ratify and give our reasons for this decision. He pointed out that it was up to Treasury to prepare a memorandum which we could use in circularizing other governments. Mr. Bevans suggested that in the preparation of such memorandum, care be taken that it contain specifics rather than general conclusions.

Mr. Cleveland felt that a new conference might be held at a later date at which a new Single Convention might be negotiated.

Mr. Bevans pointed out that, even if the 1953 Protocol comes into force, we will only have 40 countries parties to it, and that this was less than half the present number of countries in the world. He stated that at the conference in New York at which the Single Convention was adopted, the African states had made it quite clear that they would not become parties to the 1953 Protocol, and it was equally clear that neither the UK nor any members of the Soviet Bloc would ratify it.

To sum up, Mr. Cleveland decided:

1. That since Treasury was opposed to the Single Convention, we would not seek ratification of it.

2. That we would again seek to obtain information as to whether Greece or Turkey is planning to ratify the 1953 Protocol. Mr. Flues will attempt to have a talk with Ambassador Labouisse before he leaves for Athens and brief him on this. He also indicated that he would communicate with Ambassador Hare.

3. That we would circularize other governments informing them that we did not plan to seek ratification of the Single Convention, and giving them our reasons for not doing so. In this connection, it was up to Treasury to provide State with a memorandum giving specific reasons which we might use. Mr. Bevans, Mr. Mulliken and Miss Dougherty were to work with Treasury in seeing that this memorandum is obtained.

---

336.   Editorial Note

Circular telegram CW–7653, March 28, 1962, set forth the U.S. position on the Single Convention as follows: "The Mission is instructed, at its discretion, to inform the host government that after a thorough study of the document, this Government has concluded it should not seek ratification of the Single Convention on Narcotic Drugs. It believes the

Convention in its present form contains defects which are material and important, and which, if the Convention were to come into legal effect, would seriously weaken the control and restrictive systems which presently govern the production and distribution of narcotic drugs. In its opinion, one of the harmful results would be an increase in the illegal traffic in narcotic drugs, and a compounding of the world problem of law enforcement in the narcotics field." The rest of the telegram provided background information and guidance to diplomatic missions. (National Archives and Records Administration, RG 59, Central Files 1960–63, 341.9/3–2862)

---

337.   Airgram From the Embassy in Turkey to the Department of State[1]

A–906   Ankara, April 7, 1962.

SUBJECT

1961 Single Convention on Narcotic Drugs

REF

Deptel 735 and Embtel 1060[2]

Following discussions with the Ambassador and the Economic Counselor, former Assistant Secretary of the Treasury Flues, now Special Consultant to Secretary Dillon, and Mr. John Cusack, District Supervisor, U.S. Bureau of Narcotics, conferred during the week ending March 24 concerning the 1961 Single Convention on Narcotic Drugs and the 1953 Protocol on Opium, with Turkish Government Ministers and key officials responsible for this subject. Accompanied by the Financial Attaché and Embassy Economic Officers, Mr. Flues and Mr. Cusack met with, among others, the following:

Ihsan Gürsan, Minister of Commerce
Majhar Özkol, Under Secretary, Ministry of Commerce

---

[1] Source: National Archives and Records Administration, RG 59, Central Files 1960–63, 341.9/4–762. Confidential. Drafted by Flues and V.W. Mitchell, and cleared by L. Wade Lathram, William M. Kerrigan, and Elaine D. Smith (the latter two in draft). Repeated to Athens and Rome.

[2] Telegram 735 notified the Embassies in Ankara and Athens of Flues' travel plans. Telegram 1060 from Ankara summarized the meetings that Flues and Cusack had with Turkish officials. (Ibid., 102.102/3–1562 and 341.9/4–662, respectively)

Ekrem Geris, President, Foreign Trade Department, Ministry of Commerce

Cahit Hayta, Deputy Secretary General for Political Affairs, Ministry of Foreign Affairs

Vahap Asiroglu, Director General, Third Department, Ministry of Foreign Affairs

Osman Derinsu, Director General, Fifth Department, Ministry of Foreign Affairs

Ahmet Topaloglu, Minister of Interior

Fethi Celikbas, Minister of Industry

Mr. Flues informed the GOT officials that the United States will not ratify the Single Convention on Narcotic Drugs in its present form and will seek to obtain support from other countries for its position.

The major conference of the week was held under the Chairmanship of Under Secretary of Commerce Ozkol, who has been the permanent Turk expert on narcotics and represented Turkey in that capacity at international meetings. Under Secretary Ozkol will lead the Turkish delegation at the Geneva session of the United Nations Commission on Narcotic Drugs in May, and it is expected that he will probably be elected to preside over the session. On the Turkish side, this meeting was attended also by the President and other representatives from the Foreign Trade Department and representatives from Toprak, including Huran Balkan, who has acted as GOT opium monopoly salesman abroad. No representatives from the Ministry of Foreign Affairs or other Ministries participated. The major presentation by Mr. Flues was made to the Ministry of Commerce at that meeting since conversations earlier with other Ministries indicated that they normally defer to Commerce at the technical level as the Ministry directly responsible for narcotic matters.

During the course of the meeting, Under Secretary Ozkol stated the GOT position and views as follows, in summary:

a) Turkey agrees that the Single Convention is defective, should be corrected, and Turkey would not ratify it in its present form; but it believed that some 37 countries will ratify the Convention, including three already in.

b) The GOT considered the 1953 Protocol a good treaty and consequently has already put its provisions into effect internally, but believes its scope to be too narrow. Ignoring the 1948 convention, Ozkol made his usual lengthy statement regarding the need for better controls on synthetics and marijuana, and indicated his belief that the U.S. is not sufficiently interested in this area.

c) The GOT would not ratify the 1953 Protocol now but would reexamine it as an interim opium agreement if Geneva produced no prospect of meaningful changes in the Single Convention in the near future. Ozkol believes that ratification of the Protocol before the Geneva session would indicate that Turkey had been pressed by the U.S., and would thereby create a basis for adverse propaganda. He believes the prospects for obtaining support from other missions for making changes in the Single Convention are better if Turkey is not committed to the Protocol in advance.

d) Mr. Ozkol suggested use of the Geneva session to press for modification of the Single Convention, and urged that the GOT and the U.S. present a common approach and seek support meanwhile from other countries. He stated a readiness to discuss the Protocol with Mr. Anslinger at Geneva in this context. He stated also that if Geneva was a failure in generating support for modification of the Single Convention, then he would immediately discuss the situation with Anslinger and could use the full discussion of Geneva as a basis for a new look at the Protocol.

e) During the conversation, Mr. Ozkol pointed out that the United States purchased 191 tons of opium from India last year. Mr. Flues advised him that the United States also bought 20 tons from Yugoslavia, its first purchase from that source in 25 years, and stated that the GOT price was not competitive on the world market. It appeared that the GOT and Ozkol were under economic pressure with Toprak reporting 350 tons of uncommited stocks of opium on hand and prospect of a bumper crop of 250/300 tons this year. Mr. Flues requested Toprak's latest price quote and was informed that it was $18 per kilo. Mr. Flues requested that Toprak reexamine this price, with the possibility that U.S. business could help GOT clear its stock overhang if Turkey's price were more competitive.

It was the impression of Mr. Flues and the Embassy officers present at these conversations that the Foreign Office sees the narcotic problem and the U.S. position with respect to the Single Convention in a broader context and desires closer GOT/US collaboration on the subject. The Ministry of Foreign Affairs indicated that, while the Ministry of Commerce is the Ministry technically responsible for the subject, other Ministries also are involved in other aspects of the problem, such as control and enforcement, agricultural reform, etc., and that the Ministry of Foreign Affairs assumes a coordinating role, particularly with respect to international negotiations and broader considerations which may affect those negotiations. It was evident that there was some Foreign Office irritation with the Ministry of Commerce. Other Ministries appeared to have a somewhat similar attitude in looking at the problem more broadly and desiring closer Turk-American collaboration.

Summarizing the results of his conversations on the United States position with respect to the Single Convention, Mr. Flues stated the following to the Ministry of Commerce and Foreign Affairs:

a) The discussions revealed a clearer area of agreement than previously and remaining differences relate largely to strategy/emphasis.

With respect to strategy, however, the U.S. believes that changes in thinking about the Single Convention at Geneva are more likely if other nations are confronted with the 1953 Protocol in legal effect.

b) The Protocol has already been overwhelmingly ratified by other nations and thus it appears that Turkey should support world opinion by taking action to seek international adoption of effective opium controls. Moreover, as Mr. Ozkol has indicated, Turkey itself had already adopted the provisions of the Protocol for its own internal use.

c) Geneva at best has a limited role since it can only promote a better climate for changes in the Single Convention, which may take time. Meanwhile, the present opium control system needs strengthening by bringing the Protocol into legal effect.

d) While expressing gratification for the progress made during the talks, the United States, in supporting the combined effort at Geneva, will not cease its present efforts to bring the Protocol into effect.

Assessing the results and implications of the week-long series of discussions with GOT officials, Messrs Flues and Cusack, and Embassy representatives concluded:

a) The combination of the U.S. position on the Single Convention; the enlarged responsibilities of Ozkol as Under Secretary of Commerce; the Toprak stock problem; pressure from other interested Ministries, especially the Foreign Office; etc., may have influenced the Ministry of Commerce to a more responsible position. Mr. Ozkol may wish to use his suggested approach at Geneva as a more responsible and yet a fact-saving tactic; however, we doubt if he likes the Protocol any better than he did as a GOT technical narcotics expert.

b) Opinions can differ as to what meaningful results Geneva produces regarding the Single Convention. Mr. Ozkol can drag further on the Protocol by claiming that the GOT is satisfied with the progress at Geneva; Ozkol still appears to be the key GOT figure with regard to this question.

c) In view of the limited time before the Geneva sessions, it is not likely that there will be any parliamentary action on the Protocol before then in either Greece or Turkey. As a consequence, probably little would be lost by expressing respect for Ozkol's strategy, while not abating pressure for Protocol ratification as soon as possible. In light of his statements, however, it could be difficult for Ozkol to assume a completely negative position after Geneva.

After assessment of the real effect of the concessions made by Ozkol, in his final visit with Mr. Hayta, Mr. Flues suggested that he (Mr. Flues) might try to obtain a Greek concert on the Protocol so that Turkey need not feel alone.

Hare

338.   **Airgram From the Embassy in the United Kingdom to the Department of State[1]**

A–1191   London, April 30, 1962, 2 p.m.

SUBJECT

British Comments on US Position Relating to Single Convention on Narcotic Drugs

REF

CW 7653, dated March 28, 1962[2]

The Embassy has received a statement of British views regarding the reference subject, which was prepared by Mr. Green of the Drugs Branch in the Home Office. In forwarding these comments the Foreign Office indicated that it was instructing its Embassy in Washington to raise the question with the Department. The verbatim text of the British note is reproduced below.

Begin Verbatim Text

THE SINGLE CONVENTION ON NARCOTIC DRUGS, 1961

Although it is now nearly nine years since the 1953 Protocol was drawn up it has still not come into force. While it is true that all that is required to bring it into force is ratification by one other opium producer, it is most unlikely that the Protocol will ever be as widely accepted as most of the other international narcotic Conventions have been. This was perfectly clear at the plenipotentiary conference which drafted the new Single Convention, where many countries explained that they were not prepared to accept several of the provisions of the 1953 Protocol.

There would indeed be objections to pursuing a policy that would bring the 1953 Protocol into effect. The only other opium producer now likely to ratify the Protocol is Greece. If Greece were to ratify, the treaty would then be ratified by three producers, India, Iran and Greece. Greece has not for many years produced opium in significant quantities. Iran has not produced any opium for the last six years or so. India would therefore be the only effective producer, but all the other countries which had ratified the Protocol would be bound by it to obtain their opium from India. This would establish a monopoly of the supply of opium for India so far as countries parties to the Protocol were concerned. The other producers would, however, continue to trade with

[1] Source: National Archives and Records Administration, RG 59, Central Files 1960–63, 341.9/4–3062. Official Use Only.

[2] See Document 336.

non-parties and there would be no incentive for any of them to come into the Protocol.

Objection has been taken to the provision in the Single Convention which would allow a country to produce and export as much as five tons of opium without obtaining international authority. Although it is true that this would not be possible under the 1953 Protocol, it is also true that under that Protocol any country can produce opium for its own use. Moreover, the comparison should not be with a protocol which is unlikely to come into general effect, but with the present situation, in which any country can grow as much opium as it wishes without obtaining anyone's authority. There would not appear to be any reason why, if the Single Convention comes into effect, countries which could at present produce and export opium but do not do so should suddenly decide to do so. Indeed the Single Convention should discourage them from doing this since they would first have to satisfy themselves that their production of opium would not lead to overproduction in the world as a whole, and they would have to establish a national monopoly to control production. The Single Convention would therefore impose additional safeguards which do not exist at the present time.

It is true that the reservations clause of the Single Convention was, in the rush of the last week of the plenipotentiary conference, drafted in somewhat wider terms than had been intended. There does not appear, however, to be any reason to think that the provision will be abused. If the scope of possible reservations is studied carefully it will be seen that they can be of only a limited nature. What is more important, however, is that there is no reason to expect that any signatory is going to make unreasonable reservations. Such reservations as have already been made under this Article are in accord with the intentions expressed by the plenipotentiary conference and do not go beyond what the conference envisaged.

As regards reservations being made about the Board's power of imposing sanctions, the arguments in the previous paragraph would again apply. In this connection it may be noted that the Board has never made use of its present powers of sanction and it seems very improbable that it will ever wish to make use of the more drastic powers given to it.

The United Kingdom Government expects to be able to ratify the Single Convention in due course, but some further consideration of one or two points is necessary. It will probably also be necessary to have some minor legislation before the Convention can be ratified, and in view of the congested parliamentary time-table, it may take a little time for this legislation to be passed.

The United Kingdom Goverment takes the view that the Single Convention is in many respects an improvement on the existing narcotics treaties, and it hopes that the Convention will come into effect in the near future.

End Verbatim Text.

Bruce

---

339.   Telegram From the Mission in Geneva to the Department of State[1]

Geneva, May 28, 1962, 7 p.m.

1269. From USDel NARCOM. During today's session of Commission on Narcotic Drugs, Greek observer announced his government's intention seek ratification 1953 Opium Protocol. UK Delgate angrily asked Greek observer for explanation why Greece, after lapse of nine years, now seeking ratification. After explanation, apparently acceptable to other delegates, was given UK Delegate asked for formal explanation from Greek Government, which was ignored by Greek observer.

FYI. Purpose this cable inform Embassy Athens officers who worked with Treasury Dept officers and Greek officials to bring about ratification 1953 Protocol, to be alert for possible pressure on part UK to have Greek Govt shelve plans for ratification. End FYI.

Message Unsigned

---

[1] Source: National Archives and Records Administration, RG 59, Central Files 1960–63, 341.9/5–2862. Limited Official Use. Repeated to Athens.

340.   Report of the U.S. Delegation to the Seventeenth Session of the UN Commission on Narcotic Drugs[1]

Washington, August 15, 1962.

[Here follow Section 1, Background of Conference; Section 2, Agenda for Conference; Section 3, Participation in Conference; Section 4, United States Delegation; and Section 5, Organization of the Conference.]

6. Work of the Committee on Illicit Traffic.

The Committee on Illicit Traffic reviewed the illicit narcotic traffic for the year 1961. In its work the Committee was guided by summaries of illicit transactions and seizures, by annual report documents, by discussion of international investigations, and by special documents prepared for study by the Committee. Among the Committee's conclusions were the following:

Opium and the opiates, cannabis and cocaine continued to predominate in the illicit traffic. However, it was reported that in Thailand the major problem since shortly after opium was prohibited in 1959, was diacetylmorphine. There were also indications the traffic in cocaine was spreading through Latin America and thence to other parts of the world.

Canada, the United States, Hong Kong, Japan and Thailand continued to be targets for the illicit traffic in diacetylmorphine.

There was evidence that clandestine conversion of opium into white drugs was being carried out in closer proximity to producing areas.

Governments in the Near and Middle East, and in the Far East, were urged to make every effort to bring about closer working relationships for the implementation of control measures.

The Representative of the United States expressed his Government's appreciation of the cooperation extended by Canada, France, Italy, Lebanon, Mexico, Spain, Syrian Arab Republic and Turkey.

The subject of acetic anhydride and acetyl chloride was discussed at the request of the United States. The Representative of the United

---

[1] Source: National Archives and Records Administration, RG 59, Central Files 1960–63, 341.9/8–1562. No classification marking. The session was held in Geneva May 14–June 1. Harry J. Anslinger of the Treasury Department led the U.S. Delegation. His signature on the report, which was submitted to the Secretary of State, appears on the title page. The position papers that the State Department provided to Anslinger are ibid., 341.9/5–462.

States stated that experience over the past 30 years indicated that countries which had a problem of illicit manufacture of diacetylmorphine and which were not themselves producers of acetic anhydride could promptly bring the situation under control by placing import and internal restrictions on this chemical. He also called attention to the important contribution which manufacturers of acetic anhydride and acetyl chloride could make in maintaining surveillance over the distribution of their products.

7. Work of the Conference.

The Commission adopted three resolutions for submission to the Economic and Social Council, as follows:

A resolution, sponsored by Canada, India and the Netherlands, inviting governments to ratify the Single Convention on Narcotic Drugs, 1961. The vote was 12 for (Brazil, Canada, Hungary, India, Japan, Morocco, Netherlands, Poland, Switzerland, USSR, UK, Yugoslavia), 2 against (Mexico, US), with 5 abstentions (China, France, Iran, Turkey, UAR). The Mexican Representative voted against because he felt the resolution was premature, the United States because the Single Convention was unacceptable in its present form. Of those abstaining, several did so because their governments had not yet completed their study of the Single Convention.

A resolution requesting the Secretary General to prepare a legal commentary on, and to draft an administrative guide for the application of, the Single Convention. The vote was 10–0–8.

A resolution inviting the Government of Lebanon to cooperate more fully with the Commission on Narcotic Drugs in its work and, in particular, to be represented by an observer at the 18th session of the Commission and at the meetings of its Committee on Illicit Traffic.

In addition to the above, the Commission adopted the following:

A resolution noting the resolutions of the Inter-American Consultative Group which met at Rio de Janeiro in 1961, and drawing the attention of the ECOSOC to the desirability of stationing an officer of the Secretariat in Latin America with a view to facilitating regional cooperation in the field of narcotics control in that part of the world.

A resolution proposed by the United Arab Republic and co-sponsored by Brazil and the United States, requesting States Members of the United Nations or of the Specialized Agencies to encourage research into the socio-economic and medical aspects of drug addiction and illegal drug consumption, and to furnish the Secretary General with reports on the results and findings thereof.

A resolution requesting countries mentioned in paragraph 2 of resolution VII (XIII) and paragraph 3 of resolution 6 (XIV) to send to the

United Nations Laboratory authenticated samples of seized opium, and if that is impossible, authenticated samples obtained from poppies cultivated under natural conditions and under control of the government.

The United States Delegation to the 16th Session of the Commission had been successful in having consideration of a resolution on Control of Barbiturates, reading as follows:

The Commission on Narcotic Drugs

Recalling resolutions VI and VII adopted by the Commission at its twelfth session,

Considering the social danger and the danger to public health arising from the abuse of barbiturates, as reported by the World Health Organization,

Recommends

1. that governments should take appropriate measures to place the production, distribution and use of such drugs under strict control;
2. that the competent organs of the United Nations and the World Health Organization should examine the necessity and the possibility of adopting adequate measures for the international control of such drugs.

postponed until the 17th Session. The resolution was taken up by paragraphs and then as a whole. The first paragraph was changed to read "resolution VI adopted by the". Operative paragraph 1 was adopted by a vote of 17 for, none against, with 2 abstentions (Poland, US). Operative paragraph 2 was defeated by a vote of 8 for, 10 against (Canada, China, Hungary, Iran, Japan, Mexico, Netherlands, Switzerland, UK, US), with 1 abstention (Poland). The resolution was adopted in the following form:

The Commission on Narcotic Drugs

(a) *Recalling* resolution VI adopted by the Commission at its twelfth session,

(b) *Considering* the social danger and the danger to public health arising from the abuse of barbiturates, as reported by the World Health Organization,

Recommends that governments should take appropriate measures to place the production, distribution and use of such drugs under strict control.

by a vote of 16 for, none against, with 3 abstentions (Poland, Turkey, US). During the debate on the resolution the United States Representative stated that there was no illicit traffic in barbiturates and the establishment of international control would place an enormous additional administrative burden on governments. In his opinion, the problem could best be handled by educating the medical profession in the matter, and particularly to ensure that the medical profession did not issue prescriptions that could be filled more than once.

At the beginning of the discussion on Preparations for the Coming into Force of the 1961 Convention, the observer for Greece announced that his Government would ratify the 1953 Opium Protocol. The United States Representative and the Representative of the UAR expressed satisfaction with this announcement, but it was not met with any great enthusiasm by the majority of the Commission, and it was stated that the announcement could have the effect of accelerating ratification of the Single Convention. It was pointed out that when the 1953 Protocol enters into force, India will enjoy a monopoly on the licit production of opium for export to the parties to the 1953 Protocol. The Observer for Italy stated that the announcement had altered the situation and his Government would have to review the Single Convention in the light of the entry into force of the 1953 Protocol.

The United States Representative stated that for a number of reasons his Government could not ratify the Single Convention. It would encourage opium production, which would go completely out of control, and thus result in an increase in illicit production. He pointed out that in addition to permitting any country to produce up to 5 tons of opium for export, the Single Convention permitted the export of opium seized in the illicit traffic without limitation, and permitted any country to grow and stockpile as much opium as it wished. Also, under the Single Convention the effectiveness of the estimates and statistics systems of the 1931 Convention had been destroyed. Any party to the Single Convention could by reservation prevent examination of its statistics. He stated that under the Single Convention the powers of the International Narcotics Control Board, which would replace the present Permanent Central Opium Board and Drug Supervisory Body, would be seriously limited and weakened. The United States Government urged governments to consider carefully all provisions of the Single Convention before deciding to ratify it. It hoped that at some time in the future the Single Convention could be revised so as to retain and strengthen, rather than weaken, the control measures of the existing treaties, including the 1953 Protocol.

The majority of the Commission, however, spoke in favor of the Single Convention and urged its ratification. The Representative of the United Kingdom stated his Government intended to ratify as soon as the necessary domestic legislation to implement the provisions of the Single Convention could be enacted. The Representative of Canada pointed out that his Government had already ratified. The Representative of India stated that the provisions of the Single Convention were realistic and wider than those of the 1953 Protocol, and urged that the Single Convention be brought into force as quickly as possible. The Representative of the Netherlands stated it was essential that the Single Convention be brought into force at an early date. The Representative of Yugoslavia disagreed with the United States Representative and felt the Single Convention was a step forward. The Representative of Switzerland stated that his Government had the Single Convention under study and there appeared [to be] no objection to its ratification. The Representative of Morocco pointed out that while his Government was not a signatory to the Single Convention, it was one of the first to ratify it. The Representative of Poland said that his Government considered the Single Convention a progressive measure.

The Observer for Afghanistan stated that his Government considered the Single Convention a major United Nations achievement. He expressed the hope that the Single Convention would enter into force as soon as possible. The Observer for Burma stated that his Government had the Single Convention under examination and would not hesitate to ratify it if it were found that it would contribute to the effectiveness of the anti-narcotic campaign.

A resolution, addressed to the Economic and Social Council, inviting governments to ratify the Single Convention, was introduced and adopted.

A resolution, addressed to the Economic and Social Council, requesting the Secretary General to prepare a legal commentary on, and an administrative guide for the administration of, the Single Convention, was introduced and adopted.

In addition, the Commission decided to request the Secretariat to prepare, for consideration at the 18th session,

(a) a draft document indicating the form, manner and dates of government communications containing the information required in respect of annual reports, seizure reports, laws and regulations, manufacture of drugs, and offices charged with authorizing international transactions;
(b) a draft import certificate; and
(c) a document, for submission to the Council, describing the procedure for the election of members of the new International Narcotics Control Board.

The Commission also decided to invite the WHO Expert Committee on Addiction-Producing Drugs to make recommendations regarding the necessary amendments to the Schedules to the Single Convention in preparation for its coming into force.

The Commission decided to request the Secretary General to take such Secretariat action as he deemed necessary in the event of the coming into force of the 1953 Protocol.

8. Future Meetings.

The Commission decided to each year give special emphasis to a particular region of the world, beginning with the Far East, in documents prepared by the Secretary General reviewing the illicit traffic, and in the work of the Committee on Illicit Traffic.

It was also decided to recommend to the technical assistance authorities that they give favorable consideration to the Peruvian request for organization of a regional seminar on the problems of the coca leaf. The Commission felt that the Secretary General should explore the question of preparation of a report by the Food and Agriculture Organization on the possibility of replacing the licit and illicit cultivation of the coca leaf, cannabis or opium by other crops.

A provisional agenda for the Commission's 18th session was adopted.

It was agreed to invite Afghanistan, Argentina, Bolivia, Burma, Cuba, Federation of Malaya, India, Israel, Italy, Laos, Lebanon, Pakistan, Philippines, Portugal, Republic of Viet Nam, Spain and Thailand to send observers to the Commission meetings on the illicit traffic and to meetings of the Committee on Illicit Traffic.

It was agreed to invite the following countries to send observers: Italy and the Netherlands to the Commission's meetings on opium and opiates; Argentina, Bolivia, and Colombia to the meetings on the coca leaf; Lebanon and Pakistan to the meetings on cannabis; Belgium, Israel, Italy and the Netherlands to the meetings on control of other substances, including barbiturates.

9. Conclusions.

Generally, Soviet Bloc action during the session was at a minimum. The question of Chinese representation was raised by the Representative of Poland, supported by the Representatives of Hungary and the USSR. The United States Representative regretted that the question had been raised and pointed out that technical commissions were not competent to consider the issue. The Representative of China stated that his was the only legal government of China.

The United States was able to maintain leadership and substantial support throughout the session except for the discussions on the Single Convention.

Mr. James P. Hendrick, Deputy Assistant Secretary of the Treasury, was assigned to assist the delegation during the last two weeks of the session. He and Mr. Cusack conferred with numerous delegations in relation to the Single Convention. They talked with those delegations who were known to be unfavorable to the Convention and also with those who indicated a considerable degree of doubt as to whether the instrument would result in stricter international controls in suppressing the abuse of narcotic drugs. They stressed the two major weaknesses; lack of limitation of opium production and the reservations which would destroy controls under the 1931 Convention. It was pointed out that many improvements found in the Single Convention could be maintained in case of revision of that document or through revision of the 1953 Opium Protocol after it goes into effect.

341. Airgram From the Department of State to the Mission to the United Nations[1]

A–176   Washington, November 30, 1962, 5:33 p.m.

SUBJECT

United States position in General Assembly plenary on resolution urging ratifica tion of Single Convention on Narcotic Drugs, 1961

The United States Delegation should continue to vote against the resolution.[2] It is recommended that the Delegation make the following explanation of its negative vote:

"The United States has opposed passage of this resolution in the Third Committee and in the Economic and Social Council for reasons which were explained at that time. Since then, the Government of Greece has ratified the 1953 Protocol, an event which the United States believes is a major new development in the field of international control of narcotic drugs. As a result of this ratification it is expected that the 1953 Protocol will soon enter into force. [In the event that Greece deposits its ratification before the explanation is given by the Delegation, the preceding sentence should be replaced by one reading

---

[1] Source: National Archives and Records Administration, RG 59, Central Files 1960–63, 341.9/11–3062. Official Use Only. Drafted by Helen E. Dougherty; cleared by James P. Hendrick (Treasury), Bevans, and James M. Ludlow (NEA); and approved by Robert Rossow, Jr. (IO/OES).

[2] Reference is to a resolution that the UN General Assembly adopted on December 7 as resolution 1774 (XVII) by a vote of 92 to 1 with 4 abstentions. The resolution invited member states to take such steps as might be necessary to ratify or accede to the Single Convention and noted that by October 12, 64 countries had signed the Convention and 11 had ratified or acceded to it.

'As a result of the deposit of the instrument of ratification by Greece, the 1953 protocol will enter into force on————.']³

"I shall not take your time at this point to give what would be a very technical explanation of what this development means. But I am convinced that further action at this time towards implementing the Single Convention, in the absence of experience with the operation of the 1953 Protocol, is premature. I hope other governments may come to share this view once they have had the opportunity to evaluate this new development."

USUN should not lobby for the US position. It should consult with the Greek delegation and if possible prevent any lobbying on its part. Agreement should be reached with the Greek delegation on the statements to be made by the United States and Greece. The United States Delegation should request both the Greek Delegation and the Secretariat to inform the USDel the minute the Greek instrument of ratification is deposited and the date the Protocol will enter into force.

Discussion

In explaining our negative vote on this resolution in the Third Committee we stated that our opposition to the Single Convention was: (1) because it permitted any country to produce up to 5 tons of opium for export; and (2) because it permitted ratification subject to reservations which allowed countries to gain the benefits of adherence with few, if any, of the liabilities.

Greek ratification of the 1953 Protocol furnishes a third reason. The terms of the 1953 Protocol are sufficiently rigid to provide for the first time the legal control over opium production which has been sought by all persons seriously concerned with the problem since it was first discussed on an international level. It would be highly desirable, now that this system of control is at last to be put into effect, to allow nations to experience the benefits which should accrue from this system over a period of time. It can be confidently predicted that this experience will be rewarding and the chances of getting even broader international agreement on this basis after a trial period are considered good.

While this new development presents a strong reason why member countries should not ratify the Single Convention, USUN should not attempt to change the vote of other countries at this time. A very substantial number of delegations voted in favor of the resolution in the Third Committee. Presumably most of these did so under instructions, and it is unrealistic to hope that other delegations could get their instructions changed in time for a negative vote or abstention in plenary. Also, should the United States make this attempt and should the

³ Brackets in the source text.

plenary vote be overwhelmingly in favor of the resolution, then the United States' new argument will appear to have been publicly repudiated. In addition, argument at this point might harden the position and thus make it more difficult to persuade other governments to change their position in the future.

Rusk

---

342. **Editorial Note**

On February 6, 1963, Greece deposited its instrument of ratification of the 1953 Opium Protocol. The Protocol then entered into force on March 8. (Circular airgram CA–8445, February 7; National Archives and Records Administration, RG 59, Central Files 1960–63, SOC 11–5)

---

343. **Airgram From the Embassy in the United Kingdom to the Department of State[1]**

A–1817   London, February 15, 1963, 2 p.m.

SUBJECT

Narcotics—1953 Protocol vs Single Convention

REF

CA–7714 of January 22, 1963[2]

The United States point of view in support of the 1953 Opium Protocol vis-à-vis the 1961 Single Convention on Narcotic Drugs (reference airgram) was presented on February 13 to the United Kingdom during an interview with Mr. T.C. Green of the Home Office, which

---

[1] Source: National Archives and Records Administration, RG 59, Central Files 1960–63, SOC 11–5. Official Use Only. Drafted by Donald R. Lesh and cleared by Dougherty. Repeated to USUN and the Mission in Geneva.

[2] Airgram CA–7714 encouraged Missions to urge host governments to join in implementing the narcotics control system provided for by the 1953 Opium Protocol rather than to ratify the 1961 Single Convention on Narcotic Drugs. (Ibid., 399.53/1–2263)

bears primary responsibility in all matters pertaining to narcotics control. Mr. Green expressed considerable disagreement with the American position, and his arguments are summarized below. He hastened to add, however, that the United Kingdom fully shares the United States concern for securing a workable international agreement to facilitate control over illicit production and traffic in narcotics. Mr. Green felt that our disagreements stem only from honest differences of opinion as to the best means to achieve that end.

The following matters were discussed:

(1) *Closed List of Producers.* In regard to the United States contention that the 1953 Opium Protocol provides superior control over narcotics production through the use of a closed list of seven countries permitted to produce for export, Mr. Green argued that even before the Protocol comes into force on March 8 of this year the list will be outdated, and that in any case the list could never serve as a practical working device. Of the seven producing countries, three (USSR, Bulgaria, and Yugoslavia) have long since made clear their opposition to the 1953 Protocol and their intention not to ratify or support it. Of the other four countries (Greece, India, Iran, and Turkey), only Greece, India, and Iran have ratified the Protocol. However, since 1953 Iran has ceased production of opium for export, and Greece, according to Mr. Green, has not produced opium for export for many years. Therefore, since the manufacturing parties to the 1953 Protocol soon will be obliged to import only from one of the producing parties on the closed list, the result will be that India will have a monopoly on legal international trade in opium. Possible future ratification by Turkey would provide only one alternative legal market for the opium manufacturing countries who adhere to the Protocol. The United Kingdom opposes this very severe restriction on the legal sources of supply, and feels that other countries which might otherwise support the 1953 Protocol are discouraged from doing so by this situation. As for the countries which do not adhere to the agreement, they are not subject to any form of production control now, and will not be any more circumscribed even after the 1953 Protocol comes into force.

Furthermore, the Home Office rejects the United States argument that the provisions of the 1961 Convention, authorizing any state to produce up to 5 tons annually for export, will encourage new countries to enter the opium export trade. Those desiring to do so at present are already producing as much opium as they wish, and the introduction of an international agreement legalizing exports up to 5 tons a year will not necessarily serve to spark new production.

(2) *Limitations on Stocks.* On the closely related problem of establishing limits on the total stock of opium which may be held by a nation,

the United Kingdom is again opposed to the United States view. The specific percentage limitations on stocks set forth in Article 5 of the 1953 Protocol are actually, in Mr. Green's words, "a farce." Since a producing nation may select any year after January 1, 1946 as the base for the computation of its total medical and scientific needs for opium, and presumably will select the year of highest volume, the limit thus established will be so high as to be meaningless. It was in recognition of this fact that the nations which participated in the drafting of the Single Convention in 1961 omitted any reference to stock limitations. Considering the other provisions for supervision of international narcotics trade contained in the 1961 Convention, the Home Office believes that there need be no fear or expectation that any country will amass an unduly large amount of opium. Mr. Green commented that at present by far the largest single stock of opium in the world is held by the United States.

The matter of disposition of seized shipments of illicit narcotics was raised in this regard. The British here too support the terms of the 1961 Convention over the 1953 Protocol. They contend that the Single Convention actually offers greater incentive for non-producing countries to increase their surveillance over illicit traffic in narcotics. Under Article 7 paragraphs 4 and 5 of the 1953 Protocol, a non-producing nation which has confiscated an illicit narcotics shipment, and which requires no additional narcotics for its own use, is compelled either to return the narcotics to the lawful owner, if possible, or to destroy the shipment. The 1961 Convention, on the other hand, allows such a country the further option of exporting the narcotics to a manufacturing country, under normal control provisions, for a profit. It therefore will be clearly in any nation's self-interest to search out and confiscate illegal shipments of drugs.

(3) *Reservations.* While conceding that the reservations section of the 1961 Convention is broader than the United Kingdom would wish, Mr. Green explained that it had been designed primarily to obtain the support of the Soviet Bloc countries for the final draft. The Bloc countries had raised a serious objection concerning so-called "Third Countries," or countries outside the United Nations (particularly Outer Mongolia at that time, Red China, North Korea, and North Viet-Nam). Since the 1961 Single Convention would be administered solely by the United Nations, the Soviet Bloc countries insisted that they would not support the extension of the control mechanism to "Third Countries" who were unable to secure United Nations membership. This objection was met by allowing the reservation in respect to Article 12 paragraphs 2 and 3, and Article 13 paragraph 2, of the Single Convention. Mr. Green asserted that since then the Soviet Bloc countries have in fact made clear that they do not intend to make any broader use of the reser-

vations, and he believes that it is doubtful that other nations will do so to thwart the purposes of the agreement. If that is their intention, they would find it simpler to remain completely outside any international narcotics agreement. The participation of the Soviet Bloc countries, is, however, so vital to any system of narcotics control that the United Kingdom feels that to attain that end the concession on reservations is well worth any risk that may be involved.

(4) *Possible Amendments to 1953 Protocol.* Mr. Green called attention to the fact that the 1953 Protocol deals only with opium, while the 1961 Single Convention covers the entire range of narcotics, most especially coca leaf and cannabis (marijuana). In accordance with the reference airgram, the view was expressed that the United States shares the same concern, and would be happy to consider means of amending the 1953 Protocol in due course to cover all drugs, just as we would be prepared to discuss possible limited modification in the closed list of producers, and some alteration in the provisions for local inquiry and mandatory embargo. It is the opinion of the Home Office, however, that to achieve these worthwhile ends it would be necessary to convoke an international conference almost identical to that which produced the 1961 Single Convention, and that it would be most unrealistic to expect that the final agreement would be materially different from that document. Mr. Green volunteered his belief that a United States attempt to gather international support for a conference to discuss only the change we desire, and no others, would not be successful.

On the basis of these convictions, Mr. Green stated that the United Kingdom remained convinced that the 1961 Single Convention on Narcotic Drugs would prove to be a more practical instrument of narcotics control than the 1953 Opium Protocol. Therefore it is still the intention of the Government to seek enabling legislation, possibly in 1964, to permit ratification of the Single Convention. He expressed his hope that the United States, regardless of its misgivings in this matter, would cooperate in administering the 1961 Single Convention when and if it comes into force.

For the Chargé d'Affaires ad interim:
Donald R. Lesh
Third Secretary of Embassy

344. Airgram From the Embassy in Turkey to the Department of State[1]

A–1136   Ankara, June 24, 1963.

SUBJECT

    Narcotics: Turkey Ratifies 1953 Opium Protocol

REF

    CERP D–15; Embassy A–543, November 29, 1962[2]

SUMMARY

The draft bill proposing GOT ratification of the 1953 Opium Protocol which was submitted to the Turkish House of Representatives late in March, became law on June 4, 1963 (Law 245), and appeared in the *Official Gazette* of June 11, 1963 (No. 11425). The Embassy believes that the low level of opium exports and large stocks have been influential in promoting the ratification of the Protocol. The export price of Turkish opium is still not competitive with the Indian product. The Ministry of Foreign Affairs is preparing a draft bill proposing GOT ratification of the 1961 Single Convention, but according to the Ministry, present plans do not include its submission to Parliament during this session. Representations explaining U.S.G. opposition to this Convention have been made to the Ministry. *End of Summary*

Following the visit of Assistant Secretary James A. Reed to Ankara during November 1962 (see A–543 under reference), the Embassy has made frequent follow up representations during December, January and February urging GOT ratification of the 1953 Opium Protocol. Despite these representations, which received polite attention, effective action on the part of the GOT did not seem to be forthcoming. As a result of the Greek ratification and the UN announcement on February 6, 1963, the Embassy sent a formal note to the Turkish Foreign Office on March 1 (Enclosure 1)[3] notifying the Government of Turkey that with the deposit of the Greek instrument of ratification, the United Nations had announced that the Protocol would enter into force on March 8, 1963. The only reaction received by the Embassy was a note acknowledging receipt of our Note (see Enclosure 2).

---

[1] Source: National Archives and Records Administration, RG 59, Central Files 1960–63, SOC 11–5. Confidential. Drafted by Elaine D. Smith and approved by Edward P. Prince. Repeated to Istanbul, Izmir, Adana, Paris, and Rome.

[2] Neither found.

[3] The enclosures are not printed.

However, soon afterward a draft bill proposing GOT ratification of the 1953 Protocol was submitted to the Turkish House of Representatives and was referred to the Temporary Legislative Committee where it remained for almost a month. It was reported out of Committee and approved by the House on April 29 just prior to its recess. The Bill was then sent to the Senate and the Minister of Commerce requested that it be discussed on an urgent basis by the Senate when it reconvened on May 14. Senate discussion was delayed due to political disturbances but the Bill was approved by the Senate on June 4 and became Law 245. The Protocol appeared in *Official Gazette* 11425 of June 11, 1963.

The Embassy believes that the low level of opium exports has been an influential factor in promoting the ratification of the 1953 Protocol. Mr. Hurem Balkan of TOPRAK, without giving specifics, described opium exports as very "disappointing," adding that stocks are currently at the high level of 400 tons and after the new crop is harvested may reach 700 tons. This may be a conservative figure since TOPRAK in the past has not disclosed complete stocks. The Embassy has pointed out to Mr. Balkan that the relatively high price of Turkish opium was harmful to Turkish exports. He replied that costs were such that Turkish opium could not be sold for less, but as in the past, Embassy requests for cost data were refused.

On May 12 the press carried the story that opium purchase prices would be reduced. The press claimed that TOPRAK had decided to reduce purchase prices for opium by 10% and that the decision would be officially announced after Cabinet approval. The reason given was the low price of Indian opium and competition from synthetics. Decree #6/1785 of May 29, 1963 (*Official Gazette* of May 31, 1963) determined the raw opium domestic sales prices for 1963 substantially at 1962 levels. The price, depending upon the class, ranges from TL 80–100 per kilo with an additional 10% premium for the best qualities of each class.

Along with the favorable developments regarding the 1953 Protocol, there is an unfavorable development in GOT narcotic policy which the Embassy is continuing to watch closely. The Turkish Ministry of Foreign Affairs is preparing a draft bill proposing ratification of the 1961 Single Convention. This bill has not been submitted to the House of Representatives and according to an official of the Ministry of Foreign Affairs, present plans do not include its submission to Parliament during this session. In addition to the presentation made to the Ministry reported in Airgram under reference, the Embassy has made follow-up calls explaining the reasons for United States Government opposition to the ratification of the 1961 Single Convention. These representations always receive polite attention and assurances are given that the USG viewpoint will be taken into consideration, but no definite commitment is ever made.   With the 1953 Protocol ratified, and the GOT proclivity for delay, it is hoped that the Bill proposing ratification of the 1961 Single Convention will get pigeon-holed in the Ministry.   Unless otherwise instructed, the Embassy will not raise the matter with the Ministry again because such action might be counterproductive, but will endeavor by other means to keep abreast of any developments regarding the progress of this Bill.

For the Ambassador:
L. Wade Lathram
Counselor of Embassy
For Economic Affairs

345.   Report of the U.S. Delegation to the Eighteenth Session of the UN Commission on Narcotic Drugs[1]

Washington, June 28, 1963.

[Here follow Section 1, Background of Conference; Section 2, Agenda for Conference; Section 3, Participation in Conference; Section 4, United States Delegation; and Section 5, Organization of the Conference.]

6. Work of the Committee on Illicit Traffic:

The Far East and South-East Asia were the most important areas under discussion because of the enormous traffic involving Burma, Thailand, and Hong Kong.   The United States representative particularly urged the governments of the Far East to ascertain the source of "999" morphine blocks which caused a substantial part of the illicit traffic.   It was evident that they were all dragging their feet in locating the source.

Hong Kong sent its chief of the Narcotics Bureau, who painted a picture of gravity but in no case mentioned Communist China as a source.

---

[1]   Source: National Archives and Records Administration, RG 59, Central Files 1960–63, SOC 11–15 UN.   No classification marking.   The Commission met in Geneva April 29–May 17.   Harry J. Anslinger of the Treasury Department led the U.S. Delegation. His signature on the report, which was submitted to the Secretary of State, appears on the title page.   The position papers that the State Department provided to Anslinger are ibid., SOC 11–5 ECOSOC.

The observer of Thailand for the first time presented a case of increased and vigorous enforcement, which brought commendation from the Commission.

The observer of Burma showed that his country was in the throes of helplessness in dealing with the hill tribes in the Shan State. He presented a resolution for technical cooperation in the nature of a survey of opium-producing regions in Burma with the idea of crop substitution. He stated that the situation was practically out of control of the Central Government.

Thailand, Turkey, France, and Mexico commended the United States for its cooperative effort in dealing with illicit trafficking.

The United States representative commended the Governments of Thailand, Turkey, France, Mexico, Lebanon, Italy, and Japan for efforts put forth to suppress the illicit narcotic traffic and for the excellent coopcration extended to our U.S. Bureau of Narcotics by their police authorities.

Illicit trafficking in synthetic drugs presented no problem.

The USSR representative stated that there was no illicit traffic in her country. The United States representative presented three press clippings with Moscow datelines reporting illicit trafficking whereupon the USSR representative admitted there had been cases of hashish trafficking but stated that they had been dealt with severely.

Cannabis was the subject of considerable discussion, as this traffic is growing throughout the world and very little can be done at this time except increased police measures.

A proposal some years ago by the United States representative to bring the clandestine heroin manufacture under control by watching the trade in acetic anhydride and acetyl chloride was producing results in some countries.

There were sharp exchanges among the representatives of the Near and Middle East, with charges and counter charges. The situation in that area is not one where there is close cooperation, in spite of the Middle East Regional Conferences. Each time one of the countries was mentioned as a source of illicit narcotics the representative of that country would go on the defensive and attempt to obscure the problem. This is one of the unfortunate situations prevailing in the Commission, where most of the countries try to conceal the traffic by making long statements that there is no illicit trafficking.

The United States representative gave incontrovertible evidence of large illicit cocaine trafficking from Cuba to the United States. The Cuban observer stated in his reply that there was no illicit trafficking and that the Revolutionary Government of Cuba brought about social reforms and preventive measures against drug addiction. He launched into a long political tirade against the United States, whereupon the United States representative called a point of order and the Chairman insisted that the Cuban observer confine his remarks strictly to technical matters.

The Cuban observer made serious allegations about the smuggling of narcotic drugs to Cuba which he stated were sent along with other medicines from the United States in exchange for prisoners from Cuba. The United States representative replied that these drugs had been requested by the Cuban Red Cross and that the Cuban Ministry of Health had given a receipt for them; that these drugs were desperately needed for the sick in Cuba, and that no smuggling was involved. The Cuban observer also stated that these narcotics had been returned to the United States. This is not true, with the exception of a small amount of codeine compound which had deteriorated.

The United States representative stated that a list of fifty traffickers, against whom cases had been made some years ago by agents of the U.S. Bureau of Narcotics in cooperation with the Cuban police authorities, had been sent to the Revolutionary Government of Cuba and that nothing had been heard about the action taken. The Cuban observer stated that all of these traffickers had been expelled to the United States.

The United States Government's decision to send narcotic drugs along with other medicines to Cuba in exchange for prisoners was unfortunate. As a result it enabled the Cuban Government to make charges to the Permanent Central Opium Board claiming that our action in doing so was in violation of narcotic treaties to which both Governments are parties. The narcotic drugs in question were sent at the urgent request of the Cuban Red Cross that they were desperately needed. In a spirit of cooperation and as a matter of expediency the United States Government authorized shipment of the narcotics only after being assured that an official Cuban import permit had been issued which would be delivered to an American Red Cross representative when the narcotics arrived in Cuba. This permit had, in fact, not been issued but a receipt was given by the Cuban Minister of Health for the narcotic drugs.

7. *Work of the Conference:*

Election of Officers

The United States representative placed in nomination as Chairman the name of Dr. J.F. Mabileau of France, who was elected by acclamation.

The Yugoslav representative proposed Dr. I. Vertes of Hungary as First Vice-Chairman. He was evidently a popular choice, as his nomination was supported by the representatives of Turkey, USSR, Poland,

India, Iran, France, the United Kingdom, Canada, Japan, Mexico, Switzerland, the Federal Republic of Germany and the United Arab Republic.

The United Kingdom representative nominated Mr. B.N. Banerji of India as Second Vice-Chairman. His nomination was supported by the representatives of the United States and many other countries.

The representative of Canada, supported by the representatives of the United States and many other countries, proposed Dr. M. Dadgar of Iran as Rapporteur.

Question of Chinese Representation

The representative of the USSR, supported by the representatives of Poland and Hungary, said the right to represent China in the Commission belonged exclusively to the Government of the People's Republic of China.

The representative of China, supported by the representative of the United States, regretted that the question had been raised, as it had already been settled by the General Assembly in October 1962.

The representative of India maintained that the People's Republic of China should obtain its rightful place in the United Nations but considered that the question should not be voted upon or decided in the Commission.

Report of the Permanent Central Opium Board to the Economic and Social Council on the work of the Board in 1962

The consumption of codeine was increasing in keeping with the increase in population. The United States representative pointed out that since there were three generations of medical practitioners and one generation in the medical schools, it would not be likely during the next ten years that consumption of codeine, a drug with little addiction liability, would decrease to any marked extent.

The USSR representative made an interesting statement that in her country they had been working with some chemicals to produce a codeine synthetic and that results were promising.

The considerable increase in the manufacture of morphine from poppy straw was of concern, as it would tend to bring about over-production of opium. So far no illicit traffic has been reported, as the countries manufacturing morphine from poppy straw had shown proper control.

The United States representative pointed out that manufacture of morphine from poppy straw was not economically advantageous; also, that many useful alkaloids from opium could not be obtained from poppy straw.

Statement of the Drug Supervisory Body on estimated world requirements of narcotic drugs in 1963

The Hungarian representative challenged the right of the Nationalist Chinese Government to submit estimates for narcotic drugs for Communist China. It is incredible that the Nationalist Chinese Government would make an estimate for 800,000,000 people for a total of about 290 kilograms of codeine. Countries like Denmark and Sweden consume this amount. The Soviet Bloc missed a big opening here to show the stupidity of the Nationalist Chinese Government for making such a ridiculous estimate.

Appointment of a member of the Drug Supervisory Body

There had been considerable doubt that the Indian Government would permit Mr. E.S. Krishnamoorthy of the Permanent Central Opium Board to represent the Commission on the Drug Supervisory Body. One high Indian official pointed out to the United States representative that if another Indian was appointed to a prominent position in the United Nations there would be strong voices of disapproval. However, at the last moment the Indian Government decided to allow his name to be placed in nomination. In the meantime the representative of France made a strong plea for the United States representative to place the name of Mr. Charles Vaille in nomination, even though this was not consistent with the resolution of the Economic and Social Council that there should be a personal union in the membership of the Permanent Central Opium Board and the Drug Supervisory Body. As the Bureau of Narcotics now has a man stationed in Paris and one in Marseille who are assisting in making large cases of illicit heroin trafficking which is aimed at the United States, it was strongly felt by both the French and United States representatives that not to follow the wishes of the French Government might result in a lessening of cooperation which had been laboriously built up for many years. The United States representative placed the name of Mr. Charles Vaille in nomination. The vote was 14 for Mr. Krishnamoorthy and 6 for Mr. Vaille, with one abstention. However, it should be pointed out that the 4 votes which swung the election were from the Soviet Bloc.

Mr. Vaille's election would have been of great importance to the world, as he was the author of the 1953 Opium Protocol and he unquestionably is one of the world's outstanding experts on every phase of narcotics outside of the illicit traffic.

Illicit Traffic

The Commission adopted a resolution on the illicit traffic in the Far East, sponsored by Canada, India, and the United Kingdom, urging that the Governments concerned take all necessary measures to deal with the situation, in particular by

(i) obtaining more precise information about the areas in which the opium poppy is illicitly cultivated and about the location of illicit laboratories for the manufacture of morphine and heroin;

(ii) registering opium smokers, where such smoking is still permitted, with a view to the eventual elimination of the practice;

(iii) strengthening wherever necessary their enforcement services and improving the training and methods of operation of those services so that they may be able to deal more effectively with the illicit cultivation of the opium poppy, the illicit manufacture of morphine and heroin, and illicit traffic in these drugs;

(iv) controlling to the extent necessary and practicable the import and internal distribution of acetic anhydride and acetyle chloride;

(v) studying the problem of eliminating the cultivation of the opium poppy by hill tribes or other less-developed groups as a means of livelihood, and taking any necessary measures to achieve that end.

(vi) cooperating closely with other countries in the area in the direct and coordinated exchange of information useful in countering the illicit traffic;

(vii) including in their applications for technical assistance provision for appropriate assistance which may be required with a view to facilitating the implementation of plans for countering the illicit traffic, whether by way of training personnel, obtaining expert advice, or for any other purpose.

The vote on this resolution was 18 for, 1 abstention (China), 2 absent.

Abuse of drugs (drug addiction)

Government reports showed great variations in form and substance and indicated that many countries are now submitting more extensive information.

No developments were reported in progress toward finding a cure for addiction as for alcoholism. Some governments felt that the approach should be psychiatric. The United States representative said that there should be both treatment and rehabilitation and prevention by way of heavy penalties for trafficking, which was supported by several delegations.

In referring to the quasi-medical use of opium in India, the United States representative pointed out that one of the most remarkable developments in the history of narcotics was the reduction in opium consumption in India for smoking and eating purposes from 500 tons twenty years ago to some 2 tons in 1961.

Heroin addiction in Hong Kong was regarded as being of a serious nature.

Addiction among the medical profession was considered of great concern but no decision was reached as to how this was to be approached.

Program of scientific research on opium

The United Nations Laboratory continues to produce excellent reports on determination of opium origin which are always challenged by the country of origin.

The coordination of the scientific research in many laboratories throughout the world was particularly gratifying. The United States representative, however, pointed out that now is the time to begin work on the source identification of heroin and that the Oak Ridge Laboratory has already produced some interesting data.

The question of the coca leaf

The work of the Consultative Group on Coca Leaf Problems which met at Lima, Peru, in November–December 1962 was reviewed.

The Bolivian observer made a strong statement that chewing of the coca leaf was harmless. The United States representative pointed out that the Bolivian Minister of Health and all of the Bolivian officials present at the Lima conference had condemned its use. The United States representative apologized for having brought this division of opinion within the Bolivian Government to the attention of the Commission. The decision of the Commission was unanimous that coca leaf chewing was dangerous and should be eliminated. Accordingly, the Commission adopted a resolution (sponsored by Brazil, Mexico, Peru, and the United States) addressed to the Economic and Social Council which recommends to the General Assembly the exceptional appropriation, if necessary for 1964, of sufficient funds for an Inter-American Seminar on the Coca Leaf in 1964.

The question of cannabis

An article entitled "The Cannabis Habit" by Dr. H.B.M. Murphy of Ottawa, Canada, in Volume XV, No. 1, of the *Bulletin on Narcotics* drew criticism from the United States representative because it placed too much emphasis on the supposedly harmless effects of cannabis. After discussion, which included reference to an opinion of the World Health Organization that cannabis is harmful and addicting, the Commission decided that the drug is dangerous.

Program of scientific research on cannabis

Little or no progress was reported in this field. The United States representative pointed out that it was of urgent importance that a cannabis test be developed for field law enforcement use and that present identification was not satisfactory. Also, in relation to road accidents, in contradistinction to the possibility for police to determine that a driver was under the influence of alcohol, their only means of determining that a driver was under the influence of cannabis would be for the driver to admit his use of it. With the growing increase in cannabis abuse throughout the world and increase in road accidents, it was necessary to have scientific research pointed in that direction.

The question of synthetic and other new narcotic drugs

The United States representative raised the question of Hexalgon, a substance developed many years ago in Germany, which had been distributed in Hungary, Argentina, and other countries and had not been placed under international control. He pointed out that there had been cases of addiction; that this could be a mad dog run loose in the world, and it was up to the Commission to take the necessary action. It was decided to have the drug tested for addiction liability so that the proper control action could be instituted on recommendation of the World Health Organization. It is evident that in this instance the international control machinery did not function properly.

Barbiturates and Amphetamines

While the discussion on these items was rather brief, it was decided not to take any action but to keep these problems under constant surveillance.

The United States representative stated that in its interim report the committee of experts appointed after the White House Conference on Narcotic and Drug Abuse had advised against subjecting the manufacture, sale and distribution of barbiturates and amphetamines to the narcotic laws; if they were so subjected, the medical use of those drugs would be seriously hampered. Legislation had been introduced for their control, but the controls applicable to dangerous drugs were not so strict as those applicable to narcotics. There was no illicit traffic in barbiturates, and the establishment of international control would place enormous additional administrative burdens on governments as well as on the Permanent Central Opium Board and the Drug Supervisory Body.

Technical Cooperation in Narcotics Control

In addition to the resolution on technical cooperation in the field of the coca leaf, the Commission adopted a resolution (sponsored by India, United Kingdom, and Yugoslavia), addressed to the Economic and Social Council, calling for a survey of economic and social requirements of an opium-producing region in Burma to see whether any progress could be made in substituting other crops for opium cultivation among the hill tribes.

The 1961 Single Convention

At the time of the Eighteenth Session of the Commission on Narcotic Drugs seventeen nations had ratified the 1961 Single Convention. All of these, with the exception of Canada and Thailand, are small nations of minor importance in respect to narcotic problems.

An Administrative Guide for the 1961 Convention had been prepared by Mr. Bertil A. Renborg, former head of the Opium Section under the League of Nations. His voluminous work was not regarded with favor by any delegation.

The question of preparing a commentary was raised. The task had been offered to Sir Samuel Hoare, the United Kingdom representative on the Economic and Social Council. The fee will be $34,000 and the work will take about four years. Sir Samuel Hoare wisely rejected the task, as he does not have the legal or technical knowledge to produce such a document on the Single Convention. Apparently there is no one in sight who can take on this work.

A number of the delegations announced their intention to ratify the 1961 Single Convention, but evidently with tongue in cheek, as they privately stated that they would await action of the United States Government.

There was very little discussion on the subject, as previously the United States, Canada, and the United Kingdom decided to limit the discussion to bare essentials.

The United States representative pointed out that at the last meeting of the Permanent Central Opium Board a comment on the 1961 Single Convention had been prepared by the Secretariat which took a position parallel with that of the United States—that the reservations could have a substantial effect on the success of the Convention. The secretary of the Board declined to disclose the document in question.

The 1953 Opium Protocol

The Government of Turkey announced that ratification of the 1953 Opium Protocol was in process and would soon be accomplished. This caused keen disappointment among proponents of the 1961 Single Convention.

The Yugoslav representative raised the question that the 1953 Opium Protocol might not be legal and asked what proper legal steps could be taken to have a decision handed down by the International Court of Justice.

The question of an international body to administer both the 1953 Opium Protocol and the 1961 Single Convention, if it came into force, caused no difficulty as it was felt that the present two bodies could carry on this work satisfactorily, especially since the 1953 Protocol would have to be in operation for the next five years.

Work of the Commission

The Commission unanimously adopted a resolution (sponsored by Brazil, Canada, India, United Arab Republic, and the United States) requesting the Secretary-General to present to the 20th session of the Commission a report which will cover and evaluate the work done and the results obtained during the preceding 19 years.

8. Future Meetings:

The decision of the Economic and Social Council that the next session of the Commission on Narcotic Drugs last only three weeks was an excellent one. Unquestionably the Commission, if it worked full time, could dispose of all of its work in three weeks without loss of effectiveness. Most of the representatives are experts and little time is lost in arriving at a decision.

A provisional agenda for the Commission's 19th session was adopted.

It was agreed to invite Afghanistan, Argentina, Bolivia, Burma, Cuba, Cyprus, Greece, Israel, Italy, Laos, Lebanon, Federation of Malaya, Netherlands, Pakistan, Portugal, Spain, Syria, Thailand, and Viet Nam to send observers to the Commission meetings on the illicit traffic and to meetings of the Committee on Illicit Traffic.

It was agreed to invite the following countries to send observers: Argentina, Bolivia, Burma, Greece, Israel, Italy, Lebanon, Netherlands, Pakistan, and Thailand to the Commission meetings on abuse of drugs (drug addiction); Greece, Italy, and the Netherlands to the meetings on opium and scientific research on opium; Argentina, Bolivia, and Colombia to the meetings on the coca leaf; Greece, Lebanon, Nepal, Netherlands, Pakistan, and South Africa to the meetings on cannabis and scientific research on cannabis; Belgium, Ethiopia, Greece, Israel, Italy, Kenya, Netherlands, Somalia, and Yemen to the meetings on questions relating to other substances, including khat; Greece, Israel, Italy, Netherlands, and Poland to the meetings on the 1961 Single Convention.

9. Conclusions:

Mr. Otis E. Mulliken, Adviser from the Department of State, was extremely helpful in guiding the policy of the delegation in accordance with the position papers.

Commissioner of Narcotics Henry L. Giordano represented the United States in the Committee on Illicit Traffic and conducted his debates with force and courtesy.

The Honorable James A. Reed, Assistant Secretary of the Treasury, assisted the delegation during the first week of the Commission meetings. He conferred with the delegations of the United Kingdom, Canada, Switzerland, Federal Republic of Germany, Sweden, Finland, China, and others about the undesirability of ratifying the Single Convention of 1961 and urged action to make the Opium Protocol of 1953 a success.

Mr. John T. Cusack, District Supervisor of the Bureau of Narcotics in Rome, Italy, assisted the delegation in the handling of many necessary details.

The entire Eighteenth Session was a modicum of harmony, coordination, and efficiency. With few exceptions there was no acrimony and debate.

The Soviet Bloc behaved particularly well and did not place any technical obstacles to halt the work. It showed every indication of wanting to help and took advantage of the information which was presented by many delegations.

The future work of the Commission will be seriously affected by the following developments:

The departure of Mr. Gilbert E. Yates as Director of the Division of Narcotic Drugs and the transfer of Dr. Adolf Lande to head the secretariat of the Permanent Central Opium Board to succeed Mr. L. Atzenwiler who has retired, left a very serious gap in the Division to maintain the high standards of former years. With the departure of Dr. Lande, no one in the Division is qualified as a legal expert on the nine treaties and protocols and the Single Convention.

Mr. Daniel A. Chapman of Ghana took over the directorship of the Division. Representatives expressed their unanimous wish to support him in his difficult task. Neither Mr. Chapman nor three top assistants recently appointed have the slightest knowledge of narcotics. Thus the quality of the United Nations work on narcotics will be seriously hampered. There is no question that the appointments were of a political nature and without regard to efficiency. At least four of the high officials in the Division have not the slightest knowledge of the many intricate and manifold problems of narcotics. The new director, highly conscious of his disability in staff, is going to take steps to correct the situation.

International Science Issues

346. **Letter From President Kennedy to the President's Special Assistant for Science and Technology (Wiesner)**[1]

Washington, January 23, 1961.

Dear Dr. Wiesner:

Within the over-all area of your responsibility as my Special Assistant for Science and Technology, I should appreciate your finding, developing, and presenting to me facts, evaluations, and recommendations respecting matters related to science and technology and the progress of scientific endeavor in the various agencies of Government, giving particular attention to trends and developments as they affect national security and welfare, to the relative progress of Soviet and U.S. science and technology, to scientific and technological cooperation with our allies, and to the encouragement and utilization of science in the free world.

It is my desire that you advise on scientific and technological matters in top-level policy deliberations, making yourself available to Cabinet members and other officers of Government holding policy responsibilities, when appropriate and practical, and working in close association with other members of the White House staff and the Director of the Bureau of the Budget. You are authorized to attend the meetings of the National Security Council, the Cabinet, and the National Aeronautics and Space Council.

In carrying on these activities, you may retain the services of such staff and special consultants as you may require.

The foregoing is intended to serve as an aid to you in organizing your work and is not designed specifically to define your responsibilities. In carrying out your task, you will have full access to all plans, programs, and activities involving science and technology in the Government.

As my Special Assistant for Science and Technology, and thereby a member of the Federal Council for Science and Technology, I designate you as Chairman of the Council.

---

[1] Source: Kennedy Library, Jerome Wiesner Papers, White House—President Messages and Congrates, 1962, Box 10. Confidential. Jerome B. Wiesner, director of the electronics research laboratory of the Massachusetts Institute of Technology, was appointed Special Assistant to the President for Science and Technology on January 11, 1961.

It is my hope that your work will be of great value in developing information for me and in giving a greater sense of direction to all who are concerned in our nation's scientific and technological efforts.

Sincerely,

John F. Kennedy

---

347.   **Memorandum From Secretary of State Rusk to the Chairman of the Policy Planning Council (McGhee)**[1]

Washington, July 22, 1961.

SUBJECT

Population Problem

1. The Policy Planning Council's paper of June 16[2] is an excellent presentation of the population problem, although it could use certain filling out at particular points. Nevertheless, I generally agree with the main lines of the presentation.

2. I am sure that the Policy Planning Council recognizes that the policy issue goes far beyond religious, political and social attitudes in the United States. It would be easy to be naive on this matter. Nor is it helpful to project population curves into "standing room only" on the earth a century or two hence. Both population growth and the development of resources have many variables. The territory of the United States was probably more overpopulated at the time of the landing of the first white man than it has been at any time since. But even today, if one thinks of the Paley Report,[3] we would be overpopulated were we not able to suck into our productive system vast resources from other continents. I am also troubled by the question which arises if some nations take action in this field and others do not. A distortion of the make-up of the human race could occur which would not necessarily be in the interest of the American people.

3. My suggestions with respect to the recommendations are:

---

[1] Source: National Archives and Records Administration, RG 59, Rusk Files: Lot 72 D 192, Chron. File, July 1961. Confidential.

[2] Reference is to a report entitled "Foreign Policy Implications of the World Population Explosion." (Ibid., S/P Files: Lot 67 D 548)

[3] Not further identified.

1. Approved, but requires some spelling out.

2. There should be an officer in IO who gives a good deal of attention to such matters as our backstop for the United Nations Population Commission.

3. Throwing a lot of money into research programs does not necessarily speed up the right answers. The National Academy of Sciences, with the financial support of the Rockefeller Foundation, has had for thirty years a committee for research on sex which has stimulated basic research on the physiology of reproduction. Similarly, the Population Council in New York is engaging in specific, basic and applied research directly related to population contol. My impression is that the bottleneck is not money but ideas. These two organizations might be consulted by S/P to get their assessment of the research situation.

4. Agree.

5. I would not agree at this time. In a certain sense, the policy question does not arise because we have no satisfactory answers to provide these other countries. Private organizations which have been working in this field have encountered economic and sociological obstacles which are unlikely to be overcome until present and rather promising research comes up with more effective answers for the individual family. In some countries means are being adopted which would be contrary to our own public policy, such as abortion and sterilization. If foreign governments are interested (and a number of them are), it is relatively easy for them to get "information regarding human reproduction and population problems" without involving AID.

6. A good idea, but too simply stated. Again, there are private agencies which are working intensively with governments which show an interest in the problem.

7. It is easy to agree in principle but more difficult to agree about what would be the right and wise thing to say.

Let me conclude with the remark that this is not a problem for which the answers are merely inhibited by religious or political considerations. There are some real problems as to what the right answers are.

Dean Rusk[4]

---

[4] Printed from a copy that bears this typed signature.

348.   Memorandum From the President's Special Assistant for
        Science and Technology (Wiesner) to Secretary of State
        Rusk[1]

Washington, March 16, 1962.

The President's Science Advisory Committee (PSAC), as I know
you are aware, has been involved frequently in various aspects of the
interaction between foreign relations and science and technology, and
has always been interested in the effectiveness with which technical factors are included in the formulation and execution of foreign policy.

You recently mentioned your concern regarding the scientific activities in the Department of State, and I told you of the study being conducted by our International Science Panel chaired by Dr. Bronk.[2] We have
focussed in some detail on the representation of science and technology
within the Department on policy matters and on the needs, as we see
them, for increasing State Department guidance of the growing overseas
scientific and technical programs of the Government as a whole.

During the course of this study, we have held discussions with
many representatives of the Department, and have now transmitted
informally, through Mr. Alexis Johnson, our conclusions and recommendations. I am very pleased at this time to forward to you for your
consideration the formal report we have prepared.

I hope you will find this useful to you. We attach great importance
to the manner in which science and technology are integrated into the
work of the Department, and thus can be enabled to serve effectively
our national and foreign policy objectives. I would be pleased to discuss this with you at your convenience.

JB Wiesner

Attachment

Washington, February 27, 1962.

INTERNATIONAL SCIENCE PANEL

SCIENCE AND TECHNOLOGY IN THE DEPARTMENT OF STATE

The relations between nations, and hence the formulation and execution of foreign policy, are today increasingly affected by scientific and

---

[1] Source: National Archives and Records Administration, RG 59, Central Files,
1960–63, 110.10/3–1662. Official Use Only.

[2] Dr. Detlev W. Bronk, President of the National Academy of Sciences.

technical considerations that in the past were only of peripheral interest to the statesman and diplomat. Many foreign policy issues require sophisticated technical analysis and understanding of the political implications of the technical facts before policy can be effectively determined or carried out. In some areas, the international operations of the Government or the private community in science and technology are now on a scale such that they have an important impact on our relations with others. And science and its technological fruits also offer opportunities for international initiatives that can contribute in significant ways to our national objectives.

With this in mind, this Panel of the President's Science Advisory Committee considered the way these relationships are at present represented in the foreign policy organs of the United States Government and what further steps may be desirable. In the discussion that follows, we have outlined in some detail the needs as we see them, and the responsibilities we believe should fall to a strengthened and expanded science office in the Department of State.

Discussion

In 1950, an important study of the relation of science to international relations was carried out for the Secretary of State.[3] The study outlined the many interactions between science and the formation and execution of foreign policy, and presented the need for a better mechanism within the Department to reflect this relationship. As a result, a Science Adviser to the Department of State was named, and a series of Science Attachés were appointed at major overseas posts.

The new posts were allowed to lapse in the mid-50s until the shock and surprise of the launching of an artificial earth satellite by the Soviet Union, with its subsequent repercussions, indicated once again that better technical inputs into policy formulation and planning were required. Accordingly, the post of Science Adviser was filled again, this time reporting directly to the Secretary of State; the attaché program was renewed at the same time.

Since 1958, the scope and involvement of the Science Adviser and his Attachés have steadily grown and broadened. But what is most striking to this Panel is the development since the original report of 1950 of a steadily more pervasive and significant relationship between science and foreign affairs, across a broad spectrum of activities and foreign policy concerns.

---

[3] *Science and Foreign Relations*, a report by Lloyd Berkner, Special Consultant to the Secretary of State, Department of State Publication 3860, General Foreign Policy Series 30, May 1950. [Footnote in the source text.]

Probably the most noticeable, though not necessarily the most important, change has been the growing volume of international activities of scientists and engineers, and of international programs of a technical nature of the Federal Government:

—U.S. agencies now sponsor applied and fundamental research by foreign scientists in foreign countries amounting to more than $60 million per year;
—many of our domestic programs are carried out partly in an international environment: notably the space program, the oceanographic program, the Antarctic program, Atoms-for-Peace, and significant parts of others, such as research programs in the atmospheric sciences, medical sciences, agriculture, and geophysics;
—special international cooperative programs have arisen such as the IGY and cooperative space programs; many more are planned or proposed; for example, the Indian Ocean Oceanographic Expedition, an international hydrology program, the UN atmospheric sciences program, the US/Japanese scientific cooperation committee;
—almost all international organizations now have science programs of one kind or another while some organizations—for example, the IAEA—are largely technical in nature; the U.S. contributions to the technical portions of the budgets are now in the neighborhood of $25–30 million per year;
—many Federal agencies conduct special programs in the United States for the technical training of foreign nationals, especially the AEC, NASA, the Department of HEW, and the Department of State, while others devote substantial resources to the collection and dissemination of technical information abroad;
—many agencies have their own programs to foster the exchange of scientists, and several provide technical missions to assist technical operations in other countries;
—and, of course, the U.S. foreign aid program has a large technical and scientific component.

This is only a partial list, and one for which it is difficult to attach a meaningful dollar tag. Moreover, most of the activities listed are growing, some very rapidly. Clearly, direct scientific and technical activities overseas today command budgets on the order of hundreds of millions of dollars, and programs with important international implications in their operation and of a highly technical nature, are many times that size. But that, too, is misleading for the activities that may be in many ways the most significant for foreign policy may, in fact, cost very little.

The scientific community itself has greatly expanded its own international activities, with a growing number of international associations, international conferences and travel and visits to all parts of the world. These international contacts are a necessary part of science today and are required for the health and vitality of American science. The Department of State has a direct role, and not always a passive one, in safeguarding and assisting the scientific community in its international activities.

It seems to us that these extensive and intensive scientific and technical relations among governments and scientists have made it necessary to think in terms of a "foreign policy for science", to help make these relations fruitful for U.S. international and domestic interests by providing guidance and assistance, by defining political objectives, and by monitoring programs and their international effects. This is not always being achieved today primarily, in our judgment, because there has not been sufficient recognition of the breadth of these activities, of the opportunities for U.S. objectives they provide, and of the obligations they demand.

There are other quite different aspects of this relationship between science and foreign policy as well. For example, we depend on American scientific and technical achievement more than ever before for the realization of foreign policy objectives. Obviously this is so for military strength. But more directly, the Atoms-for-Peace program, U.S. initiatives on outer space in the UN, the foreign aid program, international health programs, exchange programs with iron-curtain countries, information efforts to project a U.S. "image", and many others all rely on using the excellence of American science as a basis for international operations where the political objectives are dominant. The State Department has the obvious need to utilize these achievements effectively and properly, and to take advantage of the many additional opportunities as they arise.

There is, in addition to these "overt" relations between foreign policy and science, the much more subtle and difficult, but perhaps more significant, implicit technical content of many of the areas in which policy must be developed. Obviously, our basic relations with other nations are determined in part by the technical capabilities of our military weapons, and by the weapons now in the development or research stage. Our disarmament policy, and studies necessary to develop that policy, have large technical components. The same is true of foreign aid efforts in which the prospects for economic development of Pakistan may depend on understanding and ameliorating the waterlogging problem, or in which the creation of a viable economic base for a one-crop nation may depend on the ability to locate new mineral resources or to develop new crop strains for special environments. Similar comments may be made about other policy areas, many of which simply cannot be adequately considered without understanding the often very intimate relationship between the technical and political factors.

A special case of the implicit technical content of foreign policy issues is the need to plan ahead in the development of policy to prepare for the changes being wrought by an exploding technological age. It is trite to say that the revolutions in communications, transportation, health, and a host of other fields have changed the relations among nations. How are the changes of tomorrow and of the day after going to alter further our international environment, and what should we be doing now to prepare for them? The issues can be as large as the effects of the development of simple, inexpensive means for any nation to produce atomic weapons, to the effect on a one-export nation of the development of an inexpensive synthetic substitute for its single export. The Department of State has the need to anticipate these developments, understand their likely effects, and lay the groundwork for the measures necessary to cope with them.

Conclusions

With this view of the inextricable and intense linking of science with foreign policy today, the Panel has come to the conclusion that it is time to plan for another step in the organization for science in the State Department. Working from outside the Department, we are obviously not familiar with the subtleties of Departmental organization and hence cannot recommend in detail a specific structure. However, we believe we can lay out the framework that is required based on our view of the needs and our knowledge of present organization and procedures.

It seems to us that it is necessary to have in one office in the Department the competence and the staff support to be aware of the breadth of activities and interests discussed above, and the responsibility, working with other desks in the Department and with other Federal agencies, to develop specific policy guidance. Where the issues are predominantly technical or scientific, we would expect the office to have primary responsibility; where the technical or scientific component is subsidiary, we would expect the office to play a secondary role, though it should be mandatory that they be consulted.

In effect, we are suggesting that the science office have staff responsibility in the formulation of general policy and primary or line responsibility for the formulation of policy in certain defined areas. The existing office of The Science Adviser has of course been performing well a good part of this function, but with existing staff support and lack of delineation of authority, many of the important tasks we see cannot now be fully discharged. The Office of the Special Assistant to the Secretary for Space and Atomic Energy has also been performing part of this role well for its specialized areas, and we would expect that the two offices would be combined into one. In fact, one of the tasks the Science Office should perform is to give more of the kind of guidance, support, and initiative in the technical areas of health, agriculture, geophysics, etc. that is now being provided in detail for space and atomic energy.

We recognize in this recommendation that along with line responsibility goes, inevitably, responsibility for a considerable amount of detailed work, e.g., negotiating or preparing complicated technical agreements or reviewing programs of international organizations in detail. Though this may be time-consuming and require a sizable staff, it is a necessary part of the policy process, without which "policy responsibility" would be an empty phrase.

An important phase of a Science Office's responsibility, as is the case now, is as a focus of relations between the State Department and other agencies of the Government and with the non-government scientific community on scientific matters. One of the advantages of a well-staffed office with clear responsibility will be to provide a single, authoritative voice in the Department able to give detailed guidance and support for the international scientific programs of Federal agencies. This relationship will always be a delicate one, for the State Department must not become a bottleneck to action, but at the same time must have clearly-formed policies and knowledge of foreign situations to be able to provide prompt decisions and adequate support when required. More positively, the State Department should be in the position more often than it has to date of proposing new international programs in science and technology to further U.S. foreign policy objectives, and of acting on those proposals generated by scientists throughout the country.

The relations with the private scientific community are of course of great importance; the creation of the present Office of the Science Adviser has proven to be very significant in helping to understand the effect of foreign policy decisions on science in the United States, and in providing a link for the ideas and concerns of the scientific community to be brought to the attention of the Department of State. As the international activities and interests of scientists grow, so too does the need to increase the contacts between them and the Department. The opportunities are great, for example, in more effectively tapping the scientific community to provide a manpower resource for our mushrooming overseas needs. The interest of the scientists is there, but we have not yet learned how to make effective use of it.

The Science Office can also provide, through ad hoc panels or consultants, more extensive technical advice to the Department on the specific technical-political issues it faces. This device has been relatively little used in the past and could be considerably expanded.

We would note as a final point that for an expanded science office to carry out its functions adequately, also implies a strengthened and enlarged Science Attaché program in the field. Only in that way could the office obtain the detailed information about situations in other countries, and the necessary evaluations to enable wise formulation of policy.

Detailed Functions

An expanded science function in the Department will probably require some organizational changes, though the Panel does not feel competent to advise on the exact form within the Department. We believe the head of a science office should be designated a Principal Officer of the Department, with the rank of Assistant Secretary, but whether he should have the title of Assistant Secretary or Director of an Office of Scientific Affairs, or some other designation, must depend on other considerations. We would recommend that in time it would be advisable to establish the post by statute as a means of alerting Congress to the changing requirements of foreign policy.

To sum up the responsibilities we feel should be exercised by an office for science, we list below nine major categories of responsibility drawn from this discussion:

1. *Development of a national foreign policy for science*

Here we have reference to the need to define an effective role for science in the evolution and execution of foreign policy, to bring greater coherence and policy guidance into the myriad international scientific activities of Federal agencies—many of which are only superficially known in the Department now—to enlist the technical resources of Government more effectively and widely in the support of foreign policy objectives, to encourage private scientific activities when in the nation's interest, to be aware of deficiencies as well as excesses, and to represent in the Department the relatively new awareness that the international contacts of scientists have become one of the significant interfaces between this and other nations. The relationship between the private scientific community and the foreign policy organs of Government can be yet closer and more extensive than they are today, and offer opportunities as well as responsibilities to the Department which make it necessary to have a more thoroughly developed and understood foreign policy for science.

2. *Specific programs for international cooperation*

This Government has a general policy that international cooperative programs carried out properly can contribute significantly to the nation's objectives. To bring these about, the Government must usually take the lead, but each proposal takes extensive thought and preparation, scientific planning, intragovernment arrangements, tactical planning, international discussions and negotiations, and finally monitoring and guidance during the operations. Relatively few such programs have emerged because of the time and effort each takes. But many additional proposals and ideas exist that require an interested and well-staffed office in the State Department to reach fruition.

3. *UN and Other International Governmental and Non-Governmental Organizations*

Almost all of the UN Specialized Agencies have scientific or technical programs of one kind or another; some in fact such as WHO and

WMO are largely technical in nature. The science office should provide major inputs into the determination of U.S. policy towards all of these technical programs, and is the logical point at which to tie in the private scientific community and the technical resources of the other agencies of government.

4. *Scientific Exchange and Fellowship Programs*

These areas of State Department interest necessarily involve the private scientific and academic community very heavily, and require a knowledgeable, and accepted, point of contact in the Department to work between the non-Governmental community and the Department. Only with an effective relationship can the programs serve U. S. policy well; it is instructive to note the reduction in difficulties and misunderstandings during the last few years since the appointment of the Science Adviser. These programs are sure to be increased in the future, and good advice and initiative on the scientific side will be crucial.

5. *Foreign Aid*

The foreign aid program will require particularly intensive effort in the future to increase the quality and quantity of its scientific programs, to ensure the technical quality of its work, and to embark on a meaningful research program. This cannot be the job of the State Department's science officer; the AID must have its own scientific and technical personnel. But the science officer in State may in fact be of invaluable assistance in helping AID mount its own efforts (particularly needed now) in utilizing the Science Attachés in those countries receiving U.S. assistance to help the USOMs, and, most important, in integrating the overseas science efforts of other Federal agencies to assist in the development objectives.

6. *Scientific Image of the United States*

As with the foreign aid program, the Information Agency requires greater scientific input in their activities. They, too, need their own scientific personnel, but the ability to call on a well-staffed office also within the State Department for help overseas, for contacts with the scientific community, for advice about U.S. Government activities, and for independent evaluation of their activities, would be of great use.

7. *Anticipated Technical Developments*

The science officer of State, through his general familiarity and contacts with the technical communities, is the most logical one to become aware of the trends of technical development and their implications for international relations and foreign policy. We can imagine a representative of the office meeting with the Policy Planning Staff regularly, but, in addition, what is needed is an awareness in affected areas of the Department of developments likely to be of importance in their countries or regions.

8. *Monitoring and information through Science Attachés*

To carry out all of these functions adequately and to monitor and guide government programs will require better information on the situation in each country, and more day-to-day contact with overseas U.S. activities. The Science Attaché program must provide much of this, and to do so it will have to be strengthened. In bringing this about, we should not overlook the reservoir of scientific talent from other U.S. agencies that could be available for this purpose to the benefit of both the State Department and the agencies. In addition, agency personnel already stationed abroad could be used to assist the State Department in this function. We would also note that a strengthened Attaché program would require additional funds for travel, and particularly for regular meetings in Washington.

9. *Representation in General Policy Formulation*

Perhaps the single most important of all the functions a science officer can perform we have left for the last of those we will list here. We have done this because we believe that the usefulness of the man in the science post to the Secretary and to the Department on the formulation of general foreign policy matters depends much more on the man and his relation to the Secretary than on his title or size of office.

We are referring under this heading to the part such a science officer would or could play in discussions on political-military policy matters in, let us say, the implications of new weapons or of a domestic shelter program, and to his potential role in discussions of nuclear test cut-off or atmospheric testing, or to his role in disarmament policy. Obviously, the individual's own background and interest, his relationship with the Secretary, and his usefulness in such discussions will determine in large part the extent of his participation. But it is also worth noting that with the many other responsibilities we see for this post, unless there is adequate staff it would not be possible for the incumbent to maintain the contact and knowledge necessary to be useful in this role.

We have presented our concept, as seen from outside the Department, of a strengthened and expanded science section of the Department of State, and have suggested that the science officer be designated a Principal Officer of the Department as a recognition of his extensive responsibilities in policy formulation and execution. Such an office to perform well the functions we have outlined would, we believe, have additional staff requirements in Washington and in the field; some of the staff, both at home and overseas, should, in our view, be provided from other Federal agencies for the advantage of both the Department of State and those agencies.

It is our judgment that this proposal is a logical recognition of the changing character of international relations, and of the need for organizational changes within the Department to keep up to those changes.

349. **Letter From the Deputy Under Secretary of State for Political Affairs (Johnson) to the Chairman of the Atomic Energy Commission (Seaborg)[1]**

Washington, May 16, 1962.

Dear Dr. Seaborg:

As an initial step in a planned program to strengthen the Department of State's ability to deal with matters related to international scientific affairs, it is our intention to announce near the end of this week abolishment of the Office of the Special Assistant for Atomic Energy and Outer Space, and the transfer of its functions and responsibilities relating to peaceful uses of atomic energy and outer space to the Office of the Science Adviser. State's responsibilities relating to military aspects of work in these fields will be assigned to the Deputy Assistant Secretary for Politico-Military Affairs.

Working relationships between the Department of State and the Atomic Energy Commission have been excellent. Your cooperation, and that of members of your staff, has contributed immeasurably to the resolution of important problems of international significance in which we have a mutual interest.

I am confident the organizational changes we are making will not impair in any way the effectiveness of planning and action on matters affecting foreign policy as it relates to the work of your agency. Consolidation of related responsibilities here should reduce points of contact and clearance and result in moving forward with greater facility and expedition.

Officers to whom these responsibilities are being assigned will be in touch with appropriate officials of your agency as matters arise requir-

---

[1] Source: National Archives and Records Administration, RG 59, Central Files 1960–63, 110.10/5–1662. No classification marking. Drafted by Deputy Assistant Secretary of State for Management Ralph S. Roberts. An identical letter was sent to James E. Webb, Administrator of the National Aeronautics and Space Administration.

ing consultation or joint action. However, I thought it only proper that you should know in advance of our plans since they will have a bearing on our inter-agency relationships.

Sincerely,

U. Alexis Johnson[2]

---

[2] Printed from a copy that indicates Johnson signed the original.

---

350. **Memorandum From the Deputy Under Secretary of State for Management (Orrick) to Secretary of State Rusk[1]**

Washington, September 4, 1962.

SUBJECT

Director of International Scientific Affairs—Approval Requested

Purpose

To establish the position of Director of International Scientific Affairs; to abolish the Office of the Science Adviser; and to establish the Office of International Scientific Affairs in the Department of State.

Discussion

The attached circular[2] describes arrangements for a strengthened role for science in the Department. It provides for active participation by the Director of International Scientific Affairs in foreign policy development and application, integration of science and technology into the work of the Department at all levels, and for the Department's foreign affairs leadership and guidance on matters relating to the growing overseas scientific and technical programs of the Government as a whole.

A first step in reorganization of the Department's activities in science and technology was taken May 16, 1962, when the Office of the Special Assistant for Atomic Energy and Outer Space (S/AE) was abolished and its functions concerned with non-military uses were trans-

---

[1] Source: National Archives and Records Administration, RG 59, Management Staff Files: Lot 69 D 434, Management Staff, Miscellaneous Subject Files, Scientific Attaché. No classification marking. A handwritten note on the memorandum indicates that it was signed on September 4.

[2] Not printed. Foreign Affairs Manual Circular No. 84 of September 14 established the position of Director of International Scientific Affairs and replaced the Office of the Science Adviser (S/SA) with an Office of International Scientific Affairs (ISA).

ferred to the Office of the Science Adviser (S/SA). The proposed staff of the new office will be 32, one less than the original combined strength or S/AE and S/SA before merger.

The functions and organizational arrangements are consistent with the conclusions and recommendations of the President's Science Advisory Committe (Bronk) report, on "Science and Technology in the Department of State," dated February 27, 1962. They are also in harmony with Part I of Reorganization Plan No. 2 of 1962 which establishes the Office of Science and Technology as a new element within the Executive Office of the President.[3]

Paragraph 4 of the circular has been included to make clear the intention that the new office will serve all bureaus and offices on scientific matters in the same manner that the Office of the Legal Adviser serves the entire Department on legal work. Thus, there should be no valid basis for appointment of scientists to other bureaus or offices.

The press release announcing the appointment of Dr. Ragnar Rollefson as the Director of International Scientific Affairs will be timed for simultaneous issuance with this circular on the day Dr. Rollefson is sworn in, about September 14.

Recommendation

It is recommended that you approve the attached circular.

---

[3] For text of Reorganization Plan No. 2, see 76 Stat. 1253. The Bronk report is Document 348.

---

351. Memorandum From the Executive Director of the Office of International Scientific Affairs (Pardee) to August Velletri of the Office of Management [1]

Washington, October 31, 1962.

SUBJECT

Criteria for Science Attaché Positions

In making a determination as to whether a position for a Science Attaché should be established and where it should be located

---

[1] Source: National Archives and Records Administration, RG 59, Management Staff Files: Lot 69 D 434, Miscellaneous Subject Files, Scientific Attaché. No classification marking. Copies sent to Charles H. Baldwin and Frank M. Bryan of the Division of Program Review, Office of Finance and Budget.

depends on a number of factors. Each factor is weighed against the impact it will make on the foreign policy of the United States, the furthering of U.S. policy objectives, and the improvement it would make in the relations between the U.S. and a particular country, region or continent.

Criteria

The factors which are examined include:

1. The unique opportunity which such a position would provide for analyzing the political implications of scientific developments;

2. The number of possibilities which such an avenue of communication would offer in establishing relationships with a particular foreign scientific community;

3. The possible ways these associations can be used to further this Government's foreign policy objectives;

4. Psychological and social influences which can be caused through the application of American technology;

5. Opportunities to expand scientific exchanges and associations as a means to improving the understanding of U.S. foreign policy;

6. The need for coordination of U.S. scientific efforts overseas, i.e., places where there are a large number of U.S. agencies engaged in scientific programs;

7. The need for providing technical advice and guidance to the Ambassador and Embassy staffs in those areas or countries where science and technology plays a significant role in foreign policy;

8 The requirement for establishing a regional Scientific Attaché position in less developed areas for the purpose of initiating early communication with foreign governments as they make their initial ventures into the field of science and technology.

Need for more than one position at a post.

The decision to have more than one Attaché at a post is based on two factors, (a) regional responsibility, and (b) workload. An example of regional responsibilities would be the Attaché Office in Stockholm which also covers scientific developments in Finland, Norway and Denmark. An example of where workload requires more than one officer would be in those countries where science and technology is quite sophisticated, where scientific relationships are extensive and where the need for technical advice is closely related to daily foreign policy operations. This would include such places as Germany, France, England, Italy and Japan.

Procedures for establishing an Attaché position.

The procedures which are followed in establishing an Attaché position generally follow this pattern. After ISA has considered all of the factors, has discussed the matter in detail with other interested U.S. agencies, has gathered and analyzed supporting data from scientific reports and programs or private studies, a recommendation is prepared and forwarded to the regional bureau concerned. After collaboration with the regional bureau, a recommendation is submitted to the Embassy in the field for their comments. After all comments are received and final approval obtained, a request for funds for establishing such a position is submitted in collaboration with the regional bureau to the Office of Budget.

AP

---

352.   National Security Action Memorandum No. 235[1]

Washington, April 17, 1963.

TO

The Secretary of State
The Secretary of Defense
The Secretary of the Interior
The Secretary of Commerce
The Secretary of Agriculture
The Secretary of Health, Education, and Welfare
The Chairman, Atomic Energy Commission
The Administrator, National Aeronautics and Space Administration
The Director, National Science Foundation
The Special Assistant to the President for National Security Affairs
The Special Assistant to the President for Science and Technology

SUBJECT

Large-Scale Scientific or Technological Experiments with Possible Adverse
Environmental Effects

I have approved the following policy guides governing the conduct of large-scale scientific or technological experiments that might have

---

[1] Source: Kennedy Library, National Security Files, Departments and Agencies Series, Space Activities, General, 1/63–5/63, Box 307. Confidential. Copies were sent to the Directors of the Central Intelligence Agency, the Bureau of the Budget, and the U.S. Information Agency.

significant or protracted effects on the physical or biological environment. Experiments which by their nature could result in domestic or foreign allegations that they might have such effects will be included in this category even though the sponsoring agency feels confident that such allegations would in fact prove to be unfounded.

1. The head of any agency that proposes to undertake a large-scale scientific or technological experiment that might have significant or protracted effects on the physical or biological environment will call such proposals to the attention of the Special Assistant to the President for Science and Technology. Notification of such experiments will be given sufficiently in advance that they may be modified, postponed, or cancelled, if such action is judged necessary in the national interest.

2. In support of proposals for such experiments, the sponsoring agency will prepare for the Special Assistant for Science and Technology a detailed evaluation of the importance of the particular experiment and the possible direct or indirect effects that might be associated with it.

3. The Special Assistant for Science and Technology will review the proposals and supporting materials presented by the sponsoring agency in order to assure that the need for the experiment has been properly weighed against possible adverse environmental effects.

4. On the basis of this review, the Special Assistant for Science and Technology will recommend to me what action should be taken on the proposed experiment. If the Special Assistant judges that inadequate information is available on which to make a judgment, he may request that additional studies be undertaken by the sponsoring agency or he may undertake an independent study of the problem.

5. Any experiment that may involve significant or protracted adverse effects will not be conducted without my prior approval.

6. In the case of experiments (such as atmospheric nuclear tests) that have major national security implications, the head of the sponsoring agency will notify the Special Assistant for National Security Affairs as well as the Special Assistant for Science and Technology and will supply both with an evaluation of the importance of the particular experiment and the possible direct or indirect effects that might be associated with it. The Special Assistant for National Security Affairs will determine on an individual case basis the procedure to be followed in reviewing these experiments in order to assure that the need for the experiment has been properly weighed against possible adverse environmental effects.

7. To the extent that it is consistent with national security and subsequent to approval, there should be early and widespread dissemination of public information explaining experiments of this type.

8. While the final decision to conduct such experiments must continue to reside with the government, the National Academy of Sciences and where appropriate international scientific bodies or intergovernmental organizations may be consulted in the case of those experiments that might have adverse environmental effects beyond the U.S. Recommendation on the advisability of this course of action will be made by the Special Assistant for Science and Technology in consultation with the sponsoring agency and the State Department.

John F. Kennedy

353. Report by the Department of State to the President's Special Assistant for National Security Affairs (Bundy)[1]

Washington, August 20, 1963.

SUBJECT

Progress Report on International Programs in Atmospheric Science

In the President's address to the General Assembly of the United Nations on September 25, 1961, he stated that we would "propose cooperative efforts between all nations in weather prediction and eventually in weather control."[2]

As a follow-up of this statement, the United States Delegation to the General Assembly submitted a draft resolution which was adopted unanimously in December 1961 stressing the world-wide benefits to be derived from international cooperation in weather research and analysis.[3]

At the next General Assembly, the United States Delegation submitted another draft resolution which was adopted unanimously in December 1962 calling upon Member States to strengthen weather forecasting services and to encourage their scientific communities to coop-

---

[1] Source: Kennedy Library, National Security Files, Subjects Series, Space Activities, General, 7/63–9/63, Box 308. No classification marking. A covering memorandum from Benjamin H. Read, Executive Secretary of the Department of State, transmitted the report to Bundy on August 20.

[2] See *Public Papers of the Presidents of the United States: John F. Kennedy, 1961*, p. 622.

[3] Reference is to Section C of Resolution 1721 (XVI), adopted by the UN General Assembly on December 20, 1961.

erate in the expansion of atmospheric science research. In addition, the World Meteorological Organization (WMO) was urged to develop in greater detail its plans for an expanded program to strengthen meteorological services and research, placing particular emphasis on the use of meteorological satellites and on the expansion of training and educational opportunities in these fields.[4]

Two groups were established in the United States in 1962 to prepare recommendations in this field: one by the National Academy of Sciences and the other by the Department of State.

The National Academy of Sciences appointed an ad hoc Committee on International Programs in Atmospheric Sciences and Hydrology which prepared the outline of an international program in the atmospheric sciences (and later in hydrology). Its recommendations reflected the views of scientists in the United States and was of great assistance to the federal government in the preparation of its program.

An Interagency Group on International Programs in Atmospheric Sciences was established by the Department of State in August 1962 consisting of representatives of the Departments of Commerce, Defense and State, the Office of Science and Technology, the National Aeronautics and Space Administration and the National Science Foundation, with J. Herbert Hollomon, Assistant Secretary of Commerce for Science and Technology, as Chairman. This Group completed its report in March 1963.[5]

Follow-up action was taken by the United States Delegation at the Fourth Congress of the WMO in Geneva in April 1963 and by an accelerated national program consistent with the action taken at the WMO Congress.

In response to United States initiative, the WMO Congress initiated a comprehensive study looking toward the improvement of the worldwide weather system, including an analysis of national requirements and advances in technology. An Advisory Committee was established to consist of twelve highly qualified scientists and experts, a Planning Unit was set up in the WMO Secretariat and increased funds were voted to assist in the proposed world-wide weather system study.

With the assurances of a substantial participation in the proposed weather study by the international community, steps are now being taken by various United States agencies to enable them to contribute to this program, as recommended by the Interagency Group, including the following action:

---

[4] Reference is to Section III of Resolution 1802 (XVII), adopted by the UN General Assembly on December 14, 1962.

[5] For information on the group's report, which included proposals for an atmospheric research program, see Department of State *Bulletin*, May 13, 1963, pp. 742–743.

a. United States Weather Bureau

The United States Weather Bureau has requested a supplemental appropriation for FY 1964 of $700,000 for a systems analysis of the global weather system. This study will include an analysis of the role which satellites can play in meeting global observation and communication requirements of the system. The Weather Bureau is considering additional research and development activities costing $400,000 in FY 1965.

b. National Science Foundation

The National Science Foundation is planning to support, in FY 1964, research planning conferences costing $200,000 and an international manpower survey costing $50,000. The NSF is considering, for FY 1965, a university program with other countries costing $950,000 and the translation and distribution to less developed areas of technical literature costing $200,000.

c. Agency for International Development

Discussions will be undertaken with the Agency for International Development concerning the possibility of sponsoring a conference of high-level representatives of South American weather services to consider regional climatological problems and to outline a plan for a regional climatological center and network.

We intend to continue to press ahead with cooperative programs with other countries to achieve an improved world-wide weather system. The success of our meteorological satellites is contributing significantly to the possibilities in this field, but world-wide cooperation of other countries continues to be indispensable to an effective global weather system. We are pleased with the excellent cooperation we are receiving under the auspices of the World Meteorological Organization; this is a small organization in personnel and financing, but its prestige is high with weather services throughout the world and its impact is accordingly highly significant.

354.   Circular Airgram From the Department of State to All Posts[1]

CA–3094   Washington, September 18, 1963.

SUBJECT

   Duties and Responsibilities of Science Officers

This airgram supersedes the Department's Instruction CW–4414, November 22, 1961, subject: "Duties and Responsibilities of Science Officers".[2]

Mission of Scientific Attachés

Science Officers, with the diplomatic title of Attaché, are assigned to diplomatic posts at which science and technology are playing or will play a significant role. Science Officers are integral parts of the Ambassador's Staff at such posts. They provide advice of the Chief of Mission and to other officers on scientific and technical matters, participate in the reporting program of the Embassy, and assist in the representational and negotiating activities of the Embassy. A Science Officer is normally accredited to a single post but often has regional responsibilities for performing the functions listed below in nearby countries where there is no similar science representative.

Functions of Scientific Attachés

The Scientific Attaché reports to the Chief and Deputy Chief of Mission. Although his detailed functions will necessarily vary from post to post, depending upon the local situation, they will in general fall into the three categories of *advising, reporting,* and *representing,* under the direction of the Chief of Mission.

   Advising

   1. Serves as adviser to the Chief of Mission and Staff on scientific and technical matters.

   2. Coordinates for the Chief of Mission U.S. scientific programs and activities in the areas of assignment, and in providing advice and recommendations to the Department of State and other government agencies with respect to such programs and activities.

   3. Assists the Chief of Mission in assuring that scientists from the U.S. in his area of assignment are cognizant of the foreign policy implications of their scientific and technical activities.

---

   [1] Source: National Archives and Records Administration, RG 59, Central Files 1960–63, ORG 8. Unclassified. Drafted by Pardee; cleared by J.H. Lennon (AF), Marshall P. Jones (FE), Melbourne L. Specter (ARA), Millan L. Egert (NEA), and Seaborn P. Foster (EUR); and approved by Pardee.

   [2] Not printed. (Ibid., 110.17/11–2261)

4. Maintains liaison with visiting U.S. officials who are on scientific missions abroad. Arranges appropriate visits and briefings.

5. To the extent feasible, provides advice and assistance to representatives of scientific non-governmental organizations in the U.S.

Reporting

1. Evaluates and reports significant developments and trends in science within his area of assignment especially those affecting U.S. interests, relationships or policies.

2. Reports such other scientific and technical information which would be of value to the U.S. scientific community and as may be requested from time to time by the Department of State.

Representing

1. Represents the Chief of Mission, the Department of State or other agencies of the government, at scientific meetings, conferences, ceremonies, and similar activities. Ordinarily this is within the area of assignment.

2. Promotes the exchange of scientific information between the U.S. scientific community and the scientific community of the area of assignment.

3. Advises and informs scientific groups and organizations in the area of assignment of the scientific policies and programs of U.S. governmental and non-governmental organizations.

Regional Responsibilities

Depending on available funds and workload requirements at the principal post of assignment, the Scientific Attaché will also cover scientific developments in certain nearby countries. Such countries to be covered will be agreed upon between the Embassy, the Geographic Bureau and the Office of International Scientific Affairs.

Regional responsibilities will include the functions listed above and will be carried out by periodic trips to such countries and by maintaining liaison and working relationships with a designated officer at such posts on scientific and technological matters. These designated officers, in submitting their scientific and technological reports to the Department of State, will also send information copies to the Scientific Attaché.

Support and Guidance From the Department of State

Within the Department of State, the Office of International Scientific Affairs, whose functions are outlined in Foreign Affairs Manual Circular #84 dated September 14, 1962,[3] is the focal point for providing support and guidance to the Scientific Attachés. In carrying out this

---

[3] See footnote 2, Document 350.

responsibility the Office of International Scientific Affairs works in cooperation and collaboration with the appropriate geographic bureaus and offices in the Department, as well as with other government agencies concerned with scientific matters. The Office of International Scientific Affairs also maintains contact with leading non-governmental scientific organizations.

Rusk

355. Memorandum of Conversation[1]

Washington, November 8, 1963.

SUBJECT

Meeting between SCI and NSF, November 8, 1963

PARTICIPANTS

NSF: Dr. John T. Wilson   OST-Mr. Irwin Tobin
Dr. Arthur Roe

State: Dr. R. Rollefson
Dr. Edwin M. J. Kretzmann
Dr. Eugene G. Kovach
Col. Wm. R. Sturges, Jr.
Mr. August Velletri
Mr. Arthur E. Pardee, Jr.

Dr. Rollefson opened the meeting by saying that we wished to discuss four general items which were: (1) NSF support for OECD science activities; (2) NSF's support of the U.S.-Japan Committee on Scientific Cooperation; (3) publication and distribution of *International Science Notes* and *International Science Reports;* and (4) NSF science representation overseas.[2]

---

[1] Source: National Archives and Records Administration, RG 59, Management Staff Files: Lot 69 D 434, Miscellaneous Subject Files, Scientific Attaché. No classification marking. Drafted by Pardee on November 29.

[2] In June 1963 the Department of State submitted its balance-of-payments proposals to the Bureau of the Budget. These included "plans to examine all science functions presently assigned to various Federal Agencies at Embassies in Toyko, Rio de Janeiro, Paris, and New Delhi, with the view of avoiding duplication and overstaffing, and centralizing responsibility in the Science Attaché." (Memorandum from Pardee to Lee Dashner, Chief of the Program Review Division, Office of Budget, October 29; ibid.)

Dr. Wilson spoke to the first question by saying that his recollection was that the Department of State had sent a letter to the Foundation for continuing support of OECD during FY-1962. He did not recall any formal requests for this continued support since that date. His recollection also was that NSF, in replying to the Tyler letter from State, did limit NSF's support to FY-1962. The general recollection by State representatives was that they did not recall this limitation. Dr. Wilson believed that some formal arrangements were needed to clarify this relationship. Dr. Wilson said that in 1962 when the ICA support was withdrawn from OECD science activities in Paris, NSF proceeded to station personnel in Paris to continue these activities. He related that the Bureau of the Budget had raised with NSF the question as to why the support of such activities required the presence of representatives in Paris since such support prior to 1962 was accomplished without such representation. In the light of NSF's budget situation for FY-1964, Dr. Wilson's position was that NSF had no alternative but to withdraw the representation in Paris.

Dr. Rollefson stated that we had considered this possibility and that as soon as Dr. Walske had more experience in Paris that we would like to raise the possibility of his assuming this responsibility with the assistance of Dr. Scott's replacement. This discussion led to the question of which agency should provide leadership on the question of OECD science. Dr. Wilson said that NSF was quite willing to listen to any legitimate requests for support which were within NSF's competence and mission. However, a number of matters such as "fouling of ships' hulls" did not fit this category. In the course of time, other agencies of government should be responsible for providing U.S. support for such matters. Dr. Rollefson suggested that the International Committee of the Federal Council might be used for channeling these responsibilities to the appropriate agency. Mr. Tobin from the White House agreed that the Committee might be a useful channel or umbrella but that it should not be considered as the only channel for carrying forward this responsibility. Leadership with responsibility should be designated outside and above the International Committee. He felt that back-stopping could change in light of each matter being considered. Col. Sturges suggested SCI be designated as leader in this matter. There was general agreement that this could be done.

Under the general question of providing funds for OECD science support, Dr. Kovach believed that the present arrangement on U.S. support often had gaps in obtaining adequate coverage. Dr. Wilson did not see where this was a problem. He believed that so long as it pertained to the work of OECD that OECD should certainly pay for it. Dr. Kovach pointed out that this had certain limitations. He said that often additional or special studies were required which did not fit this arrangement. Consequently it is often difficult to find an agency to pay for these projects. Mr. Tobin felt that the present funding structure for OECD in the Department was quite adequate and that it only required asking for sufficient funds to cover these matters. Mr. Pardee pointed out that the obtaining of agreement to request additional funds was often difficult to accomplish. There was general agreement that the present funding system was haphazard.

On the general question of the U.S.-Japan Committee, the general discussion was opened on the question of the Advisory Panels in that the present ones were being dissolved and new Panels would be appointed by the Foundation to serve for one year. Dr. Wilson brought up the fact that the Foundation was recommending to SCI that Panel Chairmen also be designated as members of the Joint Committee, and that a letter would be coming from the Foundation on this. Dr. Rollefson pointed out that this arrangement would have certain disadvantages. The various vested interests would be represented on the Committee which might cause a certain lack of flexibility in either expanding or contracting certain of the programs. Since we propose to limit the Committee to eight (8) members, if we appointed all of the Panel Chairmen there would not be room for any other members. If only certain Panel Chairmen were appointed, this would cause difficulties with those Panel Chairmen who were not appointed. It was certainly agreed that this arrangement might improve the coordination between the Panels and the work of the Committee. Dr. Wilson said that this was only a recommendation of the Foundation and they were not pushing for it.

The Foundation's further position on the subject of Panels was that this management approach was an awkward and top-heavy arrangement and they would like to look to the day when the Panels could be dissolved. It was decided that this possibility should be discussed informally with Dr. Kaneshige through Harry Kelly. Dr. Roe said he would call Dr. Kelly to this effect.

On the third question dealing with the *International Science Notes*, Dr. Wilson said that they really believed that the publication of such notes, since the information came basically from State Department sources, should be published by SCI. Dr. Kretzmann disagreed saying that it was not the business of the State Department to be informing U.S. scientists about such matters. Dr. Wilson disagreed with this position saying that if you follow this rationale, the Foundation should also be publishing information sent into the Department of Agriculture by Agriculture Attachés. He reiterated that this should be done by SCI. Mr. Pardee said that he would have difficulty arguing with Dr. Wilson's position since he had been using the statement with the Bureau of the Budget that our Attachés were the sole source of such information and that it did not flow back into this country by any other source. Dr. Kretzmann suggested that this matter be raised with State's Bureau of Public Affairs as to whether this could be done by the Department of State. Mr. Pardee agreed to do this.

On the last question about NSF representation overseas, Mr. Pardee said that it basically referred to the situation that existed in Tokyo on the policy position taken by Dr. Oetjen. Col. Sturges went on to explain some of the internal difficulties in Tokyo in terms of philosophy of NSF representative as to his responsibility, viz-à-viz, those of the Scientific Attaché but it was obvious in recent months that the situation had been much improved. Dr. Wilson said that as far as the Foundation was concerned, there is no question as to supremacy of the Scientific Attaché in terms of representing U.S. science abroad. As a matter of fact, he said he at one time prepared a paper on the subject. Because of the shortness of time, it was agreed that the question would be put off to be examined in more detail at a later meeting.

U.S. Space Program

356. Report by the Ad Hoc Committee on Space to President-Elect Kennedy[1]

Washington, January 10, 1961.

[Here follow Section I, Introduction; Section II, The Ballistic Missile Program; Section III, Organization and Management; and Section IV, The Booster Program.]

V. Military Space Programs

We have a large military space program in being and continuing to grow. In addition, each of the three major military services plus the Advanced Research Projects Agency (ARPA) is clamoring for a major role in space. The organizational hiatus posed by these conditions is treated elsewhere in this paper.

There are important and unique uses of space for national security and in support of our treaty alliances throughout the world. There are also important uses of space systems for arms-control purposes.

There are also many uses of space for military purposes which are now in the planning or study stage which, if allowed to continue, will jeopardize the value we can derive from valid military space programs. It is necessary that these projects and concepts be eliminated at an early date.

In absence of treaties preventing all nations from exploiting space for military advantage, the United States' policy on this matter must be that we take no new action which will foreclose development of space systems in support of our legitimate military needs.

The most urgent and immediate use of space systems for military purposes is for surveillance and target reconnaissance over the land masses of the world with particular emphasis on the Sino-Soviet bloc of nations. The technical progress we have made in this area will be discussed separately. This program is presently organized with a special

---

[1] Source: Johnson Library, Vice Presidential File, Space and Space Program. Confidential. The members of the Committee were Jerome B. Wiesner (Chairman), Kenneth BeLieu, Trevor Gardner, Donald F. Hornig, Edwin H. Land, Maxwell Lehrer, Edward M. Purcell, Bruno B. Rossi, and Harry J. Watters. The full text of the report is printed in *Exploring the Unknown: Selected Documents in the History of the US. Civil Space Program*. Volume I: *Organizing for Exploration* (National Aeronautics and Space Administration History Office, Washington, D.C., 1995), pp. 416–423.

security organization in such a manner that our other military space programs and plans are subordinated and to an extent interfered with. This can and must be corrected.

Perhaps the most disturbing and potentially dangerous part of the space program is the international aspect of the Samos and Midas programs. Our present policy concerning the use of these devices is criticized in an article by G. Zhukov—"Space-Espionage Plans and International Law"—published in the English edition of *International Affairs* in October of 1960. This publication originates with the Soviet Society for the Popularization of Political and Scientific Knowledge. It is suggested that members of the incoming administration read this article and seriously consider taking emergency steps to salvage the Samos program from destruction by international political action on the part of the Soviets. Many suggestions have been advanced in this connection. One such suggestion is that we unilaterally announce the Samos flights to the U.N., invite U.N. inspection (technical details of inspection to be defined by the U.S.), and that we make available the data obtained from Samos to all the nations of the U.N. The urgency of arriving at a *new solution* to the Samos international relations problem is of the highest order of priority for our national security.

The U.S.A.F. provides 90 percent or more of the resources and physical support required by the space programs of other agencies and is the nation's principal resource for the development and operation of future space systems, except those of a purely scientific nature assigned by law to NASA.

In view of the likely need of large boosters for military purposes, the military establishments have a vital interest in the development of such boosters. This emphasizes again the necessity of a really effective national effort for the development of large boosters. The question should be re-examined whether this program should or should not be carried out entirely by a civilian agency.

[Here follow Section VI, Science in Space and Space Exploration; Section VII, Man in Space; Section VIII, Non-Military Applications of Space Technology; and a Summary of Recommendations.]

357.   Memorandum From Charles A. Haskins of the National
        Security Council Staff to the President's Special Assistant
        for National Security Affairs-Designate (Bundy)[1]

Washington, January 19, 1961.

SUBJECT

National Aeronautics and Space Council

The National Aeronautics and Space Act of 1958,[2] besides establishing the National Aeronautics and Space Administration (NASA), established the National Aeronautics and Space Council. The statute provides that the Council shall be composed of—

"(1) the President (who shall preside over meetings of the Council);
(2) the Secretary of State;
(3) the Secretary of Defense;
(4) the Administrator of the National Aeronautics and Space Administration;
(5) the Chairman of the Atomic Energy Commission;
(6) not more than one additional member appointed by the President from the departments and agencies of the Federal Government; and
(7) not more than three other members appointed by the President, solely on the basis of established records of distinguished achievement, from among individuals in private life who are eminent in science, engineering technology, education, administration, or public affairs."

As the additional member from Government, the President designated Dr. Alan T. Waterman, Director of the National Science Foundation. As members from private life, the President first designated Dr. Detlev W. Bronk, Mr. William A. M. Burden and General James H. Doolittle. In May 1959, after General Doolittle resigned, Dr. John T. Rettaliata was designated in his stead. In October 1959, Mr. Burden resigned to accept appointment as Ambassador to Belgium and the vacancy thereby created on the Council has not been filled.

On August 19, 1958, in a letter to the Administrator of NASA, the President stated that it was important that appropriate working relations be established between the NSC and the Space Council. He invited Mr. Gordon Gray to attend all Space Council meetings as a participant; Mr. Lay attended informal meetings with him or as his alternate. (See pertinent correspondence, Tab A)[3]

---

[1]   Source: Kennedy Library, National Security Files, Departments and Agencies Series, NASA, 1961, Box 282. Confidential.

[2]   P.L. 85-568, 72 Stat. 426, approved July 19, 1958. [Footnote in the source text.]

[3]   Tabs A–C are not printed.

The statute authorizes the Council to employ a staff to be headed by a civilian executive secretary, appointed by the President by and with the advice and consent of the Senate and compensated at the rate of $20,000 a year. The executive secretary is authorized to appoint and fix the compensation of necessary personnel, including not more than three persons who may be compensated at the rate of $19,000 a year.

The President never filled the post of executive secretary. In September 1958, Mr. Robert O. Piland from the staff of the Special Assistant to the President for Science and Technology was designated Acting Secretary. In January 1959, he was succeeded as Acting Secretary by Mr. Franklyn W. Phillips of NASA. In February 1960, Mr. Phillips was succeeded by Mr. David Z. Beckler, Secretary of the Science Advisory Committee.

The Space Council held eight meetings: three in 1958, four in 1959 and one on January 12, 1960. The Council has not met since the last mentioned date. Meetings were held in the Cabinet room at the White House.

By way of preparation for formal meetings with the President, the Space Council frequently held so-called informal meetings attended by members (except the President) or their alternates, accompanied by staff. The purpose of the informal meetings was to discuss the items scheduled on the upcoming Council agenda with a view to disposing of unnecessary details and clarifying issues for later discussion at the Council itself. The informal meetings were usually held in a conference room in the Executive Office Building.

At the January 12, 1960 meeting of the Space Council, U.S. Policy on Outer Space (NSC 5918 which was prepared by an Ad Hoc Working Group from the interested agencies and then processed through the Planning Board) was adopted, subject to certain revisions. The policy paper as approved by the President was distributed to the Space Council members by the Acting Secretary. It was also distributed to the National Security Council by its Executive Secretary, although not issued as a numbered NSC paper. It superseded the August 1958 paper "Preliminary U.S. Policy on Outer Space," NSC 5814/1. (Tab B)[4]

At the January 12, 1960 meeting the President also stated that the transitional period of the Space Program seemed to be over and that the Space Council had completed its assignment. (Minutes, 1/12/60 Meeting, Item 5) (Tab C)

CAH

[4] For text of NSC 5814/1, August 18, 1958, and NSC 5918, January 26, 1960, see *Foreign Relations*, 1958–1960, pp. 845–863 and 920–936.

358.   Memorandum of Conversation[1]

Washington, March 8, 1961.

SUBJECT

Outer Space

PARTICIPANTS

Mr. James Webb, NASA
Dr. Hugh Dryden, NASA
The Secretary
Mr. W. Wallner, IO
Mr. W.I. Cargo, UNP
Dr. W. Whitman, S/SA
Mr. P.J. Farley, S/AE

The Secretary said that there was keen interest in the possibility of a productive approach to the Soviet Union for outer space cooperation. The question arose whether the United Nations was the place for this or whether it should be done bilaterally. Mr. Webb said that he had been examining our outer space goals and objectives intensively. We have a big program on the order of $1 billion a year. The implications are tremendous, not only scientifically, but also militarily and commercially. In the communications field particularly we have a major new technology which gives great opportunities for international action if we wish to use it creatively. He thought that decision on approaches to the Soviets was incidental to deciding what we want to do in the space field.

The Secretary observed that there are really only a few countries which are "producers" in the space field and that most of the others are "consumers". The United Nations might be a good place in which to handle exchange of information between the producer and consumer countries, rather than the place to arrange cooperation between the producers. Dr. Dryden reviewed briefly the course of consideration of a U.N. Outer Space Scientific Conference and establishment of a U.N. Outer Space Committee. He said that it was important to NASA to have a decision as to whether or not there would be a United Nations Conference. He remarked that, outside the United Nations, he saw Blagonravov perhaps twice a year and talked about possibilities for scientific cooperation between the United States and the Soviet Union in outer space. Blagonravov was always interested but nothing ever seemed to happen.

---

[1] Source: National Archives and Records Administration, RG 59, Central Files 1960–63, 701.022/3–861. Confidential. Drafted by Philip J. Farley and approved in S on March 17.

The Secretary said that perhaps we had held up action in the United Nations unnecessarily. Mr. Farley said that the United Nations activity ought to go ahead and referred to the telegram just received from Ambassador Stevenson.[2] He pointed out that the terms of reference of the U.N. Committee are carefully drafted and that we will retain freedom of action to approach the Soviet Union in whatever way we decide to after current studies have been considered. In response to the Secretary's question, he said that Dr. Rossi had completed the report of the outer space task force on the previous day and it would be distributed shortly for review by the agencies concerned and agreement on recommendations for the President.[3] Dr. Dryden said that he understood that this outer space task force report might not be considered until broader studies by Dr. Wiesner regarding scientific relations between the United States and the Soviet Union were completed. Mr. Farly said that, while decisions might not be taken until the whole group of scientific studies were in hand, he thought that staff work on outer space could and should begin immediately. Dr. Whitman endorsed the idea of convening the U.N. Outer Space Scientific Conference as soon as possible, citing the usefulness of the two U.N. Atoms for Peace Conferences.[4] He urged also that an effort be made to give scientists as free a hand as possible in working out arrangements. Mr. Wallner said that we hoped it would now be possible to get organizational details agreed with the Soviet Union but warned that the Soviet approach was highly political and one could not realistically expect a purely scientific exercise.

Mr. Webb spoke further of the opportunities for foreign relations inherent in the space program and particularly communications and meteorology. He said that he was re-examining in particular the role of NASA in the immediate future in developing space communications techniques and systems. He felt that the implications of space communications were so great and the stake of the Government in development costs to date so considerable that the Government ought to take the lead in developing and testing space communications systems, leaving aside for the time being the question of the ultimate mode of operation. Such an active Government role would provide greater opportunities for using this new tool internationally. He mentioned also that a preliminary review had indicated the desirability of further acceleration and funding of the NASA program by a substantial amount and asked

---

[2] Not found.

[3] Not further identified.

[4] The First International Conference on the Peaceful Uses of Atomic Energy was held in Geneva August 8–21, 1955. The second Conference was also held in Geneva September 1–14, 1958.

what the attitude of the State Department would be toward such an increase. The Secretary said that he wondered what the purpose was of activities in space on this major scale. Should not the objectives be clearly identified and undertaken not competitively but on behalf of the human race as a whole. With our many skills and forms of power, the human race in its pride is rapidly approaching a point where we may destroy ourselves. This was peculiarly an area where we might be able to stand aside and take a different and more rational approach to whatever was most worth doing in space. Mr. Webb endorsed the idea that we should look urgently at our objectives and, if necessary, re-define them. At present the spirit which he found was primarily one of exploring all possibilities for development of a new technology. The Secretary said that the State Department ought to be addressing itself to all aspects of these problems. He asked Mr. Farley to work with the Policy Planning Council and other interested parts of the Department in identifying the questions which ought to be considered and recommending answers. Mr. Farley said that this was essential in developing recommendations on the basis of the Rossi task force report. We could not sensibly address ourselves to cooperation with the Soviet Union and other countries unless we had defined our own objectives and programs. A good deal of preliminary thinking was already underway in the Department in the communications, legal and other policy aspects of outer space and could be drawn on in formulating the recommendations requested by the Secretary. Mr. Webb said that he was going to look particularly to Dr. Dryden in this area.

Dr. Dryden then reviewed some of the cooperative activities which NASA has had under way in the past in COSPAR, with the British and Canadians, and more recently with other European countries. He emphasized that there was much which the United States could do with free countries aside from what could be done with the Soviet Union or in the United Nations, and pointed out that NASA had a statutory charge to engage in international cooperation. The Secretary asked whether we had the kind of restrictions on international cooperation in this area that we did in the atomic energy field. Dr. Dryden said that the principal limitation was the classification of some of our large boosters which had missile application. Mr. Farley said we did not have the restrictions and procedural requirements in outer space that were laid down by the Atomic Energy Act for atomic energy cooperation. Referring to Dr. Dryden's summary of present cooperation, he called attention to the recent emergence of European interest in an integrated space research organization. He said that the Department with the concurrence of NASA was actively encouraging this development. It was politically advantageous as a form of European cooperation cutting across the Community of Six and the Outer Seven. It also made sense in view of the cost and complexity of space research. Furthermore, the United States did not want to encourage individual national space programs on a competitive basis primarily for prestige considerations, and we did not want to start a rush among individual countries to enter into bilateral cooperation with the United States regardless of practical importance. Dr. Dryden said that NASA was of course glad to cooperate with such a multilateral venture.

The Secretary said that it was important that we think out what we are doing in this field. He asked that action be taken in the meanwhile to resume efforts in New York to activate the U.N. Committee, since that would be desirable in any event and would not prejudice decisions on other matters.

359.   Presentation by the Administrator of the National Aeronautics and Space Administration (Webb) to President Kennedy[1]

Washington, March 21, 1961.

Administrator's Presentation to the President

The U.S. civilian space effort is based on a ten year plan. When prepared in 1959, this ten year plan was designed to go hand in hand with our military programs and permit a steady closing of the gap caused by Russian successes. Prior to this plan, U.S. procrastination for a number of years had been based in part on a very real skepticism by President Eisenhower personally as to the necessity for the large expenditures required, and the validity of the goals sought through the space effort.

In the preparation of the 1962 budget, President Eisenhower reduced the $1.35 billion requested by the Space Agency to the extent of $240 million and specifically eliminated funds to proceed with manned space flight projects beyond Mercury. This decision emasculated the ten year plan, before it was even one year old, and unless reversed guaran-

---

[1] Source: Kennedy Library, National Security Files, Departments and Agencies Series, NASA, 1961, Box 282. No classification marking. According to President Kennedy's Appointment Books, Webb attended a meeting with the President between 6:10 and 7:20 p.m. on March 22. Vice President Johnson, Deputy Administrator Hugh Dryden, David Bell, and McGeorge Bundy also attended the meeting. (Ibid.)

tees that the Russians will, for the next five to ten years, beat us to every spectacular exploratory flight.

We have already felt the effects of the fact that they were the first to place a satellite in orbit, have intercepted the moon, photographed the back side of the moon, and have sent a large spacecraft to Venus. They can now orbit 7-1/2 ton vehicles about the earth, compared to our 2-1/2 tons, and they have successfully recovered animals from orbital flights lasting as much as 24 hours. Their present position is one from which further substantial accomplishments can be expected, and our best information points to a steadily increasing pace of successful effort, on a realistic timetable.

The budget levels of the previous administration did permit extensive scientific investigation, the application of satellites to meteorological and communication systems, the Mercury man-in-space effort, and the support of these through advanced research and technological development. However, these levels have not been sufficient for the successful conduct of programs calculated to give us any substantial initiative in space exploration.

The first priority of this country's space effort should be to improve as rapidly as possible our capability for boosting large spacecraft into orbit, since this is our greatest deficiency. The present Russian booster has a 750,000 pound thrust compared with an Atlas thrust of 320,000 pounds. We are developing a cluster of 8 Atlas engines, known as Saturn, which will have a thrust of 1,500,000 pounds. Our request for additional funds to advance its available date one year (to 1966) has not been recommended to you by the Budget Bureau. In addition, we are asking funds to speed up work on the engines for a more advanced vehicle with 8 to 9 million pounds thrust, which we call Nova. Our information shows that the Russians are continuing with booster developments, and we should not put ourselves in the position of having to start such a major project with its long lead time after they are in a position to exploit their possession of such a development.

The funds we have requested for an expanded effort will bring the entire Space Agency program up to $1.43 billion in FY 1968 and substantially restore the ten-year program. The future effect of our recommendations will be to increase expenditures to an annual rate of $2.0 billion by 1965 or 1966.

The Department of Defense benefits from the NASA space program just as NASA does from the military space program. NASA research centers are investigating re-entry physics, high temperature structures, and propulsion techniques for both military and civilian needs, to mention only a few major technical areas of common interest and effort. In addition, NASA-developed electronic equipment for telemetry, tracking, data processing, stabilization and guidance will have application to military systems. Most important of all, the boosters now under development and the launching facilities to be constructed will be used directly by the Department of Defense. NASA's Centaur launch vehicle will be used to place the Defense communications satellite, Advent, in orbit and ultimately it can be expected that NASA's Saturn will make possible military missions not even foreseen at this time. We feel it is important to proceed aggressively with our program not only for civilian considerations but also to provide improved technological capability for the DOD.

Under the NASA ten-year program, we will need the large boosters we are requesting sooner than the military will need them in order to achieve a number of major space exploration milestones. Among these milestones are unmanned exploration of the moon and planets as well as manned space flight beyond Project Mercury. The Mercury vehicle carries a single man and can remain in orbit for but a few hours. For important biomedical studies, we wish to make modifications that will extend the possible flight time to one day.

To make flights about the earth with multiple crews or trips to the vicinity of the moon, we must develop a new space vehicle and team it up with the Saturn booster. President Eisenhower eliminated from his budget the preliminary design studies required to begin this effort. Unless research and development funds for an advanced design of this type are restored, the important milestone flights will be delayed at least a year.

The United States space program has already become a positive force in bringing together scientists and engineers of many countries in a wide variety of cooperative endeavors. Great Britain, France, Italy, West Germany, Japan, Australia, Canada, Sweden, Norway, Argentina, all have in one way or another taken action or expressed their will to become a part of this imaginative effort. We feel there is no better means to reinforce our old alliances and build new ones.

The Soviets have demonstrated how effective space exploration can be as a symbol of scientific progress and as an adjunct of foreign policy. Without necessarily following the Soviet lead in this kind of exploitation, we should not fail to recognize its potential. We cannot regain the prestige we have lost without improving our present inferior booster capability, and doing it before the Russians make a major break through into the multi-million pound thrust range.

Looking to the future, it is possible through new technology to bring about whole new areas of international cooperation in meteorological and communication satellite systems. These new systems will be superior to present systems by a large margin and so clearly in the interest of the entire world that there is a possibility all will want to cooperate—even the USSR. However, the extent to which we are leaders in space science and technology will in some large measure determine the extent to which we, as a nation, pioneering on a new frontier, will be in position to develop this emerging world force as a basis for new concepts and applications in education, communication and transportation, looking toward more viable political, social and economic systems for nations willing to work with us in the years ahead.

360.   Memorandum From the Secretary of State's Special Assistant for Atomic Energy and Outer Space (Farley) to the Under Secretary of State (Bowles)[1]

Washington, April 7, 1961.

SUBJECT

Hazardous Launch Trajectories

Twice in the past six months, pieces of U.S. space vehicles have landed on foreign territory. On September 26, 1960, a malfunction in the second stage of an attempted NASA lunar probe caused its premature re-entry over Africa and the impact of some metal pieces upon the Union of South Africa. On November 30, 1960, a failure in the Thor booster rocket attempting to place a Transit satellite in orbit caused the rocket motor and tank pieces to fall upon Cuba. Fortunately, with the reported exception of one Cuban cow, these impacts caused no known casualties or property damage. Fortunately, too, the reaction of the South Africans was phlegmatic curiosity and that of the Cubans overplayed histrionics. As a result, neither impact has produced a significant international demand for curtailment of our space program. There has been created, however, a certain undercurrent of international uneasiness and, in conjunction with our much-publicized launching failures, some feeling that the United State is insufficiently cautious in pursuing its space goals.

---

[1] Source: National Archives and Records Administration, RG 59, Central Files 1960–63, 701.56311/4–761. Confidential. Drafted by Richard V. Hennes, and cleared by Assistant Secretary G. Mennen Williams (AF), Wymberley DeR. Coerr (ARA), George S. Newman (G), and Leonard C. Meeker (L).

In my judgment, we must, in the interests of the future conduct of the U.S. space program, make every effort to prevent impacts of space vehicles on foreign territory. The cumulative effect of such impacts would be likely to arouse substantial opposition to our space program as a whole, would render already unpopular U.S. space projects like SAMOS more vulnerable to propaganda attack, and could be expected to foster powerful resistance to future experiments with nuclear power in space and launch vehicles. Additional impacts on foreign territory would also provide justification should proposals be made (e.g., in the UN) for requiring prior consent to overflight of countries by satellites, particularly in the case of experimental launches.

At present, we are especially concerned at the chances of impact afforded by three space programs. One is the forthcoming Mercury abort shot, scheduled for April 20, in which an empty Mercury capsule is intended to be recovered at sea in the vicinity of the Canary Islands. Malfunction of the retro-rockets, which have not been flight-tested at orbital velocity, could bring the capsule down in Africa. Malfunction of the launching vehicle at a critical stage in its burning period could cause an African or an Australian impact.

A second hazardous program involves one or two additional launches of the Transit satellite over the same ill-fated trajectory that produced the impact of November 30 on Cuba. Mr. Nitze has written you about these launches and has asserted that the statistical odds against a Cuban impact were 2,100 to 1 last November when the impact occurred. Although last November's failure raises doubt as to the validity of the Cuban odds, our principal concern has always been for an impact on South America. Transit's pre-orbital trajectory traverses the entire continent from Venezuela to southeastern Brazil with estimated impact odds of one in twenty-one.

The third program of a hazardous nature is Centaur, in which this unique hydrogen-oxygen fueled second-stage rocket is tested over a trajectory crossing the width of Africa from northwest to southeast. To our knowledge, this is the first time it has been proposed to flight-test an untried launch vehicle over a land route.

Recommendations:

It is admittedly difficult to strike a balance between the technical requirements of present space programs and the necessity to preserve opportunities for our programs in the future. Nevertheless, with respect to the foregoing programs, I recommend:

1. Because the Mercury program has the highest national priority, has proceeded thus far at great expense and effort, and would presumably bring substantial prestige rewards if successful in first placing a

man in orbit and recovering him, I recommend that, despite the hazards involved, you interpose no objections to the April 20 and subsequent Mercury flights.[2]

2. Because the Transit program has no overriding priority (while taking fully into account the value of the associated pickaback experiment) and would be delayed at the most one year by our non-concurrence in the requested research and development launches over South America, I recommend that you sign the attached letter to Mr. Nitze (Tab A)[3] regretting that the political risks are too great to permit you to concur in the launces over South America.

3. Because the important Centaur program is still in the planning stage and susceptible of modification, I recommend that you sign the attached letter to Mr. Webb (Tab B)[4] requesting that the dangers to our over-all space program and to our political relations with Africa be carefully considered before a final technical decision is made to test the Centaur vehicle over Africa or other major land areas.

---

[2] Bowles approved recommendation 1 on April 17.

[3] Not printed. The Transit communications satellite was successfully launched from Cape Canaveral on June 29, together with two satellites that were intended to study, respectively, the Van Allen radiation belts and the effects of solar X-rays on the Earth's ionosphere.

[4] Document 361.

---

361.   Letter From the Under Secretary of State (Bowles) to the Administrator of the National Aeronautics and Space Administration (Webb)[1]

Washington, April 17, 1961.

Dear Mr. Webb:

I am writing you in reference to the Centaur program as recently described to officers of this Department by officials of the National Aeronautics and Space Administration.

I am told that the presently conceived Centaur program calls for initial test flights of this hitherto untried vehicle over the continent of

---

[1] Source: National Archives and Records Administration, RG 59, Central Files 1960–63, 701.56311/4–1761. Confidential. Drafted by Hennes and cleared by George S. Newman, Assistant Secretary Williams (AF), and Leonard C. Meeker.

Africa and that utilization of the customary water range for testing would yield less complete performance data. In view of the volatile and highly unstable political situation currently prevailing in Africa, it would seem to me unwise to risk an impact on the Congo or elsewhere along the trajectory for anything but a project of the greatest national importance for which no alternative flight path could suffice.

In the light of two recent impacts of U.S. space vehicles upon foreign territory,[2] I am also concerned at the cumulative effect of repeated impacts upon our space program as a whole. At some point, particularly if we should suffer an especially unlucky hit causing damage or casualties, substantial international opposition to our space program as a whole would arise. Not only would this provoke proposals in the United Nations and elsewhere for requiring prior consent to overflights of countries by U.S. satellites, particularly in the case of experimental launches, but also it would render already unpopular U.S. space projects like Samos more vulnerable to propaganda attack. Of especial interest to NASA would seem to be the predictable unfavorable response to an impact upon their territory of those African countries who have granted NASA tracking and communications facilities and staging privileges for contingency recovery of the Mercury capsule. In addition, a pattern of impacts upon foreign territory could be expected to foster powerful resistance to future experiments involving the use of nuclear power in space and launch vehicles.

Admittedly, risks must be run in the vigorous pursuit of our national space program. It is this realization that has caused us to evaluate the very real hazards of the Mercury program as being outweighed by its overriding importance. However, I hope that you will agree that the interests of our space program as a whole demand that we accept risks of impact upon foreign territory only in those rare instances involving projects of the highest national priority. Accordingly, I should very much appreciate your assistance in assuring that the foregoing considerations are taken into account before NASA makes its technical decision to propose testing of the Centaur vehicle over Africa or other major land areas.[3]

Sincerely yours,

Chester Bowles[4]

---

[2] See Document 360.

[3] On April 28 Webb replied, in part: "You have my assurance that each of the considerations which you mention will be taken fully into account in the selection of trajectories required for this test program. We shall, in addition, maintain liaison with your Department, as has been the case in all flight testing, through the usual channels." (National Archives and Records Administration, RG 59, Central Files 1960–63, 701.56311/4–1761)

[4] Printed from a copy that indicates Bowles signed the original.

362. Discussion Notes by the Deputy Administrator of the National Aeronautics and Space Administration (Dryden)[1]

Washington, April 22, 1961.

1. *"Do we have a chance of beating the Soviets?"*

 a. *"By putting a laboratory in space?"*

There is no chance of beating the Soviets in putting a multi-manned laboratory in space since flights already accomplished by the Russians have demonstrated that they have this capability. The U.S. program must include the development of a multi-manned orbiting laboratory as soon as possible since it is essential for the accomplishment of the more difficult flights to the moon.

 b. *"Or by a trip around the moon?"*

With a determined effort of the United States, there is a chance to beat the Russians in accomplishing a manned circumnavigation of the moon. The Russians have not as yet demonstrated either the booster capability or the technology required for returning a man from a flight around the moon. The state of their booster technology and other technology required for such a difficult mission is not accurately known. With an accelerated program, it is not unreasonable for the U.S. to attempt a manned circumlunar flight by 1966.

 c. *"Or by a rocket to land on the moon?"*

On September 12, 1959, the Russians crash-landed a small package on the moon. This package did not transmit any information from the surface of the moon. The NASA program currently includes impacting instruments on the moon in such a way that they may survive the impact and transmit scientific information back to earth. The first flight in this program is scheduled for January 1962. Close-up television pictures will be obtained of the surface of the moon, as the spacecraft descends to the moon. In August 1963 the current NASA program also includes a soft landing of instruments on the moon. Several flights in succeeding months are included in this program to insure the possibility of success. The Russians can accomplish this mission now if they choose.

---

[1] Source: Johnson Library, Vice Presidential File, Space and Space Program. Confidential. An attached note by Claudia Anderson, archivist at the Johnson Library, reads: "May 4, 1979: During the course of a reference request, we found that these discussion notes were used by Dr. Hugh L. Dryden, NASA scientist, with Vice President Johnson in response to President Kennedy's memorandum, 'Do we have a chance of beating the Soviets?' April 22, 1961. This information is noted on a carbon copy retained by NASA." For text of President Kennedy's memorandum of April 20, see *Exploring the Unknown*, p. 424.

d. *"Or by a rocket to go to the moon and back with a man?"*

There is a chance for the U.S. to be the first to land a man on the moon and return him to earth if a determined national effort is made. The development of a large chemical rocket booster, the spacecraft for landing and return, and major developments in advanced technology are required to accomplish this most difficult mission. The Russians initiated their earth orbiting program probably as early as 1954 as evidenced by their flight of a dog in November 1957. In the earth orbiting competition the United States was attempting to accomplish in less than three years what the Russians had worked on for seven years. It is doubtful that the Russians have a very great head start on the U.S. in the effort required for a manned lunar landing. Because of the distinct superiority of U.S. industrial capacity, engineering, and scientific know-how, we believe that with the necessary national effort, the U.S. may be able to overcome the lead that the Russians might have up to now. A possible target date for the earliest attempt for a manned lunar landing is 1967, with an accelerated U.S. effort.

e. *"Is there any other space program which promises dramatic results in which we could win?"*

(1) The current NASA program provides the possibility of returning a sample of the material from the moon surface to the earth in 1964. An experiment of this kind would have dramatic value and may or may not be a part of the Russian program. The Russians could carry out such an experiment in the same time period or earlier if they choose.

(2) The lead the U.S has taken in developing communications satellites should be exploited to the fullest. Although not as dramatic as manned flight, the direct benefits to the people throughout the world in the long term are clear. U.S. national prestige will be enhanced by successful completion of this program. The current program will provide for the flight of an active communications satellite in mid-1962. The experiment will enable live television pictures to be transmitted across the Atlantic. The continuing program will lead to the establishment of worldwide operational communications systems.

(3) The U.S. lead established in our successful meteorological experiments with the Tiros satellites, should be maintained with a vigorous continuing program. The whole world will benefit from improved weather forecasting with the possibility of avoiding the disastrous effects of major weather disturbances such as typhoons, hurricanes and tornadoes.

2. *"How much additional would it cost?"*

An estimate of the cost of the 10-year space exploration program as planned under the Eisenhower Administration was 17.91 billion dollars, as shown in Table A–1, attached.[2] In this program it was planned that manned lunar landing and return to earth would occur in the time period after 1970 but before 1975. Re-evaluation of the cost of this program based on providing adequate back-ups in all areas of the work has recently been made and the original cost estimate revised to 22.3 billion dollars for the ten-year period through 1970. (Table D–1) For an accelerated national program aiming toward achieving manned lunar landing in the 1967 period, it is estimated that the cost over the same ten-year period will be 33.7 billion dollars, as shown in Table E–1. The additional 10 billion dollar cost of the program is due largely to paying for the program in the shorter time period. The resulting annual costs are naturally higher.

A list of the major items that would be initiated in 1962 with an accelerated program is shown in Attachment F. The total FY-62 funds, $1,744 millions, shown in Table E–1 is $509 million more than the approved current FY-62 budget.

3. *"Are we working 24 hours a day and, if not, why not?"*

There is not a 24 hour a day work schedule on existing NASA space programs, except for selected areas in Project Mercury, the Saturn C-1 booster, the Centaur engines, and the final launching phases of most flight missions.

a. *Project Mercury* at Cape Canaveral has been since October 1960 on a three-shift, seven-day-a-week basis plus shift overtime for all phases of capsule checkout and launch preparations. The McDonnell St. Louis plant, where the capsules are made, has averaged a 54-hour week on Mercury from the beginning, but also employs two or three shifts as needed in bottleneck areas. It now runs three shifts in the capsule test and checkout areas.

b. *Saturn C-1* project operates at Huntsville around-the-clock throughout any critical test periods for the first-stage booster; the remaining Saturn work is on a one-shift basis plus overtime which results in an average 47 hour week.

c. *Centaur* hydrogen engine, which also is needed for the Saturn upper stages, is on three shifts in Pratt & Whitney's shops and test stands.

d. Lastly, the final launch preparations of most flight missions require around-the-clock work at the launch sites at Cape Canaveral, Wallops Station, or the Pacific Missile Range. In addition, NASA computer installations at Goddard and Marshall Centers operate continuous shifts in order to handle launch vehicle test analyses promptly, and determine orbital and trajectory data, and provide tracking and telemetry of space vehicles in flight.

NASA and its contractors are not working 24-hour days on the rest of its projects because:

---

[2] The tables and attachments are not printed.

a. Certain projects are at an early stage of experimental study or design engineering where exchange of ideas is difficult to accomplish through multi-shifts.

b. The schedules have been geared to the availability of facilities and financial resources. The funding levels for both contractors and government laboratories have been sufficient only for single-shift operations plus overtime (generally from 5 to 20%) as required to keep up the schedules.

c. The limitations on manpower and associated funding determine the extent to which the NASA flight development centers may employ extra shifts.

In a number of areas in the national space program, the work could be accelerated if more manpower and more facilities were to be provided and funded in the immediate future. Recommendations to accomplish this are made elsewhere in this memorandum.

4. *"In building large boosters should we put our emphasis on nuclear, chemical or liquid fuel, or a combination of these three?*

In building the large launch vehicles required for the manned lunar landing mission, the immediate emphasis must be on the development of large solid and liquid rockets. It is believed that, in order to provide the necessary assurance that we will have a large launch vehicle for the lunar mission, we must have a parallel development of both a solid and liquid fueled large launch vehicle. The program on nuclear rockets must be prosecuted vigorously on a research and development basis. It is not believed that the nuclear rocket can play a role in the earliest attempt at manned lunar landing. The nuclear rockets will be needed in the even more difficult mission following manned lunar exploration. Use of the nuclear rocket for missions is not expected until after 1970 although flight test for developing the rocket will occur before then.

5a. *"Are we making a maximum effort?*

No, the space program is not proceeding with a maximum effort. Additional capability exists in this country which could be utilized in this task. However, we believe that the manpower facilities and other resources now assigned are being utilized in an aggressive fashion.

6b. *"Are we achieving necessary results?"*

Our program is directed towards unmanned scientific investigation of space, manned exploration of space, and application of satellites to communication and meteorological systems. The scientific investigation is achieving basic knowledge important for a better understanding of the universe and also provides data necessary for the achievement of manned space flight and the satellite applications. It is generally agreed that our scientific program is yielding most significant results.

The Mercury program is the first and necessary step in an ongoing program leading to the manned laboratory, circumlunar flight, and manned lunar landing discussed under Item 1. A manned ballistic flight is scheduled in May, unmanned orbital flights and orbital flights with chimpanzees are scheduled for the Spring and Summer providing the background for the manned flight planned in 1961.

Future manned flight depends upon improved launch vehicle capability as well as a new spacecraft for the crew. The Saturn will provide our first capability for large payloads but must be followed by a still larger vehicle for manned lunar landing. The launch vehicle for the first manned lunar landing will utilize either clustered F-1 liquid engines or solid propellant motors as discussed in item 4. We are achieving necessary technical data on the liquid engines but not on the large solid rocket engines. Ultimately, nuclear propulsion will be used to carry heavy payloads long distances into space. With our great capacity for engine research we have the capacity in this country to proceed more rapidly towards our objectives.

The Tiros and Echo satellites have provided important background data for meteorological and communication satellite systems. Additional experimentation is required in both fields before operational systems can be completely defined. We are continuing our meteorological program with Tiros flights and will use a newly-designed satellite called Nimbus when it is available in 1962. The first communication satellite (Echo) was a 100-ft. balloon which reflected ultra-high frequency signals between transmitters and receivers. The Echo type experiment is continuing and in addition we are instituting a program called Relay which carries microwave equipment for power amplification. This process decreases the requirements on the ground equipment but requires electronic equipment in the satellite with extremely high reliability compared to present day standards.

In summary we are achieving significant scientific and technical results. We welcome the opportunity of reviewing these results with you to ensure that these results are compatible with our national goals.

363.   Memorandum From the Secretary of State's Special
        Assistant for Atomic Energy and Outer Space (Farley) to the
        Under Secretary of State (Bowles)[1]

Washington, undated.

SUBJECT

The Mercury Program and NASA's Conduct of Public Relations

At the staff meeting yesterday morning several questions were voiced about the desirability of proceeding with the current Mercury shot in view of its having been over-publicized and the chances that it may be unsuccessful.

Although there is some basis for the concern recently expressed by Mr. Tubby, Mr. Chayes, and others about the adverse effects of failures during Project Mercury, I believe we must proceed with the Mercury ballistic and orbital flights as expeditiously as possible. The problem is not the program itself but the way it has been handled publicly.

It is apparent that the excessive and over-personalized publicity build-up surrounding NASA's Project Mercury manned ballistic launch fosters at least four undesirable impressions among foreign audiences:

1. By again violating the precept that an achievement not be publicized before the fact, such publicity contributes to a foreign image of American braggadocio and lack of restraint;

2. By providing for a microscopically detailed coverage of the astronaut, the present information arrangements encourage reporting in unfortunate terms;

3. Because our massive media coverage of the manned ballistic launch might suggest to foreign audiences that the U.S. is attempting in this way to meet the Soviet space challenge, even an entirely successful launch at this time would seem destined to appear as obviously inadequate, perhaps even a pathetic, American response to a major Soviet achievement;

4. Most importantly, the fanfare of pre-flight publicity would make a catastrophe, especially the death of the astronaut, all the more damaging to American prestige.

Despite the foregoing, the stake of the United States in achieving manned space flight argues strongly against any delay in pursuing the Mercury program. The program itself has been exhaustively reviewed by a special panel established by Dr. Wiesner and adjudged scientifical-

---

[1]   Source: National Archives and Records Administration, RG 59, Central Files 1960–63, 701.56311/5–561. Confidential.   Drafted by Howard Furnas, Wreatham E. Gathright, and Richard V. Hennes (S/AE), and cleared by Roger W. Tubby (P), Abram Chayes (L), and George A. Morgan (S/P).

ly and technically sound.[2] In this connection, the Mercury ballistic flights were determined to be an intergral part of the program.

We obviously should not cancel a project to which we are so heavily committed and which is, in any case, our first venture in the field where we are going to have to take our first step some day. On the other hand, we can try to bring public relations aspects of the project back into balance and prevent recurrrence of the circus-like atmosphere which has exaggerated tomorrow's ballistic attempt beyond all reason. There is no question here of "freedom of the press" versus "censorship." There is a question of sensible handling of the project to give out all necessary information without incurring the risks of over-publicizing events that haven't happened and that are of secondary importance when they do.

In order to minimize or prevent unfavorable foreign reactions to publicity attending NASA's space programs, the Department should be assured that the public relations connected with these programs will be fully coordinated in advance between NASA and the Department. If this were done, we would hope to influence NASA's public relations toward effectively contrasting our open space program pursued for meaningful scientific ends with Soviet secrecy, while concurrently avoiding the carnival-like atmosphere characterizing present publicity. Because of its need for favorable domestic publicity to facilitate public and Congressional support of the program, such restrictive counsels are difficult for NASA to accept without an assurance that they accurately reflect the judgment of the highest levels of the Department of State.

Recommendation:

Because of the intimate involvement of the U.S. space program with American prestige and the conduct of foreign relations, I recommend that there be close, complete coordination between NASA and the Department of State on all public relations aspects of NASA's space program. If you approve, Mr. Tubby and I will make the necessary arrangements promptly with the appropriate people in NASA.[3]

---

[2] Reference is to the Ad Hoc Mercury Panel, chaired by Donald C. Hornig, that conducted a technical review of the project and issued its report on April 12. The Panel concluded that a manned suborbital flight using the Redstone booster "would be a high risk undertaking but not higher than we are accustomed to taking in other ventures." See Loyd S. Swenson, Jr., James M. Grimwood, and Charles C. Alexander, *This New Ocean: A History of Project Mercury* (National Aeronautics and Space Administration, Scientific and Technical Information Division, Washington, 1966), p. 331.

[3] Bowles approved the recommendation on May 5.

364.   National Security Action Memorandum No. 50[1]

Washington, May 12, 1961.

TO

Dr. Edward C. Welsh, Executive Secretary, National Aeronautics and Space Council

SUBJECT

Official Announcements of Launching Into Space of Systems Involving Nuclear Power in Any Form

The President desires to reserve to himself all first official announcements covering the launching into space of systems involving nuclear power in any form. The President is especially concerned with announcements relating to the planned use of SNAP devices aboard Transit satellites which are tentatively scheduled for launching in June and July of 1961. Will you please advise members of the Space Council of the President's interest.

McGeorge Bundy[2]

---

[1] Source: National Archives and Records Administration, RG 59, S/S–NSC Files: Lot 72 D 316, NSAM–50, Signed by McGeorge Bundy. Confidential. Copies were sent to the President's Press Secretary, Director of the U.S. Information Agency, Evelyn Lincoln, and Bromley Smith.

[2] Printed from a copy that bears this typed signature.

365.   Memorandum of Conversation[1]

Washington, May 19, 1961.

SUBJECT

  United Nations Outer Space Committee and Conference

PARTICIPANTS

Dr. Hugh Dryden, NASA	Ambassador Plimpton, USUN
Dr. John P. Hagen, NASA	Mr. Peter Thatcher, USUN
Mr. Arnold Frutkin, NASA	Mr. Harlan Cleveland, IO
Mr. Philip Farley, S/AE	Mr. Richard Gardner, IO
Mr. Wreatham Gathright, S/AE	Mr. William Jones, UNP
Mr. Herbert Reis, L/UNA	Mr. William Buffum, UNP
	Mr. Oliver Crosby, UNP

Mr. Cleveland said he was pleased to have this opportunity to hear Dr. Dryden, Deputy Administrator of NASA, speak on United States space plans, expected Soviet space accomplishments and the relevance of these to the proposed Outer Space Conference. After a review of Soviet and United States space accomplishments, Dr. Dryden observed that the early Soviet development of large rocket boosters has given them an advantage in manned space flight which we can only hope to overcome over the long run. He said that while NASA hopes to put an astronaut in orbit by the end of the year, the Soviet Union has the capability to put a manned space laboratory in orbit immediately. Dr. Dryden estimated that a manned lunar orbiter or lunar landing, perhaps in 1967, offers the United States its first chance to overtake the Soviet Union in manned space flight. For this, however, the NASA budget would have to be increased to $4–5 billion a year. Dr. Dryden said President Kennedy will be sending up a message to the Congress on this in a week or so.

Dr. Dryden stated that the United States clearly leads the Soviet Union with respect to scientific research in outer space and particularly in development of meteorological and communications satellites. He indicated that the Weather Bureau's Nimbus meteorological satellite system should be operational by 1963 or 1964 and should bring great advantages in terms of weather analysis and typhoon warning as well as forecasting for military operations and reconnaissance purposes. The communications satellite is in an earlier stage, but a contract has just been signed with RCA for construction of a repeater satellite, and AT & T is making arrangements for a similar experiment at its own expense.

---

[1] Source: National Archives and Records Administration, RG 59, Central Files 1960–63, 701.56311/5–1961. Confidential. Drafted by Crosby on May 23.

Although Dr. Dryden said there was some question as to the relative value of prestige derived from scientific accomplishments and from manned flight in outer space, he expected that we would stand up well vis-à-vis the Soviet Union in an international Outer Space Conference if it were held soon. As time passes, however, the Soviet Union will have an opportunity to catch up in the scientific area, and the comparison will be less favorable for the United States. Dr. Dryden estimated that the Conference might become of somewhat dubious value if it were not held until 1962. Mr. Farley asked whether in light of this we should continue to plan for an Outer Space Conference or whether we should take advantage of the difficulties with the Soviet Union to let the matter die. Dr. Hagen said that if the Conference can be held by the end of 1961, we will be able to meet our major objectives and demonstrate the significance of our outer space achievements.

Mr. Thatcher asked how important the intelligence aspects of such a Conference might be. Dr. Dryden said there would be some possibility of intelligence value, but this would have to be judged together with prestige aspects. Mr. Gardner observed that since Soviet space accomplishments are bound to produce publicity harmful to United States prestige, an Outer Space Conference might offer us a countering opportunity to draw attention to our scientific accomplishments, which have too often been eclipsed by Soviet spectaculars.

Brief mention was made of the possible desirability of going ahead with the United Nations Space Conference without Soviet participation. Dr. Dryden said opinion was divided within NASA on this score, and he was skeptical of the idea.

Mr. Frutkin pointed out that we cannot wait for agreement on a United Nations Space Conference to capitalize on our space accomplishments, and Dr. Dryden indicated that NASA is examining the question of the comparative utility of an overall Outer Space Conference versus individual conferences of a more specialized nature. If there is no action on the United Nations Outer Space Conference by the middle of this year, Dr. Dryden said NASA will have to abandon its preparations for such a conference and salvage what it can for use in other conferences. NASA plans on June 6th to release the findings from the Freedom Seven ballistic flight of Commander Shepard. Over the longer range, NASA plans to play an active role in the International Astronautical Federation Congress in Washington this October, plans a conference on meteorological satellites in the next six months, and plans a space research conference in the Spring of 1962. Mr. Gardner suggested that the theme of a meteorological conference should be the use of outer space for the benefit of humanity, for this would point up the contrast between the open United States and closed Soviet approaches.

Ambassador Plimpton said it was difficult to tell from his conversation with Zorin on May 11 whether the Soviet Union is really interested in the Outer Space Committee and Conference. The Indian Representative at the United Nations, after talking with Zorin, has advocated agreement on a unanimity rule in the Outer Space Committee, but Ambassador Plimpton stated that we would be willing only to make a statement expressing the hope that the Committee will be able to perform its work without the need for voting.

Dr. Hagen asked if USUN had sounded out our friends on the question of convening the Space Committee despite a possible Soviet boycott. Mr. Thatcher said that conversations with the friendly members of the Outer Space Committee had indicated they might be reluctant to proceed in the face of Soviet boycott. Mr. Farley commented that it might nevertheless be possible to bring about a meeting of the Committee without the Soviets if this is necessary.

With regard to the work of the Outer Space Committee, Mr. Cleveland said the two central questions are: a) what outer space projects will we be pursuing in which international cooperation is possible, and b) what pressures can we bring to bear on the Soviets to internationalize those aspects of their space program in which they are ahead of us?

There followed some discussion of present international cooperation in connection with the United States Tiros meteorological satellite program, the Mercury program and other operations. Mr. Frutkin asserted that NASA has opened up its programs to the maximum foreign cooperation possible, and he added that the bilateral cooperative programs which we now have with Italy, Japan, and various other states figure prominently in the reports of the Committee on Space Research (COSPAR) of the International Council of Scientific Unions (ICSU), representing pressure on the Soviets to adopt a more cooperative approach.

The meeting closed with some discussion of the institutional aspects of international cooperation in outer space. Dr. Dryden hesitated to suggest any specific cooperative proposals for submission to the Outer Space Committee until the role envisioned for the Committee is clarified. Mr. Cleveland stated that the United States should decide soon how it wants to proceed in international space cooperation, for we are the leaders in building international institutions and should be in the forefront in promotion of an international regime for outer space. Mr. Gardner suggested that a beginning might be made by pressing for agreement on the legal status of outer space and celestial bodies. He also pointed out that the operational problems of communications or other satellite systems would be simplified if the operating agency were of an international character. Mr. Farley said he envisioned that the communications satellite system would be a joint, cooperative project in which United States participation would be by private companies and that of most other countries by public agencies. Mr. Cleveland observed that establishment of an international regime for outer space calls for a broader jurisdiction and competence than that available in the ITU or WMO, and he envisioned establishment of an international body which would move toward assumption of an administrative role with respect to outer space activities. Dr. Dryden expressed the view that it would be very difficult to establish a workable international agency for outer space cooperation and questioned whether the United Nations has operational capabilities which would permit it to play such a role. Mr. Cleveland agreed that most problems of international administration have become tremendously complex, but he cited the successful operation of the European Coal and Steel Community and expressed the conviction that this is the kind of approach that will be called for in the field of outer space in the next twenty years. As far as United Nations capabilities are concerned, Mr. Cleveland pointed to the operation in the Congo as an example of its executive potential and drew attention to the relative success we have enjoyed in the Congo in contrast to the experience in other areas where we have relied on a unilateral approach.

---

366. Memorandum From Secretary of State Rusk to President Kennedy[1]

Washington, July 17, 1961.

SUBJECT

Space Launcher Assistance to Other Countries

This Department, in close cooperation with Defense and the National Aeronautics and Space Administration, has formulated a proposed approach to answering queries from the Europeans about the degree to which we will assist them in the space launcher field. The

---

[1] Source: Kennedy Library, National Security Files, Departments and Agencies Series, Space Activities, General, 7/61–12/61, Box 307. Top Secret. According to a July 24 attached memorandum from Bromley Smith to Executive Secretary Lucius D. Battle, the President gave his approval, through Bundy, to the recommendation in the last paragraph.

urgency of replying to such queries is dictated by British efforts to persuade European countries to participate in the development of a space launcher using the British Blue Streak as the first stage, a French rocket as second stage, and possibly a German rocket as third stage.

We believe Blue Streak would be an unwise project for the Europeans because it would require large investments of money, time, and effort and would be obsolescent (although usable) by the time of its operational readiness. Moreover, its development might facilitate the acquisition by the Europeans of independent capabilities to develop and produce ballistic missiles.

Apart from the question of a French capability, the chance of an independent German nuclear capability could be increased since missiles are an essential and expensive part of such a capability. We believe that German entry into the nuclear weapons field would have profoundly divisive effects in NATO in addition to the other disadvantages of further national nuclear weapons capabilities: increased risk of war by accident or miscalculation, greater likelihood that any conventional clash would escalate quickly into nuclear war, lessened ability to have a controlled nuclear response, and heightened obstacles to arms control.

We would therefore propose to offer for sale certain United States space launchers (Scout and Thor), in order to offer other countries an alternative to the Blue Streak proposal as well as to assist in legitimate space science activities. We would carry out any sales in a manner which would minimize any contribution to the development of independent ballistic missiles capabilities.

I believe this approach would be consistent with your June 5 conversation with Prime Minister Macmillan. The record of that conversation indicates that it might be possible to give the French some military information, particularly about aircraft, and that this might be done ostensibly by the United Kingdom possibly in connection with a "European Space Project." We assume that this conversation should not be interpreted as contemplating any general relaxation of our policy against facilitating the acquisition of independent nuclear weapons delivery capabilities, including ballistic missiles, by other countries, or as representing an endorsement of the Blue Streak proposal.

If our interpretation above is in accord with your views, I recommend that you authorize me to proceed with an appropriate instruction to the United States Embassies in the countries concerned setting forth our approach to the sale of space launchers.

Dean Rusk

367.   Summary Minutes of the Meeting of the National
         Aeronautics and Space Council[1]

Washington, August 18, 1961.

This meeting of the National Aeronautics and Space Council was convened by the Chairman (Vice President Johnson) at 4:00 p.m. August 18, 1961 in Room 274 of the Executive Office Building. In addition to the Vice President, the principals attending the meeting were: the Secretary of State, the Secretary of Defense, the Administrator of the National Aeronautics and Space Administration, the Chairman of the Atomic Energy Commission, and the Executive Secretary of the National Aeronautics and Space Council.

Those who participated in the briefing were: Colonel Earl McFarland, Jr., representing the Intelligence Community; Dr. Harold Brown, representing the Department of Defense; Dr. Hugh L. Dryden, representing NASA.

Others present at the meeting were: Mr. Howard Furnas, Department of State; [less than 1 line of source text not declassified] Central Intelligence Agency; Dr. Lawrence Kavanau, Department of Defense.

The Chairman opened this meeting of the Council with reference to some of the major actions which had been taken through the Space Council mechanism. He referred to the coordination of the new space program, which the President had sent to the Congress on May 25; the policy recommendations on communication satellites which the President had announced on July 24; and the development of the Government position on the West Ford project, which the President had approved on August 11. He then stated that, in addition to developing policy recommendations, he planned to have the Council meet from time to time to discuss some major aspect of the space program. He illustrated this point by reference to such topics as the lunar project, potentialities of nuclear power in space, the space position of the United States before the United Nations, and problems of management and interagency coordination in space matters.

The Chairman then announced that the purpose of this meeting was to examine this country's space position vis-à-vis that of the USSR.

The first portion of the briefing was devoted to intelligence information regarding the Soviet space program. It was pointed out that most of the hard evidence regarding their program was derived from

---

[1] Source: Johnson Library, Vice President's Science File, National Aeronautics and Space Council. Top Secret. Edward C. Welsh, Executive Secretary of the Council, kept the minutes.

knowledge of their actual accomplishments, while evidence regarding specific future shots and timing, as well as regarding their military space plans, was "soft." It was emphasized, however, that there was no question that since 1955, the Soviets had established a firm objective of manned interplanetary travel.

A chart was displayed to point out graphically the number of Soviet launchings and the approximate size of the payloads in each successful shot. It was noted that through mid-1960 all of the shots, including the ICBM tests, had been made from the same launching site. (This should not be interpreted to mean that the Soviets do not have a number of operational ICBM launching pads at various locations.) The figures displayed indicated 46 successful space orbits by the U.S. and 14 by the USSR. The approximate total payload weights were 55,000 pounds for the U.S., and 110,000 pounds for the USSR. At this point, it was stated that the individual shot capability was deemed more important than the number of successful shots.

Attention was directed to the following about the Soviet program: the steady rate of increase in payload weight from about 185 pounds in Sputnik I to about 14,000 pounds in Sputnik VII; estimated that by 1962 they might orbit 25,000 pounds, and by 1965 from 50 to 100 tons; they have used essentially the same booster thrust, with some question as to Sputnik I and II, and have used military vehicles for the larger vertical firings.

As for the military aspects of the USSR space program, it was pointed out that there was little evidence of their immediate intent to use space for military purposes, although there was always the capability with their large boosters. In this regard, it was suggested that there was less USSR need for many of the types of military space projects such as the ones we are developing. Hence, it appeared that they had done little in space for reconnaissance, early warning, communications, meteorology, or navigation. (These are all projects in which the United States has shown progress, and in some cases operational accomplishment.)

One view was expressed that the U.S. was ahead in space programs except for boosters. However, others pointed out that they were at least equal to us on guidance capabilities and had possibly done more in their bio-medical program. It was further added that we should not overlook their demonstration of manned multi-orbit flight and recovery.

Some of the broad features of the USSR space program are that they focus on few objectives; they aim toward actions which will build world prestige and give indications of strength; they have integrated their ICBM development and their space program, in a single disciplined management chain; they have been particularly adroit in obtaining propaganda value on their space activities, in building a world image of military strength and technical competence; and ability to orbit large payloads, giving implication of growing capability toward using man in space for maintenance of space vehicles, for intercepting satellites of other nations, and in possibly demonstrating bombardment competence. (In regard to this latter, it was pointed out that this would be more of a threat than an efficient method for bombing.)

The comparison of U.S. and USSR space programs also brought out the following points regarding space science: (a) the Soviets failed to capitalize on their early fast start, particularly Sputnik III. This was contrasted to their outstanding achievements in technology as represented by their Luniks and the manned flights. (b) The average quality of scientific research is about the same in both countries, although nearly all of the highly original work has come from the United States. (c) The U.S. has led in the publication of scientific papers by a ratio of about 6 to 1, although there is some indication that the USSR plans to release more of its scientific data. (d) The openness and international cooperativeness features of our program have been difficult for the Soviets to counter. This may cause them to be more generous in the public exposure of their work, although there is little evidence that they are withholding much substantive scientific information. (e) Their ability to launch large payloads enables them to perform more comprehensive planetary probe experiments than the U.S., and they will have advantage in this regard until we have larger boosters in operation. (f) They have done some research in hydrogen technology but are probably not as far advanced as the U.S. (g) There is limited evidence that they are engaged in atomic power technology for interplanetary payloads. Their earliest test flight is not expected before 1970.

The United States is expected to run behind the USSR in manned earth orbital flights for some time, because of our limited launch vehicle capability. How long this U.S. disadvantage will continue depends on the relative rates of the U.S.–USSR big launch vehicle programs. It is estimated, however, that we will have a successful manned round trip to the moon in the 1967–68 period, while intelligence data for a Soviet accomplishment of this nature is about 1970. The latter estimate, however, cannot be considered firm. It is believed, however, that the Lunar program is the point at which the U.S. has reason to hope to overtake the USSR.

In a more detailed exposition on the U.S. space accomplishments, the following points were made: (a) We have definite military requirements, and have made substantial progress in the reconnaissance, communications, early warning, navigation, weather, and rendezvous and inspection areas.

[1 line of source text not declassified] (It was pointed out that some space programs such as those in weather and communications, were also being developed outside the Department of Defense, but would also have value to the military.) (b) As for our large boosters, the Saturn first stage will be flight-tested this year, with a 3-stage C-1 in 1963; the F-1 will be qualified for flight in 1964; and the C-3 or the C-4 flight test will take place in 1965. (c) For military purposes, as for non-military purposes, larger payloads are always important, but for certain types of projects the rate of increase is of decreasing importance.

It was pointed out that there is a probable role for military men in space as well as for men in space for scientific and other purposes. The advantage of having men in a space vehicle is the opportunity to use judgment and to adapt to unprogrammed or unexpected conditions. To some extent this advantage is offset by the increased vulnerability of man and the substantial weight and additional equipment which needs to be given over to the problem of survivability. However, many of the problems of vulnerability also exist as regards advancing electronic systems or films in space vehicles. Reference was made to the Dina Soar as a manned military space project. It was pointed out that this needs to be given further careful examination, to ascertain the military reasons for the space flight reentry capability. Further on the military space side, it was pointed out that there is need of a capability to maintain complex electrical equipment of at least 5000 pounds in space for extended periods of time. Little value was given to the use of space vehicles for bombardment purposes. On this aspect of military use of space, some question was raised as to whether there was significant military importance to this competence and as to whether very large payloads in space were needed for defense. It was emphasized, however, that the R & D program should be maintained to make certain that we had the competence to meet all military space requirements. At this time, there is only one manned Lunar flight program, and that is under NASA management.

Brief reference was made to the relative percentages of the respective GNP's which are being devoted to space by the U.S. and the USSR. It was stated that the U.S. will be spending about .6 of 1% of its GNP in FY 1962 while the Soviets were undoubtedly spending "very much less." This latter was explained on the basis of their smaller number of shots, lesser variety of projects, highly integrated management structure, and economy on the number and use of launching facilities. [Note: The .6 of 1% reference was undoubtedly to new obligational authority, not spending, and was probably a little high even so. The GNP for FY 1962 should be close to $520 billion; the NOA for space is about $2.9 billion; and the expenditure estimate is about $2.4 billion. Hence, the percentages would approximate .56% (NOA) and .46% (exp.)][2]

In the questions and discussion by the principals at the briefing, the following points were made: (a) Warning against spreading our resources too thinly and thereby creating inefficiency in the overall

___

[2] Brackets in the source text.

space program; (b) Statement of the Defense Department position to have the military concentrate on those projects of defense significance and not to have them duplicate or overlap with NASA; (c) Question of the adequacy as well as the fragmentation of our life sciences effort; (d) Coordination between NASA and DOD is excellent, with every intention to keep it that way; (e) Announcement that NASA is working actively to gear its organization to the new and accelerated space program; (f) Reaction of officials of other nations as to whether the U.S. should be spending upwards of $40 billion on a Lunar space effort was that the U.S. just had no choice but to spend the resources and try to win the race; (g) Substantial impetus given to the U.S. space efforts by the basic policy decisions made by the President and the increased funds approved by the Congress.

E.C. Welsh[3]
Executive Secretary

---

[3] Printed from a copy that bears this typed signature.

---

368.   **Letter From the Deputy Under Secretary of State for Political Affairs (Johnson) to the Administrator of the National Aeronautics and Space Administration (Webb)[1]**

Washington, September 12, 1961.

Dear Mr. Webb:

Mr. Bowles' letter of April 17 called attention to the undesirability of launching Centaur over a trajectory involving hazard of possible impact in an extensive region of mid-continent Africa. Your acknowledgment of April 28 stated that political considerations would be taken into account.[2] I am now writing you to confirm the understanding on the Centaur program reached with your staff and to express our continuing interest in timely consultation respecting such matters.

On the basis of discussions with NASA staff we understand that a year's delay would be involved in changing launching trajectory and

---

[1] Source: National Archives and Records Administration, RG 59, Central Files 1960–63, 701.56311/4–1761. Confidential. Drafted by Wreatham E. Gathright (S/AE), and cleared by J. Wayne Fredericks (AF) and Stephen M. Schwebel (L).

[2] See Document 361 and footnote 3 thereto.

that such a delay is considered unacceptable by NASA because of the relationship of Centaur to the Saturn and Nova developments. We also understand the the Centaur test program has been altered to include an initial ballistic flight which is to provide additional data before the first orbital attempt is made. According to NASA staff, there remains a chance of impact, but all practicable precautions will be taken.

It remains this Department's considered view that the United States must make every effort to hold to the minimum hazards to other countries arising from the conduct of our space programs. However, we appreciate that occasions will arise necessitating the use of launching trajectories not completely free of risk, and we are prepared to make exceptions where clearly necessary.

In the present case, we recognize that the key role of Centaur in our future space effort makes undesirable the further delay we are told would result from a change in trajectory. With this in mind and with the understanding that all precautions will be taken, this Department will not interpose objection to the two Centaur launchings planned for the mid-continent trajectory. Accordingly, we shall, as requested, seek arrangements so that Project Mercury facilities in Bermuda, the Canary Islands, and Australia can be employed in support of the Centaur tests. We have been informed that the other Mercury facilities will not be used.

Although we shall proceed as indicated, the information available to us points toward the conclusion that selection of the proposed trajectory was dictated by the location of existing NASA ground facilities rather than by mission and safety of flight considerations. In the circumstances, it seems clear that NASA should seek greater flexibility in its ground launching and support arrangements to make possible the avoidance of hazardous trajectories. If failure to achieve such flexibility should result in additional impacts in other countries, the political cost and the cost in possible limitations on our space activities would appear likely to outweigh the monetary costs involved.

Timely consultation is a crucial factor in minimizing problems such as the present one. We hope that as NASA proceeds with planning for the testing of new systems (such as Saturn, Nova, and Rover) and for new missions (lunar and interplanetary missions as well as further space research), this Department will be informed of such plans at a time which will permit any necessary changes to be made without undue program delays.

Sincerely yours,

U. Alexis Johnson[3]

---

[3] Printed from a copy that bears this typed signature.

369.   Circular Telegram From the Department of State to Certain Posts[1]

Washington, February 23, 1962, 6:49 p.m.

1465. For Principal Officer.   Department requests you arrange appointment with Foreign Minister or other appropriate official at your discretion to express deep gratification US Government and specifically National Aeronautics and Space Administration (NASA) for effective cooperation extended by host country in behalf Project Mercury manned space program. Successful orbital flight of astronaut just concluded due in no small degree presence tracking facilities in host countries. This participation by other lands in American space program deeply appreciated. Posts may wish stress again that Project Mercury is open peaceful scientific experiment designed further man's exploration of space and results of which available world. Posts may wish note that US will continue conduct its manned space program in open cooperation with other nations to benefit of mankind. You may wish inform officials US proposes launch manned space missions approximately every 60 to 90 days beginning April.

Department pouching text statements made US expressing gratification for participation your country in Project Mercury.

Rusk

---

[1] Source: National Archives and Records Administration, RG 59, Central Files 1960–63, 911.802/2–2362. Official Use Only. Drafted by Emery P. Smith (S/AE); cleared by Kerrigan (NASA), Alf E. Bergesen (BNA), Francis W. Herron (P), H. Freeman Matthews, Jr. (WE), Henry C. Ramsey (S/P), and Theo C. Adams (AF/W); and approved by Robert G. Packard (S/AE).

370.   Memorandum From the Administrator of the National
        Aeronautics and Space Administration (Webb) to the
        Chairman of the National Aeronautics and Space Council
        (Johnson)[1]

Washington, March 13, 1962.

SUBJECT

    Request for Highest National Priority for the Apollo Program

1. The programs that now enjoy the highest (DX) national priority are: Atlas, Titan, Minuteman, Polaris, BMEWS, Samos, Nike-Zeus, Discoverer, Mercury, and Saturn. Of these, the first eight are managed by the Department of Defense, and the last two by the National Aeronautics and Space Administration. The prescribed criteria under which the President has made these determinations is that these programs have objectives of key political, scientific, psychological or military import.

2. The NASA is requesting that the Apollo program be added to this list. Recognizing the need to restrict the number of projects on the list to the absolute minimum, NASA is prepared to drop Project Mercury from the list by the end of Calendar Year 1962, at which time its mission should be essentially complete. NASA will also expect to drop the Saturn vehicle project from the list except insofar as it pertains to the Apollo mission. In adding Apollo, the NASA would be requesting a DX priority for all of these elements of the Apollo program that are essential to its ultimate mission: to effect a manned lunar landing and return in this decade. The essential elements of the Apollo program would include development of the spacecraft and launch vehicles as well as the facilities which are required for their development, testing and use. Elements of certain other name projects would thus be included, such as Saturn and Gemini, but only insofar as they are directly applicable to the manned lunar landing.

3. Decisions on the assignment of highest national priority are made by the President and in the case of space program projects, he takes into consideration the advice of the National Aeronautics and Space Council. Therefore, I ask that this matter be placed before the Council at an early date.

4. I shall be pleased to supply any further information you think is essential to the Council's consideration.

James E. Webb[2]

---

[1] Source: Kennedy Library, National Security Files, Meetings and Memoranda Series, NSAM 144, Box 335. No classification marking.

[2] Printed from a copy that indicates Webb signed the original.

371.   Letter From Vice President Johnson to President Kennedy[1]

Washington, March 23, 1962.

Dear Mr. President:

At the National Aeronautics and Space Council meeting on March 21, 1962, consideration was given to the merits of assigning the highest (DX) priority to the Apollo space program. Administrator Webb had requested that this matter be taken up by the Council, so that appropriate recommendation might be made to the President.

It was made clear by Administrator Webb that, if such priority were assigned, it would be employed only to the extent necessary and only to those elements in the program which would otherwise be delayed in performance and which would consequently postpone a successful manned lunar flight. He stated further that NASA was prepared to remove the Mercury program from the DX priority list by the end of calendar year 1962, and also that the Agency planned to drop from such list all elements of the Saturn project, except those applicable to the Apollo program.

Based upon the premises referred to in the preceding paragraph, Defense and NASA urged that recommendation be made by the Council to the President that a DX priority be so assigned. State and AEC concurred, with the statements that they agreed with the urgency and importance of the program and had no objection to the assignment of a DX priority to it. The Chairman also expressed his agreement with these views.

In light of this unanimity, I respectfully advise that it is the sense and the recommendation of the Council that the highest (DX) national priority be assigned to the Apollo space program.

I do this with the expressed understanding that this recommendation is intended to be of assistance to you in this policy matter and is not a means to short-circuit or otherwise take the place of any essential procedures which may be required in the matter of assigning priorities.

Sincerely,

Lyndon B. Johnson

---

[1] Source: Kennedy Library, National Security Files, Meetings and Memoranda Series, NSAM 144, Box 335. No classification marking.

372.   **National Security Action Memorandum No. 144**[1]

Washington, April 11, 1962.

TO

The Vice President (as Chairman, National Aeronautics and Space Council)
The Secretary of Defense
The Secretary of Commerce
Administrator, National Aeronautics and Space Agency
Director, Bureau of the Budget
Director, Office of Emergency Planning

SUBJECT

Assignment of Highest National Priority to the Apollo Manned Lunar Landing
Program

In response to a recommendation by the National Aeronautics and Space Council, which approved a proposal by the Administrator, National Aeronautics and Space Agency, the President under the authority granted by the Defense Production Act of 1950 today established the program listed below as being in the highest national priority category for research and development and for achieving operational capability.

Apollo (manned lunar landing program, including essential spacecraft, launch vehicles, and facilities).

McGeorge Bundy

---

[1] Source: Kennedy Library, National Security Files, Departments and Agencies Series, Space Activities, General, April–May 1962, Box 307. Confidential. A copy was sent to General Maxwell Taylor.

373.   Memorandum From the Chief of the Political Research and
        Analysis Division, Arms Control and Disarmament Agency
        (Gathright) to the Deputy Director of the Arms Control and
        Disarmament Agency (Fisher)[1]

Washington, June 7, 1962.

SUBJECT

Evolution of and Reflections on the U.S. Approach to Political Aspects of the
Reconnaissance Satellite Program

I do not wish to burden a busy official with more reading matter.
However, I thought you might find it at least of historical interest to
review the attached papers,[2] which relate to certain past stages in the
development by the U.S. of its approach to political aspects of the reconnaissance satellite program. In this connection, I have summarized
below, largely from memory, some of the principal developments in this
regard and have offered some personal reflections on the matter.

Historical background

Technical consideration of the potentialities of satellites for reconnaissance purposes dates back at least to 1946. However, in what may
not unfairly be called a classic example of the lag of political planning
behind technological developments, it was not until late 1958 and early
1959 that the Department of State began examining in some depth political aspects of the problem. By that time certain developments had
already taken place which had set the framework which has affected the
flexibility of political movement ever since.

As was the case with other space programs, the reconnaissance
satellite program had derived substantial impetus from the successful
demonstration by Sputnik I of the feasibility of placing satellites in orbit
about the earth. What had previously been a single program was divided into three projects: Discoverer, Samos, and Midas. Treatment of
Discoverer as an entirely developmental effort was probably helpful.
However, a developmental effort involving over 30 launchings has not
passed unnoticed, and Discoverer as well as Samos and Midas has been
identified in the public press and by foreign propagandists as a "spy in
the sky" program. This identification, particularly in the case of Samos,
found support in public statements by military spokesmen and in official releases (see Tab A as an example of one of the least ostentatious of

---

[1] Source: National Archives and Records Administration, RG 383, ACDA/DD Files:
Lot 69 D 396, Outer Space. Secret.

[2] The attachments were not found.

these public pronouncements). Finally, the program was oriented entirely to intelligence purposes rather than to a logical extension of space observation capabilities.

The first major political effort led to consideration within the government of a position calling for prohibition of "weapons" in orbit combined with "no weapons aboard" inspection and with affirmation of the right of transit of other types of space vehicles (including reconnaissance satellites). The position was rapidly rejected although it was later to emerge in modified form in the "no bombs in orbit" proposal of 1960.

During the summer of 1959, meetings of the UN Ad Hoc Committee on the Peaceful Uses of Outer Space provided an opportunity to advance to a degree the concepts that the passage of satellites does not violate national sovereignty and that outer space is free for exploration and use. Both arguments became standard features of U.S. contingency position papers on the reconnaissance satellite program. A defensive approach was gradually elaborated including such features as argumentation that observation from space is permissible and desirable, noting a linkage between observation satellites and arms control and disarmament (see Tab B), drawing on "precedents" (such as Tiros and, subsequently, Titov's amateur photography) as they occurred, and contrasting the urgency of prohibiting the placing of weapons of mass destruction in orbit with the undesirability of attempting to prohibit observation of the earth from space. The foregoing represented essentially a collection of debating points rather than an attempt to meet basic issues.

The U-2 affair lent the then impending launch of the first experimental Samos a fearsome prospect, and an especially agonizing reappraisal of the U.S. approach to political aspects of the reconnaissance satellite program was conducted during the summer and early fall of 1960. The paper attached under Tab C was prepared by State Department staff and circulated for simultaneous consideration by higher officials within the Department and by other interested agencies. The position recommended by the paper (one of "responsible openness") was in due course rejected by the Department as well as other agencies. However, in my view, the issues outlined by the paper remain substantially the same today as two years ago except for the fact that an additional period of procrastination in facing up to basic issues has made the problem more difficult to resolve on a timely basis.

The approach finally adopted in 1960 is presented in the paper attached under Tab D. The central feature of the approach was to be an attempt to handle Samos "in extremely low key with minimum disclosure." The experimental character of the program was to be emphasized (as it had been with a degree of success in the case of the Discoverer program) and achievement of an operational capability was to be presented as a distant possibility rather than an imminent reality. Only limited public statements were to be made, but these were to be factual in character in order to avoid replaying at least part of the U-2 scenario. The product of the program was to be in the hands of the intelligence community absent specific contrary decision by the Secretaries of State and Defense and the Director of CIA. The approach was inaugurated upon the first attempted Samos launching (see Tab E). As it turned out, the first attempt failed, and the schedule slipped to the extent the new administration found itself confronted with a Samos launching during its first weeks of office.

From the outset, the present administration clearly believed that too much had been said about the program by military spokesmen (which was correct) and initiated a trend toward even less disclosure than that contemplated under the 1960 approach. This trend ultimately led not to an approach of remaining silent about launchings but of refusing to identify what object had been launched. It is not clear why it was believed that such an approach would be politically advantageous. In any case, as you know, this approach ran head on into the simultaneous U.S. effort at the UN to inaugurate a procedure for registering space vehicles.

It will be clear that the foregoing account is necessarily limited by the extent of my involvement in staff level consideration of this problem. However, I believe the main trends are accurately identified.

Some reflections on political aspects

Under the continuing impact of the U-2 affair, political handling of the reconnaissance satellite program has to date reflected primarily the desire to avoid in the short-term precipitating a similar direct clash with the Soviet Union. The goal is an understandable but not necessarily an attainable one. In view of the basic conflict of interests involved, it has always been questionable how long a clash could be postponed. However, the approach taken by the U.S. can be said to have bought time but possibly at the expense of placing the program on a sounder long-term footing.

The Soviet Union appears to have faced up to the issue sooner than the U.S. and to have embarked on a political offensive against reconnaissance satellites. At the time of this writing, it remains to be seen whether (or perhaps more accurately when) this offensive will be carried to the point of a major clash. Although we have no interest in hastening such a clash, it would be illogical for us to continue to refrain from taking steps to place the program in a more defensible position if such steps can be developed and implemented in a manner calculated to place the least strain on our relations with the Soviet Union.

If the reconnaissance satellite program could have been conducted entirely in secret, that might have been the safest approach. The steps that would be required to achieve complete secrecy now would be difficult, if not impossible, to carry out with credibility. In the long-term, steps in this direction would be headed for collision with arms control and disarmament arrangements affecting outer space and involving the inspection of space vehicles.

Even if apparently practical steps toward increased secrecy could be devised, they would involve certain hazards. We would be fighting on the Soviet Union's terms rather than our own by acting as if we accepted their view that the activities involved were not legitimate. Moreover, we are always embarrassed when we are "caught in the act", a handicap the Soviet Union does not share. Our conscience plagues us, and we are likely to border on incoherence or actually to become incoherent, as in the U-2 affair. If we need to undertake certain types of activities, we ought to conduct them, where possible, in the manner we feel most comfortable about. We are generally somewhat ill at ease with excessive secrecy. It may be a flaw in our national character, but it is there nonetheless.

In the long-term conflict with the Soviet Union, "openness" would seem as a general matter to be advantageous to the United States. Obviously, we cannot conduct all activities openly, but where we can (or where we can approach "openness"), we relieve ourselves of some of the burdens outlined above, act more consistently with our political and social philosophy, and provide an effective contrast with the Soviet way of doing things. Moreover, although we are not likely to pry the Soviet Union away from its philosophy of secrecy, it would seem in our interest to do what we can to convince it that the trend is in the direction of "openness". As long as we remain on the defensive in the reconnaissance satellite field, we cannot play what might in time prove to be one of our best cards in this game, and the Soviet Union can feel warm, if not completely safe, in its cocoon. We do not want to arouse fear, but it might be helpful if the tenant of the cocoon were to become gradually aware that its hiding place is exposed to the sun.

The problem, of course, would be to develop in considerable detail (sufficient for fair assessment) an operational approach which might enable us to move, in low-key, toward gradually increasing openness in the conduct of "observation" satellite programs. Under such an approach, observation from space would be emphasized. Military intelligence would not be curtailed but would be derivative rather than paramount. The unfolding of capabilities would take place at a deliberate pace. The issues confronting us today in both forums in Geneva we will have to deal with as best we can. But I hope the present review will provide an opportunity to consider possibly more constructive alternatives for the future.

374.   **Record of Action at the 502d Meeting of the National Security Council**[1]

Washington, July 10, 1962.

RECOMMENDED POLICY

1. The United States should maintain the legal position that the principles of international law and the UN Charter apply to activities in outer space and, specifically, that outer space is free, as are the high seas.

2. The US should therefore continue to avoid any position implying that reconnaissance activities in outer space are not legitimate. Similarly, we should avoid any position declaring or implying that such activities are not "peaceful uses."

3. The US should, to the extent feasible, seek to avoid public use of the term "reconnaissance" satellites, and where appropriate use instead such broader and more neutral terms as "observation" or "photographic" satellites.

4. Further studies should be made on an urgent basis to determine whether there are releaseable data, such as mapping information, or procedures such as occasionally calling Tiros and Nimbus vehicles "photographic" satellites, which would help create wider public acceptance of space observation and photography.

5. NASA should study urgently the possibilities of accelerating bilateral international cooperation to develop non-military space activities involving space observation, perhaps including photography.

6. It is recognized that the US cannot entirely avoid or disclaim interest in reconnaissance, so that where feasible the US should also seek to gain acceptance of the principle of the legitimacy of space reconnaissance.

7. When confronted by specific Soviet pressure to outlaw reconnaissance activities in space, the US should continue to take a public stand for the legitimacy of the *principle* of reconnaissance from outer space, the precise form and extent of which would depend upon the circumstances of the confrontation.

8. The US should not at this time attempt to conduct a truly clandestine program (by which we mean a program with covert and unregistered launchings, and public denial that the US is engaged in reconnaissance). However, the US should pursue the research and develop-

---

[1]   Source: National Archives and Records Administration, RG 59, S/S–NSC (Miscellaneous) Files: Lot 66 D 95, NSC Records of Actions. Top Secret.

ment for a stand-by capability for clandestine operations in case circumstances ever make such operations necessary.

9. The present practice of not identifying individual military space launchings by mission or purpose is sound. We believe, however, that there should also be a more open (but not more detailed) public reference to the general over-all military program. An appropriate nickname for public identification should be given to the over-all military program, with its objectives intentionally stated in broad and general terms. All military launchings would be described in terms of the general objectives of the over-all military program. No specific mission would be ascribed to any particular launch.

10. The US should not, at this time, publicly disclose the status, extent, effectiveness or operational characteristics of its reconnaissance program.

11. Strict control over public statements and backgrounding concerning reconnaissance satellites should be exercised to ensure consistency with the policy guidelines suggested in these recommendations.

12. No public attention should be directed toward development of anti-satellite capabilities, and any publicized demonstration of developmental work and any actual test of such a capability should require White House approval, with full account given to the adverse effects for our reconnaissance satellite program. We should avoid any indications that physical countermeasures to reconnaissance vehicles would be justified, and as appropriate the US should make a positive effort to propagate the idea that interference with or attacks on any space vehicle of another country in peacetime are inadmissible and illegal.

13. The US should discreetly disclose to certain allies and neutrals selected information with regard to the US space reconnaissance program, making each disclosure orally and at a time and in a manner that will preserve the essential security of our program while impressing upon them its importance for the security of the Free World. Disclosures should be made in a manner that will preclude acquisition by the Communist Bloc of usable evidence of an official US acknowledgment that we are conducting a satellite reconnaissance program. Proposals for such disclosures should include clearance by the National Reconnaissance Office.

14. The US should in private disclosures emphasize the fact of our determination and ability to pursue such programs because of their great importance to our common security, despite any efforts to dissuade us.

15. The US should note in connection with private disclosures that, except in some cases for specifically defined disarmament agreements, the US cannot agree to (a) declarations of the precise purpose of all

satellites, (b) declarations of the equipment of all satellites, (c) general requirements for advance notification of all satellite launchings and the tracks of satellites, (d) pre-launch inspection of the satellites, or (e) a specific definition of peaceful uses of space which does not embrace unlimited observation.

16. The possible roles of space reconnaissance in disarmament inspection arrangements or in creating military stability should be further studied.

17. The US should stand by the disarmament proposal for a provision in Stage One of a Treaty on General and Complete Disarmament banning weapons of mass destruction from being carried in satellites, and providing for advance notification and inspection of all missile and space launchings to insure that ban. The US should continue to exclude any ban on reconnaissance satellites.

---

375. Memorandum From the Deputy Assistant Secretary of State for European Affairs (Tyler) to Secretary of State Rusk[1]

Washington, September 7, 1962.

SUBJECT

Cooperation with Europe in the Development and Production of Space Launch Vehicles

The Problem:

The recent establishment of the ten-nation European Space Research Organization (ESRO) and the seven-nation European Launcher Development Organization (ELDO)[2] reflects European aspirations in the field of outer space and raises questions of long-range United States policy toward a potentially vigorous and sustained European effort in space science and technology. Current US policy foresees, and NASA has already offered, cooperation with ESRO in

---

[1] Source: National Archives and Records Administration, RG 59, SCI Central Files: Lot 65 D 473. Official Use Only. Drafted by D.R. Morris and R.F. Packard (S/SA).

[2] *ESRO* now includes the UK, France, West Germany, Italy, The Netherlands, Belgium, Spain, Sweden, Switzerland and Austria. It is expected that Norway and Denmark will join within a year or two. *ELDO* includes the UK, France, West Germany, Italy, The Netherlands, Belgium and Australia. [Footnote in the source text.]

space research as well as in launching its satellite experiments. There are many indications, however, that the Europeans will not be content, for economic and political reasons as well as for considerations of prestige, to continue to be dependent upon US launch vehicles. We have been told specifically that ESRO planning looks to the launching of European-developed space satellites by European-built launch vehicles as soon as technically possible. ELDO, with its mandate to develop a European space launch vehicle, is the most obvious expression of this determination. We believe, therefore, that the United States must look beyond cooperation with ESRO to the more complicated question of our cooperation with ELDO in the development of European launch vehicle technology.

Discussion:

The formation of ESRO and particularly of ELDO (despite US offers to supply launch vehicles for the scientific payloads of individual European countries) reflects the force of European determination to mount an active space program and to develop an indigenous capability not dependent upon US technology and US launch vehicles. In addition to considerations of prestige and pride, there is widespread view among European industrial and government leaders that space technology is a frontier of modern industry and of applied science which cannot be left unexploited, if the dynamics of European industry and science are to be maintained in the future. Visits to the United States by representatives of European industry and reports from representatives of American industry abroad point to an impressive level of enthusiasm, activity, and technical progress. It is clear that the Europeans intend to forge ahead in this new technology.

The military implications of a growing European space capability are inescapable, given the fact that the technology of launch vehicles for placing satellites in orbit can be applied in varying degrees to the development of missiles. The extent to which this application will actually occur will depend in part on the general direction in which European space technology develops. It is during the present stage of initial formulation of the European effort that the United States has the best opportunity to influence the direction of that effort, not only toward projects less directly related to military applications, but also toward an integrated, multinational program which would reinforce our broad policy objectives in Europe in other fields. If we exhibit now a willingness to cooperate, it may also be possible to steer the European Community toward a capability in space technology which would complement our own (i.e., one which would avoid duplication of our efforts and would encourage the most effective use of limited Western scientific and industrial resources).

If, however, we stand aloof from the development of European space technology, the Europeans will clearly go it alone. Their capability for doing so is unquestioned. There is considerable evidence that they already possess a large body of knowledge gained from our technical literature, from visits to and from American industry and space laboratories, from exchange of information between American and European industrial representatives, from US military contracts, from the Blue Streak technology, and from their own growing efforts. (A summary of European programs in this field is attached at Tab B.)[3]

Given such an informational base and the enthusiasm displayed in industrial, scientific and engineering circles, there is no doubt that the Europeans will develop an independent space technology. At the same time, despite the fact that the Europeans realize that they must to some extent enter this new field of technology from the ground up, they hope that they may build upon experience already extant in the United States so as to avoid useless duplication and to make it possible for them to advance the over-all Western capability at an early stage. Cooperation to this end in the foundation of an independent European Community capability in space technology would be consistent with our broader goals in Europe. It would parallel the similar developments which we are encouraging in the field of nuclear energy.

The United States has welcomed the formation of ESRO and has indicated its willingness to cooperate with the Organization in the space sciences as well as to provide launch assistance for the Organization's experiments. We have not been enthusiastic about the separate establishment of ELDO since its initial program calls for the development of a space launch vehicle which will largely duplicate existing US vehicles. We have agreed, however, to assist ELDO indirectly in one respect, i.e., we have agreed that the British may pass on to the other members of the Organization certain data (other than information on guidance and re-entry) which we had previously provided to the British and which they have used in the development of the Blue Streak missile (Blue Streak was developed initially by the British as a prototype intermediate-range ballistic missile, but is now to be converted into the first stage of the proposed three-stage ELDO space launch vehicle.)

US policy limits cooperation in space launch technology to that which would not significantly enhance any national ballistic missile delivery capability. As a practical matter, however, no specific guidelines have been agreed as to what areas of cooperation would be permissible; nor has the question whether some cooperation of this sort would be desirable been considered carefully in the broader context of

---

[3] Not printed.

over-all policy toward the European Community. Such guidance is being sought by NASA and by representatives of the American aerospace industry. In the absence of specific guidelines reflecting an over-all policy, we have had to deal with requests for cooperation or assistance in this field on an ad hoc basis, applying as the over-riding criterion for decision in each case the lowest common denominator (i.e., the question whether such a release or license approval would appear to assist in any way the development of a national missile delivery capability) without regard to other desiderata or policy considerations. Reliance on this procedure is not only inadequate for NASA and our own industry, but precludes any advantageous initiative on our part and forces us to stand aside from these European developments. It creates the impression that we are unable to cooperate or that our cooperation is grudging at best.

There is attached at Tab A for your consideration a suggested draft United States Position on Cooperation with Europe in the Development and Production of Space Launch Vehicles.[4] It reaffirms our own national interest in such cooperation, sets forth criteria for judging the general acceptability of any proposed area of cooperation, and charges the Department in conjunction with NASA and the Department of Defense to identify specific projects involving space launch technology which would contribute to Atlantic Community aims and would not at the same time contribute significantly to the development of national military missile capabilities.

---

[4] Not printed. An excerpt from the October 3 Staff Record from the Executive Secretariat indicates that the Department approved the draft position paper on October 1. The Assistant Secretary for European Affairs was designated to represent the Department in discussions with NASA, the Defense Department, and the President's Science Adviser. (National Archives and Records Administration, RG 59, SCI Central Files: Lot 65 D 473)

376.   **Letter From the Administrator of the National Aeronautics and Space Administration (Webb) to President Kennedy[1]**

Washington, November 30, 1962.

Dear Mr. President:

At the close of our meeting on November 21, concerning possible acceleration of the manned lunar landing program, you requested that I describe for you the priority of this program in our over-all civilian space effort. This letter has been prepared by Dr. Dryden, Dr. Seamans, and myself to express our views on this vital question.

The objective of our national space program is to become pre-eminent in all important aspects of this endeavor and to conduct the program in such a manner that our emerging scientific, technological, and operational competence in space is clearly evident.

To be pre-eminent in space, we must conduct scientific investigations on a broad front. We must concurrently investigate geophysical phenomena about the earth, analyze the sun's radiation and its effect on earth, explore the moon and the planets, make measurements in interplanetary space, and conduct astronomical measurements.

To be pre-eminent in space, we must also have an advancing technology that permits increasingly large payloads to orbit the earth and to travel to the moon and the planets. We must substantially improve our propulsion capabilities, must provide methods for delivering large amounts of internal power, must develop instruments and life support systems that operate for extended periods, and must learn to transmit large quantities of data over long distances.

To be pre-eminent in operations in space, we must be able to launch our vehicles at prescribed times. We must develop the capability to place payloads in exact orbits. We must maneuver in space and rendezvous with cooperative spacecraft and, for knowledge of the military potentials, with uncooperative spacecraft. We must develop techniques for landing on the moon and the planets, and for re-entry into the earth's atmosphere at increasingly high velocities. Finally, we must learn the process of fabrication, inspection, assembly, and check-out that will provide vehicles with life expectancies in space measured in years rather than months. Improved reliability is required for astronaut safety, long duration, scientific measurements, and for economical meteorological and communications systems.

---

[1] Source: Johnson Library, Vice President's Science File, National Aeronautics and Space Council, T.S. Official Use Only. A covering memorandum, also dated November 30, from Edward C. Welch, Chairman of the National Aeronautics and Space Council, indicates that the letter was also sent to Vice President Johnson.

In order to carry out this program, we must continually up-rate the competence of Government research and flight centers, industry, and universities, to implement their special assignments and to work together effectively toward common goals. We also must have effective working relationships with many foreign countries in order to track and acquire data from our space vehicles and to carry out research projects of mutual interest and to utilize satellites for weather forecasting and world-wide communications.

Manned Lunar Landing Program

NASA has many flight missions, each directed toward an important aspect of our national objective. The manned lunar landing program requires for its successful completion many, though not all, of these flight missions. Consequently, the manned lunar landing program provides currently a natural focus for the development of national capability in space and, in addition, will provide a clear demonstration to the world of our accomplishments in space. The program is the largest single effort within NASA, constituting three-fourths of our budget, and is being executed with the utmost urgency. All major activities of NASA, both in headquarters and in the field, are involved in this effort, either partially or full time.

In order to reach the moon, we are developing a launch vehicle with a payload capability 85 times that of the present Atlas booster. We are developing flexible manned spacecraft capable of sustaining a crew of three for periods up to 14 days. Technology is being advanced in the areas of guidance and navigation, re-entry, life support, and structures—in short, almost all elements of booster and spacecraft technology.

The lunar program is an extrapolation of our Mercury experience. The Gemini spacecraft will provide the answers to many important technological problems before the first Apollo flights. The Apollo program will commence with earth orbital maneuvers and culminate with the one-week trip to and from the lunar surface. For the next five to six years there will be many significant events by which the world will judge the competence of the United States in space.

The many diverse elements of the program are now being scheduled in the proper sequence to achieve this objective and to emphasize the major milestones as we pass them. For the years ahead, each of these tasks must be carried out on a priority basis.

Although the manned lunar landing requires major scientific and technological effort, it does not encompass all space science and technology, nor does it provide funds to support direct applications in meteorological and communications systems. Also, university research and many of our international projects are not phased with the manned lunar program, although they are extremely important to our future competence and posture in the world community.

Space Science

As already indicated, space science includes the following distinct areas: geophysics, solar physics, lunar and planetary science, interplanetary science, astronomy, and space biosciences.

At present, by comparison with the published information from the Soviet Union, the United States clearly leads in geophysics, solar physics, and interplanetary science. Even here, however, it must be recognized that the Russians have within the past year launched a major series of geophysical satellites, the results of which could materially alter the balance. In astronomy, we are in a period of preparation for significant advances, using the Orbiting Astronomical Observatory which is now under development. It is not known how far the Russian plans have progressed in this important area. In space biosciences and lunar and planetary science, the Russians enjoy a definite lead at the present time. It is therefore essential that we push forward with our own programs in each of these important scientific areas in order to retrieve or maintain our lead, and to be able to identify those areas, unknown at this time, where an added push can make a significant break-through.

A broad-based space science program provides necessary support to the achievement of manned space flight leading to lunar landing. The successful launch and recovery of manned orbiting spacecraft in Project Mercury depended on knowledge of the pressure, temperature, density, and composition of the high atmosphere obtained from the nation's previous scientific rocket and satellite program. Considerably more space science data are required for the Gemini and Apollo projects. At higher altitudes than Mercury, the spacecraft will approach the radiation belt through which man will travel to reach the moon. Intense radiation in this belt is a major hazard to the crew. Information on the radiation belt will determine the shielding requirements and the parking orbit that must be used on the way to the moon.

Once outside the radiation belt, on a flight to the moon, a manned spacecraft will be exposed to bursts of high speed protons released from time to time from flares on the sun. These bursts do not penetrate below the radiation belt because they are deflected by the earth's magnetic field, but they are highly dangerous to man in interplanetary space.

The approach and safe landing of manned spacecraft on the moon will depend on more precise information on lunar gravity and topography. In addition, knowledge of the bearing strength and roughness of the landing site is of crucial importance, lest the landing module topple or sink into the lunar surface.

Many of the data required for support of the manned lunar landing effort have already been obtained, but as indicated above there are many crucial pieces of information still unknown. It is unfortunate that the scientific program of the past decade was not sufficiently broad and vigorous to have provided us with most of these data. We can learn a lesson from this situation, however, and proceed now with a vigorous and broad scientific program not only to provide vital support to the manned lunar landing, but also to cover our future requirements for the continued development of manned flight in space, for the further exploration of space, and for future applications of space knowledge and technology to practical uses.

Advanced Research and Technology

The history of modern technology has clearly shown that pre-eminence in a given field of endeavor requires a balance between major projects which apply the technology, on the one hand, and research which sustains it on the other. The major projects owe their support and continuing progress to the intellectual activities of the sustaining research. These intellectual activities in turn derive fresh vigor and motivation from the projects. The philosophy of providing for an intellectual activity of research and an interlocking cycle of application must be a cornerstone of our National Space Program.

The research and technology information which was established by the NASA and its predecessor, the NACA, has formed the foundation for this nation's pre-eminence in aeronautics, as exemplified by our military weapons systems, our world market in civil jet airliners, and the unmatched manned flight within the atmosphere represented by the X-15. More recently, research effort of this type has brought the TFX concept to fruition and similar work will lead to a supersonic transport which will enter a highly competitive world market. The concept and design of these vehicles and their related propulsion, controls, and structures were based on basic and applied research accomplished years ahead. Government research laboratories, universities, and industrial research organizations were necessarily brought to bear over a period of many years prior to the appearance before the public of actual devices or equipment.

These same research and technological manpower and laboratory resources of the nation have formed a basis for the U.S. thrust toward pre-eminence in space during the last four years. The launch vehicles, spacecraft, and associated systems including rocket engines, reaction control systems, onboard power generation, instrumentation and equipment for communications, television and the measurement of the space environment itself have been possible in this time period only because of past research and technological effort. Project Mercury could not have moved as rapidly or as successfully without the information provided by years of NACA and later NASA research in providing a base of technology for safe re-entry heat shields, practical control mechanisms, and life support systems.

It is clear that a pre-eminence in space in the future is dependent upon an advanced research and technology program which harnesses the nation's intellectual and inventive genius and directs it along selective paths. It is clear that we cannot afford to develop hardware for every approach but rather that we must select approaches that show the greatest promise of payoff toward the objectives of our nation's space goals. Our research on environmental effects is strongly focused on the meteoroid problem in order to provide information for the design of structures that will insure their integrity through space missions. Our research program on materials must concentrate on those materials that not only provide meteoroid protection but also may withstand the extremely high temperatures which exist during re-entry as well as the extremely low temperatures of cryogenic fuels within the vehicle structure. Our research program in propulsion must explore the concepts of nuclear propulsion for early 1970 applications and the even more advanced electrical propulsion systems that may become operational in the mid-1970's. A high degree of selectivity must be and is exercised in all areas of research and advanced technology to ensure that we are working on the major items that contribute to the nation's goals that make up an over-all pre-eminence in space exploration. Research and technology must precede and pace these established goals or a stagnation of progress in space will inevitably result.

Space Applications

The manned lunar landing program does not include our satellite applications activities. There are two such program areas under way and supported separately: meteorological satellites and communications satellites. The meteorological satellite program has developed the Tiros system, which has already successfully orbited six spacecraft and which has provided the foundation for the joint NASA-Weather Bureau planning for the national operational meteorological satellite system. This system will center on the use of the Nimbus satellite which is presently under development, with an initial research and development flight expected at the end of 1963. The meteorological satellite developments have formed an important position for this nation in international discussions of peaceful uses of space technology for world benefits.

NASA has underway a research and development effort directed toward the early realization of a practical communication satellite system. In this area, NASA is working with the Department of Defense on the Syncom (stationary, 24-hour orbit, communications satellite) project in which the Department of Defense is providing ground station support for NASA's spacecraft development; and with commercial interests, for example, AT&T on the Telstar project. The recent "Communications Satellite Act of 1962" makes NASA responsible for advice to and cooperation with the new Communications Satellite Corporation, as well as for launching operations for the research and/or operational needs of the Corporation. The details of such procedures will have to be defined after the establishment of the Corporation. It is clear, however, that this tremendously important application of space technology will be dependent on NASA's support for early development and implementation.

University Participation

In our space program, the university is the principal institution devoted to and designed for the production, extension, and communication of new scientific and technical knowledge. In doing its job, the university intimately relates the training of people to the knowledge acquisition process of research. Further, they are the only institutions which produce more trained people. Thus, not only do they yield fundamental knowledge, but they are the sources of the scientific and technical manpower needed generally for NASA to meet its program objectives.

In addition to the direct support of the space program and the training of new technical and scientific personnel, the university is uniquely qualified to bring to bear the thinking of multidisciplinary groups on the present-day problems of economic, political, and social growth. In this regard, NASA is encouraging the universities to work with local industrial, labor, and governmental leaders to develop ways and means through which the tools developed in the space program can also be utilized by the local leaders in working on their own growth problems. This program is in its infancy, but offers great promise in the working out of new ways through which economic growth can be generated by the spin-off from our outer space and related research and technology.

International Activity

The National Space Program also serves as the base for international projects of significant technical and political value. The peaceful purposes of these projects have been of importance in opening the way for overseas tracking and data acquisition sites necessary for manned flight and other programs which, in many cases, would otherwise have been unobtainable. Geographic areas of special scientific significance have been opened to cooperative sounding rocket ventures of immediate technical value. These programs have opened channels for the introduction of new instrumentation and experiments reflecting the special competence and talent of foreign scientists. The cooperation of other countries—indispensable to the ultimate achievement of communication satellite systems and the allocation of needed radio frequencies—has been obtained in the form of overseas ground terminals contributed by those countries. International exploitation and enhancement of the meteorological experiments through the synchronized participation of some 35 foreign nations represent another by-product of the applications program and one of particular interest to the less developed nations, including the neutrals, and even certain of the Soviet bloc satellite nations.

These international activities do not in most cases require special funding: indeed, they have brought participation resulting in modest savings. Nevertheless, this program of technical and political value can be maintained only as a extension of the underlying on-going programs, many of which are not considered part of the manned lunar landing pro gram, but of importance to space science and direct applications.

Summary and Conclusion

In summarizing the views which are held by Dr. Dryden, Dr. Seamans, and myself, and which have guided our joint efforts to develop the National Space Program, I would emphasize that the manned lunar landing program, although of highest national priority, will not by itself create the pre-eminent position we seek. The present interest of the United States in terms of our scientific posture and increasing prestige, and our future interest in terms of having an adequate scientific and technological base for space activities beyond the manned lunar landing, demand that we pursue an adequate, well-balanced space program in all areas, including those not directly related to the manned lunar landing. We strongly believe that the United States will gain tangible benefits from such a total accumulation of basic scientific and technological data as well as from the greatly increased strength of our educational institutions. For these reasons, we believe it would not be in the nation's long-range interest to cancel or drastically curtail ongoing space science and technology development programs in order to increase the funding of the manned lunar landing program in fiscal year 1963.

The fiscal year 1963 budget for major hardware development and flight missions not part of the manned lunar landing program, as well as the university program, totals $400 million. This is the amount which the manned space flight program is short. Cancellation of this effort would eliminate all nuclear developments, our international sounding rocket projects, the joint U.S.-Italian San Marcos project recently signed by Vice President Johnson, all of our planetary and astronomical flights, and the communication and meteorological satellites. It should be realized that savings to the Government from this cancellation would be a small fraction of this total since considerable effort has already been expended in fiscal year 1963. However, even if the full amount could be realized, we would strongly recommend against this action.

In aeronautical and space research, we now have a program underway that will insure that we are covering the essential areas of the "unknown." Perhaps of one thing only can we be certain; that the ability to go into space and return at will increases the likelihood of new basic knowledge on the order of the theory that led to nuclear fission.

Finally, we believe that a supplemental appropriation for fiscal year 1963 is not nearly so important as to obtain for fiscal year 1964 the funds needed for the continued vigorous prosecution of the manned lunar landing program ($4.6 billion) *and* for the continuing development of our program in space science ($670 million), advanced research and technology ($263 million), space application ($185 million), and advanced manned flight including nuclear propulsion ($485 million). The funds already appropriated permit us to maintain a driving, vigorous program in the manned space flight area aimed at a target date of late 1967 for the lunar landing. We are concerned that the efforts required to pass a supplemental bill through the Congress, coupled with Congressional reaction to the practice of deficiency spending, could adversely affect our appropriations for fiscal year 1964 and subsequent years, and permit critics to focus on such items as charges that "overruns stem from poor management" instead of on the tremendous progress we have made and are making.

As you know, we have supplied the Bureau of the Budget complete information on the work that can be accomplished at various budgetary levels running from $5.2 billion to $6.6 billion for fiscal year 1964. We have also supplied the Bureau of the Budget with carefully worked out schedules showing that approval by you and the Congress of a 1964 level of funding of $6.2 billion together with careful husbanding and management of the $3.7 billion appropriated for 1963 would permit maintenance of the target dates necessary for the various milestones required for a final target date for the lunar landing of late 1967. The jump from $3.7 billion for 1963 to $6.2 billion for 1964 is undoubtedly going to raise more questions than the previous year jump from $1.8 billion to $3.7 billion.

If your budget for 1964 supports our request for $6.2 billion for NASA, we feel reasonably confident we can work with the committees and leaders of Congress in such a way as to secure their endorsement of your recommendation and the incident appropriations. To have moved in two years from President Eisenhower's appropriation request for 1962 of $1.1 billion to the approval of your own request for $1.8 billion, then for $3.7 billion for 1963 and on to $6.2 billion for 1964 would represent a great accomplishment for your administration. We see a risk that this will be lost sight of in charges that the costs are skyrocketing, the program is not under control, and so forth, if we request a supplemental in fiscal year 1963.

However, if it is your feeling that additional funds should be provided through a supplemental appropriation request for 1963 rather than to make the main fight for the level of support of the program on the basis of the $6.2 billion request for 1964, we will give our best effort to an effective presentation and effective use of any funds provided to speed up the manned lunar program.

With much respect, believe me

Sincerely yours,

James E. Webb[2]

---

[2] Printed from a copy that indicates Webb signed the original.

377. Memorandum From the President's Special Assistant for Science and Technology (Wiesner) to President Kennedy[1]

Washington, January 10, 1963.

SUBJECT

> Need for DOD–NASA Coordination and Consolidation in Earth-Orbit Space Activities

At the present time the United States is supporting two more or less independent and growing efforts in the development of earth-orbit space capabilities. These include both the near term developments of DynaSoar and Gemini and the longer term development of orbiting space stations for research and reconnaissance purposes. I believe that earth orbit activities will become an increasingly important and costly part of both the military and scientific space efforts, therefore we should make a major effort to unify them now before we become further committed to two large programs.

In addition to the long-term desirability of a single effort, there are a number of possible short-term gains which would be worthwhile. These would include the savings made possible by a major cutback in the DynaSoar program, which would be possible if the Air Force were given a significant role in the Gemini program, and some relief from the technical manpower needs of NASA. Furthermore, I am convinced that you will be increasingly faced with criticism for allowing this duplication to persist. In this memorandum I present a series of arguments for assigning a major responsibility in this area to the Air Force, as follows:

1) There be created a joint NASA–DOD development effort for development of an earth orbiting space station as a national space program facility and that the DOD be the executive agent for the program.
2) Arrangements be initiated for a major investment of the DOD, including funding, in the Gemini program and that the DynaSoar effort be collaterally reprogramed to a small fraction of its current level.

I believe that Secretaries McNamara and Gilpatric would concur in the desirability of these proposals and support such an effort. Mr. Webb would also agree on the philosophical desirability of such steps, but probably would vigorously oppose such a proposal because of his past experiences with the Air Force, because of the problems which may be created for the tracking network, and because of the peaceful image

---

[1] Source: Kennedy Library, President's Office Files, Staff Memoranda, Wiesner, Jerome B., Box 67C. Secret. A note dated January 10 requested permission to give copies of the memorandum to Webb and to Secretary Gilpatric.

problem which he believes would be created by the direct involvement of the DOD. There is more than a little justification for his attitude.

During the last few days there have been discussions between Secretary McNamara and Mr. Webb regarding joint support of Gemini. While this would be less sweeping than I regard as desirable, it would nonetheless be an important start in changing the present trend. It is important to move rapidly if we are to affect the Gemini program.

Relevant Components of Present NASA and DOD Manned Space Flight Programs

Attention is focused in this memorandum on only four components of the National Space Program; two in NASA and two in DOD. Although other projects could no doubt be included in this analysis, those to be described below are probably the largest in the resources required and in their potential importance for growth of general technological capability for manned space flight.

a) *Gemini (NASA)*. Intended to provide long-duration experience (up to two weeks) with manned flights in earth orbit and to develop rendezvous, docking, and controlled land landing techniques. Because of overlapping time schedules, the development of Apollo rendezvous and docking technology will proceed largely independently of Gemini.

b) *DynaSoar (USAF—X-20)*. Principal objectives are to demonstrate flexible, controlled recovery and landing from space flight, to test vehicle equipment, and to explore man's functions in near earth space flight. Because the X-20 is a winged vehicle, its development is substantially more difficult than that of spacecraft such as Gemini, and the effective orbital payload for a given launch capability is substantially smaller. On the other hand, it would be maneuverable during re-entry, capable of choosing a landing site over a large area, and to execute a landing, more or less, as a conventional aircraft.

c) *Military Orbital Development System ("MODS" USAF-648C)*. The objective is to provide a manned, long-duration orbital base for the conduct of military tests and experiments, under laboratory conditions, in the space environment. The base would be assembled from modules delivered to orbit by the Titan III, and serviced by modified Gemini-type personnel carriers.

d) *Manned Space Station (NASA)*. The objective (as in MODS, above) is to provide a near earth capability for conducting experiments in space, and for testing of spacecraft components. In addition, the station would be used for "maintaining and refueling spacecraft engaged in lunar and deepspace missions." The Space Station would be orbited by a Saturn C-5 rocket, and would have a supply and personnel transfer system based on a variety of launch vehicles as required.

The present budgetary plans for the above four projects are as follows *(to date, MODS has only been approved by the Headquarters, USAF Systems Review Board, and a request for emergency funding to conduct a "Phase I Program Definition" during 1963 is being forwarded to DOD)*:

Fiscal Years (In Millions of Dollars)

	1963	1964	1965	1966	1967
Gemini (NASA)	55	249	312	28	—
DynaSoar (DOD)	131	125	135	135	50
MODS (DOD)	15	125	324	179	37
Space Station (NASA)	—	4	10	150	350

Past experience would lead me to believe that projections for 1965 and later are probably low.

Suggested Program Considerations and Realignments

a) *MODS—Manned Station.* In general, a major problem in the development of useful and reliable space systems is the great difficulty in realistic reproduction in earth surface laboratories of the stresses due to extended space operations. There is little question that a most important step in accelerating technological development of systems suitable for prolonged space missions, manned or unmanned, will be in providing laboratory and testing facilities in earth orbit. The USAF proposal for a Military Orbital Development System (MODS) and the NASA plan for a Manned Space Station are both principally intended to provide such capabilities. However, it is difficult to see any differences in the basic requirements for an engineering space laboratory for the DOD or NASA—substantially the same technological problems involved in developing equipment suitable for extended operations in space will be met by both agencies, and the same will be true of crew conditioning and training problems. Accordingly, it seems clear that a single Manned Space Station Program, designed to meet all national needs, would be feasible.

Since both the DOD and NASA projects for a Space Station are now in their early planning stages, *a decision at this time to the effect that a single development for all national needs will be undertaken would inhibit growth of parallel efforts in both agencies—and would insure future savings not only of funds, but of the relatively scarcer resources in technological and managerial skills.*

In view of previous remarks, *it would seem advisable that the DOD be assigned responsibility for this development.* This step, aside from the important advantage of allowing greater NASA concentration of skills and energies on the Manned Lunar Landing Program, should also serve to advance the rate of growth in the technical maturity of military approaches to the space medium. In addition, it might also result in diminished political pressure for more vague and less rational approaches for expansion of military operations in space.

b) *Gemini-DynaSoar.* There seems to be general agreement that the use of space for reconnaissance and surveillance activities is a high-priority element of the DOD Space Program. More recently, such agreement has been extended to include communications, navigation and geodesy. Aside from these fairly well defined areas, there is little general agreement either as to the character of worthwhile missions or as to their suitability for DOD implementation.

However, if surveillance of Soviet territory is to be a high-priority element of the national space program, then it can be argued that U.S. surveillance of near-earth space should also have high priority. For example, it must be assumed that if, and as soon as, it becomes technically possible and militarily advantageous, the Soviet Union will use space for military purposes. The fact that no such purposes can now be described as probable is not an argument against research and development of the capabilities for defensive measures; it implies, rather, that such preparations must be flexible, non-specific and not on a crash basis—concerned, for example, with developing the technology of operations in space and the physical capability of discovering and identifying threats if and when these should appear. With respect to initial emphasis in such technological developments, it is now reasonable to say that. (1) development of rendezvous, docking, maneuver, and refueling techniques in earth orbit and of routine recovery from earth orbit are prerequisite objectives; (2) such operations must, at least initially, be based on the utilization of manned spacecraft since technical reliability and instrumentation considerations both imply that useful, fully automatic systems will probably take considerably longer to develop.

The current space program of the Department of Defense largely reflects the above line of argument; the purpose of the immediately following remarks is to focus it on the interaction between the DOD X-20 and NASA's Gemini projects.

The X-20 (DynaSoar) vehicle, in view of its relatively greater sophistication, will mature substantially later than Gemini. Moreover, it is not clear that boosters provided by the current national program will be able to support useful military operational versions of glider-type manned spacecraft in this decade. In view of the evident desirability of establishing at an early date the existence (if any) of military potential of manned applications in space reconnaissance and surveillance, the question naturally arises as to *whether growth in national space capability would not be accelerated by diversion of technical effort (and funds) from the*

X-20 to Gemini, which should be available at least 18 months sooner than the X-20. Such diversion in addition to allowing earlier military experience in space, with rudimentary capability for controlled land landings, would complement and accelerate development of techniques for effective use of an orbiting space laboratory—particularly if responsibility for this program is assigned to DOD as suggested above.

Furthermore, because the Gemini project is not integrally related to the Apollo in any important technological respect, and the resources of NASA's Manned Spacecraft Center will obviously be strained to an increasing degree in Apollo technical management, *the question must also be asked as to whether greater success in the national space program would be achieved by shifting part of the responsibility for Gemini from NASA to the DOD.* In addition to direct management benefits, such reassignment of responsibility would enable more effective and rapid exploration of the military utility of the space medium, as well as have obvious domestic political advantages. On the other hand, in view of the fact that the USSR Space Program is entirely military in character, and because of recent increasingly frequent public utterances in the USSR about the importance of military applications in space, it would not seem likely that seriously damaging political criticism would result from such a step.

Jerry

---

378. Circular Airgram From the Department of State to All Posts[1]

Washington, February 18, 1963.

SUBJECT

NASA–DOD Project Gemini Agreement

SUMMARY

The recently concluded agreement between the DOD and NASA provides for certain participation in the NASA Project Gemini and as a

---

[1] Source: National Archives and Records Administration, RG 59, Central Files 1960–63, SP 10 US/GEMINI. Limited Official Use. Drafted by Trevanion H.E. Nesbitt; cleared by Under Secretary McGhee and Rollie H. White (M), William L.S. Williams (ARA), Hanson (USIA), Deputy Under Secretary Johnson (G), Richard Friedman (EUR), Guy A. Lee (NEA), Richard E. Usher (FE), Dana Orwick (G/PM), Arnold W. Frutkin (NASA), Eric E. Oulashin (AF), George Moffitt (UNP), Francis W. Herron (P), Laurence L. Kavanau, and Colonel John (DOD); and approved by Edwin M.J. Kretzmann (SCI).

consequence may pose certain questions. The following background and talking points are for the Missions' information and use in answering questions about the agreement.

On January 22 the Department of Defense and NASA announced that an agreement has been reached between the two agencies under which the Department of Defense will participate in the Gemini Program. Gemini, a two-man follow-up of the single-man Mercury manned space flight program is an experimental program to advance the technology of manned space flight, including rendezvous and docking, and to study the effect of weightlessness for a period of up to two weeks. This NASA–DOD agreement is intended to assure the most effective utilization of Project Gemini. It supplements the NASA–USAF management agreement that has been in effect since the spring of 1962 and which, among other things, provided space vehicle development support, Air Force assistance in contingency recovery of capsules, use of Air Force tracking facilities and the provision of logistic support. Under this new agreement, the Department of Defense will assist in the development, pilot training, pre-flight checkout, launch operations and flight operations of the Gemini Program so as to meet both DOD and NASA objectives. (Enclosure)[2]

Under the terms of the new agreement, NASA will continue to be responsible for managing the Gemini Project. A Gemini Program Planning Board has been established under the co-chairmanship of Dr. Robert Seamans, Associate Administrator for NASA and the Honorable Brockway McMillan, Assistant Secretary of the Air Force for Research and Development. Other Board Members are Mr. Brainerd Holmes, Deputy Associate Administrator (for Manned Space Flight Centers), NASA, Admiral W.F. Boone, USN (Ret), Deputy Associate Administrator (for Defense Affairs), NASA, Lt. General B.A. Schriever, USAF, Commander, Air Force Systems Command, and Dr. Lawrence Kavanau, Special Assistant (Space) to the Director, Defense Research and Engineering. The Board will report jointly to the Administrator of NASA and to the Secretary of Defense. The Board will insure that the Gemini Program is planned, executed and utilized in the over-all national interest in accordance with policy direction of the Administrator of NASA and the Secretary of Defense, so as to avoid duplication of effort in the field of manned space flight.

FYI. As specified in the agreement, the US will utilize the Gemini for the acquisition of scientific and engineering data which, while of potential interest to our national security, has not been permitted to justify the establishment of a parallel program under military direction. End FYI.

---

[2] Not printed.

The public announcement of the conclusion of this agreement may pose certain questions regarding international relations generally and in particular, the retention of certain foreign support which will be required for Mercury, Gemini, and other space projects.

Department, NASA and Defense unaware extent foreign press coverage given to foregoing agreement and whether unwarranted conclusions reached concerning nature DOD participation in program. Misimpressions that Gemini Program now being converted to military objectives could be particularly undesirable at present time when extension of manned flight tracking station agreements under urgent renegotiation.

Embassies should not take initiative at this time to discuss USAF participation in program, but should be guided by following points in responding any questions which may be raised:

a. Gemini objectives remain unchanged. Project is experimental program to advance technology of manned space flight, including rendezvous and docking, and to study effect weightlessness for periods up to two weeks.

b. As is well known, DOD has in past supported manned flight program through provision of test pilots as astronauts, astronaut recovery operations, boosters, availability of launch sites, and tracking by down-range instrumentation stations. The new agreement provides additional support.

c. Participation of DOD (which is, of course, civilian controlled) will not alter peaceful scientific and engineering character of Gemini program in future any more than in past.

d. NASA continues responsible for management Gemini Project, including planning for and operation of NASA tracking stations.

e. As in the case of the Mercury program, scientific data received from Gemini program will be made available to the world scientific community through customary channels.

f. The total U.S. space effort seeks to exploit to the fullest extent possible the national resources of the U.S. without duplication by individual agencies. The planned cooperation by NASA and DOD on Project Gemini is designed to accomplish this end.

Missions now engaged negotiations extension Mercury tracking station agreements will receive supplemental instructions.

Rusk

379.   Letter From the Deputy Under Secretary of State for Political
        Affairs (Johnson) to the Deputy Assistant Secretary of
        Defense for International Security Affairs (Bundy)[1]

Washington, May 1, 1963.

Dear Bill:

Thank you for your letter of March 28, 1963 requesting policy guidance on actions to be taken in the event of a contingency landing during the forthcoming Mercury 9 flight and future Gemini operations.[2] An instruction to our embassies in countries under the orbital path describing in detail the procedures to be followed in contingency situations is attached for your information. This message, drafted in consultation with DOD and NASA, is also being sent to the appropriate military commanders and to posts in intermediary countries.[3]

The Department has given careful consideration to the implications of a contingency landing and our objective has been to develop guidance which will secure for us maximum opportunity to effect recovery of the astronaut and his space vehicle. It is our view that the more forthcoming we are with governments in giving them advance notification on the details of the flight, the more cooperation we will receive in an emergency situation. I have therefore outlined in some detail the procedures we will follow so you will have a clear idea of how our planning has developed.

In anticipation of contingencies which might arise during the expanded Mercury and Gemini programs, the U.S. delegation to the UN introduced a resolution in early 1962 in the Legal Subcommittee of the Outer Space Committee which, if adopted by the United Nations General Assembly, would establish the broad, general principle providing for assistance to and safe return of the astronaut and the spacecraft to the launching country. While there was no disagreement with the Soviets or any other country on this principle, Soviet instransigence on other points blocked the adoption of this resolution thus far.

---

[1] Source: National Archives and Records Administration, RG 59, Central Files 1960–63, SP 10 US/GEMINI. Secret. Drafter by Trevanion H.D. Nesbitt, and cleared in draft by George S. Newman and George Warren (G/PM), Richard D. Kearney and Allan I. Mendelsohn (L), Edward E. Rice and Captain Robert E. Wood (FE), and Edward M.J. Kretzmann (SCI). Copies were sent to Charles Johnson (NSC), James E. Webb, and Edward Welsh.

[2] In this letter, Bundy transmitted a memorandum from the Joint Chiefs of Staff pointing out the need for such policy guidance. (Ibid.)

[3] Attached but not printed.

Consideration has also been given to the negotiation of separate bilateral agreements outside the UN framework. Practical political reasons argue against this procedure.

It is, however, our intention to inform governments of the spaceflight in advance. The Department feels that prior advice would pave the way for their assistance in effecting immediate recovery. As you know we hold the view that outer space is not an extension of sovereign air space. National sovereignty is not therefore involved and no prior approval to orbit spacecraft over any territory is to be requested.

We plan to follow a similar procedure with the Chinese Communists, where we are instructing Ambassador Cabot to forward a letter to the Chinese Ambassador in Warsaw. In the case of the North Vietnamese, we are exploring the question of whether the International Control Commission in Saigon with access to Hanoi could give the necessary assistance. With respect to Cuba, we shall inform the Swiss in advance.

The Department will be informed by NASA of the possibility of any contingency landing. In anticipation of a contingency landing in non-Communist controlled territory, Search and Rescue or Naval recovery units will proceed to the spacecraft landing area. NASA will inform the Department of such a landing and the mission concerned will be contacted by telephone and Flash precedent telegram to request necessary clearance for Search and Rescue aircraft underway. If known, the coordinates of the landing will be furnished at this time.

Search and Rescue (SAR) aircraft should be instructed to observe ICAO regulations and aircraft commanders should follow all instructions issued by Air Route Traffic Control. In the event they are unable to contact the country's Air Route Traffic Control, they should be instructed to proceed according to their flight plan. In the case of a few countries such as Indonesia it may be necessary to modify this policy and we are currently examining this matter.

In the event of an emergency landing within territorial waters of a friendly power, appropriate Naval commanders are authorized to order naval ships, or to request friendly merchant ships, to enter these waters to effect recovery. Embassy and Naval authorities should notify appropriate authorities of host country concerned if this contingency arises.

It should be noted that there are large gaps in the tracking and communications facilities used to track the spacecraft and that an emergency landing could occur in areas outside the range of tracking facilities which could precipitate a search over a vast area. On certain orbits this could include Communist held territory.

Should a known contingency landing take place in Communist China, North Viet Nam or Cuba those countries will be requested through intermediaries to give assistance to and effect the early return of the astronaut and spacecraft. In the case of Communist China, the Department plans to enlist the aid of the British Mission in Peiping in addition to the Ambassadorial channel in Warsaw. Similarly, the British Mission in Hanoi, in addition to the International Control Commission at Saigon, will be asked to intervene with North Viet Nam. The Government of Switzerland will be asked to intervene in the case of Cuba. Prior arrangements will be made with the intervening countries.

SAR aircraft will not be permitted to enter the airspace of or land in Communist China, North Viet Nam or Cuba. In the case of a landing known to be within the Communist-controlled areas of Laos, the ICC will be requested to use its aircraft to assist in locating and retrieving the astronaut and spacecraft. Because of the openness and world-wide interest in the type of flight, it is our judgment that should the astronaut land in Communist territory and be turned over to the governmental authorities he will be returned to the United States. However, little hope is held for return of the spacecraft.

SAR aircraft and Naval forces should be authorized to penetrate the territorial waters of Communist China, North Viet Nam and Cuba for the purpose of locating, rendering assistance to and retrieving the astronaut and the spacecraft. In the event the SAR forces are opposed or fired upon the rescue forces are authorized to proceed to recover the astronaut and spacecraft, if in the judgment of the on-scene commander the recovery is militarily feasible and can be expeditiously accomplished without unduly endangering the life of the astronaut.

If the astronaut or spacecraft is recovered by foreign forces within their territorial waters, SAR and Naval forces should make every effort to effect recovery by peaceful means. The use of force should not be authorized without prior consultation with the Department of State.

In the event the spacecraft lands on the high seas and the astronaut or spacecraft is recovered by a foreign vessel, U.S. forces should be directed to request the transfer of the astronaut and the spacecraft to American control. In the event the foreign vessel refuses to return the astronaut and spacecraft, the American commander should so report through his chain of command to the DOD which should consult the Department of State before issuing further instructions. He should not be authorized to use force but should be directed to keep the foreign vessel under surveillance pending receipt of instructions.

As you will note from the attachment, the Department of State will maintain an around-the-clock watch during the entire course of the flight and will have available facilities providing direct communications with the NMCC, NASA headquarters and Mercury Control Center at Cape Canaveral. Throughout the flight, Embassies and Mission located in countries orbited will have a senior officer available on an 24-hour alert basis and will maintain a supporting communications watch. Every effort possible is being made by the Department of State to assure that adequate means of communication will be available to all posts involved.

With regard to the suggestion contained in the JCS memorandum of March 15, 1963 to the Secretary of Defense the press as well as the Voice of America, as in the case in previous flights, will provide the world with information on the progress of the flight.

Sincerely,

Alex[4]

---

[4] Printed from a copy that indicates Johnson signed the original.

---

380.   National Security Action Memorandum No. 237[1]

Washington, May 3, 1963.

TO

> The Secretary of State
> The Secretary of Defense
> The Director of Central Intelligence

SUBJECT

> Project Mercury Manned Space Flight (MA-9)

The President is aware of the contingency planning with respect to the possibility of the landing of Mercury 9 or future Gemini flights in the territorial waters of Communist China, North Vietnam, or Cuba, as described in the letter dated May 1, 1963, from the Deputy Under Secretary of State to the Deputy Assistant Secretary of Defense for International Security Affairs.

The President agrees that the Secretary of Defense has adequate authority to authorize the penetration of the territorial waters of the above countries for the purpose of locating, rendering assistance to, and retrieving the personnel and spacecrafts.

McGeorge Bundy

---

[1] Source: National Archives and Records Administration, RG 59, S/S–NSC Files: Lot 72 D 316, NSAM 237. Secret. Copies were sent to the Director of the Bureau of the Budget and the Administrator of NASA.

381.   National Security Policy Planning Paper[1]

Washington, undated.

IMPLICATIONS OF OUTER SPACE IN THE 1970's

Conclusions

A. The United States should continue to place its main emphasis in the field of space exploration on broadening our horizon of knowledge and breadth of competence in this new medium, with particular attention to the political implications of our achievements measured against those of the USSR, and the assurance of our national security. We should continue to encourage international cooperation in space activities, including bilateral arrangements with the USSR, and including the development of space law. We should continue to stand on the general principle of freedom of space. We should actively seek arms control or disarmament arrangements which enhance national security. At the same time, we should continue to pursue vigorously the development and use of military support activities in space, and to develop the capability to meet as necessary possible Soviet exercise of options for military weapons in space.

B. Military activity in outer space will not be sui generis; rather, it will relate to the character of, and balance among, earth-based military systems, and should not be considered in a vacuum. The occasionally voiced axiom that he who controls outer space will control the earth appears illusory, and at the least is unproven.

1. The essential requirement for military capabilities in outer space will be the need for research, development, testing and operational activity sufficient to enable the US to avoid technological surprise in outer space, and to achieve and maintain that margin of superiority in space activity necessary as insurance to offset possible Soviet military uses of space.

2. We should study fully the possibilities of relatively low cost launching and in-flight propulsion systems which could alter cost efficiency criteria for various civil and military uses of space, and provide maneuverability, range and speeds which would have important scientific and potential military uses.

---

[1] Source: Kennedy Library, National Security Files, Subjects Series, Space Activities, General, 6/63, Box 308. Secret. A covering memorandum from Raymond L. Garthoff, Special Assistant for Politico-Military Affairs, to Walt W. Rostow, Counselor and Chairman of the Policy Planning Council, was dated May 31, 1963. Only the conclusions of the paper (pp. iii–xi) are printed.

3. [3 *lines of source text not declassified*]

4. [5 *lines of source text not declassified*]

C. There may be a substantial change of pace of over-all US outer space activity during the 1970's. Such a change of pace may begin shortly after a manned lunar landing, or sooner if events indicate that the Russians either are not in a race or disengage from this "race." The "newness" of space may have passed away to some extent. This change of pace will apply to both the character and scheduling of our over-all program, and in differing degree to various parts of the program: to further lunar exploration, to subsequent interplanetary exploration, to space applications involving satellites in earth orbit (e.g., communications satellites, meteorological satellites, navigational satellites), and to the general balance between scientific investigation and practical application. There may be less emphasis on spectaculars; less urgency in our program.

D. The nature of outer space activities themselves, and of the international context in which they will develop, will necessarily lead to increased international interdependence in this field. International cooperation in space and space-related activities should be sought from the points of view both of the foreign support which the US program will need, and of the foreign policy objectives which can be served. The character of this cooperation will, however, change in the following significant respects:

1. There will be an increasing dependence upon tacit or negotiated international agreement for the conduct of our space program (frequency allocation, rescue and return of astronauts and spacecraft, effective channels for the exchange and analysis of data, etc.). Space law, at least through customary usages of space, will continue to develop.

2. We will have to take account of active space programs conducted by other countries, particularly the Western European countries and Japan. Substantial involvement of these countries in space programs will afford a greater opportunity to encourage multinational or regional programs as opposed to purely national programs.

3. Communications satellites will facilitate international intercourse, and will probably be capable of serving either cooperative or adversary use for direct communication to the homes of populations in other lands. The opportunities, and dangers, of this technique deserve further careful study.

4. Outer space developments will accentuate, rather than mitigate, the differences between the industrial countries on the one hand and developing countries on the other. This increasing divergence will in itself argue that the US may find it desirable to be responsive to the worldwide desire for international participation in some outer space

programs. There may be an increasing reaction in the economically underdeveloped countries against great expenses in space exploration while millions on earth barely subsist.

5. It is possible that by or during the 1970's some disarmament and/or UN peacekeeping arrangements will come to use spaceborne observation. The US should consider ways to facilitate such international uses of observation satellites without affecting essential unilateral capabilities.

E. The United States should consider the feasibility and desirability—technical and political—of proposing or accepting a joint US-USSR effort to land on the moon, in lieu of a competitive race to the first lunar landing.[2] It should be noted that the USSR has not, so far as we know, committed itself to a race for a manned lunar landing, and may in fact have set other space goals. In the impression of most people, however, there is a "race," even if it is unacknowledged by the Soviets.

Preferred Formulations of Conclusions A and B from the Working Group Member of the Department of Defense

1. *Conclusion A.* Expand last sentence as follows:

"A. . . . At the same time, we should continue to pursue vigorously the development and use of military support activities in space, and the development of capabilities to meet possible Soviet exercise of options for military weapons in space or to develop other operational military space systems necessary for our national security."

Reason: To remove the inference that future US military requirements in space will be determined solely by Soviet space applications. The prime determinant of US military space requirements will be our national security needs rather than merely reactions to Soviet military space uses.

---

[2] It does not appear likely that such a joint effort could be agreed upon or arranged, nor sure that it would be desirable. In order to impress the world favorably, and to have greatest chance of acceptance, such an offer by the US could only be made after we had demonstrated at least the impression of equality with the USSR in the present "moon race," which would probably only be at a time when in fact our chances for winning the race were quite good. At such a juncture, probability of victory in the race would be an incentive to go on and win. But it is necessary to consider whether giving up the political assets of winning the race would be overweighed by the less certain but possibly greater long-run political gains of momentum for cooperation and for influencing the basic US-Soviet relationship. The same consideration would, of course, apply to the case where the USSR judged it would not win the race, and then itself took the initiative in offering to merge efforts—but it would be better if we made the offer first. If we made such an offer and it were rejected, and we then won the race, we would gain doubly. There would, however, be formidable and very possibly prohibitive technical problems to effecting such collaboration, and this consideration requires careful study. The Committee is sharply divided on this question, which goes beyond (though in terms of time "before") the scope of this study, but its resolution could affect significantly national security aspects of space in the 1970's.—R.G. [Footnote in the source text.]

2. *Conclusion B.* Replace as follows:

"B. The essential requirements for military capabilities in outer space are research, development, testing and operational activity sufficient to enable the United States to avoid technological surprise, to offset possible Soviet military uses of space, and to ensure superiority both in space technology and in operational applications as specific military requirements are identified and established. [*2-1/2 lines of source text not declassified*] We should also continue to seek relatively low cost launching and in-flight propulsion systems which could alter cost efficiency criteria and which would provide the maneuverability, range [*2 lines of source text not declassified*].

Reason: Deletion of the two introductory sentences of the majority formulation is desired to remove the essentially negative connotation these sentences place on the Conclusion regarding military space requirements. Moreover, the observation that military activities in space are related to the character and balance among earth-based systems is unchallenged and therefore both unnecessary and misleading, in that it suggests the existence of a strong body of official opinion which holds the contrary view. Reference to the so-called "axiom" regarding the relationship between control of space and earth is similarly inappropriate as it also erroneously suggests the existence of a body of official opinion in need of negation. Other modifications set forth in the DOD preferred formulation are intended to (1) remove the inference that future military space requirements will be determined solely by Soviet military uses of space, (2) remove reference to military space developments as purely a form of "insurance" and (3) delete the inclusion of [*less than 1 line of source text not declassified*] from the Conclusion regarding military space requirements. In the latter connection, although use of space [*4 lines of source text not declassified*].

Comments of the Working Group Member from the Joint Staff

I am unable to concur in the report as presently written for the following basic reasons:

a. The military aspects of space in the 1970's continue to be disposed of as of little significance other than as a need for "insurance" to offset possible Soviet military uses of space. In my view this does not take sufficient account of technological possibilities of the 1970's.

b. Conclusion A suggests that, in the 1970's, the United States "should continue to place its main emphasis . . . on broadening man's horizon of knowledge and breadth of competence . . . with particular attention to the political implications . . . and the assurance of our national security." This formulation does not, in my view, lend sufficient weight to the fact that, by that time, additional emphasis should have been devoted to those measures necessary to enhance and preserve our national security.

c. As previously noted, a major section of the paper devoted to the lunar landing is predicated on the assumption that the Soviet Union is publicly committed to a moon race at the present time, whether it wishes to be or not. Although it certainly is wise in a paper which considers the implications of outer space in the 1970's to assume that a moon race between the United States and the Soviet Union is in progress, it is considered both inappropriate and dangerous not also to explore fully other courses of action on the assumption that there is *no* moon race in progress. For one thing, our national strategy probably would be quite different if the United States possessed a unilateral capability for manned exploration and use of the lunar surfaces. A more disturbing possibility is that the USSR may have chosen an alternate national space objective which could be achieved sooner and, at the same time, have more significance from a national security standpoint. Failure fully to explore the possibility of such a course of action could result in major loss of US prestige by default in the USSR version of a space race as well as significant imbalance in the relative military support capabilities in space. In the Report, the "race" theme is the only one afforded substantial consideration.

d. In the discussion and conclusion concerning a possible joint US-USSR lunar effort, I believe insufficient treatment is afforded to the "cons"—both technically and politically.

[Here follows the 72-page text of the paper.]

---

382. Action Memorandum From the Director of the Office of International Scientific Affairs (Rollefson) to Secretary of State Rusk[1]

Washington, July 11, 1963.

SUBJECT

Meeting of the National Aeronautics and Space Council to be held at 2:30 p.m. July 17 in Room 274 of the Executive Office Building

Vice President Johnson, the Chairman of the National Aeronautics and Space Council, is convening a meeting of the Space Council, the purpose of which is to explore the status and progress of coordination in space activities. More specifically, coordination between NASA and DOD in project Gemini and in the establishment of space stations will be discussed.

---

[1] Source: National Archives and Records Administration, RG 59, Central Files 1960–63, SP 10 US. Limited Official Use.

On January 22 the DOD and NASA announced that agreement had been reached between the two agencies under which the DOD would participate in the Gemini program. Gemini, a two man follow-up of the single-man Mercury manned space flight program is an experimental program to advance the technology of manned space flight including rendezvous and docking and to study the effect of weightlessness in a period of up to two weeks. The Gemini program, in part, will prepare for the Apollo lunar missions which will land US astronauts on the moon.

The NASA–DOD agreement is intended to assure the most effective utilization of Project Gemini and to provide for Air Force participation in what was originally conceived by NASA to be a purely civilian project.

Under the terms of the agreement NASA will continue to be responsible for the management of the Gemini project but coordination will be effected through a Program Planning Board composed of representatives from NASA and the DOD.

While it is understood that Secretary McNamara and Mr. Webb are in general agreement with regard to the degree of Air Force and NASA participation in the project, it is understood that lower echelons in NASA and in the Air Force are still dissatisfied with the extent of each other's detailed participation. The purpose of the meeting is to attempt to clarify these issues.

The Department, at the request of NASA, recently negotiated the extension of the Mercury tracking agreements for use in the Gemini program with the U.K., Spain, Nigeria and Mexico. Negotiations with respect to the extension of the Mercury agreement with Zanzibar are continuing. In obtaining renewal of the agreements with Mexico, Spain and Nigeria the Department, with the concurrence of NASA and DOD, agreed that acceptance of the agreement by the other governments was based on the understanding that the tracking stations would be used only in experiments of a strictly scientific and technical character without military objectives. The U.S. would notify those countries in advance of Gemini flights which would have objectives other than those stated above if the stations were to be used. It is highly doubtful that these countries would permit the use of the tracking stations for Gemini flights if the military role in the flight were significant.

Deputy Under Secretary U. Alexis Johnson is familiar with the DOD–NASA Gemini agreement and the problems it could raise with respect to U.S. tracking stations operated abroad. Under the circumstances it would appear appropriate that Mr. Johnson represent you at the meeting of the Space Council on July 17.[2]

---

[2] A handwritten note below the last paragraph reads: "Mr. Johnson concurs." Rusk approved the recommendation on July 13.

383.   **Memorandum From Maxwell W. Hunter II of the National Aeronautics and Space Council to Robert F. Packard of the Office of International Scientific Affairs[1]**

Washington, July 18, 1963.

SUBJECT

Thoughts on the Space Alien Race Question

During recent discussions the question has occasionally, though rarely, arisen that perhaps we should consider the policy question of what to do if an alien intelligence is discovered in space. Some discussion of this occurred, as you will recall, during deliberations on BNSP Task I. This memo contains some miscellaneous thoughts on the question.

The consensus of scientific view says, with quite good reasons, that the possibility of running across an alien intelligent race in our solar system is negligible. This is due primarily to the presumed unsuitability of conditions upon other planets to support life as we know it. The flying saucer advocates claim, of course, that the scientific viewpoint is nonsense, and that there is overwhelming evidence of such beings. In my own mind, I find it difficult to side with the flying saucer advocates, but the almost total impossibility envisioned by most scientists also is disturbing. Therefore, I present the problem in current perspective, as I see it.

Up until a few decades ago it seemed very improbable that intelligent life existed anywhere outside of the solar system. The chief reasons for this were a combination of scientific theory, scientific knowledge, and religious belief. The most widely accepted scientific theory as to the formation of the solar planetary system held that it was a result of the near collision of two stars. Since such a precise near-miss of two stars would be an extremely rare event, it followed that there would be very few other planetary systems in the universe and, indeed, perhaps this was the only one. Religious belief said, furthermore, that life was a gift bestowed by God. This was a relatively undisputed point since no scientific data existed to bridge the gap between non-living and living materials.

The situation today is vastly changed in these respects. The most widely held theory of stellar formation would predict the formation of planetary systems to be a natural consequence of stellar evolution. On this basis, most stars would possess planetary systems, and the number

---

[1] Source: National Archives and Records Administration, RG 59, Central Files 1960–63, SP 16. Official Use Only.

of habitable planets in our galaxy would be tremendous. Our biggest telescopes cannot resolve planets at the distances even of the nearest stars, so no direct confirmation is yet available. In my own mind, however, the wide prevalence of multiple stars is an overwhelming hint in support of this theory. In addition, the biological sciences have almost completely traced a series of natural occurrences which lead from inanimate molecules to elementary living viruses. Thus, we have the current scientific theory and data not only that there are a huge number of planets in the galaxy, but that life is quite likely to arise spontaneously on a large number of these. This, of course, does not necessarily imply intelligent life. Modern theology is not necessarily incompatible with this. The description in Genesis of the Creation certainly is a better picture of the current theory than of a stellar collision, and since God only spent seven days on this system, He has clearly had lots of time to create many more systems.

Even granting a probable existence of much life in the galaxy, there is still the question of whether another intelligent race exists in our solar system. There are, of course, two methods of its establishment in our system. One of these is that it originated on some other planet, for instance, Mars. Some of the spectacular markings of Mars have been interpreted as indicating intelligence. In particular, the famous "Canali" are rather narrow, and always run from one prominent marking to another, frequently with round splotches at intersections. As far as I know, no one has discovered a "Canali" which goes nowhere. This has quite understandably stimulated much conversation. In fact, a number of decades ago, when scientists thought that any life on other stellar systems was very remote, they seemed to feel that intelligent life probably existed on our other planets. Some of the discussions about life on Mars at the turn of the century seem to indicate a strong urge to want to find intelligent life elsewhere. Today, the situation is completely reversed, and although intelligent life is considered quite probable among the stars, it is held to be quite unlikely within the solar system. We seem more eager to listen with Ozma than to look closely at Canali.

One school of flying saucer advocates claims that the Martians have been mining our moon for natural resources for some time. At first thought, one would think they would rather mine earth. It is interesting to speculate, however, upon space flight from the point of view of a Martian. The escape speed of Mars is only 16,500 fps, and, of course, braking speed on our moon is less than 10,000 fps. Thus, Martians looking at earth would tend to view it the same way Terrestrials look at Jupiter. Our moon might not be less work to get to, since atmospheric braking to earth is possible, but would be very much easier to return from, while the energy requirements to go to and return from the surface of the earth might well be so high as to discourage interest, at least initially. Interestingly enough, even a normal high energy chemical rocket could make a trip from Mars to our moon at favorable times while carrying almost 10% of its gross weight in payload. Space flight starting from Mars, then, is a much easier prospect than starting from Terra. If a suitable refueling base had been painfully established on our moon, the operation could be done quite commendably with merely chemical energy. (The aforementioned high energy chemical rocket could carry at favorable times almost 50% payload back to Mars.) Of course, many flying saucer advocates claim that the discovery of both Martian moons within a week in the latter part of the Nineteenth Century indicates that they are large artificial space stations, otherwise they would have been found earlier. If we were to discover Martians on the moon, it would result in surprisingly little readjustment of our scientific thinking. The biggest question would be why they were there rather than among the Asteroids.

In fact, if we were not as scientifically sure of ourselves as we are, three recent events would be hailed as broad hints of intelligent life on the moon. (1) The discovery of hot gasses eminating from the crater Alphonsus when the moon was supposedly dead. This would be considered evidence of civilization and, since Alphonsus is close to the visible edge, interpreted to mean that the other side of the moon was teeming with population which had begun to spill around to this side. (2) The infra-red scans which show hot spots. These would be interpreted as indications of cities or at least mining camps. (3) The fact that no lunar or planetary probe of significance has been successful, in spite of major efforts on the part of two very successful earth orbitfaring nations. It would be supposed that someone was denying us deep space. (The other-side-of-the-moon pictures from Lunik III show no details of consequence, and the same can be said of the data from Mariner II compared to what we had already known about Venus from earth-based measurements.) Should the Martians have colonized the moon without discovering nuclear energy, then they represent no real problem, and our current national policy would be made to order for the situation. If all of this were true, of course, I would expect the Martians to be scared to death of what they have seen recently on this planet, and would expect that the highest priority development program in the solar system is being conducted by the Atomic Energy Commission of Mars.

Even if we are secure in our belief that intelligent life never would develop on Mars or some other solar planet, there is still the question of visitors to the solar system from other stellar systems. This is normally written off as an extremely low probability, due to the tremendous distances between stars, and the Einstein limitation on travel faster than the speed of light. Therefore, even if there are a large number of intel-

ligent life forms in the galaxy, and even if they are continuously searching for other races, the frequency of investigation of any stellar system
would be only once in many thousands of years and contact would
rarely, if ever, be achieved. It might never be achieved, since presumably intelligent races die out. (What happened to the planet whose
pieces now are spread around the Asteroid Belt? Or, for that matter,
why is Uranus lying on its side?) I am not sure that this travel restriction is quite as infallible as it sounds. I believe that it is possible with
what we now know about nuclear energy to envision ships driven at
half to three-quarters of the speed of light. This, since the galaxy is
100,000 light-years across, still does not make a search of the entire
galaxy feasible within the life span of the average man. But suppose
some race under pressure of population explosion were expanding as
fast as technically feasible from star to star throughout the galaxy. If
their ships averaged half the speed of light, and if, on the average, they
stopped every 10 light-years for a twenty-year stay at a stellar system to
deposit colonists, refuel, and build extra ships, they would only take
two hundred thousand years, starting at the center of the galaxy, to
spread throughout the whole system. Since the earliest known remains
of man have recently been dated at approximately one million seven-
hundred thousand years, a sustained drive for merely two hundred
thousand years may not be unreasonable. Of course, if we were to run
across representatives of this kind of interstellar race, they would not be
nearly as tame as the previously hypothesized chemical Martians, and
our policy would need to be revised accordingly. Fortunately, travel
time restrictions would inhibit their ability to bring all forces to bear, in
case we should develop differences of viewpoint.

The third possibility, scientifically abhorrent, is that the Einstein
theory may only be an approximation, and an alien race which actually
travels faster than light exists. If we were to meet such a race, our policy had better be to negotiate fast, because the implications of their far
better understanding and control of the fundamental forces of nature
would be obvious. If all the scientific speculation were to turn out
wrong and we were to stumble across an alien race, we would want to
know as quickly as possible which of the three types I have indicated it
was, as our diplomatic policy would damned well be influenced by the
results.

Conclusions

Although all plausible scientific thinking suggests that we will not
find any other intelligence race, the probability that we will is finite, and
perhaps should not be completely ignored. Were we to find one, the
question of whether it was a race with primitive chemical space flight,
space flight equivalent to our best understanding of nuclear energy, or

space flight based on physics beyond Einstein should be ascertained as rapidly as possible, since our policies would be affected in the most drastically possible way. In any event, a policy of the immediate burying of all Terrestrial hatchets would likely be in order. Even if we only found tame chemical Martians, or merely the debris from some intragalactic survey mission, it would be a good idea to proceed on the assumption that the human race would finally have found a bigger problem than the ones it has created for itself. There likely is nothing to be done at the moment to prepare for these possibilities (the only body of writing on the subject available in an emergency is science fiction), because no one of consequence is going to take this rubbish seriously unless it happens. At that point, our policy will be determined in the traditional manner of grand panic.

Maxwell W. Hunter, II

---

384. **Letter From the Director of the Bureau of the Budget (Gordon) to the Administrator of the National Aeronautics and Space Administration (Webb)[1]**

Washington, July 19, 1963.

Dear Mr. Webb:

As you know, the chronic balance of payments deficit of the United States has become a source of increasing concern to the President. The urgency which he attaches to the program has been manifested in his public statements, in meetings with business and labor leaders, and in his instructions to officials of the executive branch to take positive steps to reduce wherever possible the level of Government expenditures abroad. As part of this effort, the Bureau of the Budget has recently conducted a special review of all offices and missions overseas based on reports submitted by agencies under Bulletin 63–13. We believe that we have identified a number of actions which, if taken, might have a favorable impact on our balance of payments. Although these various agency actions may not, in all cases, appear to offer dramatic balance of payments savings individually, in the aggregate they could result in a

---

[1] Source: National Archives and Records Administration, RG 59, Management Staff Files: Lot 69 D 434, Interagency Liaison Files, 1962–1968, NASA. No classification marking.

significant reduction in our overseas expenditures. For this reason, I commend the issues noted below to your personal attention.

I realize that, with one or two exceptions, all NASA offices and missions abroad are comprised of tracking and data acquisition stations which have been established to support NASA space flight missions, and that very limited flexibility exists within which action can be taken to reduce these activities without affecting the flight programs. I also realize that any substantial changes may have an impact on existing international agreements or negotiations now in progress. Nevertheless, in view of the gravity of our balance of payments problem, serious consideration should be given at this time to actions affecting the balance of payments despite the circumstances noted above.

Therefore, it is requested that you have your staff conduct a detailed study to identify the effects on NASA programs, total FY 1964 costs, and on the balance of payments, of the actions listed below, plus any others which you may suggest as promising some alleviation of the balance of payments problem. Such studies should be completed by September 15, 1963. These studies, together with parallel information on the international relations aspects of the suggested actions, would provide us with better information on which to base judgment than that developed to date. The actions which we suggest, based on the preliminary information currently available, are as follows:

1. Reduce the tracking stations at Kano, Nigeria, and Zanzibar in Africa to standby status in view of the termination of the Mercury series of flights and the stated NASA plan to place primary reliance on other stations for the Gemini flights.

2. Defer the planned personnel increase at the Johannesburg, South Africa, Minitrack station until FY 1965 or later, retaining the station at its present complement of about 59 employees.

3. Abandon the present plan for establishing a NASA office in Paris.

4. Close the Mercury tracking station in Muchea, Australia, in view of the termination of the Mercury program and the construction of a new primary Gemini station at Carnarvon.

5. Close the Mercury station at Quaymas, Mexico, in favor of conducting the Gemini tracking from some point within the borders of the United States, such as Point Arguello, California, White Sands, New Mexico, or Corpus Christi, Texas.

6. Close the Minitrack station at Autofagusta, Chile, in favor of tracking from other stations in the Minitrack net.

Our preliminary estimates are that these suggestions, if implemented soon, could reduce our balance of payments deficit by $1.2 million in FY 1964 and almost twice that amount annually in future years. I understand that some of these actions are already under consideration within NASA for program reasons, but that others would involve totally new studies. However, my hope is that these suggestions, plus whatever additional suggestions you may have, can be acted upon by October 1, 1963.

Sincerely,

Kermit Gordon[2]

---

[2] Printed from a copy that indicates Gordon signed the original.

---

385.   Memorandum From the Administrator of the National Aeronautics and Space Administration (Webb) to the Deputy Under Secretary of State for Political Affairs (Johnson) and the President's Special Assistant for National Security Affairs (Bundy)[1]

Washington, November 15, 1963.

As you know, the last Project Mercury flight is behind us, and we may have upwards of a year before our next manned flight which will occur in the Gemini program. In the interval, we will be conducting unmanned Gemini flights and frequent scientific and vehicle development flights. At the same time, we are conscious that there is overseas a great reservoir of good will toward our astronauts. Putting these two considerations together, there may be advantages in the near future to sending a small team of NASA astronauts, scientists, and technicians abroad to convey directly and by personal appearances to other nations the character and results of the U.S. manned flight program and to afford our friends overseas an opportunity for the expression of their good will.

The format which suggests itself to us for such a team effort is quite different from the parade and publicity type tours of the Soviet cosmonauts and would be designed to emphasize the seriousness, openness, and carefully balanced character of U.S. space activities. We have in mind the following approach: We would establish some reasonable but limited objective for a single visit abroad, such as interest in inspecting the San Marco platform now being prepared by Italy for launching of an equatorial satellite. We would then contact appropriate European agencies with which we regularly deal to apprise them of the possibility of

---

[1] Source: National Archives and Records Administration, RG 59, Central Files 1960–63, SP 10 US/MERCURY. Confidential. A copy was sent to USIA Director Edward R. Murrow.

such a visit and of the availability of the visiting team for one or more de-briefings on the manned flight program and its place in our total space effort. These first contacts would seek to arrange for proper forums under appropriate sponsorship in each area where a stopover might be made (e.g., Madrid, Rome, Paris). The central element of each stopover would be a responsible professional report, followed by extensive questions and answers. Undoubtedly, there would be occasion for public appearances of a more visible character by the astronauts in conjunction with each stopover, and we would endeavor to accommodate a reasonable number.

The details can be arranged following a judgment that an initial trip is indeed desirable, but it may help to provide a few illustrations to facilitate consideration of the matter. The team would involve one or two astronauts and a supporting group of perhaps half-a-dozen persons, including an engineer, aeromedic and scientist, as well as support personnel. (Colonel Glenn would be available and is anxious to contribute to an effort of this kind.) Three to five days could be devoted to each country, with travel by commercial or special aircraft, with a total cost of $15–25,000 per country. For reasons which are indicated below, the timing would be as soon after the first of the coming year as feasible.

In the interests of a balanced final judgment, I would point out that we do not have new material in the area of manned space flight beyond what has already been published or reported in this country and that, as here, there are elements of the scientific community abroad with only limited interest and sympathy for manned space flight. And we always run the risk of a Soviet space spectacular occurring between the planning and execution of a trip such as this. However, bringing the Mercury story graphically into foreign countries, with questions and answers in depth, may be counted upon to attract wide interest, to discharge our obligations to share data, and to help educate the foreign scientific community in the values of manned space flight. A short trip would reduce the hazard of coincidence with a major Soviet spectacular.

I would appreciate your comments on the prospect suggested here. If positive, we will proceed to provide a detailed prospectus and develop, discreetly, the necessary interest and preparations abroad. In this connection, the assistance of the Science Attachés abroad would be most helpful.

James E. Webb

U.S.-Soviet Space Cooperation

386. **Memorandum From the President's Special Assistant for Science and Technology (Wiesner) to President Kennedy[1]**

Washington, February 20, 1961.

Following up on our conversation of the other evening, I would like to elaborate on the questions posed by the Russian Venus shot and our relative positions in the general fields of space exploration and science. The most significant factor, as we have said many times, is that the Soviets have developed a rocket as part of their ballistic missile program with considerably more thrust or lifting power than anything we have available. We know that the Soviet booster can put payloads of the order of several tons (the most recent one was announced to be seven tons) in a low orbit, while the best we can do at the present time, using our latest combination rocket Atlas-Agena, is approximately 5,000 pounds. This combination was used to launch the recent Samos shot. These figures indicate that the Soviets have approximately a three-to-one advantage in weight-lifting capability at this time. This corresponds roughly to the difference we believe to exist in the payload capability of the USSR vs. U.S. ballistic missiles.

We do not fully understand why the Soviets chose to make so large a ballistic missile, because it is undoubtedly a nuisance to operate. We suspect that the design was well under way before the feasibility of thermonuclear bombs was proven and that it was probably designed to carry ordinary nuclear weapons which are much heavier. Also, the Soviet Union has been developing ballistic missiles for a considerably longer period of time than has the U.S., so they have had the advantage of an orderly evolutionary program. They began with a relatively short-range missile (200 to 300-mile range), went to a 600-mile missile, then a 900-mile missile, and on up to the IRBM stage, and finally to the present long-range missile. By doing this they were in position to use many of the components developed in one stage for successive stages, possibly making only minor changes and improvements. We, on the other hand, because of our late entry in the missile field, have found it necessary to develop complete missile systems with entirely new components. This has resulted in more duplications in our experimental

---

[1] Source: Kennedy Library, National Security Files, Departments and Agencies Series, Space Activities, General, 1/61–3/61, Box 307. Confidential.

program than has been the case in the Soviet program. It is my personal opinion, as a matter of fact, that some of this duplication and accompanying difficulty could have been avoided had our program been somewhat better integrated.

We do not expect to have boosters comparable to the present Soviet booster for approximately three years, though I believe we should be able to speed this up with hard work, so that we must expect continued embarrassments of the present type for some time, because in any space exploit requiring large payload capability the Soviet Union is ahead. On the other hand, as we have frequently said, the U.S. has done by all odds the most impressive job of exploiting its payload capability for scientific purposes. The Soviets have done surprisingly little with the opportunities they have had. The most impressive things that they have done were photographing the back side of the moon and transmitting the photographs back to earth (and this was a superb technical performance) and the return of the dogs from orbit. The U.S. has to its credit the discovery and definition of the Van Allen belts; the first precise geodetic use of an artificial earth satellite to obtain refined information on the size and shape of the earth; the first achievement of both active and passive communications satellites; discovery of a large electrical current system about the earth; successful use of weather satellites with cloud cover pictures and earth heat balance measurements; the first measurements of interplanetary magnetic fields; radio communications at inter-planetary distances; and the first simultaneous observation of solar disturbances and associated magnetic storms from interplanetary space and on earth. Unfortunately, it is much more difficult to dramatize these things than it is the massive performances by the Soviet Union.

One of the things we must realize is that in dramatizing the space race we are playing into the Soviet's strongest suit. They are using this accomplishment at home and around the world to prove the superiority of Soviet science and technology and to divert attention from many of their more mundane difficulties. The fact of the matter is that Western science, and particularly American science, is still vastly superior in most fields to Soviet science and they know this as well as we do. Furthermore, in almost any other arena in which we would elect to compete, food, housing, recreation, medical research, basic technological competence, general consumer goods production, etc., they would look very bad. We should attempt to point this out rather than assist them by an official and press reaction which supports their propaganda.

J.B. Wiesner[2]

---

[2] Printed from a copy that bears this typed signature.

387.   Paper Prepared in the Department of State[1]

Washington, April 13, 1961.

DRAFT PROPOSALS FOR US-USSR SPACE COOPERATION

General Objectives

The general objectives of scientific cooperation between the United States and the Soviet Union are to demonstrate the possibility of cooperative enterprise between the U.S. and the USSR in fields of wide interest, to achieve the practical advantages of sharing the work and cost on major projects, and to establish early cooperation in fields (e.g. meteorological activities that might eventually lead to weather control or manned exploration of the moon) in which unchecked competition may ultimately be dangerous as well as wasteful.

Guidelines

The proposals herein seek to (a) maximize acceptability by the USSR, and (b) minimize the potential for misunderstanding and obstruction which must be recognized to exist in any joint program with the Soviet Union. The proposals therefore have, in general, the following character:

(1) Valid scientific objectives
(2) Comparable contributions by the U.S. and USSR.
(3) Technical and economic feasibility for the U.S.
(4) Minimal interference with on-going U.S. programs.
(5) Minimal grounds for Soviet suspicions of U.S. motives (access, surveillance, etc.)
(6) Opportunities for third-nation participation at appropriate time.

The proposals fall into three categories:

(a) The employment of existing or easily attainable ground facilities for exchange of information and services in support of orbiting experiments.

---

[1] Source: National Aeronautics and Space Administration, Office of International Affairs. Confidential. The paper is marked "Redraft." An April 14 covering memorandum from Philip J. Farley, Special Assistant to the Secretary of State for Atomic Energy and Outer Space, transmitted the paper to Eugene B. Skolnikoff, Technical Assistant in the Office of the President's Special Assistant for Science and Technology, and Marvin W. Robinson of NASA's Office of International Programs. Robinson in turn sent it to Deputy Administrator Dryden on the same date. The paper is also printed in John M. Logsdon, Dwayne A. Day, and Roger D. Launius (eds.), *Exploring the Unknown: Selected Documents in the History of the U.S. Civil Space Program*, Volume II: *External Relationships* (Washington, 1996), pp. 143–147.

(b) The coordination of independently-launched satellite experiments so as to achieve simultaneous but complementary coverage of agreed phenomena.

(c) Coordination of or cooperation in ambitious projects for the manned exploration of the moon and the unmanned exploration of the planets.

The three categories of proposals are advanced in order to offer the Soviet Union a wide range of choice and avoid the appearance of "pushing" a pre-selected objective. While the costs are estimated to range from relatively insignificant levels in Category (a) to $15–20 million in Category (b) and, very roughly, $10 to $30 billion in Category (c), it may be assumed that the Soviet Union as well as ourselves is likely to pursue the more costly programs in any event.

Such cooperation as is discussed here should be proposed and carried out on the basis of an expanding U.S. program of space science and exploration, and without prejudice to continuing joint enterprise with and assistance to the free world.

Procedure

Overtures should be made at a high Governmental level to be decided at the time, inviting the USSR to engage in cooperative enterprises such as the proposals made below. Soviet counter-suggestions of areas of cooperation would also be invited. The initial discussions would seek a go-ahead for exploratory technical talks preliminary to agreement in principle. Privacy in all such discussions would appear to enhance the chances of success. Technical advice should be available at all times. Our major allies would be informed in advance of the overtures.

Proposals

Category (a)

These proposals for the most part call for the use of ground facilities for mutual services:

(i) The U.S. and the USSR might agree to provide ground-based support on a reciprocal basis for space experiments, e.g.,

—When either nation launches a satellite or probe carrying a magnetometer experiment, the other would collect rapid-run magnetograms at its ground observatories. (A Soviet scientist has recently promised to do this in connection with the U.S. P-14 probe, following a private request.)

—When either nation launches a meteorological satellite, the other would carry out routine and special (airborne, balloon-borne, all-sky camera) weather observations synchronized with the passes of the satellite, analyze the data from both sources, and participate in scientific exchanges of the results.

—Similar arrangements would be useful in connection with ionospheric, auroral, and other geophysical researches.

(ii) The U.S. and the USSR could agree to record telemetry from each other's satellites, exchanging the resulting tapes as requested. Each would furnish the necessary orbital information and telemetry calibrations to the other. This would be of particular value in sun-related experiments and could extend to the exchange of command signals to permit the best-situated nation to energize a given experiment under certain conditions of solar activity.

(iii) In the communications field, the USSR may wish to employ a ground facility for long-distance experimental transmission of voice or TV signals by means of communications satellites to be launched by NASA after mid-1962 (Projects Relay/Rebound). Such facilities are being prepared also by the U.K. and France. Transmissions may be effected between the latter and the USSR (by means of a U.S. satellite) as usefully as between the U.S. and the USSR. (If *supplementary* equipment peculiar to such experimental testing in this case is required by the USSR, NASA could provide it at costs ranging up to $2 million.)

(iv) Another type of cooperation can be envisaged in the field of *space medicine. Summer institutes* in various fields of space science also might be proposed.

The exchanges proposed in (a) have been sought, almost with complete unsuccess, at government agency and scientific society levels since the beginning of the IGY. They are included because of their inherent desirability and because a somewhat greater chance of acceptance may follow if initiated at higher levels. (The program in Categories (b) and (c) have not yet been proposed to the Soviet Union.)

The proposals made in Category (a) are for *coordinated* rather than *interdependent* efforts and thus would avoid difficulties which may be associated with the latter type of cooperation with the USSR. Activities in this category are within the capability of many nations, and participation by interested countries should be provided for.

Category (b)

(i) Weather satellites promise broad near-future benefits as a meteorological tool. Equal participation by the U.S. and the USSR in coordinated launching of experimental satellites capable of providing typhoon warnings, etc., would have great impact.

One specific proposal[2] is that the U.S. and the USSR each place in polar orbit a meteorological satellite to record cloud-cover and radiation-balance data, such that

---

[2] Broader cooperation in meteorology is possible and desirable. A specific proposal for a major world-wide cooperative meteorological program, in which satellites would be a part, is being developed separately. [Footnote in the source text.]

—The two satellites have reasonably overlapping lifetimes (at least three months).
—The satellites orbit in planes at right angles to each other, providing at least six-hour coverage of the earth.
—The data characteristics permit reception and analysis interchangeably, if possible.
—Each country may receive telemetry from the other's satellite through continuous readout if power sources permit or by command if otherwise.
—Camera resolutions are appropriate only for the objective—photographs of cloud cover.
—The results are to be made available to the scientific community (World Data Centers and WMO).

(ii) Coordinated programs including experimental or research satellite launchings in other fields than meteorology (e.g., communications) could also be of value. In the field of geophysics, for example, there are possibilities for the useful coordination of the orbits of contemporaneous satellites so as to obtain measurements under contrasting or complementary conditions.

(iii) Simultaneous and coordinated rocket launchings from a number of stations covering a wide range of latitudes and longitudes would for the first time provide a global picture of the properties of the atmosphere at a given instant of time, if conducted on a scale greater than now done during International Rocket Weeks.

The first proposal in Category (b) above falls in the meteorological field, in which the U.S. appears to lead. While the USSR has not yet done anything in this field, it has on one occasion indicated at the highest scientific level that space meteorology is favorably viewed as an area for cooperation. A generous timescale (or offer to provide instrumentation) might moderate the negative factor.

The proposals made in Category (b) are, like those in Category (a), for *coordinated* rather than *interdependent* efforts and thus would avoid difficulties which may be associated with the latter type of cooperation with the USSR.

Category (c)

These proposals relate to the exploration of celestial bodies.

(i) Mars or Venus programs.

Planetary investigations are immensely difficult undertakings requiring protracted programs of great complexity and variety, progressing through fly-bys, orbiters, hard and soft landings, and surface prospecting. The U.S. and the USSR could coordinate their independent programs so as to provide for a useful sequencing and, perhaps, sharing of experimental missions, with scientific benefits and economics. Full data exchange, guaranteed by provision of telemetry calibrations, should be provided. If cooperation is interrupted, no loss is sustained and the programs may proceed independently.

The U.S. and USSR could, alternatively, enter into a joint program that would mean more intimate involvement; such a program would include cooperative development of equipment and sharing of experimental missions, and would point toward eventual joint launching of probes.

(ii) Manned Exploration of Moon.

The exploration of the surface of the moon is the first space endeavor where we think that the presence of man will add greatly to what could reasonably be done with instrumented packages.

As a first step in non-limited cooperative effort, the U.S. and the USSR would each undertake to place a small party (about 3) of men on the moon for scientific purposes and return them to earth.

As in planetary programs, a more extensive cooperative program could also be envisaged in which the U.S. and USSR enter into a joint manned lunar program, including cooperative development, planning, and international exploration.

The proposals made in Category (c), in the lunar and planetary fields, suggest programs for which the USSR has demonstrably greater existing capability. Inclusion of both categories in proposals to the USSR may therefore be effective.

No significant Mars probe capability now exists in the U.S. By 1964, Centaur should permit significant fly-bys only, while Saturn C-1 would put about 300 pound payloads in orbit after 1964.

The Mars/Venus program is a long-range one whose cost varies widely with numbers of launchings, nature of payloads, and extent of back-up. A balanced program (unmanned), including some 15 Venus shots and 8 Mars shots in the next decade, may cost in the order of $1 billion.

Neither country now possesses a capability for a manned lunar project. It will require boosters of the order of Saturn C-2 using orbital rendezvous and refueling techniques (still to be attempted and perfected) for the upper stages. At least six Saturn C-2's would be required for a single mission, plus appropriate back-up. The time-scale is probably a decade, during which some 70–80 Saturns would be required for developmental purposes, and the cost is roughly of the order of $10 to $30 billion. During the decade, alternative vehicle systems may conceivably become available, obviating the difficult rendezvous requirement.

In the suggestions for cooperation given above, it can be seen that the degree of involvement between the U.S. and the USSR can in principle be varied from coordination of national programs to full coordination on joint endeavors;

It is possible to *restrict* proposals which may be made to the Soviet Union to the level of coordination of essentially independent programs. Benefits would derive from joint planning and organization of such coordinated efforts. This might have the advantages of greater acceptability in the U.S. and in the Soviet Union (where suspicions of U.S. motivations would be present in any case). It may also be more realistic in terms of the technical exchanges and access which may be feasible.

On the other hand, it would be possible to indicate *a range* of possible relationships to the Soviet Union, extending to interdependent programs and leaving it to them to select the starting level.

As we contemplate programs that involve greater degree of cooperation, positive factors would be the impact on U.S./USSR relations growing out of intimate cooperation on large and meaningful projects, and the advantages accruing to both countries in carrying out space programs utilizing the best of what each has to offer without unnecessary time pressures. We must also anticipate certain increased difficulties. These would include the risk that the whole program would be lost if one or the other participant withdrew because of political or other reasons; the fact that we would have to be prepared to admit Russians to installations such as Cape Canaveral and to show them details of our booster and payload systems (of course, the Russians would have to do the same if they agreed to intimate cooperation), and the possibility that Congressional, scientific and public support might also be more difficult because of the very high costs involved, coupled with the potential damage to our program if the Soviets became obstructive or withdrew.

At any level of relationships, proposals for cooperation in Category (c) have the greatest potential for matching the President's theme that "Both nations would help themselves as well as other nations by removing these endeavors from the bitter and wasteful competition of the Cold War." The United States considers exploration of the celestial bodies, particularly manned space exploration, to be perhaps the most challenging adventure of this century. This venture should be conducted on behalf of the human race and the earth as a whole, not on behalf of any single nation. The vigorous and accelerating United States space exploration program is proceeding in this spirit. If the Soviet Union shares this conception, then planning should be undertaken promptly for cooperative manned exploration of the moon and unmanned exploration of Mars and Venus. These projects should of course be open to the participation of all interested countries, conceivably under the auspices of the United Nations. They could, however, be undertaken most constructively only if the United States and the Soviet Union agree on objectives and on coordination of their efforts for the most rapid progress and the most efficient use of human and natural resources.

---

388.   National Security Action Memorandum No. 129[1]

Washington, February 23, 1962.

TO

The Secretary of State

SUBJECT

U.S.-U.S.S.R. Cooperation in the Exploration of Space

The President has responded to a message of congratulation from Chairman Khrushchev by indicating his desire that the U.S. and U.S.S.R. should cooperate in the exploration of space.[2] While emphasizing his belief in strong support of the work of the United Nations in this same field, he told the Chairman that he was "instructing the appropriate officers of this Government to prepare new and concrete proposals for immediate projects of common action." He also expressed his hope that "at a very early date representatives of our two space teams may meet to discuss our ideas and yours in a spirit of practical cooperation."

Accordingly, the President requests that in cooperation with the Administrator of the National Aeronautics and Space Administration, the Executive Secretary, National Aeronautics and Space Council, and the Special Assistant to the President for Science and Technology, the Department of State promptly develop such new and concrete proposals, together with recommendations as to the best way of opening discussion with Soviet representatives on these matters. These recommen-

---

[1] Source: Kennedy Library, National Security Files, Meetings and Memoranda Series, NSAM No. 129, U.S.–USSR Space Cooperation, Box 334. No classification marking. Copies were sent to the Administrator of NASA, Director of the Bureau of the Budget, the Director of USIA, Executive Secretary of the NASC, and the Special Assistant to the President for Science and Technology. A typed notation indicates that this NSAM was revised on February 27. An attached memorandum from Bundy to Webb, dated February 23, urged NASA to "go a little out of their way to find good projects" in view of the political advantages that could be derived from being "forthcoming and energetic in plans for peaceful cooperation with the Soviets in this sphere."

[2] For texts, see *Foreign Relations*, 1961–1963, vol. VI, Documents 35 and 36. See also Document 389.

dations should, of course, be consistent with continued support of the work which has begun in the UN, but the President does require that there be a prompt and energetic follow-up of his message to Chairman Khrushchev.

The President further requests that you designate one officer of the Department of State to have general charge of this project and inform us when this designation has been made.[3]

McGeorge Bundy[4]

---

[3] On February 27 Executive Secretary Lucius D. Battle informed Bundy that Under Secretary of State for Political Affairs George C. McGhee had been designated as the officer in charge of preparing proposals for space cooperation with the Soviet Union. (Kennedy Library, National Security Files, Meetings and Memoranda Series, NSAM No. 129, U.S.–USSR Space Cooperation, Box 334)

[4] Printed from a copy that bears this typed signature.

---

389.   Editorial Note

President Kennedy sent two letters to Chairman Khrushchev that suggested that the United States and the Soviet Union should seek areas in which they might cooperate in the exploration of outer space. The first, dated February 21, 1962, acknowledged Khruschchev's congratulations following the orbital flight of Colonel John Glenn, and concluded, "I am instructing the appropriate officers of this Government to prepare new and concrete proposals for immediate projects of common action, and I hope that at a very early date our representatives may meet to discuss our ideas and yours in a spirit of practical cooperation." The second, dated March 7 and released on March 18, suggested certain areas for possible cooperation, including: joint establishment of a weather satellite system, establishment of a satellite tracking system in each other's country, mapping the earth's magnetic field, communications satellite technology, and space medicine. Secretary of State Rusk submitted a draft copy of this letter to the President on March 6. For texts of these messages, see *Foreign Relations, 1961–1963*, volume VI, Documents 36 and 41.

On March 16 Acting Secretary of State George Ball recommended to President Kennedy that Dr. Hugh L. Dryden, Deputy Administrator of NASA, be designated as the principal U.S. technical representative should the Soviets agree to discuss areas for cooperation. (Kennedy Library, National Security Files, Meetings and Memoranda Series, NSAM No. 129, U.S.–USSR Space Cooperation, Box 334)

390.   Paper Prepared in the National Aeronautics and Space Administration[1]

Washington, April 21, 1962.

STATUS OF US/USSR BILATERAL SPACE TALKS

1. Dr. Dryden and Professor Blagonravov, with small technical and political staffs, met in New York on March 27th, 28th and 30th.

2. It was agreed that the talks would be preliminary and exploratory and that formal negotiations would begin either at the time of the COSPAR meeting in Washington April 30th to May 9th or at the time of the meetings of the technical and legal subcommittees of the UN Committee on the Peaceful Use of Outer Space in Geneva beginning May 28th. A letter has since gone from Dr. Dryden to Professor Blagonravov through the U. S. Embassy in Moscow requesting an early indication of the Soviet choice of these two alternatives.

3. The New York talks were very relaxed in character with an almost total absence of cold war atmosphere. The exceptions were as follows:

(a) At one point Blagonravov stated that he had been requested to state the desirability of a joint pledge by US and USSR scientists to reserve space for peaceful purposes and prohibit "spy-in-the-sky" satellites. Dr. Dryden stated that this subject fell outside the scope of the discussions. At the conclusion of the talks, an issue arose as to whether a joint press release should cite the subjects which it was agreed would be developed first. Blagonravov objected unless all subjects discussed, including the spy-in-the-sky matter, were included. It was agreed that no subjects would be specified, and the press release indicated that current and future discussions would follow the items developed in the Kennedy–Khrushchev correspondence.

(b) Blagonravov repeated the line that more far-reaching cooperation would be contingent upon agreement on disarmament.

In both of the above cases, Blagonravov was very relaxed and almost apologetic.

4. With regard to the content of the discussions, Blagonravov indicated:

---

[1] Source: Kennedy Library, National Security Files, Meetings and Memoranda Series, NSAM No. 129, U.S.–USSR Space Cooperation, Box 334. No classification marking. An attached routing slip from Arnold W. Frutkin of NASA to Bromley Smith, also dated April 21, reads: "Attached is brief status report you requested. It was not possible to get into my safe for Dr. Dryden's own summary. I will provide this Sunday or Monday a.m. to supplement the attached."

(a) The USSR will very likely launch meteorological satellites and is willing to coordinate their orbits and exchange the data much as suggested in the President's letter.

(b) While prepared to carry out experimental communications with the U.S. by means of a passive reflector satellite (ECHO or an ECHO follow-on), the USSR is not ready to discuss general cooperation in satellite communications yet.

(c) The USSR is ready to cooperate in a coordinated survey of the earth's magnetic field by satellites in complementary orbits.

(d) While not prepared to exchange tracking stations, the USSR would be willing to exchange tracking and telemetry services, even to the extent of providing equipment to U. S. specifications.

(e) Other subject areas were discussed in general terms, nothing being excluded, although there was some indication of unwillingness to exchange laboratory visits at this time. With regard to disturbances and contamination in space, Blagonravov's objective seemed to be simply that experiments with such potential would be brought to the notice of the interested countries in order to avoid interference with their experiments.

5.   The US side prepared three short papers expanding upon the President's proposals in the meteorological, magnetic survey, and telemetry exchange fields. These were presented to Blagonravov for consideration for more detailed negotiations at the next meeting. Blagonravov hoped that similar papers might be prepared by Soviet scientists for the same purpose. Dr. Dryden's letter, mentioned above, asks that such papers be made available as soon as possible. (The US side is preparing additional papers on the remaining subjects.)

6.   With regard to future procedure, at the request of Dr. Dryden, Blagonravov indicated a strong preference for agreement on individual projects if agreement can be reached rather than deferral of agreement until a total package can be achieved. To the extent that this position is maintained, it should minimize roadblocks in the form of political conditions.[2]

---

[2]   A handwritten note at the bottom of the page reads: "A summary of the 3 U.S.–USSR meetings is attached." The attached summary is not printed. For text of the "Record of the US-USSR Talks on Space Cooperation," see *Exploring the Unknown*, Volume II: *External Relationships*, pp. 153–162.

391. Memorandum From Secretary of State Rusk to President Kennedy[1]

Washington, May 15, 1962.

SUBJECT

Bilateral Talks Concerning US-USSR Cooperation in Outer Space Activities

While in Washington for the Symposium of the International Committee on Space Research (COSPAR), Professor Blagonravov has said that he will be prepared to continue his discussions with Dr. Dryden at Geneva in June during the meetings of the subcommittees of the UN Outer Space Committee. You will recall that Professor Blagonravov is the Soviet scientist who was designated by Khrushchev to discuss with your designee the proposals which were contained in your exchange of letters with Khrushchev on cooperation in outer space activities. The first such discussions between Professor Blagonravov and Dr. Dryden were held in New York City on March 27–30.

As a result of those talks Dr. Dryden feels, and we agree, that the Soviets clearly prefer to develop such arrangements on a step-by-step basis, not on the basis of an overall formal agreement between the two governments. Further, the Soviets are apparently interested in working primarily within multilateral programs (e.g. those of the World Meteorological Organization and the International Telecommunications Union), but on the basis of prior US-USSR agreement. It appears unlikely that significant joint effort in outer space activities will develop in the near term, but there is a prospect that the Soviets will agree to some modest cooperation in the form of coordinated satellite launch schedules, compatible instrumentation, and some additional exchange of technical information.

The talks in New York were preliminary and exploratory. They were limited to the specific proposals contained in your letter to Khrushchev and his reply. It was clear that Professor Blagonravov was not fully prepared on the detailed technical aspects of several of those proposals and was not authorized to make commitments, however preliminary. Thus the June Geneva talks should be more revealing of Soviet willingness to take concrete steps.

At one point in the talks Professor Blagonravov suggested that progress toward cooperation would be greatly facilitated if the US and the USSR would agree to ban all military reconnaissance activities in

---

[1] Source: Kennedy Library, National Security Files, Meetings and Memoranda Series, NSAM 129, U.S.–USSR Space Cooperation, Box 334. Confidential. A handwritten note by Bundy on the memorandum reads: "Hold for Standing Group this p.m."

outer space. (He suggested that Dr. Dryden, as a scientist, should prevail upon his Government to this end.) We have since learned from the Soviet Mission in New York that this proposition is more than a suggestion; that it is in fact a formal Soviet proposal which they are likely to press in the UN Outer Space Subcommittee meetings at Geneva. So far agreement on this point has not been made a precondition to technical cooperation. The Soviets continue to cite the need for disarmament as a precondition to intimate and extensive space cooperation but not necessarily to more modest cooperation.

Following the recent talks, Under Secretary McGhee, who is coordinating this matter for the Department, convened a meeting of the interested agencies of government in which Mr. Webb, Dr. Wiesner, and Dr. Welsh, among others, participated.[2] A review of the conduct of these talks during this meeting resulted in an agreement that the present low-key, step-by-step approach through informal talks by scientific representatives holds the most promise of breaking through Soviet reservations and initiating cooperation. For the time being we do not feel it necessary or wise to set a specific deadline by which these talks should be completed successfully or terminated. There will, of course, have to be agreed arrangements covering each project undertaken.

Dean Rusk

---

[2] No other record of this meeting has been found.

392.   Memorandum From the Under Secretary of State (Ball) to
        President Kennedy[1]

Washington, July 5, 1962.

SUBJECT

Bilateral Talks Concerning US-USSR Cooperation in Outer Space Activities

On May 15 the Secretary wrote to you describing the developments in this matter prior to the recent talks in Geneva between Dr. Dryden and Professor Blagonravov.[2] These talks commenced on May 29 and continued concurrently with meetings of the subcommittees of the UN Outer Space Committee. As a result, technical arrangements for three specific cooperative projects were agreed ad referendum to the US and Soviet Governments in a joint memorandum signed by Dr. Dryden and Professor Blagonravov on June 8. (See Enclosure 1.)[3] On the same day, Dr. Dryden and Professor Blagonravov issued a joint Press Communiqué summarizing briefly the results of these discussions. (See Enclosure 2.)[4]

The three projects involve (1) exchange of weather data from satellites and the eventual coordinated launching of meteorological satellites, (2) a joint effort to map the magnetic field of the earth by means of coordinated launchings of geomagnetic satellites and related ground observations, and (3) cooperation in the experimental relay of communications via the Echo satellite. It was also agreed that there should be further discussion of the possibility of broader cooperation in experiments using active communications satellites to be launched in the future. These arrangements are quite limited in scope and have been drawn carefully to assure reciprocal benefit. They have been developed in the context of multilateral programs (e.g., the program of the World Meteorological Organization for the acquisition and world-wide distribution of weather data, and the program being planned by the

---

[1] Source. Kennedy Library, National Security Files, Meetings and Memoranda Series, NSAM No. 129, U.S.-USSR Space Cooperation, Box 334. Confidential. Also printed in *Exploring the Unknown*, Volume II: *External Relationships*, pp. 163–164. In a July 13 attached memorandum to the President, Bundy noted that the three projects described in this memorandum had been reviewed by the CIA, the Defense Department, and various members of Congress and were "quite safe." "In essence they provide for the kind of cooperation in which we get as much as we give, and in which neither our advanced techniques nor our cognate reconnaissance capabilities will be compromised."

[2] Dryden and Blagonravov held their first meetings to discuss U.S.-Soviet space cooperation May 29–June 8 in Geneva, Switzerland.

[3] For text of the Summary of Understandings, signed by Dryden and Blagonravov on June 8, see *American Foreign Policy: Current Documents, 1962*, pp. 1328–1332.

[4] Not printed.

International Union of Geodesy and Geophysics for a world geomagnetic survey). The Soviets appeared quite anxious to achieve these agreements.

The arrangements proposed in the joint Dryden–Blagonravov memorandum represent a sound way of proceeding so long as they are adhered to by the Soviet Government and are developed in such a way as not to foster an impression abroad that they represent a more significant step toward US-Soviet cooperation than they actually do or that US-USSR cooperation will in any way preempt the cooperation already being developed with other countries.

There remain three other specific projects which were suggested in your exchange of correspondence with Chairman Khrushchev last March, but on which no specific conclusions or proposals have been reached during the technical discussions so far, i.e.: (1) the acquisition of data obtained through tracking facilities located in each other's countries but operated by the host governments, (2) joint observation of solar and interplanetary probes, and (3) space medicine. Although it seems clear that the Soviets are not interested in cooperating in tracking and it appears doubtful that they are really interested in joint observation of space probes, it would be well to afford them the opportunity to discuss all these projects further.

Upon Dr. Dryden's return from Geneva, Under Secretary McGhee, who is coordinating this matter for the Department, convened a meeting of the interested agencies of government in which Dr. Dryden, Dr. Welsh, Dr. Reichelderfer and representatives of Dr. Wiesner, Mr. Bundy, the Defense Department, the Air Force and CIA participated. A review of the recent discussions in Geneva and of the specific proposals contained in the joint Dryden–Blagonravov memorandum resulted in agreement to proceed as follows:

1. After a reasonable interval and if no serious objections have been raised by any of the interested agencies, Dr. Dryden will inform Professor Blagonravov that we have no changes to suggest in their joint memorandum.[5] (The memorandum provided for a two-month waiting period during which either party could propose changes.)

2. Upon notification from Professor Blagonravov that the Soviets do not desire changes which would be unacceptable to us (or at the conclusion of the two-month waiting period), we will, assuming the Soviets still wish to proceed, exchange notes with the Soviet Government to confirm government-level agreement to these proposals.

---

[5] On July 9 Dryden sent a letter to Blagonravov, informing him that he had no changes to suggest in the text of the Summary, that Congressmen George P. Miller and James G. Fulton had been added to the list of U.S. advisers, and that a selection process for the U.S. members of the joint working groups was being devised. (NASA Historical Reference Collection, Folder 003296, US-USSR Peaceful Uses Outer Space, 1962)

3. It was suggested that when that agreement has been obtained, you may wish to write to Chairman Khrushchev noting both the agreement to proceed with the specific arrangements at hand and the prospects of further technical discussions on additional topics. A draft of such a letter will be submitted for your approval.

4. Meanwhile, Under Secretary McGhee and Dr. Dryden will report these developments to members of Congress who have a specific interest and responsibility in this field, and the Department will prepare a report to be sent to the Secretary General of the United Nations when formal agreement has been reached with the Soviets.

5. Dr. Dryden will, in cooperation with the interested agencies, proceed now to arrange nominations for US membership in the joint US-Soviet working groups which are to develop the detailed implementation of the meteorological and geomagnetic proposals. These working groups will not, however, be activated until formal agreement has been reached with the Soviet Government.

6. The joint Dryden–Blagonravov memorandum will be treated as Confidential, pending government-level agreement by the Soviets or earlier Soviet public release.

7. After formal agreement has been obtained, Dr. Dryden will arrange directly with Professor Blagonravov for further technical discussions, possibly in Moscow this fall, concerning broader cooperation in communication via satellites and the possibility of cooperation in such of the remaining topics dealt with in your exchange of letters with Chairman Khrushchev as may seem worthwhile to pursue further.

It is our feeling that the present low key, step-by-step approach through informal talks by scientific representatives continues to be the preferable means of moving toward further cooperation and that we should plan to proceed on this basis after government-level agreement has been reached on the specific arrangements already proposed.

George W. Ball

393. National Security Action Memorandum No. 172[1]

Washington, July 18, 1962.

TO

Secretary of State
Administrator, National Aeronautics and Space Administration

SUBJECT

Bilateral Talks Concerning US-USSR Cooperation in Outer Space Activities

The President has reviewed the report on the current state of these conversations sent to him by the Under Secretary of State on July 5, 1962.[2]

The President concurs in the general approach described in the report and has requested that the responsible agencies proceed to carry out the steps described in paragraphs one through seven of pages three and four.

McGeorge Bundy

---

[1] Source: Kennedy Library, National Security Files, Subjects Series, Space Activities, U.S.-U.S.S.R. Space Cooperation, 1961–63, Box 308. Confidential. Copies were sent to the Secretary of Defense, the Director of the Office of Science and Technology, and the Director of Central Intelligence.

[2] Document 392.

---

394. Memorandum From the Director of the Office of International Scientific Affairs (Rollefson) to the Under Secretary of State for Political Affairs (McGhee)[1]

Washington, October 29, 1962.

SUBJECT

Bilateral Cooperation with the USSR in Outer Space Activities

Last week we received notification from the Soviets accepting the technical proposals for cooperative projects in outer space activity

---

[1] Source: National Archives and Records Administration, RG 59, SCI Files: Lot 65 D 473, SP 1–1, International Cooperation, USSR. Confidential. Drafted by Robert F. Packard (ISA), and concurred in by Ambassador at Large Llewellyn E. Thompson. Copies were sent to Thompson, Robert J. Manning (P), Leonard C. Meeker (L), Richard N. Gardner (IO), John C. Guthrie (EUR/SOV), Raymond L. Garthoff (G/PM), George Moffitt (IO/UNP), and Arnold Frutkin (NASA). The date of this memorandum was changed by hand from October 25 to October 29.

which had been worked out between Dr. Dryden and Academician Blagonravov last June. This notification was in the form of a note dated October 12 from the Ministry of Foreign Affairs to our Embassy in Moscow (Tab A)[2] and a letter dated October 12 to Mr. Webb as Administrator of NASA from M.V. Keldysh, President of the Academy of Sciences of the USSR (Tab B).[3]

It was agreed within the Department (in consultation with Ambassador Thompson, Mr. Davis, and Mr. Garthoff on behalf of Deputy Under Secretary Johnson) that the note and the letter from Keldysh together constitute an adequate basis of agreement with the USSR for proceeding with the projects proposed by Dryden and Blagonravov.

NASA prepared, and we cleared within the Department, a press release to be issued by NASA (Tab C).[4] The White House has directed, however, that the Government should not make any public statement on these developments at this time. Notwithstanding the White House "Hold" on the press release, the story leaked and appeared in this morning's issue of the *Washington Post* (Tab D).[5]

Dr. Dryden has offered to notify the Senate and House Space Committees indicating that you and he would be pleased to discuss the matter personally with members of either Committee, if they should so desire. It seems appropriate that this be done as soon as convenient.

All the agencies who were represented in the several earlier meetings which you held on this subject have been notified.

NASA, as the agency responsible for proceeding with these projects on behalf of the U.S. Government, will when appropriate make arrangements directly with the Soviet Academy or Blagonravov for meetings of the technical working groups which will develop the detailed arrangements for proceeding with these projects.

You will recall that, at the meeting on this subject which you chaired in mid-June, it was agreed that the President might write to Chairman Khrushchev noting both the agreement to proceed with the specific projects at hand and the prospects of further technical discussions on additional topics. The President was so informed in a memo-

---

[2] Not printed. In the note the Ministry of Foreign Affairs informed the Embassy that, on September 13 Academician A. A. Blagonravov had informed NASA Representative Frutkin of Soviet approval of the recommendations. Their meeting took place during a session of the UN Committee on the Use of Outer Space for Peaceful Purposes.

[3] Not printed. In the letter, Keldysh informed Webb that the Soviet Union considered the agreement to have entered into effect and that Soviet scientists were ready to implement it.

[4] Not printed.

[5] Not printed. The story, entitled "Crisis Threatens Plan for Space Cooperation," appeared in the October 25 edition of the *Washington Post*.

randum of July 5 from the Acting Secretary (Tab E).[6] It seems to us now that this need not, and should not be done.

The remaining step will be for Mr. Cleveland, at an appropriate time, to inform the UN Outer Space Committee of these developments through the Acting Secretary General.

These are the steps which were agreed at your meeting on June 15 and were reported to the President on July 5.

Recommendation

If you agree, I will see to it that they are taken as soon as it seems appropriate to Ambassador Thompson and Assistant Secretaries Tyler and Cleveland to do so., i.e.:

1. That the Senate and House Space Committees be notified by Dr. Dryden as soon as the White House withdraws its "Hold" on the NASA press release.

2. That NASA proceed to arrange with the Soviet Academy and Professor Blagonravov the steps to get underway the specific projects which have been agreed.

3. That the UN Outer Space Committee be informed through the Acting Secretary General of the United Nations.

4. That the White House (Mr. Bundy) be notified that, subject to his concurrence, we do not believe a letter on this subject from the President to Premier Khrushchev is necessary or appropriate at this time.[7]

---

[6] Document 392.

[7] A handwritten note at the end of the memorandum indicates that McGhee approved all four recommendations on October 31.

395. Memorandum From the Under Secretary of State for Political Affairs (McGhee) to the President's Special Assistant for National Security Affairs (Bundy)[1]

Washington, December 7, 1962.

SUBJECT

Bilateral Cooperation with the USSR in Outer Space Activities

As you know the Secretary General of the United Nations was informed today in a joint memorandum from Ambassadors Stevenson and Zorin of the agreement which has been reached between the Soviets and ourselves to cooperate in three outer space projects (the Dryden–Blagonravov proposals). That memorandum appended copies of the technical agreement reached between Dryden and Blagonravov at Geneva in early June (Tab B), copies of the correspondence exchanged in October between Mr. Webb and M. V. Keldysh, President of the Academy of Sciences of the USSR (Tabs C and D), copies of the notes exchanged between our embassy in Moscow and the Soviet Ministry of Foreign Affairs in August and October (Tabs E and F).[2]

I understand that yesterday afternoon Deputy Assistant Secretary Gardner spoke to you by phone to point out that the release of this correspondence—particularly Webb's letter to Keldysh of October 30— would have the effect of committing the United States to proceed directly with the implementation of these proposals, and that you agreed to the release on that understanding.

Accordingly Dr. Dryden proposes to send to Blagonravov a letter (Tab A) suggesting that they proceed now with the steps called for in their technical agreement. We find the letter entirely satisfactory and see no reason why it should not be sent. I am suggesting to Dr. Dryden that he do so on Friday or early next week.[3]

George C. McGhee

---

[1] Source: Kennedy Library, National Security Files, Meetings and Memoranda Series, NSAM 129, U.S.-USSR Space Cooperation, Box 334. Official Use Only.

[2] For the June 8 agreement, see footnote 3, Document 392. The correspondence and notes are printed in Department of State *Bulletin*, December 24, 1962, pp. 963–965.

[3] The letter at Tab A, not printed, is dated December 5. On December 10 Bundy replied that Dryden's letter appeared "entirely satisfactory," and he agreed that Dryden should proceed with the next steps of the technical agreement. Charles E. Johnson of the NSC Staff indicated his agreement in a separate memorandum of the same date. (Kennedy Library, National Security Files, Meetings and Memoranda Series, NSAM 129, U.S.-USSR Space Cooperation, Box 334) The final text of the letter is dated December 11. (Ibid.)

396.   Telegram From the Embassy in Italy to the Department of State[1]

Rome, March 12, 1963, 8 p.m.

1831. Department pass NASA and USIA. After welcome by Ambassador Kozyrev in his office at 9:30 both groups consisting of US Delegates Dryden, Stelter, Hornig, Burnett, Porter, Frutkin, Tepper, Malone, Townsend, Johnson, Butler, and Soviet Delegates Blagonravov, Kalinin, Evseyev, Bugayev, Milovidov, Stashevskiy, Klokov, Talyzin, Krupin, and Kolokatov and Ramberg of two Embassies, met in Orangerie for general discussion of program on weather satellites and communication links for data exchange.[2] After hour of general discussion decided to separate into two groups, one on weather satellites and other on adequate communication links for transfer satellite data. During recess Blagonravov reiterated invitation of Ambassador for meeting at Ambassador's summer residence Via Aurelia Antica 12 beginning Thursday morning.[3] Dryden agreed meet there Thursday and suggested deciding at end of meeting whether or not continue meeting there Friday or return Via Abruzzi 25 closer to Chanceries' facilities. Group on weather satellites started meeting 10:45 with following attending: Dryden, Hornig, Tepper, Burnett, Townsend, Butler, Johnson, Malone, Bugayev, Evseyev and Milovidov. Group on communication links consisting of Stelter, Porter, Frutkin, Blagonravov, Klokov, Stashevskiy, Krupin, Talyzin met at same time for detailed discussion.

Discussions were amicable frequently developing into simultaneous give and take conversation, mostly in English, between various delegates to clarify difficult technical points.

In general discussion Soviets emphasized initiating data exchange with conventional data. Dryden made clear US requirement communications link be used primarily for satellite data, that link should be established no earlier than few months in advance availability Soviet satellite data, this interval being provided for test and shakedown purposes. In group discussions Soviets generally agreeable US proposals

---

[1] Source: National Archives and Records Administration, RG 59, Central Files 1960–63, SP 1–1 US–USSR. Limited Official Use. Repeated to Moscow.

[2] On January 7 Blagonravov suggested to Dryden that the working groups meet in Rome before the conference of the Committee of the "International Year of the Quiet Sun." On January 21 Dryden proposed a preliminary meeting in March at the U.S. Embassy in Rome. In February they agreed to hold the first meeting at the Embassy on March 11, the second at a location of Blagonravov's choosing the next day, and the third at the Embassy. (Ibid.)

[3] The meeting took place on March 14.

for character of data, communication link and terminal equipment. Decision for groups to recess and draft summary of discussions to date.

Questions outstanding are date of availability Soviet satellite data and routing of communication link. Bugayev stated such data available December 1963 on experimental but not operational basis. Again, no overt or legal issues raised.

Two groups to meet jointly Via Abruzzi 25 Wednesday morning 9:30.

Reinhardt

---

397.   Telegram From the Embassy in Italy to the Department of State[1]

Rome, March 15, 1963, 7 p.m.

1858. Department pass NASA, USIA, and FCC. Joint meeting summer residence 6 PM yesterday attended by Dryden, Frutkin, Hornig, Townsend, Malone, Tepper, Stelter, Porter, Burton, Johnson, Burnett, Blagonravov, Klokov, Bugayev, Evseyev, Milovieov, Stashevskiy, Krupin, Talyzin and interpreters Edmundson, Pavlov, Ustinov. Meeting devoted to comparison Russian and English texts on meteorological program. Minor changes style resulted. Statement on implementation this program put aside till all statements ready when they will be incorporated in single document subject to review and exception within 60 days.

Meetings resumed Via Abruzzi 9:30 Friday morning with communication satellite and geomagnetism groups meeting separate rooms.

Communication satellite meeting attended by Dryden, Jaffe, Mazur, Porter, Hornig, Siry, Stelter, Klokov, Stashevskiy, Krupin, Talyzin with Ustinov, Sawicki, interpreting. At meeting US Delegation gave USSR Delegation technical information in writing covering expected characteristics Echo II satellite and radio equipment at Goonhilly Downs, and presented proposed draft agreement which provides for communication experiments between USSR and UK on 162 MC and for demonstration between USSR and USA using Echo as "part

---

[1] Source: National Archives and Records Administration, RG 59, Central Files 1960–63, SP 1–1 US–USSR. Limited Official Use. Repeated to Moscow.

of link." Draft also calls for consideration both sides of communication experiments USSR to UK at higher frequencies in addition to or instead of 162 MC. Soviet Delegation refrained from substantive comment on draft but agreed make comments Saturday morning. Questions of higher frequencies regarded by them as "delicate" because of forthcoming ITU meeting.

Meeting adjourned 11:30 to be resumed 9:30 Saturday morning summer residence.

Geomagnetism meeting attended by Cahill, Frutkin, Townsend, Heppner, Cain, Vestine, Kalinin, Blagonravov, Milovidov, with Edmundson, Pavlov interpreting. Meeting considered US paper. USSR reluctant to promise elliptical or polar orbit, to separate out instrumental and positional errors, to hold to minimal observational error recommended by IUGG, or to agree direct exchange raw data. However, general agreement indicated on over-lapping orbits in time and space, provision for launch US and USSR satellites within same three month period, adequate indication over-all data error, extensive exchange important ground observations, and absolute magnetometer instrumentation. New USSR draft due Monday. Meeting adjourned around need to reconvene Via Abruzzi 9 AM Monday.

Williamson

---

398.   Telegram From the Mission in Geneva to the Department of State[1]

Geneva, May 16, 1963, 11 p.m.

1440. For Frutkin NASA. Outer Space Bilaterals. At first meeting today Blagonravov stated Soviet Academy had not yet approved Rome memo of understanding,[2] wishing to await inclusion of geomagnetic portion. Handed Dryden following statement:

Begin Verbatim Text.

The Delegation of the Academy of Sciences of the USSR, appointed to continue bilateral negotiations between NASA of the USA and the

---

[1] Source: National Archives and Records Administration, RG 59, Central Files 1960–63, SP 1–1 US–USSR. Confidential; Priority. Repeated to USUN.
[2] See Document 400.

Academy of Sciences of the USSR on questions of magnetic survey by means of artificial earth satellites, has been authorized by the Academy of Sciences of the USSR to announce the following change in the text of the recommendations agreed upon in Rome:

In Section VI, the period of coming into effect, instead of the words: "In a two-months period beginning from today" to insert the words: "In the shortest possible time after the completion of negotiations on the conduct of a world magnetic survey by means of artificial satellites."

Academician A. Blagonravov

End Verbatim Text.

Turning immediately to geomagnetic question, Kalinin said he had reviewed whole matter with colleagues in Moscow and concluded their Rome position sound. Proposed, therefore, that satellite data be exchanged in form most useful and economical of each sides' time and effort, i.e., in scientific reports and articles with data processed by experimenter from whose satellite they came. Since both sides had equal interest in success of venture, this should be satisfactory. Proposed prior agreement on recommendations for procedures for correcting data.

We will probe Soviet position more fully tomorrow after reviewing Kalinin's prepared statement. Geomagneticians meeting at 10, to be joined by principals at noon. We intend review in detail our plans for data handling and processing in order make absolutely clear reasons for our position on need for raw data.

After meeting, Stashevsky handed DelOff without comment copy letter "which was mailed today to Dryden." Our translation follows:

Begin Verbatim Text.

Dear Dr. Dryden:

In accordance with our understanding in Rome, I have informed the authorities of the Academy of Sciences of the USSR of the recommendations pertaining to certain questions of cooperation in the field of space research between the Academies of Sciences of the USSR and NASA which we had agreed upon.

The above-mentioned recommendations have been carefully studied. I have not been successful, however, in obtaining their definite approval prior to my departure for Geneva. Our Academy attaches great importance to the fact that during our meeting in Rome we had not succeeded in reaching an agreement on questions of cooperation in the conduct of a world magnetic survey by means of satellites even though, in our opinion, rather good possibilities exist for such an agreement.

Very recently some discouraging results have also come to light concerning negotiations held last April in New York on the legal prob-

904 Foreign Relations, 1961–1963, Volume XXV

lems of space. Under these circumstances, it seems necessary to think over once more in detail the entire problem as a whole, since, as you understand, the legal and scientific-technical problems of space cooperation are, at the present time, closely linked together by life itself.

Upon my return from Geneva I shall once again bring up the question of approval of the Rome recommendations to the authorities of the Academy of Sciences of the USSR, taking also into consideration results of negotiations which we hope shall be continued here in Geneva.

Respectfully,

Academician A. Blagonravov

Geneva, May 16, 1963.

End Verbatim Text.

Also present from USSR were Dr. Peter Evseev, Dr. Nicolai Talizin and interpreter from local Mission.

Tubby

---

399.   **Telegram From the Mission in Geneva to the Department of State**[1]

Geneva, May 27, 1963, 9 p.m.

1525. For Frutkin NASA. Outer Space Bilateral. At final meeting May 24 Dryden and Blagonravov exchanged English and Russian texts of geomagnetism agreement reported Mission tel 1453[2] with editorial changes: In numbered para 8 "an attachment" should read "attachments" and word "survey" following thereafter should be plural. In para 9 final clause first sentence should read "and of analysis of the results."

As reported telcon with NASA,[3] Blagonravov stated he had tried unsuccessfully to obtain agreement on all three areas of agreement prior Friday's mtg.[4] But Soviet Academy had said in view of internal problems in Academy they wished have personal report by Blagonravov

---

[1]   Source: National Archives and Records Administration, RG 59, Central Files 1960–63, SP 1–1 US–USSR. Limited Official Use.

[2]   Not printed. (Ibid.)

[3]   No other record of this telephone conversation has been found.

[4]   May 24.

prior to acting. He felt two weeks would be sufficient for Academy review and that approval might come during time of COSPAR mtg. In lieu of signed covering statement as reported reftel, Blagonravov proposed exchange of letters, noting each side would refer matter back home for review, and referring to earlier agreement that Section VI of Rome memo be amended to provide notification of any changes "in shortest possible time after conclusion" geomagnetic discussion here. Was agreed that new geomagnetic text should replace Para IV in Rome text. He obviously instructed handle this in low key and avoid implication of anything beyond completion of job begun in Rome.

Texts of letters follow:

May 24, 1963

Dear Dr. Dryden:

During our meeting last May 16, I informed you, on the instruction of the Academy of Sciences of the USSR of the following changes in the text of the recommendations we had agreed upon in Rome: In Section VI, the period of coming into force, instead of the words "in a two-month period beginning with today" to put in the words "in the shortest possible time after the conclusion of discussions concerning the conduct of a world magnetic survey by means of artificial satellites."

As I had already informed you in my letter of May 16, 1963,[5] in connection with the conclusion of our negotiations in Geneva, I shall, upon my return to Moscow, inform the Academy of Sciences of the USSR of the mutual understanding we have reached on the question of a magnetic survey by means of artificial earth satellites. The decision of the Academy of Sciences of the USSR on this question shall be communicated to NASA of the United States of America according to the arrangements concerning the recommendations we had agreed upon in Rome.

Academician A. Blagonravov

May 24, 1963

Dear Academician Blagonravov:

The proposal of the Academy of Sciences of the USSR, which you communicated to me on May 16, to make certain changes in Section VI of the recommendations we made in Rome, is accepted. In Section VI the words "in a two-month period beginning with today are replaced by "in the shortest possible time after the conclusion of discussions concerning the conduct of a world magnetic survey by means of artificial satellites."

At our meeting today we exchanged English and Russian texts of the mutual understanding we have reached on the question of a mag-

---

[5] See Document 398.

netic survey by means of earth satellites, which completes our discussion of this question begun in Rome and reported in Paragraph IV of the Rome recommendations. On my return, I will report this recommendation to NASA and inform you promptly of our decision on acceptance.

Hugh L. Dryden

Tubby

---

400.   Editorial Note

The Memorandum of Understanding between NASA and the Soviet Academy of Sciences on implementation of a cooperative space program, drafted at Rome in March 1963 and at Geneva in May 1963, was made public by NASA on August 16, after an exchange of letters between Dryden and Blagonravov. For text of the Memorandum of Understanding and the NASA announcement, see *American Foreign Policy: Current Documents, 1963*, pages 1069–1080. For text of the July 8 letter from Dryden and the August 16 letter from Blagonravov indicating Soviet readiness to proceed with implementation of the agreement, see Department of State *Bulletin*, September 9, 1963, page 405.

401.   Memorandum Prepared in the Central Intelligence Agency[1]

Washington, July 31, 1963.

SUBJECT

Soviet Views on Future Space Operations

Dr. Hugh Dryden of NASA has received a letter, date 23 July 1963, from Sir Bernard Lovell, Director of the Jodrell Bank Radio—astronomical observatory, forwarding the suggestions of Matislav Keldysh, President of the Academy of Sciences USSR.[2]

During his talks with Lovell, Keldysh suggested that plans for an early manned lunar landing should be developed on an international basis. Keldysh claimed that Soviet scientists had rejected any manned lunar landing mission for the time being because of the hazards of solar flares, the tremendous launch propulsion requirements, and the ability of unmanned instrumented probes to solve the scientific problems involved in lunar exploration more cheaply and quickly.

Lovell concluded during his conversations with Keldysh that decisions had been made by the Soviets to continue instrumented probes to Mars, Venus, and the moon; that the apparatus for a soft landing of instruments on the moon will be ready for launch in a matter of months; and that rendezvous and docking techniques would be developed "with an immediate aim (perhaps 1965–66)" of establishing a manned space platform for astronomical observations. Lovell also forwarded the details of a cooperative program arranged between Jodrell Bank and the Deep Space Tracking Center at Yevpatoriya, which he visited during his recent trip to the USSR.

We believe that the proposal submitted by Keldysh—that a manned lunar enterprise be considered on an international basis—is another step in a Soviet move to internationalize manned lunar exploration. This step closely coincides with one taken during an early July 1963 meeting of the Executive Committee of the International Astronomical Union (IAU) in Liege, Belgium. According to a US scientist, V.A.

---

[1] Source: Kennedy Library, National Security Files, Departments and Agencies Series, Space Activities, U.S.-USSR Cooperation, 1961–63, Box 308. Confidential. The memorandum gives no addressee and is unsigned, but is attached to a covering memorandum from Cline to Bundy, which reads: "1. Mr. McCone and I think you may be interested in the attached memorandum. 2. The President of the USSR Academy of Sciences has suggested that an international program be launched for an early-manned lunar landing mission. The memorandum summarizes and comments on his suggestions, forwarded to Hugh Dryden of NASA in a letter from Sir Bernard Lovell following the latter's visit to the USSR. 3. We have made no distribution of this memorandum."

[2] See footnote 3, Document 404.

Ambartsumyam—a member of the Academy of Sciences USSR and President of the IAU—told foreign scientists that both he and Keldysh are of the opinion that any attempted manned flight to the moon should be deferred at this time in favor of deep space probes. He stated that the potential scientific results that might be obtained from a manned lunar mission do not justify the great expenses necessary to achieve it.

---

402. Letter From the Deputy Administrator of the National Aeronautics and Space Administration (Dryden) to the Chairman of the Commission on Exploration and Utilization of Outer Space, Academy of Sciences of the USSR (Blagonravov)[1]

Washington, August 23, 1963.

Dear Academician Blagonravov:

I am glad to have your letter of August 1 conveying the consent of the Academy of Sciences of the USSR to the Memorandum of Understanding completed by us on May 24 in Geneva.[2] With the Memorandum in force, we can now proceed to implement the program set forth in the bilateral agreement of June 8, 1962.[3]

The following matters require the earliest possible action if the program is to proceed according to the agreed time schedule:

(1) Section II.D of the Memorandum provides that NASA and the Academy of Sciences of the USSR are to agree upon a suitable mechanism for equal sharing of the costs of the meteorological communications link, and are to designate representatives to carry out continued technical coordination of details concerning this link. In my letter of April 15, I proposed an arrangement whereby the General Post Office of the United Kingdom would be asked to act as the collection and disbursing agent for all charges relating to the Washington–Moscow link.[4]

---

[1] Source: National Archives and Records Administration, RG 59, SCI Files: Lot 65 D 473, SP 1–1, International Cooperation, USSR. No classification marking. Drafted by D.R. Morris (AI) on August 23, and concurred in by Morris, Dillery (D/S), Homer E. Newell (S), Townsend (G), Morris Tepper (FM), and Leonard Jaffe (FC).

[2] See Document 400.

[3] See footnote 3, Document 392.

[4] The April 15 letter was not found.

If my proposal as set forth in that letter is acceptable, agreement on this matter should be reached as soon as possible and consultations begun immediately with U.K. authorities.

(2) We hope to receive your designation of a Soviet counterpart to Mr. Laverne R. Stelter, Head of the NASA Communications Division at the Goddard Space Flight Center, whom I designated in my letter of April 18 as the NASA technical representative for coordination of details concerning the link.[5] An early meeting between the two representatives must be arranged. It should be borne in mind that the common carriers involved between Washington and Berlin require 30 days advance notice before the establishment of an operational link.

(3) Aside from the technical details of the communications link itself, there will be details relating to the data and information to be transmitted which will require coordination. I suggest you designate a central point of contact in the USSR with whom Dr. Morris Topper, Chairman of the US Working Group on Meteorology, may correspond concerning such matters.

(4) Mr. Leonard Jaffe, whom I designated in my April 18 letter as the NASA representative for technical coordination of the planned communications experiments with Echo II, has reported that his meeting in the United Kingdom with Dr. Chetmantshev and Zhulin in late May left several questions unresolved. Those were set forth, I understand, in a memorandum prepared on May 28 by Dr. Chetmantshev and the UK representatives, Mr. Taylor and Dr. Davies.[6] In order to permit adequate preparation and planning for the experiments, it is necessary to schedule a meeting as soon as possible between Mr. Jaffe and Soviet technical representatives knowledgeable about the communications aspects of the proposed experiments to decide on details, particularly with regard to questions of frequency and plans for transmissions from Gorki. In this case also, we hope to receive your designation of a Soviet counterpart to Mr. Jaffe.

(5) Section III.C of the Memorandum of Understanding raises the possibility of extending the tests with Echo II into the microwave region of the frequency spectrum and also of arranging radar and optical observations by the USSR of the Echo II satellite during the period of its inflation and thereafter. Please advise us of the results of your consideration of these two possibilities, both of which appear highly desirable to NASA.

(6) With regard to the magnetic field survey, the Memorandum of Understanding foresees the exchange of ground observations from various observatories in the US and the USSR, as well as of data from

---

[5] The April 18 letter was not found.
[6] The May 28 memorandum was not found.

ground, sea, and aerial surveys. Would it not be most practical for the experimenters in each country to correspond directly concerning such matters? If this appears to be a suitable arrangement, please designate a central point of contact in the USSR for such correspondence.

Possibly, we shall meet again in New York in September during the meeting of the United Nations Committee on the Peaceful Uses of Outer Space. Meanwhile, I shall look forward to hearing from you concerning the immediate questions raised above.

Sincerely yours,

Hugh L. Dryden[7]

---

[7] Printed from a copy that indicates Dryden signed the original.

---

403. Memorandum From the Principal Deputy Assistant Secretary of State for International Organization Affairs (Sisco) to the Deputy Assistant Secretary of State for International Organization Affairs (Gardner)[1]

Washington, September 3, 1963.

SUBJECT

Outer Space Problems in the Proposed GA Speech

I. Concrete Proposals for Cooperation in Outer Space

A) *Cooperative Studies on the Medical Aspects of Manned Space Flight*

1. Description. The U.S. and USSR might agree to exchange complete data on the post-flight examinations of their astronauts in an effort to compile the maximum amount of information on the effects of space flight on man as rapidly and economically as possible.

2. History

a. Suggested as possible Presidential offer to Khrushchev for Vienna meeting, 1961.[2]

---

[1] Source: National Archives and Records Administration, RG 59, Central Files 1960–63, UN 3 GA. Confidential. Drafted by R. McKelvey (IO/UNP) on August 30.

[2] A background paper, dated May 25, 1961, prepared by the State Department in preparation for the meeting, suggested that Khrushchev might revive "some earlier US proposal on bilateral cooperation in scientific or medical endeavors (though probably not in the exploration of outer space)." See *Foreign Relations*, 1961–1963, vol. V, Document 76.

b. Firm offer by U.S. to USSR to "pool our efforts and exchange our knowledge in the field of space medicine" in Kennedy letter to Khrushchev, March 7, 1962.[3]

c. Khrushchev reply, March 20, 1962, notes: "I can say that Soviet scientists are prepared to cooperate in this and to exchange data. . ."[4]

d. Space medicine was not one of the subjects that Soviets were prepared to discuss in context of Dryden–Blagonravov talks although it was proposed by the U.S.

e. The Secretary raised the possibility of cooperation in space medicine during his talks in Moscow.

3. Cost. If limited to exchange of data, the costs would be small. If joint experimentation was involved, however, costs could be much larger according to the extent of the program, but the value for money should be good since Soviets would pay half presumably.

B) *Cooperative Tracking of Flights*

1. Description. This arrangement could take several forms. It might include a tracking station with U.S. equipment on Soviet territory run by specially trained Soviet personnel with a similar Soviet station here. Or it could be limited to exchange of information from existing tracking facilities. Cooperative tracking could cover manned flights to increase the safety of the astronauts, deep space probes, specially agreed flights, or all flights.

2. History

a. President Kennedy's letter to Khrushchev of March 7, 1962 suggested the establishment of a tracking station with U.S. equipment on Soviet territory run by specially trained Soviet personnel and a similar Soviet station here.

b. Chairman Khrushchev replied cautiously (March 20, 1962) that a joint program of observation would be of value, but he mentioned it only in the context of deep space and lunar probes.

c. Sir Bernard Lovell, Director of the Jodrell Bank Observatory, recently negotiated an agreement with the Soviets for "an extension of our cooperative work with the Soviet Union in the tracking of lunar and deep space probes." The agreement appears to be limited to a more rapid and more complete exchange of data. A British offer to accommodate a small number of Soviet scientists at Jodrell Bank to track probes is apparently being considered by the USSR. (Two Soviet scientists came to Jodrell Bank in June 1961 to search for signals from the Venus probe.)

3. Cost. The extent of the program agreed would determine the costs. Exchange of information or observers would cost little; establishment of a tracking station and equipment could involve $5–$10 million expenditure.

---

[3] See ibid., vol. VI, Document 41.

[4] See ibid., Document 43.

C) *Network of Earth and Space-Based Observatories*

1. Description. Several types of programs could be involved. A cooperative program of observation from earth would be of great value since study of the same event from different angles improves the results obtained. Observation from space might include one nation providing technical equipment and the other putting it into orbit much as the U.S. has done with experimental equipment of its allies. A cooperative program might be negotiated to launch a space platform for extended observations from space.

2. History

a. Both the Kennedy and Khrushchev letters contain references along the lines of "cooperation to unlock the secrets of the universe" but no concrete programs were put forward.

b. The Lovell agreement includes a three point program for joint observation between the UK and the USSR on flare star radio emission, bi-static radar observations, and study of angular diameters and structure of radio sources.

3. Cost. The cost of a program would be governed by the projects involved. Exchange of information or observers would cost little. If an intensive program were agreed upon, including the establishment of new observation facilities on earth or extensive satellite launchings, the cost could be considerable. Language problems and resolution of technical details in construction might raise the total cost above that of a single nation's program.

D) *Cooperative Program of Space Exploration by Instruments and Men*

1. Description. This proposal could be as limited as an exchange of information from instrument probes of space or it could be as extensive as joint unmanned landings on the lunar surface or, perhaps, joint flights by Soviet and American astronauts.

2. History

a. The Kennedy letter of March 7, 1962 spells out a far reaching program of space research as a hypothetical example of the type of cooperation the U.S. and the USSR might someday achieve. He specifically mentions an unmanned lunar landing and probes of Venus and Mars and even suggests the "possible utility of manned flight in such programs."

b. Khrushchev's reply (March 20, 1962) speaks in general terms about the need for extensive cooperation in space experiments.

3. Cost. The cost for an extensive joint program might exceed the total costs of a U.S. program alone due to the problems of language and achieving joint technical specifications in production.

Problem: There is little disagreement that increased and improved cooperation with the Soviet Union on outer space matters, including the four issues noted above, is in the best interests of the U.S. Government. NASA and others have pointed out, however, that mentioning these and other specific items in the GA speech may not further this end. Some of the reasons cited are:

1. As the speech is worded, there is an implication that the three offers represent a new initiative by the U.S. when in fact they have all been put forward in one form or another previously and have not been picked up by the USSR.

2. By repeating these offers we are, in effect, asking the Soviets to cooperate on something we know they have let pass before. At the extreme this might be misinterpreted as a cold war tactic of "offering the unacceptable" to win favor with world opinion. We do not want to return the cold war to an area that has been so painstakingly defrosted.

3. Usually, these negotiations have been conducted bilaterally with a minimum of publicity. Dr. Dryden of NASA has recently written to Mr. Keldysh of the Soviet Academy to reopen the dialogue and seek new areas of agreement. NASA is reluctant to mention specific items, especially points to which the Soviets have not responded previously, when a general offer of cooperation has been made. Further, they are especially reluctant to do this in a public and multi-lateral forum when a private and bilateral suggestion has been made.

4. Some of these proposals create serious problems at the present time. Medical data: the U.S. has published its data and we have little to trade with the Soviets until the next manned flight 18 months away. Tracking: the Soviets are reluctant to engage in any operations that will reveal their tracking capabilities. Their hedging on the geomagnetic data and delayed response to the Echo II experiments are cases in point. Moreover, the U.S. tracking facilities are carrying a heavy load and we have been discouraging requests from ESRO to track for them when their program is operational. A UN offer might bring requests from our allies as well as the Soviets that we cannot fill. Space-based observatories: our platform requires sophisticated techniques that we do not wish to reveal for security reasons, although this problem probably might be overcome if an agreement with the Soviets seemed possible.

5. An important question of policy should be decided. Are we prepared actively to seek new agreements with the Soviets before we have lived within the present agreements for some time?

Proposal: Presuming a favorable response to point 5 above, the President should convey to the Soviets and the General Assembly the strong desire of the U.S. Government to seek further agreement on projects of mutual benefit. He could note the specific projects as suggestions to revive discussion, not as new initiatives. Suggested language follows:

"As you know, Premier Khrushchev and I corresponded last year about a number of projects in outer space on which mutual agreement might be possible. Among them were the three projects on which we now have a signed agreement.

"I hope these three items will be but the first of a growing list of joint efforts—that we can search out other specific projects. We might begin, perhaps, with proposals which Premier Khrushchev and I discussed in our correspondence, such as cooperative studies of space medicine and cooperative tracking of manned flights and space probes. An additional example would be a cooperative network of observation stations on earth and in space to help us to unlock the secrets of the universe. Exploration of outer space, first by instruments and eventually by man, is a task of such challenge and magnitude that common sense dictates the maximum degree of cooperation that we can achieve. What I wish to convey to this Assembly is my government's genuine and earnest desire to explore with the Soviet Union and other countries any projects that will promote the interests and progress of man in space."[5]

II. Space Law

A second outer space problem in the speech relates to the statement: "Let us embody them [legal principles on which there is agreement][6] in a declaration of Space Law at this Assembly." If we have reached an arrangement with the Soviet Union in the bi-lateral negotiations, then this statement poses no problem. If not, then a decision must be made whether to seek a GA resolution. Our present position as stated in the strategy paper is that:

". . . the United States should consider putting forward such a Declaration in the Assembly and pressing it to a vote even without Soviet support, although we would have to weigh carefully the risks that this might open up debate on such matters as a ban on all military uses of space."

---

[5] Regarding the speech President Kennedy delivered to the General Assembly, see footnote 2, Document 406.

[6] Brackets in the source text.

404.   Memorandum for the Record[1]

Washington, September 17, 1963.

SUBJECT

Luncheon with Academician Blagonravov in New York, September 11, 1963

The objective of the luncheon was to discuss with Academician Blagonravov the plans and progress within the Soviet Academy of Sciences for implementation of the agreement recently signed for cooperation in meteorological satellites, passive communications experiments, and magnetic field survey. Those present at the luncheon were Academician A. Blagonravov, Mr. G.S. Stashevsky, Dr. Hugh L. Dryden and Mr. Arnold Frutkin from NASA, and Peter Thatcher from the U.S. United Nations Mission in New York.

I first asked how things were going with regard to the implementation of the agreement. Blagonravov replied that he was having some difficulty with the Soviet Ministry of Communications, who had been so busily occupied with the "hot line" between the Kremlin and the White House that they had not yet undertaken to deal with the problems of the communication link for exchange of cloud pictures as provided in our negotiations. My letter of August 23rd,[2] which outlined the next steps as we foresaw them and gave names of NASA representatives who were prepared to proceed with the discussions and detailed planning in specific areas, had not yet been received, since Blagonravov left Moscow early in September. I gave Blagonravov a copy of my letter of August 23rd, and he read it without detailed comment except to again refer to his problems with the Ministry of Communications. I requested him to move as rapidly as procedures within the Academy permitted and said that we were prepared to move as fast as he could.

I then congratulated him on his appointment as Chairman of the Commission on the Exploration and Utilization of Outer Space, as successor to Federov, who has become Chief of the Hydro Meteorological Service.

I then asked Blagonravov whether he was present at the Lovell discussion, and he replied "no, that he couldn't be there."

---

[1] Source: National Archives and Records Administration, RG 59, Central Files 1960–63, SP 10 US/USSR. Confidential. Dryden forwarded the memorandum under cover of a memorandum of the same date to U. Alexis Johnson, with copies to McGeorge Bundy and the Director of the President's Office of Science and Technology. Assistant Secretary Cleveland forwarded the memorandum and attached correspondence under cover of a September 30 memorandum to Under Secretary Ball.

[2] Document 402.

We then discussed the problems of the manned lunar program as outlined in the Lovell letter,[3] which had to be solved in advance of the lunar landing.   These included the radiation and other problems. Blagonravov stated that these were problems which had to be solved as a basis for the manned program. Although there was some intimation in the way in which this was said that he might be thinking of solving these problems first before proceeding with the manned lunar project, I do not think that concurrent action was excluded by the language used. He mentioned specifically that rocket power was not a problem, but in the context of this exchange and others which occurred later I interpret this to mean that there are no unknown problems in rocket technology similar to the radiation and weightlessness problems in outer space. We shall return to this subject later.

We then referred to Lovell's account of the Keldysh discussion of "why go to the moon" which was said to be occurring within the Soviet Academy of Sciences. It is my impression from the brief discussion that there are factions within the Soviet Academy who have been discussing the reasons for and against going to the moon. Especially there are scientists in the Soviet Union, as in the U.S., who wish a greater emphasis on science. At one point Blagonravov raised his chin and stated that he personally was the champion of the manned lunar program. As the translator spoke the word "champion," Blagonravov became slightly uneasy and said that perhaps he had not chosen his words very well, that he was a "supporter" of the manned lunar program. I gained the impression that there is a temporary hold in the manned lunar program pending the attainment of soft landing of instruments on the moon. Blagonravov stated that "Lovell's statement (i.e., that there was a temporary hold in the lunar program) might be true as of today."

I advanced the view that it was not necessary to use Lovell as a channel to convey Soviet desires to the U.S., and Blagonravov seemed to agree with this observation. He went so far as to state that it might be advisable for the Blagonravov/Dryden groups to have discussions later of the possibility of cooperation in manned lunar exploration after

---

[3] On July 23 Sir Bernard Lovell, Director of the Jodrell Bank Radio Observatory in England, sent a letter to Dryden describing a visit that he had made to Soviet observatories between June 25 and July 15, as a guest of the Soviet Academy of Sciences. Soviet scientists had told Lovell that while they wanted to establish a manned orbiting observatory, they did not believe that a manned flight to the moon would be practicable in the near future. They also said that international cooperation would help determine how the technical problems might be overcome and what scientific tasks would require a human presence on the moon. Dryden was on vacation when Lovell's letter arrived, so NASA Administrator Webb responded on his behalf in an August 6 letter. Webb suggested to Lovell that Dryden and Blagonravov might explore these matters within the context of the agreement between NASA and the Soviet Academy of Sciences. Both letters are attached to this memorandum.

instrumented landings on the moon had been made. This is a real change from previous discussions in which he had taken the point of view that there was no use in discussing cooperation in this area because of the political climate.

I offered to answer questions with regard to our own program. He seemed to know the names of most of the projects and was particularly interested in Ranger.

We then turned to the subject of the cooperative program on mete-orological satellites, and I asked whether the date of mid-1964 would be met for the exchange of pictures. Blagonravov said that he still hoped to meet the mid-64 date, although there were problems. He did not say whether these were technical or political. He did say that "industry" was not greatly interested in meteorological satellites. By industry I assumed he meant those persons who were interested in the exploita-tion of power development, consumer goods, et cetera, as contrasted with space.

With respect to the lunar landing, he pointed out again that rocket thrust was not a problem, that capsules have to be designed and built. He made the statement that he was satisfied that with Saturn V we could go to the moon. I made every attempt to find out whether he felt that the present Soviet booster capacity would enable lunar missions. He did not say that it would or would not, but he again repeated the phrase that present rocket technology would permit going to the moon.

Finally, he supported the suggestion in Lovell's letter, attributed to Keldysh, that there be an international discussion of the desirability of going to the moon. (We have elsewhere noted the disadvantages of such discussions from our own point of view.)

In summary, I believe that the Russians as well as we are having discussions on the value of manned lunar landing. I think it would be very dangerous to interpret what was said by Blagonravov at this lun-cheon as indicating that the Russians in fact had no lunar program but were just now discussing the possibility of beginning one. I do not believe that the manned lunar program is under the direction or control of the Soviet Academy of Sciences. Quite to the contrary, I am con-vinced that it is a program originated and operated by the military. Therefore we must be very cautious in interpreting statements which come only from the Soviet Academy of Sciences.

Hugh L. Dryden[4]

---

[4] Printed from a copy that indicates Dryden signed the original.

405.   Memorandum From the President's Special Assistant for
        National Security Affairs (Bundy) to President Kennedy[1]

Washington, September 18, 1963.

SUBJECT

Your 11 a.m. appointment with Jim Webb

Webb called me yesterday to comment on three interconnected aspects of the space problem that he thinks may be of importance in his talk with you:[2]

1. *Money.* The space authorization is passed at $5,350 billion, and he expects the appropriation to come out at about $5,150 billion. While the estimates are not complete, his current guess is that in early 64 he will require a supplemental of $400 million ($200 million requiring authorization and $200 million appropriation only) in order to keep our commitment to a lunar landing in the 1960's.

2. *The Soviets.* He reports more forthcoming noises about cooperation from Blagonravov in the UN, and I am trying to run down a report in today's *Times* (attached) that we have rebuffed the Soviets on this.[3] Webb himself is quite open to an exploration of possible cooperation with the Soviets and thinks that they might wish to use our big rocket, and offer in exchange the advanced technology which they are likely to get in the immediate future. (For example, Webb expects a Soviet landing of instruments on the moon to establish moon-earth communications almost any time.)

The obvious choice is whether to press for cooperation or to continue to use the Soviet space effort as a spur to our own. The *Times* story suggests that there is already low-level disagreement on exactly this point.

3. *The Military Role.* Webb reports that the discontent of the military with their limited role in space damaged the bill on the Hill this year, with no corresponding advantage to the military. He thinks this point can and should be made to the Air Force, and he believes that the thing to do is to offer the military an increased role somehow. He has already had private exploratory talks with Ros Gilpatric for this purpose.

---

[1] Source: NASA Historical Reference Collection. No classification marking. Also printed in *Exploring the Unknown,* Volume II: *External Relationships,* pp. 165–166.

[2] Webb's meeting with the President took place between 11:30 a.m. and 12:20 p.m. (Kennedy Library, President's Appointment Books.) No record of this meeting has been found.

[3] Not printed. The article, entitled "U.S. Aide Rebuffs Soviet's Moon Bid," mentioned that Dr. Robert R. Gilruth, Director of NASA's Manned Space Flight Center, had called a joint U.S.-Soviet lunar expedition impractical.

Webb thinks the best place for a military effort in space would be in the design and manning of a space craft in which gravity could be simulated, in preparation for later explorations. He thinks such a space craft may be the next logical step after Gemini. On the other hand, he is quite cool about the use of Titan III and Dinosoar and would be glad to see them both cancelled. You will recall that McNamara has just come out on the other side on Titan III.

My own hasty judgment is that the central question here is whether to compete or to cooperate with the Soviets in a manned lunar landing:

1. *If we compete,* we should do everything we can to unify all agencies of the United States Government in a combined space program which comes as near to our existing pledges as possible.

2. *If we cooperate,* the pressure comes off, and we can easily argue that it was our crash effort in '61 and '62 which made the Soviets ready to cooperate.

I am for cooperation if it is possible, and I think we need to make a really major effort inside and outside the government to find out whether in fact it can be done. Conceivably this is a better job for Harriman than East-West trade, which might almost as well be given to George Ball.

McG. B.

---

406. Letter From the Deputy Under Secretary of State for Political Affairs (Johnson) to the Administrator of the National Aeronautics and Space Administration (Webb)[1]

Washington, October 14, 1963.

Dear Jim:

With reference to our conversation on how best to follow up on the President's proposal before the United Nations General Assembly that we should explore the possibilities of cooperation with the Soviets in manned exploration of the moon,[2] I suggest we should have as clear an

---

[1] Source: National Archives and Records Administration, RG 59, Central Files 1960–63, SP 10. Confidential. Drafted by Richard F. Packard on October 10 and retyped in S/S-S on October 14.

[2] President Kennedy addressed the 18th UN General Assembly on September 20. During his speech, he suggested that a joint U.S.-Soviet expedition to the moon might be possible. See *Public Papers of the Presidents of the United States: John F. Kennedy, 1963,* p. 695.

understanding of the broad technical and programmatic aspects as is possible at this time.

We have as yet not received any official response to the President's proposal, and it seems doubtful that the Soviets will soon bring themselves to face up to the severe security, programmatic and political problems involved in discussing such a joint undertaking. Nonetheless we should be as fully prepared to deal with any response which may be forthcoming from them as we have been throughout the Dryden–Blagonravov discussions to date.

We would therefore appreciate receiving NASA's views as soon as possible. We have in mind, for example, such considerations as the following:

1. What modes of cooperation would be useful? Which would be practicable? Which would be most advantageous from the viewpoint of our national program? Which would appear to be most likely to evoke a constructive response from the Soviets?

2. What significant effects upon our Gemini and Apollo programs should we anticipate? What measure of commitment or diversion of our national program should be entailed?

3. What assurances ought we to require? How could cooperation be developed so as to provide adequate assurances at each significant step before proceeding to the next, or so as to be able to disengage with minimum adverse effects?

4. Should we proceed along the lines already laid out for the Dryden–Blagonravov discussions, or should we proceed on a different basis in this instance?

I would propose that after you have had an opportunity to formulate your views on the foregoing questions and any others that you may consider pertinent, to call a meeting to include other interested agencies at which we would seek to formulate general terms of reference for dealing with any Soviet response.

Sincerely,

Alex[3]

---

[3] Printed from a copy that indicates Johnson signed the original.

407. **Memorandum From the Deputy Director (Intelligence), Central Intelligence Agency (Cline) to the President's Special Assistant for National Security Affairs (Bundy)**[1]

Washington, October 29, 1963.

SUBJECT

Khrushchev and the Soviet Lunar Program

The Khrushchev Statement on 25 October

1. The reports published in the US press on 27 October stating that Khrushchev has "withdrawn" from the "moon race" not only distorted the import of his actual remarks but conveyed a misleading impression that a major change in Soviet lunar plans had recently taken place.[2]

2. In reply to a question that had been submitted in advance as to whether a Soviet flight to the moon "is planned for the not too distant future," Khrushchev said, "I cannot at present say when this will be done." He added that the USSR is not "at present planning" such an operation, but indicated that Soviet scientists are working on the problem and that the necessary research is being done." Khrushchev noted that the Americans "want to land a man on the moon by 1970" and wished them success. After saying the Soviets would observe US experience, particularly how the Americans contrive to "return home," Khrushchev indicated that the USSR did not want to compete in "sending people to the moon without careful preparation." He contended that no benefits would be derived from competition which might result in the "destruction of people." He concluded with a statement that "much work will have to be done and good preparations made for a successful flight to the moon by man."

3. This is not the first time that Khrushchev has voiced skepticism regarding the feasibility of a manned lunar landing. Khrushchev's remarks on 25 October bear a close resemblance to views he has expressed over the past two years. In an interview with Cyrus Sulzberger in September 1961, he said the USSR had no fixed schedule and that the problem was not landing a man on the moon

---

[1] Source: Kennedy Library, National Security Files, Departments and Agencies Series, Space Activities, General, 10/63–11/63, Box 308. Secret.

[2] On October 26 Chairman Khrushchev told the Third World Meeting of Journalists in Moscow that the Soviet Union had no plans for a manned flight to the moon, although Soviet scientists were studying the problems involved. See *Current Digest of the Soviet Press*, Vol. XV, No. 43, p. 19.

but "getting him off again."[3] Khrushchev told Gardner Cowles in April 1962 that he could "not give any date" for a manned lunar flight and spoke of the "many different problems" and great cost involved in this mission.[4] Khrushchev's remarks last Friday also parallel views deliberately given to Western scientists by Soviet scientific officials earlier this year. These views alleged that Soviet scientists, at least for the time being, regard manned lunar missions as unfeasible.

4. The similarity between Khrushchev's remarks to Sulzberger and Cowles and his statements last Friday casts doubt on the assumption that the Soviet leaders have taken some major decisions in recent weeks affecting the scope or pace of their lunar program. In these interviews, Khrushchev indicated that Soviet scientists were working in this field and that they were encountering many problems. In effect, he attempted to create the impression that the Soviets were not engaged in an extensive high-priority program along the lines, for example, of Project Apollo.

Political Aims

5. Since all the questions answered by Khrushchev in his press conference were submitted in advance, it must be assumed that he had some specific purpose in mind in commenting on the Soviet lunar program at this time. Internally, the Soviet consumer's current situation and prospects are poor, and Khrushchev may have wished to reassure the population that large sums were not being spent in non-productive projects. Externally, one of Khrushchev's main objectives in agreeing to the test ban treaty and encouraging a détente atmosphere in East-West relations is to retard the pace of the arms and technological race, thereby relieving some of the pressures on Soviet resources. Against this background of general Soviet policy, we would interpret Khrushchev's deliberate effort to downgrade the urgency of a manned lunar landing as being aimed at influencing US Congressional and public opinion on the question of the expenditures and pace of the US lunar program. Khrushchev also is making it clear that the Soviet Union is unwilling to allow the United States to set the terms for competition in space.

Scientific and Technical Factors

6. The USSR has been energetically pursuing a space program which includes lunar exploration. However, launch capabilities still depend on the only large boost vehicle so far developed in the USSR.

---

[3] This interview took place in Moscow on September 5, 1961. See *The New York Times,* September 8, 1961, p. 1.

[4] This interview took place in Moscow on April 20, 1962. See ibid., April 25, 1962, p. 1.

This booster is not powerful enough for manned lunar landing missions, nor can it serve as a building block for such missions.

7. We have not detected development or testing of a larger vehicle. We believe that a larger engine is under development but we do not know whether it will be suitable for a manned lunar landing. In any case, we believe we would know if it were approaching flight testing. Other technical indicators of a high priority lunar landing program are also lacking.

8. At the same time, Soviet efforts to carry out the unmanned space reconnaissance which could relate to a manned lunar landing continue, despite repeated failures.

Economic Factors

9. Khrushchev and other Soviet officials have often expressed concern in the past over the high cost of a manned lunar landing program. In recent years Soviet military and space expenditures have placed a heavy burden on the economy. Moreover, these expenditures have grown at a considerably faster pace than the economy as a whole. The impact has also been severe in terms of competition for high quality manpower and materials. Even though some costly military programs are approaching completion, pursuit of a high-priority manned lunar landing program would aggravate and prolong the present period of serious economic strain in the USSR. Unless the Soviets have made greater technical progress toward a manned lunar landing than we now perceive, we believe that present economic stringencies are a considerable argument against attempting to compete with the US Apollo program.

Conclusion

10. We think that the primary intent of Khrushchev's statement was to change the focus of the space race. Present evidence, while far from conclusive, suggests that the USSR is not now trying to land a man on the moon in advance of the Apollo program. If this is so, then Khrushchev is trying to discount this American achievement in advance, and perhaps delay it as well, while intending to sustain Soviet prestige with a series of earlier, less expensive but still spectacular projects, such as the orbiting of a manned space station and a manned circumlunar flight.

Ray S. Cline

408.   Memorandum From the President's Special Assistant for Science and Technology (Wiesner) to President Kennedy[1]

Washington, October 29, 1963.

SUBJECT

   The US Proposal for a Joint US-USSR Lunar Program

I believe that Premier Khrushchev's statement of October 26 that the USSR does not plan to land a man on the moon gives us a unique opportunity to follow through on your UN proposal for a joint US-USSR program in a way that will not only be in accord with U.S. objectives for peaceful cooperation if accepted by the USSR, but will also decisively dispel the doubts that have existed in the Congress and the press about the sincerity and feasibility of the proposal itself. Specifically, I would propose a joint program in which the USSR provides unmanned exploratory and logistic support for the U.S. Apollo manned landing. I believe such a program would utilize the combined resources of US and USSR in a technically practical manner and might, in view of Premier Khrushchev's statement, be politically attractive to him.

The manned lunar program encompasses much more than the manned landing vehicle itself. The PSAC space panels have consistently emphasized the importance of the unmanned lunar exploration program to develop technical information about the lunar surface. This information appears critical to a successful manned landing. The U.S. unmanned program hinges around the Surveyor program which at best is a marginal one. At the present time its estimated payload had dropped to 65 pounds and its schedule is unreliable. The Soviet Union, however, apparently has a substantial capability at this time for this type of exploratory mission. A joint program which would use this capability would be very valuable to us.

More directly involved with the manned landing itself is a vehicle and spacecraft for placing a large stock of supplies and equipment at the site of the manned landing. NASA and the PSAC space panels all agree that the 24–48 hours staytime provided by Apollo does not permit the astronauts to conduct significant scientific exploration. It is agreed that to make Apollo a useful scientific endeavor an additional 7000

---

[1] Source: Kennedy Library, National Security Files, Departments and Agencies Series, Space Activities, General, 10/63–11/63, Box 308. Confidential. In an October 30 covering memorandum to Bundy, Wiesner noted that it might be advantageous for the President to reply as soon as possible, and that it should be possible for NASA to produce an outline of a joint program.

pounds of equipment and supplies must be landed at his site to permit him 5 to 7 days of useful scientific exploration before he returns to earth. This logistic support requires another large vehicle and spacecraft to be available on about the same time schedule as Apollo. The U.S. development program to provide this capability has not yet been initiated. If the Soviet Union could be convinced that the logistic support was indeed an essential and integral part of the manned landing and persuaded to provide this support system, the resulting program would again result in an effective use of combined resources. The Apollo program would remain a purely U.S. technical program without modification of present plans. A Russian could easily be included as a member of the landing team without complicating the engineering effort. In addition, the proposal would have the practical value of minimizing requirements for complicated joint engineering projects and launching operations and would emphasize the exchange of plans, information and possibly people.

If we assume that Premier Khrushchev is telling the truth (and I believe that he is), this proposal will give the USSR the opportunity of sharing in the credit for a successful lunar mission without incurring major expenditures much beyond those that they probably plan to undertake as part of their present space program. By not including joint engineering and launching activities, the proposal minimizes the security impact on the USSR that undoubtedly acts as a restraint on joint activities because of the close association of the Soviet space and military missile programs.

It is true that the above proposal assumes that the USSR would be willing to follow the now well established U.S. operational plan for manned lunar exploration. This did not seem reasonable as long as it appeared likely that Russia had a well developed program of her own. Now, however, Premier Khrushchev's statement, whether it is true or not, makes such a proposal by the United States reasonable from every standpoint. The proposal now not only offers a program which truly enhances the manned lunar exploration effort while leaving the Apollo program intact, but also one which ought to be acceptable to the USSR.

It might be extremely advantageous for you to publicly offer this plan to the USSR as a specific proposal for a joint program, formulated in the light of Premier Khrushchev's statement and designed to effectively combine the resources of both countries. The effectiveness of the offer would be enhanced if it were made while Khrushchev's statement is still fresh in the mind of the public. If the proposal is accepted we will have established a practical basis for cooperative program. If it is rejected we will have demonstrated our desire for peaceful cooperation and the sincerity of our original proposal.

If you believe this proposal has merit, I suggest that you request that NASA prepare as soon as possible a specific plan along these lines for your consideration.[2]

Jerome B. Wiesner[3]

---

[2] During his news conference of October 31, President Kennedy expressed skepticism about Premier Khrushchev's claim that the Soviet Union was no longer in a race to the moon. He also said, "I think we ought to stay with our program. I think that is the best answer to Mr. Khrushchev." See *Public Papers of the Presidents of the United States: John F. Kennedy, 1963,* p. 832.

[3] Printed from a copy that bears this typed signature.

---

409.   Memorandum From the President's Special Assistant (Schlesinger) to the President's Special Assistant for National Security Affairs (Bundy)[1]

Washington, November 7, 1963.

In view of Moscow's #1542[2] (discussing Khrushchev's apparent acceptance in principle of the idea of a joint moon shot), it would seem important that NASA undertake serious studies as to how lunar collaboration might be worked out. On Tuesday, Harlan Cleveland, Dick Gardner and I met with Hugh Dryden and a number of his colleagues. My impression is that NASA remains rather negative about the whole idea, and that an expression of Presidential interest in their progress in planning for it might be appropriate.[3]

At present they have under way a paper, prepared at State's request, analyzing the stages which might be involved in exploring whether collaboration might be possible. This paper is procedural rather than substantive in character. It proposes three stages:

---

[1] Source: Kennedy Library, National Security Files, Departments and Agencies Series, Space Activities, General, 10/63–11/63, Box 308. Confidential.

[2] Not printed.

[3] On November 9 Schlesinger sent Bundy a second memorandum reading: "I think it might help the current State Department–NASA debate if you could send a memorandum along the following lines to Harlan Cleveland: 'I trust that Governor Stevenson's speech in the UNGA space debate will include an adequate follow-up of the President's moon proposal.'" (Kennedy Library, National Security Files, Departments and Agencies Series, Space Activities, General, 10/63–11/63, Box 308) Regarding Stevenson's speech, see footnote 3, Document 412.

a) full and serious exchange of information on existing experience with manned space flight;

b) exchange of "gross information" regarding planning for manned lunar flight;

c) more specific description by both sides of their manned lunar programs.

The distinction between (b) and (c) was not clear to Cleveland and me, even when explained by Dryden. NASA points out that none of these stages involves significant security problems for us, since we have published a good deal of the information anyway; but that they would all involve more or less significant security problems for the USSR.

The NASA view is that eventual substantive steps would depend on the confidence established by these early procedural steps. The substantive steps, they say, would involve significant security questions for us. And, in general, they were most bearish about the technical feasibility of what they called "integration of hardware"—i.e., the "marriage" of the American and Soviet programs on the "hardware level." When Cleveland suggested that "integration of personnel" might be an alternative means of carrying out (sorry, "implementing") the President's suggestion, the NASA people acted almost as if this were a new thought. However, they rallied gamely and were soon pointing out how impossible this would be too.

Eventually Dryden thought that it might be a good idea to have a General Assembly resolution endorsing the idea of a joint moon expedition, thereby tacitly bringing pressure on the Soviet Union to join up. This suggests that the NASA mind is not totally closed to the President's proposal. But I would think that a call from you to Dryden and an expression of White House interest in *substantive* planning as well as in exploratory procedures would be a good idea.

Arthur

410.   **National Security Action Memorandum No. 271**[1]

Washington, November 12, 1963.

MEMORANDUM FOR

The Administrator, National Aeronautics and Space Administration

SUBJECT

Cooperation with the USSR on Outer Space Matters

I would like you to assume personally the initiative and central responsibility within the Government for the development of a program of substantive cooperation with the Soviet Union in the field of outer space, including the development of specific technical proposals. I assume that you will work closely with the Department of State and other agencies as appropriate.

These proposals should be developed with a view to their possible discussion with the Soviet Union as a direct outcome of my September 20 proposal for broader cooperation between the United States and the USSR in outer space, including cooperation in lunar landing programs. All proposals or suggestions originating within the Government relating to this general subject will be referred to you for your consideration and evaluation.

In addition to developing substantive proposals, I expect that you will assist the Secretary of State in exploring problems of procedure and timing connected with holding discussions with the Soviet Union and in proposing for my consideration the channels which would be most desirable from our point of view. In this connection the channel of contact developed by Dr. Dryden between NASA and the Soviet Academy of Sciences has been quite effective, and I believe that we should continue to utilize it as appropriate as a means of continuing the dialogue between the scientists of both countries.

I would like an interim report on the progress of our planning by December 15.

John F. Kennedy

---

[1] See Document 407. Source: National Archives and Records Administration, RG 59, S/S–NSC Files: Lot 72 D 316, NSAM No. 271. Confidential. Copies were sent to the Chairman of the National Aeronautics and Space Council, the Secretaries of State and Defense, the Director of Central Intelligence, the Chairman of the Atomic Energy Commission, the Director of the National Science Foundation, the Special Assistant to the President for Science and Technology, the Director of the Bureau of the Budget, and the Director of the U.S. Information Agency. Also printed in *Exploring the Unknown*, Volume II: *External Relationships*, pp. 166–167.

411.   Memorandum From the Assistant Secretary of State for International Organization Affairs (Cleveland) to Acting Secretary of State Ball[1]

Washington, November 20, 1963.

SUBJECT

In Outer Space, Too, It Takes Two To Tango

As I mentioned in our recent conversation, my colleagues and I have tried to sort out what Adlai Stevenson could appropriately say, in his basic General Assembly speech on Outer Space next week, about the President's September 20 proposal that manned flight to the moon be a cooperative, rather than competitive, affair.[2] The following is a suggested line of approach on which I should appreciate your comments:

1. Last September the President made a formal and consciously dramatic public offer to the Soviet Union to cooperate in putting men on the moon, saying:

"Finally, in a field where the United States and the Soviet Union have a special capacity—in the field of space—there is room for new cooperation, for further joint efforts in the regulation and exploration of space. I include among these possibilities a joint expedition to the moon. Space offers no problems of sovereignty; by resolution of this Assembly, the members of the United Nations have forsworn any claim to territorial rights in outer space or on celestial bodies and declared that international law and the United Nations Charter will apply. Why, therefore, should man's first flight to the moon be a matter of national competition? Why should the United States and the Soviet Union, in preparing for such expeditions, become involved in immense duplications of research, construction, and expenditure? Surely we should explore whether the scientists and astronauts of our two countries—indeed, of all the world—cannot work together in the conquest of space, sending some day in this decade to the moon not the representatives of a single nation but the representatives of all of our countries."

2. This month, the United States and the Soviet Union have completed negotiations on an agreed statement of legal principles for outer space which, among other things, solemnly declares":

—that "in the exploration of outer space States shall be guided by the principle of cooperation and mutual assistance . . ."; and

---

[1] Source: National Archives and Records Administration, RG 59, Central Files 1960–63, SP 6 UN. Confidential. Drafted by T. Wilson (IO) on November 19. Copies were sent to Ambassador Llewellyn E. Thompson, William R. Tyler, Walt W. Rostow, and Ragnar Rollefson.

[2] See footnote 3, Document 412.

—that "States shall regard astronauts as envoys of mankind in outer space . . ."

These principles reflect the semantic value—and the political force—of "international cooperation".

3. In the meantime, Chairman Khrushchev has maneuvered himself into this public position: he is not racing the Americans to the moon because life on earth is so good that he is not in that much of a hurry and, because he doesn't want to risk human life; he has a large and active moonlanding project on the boards which he fully expects to succeed but which is unencumbered by a rigid time schedule; he sees limits to the possibility of cooperation because of the secrecy unhappily engendered by the arms race, but he is interested in the President's offer. This would seem to rule out the possibility—suggested by the President—of "a joint expedition to the moon".

Mr. Khrushchev's somewhat erratic statements no doubt reflect internal differences in the Soviet leadership over the desirability of cooperation with the U.S. They may also reflect financial difficulties. And they may reflect indecision about scientific problems in connection with a lunar landing—or even a conviction that the Soviet Union cannot get there first.

4.   Nevertheless, this is a well-thought-out position from Khrushchev's point of view. If the Americans succeed in landing and recovering the first man from the surface of the moon by 1970, the resulting national prestige will be modified by the fact that we did not win "victory" in a "race" against the Russians; we simply—if dramatically—met a self-imposed deadline—and self-restraint would inhibit global gloating about that.

If the Americans put the first man on the moon *after* 1970 the resultant prestige will be further modified by the fact that we got there late according to our own timetable.

If the Soviets put the first man on the moon, the resultant prestige for the Soviets would be greatly amplified by the fact that they did not get there first because they were racing with the Americans but because their technology was so far ahead that there was no point in waiting around.

If the Americans should try first and fail—and especially if this involved loss of life—Khrushchev not only would appear to have better judgment but could express his sympathies in the garb of the true humanitarian.

By postulating that it takes two to make a race, Khrushchev has put himself in the best position available in the circumstances—unless it can be demonstrated that it is he who is declining international cooperation.

5. Given the alternative outcomes it seems clear that net national U.S. advantage lies in sticking with the policy of going to the moon as quickly as possible—alone if need be but preferably with the maximum feasible international cooperation—without the Russians if need be but preferably with them. Credit would accrue to the U.S. for national success in sending an American to be the first man on the moon; even greater credit, in the minds of most non-Americans, would accrue to the nation which leads a cooperative enterprise and makes the leading contribution to it.

6. But if it takes two to race, it also takes two to cooperate. The President has committed the United States to try to pursue that course; the door has not been closed on all hope for cooperation; the ball is back in our court; the U.S. Delegate is scheduled to speak in the U.N. Outer Space Committee next week; and if the U.S. were to go silent on a dialogue initiated by the President, the conclusion no doubt will be drawn that the President has given in to advocates of noncooperation. So having made an offer of maximum cooperation—a joint U.S.-USSR flight to the moon—the U.S. can hardly fail to push for lesser forms of cooperation.

7. The principal objections raised to cooperation on our side—and no doubt on the other—seem to be (a) that technology is too far advanced to marry up U.S. and Soviet space exploration systems; (b) that joint teams of astronauts are not feasible for technical and training reasons; (c) that there are military security problems; and (d) that the U.S. [the USSR] cannot be in a position of having its program stymied by the failure of the Soviets [the Americans][3] to carry out projects allocated to it under a cooperative program.

8. These objections—even when accepted at full face value—do not themselves preclude effective steps toward achievement of the President's stated objective of exploring "whether the scientists and astronauts of our two countries—indeed of all the world—cannot work together in the conquest of space . . ."

9. It is assumed that the Soviet Union has much more difficulty with the mere thought of cooperation than we do and that they will have more serious "security problems" at any realistic level of cooperation than we will have—for all the reasons flowing from the fact that they run a closed society and we run an open society. We therefore can take it for granted, with considerable confidence, that the Russians will in no event be willing to go so far as to raise serious military security problems for us: we are safe in shooting for the maximum amount of cooperation that the Soviets can be talked into yielding.[4]

---

[3] Brackets in the source text.

[4] A handwritten marginal note reads: "depends on who is to do what in coop. venture."

It therefore is important that—while detailed negotiations would be largely bilateral—we egg on the Russians to cooperate in an open forum where the maximum influence of the on-looking world community could be brought to bear.[5]

10. To pursue U.S. policy of going to the moon with the maximum amount of international cooperation that will not interfere with our program, our next objective should be not to *integrate* the two national lunar programs but to *add them up* together with the efforts of other nations, into a *world program of lunar exploration* in which both prestige and failure could be to some extent shared—in which the scientists and astronauts of all participating nations can "work together in the conquest of space" as "representatives of all our countries". This would have to be done in a way which does not require us to weld a U.S. capsule on a Russian rocket, or to mate a clean-cut American astronaut with a chubby Soviet cosmonette, or to compromise the security of either state, or to make progress of one national program dependent upon progress in the other.

The point is to put a largely symbolic international umbrella over *both* national programs, plus the contributions of other countries, and to create the image of a mutually cooperative world program to put men on the moon as "representatives of all our countries" regardless of the nationality of the first arrivals.

A good analogy is the "World Weather System" which will depend very largely upon U.S. and Soviet technology, which will maintain World Data Centers under national control in Washington and Moscow, but which enjoys the blessing and the nominal parenthood of the World Meteorological Organization and which draws into the program whatever supporting resources can be contributed by other countries.

Once the protective mantle of the international community is thrown over a project, symbolism and terminology can reinforce the desired impression. For example, if the Americans are ready to send out the first team, and the Russians the second and third teams, we could begin to refer to them as Moon Teams I, II, and III in the World Program for Lunar Exploration.

11. Neither nation would put aside its national program to work this out; negotiations could proceed on a subject-by-subject basis, taking the easiest ones first; national chips could be tossed into the international pot one at a time; and both sides could reserve the right to get acclimated to cooperation gradually. Cooperation could take the form of mutual support through coordinated national activities—cooperative tracking of astronauts, coordinated observation and sampling of the lunar surface, exchanges of information on man's biological performance in space.

---

[5] A handwritten marginal note reads: "not necessity."

If this approach does not work, the U.S. would get political credit for trying.

If it does work, U.S. interests would be furthered generally by another step toward de-fuzing the cold war, toward keeping outer space peaceful, toward engaging the Soviet Union in responsible mutual enterprise, toward building international institutions, toward an atmosphere more conducive to genuine measures of arms control and disarmament. More specifically, U.S. interests would be furthered by promoting that alternative outcome of the moon project in which net national advantage resides.

12. Meanwhile, and in any event, we should certainly get on with our own Apollo program. The fundamental reason for getting to the moon is not to beat the Russians but to get to the moon. Neither Congress nor the Administration should let Chairman Khrushchev influence the level of our appropriations or the degree of our resolve.

---

412. Memorandum From the Deputy Legal Adviser of the Department of State (Meeker) to the Deputy Under Secretary of State for Political Affairs (Johnson)[1]

Washington, December 4, 1963.

SUBJECT

Cooperation with the Soviets on a Joint Expedition to the Moon

In accordance with the suggestion of SCI, we are addressing to you our comments on the NASA paper of November 19, concerning cooperation with the Soviets on a joint expedition to the moon.[2]

President Kennedy in September included in his speech to the United Nations General Assembly a generalized proposal of United States-Soviet cooperation on a manned lunar landing. The proposal was referred to by Ambassador Stevenson in his speech of December 2 to the General Assembly's Political Committee. He said: "President Johnson has instructed me to reaffirm that offer today."[3]

---

[1] Source: National Archives and Records Administration, RG 59, Central Files 1960–63, SP 1–1 US–USSR. Confidential.

[2] Not found.

[3] For text of Ambassador Stevenson's speech, see Department of State *Bulletin*, December 30, 1963, pp. 1005–1012.

It is possible that the Soviets do not feel that they are called upon to make any particular reply to a proposal set forth and repeated in speeches before the United Nations. Therefore, it would seem advisable at some time early in 1964 to make a private bilateral approach to the USSR, asking whether the Soviets would like to discuss the possibilities of cooperation on a manned lunar landing.

Since Soviet performance is already overdue under the Dryden–Blagonravov Agreement, we would presumably not wish to propose further agreements until the Soviet attitude toward the existing arrangements has been clarified. This might be done in a high-level approach, by Ambassador Kohler or perhaps in a Presidential letter to Chairman Khrushchev, embodying the following elements:

1. The United States remains committed to the principle of international cooperation in outer space and believes that the United States and the USSR should work together constructively in the exploration of space;

2. The new Administration in this country fully intends to carry forward the implementation of the Dryden–Blagonravov Agreement, and wishes to confirm that the Soviet Government will do likewise;

3. If the Soviet Government shares these views, the United States proposes that there should be bilateral discussions to consider further prospects for United States-Soviet cooperation in space, to include, if the Soviet Government desires, a discussion of ways in which the two countries could work together toward a manned lunar landing.

We would want to know that the Soviets intend to go ahead with the Dryden–Blagonravov Agreement before we enter into discussions with them of more ambitious cooperative projects. And we would want to see actual performance by the Soviets under their existing commitments before we embarked on other programs of cooperation in space.

413.   **Letter From the Administrator of the National Aeronautics and Space Administration (Webb) to the Deputy Under Secretary of State for Political Affairs (Johnson)**[1]

Washington, December 18, 1963.

Dear Alex:

As you know, the President, in a National Security Action Memorandum dated November 12, directed me to take personal responsibility for the formulation of proposals for possible cooperation in space matters with the Soviet Union and for coordinating with other agencies as appropriate.

To establish a basis for a report to the President, I asked that a staff paper be prepared and circulated informally among several of the interested agencies, including your office. A number of helpful comments have now been received and incorporated. As it now stands, I believe the paper is responsive to your own letter of October 14. Accordingly, I am forwarding it to you herewith.[2]

I am asking Dr. Dryden to convene an interagency meeting as early as possible in January in order to provide for formal coordination of all interested offices, prior to forwarding a final report to the President.

While the enclosed paper is primarily concerned with the technical content of, and suitable framework for, possible discussions with the Soviet Union, some thought has also been given to the timing and channels appropriate for such discussions. I want to assure you, however, that we recognize fully the Department of State's responsibilities in this regard.

Sincerely yours,

James E. Webb

---

[1] Source: National Archives and Records Administration, RG 59, SCI Files: Lot 65 D 473, Box 1, SP 1–1, International Cooperation USSR. Confidential.

[2] For text of Webb's report, "US–USSR Cooperation in Space Research Programs," see *Exploring the Unknown*, Volume II: *External Relationships*, pp. 170–182.

Peaceful Uses of Outer Space

414. Memorandum From Secretary of State Rusk to President Kennedy[1]

Washington, February 2, 1961.

SUBJECT

United Nations Outer Space Activities

One matter on which I believe we might proceed promptly to probe Soviet willingness to set up reasonable arrangements for cooperation is the organization of the United Nations Committee on the Peaceful Uses of Outer Space, and initiation by the Committee of the planning of a U.N. scientific conference on the exploration and use of outer space, patterned on the Atoms-for-Peace conferences which have been successfully held in the past.

The General Assembly resolution which established the Committee and called for the conference was adopted in December 1959. A copy is enclosed.[2] The vote was unanimous since the resolution combined the U.S.-proposed Committee, which had an agreed membership, and the Soviet-proposed conference. In addition to planning the conference, the Committee is charged with studying scientific and technical cooperation and legal problems. The Committee does not have responsibilities in the disarmament field.

The Committee has not met because the Soviet Union has sought East-West parity in Committee and Conference offices and has held out for voting arrangements which would make possible Soviet obstruction of the Committee's work. Before the pre-Christmas recess of the General Assembly, agreement had been reached to postpone some of these issues, and only the voting issue was delaying the convening of the Committee. Early discussions by Ambassador Stevenson and Soviet Ambassador Zorin might result in further progress.

Pressing ahead with this matter is desirable. It is useful for the U.S. to continue to take the lead in space cooperation and to support implementation of the resolution which the General Assembly adopted. The

---

[1] Source: Kennedy Library, National Security Files, Subjects Series, United Nations, General, 1/61–7/61, Box 210. Confidential.

[2] Not printed. Resolution 1472 (XIV) was adopted unanimously by the UN General Assembly on December 12, 1959.

Committee would be the logical place to discuss the types of cooperative outer space proposals included in your State of the Union Message,
and we are now working out positions and detailed proposals. While
troublesome issues can of course be introduced by others in either the
technical or legal aspects of the Committee's work, such issues can in
any event be raised in the U.N. if there is a determination to do so, and
the Committee might provide a more favorable forum than the General
Assembly itself in which to rule such issues out of order or deal with
them on their merits.

The proposed conference has been considered in the interest of the
U.S. especially if we are successful in arranging for a broad agenda of
scientific and technical reports. A broad agenda would give the best
opportunity for the U.S. to make a favorable showing in the inevitable
competition with the Soviet Union since it would permit fuller appreciation of the variety of programs the U.S. has under way and of our freedom to discuss both our technology and the scientific results achieved.
The conference is not intended to take up legal and political issues.
Scientific and technical preparations for U.S. participation in the conference have been initiated by the National Aeronautics and Space
Administration in cooperation with the Department of Defense and
other agencies active in the peaceful exploration and use of outer space.
However, since about eight months would be required to complete
preparations, it will be necessary to proceed promptly with conference
planning and arrangements to meet the General Assembly's desire that
the Conference be held before the end of 1961.

In view of the nature of the work of the U.N. Committee and of the
proposed conference, we can proceed with these activities without prejudice to future reviews of our outer space programs, objectives, and
policies. This conclusion has the concurrence of the Department of
Defense, the National Aeronautics and Space Administration, and your
Special Assistant for Science and Technology.

If you approve, I will instruct Ambassador Stevenson to proceed
immediately with discussions with Ambassador Zorin and others in
New York in an attempt to get the U.N. Committee organized and conference planning under way.

Dean Rusk[3]

---

[3] Printed from a copy that bears this stamped signature.

415.   **Memorandum From the President's Special Assistant for National Security Affairs (Bundy) to Secretary of State Rusk**[1]

Washington, February 28, 1961.

SUBJECT

UN Outer Space Activities

We have been very slow in responding to your memorandum to the President dated February 2, 1961, which he handed to me for consideration, in the light of his State of the Union Message and its proposal of joint US-Soviet cooperation in space activities.

Since your memorandum was prepared, events in the United Nations, and in particular the Soviet Union's attitude toward that organization, have raised a question over here as to whether we really want to take active steps in that particular forum on this particular issue, with the Soviet Union, at this time. My own feeling is that the President would be reluctant to see us move in this direction now.

In our planning meeting with George McGhee, it was agreed that Jerry Wiesner should be asked to take the lead in planning on the general problem of relations with the Soviet Union in this and other scientific fields, and I believe he is at work on this business now, in cooperation with Whitman and others in the Department of State. Unless you press again, therefore, I think we might wait until we hear from this group.

Obviously, if you people feel that this matter is more urgent and that we have not understood it correctly, the matter can be put to the President again.

McGeorge Bundy[2]

---

[1] Source: Kennedy Library, National Security Files, Departments and Agencies Series, Space Activities, General, 1/61–3/61, Box 307. Confidential.

[2] Printed from a copy that bears this typed signature.

416.   Letter From the President's Special Assistant for Science and Technology (Wiesner) to the Assistant Secretary of State for International Organization Affairs (Cleveland)[1]

Washington, August 30, 1961.

Dear Harlan:

I am enclosing a summary of the meeting held in this office on Monday to review planning for the UN Assembly.[2] This memorandum was prepared by Dr. Robert F. Bacher in his capacity as Chairman of the ad hoc group and represents conclusions drawn from the day-long review, primarily relating to outer space, which you attended.

These conclusions suggest that at least two significant policy changes are called for in current planned positions, and they are indicated as comments to a marked-up copy of the Draft Resolution on Outer Space.[3] The first change would eliminate the attempt to stigmatize carriers of weapons of mass destruction, and thereby develop a legal distinction on orbiting satellites that would be patently favorable to the U. S.; in its comments, the group indicated that such an attempt would be ineffectual and inappropriate in its present context.

A second suggested change involves the procedure for developing a competent UN body to effectuate international cooperation in space: the group would have the Secretary General's Science Advisory Committee conduct the essential preliminary planning and aid in the process of securing Assembly support.

Behind the group's dissatisfaction with the reference in the Draft Resolution to weapons of mass destruction was a strong feeling that there is no evidence of adequate political-military planning to prepare for the availability of the U. S. satellite reconnaissance systems, Midas and Samos. Accordingly, the group recommends that "the Department of State and other interested agencies should prepare a thorough analysis of situations in which the Midas–Samos issue is likely to arise and a study of the gains and losses of alternative U.S. responses." I have raised this proposal in conversation with Arthur Schlesinger.

The comment on other subjects for initiative is limited, although some judgments are made. Most members of the group thought that a

---

[1] Source: Kennedy Library, Cleveland Papers, Outer Space, 18th GA Initiative, Box 20. Confidential.

[2] Not printed. The discussion centered around a position paper prepared in the Bureau of International Organization Affairs entitled "An Initiative on Outer Space at the 16th Session of the General Assembly." See Document 417.

[3] The draft resolution was Tab A of the position paper, Document 417.

more detailed position on meteorology would have been helpful for an adequate review, especially in the case of the proposed Meteorological Commission. If you think it would be helpful, this Office would be prepared to convene an ad hoc working panel within the next few days to consider the nature and functions of a competent UN body.

Perhaps two additional nuances to the current plans are worth consideration. There is a possibility, which we are exploring, that a useful role through the UN could be worked out for U.S. navigational satellites for ships. The Navy is responsible for our program and will be sounded out by this Office.

In addition, it is possible that the marked-up Draft Resolution or another without reference to the weapons question could be acceptable to the Russians. Would there be any value to introducing it with them, as a *joint resolution*, if they could be brought along?

Sincerely,

Jerry

417. Position Paper Prepared in the Bureau of International Organization Affairs[1]

Washington, undated.

AN INITIATIVE ON OUTER SPACE AT THE 16th SESSION OF THE GENERAL ASSEMBLY

The attached plan for United Nations Consideration of Outer Space matters outlines a number of initiatives which the United States has the opportunity to take in this field at the Sixteenth Session of the General Assembly. These would represent an important step in implementation of the position the President has taken with respect to international cooperation in outer space and in connection with meteorological and communications satellite systems.

In his January 30th message, the President stated "this Administration intends to explore promptly all possible areas of coop-

---

[1] Source: Kennedy Library, National Security Files, Subjects Series, United Nations, General, 9/61, Box 310. Confidential. Drafted by Richard N. Gardner, Oliver S. Crosby, Elmore Jackson (all of IO), and Herbert L. Reis (L).

eration with the Soviet Union and other nations 'to invoke the wonders of science instead of its terrors'".[2] He then extended an invitation to all nations to join with the United States in developing a weather prediction program and a new communications satellite program. Later, in his statement on communications satellite policy, he again invited "all nations to participate in a communications satellite system, in the interest of world peace and closer brotherhood among peoples throughout the world."[3]

The attached plan, in brief, calls for the United States to: a) outline to the General Assembly our efforts in the development of communications and meteorological satellites and our plans for international cooperation in their use, and b) present a set of proposals relating to the establishment of a regime of peace and law in Outer Space.

United States proposals relating to peace and law in outer space will serve to strengthen the role of the United Nations in this new field and will represent an effort to curb extension of the harmful consequences of the cold war to the dimension of space. These proposals, together with United States initiatives with regard to cooperative sharing in the field of communications and weather satellites, will contrast strongly with the approach the Soviets have adopted in outer space thus far and will help build legitimacy for outer space activities which the United States wishes to undertake. It is important, for example, to set the stage now for general acceptance of the world-wide communications system which the United States will want to establish by the middle of the present decade and to elicit essential foreign cooperation in regard to allocation of frequencies, establishment of ground terminals, financial support, rate-making, etc.

By taking the initiative in the sharing of its achievements in these areas, the United States can demonstrate that it has the vision and generosity to match its technical accomplishments.

The principal cautionary consideration in developing such an initiatives plan is that the United States should not overcommit itself. In this interest various modifications have been made to an earlier draft of the proposal in an effort to bring it in line with present and estimated future capabilities in these fields.

---

[2] See *Public Papers of the Presidents of the United States: John F. Kennedy, 1961*, p. 26.
[3] See ibid., p. 530.

Attachment

PLAN FOR UNITED NATIONS CONSIDERATION OF OUTER SPACE MATTERS

During the 16th session of the General Assembly the United States would set forth its view of the importance of the role of the United Nations in outer space, would outline United States plans and efforts regarding projects of direct interest to all nations, and would present a set of proposals relating to outer space.

A. Advocacy of a Regime of Peace and Law in Outer Space.

The United States would make clear that we seek a regime of peace and law in outer space and the development of practices, principles and agreements on which such a regime can rest. In this connection, the United States would make the following points:

1) Outer space begins at least as close to the surface of the earth as the region in which satellites may be maintained in orbit.

2) International law, and, in particular, the Purposes and Principles of the United Nations Charter, have application to outer space and celestial bodies.

3) Outer space and celestial bodies are available for exploration and use by all States, in conformity with the principles of international law, and are not subject to national appropriation by claim of sovereignty or otherwise.

4) The benefits of the peaceful exploration and use of outer space should accrue to all mankind. To this end, international cooperation in Outer Space should be maximized.

5) As a first step to keep the arms race from extending to outer space, States examining the question of disarmament should include in their discussions the desirability of the early establishment of effective measures to ensure that weapons of mass destruction are not stationed in outer space or on celestial bodies.

6) The United Nations has an important role to play in facilitating and regulating outer space activities.

7) States launching objects into orbit or sustained space flight should transmit to the Secretary-General, as early as practicable, information concerning such launchings together with data relevant for the purpose of identification of such objects.

8) There should be established within the United Nations Secretariat a small expert group which would:

a) Register all objects launched into orbit or sustained space transit, together with a record of information relating to such objects and facilitating their identification;

b) Communicate, upon request, available information concerning launchings, together with data relevant for identification, to Members of the United Nations and of the Specialized Agencies;

c) Serve as a clearing house of the exchange of scientific, technical and other information relating to outer space activities;

d) Assist in formulating proposals for the promotion of international cooperation in outer space activities;

e) Advise the Secretary-General in matters pertaining to outer space activities;

f) Perform such other functions of a technical nature as may be relevant to the international use of outer space;

g) To these ends, maintain contact with Members of the United Nations and of the Specialized Agencies and with governmental and non-governmental organizations concerned with outer space.

The attached draft resolution (Tab A)[4] embodying the points outlined above would be submitted for General Assembly consideration.

B. Fostering of Other International Cooperation in Outer Space.

Reemphasizing our view that the exploration and use of space are ultimately a venture on behalf of the human race as a whole, the United States should inform the General Assembly that we are devoting special attention to space activities which are fully expected to become, over a period of years, of widespread practical benefit. We would point out that both in the case of meteorological and communications applications of satellites, we will need not only to perfect the complex ground and space-borne instruments; we will also need to develop workable international cooperative arrangements.

1) In the field of communications, it should be stated that:

a) The United States views the communications satellite as a tool for improving communications and thereby mutual understanding throughout the world. We wish to see our research efforts lead to the establishment of a system which will over a period of years achieve global coverage and maximum linking of the countries of the world. We wish to see United Nations Members not only use the system, but also participate in its ownership and operation if they so desire. We are seeking practical ways to do this. We have already begun to enlist the aid of other countries in the experiments we are now planning, and we shall extend our efforts to include additional countries as this becomes practical.

b) Bearing in mind the importance of preventing space activities from widening the gap between the technologically advanced nations and other nations, we hope that the communications satellite can help meet the needs of developing as well as developed areas. To this end,

---

[4] Not printed.

the United States stands ready to support the technical assistance program of the International Telecommunication Union and to take other appropriate measures to give technical and financial assistance to less developed countries for the development of their domestic communications facilities so that they can take advantage of the world-wide system of space communications.

c) We believe that the United Nations will itself play a constructive role. As the problems of using this new tool are identified, the United Nations should deal effectively with them. A pressing problem which can be met by an existing specialized agency (the International Telecommunication Union) is the allocation of radio frequencies. We believe the ITU conference now *tentatively* scheduled for 1963 should in fact be called and that sufficient progress will have been made by that time to provide the basis for action which will accommodate the interests of all nations in ensuring the optimum use of the limited radio frequencies.

d) In our view special arrangements should be made to service the communications needs of the United Nations through this new system. This might be done in many ways. Communications satellites could provide rapid, reliable communications for United Nations emergency operations such as that in the Congo. They could provide for direct television contact between the United Nations Secretary General and foreign government leaders; conferences between heads of government might be conducted through this medium if the necessity arose. To generate world-wide understanding of vital issues before the United Nations, provision should be made for television and radio relay of United Nations Security Council and General Assembly sessions and information programs of the United Nations Department of Public Affairs. The United States hopes that by the Fall of 1962 one of our experimental satellites will be capable, for brief periods, of transmitting across the Atlantic live television reports of debates in the General Assembly.

2) In the field of *meteorology*, The United States would state that:

a) Scientific and technological developments in the atmospheric sciences have been extraordinarily rapid in recent years, due in large part to applications of electronic computers, instrumented balloons, rockets, satellites, and several indirect methods for probing the atmosphere. Furthermore, advances in physical theory and computer techniques make it now possible to study the atmosphere in unprecedented scope and detail. This progress opens the way for improvement of the scientific basis of weather forecasting and for examination of the possibilities of large scale weather modification. These prospects hold great promise for both developed and underdeveloped countries. By making natural phenomena more predictable, they would foster progress in industry, agriculture, and health, and open the way to a rising standard of living around the world.

Much of the progress already achieved has resulted from international scientific cooperation, and further progress depends in large measure on the services of the World Meteorological Organization. This Specialized Agency of the United Nations has defined for itself a valuable role which should be maintained and strengthened.

b) To make best use of existing resources and new opportunities for progress, the United States advocates that consideration be given by the United Nations, through UNESCO and WMO as appropriate, to the establishment of an International Atmospheric Science Program (IASP) and an International Meteorological Service Program (IMSP), coordinated to achieve the following purposes on a systematic world-wide basis:

1) To obtain, through IASP, global coverage in atmospheric data gathering and improved understanding of higher altitude conditions through the coordinated international use of rocket firings, indirect probes, and meteorological satellites in a World Weather Watch (WWW). By extending the coverage of existing data-gathering networks, the WWW would encourage a firmer scientific basis for weather forecasting, greater knowledge of basic physical forces affecting climate, and the possibility of investigations of large-scale climate modification.

2) To assist member nations, or groups of nations, to make effective use of currently existing meteorological techniques and data by establishing, under IMSP, Regional Weather Analysis Centers. Such Regional Centers could be established in underdeveloped areas through intergovernmental agreement, in part fostered by WMO's technical assistance and communication programs.

c) To facilitate these international programs, the U.S. is prepared to make available the new opportunities for significant improvement in data gathering and transmission techniques achieved by its meteorological and communications satellites. The U.S. is conducting research on methods which would permit direct read-out of satellite cloud photography in any part of the world. If this is successful, the way will be opened for a marked increase in the timely availability of useful data. The U.S. is further planning an international workshop in which technical experts from 104 weather services will be able to develop skills for analyzing cloud cover photographs and other meteorological satellite observations. In addition, the U.S. envisions that the facilities of its communications satellite program, currently in the process of development, could be made available to improve the timely interchange of meteorological data on a regular basis.

d) To achieve these ends, the United States recommends that the General Assembly

1) Invite the International Council of Scientific Unions to constitute an appropriate body for continuing high level scientific advice and innovation in the field of Atmospheric Sciences in the form of a Special Committee on the Atmospheric Sciences.

2) Invite UNESCO to constitute an Atmospheric Sciences Commission (ASC) to focus the resources of governments on the IASP and IMSP and to achieve their implementation.

3) Commend the WMO for its effective service activities in communication and technical assistance and encourage the continued expansion of these functions to facilitate the objectives of the IMSP.

3) In the field of navigation, the U.S. would state that it is currently developing a navigational satellite system that will provide precise and frequent positional information at any point on the earth's surface. This system, which utilizes four transit satellites in polar orbits at 600 nautical miles altitude, has been successfully tested and is planned to become fully operational in 1962 or 1963. The U.S. will make available the specifications for the shipborne navigational equipment which will enable ships of all nations to share in this advance in navigational science. The U.S. is currently exploring ways in which the services of the appropriate Specialized Agencies of the United Nations might be utilized in extending the benefits of this system to all members of the United Nations.

Activities of the Outer Space Committee.

The United States should refer to the foregoing and to the rapidly accelerating pace of outer space activities. We should note that two years have elapsed since a committee representing the General Assembly reviewed outer space matters. We are keenly disappointed that the Committee established by the General Assembly at its 14th Session has never met to undertake the work assigned it. We attach great importance to the United Nations role in outer space matters and to the constructive work which the Outer Space Committee should perform. In this regard the United States therefore strongly urges the activation of the Outer Space Committee, recommends that since its current members have not yet been able to exercise their functions as such their terms should be extended for the years 1962–1963, and calls upon all members of this committee to participate in its work in a spirit of international cooperation.

418.   Memorandum From the Deputy Under Secretary of State for Political Affairs (Johnson) to the President's Special Assistant for National Security Affairs (Bundy)[1]

Washington, May 25, 1962.

SUBJECT

16 May Letter to the President from the Foreign Intelligence Advisory Board

The points raised by Dr. Killian in his 16 May letter to the President[2] are well taken and I can assure you that the Department shares the concern expressed by Dr. Killian's Board and is fully conscious of the impact our outer space negotiations in the UN and elsewhere can have on the national security. All the position papers prepared to date for UN, Disarmament or other negotiations have been designed to protect our current reconnaissance satellite capabilities.

With regard to point (a) in Dr. Killian's letter, the Department believes that a thorough re-examination of US policy for the political handling of our reconnaissance satellite program is necessary and suggests that the President direct the issuance of a National Security Action Memorandum calling upon the Departments of State and Defense, ACDA, CIA and NASA to develop urgently recommendations on this subject for approval by the President. The Department of State would be ready to accept the chairmanship of the drafting group. (It would be desirable to discuss with Jim Webb the way in which NASA could best participate.)[3]

The other problems noted by Dr. Killian have already been dealt with or are in the process of settlement. Specifically, the position papers for the UN outer space meetings that open in Geneva on May 28 have been fully coordinated with the Department of Defense, NASA, ACDA, and where appropriate, with CIA. In the case of the particularly sensitive issue of a possible Soviet initiative for a joint declaration banning the use of outer space for reconnaissance, the position paper was also reviewed by the Special Group. I am not aware of any difference of views among the agencies concerned.

In this connection, all the agencies are aware of the importance of consultation and coordination on outer space problems. The Special Group, USIB and its subcommittees, and the individual agency liaison channels provide a sensitive mechanism for thorough and responsible

---

[1] Source: Kennedy Library, National Security Files, Meetings and Memoranda Series, NSAM No. 156, Negotiations on Peaceful Uses of Outer Space, Box 336. Top Secret.

[2] Not found.

[3] See Document 420.

review of position papers touching on reconnaissance satellite problems, and I am confident that, while improvements can and will be made, it is basically adequate for the job. In the special case of ACDA, which is not a member of the Special Group or of USIB, Bill Foster and I have taken steps to establish an effective liaison channel for all matters pertaining not only to satellite reconnaissance but to intelligence of all kinds. I believe such liaison already exists between ACDA and CIA and the Department of Defense.

On the question of briefing key US representatives involved in discussions on the uses of outer space at the UN or elsewhere on US satellite programs, the Department has already indoctrinated most of these officials. Ambassador Stevenson, Ambassador Francis Plimpton, senior US delegate, and Leonard Meeker, US representative to the Legal Subcommittee have been cleared and briefed in connection with the forthcoming meetings in Geneva.

Since the negotiating forums and issues in the outer space field are growing in number and complexity, the Department foresees a need to brief more policy-making officers on the facts of our satellite reconnaissance programs than can reasonably be accommodated under the strict rules governing authorization for clearances. These officers would seldom have any requirement for access to operational details of these programs or to their intelligence product and thus could not qualify on a need-to-know basis for any of the existing clearances. I believe that a new clearance should be created for these cases which would provide maximum protection for the source but permit certain policy-making officials to know something of the US satellite program. I have submitted to the Special Group proposals for the establishment of such a clearance.

I enclose a draft for a reply by the President to Dr. Killian in the sense of this memorandum.[4] The members of the Special Group have concurred in this draft.

U. Alexis Johnson

---

[4] See Document 419.

419.   Letter From President Kennedy to the Chairman of the President's Foreign Intelligence Advisory Board (Killian)[1]

Washington, May 26, 1962.

Dear Dr. Killian:

Thank you for your letter of May 16th.[2] I welcome your thoughtful suggestions on the difficult policy and security problems we face in fulfilling the various international commitments we have assumed or are negotiating in the field of outer space. I have issued a National Security Action Memorandum calling on the appropriate Departments to reexamine our position on this matter and give me recommendations for a national policy which gives full consideration to the needs of our reconnaissance satellite programs.[3]

The other points you have raised have been examined and I am satisfied that they have been dealt with satisfactorily. Specifically, the Department of State has assured me that the key negotiating officials at the UN and elsewhere have been fully cleared and briefed on our satellite reconnaissance program. Steps have also been taken to establish a special clearance for use in the future for those officials who cannot meet the strict need-to-know criteria for any of the existing clearances but who require some general orientations as to our program.

The position papers for the forthcoming Geneva meetings on outer space have been fully coordinated and cleared by the appropriate agencies. They have been carefully designed to protect our national security interests both for the present and future. I am confident they fully serve this purpose.

I am looking forward to our meeting on June 26th and the opportunity it offers to discuss these matters further.

Sincerely,

John Kennedy[4]

---

[1] Source: Kennedy Library, National Security Files, Meetings and Memoranda Series, NSAM No. 156, Negotiations on Peaceful Uses of Outer Space, Box 336. Top Secret. A copy of the letter was sent to General Taylor. A typed note at the end of the letter reads: "Signed ltr picked up by Mr. Coyne's office 5/28/62 w/cc and orig of incoming ltr 5/16/62 fm FIAB to President."

[2] Not found. See Document 418.

[3] Document 420.

[4] Printed from a copy that indicates Kennedy signed the original.

420.   National Security Action Memorandum No. 156[1]

Washington, May 26, 1962.

TO

The Secretary of State
The Secretary of Defense
The Director of Central Intelligence
The Director, National Aeronautics and Space Administration
The Director, Arms Control and Disarmament Agency

1. We are now engaged in several international negotiations on disarmament and peaceful uses of outer space. These negotiations are likely to continue for a long time, and may well grow in scope. They raise the problem of what constitutes legitimate use of outer space, and in particular the question of satellite reconnaissance.

2. In view of the great national security importance of our satellite reconnaissance programs, I think it desirable that we carefully review these negotiations with a view to formulating a position which avoids the dangers of restricting ourselves, compromising highly classified programs, or providing assistance of significant military value to the Soviet Union and which at the same time permits us to continue to work for disarmament and international cooperation in space. Accordingly, I request that the Department of State organize a committee for this purpose, with representatives of all addressees with sufficient standing to permit them to be fully cognizant of all our programs in this area.[2]

I wish to receive your report and recommendations by 1 July.

John F. Kennedy

---

[1] Source: Kennedy Library, National Security Files, Meetings and Memoranda Series, NSAM No. 192 Re: "A Separate Arms Control Measure for Outer Space," Box 339. Top Secret. A copy was sent to Arthur M. Schlesinger.

[2] On May 29 Lieutenant General Marshall S. Carter, Acting Director of the CIA, informed Secretary Rusk that either the Director or the Deputy Director for Research would represent the Agency in committee meetings. On May 31 Deputy Secretary of Defense Gilpatric informed Alexis Johnson that Paul Nitze would be the Defense Department's representative. On May 29 Johnson informed the Secretary of Defense, the Director of the CIA, the Administrator of NASA, and the Director of ACDA that the committee would hold its first, organizational meeting in his office on June 1. (National Archives and Records Administration, RG 59, S/S–NSC Files: Lot 72 D 316, NSAM No. 156) For the committee's report, see Document 421.

**421.   Report by the Committee on Satellite Reconnaissance
Policy[1]**

Washington, undated.

REPORT ON POLITICAL AND INFORMATIONAL ASPECTS OF SATELLITE RECONNAISSANCE POLICY

Note

This report and its recommendations do *not* include examination of possible private disclosure of US reconnaissance satellite capabilities to the Soviet leadership.

The Problem

To develop a policy with respect to United States reconnaissance programs which will:

A. Maintain our freedom of action unilaterally to conduct reconnaissance satellite operations.

B. Prevent foreign political and physical interference with the conduct of these operations.

C. Prevent accidental or forced disclosure of details of the operations or end products of the US satellite reconnaissance program.

D. Avoid situations, statements or actions which, in the context of our satellite reconnaissance program, could later be exploited as evidence either of alleged US aggressiveness or duplicity.

E. Facilitate the resolution of any conflicts which might arise between the essential technical and security requirements of the US satellite reconnaissance program and the international commitments and foreign policy objectives of the United States in a manner which is in the over-all best interests of the national security of the United States.

Discussion

1. The reconnaissance satellite program is extremely important to Free World security, and will continue to be necessary to provide crucial information about Soviet activities, capabilities, and targets.

2. Complex international attitudes toward this program pose significant problems for the US. In the first place, other governments and peoples are in varying degrees of ignorance about whether the US has

---

[1] Source: National Archives and Records Administration, RG 59, S/S–NSC Files: Lot 72 D 316, NSAM No. 156. Top Secret. The report was forwarded under cover of a July 2 memorandum from Secretary Rusk to President Kennedy. Rusk observed that the committee had not reached an agreement on Recommendations 18 and 19, and recommended that the President's principal advisers on national security and arms control meet for further discussion of these points.

a reconnaissance satellite program, about the capabilities of such satellites, about the implications of such a program, about its relation to various space and disarmament negotiations, and about the propriety and
justification for peacetime reconnaissance activities. There are, of
course, differences both of knowledge and attitude on the part of various allied, neutral and Communist states. Regardless of what the US
does, or does not, say about this program, it is clearly military and it is
related to the "Cold War." There are confused views on pairing the distinction between "peaceful," "military," "non-prohibited" and "legal"
on the one hand, and "aggressive," "civilian," "prohibited" and "illegal," on the other. For example, the connotations of the UN General
Assembly Resolution 1721 (XVI) on "International Cooperation in the
Peaceful Uses of Outer Space," as distinguished from its actual operative provisions, may seem to many to militate against any "military"
use of space.

3. There is, strictly speaking, no settled regime of law governing
activities in outer space. There have been no authoritative statements by
authoritative bodies. This is a developing field and the legitimacy of the
use of observation satellites in outer space, like other space activities,
must, consequently, be argued largely on the basis of analogies from
other areas of international law and of emerging practice.

Arguments have been advanced, on the premise that a reconnaissance satellite program is a "military" (as opposed to "peaceful") program, that the use of such satellites in outer space is an aggressive act
and thus a violation of international law. The confusions over legality,
propriety and peacefulness earlier noted can be exploited for use
against space reconnaissance. Thus it could be argued, with considerable appeal, that the military uses of outer space, such as satellite reconnaissance, should be proscribed as non-peaceful.

On the other hand, strong arguments are available to support the
conclusion that the gathering of information by means of reconnaissance satellites is permissible:

(a) There is no reasonable basis for considering unarmed satellites
as constituting either a threat or the use of force (proscribed by Article
2(4) of the UN Charter), and there is nothing in the Charter which could
be construed as prohibiting the essentially non-aggressive activities of
an observation satellite.
(b) It is well established that areas subject to the jurisdiction of a
state may be freely observed from points outside that jurisdiction, e.g.,
from a ship on the high seas. Observation from outer space, which is not
subject to territorial claims, also cannot be considered to constitute a
violation of international law.
(c) In terms of practice to date, there have been no objections to
visual and photographic observation during manned space flights; nor
to Tiros photographic satellites. Although there is a difference in the

degree of performance, this practice helps us to sustain the argument that photographic satellites of any kind are permissible.

On balance, the arguments in favor of the legitimacy of satellite reconnaissance are sounder from a technical legal standpoint.

4. The US is not at present *legally* bound to observe any commitments regarding the use of outer space. However, as a matter of national policy, the US does consider itself bound to comply with the United Nations General Assembly Resolution 1721 (XVI), which the US drafted and sponsored and which was unanimously adopted by the UNGA on December 20, 1961. That Resolution "commends to States for their guidance in the exploration and use of outer space" two principles:

(a) International law, including the Charter of the United Nations, applies to outer space and celestial bodies;
(b) Outer space and celestial bodies are free for exploration and the use by all States in conformity with international law, and are not subject to national appropriation.

Pursuant to UNGA Resolution 1721, the United States now registers all satellite launchings with the UN. There is no internationally agreed formula governing the data provided for registration with the United Nations.

5. At the recent meetings of the UN Outer Space Committee's Legal Subcommittee in Geneva,[2] the US proposed:

(a) A draft General Assembly resolution regarding assistance to and return of space vehicles and their occupants, and
(b) A draft resolution requesting the Secretary General of the United Nations to constitute a panel of experts to draft an international agreement dealing with liability of launching states and international organizations for injury, loss or damage caused by space vehicles.

Those proposals were carefully framed so as not to affect the US reconnaissance satellite program. It should be noted, however, that the issue of banning reconnaissance satellites was specifically raised by the Soviets in a Draft Declaration of Principles. The question of exempting reconnaissance satellites from any agreement to return space vehicles inadvertently landing on the territory of other states was also raised not only by the Bloc, but by some other countries as well. The Legal Subcommittee was unable to reach agreement on any substantive issues. The US Delegation in the Outer Space Technical Subcommittee, which met concurrently, proposed that reports on general national plans for international space activities be submitted to the Outer Space

---

[2] The classified report of the U.S. Delegation to the Legal Subcommittee of the UN Committee on the Peaceful Uses of Outer Space is ibid., SCI Files: Lot 65 D 473, September 1962–December 1963.

Committee and agreement was reached on this point. It was made clear by the United States (and by the Soviet Union) that such information will be submitted on a purely voluntary basis and at the discretion of the reporting state.

6. The US proposed Treaty Outline on General and Complete Disarmament of April 18, 1962,[3] includes as a measure in Stage One provision for prohibition of "the placing into orbit of weapons capable of producing mass destruction." For verification of this measure, inspection of vehicles and advance notification of all launchings of space vehicles or missiles, would be provided. In addition, the International Disarmament Organization would establish any arrangements necessary for detecting unreported launchings. Finally, the production, stockpiling and testing of boosters for space vehicles would be subject to agreed limitations. The US is also committed to consideration of a possible separate disarmament agreement limited to banning weapons of mass destruction from outer space along the general lines of the provisions contained in the April 18 Treaty Outline.

7. It is clear that in negotiations involving outer space and disarmament certain issues have been or will be raised that have serious implications for the US reconnaissance satellite program and on which the US position must be carefully formulated and vigorously defended. Our negotiating posture is weakened, however, by current practices with respect to security that prevent us from making a convincing explanation of our position to allies and friendly neutrals. We are increasingly in danger of being isolated in negotiations on seemingly minor issues, whose implications are better understood by our enemies than by our friends.

A careful review of official statements on US plans for a reconnaissance satellite program, of present free world attitudes toward the concept of satellite reconnaissance, and of the probable extent of Soviet knowledge of our program, indicates that the US might privately seek support from allies and certain neutrals by impressing upon them the importance of the program to the free world, the requirements it imposes on US negotiating positions on outer space and disarmament matters, and US determination to protect and pursue the program.

8. Public official statements, budgetary funding of the reconnaissance satellite program, and limited publicity about launching of developmental vehicles associated with the program, have committed the US to some degree of public acknowledgment of this program, and in addi-

---

[3] For text of the U.S. treaty outline submitted to the Eighteen-Nation Disarmament Committee on April 18 (UN doc. ENDC/30), see *Documents on Disarmament, 1962*, pp. 351–382. U.S. Representative Dean's statement before the Committee when he presented the outline is printed in *American Foreign Policy: Current Documents, 1962*, pp. 1156–1165.

tion there has been an undesirable amount of press commentary and speculation on US reconnaissance activities. Intent to develop a reconnaissance capability is on record. No official statement has indicated what results might have been achieved or information obtained from satellite reconnaissance.

9. The existence of a US requirement for effective intelligence on the Sino-Soviet bloc is generally clear to the leaders of the principal countries of the free world, as well as the official, military and some other groups in those countries. Available evidence indicates that these elements generally support US efforts to develop reconnaissance satellite systems. In some cases, US activities in connection with satellites (not specifically reconnaissance satellites) have elicited concern. In Japan, for example, there has been reluctance to cooperate with NASA on the establishment of US tracking facilities because of suspicion that military activities might be or become involved. In Zanzibar and Nigeria also some groups have argued that the presence of US tracking stations is inconsistent with a neutralist posture since the stations may involve US activities of a military nature. These scattered evidences of concern suggest that a concerted Sino-Soviet bloc campaign attributing sinister and threatening motives to US military (including reconnaissance) satellite programs might elicit a favorable and sympathetic reaction not only from anti-US elements, but also from some others concerned over heightening of international tension. US private diplomatic efforts to gain support for the concept of the right of space reconnaissance would probably counteract the Soviet campaign to some degree, though it is unlikely that the US could at this time gain widespread support for a positive affirmation in the UN or other international forum of the right to conduct space reconnaissance.

10. It is particularly important that the US avoid public statements about our satellite operations that would pose a direct political challenge to the Soviet Union on the sensitive issue of reconnaissance. The Soviets would feel compelled for reasons of prestige to react very strongly by any of a variety of political means to such statements. Similarly, if the Soviets were able to obtain any convincing evidence of the US activity they might, even if not compelled to do so, use the opportunity to launch a major political offensive against the US in an effort to end the reconnaissance program.

11. There can be little doubt that the USSR is aware that the US is engaged in a reconnaissance satellite program, though they are probably in some doubt as to its precise effectiveness. Even in this respect, by extrapolating from known U-2 photographic equipment, they can probably make a reasonable estimate of the resolution of cameras that such a satellite could have. There is reason to believe that the Soviets are developing an anti-satellite weapons system and they may have some capability for anti-satellite operations by 1963. While the US probably cannot

keep the Soviets from attempting physical anti-satellite measures if they decide to do so, our objective should be to create conditions in which the Soviets will not attempt this or would pay a political price for doing so by creating a climate of acceptance of the principle of freedom of space and the unacceptability of forcible interference with the exercise of that freedom. US handling of its public relations on reconnaissance operations, and on US development of anti-satellite capabilities, will have an important bearing on this question. Moreover, there are a series of technical measures which the US can use to counter hostile active countermeasures. On balance, it seems probable that from a technical point of view it should be possible by concerted efforts to maintain an effective reconnaissance program despite hostile countermeasures.

Recommended Policy

1. The United States should maintain the legal position that the principles of international law and the UN Charter apply to activities in outer space and, specifically, that outer space is free, as are the high seas.

2. The US should therefore continue to avoid any position implying that reconnaissance activities in outer space are not legitimate. Similarly, we should avoid any position declaring or implying that such activities are not "peaceful uses."

3. The US should, to the extent feasible, seek to avoid public use of the term "reconnaissance" satellites, and where appropriate use instead such broader and more neutral terms as "observation" or "photographic" satellites (See Tab A).[4]

4. Further studies should be made on an urgent basis to determine whether there are releaseable data, such as mapping information, or procedures such as occasionally calling Tiros and Nimbus vehicles "photographic" satellites, which would help create wider public acceptance of space observation and photography.

5. NASA should study urgently the possibilities of accelerating bilateral international cooperation to develop non-military space activities involving space observation, perhaps including photography.

6. It is recognized that the US cannot entirely avoid or disclaim interest in reconnaissance, so that where feasible the US should also seek to gain acceptance of the principle of the legitimacy of space reconnaissance.

7. When confronted by specific Soviet pressure to outlaw reconnaissance activities in space, the US should continue to take a public stand for the legitimacy of the *principle* of reconnaissance from outer space, the precise form and extent of which would depend upon the circumstances of the confrontation.

---

[4] The tabs were not found.

8. [*6 lines of source text not declassified*]

9. The present practice of not identifying individual military space launchings by mission or purpose is sound. We believe, however, that there should also be a more open (but not more detailed) public reference to the general over-all military program. An appropriate nickname for public identification should be given to the over-all military program, with its objectives intentionally stated in broad and general terms (See Tab B, which is illustrative). All military launchings would be described in terms of the general objectives of the over-all military program. No specific mission would be ascribed to any particular launch.

10. The US should not, at this time, publicly disclose the status, extent, effectiveness or operational characteristics of its reconnaissance program.

11. Strict control over public statements and backgrounding concerning reconnaissance satellites should be exercised to ensure consistency with the policy guide-lines suggested in these recommendations.

12. No public attention should be directed toward development of anti-satellite capabilities, and any publicized demonstration of developmental work and any actual test of such a capability should require White House approval, with full account given to the adverse effects for our reconnaissance satellite program. We should avoid any indication that physical countermeasures to reconnaissance vehicles would be justified, and as appropriate the US should make a positive effort to propagate the idea that interference with or attacks on any space vehicle of another country in peacetime are inadmissible and illegal.

13. The US should discreetly disclose to certain allies and neutrals selected information with regard to the US space reconnaissance program, making each disclosure orally and at a time and in a manner that will preserve the essential security of our program while impressing upon them its importance for the security of the Free World. Disclosures should be made in a manner that will preclude acquisition by the Communist Bloc of usable evidence of an official US acknowledgment that we are conducting a satellite reconnaissance program. Proposals for such disclosures should include clearance by the National Reconnaissance Office.

14. The US should in private disclosures emphasize the fact of our determination and ability to pursue such programs because of their great importance to our common security, despite any efforts to dissuade us.

15. The US should note in connection with private disclosures that, except in some cases for specifically defined disarmament agreements, the US cannot agree to (a) declarations of the precise purpose of all satellites, (b) declarations of the equipment of all satellites, (c) general requirements for advance notification of all satellite launchings and the tracks of satellites, (d) pre-launch inspection of the satellites, or (e) a

specific definition of peaceful uses of space which does not embrace unlimited observation.

16. The possible roles of space reconnaissance in disarmament inspection arrangements or in creating military stability should be further studied.

17. The US should stand by the disarmament proposal for a provision in Stage One of a Treaty on General and Complete Disarmament banning weapons of mass destruction from being carried in satellites, and providing for advance notification and inspection of all missile and space launchings to insure that ban. The US should continue to exclude any ban on reconnaissance satellites.

18. The US should not make or endorse in the disarmament negotiations any proposal for advance notifications of missile and space launchings as one of a separate group of measures to "reduce the risks of war."

The ACDA does not concur in this recommendation. All members of the Committee recognize that there are arguments pro and con on this proposition, but the other members believe the advantages of such a proposal as an arms control measure are not great enough to outweigh the disadvantage to the reconnaissance satellite program from assistance to passive (and potentially to active) countermeasures which would be provided by advance notification. The ACDA member believes that the value of the whole group of measures to reduce risks of war should be considered, since *omission* of missile and space launchings would appear to represent an undue and even a suspicious concern by the US. In his view, this consideration outweighs possible ill consequences for the reconnaissance program.

19. It is recommended that a decision be made now as to whether to propose a *separate* arms control agreement banning weapons of mass destruction from being carried in satellites, with appropriate verification controls. The US has proposed discussion of such an agreement along the general lines of the provisions contained in the April 18 Treaty Outline. The members of this Committee are not agreed on the net advisability of making such a proposal, which of course depends on political considerations apart from its effect on the reconnaissance satellite program. (See Tab C for a summary of the considerations pro and con.) They are agreed that no such proposal should be tabled until the question has been reviewed with you.[5]

---

[5] Following NSC discussion of this report on July 10, President Kennedy issued NSC Action No. 2454, which accepted the Committee's recommendations and referred the question of a separate arms control accord back to the Committee for further study. (National Archives and Records Administration, RG 59, S/S–NSC (Miscellaneous) Files: Lot 66 D 95, Records of Action by the National Security Council) For further information, see *Foreign Relations*, 1961–1963, vol. VII, Document 226.

The foregoing Report has, in compliance with National Security Action Memorandum No. 156 of May 26, 1962, been prepared and is concurred in by:

Paul H. Nitze
Representative of the Department of the Defense

Joseph Charyk
National Reconnaissance Office

Herbert Scoville, Jr.
Representative of the Director of Central Intelligence

Robert C. Seamans, Jr.
Representative of the National Aeronautics and Space Administration

Adrian S. Fisher
Representative of the Arms Control and Disarmament Agency

Carl Kaysen and Jerome Wiesner also were
consulted in the work of the Committee

U. Alexis Johnson[6]
Representative of the Department of State

---

[6] Printed from a copy that indicates Johnson signed the original; all the other signatures are typed.

---

422. Memorandum From the Director of the Arms Control and Disarmament Agency (Foster) to President Kennedy[1]

Washington, July 6, 1962.

SUBJECT

Arms Control Aspects of Proposed Satellite Reconnaissance Policy

Recommendations 18 and 19 of the "Report on Political and Informational Aspects of Satellite Reconnaissance Policy" call attention to two issues on which the agencies concerned have been unable to reach agreement.[2] The views of the Arms Control and Disarmament Agency are summarized below.

---

[1] Source: Kennedy Library, National Security Files, Meetings and Memoranda Series, NSAM No. 156, Negotiations on Peaceful Uses of Outer Space, Box 336. Top Secret.

[2] See Document 421 and footnote 1 thereto.

Advance Notification of Launchings

The Geneva Conference has agreed to discuss separate measures to reduce the risk of war through accident, miscalculation or failure of communication. The purpose of such measures would be to provide reassurance among states and to hold to the minimum the hazards that might arise from misinterpretation of abrupt acts of a military but non-belligerent character. Measures designed for this purpose might involve arrangements for advance notification of certain types of military movements and maneuvers, including advance notification of missile launchings, a measure already suggested by the Swedish Delegation, and possibly advance notification of space vehicle launchings as well.

Recommendation 18 of the Satellite Reconnaissance Report would preclude the United States from making or endorsing proposals for advance notification of missile and space vehicle launchings. In the case of space vehicle launchings, the recommendation is based on the contention that advance notification would facilitate passive and active countermeasures against reconnaissance satellites. Advance notification of missile launchings is presumably ruled out because space vehicle launchings might become a collateral issue.

ACDA does not wish to underestimate the countermeasures problem, but we have difficulty in assigning it over-riding significance. Past and continuing publicity respecting reconnaissance satellites is sufficient to have aroused Soviet interest in the possibility of countermeasures. If passive countermeasures are practical, it is not unreasonable to suppose that the Soviet Union may undertake them whether or not advance notification is provided. In so far as active countermeasures are concerned, it is not evident that advance notification need be so precise as to result in the pin-pointing of targets in outer space. To the extent that such notification might serve to place a Soviet anti-satellite system on the alert, such maneuvers as plausible changes in launching schedules might be employed by the United States with a view to effecting some attrition of the Soviet system through profitless alerts. If the Soviet Union should succeed in taking advantage of an agreed measure to reduce the risk of war in order to destroy or neutralize a peaceful United States satellite, a variety of responses would be available, including a strengthened basis for United States political opposition to such acts.

We may not, in fact, be able to reach agreement with the Soviet Union on any type of advance notification. However, an affirmative United States position would be consistent with our view that the objects we place in orbit represent legitimate uses of outer space. By carrying our concern regarding our space vehicles to the point where we are unwilling to discuss advance notification of missile launchings, we may encourage the conclusion that we are attempting to shield activities which we ourselves regard as suspect. It is difficult to see how such an approach could contribute to the political and legal defense of satellite reconnaissance.

Furthermore, a separate measure for advance notifications of missile and space launchings, if agreed to by the United States and the Soviet Union, would constitute an important step in the arms control field. First, it would give greater assurance that a surprise missile attack could not take place in a way that would catch the U.S. off guard. Secondly, by having advance notifications of such launchings, each party to the agreement would have a good record of the other party's planned programs in the space and missile fields, including both test programs and possible programs for the further deployment of missiles. Third, advance notifications of missile and space launchings would decrease tension that is bound to come as the United States and the Soviet Union, and possibly other countries as well, increase the number of missiles at their disposal. The more information that can be obtained about the intentions of potentially hostile parties, as the United States and the Soviet Union increase their dependence on missiles for military purposes, the less likely it will be that one or the other party will miscalculate and possibly start or escalate a war with missiles.

There are issues of greater consequence than measures "to reduce the risk of war." However, other things being equal, it would seem desirable that the United States seek limited gains in the arms control field as well as major ones. ACDA is not convinced that the arguments supporting Recommendation 18 outweigh these against it, and recommends that it be disapproved.

Prohibition of Bombs in Orbit

The Canadian Foreign Minister has pressed at Geneva for consideration of a separate measure to prohibit the placing in orbit of weapons of mass destruction (it is perhaps worth noting that the United States is currently pressing for a tracking station in Canada to support military space programs). The United States has expressed willingness to discuss the possibility of such a separate measure, provided that it take the form of an agreement which would be subject to inspection. To date, the Soviet Union has opposed consideration of the matter except in connection with general and complete disarmament. Recommendation 19 of the Satellite Reconnaissance Report raises a question as to whether we should continue to pursue our present course.

ACDA believes that if an agreement could be reached to prohibit the placing in orbit of weapons of mass destruction, such an agreement would be in the interest of the national security. To prevent extension of the arms race to outer space should be an important objective of arms control, and hence national security policy. This conclusion appears valid even if such an agreement were fully effective only against very large and hence very high yield weapons such as those tested by the Soviet Union in its last test series. The fact that the Soviet Union would gain increased knowledge of our satellite reconnaissance capabilities does not seem a compelling argument against our acceptance of inspection procedures, particularly in view of the present Soviet ability to estimate these capabilities with a substantial degree of accuracy, a fact that is noted in the Satellite Reconnaissance Report.

The basic objection to the present United States position of willingness to consider a separate outer space agreement appears to rest primarily on the argument that discussion of a separate agreement might involve the United States, to its tactical disadvantage, in a public airing of the satellite reconnaissance issue.

The Soviet Union has, of course, already raised this issue not only in its propaganda output but also in private conversations with the United States and in discussions in the context of the United Nations Outer Space Committee. Ambassador Stevenson is concerned that the issue may be raised in the General Assembly. There is good reason for such concern since the public record affords ample "evidence" to support a strong political attack. Under these circumstances, the question may be where, not whether, the United States may have to debate the matter.

We may not be able to prevent the Soviet Union from speaking out in the forum of its choice, but if we continue to maintain that limitations on military uses of outer space are arms control matters and that Geneva is the proper place to discuss them, we will have a reasonable tactical basis for declining to join issue in the Outer Space Committee or the General Assembly. We will also have reasonable procedural grounds for ignoring, if not defeating, condemnatory principles of space law or hortatory resolutions which might embarrass the satellite reconnaissance program.

In view of the foregoing considerations, ACDA strongly urges that approval be given to an effort on the part of the United States to seek a separate agreement to prohibit the placing in orbit of weapons of mass destruction.

William C. Foster

423. **Memorandum From the President's Special Assistant for National Security Affairs (Bundy) to Secretary of State Rusk[1]**

Washington, July 23, 1962.

SUBJECT

Recommended U.S. Position on a Separate Ban on Weapons of Mass Destruction in Outer Space

The President reviewed your memorandum of July 12th and asked me to report to you that he was not prepared to accept paragraphs 2, 3 and 6 of the recommended position insofar as they imply a total rejection of any possible declaratory ban on weapons of mass destruction in outer space.[2] His present belief is that at a certain stage such a declaratory ban might be in our interest if nothing better can be achieved. He would like an examination of the possibilities of nationally operated systems for the detection and identification of any such weapons. Moreover, he questions whether our position on insistence on inspection must be maintained on all subjects, regardless of our own possible interest in declaratory agreements in special cases.

The President hopes that the matter will be reviewed in the light of these comments and that a further recommendation can be presented to him soon.

McGeorge Bundy[3]

---

[1] Source: Kennedy Library, National Security Files, Meetings and Memoranda Series, NSAM No. 156, Negotiations on Peaceful Uses of Outer Space, Box 336. Top Secret.

[2] This July 12 memorandum transmitted the recommendations of the Committee on Satellite Reconnaissance Policy, Document 421. The three paragraphs recommended that the United States oppose a declaratory ban on weapons of mass destruction in outer space, while stressing the need for adequate means of verification. (Kennedy Library, National Security Files, Meetings and Memoranda Series, NSAM No. 156, Negotiations on Peaceful Uses of Outer Space, Box 336)

[3] Printed from a copy that bears this typed signature.

424. **Memorandum From the President's Special Assistant for Science and Technology (Wiesner) to President Kennedy**[1]

Washington, August 9, 1962.

At your request, I have examined the problem of a declaratory ban on weapons of mass destruction in outer space. It is my general conclusion that such a declaratory ban would not involve any real risks to this country from a military security point of view. However, this conclusion is based on relatively sophisticated considerations and the proposal would certainly prove to be very controversial domestically.

There is no question that it would be technically feasible to design a variety of weapons systems employing nuclear weapons in space. These weapons systems could be designed either for target bombardment with accuracies approaching those obtaining with ballistic missiles or for the detonation of extremely high yield warheads—possibly as large as 1000 Megatons—directly in orbit. The latter possibility has been widely discussed as a possible terror weapon since a single such device detonated at altitudes of a few hundred miles would on a clear day probably cause lethal burns and produce fires over areas extending to several tens of thousands of square miles. Despite the very impressive effects associated with such weapons systems, it can be shown on the basis of rather general considerations that these same effects can be achieved much more effectively and economically by earth-based weapons systems. When practical considerations such as payload, component reliability, command and control, vulnerability, and cost are taken into account, space-based weapon delivery systems as presently visualized compare poorly with comparable earth-based weapon delivery systems.

I believe the following general comments summarize the various factors that are unfavorable to the deployment of weapons of mass destruction in space:

1. *Payload:* A given rocket can deliver a substantially larger payload to a target as a ballistic missile than it can place into orbit. For example, a 2 stage rocket can deliver almost twice the payload to 6,000 miles as a ballistic missile as it can place in a low orbit (100 to 200 miles). Weapons systems in higher orbits involve progressively greater payload penalties; and, as an extreme case, a weapon system based on the moon would permit payloads of only a few percent of comparable 6,000 mile ballistic missile systems for comparable expenditure of energy.

2. *Reliability:* Component reliability is a major problem in the design of nuclear weapons delivery systems and a mean life to failure in these

[1] Source: Kennedy Library, President's Office Files, Staff Memoranda, Jerome B. Wiesner, Box 67C. Secret.

complex systems is often disturbingly short. However, in the case of earth-based systems, there can be a continuous checkout and periodic repairs or replacement. In the case of a space based weapon failure of even a minor component could make the system inoperable and possibly also unsafe. Any effort to increase reliability of a space system by redundancy in components would further penalize the payload of the space system as compared with a comparable earth-based system.

3. *Command and Control:* The maintenance of command and control of a satellite weapons system would be much more difficult than in the case of an earth-based system. This is true not only because of poor component reliability in the satellite, but also because of the possibility that the enemy might jam communication circuits or even take control of the system by breaking the control code.

4. *Vulnerability:* In general, a satellite in orbit would appear to be a very insecure place to store nuclear weapons for any appreciable length of time since the satellites would be vulnerable to enemy action and peacetime attrition. Unless a special countermeasure were taken, a normal satellite would be extremely vulnerable to ground fire from a Nike Zeus type AICBM system or modified ballistic missiles such as Minuteman since the satellite could be tracked over a period of time and its orbit calculated with extreme accuracy. While the vulnerability of a satellite could be reduced somewhat by a variety of sophisticated countermeasures, it would appear to be extremely difficult and expensive to achieve a high level of confidence that such a weapons system would be immune to enemy action since the defender would have an extended period of time to identify the hostile satellite Specifically, it does not appear to be feasible to make a large satellite weapon carrier simultaneously invisible to both radar and optical observation. Although the vulnerability of the satellite could certainly be reduced by introducing controlled or random steering in the satellite, this would further reduce the effective payload of the weapon carrier. The most significant reduction in vulnerability would probably result from the use of decoys. However, given the possibility of extended observations, techniques could probably be developed to sort out light decoys in space. In addition to the satellite vehicle itself, the communication and tracking equipment with its large radars necessary for the operation and control of a satellite weapon system would be extremely vulnerable to enemy attack.

5. *Cost:* For all the above reasons, the cost of a satellite based weapon system would be much greater than that of a comparable earth-based system. For example, considering some of the obvious problems, the Rand Corporation has estimated that a bombardment satellite system would be at least 5 times as expensive as earth-based system with comparable effectiveness.

I believe that the arguments in support of space based weapons systems appear to be essentially limited to the following areas:

1. *Psychological:* It is argued that the general fear induced by the knowledge that nuclear weapons were actually orbiting overhead would be so great as to destroy the will of the people to resist the demands of an aggressor. I find it difficult to evaluate this psychological problem since the actual danger of large scale nuclear attack exists and is much greater from the more effective earth-based weapons system from satellites. The existence of a space based weapons system would add to the international technical-military prestige of its possessor.

2. *Dispersal:* Stationing of weapons of mass destruction in orbit, particularly as part of a deterrent system, would have the advantage of removing military targets from a country and thereby avoiding the destruction associated with a counter force attack. It might also make the deterrent more effective by complicating and diversifying the requirements for a counter force attack. However, all of the earlier technical considerations, especially vulnerability in peacetime and component reliability, argue against the use of space for long lived systems which would be needed to establish a recognized deterrent capability.

3. *Surprise:* It is argued that a satellite based weapons system could attack without warning. While it is true that satellites in low orbit over the U.S. could be detonated simultaneously or could descend from orbit and attack targets with warning as short as those associated with submarine attack, the fact that large numbers of satellites were programmed to arrive over the U.S. simultaneously could be detected quite early and would provide days of strategic warning of a possible attack. An attack by bombardment satellites, which were not programmed to arrive over the U.S. simultaneously, could probably be detected so as to provide warning comparable to that of an ICBM attack. Such an attack would consist of a small first strike with relatively short warning followed by successive detonations for perhaps an hour due to variable times of descent. In any event, a rapid build-up of satellites would certainly be known to the other side and would remove the surprise element from the first strike attack.

On the basis of these considerations, I have concluded that, while technically feasible, a satellite weapons system would constitute a very ineffective approach to the development of a first-strike capability and would also represent a poor approach to long lived, confident weapon system for deterrent strategy. I believe that most military planners who have critically considered this problem would not take exception to this conclusion. It is significant to note that the Air Force at the present time is not calling for any specific space based weapons systems but rather desire a program to develop a capability to place payloads in space in the event some undetermined requirement arises. Nevertheless, despite the strong technical arguments against satellite weapon systems, the Soviet Union may still decide to deploy such a system because of its psychological effect or as a means of achieving what the Soviets might consider to be a more effective deterrent in view of their relatively inferior strategic position.

The verification of a declaratory ban would, of course, be dependent upon our unilateral monitoring and intelligence capabilities. We have an excellent unilateral capability to monitor space launches and to track satellites. We do not however, at present, have a unilateral capability to determine whether a given satellite contains a nuclear weapon. Nevertheless, the launching of a large number of satellites for which no scientific research or other explanation was available coupled with efforts to reduce vulnerability, (such as maneuverability or decoys) would create a strong suspicion that a military satellite system which might be associated with weapon delivery was being deployed. In the period after 1965, it would also be possible to develop unmanned satellite inspection systems that might be capable of determining whether unidentified satellites contained nuclear weapons.

A simple declaratory ban of weapons for destruction in space has several attractive features. It might be easily agreed upon with the USSR since it does not involve inspection; it would deal with a type of armament which neither side has deployed; and it might result in the saving of vast sums of money which both sides may be compelled to spend on these developments in the absence of an agreement for reasons of fear or military prestige. Such a proposal would, however, also involve international and domestic and political problems, which must be given careful consideration. It would be argued that, as a first step to arms control, it would tend to set a precedent against inspection, especially as it would be noted that a ban on weapons of mass destruction in space could be easily and reliably monitored by a mutual agreement to require inspection of the payloads of all declared space launches. The question as to whether all launches had, in fact, been declared could be monitored by either an international radar system or by our existing "national" radar monitoring system. It is difficult to imagine any separate arms control agreement that could be monitored more effectively than this and at less cost than this if national radar monitoring systems were utilized.

A much more serious practical problem however, would be the question of domestic acceptance. Given the popular enthusiasm and confusion about space and the powerful lobby interest in this field, it is hard to imagine that there would be easy acceptance of the rather sophisticated arguments as to why such a ban would not involve a significant military risk to this country. If public and Congressional acceptance requires a major campaign to minimize the military significance of space, it would substantially reduce the rationale of undertaking a major campaign to advance such a proposal as a separable disarmament measure.

In summary, I believe that a declaratory ban of weapons of mass destruction would not involve any real military danger to the U.S. At the same time and for the same reason, it would not be a major step toward the control of armaments. Nevertheless, it could serve as a tactic to initiate some activity in the field of disarmament and could prevent a very expensive new dimension to the arms race with its unpredictable psychological reaction which might affect the overall level of military activities of both sides. As a disarmament measure I would be in favor of a declaratory ban; however, I recognize that such a proposal would involve significant domestic political problems. The question of whether the advantages of such a proposal as a disarmament measure outweigh these domestic disadvantages should be thoroughly explored.

Jerry

425. National Security Action Memorandum No. 183[1]

Washington, August 27, 1962.

MEMORANDUM TO

Secretary of State
Secretary of Defense
Director of Central Intelligence
Administrator, National Aeronautics and Space Administration
Director, Arms Control and Disarmament Agency
Chairman, Atomic Energy Commission
Director, Office of Science and Technology

SUBJECT

Space Program of the United States

The President desires that the space program of the United States be forcefully explained and defended at the forthcoming sessions of the

---

[1] Source: Kennedy Library, National Security Files, Meetings and Memoranda Series, NSAM No. 183, Space Program for the United States, Box 338. Top Secret. An August 28 memorandum by Charles E. Johnson of the NSC Staff indicates that NSAM No. 183 was distributed as an unnumbered memorandum before its inclusion in the NSAM series.

UN Outer Space Committee and the General Assembly. The Department of State is requested to consult with the Department of Defense, CIA, NASA, AEC, ACDA and the Office of the Science Adviser to develop positions which meet the following objectives:

1. To show that the distinction between peaceful and aggressive uses of outer space is not the same as the distinction between military and civilian uses, and that U.S. aims to keep space free from aggressive use and offers cooperation in its peaceful exploitation for scientific and technological purposes.

2. To build and sustain support for the legality and propriety of the use of space for reconnaissance. This position should proceed from the approved recommendations of the report submitted on this subject on June 30, 1962.[2]

3. To make it plain that neither U.S. nuclear tests nor other U.S. experiments in space were undertaken without a proper sense of scientific responsibility, and that, in the case of the nuclear tests, these were a response to previous Soviet tests.

4. To demonstrate the precautionary character of the U.S. military program in space.

5. To show that U.S. policies for communication satellites are fully consistent with cooperative international arrangements.

McGeorge Bundy[3]

---

[2] Document 421.

[3] Printed from a copy that indicates Bundy signed the original.

426.   Report of the U.S. Delegation to the Second Session of the
        Scientific and Technical Subcommittee of the UN
        Committee on the Peaceful Uses of Outer Space[1]

Washington, June 24, 1963.

[Here follow sections 1–8.]

9. Conclusions.

(1) The work of the Second Session of the Scientific and Technical
Subcommittee consisted largely of a review and continuation of the
work begun at its first session a year ago. In one sense it might be said
that the Subcommittee was still feeling its way toward practical means
of fulfilling its generally understood role as a catalyst in the process of
cooperation among nations in the peaceful exploration of outer space.
Reflected in the final report of the Subcommittee was a more refined
appreciation of areas where its recommendations can most property
and effectively be addressed and a better understanding of its limitations, both with regard to scientific competence and quasi-political
judgments. At the same time, however, a general characteristic of this
session was the lack of any real demonstrated interest in most of the
proceedings on the part of the noncommitted and smaller countries.
The single exception to this was their great interest in the subject of
training and assistance in space fields.

(2) Of the six Middle Eastern and African countries which are members of the Subcommittee, only Iran and the United Arab Republic were
represented at this Session. Representatives of Sweden and Brazil were
present only during the last few days of the Session and took no part in
the work of the Subcommittee.

(3) The United States Delegation played a major role in consideration of the problem of making available to Member States information
about outer space activities which would help them keep informed
about such activities in other countries, assist them in evaluating their
own plans for activity in space work, and indicate to them sources of
further information and facilities for assistance. In its Report, the
Subcommittee adopted most of the proposals suggested by the United
States. The Delegation was unsuccessful, however, in its efforts to have
the Subcommittee reinforce its earlier recommendation that the United
Nations Secretariat compile information received by it on a voluntary

---

[1] Source: Kennedy Library, National Security Files, Departments and Agencies
Series, Space Activities, General, 1/63–5/63, Box 307. No classification marking. The session was held in Geneva May 14–29. Homer E. Newell led the U.S. Delegation.

basis by Member States in concise tabular form so that such information would be most useful to those requiring it. It seemed clear that the Soviet Delegation wished to avoid any action which would serve to highlight Soviet failure to provide any information at all concerning its national space program. Similarly, in formulating the Subcommittee's recommendation that a survey be prepared of national and cooperative international space activities, the Soviet Delegation insisted that this matter be considered once again in the parent Committee prior to the actual preparation of such a survey.

(4) The Subcommittee's recommendations on education and training fell far short of a reflection of the interest and enthusiasm exhibited by the developing countries which participated in the session. Soviet refusal to accept any recommendation which would in any way imply a commitment on the part of the Soviet Union to assist others in the field of space activities was so insistent that several other Delegates in drafting session became visibly upset. This was in marked contrast to the attitude of the United States Delegation, which, although not represented in the drafting session, submitted two informational working papers setting forth the various possibilities for education and training supported by NASA, and those activities supported by the United States Weather Bureau in the field of satellite meteorology. The substantive recommendation finally adopted is a useful first step in identifying for those Member States desiring help in education and training the existing facilities for such assistance in other countries.

(5) While the United States Delegation did not encourage substantive consideration of the problem of potentially harmful interference with space activities and pointed out that effective consideration of this problem lay with the Legal Subcommittee, I believe the discussions on this matter and the recommendations adopted by the Subcommittee reflect a step forward in the Subcommittee's definition of its role. For the first time in the history of the Committee and the Scientific and Technical Subcommittee, it was recognized implicitly and unanimously that the question of ending nuclear weapons tests lay beyond the competence of the Subcommittee and that the only proper action was to point out the potential hazards of nuclear testing to other space experiments. Similarly, there was a general understanding that the Subcommittee was not qualified to pass quantitative judgment on national space activities which could interfere with other peaceful uses of outer space. Specific mention was drawn to the existence of the independent scientifically qualified body established by COSPAR which is available for quantitative analysis of the potential effects of planned space experiments when such assistance is needed.

(6) As described earlier in this report, the Soviet Delegate sought energetically to evoke a statement by the Subcommittee to the effect

that lack of progress in formalizing general principles governing the conduct of man's activity in outer space seriously prejudiced the work of the Scientific and Technical Subcommittee in its efforts to encourage international cooperation in this field. With the exception of the other Bloc Delegations there was no support for this point of view. Indeed, most of the Delegations which spoke in the general debate rejected the Soviet contention that the Scientific and Technical Subcommittee was hamstrung in its work because of lack of formal agreement in the Legal Subcommittee. At the close of the general debate, the United States spoke again in defense of this latter point of view, rehearsing the large measure of understanding reached during the meetings of the Legal Subcommittee even though no formal agreements had been registered, and suggesting that the Subcommittee proceed with its own work without becoming preoccupied with matters which had been directed by the Committee on the Peaceful Uses of Outer Space to another Subcommittee. The Soviet Delegation received no effective support for inclusion of its proposals on this matter in the final report of the Subcommittee, although the Soviet Delegate did make a final statement for the record decrying the failure of the Subcommittee to address itself to this matter.

(7) I recommend that full United States support be given to adoption by the Committee on the Peaceful Uses of Outer Space of the various recommendations and proposals forwarded to it by the Scientific and Technical Subcommittee. I further recommend that the United States continue its participation in the work of the Subcommittee, seeking to encourage those impulses toward international cooperation in the peaceful exploration of outer space which motivate the basic United Nations interest in this field.

[Here follows a list of Annexes: Annex I, Report of the Subcommittee; Annex II, Summary Records; Annex III, Working Papers; Annex IV, Major U.S. Statements; and Annex V, U.S. Informational Working Papers on Education and Training. None of the Annexes is printed.]

427. Memorandum From the Assistant Secretary of State for International Organization Affairs (Cleveland) and the Deputy Legal Adviser (Meeker) to Secretary of State Rusk[1]

Washington, July 19, 1963.

SUBJECT

Further Approach to Soviets on Outer Space Legal Questions

Discussion

The United States Delegation to the UN Legal Subcommittee on Outer Space recommended in its report that a further approach be made to the Soviets on questions of outer space law prior to the September 1963 session of the parent UN Committee on the Peaceful Uses of Outer Space.[2] A draft paper on questions of space law was attached to the Delegation's Report, and was circulated within the Department of State and to Defense and NASA for clearance.[3] There has been general agreement on this paper and on the desirability of handing it to the Soviets some time before September. Decision was reserved as to timing.

We think it is now timely to go forward with the approach. Developments in Moscow in connection with the test ban talks and the Sino-Soviet breach suggest improved prospects for our being able to reach some agreements with the Soviets on matters of outer space law. This is an area where the U.S. has long felt that cooperation with the Soviet Union is of mutual interest and is possible.

These developments may not, of course, portend any change in Soviet policy on reaching a space law agreement. Recently, the Soviets replied to Ambassador Stevenson's letter of June 6, to the United Nations Secretary-General, in which we called attention to Soviet failure to register six space launchings.[4] The reply, while hostile in tone, is milder than earlier Soviet propaganda on some points. So far, the

---

[1] Source: National Archives and Records Administration, RG 59, Central Files 1960–63, SP 6 UN. Confidential. Drafted by Meeker and concurred in by Robert F. Packard (SCI), Raymond L. Garthoff (G/PM), and John C. Guthrie (EUR). An attached note by Rusk reads: "If this has not been cleared with NASA & Space Council, it should be." Another attachment noted that Welsh of the Space Council approved the paper on July 22, and noted the approval of the Defense Department and NASA representatives.

[2] The report of the U.S. Delegation is in the Kennedy Library, National Security Files, Departments and Agencies Series, Space Activities, General, 1/63–5/63, Box 307.

[3] The text of this undated draft paper was very similar to the text attached as Tab A to this memorandum; see footnote 5 below.

[4] For text of Stevenson's letter, see Department of State *Bulletin*, July 15, 1963, pp. 104–105. The Soviet reply has not been found.

Soviets have chosen not to circulate it as an official UN document, leaving the reply as a USSR Mission press release.

In sum, we think the prospects of a shift in Soviet attitude worth exploring.

There is sentiment among UN Members favoring a further effort by the United States and USSR to arrive at some agreements in the field of outer space law. It would be to our advantage to make an approach before the September session of the UN Outer Space Committee, and to do so far enough in advance of that session so that we will be in a position to refer publicly to our approach if this should become desirable.

USUN reports from New York that Austrian Ambassador Matsch (Chairman of the Outer Space Committee) has this week commenced talks with the Soviets on outer space. Ambassador Fedorenko is reported to have said the USSR was "eager for consultations with the U. S. on legal matters". If we do not respond directly, there is a risk that Matsch will take the initiative in proposing some compromises which would not be in our interest.

At the end of June we gave the United Kingdom a copy of the attached paper (Tab A)[5] for their comments, and we plan to inform the other friendly members of the Outer Space Committee of our approach to the Soviets.

Recommendation

That you approve a further approach to the Soviets in New York on outer space law questions, along the lines of the paper attached at Tab A.[6]

---

[5] Not printed. Elements of this paper were included in Resolution 1962 (XVIII), "Declaration of Legal Principles Governing the Activities of States in the Exploration and Use of Outer Space," which was adopted unanimously by the UN General Assembly on December 13. For text, see *American Foreign Policy: Current Documents, 1963*, pp. 1087–1089.

[6] Secretary Rusk approved the recommendation.

428.   Telegram From the Mission to the United Nations to the Embassy in Yugoslavia[1]

New York, September 9, 1963, 8 p.m.

2. Belgrade for Daddario. Outer Space.

US delegation to outer space committee met privately with Soviet today at Soviet request.[2] Soviets read from lengthy paper indicating possibilities of compromise and areas where they continue to insist on their position.

Soviets said they could accept US views to effect that: Fact that programs of scientific cooperation are not dependent upon agreement on legal issues; jurisdiction over space vehicles in flight should belong to state of registry; state in which space vehicle accidentally lands should have right to seek identifying data from launching state; international organizations may share with their member states responsibility for their space activities.

Soviets continue to stress necessity of prohibition on space observation activities and on war propaganda.

Not possible to evaluate yet whether achievement of consensus is possible. Tone of Soviet presentation was moderate. Seems clear Soviets did wish to begin negotiations prior to opening outer space committee, and that negotiations will require considerable amount of time. At this point, US delegation believes it not likely that committee report will be able indicate areas of progress beyond Lachs consensus statement made on May 3 at conclusion legal subcommittee session (see paragraph 10 and 11 of legal subcommittee report).[3]

Please treat above as confidential.[4]

---

[1] Source: National Archives and Records Administration, RG 59, Central Files 1960–63, SP 6 UN. Confidential. Repeated to the Department of State as telegram 743. The text printed here is the Department's copy.

[2] The U.S. position paper is ibid., SCI Files: Lot 65 D 473, SP 6, June–Dec. 1963.

[3] UN doc. A/AC.105/12, pp. 3–4.

[4] Printed from an unsigned copy.

429. Telegram From the Mission to the United Nations to the Department of State[1]

New York, September 10, 1963, 9 p.m.

755. Outer space—consultations with Soviets. USUN's 744.[2]

1. We believe Soviet paper received yesterday is moderate, businesslike document which provides basis for useful consultations in coming weeks. Fact that response to our July 26 paper delayed until morning of Outer Space Comite meeting indicates Soviets probably do not anticipate concrete agreement on legal principles during course of meeting, but would envisage progress, if any, to be recorded later, possibly during GA debate. See separate report of conversation with Morozov. Due delay in translations, caused by debate, have been unable compare language with Fedorenko statement in Comite.

2. We do not feel that Space Comite meeting should be suspended or delayed on account of bilateral consultations with Soviets. To do so would place other members Comite in awkward, secondary role, and, as practical matter, would be difficult to convene Comite and produce its report to GA later than this week. Consultations with Soviets may require months before results are known. Accordingly, we are maintaining line that Comite seek finish work this week. Matsch and friendly members are in agreement.

3. Believe legal portion of Comite report should be limited to recording results of Legal Subcomite meeting as indicated in para 11 of Legal Subcomite report and taking account consultation by modifying last para along fol lines:

"With a view to the desirability of reaching full agreement on the issues on the agenda of the Committee, the delegations taking part in its work recommend that the consultations and exchanges of views between members which have been undertaken should continue. It is hoped that these will result in a wider consensus before the GA takes up the Outer Space item during its 18th session."

4. If Dept agrees, we will respond to Soviet paper early 12 Sept as follows:

A. Present Soviets with our translation their paper and ask if translation is accurate; and

---

[1] Source: National Archives and Records Administration, RG 59, Central Files 1960–63, SP 6 UN. Confidential.

[2] Telegram 744 from USUN described at greater length the Soviet paper outlined in Document 428. (National Archives and Records Administration, RG 59, Central Files 1960–63, SP 6 UN)

B. Seek clarification of Soviet paper with following questions:

(1) With ref 3(A), does revision of preamble Soviet text include dropping para 1, as well as revision para 5?

(2) 3(D), what does joint responsibility of international orgs and "states participating" mean? How is responsibility divided? Are all member states participating or have Soviets some other idea? What orgs have Soviets in mind?

(3) 3(E), When do Soviets envisage Legal Subcomite would determine composition study groups? When would study groups meet?

(4) Do Soviets envisage in their para 4 that state itself would determine potential danger its experiments before seeking consent other states? If not, how is potential danger to be determined?

(5) With regard to compromise formula for unresolved problems, such as, for example, banning use of satellites for purposes of war propaganda, etc., and activity in outer space of private companies, what language have Soviets in mind?

(6) Do Soviets believe that declaration must represent agreement on all outstanding issues, e.g., war propaganda, or might it be limited to areas on which agreement has already been reached, as outlined Fedorenko's address?

5. Although we might not pose all of above questions in next bilateral meeting, believe it would be useful to signal to USSR by 12 Sept. that we consider their response businesslike and will give it serious study in coming weeks. At same meeting we would also plan discuss with them above ideas for formulating legal portion of Comite report to GA.

6. Unless we hear to contrary we plan give text of Soviet note to UK, Canadian and Australian Dels late 11 Sept with request that it be maintained strictly confidential as has been case with our 26 July note to Soviets.[3]

Stevenson

---

[3] This note was transmitted to USUN in telegram 197, July 23. (Ibid.)

430. Memorandum From the Deputy Legal Adviser of the Department of State (Meeker) to Secretary of State Rusk[1]

Washington, October 8, 1963.

SUBJECT

Status of Discussions with Soviets on Outer Space Legal Questions

In the last two weeks, we have had five meetings with the Soviet Delegation in New York to discuss outer space legal questions, on which previously no progress had been made in the United Nations because of Soviet intransigence.[2] The meetings have been held to pursue further (1) a set of suggestions advanced by the United States in a memorandum handed to Ambassador Fedorenko on July 26, 1963, and (2) an aide-mémoire received from the Soviets on September 9.

For the first time in the nearly two years of international discussion of outer space legal questions, the Soviets have seemed affirmatively interested in arriving at a meeting of minds with us. Our recent talks have gone well. At the end of this morning's session, Ambassador Morozov said he planned to refer unagreed points to Foreign Minister Gromyko, and he said he assumed that we on our side would be reporting to you. This memorandum is written to summarize the negotiating situation, in case Gromyko should raise the subject.

1. The Soviets have sought a treaty or international agreement setting forth principles of outer space law. We have argued strongly for a General Assembly resolution, following the pattern of General Assembly resolution 1721 (XVI). The question of *form* of declaration remains an issue with the Soviets, but they have intimated probable acceptance of General Assembly resolution form if the United States would make an appropriate statement on the character and effect of legal principles in a resolution voted unanimously by the Assembly. The text of a statement authorized by the Department for this purpose is given at Tab A.[3] We have not shown this text to the Soviets.

---

[1] Source: National Archives and Records Administration, RG 59, Central Files 1960–63, SP 5 UN. Confidential.

[2] The U.S. position paper for negotiations with the Soviets on legal problems of outer space was transmitted in airgram A–91 to USUN, September 24. (Ibid., SP 6 UN)

[3] Tabs A–C are not printed. This draft statement in Tab A reads: "The legal principles set forth in this resolution clearly reflect international law as it is accepted by the Members of the United Nations. The United States, for its part, will respect those principles in the same way as the United States respects international law generally. We hope that the conduct which the resolution commends to nations in the exploration of outer space will become the practice of all nations."

We recommend that you maintain our position in favor of a General Assembly resolution, with appropriate accompanying statements in the Assembly.

2. The text of a declaration setting forth legal principles in resolution form is largely agreed. The current United States draft is given at Tab B. A few significant differences remain:

a. Operative paragraph 6 in Tab B gives the United States position on the subject of "interference" and "harmful experiments". The Soviet proposal on this subject appears as operative paragraph 6 in their draft (Tab C). The Soviet position is entirely unrealistic and unacceptable as it would purport to give a veto to any of the more than 100 States around the world over any space project which the Unites States, the USSR, or another country might be contemplating. We have let the Soviets know that their proposal is non-negotiable, and have indicated that our suggested paragraph 6 (Tab B) is as far as we are prepared to go.

We recommend that you maintain this position.

b. The Soviets have pressed to insert the words "sovereign rights of" before the words "jurisdiction and control" in operative paragraph 7 of the US draft (Tab B). There is not an essential difference of meaning between the Soviet formulation and our own, but we have resisted the inclusion of a reference to sovereignty on the ground that this is inappropriate to a declaration of outer space legal principles and is not in conformity with the analogous provisions in the Antarctic Treaty and the Convention on the High Seas.

We recommend that on this point you indicate simply that it should be possible to work out some appropriate language. (We can accept the Soviet formulation if necessary.)

c. Throughout our recent discussions the Soviets have referred in a perfunctory way, from time to time, to the necessity of including in the declaration a provision banning reconnaissance satellites. We have stated flatly that we would not accept any such provision, and there has been no serious discussion of the subject. While the Soviets have not conceded on this, we think they will probably agree to a declaration which says nothing about the use of observation satellites.

In any event, we recommend that you dismiss summarily any suggestion by Gromyko that some compromise should be sought in this area.

3. We have agreed with the Soviets on the desirability of treating the current series of discussions as confidential for the present. We have, of course, made it plain that any text which our two delegations might come together on would next have to be submitted for consideration by the other members of the United Nations Outer Space Committee and

the General Assembly as a whole. We plan in the next few days to brief a few selected delegations in New York, on a confidential basis, concerning the general course of the bilateral talks we have been having with the Soviets.

---

431.   Telegram From the Department of State to the Embassy in Japan[1]

Washington, November 13, 1963, 7:48 p.m.

1244. UN General Assembly Resolution on Outer Space Legal Principles.

After long negotiations, US has reached working agreement with USSR in New York on text declaration outer space legal principles in form GA resolution. Negotiations were undertaken at request UN Committee on Peaceful Uses of Outer Space. We and Sovs have now initiated consultation with other 26 members Space Committee to gain their cosponsorship of res before item discussed in Committee One, probably about Nov. 18. (We have indicated Sovs that we should consider suggestions by other members, although acceptance by Sovs also necessary.) We attach considerable importance to Japanese support and cosponsorship.

Minister Nakagawa explained to Dept today that Japanese cosponsorship is dependent on acceptance three amendments: (1) Preambular reference in declaration to resolution 1884 (XVIII)[2] calling upon all states to refrain from orbiting nuclear and other weapons mass destruction in space; (2) Language in operative para limiting outer space to "peaceful purposes"; and (3) Provision requiring prior registration and notification by launching state as condition for returning space vehicle or parts should such land accidentally in another state.

You should present our position to FonOff at appropriately high level soonest along following lines taken by Dept today: (As Embassy

---

[1] Source: National Archives and Records Administration, RG 59, Central Files 1960–63, SP 6 UN. Confidential; Priority. Drafted by Craig R. Eisendrath (IO/UNP); cleared by William B. Buffum, Raymond L. Garthoff, Louise McNutt, and Meeker; and approved by Richard N. Gardner. Repeated to USUN.

[2] This resolution was adopted by the General Assembly by acclamation on October 17. For text, see *American Foreign Policy: Current Documents, 1963*, pp. 1082–1083.

will recall some of these arguments were discussed last year with FonMin in Tokyo.)

(1) US prepared accept preambular reference to res 1884. We are not sure Sov reaction, although they have taken negative attitude toward any amendments.

(2) Meaning "peaceful purposes" is not clear, and inclusion in legal principles would be confusing. We interpret "peaceful purposes" as meaning non-aggressive, rather than non-military uses as apparently do Japanese.

We believe res 1884 and nuclear test ban have accomplished principal objectives of proponents for "peaceful purposes only" provision. If other military uses of outer space are intended to be excluded, such as observation from space for military intelligence, this would impinge on programs necessary to defense US and entire free world, of which Japan is important member.

We are sure that if phrase means non-military, it would be unacceptable to Sovs as well as US. Both US and USSR have military space programs. Moreover, satellites like many objects common to all countries serve both military and non-military purposes, and carrying distinction into effect would be impracticable. For example, without adequate inspection it is impossible determine if satellite is photographing clouds or military installations. Satellites which help navigate commercial vessels may also steer warships and submarines.

(3) Providing advance notification and data, as suggested by Japanese, would facilitate Sov counter measures against US observation satellite program. While we have provided for advance notification of satellite launching in our general and complete disarmament proposals, this is coupled with pre-launch inspection of satellites. Until Sovs willing accept this and world moves into period of greater security and trust under GCD, we cannot accept obligation provide advance notification and registration.

Moreover there is every indication Sovs would not comply. While US, for example, has registered every object launched into space or beyond with UN, Sovs have not fully complied with this obligation. They have not registered launching of six satellites of Cosmos series.

(4) Text of declaration represents best we could obtain from Sovs after months hard negotiations. We believe it important step toward legal order in space and would greatly appreciate Japanese support and cosponsorship. Reservations Japanese might have could be brought up during framing future international agreements. Opportunity would be presented next spring during framing agreements on liability and return of astronauts and space vehicles. Japanese might also make comments, to reserve their position on certain points, during their speech on

outer space item. Declaration of legal principles is not last word on sub-ject and, as more experience is gained, there will be continual opportu-nities refine and improve these first general principles.

FYI. Nakagawa requested he not be mentioned as suggesting con-sultations with Japanese FonOff, although he indicated private agree-ment with US position and in fact suggested we raise matter at high level with Foreign Office. He suggested Japanese sensitivity on peace-ful purposes question was related to attacks on government by Socialists. Position was moreover traditional one for Japanese. End FYI.

Rusk

---

432.   Editorial Note

On December 13, 1963, the UN General Assembly unanimously adopted Resolution 1962 (XVIII), "Declaration of Legal Principles Governing the Activities of States in the Exploration and Use of Outer Space," and Resolution 1963 (XVIII), "International Cooperation in the Peaceful Uses of Outer Space." Both resolutions are printed in *American Foreign Policy: Current Documents, 1963*, pages 1087–1092.

Communications Satellites

433.   Editorial Note

The outline of U.S. policy on communications satellites was set by President Kennedy's public release on July 24, 1961, of recommendations of the National Aeronautics and Space Council, which invited all nations to join with the United States in a commercial satellite program. See *Public Papers of the Presidents of the United States: John F. Kennedy, 1961,* pages 529–531. One of the main objectives of promoting international cooperation was to forestall development of competing systems by the United States, the Soviet bloc, Western Europe, and others. Coordination of U.S. policy was handled by a special Subcommittee on Communications Satellites of the NSC Subcommittee on Communications. The special Subcommittee was established on January 28, 1963, with W. Michael Blumenthal as Chairman. (Memorandum from Orrick to Department of State Principals, January 28; National Archives and Records Administration, RG 59, IO Files: Lot 67 D 378, ITU)

434. National Security Action Memorandum No. 175[1]

Washington, July 21, 1962.

MEMORANDUM FOR

The Secretary of State
The Secretary of Defense

SUBJECT

DOD–State Concept for Communication between National Leaders

1. The May 25, 1962 memorandum for the President from the Deputy Secretary of Defense and its attachment, outlines a series of measures proposed by the Joint Chiefs of Staff to improve our means of maintaining communications with foreign national leaders during emergency conditions.[2] While recognizing that adjustments may be required as detailed planning and development progresses, the general concept in the Joint Chiefs of Staff's plan is approved for planning purposes.

2. All actions taken should be consistent both with planning for the National Military Command System (NMCS), which will be designed as the unified survivable national communications system, and with the integration of State–CIA communications facilities. Also, cognizance should be taken of studies presently under way in government which may lead to a proposal for improved communication links between the national leaders of the US and the USSR. All planning should be accomplished with the view that this additional requirement at some future date may be imposed upon the National Military Command System.

3. The Secretaries of State and Defense are requested to initiate planning based upon the proposed concept with the assistance of such other government agencies as may be required. The detailed plan with estimates of cost will be submitted to the President for approval prior to implementation.

McGeorge Bundy

---

[1] Source: National Archives and Records Administration, RG 59, S/S–NSC Files: Lot 72 D 316, NSAM 175. Top Secret.

[2] The memorandum is attached but not printed. Its attachment was not found.

435.   **Memorandum From the Deputy Assistant Secretary of State for International Organization Affairs (Gardner) to the Deputy Assistant Secretary of State for Economic Affairs (Blumenthal)[1]**

Washington, October 4, 1962.

SUBJECT

U.S. Policy on the Organization of Global Satellite Communications

This memorandum, written in haste amid the usual distractions of a General Assembly, seeks to outline a U.S. position on the organization of an international satellite communications system—a position which will be needed in forthcoming talks with the United Kingdom and Canada and subsequently in consultations with other countries.

I. Objectives

The President's policy statement of July 24, 1961,[2] Part D of the U.S.-sponsored General Assembly Resolution 1721 (XVI),[3] the Communications Satellite Act of 1962,[4] and other official statements have identified the basic objectives of U.S. policy in the field of satellite communications. For the purpose of this memorandum, the most important of these objectives are the following:

(1) To get a communications satellite system operating as soon as possible, for reasons of prestige and foreign policy;

(2) To realize the economic and technical benefits from this improvement in communications (more channels, intercontinental television, possibly lower costs);

(3) To achieve political gains resulting from increased international communication, including communication with Communist countries;

(4) To augment the economic development of less developed countries and our political relations with them by means of a global system which links low traffic areas as well as the main industrial countries;

(5) To make the most efficient use of the limited number of radio frequencies available for space communications as well as other communications.

---

[1] Source: National Archives and Records Administration, RG 59, IO/OES Files: Lot 68 D 379, K-11, Negotiations on International Organization, 1963. Official Use Only. Drafted by Gardner on October 3. Copies were sent to Assistant Secretary Cleveland, OES, and Gil Carter (E).

[2] See Document 433.

[3] This resolution was adopted unanimously by the UN General Assembly on December 20, 1961. For text, see *American Foreign Policy: Current Documents, 1961*, pp. 1202–1205.

[4] Public Law 87–624 of August 31, 1962. (76 Stat. 419)

II. The Central Question

One of the primary issues to be resolved at an early stage is whether there will be one global satellite communication system or several competing systems organized by the Communist Bloc, the Commonwealth and Europe, the U.S. and others.[5]

All but the first of the five policy objectives outlined above argue for a single satellite system:

1. From the *economic* and *technical* point of view, satellite systems offer such a vast increase in the capacity for communications that it is doubtful that the capacity of several systems could be fully utilized in the foreseeable future. Moreover, several systems with different kinds of equipment would require the duplication of ground installations. Finally, the use of several systems would reduce the flexibility which one system offers for routing communications in the most efficient possible way. For all of these reasons, the establishment of several different systems might prejudice opportunities for substantial reductions in communications rates.

2. From the point of view of the *political* gains resulting from increased communications, a number of different systems would reduce the possibility for the worldwide exchange of programs. The opportunity to link the Soviet Bloc into a global communications network would be lost. There would be competition between the Soviet Bloc, the U.S., the Commonwealth and Europe to link less developed countries on an exclusive basis. United States access to certain less developed countries might thereby be lost.

3. From the point of view of our relations with *less developed countries*, a number of competing systems may result in uneconomic expansion in the communication facilities of certain politically favored countries and the neglecting of less favored ones. Instead of having access to all countries, the less developed countries will be "adopted" as members of more or less exclusive communications clubs.

4. From the point of view of the scarce *frequency spectrum*, several competing systems would be extremely wasteful and would be likely to get in the way of one another as well as other communication needs.

If, for all the reasons given above, we are to achieve a single international satellite system, this has important implications for U.S. policy. Our position on the host of organizational questions which arise in the establishment of a satellite system must be sufficiently attrac-

---

[5] It is generally agreed that U.S. needs for military communications will require a separate U.S. system for this purpose. [Footnote in the source text.]

tive to other countries so as to dissuade them from establishing competing systems and to persuade them to join us in the establishment of a single network. If the U.S appears to be seeking a satellite network which is essentially U.S. owned and managed, there is little doubt but that the Soviet Union and the Commonwealth (possibly in conjunction with Western Europe) will develop their own self-centered satellite systems. Thus the devising of a genuine international arrangement with widespread participation in ownership and management is a prerequisite to the achievement of a single system.

There are at least two reasons why the U.S. should express its views *now* about establishing a genuine international arrangement:

In the *first* place, this will help foreclose the establishment of competing systems. The possibility of a Commonwealth satellite system is now under consideration. The forthcoming talks with the United Kingdom and Canada provide an important opportunity to influence Commonwealth policy. The same is true of any further discussions we may have with the Soviet Union either in the International Telecommunications Union (ITU) or pursuant to the Dryden–Blagonravov talks.

In the *second* place, this will help us secure the necessary frequency assignments for space communications at the International Telecommunications Union (ITU) conference in October 1963. Other countries will be more likely to accept a self-denying ordinance not to use certain frequencies for conventional communications (as well as reasonable ground rules for space communications) if they think they are "going to get something" through participation in an international arrangement on the basis of mutual benefit.

Bearing all these points in mind, there is nevertheless an outer limit to United States willingness to "internationalize" satellite communications. This limit is set primarily by our concern with the first objective mentioned above, namely, the achievement of an operating system as soon as possible. Multilateral participation in satellite communications must not be pressed to the point where it delays the establishment of the system. This could easily happen if American efforts in research and development were held back by an excessive "farming out" of tasks to other countries or if negotiations bogged down in political controversy. Moreover, the United States domestic satellite corporation will be unwilling to invest the necessary financial and human resources if the international arrangements prove unacceptable.

The central question, therefore, is to develop a satellite arrangement which is "international" enough to assure foreign participation in a single enterprise and yet which safeguards the U.S. position sufficiently to assure rapid progress and vigorous participation by the U.S. corporation. It may turn out that an arrangement achieving both these purposes is not capable of achievement, but we have the obligation to try.

III. Policy Issues

In reality, there are not simply the two alternatives of a United States system versus an international system. There is a whole spectrum of conceivable arrangements between the two extremes. The variety of arrangements can be seen only when we have identified the principal questions which may call for international negotiations. A summary of these questions follows:

A. Questions relating to participation before establishment of the system.

1. *Research and development.* Is the United States to do all the research and development, or is this to be "farmed out" to the Commonwealth, the Europeans and the Soviet Bloc on some basis of comparative advantage?

2. *Manufacture.* Is the United States to manufacture all of the components of the system (ground equipment, satellites, boosters) or are foreign countries to participate?

3. *Launch.* Is the United States to launch all the satellites, or is the Soviet Union (and eventually Europe) to launch some of the satellites?

4. *System design.* To what extent is the type of system to be employed (e.g., Telstar versus Syncom) to be determined unilaterally by the United States or on the basis of agreement with other countries? (This decision has important consequences for foreign interests: Syncom means cheaper and simpler ground installations, and thus less burdens on the less developed countries; Telstar offers greater opportunities for frequency-sharing.)

5. *Global coverage.* How rapidly and to what extent is there to be global coverage of low traffic areas?

B. Questions relating to ownership and management of satellites.

1. *Investment.* Who is to contribute, and on what basis, to the cost of the satellite portion of the system? (The cost of constructing and launching the satellites accounts for over half the cost of the satellite system.)

2. *Revenue sharing.* Who is to share, and on what basis, in the revenue to be attributed to the satellite portion of the system?

3. *Control.* Who is to allocate the voice channels in the satellites to different uses (e.g., 600 telephone channels versus one TV channel)? Who is to allocate the channels as between different countries capable

of using them at the same time? Who is to determine when satellite service is to be discontinued or when satellites are to be replaced?

C. *General operating problems.*[6]

1. *Rate-making.* How are rates to be established? Is there to be a unitary rate system, i.e. one rate between any two points of the system, regardless of the volume of traffic (a subsidy to communication with low traffic areas)? Will rate-making policy take into account the desire to protect existing investment in cables? Will the emphasis be on relatively high rates to recoup existing investment quickly, or on relatively low rates with a view to the long-term elasticity of demand and the political benefits of increased communication? How will decision-making on these various subjects be shared as between participants in the system?

2. *Technical ground rules.* How will technical compatibility of different system components be assured (e.g. between ground stations and satellites and between different satellites where manufacturing has been done in different countries)? What ground rules with respect to non-interference and cooperation will be required and how will they be enforced? For example, what collective sanctions might be undertaken to deal with countries seeking a "free ride" on the system?

D. *Questions relating to ground terminals.*

1. *Ownership.* Who is to own (invest in, derive revenue from, control) the ground stations?

2. *Location.* Who is to determine the location of a ground terminal in a region where only one is economically justified? (Quite apart from advantages in terms of prestige and technology, the location of a ground terminal in a specific country enables that country to "black-out" its neighbors from the global system for political and military purposes.)

E. *Questions relating to assistance to less developed countries.*

1. *The construction of ground terminals.* Who is to pay for (and supervise the construction of) ground installations in less developed countries which lack the financial and other means to construct them?

2. *Operating ground terminals.* Who is to supply the personnel (or train indigenous personnel) to operate the ground terminals in less developed countries?

3. *Assistance to internal communications.* Who is to supply technical assistance and capital aid to develop the internal communications networks of less developed countries to the point where they can be meaningfully linked into the satellite system?

---

[6] The problem of frequency allocation is not discussed here on the assumption that it will continue to be handled in the ITU. [Footnote in the source text.]

F. Public uses of the system.

1. *National information activities.* Will the USIA, Moscow Radio and other national institutions be permitted to use the system for broadcasts serving national political objectives? Will they pay the commercial rate or a specially low rate?

2. *United Nations.* Will the United Nations and its Specialized Agencies be permitted to use the system? Will they pay the commercial rate or will they be given a specially low rate? (During the experimental phase of another year or two the UN will be using Telstar without charge to broadcast its proceedings, but what happens afterwards?)

G. Questions relating to broadcasting.

1. *The exchange of broadcasts between nations.* What agreements will be made as to the dissemination of foreign broadcasts on national networks?

2. *Control of content.* Will there be any restrictions whatever on the content of programs that are sent out by means of the system? (See, e.g., the Soviet proposal to outlaw "war propaganda in outer space".)

IV. Institutional Alternatives

As noted earlier, the choice is not simply between a "U.S. system" and an "international" system. The various questions outlined above are susceptible to a wide variety of answers—answers which represent—many points in the spectrum between the "U.S." and "international" extremes. As a practical matter, however, certain extreme possibilities can be eliminated at the outset. For example, no one seriously advocates United States domination of the entire satellite system, since it is generally agreed that foreign countries will want to own and operate the ground stations located on their territories. On the other extreme, no one seriously advocates establishing a United Nations agency in which management of the system would be shared on the basis of one country, one vote.

As a practical matter, there are three principal institutional alternatives for dealing with the questions listed above:

A. *A "United States-controlled" system.* One possible alternative would be a system which, for want of a better name, could be described as "United States controlled." Foreign countries would own and manage the ground stations in their territories. The ground stations in the United States would be owned and managed either by the U.S. corporation itself or by the common carriers. But the satellites would be owned by the U.S. corporation. The U.S. corporation, under government regulation, would carry on the research and development; would determine the most satisfactory system to be established and the extent to which it would be global; would control procurement of system components; and would arrange for launching with the U.S. Government. It would put up the money for the manufacture and launch of the satellites; would collect the revenue attributable to them; and would control the allocation of the voice channels by renting them out to different users in the U.S. and abroad. For the most part, questions of rate making and technical ground rules would be negotiated bilaterally with individual foreign countries linked into the system, although some of these questions might be discussed in the ITU. The construction of ground terminals in less developed countries and capital aid to these countries would be the responsibility mainly of the U.S. corporation and the United States Government.

B. *International system: functional approach.* This is not really one alternative but a group of alternatives. The approach would be unilateral, bilateral, regional and multilateral (through the ITU or elsewhere) in accordance with the particular functional problem. Ownership would be shared, either on an undivided basis (each country would have a percentage share in *all* the satellites) or on a divided basis (each country would own particular satellites which might finance, manufacture or launch). The allocation of channels as between uses and users might be carried out bilaterally and regionally for particular satellites at particular times. The decision as to the allocation of ground stations in a particular region might be left to the countries of the region. Questions of technical and financial assistance might be taken up in institutions such as UN Expanded Program of Technical Assistance (ETAP), the Special Fund, International Development Association (IDA) or the Organization for Economic Cooperation and Development (OECD).

C. *International system: corporate approach.* Under this alternative, there would be an international institution to handle most of the specific problems enumerated in Section III. Since U.S. participation will be in the form of a private corporation, an inter-governmental agency would not be desirable. Instead, there would be created an international corporation on the model of Eurochemic, the European company established for the processing of chemical fuels. Eurochemic was chartered by the Organization for European Economic Cooperation (OEEC), but its shares are held by governments and private firms. An international satellite corporation could be established on the same model. Its charter could be worked out through inter-governmental negotiations either in the ITU or elsewhere. Some of the shares of the corporation would be held by the United States satellite corporation. The remainder of the shares would be held by foreign public corporations such as the British Post Office or foreign government departments as in the case of the Soviet Union. A small Board of Directors would make fundamental management decisions, but there could be periodic meetings of all interested governments to review the operations of the corporation and make general recommendations. The latter function might be served by the ITU Plenipotentiary Conference. Voting in the Board of Directors could be based in part on financial contribution, in part on use of the system, and in part on other criteria which would give some voice to small and less developed countries. Under any rational formula, the United States would have at least one-third to two-fifths of the votes and would have a majority in conjunction with its European allies. For political reasons qualifying majorities might be necessary to safeguard what the Soviet Union and other countries might regard as fundamental interests.

The difficulties with all three of these alternatives are readily apparent. Alternative A is almost certainly destined to produce competing systems from the Soviet Bloc and the European-Commonwealth group. Alternative C poses political and organizational problems of great difficulty. In the present political climate, it is not easy to imagine an effective working relationship on the Board of Directors between Soviet and American representatives. Alternative B, for all its advantages of flexibility, may fail to provide an adequate structure for an efficient international approach.

V. Future Strategy

The choice between the three principal alternatives outlined above is of great importance. All of its implications will not be clear until we know more about the technical details of the system. It is obvious that we cannot commit ourselves to any institutional design at this early date. There are, however, some things that can be done in our conversations with other countries even at this stage:

1. We can impress other countries with our technical superiority in satellite communications and our determination to press ahead with the speediest development of the system. This will strengthen our bargaining power.
2. We can say that we desire a single commercial system rather than competing systems. We can cite all the reasons given in Part II of this memorandum and emphasize that these are not just matters of U.S. interest but of interest to all countries.
3. We can say that we favor a truly international system, with foreign participation in ownership and management of the satellites as well as in ownership of ground stations in other countries.
4. We can spell out the major questions which will have to be decided in the years ahead along the lines of Part III above and invite an exchange of views as to different ways of dealing with them.
5. We can outline alternatives B and C—the functional approach and the corporate approach—while indicating that the United States has not reached a decision between them.

These above points should be the major themes in our conversations with the United Kingdom and Canada and with other countries in the months ahead. Points 1 through 4 should also be outlined in our speeches on outer space at the current United Nations General Assembly and in the report to the International Telecommunications Union which we are requested to submit by December 31.

---

436.   Memorandum From the President's Special Assistant for Science and Technology (Wiesner) to President Kennedy[1]

Washington, October 25, 1962.

RE

> Your Directive Concerning Improvements in the U.S. World-wide Communications Capabilities

1. At a meeting called by Mr. Bundy and Secretary McNamara, a National Communications Systems Working Group was created. The members are to be: W.H. Orrick, Jr., Department of State (Chairman); Admiral William Irvin, Department of Defense (Vice Chairman); [*less than 1 line of source text not declassified*] CIA; Dr. Irvin Stewart, OEP, Special Assistant to the President for Telecommunications; and Dr. David Robinson, OST Staff (Observer).

2. The committee was given the following tasks:

a. On the highest urgency make plans for correcting communication deficiencies to Latin America, with particular emphasis on the needs of CINCCARIB.

b. Make a comprehensive survey of requirements of government agencies and a survey of available facilities.

c. To plan an integrated national communications facility to meet these needs.

3. A task force concerned with communications in the [*less than 1 line of source text not declassified*] area has made a preliminary survey of communications needs and additional facilities required to meet them for CINCCARIB and for general DOD, State and CIA communications to [*less than 1 line of source text not declassified*] countries and is attempting to do the following:

a. Increase the circuit capability from the U.S. to Panama. Several techniques are being explored, including the crash installation of a tropospheric scatter system, additional commercial facilities and the expe-

---

[1] Source: Kennedy Library, National Security Files, Meetings and Memoranda Series, NSAM No. 201, Box 339. Secret.

dition of a planned submarine cable to Panama. Because of CINCCARIB's requirements, this project has the highest priority.

b. Mr. McCone has directed augmented staffing of the CIA communications centers in Latin America. The CIA and DOD are undertaking to provide the necessary manpower.

c. The State Department has prepared a resolution on communications, recommending that member states of the OAS cooperate to strengthen their communications capabilities by entering into bilateral and other arrangements. A draft copy of the resolution is being forwarded to our Ambassadors to Latin America with the request that they consult local governments regarding the resolution. It is hoped that the resolution could be acted upon in the very near future and pave the way for the introduction of additional communication equipment, particularly by the Department of Defense. A draft copy of the resolution and a circular for our Ambassadors is attached.[2]

d. The Department of Defense has located equipment which can be air transported if needed once agreements permitting its use have been obtained.

e. A survey is being made of the availability of additional commercial service to the U.S. embassies in the area.

4. The National Communications Systems Working Group is beginning a review of U.S. Government requirements on a worldwide scale. In parallel they will also survey the existing facilities and attempt to plan needed corrective measures. It is hoped that a preliminary report will be available for Mr. McNamara and Mr. Bundy on Friday, October 26. The group has organized five regional subcommittees on Africa, Latin America, Europe, the Near East and South Asia, and the Far East and Pacific, with members from DOD, State Department and CIA. The assignment sheet for regional subcommittees is attached.[3]

5. It is generally agreed the most serious deficiencies in the communications systems are lack of integration and the fact that the State–CIA net has not been planned to meet crisis loads. It is our understanding of the present assignment that the facilities are to be modified and augmented so that it will be adequate for peak loads. This will involve the introduction of additional equipment and staffs at numerous points around the world. We are proceeding on the understanding that this is your desire.

JB Wiesner

---

[2] See Document 437.

[3] Not found.

437. Circular Telegram From the Department of State to Certain Posts[1]

Washington, October 25, 1962, 8:03 p.m.

760. For Ambassador from Martin. President has directed that most urgent action be taken improve US communications facilities particularly in American Republics area. Numerous and serious communications shortcomings encountered last several days prior President's statement on Cuba demonstrate unequivocal, immediate, and continuous need for effective overt US Govt-controlled radio communications system with facilities in each ARA country.

Request you immediately seek from Fonmin, or higher level, oral agreement in principle to necessity for such radio communications system (in light its crucial importance to hemispheric cooperation and defense) and willingness of Govt to which you accredited to explore with us immediately means for putting it into effect. FYI. If necessary, pursuant to recently enacted legislation US Govt prepared consider granting radio operations privileges in Washington, D.C.

Reply urgently by cable giving your estimate time required for conclusion successful negotiations.

Rusk

---

[1] Source: Kennedy Library, National Security Files, Meetings and Memoranda Series, NSAM No. 201, Box 339. Top Secret; Niact; Limit Distribution. Drafted by Clarence E. Birgfeld and Melbourne L. Spector (ARA/EX) on October 25; cleared by Assistant Secretary Edwin M. Martin (ARA), Colonel Hill (DOD/ISA), Bromley Smith (White House), Jordan T. Rogers (S/S), Robert G. Kreer (DC), Warde L. Cameron (L), and Colonel William B. Robinson (G/PM); and approved by Deputy Under Secretary William H. Orrick, Jr. This telegram was sent to all posts in Latin America except La Paz, with information copies to the POLADs at CINCCARIB and CINCLANT.

438.   National Security Action Memorandum No. 201[1]

Washington, October 26, 1962.

TO

The Vice President
The Secretary of State
The Secretary of Defense
The Secretary of the Treasury
The Attorney General
The Chairman, Joint Chiefs of Staff
The Director of Central Intelligence
The Under Secretary of State
The Deputy Secretary of Defense
The Ambassador at Large
The Special Counsel to the President
The Acting Director, U.S. Information Agency
The Director, National Security Agency
The Administrator, National Aeronautics and Space Administration
Chairman, Federal Communications Commission
Administrator, Federal Aviation Agency
Administrator, General Services Administration
Director, Office of Emergency Planning
Assistant Secretary of Defense (International Security Affairs)
The Counselor of the Department of State

SUBJECT

Establishment of Subcommittee on Communications

There is hereby established a Subcommittee on Communications of the Executive Committee of the National Security Council. It shall be the responsibility of this subcommittee, under the direction of the Executive Committee, to ensure the establishment of a national communications system which will make the worldwide communications available to the United States Government as prompt, reliable, and secure as possible. The President has designated William H. Orrick, Jr., Deputy Under Secretary of State for Administration, to be Chairman of this subcommittee. Mr. Orrick will take whatever action is necessary to eliminate deficiencies which presently exist. He will look to all agencies for prompt and immediate support. He will have as Vice Chairman an officer designated by the Secretary of Defense, who shall be the representative of the Department of Defense, who has undertaken to give particular support to the pursuit of this objective.

In this task, Mr. Orrick should consult with and secure the cooperation of other departments, agencies, and the public sector as appropri-

---

[1] Source: National Archives and Records Administration, RG 59, S/S–NSC Files: Lot 72 D 316, NSAM 201.   Confidential.

ate, drawing to the extent necessary upon the work done by the Emergency Planning Committee under NSAM 127.[2] By copy of this memorandum, other agencies are instructed to cooperate with Mr. Orrick in this mission to the fullest extent. If Mr. Orrick encounters difficulties or resistance, he will report at once to the President.

McGeorge Bundy

---

[2] Not printed. (Ibid.)

---

439.   Memorandum From the Special Assistant to the Assistant Secretary of State for International Organization Affairs (Wilson) to the Assistant Secretary (Cleveland)[1]

Washington, March 11, 1963.

SUBJECT

Space Communications

I was stunned yesterday to overhear Dick's comments which suggested that the State Department is on top of space communications like NASA is on top of SYNCOM; or maybe it's worse, since NASA at least has a pretty good idea of where SYNCOM is.

Can it possibly be that the Department of State still thinks that "science" is a peculiar branch of metaphysics on which the Secretary should be "advised" from time to time—that outer space is beyond the pale of politics—that international telecommunications has no more to do with international relations than has IT&T in Brazil—that a global satellite communications system will somehow be fathered by the FCC out of the Space Council with Edward R. Murrow serving as Godfather?

After the flap last year about "peaceful uses" (muted only by the hullabaloo of the Cuban crisis); after dashing up to the Hill to testify that the communications satellite bill fully protected the foreign policy interests of the United States (a highly dubious proposition); and after publicly, formally and explicitly stating a U.S. policy commitment to a truly universal satellite communications system managed by a truly international organization (which was followed up so effectively that

---

[1] Source: Kennedy Library, Cleveland Papers, Outer Space, Communications Satellites, Box 20. Personal and Confidential.

the British appear to be far gone toward a decision to establish a Commonwealth satellite system)—I should have thought that the State Department at long last would have taken charge of this subject.

At the risk of being accused of empire-building, don't you think IO should now move in and take the responsibility? After all, whatever else it is, *this is a problem in international organization.*

---

440. **Telegram From the Embassy in the United Kingdom to the Department of State**[1]

London, May 8, 1963, 6 p.m.

4429. Deptel 5888.[2] Substance report contained reftel confirmed by FonOff source (Hope-Jones). In extremely frank discussion on current developments in space communications Hope-Jones indicated the following:

1. There has been considerable pulling and hauling among European countries as to how to proceed in space communications. FonOff has been attempting take the lead in organizing European countries to focus on this question. Unfortunately Cabinet indecision led to delays and in end French seized initiative. As result first meeting will be held at invitation of French in Paris at Ambassadorial level on May 20. British Minister in Paris, Sir Algernon Rumbold, will head UK Delegation which will include Hope-Jones, Sir Robert Harvey and MOA representatives. The British were successful in arranging for a second meeting at Ministerial level to be held in London in July.

2. French wish primary point on Paris agenda to be "forms of European cooperation" but British have indicated they intend enlarge scope this item to include general international concept of space communications since obvious some understanding on this point must be reached prior to discussion of European forms of cooperation. Other agenda items include (A) machinery for handling space communica-

---

[1] Source: National Archives and Records Center, RG 59, IO/OES Files: Lot 68 D 379, K-11, Negotiations on International Organization, 1963. Secret; Priority; No Distribution Outside Dept.

[2] In telegram 5888 to London, May 7, the Department asked for information on meetings to be held in Europe concerning commercial communications satellite planning. (Ibid., Central Files 1960–63, TEL 3 CEPT)

tions matters between European countries on both industry and government levels; (Hope-Jones indicated UK plans propose standing committee as initial inter-governmental organization until clearer idea obtained as to type international organization required.) (B) relations with the UN; (C) relations with under-developed countries, and (D) provision of guidance to CEPT.

3. UK expects Paris meeting will identify problems and determine general scope of substantive statement to be presented US following July meeting. During July meeting governments will present positions on points developed during Paris discussion and presumably agree on details of statement.

4. With respect to CEPT European governments concerned with implications of CEPT questionnaire and presumably have decided against sending questionnaire to US. Hope-Jones implied that hereafter CEPT discussions and actions will be directed by governments. This has apparently generated considerable adverse reaction on part GPO and PTT administrations. GPO has informed FonOff that US Communications Satellite Corporation taking over responsibility for international dealings involving space communications and State Department activities in this area are phasing out. On basis this report GPO attempting persuade HMG that there is no need for FonOff involvement since matters can now be resolved between technical administrations, i.e. GPO, PTT and Communications Satellite Corporation. (Department may wish comment on this.)

5. Hope-Jones said there was some feeling in Europe that French were trying to dominate European space communications scene. French are reported to have indicated they would go into cooperative arrangement with US on space communications only for limited period of five years "to learn the business" and then withdraw to form independent system. When asked with whom the French could establish independent system, Hope-Jones replied presumably there would always be specific links which might lie outside the main axis of a global system, e.g. France–Africa.

6. In conclusion Hope-Jones stated FonOff position favoring single global system substantially represents UK posture today but, at instigation MOA, UK is keeping as alternative course possibility of independent system in event global system advocated by US did not permit UK adequate opportunity to participate in all phases.

Comment: In view Hope-Jones' frankness and sensitivity of this material, Department requested protect source. UK position for Paris meeting on May 20 expected to be formulated end next week. Embassy will attempt learn substance and report.

Bruce

441. Resolution Adopted by the Conference on Satellite Communications[1]

Paris, undated.

CONFERENCE ON SATELLITE COMMUNICATIONS—
PARIS, MAY 20–21, 1963

Resolution adopted by the Conference

The preliminary consensus of view of the Conference is that satellite communications should be organized on an international basis in such a way as to enable European countries:

(a) to participate in the design of the system
(b) to share in the ownership of the system
(c) to play a full part in the management of the system
(d) to have an opportunity, as the system is expanded and developed, to provide satellites, launchers and other necessary equipment, for inclusion in the system

The Conference requests the British and French Authorities to bring to the attention of the United States Authorities, on behalf of the whole Conference, this summary of the views expressed during the first session of the Conference held at Paris on May 20 and 21. The Conference emphasizes the importance it attaches to the views of the American Authorities on these principles being made known in time for them to be considered by the Conference in London in mid-July.

The Conference also thinks it necessary for the American Authorities to be informed of the interest it has in the enquiries which the CEPT ad hoc Committee is to make for its part.

The Conference also invites the Governments represented at the present Meeting to submit papers expanding their views on these subjects in time for the London Meeting.

---

[1] Source: National Archives and Records Administration, RG 59, IO/OES Files: Lot 68 D 379, K-11.1, Structure of International Organizations. Limited Official Use. The resolution is Annex A to circular airgram CA–14556, June 27. For Annex B, see Document 443.

442.   **Memorandum From the Chairman of the Subcommittee on Communications of the National Security Council (Orrick) to the Executive Committee of the National Security Council**[1]

Washington, May 21, 1963.

SUBJECT

Final Report of the Sub-committee on Communications

Submitted herewith (Tab A)[2] is the final report the Sub-committee on Communications of the Executive Committee of the National Security Council. This Sub-committee was established by National Security Action Memorandum No. 201 of October 26, 1962, which stated that "It shall be the responsibility of this subcommittee, under the direction of the Executive Committee, to ensure the establishment of a national communications system which will make the worldwide communications available to the United States Government as prompt, reliable, and secure as possible."[3]

Scope of Sub-committee's Activities

For several weeks following the issuance of NSAM No. 201, the Sub-committee met in continuous session. The initial phase of its activities was concerned with an appraisal in detail of existing communications facilities, an identification of major deficiencies, and the issuance of directives for the expeditious carrying out of the required improvements. The Sub-committee then turned its attention to an intensive examination of ways in which longer-range improvements could be achieved through the upgrading of existing facilities or new installations.

The Sub-committee's decisions and objectives were embodied for the most part in the form of "action directives," and 125 such directives were issued. Within a relatively short time substantial progress was realized with respect to solving some complicated technical, administrative and diplomatic problems. As of this date, 97 of the actions requested have been completed. Thus, 78 percent of the specific measures directed by the Sub-committee have been taken. Most of the remaining directives involve actions which are not scheduled for completion until later in 1963 or in 1964.

Areas of Major Improvement

Particularly noteworthy is the marked improvement brought about in the facilities for communicating with Latin America, the lack of

---

[1] Source: Kennedy Library, National Security Files, Meetings and Memoranda Series, NSAM No. 201, Box 339. Secret.

[2] None of the tabs is printed.

[3] Document 438.

which loomed so large in the crisis that gave rise to the establishment of the Sub-committee. In Latin America, and at most key posts in other areas, a 24-hour, seven-days-a-week communications response capability is now in being. "On-line" cryptographic equipment has been installed, or planned, for all major diplomatic missions and will result in providing more rapid, reliable and secure communications. Slower, but measurable progress has been witnessed in the construction of the European and Trans-Mediterranean tropospheric scatter systems, as well as in communications improvements in other areas of the world.

Programs for improving relay and switching centers at key points throughout the world have been initiated. Major steps have also been taken to improve radio transmitting equipment and to obtain, where necessary, transmitting rights for US embassies in foreign countries so that improved communications or emergency back-up facilities will be available. Under the auspices of the NSC Sub-committee a special working group has completed a study of the potential impact of the communications satellites on a national communications system. In addition, the following basic reports resulting from Sub-committee directives have been completed: (1) acceptability of certain "off-line" cryptographic systems, (2) physical and technical security problems and precautions, and (3) manpower requirements resulting from the actions of the NSC Sub-committee.

Secure communications facilities among top officials in Washington have been expanded and studies have been completed for the installation of still more sophisticated equipment. The Department of State message precedence system has been revised to ensure conformity with that employed by the Department of Defense and CIA.

The work of the Sub-committee, briefly summarized above, is described in more detail in the enclosed Final Report.

Remaining Issues To Be Resolved

There remain a few problems of major importance to be solved:

(1) The extent to which separate Defense, State or CIA communications centers at Foreign Service posts abroad can be consolidated or centralized;
(2) Budget planning for and financing of the national communications system; and,
(3) The question of "privacy," which includes the need for a thorough review of the present systems for allocation of available circuits to various governmental users.

These issues are discussed at greater length on pages 13–14 of Tab A.

Recommendation

The most pressing immediate requirement, however, is to proceed with the creation of a permanent organizational framework for a national communications system, upon which the solution of these remaining major problems depends. To provide for such a framework, a draft National Security Action Memorandum is enclosed (Tab B). This memorandum proposes the designation of the Director of Telecommunications Management as Special Assistant to the President for Telecommunications and of the Secretary of Defense as Executive Agent for the NCS, each with specific responsibilities as set forth therein.

The Sub-committee urges strongly that the Action Memorandum be approved at the earliest possible date.

The Sub-committee notes that the position of Director of Telecommunications Management is now vacant. The Sub-committee is unanimously of the opinion that the issuance of the above-mentioned Action Memorandum need not, and should not, await the filling of the above position. Moreover, it recommends that every effort be made to fill this vacancy at the earliest possible date to permit the newly designated Special Assistant to the President for Telecommunications to assume his responsibilities expeditiously.

The Sub-committee is in disagreement on one point. Three participants[4] recommend that the Sub-committee on Communications continue in existence to give policy direction to the NCS until the future Special Assistant to the President for Telecommunications notifies the Sub-committee that he is ready to assume his responsibilities. This majority recommendation stems from the following considerations: (1) NSAM No. 201 placed responsibility on the Sub-committee to ensure the establishment of an NCS; (2) a serious gap in the organizational structure of such a system would initially result if the Sub-committee is dissolved before a Special Assistant to the President is appointed; (3) the functions of the Sub-committee would not, therefore, be wholly fulfilled; and (4) in any event, the Sub-committee could serve a useful purpose in the interim as a means through which over-all policy guidance could be obtained, and as a forum to air any interagency differences which might arise.

Two members[5] consider that, with the issuance of the Action Memorandum, the Sub-committee should be dissolved. This view is set forth in the enclosed statement of the Vice Chairman, Lt. General Starbird (Tab C).

William H. Orrick, Jr.
Chairman

---

[4] Deputy Under Secretary of State Orrick, Sub-committee Chairman; Dr. William O. Baker; Dr. David Z. Robinson. [Footnote in the source text.]

[5] Lt. General Alfred D. Starbird, Sub-committee Vice Chairman; [*less than 1 line of source text not declassified*]. [Footnote in the source text.]

443. Aide-Mémoire From the Government of the United States to the Governments of the United Kingdom and France[1]

Washington June 26, 1963.

AIDE-MEMOIRE

On June 12, 1963, the British Embassy and the Embassy of the French Republic delivered to the Department of State a copy of a Resolution adopted by the Conference on Satellite Communications held in Paris on May 20–21, 1963, requesting, on behalf of the Conference, the written views of the United States on the principles set forth in the Resolution.

The United States Government is pleased to have the opportunity to state that it shares the view of the Conference set forth in the Resolution that commercial satellite communications should be organized on an international basis in such a way as to enable European countries to participate in the design, ownership and management of the system and, in addition, to provide, as the system is expanded and developed, satellites, launchers and other equipment for inclusion in the system. It is noted that the same considerations would also apply to other participants.

Believing that additional information may be of use to the countries participating in the Satellite Communications Conference to be held in London in July, the United States Government offers the following additional comments:

Persuasive technical, economic and political considerations indicate that commercial communications satellites should be planned, developed and operated on the basis of a single global system. The concept of a single global system for commercial purposes contemplates that the organization of the system will be such that all parties are engaged in a single coordinated effort to provide global communications and that competition for traffic through independently established or managed systems be avoided. The technological development of the single system will be evolutionary.

In the interest of efficient and expeditious establishment of an operational system, the original participants should be those countries or regions having the desire and the means to make significant economic

---

[1] Source: National Archives and Records Administration, RG 59, IO/OES Files: Lot 68 D 379, K-11.1, Structure of International Organizations. Limited Official Use. The aide-mémoire is Annex B to circular airgram CA–14556, June 27. For Annex A, see Document 441.

and technical contributions to the development and use of the system. The original participants should, however, acknowledge the goal to be global coverage and, while recognizing that there will be differing modes of participation, should adopt the principle of non-discriminatory access to the system by all countries or regions wishing to participate.

Although most of the traffic in the early stages will be within the Atlantic and Far Eastern areas, the initial operating system should permit service to be provided at some points in all major geographical areas of the world.

This Government would expect that the voice of participants in questions of management, finance, technology, operations and supply will be related to capital invested and use of the system, recognizing, however, that all participants should be able to make appropriate contributions to such decisions.

The United States Government considers that such financial assistance to the developing nations as may be required to bring their communications system to a point permitting meaningful participation in the global system would be the responsibility of national and international sources of capital assistance and not of the entities participating in the satellite system in their capacity as such. The responsibility in this connection of such participating entities would extend only to assuring, on an equitable basis, the opportunity for future participation by such nations.

An identical aide-mémoire has been delivered this day to the Embassy of the French Republic.

444.   National Security Action Memorandum No. 252[1]

Washington, undated.

TO

The Vice President
The Secretary of State
The Secretary of Defense
The Secretary of the Treasury
The Attorney General
The Director of Central Intelligence
The Director, U.S. Information Agency
The Administrator, National Aeronautics and Space Administration
The Chairman, Federal Communications Commission
The Administrator, Federal Aviation Agency
The Administrator of General Services
The Director, Bureau of the Budget
The Director, Office of Emergency Planning
The Director, Office of Science and Technology
The Director of Telecommunications Management

SUBJECT

Establishment of the National Communications System

Concept and Objectives

In furtherance of the general objectives stated in NSAM 201, dated October 26, 1962,[2] a National Communications System (NCS) shall be established and developed by linking together, improving, and extending on an evolutionary basis the communications facilities and components of the various Federal agencies. The organizational arrangements set forth in NSAM 201 are superseded by those established in this memorandum.

The objective of the NCS will be to provide necessary communications for the Federal Government under all conditions ranging from a normal situation to national emergencies and international crises, including nuclear attack. The system will be developed and operated to be responsive to the variety of needs of the national command and user agencies and be capable of meeting priority requirements under emergency or war conditions through use of reserve capacity and additional private facilities. The NCS will also provide the necessary combina-

---

[1] Source: National Archives and Records Administration, RG 59, S/S–NSC Files: Lot 72 D 316, NSAM 252. Confidential. An attached memorandum from Bundy to all recipients, dated July 12, indicates that NSAM No. 252 was dated July 11. The memorandum also states that the President's Special Assistant for Science and Technology would perform the functions assigned to the Special Assistant for Telecommunications.

[2] Document 438.

tions of hardness, mobility, and circuit redundancy to obtain surviv-ability of essential communications in all circumstances.

Initial emphasis in developing the NCS will be on meeting the most critical needs for communications in national security programs, partic-ularly to overseas areas. As rapidly as is consistent with meeting criti-cal needs, other Government needs will be examined and satisfied, as warranted, in the context of the NCS. The extent and character of the system require careful consideration in light of the priorities of need, the benefits to be obtained, and the costs involved.

Although no complete definition of the NCS can be made in advance of design studies and evolution in practice, it is generally con-ceived that the NCS would be comprised primarily of the long haul, point-to-point, trunk communications which can serve one or more agencies.

The President has directed the following organizational arrange-ments relating to the establishment and effective operation of the NCS.

Executive Office Responsibilities

In carrying out his functions pursuant to Executive Orders 10705 and 10995[3] and under this memorandum, the Director of Telecommunications Management shall be responsible for policy direc-tion of the development and operation of a National Communications System. In this capacity, he shall also serve as a Special Assistant to the President for Telecommunications and shall:

a. Advise with respect to communication requirements to be sup-plied through the NCS; the responsibilities of the agencies in imple-menting and utilizing the NCS; the guidance to be given to the Secretary of Defense as Executive Agent for the NCS with respect to the design and operation of the NCS; and the adequacy of system designs developed by the Executive Agent to provide, on a priority basis and under varying conditions of emergency, communications to the users of the NCS.

b. Identify those requirements unique to the needs of the Presidency.

c. Formulate and issue to the Executive Agent guidance as to the relative priorities of requirements.

d. Exercise review and surveillance of actions to insure compliance with policy determinations and guidance.

---

[3] Executive Order 10705 of April 17, 1957 (22 FR 2729), delegated authority vested in the President by Subsections 305(a) and 606 (a), (c), and (d) of the Communications Act of 1934, as amended, to the Director of the Office of Defense Mobilization in time of war. Executive Order 10995 of February 16, 1962 (27 FR 1519), established a Director of Telecommunications Management to be in charge of federal telecommunications activi-ties, policies, and standards. The Director would be one of the Assistant Directors of the Office of Emergency Planning and would assume the functions vested in the Director of the Office of Emergency Planning under Executive Order 10705, as amended.

e. Ensure that there is adequate planning to meet future needs of the NCS.

f. Assist the President with respect to his coordinating and other functions under the Communications Satellite Act of 1962 as may be specified by Executive Order or otherwise.

In performing these functions, the Special Assistant to the President for Telecommunications will work closely with the Special Assistant to the President for National Security Affairs; he will consult with the Director of the Office of Science and Technology and the Director of the Bureau of the Budget, as appropriate; will establish arrangements for inter-agency consultation to ensure that the NCS will meet the essential needs of all Government agencies; and will be responsible for carrying on the work of the Subcommittee on Communications of the Executive Committee of the National Security Council which is hereby abolished. In addition to staff regularly assigned, he is authorized to arrange for the assignment of communications and other specialists from any agency by detail or temporary assignment.

The Bureau of the Budget, in consultation with the Special Assistant to the President for Telecommunications, the Executive Agent and the Administrator of General Services, will prescribe general guidelines and procedures for reviewing the financing of the NCS within the budgetary process and for preparation of budget estimates by the participating agencies.

Executive Agent Responsibilities

To obtain the benefits of unified technical planning and operations, a single Executive Agent for the NCS is necessary. The President has designated the Secretary of Defense to serve in this capacity. He shall:

a. Design, for the approval of the President, the NCS, taking into consideration the communication needs and resources of all Federal agencies.

b. Develop plans for fulfilling approved requirements and priority determinations, and recommend assignments of implementation responsibilities to user agencies.

c. Assist the user agencies and the General Services Administrator with respect to the Federal Telecommunications System to accomplish their respective undertakings in the development and operation of the system.

d. Allocate, reallocate, and arrange for restoration of communications facilities to authorized users based on approved requirements and priorities.

e. Develop operational plans and provide operational guidance with respect to all elements of the NCS, including (1) the prescription of standards and practices as to operation, maintenance, and installation; (2) the maintenance of necessary records to ensure effective utilization of the NCS; (3) the request of assignment of radio frequencies for the

NCS; (4) the monitoring of frequency utilization; and (5) the exercise and test of system effectiveness.

f. Within general policy guidance, carry on long-range planning to ensure the NCS meets future Government needs, especially in the national security area, and conduct and coordinate research and development in support of the NCS to ensure that the NCS reflects advancements in the art of communications.

Within the framework of the NCS, the Executive Agent will provide for the requirements for survivable communications of the President and civilian agencies. A statement of such requirements is set forth in the report of the Task Group on Survivable Communications Requirements of the President and Top Civil Leaders, dated August 20, 1962[4] which is approved for planning purposes.

The Secretary of Defense may delegate these functions within the Department of Defense subject at all times to his direction, authority, and control. In carrying out his responsibilities for design, development and operation of the NCS, the Secretary will make appropriate arrangements for participation of staff of other agencies.

Responsibilities of the Administrator of General Services

The Federal Telecommunications System, established with the approval of the President under authority of the Federal Property and Administrative Services Act of 1949, as amended, to provide communications services to certain agencies in the Fifty States, the Commonwealth of Puerto Rico and the Virgin Islands, shall be a part of the NCS and shall be implemented and developed in accordance with approved plans and policies developed pursuant to this memorandum. The Executive Agent and the Administrator of General Services shall be responsible for establishing arrangements to avoid duplication in requests for cost, traffic, and other information needed from agencies served by the FTS.

Nothing contained herein shall affect the responsibilities of the Administrator of General Services under the Federal Property and Administrative Services Act of 1949, as amended, with respect to the representation of agencies in negotiations with carriers and in proceedings before Federal and state regulatory bodies; prescription of policies and methods of procurement; and the procurement either directly or by delegation of authority to other agencies of public utility communications services.

Responsibilities of Other Agencies

All agencies are directed by the President to cooperate with and assist the Special Assistant to the President for Telecommunications, the

---

[4] Not printed. (Kennedy Library, National Security Files, Departments and Agencies Series, Office of Emergency Planning, Box 283)

Executive Agent, and the Administrator of General Services in the performance of the functions set forth above.

McGeorge Bundy

---

445.   Letter From Secretary of Defense McNamara to Secretary of State Rusk[1]

Washington, July 15, 1963.

Dear Dean:

Recently, the Joint Chiefs of Staff forwarded for my approval a Master Plan for the National Military Command System (NMCS) designed to improve the responsiveness of the NMCS to National Command Authorities. Copies are attached.[2] I have approved the Master Plan for planning purposes and implementation, as appropriate, within the Department of Defense.

National Security Action Memorandum No. 166 of 25 June 1962[3] requires that the NMCS form the basis of a system to serve the needs of the President and the top civilian leaders as well as those of the Department of Defense over a spectrum of emergency conditions. To fulfill this assignment, you will note that the Master Plan provides for participation by Department of State personnel in the activities of the National Military Command Center and the alternate command centers. Our proposal is to test this arrangement initially in the National Military Command Center and in the alternates on land and at sea. Later we plan to expand the arrangement to include the National Emergency Airborne Command Post. In addition, the Plan proposes that the Department of Defense provide representation in the Department of State Operations Center.

I am also attaching a draft State–Defense Agreement recommended by the Joint Chiefs of Staff pertaining to this exchange of personnel which I understand was worked out informally with your people.[2] If

---

[1]   Source: National Archives and Records Administration, RG 59, Central Files 1960–63, ORG 1 OSD–STATE. Secret.

[2]   Not printed.

[3]   Entitled "Report on Emergency Plans and Continuity of the Government." (National Archives and Records Administration, RG 59, S/S–NSC Files: Lot 72 D 316, NSAM 166)

the proposed Agreement meets with your approval, we will take the necessary steps to put it in final form and obtain formal Department of State authentication. We are in the process of negotiating similar agreements for participation in the activities of the command centers by representatives of the Director of Central Intelligence and the Director of the Office of Emergency Planning.

Subsequent to securing your approval of the proposed State–Defense Agreement, and approval by other agencies of agreements, as appropriate, I propose to promulgate the Master Plan as a Department of Defense directive. In this regard, I welcome your comments on the Plan as it pertains to the Department of State.

Response at your earliest convenience would be greatly appreciated.

Sincerely,

Bob

---

446. **Memorandum From the President's Special Assistant for National Security Affairs (Bundy) to the Heads of All Executive Departments and Agencies[1]**

Washington, August 21, 1963.

SUBJECT

Establishment of the National Communications System

The President has directed the establishment of a National Communications System (NCS) to provide better communications support to critical functions of government. Attachment I advises the Heads of Departments and Agencies of this action and designates the Director of Telecommunications Management as Special Assistant to the President for Telecommunications to advise and assist him with respect to communications requirements and plans for the NCS.[2]

The President has further directed that on an interim basis his Special Assistant for Science and Technology shall perform the func-

---

[1] Source: Kennedy Library, National Security Files, Bundy Chron Files, Aug. 1963, Box 404. No classification marking.

[2] Not printed.

tions assigned to the Director of Telecommunications Management concerning the establishment of a National Communications System.[3]

McGeorge Bundy[4]

---

[3] Attachment 2, "Procedures and Working Relationships for the National Communications System," August 21, and Attachment 3, "Statement of Initial Tasks Assigned to the Manager of the National Communications System," August 6, are not printed.

[4] Printed from a copy that bears this typed signature.

---

447. Airgram From the Mission to the United Nations to the Department of State[1]

A–587 New York, November 8, 1963.

SUBJECT

Outer Space

1. Jean D'Arcy, Director of Radio and Visual Services Division, of the UN Office of Public Information, and former Director of Eurovision, feels that the USSR is not alone in its apparent fear about direct broadcasting from communications satellites to the home receiver, further that the technology in this field is more advanced than commonly realized, even with regard to TV signals.

2. D'Arcy had just returned from the ITU Conference in Geneva at which it was decided not to go into the question of direct broadcasting. The French position, which he said was dictated by the Quai d'Orsay, was to call for a prohibition of direct broadcasting from satellites. D'Arcy talked with members of the French Delegation but was unable to find precisely what lay behind this position other than that it was political in nature. He was convinced, however, that the French would find strong support if they switched to a more reasonable position which requested study of the question.

3. D'Arcy felt that many of the less developed states, who lacked conventional transmission facilities outside of major urban centers, were properly fearful of the ability of the space powers to communicate directly to their citizens. For example, one of the Indonesian represent-

---

[1] Source: National Archives and Records Administration, RG 59, Central Files 1960–63, SP 6 UN. Confidential. Drafted by Peter S. Thacher on November 8, cleared by Zachary P. Geneas and Craig Eisendrath, and approved by Eisendrath.

atives at the Geneva Conference had said that it would be intolerable if President Kennedy used a communication satellite to speak directly to large numbers of Indonesians to whom President Sukarno wished to speak but could not for lack of conventional facilities. D'Arcy thought that similar considerations lay behind the Brazilian favor for UN censorship over the content of mass media relayed by satellite. A country like Brazil, or for that matter the USSR, might never find it economically feasible to develop conventional transmission facilities sufficient to provide coverage throughout the entire country. Thus, at such time as satellites have a direct TV transmission capability, the situation would arise in which an outside state could develop an audience which was denied to the television studios within that country.

4. D'Arcy noted that when Eurovision was being established it was thought of principally in terms of its usefulness for those states whose television facilities were highly developed, i.e., France, Germany and Great Britain. But in actual fact the countries which today make greatest use of Eurovision are just the opposite, namely those who, because they are less developed, are greatly in need of program content. Today Eurovision programs are only rarely seen in the most developed states because they have their own programming. D'Arcy foresaw a similar trend in space. He could imagine the situation in which many countries would be forced to rely in large part on programs beamed via satellite. Countries unable to satisfy audience demand by local programming would in effect be open to propaganda and commercial advertising by outside states, thus opening up long-term domestic and economic effects beyond their control.

5. On the basis of conversations with Americans active in the communications field, D'Arcy was convinced that there were no serious obstacles to direct radio broadcasts from satellites in the immediate future, and that it was probably only a matter of time before there could be direct TV transmission to home receivers. Although the technology might never be attractive from an economic point of view, its mere existence created the fear that major powers like the US might decide on its employment for political reasons. It was this possibility which D'Arcy felt is of real concern to many representatives who attended the ITU Conference.

6. D'Arcy said it seemed clear to him that the ITU was not the forum in which to consider what is essentially a non-technical problem. He therefore hoped that the US was giving thought to its consideration in the context of the Outer Space Committee of the General Assembly. He said he would welcome further discussion on this topic.

Stevenson

448.   **Memorandum From the Director of the Office of International Economic and Social Affairs, Bureau of International Organization Affairs (McKitterick) to the Assistant Secretary of State for International Organization Affairs (Cleveland)**[1]

Washington, November 22, 1963.

SUBJECT

Establishment of Intergovernmental Agency for Satellite Communications

At Mr. Gardner's request, Jim Simsarian accompanied Mr. Chayes and Mr. Carter to a meeting with Mr. Welch, Mr. Charyk, Mr. Throop and Mr. Cutler of Communications Satellite Corporation yesterday afternoon.

The following significant decisions were reached in principle:

1. We will go ahead with the negotiation and establishment of an intergovernmental agreement to set up an intergovernmental agency on satellite communications.

2. We will try to have a caucus with the Europeans in Europe in early January 1964.

3. We will propose convening an interim intergovernmental conference in February or March 1964 in the United States with Europeans plus a representative group of other countries (including Japan, Canada, Australia) to complete and sign an intergovernmental agreement to set up a provisional intergovernmental agency on satellite communications. This would be an executive agreement and only an interim arrangement pending the completion of an intergovernmental convention later which would be submitted to the Senate for approval. However, the interim agency would go ahead in the meanwhile with the financing and establishment of a communications satellite system. The date of the interim conference will depend upon the date of issue of the Corporation stock in early 1964.

4. We contemplate convening an intergovernmental conference to draft and complete an intergovernmental convention in September 1964 (or later, depending on developments). This convention would be submitted to the Senate for approval.

Mr. Chayes presented the State Department position very well, and in the light of talks that Mr. Welch and Mr. Charyk have had in Europe, they agreed along the above lines. However, agreement was in principle, and these points have to be pinned down.

---

[1] Source: National Archives and Records Administration, RG 59, IO/OES Files: Lot 68 D 379, K-11, Negotiations on International Organization, 1963. Limited Official Use. Drafted by James Simsarian (IO/OES). Copies were sent to Richard N. Gardner and Thomas W. Wilson (IO).

Mr. Throop and Mr. Cutler are preparing a CSC draft of an agreement to be negotiated with other countries (we hope it is in terms of negotiations with other countries rather than Postal Administrations). We are hoping to see this soon. In the meanwhile, Mr. Chayes believes we should be lining up our own views in the Department of State on organizational issues.

Accordingly, at the request of Mr. Gardner, Jim Simsarian has prepared the attached draft which he is discussing with Mr. Carter and Mr. Chayes and others in Legal.[2] Jim's draft includes the principles set forth in earlier CSC proposals, a General Assembly and Administrative Council suggested by the CSC, and the CSC as Managing Firm of the new intergovernmental agency (at least in its interim stage). The draft is in terms of a provisional arrangement pending a more detailed convention to be prepared at the later intergovernmental conference. We need a draft agreed in the Department of State, with other agencies and the Corporation before the end of December for purposes of discussion (at least in terms of principles) with the Europeans at our proposed meeting in early January. This is a tight schedule, but because of the proposed early stock issue and other pressures on the Corporation, we will have to move ahead quickly both here and in negotiations with other countries.

Jim's draft is based on the structure of the World Bank and EURO-CHEMIC in Europe; the Europeans have repeatedly urged the establishment of an agency structured along these lines.

---

[2] Not printed.

449.   Memorandum From the Assistant Secretary of State for
         Economic Affairs (Johnson) to the Under Secretary of State
         (Ball)[1]

Washington, December 4, 1963.

SUBJECT

Communication Satellites—Report of Plenary Meeting of European Conference on
Satellite Communication, Rome, November 26–29, 1963

The Third Plenary Meeting of the European Conference on Satellite
Communication reached a number of important decisions, summarized
below.

1. *Cables vs. Satellites.* The Conference discussed this question at
length. The Europeans seemed to feel that for them it is an either-or
choice in terms of providing the circuits necessary to meet anticipated
traffic in the period of 1965–67. They are far from satisfied that satellites should be chosen over cables. The Conference authorized their
Telecommunications Committee to invite officials of the American
Telephone and Telegraph Company to an intensive discussion of the
relative merits of cables and satellites to be held in Bonn on January
13. The Conference will also inform the United States Government of
the meeting in order that we may send officials of appropriate agencies, to attend together with the AT&T representatives. The interested
bureaus of the Department are in agreement that representatives of
the   Communications   Satellite   Corporation,   the   Federal
Communications Commission, and the Department should attend the
meeting.

It is important that the Corporation, the Government, and the
AT&T be in complete agreement on the positions to be adopted in the
meeting. It may be desirable for you and other Executive Branch officials to meet with AT&T officials in the near future.

2. *European Organization.* It was agreed that the 19 countries participating in the Conference should form a new regional organization, in a
corporate form, to be the European partner of the United States
Communications Satellite Corporation in a global system of communication satellites. The Conference declared itself to be the provisional
European organization. The primary organizational questions not yet
resolved are:

---

[1] Source: National Archives and Records Administration, RG 59, SCI Central Files:
Lot 65 D 473, TEL 6, August–December 1963. No classification marking. Drafted by
William G. Carter. Copies were sent to Abram Chayes, Harlan Cleveland, and Ragnar
Rollefson.

(a) Whether the commercial organization (to be formed by treaty) should have a regularly constituted governmental supervisory council to deal with "political" questions in addition to its regular board of directors.

(b) Whether voting on "political" questions should be weighted in proportion to investment of each participating country or be on a one-country-one-voice basis. It is agreed that on commercial questions voting should be weighted in direct proportion to investment.

The Organizational Committee of the Conference will attempt to solve these problems at meetings to be held in the coming months.

3. *Discussions and Negotiations with the United States.* The Conference decided to invite the Governments of the United States and Canada to an exploratory meeting to be held in Rome the first week in February. The purpose of the meeting will be to determine if a basis for agreement exists between Europe and North America and to plan the terms of reference of a first negotiating conference to be held in March or April with the view toward concluding provisional intergovernmental agreements permitting progress to be made in the design, installation and operation of an initial system.

A cooperative attitude on the part of the Europeans was reflected in their willingness to accede to the timetable proposed by the United States.

It is anticipated that a formal negotiating conference to conclude a multilateral treaty providing a framework for a permanent organization will be held in the fall of 1964. The Europeans are agreeable that both the formal conference and the conference to agree on provisional arrangements be held in the United States if we so desire.

4. *Industrial Participation by the European Countries in the Global System.* On the one hand, the Europeans are most anxious to be in a position to make the maximum industrial and technical contribution to the global system. As they are considerably behind the United States in this field there is a tendency for them to attempt to delay implementation of an operational system to give them time to catch up. On the other hand, they also recognize the desirability, as a general political objective, of participating from the beginning in the structuring and management of a global system.

The really difficult area concerning industrial participation is their desire to provide launching services. Here, they are very far behind the United States and yet this is the "big money" in the field. Negotiations in this area will be difficult.

Antarctica

450. Editorial Note

The Antarctic Treaty was negotiated at the Conference on Antarctica held in Washington October 15–December 1, 1959; it was signed by 18 nations on December 1, 1959. For documentation on the sessions of the Conference, see *Foreign Relations,* 1958–1960, volume II, pages 580–632. For text of the Treaty, see 12 UST 794 or *American Foreign Policy: Current Documents, 1961,* pages 452–458. The United States ratified the treaty on August 18, 1960, and it came into effect on June 23, 1961, after ratification by all the signatories.

451. Memorandum of Conversation[1]

Washington, January 31, 1961.

SUBJECT

　　Antarctica

PARTICIPANTS

　　Members of Foreign Embassies: Dr. Guyer (Argentina); Mr. Morrison (Australia); Mr. Steyaert (Belgium); Mr. Bianchi (Chile); Mr. Barthelemy (France); Mr. Sugihara (Japan); Mr. McLean (New Zealand); Mr. Blaksted (Norway); Mr. Franklin (Union of South Africa); Mr. Filippov (U.S.S.R.); Mr. McCall-Judson (United Kingdom)

　　George R. Owen, IO; Wayne W. Fisher, IO

The Chairman of the Twenty-seventh Interim Meeting of representatives of Antarctic Treaty signatories, held today, was Mr. Morrison of Australia.[2]

---

[1] Source: National Archives and Records Administration, RG 59, IO Files: Lot 69 D 169, Antarctica Files, Chronology, January–March 1963. Official Use Only. Drafted by Fisher.

[2] Reports on the Interim Meetings of the Antarctic Treaty signatories during 1960 are ibid., Central Files 1960–63, 397.022.

Ratification of Antarctic Treaty

The Chilean representative, who returned recently from a visit to Santiago, stated that the only reason the Treaty has not been pushed is that the Committee on Foreign Affairs of the Chilean Senate has been "occupied with other urgent and pressing matters." He said Parliament is now in recess to permit campaigning for the March elections, and will reconvene on March 14. The Foreign Office, he said, would make every effort to have the Treaty considered between mid-March and the end of April.

Agenda of the Canberra Meeting

The French representative distributed copies of an explanatory note (copy attached)[3] to accompany Item 12 of the list of 17 tentative agenda items. Item 12, which relates to reciprocal assistance among expeditions, was proposed for the agenda by France. He said France had no intention of attempting to define a code of conduct for expeditions, but hoped for some definition of the measures the head of an expedition could take in an emergency without consulting with his Government. He did not envisage the establishment of any special group to study this question at Canberra, although the matter could be discussed at the meeting if there were experts on the question present.

The Japanese representative said he had received instructions from his Government stating that after consideration it does not wish to propose an agenda item on the subject of cooperation in joint scientific research projects, joint management of bases, and joint logistic support. He had raised this matter at the Twenty-fourth Interim Meeting on December 6, 1960 when he had announced that Japan was considering abandoning its Antarctic operations next year (memorandum of conversation, IO: WWFisher, December 6).[3]

Referring to Item II of the proposed agenda (preservation of historic sites), the New Zealand representative said that this year's New Zealand expedition was making an effort to restore the two huts used by Captain Scott on his expeditions, and would also try to restore Shackleton's hut. This action was being carried out in full consultation with the Royal Geographic Society and would provide experience which might be useful in consideration of this Item.

Rules of Procedure for Canberra Meeting

In a discussion of this subject, the French representative said that the draft Rules (distributed by the Australian representative at the Twenty-fifth Interim Meeting on December 14, 1960) should be amend-

---

[3] Not printed.

ed to refer to "recommendations" rather than "decisions" of the meeting, to accord with the wording of Article IX. Otherwise France approved of the draft Rules. France, he said, believed that the final report of the meeting should contain only these recommendations unanimously adopted. If all decisions were reported, however, minority opinions should also be included.

Speaking as the Australian representative, the Chairman said his Government hoped to be able to avoid majority and minority reports and wanted the final report of the meeting to be unanimous. Hopefully, the drafting committee would be able to agree unanimously on a form of words, which the plenary would then adopt. Any differences could be ironed out in the plenary session, or deleted from the report entirely.

Mr. Owen said the main question was not how decisions of the meeting are to be reached, since the meeting was, under Article IX, intended to be consultative and to recommend "measures" that would in any event become binding only if approved by the Governments. The actual problem was what kind of report it was desired to have the meeting produce; a report could be in narrative form. He recommended that this be given further thought.

Exchange of Information on Expeditions and Stations

The Chairman acknowledged the receipt, since the last meeting, of papers distributed by the Belgian and Chilean representatives. With reference to the Chilean paper, which referred several times to "the Chilean Antarctic Territory," the Argentine representative distributed a statement in Spanish (copy attached)[4] reaffirming Argentina's "rights of sovereignty throughout the totality of its Antarctic territory." He then translated the statement aloud in English. Referring to both the Chilean paper and the Argentine statement, Mr. Owen recalled the traditional position of the United States which does not recognize the validity of any territorial claims in Antarctica. The Chilean representative stated that the mention of "Chilean Antarctic Territory" in the Chilean paper had not been intended as a reaffirmation of Chilean claims in Antarctica, and that he did not understand why there was objection to it. The Argentine representative pointed out that in the paper he had distributed previously on Argentine Antarctic activities, there had been a conscious effort to refrain from using any language that would bring up the problem of sovereignty in Antarctica. (Mr. Bianchi has been handling Antarctic matters for the Chilean Embassy since 1958. Had he been in Washington at the time the Chilean paper was distributed it is quite possible that he would have favored removing the controversial reference prior to distributing the paper.)

---

[4] Not printed.

452. Draft Guidance Paper Prepared by the Antarctica Staff of the Bureau of International Organization Affairs[1]

Washington, February 10, 1961.

PRELIMINARY GUIDELINES FOR IMPLEMENTATION OF ANTARCTIC TREATY FOR USE OF OCB WORKING GROUP

I. Exclusively Peaceful Use of Antarctica (Article I)

A. U.S. Programs

Discussion

U.S. practice has consistently been in accordance with Article I of the Treaty and will continue to be so. Beyond this, in order to maintain U.S. initiative, enhance U.S. prestige in connection with this Treaty that resulted from a U.S. proposal, and promote world-wide recognition of the provisions of this Treaty, it is desirable to give emphasis to the peaceful nature and nonmilitary purpose of our programs. In this connection, the use of military personnel to assist in peaceful scientific efforts has been traditional in the United States.

Guidance

All agencies concerned will give proper emphasis, in public pronouncements and press releases, as well as in organizational and administrative procedures, to the peaceful and nonmilitary purpose of our programs.

B. Activities of Other Countries

Discussion

To date there is no evidence of non-peaceful activity by other countries. However, it should be noted that a major difficulty exists in the identification of what constitutes a non-peaceful activity. Current U.S. estimates indicate that Soviet and other interests in Antarctica are primarily scientific. Under Communist ideological concepts, however, such Soviet research has long-range utility for military as well as peaceful purposes. These research activities, however, cannot be excluded or prevented under the terms of the Treaty.

---

[1] Source: National Archives and Records Administration, RG 59, IO Files: Lot 69 D 169, Antarctica Files, 1961–1962, U.S. Policy Matters, Department of State, January–July 1961. Secret. A covering reference slip dated February 20 indicates that the paper was transmitted to Alexander Akalovsky, Officer in Charge of General Disarmament Negotiations, U.S. Disarmament Administration. The draft printed here bears several handwritten revisions, but there is no indication who made them or when they were made. See footnotes 2–5 and 8 below.

Since Soviet basic research already serves long-range military interests and in the face of the unlimited inspection terms of the Treaty, it is
not expected that the Soviets will undertake any overt military activities
and none have been observed to date.

In this connection, there are in particular three types of scientific
activity, permitted under the treaty, which could have possible non-
peaceful applications of significance in the present state of military technology.

First, known Soviet interest in satellite tracking could make such
data usable against the U.S. reconnaissance satellite, and, in the event of
war, such facilities could even provide midcourse guidance for an
extended range ballistic missile attack against the United States.
Second, ionospheric and magnetic research, both important in Soviet
programs, may prove useful to controlled blackouts of communications
at conjugate points in the Northern Hemisphere. Third, the large
expansion of Soviet whaling (to four flotillas by the 1961–62 season)
could provide a fleet of 60 or more ships to serve as auxiliaries to Soviet
Southern Hemisphere submarine operations.

The measures to be taken in regard to the foregoing and the means
by which covert military activity could be detected are discussed in connection with the inspection system.

Guidance

In the event of activities contrary to Article I (or of any other of the
Treaty provisions), the United States will consider what course of action
is most suitable, in the light of the circumstances, including consultation
with other parties and implementation of the Treaty provisions concerning disputes and activities of non-parties.

II. Matters Related to the Inspection System (Article VII)

A. Exercise of Rights of Inspection by the United States.

Discussion

We are satisfied with the inspection provisions established by
Article VII of the Treaty which ensure absolute unilateral rights of
inspection and over-flight.

The inspection provisions relate to ensuring observance of the various other provisions of the Treaty. The major objectives in the U.S. exercise of the rights of inspection is to forestall and detect the use of
Antarctica for military purposes, chiefly by the Sino-Soviet Bloc.
Whereas, inspection for other activities prohibited by the Treaty present
no insurmountable obstacles, there are complications relative to inspection for evidences of military activity, part of which have been outlined in
Section I above. In addition to these, the following factors are pertinent:

Inspection planning and operations are confronted with environmental characteristics unique to Antarctica: extremely low temperatures and high winds, the predominance of ice in the interior, widespread coastal inaccessibility because of heavy sea ice conditions. These will lend a distinctive and unique character to the inspection system and program that will evolve. These unique characteristics will both complicate and facilitate inspection planning and operations. Activities currently are generally limited to a few stations. Main stations are dependent on ships operating out of non-Bloc controlled ports. In the future, accessibility may be significantly increased by the USSR employment of the atomic icebreaker, and jet air power which could broaden Bloc station deployment. In this connection, Soviet interest in the mapping of one-half of the ice-free areas is noteworthy.

The complexity of identifying Soviet activities which may violate any of the Treaty provisions and the harsh environmental conditions make an absolutely fool-proof inspection system all but impossible. Nevertheless, because of the elaborate logistic arrangements presently required for Antarctic operations, it will be possible, in the immediate future, to keep track of the establishment of stations and support operations therefor by other countries, by means of relatively few overflights and normal procedures for observation of shipping.

Moreover, to a considerable extent, observation of the activities of other nations at existing facilities may be accomplished through continuation of certain practices without necessarily resorting to all of the procedures for inspection provided by the Treaty. Among these practices are:

1. The exchange of resident scientists, such as has been practiced with other countries, including the USSR. It is, indeed, more difficult to hide a covert military operation from a technically qualified inspector who is spending his entire time at a station than from a similarly qualified inspector who visits the site on a periodic basis. This does not mean that U.S. scientists assigned to foreign stations need be designated observers under the Treaty procedures, nor that they should become clandestine observers. Their presence, in the normal performance of their scientific functions, provides, in effect, a first-hand opportunity to become aware of many of the types of activities which might result in possible violations of the Treaty.

2. Visits to other stations by air, sea, or overland will also provide opportunity to observe foreign activities.

3. Continuation of the program of exchanging persons to accompany resupply expeditions (who have heretofore been designated "official observers") will provide a similar opportunity. In certain situations, it may be found useful to designate these persons observers under the

Treaty procedures. However, the practice has been to exchange them by agreement, through State Department channels. An observer under the Treaty does not, of course, require prior agreement for his presence. It is noted that the USSR has not, to date, agreed to exchange these "official observers."

4. Implementation of the observer codicil[2] to the international whaling convention might also provide a means outside the Treaty machinery to keep informed of Soviet activities in Antarctic waters.

In view of the foregoing considerations and the conditions peculiar to Antarctica, it is believed that the establishment of an elaborate inspection system is not an absolute necessity at this time.[3] However, there are certain factors which make it both necessary and desirable to conduct a program of inspections of activities, facilities, equipment, ships, aircraft and ground stations by observers specifically designated in accordance with the Treaty:

1. Exercise of the inspection procedures set forth in the Treaty will provide information on the activities of other countries which might be unobtainable either by the methods outlined above or otherwise.

2. There is the likelihood that the right of inspection will be impaired if it is not exercised. It is desirable that inspections be made as a matter of course, whether or not there is evidence indicating a special need for inspection. Establishing the routine of inspection during the early stages of the Treaty will minimize the probability of interference with inspection at a later date.

3. Because the Antarctic Treaty is the first that grants the right of inspection, the Treaty may come to be viewed as a precedent which should influence our position in negotiations on inspection arrangements in other fields. It would be dangerous to our long established position on arms controls if we fail to exercise the right of inspection granted by the Treaty.[4]

4. The conduct of inspections under the Treaty might serve as a deterrent of violations.

5. The actual conduct of operations may provide useful experience in inspection procedure, which might be helpful in the future development of inspection arrangements relating to arms controls, under [sea] nuclear testing, and outer space.

---

[2] "codicil" was changed to "Protocol of 1950."

[3] Inserts have changed the phrase to read: "it is not believed that very extensive inspection is likely to be an absolute necessity in the near future."

[4] A final sentence of this paragraph was added by hand: "The Soviets might argue that our failure to exercise a treaty given inspection right demonstrates that our insistence on inspection rights in other countries in insincere."

On the other hand, it should be noted that the logistic support required for large-scale official inspection, involving visits on an unannounced or minimum notice basis, is substantial, and must be weighed against the benefits to be gained. To transport an observer to Mirnyy or Lazaryev requires caching of fuel at Pole or other stations and special logistic arrangements. In order to avert undue diversion of present resources from support of scientific programs, present resources, appropriately supplemented, should be used for inspections, or sizable increases in the men, planes, and ships committed to Antarctic operations will be required.

Although the U.S. may, for reasons of economy, rely primarily on over-flights, the observation of shipping, and other practices already described to prevent[5] or detect violations of the Treaty, at least in the initial stages, these measures alone cannot satisfy the inspection requirements and the U.S., in the interests of security should also conduct land, sea, and air inspections of ground stations, installations, facilities, equipments, ships, and aircraft. These inspections should be instituted during the first Antarctic season after the Treaty enters into force, and should be applicable as a minimum to the main Soviet station and to stations of one or two other countries.

The assignment of tasks to establish a U.S. inspection program in Antarctica should be consistent with the alignment of functions implicit or specifically designated within the mission of the various agencies of the Executive Branch as well as with the special arrangements made for conduct of U.S. operations in Antarctica. Whereas the Department of Defense is responsible for the conduct of arms control inspections, the *Department of State is responsible for conduct of relations with other countries, and hence has an interest in scheduling Antarctic inspections so as to maintain the best climate for these and other foreign relations.* [The Department of State being responsible for conduct of relations with other countries would have to determine when a specific inspection or program of inspection would be undertaken.][6] The inspection provision of the Antarctic Treaty is not limited to scrutiny of activities to determine their military application alone, but extends to other prohibited actions, such as the disposal of nuclear waste, in which the Department of Interior and National Science Foundation, among others, will have an interest. Finally, any sizable inspection effort will impinge on other U.S. Antarctic programs and hence become subject to the coordination control of the Operations Coordinating Board, the agency presently charged with the over-all direction of U.S. operations in Antarctica.

---

[5] "Prevent" was changed to "deter."

[6] Bracketed portion is Department of State wording. Department of Defense wording, underscored, is not acceptable to Department of State. [Footnote and brackets in the source text. The underscored text is printed as italics.]

Guidance

1. Appropriate agencies involved shall continue to collect, evaluate and maintain information on the activities of other nations in Antarctica through utilizing the information provided by the means above, in addition to any other sources available. The need to keep informed of activities of other countries will be taken into consideration in the plans of agencies conducting operations in Antarctica and they shall advise the Department of State when violations are suspected or detected.

2. The Department of State will accumulate from participating agencies all information concerning activities of other countries in Antarctica, pertinent to their observance of the Treaty provisions. The evaluation of the information in relation to military or other significance will continue to be responsibility of the appropriate agencies.

3. The Department of Defense shall have continuing responsibility for developing and maintaining capabilities to conduct inspection operations. Supporting agencies will be CIA, AEC, and others with demonstrated interest. In particular, the Department of Defense should develop specific plans for the conduct of over-flights and air, sea, and ground inspections to be initiated as early as possible after the Treaty enters into force, and maintained on a continuing basis.

4. The persons to be designated as observers under the Treaty provisions shall be recommended by interested agencies, selected by the Department of Defense in consultation with the Department of State, which shall designate them as such, and inform the other Governments, in accordance with the Treaty.

5A. *The Operations Coordinating Board (or successor agency) will determine the scope of the inspections on an annual basis, specifying the foreign installations and activities to be officially observed, as well as other measures that may be required. The Senior U.S. Representative in Antarctica will be authorized to depart from this schedule to the extent that unforeseen contingencies necessitate, and when timely action would be aborted by referral of the matter to higher authority.*

[5B. Specific Inspections and Programs of Inspection of foreign installations in Antarctica will be initiated by the Department of State at the recommendation of, or in consultation with agencies conducting operations in Antarctica and carried out by the Department of Defense in accordance with paragraph 3 above.][7]

---

[7] Agreement not reached on substance; para 5A is DOD recommendation; para 5B represents Dept. of State position. [Footnote and brackets in the source text.]

B. Inspection of U.S. Facilities by Other Countries.

Discussion

No particular difficulty is envisaged here since the United States does not engage in activities contrary to the Treaty provisions. Instructions are being prepared for the Task Force to permit the admission of observers of foreign nations to all installations, stations, and ships in the Antarctic area in accordance with the Treaty. The inspection of ships and aircraft by foreign observers is limited to those discharging or embarking cargo or personnel in the Antarctic area. The purpose of this latter qualification is to be sure that we do not permit the establishment of a precedent whereby our ships on the high seas could be halted.

At the present time, except for cryptographic gear, and a limited amount of classified material aboard ships and aircraft (such as sonar, ECN), there is nothing maintained in Antarctic stations or placed aboard ship which, if made open to inspection by the Soviets, or others, would compromise the national interest. The Department of Defense has the principal interest in this area, and is prepared to take administrative action to eliminate from ships and aircraft participating in the Antarctic operations, all classified matter, except written material.[8]

Guidance

The Department of Defense and other agencies concerned should take such measures as may be necessary to insure that facilities, equipment, aircraft, and ships are open for inspection to foreign observers officially designated for this purpose by the signatory power concerned. The Department of State is to keep all agencies involved informed as to the names of officially designated observers and those empowered to appoint observers. The United States position should be that we are open to inspection.

C. Attitude of the United States in International Consultations Regarding the Inspection System

Discussion

We are satisfied with the Treaty provisions as they stand and see no advantage in multilateral discussion of inspection procedures at the present time. However, several friendly countries maintain that in view of public interest in the inspection feature of the Treaty (as a deterrent, not only of military, but also other, e.g., nuclear, activities), matters related to the inspection system should appear on the agenda of the Canberra meeting to be held under Article IX of the Treaty, which refers

---

[8] A sentence is written above this paragraph: "Instructions and regulations in this regard shall be approved by the Dept. of Defense and the Dept. of State."

to measures regarding the "facilitation of the exercise of the rights of inspection" as a matter to be considered at such meetings.

Guidance

If matters related to inspection procedures are raised by other countries for multilateral discussions among the Treaty countries, the U.S. position will be:

1. To prevent any impairment of the unilateral inspection rights as set forth in the Treaty.
2. To support discussion and recommendations concerning agreement on the scope and nature of information to be exchanged under Article VII, paragraph 5.

III. Nuclear Explosions and Waste Disposal (Article V)

A. U.S. Installations

Discussion

The extent to which the operation of our planned reactor may involve disposal or emission of waste may be questioned. The United States has consistently maintained that Article V does not preclude the installation and operation of a reactor. The United States must be prepared to show that a reactor can be operated in strict compliance with Article V and also should be able to reassure any Government which may be concerned with the effect that a reactor may have on scientific programs.

Guidance

Present and planned installation of nuclear reactors in the Antarctic under U.S. sponsored programs should provide means whereby disposal of waste would be accomplished outside Antarctica and all prudent measures taken to insure against the possibility of nuclear accidents. The United States should make available to other signatory powers such information that may be helpful in understanding the plan to avoid nuclear contamination from nuclear power plants.

B. Nuclear Activities of Other Countries

Discussion

At the present time there is no foolproof means by which we could monitor against the occasion of a nuclear explosion or disposal of nuclear waste in Antarctica. However, through normal seismic observations and air sampling for radioactive particles, it is fairly certain that any open nuclear explosion that took place in Antarctica would be detected. The question of where it took place would be difficult to determine. In any event, this does not seem to be an immediate problem or one for which we should take special measures. Rather, the United States should encourage the dissemination and exchange among signatory powers of information relative to nuclear activities in Antarctica.

Guidance

The U.S. position should be to encourage strongly the exchange of information among signatory countries regarding nuclear activities in Antarctica. Agencies involved in Antarctic operations should keep alert to the possible use of nuclear devices by other nations.

IV. Scientific Cooperation (Article III)

Discussion

Article III of the Treaty sets forth the obligation of the parties to promote scientific cooperation, in particular, by means of (1) exchange of information regarding programs, (2) exchange of scientists, and (3) exchange and making available of scientific observations gathered in Antarctica. The United States favors scientific cooperation among the Treaty parties. The Special Committee on Antarctic Research (SCAR), the nongovernmental sub-body of International Council of Scientific Unions, which sponsored the IGY, now serves as a nongovernmental mechanism for the free exchange of views among scientists and for the development of scientific cooperation in an advisory capacity. There is no current need for the Governments to set up a new mechanism for the discussion of scientific problems nor is it desirable to convert SCAR into an official body, since this would inhibit the free discussion of scientific programs. However, the United States should be prepared to support inter-governmental action and arrangements in the field of scientific cooperation in circumstances where such official action would be more effective in relation to U.S. policy objectives.

In inter-governmental discussion of scientific cooperation, the United States should be in a position to demonstrate its active interest therein.

Guidance

1. The United States favors full exchange of information regarding scientific programs among the Governments who are parties to the Antarctic Treaty or among their scientists, including information as to scientific work being done and being planned, and information regarding equipment that is being used, and also by encouraging our participation in meetings and symposia on Antarctic scientific research.

2. The United States favors increasing the exchange of scientific personnel and joint research among scientists with other countries in Antarctic operations. The National Science Foundation, in consultation with the Department of State, shall coordinate and make arrangements regarding the conduct of joint scientific work with other countries; and may seek the assistance of public and private scientific organizations, when appropriate, in making these arrangements.

3. The United States favors the broadest possible exchange of scientific data gathered in Antarctica and should be prepared to support appropriate inter-governmental arrangements which would assure the availability of scientific data gathered by other countries, including arrangements for systematic reporting on ice conditions and weather conditions by vessels and aircraft operating in the Antarctic area.

V. Matters Related to the Question of Claims of Sovereignty

Discussion

The Treaty, by virtue of Article IV, does not, of course, modify the U.S. policy of nonrecognition of any of the territorial claims which have been asserted. On the other hand, the Treaty does not either imply renunciation of these claims by the claimant countries. Although the Treaty precludes the assertion of new claims, it is nevertheless useful, from the standpoint of maintaining a leading U.S. position in Antarctica, that a convenient legal record of current U.S. activities in exploration and discovery be available.

Guidance

1. The agencies concerned with Antarctic affairs shall continue to avoid any action that might be construed as evidence of recognition of any claim of sovereignty over any part of Antarctica by a foreign country and shall reaffirm, whenever appropriate, the U.S. policy of nonrecognition of such claims and of reservation of all U.S. historic rights.

2. The agencies having responsibility for operations in Antarctica shall, insofar as practicable, assure that orderly and convenient public records be established of future instances of discovery and exploration by persons participating in U.S. operations.

453.   Memorandum From the Assistant Secretary of State for International Organization Affairs (Cleveland) to the Under Secretary of State (Bowles)[1]

Washington, April 12, 1961.

SUBJECT

Antarctica: Inter-Agency Coordination of Activities and Policy Guidance

Pursuant to the abolition of the OCB and the Department's responsibility to "provide policy guidance and ensure coordination for all activities in Antarctica," IO has been holding regular weekly meetings (Wednesdays, 2:00 p.m.) with representatives of the agencies concerned (list attached, Tab A).[2] This function is carried out by George H. Owen, Antarctica Staff, IO. There have been five such meetings to date.

You may be interested in the manner in which this non-crisis function of the Department is being carried out, and I have enumerated, by way of illustration, matters of both long-term and short-term import which have been dealt with at the meetings referred to above (Tab B).

The main reasons why coordination is necessary, are:

(1) Our scientific programs in Antarctica are conducted by the National Science Foundation through grants to other agencies or universities. The Navy furnishes logistic support therefor. The two agencies budget separately for their respective functions. Scientists have said that the scientific program sometimes receives secondary consideration in the use of logistic facilities. The weekly meetings provide a forum in which these problems, big and small, can be aired.

(2) In countless ways our Antarctic programs affect U.S. foreign relations. There is international cooperation in science, joint programs with certain other countries, and the scope, nature and "image" of the U.S. presence in Antarctica must conform to U.S. policy and the Antarctic Treaty.

---

[1] Source: National Archives and Records Administration, RG 59, Central Files 1960–63, 702.022/4–1261. Confidential. An April 22 covering memorandum by Samuel W. Lewis indicates that the memorandum was forwarded to Deputy Under Secretary U. Alexis Johnson.

[2] Not printed.

Tab B

MATTERS DEALT WITH AT THE INTER-AGENCY
COORDINATION MEETINGS

1. Future usefulness of Byrd Station for the scientific program. The question has been raised as to whether scientific programs in the future require the elaborate logistic facilities which the Navy is setting up there.

2. The suggestion of NSF that consideration be given to establishing a new base to provide airlift support to a planned mobile station in a particular area for a particular project in ionospheric physics.

3. The question of whether we should make arrangements, bilateral or otherwise, to ensure continuation of scientific work at the Belgian and Japanese stations which are about to be abandoned. The Soviets maintain aviation gas depots at both of these locations.

4. Ensuring that no foreign scientists, VIP's or correspondents are invited by either NSF or Navy without knowledge and concurrence of the Department of State. In the past this has not been properly coordinated.

5. Coordinating the manner in which foreign correspondents are selected to accompany our operation. USIA is suggesting a planned program of selecting those who will produce the most from a USIA standpoint.

6. Ensuring that publications of the U.S. Antarctic Projects Office of DOD are cleared with State as regards references affecting our position toward foreign countries.

7. Obtaining preliminary but official views from the agencies concerned on the matters we are discussing with representatives of other Antarctic Treaty signatory Governments at the "Interim Meetings," which have been held regularly since the Antarctic Conference, pending entry into force of the Treaty; in particular, with reference to the agenda of the meeting which is to take place in Canberra after the Treaty enters into force. (Of the 12 signatories, only two have not yet ratified, Argentina and Chile. As of now, they are expected to do so before the middle of the year.)

8. Ensuring that NSF distributes to other agencies concerned matters referred to it by the scientists designated by the National Academy of Sciences, who participate for the United States in SCAR (Special Committee on Antarctic Research, a sub-body of the non-governmental International Council of Scientific Unions), in order that a coordinated U.S. Government view can be worked out.

9. A Navy initiative to organize a symposium in the United States of logistic support experts with representatives of other countries under the aegis of SCAR.

10. A further effort of coordination will have to be made regarding the separate funding of NSF requirements and Navy support activities, season by season. By working closely with the Bureau of the Budget in this connection, it may be desirable to establish procedures where the Department could assist in coordinating these budgetary operations in the light of a long-term plan which reflects the real objectives of our presence in Antarctica.

11. A variety of other problems are also dealt with, such as the recent illness of the Soviet exchange scientist at Byrd Station which required his evacuation on an emergency basis; problems related to transmission through Navy communications facilities of scientific reports between stations, et cetera.

454.   **Memorandum From Wayne H. Fisher of the Office of the Special Assistant for Antarctic Affairs, Bureau of International Organization Affairs, to the Assistant Secretary of State (Cleveland) and the Deputy Assistant Secretary of State for International Organization Affairs (Gardner)**[1]

Washington, July 10, 1961.

SUBJECT

Recent Antarctic Developments

The Antarctic Treaty, which was signed at Washington on December 1, 1959, entered into force on Friday, June 23, 1961 upon the simultaneous deposit at noon on that day of the instruments of ratification of Argentina, Australia and Chile. Attached is a White House announcement made on the occasion of the entry into force of the Treaty.[2]

The Treaty provides that a Consultative Meeting shall be held at Canberra within two months after the date of entry into force of the Treaty. The Canberra Meeting convenes today and is expected to last

---

[1] Source: National Archives and Records Administration, RG 59, IO Files: Lot 69 D 169, Antarctica Files, 1961–1962, Administrative Within USG, 1961. No classification marking.

[2] Not printed. For text, see *Public Papers of the Presidents of the United States: John F. Kennedy, 1961*, pp. 471–472.

about two weeks. Ambassador Sebald is the U.S. Representative to this Meeting. George Owen is the Alternate U.S. Representative. Attached is a press release listing the members of the U.S. delegation.[3]

At the Interim Meetings of representatives of Antarctic Treaty signatories which have been held regularly in Washington since January of 1960, a proposed agenda (copy attached) for the Canberra Meeting was developed.[4] U.S. position papers on Items 6 through 20 were prepared and cleared with the various interested offices in the Department, as well as with other Government agencies concerned with Antarctica.

The Canberra Meeting is expected to be of a more technical nature than was the Conference on Antarctica. We have had no indication up to now that the Soviet Union or any other country plans to raise highly controversial questions at the Meeting. The proposed agenda does not include items that directly concern such important Treaty provisions as nonmilitarization and inspection in Antarctica, but several countries, including the United States, may make reference in their opening statements to the inspection provision and to their intention to exercise their inspection rights, not necessarily as a result of suspicion but as a normal activity under the Treaty.

Poland acceded to the Treaty on June 8, 1961. She has not, however, sought to be included among the countries participating in the Canberra Meeting. In the event of such a request, our position has been that Poland is not entitled to participate in the Meeting since she is not engaged in "substantial scientific research activity" in Antarctica, which is a Treaty requirement that acceding countries must fulfill before they are entitled to participate in the Consultative Meetings.

---

[3] Not printed. For text, see Department of State *Bulletin,* July 24, 1961, p. 167.

[4] Not attached. A copy is in the National Archives and Records Administration, RG 59, IO Files: Lot 69 D 169, Antarctica File, 1961–1962, U.S. Policy Matters, Department of State, January–July 1961. Agenda items 6 through 20 were: exchange of information regarding plans for scientific programs; exchange of scientific personnel; exchange and making available of scientific observations and results; relations with SCAR, relations with other international organizations having a scientific or technical interest in Antarctica; exchange of information concerning expeditions and stations under Article VII, Paragraph 5; matters relating to logistic support; preservation and conservation of living resources; preservation of historic sites; reciprocal assistance among expeditions; arrangements for radio communications; cooperation in mail services; exchange of information and advice relating to the application of nuclear energy in the treaty area; administrative arrangements; and date and place of the next meeting.

455.   Memorandum From the Executive Secretary of the
        Department of State (Battle) to the President's Special
        Assistant for National Security Affairs (Bundy)[1]

Washington, July 28, 1961.

SUBJECT

Recent Antarctic Developments

The Antarctic Treaty was signed at Washington on December 1, 1959 by the following 12 countries: Argentina, Australia, Belgium, Chile, France, Japan, New Zealand, Norway, South Africa, U.S.S.R., United Kingdom, and United States. The Treaty entered into force on June 23, 1961 upon the simultaneous deposit on that date of the ratifications of Argentina, Australia and Chile.

The Treaty provided that a Consultative Meeting be held at Canberra within two months after the date of entry into force of the Treaty. The Canberra Meeting was held July 10–24, 1961.[2]

At Canberra 16 recommendations in furtherance of the principles and objectives of the treaty were unanimously approved. These recommendations will now be submitted to the Governments concerned for approval.

On the whole, the recommendations conformed to United States positions adopted prior to the Meeting. They relate mainly to scientific and logistic cooperation in Antarctica, conservation of living resources, and preservation of historic sites. A recommendation was also approved that the Governments exchange information on the application of nuclear equipment and techniques in Antarctica. An Australian proposal to create a secretariat to service the Antarctic Treaty and to locate it at Canberra was rejected. We believe that there is as yet no demonstrated need for such a secretariat, and that if there is to be one, it should be in Washington. Antarctic discussions have been centered here for the past several years and all the Treaty signatories are adequately represented here.

It was decided to hold the next meeting at Buenos Aires, approximately a year from now.

---

[1] Source: National Archives and Records Administration, RG 59, IO Files: Lot 69 D 169, Antarctica Files, 1961–1962, Administrative, Within USG, 1961. Official Use Only. Drafted by Fisher on July 27 and cleared by Wilson (IO).

[2] For text of the report of the U.S. delegation to the First Consultative Meeting, see ibid., Antarctica Public Relations, Congressional, 1962. Recommendations adopted at the Consultative Meeting are printed in *American Foreign Policy: Current Documents, 1961*, pp. 458–465.

The Canberra Meeting was more of a technical meeting than was the Conference on Antarctica. The agenda did not include items that directly concerned such important Treaty provisions as nonmilitarization and inspection in Antarctica.

The attitude of the Soviet delegation was friendly and cooperative throughout. This is in keeping with the generally cooperative attitude they have shown in Antarctica since the days of the IGY. The Soviets raised no controversial issues, nor did they raise the question of Polish participation in the Meeting.

Poland acceded to the Treaty on June 8, 1961. She did not, however, seek to be included among the countries participating in the Canberra Meeting. We would have opposed such a request on the grounds that Poland is not entitled to participate in the meetings since she is not engaged in "substantial scientific research activity" in Antarctica. This is a Treaty requirement that all acceding countries must fulfill before they are entitled to participate in the Consultative Meetings.

Following the abolition of the OCB by Executive Order on February 18, 1961, the Department of State assumed the responsibility of providing policy guidance on Antarctica and ensuring coordination for all activities in Antarctica. Since March 3 weekly meetings for this purpose have been held under the chairmanship of Mr. George H. Owen, Special Assistant for Antarctica in the Department of State.

These meetings are attended by representatives of Department of Defense, National Science Foundation, Department of Commerce, Department of the Interior, CIA, USIA, and Bureau of the Budget. At the meetings there is discussion and decision on action with respect to the great variety of problems that arise in connection with Antarctic operations and planning. The main purpose is coordination in specific matters as well as long-term plans. Participants are the officials mainly concerned with Antarctic operations in each agency.

Donald B. Easum[3]

---

[3] Easum signed for Battle above Battle's typed signature.

456.   Memorandum From the Special Assistant for Antarctica Affairs, Bureau of International Organization Affairs (Owen) to the Deputy Director of the Arms Control and Disarmament Agency (Fisher)[1]

Washington, October 2, 1961.

SUBJECT

Exercise of Rights of Inspection under Antarctic Treaty

Article VII of the Antarctic Treaty provides that "in order to promote the objectives and ensure the observance of the provisions" of the Treaty, each party has the right to designate observers to (1) inspect, in effect, the activities of others, and (2) carry out overflights anywhere in Antarctica.

Among the main provisions of the Treaty are: (1) Antarctica is to be used for peaceful purposes only; (2) a prohibition of nuclear explosions and disposal of nuclear waste; (3) cooperation in science.

The Treaty was signed December 1, 1959, entered into force June 23, 1961, and the First Consultative Meeting under the Treaty was held at Canberra in July 1961.[2] The inspection provisions (other than paragraph 5 of Article VII referred to below) have not been the subject of discussions either during the "interim talks" (between the signature and the entry into force of the Treaty) or at the Canberra Meeting. However, the opening statement of the United States at the Canberra Meeting contained the following:

"The provisions of the Treaty are complemented by a system of inspection designed to promote the Treaty's objectives and ensure the observance of its provisions. We expect that the exercise of the rights of inspection established by the Treaty will be a normal activity under the Treaty. We would not regard the exercise of these rights as necessarily indicating that there is suspicion of activities contrary to the Treaty. Indeed, the practice of inspection is the best way of assuring the absence of suspicion. The inspection system is a useful and practical feature which will contribute to the effectiveness of the Treaty and the realization of its basic objectives, which are peace and co-operation."

In the course of the "interim talks" and at the Canberra Meeting, the Soviets have hardly commented at all on the inspection provisions. In a published article (in February 1960), G.I. Tunkin, Legal Adviser of the Soviet Foreign Office, who participated in the Antarctic Treaty

---

[1] Source: National Archives and Records Administration, RG 59, IO Files: Lot 69 D 169, Antarctica Files, Inspection 1962–63. Confidential. Copies were sent to Cleveland, Wallner, the Science Adviser, the Special Assistant for Atomic Energy and Outer Space, and the Office of Soviet Union Affairs.

[2] See Document 455.

Conference, briefly outlined the inspection provisions and discussion thereof at the Conference and concluded with this statement:

"Thus, the specific conditions prevailing in the Antarctic, where inspection cannot be used against national security, permitted agreement on unlimited inspection."

The present question is whether or not it would be advantageous to exercise our rights of inspection under the Treaty, in particular of Soviet activities. Since this is the only Treaty with the Soviets providing for inspection to control its observance, the exercise of our rights thereunder may significantly relate to our attitude or policy in other negotiations where inspection rights are important.

In Antarctica, the Soviets have three year round stations. As regards Soviet activities in Antarctica itself, we have received no evidence that the Soviets are engaged in any activity in violation of the Treaty's provisions.

Moreover, during five of the six years in which the Soviets have been active there, a U.S. resident exchange scientist has wintered over at Mirny, while a Soviet scientist was assigned at our McMurdo Station.

Logistic problems being what they are in Antarctica, observers' inspection visits, whether by ship or aircraft, would inevitably require diversion of transport facilities for that purpose from our own regularly scheduled activities there, i.e., logistics support of scientific programs. Our resources in ships and aircraft are usually fully committed to these programs. It would be most appropriate if the Navy could spare an icebreaker for a trip along the Antarctic coast, visiting the two Soviet coastal stations, Mirny and Lazarez—which are over 2,000 miles apart—as well as Australian and other stations in between. Designated observers could be aboard and perform inspections at places visited. But we have hardly enough icebreakers for our regular programs.

About the only inspection trip which our logistic capability would allow this year would be to have an officially designated observer accompany a flight that is planned (subject to weather and other logistic considerations) to go from McMurdo to Mirny Station in connection with a gravity research program. The purpose of the flight is to transport a U.S. physicist to Mirny Station to make gravity measurements. The type of aircraft which will probably be used would require refueling at Mirny. The flight may be feasible in November or as late as January 1962.

The question of whether the time is appropriate for the United States to exercise its inspection rights under the Treaty has been discussed with DOD, NSF, and CIA. In these discussions the following points have been considered:

(1) The argument has been made that it may be desirable that inspections be carried out under the Treaty, whether or not there is evi-

dence indicating a special need for inspection. Establishing the "routine of inspection" during the early stages of the Treaty would minimize the probability of interference with inspection at a later date.

(2) The argument has also been advanced that this being the first treaty providing for inspection, the Soviets might argue that our failure to exercise Treaty given inspection rights would demonstrate that our insistence on inspection in other contexts is insincere.

(3) The actual conduct of an inspection operation might provide useful experience in inspection procedures.

(4) On the other hand, the advantages to be gained by exercising the Antarctic Treaty inspection rights, may not be substantial enough to outweigh the possible risk of arousing suspicion and adversely affecting the climate of friendly cooperation by "bringing the cold war" to Antarctica. Relations among the scientists in Antarctica, and also in the diplomatic field with the Soviets on negotiations concerning Antarctica as late as the Canberra Meeting in July, have been outstanding in the absence of Soviet cold war tactics and maneuvers and recriminations.

(5) It might also be borne in mind that to exercise inspection rights when there is no evidence of wrongdoing, may provide the Soviets with an argument that our predilection for inspection systems is based on inspection-for-its-own-sake.

In any event, I would not wish to proceed further in a decision to undertake an inspection under the Treaty without thorough consideration being given to the relationship of such action on our part to our attitude and policy in other fields where inspection is important.

Article VII also provides that each party inform the others of its expeditions and stations in Antarctica and any military personnel or equipment it introduces there. This feature has been the subject of discussion both at the "interim talks" and at the Canberra Meeting. In fact, representatives of the signatories agreed to exchange this information before the Treaty entered into force, and we provided the most comprehensive information on our expedition. The Canberra Meeting approved a recommendation (Recommendation VI) listing in some detail the kind of information that should be provided. We are compiling the information we will distribute to the other Governments this year, and when we do so will state to the others, including the Soviets, that we expect them to provide us with similar information.

There are attached copies of the Antarctic Treaty and of the Report of the Canberra Meeting. There is also attached an excerpt of Tunkin's article in which he dealt with the inspection provisions.[3]

---

[3] The attachments are not printed.

I would appreciate discussing this problem with you at your earliest convenience.

---

457. **Memorandum From the Deputy Director of the Arms Control and Disarmament Agency (Fisher) to the Special Assistant for Antarctica, Bureau of International Organization Affairs (Owen)**[1]

Washington, October 13, 1961.

SUBJ

Exercise of Rights of Inspection under Antarctic Treaty

I believe there are strong arguments in favor of exercising our rights of inspection of the Antarctic Treaty regardless of any suspicion of activities contrary to the treaty. These reasons are sufficiently well adduced in your memorandum to me dated October 2, 1961[2] and require no further amplification by me.

I believe, however, that the timing of the exercise of these rights of inspection ought to be considered in light of other aspects of Soviet-American relations and in light of the time required to mount an inspection trip of more than a perfunctory character. I can see no immediate need to exercise our right of inspection on strictly disarmament considerations and I do not think it would be harmful if the Soviet Union were the first to ask for an inspection. Specifically, I believe that the period November 1961 to January 1962, the time mentioned in your memorandum, is too early. It is too early considering the many other difficulties we can expect to find besetting Soviet-American relations at that time and it is too early to set up an inspection trip properly manned and equipped. I would suggest, therefore, that we contemplate an inspection trip sometime in late 1962, which is presumably the next earliest feasible time.

In connection with plans for mounting the inspection, I would refer you to Section 34(c) of the Arms Control and Disarmament Act. This provision is as follows:

---

[1] Source: National Archives and Records Administration RG 59, IO Files: Lot 69 D 169, Antarctic Files, 1961–62, U.S. Policy Matters 1961, Department of State, August–December. Confidential. Drafted by James E. Goodby.

[2] Document 456.

"(c) the Director is authorized (1) to formulate plans and make preparations for the establishment, operation, and funding of inspection and control systems, which may become part of the United States arms control and disarmament activities, and (2) as authorized by law, to put into effect, direct, or otherwise assume United States responsibility for such systems."

We will be in touch with you further concerning the inspection operation. Our preliminary opinion is that we should think of the inspection operation in terms of its precedent-setting value as a model for other inspection arrangements. From this standpoint, the inspection might be more elaborate than might otherwise be required.

458. **Memorandum From the Special Assistant for Antarctica, Bureau of International Organization Affairs (Owen) to the Deputy Director of the Arms Control and Disarmament Agency (Fisher)**[1]

Washington, October 23, 1961.

SUBJECT

Inspection under Antarctic Treaty

U.S. Navy ships participating in the Deep Freeze operation which are likely to find themselves in circumstances where they would be subject to inspection under Article VII of the Antarctic Treaty, now carry only such cryptographic equipment and materials, the "viewing" of which gives rise to no problem of "compromise" or only to such "compromise" as may be eliminated.

One of the ships has, in effect, inquired what should be done in relation to inspection procedures as regards classified papers, documents, and books, other than cryptographic materials. The Navy has asked for an "interpretation" from the Department (see Navy messages on this case, State Department Control Nos. 8677 and 8816).[2]

---

[1] Source: National Archives and Records Administration, RG 59, IO Files: Lot 69 D 169, Antarctic Files, 1961–62, U.S. Policy Matters 1961, Department of State, August–December. Secret. Drafted by Owen.

[2] Neither printed. The first message (No. 8677, October 13, 1961) said that the Navy was seeking an interpretation from the State Department that would allow classified, non-cryptographic materials to remain aboard ships taking part in Antarctic missions. The second (No. 8816, October 16, 1961) said that one such vessel, the USS *Arneb*, had received instructions concerning reduced allowances of cryptographic materials, but carried non-cryptographic materials of all classifications and would continue to do so unless otherwise directed (UNODIR).

Apparently there are some such classified papers which have to remain on board. The Navy would like us to interpret the inspection provisions in the sense that, as far as papers are concerned, inspection may go no further than to determine that they are, in fact, papers.

A statement of this position might be made as follows:

1. The United States maintains the position that the inspection provisions of the Antarctic Treaty do not establish the right of a foreign observer to examine the contents of written materials, whether in the form of books, documents or other papers. The right of inspection of these materials is confined to such examination as is reasonably necessary to ascertain that they are papers.

2. U.S. personnel in Antarctica shall prevent the examination by a foreign observer of any documents classified "Secret" or "Confidential" except to the extent reasonably necessary to ascertain that they are documents.

3. U.S. stations in Antarctica and ships that may be subject to inspection under the Antarctic Treaty shall retain only the essential minimum of classified documents.

I would appreciate ACADA's expression of concurrence or other views. This is one of the first instances of development of "inspection law."

I am also sending a copy of this memorandum to L (Mr. Neidle) for comment.

459. **Memorandum From the Deputy Director of the Arms Control and Disarmament Agency (Fisher) to the Special Assistant for Antarctica, Bureau of International Organization Affairs (Owen)[1]**

Washington, October 25, 1961.

SUBJ

Inspection Trip to Antarctica

We believe that the trip referred to in Naval Message R220130Z should not be designated as an inspection trip.[2] We would have no objection at all to other work being performed by the mission as may be appropriate under the terms of the Antarctica Treaty. In particular, we have no objection in principle to the taking of aerial photographs during the trip as suggested in paragraph 2 of the referenced message.

Our reasons for recommending that this particular flight not be designated as an inspection trip are as follows.

First, we do not believe that the right of inspection under the Antarctica Treaty will atrophy if it is not utilized during the current summer season in Antarctica.

Secondly, we see no useful purpose from the standpoint of disarmament negotiations which would be served by an inspection trip at this time; on the contrary, we would be concerned that an inspection trip now would have the appearance of an over-eagerness to conduct inspection and thus lend credence to the Soviet charges that the U.S. seeks nothing but espionage privileges in disarmament negotiations.

Thirdly, we think the general state of Soviet-American relations at the present time should not be exacerbated needlessly as might be the case with this particular inspection trip.

Fourthly, when the inspection trip is made, we believe it should be mounted with more thoroughness and greater attention to the expected results of the inspection than appears to be possible in the case in question.

---

[1] Source: National Archives and Records Administration, RG 59, IO Files: Lot 69 D 169, Antarctica Files, Inspection 1962–63. Confidential. Drafted by Goodby.

[2] The flight mentioned in the message to the U.S. Antarctic Project office in Washington involved taking gravity and magnetic measurements as requested by the National Science Foundation, and required overnight stops at the Mirny and Wilkes Stations and an overflight of the Soviet Union's Vostok Station. Since a Navy aircraft would be used, the Navy wondered whether the flight should be designated as an inspection trip and whether photographs should be taken of the stations to be visited. (Ibid.)

460. Memorandum From the Assistant Director for International Relations, Arms Control and Disarmament Agency (Beam) to the Special Assistant for Antarctica, Bureau of International Organization Affairs (Owen)[1]

Washington, May 4, 1962.

SUBJECT

Treaty Inspection Rights in Antarctica

Your memorandum of April 24, 1962,[2] requested our views on whether the United States should include an inspection trip in its plans for Antarctica operations during the 1962–63 season. As this Agency has stated in its previous correspondence with you, and particularly in Mr. Fisher's memorandum of October 25, 1961,[3] we think it would be useful to exercise our right of inspection but we have also felt that the timing has not been propitious for such an inspection. We are not inclined to think that these rights would atrophy if not exercised in the near future. It seems to us that there is no pressing need this year for an inspection and therefore we would recommend that no plans be made for such a trip during the 1962–63 season.

It is our understanding that in the course of normal contacts between the personnel of various countries engaging in Antarctic operations, the United States is acquainted with all activities being carried out in Antarctica. If, however, there is some Soviet activity in the Antarctic with which we are unfamiliar, it would be reasonable to suggest that an inspection of that particular activity be carried out. We would therefore suggest that in your discussions with Admiral Tyree you should ascertain whether there are any activities with which we are unfamiliar and which might justify a request by us for an inspection. If there is any such activity, we would be happy to reconsider our decision that no inspection should be contemplated this year.

---

[1] Source: National Archives and Records Administration, RG 59, IO Files: Lot 69 D 169, Antarctica Files, Inspection 1962–63. Confidential.

[2] Not printed. (Ibid.)

[3] Document 459.

461. Memorandum From the Special Assistant for Antarctica,
      Bureau of International Organization Affairs (Owen) to the
      Assistant Secretary of State for International Organization
      Affairs (Cleveland)[1]

Washington, June 13, 1962.

SUBJECT

Antarctica: Questions related to Internationalization as Long-term Objective

Supplemental to the tactical problems attendant upon U.S. advocacy of a secretariat for Antarctica (my memorandum of June 7, 1962),[2] following are some more fundamental considerations on the merits of internationalization as an objective and the usefulness of a secretariat as a means to that, or some other desirable, end, assuming that somehow a secretariat would be agreed to by all.

Our present position is based on the consensus of opinion among U.S. agencies concerned, as developed in our running interagency coordination. It is therefore the position of the Department making judgments on the basis of consultation principally with NSF, DOD, and CIA. A reassessment of this position would require careful consideration of the following:

1. Would a secretariat lead to greater internationalization with eventual surrender of claims? Actually, there is reason to expect that, even if the Latins, by inadvertence or under pressure, accepted a secretariat, the result might well be to aggravate their attitude on the claims issue.

2. More fundamentally, although we do not recognize any of these claims and have made none of our own, does it necessarily follow that renunciation by all claimants is a good thing for us? We did consider various formulas of "pooling claims" in the past. But this was before it became necessary to make the Soviets full partners in a treaty on Antarctica. There is much crystal gazing involved here, but are we cer-

---

[1] Source: National Archives and Records Administration, RG 59, Central Files 1960–63, 702.022/6–1362. Confidential. Drafted by Owen. A copy was sent to Wallner.

[2] In this memorandum Owen reported that the British regarded "an embryonic secretariat" as a means to internationalize Antarctica and divest themselves of territorial claims. A secretariat would be strongly opposed by Argentina, Chile, and France, which were most vocal in their territorial claims. Norway, New Zealand, Japan, and South Africa would probably support a secretariat. Australia hoped to provide a headquarters for it. The Soviet Union would only support a secretariat if it contained "a built-in veto" and could be exploited. Owens recommended that the United States should support "intensifying multilateral consultations" and wider international scientific cooperation as a more feasible means to internationalize Antarctica. (Ibid., 702.022/6–762)

tain that it is in our interest to persuade countries like Australia or Argentina to surrender their claims (albeit unrecognized by us) in exchange for a joint tenancy which includes the Soviets?

3. Aside from eventual surrender of claims, are there other advantages for the United States in a secretariat? There is practically no function which requires a secretariat. A real international secretariat would cost money, involve problems of getting the right officials selected, and, since the proponents apparently refuse to consider Washington as the situs, would probably close the door to our objective of retaining Washington as the center of consultations.

4. We might successfully strive either to (1) control such a secretariat or (2) keep it innocuous and useless. Otherwise, a secretariat as well as any attendant expansion of international administrative measures is likely to restrict our freedom of action beyond what is now in the Treaty. It would tend to create pressures for such things as coordination of our science programs with those of others, and U.S. logistic support to others. In the present state of knowledge about Antarctica, the possible future uses of the area that we may have to engage in or prevent, will become identifiable only with scientific and technological progress. For instance, we may find it necessary to set up a system of tracking stations there, or engage in some other activity which, while within the terms of the Treaty, is nevertheless one in which interference or the restrictions resulting from a secretariat may be undesirable.

5. It is true that retaining our freedom means leaving others with theirs. But we already have a Treaty prohibiting nonpeaceful use and nuclear explosions, with rights of inspection. We believe it is too early to state with confidence that, on balance, we would gain with further restrictions on the freedom of action that remains. While we would, as usual, abide by new restrictions, there is doubt whether a secretariat would effectively limit, any more than does the present provision for inspection, *that* kind of action by *those* others which we, precisely, would have reason to be concerned about. The only countries whose freedom of action we may have to worry about are (1) the U.S.S.R. and (2) the Latin Americans in the event of political changes unfriendly to us in their governments.

6. Would the halfway step suggested by the British for a secretariat, not truly international, but provided by one of the countries (Australia), really be a step towards internationalization? As a practical matter, such a secretariat would be subservient to the government which provides it. The Australians are nice people, but would they always consult us in time in connection with eventual initiatives a secretariat would undertake?

7. On the other hand, international administration on a basis broader than the countries that have been active in Antarctica would present

other factors: It is easier for us to deal on Antarctic affairs with those actually concerned than with all comers.

8. I should add that there are implications of domestic politics to be considered in adopting a pro-internationalization position. The minority in Congress that opposed the present Treaty as going too far in pooling our interests with the Soviets, would be even more adamant. In the Senate, besides the "southern bloc" led by Byrd and Russell, and Mr. Goldwater, this group included Messrs. Engle, Gruening, and Dodd.

So, the objections to a shift of position boil down to (1) tactical difficulties and (2) uncertainty as to the future significance of Antarctica. I know that having to deal with trees should not obscure one's sight of the forest, and it would be a pity to forego a good opportunity to push for an experiment in international government when it comes along. So far, I sincerely wish I could think of good reasons why we should advocate a secretariat, or internationalization, but I cannot think of any which do not involve complications or unknowns.

---

462.   Paper Prepared in the Department of State[1]

Washington, July 12, 1962.

STATEMENT OF U.S OBJECTIVES REGARDING ANTARCTICA AND COURSES OF ACTION DURING THE NEXT SEVERAL YEARS

The basic objective of the United States with respect to Antarctica may be stated as follows: To take advantage of present and possible future uses of Antarctica (political, scientific, economic, and other) that benefit the security and welfare of the United States and to prevent any use of Antarctica which would be detrimental thereto.

---

[1] Source: National Archives and Records Administration, RG 59, Central Files 1960–63, 702.022/4–262. Confidential. Attached to an August 22 letter from Special Assistant George H. Owen to Leonard H. Dykes of the CIA, requesting CIA's concurrence. An earlier version of this paper, dated February 14, was sent on March 2 by Assistant Secretary Cleveland to Under Secretary McGhee for transmittal to the Defense Department, the National Science Foundation, the CIA, the Commerce Department, and the Bureau of the Budget. (Ibid., 702.022/3–262) This version was approved by the CIA on April 2 and by the Defense Department on April 13. The revised statement of policy was approved by all interested agencies at the beginning of March 1963.

This basic objective is the underlying reason for our having undertaken a program of Antarctic activities at the time of the IGY, and of having proposed and concluded an international treaty providing for freedom of scientific research and for the peaceful use of Antarctica.

At the present time, the principal and clearly identifiable profitable use or "resource" of Antarctica is the scientific information which can be gathered there. The benefit derived from this information is increased knowledge in the United States a) of the physical characteristics of Antarctica and b) in those branches of science to which observations conducted in the unique location of Antarctica are especially useful.

Consequently, United States activities in and concerning Antarctica should, first of all, be those of carrying out, providing logistic support for, and promoting international relations which facilitate, a long-term program of scientific observations and studies in Antarctica. However, the operations of United States agencies conducted for this purpose in Antarctica, as well as activities in diplomacy and scientific exchange concerning Antarctica, should, wherever practicable, serve the broader scope of the basic objective.

The nature of future activities which United States agencies may be required to perform in Antarctica to meet this broad objective will be determined in the light of scientific and technological progress, particularly in fields where utilization of the Polar areas is significant, of unpredictable political developments, and of the significance of the area in relation to economic and population growth. As in the case of unknown or unoccupied areas in the past, it is reasonable to assume that the ability to "have things our own way" is more likely to be enhanced by a position of leadership in Antarctic affairs than by letting others overtake us in the scope of what they do regarding Antarctica.

In this connection, the present objectives of Soviet activities in Antarctica apparently are: (1) to increase their scientific knowledge through data obtainable in Antarctica (including that of military value) as a part of their systematic investigations of the earth as a whole from its core to outer space, and (2) to demonstrate superior Communist capabilities by their achievements in Antarctica. In pursuit of these objectives Soviet activities are expected to include as they do now: (a) gradually expanding scientific research and exploration, with long-range planning, and permanent occupation of sites; (b) participation in international scientific cooperation to obtain as much scientific data as possible; (c) increasing participation by bloc countries; (d) expansion of whaling and interest in potential mineral resources; (e) possible use of Antarctica for satellite monitoring; (f) propaganda exploitation of their activities in discovery, scientific findings and in production of reports and maps.

United States activities of exploration, discovery, mapping, the permanent occupation of a certain number of sites, the movement of personnel and equipment to, from and within the Antarctic area, cooperative scientific efforts with other countries, and instances of assistance to other expeditions, besides being a necessary element of a long-term scientific program, are of the kind that maintain the leadership and increase the experience of the United States in Antarctica. We should continue to engage in them, even when the return is not immediately apparent in terms of specific scientific data, so long as they do not disproportionately detract from the carrying out of the scientific research programs and provided the cost of any such particular undertaking is not out of proportion to the reasonably foreseeable benefits to be derived therefrom.

In the light of the foregoing, the following policies concerning Antarctica shall be pursued:

Statement of Policy

(1) To conduct, with adequate logistic support, a long-term program of scientific observations and studies in Antarctica.

(2) In combination with the effort of supplying logistic support for the foregoing, to engage in and encourage other activities that contribute to maintaining United States leadership in Antarctic affairs in view of the basic objective concerning the use of Antarctica.

(3) To observe the provisions of the Antarctic Treaty, make certain their observance by governments and persons of all countries that engage in activities in Antarctica, and conduct our relations with other nations, in particular the consultations under the Antarctic Treaty, with a view to securing the basic U.S. objective concerning present and possible future uses of Antarctica.

(4) To continue the policy of not recognizing any of the claims of territorial sovereignty in Antarctica which have been or may be asserted by other countries, and reserving our rights throughout Antarctica.

(5) To continue the tradition of scientific cooperation in Antarctica and maintain and develop the kind of contacts with foreign governments and their nationals which are advantageous to the United States whether in Antarctic scientific work, or otherwise.

(6) To plan for and conduct all activities in and concerning Antarctica in a manner which assures effective coordination among the agencies having responsibility for funding or executing them, or of formulating policy with respect to Antarctica.

It is assumed that in the absence of developments of overriding importance, the foregoing objectives can be adequately pursued during the next few years without any major change in the level of activities

1050 Foreign Relations, 1961–1963, Volume XXV

conducted at the present time. The following courses of action should be undertaken or continued during the next several years:

Statement of Courses of Action concerning Antarctica to be Pursued by the United States during the Next Several Years

1. Continue permanent occupation of McMurdo Sound Station, so long as it can profitably be used as:

(a) a supply base for activities in other locations in Antarctica (administrative services, transportation, communications, storage, quarters, and utilities including nuclear power supply),
(b) a site for year-round scientific studies, such as meteorology, marine biology, and a number of upper atmospheric physics programs,
(c) a site from which to carry out scientific summer studies, such as programs in biology, geology, limnology, pedology, etc., in the surrounding area.

2. Continue permanent occupation of Pole Station, so long as it can profitably be used:

(a) as a site for scientific studies, such as upper atmospheric physics, meteorology, and geophysics, and as a site to carry out specialized programs in the surrounding area,
(b) for its value, because of its unique location, to United States prestige in Antarctic affairs.

3. Continue permanent occupation of Byrd Station, so long as it can profitably be used as:

(a) a site for scientific studies, such as upper atmospheric physics, meteorology, geophysics, and other sciences,
(b) an advance supply base for activities at other locations which can be supplied from Byrd Station.

4. Establish a small, preferably relocatable, year-round site (Eights Station) in the Ellsworth Land area south of the Bellingshausen Sea for use primarily for upper atmospheric physics and meteorological studies to take advantage of a favorable location with respect to the auroral zone, and magnetic conjugateness to accessible land areas of the northern Hemisphere.

5. Investigate the feasibility of establishing a station in the Palmer Peninsula area, possibly in cooperation with one or more of the countries already operating in the area, to be used as:

(a) a site for scientific observations in marine and land biology, meteorology and upper atmospheric physics, the installations to include a biological laboratory facility,
(b) to serve as a supply base for inland geological and biological operations in that area.

6. Continue to maintain advance headquarters in New Zealand with facilities for the conduct of supply operations there and conduct

relations with New Zealand in a manner conducive to securing the continued cooperation of that country for this purpose.

7. Secure observance of the agreements with Argentina and Australia concerning operations at Ellsworth and Wilkes Stations, continue arrangements for joint operations at Hallett Station with New Zealand, and participate in activities at these stations to the extent that is useful in the light of the policy directives stated above.

8. Continuation of a coordinated program of aerial photography, geodetic control and cartography.

9. Undertake, as practicable, geographic exploration in Antarctica, by ship, air, and on the surface of the continent, in combination with suitable scientific or supply operations and in cooperation with other countries when desirable, and visits to stations of other countries.

10. Be prepared to exercise rights of inspection under the Antarctic Treaty, exercise these rights at appropriate times and places, and make apparent, as a deterrent, our capability to exercise these rights.

11. Encourage the participation in Antarctic programs of countries friendly to the United States.

12. Engage in programs for the exchange of scientific or other appropriate personnel to participate in the activities of other nations concerning Antarctica and, in particular, assure continuation of the exchange of scientists with the USSR. Within the transportation facilities to and from Antarctica that are available for the purpose of conducting U.S. activities there, maintain the capability of transporting a number of scientists, representatives or invitees of other countries which it is desirable to accommodate to carry out personnel exchange programs, or in view of any other objectives stated herein, including a small number of foreign journalists for the purposes of paragraph 14 below.

13. Continue to participate in international cooperative arrangements furthering the collection, dissemination and analysis of scientific information, both concerning Antarctica and that related to the Antarctic aspects of global scientific studies and programs.

14. Promote publicity concerning U.S. activities in Antarctica which enhances the prestige of the United States.

15. Promote the systematized study of the scientific data gathered through Antarctic operations.

16. Assign responsibilities among appropriate United States agencies for the planning, funding, management, execution and coordination of all activities undertaken in fulfillment of the foregoing courses of action in conformity with the statement of policies set forth above.

463. Memorandum From the Special Assistant for Antarctica, Bureau of International Organization Affairs (Owen) to the Assistant Secretary of State for International Organization Affairs (Cleveland)[1]

Washington, August 20, 1962.

SUBJECT

Buenos Aires Antarctic Meeting

I wrote all the telegrams from Buenos Aires during the Antarctic Meeting except the last one, No. 300 of July 30,[2] which apparently was sent after I had left. I believe the following comments may be useful:

It is true that the Soviet delegation was, as at Canberra, displaying the utmost cordiality. The Soviet Ambassador made a point of telling me at great length how he thought the Antarctic Treaty should be an "example" for other agreements. Their Foreign Office man, Movchan, who had been at Canberra, was also cooperative. However, there was a marked difference in his attitude in conversation with me, depending on whether his Ambassador was present or not. At all receptions the Soviets stuck together like particles of an atomic nucleus so long as the Ambassador was with them. When on their own they relaxed and talked quite freely.

As for the other remarks in the telegram, I feel I am not familiar enough with UNESCO meetings to comment on the simile, but I believe the remark about delegates taking in "each other's laundry" may be misunderstood. The delegates did make much use of references to the cordiality that marked earlier meetings. If there was less disagreement than there had been at Canberra, this appeared to be due to the fact that several of the delegations that had opposed us on some issues at Canberra were coming around to the U.S. views, in particular the British and Australians, on such questions as the immediate creation of an all Australian secretari-

---

[1] Source: National Archives and Records Administration, RG 59, IO Files: Lot 69 D 169, Antarctica Files, Multilateral, General, 1962. Confidential.

[2] Reference is to telegram 180, July 19, telegram 236, July 25, and telegram 287, July 28, from Buenos Aires. (Ibid., Central Files 1960–63, 397.022/7–1962, 397.022/7–2562, 397.022/7–2862, respectively) In telegram 300 from Buenos Aires, July 30, Ambassador McClintock wrote: "My overall impression is that this is a sort of minor 'UNESCO on Ice' with tendency of members of same Penguin Club [an informal group of diplomats stationed in Washington from countries with Antarctic claims] to take in each other's laundry. I see no reason for consultative meetings at intervals of less than two years. In my closing speech while lauding delegates for their not very memorable achievements, I stressed that thanks of conference should go not to cozy diplomats but to the scientists, seamen, and airmen who were living in a more rigorous environment in the Antarctic Continent and the Southern Ocean." (Ibid., 397.022/7–3062)

at or the adoption of additional multilateral regulations on a variety of subjects. But no special favors were made as among any delegates.

As to the desirability of not having these meetings too frequently, this, as you know, is well known to us. However, I advised against making a public statement to that effect since the United States is already accused of "holding back" too much. We can negotiate as to the date of the next meeting as we see fit. That the achievements of the meeting were "not very memorable" is true, but the main thing is that this was in accordance with the U.S. position papers.

The British acted too quickly in withdrawing their "jurisdiction" item. This was the result of Chilean pressure. The Argentines really did not want to make an issue of its inclusion in the agenda. We formally stated our approval of its inclusion and even suggested to the British that they should not cave in so easily.

---

464.   Report on the Second Consultative Meeting Under the Antarctic Treaty[1]

Washington, undated.

REPORT ON SECOND CONSULTATIVE MEETING UNDER THE ANTARCTIC TREATY

There is attached a report of the proceedings of the Second Consultative Meeting under Article IX of the Antarctic Treaty, held at Buenos Aires from July 18 to July 28, 1962. It is arranged by topic in the order of the agenda adopted for the meeting. There is also included a summary of the manner in which the question of "jurisdiction" was dealt with, which was not included in the approved agenda.

As at the Canberra Meeting, the Rules of Procedure provided that neither minutes nor a summary record of the debates should be pro-

---

[1] Source: National Archives and Records Administration, RG 59, IO Files: Lot 67 D 378, Antarctica. Confidential. Attached is a September 6 memorandum by Owen transmitting the report to Assistant Secretary Cleveland. It contained a handwritten note reading, "Also attached is a copy of the Final Report containing the recommendations adopted." The Final Report is not printed. The Recommendations of the Second Consultative Meeting are printed in *American Foreign Policy: Current Documents, 1962*, pp 534–537.

duced. The Argentine Government as host may, however, have a taped recording of the proceedings. In the attached summary of the proceedings an account is given of the background of each topic as well as of the manner in which it was dealt with at the meeting.

Noteworthy features of the meeting may be summarized as follows:

(1) Unlike the Canberra Meeting, no efforts were made at Buenos Aires to convert SCAR into the official instrument for discharging the Governments' responsibilities regarding scientific cooperation. In this regard, the British had obviously changed their earlier position. They appear to agree that it is best not to convert SCAR into an official body indirectly by delegating to that body the responsibilities of governments. However, the British, Australians and New Zealanders did oppose certain features of the Soviet proposal regarding exchange of scientific information (Item 6 of Agenda) on the grounds that the Governments would seem to be "dictating" to SCAR. In the main this view was shared by the United States, since the U.S. Government, although it finances the U.S. scientists engaged in Antarctic research, does not control them so that it can commit itself to meet deadlines on scientific exchange.

(2) On the question of the secretariat, the chief proponents of the establishment of one at the Canberra Meeting, namely, the United Kingdom and Australia, were practically silent. The opponents of a secretariat made lengthy speeches on the subject. The British and Australians did not put forward any arguments in favor of a secretariat. Nor did the British and Australians make any overt statements against resuming consultations in Washington (as they had at the Canberra Meeting). Washington as a site for interim consultations was favored not only by Belgium (as at the Canberra Meeting), but also by New Zealand, Norway, and Japan.

(3) The Soviet attitude, as at the Canberra Meeting and at the Washington Conference, was on the whole friendly and cooperative. It may be noteworthy that while the Soviets have up to now avoided any references to the inspection provisions, one of their representatives in a working group meeting emphasized the fact that the topic, "Exchange of Information under Article VII, Paragraph 5" (Item 9 of Agenda), was a "political" topic and related to the inspection system of the Treaty. The same Soviet delegate in the course of discussions of the press communiqué of the meeting, stressed the need to include a reference to the spirit of harmony and cooperation in which the meeting was conducted. The Soviet Ambassador made a point of telling the U.S. delegation what a fine thing the Antarctic Treaty was and that it should be an "example" to other agreements.

(4) There appeared to be general recognition of the fact that there had been insufficient consultation among the Governments in preparation for this meeting, and that as a result the meeting "accomplished" very little. Actually, the Governments that had so emphatically expressed their desire for the adoption of more "measures" at and after the Canberra Meeting, especially the United Kingdom, had not responded to efforts of the United States to consult on these matters prior to the Buenos Aires Meeting; and at the meeting, they did not press for even an exchange of views on some of their favorite topics. For instance: The British took steps to withdraw their modest proposal on jurisdiction at the first rumblings of Chilean opposition. The Australians did not avail themselves of the opportunity to present their reasons for the early convening of a meeting on communications.

(5) The recommendations adopted were in accord with the U.S. position for the several topics. The United States did not seek the adoption by this meeting of any recommendations for new measures or agreements beyond existing ones and believes that additional measures (for instance, on conservation, logistics, et cetera) require considerable consultation among governments prior to their formulation by meetings such as this.

---

465. Letter From the Director of the Arms Control and Disarmament Agency (Foster) to the Assistant Secretary of State for International Organization Affairs (Cleveland)[1]

Washington, January 29, 1963.

Dear Harlan:

Your letter of January 25, 1963,[2] recommends immediate implementation of the inspection provisions of the Antarctica Treaty and transmits a draft memorandum concerning a method for carrying out an inspection during the 1963–1964 austral summer season. In considering this matter, I believe that we should differentiate between two questions: first, whether it would be desirable to prepare an inspection plan; and second, when such a plan might best be implemented.

---

[1] Source: National Archives and Records Administration, RG 59, IO Files: Lot 69 D 169, Antarctica Files, Inspection 1962–63. Confidential.

[2] Not printed. (Ibid., Chron Files, Jan–Feb. 1963)

Insofar as preparation of a plan is concerned, I believe that it is important to proceed with the necessary planning effort. In this regard, the draft memorandum prepared by your staff outlines some of the elements involved in one possible approach. However, it will be necessary, in our view, to consider some aspects of the matter in greater depth on an interagency basis in order to identify more specifically the objectives of an inspection (that is, what we are looking for), to determine the feasibility of various techniques (including, in particular, the extent to which aircraft can be used), to evaluate the effectiveness of a multilateral inspection team in contrast with a unilateral inspection team, and to develop additional information concerning skills required, method of financing, and related aspects. Although the informal staff-level consultations that have taken place have been useful in focusing attention on some of these problems, we think that additional effort is required to be certain that the most satisfactory approach has been selected.

The timing of an inspection presents problems of a different character. As you know, we have had some difficulty in convincing others that the United States does not desire inspection for inspection's sake. Particularly at a time when we may be able to make some progress toward an agreement on nuclear inspection, I am inclined to think that it might be counter-productive for us to commit ourselves to an early Antarctica inspection. At the same time, if an agreement on nuclear testing is reached and presented to the Senate for ratification, I would not wish us to be vulnerable to possible charges arising from the fact that we had not implemented inspection provisions of the Antarctica Treaty. In the event of such charges, it would be helpful to have prepared a contingency plan and possibly set a schedule for its implementation. We might possibly mention it in our annual submission of the U.S. Antarctica plan to the other signatories due by the end of November 1963.

With more specific references to the Antarctica situation, I am concerned to learn that the scientific community has not been taking full advantage of Soviet invitations to visit their activities. Such visits could be an important source of continuing reassurance in the absence of formal inspections. Moreover, they could assist in defining inspection objectives and limiting inspections to areas of greatest potential concern, thereby minimizing possible disruptive effects. I understand that we hope to take fuller advantage of such opportunities in the future, and I would like to stress the value of doing so.

In view of the foregoing considerations, I would like to reserve for the time being judgment on the scheduling of an inspection. However, as previously indicated, I favor proceeding with development of an inspection plan without prejudice to the question of timing. With this in view, I am requesting the ACDA staff to complete study of various aspects of an Antarctica inspection as rapidly as possible in consultation with your staff as well as staff of other interested agencies. In view of the progress that has already been made, we should be in a position to resolve any outstanding differences in the near future.

Sincerely yours,

Bill

466. **Memorandum From the Director of the Office of International Economic and Social Affairs, Bureau of International Organization Affairs (McKitterick) to the Deputy Assistant Secretary of State for International Organization Affairs (Gardner)**[1]

Washington, February 27, 1963.

SUBJECT

Proposed Meeting with ACDA on Inspection in Antarctica

In proceeding with the proposed meeting with ACDA concerning inspection in Antarctica, you will no doubt wish to keep the following points in mind:

1. The inclusion of the inspection provision in the Antarctic Treaty played an important part in obtaining the necessary two-thirds vote in the Senate. At the time of the approval of the Antarctic Treaty by the Senate, the Department spokesman assured the Senate that we would proceed with the implementation of the inspection provision of the Antarctic Treaty. For Mr. Phleger's statement see Tab D of the proposed memorandum to the Secretary.[2]

2. The only effective way to assure compliance with the Antarctic Treaty is through the implementation of the inspection provision of the Treaty.

3. The Department regional bureaus, G/PM and Legal have expressed agreement with the view that we should proceed promptly with inspection in the Antarctic, beginning with the next summer period.

---

[1] Source: National Archives and Records Administration, RG 59, IO Files: Lot 67 D 378, Antarctica. Confidential. Drafted by James Simsarian.

[2] Document 468.

4. According to informal consultations we have already had with other agencies concerned with United States activities in the Antarctic (including the Department of Defense and the Department of the Navy), they agree that we should proceed promptly with inspection in the Antarctic, beginning with the next summer period.

5. The two Admirals in charge of United States Naval Support in the Antarctic are of the opinion that we should proceed promptly with inspection in the Antarctic, beginning with the next summer period. Mr. Simsarian has discussed this matter with Admiral Tyree who just retired after four years in the Antarctic; and Mr. Mills has discussed this matter with Admiral Reedy now in charge in the Antarctic.

6. We need an early decision to proceed with inspection in order to carry out an inspection program in November 1963. The Department of the Navy has already urged us to resolve this matter now in order that planning can proceed at this time with respect to the utilization of the few icebreakers available. In fact Admiral Tyree has pointed out that the *Glacier* should be used for this purpose, and there will be a number of demands on this ship.

7. Admiral Tyree and Admiral Reedy have both pointed out that inspection by planes is not feasible at this time, and that a ship would have to be used for the 1963–64 season. Landing facilities at foreign bases are not safe for use by American planes at this time, according to Admiral Tyree, who certainly is knowledgeable on this subject.

8. An immediate decision on this matter is also necessary to enable the National Science Foundation to proceed with arrangements it already has underway for the recruitment of scientists to be sent to the Antarctic during the 1963–64 season. This program will have to be meshed with logistics arrangements for the inspection program.

9. Since starting our own discussions relating to an inspection program in the Antarctic, the United Kingdom has proposed to the Department the desirability of proceeding immediately with the implementation of the inspection provisions of the Treaty. We have informed the United Kingdom that we are studying this matter and will provide a United States response as soon as possible.

10. All of the above points relate to the urgent need to reach an early decision to proceed promptly with a plan for inspection in Antarctica, beginning with the 1963–64 season. There of course is the separate question of whether we should proceed unilaterally or multilaterally. On this issue there is a difference of opinion that should be resolved. While IO and EUR favor the multilateral approach, Legal and ACDA are pressing for the unilateral approach.

467.   **Editorial Note**

The first preparatory meeting for the Third Consultative Meeting of signatory governments to the Antarctic Treaty was held in Brussels on March 7, 1963. The delegates could not agree on when to hold the meeting, but would request instructions from their governments prior to the next preparatory meeting, scheduled for April 4. No agreement was reached as to whether measures to protect Antarctic wildlife would take the form of a code or a convention (some delegates preferred a code since a convention would require legislative approval). No action needed to be taken to arrange a technical meeting on radio communications in the Antarctic, since one was scheduled in Washington between June 24 and 28. No need was seen for a symposium on logistics until after the Third Consultative Meeting had taken place. (Airgram A–1109 from Brussels, March 22, 1963; National Archives and Records Administration, RG 59, Central Files 1960–63, SCI 11–1 ANT)

468.   **Draft Memorandum Prepared in the Department of State[1]**

Washington, undated.

SUBJECT

Exercise of the Right of Inspection Under the Antarctic Treaty

Discussion

In reviewing United States interests and objectives in Antarctica, it is gratifying to note the progress made there and the continuing spirit of friendly cooperation between the United States and the other signatories of the Antarctic Treaty; Argentina, Australia, Belgium, Chile, France, Japan, New Zealand, Norway, South Africa, the Soviet Union,

---

[1] Source: National Archives and Records Administration, RG 59, Central Files 1960–63, SCI 11–1 ANT. Confidential. According to covering memoranda from Secretary Rusk and Executive Secretary Brubeck, the memorandum was sent to Secretary of Defense McNamara on March 29 and to McGeorge Bundy on April 5.

and the United Kingdom (Tab A).[2] To the best of our knowledge, Treaty provisions reserving the continent for peaceful purposes only and prohibiting any measures of a military nature have been observed by all countries active in Antarctica. It is in the interest of the United States to foster this situation by continuing to implement the unique provisions of the Treaty which ensure continued use of Antarctica for peaceful purposes only.

Article VII of the Antarctic Treaty (Tab B) provides that "In order to promote the objectives and ensure the observance of the provisions" of the Treaty, each Contracting Party which conducts substantial scientific research in Antarctica has the right to designate observers to inspect all areas of Antarctica. It seems to us that this inspection provision should be implemented beginning with the 1963–64 season by arranging for the inspection of bases in Antarctica. Extensive logistic requirements do not permit an inspection of all Antarctic bases in any one year, but routine annual inspections should be initiated. (Tab C).[3]

In Senate hearings on the Antarctic Treaty it was made clear that inspections would be carried out. On June 14, 1960 before the Foreign Relations Committee, Mr. Herman Phleger, representing the Department of State, said ". . . it would be contemplated that upon ratification of the treaty and its coming into force the parties, including the United States would designate observers who would see to it that the provisions were respected." (Tab D).[4]

The inspection provision of the Treaty has not been a controversial subject between signatory countries since the signing of the Treaty. In his opening statement at the Canberra Consultative Meeting under the Antarctic Treaty, on July 24, 1961, the United States representative spoke of inspection as "a normal activity under the treaty." A Soviet legal adviser has stated that "any State with the right to attend consultative conferences may appoint observers. They are free to travel to any part

---

[2] The tabs are not printed. The list of contracting parties was updated to include the accessions of Poland (June 8, 1961) and Czechoslovakia (June 14, 1962). These most recent signatories had not yet met the requirements that would permit them to delegate observers.

[3] According to the memorandum at Tab C, the United States intended to designate about six observers, who were to have appropriate scientific backgrounds as well as proficiency in Russian, Spanish, or French. Three or four would be selected to inspect that sector of Antarctica that included French, Australian, and Soviet bases. If logistic support was available, Argentinian, Chilean, and British bases on the Palmer Peninsula would also be inspected during the 1963–1964 austral summer season. Transportation would be provided by ships or aircraft of the U.S. Naval Support Force, Antarctica. The United States would in turn be willing to open its Antarctic bases to inspection, and expressed the hope that other signatory powers would designate observers and carry out inspections.

[4] See *The Antarctic Treaty: Hearings Before the Committee on Foreign Relations, United States Senate, Eighty-Sixth Congress, Second Session* (Washington, 1960), p. 67.

of the Antarctic at any time. The signatories must admit them for inspection of all stations, installations, equipment, and ships and planes at points of discharge and loading in the Antarctic."[5]

United States agencies and departments active in Antarctica are complying with the obligations of the Antarctic Treaty, and they of course do not object to their activities being inspected should another signatory choose to inspect.

The Treaty does not prescribe procedures for carrying out inspection. The precise manner in which inspection is to be carried out will depend upon the procedures which are developed and the precedents established as the Treaty is implemented. Since we do not believe that the Soviet Union, or any other Contracting Party, is presently engaging in improper activities, it should be relatively simple to develop inspection procedures at this stage. It will become more difficult to procure adequate inspection if we wait until the Soviets may have something to hide. Moreover, while we have no reason to believe that the Soviet Union is acting in violation of the Treaty, inspection would provide additional assurance that the objectives of the Treaty are being fulfilled. Finally, inspection would, if properly executed, deter possible violations, and provide a body of experience which might be applicable elsewhere.

Inspection parties would be transported by ship or aircraft of the U.S. Naval Support Force in Antarctica. Since both ships and aircraft are tightly scheduled to carry out existing projects, careful and early planning and coordination will be required in order to carry out effective inspections without disrupting scientific projects. Planning and logistics for 1963–64 are set forth in Tab C.

Recommendation

It is recommended that the United States plan and carry out inspections in accordance with Article VII of the Antarctic Treaty of areas in the Antarctic, including bases of the Soviet Union, on a routine annual basis, starting with the 1963–64 austral summer season. It is further recommended that arrangements for carrying out these inspections begin immediately.

---

[5] The Soviet statement, "An Example of International Co-Operation," by Professor G. I. Tunkin, Legal Adviser of the Soviet Foreign Office, was published in *International Affairs* (USSR), No. 2, February 1960.

469. Editorial Note

The second preparatory meeting for the Third Antarctic Treaty Consultative Meeting took place in Brussels on April 4, 1963. The Consultative Meeting was scheduled for the first 2 weeks of June 1964 in Brussels. The delegates discussed a British draft convention for the protection of Antarctic wildlife; representatives of Chile and the Soviet Union said that their governments were preparing drafts of their own. Chairman A. van der Essen said that a convention was preferable to a code since a code would apply only to signatories of the Antarctic Treaty, while a convention could be ratified by other countries. Before adjourning, the delegates discussed representation at the telecommunications conference scheduled for Washington in June, and agreed to ask their governments to submit a list of topics for the agenda of the Third Consultative Meeting. (Airgram A–1262 from Brussels, April 26, 1963; National Archives and Records Administration, RG 59, Central Files 1960–63, SCI 11–1 ANT)

470. Memorandum From William H. Mills of the Office of International Economic and Social Affairs, Bureau of International Organization Affairs, to George M. Fennemore of That Office[1]

Washington, April 15, 1963.

SUBJECT

Antarctic Inspection

You will recall from your brief conversation with Ambassador Daniels that he continues to believe we should go ahead with picking a person to represent State on a selection board which will designate the persons to be named as inspectors in Antarctica.

Recalling your comment that planning should be more definite so we will know what sort of person to designate, I have listed below the criteria which the selection board will use. These criteria were agreed

---

[1] Source: National Archives and Records Administration, RG 59, IO Files: Lot 69 D 169, Antarctica Files, Inspection 1963. Confidential.

upon tentatively at several meetings of Ambassador Daniels' subgroup. Admittedly it is something less than firm written planning but I believe all the points will be in any written plan produced:

1. The panel of inspectors, from which teams of 2, 3 or 4 will be chosen, will be about 20 persons.

2. NASA, CIA, DOD, NSF, ACDA and State will be asked to submit names of qualified persons as candidates. Any other agency is welcome to submit names. Agencies submitting names are not limited to their own personnel.

3. Persons not qualified are:

a. Any individual who has served as an exchange scientist in Antarctica. This will prevent present exchange scientists from being viewed as potential inspectors.

b. Any present member of the United States Naval Antarctic Support Force. It is believed that their inclusion might impair the friendly working relationship to personnel of other countries in Antarctica.

c. Any present member of the United States Antarctic Research Program (the scientists). This is for the same reason as b above.

d. Any person known to be connected with CIA.

4. The selection board will consist of one member each from NASA, ACDA, State, DOD, NSF, and CIA.

5. Inspectors chosen by the selection board will be appointed by ACDA. (Probably with some sort of written commission from the Secretary of State and the President).

6. The 20 man panel of inspectors should possess the following qualifications:

a. Fluent knowledge of Russian, Spanish and French.
b. Knowledge and/or experience of Antarctica.
c. Competence in some of the earth sciences studied in Antarctica.
d. Competence in electronics, and space science and (probably) in the use of a camera.
e. An affable, diplomatic personality.

As to the inspection itself, it is pretty firm that we plan to inspect by ship coastal bases between 180° and 90°E i.e. the French base Dumont D'Urville, the Australian-United States Wilkes base, and the Russian Mirnyy base. If logistics permit, this inspecting group might go on to the Australian Mawson base and Russia's Molodezhnaya base.

Still tentative is a plan to inspect bases of Chile, Argentina and the U.K. in the Palmer Peninsula area. Whether or not we do depends upon political considerations—the nationalist sensitivity of Argentina and Chile. Logistics here is no problem since inspectors could get a "free ride" on a United States ship which plans to go there for scientific purposes.

Also being considered is the possibility of inspection of some bases by overflight. Bases which have so far been discussed for such inspection are Vostok, Sovetskaya and Komsomolskaya, all Russian.

This leaves a number of things still to be decided, but should be enough to permit designation of a State member for the selection board.

I suggest that we contact the Office of Personnel, explain the problem and ask them to produce about 15 or 20 individuals, each of them possessing one or more of the necessary qualifications, and each of them available for any six week period between November 1, 1963 and March 1, 1964.

This is a very big order indeed and needs corresponding justification.

The job of inspecting foreign bases in Antarctica is a very delicate one. A mistake in judgment could have serious adverse consequences for our presently cordial relations there. I believe that the only way we can discharge our responsibility with regard to Antarctica is by having representatives on any group undertaking inspection of foreign bases there and I also believe that any United States inspection team should not be predominately military because of the emphasis on peaceful activities only in the Antarctic Treaty. This might occur naturally simply because DOD has so many more people to draw upon, unless we are able to submit the 15 or 20 names I have suggested.

---

471. Memorandum of Conversation[1]

Washington, April 17, 1963.

SUBJECT

Inspection of Bases in Antarctica

PARTICIPANTS

Mr. Viktor Karpov, First Secretary, Soviet Embassy
Ambassador Paul Daniels, ACDA
Mr. William Mills, OES

Ambassador Daniels explained that because of his Antarctic background he had been asked to help in the planning for implementing the inspection provision of Article VII of the Antarctic Treaty, the article

---

[1] Source: National Archives and Records Administration, RG 59, IO Files: Lot 69 D 191, Antarctica Files, Inspection 1963. Confidential. Drafted by Mills.

included to ensure no violations of the treaty. He said that there has never been any need to inspect and is none now so far as he knew, but it wasn't desirable to let this valuable article atrophy through disuse. In any case, inspections might well serve to inspire confidence. He said that it seemed a good idea to inform other governments—especially the USSR—of our planning, to maintain the mutual confidence and cordial relations which exist in Antarctica. He said it is too early to make definite statements about details of the inspection since we are in the planning stage. He hoped that Mr. Karpov's government would look upon any inspection in Antarctica as the United States does, namely as a routine Antarctic operation. The United States would, of course, welcome inspection of any of our bases. The Ambassador said that he did not anticipate an immediate response from Mr. Karpov, but would like to exchange views as soon as Mr. Karpov could report this conversation to his government.

Mr. Karpov asked whether it was visualized that each nation active in Antarctica should inspect all other bases.

Ambassador Daniels responded that that would be too expensive but we might inspect, say, the French D'Urville base, Mirnyy, where we would expect a cordial welcome, and the Australian base at Mawson with possibly inclusion of bases of Argentina, Chile and the U.K. in the Palmer Peninsula.

Mr. Karpov asked whether United States scientists working in Antarctica would be included in the United States inspection program.

Ambassador Daniels said that they would not, emphasizing that any inspection would be completely separated from the scientific program in Antarctica. He said that later on we will inform all treaty signatories of the names of our observers as required by the treaty.

Mr. Karpov asked whether all governments would be informed simultaneously. Ambassador Daniels said yes.

Mr. Karpov asked how long inspectors would stay at any one base.

Ambassador Daniels said that no very lengthy stay was planned and there was no desire to abuse anyone's hospitality. He added that we have made no announcement about this matter and do not plan to do so. We hope that any inspection would be a "low key" matter not to be "glamorized." The United States views this inspection strictly in the Antarctic context without any connection to the rest of the world.

Mr. Karpov asked whether there was any special reason for planning the inspection now.

Ambassador Daniels said there was none but that we did not want this valuable treaty provision to atrophy from disuse. The Ambassador added that if nobody used the inspection provision until six or eight years had passed, then initiation of an inspection would indeed cause comment and speculation.

Mr. Karpov asked if any procedures had been worked out, noting that there could be many important practical considerations. He also asked whether detailed procedures would be decided by consultation among governments.

Ambassador Daniels said that presumably there will be conversations on this subject, and procedures would be the same for all countries. He noted that there were no rules for the details of inspection and expressed the belief that the matter would resolve itself with the use of common sense.

Mr. Karpov said that he would inform his government and see if we could reach an agreement on detailed procedures.

Ambassador Daniels said that there was no need to reach an agreement about inspection but that we would be interested in any comments on procedural matters. He added that it might be good if Soviets inspect United States bases and others. The Ambassador reiterated that we view this inspection as purely an Antarctic matter, unrelated to other parts of the world. Mr. Karpov proposed "a hypothetical case" in which only the United States and the USSR designated inspectors. He then asked whether we would agree upon procedures to be used. Ambassador Daniels said that there would not be much to agree upon because the right to inspect is established.

Mr. Karpov asked whether the United States would go ahead and inspect if no other country did so because of costs involved and so forth.

Ambassador Daniels said yes.

Mr. Karpov asked whether we had any procedures to avoid overcrowding the base being inspected.

Mr. Mills said that we would not abuse anyone's hospitality.

Mr. Karpov asked whether these things will be subject to agreement "on the spot."

Ambassador Daniels said in most cases, yes. He reiterated that we hope any inspection will be viewed as a routine non-glamorous operation.

Mr. Karpov said that he could not assume a very quick response to this conversation.

Ambassador Daniels reiterated the fact that we have no suspicions about any present activity in Antarctica and are very happy about the cordial relations there.

472. Summary Record of Meeting[1]

Washington, May 8, 1963.

SUMMARY RECORD OF MAY 8 ANTARCTICA PERSONNEL
ADVISORY GROUP (PAG) MEETING

1. Those present at the May 8 meeting of Antarctica PAG were Commander Kline (DOD), Mr. Dykes (CIA), Col. Pozinsky (NASA), Mr. Fennemore (State), Mr. Mills (State) and Mr. Freund (ACDA) in whose office the meeting took place.

2. It was agreed that in drawing up the lists of qualifications for inspectors two lists would be needed. One will be a list of general qualifications that would be needed in light of Tab A of the Committee of Antarctica Working Paper dated April 18 ("Possible activities in Antarctica which would be inconsistent with the treaty").[2] The other list would be based on our knowledge of the specific significant activities known to be carried on at each of the bases we are considering inspecting. Messrs. Mills and Dykes and Commander Kline agreed to collaborate in furnishing for the next meeting of the PAG a list of known activities for each base.

3. It was further agreed that no matter how uninteresting a base might be from the point of view of U.S. national security or how elementary its activities are, the make-up of the group inspecting would take into account both the sensibilities of the government operating the base and of the Soviets. By this it was meant that there would be serious explorations made by fully qualified U.S. personnel and that we would avoid too great contrasts between the groups inspecting, for example, Soviet and Chilean bases. As Mr. Mills suggested, we would in fact have two categories of inspection groups, one where our national security interests are involved and the other where they are not, but this would not be apparent to the hosts.

4. The question of whether military personnel would be included among the inspectors was put off for later consideration, although no group would, in any case, be predominantly military.

5. The question of numbers in each group was also left open, pending examination of the qualifications mix required in each case and the

---

[1] Source: National Archives and Records Administration, RG 59, IO Files: Lot 69 D 169, Antarctica Files, Inspection 1963. Confidential. Drafted on May 10 by Richard B. Freund (ACDA/IR).

[2] Reference is to a working paper prepared by the Committee on Antarctica of the Arms Control and Disarmament Agency; not printed.

possibilities of finding individuals who combine a variety of capabilities.

6. It was agreed that special efforts both in the selection of inspectors and their training will be necessary to avoid any impression that we are carrying out intelligence activities. For example, former service attachés would be excluded.

7. Inspection groups will be asked to submit serious unclassified reports for later submission to the other signatories. By "serious" we mean that the reports on both the above-mentioned categories of bases will be equally thorough though commensurate with the numbers and kinds of activities going on at any given base.

8. The draft document of April 18 on "Qualification and Selection of Personnel" was briefly reviewed. It was agreed that a thorough review would await the availability of the promised revised draft. Nevertheless, the following points in the paper were considered:

a. Near the top of Page 2 provision will be made for State Department suggestion that the inspection will be designed as a precedent for subsequent inspections.

b. Proficiency in language (Page 3) will be secondary to expertise in substantive fields.[3] In fact, Soviet suspicion could be aroused if we include an inspector fully fluent in Russian who is not also highly qualified in one of the technical fields of Soviet activity at the bases inspected.

c. Observer qualifications (Page 3) should include at least one inspector in each group with good amateur photographic ability. There would still be special training (Page 5) in the peculiarities of photography in Antarctica.[4] We would also consider how much aerial photography can be accomplished by the aircraft carrying the inspector groups in and out of the bases.

d. If there is considered to be any possibility at all that nuclear materials are at or near any of the bases to be inspected, we will consider as a qualification ability to operate detection devices of a relatively simple nature. Mr. Dykes undertook to explore this point in his own Agency and with other Agencies as appropriate.

e. Mr. Dykes pointed out that the last clause of the first paragraph on Page 4 is unnecessary.[5]

9. It was agreed that the next meeting will take place at 2 p.m., May 21 in Mr. Freund's office. Among other things, the PAG will consider (a) a draft paper giving the list of functions at each base being considered

---

[3] On page 3 of the working paper, language proficiency preceded polar experience and scientific background among observer qualifications.

[4] The section dealing with training and equipment of observers included the following: "In particular, instruction in the acquisition of photography both from the air and on land would be provided."

[5] This clause listed "an overt connection with a US intelligence agency" among the "negative qualifications."

for inspection and related qualifications for inspectors, (b) the revised version of the "Qualifications and Selection of Personnel" paper, and (c) a draft list of qualifications related to Tab A of the April 18 Antarctica Working Paper.

473.   Editorial Note

The third preparatory meeting prior to the Third Antarctic Treaty Consultative Meeting was held in Brussels on June 6, 1963. Participants discussed Chilean proposals to modify a British draft convention on the protection of Antarctic flora and fauna. They agreed that the Third Consultative Meeting should decide whether measures to protect wildlife should be in the form of a code or a convention, although preparatory meetings could draft the text. Participants then discussed agenda items for the Third Consultative Meeting, and tentatively agreed to include: a draft text of the convention for the protection of Antarctic flora and fauna, exchange of scientific information, the result of the Washington telecommunications meeting, administrative arrangements between consultative meetings, and creation of a regional meteorological establishment. (Airgram A–1439 from Brussels, June 13, 1963; National Archives and Records Administration, RG 59, Central Files 1960–63, SCI 11–1 ANT)

474.   Memorandum From Richard Bilder of the Office of the Legal Adviser to the Officer in Charge of International Scientific Organizations, Bureau of International Organization Affairs (Simsarian)[1]

Washington, June 21, 1963.

SUBJECT

Control of United States Nationals in Antarctica

Mr. Owen's memorandum of November 28, 1961 on "Privately Sponsored Activities in Antarctica",[2] which you have transmitted to me for my information, asks whether authority exists under United States law to control the conduct of United States nationals in Antarctica, and if not, whether legislation to accomplish this result is desirable. I understand that these questions have not as yet been explored.

As you know, I have not yet had time to become thoroughly acquainted with Antarctic problems, or to research such questions in depth. However, as a basis for further discussion, some preliminary thoughts and comments on the questions raised by Mr. Owen may be useful.

1. *U.S. International Legal Obligations Respecting the Conduct of Individuals in Antarctica.*

As a Party to the Antarctic Treaty, the United States has an obligation to ensure that the provisions of the Treaty are not violated either by the United States Government or by United States nationals. Article X of the Treaty casts this obligation in the broadest possible terms:

Each of the Contracting Parties undertakes to exert appropriate efforts, consistent with the Charter of the United Nations, to the end that no one engages in any activity in Antarctica contrary to the principles or purposes of the present Treaty.

Article X appears to impose an obligation on each Party not only to prevent violations by its own citizens, but also to prevent violations by other Parties or their citizens and even by non-Parties or their citizens.

---

[1]   Source: National Archives and Records Administration, RG 59, Central Files 1960–63, SCI 11–1 ANT. Limited Official Use.

[2]   In this memorandum, Owens wrote that private activities in Antarctica had to be coordinated with government operations, if only to avoid duplication of or interference with scientific activities. This in turn raised the question of jurisdiction over economic activities or crimes committed in what was "a terra nullius as far as the U.S. is concerned." He therefore sought the views of the Legal Adviser and the Justice Department about what legal authority presently existed for "(1) some reasonable control of private activities in Antarctica as well as for (2) the exercise of criminal jurisdiction," and whether legislative action would be necessary. (Ibid., 702.022/11–2861)

In fact, few provisions of the Treaty appear to be presently capable of violation by individuals, as opposed to Governments. Thus, it is difficult to conceive of individuals carrying on military or nuclear activities in Antarctica. The principal provisions which might relate primarily to conduct by individuals are those of Article IX(1)(f), concerning the preservation and conservation of living resources in Antarctica. Though these do not in terms impose any positive obligations on individuals, it may be noted that the First Consultative Meeting under the Treaty recommended the issuance of specified general rules of conduct to protect living resources, as well as the adoption of adequate measures to protect tombs, buildings and objects of historic interest from damage or destruction (see pages 8 and 9 of Report of the meeting).[3] A Convention to Protect Living Resources in Antarctica is currently under consideration by the Preparatory Committee for the Third Consultative Meeting. The adoption of such a Convention will doubtless require the assumption by the United States of specific obligations to forbid certain types of conduct or activities by United States nationals.

2. *Practical Need for Authority to Control Conduct of United States Nationals.*

Authority to control the conduct of United States nationals in Antarctica may as a practical matter be desirable in at least three areas:

(a) If the United States becomes party to a Convention to Protect Living Resources in Antarctica, we will probably need legal authority to ensure that United States nationals do not violate its provisions;

(b) Substantial numbers of United States nationals, both military and civilian, are currently present in Antarctica as part of our Antarctic expeditions. Some measure of regulation of personnel on such expeditions seems highly desirable. Especially in view of the strains of Antarctic life, it is not unlikely that serious criminal conduct may occasionally occur;

(c) It is not impossible that non-Governmental expeditions, financed by private United States individuals or institutions, may in the future attempt to go to the Antarctic. In the absence of any governmental regulation of entry into Antarctica by such expeditions, or control of them while there, they could conceivably interfere with or constitute a burden upon our governmental efforts in this field (e.g. by requiring diversion of official expedition resources for rescue efforts).

Since foreign nationals usually accompany our expeditions as observers or exchange scientists, or may otherwise operate with or in

---

[3] These recommendations were approved by the U.S. as well as by all other treaty parties. (See para. I–VIII, TIAS 5094.) They were reaffirmed in the recommendations of the 1962 Buenos Aires Meeting which were similarly approved. (See para. II–II of TIAS 5274.) Such approval by the U.S. probably comes close to an international commitment to ensure compliance with these general rules. [Footnote in the source text.]

the vicinity of our own personnel, authority to control their conduct might also be desirable. However, measures to control foreign nationals appear to raise substantially more serious problems than measures to control United States nationals, and are probably of a lower order of priority.

3. *Existing Legal Authority to Control Conduct of United States Nationals.*

I have found no United States legislation by its terms specifically applicable to Antarctica. Moreover, since federal legislation is usually construed to apply only to conduct taking place within the territory of the United States, our criminal and other laws would not, in general, be regarded as applicable in Antarctica unless they specifically so provided. As a general rule, therefore, United States law does not apply in Antarctica.

There are, however, several important exceptions to the above rule.

(a) The Uniform Code of Military Justice (UCMJ) is applicable to all military personnel wherever they may be. Thus, all naval and other military personnel in Antarctica are presently subject to a complete code of United States disciplinary and criminal law. However, a series of Supreme Court decisions has severely limited the reach of provisions of the Code purporting to extend it to civilians accompanying our armed forces in peacetime. It seems virtually certain that the Code could not be regarded as applicable to civilians in Antarctica.

(b) 18 U.S.C. Section 7 defines the "Special Maritime and Territorial Jurisdiction" of the United States to include:

(1) The high seas, any other waters within the admiralty and maritime jurisdiction of the United States and out of the jurisdiction of any particular State, and any vessel belonging in whole or in part to the United States or any citizen thereof, or to the United States, or of any State, Territory, District, or possession thereof, when such vessel is within the admiralty and maritime jurisdiction of the United States and out of the jurisdiction of any particular State.

(3) Any lands reserved or acquired for the use of the United States, and under the exclusive or concurrent jurisdiction thereof, or any place purchased or otherwise acquired by the United States by consent of the legislature of the State in which the same shall be, for the erection of a fort, magazine, arsenal, dockyard, or other needful building.

(5) Any aircraft belonging in whole or in part to the United States, or any citizen thereof, or to any corporation created by or under the laws of the United States, or any State, Territory, district, or possession thereof, while such aircraft is in flight over the high seas, or over any other waters within the admiralty and maritime jurisdiction of the United States and out of the jurisdiction of any particular State.

Other provisions of the Criminal Code provide that certain types of conduct within this special jurisdiction as so defined shall constitute crimes. See e.g. 18 USC 81 (arson); 18 USC 113 (assault); 18 USC 2111 (burglary); 18 USC 791 (espionage); 18 USC 2032 (carnal knowledge); 18 USC 661 (larceny); 18 USC 114 (maiming); 18 USC 1363 (malicious mischief); and 18 USC 2031 (rape); and 18 USC 2111 (robbery). The District courts of the United States have jurisdiction over such offenses (18 USC 3231); under 18 USC 3238, "The trial of offenses begun or committed upon the high seas, or elsewhere out of the jurisdiction of any particular state or district, shall be in the district where the offender is found, or into which he is first brought".

These provisions may be applicable to such part of the Antarctic Treaty Area as may be considered to constitute part of "the high seas" or "any land reserved or acquired for the use of the United States, and under the exclusive or concurrent jurisdiction thereof". Since we do not recognize any territorial sea in Antarctica, the "high seas" can probably be regarded as extending at least to the edge of the ice. It could even be argued that the "high seas" within the meaning of the statute reached even onto the ice, so long as it was definitely sea ice; certainly this would not appear to do violence to the purpose of the statute. It is also conceivable that paragraph (3) of 18 USC 7 might conceivably be construed to include an Antarctic base; this point may warrant further research.

(c) A few statutes, of relatively minor importance to the question of control of conduct in Antarctica, are applicable to United States nationals wherever they may be, including Antarctica. This is the case, for instance, respecting the treason law (18 USC 2381), the income tax law (See Int. Rev. Code of 1954, Sec. 911, 2001), and the Universal Military Training Act (50 USC 453).

The legal situation respecting United States nationals in Antarctica would in summary, therefore, appear to be as follows:

All naval and military personnel are fully covered by the UCMJ, and there is no special need for further legislation controlling the conduct of such persons;

United States civilian nationals in Antarctica and aliens accompanying United States expeditions are in general not covered by the United States criminal laws or other United States statutes, except when they are within the limited "special maritime and territorial jurisdiction of the United States", in which case they are subject to laws proscribing only the most serious crimes.

There does not appear to be any general authority to prohibit or control travel of United States nationals to Antarctica. While in certain circumstances the Government might conceivably seek injunctions to prevent private citizens from journeying to Antarctica for the purpose of conducting activities violating the Treaty (on the analogy of the injunctions successfully obtained against persons intending to sail into prohibited atomic testing zones), this remedy would seem limited.

4. *Consistency of United States Legislation Controlling Conduct of United States Nationals in Antarctica with International Law and the Antarctica Treaty.*

The principal Article of the Antarctic Treaty dealing with the question of jurisdiction is Article VIII, which provides:

1. In order to facilitate the exercise of their functions under the present Treaty, and without prejudice to the respective positions of the Contracting Parties relating to jurisdiction over all other persons in Antarctica, observers designated under paragraph 1 of Article VII and scientific personnel exchanged under subparagraph 1(b) of Article III of the Treaty, and members of the staffs accompanying any such persons, shall be subject only to the jurisdiction of the Contracting Party of which they are nationals in respect of all acts or omissions occurring while they are in Antarctica for the purpose of exercising their functions.

2. Without prejudice to the provisions of paragraph 1 of this Article, and pending the adoption of measures in pursuance of subparagraph 1(e) of Article IX, the Contracting Parties concerned in any case of dispute with regard to the exercise of jurisdiction in Antarctica shall immediately consult together with a view to reaching a mutually acceptable solution.

Article IX(1)(e) requires the parties to consider measures concerning "questions relating to the exercise of jurisdiction in Antarctica". It is apparent from these articles that the question of jurisdiction was a troublesome one on which no clear decision was reached in the negotiations, and that it was the intent of the drafters that any problems which might arise be dealt with subsequently by mutual accommodation.

There would appear to be no legal barrier, however, under either international law or the Antarctic Treaty, to United States legislation aimed at controlling the conduct solely of United States nationals in Antarctica so long as such legislation is based upon such United States nationality. It is a recognized principle of international law that every state has the right to control the conduct of its own nationals wherever they may be, and the Antarctic Treaty in no way restricts this principle.

The case would be otherwise were we to attempt to base legislation aimed at controlling particular conduct by our nationals or foreign nationals on a claim of territorial jurisdiction. Any such attempt on our part would be inconsistent with what I understand to be our policy of refraining from making any territorial claim in Antarctica. Moreover, such legislation might be interpreted as a "new claim . . . to territorial sovereignty" inconsistent with Article IV of the Treaty, and, under Article IV, need not in any case be recognized by other states.

The right of each state to control its own nationals in Antarctica was expressly stated by Mr. Phleger during the Senate Hearings as follows:

Mr. Phleger. By virtue of recognizing that there is no sovereignty over Antarctica we retain jurisdiction over our citizens who go down there and we would deny the rights of the other claimants to try that citizen. (*Hearings*, p. 62)

This right is also implicit in the provisions of Article VIII(1) of the Treaty, which makes it clear that observers and scientific personnel of one country present with another country's expedition are to be subject only to the jurisdiction of their national state.

As Mr. Phleger's statement indicates, there is always the possibility of a conflict of jurisdictional claims, e.g. where one nation asserts jurisdiction on the basis of nationality and another asserts jurisdiction on the basis that the act occurred in its territory. Theoretically, both claims may be legally valid and the question simply one of priority of concurrent jurisdictions. However, given the confused situation as to territorial claims in the Antarctic, and the clear recognition of this problem and intent to create a moratorium respecting it in Article IV of the Antarctic Treaty, it seems most likely that states will in practice permit the exercise of jurisdiction by a state over its own nationals on the undisputed basis of nationality, without asserting possible conflicting claims to exercise jurisdiction over such persons based solely on claims to territorial jurisdiction.

A more difficult question is the right to control the conduct of persons who are not nationals of the United States accompanying a United States expedition. It is clear under Article VIII(1) that if such persons are either foreign observers or exchange scientists or their staffs, the United States cannot exercise jurisdiction over them, and that they are subject only to the jurisdiction of their own states. Since aliens present with United States expeditions will ordinarily fall into one of the above specified categories, the scope of the problem insofar as we have authority to deal with it seems minimal and perhaps best ignored.

5. *Possible form of United States legislation.*

I would think that legislation to control serious criminal conduct by United States nationals in the Antarctic could be reasonably brief and simple. One possibility would be to incorporate by reference into an Antarctic criminal statute crimes already so defined for the purposes of the "Special Maritime and Territorial Jurisdiction of the United States". The statute might provide, for instance, that:

Any national of the United States who commits within the area south of 60º South Latitude an act which would constitute (as defined in 18 USC 81, 113, 2111, 791, 2032, 661, 114, 1363, 2031, and 2111) a crime if committed within the special maritime and territorial jurisdiction of the United States (18 USC 7), shall be subject to the same penalties provided for such act if committed with the special maritime and territorial jurisdiction of the United States.

This draft is, of course, suggestive only, and would require much more work. It would be easier from a drafting standpoint to define the Special Maritime and Territorial Jurisdiction of the United States as including Antarctica; however, this would not seem practical since such action by the U.S. might be interpreted as an exercise of territorial jurisdiction on our part. As a possible alternative, the crimes defined with respect to the Special Maritime and Territorial Jurisdiction of the United States could be completely spelled out with respect to U.S. nationals in Antarctica, though this would, of course, mean a more lengthy statute. In either case, no special legislation would appear required to either make such offenses triable by United States District Courts (18 USC 3231) or to permit trial in the court of the District into which the accused is brought (18 USC 3238).

The drafting of legislation to implement any Convention on the Protection of Living Resources in Antarctica must obviously await the final form of such a Convention and the defining of U.S. obligations therein. It may be noted, however, that conservation legislation of this general sort already exists in U.S. law (see 16 USC 715 [Migrating birds] and 16 USC 631 [seals])[4] and should not pose any special problems. Even in the absence of such a Convention, unilateral legislation to implement the recommendations of the First Consultative Meeting and protect these resources from harm by United States nationals might be desirable.

More generally, some thought might be given to the seeking of legislation vesting a general power in the Secretary of Interior generally to administer United States bases and expeditions in Antarctica and to make such rules and regulations as may be required for the government of U.S. nationals in the Treaty area. (See e.g. 48 USC 1661 [American Samoa] and 48 USC 1681 [Trust Territory of the Pacific] and Exec. Orders 10264 and 10265). Any such general grant of authority would, of course, have to be cast in a form consistent with the Treaty provisions creating a moratorium on territorial claims so as not to raise any disputes with our Treaty partners.

6. *Concluding Comments.*

A decision whether actively to seek legislation to control United States nationals in Antarctica will need to take into account the fact that no significant problems in this respect have as yet arisen and the possibility that any attempt to seek such legislation may conceivably give rise to some controversy in Congress and with our Treaty partners.

On the other hand, account must be taken of the possibility that sooner or later a United States national in Antarctica may commit a seri-

---

[4] All brackets in the source text.

ous crime not punishable under present law. If this occurs, the Department and other Government agencies concerned might be subject to criticism if steps have not been taken to anticipate and deal with this situation. Moreover, if a Convention to Protect Living Resources in Antarctica is drawn up in the near future, and if we have in any case to seek legislation to implement its provisions, it would not be much more arduous or difficult to at the same time seek additional legislation dealing with related jurisdictional problems. Mr. Phleger's testimony to the Senate indicates that this problem was anticipated, and no reason is apparent why Congress would resist granting such legislation. I would think it at least desirable that this matter be further explored by a small group consisting of representatives of State, Navy, Interior, and Justice.

475. Editorial Note

The Antarctic Treaty Meeting on Telecommunications was held in Washington June 24–28, 1963. For text of the final communiqué, see Department of State *Bulletin*, July 15, 1963, pages 107 108. The Report of the U.S. Delegation is in the National Archives and Records Administration, RG 59, IO Files: Lot 69 D 169, Antarctica Files, Multilateral, General, 1963. The Recommendations of the meeting are printed in *U.S. Policy and International Cooperation in Antarctica, Message From the President of the United States Transmitting Special Report on United States Policy and International Cooperation in Antarctica, 88th Congress, Second Session, House Document No. 358* (Washington, 1964), Annex III, Document No. 6.

476.   Memorandum From Richard Bilder of the Office of the
        Legal Adviser to the Officer in Charge of International
        Scientific Organizations, Bureau of International
        Organization Affairs (Simsarian)[1]

Washington, June 25, 1963.

SUBJECT

Appropriate Subjects for Observation in Antarctica Inspection

In connection with the proposed United States inspection in Antarctica during the coming austral summer, you have asked our views as to what the observers should seek in particular to observe.

As we previously discussed, it seems important that the observers simply observe and report their observations, and not attempt in the course of their inspection to draw any definitive legal conclusions as to whether any of the facts or activities observed constitute a violation of the treaty. The judgment whether a violation may be involved and whether an international complaint is justified should only be reached subsequently by the appropriate United States Government agencies on the basis of the observers' report.

Nevertheless, the observers will need a general idea of what to look for in their inspection and what facts or activities merit report or comment. This memorandum therefore gives some general guidance as to what legal obligations the Treaty imposes on parties. It is impossible, however, to completely catalogue or list the acts or failures to act which might constitute violations of these obligations. While principal guidelines can be given, and technical instructions will be required, the subjects to which the observers direct particular attention may in the last analysis have to be dictated by their good judgment in the light of what they see during the inspection.

DISCUSSION

Article VII of the treaty sets forth the purposes and describes the general procedures and scope of inspection.[2] The purpose of inspection is stated in the first clause of Article VII to be "to promote the objectives and ensure the observance of the provisions of the present Treaty." It

---

[1] Source: National Archives and Records Administration, RG 59, IO Files: Lot 69 D 169, Antarctica Files, U.S. Activities, Legal, 1963. Secret.

[2] In a previous memorandum from L/UNA–Mr. Schwebel to OES–Mr. William Mills on the subject of "Scope of Inspection under the Antarctic Treaty", dated April 25, 1963, we express the opinion that the physical scope of such an inspection is virtually unlimited, except as regards documents. [Footnote in the source text.]

may be noted that the purpose of the inspection is in terms broader than simply checking for treaty violations; it is designed also to promote the treaty's objectives. Since the Treaty's objectives are very broad, the appropriate scope of concern of the observers would appear likewise extremely broad, and it would not be technically necessary to justify particular desired observations in terms of specific treaty obligations. However, for all practical purposes, the observers will be primarily concerned with matters linked with express treaty obligations. It may therefore be useful to examine these obligations seriatim.

1. *Peaceful Purposes.*

Article I of the Treaty provides that Antarctica shall be used for peaceful purposes only and that there shall be prohibited inter alia any measures of a military nature such as the establishment of military stations and fortification, the carrying out of military maneuvers, or the testing of any type of weapons. It is expressly provided, however, that military personnel and equipment may be used for scientific research or for any other peaceful purposes.

The observers should therefore pay particular attention to any indications of the following:

(a) The establishment of military bases and fortifications;
(b) The carrying out of military maneuvers;
(c) The testing of any type of weapons;
(d) Any other measure which might be construed as one of a military nature.

If military personnel or equipment are in use, the purpose and scope of their use should be carefully noted, and, if possible, the reason for the use of military instead of civilian personnel or equipment enquired into.

2. *Exchange of Scientific Information.*

Article III provides, inter alia, that to the greatest extent feasible and practicable, information regarding plans for scientific programs in Antarctica shall be exchanged and scientific observations and results from Antarctica should be exchanged and made freely available.

The observers should, therefore, pay particular attention to the following:

(a) What scientific programs are being carried on?
(b) What scientific observations and results are being obtained?

Of course, the observers will not be in a position to verify whether information regarding the programs, observations, and results has in fact been exchanged and made freely available; this will have to be done by comparing information from their report with information previously or subsequently made available by the foreign government. However, the observers should attempt to obtain as detailed a sense of the scope of scientific activity as feasible in order that an evaluation can be later made in this respect.

3. Nuclear Ban.

Article V of the Treaty prohibits any nuclear explosions in Antarctica or the disposal there of any radioactive waste material.

The observers should, therefore, look for any indications either of:

(a) the carrying on of nuclear explosions, or
(b) the disposal of radioactive waste material.

4. Advance Notification concerning Expeditions, Stations, Personnel and Equipment.

Article VII(5) provides that each Contracting Party will inform the other Contracting Parties and give them advance notice of all expeditions to and within Antarctica, all stations in Antarctica occupied by its nationals, and any military personnel or equipment intended to be introduced by it into Antarctica. Paragraph I-VI of the 1961 Canberra Recommendations, which were approved by all the Contracting Parties (TIAS 5094), recommends a more detailed list of such information which should be furnished.

The observers should observe and record information regarding the detailed matters specified in Paragraph I-VI, in order to permit subsequent verification as to whether the provisions for advance notification have been in fact complied with.

5. Preservation and Conservation of Living Resources and Protection of Historical and other Monuments and Objects.

Article IX provides that the Parties may, in Consultative Meeting, recommend to their governments measures in furtherance of the principles and objectives of the Treaty, including measures regarding the preservation and conservation of living resources in Antarctica. These measures are to become effective when approved by all the Contracting Parties.

The Contracting Parties, at the 1961 Canberra meeting, recommended that, as an interim measure, and to the extent possible under national legislation and binding international convention, they issue general rules of conduct for the preservation and conservation of living resources in Antarctica on the lines of the 1960 SCAR recommendations, annexed to the recommendation. This recommendation, inter alia, was approved by the United States and the other parties (see paragraph I-

VIII of TIAS 5094) and was subsequently reaffirmed and reapproved at the 1962 Buenos Aires meeting (see para II-II of TIAS 5274). The Canberra meeting also recommended that governments adopt all adequate measures to protect tombs, buildings or objects of historical interest from damage and destruction (I-IX of TIAS 5094), and this was similarly approved by governments.

While the acceptance of these recommendations appears technically to create only an obligation to *issue* such general rules, and then only to the extent possible under national legislation, it may be argued that acceptance in practical effect comes close to importing an obligation to conform with the standards. Matters covered by the rules therefore seem an entirely appropriate subject of observation.

The observers should accordingly note whether there are any activities being engaged in inconsistent with the general rules set forth in the Canberra meeting, and in particular: (a) whether indigenous animals or plants are being unnecessarily destroyed or disturbed or injured except as provided in the general rules; (b) whether alien forms of flora and fauna are being deliberately introduced except when rigidly controlled; and (c) whether the activities specified in paragraph 3 of the general rules and conduct are being regulated with a view to preventing serious harm to wildlife (e.g. allowing dogs to run free, discharge of oil from ships, etc.).

6. Facilitation of Observation.

Article VII, as previously noted, provides in extremely broad terms for the scope of inspection. Article VIII provides that there will be no exercise of jurisdiction over the observers making the inspection.

The observers should pay particular note to any restrictions on their freedom of movement or observation or to any attempts to exercise jurisdiction over them, and should include any such activities in their report.

7. General Exchanges of Information.

The recommendations of the 1961 Canberra Consultative Meeting, accepted by all the Contracting Parties, recommended that Governments undertake to exchange information on logistic problems (para I-VIII) and that governments exchange by all means deemed advisable information on the application of nuclear equipment and techniques in the Treaty area (para I-III).

Matters relating to these subjects would therefore also be appropriate subjects for observation.

477. Memorandum From the Assistant Secretary of State for International Organization Affairs (Cleveland) to Secretary of State Rusk[1]

Washington, June 28, 1963.

SUBJECT

Responsibility for Carrying out Inspections in Antarctica

I.

Mr. William C. Foster, in a memorandum of June 26 to you,[2] recommends that ACDA have responsibility for the implementation of Antarctic inspections. He raises three questions in his memorandum:

1. That letters designating observers for the inspection operation in Antarctica be signed by you as Secretary of State. I recommend that you agree to sign these letters. (There may be about a dozen of them.)
2. That ACDA have primary responsibility for the implementation of the inspection operation in Antarctica. On this proposal I raise some questions below.
3. That the Department of State and ACDA consult with one another prior to making proposals to foreign Governments concerning inspection matters. This should of course be standard operating practice.

II.

Our relations with ACDA work very well these days, and I have no doubt that the Agency would do an excellent job of managing the Antarctic "observers" operation (we should probably stick to the Treaty language rather than by calling the "inspectors") if you ask Mr. Foster to assume responsibility for it. However, I do believe there are significant policy questions that should be considered before deciding that Antarctic Treaty responsibilities should be handled as an aspect of arms control and disarmament. I regret the need to raise an essentially jurisdictional question; I do so only because I think real matters of policy are hidden behind the issues of bureaucratic parochialism.

The policy issues are four:

1. There is no example of international harmony and cooperation anywhere in the contemporary world to compare with that presently prevailing in Antarctica. The Cold War has not intruded; the territorial

---

[1] Source: National Archives and Records Administration, RG 59, IO Files: Lot 69 D 169, Antarctica Files, Inspection 1963. Confidential. Drafted by James Simsarian and concurred in by Greenfield (P).

[2] Not printed. (Ibid.)

claims and aspirations of the Antarctic powers have been placed in abeyance; and an extraordinary tradition of scientific cooperation has been established. The achievement of this condition of international harmony and cooperation is the result of many years of patient effort on the part of the United States, and its preservation should remain a primary objective of the national policy of the United States. One of the high points of this effort was the conclusion of the Antarctica Treaty in 1959, largely as the result of United States initiative, which provides in Article I that "Antarctica shall be used for peaceful purposes only." The "observation" provision is an important element of the Treaty, and it should not be allowed to atrophy from disuse. At the same time, the exercise of this right should not disrupt the very harmony and international cooperation which it is the primary purpose of the Treaty to preserve.

2. If you now give ACDA the responsibility for "observers" in Antarctica, it would be hard to avoid the whole operation being publicly presented as an exercise on arms control. Because of the statutory objectives of ACDA and its very name, its identification with inspections in Antarctica would place the program in a military context which could do damage to United States objectives under the Antarctica Treaty. ACDA should certainly participate actively in developing and carrying out the inspection program; something of value may be learned about inspection techniques in general. But the responsibility for the implementation of this program, and for the control of public information about it, might better reside in the Department of State.

3. The inspection provisions of the Antarctic Treaty involve something quite distinct from the kind of inspections contemplated in the case of nuclear testing and disarmament. Inspections in Antarctica are bound to look rather "soft" to persons thinking in terms of disarmament inspection. The other nations will have plenty of notice, the names of the observers will be fixed well in advance, the inspection will not result from suspicious "events" as contemplated in the nuclear testing field; altogether the Antarctica inspections will not have (and in the absence of some suspicious event should not have) the character of adversary proceedings that will be inevitable in the case of nuclear testing and disarmament. Consequently to identify the Antarctica inspections too closely with arms control and disarmament might give Congress and the general public an entirely erroneous impression of the depth and seriousness of ACDA's plans in other fields.

4. We have no grounds for believing that other nations have arms of any significance in Antarctica. Indeed, the United States has more military personnel and guns in Antarctica than any other nation does. The Soviet Union reports (and there is no contrary evidence) that they

have no military personnel and are not using any armed naval ships in the area. In contrast, the United States has about 3,000 military personnel in the area and our logistic support is entirely military including seven armed ships with 6"/50, 5"/38 and 3"/50 guns as well as machine guns. The United Kingdom has one ship with two 4" guns as well as machine guns. An inspection which emphasized the arms control aspect would only serve to attract attention to United States military forces in an Antarctica dedicated by Treaty to peaceful purposes.

III.

ACDA has done excellent work in helping to develop the planning for this program, and it should continue to participate in the program. However, for the reasons cited above, the Department of State should retain the over-all direction of the program, and ACDA's role should be to assist the Bureau of International Organization Affairs in carrying out the inspection program. The Inter-Agency Coordinating Committee on Antarctica, which is chaired by our Bureau, should serve as the coordinating committee for this inspection program as it does with respect to all other United States activities in Antarctica, including the $7,000,000 scientific exploration program. The Commander of the United States Naval Support Force, Antarctica will have responsibility for logistics for this program as he does for other programs in Antarctica.

The Antarctica experts in the Departments of Defense, Commerce and Interior have separately expressed to us their concern on some or all of the above scores; my impression is that they would agree with the substance of this memorandum and with its recommendations. I am sending a copy to Mr. Foster, but making no other distribution.

Recommedations

1. That you authorize the Bureau of International Organization Affairs to carry out the recruitment and supervision of observers under the Antarctica Treaty.

2. That you request ACDA to participate actively in the development and carrying out of the inspection program in Antarctica.

3. That you direct the Bureau of Public Affairs to coordinate all public information on the plan for and activities of American observers in Antarctica.[3]

---

[3] There is no indication on the memorandum if the recommendations were approved or disapproved.

478.   Memorandum From the Commanding Officer of the U.S.
Naval Support Force, Antarctica (Reedy) to the Interagency
Coordinating Committee on Antarctica[1]

Washington, July 16, 1963.

SUBJ

Commercial Carriers in Antarctica

1. The purpose of this paper is to outline recommendations which should become prerequisites for U.S. commercial carriers to operate in or through Antarctica.

2. Matters related to personnel support and habitability:

a. *Berthing.* Facilities at McMurdo Station and satellite stations normally are utilized to capacity. Therefore, under normal circumstances, berthing facilities will not be available to commercial carrier crews and passengers. In event of an emergency, and should facilities become available, charges would be in accordance with current U.S. Navy policies and rates.

b. *Messing.* Food requirements are carefully determined in advance of the operating season to support known personnel requirements. Providing for messing civilians and issuing flight rations would raise shipping and purchasing requirements considerably. There is no provision in our budget for such additional support. In event of an emergency, limited messing would be made available and charges would be made in accordance with established procedures and prescribed rates. If the emergency persisted for more than 24 hours, the only alternative would be to evacuate crews and passengers to New Zealand in military aircraft at the expense of the carrier.

c. *Sanitation.* Facilities are limited and primitive by stateside standards and there are no special facilities available for ladies.

d. *Medical.* Facilities and assistance are generally limited, and rudimentary at satellite stations. Humanitarian treatment would be provided in emergencies. It must be understood by the carrier and his insurance company that, in event of an aircraft crash or major disaster, the U.S. Navy does not have the capability to handle a large number of casualties, and that the capability for rapid emergency evacuation is very limited. The Task Force's mission does not provide for improving the medical assistance capability beyond that required to support Deep Freeze operations.

---

[1] Source: National Archives and Records Administration, RG 59, IO Files: Lot 69 D 169, Antarctica Files, Policy 1963. Official Use Only.

3. Services:

a. *POL.* Requirements in Antarctica are computed and procured according to operational requirements with a contingency reserve for emergency. This does not provide specifically for any other operations than those directly connected with the Deep Freeze mission. Requirements beyond the present ones will necessitate increasing established POL levels with a resultant increase in shipping requirements and cost. No provisions for this is made in the Support Force budget. Therefore, prior to departing for Antarctica:

(1) Aircraft must make their exact requirements known in advance and receive confirmation that fuel is available.
(2) Ships should be required to depart for Antarctica with sufficient amounts of fuel to assure that refueling in Antarctica would not be required, and that there is sufficient reserve on board to sustain the ships' needs should tanks be damaged by ice, or should ships become beset.

b. *Water.* Supplies are extremely limited. For the foreseeable future, carriers should be self-sufficient. In an emergency, MSTS ships and ice-breakers, if in the area, probably could furnish a very limited amount of water. Here, again, ships should be required to carry sufficient reserves in event of ice damage to tanks. Temperatures and distances preclude "water lines from the beach" as ships are accustomed to arranging in most ports.

c. *Electricity.* There are no means of providing this to ships. They must provide their own.

d. *Crash.* Facilities to handle aircraft crashes are very limited generally, and practically non-existent at satellite stations. There is no proper way to provide the services needed in crashes involving large numbers of people. Therefore, the U.S. Navy cannot be responsible for providing adequate crash equipment. It is also not within the mission, or funds available to Commander Task Force 43 to provide the additional equipment necessary to support commercial carriers in this matter. Naturally, existing facilities would be made available. Additionally, there are no crash boats, tugs, etc., to assist ships which may be distressed by ice damage.

e. *Vehicular transportation.* These facilities are limited but could be made available for special occasions of short duration. There is not sufficient equipment to support "cruises" and sightseers. The Task Force is unable, under present funding, to provide proper transportation to support commercial carriers. Likewise, should commercial carriers desire to provide their own mode of transportation, the adequacy, in severe climatic conditions and rugged terrain, of such vehicles should be approved by an appropriate government agency in advance.

f. *Ground support.* Commercial ships must provide their own line handlers, make available and install their own dead men for mooring or turning, carry additional mooring lines to guard against severe weather conditions which are rather unpredictable, and provide their own brows and accommodation ladders. Air carriers are required to determine the availability of starters, engine heaters, etc., *prior* to clearing the flight. Ladders for disembarking passengers and the crew must be carried as standard equipment of the aircraft, as must all means of securing the aircraft to protect it against high winds and blowing snow.

g. *Special cold weather clothing.* Commercial carriers will be required to have adequate cold weather clothing to protect passengers and crews in Antarctica.

4. Search and Rescue: Would be provided on a humanitarian basis in accordance with established conventions. Here, again, the capability is extremely limited, and any employment for this purpose, of the aircraft or ships severely affects the Task Force Mission.

5. Control of aircraft:

a. ICAO procedures should be extended to include Antarctica.

b. U.S. commercial air carriers will be required to comply with local traffic control procedures which CTF-43 has established to protect military aircraft at its Antarctic stations.

c. U.S. Navy can make available weather and ice information on a "non-interference-with-operations" basis.

6. Special requirements:

a. Pilots of aircraft must be currently experienced in landing on ice and snow. Ship masters should be experienced in operating in waters where ice threatens the safety of a ship and its embarked personnel.

b. Aircraft must be FAA and ICAO certified.

c. Ships should be required to have reinforced hulls to protect them from ice hazards prior to certifying them for Antarctic operations.

d. Aircraft intending to land at U.S. stations other than McMurdo will be required to be ski-equipped.

e. The U.S. Navy will not accept designation as investigator for any accident involving commercial carriers in any manner other than in the case of such an accident involving the Navy anywhere else.

7. Several major problems require resolution:

a. The Department of the Navy has established rates and procedures covering services furnished by military personnel and purchases by civilian enterprises. Existing rules provide for reimbursement for use of military personnel, for POL, for landing fees, for subsistence, etc. Regulations normally require a deposit in advance to cover potential costs. The amount of the deposit would be determined according to the extent and the nature of the services to be provided. This should be resolved in advance of any flight, or trip by ship. It should further be understood that, although CTF-43 purchases these items from allocated funds, payment by the civil carrier is to the Navy Department. The Task Force is NOT, in turn, reimbursed by this amount. The Task Force stands the loss. The exception to this is messing.

b. The problem of jurisdiction regarding the protection of historic landmarks, conservation of wildlife, etc., is a much more complicated issue. Likewise, the problem of handling felonies and misdemeanors is a related problem. At present, the Uniform Code of Military Justice provides adequate jurisdiction over military personnel. On board ships and in the air, admiralty and maritime laws appear to provide adequate jurisdiction in these areas. This probably extends to the edge of the ice shelf. At this time, there does not appear to be a way of applying legal jurisdiction over civilians who might commit an offense in Antarctica. If a serious crime were committed, it would be prudent to take steps to protect others, but there does not appear to be established any means for disposing of civil criminal cases. If historic landmarks were damaged, it is considered that the matter would have to be resolved between the governments of the nationals involved. This can become complicated in the instance where U.S. carriers are carrying foreign nationals. The commission of certain offenses is not provided for in the Antarctic Treaty, and this further complicates the matter of jurisdiction over foreign nationals carried by U.S. carriers when the governments of these nationals are not signatories to the Antarctic Treaty. Therefore, at this time, Commander Task Force 43, as senior U.S. representative in Antarctica, cannot be responsible for offenses committed by civilians in Antarctica.

J.R. Reedy
Rear Admiral, U.S. Navy
Commander Task Force 43

479.   Editorial Note

The fourth preparatory meeting for the Third Antarctic Treaty Consultative Meeting was held in Brussels on September 5, 1963. The delegates still had not reached an agreement on whether measures to protect Antarctic flora and fauna should be in a code or a convention. The United States was asked to submit its views in time for the next meeting in November. The agenda for the Third Consultative meeting was discussed, and it was agreed that the establishment of a standing committee on Antarctic meteorology should be placed on the agenda. (Airgram A–270 from Brussels, September 18, 1963; National Archives and Records Administration, RG 59, Central Files 1960–63, SCI 11–1 ANT)

480.   Memorandum From Nathaniel McKitterick of the Office of International Economic and Social Affairs, Bureau of International Organization Affairs, to the Assistant Secretary of State for International Organization Affairs (Cleveland)[1]

Washington, September 13, 1963.

SUBJECT

President Approves Initiation of Antarctic Inspections

The President has approved the initiation of inspections in Antarctica during the coming austral summer season.[2] The Washington Embassies of the other eleven Governments which are signatories to the Antarctic Treaty were informed of this decision by this office yesterday and this morning. Attached is a copy of the Press Release being issued by the Department of State at noon today (with 3 o'clock as the release time).[3]

[1] Source: National Archives and Records Administration, RG 59, IO Files: Lot 69 D 169, Antarctica Files, Chron. Files, Sept.–Oct. 1963. Confidential. Drafted by Simsarian.

[2] A September 4 memorandum from McGeorge Bundy to Secretary Rusk stated that the President had given his formal approval to the Antarctic inspection plan summarized in Rusk's September 3 memorandum. (Ibid., U.S. Activities in Antarctica, Inspection 1963) The September 3 memorandum was not found.

[3] Not printed. For text of the Department of State's announcement of September 13 that an inspection would be held during the 1963–1964 summer season, see American Foreign Policy: Current Documents, 1963, pp. 1045–1046.

1090 Foreign Relations, 1961–1963, Volume XXV

Plans are considerably advanced for the inspections to be undertaken. Two teams of Observers will be sent to the Antarctic. One team of four, headed by Russian-speaking John Guthrie, Director of the Office of Soviet Affairs, will go by plane from McMurdo to two Soviet stations (Mirnyy and Vostok) and to two Australian stations (Mannon and Wilkes). This team will also visit the New Zealand Scott station and make a flight over the French station at D'Urville for aerial observation (as expressly authorized by paragraph 4 of Article VII of the Antarctic Treaty). This team will consist of four rather than three because we are including an interpreter for full coverage of the Russian language.

The other team of three, headed by Richard Hawkins, Spanish-speaking Foreign Service Officer, will travel by the Coast Guard icebreaker *Eastwind* from Valparaiso to Palmer Peninsula to inspect the stations of Argentina, Chile and the United Kingdom (two each).

Nine observers have been selected, seven of them to serve on the two teams and two serve as alternates.

The reaction of the Soviet Union to our plans has been: this is not necessary but if you wish to go ahead with inspections, you are welcome to visit Soviet Stations.

Four other countries have indicated that they also intend to designate Observers and inspect the United States station at McMurdo and the New Zealand Scott station nearby. These four are Australia, Japan, New Zealand and the United Kingdom. Each inspection will be undertaken on a unilateral basis.

---

481. **Memorandum From the Director of the Arms Control and Disarmament Agency (Foster) to Secretary of State Rusk**[1]

Washington, October 29, 1963.

SUBJECT

Appointment of U.S. Antarctic Observers

Notification of the President's formal approval for an Antarctic inspection was transmitted to you in Mr. McGeorge Bundy's memoran-

---

[1] Source: National Archives and Records Administration, RG 59, Central Files 1960–63, SCI 11–1 ANT. Confidential.

dum of September 3, 1963.[2] The selection of nominees for appointment by you as U.S. Antarctic Observers has now been completed on the basis of agreed qualifications by a special inter-agency Personnel Advisory Group. Nine nominees have passed appropriate physical examinations and have Top Secret clearances.

It is contemplated that each of two 3-Man Observer Teams will consist of a Team Leader (a Foreign Service Officer), a civilian military scientist and a biologist. An interpreter in Russian will be included in the team visiting bases of the USSR, New Zealand and Australia. The other Team, whose leader is a Spanish linguist, will visit the Palmer Peninsula bases of the UK, Argentina and Chile. There will be a photo overflight of a French base. Three Observers will be held available in the U. S. for possible use as alternates in the event that any of the regular Observers becomes incapacitated or is unable to participate for any other reason. There will be a two-week briefing for all team observers and alternates prior to the departure of the Observer Teams.

The names of the nine nominees with a brief biographic sketch for each as well as an evaluation are enclosed.[3] A Letter of Appointment and a Certificate of Appointment for each nominee are attached for your signature. The name of an additional nominee (a biologist) will be transmitted to you for appointment as a U.S. Antarctic Observer when his nomination procedure has been completed.

I recommend that you sign the attached Letters and Certificates of Appointment. After the Letters have been received by the appointed Observers, it is planned to send official notification to the diplomatic missions in Washington of the other 11 signatory Governments, at least one day before public announcement is made of the appointments.

William C. Foster

---

[2] See footnote 2, Document 480. The observers were: Dr. Charles C. Bates, Dr. John L. Buckley, John C. Guthrie, Richard H. Hawkins, Jr., Michel Ivy, Dr. George W. Rathjens, Dr. J. P. Ruina, Dr. Victor B. Scheffer, and Frank G. Siscoe. Their appointment was officially announced by the Department of State in Press Release No. 591 of November 18. For text (without the biographies of the observers), see Department of State *Bulletin,* December 16, 1963, pp. 932–933.

[3] The enclosures are not printed.

482.   Editorial Note

The fifth preparatory meeting for the Third Antarctic Treaty Consultative Meeting was held in Brussels on November 14, 1963. The delegates agreed to postpone the establishment of a standing committee on Antarctic meteorology until the Third Consultative Meeting. Most of the meeting dealt with how to formulate measures for protecting Antarctic wildlife. The United States had submitted a draft of "Agreed Measures for the Conservation of Living Resources in the Antarctic." Chairman A. van der Essen of Belgium regretted that these proposals had not been presented as amendments to a British "Draft Agreement on the Conservation of Wild Life in the Antarctic," and pointed out that a code or "Agreed Measures" would be less binding on individual citizens than a convention would be. The delegates reached no agreement on permanent administrative arrangements between meetings, and scheduled their next meeting for January 9, 1964. The meeting was later rescheduled for the week of January 20–24. (Airgram A–484 from Brussels, November 20, 1963; National Archives and Records Administration, RG 59, Central Files 1960–63, SCI 11–1 ANT)

483.   Editorial Note

The U.S. observers conducted their inspections during January 1964. Group A, comprising Richard H. Hawkins, Jr., John L. Buckley, and George W. Rathjens, visited the stations of Argentina, Chile, and the United Kingdom. Group B, comprising John C. Guthrie, Jack P. Ruina, Victor B. Scheffer, and interpreter Michel Ivy, visited the stations of France, New Zealand, and the Soviet Union. For text of their report, submitted in May 1964, see *U.S. Policy and International Cooperation in Antarctica*, Annex III, Document No. 7, or *Documents on Disarmament, 1964*, pages 195–203.

Law of the Sea

484. Memorandum of Conversation[1]

Washington, January 27, 1961.

SUBJECT

Law of the Sea—Canadian Approach to other Governments Concerning a
Multilateral Treaty

PARTICIPANTS

Mr. S.F. Rae, Minister—Canadian Embassy
Jim S. Nutt, Counselor, Canadian Embassy
Mr. Raymond T. Yingling, Assistant Legal Adviser, State Department

Mr Rae said they had come in to leave a memorandum indicating the intention of the Canadian Government to sound out a selected number of other Governments (list attached)[2] on their attitude to adherence to a multilateral Convention embodying the United States-Canadian proposal which narrowly failed to receive the necessary two-thirds vote to be adopted at the Second Conference on the Law of the Sea held at Geneva in 1960.[3] Mr. Rae stated that of course we are aware of the reasons for endeavoring to conclude a multilateral Convention on this matter. He indicated that his Government hoped that our Embassies in the countries which will be approached could be instructed to adopt a "benevolent attitude" to their efforts in the event that the Embassies were approached by the Governments to which accredited. He added that we would be given the results of the soundings at a later date.

I replied that consistent with our present policy with respect to a multilateral Convention, we were not in a position to approach the indicated Governments directly on this matter. On the other hand, as previously informally indicated to the Canadian Government, we had no

---

[1] Source: National Archives and Records Administration, RG 59, Central Files 1960–63, 399.731/1–2761. Secret. Drafted by Yingling.

[2] Not printed. The countries on the list were Australia, New Zealand, South Africa, Pakistan, Ireland, Denmark, Greece, Germany, Israel, Italy, the Netherlands, Portugal, Spain, Sweden, Switzerland, Turkey, Thailand, and Japan.

[3] During the 13th Plenary Session on April 26, 1960, the Second Law of the Sea Conference failed by a vote of 54–28–5 to adopt a U.S.-Canadian proposal for a 6-mile territorial sea plus a 6-mile contiguous fishing zone that would remain open to traditional users for 10 years.

objection to its taking soundings of the nature indicated even though we could not cooperate in this exercise.[4] Therefore, it could be assumed that we would make no statements contrary to their efforts.

I concluded that of course there has been no opportunity as yet to obtain the views of the new Administration in the Department on Law of the Sea matters.

---

[4] On January 31 the Department sent circular telegram CA–1130 to this effect to the Embassies in Turkey, Greece, Thailand, Switzerland, West Germany, Australia, Denmark, Ireland, the Netherlands, Pakistan, Portugal, Spain, South Africa, Italy, Sweden, Israel, Tokyo, and New Zealand. (National Archives and Records Administration, RG 59, Central Files 1960–63, 399.731/1–3161)

---

485.   Editorial Note

The United States ratified the Convention on the Territorial Sea and the Contiguous Zone (15 UST 1606), the Convention on the High Seas (13 UST 2312), the Convention on Fishing and Conservation of the Living Resources of the High Seas (17 UST 138), and the Convention on the Continental Shelf (15 UST 471) on March 24, 1961. All four conventions had been signed by the United States on September 15, 1958, and had received the advice and consent of the Senate on May 26, 1960. The United States deposited its ratifications with the Secretary-General of the United Nations on April 12, 1961.

486.   Aide-Mémoire From the Canadian Embassy[1]

Washington, May 15, 1961.

AIDE-MÉMOIRE

The joint assessment of Canada and the United Kingdom of the prospects of a multilateral convention based on the "six-plus-six" Geneva formula is that the support of some twenty-one countries, not including the United States, would probably be forthcoming, provided sufficient additional support could be obtained, and the support of a further nine or ten countries could be fairly readily obtained with United States assistance. This would leave only approximately a dozen countries whose support would be required in order to bring the total up to a workable figure of forty-four or forty-five. This assessment is based on the information which follows.

Results To Date of the Preliminary Survey

I. Positive support for a convention at governmental level: Australia, New Zealand, Portugal, The Republic of Ireland, Spain, Switzerland, Greece and South Africa.

II. Favourable initial reaction final replies outstanding: Italy and The Netherlands.

III. Conditional approval: Denmark.

IV. Approval dependent on reactions of other states and/or degree of support forthcoming: Germany, Israel and Japan.

V. Qualified approval, owing to special problems: Pakistan and Turkey.

VI. Hesitant or non-committal: Sweden and Thailand.

In addition to the countries which have been canvassed, Norway can be expected to support a convention.

Arguments In Support of a Convention

The arguments in favour of a convention which have been presented to other countries, and which we hope will prove equally persuasive to the United States, are as follows:

---

[1] Source: National Archives and Records Administration, RG 59, Central Files 1960–63, 399. 731/5–1561. Secret. A May 16 covering memorandum from Frank A. Mau (S/S–RO) to Jac H. Bushong (L) requested that the Office of the Legal Adviser prepare a memorandum by May 26 to Under Secretary Bowles recommending a course of action. Earlier on May 15 Assistant Legal Adviser Yingling sent a memorandum to Acting Secretary Bowles advising him that Canadian Ambassador Heeney would deliver the Aide-Mémoire to him at 6 p.m. Yingling recommended that Bowles tell Heeney "that the Department will carefully consider the results and the views of his government thereon." (Ibid.)

(A) The proposed convention, especially if it numbers amongst its signatories the chief maritime and air transport nations of the world, and includes some of the more important fishing nations, would provide an important source of law from which a universal rule of law might gradually evolve.

(B) The general desirability of reaching agreement on the two important questions left unanswered at the 1960 Geneva Conference on the Law of the Sea (i.e. the breadth of the territorial sea and fishery limits) is underlined by the present uncertainty and the likelihood of a continued drift towards chaos in the Law of the Sea. The sooner therefore that a multilateral convention can be concluded the sooner this disturbing drift can be stopped. It is hoped that if a multilateral convention is concluded in time, enough countries will accede so as to fulfill substantially the same purpose as would have been achieved at Geneva.

(C) The initiative is in no sense a cold war project or an attempt to avenge the "diplomatic defeat" at Geneva. On the contrary, it is motivated by a desire to further the orderly development of international law, and in particular to complete the codification of the Law of the Sea so nearly achieved at the last conference.

(D) Support for a multilateral convention at this stage, rather than later, would still have a good chance of building on the large measure of agreement reached at the Conference and of avoiding the loss of effort put into it.

(E) A convention would provide an agreement to which new countries could adhere when they gain their independence, and would forestall the possibility of a twelve-mile convention being the first or even the only possible one in the field.

(F) The movement to a twelve-mile territorial sea would be slowed down and countries might be restrained from making more extravagant claims. Maximum freedom of the seas would thereby be ensured for security, navigational and commercial purposes.

(G) The existence of an agreement would help to prevent disputes arising out of incidents on the seas and would encourage countries with outstanding disputes to arrive at an early solution.

(H) The conclusion of a multilateral convention on the remaining questions in issue might further encourage states to ratify the Conventions adopted by the 1958 Conference.

(I) A further argument which can now be made is that the degree of support already obtained is encouraging.

Proposed Plan of Action:

The first question to be determined, should the United States authorities agree to join actively in the survey, would be whether further approaches should be restricted to likely supporters or should be made to the international community as a whole. The answer to this would seem to depend to a large extent on whether the next phase should be kept confidential.

Since it is still too early to be certain of our objective (i.e. enough support quantitatively to open the proposed multilateral convention for signature) it would seem better to maintain the confidential character of the canvass during the second phase also. Presumably the United States, like most of the eighteen countries already canvassed, would prefer that its views not become generally known at this stage. It may be also that a number of countries to be approached would find it easier to indicate support for the scheme if it were clearly understood that they would not be committed should it transpire that the multilateral approach had to be given up. (This, after all, is the position of Canada and the United Kingdom and would presumably be that also of the United States.) Finally, abandonment of the scheme, if it were publicly undertaken, would weaken the significance of the Geneva vote on the Canada–United States proposal.

The conclusions of Canada and the United Kingdom are that Canada, the United Kingdom and, it is hoped, the United States and certain of the countries already approached, should either individually or collectively, as may be agreed, approach another group of some twenty-five to thirty countries who may be expected to react favourably. By an agreed date, the results of this second stage in the canvass would be reviewed and a decision could then be made whether further efforts should be undertaken, or the whole scheme dropped for lack of sufficient support. In making this final decision, it would, of course, be necessary to balance the risks in eliciting a reaction from the twelve milers against the possibility of attracting countries which had been hesitant until the end, or which had not been approached, which might be prepared to join "the Club" later on. In approaches to all countries it would be clearly understood that an indication of support in principle would in no sense be a final commitment to sign the proposed convention, and that a final decision would be reserved until the extent of support from other countries is known. All countries concerned would have an opportunity to consider the results of the survey before either taking any further steps or making a final decision.

The next question to be decided would be whether some or all of the eighteen countries which have been canvassed should be asked to lend their active assistance during the second phase of the survey. Such countries as France, assuming her active support could be obtained with United States assistance, and Italy and Australia could give us considerable assistance, while it would be inadvisable to request support from lukewarm countries. It is therefore suggested that the second phase of the survey should be conducted by the United States, the United Kingdom and Canada, possibly with the assistance of additional countries as might be desirable in certain cases.

Another question to be decided would be the position we should take concerning the Brazilian amendment. It would be unrealistic to include some of the Latin Americans in the next phase of the survey, while hoping that they would not raise the question of the Brazilian amendment. (Thus far only Australia, Turkey and Japan have inquired concerning the amendment, but the support of Turkey is partly conditional upon its exclusion and that of Japan almost entirely so.) In our view the only sensible course we can follow is to continue to give a non-committal answer, as we have done thus far with the initial eighteen countries, and to defer final determination of this question until a later stage. A decision either for or against the amendment is bound to involve loss of some potential signatories. It will be a question of determining which is the least expensive course. It would be for consideration, in this connection, whether Argentina, Brazil, Uruguay and Iceland, which are known to be in favour of the Brazilian amendment, should be approached in the second phase of the survey or later.

As to the question of how many supporters would be required to warrant opening a convention for signature, it is the view of the United Kingdom and the Canadian authorities that this question should be left open for the time being. By an agreed date the results of our individual and joint efforts could be reviewed and decisions made as to the next steps to be taken. It might, for instance, be preferable to line up forty countries, including all key countries from a functional point of view, which are reasonably well distributed geographically than to obtain as many as fifty countries not including the important fishing or shipping countries and not well distributed geographically. The idea would, of course, be to obtain the requisite number both as to distribution and importance, and the next phase of the survey should be devised with this in mind. The main object at this time, however, should be to obtain more supporters; a decision can always be made at a later stage as to whether enough have been obtained to open a convention for signature.

As to which country should be approached, and by whom, the following suggestions are raised for consideration by the State Department, it being understood that should the United States authorities decide to support a convention, their support and their assistance in the survey would be in no way tied to a particular plan of action and that these suggestions are made, therefore, merely in hopes of lessening delays which might otherwise result and in order to present the United States authorities with a concrete plan of action. The list of countries which Canada and the United Kingdom would put forth for consideration by the United States is as follows: Argentina (USA), Austria (USA), Belgium

(USA), Bolivia (USA), Brazil (USA), Ceylon (UK and Canada), China (USA), Colombia (USA and Canada), Costa Rica (USA), Cyprus (UK and Greece), Dominican Republic (Canada), France (USA), Guatemala (USA), Holy See (USA and Italy), Honduras (USA), Iceland (USA and Canada), Jordan (UK and USA), Korea (USA), Lebanon (USA), Liberia (USA), Luxembourg (USA), Monaco (France), Nicaragua (USA), Nigeria (UK and Canada), Paraguay (USA), Philippines (Australia and USA), San Marino (Italy), Tunisia (USA and UK), Uruguay (USA), Vietnam (USA).

As soon as the approach to the United States has actually been made, the eighteen countries included in the preliminary survey will be informed in broad terms that its results were sufficiently encouraging to justify an approach being made to the United States, and that the United Kingdom and Canada were proceeding accordingly. France, Belgium and Norway will be informed at the same time.

It is hoped that the United States authorities will agree that on the basis of the preliminary confidential survey already conducted, it would be well worthwhile to undertake a united effort to determine whether sufficient additional support for a multilateral convention based on the "six-plus-six" Geneva formula can be obtained to warrant the opening of such a convention for signature in Ottawa at a future date.

If the United States authorities agree with the course proposed, then it is suggested that three-way talks be held as soon as possible to discuss the nature and timing of the next steps in the survey.

---

487. Memorandum From the Special Assistant for Fisheries and Wildlife (Herrington) to the Assistant Legal Adviser for Special Functional Problems (Yingling)[1]

Washington, May 23, 1961.

SUBJECT

Comments on Canadian Proposals Regarding a Multilateral Convention on the Territorial Sea and Fisheries Jurisdiction

1. The proposed formula in either the 6+6 form or the 6+6 with the Brazilian-Cuban-Uruguyan amendment, would be of no substantial benefit to U.S. fishermen off the coast of the United States, particularly since

---

[1] Source: National Archives and Records Administration, RG 59, Central Files 1960–63, 399.731/5–2361. Secret.

in no event would the USSR be a party nor would Japan be a party if the Brazilian amendment is included. On the other hand, the formula would do very substantial damage to U.S. fisheries off the coast of Latin America, particularly with the Brazilian amendment included, and lesser damage off the coasts of Canada. Consequently the United States should consider accepting the Canadian proposal only if it can be demonstrated that there would be substantial, over-riding benefits in the field of national security.

2. The threat to national security interests appears to lie in the possibility of the world, with the territorial sea problem unresolved, moving increasingly to a 12-mile territorial sea. There appear to be no indications of serious threats to go beyond this distance since the Law of the Sea Conference in 1960.

At both the 1958 and 1960 Conferences the United States based its 3-mile position on the argument that this was the only rule that had been generally accepted by the family of nations and that this rule could not be changed by unilateral actions or agreements between states, except by generally agreed upon multilateral action. It would appear therefore that a multilateral convention of the type proposed would be helpful only if generally accepted by nations. The prospects of such general acceptance can be realistically evaluated on the basis of our extensive experience at the 1958 and 1960 Conferences and our bilateral consultations with most of the participating nations in the course of our preparatory work.

Judged by this background, the results of the Canadian-UK preliminary survey of some 21 nations would appear to be more discouraging than encouraging since about half of them have attached qualifications or reservations to their support. If the Brazilian amendment is included in the formula it can be expected that the response of the Europeans would be even less favorable. On the other hand, failure to include the Brazilian amendment would lose most of the coastal states. This includes practically all of Latin America and many in Africa and Southeast Asia. The resulting document then would be primarily a North Atlantic agreement including Western Europeans, Canada, the United States and a few others. Thus it appears that the prospects of general acceptance of either of these formulas approaches the vanishing point. In fact it is most likely that an attempt on our part to get support for any form of 6+6 formula would stimulate the negotiation of a rival multilateral agreement on a 12-mile territorial sea which would gain support approaching or possibly exceeding that for ours. The chief result then would be to crystalize the division of the world into two blocs with the rival claims generating comparable status. Under these circumstances any military action by the U.S. Armed Forces which did not respect the 12-mile jurisdiction of members of the rival agreement would become substantially more subject to criticism than at present if by our own action we have admitted the right of states to determine the breadth of their territorial sea by limited multilateral action. Thus a strong case can be made that the security interests of the United States would be more likely to be substantially damaged than benefited by the proposed action.

In assessing the extent of support that might be developed I have estimated that European adherence to any agreement which includes the Brazilian amendment would be very limited because of the serious threat to their fishing interests by making possible the extension of the fishing jurisdiction of the coastal states beyond 12 miles. On this assumption the possibilities of such an agreement obtaining broad and representative support are so poor as to be negligible. Should this evaluation be open to real question and it be decided that further sounding out of positions is justified, it would appear extremely desirable to first ascertain the position of the European states on the Brazilian amendment before the United States becomes publicly associated with the proposed extended exploratory project. If this check substantiates the evaluation that the European reaction to the Brazilian amendment is generally negative it should provide convincing evidence that the Canadian proposal is more likely to worsen than improve the present situation.

---

488. Memorandum From the Director of the Office of International Relations, Fish and Wildlife Service, Department of the Interior (Terry) to the Assistant Legal Adviser for Special Functional Problems (Yingling)[1]

Washington, May 23, 1961.

SUBJECT

Canadian request for United States participation in Law of the Sea canvass

Reference is made to the Canadian Aide-Mémoire of May 15, 1961, and to the meeting in your office on May 22.[2]

The Department of the Interior's position on the desirability of United States participation in a canvass to determine the attitude of various governments toward a multilateral convention incorporating the

---

[1] Source: National Archives and Records Administration, RG 59, Central Files 1960–63, 399.731/5–2361. Secret.

[2] The Canadian aide-mémoire is Document 486. No record of this meeting has been found.

essence of the United States-Canadian proposal at the Second Geneva Conference remains as it was in May of 1960 when the question first arose. The basic elements of this position are as follows:

1. The Department has been prepared to agree to certain concessions of fishery jurisdiction in a 12-mile contiguous zone in order to achieve the objectives of the United States at the Geneva Conference, i.e., agreement in the interest of United States security on a six-mile territorial sea in the context of codification or progressive development of international law. It considers that the adoption of a multilateral convention incorporating the provisions of the United States-Canadian proposal is quite another thing. It is convinced that relatively few of the governments which supported the United States at Second Geneva would become signatory to a multilateral convention. It doubts that the advantages to be obtained from a convention with the number of signatories which might be expected are the equivalent of those which might have been obtained at Geneva, and is not convinced that such advantages, whatever they may be worth, justify the same concessions. In the light of the clearly expressed doubts of the Department of Defense as to the value for security purposes of a multilateral convention, the Department of the Interior would at this time oppose a renewed offer of fishery concessions.

2. This Department has consistently opposed the offering of concessions in regard to preferential fishing rights beyond 12 miles. At the time of the Second Geneva Conference it was of the view that such concessions were neither warranted nor necessary to achievement of the objectives sought at the Conference. You will recall that the decision to offer such concessions was made over the objections of Interior's representatives on the United States Delegation. This Department continues of this view, and is firmly opposed to making such concessions for any less substantial advantages than might have been obtained at the Second Geneva Conference. Such concessions would undoubtedly be necessary in order to obtain a substantial number of Latin American signatures without which the proposed multilateral convention would be of virtually no value.

3. The Department of the Interior strongly doubts that a canvass of additional governments will prove of real value. The problem is, after all, not a new one. It and the attitudes of governments toward it have been studied and re-studied in this Government over a long period of years. These attitudes and the factors which control them are well-enough understood to permit this Government to predict with a high degree of accuracy the manner in which these governments will react to a canvass. The United Kingdom-Canadian canvass to date, for example, has revealed little if anything which could not have been predicted a

year ago. On the other hand, it is our view that participation by the United States will perhaps be counter-productive in that it will tend to produce commitments with our friends and encourage counter-moves by those whose interests run counter to ours.

4. In view of these considerations, the Department of the Interior opposes, as it did when the question arose a year ago, United States participation in a canvass, as suggested by Canada. Indeed, the Department believes that the United States should discourage further efforts by Canada and the United Kingdom in this regard.

William M. Terry

489. Memorandum by the Assistant Legal Adviser for Special Functional Problems (Yingling)[1]

Washington, May 24, 1961.

SUBJECT

Canadian Request for United States Participation in a Survey to Ascertain Support for a Multilateral Convention on the Law of the Sea Based on the Canadian-United States Proposal at Geneva in 1960

For the following reason, the Office of the Legal Adviser considers that the United States should participate in the extended survey on the above subject:

1) It is the only constructive proposal put forward to salvage something from the Geneva defeat, and to bring some semblance of law and order into the present chaotic situation. The tide is not running in our favor in this field. L cannot accept the alternative of sitting and awaiting the deluge.

2) A treaty of this kind with substantial adherence (say 40 to 45 countries) would not at that stage establish international law, but it would create a hard core to which other countries interested in a rule of law could rally, and thus international law could be made.

3) It would create a blocking one third against the adoption in the foreseeable future at another conference or elsewhere of any other rule not acceptable to its adherents.

---

[1] Source: National Archives and Records Administration, RG 59, Central Files 1960–63, 399.731/5–2461. Secret.

4) L does not consider it likely that such a treaty would result in a rival twelve-mile treaty. The principal support for a twelve-mile territorial sea at Geneva came from the Soviet and Arab blocs. It is doubted that the Soviet bloc would be willing to restrict itself by treaty to even twelve miles or if it were that the Arabs would be willing to enter into treaty relations with it. But if there were such a treaty, it would be binding on only the parties thereto. Furthermore, it is not believed that any country would adhere to such a treaty which would not itself unilaterally claim a twelve-mile territorial sea anyway so nothing is lost to us by the existence of such a treaty.

5) If the proposed survey reveals insufficient support to make the treaty feasible, the matter will be dropped. It is not seen what great harm will have been done. It is no secret that we are for a rule of law in this field, and the proposal is the same we sponsored at Geneva.

6) It is believed that failure of the United States to participate in further surveys will kill the project as such non participation will be taken as opposition to the proposal. If, therefore, we decide not to participate, it is recommended that we discourage Canada and the United Kingdom from pursuing the matter at this time.

---

490.   Letter From the Deputy Secretary of Defense (Gilpatric) to the Under Secretary of State (Bowles)[1]

Washington, May 25, 1961.

Dear Chet:

I am informed that Canada and the United Kingdom have recently completed a joint assessment of the prospects of a multilateral convention based on the "six plus six" Geneva (1960) formula. I am informed further that it is the joint conclusion and recommendation of Canada and the United Kingdom that the United States should join them in further efforts to explore the prospects for the type of convention in question.

I consider that it would be definitely against the best interests of the United States, particularly its security interests, to follow the conclusion

---

[1] Source: National Archives and Records Administration, RG 59, Central Files 1960–63, 399.731/5–2561. Confidential. The typed salutation "Dear Chester" was changed by hand to "Dear Chet".

and recommendation of the friends mentioned. The reasons for my conclusion are as follows:

If the issue for decision were regarded solely as a question of whether we should join in an effort to learn more about the prospects of such a convention, obligations of courtesy might alone dictate an affirmative answer. I do not so regard the issue. Once the United States joins such an exploratory effort, indicating thereby an active interest in promoting a multilateral on the basis indicated, the states opposed to the United States position on the territorial sea question are expected to learn of such activity and to initiate the highly detrimental countermeasures discussed hereafter. No one has suggested that the opponents of our position could be kept unaware of our activity. In other words, great potential detriment is deemed to exist in the mere act of joining "explorations" for information, wholly apart from any ultimate decision as to whether such a multilateral is to be actually opened for signature.

The real issues for decision I therefore regard as the following. Is the current state of our information on the prospects of such a multilateral adequate for decision on the ultimate question? Are the prospective benefits of promoting this multilateral substantial? Are there detriments involved in promoting this multilateral and if so, how do they compare relative to any expected benefits?

The current state of United States information on this issue is regarded as completely and uniquely adequate for a final decision on the advisability of seeking to promote the multilateral in question. This conclusion is understood to be shared by three of the four remaining sections of the interdepartmental committee which has closely studied this issue for over four years and was shared by the other section before its dissolution.

As to the question of prospective benefits to be derived from promoting the proposed multilateral, it is the considered opinion here that it would be useless from a security viewpoint, even assuming forty-five states became parties to the agreement. (This is the largest number hypothesized by anyone conversant with this subject and it is regarded here as unrealistic.) This conclusion follows from the fact that no one has suggested or would suggest that any (except Iceland) of the twenty-eight states which opposed the 1960 "six plus six" proposal would become parties to such a convention now, [2-1/2 *lines of source text not declassified*]. As to the remaining states, who voted for the "six plus six" proposal in 1960, the territorial sea breadth presents no substantial security problem and effectuation of the proposed multilateral would therefore afford United States security interests no substantial benefit.

The proposed multilateral could be, and it is judged that it would be, highly detrimental to United States security interests. At present we stand at a position where, at the last vote, the 1960 "six plus six" proposal failed of United Nations Conference adoption by only one negative vote to achieve the required two-thirds majority. No other proposal achieved even a simple majority. Thus, the "six plus six" position must be taken as the decisively marked point of prospective international compromise as matters now stand. If, however, the twenty-seven (leaving out Iceland) opponents of the "six plus six" formula, plus Cuba which now must be added, are galvanized into offensive action by our espousal of the Canada-United Kingdom multilateral, we anticipate a decisively unfavorable modification of the 1960 Geneva vote.

We anticipate, for instance, that action by the United States, Canada and the United Kingdom, proposing a solution to the territorial sea question by independent (of the United Nations) multilateral convention would force the opposition to take cohesive and all-out action to protect their position by means of an opposed multilateral offering twelve mile territorial seas. Though the 1960 opposition was heterogeneous in marked degree (Soviet bloc, Arab bloc, Chile, Ecuador, Peru, Venezuela, Mexico, Indonesia, India, Guinea), it operated with remarkable cohesion and cooperation. As unlikely as such an alliance might otherwise be, it is regarded as almost a certainty that on this particular question, the action recommended by Canada and the United Kingdom would cause the opposition to unite in an opposed multilateral.

By itself this action would greatly disadvantage United States security interests.

Instead of confronting individual states unilaterally claiming territorial seas beyond the limit we acknowledge as legitimate, we would be confronting and challenging the validity of a multilateral treaty of approximately thirty sovereign states. Furthermore, our experience indicates that this opposition would attract more supporters from among the newly emerging states than we could, thus increasing their number to approximately forty. Finally, our ground for challenging the validity of the opposed multilateral would be decimated, once we had abandoned our present position that the territorial sea issue can only be settled by a universal rule and adopted the position that it could be validly settled by a group multilateral. (The grounds for the validity of ours could not then be distinguished from the grounds for theirs.)

On the other hand, we anticipate that our support would diminish as and because the opposition became stronger or more vociferous. Much of the support for our 1960 "six plus six" proposal was not given from any preference for that proposal. In fact no state is known to prefer it. It was supported extensively as the only possible compromise exit from a bitter conflict. When it appears, as we anticipate, that the opposing multilaterals are only going to heighten the conflict, we anticipate a substantial loss of support. In all, we anticipate that our support would be reduced to about thirty-one states. This would be a drastic reduction from the fifty-four supporters in Geneva 1960 and if, as expected, the opposition easily exceeded that figure the ultimate capitulation of our multilateral would be foreordained.

I have dwelt at length on this matter because of its grave importance for the United States, I assure you that we regret advising against this affirmative proposal while being able to offer no alternative course of action at this time. We have had this specific problem under constant review for one year, however, and have consistently concluded that the independent multilateral is a course holding no substantial promise while at the same time it does hold grave potential detriment for the United States.

Sincerely,

Ros Gilpatric

---

491.   Memorandum From the Deputy Legal Adviser (Meeker) to the Under Secretary of State (Bowles)[1]

Washington, May 25, 1961.

SUBJECT

Multilateral Convention Embodying the Provisions of the United States-Canadian Proposal at Geneva regarding the Law of the Sea

On May 15, 1961, the Canadian Ambassador left with you (Tab E) an aide-mémoire giving the results of a preliminary survey made by Canada and the United Kingdom to ascertain the attitude of the eighteen countries approached on the above subject.[2] The Canadian Ambassador indicated that the two governments considered the results encouraging, and the aide-mémoire proposed that the survey be extended to twenty-five to thirty countries and requested United States participation in the extended survey. A similar aide-mémoire was delivered by the British Embassy to the Legal Adviser's Office the next day. L was requested to prepare a memorandum recommending a course of action with respect to the suggestions in the aide-mémoire.

---

[1]   Source: National Archives and Records Administration, RG 59, Central Files 1960–63, 399.731/5–2561. Secret.

[2]   Document 486.

A meeting, attended by representatives of the Department of the Navy, Department of the Interior, U/FW, EUR, FE, ARA and NEA was held in L (Mr. Yingling's office) on May 22 to discuss the subject. The discussion revealed a difference of views as to participation in the proposed survey, indeed as to the objective itself.

L considers that such a multilateral treaty as proposed is the only alternative now available to legal chaos and an ultimate situation very unfavorable to United States interests. Its reasons are briefly summarized in the attached paper (Tab A).[3] L is authorized to say that EUR, FE, ARA, and NEA concur in its views, and consider the proposed course of action not only feasible but necessary.

The Department of Defense considers that the United States should not participate in the extended survey and questions the desirability of the ultimate objective. Its views have been stated in a letter of May 25, 1961, from Deputy Secretary of Defense Gilpatric, a copy of which is attached (Tab B).[4]

The Fish and Wildlife Service, Department of the Interior and U/FW are of the view that the United States should not participate in the extended survey. They see no advantage in the proposed treaty from a fisheries standpoint, rather the contrary, and do not feel that these disadvantages are compensated by any gains in the field of national security. Their views are briefly set forth in the attached memoranda (Tabs C and D).[5]

Recommendations:

1. If you agree that the United States should participate with Canada and the United Kingdom in an extended survey to ascertain support for a multilateral treaty on the lines indicated, that you authorize L to participate in talks with representatives of Canada and the United Kingdom to plan the next steps to be taken.

2. If you do not approve participation by the United States in the extended survey that Canada and the United Kingdom be so informed, and that we attempt to discourage them from pursuing the matter further at this time. In this event, L will communicate this decision to the British and Canadians.[6]

---

[3] Document 489.

[4] Document 490.

[5] Documents 487 and 488.

[6] The memorandum bears no indication of Bowles' approval or disapproval of the recommendations.

492.   Telegram From the Department of State to the Embassy in Canada[1]

Washington, July 19, 1961, 2 p.m.

47. Your 1098, June 30, and 31, July 11.[2] Dept regrets that it has so far not reached a decision resolving viewpoints of interested agencies but matter has been under active consideration and you may so inform FonMin Green. Dept hopes to be able to furnish a more definite reply at an early date.

Dept appreciates considerations set forth by Canadian Govt but hopes FonMin realizes this not simple problem for us and appreciates our desire to be as helpful as possible in political situation he faces.

Rusk

---

[1]   Source: National Archives and Records Administration, RG 59, Central Files 1960–63, 399.731/7–1961. Confidential. Drafted by Yingling.

[2]   In telegram 1098, Ambassador Merchant described a meeting with Canadian Assistant Under Secretary and Legal Adviser Marcel Cadieux, in which Cadieux expressed the hope that the United States would soon reply to the May 15 aide-mémoire. The Canadian Government had gotten encouraging results from its survey, but feared that unless action were taken, momentum would be lost, "defections" might occur, and a country not canvassed might take unilateral action. There were also pressures from Canadian fishing interests for unilateral action. (Ibid., 399.731/6–3061) In telegram 31, Ambassador Merchant noted that on July 11 Foreign Minister Green had asked again for a reply concerning Canada's note. (Ibid., 399.731/7–1161)

---

493.   Letter From Acting Secretary of Defense Gilpatric to the Deputy Under Secretary of State for Political Affairs (Johnson)[1]

Washington, July 24, 1961.

Dear Alex:

On further consideration of the Canadian-United Kingdom proposal that we join in an assessment of the prospects of a multilateral convention concerning the breadth of the territorial sea and fisheries

---

[1]   Source: National Archives and Records Administration, RG 59, Central Files 1960–63, 399.731/7–2461. Confidential.

jurisdiction, referred to in my letter of 25 May 1961,[2] I have concluded that it might be useful to provide you with our analysis of the anticipated support for and opposition to such an endeavor.

In this analysis the following basic assumptions have been made: (1) that the provisions of the proposed multilateral, when offered for signature, would be exactly the same as the proposal which received fifty four affirmative votes at the 1960 Conference in Geneva, Switzerland (i.e., the United States-Canadian proposal plus the Brazil amendment); (2) that the United States and the West European Governments would support and strongly urge others to support a prospective multilateral on the terms mentioned; (3) that United States fishing interests and congressmen and their European counterparts' opposition to the prospective multilateral will be moderate or promptly and effectively overcome.

It is estimated that the maximum number of states which could be persuaded to sign the prospective multilateral is 30 to 35. This range is arrived at on the basis of analysis which indicates that there are 42 reasonably possible adherents. Of these 42, 12 are virtually certain adherents and 11 are substantially doubtful. We resolve the unknown factor on the basis of past experience and conclude that we might persuade 65 to 85 per cent of those in the reasonably possible category to sign the prospective multilateral.

If we attracted the maximum of 35 signatories, there would be left remaining 77 non-signatories (counting Communist China, East Germany, outer Mongolia and Kuwait).

Of the 77 who are regarded as not reasonably possible adherents to a prospective multilateral on the terms mentioned, at least 36 are known to be strongly opposed to the terms of the prospective multilateral and to be strongly in favor of a twelve mile territorial sea.

If, as is considered likely, this nucleus of 36 were to attempt to protect its position by creating a twelve mile multilateral, it is estimated that as many as 50 signatories could be achieved and the reasonable possibilities run as high as 57 to 60.

On the basis of our analysis we conclude that the United States should not engage in attempting to promote a multilateral treaty on the terms mentioned. On the contrary, it is urged that the United States should seek to dissuade Canada and the United Kingdom from further efforts in this direction.

Our conclusions are buttressed by a further consideration: even if our estimate of support for the prospective multilateral proved to be

---

[2] Document 490.

fundamentally in error, and as many as fifty signatories could be attracted, the resulting 50 state multilateral treaty would constitute no current net benefit and would very likely result in a substantial current net detriment. The reason for this conclusion is the circumstance that we could only attract the adherence of "friends", in any case. Their adherence to the treaty contemplated offers no current security advantages. The making of such a treaty, however, would surely harden the attitude of the opposition and that result could be substantially detrimental to current security interests.

Sincerely,

Roswell Gilpatric

494.   **Letter From the Assistant Secretary of the Interior (Briggs) to the Deputy Under Secretary of State (Johnson)[1]**

Washington, July 25, 1961.

Dear Mr. Secretary:

During recent weeks representatives of the Department of the Interior have been discussing with representatives of the Departments of State and Defense a proposal from Canada and the United Kingdom that the United States join them in a canvass of various foreign governments aimed at determining the attitude of those governments toward a multilateral convention on the breadth of the territorial sea and the extent of national jurisdiction over fisheries in coastal waters. The proposed convention would incorporate the essential elements of the formula which the United States supported at the Second United Nations Conference on the Law of the Sea. These essential elements are a six-mile territorial sea; an additional six-mile contiguous zone in which, at the end of ten years, the coastal nations would have exclusive jurisdiction over fisheries; and, in special circumstances, a preferential right on the part of coastal nations to fishery resources in waters seaward of the contiguous zone.

Although this Department's representatives have explained our position on this matter on several occasions, I wish now to set it forth

[1] Source: National Archives and Records Administration, RG 59, Central Files 1960–63, 399.731/7–2561. Confidential.

more formally for your benefit. We are opposed to United States participation in the proposed canvass. Indeed, we believe that the United States should not only decline to participate, but should also discourage further efforts in this connection on the part of Canada and the United Kingdom. Our opposition goes not so much to the canvass as it goes to the ultimate objective—a multilateral convention—toward which a canvass is the first step. We are not convinced that the benefits which would accrue from a multilateral convention would justify the concessions which the United States would have to make in order to obtain those benefits. It is my understanding that the Department of Defense has taken a similar position.

In our judgment an orderly approach to the problem involves three basic determinations. First, what are the benefits which will accrue to the United States from a multilateral convention incorporating a six-mile territorial sea provision with 30 signatory nations? With 40 signatory nations? With 50 signatory nations? I may say at this point that, in our view, the likelihood of any convention's attracting 50 signatures is remote. Second, what concessions will the United States be required to make in order to obtain 30 signatures, 40 signatures, or 50 signatures? Third, do the benefits which accrue in each case justify the concessions? We believe that the factors involved in these determinations have to date received insufficient attention.

In approaching the first of these determinations, while we would not presume to specify benefits, we think it reasonable to conclude that any convention which obtained substantially fewer signatures than the final proposal at the Second United Nations Conference received supporting votes would result in benefits, substantially less than those which might have been obtained at the Conference. Here again, it is my understanding that the Department of Defense has taken a similar position.

With regard to the second determination, no further canvassing is needed to enable the United States to establish at least the minimum concessions which would be necessary. We think it obvious that any multilateral convention which did not incorporate a provision for preferential rights on the part of the coastal nations to fisheries beyond twelve miles, in addition to a six-mile territorial sea and a six-mile contiguous zone for exclusive fishery jurisdiction, would fail to attract even the smallest number of signatures noted above. This is a critical issue, one which the United Kingdom and Canada have understandably avoided meeting, and one which has been glossed over in discussions in this Government. Without provision for this preferential right, the proposed convention will be acceptable to few Latin American countries. With such a provision, the convention will become most difficult for the European fishing countries and Japan to accept.

Coming to the third determination, I reiterate the position which this Department has taken previously. This Department agreed to the concession to coastal nations of exclusive jurisdiction over fisheries in a zone extending twelve miles from the coast in order to achieve the objectives of the United States at the Second United Nations Conference on the Law of the Sea, i.e., agreement, in the interest of United States security, on a six-mile territorial sea in the context of codification or progressive development of international law. This constituted a maximum concession and this Department opposed the offering of concessions in regard to preferential fishing rights beyond twelve miles. We are not now prepared to agree to the concession of jurisdiction over fisheries in a twelve-mile zone for advantages substantially less than those which might have been obtained at the Second Conference. We do not consider that such lesser advantages warrant the sacrifices which the United States will be called upon to make. It follows that we are not prepared to agree to the offering of concessions in regard to preferential fishing rights beyond twelve miles for the lesser advantages.

One further comment may be made in connection with concessions. To this point this discussion has been limited to concessions related to fisheries. It would be foolhardy, however, for us to conclude that the offering of fishery concessions would bring about the desired result. An enormous effort at persuasion was necessary prior to and during the Second Conference to bring the United States even within reach of its goal, an effort which was prodigal in its expenditure of political goodwill. A similar effort would be necessary in connection with the proposed multilateral convention. The political capital which would be expended in such an effort must be added to the suggested fishery concessions in totaling the cost.

To recapitulate, this Department does not consider the advantages from a convention with the largest number of signatures which may be expected to justify the concessions which would be required. It consequently is opposed to United States participation in the suggested canvass.

One additional factor must be taken into consideration. The attitude of the interested public in the United States to the proposal which the United States and Canada put forward at the Second United Nations Conference, i.e., a six-mile territorial sea and a six-mile contiguous fishing zone, was one of reluctant acceptance of the need for sacrifices on its part in the interest of achieving an objective vital to the security of the United States. Although fearful of the results, the industry with some exceptions supported the Government. Without this support, this Government's problems would have been multiplied immeasurably, and it is questionable in our minds that this Government would have been able to proceed as it did, without this support. Industry did not, however, agree to the additional concession involving a preferential right to fisheries beyond twelve miles, but opposed it to the end.

It is our view that industry will continue to oppose concessions involving waters beyond twelve miles, and that in addition it will oppose the lesser concessions for advantages which in its judgment will appear less substantial than those which might have been obtained at the Second Conference. We believe it essential, in coming to a decision on this matter, that the inevitability of strong opposition from industry and severe criticism of the Administration be taken into account. We think it also necessary to consider as a distinct probability, if not a certainty, a determined effort by industry to prevent ratification of any convention which the United States might sign.

Sincerely yours,

Frank P. Briggs

---

495.   Editorial Note

On August 25, 1961, Canadian Ambassador Heeney sent a letter to Legal Adviser Abram Chayes, in which he wrote that the Canadian Government would like to send a delegation to Washington to discuss the U.S. position on the proposed multilateral Law of the Sea convention. He hoped that the meeting could be scheduled before the reopening of the Canadian Parliament on September 7. On September 7 Chayes replied that although the United States had not reached a decision about the convention, he would be willing to meet with a Canadian delegation on September 8. (National Archives and Records Administration, RG 59, Central Files 1960–63, 399.731/8–2561 and 399.731/4–1612)

496.   Memorandum From the Legal Adviser (Chayes) to Secretary of State Rusk[1]

Washington, September 27, 1961.

SUBJECT

Multilateral Convention Embodying the Provisions of the United States-Canadian Proposal at the Law of the Sea Conference in Geneva in 1960

Background:

The United States-Canadian proposal which narrowly failed of adoption at Geneva in 1960 provided for a six-mile territorial sea plus a six-mile exclusive fisheries zone in which traditional users would have a ten-year phase out privilege. A Brazilian amendment accepted by the United States and Canada provided preferential fishing rights for the coastal State outside of twelve miles in exceptional cases. On May 15, 1961, the Canadian Ambassador left with the Acting Secretary an aide-mémoire giving the results of a preliminary survey of eighteen countries made by Canada and the United Kingdom to ascertain the attitude of the eighteen countries to a multilateral treaty embodying this proposal. The Ambassador indicated that the results of the survey were considered encouraging and requested United States participation in a survey of additional countries. A similar approach was made by the United Kingdom Embassy at lower level, and I believe the United Kingdom Ambassador mentioned it informally to you. The matter was referred by the Under Secretary to Mr. Johnson.

All interested parties (Defense, Interior, L, U/FW, and the political areas of the Department) have stated their respective views in ample memoranda, and around the conference table. Defense considers that such a treaty would be adhered to only by friends of the United States and not by its potential enemies and, therefore, that it affords nothing from a security standpoint. Interior and U/FW consider that it would be disadvantageous from a fisheries standpoint and that such disadvantages are not acceptable except in exchange for substantial security benefits. L considers such a treaty the only constructive proposal and perhaps our last clear chance to stem the tide running against us toward a twelve-mile territorial sea; therefore in the long range overall interest of the United States as a whole. Moreover, it considers that substantial

---

[1] Source: National Archives and Records Administration, RG 59, Central Files 1960–63, 399.731/9–2761. Confidential. Drafted by Yingling, and cleared by Daniel M. Braddock (ARA), Louise McNutt (FE), M. Gordon Knox and Wharton D. Hubbard (EUR), James M. Ludlow (NEA), and Richard N. Gardner (IO).

adherence (40 to 45 countries) to such a treaty would create a blocking one-third against the adoption at another Law of the Sea Conference of any other rule not acceptable to the parties to the treaty.

After considering the views of all parties, Mr. Johnson concluded on August 26, 1961, that there did not seem to be a sufficiently clear balance of advantage to the United States to justify our joining in the Canadian proposal for a survey. However, he suggested that if this Office (or EUR for reasons of our relations with Canada) desired to pursue the matter further, a memorandum should be sent to you.[2]

Discussion:

We can see no substantial objection to participation in a survey as requested by Canada and the United Kingdom, and the political areas of the Department support this view. Because of his past association with this problem, I have discussed it with Ambassador Arthur Dean and he also sees no objection to such a survey.

Strong representations have been made to the Department and to our Embassy in Ottawa on this matter, and a Canadian delegation headed by Deputy Under Secretary and Legal Adviser Marcel Cadieux came to Washington on September 8, and supported by a United Kingdom delegation met with the representatives of the interested agencies to present their strong view that the United States should participate in the proposed extended survey.

The Canadian Government is under strong pressure from fisheries interests to proclaim a twelve-mile fishing limit unilaterally and its representatives indicated that this possibility should not be discounted in the event the multilateral treaty approach had to be abandoned.

This Office considers that the views of Defense and the fisheries people cannot be changed, but that the decision as to United States participation in such a survey is ultimately one for the Department.

Recommendation:

If you agree that the United States should participate with Canada and the United Kingdom in a further survey to ascertain support for a multilateral treaty on the lines indicated, that you authorize L to participate in talks with representatives of Canada and the United Kingdom to plan the next steps to be taken.[3]

---

[2] Johnson's memorandum is ibid., 399.731/8–2661.

[3] The memorandum bears no indication of Rusk's approval or disapproval of the recommendation.

497.   Editorial Note

On November 8, 1961, Canadian Ambassador Heeney sent a letter to Secretary of State Rusk in which he expressed the hope that Rusk could "spare a few minutes to consider our request" and that Rusk would be willing to join with Canada in "a further confidential exploration of the prospects for a multilateral convention." Rusk replied on November 17 that he had referred the question to the Legal Adviser for coordination and further action, and hoped that he could inform Heeney of his decision soon. (National Archives and Records Administration, RG 59, Central Files 1960–63, 399.731/11–861)

498.   Memorandum From the Deputy Assistant Secretary of State for Politico-Military Affairs (Kitchen) to the Special Assistant to the Under Secretary of State for Economic Affairs (Schaetzel)[1]

Washington, December 7, 1961.

SUBJECT

Law of the Sea

Tuesday at lunch we discussed briefly the Law of the Sea and the question of our adoption of a proposal made by the Canadians in May that we join them and the British in an expanded survey to ascertain the attitude of certain countries toward a multilateral convention embodying the provisions of the U.S.-Canadian Proposal made at the 1960 Geneva Law of the Sea Conference. This question has been discussed at length, both within the Department and with other interested Agencies. While opinion within the Department is divided, the other Agencies concerned are universally against our going along with the Canadian plan.

---

[1] Source: National Archives and Records Administration, RG 59, Central Files 1960–63, 399.731/12–761. Confidential. In an attached note, dated December 8, Schaetzel asked Special Assistant Arthur A. Hartman to "(1) find out what, if anything, George [Ball] has said or done on this subject; and (2) find out where the original October petition to the Secretary stands." He added, "I am persuaded that Kitchen is right, namely, that this is basically a part of a vendetta between Yingling and the Defense Department."

On August 26, Deputy Under Secretary Johnson advised L that he did not believe that there was a sufficiently clear balance of advantage to the U.S. to justify our joining in the Canadian proposal for a survey. He indicated, however, that should L desire further to pursue the matter, a memorandum submitting the question to the Secretary should be prepared.[2] L opted to submit such a memorandum and it went forward to the Secretary on October 11.[3] As far as I know this is where the matter stands today.

In my opinion, and I think everyone would probably agree with this, the countries most likely to react favorably to representations aimed at a Law of the Sea accord would be those where there is the least clear advantage for the U.S., i.e., countries that can be expected to meet our high seas' security requirements with or without a signed convention. Conversely, the countries least likely to adopt a Law of the Sea formula agreeable to our interests are precisely those countries whose acquiescence would hold the greatest advantage for us.

It is my understanding that the proposed convention would not constitute a rule of International Law, even if the maximum conceivable number of countries signed, since it would not be the product of an International Convention bound by established rules of procedure. It would be a simple contract binding only upon the signatories in their relationships with each other.

It seems to me that acceptance of the Canadian proposal would cast us in the light of sponsoring a treaty. This role, even if we were only required to deal with those countries that share our inclinations on the Law of the Sea would require a de facto expenditure of a certain amount of political capital. On general principle, such an expenditure should be made on the basis of demonstrable evidence of significant advantages which the U.S. could reasonably expect in return for its efforts. The burden of proof should be placed upon those who advocate favorable consideration of the Canadian plan.

The opposition's case is stated in the attached letters of May 25, 1961, to Under Secretary Bowles from Deputy Under Secretary of Defense Gilpatric and of July 25, 1961, to Deputy Under Secretary Johnson from Assistant Secretary of the Interior Briggs.[4] Representatives of the Departments of the Interior and the Navy have stated orally, in terms as strong as those appearing in these letters, their sentiments against our joining in the expanded survey. In response to these representations it was clearly indicated that, should the disposi-

---

[2] See footnote 2, Document 496.

[3] Presumably a reference to Document 496.

[4] Documents 490 and 494.

tion of the Department of State be to accept the Canadian proposal, an opportunity would be given the other Agencies concerned to make a final statement of their views before we moved to implement our decision. Such consultation was deemed prudent in view of the categorical opposition of Defense, Interior and Navy to such a course of action.

499. Telegram From the Department of State to the Embassy in Canada[1]

Washington, February 8, 1962, 4:29 p.m.

774. For Ambassador from Under Secretary Ball. Endeavoring here expedite reply long standing Canadian request for U.S. participation in canvass interested nations on possibility undertaking multilateral agreement on Law of Sea. Had anticipated that Canadians would raise this subject with us in Ottawa at January 12–13 session and permit us assess strength Canadian Cabinet views this matter. Issue never raised there but before reaching final decision here wish have your personal assessment of (a) likelihood that negative response our part would result Canadian attempt through unilateral action extend territorial sea, (b) strength underlying internal political feeling this subject and extent to which local political situation, particularly in election year, is basis Canadian request; (c) whether Canadians talking in terms six-mile territorial sea and six-mile fishing zone, or three-mile sea and nine-mile zone, or twelve-mile sea; and (d) any other views you may have on this matter, including impact negative response our part on overall US-Canadian relations.

Rusk

[1] Source: National Archives and Records Administration, RG 59, Central Files 1960–63, 399.731/2–862. Confidential; Limit Distribution. Drafted by George S. Springsteen; cleared by Chayes, Delmar R. Carlson (BNA), and William H. Brubeck (S/S); and approved by Under Secretary Ball.

500.   Telegram From the Embassy in Canada to the Department of State[1]

Ottawa, February 9, 1962, 5 p.m.

757. For Under Secretary Ball from Ambassador. Greatly appreciate your attention to question US reply to long-standing Canadian request on Law of Sea.

Following are my comments seriatim on questions raised your 744.[2]

(A) Outright refusal on our part participate proposed canvass interested nations would, I assume, greatly lessen interest UK and others. If it thus became apparent to Canadians no point in pursuing multilateral possibilities, then I believe Canadians might well feel obliged take unilateral action.

(B) Issue is active in Canada today though without burning intensity which surrounds number other domestic political issues. Government has thus far avoided action by publicly implying international negotiations in progress. Liberal opposition has publicly said it stands for cooperation with other interested nations but would if necessary take unilateral action. CCF (Socialist) member Parliament has presented bill which would provide unilateral extension fishing rights to twelve miles. This bill however unlikely come to vote so long as government can indicate alternative solution being pursued. We are in heavy pre-election atmosphere and government is growing increasingly restive on this question. By coincidence ExtAff at personal request Foreign Minister Green made oral approach to us again today urging early US reply.

(C) CCF bill referred to above speaks of "12-mile fishing zone" and presumably is not concerned with other territorial rights. In its approach today ExtAff emphasized to us GOC speaking of Six plus Six formula with 10-year phase-out of historic fishing rights.

(D) I believe that by affirmative response to request participate in canvass or even response which falls short of this but indicates willingness sit down and talk (my telegram 234, September 1, 1961).[3] We would have good chance forestalling unilateral Canadian action during

[1] Source: National Archives and Records Administration, RG 59, Central Files 1960–63, 399.731/2–962. Confidential; Limit Distribution.

[2] Document 499.

[3] In telegram 234, Ambassador Merchant urged the Department to indicate readiness to discuss the Law of the Sea Convention with Canada even if it were not possible to hold a meeting before the Canadian Parliament reconvened on September 7. (National Archives and Records Administration, RG 59, Central Files 1960–63, 399.731/9–161)

present session Parliament and probably until after elections. For sake our bilateral relations with Canada I would of course hope we could participate in canvass. I cannot judge other factors involved but in this connection Canadians made clear to us again today their understanding our participation would imply no substantive commitment whatsoever.

In any event, as indicated my A-291[4] there is some reason believe Canadians are becoming concerned over state US-Canada relations and particularly over manner in which they have dealt with us in certain current bilateral issues. If we can now be moderately forthcoming on this question (and, as I believe, at same time further our interests on Law of Sea question) I think we would further encourage their remorse and would contribute to their sense of need to husband more carefully their store of goodwill in US. This would be most welcome development.

Merchant

---

[4] Not printed.

---

501. Editorial Note

On February 26, 1962, Ambassador Merchant met with Canadian Foreign Minister Green, who said that lack of progress on the Law of the Sea Convention could become an issue in Canada's national elections. Merchant replied that he would report on the Canadian Government's concerns. In telegram 815 from Ottawa, Merchant requested, "Would appreciate early report present status." On February 28 the Department replied, "Under Secretary seeing Ambassador Heeney tomorrow. Department will report later." (National Archives and Records Administration, RG 59, Central Files 1960–63, 399.731/2–2762 and 399.731/2–2862) Regarding Ball's meeting with Heeney, see Document 502.

502. Telegram From the Department of State to the Embassy in Canada[1]

Washington, March 8, 1962, 8:43 p.m.

882. Basis uncleared Memcon,[2] Under Secretary informed Ambassador Heeney today that U.S. could not accede to Canadian request contained in Canadian Embassy Aide-Mémoire of May 15, 1961 participate in expanded canvass re possibility Law of Sea multilateral treaty. Memcon follows.

Rusk

---

[1] Source: National Archives and Records Administration, RG 59, Central Files 1960–63, 399.731/3–862. Confidential. Drafted by Wharton D. Hubbard (EUR/BNA), cleared by Andre J. Navez (S/S), and approved by Milton C. Rewinkel.

[2] Not found.

---

503. Memorandum of Conversation[1]

Hyannis Port, May 11, 1963, 10 a.m.

SUBJECT

Territorial Sea and Fisheries Zone

PARTICIPANTS

US	*Canada*
The President	The Prime Minister
Ambassador Butterworth	Ambassador Ritchie
Mr. William Tyler	Mr. Edward Ritchie
Mr. Pierre Salinger	Mr. Basil Robinson
	Mr. Orme Dier

The Prime Minister presented the Canadian case on the above. He felt there was no possibility of the matter being settled by international agreement. Forty countries had increased their territorial waters beyond the 3-mile limit. Canada had favored a 6-mile fishery zone in

---

[1] Source: National Archives and Records Administration, RG 59, Conference Files: Lot 66 D 110, Memorandums of Conversation, Pearson Visit, May 10–11, 1963. Secret. Drafted by William R. Tyler (EUR) and approved in the White House on May 16. The memorandum is marked No. 3 of 8.

addition to a 6-mile limit but now was prepared to leave the 3-mile limit untouched but would declare an additional 9-mile Fishery Zone. The Prime Minister recognized that Canada must take into account the historic and treaty rights of the United States and that there must be consultations with the United States Government. He felt that the Canadian position was consistent with the Geneva negotiations. He pointed out that a 12-mile zone would affect less than one per cent of US fishing interests. The President then presented the US position, emphasizing not only the protection of US rights but the possible adverse implications of the base line principle, in so far as it might result in the closing of bays and of stretches of water of importance to US interests. The Prime Minister agreed that the application of the Canadian decision must be discussed. Canada did not want to have a row with the United States about this. He hoped that the United States would not overlook the advantage, from the security standpoint, of, for example, Canadian control of Hudson Bay. The President mentioned our difficulties with regard to US interests on the West Coast, and in relation to US shrimp fishing interests in the Gulf of Mexico. He said we would like to discuss further the Canadian proposal re the base line, and what this means in reality; also the security implications of the proposed step, for the U.S.A. The President asked the Prime Minister, in view of the latter's statement that US fishing interests would be so little affected, what great advantage there would be to Canadian fishermen. The Prime Minister was not able to answer this very convincingly. The President repeated that we would like to have talks about all these matters with the Canadian Government and see what the application of the Canadian position would mean in practice. Ambassador Butterworth pointed out that taking account of US treaty and historic rights should not mean that they were to be subject to diminution and erosion by the Canadian action. The Prime Minister said the Canadian Government could only modify these US rights in agreement with the United States. The President suggested that Canadian experts on this subject go to Washington soon, perhaps as early as next week, and the Prime Minister agreed that talks should be held very soon. He emphasized that no Canadian action would be taken without prior consultation. The President said that this was likely to be a matter on which the United States and Canada would disagree, and he then dictated some language for the communiqué on this point, which the Prime Minister accepted. The Prime Minister drew the President's attention to the security aspects of the problem which might alleviate and compensate for any disadvantages for the United States. The President told Mr. Tyler that he would like Mr. Feldman of the White House to sit in on the talks as an observer.

Index

ISBN 0-16-050885-1

9 780160 508851

90000